T0191532

Lecture Notes in Computer Science   9915

Commenced Publication in 1973
Founding and Former Series Editors:
Gerhard Goos, Juris Hartmanis, and Jan van Leeuwen

Editorial Board

David Hutchison
  Lancaster University, Lancaster, UK
Takeo Kanade
  Carnegie Mellon University, Pittsburgh, PA, USA
Josef Kittler
  University of Surrey, Guildford, UK
Jon M. Kleinberg
  Cornell University, Ithaca, NY, USA
Friedemann Mattern
  ETH Zurich, Zurich, Switzerland
John C. Mitchell
  Stanford University, Stanford, CA, USA
Moni Naor
  Weizmann Institute of Science, Rehovot, Israel
C. Pandu Rangan
  Indian Institute of Technology, Madras, India
Bernhard Steffen
  TU Dortmund University, Dortmund, Germany
Demetri Terzopoulos
  University of California, Los Angeles, CA, USA
Doug Tygar
  University of California, Berkeley, CA, USA
Gerhard Weikum
  Max Planck Institute for Informatics, Saarbrücken, Germany

More information about this series at http://www.springer.com/series/7412

Gang Hua · Hervé Jégou (Eds.)

Computer Vision –
ECCV 2016 Workshops

Amsterdam, The Netherlands, October 8–10 and 15–16, 2016
Proceedings, Part III

 Springer

Editors
Gang Hua
Microsoft Research Asia
Beijing
China

Hervé Jégou
Facebook AI Research (FAIR)
Menlo Park
USA

ISSN 0302-9743   ISSN 1611-3349   (electronic)
Lecture Notes in Computer Science
ISBN 978-3-319-49408-1   ISBN 978-3-319-49409-8   (eBook)
DOI 10.1007/978-3-319-49409-8

Library of Congress Control Number: 2016951693

LNCS Sublibrary: SL6 – Image Processing, Computer Vision, Pattern Recognition, and Graphics

Printed on acid-free paper

This Springer imprint is published by Springer Nature
The registered company is Springer International Publishing AG
The registered company address is: Gewerbestrasse 11, 6330 Cham, Switzerland

Foreword

Welcome to the proceedings of the 2016 edition of the European Conference on Computer Vision held in Amsterdam! It is safe to say that the European Conference on Computer Vision is one of the top conferences in computer vision. It is good to reiterate the history of the conference to see the broad base the conference has built in the 13 editions. First held in 1990 in Antibes (France), it was followed by subsequent conferences in Santa Margherita Ligure (Italy) in 1992, Stockholm (Sweden) in 1994, Cambridge (UK) in 1996, Freiburg (Germany) in 1998, Dublin (Ireland) in 2000, Copenhagen (Denmark) in 2002, Prague (Czech Republic) in 2004, Graz (Austria) in 2006, Marseille (France) in 2008, Heraklion (Greece) in 2010, Florence (Italy) in 2012, and Zürich (Switzerland) in 2014.

For the 14th edition, many people worked hard to provide attendees with a most warm welcome while enjoying the best science. The Program Committee, Bastian Leibe, Jiri Matas, Nicu Sebe, and Max Welling, did an excellent job. Apart from the scientific program, the workshops were selected and handled by Hervé Jégou and Gang Hua, and the tutorials by Jacob Verbeek and Rita Cucchiara. Thanks for the great job. The coordination with the subsequent ACM Multimedia offered an opportunity to expand the tutorials with an additional invited session, offered by the University of Amsterdam and organized together with the help of ACM Multimedia.

Of the many people who worked hard as local organizers, we would like to single out Martine de Wit of the UvA Conference Office, who delicately and efficiently organized the main body. Also the local organizers Hamdi Dibeklioglu, Efstratios Gavves, Jan van Gemert, Thomas Mensink, and Mihir Jain had their hands full. As a venue, we chose the Royal Theatre Carré located on the canals of the Amstel River in downtown Amsterdam. Space in Amsterdam is sparse, so it was a little tighter than usual. The university lent us their downtown campuses for the tutorials and the workshops. A relatively new thing was the industry and the sponsors for which Ronald Poppe and Peter de With did a great job, while Andy Bagdanov and John Schavemaker arranged the demos. Michael Wilkinson took care to make Yom Kippur as comfortable as possible for those for whom it is an important day. We thank Marc Pollefeys, Alberto del Bimbo, and Virginie Mes for their advice and help behind the scenes. We thank all the anonymous volunteers for their hard and precise work. We also thank our generous sponsors. Their support is an essential part of the program. It is good to see such a level of industrial interest in what our community is doing!

Amsterdam does not need any introduction. Please emerge yourself but do not drown in it, have a nice time.

October 2016

Theo Gevers
Arnold Smeulders

Preface

It is our great pleasure to present the workshop proceedings of the 14th European Conference on Computer Vision, which was held during October 8–16, 2016, in Amsterdam, The Netherlands. We were delighted that the main conference of ECCV 2016 was accompanied by 26 workshops. The workshop proceedings are presented in multiple Springer LNCS volumes.

This year, the 2016 ACM International Conference on Multimedia was collocated with ECCV 2016. As a synergistic arrangement, four out of the 26 ECCV workshops, whose topics are of interest to both the computer vision and multimedia communities, were held together with selected 2016 ACM Multimedia workshops.

We received 44 workshop proposals on a broad set of topics related to computer vision. The high quality of the proposals made the selection process rather difficult. Owing to space limitation, 27 proposals were accepted, among which two proposals were merged to form a single workshop due to overlapping themes.

The final 26 workshops complemented the main conference program well. The workshop topics present a good orchestration of new trends and traditional issues, as well as fundamental technologies and novel applications. We would like to thank all the workshop organizers for their unreserved efforts to make the workshop sessions a great success.

October 2016

Hervé Jégou
Gang Hua

Organization

General Chairs

Theo Gevers   University of Amsterdam, The Netherlands
Arnold Smeulders   University of Amsterdam, The Netherlands

Program Committee Co-chairs

Bastian Leibe   RWTH Aachen, Germany
Jiri Matas   Czech Technical University, Czech Republic
Nicu Sebe   University of Trento, Italy
Max Welling   University of Amsterdam, The Netherlands

Honorary Chair

Jan Koenderink   Delft University of Technology, The Netherlands
     and KU Leuven, Belgium

Advisory Program Chair

Luc van Gool   ETH Zurich, Switzerland

Advisory Workshop Chair

Josef Kittler   University of Surrey, UK

Advisory Conference Chair

Alberto del Bimbo   University of Florence, Italy

Local Arrangements Chairs

Hamdi Dibeklioglu   Delft University of Technology, The Netherlands
Efstratios Gavves   University of Amsterdam, The Netherlands
Jan van Gemert   Delft University of Technology, The Netherlands
Thomas Mensink   University of Amsterdam, The Netherlands
Michael Wilkinson   University of Groningen, The Netherlands

Workshop Chairs

Hervé Jégou	Facebook AI Research, USA
Gang Hua	Microsoft Research Asia, China

Tutorial Chairs

Jacob Verbeek	Inria Grenoble, France
Rita Cucchiara	University of Modena and Reggio Emilia, Italy

Poster Chairs

Jasper Uijlings	University of Edinburgh, UK
Roberto Valenti	Sightcorp, The Netherlands

Publication Chairs

Albert Ali Salah	Boğaziçi University, Turkey
Robby T. Tan	Yale-NUS College and National University of Singapore, Singapore

Video Chair

Mihir Jain	University of Amsterdam, The Netherlands

Demo Chairs

John Schavemaker	Twnkls, The Netherlands
Andy Bagdanov	University of Florence, Italy

Social Media Chair

Efstratios Gavves	University of Amsterdam, The Netherlands

Industrial Liaison Chairs

Ronald Poppe	Utrecht University, The Netherlands
Peter de With	Eindhoven University of Technology, The Netherlands

Conference Coordinator, Accommodation, and Finance

Conference Office

Martine de Wit	University of Amsterdam, The Netherlands
Melanie Venverloo	University of Amsterdam, The Netherlands
Niels Klein	University of Amsterdam, The Netherlands

Workshop Organizers

W01 — Datasets and Performance Analysis in Early Vision

Michael Goesele	TU Darmstadt, Germany
Bernd Jähne	Heidelberg University, Germany
Katrin Honauer	Heidelberg University, Germany
Michael Waechter	TU Darmstadt, Germany

W02 — Visual Analysis of Sketches

Yi-Zhe Song	Queen Mary University of London, UK
John Collomosse	University of Surrey, UK
Metin Sezgin	Koç University, Turkey
James Z. Wang	The Pennsylvania State University, USA

W03 — Biological and Artificial Vision

Kandan Ramakrishnan	University of Amsterdam, The Netherlands
Radoslaw M. Cichy	Free University Berlin, Germany
Sennay Ghebreab	University of Amsterdam, The Netherlands
H. Steven Scholte	University of Amsterdam, The Netherlands
Arnold W.M. Smeulders	University of Amsterdam, The Netherlands

W04 — Brave New Ideas For Motion Representations

Efstratios Gavves	University of Amsterdam, The Netherlands
Basura Fernando	The Australian National University, Australia
Jan van Gemert	Delft University of Technology, The Netherlands

W05 — Joint ImageNet and MS COCO Visual Recognition Challenge

Wei Liu	The University of North Carolina at Chapel Hill, USA
Genevieve Patterson	Brown University, USA
M. Ronchi	California Institute of Technology, USA
Yin Cui	Cornell Tech, USA
Tsung-Yi Lin	Cornell Tech, USA
Larry Zitnick	Facebook AI Research, USA
Piotr Dollár	Facebook AI Research, USA
Olga Russakovsky	Carnegie Mellon University, USA
Jia Deng	University of Michigan, USA
Fei–Fei Li	Stanford University, USA
Alexander C. Berg	The University of North Carolina at Chapel Hill, USA

W06 — Geometry Meets Deep Learning

Emanuele Rodolà	Università della Svizzera Italiana, Switzerland
Jonathan Masci	Università della Svizzera Italiana, Switzerland
Pierre Vandergheynst	Ecole Polytechnique Fédérale de Lausanne, Switzerland

Sanja Fidler   University of Toronto, Canada
Xiaowei Zhou   University of Pennsylvania, USA
Kostas Daniilidis   University of Pennsylvania, USA

W07 — Action and Anticipation for Visual Learning

Dinesh Jayaraman   University of Texas at Austin, USA
Kristen Grauman   University of Texas at Austin, USA
Sergey Levine   University of Washington, USA

W08 — Computer Vision for Road Scene Understanding and Autonomous Driving

Jose Alvarez   NICTA, Australia
Mathieu Salzmann   Ecole Polytechnique Fédérale de Lausanne,
                                Switzerland
Lars Petersson   NICTA, Australia
Fredrik Kahl   Chalmers University of Technology, Sweden
Bart Nabbe   Faraday Future, USA

W09 — Challenge on Automatic Personality Analysis

Sergio Escalera   Computer Vision Center (UAB) and University
                                of Barcelona, Spain
Xavier Baró   Universitat Oberta de Catalunya and Computer Vision
                                Center (UAB), Spain
Isabelle Guyon   Université Paris-Saclay, France, and ChaLearn, USA
Hugo Jair Escalante   INAOE, Mexico
Víctor Ponce López   Computer Vision Center (UAB) and University
                                of Barcelona, Spain

W10 — BioImage Computing

Patrick Bouthemy   Inria Research Institute, Switzerland
Fred Hamprecht   Heidelberg University, Germany
Erik Meijering   Erasmus University Medical Center, The Netherlands
Thierry Pécot   Inria, France
Pietro Perona   California Institute of Technology, USA
Carsten Rother   TU Dresden, Germany

W11 — Benchmarking Multi-Target Tracking: MOTChallenge

Laura Leal-Taixé   TU Munich, Germany
Anton Milan   University of Adelaide, Australia
Konrad Schindler   ETH Zürich, Switzerland
Daniel Cremers   TU Munich, Germany
Ian Reid   University of Adelaide, Australia
Stefan Roth   TU Darmstadt, Germany

W12 — Assistive Computer Vision and Robotics

Giovanni Maria Farinella	University of Catania, Italy
Marco Leo	CNR – Institute of Applied Sciences and Intelligent Systems, Italy
Gerard G. Medioni	University of Southern California, USA
Mohan Trivedi	University of California, San Diego, USA

W13 — Transferring and Adapting Source Knowledge in Computer Vision

Wen Li	ETH Zürich, Switzerland
Tatiana Tommasi	University of North Carolina at Chapel Hill, USA
Francesco Orabona	Yahoo Research, NY, USA
David Vázquez	CVC and Universitat Autònoma de Barcelona, Spain
Antonio M. López	CVC and Universitat Autònoma de Barcelona, Spain
Jiaolong Xu	CVC and Universitat Autònoma de Barcelona, Spain
Hugo Larochelle	Twitter Cortex, USA

W14 — Recovering 6D Object Pose

Tae-Kyun Kim	Imperial College London, UK
Jiri Matas	Czech Technical University, Czech Republic
Vincent Lepetit	Technical University Graz, Germany
Carsten Rother	Technical University Dresden, Germany
Ales Leonardis	University of Birmingham, UK
Krzysztof Wallas	Poznan University of Technology, Poland
Carsten Steger	MVTec GmbH, Germany
Rigas Kouskouridas	Imperial College London, UK

W15 — Robust Reading

Dimosthenis Karatzas	CVC and Universitat Autònoma de Barcelona, Spain
Masakazu Iwamura	Osaka Prefecture University, Japan
Jiri Matas	Czech Technical University, Czech Republic
Pramod Sankar Kompalli	Flipkart.com, India
Faisal Shafait	National University of Sciences and Technology, Pakistan

W16 — 3D Face Alignment in the Wild and Challenge

Jeffrey Cohn	Carnegie Mellon University and University of Pittsburgh, USA
Laszlo Jeni	Carnegie Mellon University, USA
Nicu Sebe	University of Trento, Italy
Sergey Tulyakov	University of Trento, Italy
Lijun Yin	Binghamton University, USA

W17 — Egocentric Perception, Interaction, and Computing

Giuseppe Serra   University of Modena and Reggio Emilia, Italy
Rita Cucchiara   University of Modena and Reggio Emilia, Italy
Walterio Mayol-Cuevas   University of Bristol, UK
Andreas Bulling   Max Planck Institute for Informatics, Germany
Dima Damen   University of Bristol, UK

W18 — Local Features: State of the Art, Open Problems, and Performance Evaluation

Jiri Matas   Czech Technical University, Czech Republic
Krystian Mikolajczyk   Imperial College London, UK
Tinne Tuytelaars   KU Leuven, Belgium
Andrea Vedaldi   University of Oxford, UK
Vassileios Balntas   Imperial College London, UK
Karel Lenc   University of Oxford, UK

W19 — Crowd Understanding

François Brémond   Inria Sophia Antipolis, France
Vít Líbal   Honeywell ACS Global Labs Prague, Czech Republic
Andrea Cavallaro   Queen Mary University of London, UK
Tomas Pajdla   Czech Technical University, Czech Republic
Petr Palatka   Neovision, Czech Republic
Jana Trojanova   Honeywell ACS Global Labs Prague, Czech Republic

W20 — Video Segmentation

Thomas Brox   University of Freiburg, Germany
Katerina Fragkiadaki   Google Research, USA
Fabio Galasso   OSRAM GmbH, Germany
Fuxin Li   Oregon State University, USA
James M. Rehg   Georgia Institute of Technology, USA
Bernt Schiele   Max Planck Institute Informatics and Saarland
                             University, Germany
Michael Ying Yang   University of Twente, The Netherlands

W21 — The Visual Object Tracking Challenge Workshop

Matej Kristan   University of Ljubljana, Slovenia
Aleš Leonardis   University of Birmingham, UK
Jiri Matas   Czech Technical University in Prague, Czech Republic
Michael Felsberg   Linköping University, Sweden
Roman Pflugfelder   Austrian Institute of Technology, Austria

W22 — Web-Scale Vision and Social Media

Lamberto Ballan	Stanford University, USA
Marco Bertini	University of Florence, Italy
Thomas Mensink	University of Amsterdam, The Netherlands

W23 — Computer Vision for Audio Visual Media

Jean-Charles Bazin	Disney Research, USA
Zhengyou Zhang	Microsoft Research, USA
Wilmot Li	Adobe Research, USA

W24 — Computer Vision for Art Analysis

Joao Paulo Costeira	Instituto Superior Técnico, Portugal
Gustavo Carneiro	University of Adelaide, Australia
Alessio Del Bue	Istituto Italiano di Tecnologia (IIT), Italy
Ahmed Elgammal	Rutgers University, USA
Peter Hall	University of Bath, UK
Ann-Sophie Lehmann	University of Groningen, The Netherlands
Hans Brandhorst	Iconclass and Arkyves, The Netherlands
Emily L. Spratt	Princeton University, USA

W25 — Virtual/Augmented Reality for Visual Artificial Intelligence

Antonio M. López	CVC and Universitat Autònoma de Barcelona, Spain
Adrien Gaidon	Xerox Research Center Europe (XRCE), France
German Ros	CVC and Universitat Autònoma de Barcelona, Spain
Eleonora Vig	German Aerospace Center (DLR), Germany
David Vázquez	CVC and Universitat Autònoma de Barcelona, Spain
Hao Su	Stanford University, USA
Florent Perronnin	Facebook AI Research (FAIR), France

W26 — Joint Workshop on Storytelling with Images and Videos and Large-Scale Movie Description and Understanding Challenge

Gunhee Kim	Seoul National University, South Korea
Leonid Sigal	Disney Research Pittsburgh, USA
Kristen Grauman	University of Texas at Austin, USA
Tamara Berg	University of North Carolina at Chapel Hill, USA
Anna Rohrbach	Max Planck Institute for Informatics, Germany
Atousa Torabi	Disney Research Pittsburgh, USA
Tegan Maharaj	École Polytechnique de Montréal, Canada
Marcus Rohrbach	University of California, Berkeley, USA
Christopher Pal	École Polytechnique de Montréal, Canada
Aaron Courville	Université de Montréal, Canada
Bernt Schiele	Max Planck Institute for Informatics, Germany

Contents – Part III

W09 – ChaLearn Looking at People Workshop on Apparent Personality Analysis and First Impressions Challenge

W13 – Transferring and Adapting Source Knowledge in Computer Vision

W14 – Recovering 6D Object Pose

W18 – Local Features: State of the Art, Open Problems and Performance Evaluation

W20 – The Second International Workshop on Video Segmentation

W25 – 1st International Workshop on Virtual/Augmented Reality for Visual Artificial Intelligence (VARVAI)

W04 – Brave New Ideas For Motion Representations (Continued)

Preface

In the late years Deep Learning has been a great force of change on most Computer Vision and Multimedia tasks. In video analysis problems, however, such as action recognition and detection, motion analysis and tracking, shallow architectures remain surprisingly competitive. Assuming that the recently proposed video datasets are large enough for training deep networks for video, another likely culprit for this standstill could be the capacity of the existing deep models. More specifically, the existing deep networks for video analysis might not be sophisticated enough to address the complexity of motion information. This makes sense, as videos introduce an exponential complexity as compared to static images. Unfortunately, state-of-the-art motion representation models are extensions of existing image representations rather than motion dedicated ones. Brave, new and motion-specific representations are likely to be needed for a breakthrough in video analysis.

Brave new ideas require novel insights. For this reason at this workshop we have confirmed the availability of several experts from different fields that relate to the understanding and modelling of motion and sequence data: (a) from Computer Vision Dr. I. Laptev, Research Director at INRIA Paris-Rocquencourt and a leading expert in action recognition, (b) from Machine Learning Prof. M. Welling at the University of Amsterdam, a leading expert in variational methods and ayesian modelling, (c) from Neuroscience, Dr. Aman Saleem, Senior Researcher at the University College London, working on the integration of motion and locomotion in the visual cortex of mammals.

Attempting to publish a wild, but intriguing idea in Computer Vision, Machine Learning and Multimedia conferences can be daunting, resulting in slow progress. On one hand a controversial new idea might be rejected by top-tier conferences, without the right experimental justification. On the other hand, researchers may not want to reveal a smart idea too soon in the fear of not receiving the right credit. To make amends with these two factors, the workshop will admit 4-page papers describing novel, previously unseen ideas without necessarily requiring exhaustive quantitative justifications. Moreover, to make sure proper accreditation is given in the future, the workshop relied on a successful open-review process, where all submitted papers were first uploaded to arXiv. In total, there were 13 high-quality submissions, all accepted, several of which proposed interesting new ideas.

October 2016

ECCV BNMW 2016
Basura Fernando
Efstratios Gavves
Jan van Gemert
Program Chairs

Back to Basics: Unsupervised Learning of Optical Flow via Brightness Constancy and Motion Smoothness

Jason J. Yu$^{(\boxtimes)}$, Adam W. Harley, and Konstantinos G. Derpanis

Department of Computer Science, Ryerson University, Toronto, Canada
{jjyu,aharley,kosta}@scs.ryerson.ca

Abstract. Recently, convolutional networks (convnets) have proven useful for predicting optical flow. Much of this success is predicated on the availability of large datasets that require expensive and involved data acquisition and laborious labeling. To bypass these challenges, we propose an unsupervised approach (i.e., without leveraging groundtruth flow) to train a convnet end-to-end for predicting optical flow between two images. We use a loss function that combines a data term that measures photometric constancy over time with a spatial term that models the expected variation of flow across the image. Together these losses form a proxy measure for losses based on the groundtruth flow. Empirically, we show that a strong convnet baseline trained with the proposed unsupervised approach outperforms the same network trained with supervision on the KITTI dataset.

1 Introduction

Visual motion estimation is a core research area of computer vision. Most prominent has been the recovery of the apparent motion of image brightness patterns, i.e., optical flow. Much of this work has centred on extracting the pixelwise velocities between two temporal images within a variational framework [7,13].

Recently, convolutional networks (convnets) have proven useful for a variety of per-pixel prediction tasks, including optical flow [3]. Convnets are high-capacity models that approximate the complex, non-linear transformation between input imagery and the output. Success with convnets has relied almost exclusively on fully-supervised schemes, where the target value (i.e., the label) is provided during training. This is problematic for learning optical flow because directly obtaining the motion field groundtruth from real scenes — the quantity that optical flow attempts to approximate — is not possible.

In this paper, we propose an end-to-end unsupervised approach to train a convnet for predicting optical flow between two images based on a standard variational loss. Rather than rely on imagery as well as the corresponding groundtruth flow for training, we use the images alone. In particular, we use a loss function that combines a data term that measures photometric constancy over time with a spatial term that models the expected variation of flow across the image. The photometric

© Springer International Publishing Switzerland 2016
G. Hua and H. Jégou (Eds.): ECCV 2016 Workshops, Part III, LNCS 9915, pp. 3–10, 2016.
DOI: 10.1007/978-3-319-49409-8_1

loss measures the difference between the first input image and the (inverse) warped subsequent image based on the predicted optical flow by the network. The smoothness loss measures the difference between spatially neighbouring flow predictions. Together, these two losses form a proxy for losses based on the groundtruth flow.

Recovering optical flow between two frames is a well studied problem, with much previous work founded on variational formulations [2,7,12,13]. Our loss is similar to the objective functions proposed for two-frame motion estimation; however, rather than optimize the velocity map between input frames, we use it to optimize the convnet weights over the training set of imagery.

Several recent works [3,10] have proposed convnets that learn the mapping between input image frames and the corresponding flow. Each of these approaches is presented in a supervised setting, where images and their corresponding groundtruth flows are provided. This setting assumes the availability of a large, annotated dataset. Existing flow datasets (e.g., KITTI [6]) are too small to support training accurate networks. Computer generated scenes and their corresponding flow [3,4,10] provide a means to address this issue. Although some recent efforts have attempted to semi-automate the data creation process [4], creating large, diverse imagery remains laborious. Another possibility is using the output of an existing optical flow estimator to provide the groundtruth [14]. This training approach may result in learning both correct flow prediction and the failure aspects of the flow estimator used for training. In this work, we avoid these drawbacks by learning flow in an unsupervised manner, using only the input imagery.

Concurrent work has proposed unsupervised methods to circumvent the need of vasts amounts of labeled data for training. A spatiotemporal video autoencoder [11] was introduced that incorporates a long short-term memory (LSTM) architecture for unsupervised flow and image frame prediction. Here, we present a simpler feedforward convnet model targeting flow prediction alone. Most closely related to the current paper is recent work that proposed a convnet for depth estimation trained in an unsupervised manner [5]. In a similar fashion to the proposed approach, a photometric loss warps one image to another, and a smoothness loss term is used to bias the predictor towards smooth depth estimates. Unlike the current work, the manner in which the photometric loss is handled (via a linear Taylor series approximation) precludes end-to-end learning.

Contributions. In the light of previous research, we make the following contributions. First, we present an unsupervised approach to training a convnet in an end-to-end manner for predicting optical flow between two images. The limited but valuable groundtruth flow is reserved for fine-tuning the network and cross-validating its parameters. Second, we demonstrate empirically that a strong convnet baseline trained with our unsupervised approach outperforms the same network trained with supervision on KITTI, where insufficient groundtruth flow is available for training.

2   Technical Approach

Given an RGB image pair as input, $\mathbf{X} \in \mathbb{R}^{H \times W \times 6}$, our objective is to learn a non-linear mapping (approximated by a convnet) to the corresponding optical flow, $\mathbf{Y} \in \mathbb{R}^{H \times W \times 2}$, where H and W denote the image height and width, respectively. In Sect. 2.1, we outline our unsupervised loss. Section 2.2 provides details on how the unsupervised loss is integrated with a reference convnet architecture.

2.1   Unsupervised Loss

The training set is comprised of pairs of temporally consecutive images, $\{I(x, y, t), I(x, y, t+1)\}$. Unlike prior work, we do not assume access to the corresponding velocity pixel labels, cf. [3]. Instead, we return to traditional means for scoring a given solution, via a loss that combines a photometric loss between the first image and the warped second image, and a loss related to the smoothness of the velocity field prediction [7]:

$$\mathcal{L}(\mathbf{u}, \mathbf{v}; I(x, y, t), I(x, y, t+1)) =$$
$$\ell_{\text{photometric}}(\mathbf{u}, \mathbf{v}; I(x, y, t), I(x, y, t+1)) +$$
$$\lambda \ell_{\text{smoothness}}(\mathbf{u}, \mathbf{v}), \tag{1}$$

where $\mathbf{u}, \mathbf{v} \in \mathbb{R}^{H \times W}$ are the horizontal and vertical components of the predicted flow field, respectively, and λ is a regularization parameter that weighs the relative importance of smoothness of the predicted flow. Note, the photometric loss can be replaced or augmented with other measures, such as the image gradient constancy [2].

Given the predicted flow, the photometric loss is computed as the difference between the first image and the backward/inverse warped second image:

$$\ell_{\text{photometric}}(\mathbf{u}, \mathbf{v}; I(x, y, t), I(x, y, t+1)) = \tag{2}$$
$$\sum_{i,j} \rho_D(I(i, j, t) - I(i + u_{i,j}, j + v_{i,j}, t+1)),$$

where ρ_D is the data penalty function. We consider the robust generalized Charbonnier penalty function $\rho(x) = (x^2 + \epsilon^2)^\alpha$ to mitigate the effects of outliers [13].

To compute the non-rigid backward warp, we use the recently proposed spatial transformer module [8]. This allows the learning to be performed with standard backpropagation in an end-to-end fashion. In brief, the spatial transformer can be described as two parts that work in sequence: (i) a sampling grid generator and (ii) a differentiable image sampler. (The spatial transformer localization step is not needed here as flow prediction, (u, v), provides the necessary parameters for the mapping between image points across frames.) The sampling grid is generated by the following pointwise transformation:

$$\begin{pmatrix} x_2 \\ y_2 \end{pmatrix} = W_{(u,v)} \begin{pmatrix} x_1 \\ y_1 \end{pmatrix} = \begin{pmatrix} x_1 + u \\ y_1 + v \end{pmatrix}, \tag{3}$$

where (x_1, y_1) are the coordinates in the first image and (x_2, y_2) are the sampling coordinates in the second image. The bilinear sampling step can be written in the following (sub-)differentiable form:

$$I_{\text{warp}}(x_1, y_1, t+1) =$$
$$\sum_j^H \sum_i^W I(i, j, t+1) M(1 - |x_2 - i|) M(1 - |y_2 - j|), \tag{4}$$

where $M(\cdot) = \max(0, \cdot)$. For details about backpropagating through this module, see [8].

Regions with insufficient image structure support multiple equally scoring velocities, e.g., the aperture problem. To address this ambiguity, we introduce a standard robust (piecewise) smoothness loss:

$$\ell_{\text{smoothness}}(\mathbf{u}, \mathbf{v}) =$$
$$\sum_j^H \sum_i^W [\rho_S(u_{i,j} - u_{i+1,j}) + \rho_S(u_{i,j} - u_{i,j+1})$$
$$+ \rho_S(v_{i,j} - v_{i+1,j}) + \rho_S(v_{i,j} - v_{i,j+1})], \tag{5}$$

where $\rho_S(\cdot)$ is the (spatial) smoothness penalty function realized by the generalized Charbonnier function.

A summary of our proposed unsupervised approach for flow prediction is provided in Fig. 1.

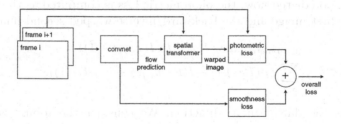

Fig. 1. Overview of our unsupervised approach.

2.2 Network Architecture

We use "FlowNet Simple" [3] as a reference network. This architecture consists of a contractive part followed by an expanding part. The contractive part takes as input two RGB images stacked together, and processes them with a cascade of strided convolution layers. The expanding part implements a "skip-layer" architecture that combines information from various levels of the contractive part with "upconvolving" layers to iteratively refine the coarse flow predictions. The FlowNet Simple architecture is illustrated in Fig. 2.

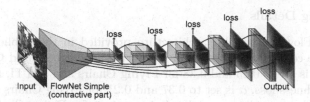

Fig. 2. "FlowNet Simple" architecture. Two images are taken as input, and an optical flow prediction is generated using a multi-stage refinement process. Feature maps from the contractive part, as well as intermediate flow predictions, are used in the "upconvolutional" part.

In this work, we use a loss comprised of a final loss and several intermediate losses placed at various stages of the expansionary part. The intermediate losses are meant to guide earlier layers more directly towards the final objective [9]. In FlowNet, the endpoint error (EPE), a standard error measure for optical flow, is used as the supervised training loss. As a proxy to per-pixel groundtruth flow, we replace the EPE with the proposed unsupervised loss, (1).

3   Empirical Evaluation

3.1   Datasets

Flying Chairs. This synthetic dataset is realized by applying affine mappings to publicly available colour images and a rendered set of 3D chair models. The dataset contains 22,232 training and 640 test image pairs with groundtruth flow. To cross-validate the hyper-parameters and monitor for overfitting in learning, we set aside 2,000 image pairs from the training set. We use both photometric and geometric augmentations to avoid overfitting. The photometric augmentations are comprised of additive Gaussian noise applied to each image, contrast, multiplicative colour changes to the RGB channels, gamma and additive brightness. The geometric transformations are comprised of 2D translations, left-right flipping, rotations and scalings.

KITTI 2012. This dataset consists of images collected on a driving platform. There are 194 and 195 training and testing image pairs, respectively, with sparse groundtruth flow. The training set is used for cross-validation and to monitor the learning progress. For training, we use the raw KITTI data from the city, residential and road classes, where groundtruth flow is unavailable. To avoid training on related testing imagery, we remove all raw images that are visually similar with the testing ones, including their temporal neighbours ±20 frames. The (curated) raw data is comprised of 82,958 image pairs. We include both photometric and geometric augmentations. We use the same type of photometric augmentations as applied to Flying Chairs. The geometric transformations consist of left-right flipping and scalings. We also use a small relative translation.

3.2   Training Details

We use the "FlowNet Simple" architecture provided in the publicly available FlowNet Caffe code [1]. For the photometric loss, the generalized Charbonnier parameter, α, is set to 0.25 and 0.38 for Flying Chairs and KITTI, respectively. For the smoothness loss, α is set to 0.37 and 0.21 for Flying Chairs and KITTI, respectively. The smoothness weight, λ, is set to 1 for Flying Chairs and 0.53 for KITTI. We use Adam as the optimization method, where its parameters $\beta_1 = 0.9$ and $\beta_2 = 0.999$. The initial learning rate is set to 1.6e–5 for Flying Chairs and 1.0e–5 for KITTI and we divide it by half every 100,000 iterations.

Fig. 3. KITTI example. (top-to-bottom) Input image frames overlaid, groundtruth flow, and predicted flow from unsupervised network overlaid on the first input image.

Table 1. Average endpoint error (EPE) flow results. The reported EPEs for supervised FlowNet are the best results of the FlowNet Simple architecture [3] without variational smoothing post-processing. "Avg. All" and "Avg. NOC" refer to the EPE taken over all the labeled pixels and all non-occluded labeled pixels, respectively.

Approach	Chairs	KITTI			
		Avg. All		Avg. NOC	
	Test	Train	Test	Train	Test
EpicFlow [12]	2.9	3.5	3.8	1.8	1.5
DeepFlow [15]	3.5	4.6	5.8	2.0	1.5
LDOF [2]	3.5	13.7	12.4	5.0	5.6
FlowNet [3]	2.7	7.5	9.1	5.3	5.0
FlowNet (ours)	5.3	11.3	9.9	4.3	4.6

The batch size is set to four image pairs. In total, we train using 600,000 iterations for Flying Chairs and 400,000 for KITTI. In initial tests, we noticed that the unsupervised approach had difficulties in regions that were highly saturated or very dark. Adding photometric augmentation compounds this issue by making these regions even less discriminable. To address this issue, we pass the geometrically augmented images directly to the photometric loss prior to photometric augmentation. Further, we apply a local 9×9 response normalization to the geometrically augmented images to ameliorate multiplicative lighting factors.

3.3 Results

Table 1 provides a summary of results. As expected, FlowNet trained with the groundtruth flow on Flying Chairs outperforms the unsupervised one. Note, however, the scenario where sufficient dense groundtruth is available is generally unrealistic with real imagery. Conversely, KITTI exemplifies an automative scenario, where abundant dense groundtruth flow with real images is unavailable. To sidestep this issue, previous work [3] used synthetic data as a proxy for supervised training. On the non-occluded (NOC) metric, the unsupervised approach improves upon the supervised one [3] on the KITTI training set. This improvement persists on the official test set. Considering all pixels (i.e., occluded and non-occluded) the proposed approach remains competitive to the supervised one. Figure 3 shows an example flow prediction result on KITTI. While the performance of the unsupervised approach lags behind the state-of-the-art, it operates in realtime with a testing runtime of 0.03 s on an NVIDIA GTX 1080 GPU.

4 Discussion and Summary

We presented an end-to-end unsupervised approach to training convnets for optical flow prediction. We showed that the proposed unsupervised training approach yields competitive and even superior performance to a supervised one. This opens up avenues for further improvement by leveraging the vast amounts of video that can easily be captured with commodity cameras taken in the domain of interest, such as automotive applications. Furthermore, this is a general learning framework that can be extended in a variety of ways via more sophisticated losses to enhance convnet-based mappings between temporal input imagery and flow.

References

1. FlowNet Caffe code (v1.0). http://lmb.informatik.uni-freiburg.de/resources/software.php
2. Brox, T., Malik, J.: Large displacement optical flow: descriptor matching in variational motion estimation. PAMI **33**(3), 500–513 (2011)
3. Dosovitskiy, A., Fischer, P., Ilg, E., Häusser, P., Hazirbas, C., Golkov, V., van der Smagt, P., Cremers, D., Brox, T.: FlowNet: learning optical flow with convolutional networks. In ICCV, pp. 2758–2766 (2015)

4. Gaidon, A., Wang, Q., Cabon, Y., Vig, E.: Virtual worlds as proxy for multi-object tracking analysis. In: CVPR (2016)
5. Garg, R., Vijay Kumar, B.G., Carneiro, G., Reid, I.: Unsupervised CNN for Single View Depth Estimation: Geometry to the Rescue. In: Leibe, B., Matas, J., Sebe, N., Welling, M. (eds.) ECCV 2016. LNCS, vol. 9912, pp. 740–756. Springer, Heidelberg (2016). doi:10.1007/978-3-319-46484-8_45
6. Geiger, A., Lenz, P., Stiller, C., Urtasun, R.: Vision meets robotics: the KITTI dataset. IJRR **32**, 1231–1237 (2013)
7. Horn, B.K.P., Schunck, B.G.: Determining optical flow. AI **17**(1–3), 185–203 (1981)
8. Jaderberg, M., Simonyan, K., Zisserman, A., Kavukcuoglu, K.: Spatial transformer networks. In: NIPS (2015)
9. Lee, C., Xie, S., Gallagher, P., Zhang, Z., Tu, Z.: Deeply-supervised nets. In: AISTATS (2015)
10. Mayer, N., Ilg, E., Hausser, P., Fischer, P., Cremers, D., Dosovitskiy, A., Brox, T.: A large dataset to train convolutional networks for disparity, optical flow, and scene flow estimation. In: CVPR (2016)
11. Patraucean, V., Handa, A., Cipolla, R.: Spatio-temporal video autoencoder with differentiable memory. CoRR, abs/1511.06309 (2015)
12. Revaud, J., Weinzaepfel, P., Harchaoui, Z., Schmid, C.: EpicFlow: edge-preserving interpolation of correspondences for optical flow. In: CVPR (2015)
13. Sun, D.Q., Roth, S., Black, M.J.: A quantitative analysis of current practices in optical flow estimation and the principles behind them. IJCV **106**(2), 115–137 (2014)
14. Tran, D., Bourdev, L.D., Fergus, R., Torresani, L., Paluri, M.: Deep end2end voxel2voxel prediction. In: Workshop on DeepVision (2016)
15. Weinzaepfel, P., Revaud, J., Harchaoui, Z., Schmid, C.: DeepFlow: large displacement optical flow with deep matching. In: ICCV (2013)

Human Action Recognition Without Human

Yun He, Soma Shirakabe, Yutaka Satoh, and Hirokatsu Kataoka[✉]

National Institute of Advanced Industrial Science and Technology (AIST),
Tsukuba, Ibaraki, Japan
{yun.he,shirakabe-s,yu.satou,hirokatsu.kataoka}@aist.go.jp

Abstract. The objective of this paper is to evaluate "human action recognition without human". Motion representation is frequently discussed in human action recognition. We have examined several sophisticated options, such as dense trajectories (DT) and the two-stream convolutional neural network (CNN). However, some features from the background could be too strong, as shown in some recent studies on human action recognition. Therefore, we considered whether a background sequence alone can classify human actions in current large-scale action datasets (e.g., UCF101).

In this paper, we propose a novel concept for human action analysis that is named "human action recognition without human". An experiment clearly shows the effect of a background sequence for understanding an action label.

1 Introduction

An effective motion representation is in demand for action recognition, event recognition, and video understanding. In human action recognition especially, several survey papers have been published in the last two decades [1,2,10,11]. We have investigated a more reliable and faster algorithm to put action recognition into practice. The target applications of action recognition can be easily imagined, for example, surveillance, robotics, augmented reality, and intelligent surgery. However, current vision-based video representations focus on the media to improve the recognition rate on UCF101 [16], HMDB51 [7], and ActivityNet [4].

Here we categorize action recognition into two types: direct and contextual approaches.

The direct approach, which is motion representation, has been studied in action recognition. Since Laptev *et al.* proposed space-time interest points (STIP) [8,9], xyt keypoint acquisition has been well established in temporal representation. STIP is significantly improved with densely connected keypoints in the dense trajectories approach (DT) [17,18]. The DT is a more natural approach for understanding whole body motions because it uses a large amount of tracked keypoints. Recently, two-stream CNN has been applied as a representative method in action recognition [15]. The two-stream convolutional neural network (CNN) uses spatial and temporal streams to extract appearance and motion

© Springer International Publishing Switzerland 2016
G. Hua and H. Jégou (Eds.): ECCV 2016 Workshops, Part III, LNCS 9915, pp. 11–17, 2016.
DOI: 10.1007/978-3-319-49409-8_2

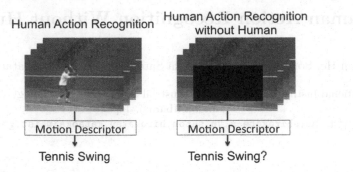

Fig. 1. Human action recognition (left) and human action recognition without human (right): We simply replace the center-around area with a black background in an image sequence. We evaluate the performance rate with only the limited background sequence as a contextual cue.

features from RGB and optical flow input. The classification scores at each stream are fused for evaluating an objective video. Other CNN-based approaches apply a dynamic scene descriptor such as a pooled time series (PoT) [14] and capture sensitive motion with a subtle motion descriptor (SMD) [6].

The contextual approach is focused around the region of a human and can provide an important cue to improve human action recognition. In related work, Jain et al. [5] and Zhou et al. [20] showed that object and scene context aid in the recognition of human actions. Jain et al. carried out an evaluation of how much object usage is needed for action recognition [5]. They combined object information with a classifier score into the improved DT (IDT) plus Fisher vectors (FVs) [12] as a motion feature from a human area. A large number of object labels (15,923 objects), e.g., computer and violin, are corresponded to an output function with AlexNet as an object prior. The response of CNN-based object information must be combined with a motion vector for a richer understanding of human actions. In their evaluation, motion + object vector allow us to obtain a better feature in an image sequence. When using object information, the performance rate rises by +3.9 %, +9.9 %, and 0.5 % on UCF101, the THUMOS14 validation set, and KTH, respectively. According to experiments, the object vector improves recognition accuracy on a large-scale action database. Zhou et al. proposed a combination of a contextual human-object interaction and a motion feature for fine-grained action recognition [20]. Object proposals are captured by using BING [3]. However, some useless proposals are generated around a human area. The pruning of extra regions is executed by referring to dense trajectories around object proposals. The recognition rate can be improved with human-object interaction as a mid-level feature. The mid-level feature records an outstanding rate 72.4 % on the MPII cooking dataset [13], which is known as a fine-grained action database. These two examples are convincing enough to integrate a mid-level feature into a motion vector.

The mid-level feature including objects and backgrounds are enough to describe the situation around human(s).

The conventional approaches have implemented video-based human action recognition from a whole image sequence including a background. However, a curious option appears:

- Human action recognition can be done just by analyzing motion of the background.

To confirm this option, we try to prove the importance of the background on a well-studied dataset [16].

In this paper, we evaluate the effect of the background in human action recognition (see Fig. 1). Our target is to measure a video-based recognition rate with a separated human and background sequence. We employ two-stream CNN [15] as a motion descriptor, and center-around image filtering to blind the human area.

2 Human Action Recognition *without* Human

The flowchart of human action recognition without human is shown in Fig. 2. The recognition framework is based on the very deep two-stream CNN [19]. We only look at the appearance and motion features of the background sequence.

Setting Without a Human (See Fig. 3 Top). In the setting without a human, we calculate the image filtering with a black background as follows:

$$I'(x,y) = I(x,y) * f(x,y) \tag{1}$$

where I' and I show the filtered and input images, respectively, and x, y are pixel elements. Filter f replaces the center-around area with a black background. (The black background is a controversial representation.) The detailed operation is shown at the top of Fig. 3.

Setting with a Human (see Fig. 3 Bottom). We confirm the importance of the human appearance and motion features from an image sequence as follows:

$$\overline{I'}(x,y) = I(x,y) * \overline{f}(x,y) \tag{2}$$

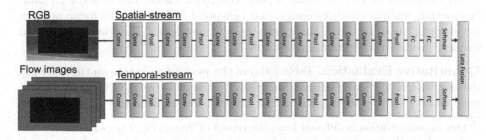

Fig. 2. Very deep two-stream CNN [19] for human action recognition without human.

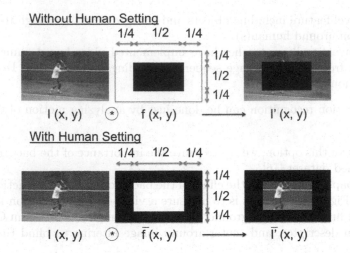

Fig. 3. Image filtering for human action recognition without human.

where $\overline{I'}$ and filter $\overline{f}$ are an inverse image and filter in the setting without a human. The background is eliminated with the inverse filter at the bottom of Fig. 3.

Training of Two-Stream CNN. The learning parameters of the spatial and temporal streams are based on [19]. Our goal is to predict the video label without additional training in the setting without a human (see Fig. 1). By using an original pre-trained model [19], we obtained the following results on UCF101 split 1: 74.86 % (spatial), 80.33 % (temporal), and 84.30 % (two-stream)[1], as shown in Table 1.

3   Experiment

Dataset. We apply the well-studied UCF101 dataset. This large-scale dataset was mainly collected from YouTube videos of sports and musical instrument performance scenes. The recognition task is to predict an action label from a given video. The dataset contains several computer vision difficulties, e.g., camera motion, scaling, posture change, and viewpoint difference. The mean average accuracy is calculated with three training and test splits. Here we calculate an average precision with training/test split 1.

Quantitative Evaluation. Table 2 shows the performance rate on the UCF101 dataset with or without a human. Surprisingly, the two-stream CNN performance was 47.42 % in the setting without a human. We understand that a motion

---

[1] Our implementation is different from the report of Wang [19]. The performance rate depends on the parameter tuning. They reported 79.8 % (spatial), 85.7 % (temporal) and 90.9 % (two-stream) on UCF101 split 1.

Table 1. Performance rate on the UCF101 dataset with baseline two-stream CNN

Stream	% on UCF101 (split 1)
Spatial stream	74.86
Temporal stream	80.33
Two-stream (S+T) [19]	84.30

Table 2. Performance rate of human action recognition with or without a human

With or without a human	Stream	% on UCF101 (split 1)
With human	Spatial stream	51.26
	Temporal stream	40.50
	Two-stream	**56.91**
Without human	Spatial stream	45.33
	Temporal stream	26.80
	Two-stream	**47.42**

recognition approach relies on a background sequence. The spatial stream is +18.53 % better than the temporal stream. Therefore, an appearance tends to classify between backgrounds. Motion features contribute slightly to the background classification; that is, the performance rate is increased +2.09 % with the temporal stream. The two-stream CNN recorded 56.91 % in the with human setting, which is +9.49 % higher than the setting without a human.

Qualitative Dataset Evaluation. Figure 4 shows examples without a human setting on the UCF101 dataset. Where we evaluated partial and complete images without a human (Figs. 4(a) and (b), respectively), the number of partial images without a human was 1,114 in 3,783 videos. The rate was 29.45 % in UCF101 split 1. The complete images without a human were not found on the videos.

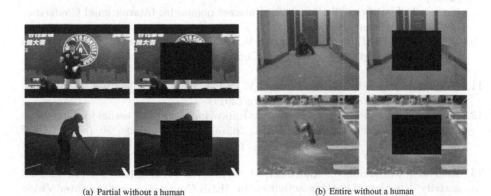

(a) Partial without a human   (b) Entire without a human

Fig. 4. Qualitative evaluation of the setting without a human on the UCF101 dataset.

4   Conclusion

To the best of our knowledge, this is the first study of human action recognition without human. However, we should not have done that kind of thing. The motion representation from a background sequence is effective to classify videos in a human action database. We demonstrated human action recognition in with and without a human settings on the UCF101 dataset. The results show the setting without a human (47.42 %) was close to the setting with a human (56.91 %). We must accept this reality to realize better motion representation.

References

1. Aggarwal, J.K., Cai, Q.: Human motion analysis: a review. Comput. Vis. Image Underst. (CVIU) **73**, 428–440 (1999)
2. Aggarwal, J.K., Ryoo, M.S.: Human activity analysis: a review. ACM Comput. Surv. (2011)
3. Cheng, M.-M., Zhang, Z., Lin, W.-Y., Torr, P.: BING: binarized normed gradients for objectness estimation at 300fps. In: IEEE Conference on Computer Vision and Pattern Recognition (CVPR) (2014)
4. Heilbron, F.C., Escorcia, V., Ghanem, B., Niebles, J.C.: Activitynet: a large-scale video benchmark for human activity understanding. In: IEEE Conference on Computer Vision and Pattern Recognition (CVPR) (2015)
5. Jain, M., van Gemert, J.C., Snoek, C.G.M.: What do 15,000 object categories tell us about classifying and localizing actions? In: IEEE Conference on Computer Vision and Pattern Recognition (CVPR) (2015)
6. Kataoka, H., Miyashita, Y., Hayashi, M., Iwata, K., Satoh, Y.: Recognition of transitional action for short-term action prediction using discriminative temporal CNN feature. In: British Machine Vision Conference (BMVC) (2016)
7. Kuehne, H., Jhuang, H., Garrote, E., Poggio, T., Serre, T.: HMDB: a large video database for human motion recognition. In: International Conference on Computer Vision (ICCV) (2011)
8. Laptev, I.: On space-time interest points. Int. J. Comput. Vis. (IJCV) **64**, 107–123 (2005)
9. Laptev, I., Lindeberg, T.: Space-time interest points. In: International Conference of Computer Vision (ICCV) (2003)
10. Moeslund, T.B., Hilton, A., Kruger, V.: A survey of advances in vision-based human motion capture and analysis. Comput. Vis. Image Underst. (CVIU) **104**, 90–126 (2006)
11. Moeslund, T.B., Hilton, A., Kruger, V., Sigal, L.: Visual Analysis of Humans: Looking at People. Springer, Heidelberg (2011)
12. Perronnin, F., Sánchez, J., Mensink, T.: Improving the Fisher kernel for large-scale image classification. In: Daniilidis, K., Maragos, P., Paragios, N. (eds.) ECCV 2010. LNCS, vol. 6314, pp. 143–156. Springer, Heidelberg (2010). doi:10.1007/978-3-642-15561-1_11
13. Rohrbach, M., Amin, S., Andriluka, M., Schiele, B.: A database for fine grained activity detection of cooking activities. In: IEEE Conference on Computer Vision and Pattern Recognition (CVPR) (2012)

14. Ryoo, M.S., Rothrock, B., Matthies, L.: Pooled motion features for first-person videos. In: IEEE Conference on Computer Vision and Pattern Recognition (CVPR) (2015)
15. Simonyan, K., Zisserman, A.: Two-stream convolutional networks for action recognition. In: Neural Information Processing Systems (NIPS) (2014)
16. Soomro, K., Zamir, A.R., Shah, M.: Ucf101: a dataset of 101 human action classes from videos in the wild. CRCV-TR-12-01 (2012)
17. Wang, H., Klaser, A., Schmid, C.: Dense trajectories and motion boundary descriptors for action recognition. Int. J. Comput. Vis. (IJCV) **103**, 60–79 (2013)
18. Wang, H., Klaser, A., Schmid, C., Cheng-Lin, L.: Action recognition by dense trajectories. In: IEEE Conference on Computer Vision and Pattern Recognition (CVPR) (2011)
19. Wang, L., Xiong, Y., Wang, Z., Qiao, Y.: Towards good practices for very deep two-stream convnets. arXiv pre-print 1507.02159 (2015)
20. Zhou, Y., Ni, B., Hong, R., Wang, M., Tian, Q.: Interaction part mining: a mid-level approach for fine-grained action recognition. In: IEEE Conference on Computer Vision and Pattern Recognition (CVPR) (2015)

Motion Representation with Acceleration Images

Hirokatsu Kataoka[✉], Yun He, Soma Shirakabe, and Yutaka Satoh

National Institute of Advanced Industrial Science and Technology (AIST),
Tsukuba, Ibaraki, Japan
{hirokatsu.kataoka,yun.he,shirakabe-s,yu.satou}@aist.go.jp

Abstract. Information of time differentiation is extremely important cue for a motion representation. We have applied first-order differential velocity from a positional information, moreover we believe that second-order differential acceleration is also a significant feature in a motion representation. However, an acceleration image based on a typical optical flow includes motion noises. We have not employed the acceleration image because the noises are too strong to catch an effective motion feature in an image sequence. On one hand, the recent convolutional neural networks (CNN) are robust against input noises.

In this paper, we employ acceleration-stream in addition to the spatial- and temporal-stream based on the two-stream CNN. We clearly show the effectiveness of adding the acceleration stream to the two-stream CNN.

1   Introduction

Highly discriminative motion representation is needed in the fields of action recognition, event recognition, and video understanding. Space-time interest points (STIP) that capture temporal keypoints are a giant step toward solving visual motion representation. An improvement over STIP is the so-called dense trajectories (DT) proposed by Wang et al. [20]. The simple purpose of DT is to have denser sampling and more various descriptors than STIP. In 2013, DT was improved by three techniques, namely, camera motion estimation with SURF, Fisher vector representation, and detection-based noise canceling [21]. The powerful framework of DT or improved DT (DT/IDT) has been cited in numerous papers as of 2016. However, the success of convolutional neural networks (CNN) cannot be ignored in image-based recognition. We project motion information into images in order to implement the CNN architecture for motion representation. The two-stream CNN is a noteworthy algorithm to capture the temporal features in an image sequence [18]. The integration of spatial and temporal streams allows us to effectively enhance motion representation. We obtain significant knowledge about the spatial information, which helps the temporal feature. The strongest approach introduced is the crosspoint of the IDT and the two-stream CNN. Trajectory-pooled deep-convolutional descriptors (TDD) [22] have achieved the highest performance in several benchmarks, such as UCF101 [19] (91.5 %) and HMDB51 (65.9 %) [11]. A more recent performance was demonstrated in the ActivityNet challenge in conjunction with CVPR2016. At this

G. Hua and H. Jégou (Eds.): ECCV 2016 Workshops, Part III, LNCS 9915, pp. 18–24, 2016.
DOI: 10.1007/978-3-319-49409-8_3

performance, the TDD-based approach surprisingly accomplished a 93.2 % mAP (94.2 % on UCF101 and 69.4 % on HMDB51).

However, the current approaches heavily rely on the two-stream architecture. To improve motion-based features, we must employ the acceleration stream for richer image representation. In physics, acceleration is the change rate of speed with respect to time. Here, acceleration images are able to extract a precise feature from an image sequence.

In this paper, we propose the simple technique of using "acceleration images" to represent a change of a flow image. The acceleration images must be significant because the representation is different from position (RGB) and speed (flow) images. We apply two-stream CNN [18] as the baseline; then, we employ an acceleration stream, in addition to the spatial and the temporal streams. The acceleration images are generated by differential calculations from a sequence of flow images. Although the sparse representation tends to be noisy data (see Fig. 1), automatic feature learning with CNN can significantly pick up a necessary feature in the acceleration images. We carry out experiments on traffic data in the NTSEL dataset [7].

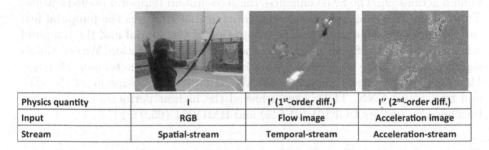

Physics quantity	I	I' (1st-order diff.)	I'' (2nd-order diff.)
Input	RGB	Flow image	Acceleration image
Stream	Spatial-stream	Temporal-stream	Acceleration-stream

Fig. 1. Image representation of RGB (I), flow (I'), and acceleration (I'').

2 Related Work

Space-time interest points (STIP) have been a primary focus in action recognition [13]. In STIP, time t space is added to the x, y spatial domain. Improvements of STIP have been reported in several papers, such as [3,14,15]. However, the significant approach is arguably the dense trajectories approach (DT) [20]. The DT is describes the trajectories that track densely sampled feature points. Descriptors are applied to the densely captured trajectories by histograms of oriented gradients (HOG) [1], histograms of optical flow (HOF) [14], and motion boundary histograms (MBH) [2].

Dense sampling approaches for activity recognition were also proposed in [6,8,21] after the introduction of the first DT. These studies incremented DT, for example, by eliminating extra flow [6] and integrating a higher-order descriptor into the conventional features for fine-grained action recognition [8].

Additionally, Wang *et al.* proposed an IDT [21] by executing camera motion estimation, canceling detection-based noise, and adding a Fisher vector [16]. More recent work has reported state-of-the-art performance achieved with the concatenation of CNN features and IDT in the THUMOS Challenge [4,5,25]. Jain *et al.* employed a per-frame CNN feature from layers 6, 7, and 8 with AlexNet [10]. Zhu *et al.* [25] extended both the representations with multi-scale temporal sampling in the IDT [12] and video representations in the CNN feature [24]. The combination of IDT and CNN synergistically improves recognition performance.

Recently, CNN features with temporal representations have been proposed [17,18,22]. Ryoo *et al.* clearly bested IDT+CNN with their pooled time series (PoT) that continuously accumulates frame differences between two frames [17]. The feature is simple but effective for grasping continuous action sequences. The feature type that should be implemented, however, is one that improves the representation so that it adequately fits the transitional action recognition. It is difficult to achieve short-term prediction by using the PoT, because it describes features from a whole image sequence. Kataoka proposed a subtle motion descriptor (SMD) to represent sensitive motion in spatio-temporal human actions [9]. The SMD enhances the zero-around temporal pooled feature. Two-stream CNN is a well-organized algorithm that captures the temporal feature in an image sequence [18]. The integration of the spatial and the temporal streams allows us to effectively enhance the motion representation. We can obtain significant knowledge about how spatial information helps the temporal feature. Moreover, the strongest approach introduced is at the crosspoint of the IDT and two-stream CNN. TDDs have achieved the highest performance in several benchmarks, such as UCF101 (91.5%) and HMDB51 (65.9%) [22].

3   Acceleration Images into Two-Stream CNN

Acceleration images. The placement of acceleration images is shown in Fig. 1. The acceleration image I'' is a second-order differential from a position image I that is RGB input. The acceleration image I'' is shown below:

$$I''_x = I'(i+1, j) - I'(i, j) \tag{1}$$

$$I''_y = I'(i, j+1) - I'(i, j) \tag{2}$$

where i and j are elements of x and y. I' indicates a flow image that is calculated with optical flow displacement (d) [18]:

$$I'_x = d^x(u, v) \tag{3}$$

$$I'_y = d^y(u, v) \tag{4}$$

where (u, v) is an arbitrary point. The acceleration and flow images are stacked 10 frames in a row as $(I''_{x1}, I''_{y1}, I''_{x2}, I''_{y2}, ..., I''_{x10}, I''_{y10})$ and $(I'_{x1}, I'_{y1}, I'_{x2}, I'_{y2}, ..., I'_{x10}, I'_{y10})$ [18].

We implement VGGNet, which is supported by Wang et al. [23]. We integrate the acceleration stream on the two-stream CNN, in addition to the spatial and temporal streams as follows:

$$f = f_{spa} + \alpha f_{tem} + \beta f_{acc} \qquad (5)$$

where f indicates the softmax function, and spa, tem, and acc correspond to the spatial, temporal, and acceleration streams, respectively. α ($= 2.0$) and β ($= 2.0$) are weighted parameters.

CNN training. The learning procedure of the spatial and the temporal streams is based on [23]. We employ a temporal net as a pre-trained model, because the 20-channel input and image values are very similar. The initial learning rate is set as 0.001 and updating is x0.1 for every 10,000 iterations. The learning of the acceleration stream terminates at 50,000 iterations. We assign a high dropout ratio in all fully connected (fc) layers. We set 0.9 (first fc layer) and 0.9 (second fc layer) for the acceleration stream.

4 Experiment

NTSEL dataset (NTSEL) [7] (Figure 2). The dataset contains near-miss events captured by a vehicle. We focused on a pedestrian's gradual changes *walking straight, turning*, which is a fine-grained activity on real roads. The four activities are *walking, turning, crossing,* and *riding a bicycle*. The dataset has 100 videos of pedestrian actions. Each of the four actions has 25 videos: 15 videos for training and the other 10 videos for testing. A difficulty of the dataset is to divide walking activities (e.g., *walking, turning, crossing*) with similar appearances from the image sequence. Primitive motion understanding is beneficial to the dataset.

Fig. 2. NTSEL dataset.

Results. The results are shown in Table 1. The performance rate is based on per-video calculations. The video recognition system outputs an action label for each video. Our proposed algorithm that adds the acceleration stream significantly outperforms the two-stream CNN with an increase of 2.5 % on the NTSEL dataset. The correct recognitions of the spatial, temporal, and acceleration streams are 87.5 %, 77.5 %, and 82.5 %, respectively. Surprisingly, the acceleration stream performs better than the temporal stream. The acceleration stream effectively recognizes the movement of acceleration in the traffic data. We confirmed that the motion feature of acceleration in an image sequence improves video recognition. Although the knowledge is based on position, speed, and acceleration in physics, we proved the existence of acceleration in the video motion. Moreover, we believe that the CNN processing automatically selected the dominant feature from the acceleration stream.

Table 1. Performance rate of three-stream architecture (spatial + temporal + acceleration; S+T+A) and other approaches on the NTSEL dataset.

Approach	% on NTSEL
Spatial stream	87.5
Temporal stream	77.5
Acceleration stream	82.5
Two streams (S+T) [23]	87.5
Three stream (S+T+A; ours)	**90.0**

5   Conclusion

In this paper, we propose the definition of acceleration images that represent a change of a flow image. The acceleration stream is employed as an additional stream to a two-stream CNN. The process of the two-stream CNN picks up a necessary feature in the acceleration images with an automatic feature mechanism. Surprisingly, the motion recognition with the acceleration stream is better than recognition with the temporal stream.

Our future work is to iteratively differentiate the acceleration images to extract more detailed motions. In particular, we hope to capture more refined features in human motion.

References

1. Dalal, N., Triggs, B.: Histograms of oriented gradients for human detection. In: IEEE Conference on Computer Vision and Pattern Recognition (CVPR) (2005)
2. Dalal, N., Triggs, B., Schmid, C.: Human detection using oriented histograms of flow and appearance. In: Leonardis, A., Bischof, H., Pinz, A. (eds.) ECCV 2006. LNCS, vol. 3952, pp. 428–441. Springer, Heidelberg (2006). doi:10.1007/11744047_33

3. Everts, I., Gernert, J.C., Gevers, T.: Evaluation of color stips for human action recognition. In: IEEE Conference on Computer Vision and Pattern Recognition (CVPR) (2013)
4. Gorban, A, Idrees, H., Jiang, Y.-G., Roshan Zamir, A., Laptev, I., Shah, M., Sukthankar, R.: THUMOS challenge: action recognition with a large number of classes (2015). http://www.thumos.info/
5. Jain, M., Gemert, J., Snoek, C.G.M.: University of Amsterdam at THUMOS challenge2014. In: European Conference on Computer Vision Workshop (ECCVW) (2014)
6. Jain, M., Jegou, H., Bouthemy, P.: Better exploiting motion for better action recognition. In: IEEE Conference on Computer Vision and Pattern Recognition (CVPR) (2013)
7. Kataoka, H., Aoki, Y., Satoh, Y., Oikawa, S., Matsui, Y.: Fine-grained walking activity recognition via driving recorder dataset. In: IEEE Intelligent Transportation Systems Conference (ITSC) (2015)
8. Kataoka, H., Hashimoto, K., Iwata, K., Satoh, Y., Navab, N., Ilic, S., Aoki, Y.: Extended co-occurrence HOG with dense trajectories for fine-grained activity recognition. In: Cremers, D., Reid, I., Saito, H., Yang, M.-H. (eds.) ACCV 2014. LNCS, vol. 9007, pp. 336–349. Springer, Heidelberg (2015). doi:10.1007/978-3-319-16814-2_22
9. Kataoka, H., Miyashita, Y., Hayashi, M., Iwata, K., Satoh, Y.: Recognition of transitional action for short-term action prediction using discriminative temporal CNN feature. In: British Machine Vision Conference (BMVC) (2016)
10. Krizhevsky, A., Sutskever, I., Hinton, G.E.: Imagenet classification with deep convolutional neural networks. In: Neural Information Processing Systems (NIPS) (2012)
11. Kuehne, H., Jhuang, H., Garrote, E., Poggio, T., Serre, T.: HMDB: a large video database for human motion recognition. In: International Conference on Computer Vision (ICCV)(2011)
12. Lan, Z., Lin, M., Li, X., Hauptmann, A.G., Raj, B.: Beyond Gaussian pyramid: Multi-skip feature stacking for action recognition. In: IEEE Conference on Computer Vision and Pattern Recognition (CVPR) (2015)
13. Laptev, I.: On space-time interest points. Int. J. Comput. Vis. (IJCV) **64**, 107–123 (2005)
14. Laptev, I., Marszalek, M., Schmid, C., Rozenfeld, B.: Learning realistic human actions from movies. In: IEEE Conference on Computer Vision and Pattern Recognition (CVPR) (2008)
15. Marszalek, M., Laptev, I., Schmid, C.: Actions in context. In: IEEE Conference on Computer Vision and Pattern Recognition (CVPR) (2009)
16. Perronnin, F., Sánchez, J., Mensink, T.: Improving the fisher kernel for large-scale image classification. In: Daniilidis, K., Maragos, P., Paragios, N. (eds.) ECCV 2010. LNCS, vol. 6314, pp. 143–156. Springer, Heidelberg (2010). doi:10.1007/978-3-642-15561-1_11
17. Ryoo, M.S. Rothrock, B., Matthies, L.: Pooled motion features for first-person videos. In: IEEE Conference on Computer Vision and Pattern Recognition (CVPR) (2015)
18. Simonyan, K., Zisserman, A.: Two-stream convolutional networks for action recognition. Neural Information Processing Systems (NIPS) (2014)
19. Soomro, K., Zamir, A.R., Shah, M., UCF101: a dataset of 101 human action classes from videos in the wild. CRCV-TR-12-01 (2012)

20. Wang, H., Klaser, A., Schmid, C., Cheng-Lin, L.: Action recognition by dense trajectories. In: IEEE Conference on Computer Vision and Pattern Recognition (CVPR) (2011)
21. Wang, H., Schmid, C.: Action recognition with improved trajectories. In: International Conference on Computer Vision (ICCV) (2013)
22. Wang, L., Qiao, Y., Tang, X.: Action recognition with trajectory-pooled deep-convolutional descriptors. In: IEEE Conference on Computer Vision and Pattern Recognition (CVPR) (2015)
23. Wang, L., Xiong, Y., Wang, Z., Qiao, Y.: Towards good practices for very deep two-stream convnets arXiv pre-print. arXiv:1507.02159 (2015)
24. Xu, Z., Yang, Y., Hauptmann, A.G.: A discriminative CNN video representation for event detection. In: IEEE Conference on Computer Vision and Pattern Recognition (CVPR) (2015)
25. Zhu, L., Yang, Y., Hauptmann, A.G.: UTS-CMU at THUMOS 2015. In: CVPR2015 International Workshop and Competition on Action Recognition with a Large Number of Classes (2015)

Segmentation Free Object Discovery in Video

Giovanni Cuffaro, Federico Becattini[✉], Claudio Baecchi,
Lorenzo Seidenari, and Alberto Del Bimbo

University of Florence, Florence, Italy
{giovanni.cuffaro,federico.becattini,claudio.baecchi,
lorenzo.seidenari,alberto.delbimbo}@unifi.it

Abstract. In this paper we present a simple yet effective approach to extend without supervision any object proposal from static images to videos. Unlike previous methods, these spatio-temporal proposals, to which we refer as "tracks", are generated relying on little or no visual content by only exploiting bounding boxes spatial correlations through time. The tracks that we obtain are likely to represent objects and are a general-purpose tool to represent meaningful video content for a wide variety of tasks. For unannotated videos, tracks can be used to discover content without any supervision. As further contribution we also propose a novel and dataset-independent method to evaluate a generic object proposal based on the entropy of a classifier output response. We experiment on two competitive datasets, namely YouTube Objects [6] and ILSVRC-2015 VID [7].

1 Introduction

Image and video analysis can be considered similar on many levels, but whereas new algorithms are continuously raising the bar for static image tasks, advancements on videos seem to be slower and hard going. What makes video comprehension more difficult is mainly the huge amount of data that has to be processed and the need to model an additional dimension: time.

We believe that focusing on relevant regions of videos, such as objects, will reduce the complexity of the problem and ease learning for models like Deep Networks. The same concept has been successfully applied to images using object proposals, which analyse low level properties, such as edges, to find regions that are likely to contain salient objects. Advantages are twofold, first the search space is considerably reduced, second, as a consequence, the number of false positives generated by classifiers is lowered.

In this work we propose a technique to include time into a generic object proposal, by exploiting the weak supervision provided by time itself to match spatial proposals between adjacent frames. This results in spatio-temporal tracks that represent salient objects in the video and can therefore be used instead of the whole sequence. To the best of our knowledge we are the first to adopt a fully unsupervised matching strategy that only relies on bounding box coordinates without any semantic content or visual descriptor apart from optical flow.

© Springer International Publishing Switzerland 2016
G. Hua and H. Jégou (Eds.): ECCV 2016 Workshops, Part III, LNCS 9915, pp. 25–31, 2016.
DOI: 10.1007/978-3-319-49409-8_4

We also introduce a novel dataset-independent proposal evaluation method based on the entropy of classifier scores.

2   Related Work

Object proposals [3] provide a relatively small set of bounding boxes likely to contain salient regions in images, based on some *objectness* measure. Different proposals, such as EdgeBoxes [12], are commonly used in image related tasks to reduce the number of candidate regions to evaluate. Recently, there have been some attempts to adapt the paradigm of object proposals to videos to solve specific tasks, by generating consistent spatio-temporal volumes. In [6] motion segmentation is exploited to extract a single spatio-temporal tube for video, in order to perform video classification. The task of object discovery is tackled in [9] by generating a set of boxes using a foreground estimation method and matching them across frames using both geometric and appearance terms. Kwak *et al.* [4] combine a discovery step matching similar regions in different frames and a tracking step to obtain temporal proposals. In [5] a classifier is learnt to guide a super-voxel merging process for obtaining object proposals. Temporal proposals have been exploited to segment objects in videos in [10] by discovering easy instances and propagating the tube to adjacent frames. Other methods to generate salient tubes have been proposed for action localization in [11] using human and motion detection.

Differently from the above approaches we do not rely on segmentation, which is a time-consuming task especially for videos. Our method is simply based on the response of a frame-wise proposal method. The weak supervision obtained from the temporal consistency of the video is exploited to generate tracks. Our method aims at generating few, highly precise, tracks containing objects in the video.

3   Video Temporal Proposals

In this section we introduce the concept of "track", describing in details how these are generated from a set of bounding boxes extracted by an object proposal in the video.

Given a video V, for each frame f_i we extract a set B_i of bounding boxes b_i^k using an object proposal. We propose a method to match boxes that exhibit a temporal consistency in consecutive frames through the video, yielding to a set T of tracks t_j. A track is defined as a succession of bounding boxes b_i^k for which the intersection over union (IoU) between two boxes b_i^m (belonging to frame f_i) and b_{i+1}^n (belonging to frame f_{i+1}) is above a defined threshold θ_τ.

Starting from the first frame, each time a match is found, the corresponding bounding box is added to the end of the track and becomes the reference box for the following frame. If no match is found the last box of the track is compared with the following frames until a good match is obtained. An example of matching is shown in Fig. 1.

Fig. 1. Example of frame matching; matched boxes are inserted into their respective track. *(left)* reference frame where the top 10 proposals extracted with EdgeBoxes are shown; *(center)* following frame with top 10 EdgeBoxes proposals; *(right)* 2 matched proposals between the two frames; these will be part of two different tracks

When one or more consecutive matches are not found, tracks become fragmented, i.e. there are frames for which a track is active but there is no bounding box. This is usually due to a lack of good bounding boxes for that frame, occlusion or appearance changes of the object. It is thus necessary to avoid matching boxes in frames too far apart that therefore do not represent the same content, but at the same time we want to be able to tolerate some missing boxes without prematurely terminating the track.

To this end we introduce a Time to Live counter (TTL) τ for each track. We define $\tau_i(t_j)$ as the number of frames, at frame i, that the method can still wait before considering the track t_j terminated. TTL starts from an initial value γ; each time a box can not be matched in a consecutive frame the TTL is decremented, otherwise is incremented (up to γ). More formally, given a track t_j and its last bounding box b_i^m we increment or decrement its TTL as follows:

$$\tau_{i+1}(t_j) = \begin{cases} \tau_i(t_j) + 1, & \text{if } \exists\, n : \text{IoU}(b_i^m, b_{i+1}^n) > \theta_\tau \\ \tau_i(t_j) - 1, & \text{otherwise} \end{cases} \tag{1}$$

When the TTL for a track reaches 0, the track is considered terminated. Missing frames caused by track fragmentation are linearly interpolated using the positions of the previous and following bounding boxes in the track.

Proposal Motion Compensation. Proposals around objects in consecutive frames are usually unaligned due to movements of the object or the camera. This causes the IoU score to decrease even if the matching is good. We work around this problem by registering the boxes with optical flow before computing the IoU. The registration is performed on the last box of each track, by computing the mean offsets along the x and y axes inside the boxes. Shifted boxes are only used for matching and tracks consist only of unaltered boxes.

Temporal NMS. As in the spatial case, temporal proposals also suffer of high redundancy. To reduce this effect we extend spatial non-maximal suppression to time, defining a temporal NMS where instead of computing IoU on areas it is computed over volumes (vIoU). If α_j^k is the area of the k-th bounding box in track t_j, then the volume v_j of the track is calculated as $v_j = \sum_{k=0}^{K} \alpha_j^k$ where K is the length of the track. Then, vIoU is defined as:

$$\mathrm{vIoU}(t_j, t_k) = \frac{v_j \cap v_k}{v_j \cup v_k} \qquad (2)$$

Using vIoU we apply the standard NMS.

Proposal Suppression. Once all the tracks are computed for a given video, we apply a post-processing to remove the ones that are unlikely to represent an object. To this end we remove those tracks which have a length smaller than a value l. In this way we exclude very short tracks that are likely to be composed by background boxes that happen to have a high IoU.

Another problem is posed by logos and writings impressed on the video. In fact both of these are very well located by an object proposal but are usually of no interest. To prevent such objects to be considered as valid tracks, we take the mean optical flow magnitude in all the boxes of the track and we discard it if under a threshold s.

Track Ranking. It is important to compute a score for temporal proposals, in order to account for the likelihood of objects in such proposal. To this end, we propose to consider two factors: the object proposal score used to generate the bounding boxes at each frame and the values given by the IoUs between frames of the tracks. For the former we define E_t as the mean of the scores given by EdgeBoxes, for the latter we define I_t as the mean of all the IoUs of the frames in the track. Using these two figures we define a track score as:

$$S_t = \lambda E_t + (1 - \lambda)I_t \qquad (3)$$

where $\lambda \in [0, 1]$ is a weighting factor used to balance the contributions of the two scores.

4 Method Evaluation

Object proposals are usually evaluated measuring how well objects are covered by the generated boxes. These kind of evaluation does not take into account unannotated objects, and therefore provide a benchmark not reflecting the real capabilities of the proposal method.

The method presented in this paper is a general framework for discovering salient spatio-temporal tracks in videos, which is built upon a generic bounding box oracle. To evaluate it, we introduce a novel method to establish the effectiveness of a generic video proposal, which is also dataset-independent since it does not rely on annotations. We evaluate whether a proposal effectively represents an instance of some object, since the goal of an object proposal is to locate good candidates and not to produce the candidate of a given class (i.e. the one of the ground truth). To this end we propose an entropy based evaluation which indicates how the proposal is likely to be recognized as an object. Given a classifier capable of providing for an image a probability distribution $X = \{x_1, \ldots, x_N\}$ over N classes, we compute the Shannon entropy H for the probability vector X, $H(X) = -\sum_{i=1}^{N} x_i \log(x_i)$.

The rationale behind this choice is that, given a good classifier, for a known object the output probability distribution will be high for the relative class and near zero for the others, thus producing a small entropy. On the contrary, for inputs that the classifier is unsure of, e.g. background patches, the output probability will be distributed non-uniformly among all the possible classes, resulting in a higher entropy. Therefore, if the classifier is able to cover effectively a sufficiently large number of classes, then the entropy can be interpreted as a measure of *objectness* for the given proposal.

5   Experiments

We experiment on the YouTube-Objects (YTO) [6] and on the ILSVRC2015-VID (VID) datasets [7], which both provide a per-frame annotation of the objects. YTO is composed by 10 classes and most videos contain a single object per video. VID instead is a more challenging dataset with 30 classes with multiple objects per video.

Here we evaluate our method using the entropy measure introduced in Sect. 4. In all experiments we use EdgeBoxes [12] as object proposal to generate bounding boxes and as baseline. For the entropy-based proposal scoring we chose the VGG-16 [8] network, trained on the ImageNet [7] dataset as image classifier, yielding a 1000-dimensional output probability vector.

For each video we classify 25 proposals and compute the entropy score. For our method we select the best 25 tracks of each video, according to Eq. 3, and for each of them we classify, as representative, the box with the best EdgeBoxes score. We compare the entropy scores against the best 25 boxes given by Edge-Boxes for the whole video. As a lower-bound reference value we run the classifier on the dataset ground truth. This value is what can be expected to be obtained when proposing only meaningful objects.

Results for YTO are shown in detail in Table 1; it can be seen that our method yields a much lower entropy than EdgeBoxes, also it is close to the ground truth reference. The same trend can be observed on the VID dataset where we measured an average Entropy of 4.73, 3.96 and 3.71 for EdgeBoxes, Our method and the ground truth respectively.

High Precision Proposals. As a further evaluation, we treated our proposal as an object detector measuring the mean Average Precision (mAP) for the YTO dataset. This aims at measuring the precision of a proposal method. Since the

Table 1. Entropy comparison (lower is better) between the proposals provided by EdgeBoxes (EB) and our method (Ours) and Ground Truth boxes (GT).

Method	✈	🐦	⛵	🚗	🐱	🐄	🐕	🐎	🏍	🚆	Mean
EB [12]	5.02	5.19	5.48	4.52	5.92	6.27	6.16	6.54	5.68	5.19	5.60
Ours	3.58	3.25	3.10	2.45	4.02	3.00	3.58	3.25	3.10	2.45	3.18
GT	0.58	1.33	1.03	1.83	2.31	2.41	2.28	2.58	2.57	2.41	1.93

Table 2. AP comparison (higher is better) for object detection between EdgeBoxes (EB) and Our method.

Method	✈	🐦	⛵	🚌	🐱	🐄	🐕	🐎	🏍	🚂	Mean
EB [12]	0.94	0.40	0.49	1.80	10.96	0.57	0.56	0.61	0.26	2.95	0.98
Ours	9.15	7.16	5.98	14.94	10.95	8.43	6.10	2.26	3.42	14.91	8.33

Fig. 2. Keyframes of the top 10 tracks in the VID dataset, compared with the top 10 EdgeBoxes proposals. Our method has less redundancy and frames objects more clearly.

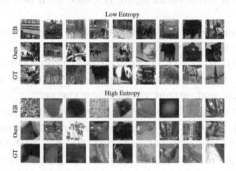

Fig. 3. Highest and lowest entropy proposals for our method (Ours), EdgeBoxes (EB) and ground truth boxes (GT).

class set of YTO is a subset of the one of Pascal VOC [1], for this evaluation we used Fast-RCNN [2], restricted to the ten common classes.

Table 2 shows a comparison between our proposed tracks and EdgeBoxes. In order to make the comparison fair, we evaluated the best 25 boxes proposed by both methods for each video, similarly to the entropy evaluation in Sect. 5. The mAP of our tracks is 8.5 times higher than EdgeBoxes, proving that our proposal is much more precise.

Qualitative Results. We report some qualitative results, showing a comparison of content extracted by our proposal with respect to EdgeBoxes. We compare the best boxes and tracks in a given video. In Fig. 2 it can be seen how our proposals are more diverse and frame an object correctly with respect to the top proposal chosen from EdgeBoxes.

In Fig. 3 we show an example of high and low entropy proposals. For our method and EdgeBoxes we report the 10 boxes with the lowest and highest entropies among the first best 25 proposals. As reference we also report high and low entropy boxes from the ground truth. It can be seen that our method is more focused on objects even in its highest entropy proposals.

6   Conclusions

We proposed a novel and unsupervised method to extract from videos, tracks containing meaningful objects. Our track proposal can build on any object bounding box proposal method. The matching process only relies on bounding box geometry and optical flow, resulting in a simple and effective method for high precision video object proposals. We also introduce a dataset independent method to evaluate the effectiveness of an object proposal, not relying on dataset annotations. The proposal has been evaluated on the YouTube Objects and ILSVRC-2015 VID datasets, showing a high precision and providing meaningful object proposals that can be used for any video analysis task without looking at the whole sequence.

References

1. Everingham, M., Van Gool, L., Williams, C.K.I., Winn, J., Zisserman, A.: The pascal visual object classes (voc) challenge. Int. J. Comput. Vis. **88**(2), 303–338 (2010)
2. Girshick, R.: Fast R-CNN. In: Proceedings of ICCV (2015)
3. Hosang, J., Benenson, R., Dollár, P., Schiele, B.: What makes for effective detection proposals? IEEE Trans. Pattern Anal. Mach. Intell. **38**(4), 814–830 (2016)
4. Kwak, S., Cho, M., Laptev, I., Ponce, J., Schmid, C.: Unsupervised object discovery and tracking in video collections. In: Proceedings of ICCV (2015)
5. Oneata, D., Revaud, J., Verbeek, J., Schmid, C.: Spatio-temporal object detection proposals. In: Fleet, D., Pajdla, T., Schiele, B., Tuytelaars, T. (eds.) ECCV 2014. LNCS, vol. 8691, pp. 737–752. Springer, Heidelberg (2014). doi:10.1007/978-3-319-10578-9_48
6. Prest, A., Leistner, C., Civera, J., Schmid, C., Ferrari, V.: Learning object class detectors from weakly annotated video. In: Proceedings of CVPR. IEEE (2012)
7. Russakovsky, O., Deng, J., Hao, S., Krause, J., Satheesh, S., Ma, S., Huang, Z., Karpathy, A., Khosla, A., Bernstein, M., et al.: Imagenet large scale visual recognition challenge. Int. J. Comput. Vis. **115**(3), 211–252 (2015)
8. Simonyan, K., Zisserman, A.: Very deep convolutional networks for large-scale image recognition. arXiv preprint arXiv:1409.1556 (2014)
9. Stretcu, O., Leordeanu, M.: Multiple frames matching for object discovery in video. In: Proceedings of BMVC (2015)
10. Xiao, F., Lee, Y.J.: Track and segment: an iterative unsupervised approach for video object proposals. In: Proceedings of CVPR (2016)
11. Yu, G., Yuan, J.: Fast action proposals for human action detection and search. In: Proceedings of CVPR (2015)
12. Zitnick, C.L., Dollár, P.: Edge boxes: locating object proposals from edges. In: Fleet, D., Pajdla, T., Schiele, B., Tuytelaars, T. (eds.) ECCV 2014. LNCS, vol. 8693, pp. 391–405. Springer, Heidelberg (2014). doi:10.1007/978-3-319-10602-1_26

Human Pose Estimation in Space and Time Using 3D CNN

Agne Grinciunaite[1], Amogh Gudi[2(✉)], Emrah Tasli[3], and Marten den Uyl[2]

[1] Vilniaus Gedimino Technikos Univ., Vilnius, Lithuania
a.grinciunaite@gmail.com
[2] VicarVision, Amsterdam, Netherlands
amogh@vicarvision.nl, denuyl@smr.nl
[3] Booking.com, Amsterdam, Netherlands
emrah.tasli@booking.com

Abstract. This paper explores the capabilities of convolutional neural networks to deal with a task that is easily manageable for humans: perceiving 3D pose of a human body from varying angles. However, in our approach, we are restricted to using a monocular vision system. For this purpose, we apply a convolutional neural network approach on RGB videos and extend it to three dimensional convolutions. This is done via encoding the time dimension in videos as the 3rd dimension in convolutional space, and directly regressing to human body joint positions in 3D coordinate space. This research shows the ability of such a network to achieve state-of-the-art performance on the selected Human3.6M dataset, thus demonstrating the possibility of successfully representing temporal data with an additional dimension in the convolutional operation.

1 Introduction

From a psychological stand point, it has been argued that humans detect real-world structures by detecting changes along physical dimensions (contrast values) and representing these changes (with respect to time) as relations (differences) along subjective dimensions [1]. More directly, it has been suggested that the temporal dimension is necessary and is coupled with spatial dimensions in human mental representations of the world [2]. This implies merit in incorporating time into a definition of structure from a computer vision modelling point of view. This forms the inspiration for this work.

This work deals with a long-standing task in computer vision - human pose modelling in 3D from monocular videos. The challenges of this task include large variability in poses, movements, appearance and background, occlusions and changes in illumination.

This paper proposes a method to estimate the body pose of a human (in terms of body joint locations in 3D) from video capture using a single 2D monocular camera via a deep three dimensional convolutional neural network. The key

---

A. Grinciunaite, E. Tasli—This research was done while the author was employed at VicarVision.

© Springer International Publishing Switzerland 2016
G. Hua and H. Jégou (Eds.): ECCV 2016 Workshops, Part III, LNCS 9915, pp. 32–39, 2016.
DOI: 10.1007/978-3-319-49409-8_5

idea behind this approach is that time, as a dimension, could be encoded as the Z-dimension of 3D convolutional operation (where the other two X and Y dimensions are along the height and width of the image). The hypothesis behind this is that temporal information can be efficiently represented as an additional dimension in deep convolutional neural networks (see [3,4] for a detailed description of 3D convolution). It is important to note here that no depth information is provided to the network as input, and the system is expected to infer the location of body joint positions in all three spatial dimensions only based on the stream of 2D frames in the video. A more detailed and complete description of this work can be found in [4].

Such a system can have applications in areas such as visual surveillance, human action prediction, emotional state recognition, human-computer interfaces, video coding, ergonomics, video indexing and retrieval, etc.

2   Related Work

There have been a number of studies carried out in the human pose estimation field using different generative and discriminative approaches. Most of the published works deal with still single [5] or depth images [6]. Also, most often it is attempting to estimate 2D full [7], upper body [8] or single [9] joint position in the image plane. Additionally, many approaches incorporate 2D pose estimations or features to retrieve 3D poses [10,11]. The work in [8] formulates 2D pose estimation as a joint regression problem, using a conventional deep CNN architecture. The predictions are further iteratively refined by analysing relevant regions within the images in higher resolution. [12] introduces a heat-map based approach, where a spatial pyramid input is used to generate a heat map describing the spatial likelihood of joint positions. [13] presents an architecture similar to [8], with a key difference being that multiple consecutive video frames are encoded as separate colour channels in the input. Although this approach appears similar to that of 3D CNNs, the key difference here is that this approach enforces the Z dimension of the '3D' kernel to be equal to the number of channels. Therefore, the kernel has no space to convolve in this dimension. The first architecture utilizing 3D CNNs was proposed in 2013 and applied to human action recognition in [14]. As in our proposed work, the third spatial dimension of the convolution operation is used to encode the time dimension on the video stream. This work also utilizes recurrent neural networks to finally predict the human action category. However, they do not explore the use of 3D CNNs for predicting the precise locations of body joints. Recent methods tested on the Human3.6M dataset include a discriminative approach to 3D human pose estimation using spatiotemporal features (HOG-KDE) [15], as well as a 2D CNN based 3D pose estimation framework (2DCNN-EM) [11]. However, one of the drawbacks of these approaches is that they utilize a large number of frames in a sequence comparing to our proposed 3D CNN method.

Our approach studies the suitability of using 3D convolutional networks for the task of 3D pose estimation from 2D videos. To the extent of our knowledge, this is the first work to do so. More fundamentally, this work explores the effects of processing spatio-temporal data using three dimensional convolutions, where the temporal dimension in data is represented as a additional dimension in convolutions.

3 Dataset

Human3.6M Dataset [16] is so far the largest publicly available motion capture dataset. It consists of high resolution 50 Hz video sequences from 4 calibrated cameras capturing 10 subjects performing 15 different actions ('eating', 'posing', etc.). 3D ground truth joint locations as well as bounding boxes of human bodies are provided. Note that we consider videos from the 4 camera positions independently, and do not combine them in any way. Our evaluation was done on 17 core joints from the available 32 joint locations. For official testing, the ground truth data for 3 subjects is withheld and used for results evaluation on the server.

4 Method

4.1 Pre-processing

The original Human3.6M video frames are cropped using bounding box binary masks and extended to the larger side to make the crop squared. Cropped images are resized to 128 × 128 resolution (chosen arbitrarily). The results of cropping can be seen in Fig. 1.

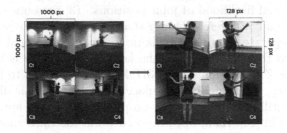

Fig. 1. Image pre-processing from 4 camera views capturing subject no. 1 performing action 'Directions'

Data Sampling. Due to the large amount of available data, limited memory and time constrains, data sub-sampling is performed. One training data sample is composed of 5 sequential colour images with resolution of 128 × 128. These were sampled from the original video to obtain a frame-rate of 13 Hz. Random selection was performed from every chosen training, validation and testing subjects' videos to ensure that all the possible poses are selected.

Data Alignment. Ground truth joint positions were centered to the pelvis bone position (first joint).

Contrast Normalization. To reduce the variability that DNN needs to account for during training, global contrast normalization (GCN) was applied to the network's input data (per colour channel).

4.2 Deep 3D Convolutional Neural Network

The final model of network's architecture was made up by starting with the small basic network with only three hidden 3D convolutional layers and building it up when testing with the small subset of data. Decisions on the construction parts and hyper-parameter selection were made by analysing experimental results and utilizing similar choices reported in related work reviewed in Sect. 2. In this network, all the activations are PReLUs [17] with p set to 0.01.

The following equation provides a mathematical expression of discrete convolution (denoted by $*$) applied to three dimensional data ($\mathbf{X}$, of dimensions $m \times n \times l$), using three dimensional flipped kernels ($\mathbf{K}$):

$$(\mathbf{K} * \mathbf{X})_{i,j,k} = \sum_{m}\sum_{n}\sum_{l} \mathbf{X}_{i-m,j-n,k-l}\mathbf{K}_{m,n,l} \tag{1}$$

In our implementation, the stride is always equal to 1 and there is no zero-padding performed. Experiments have been completed with different kernel sizes and a number of convolutional layers in the network. The best performance was achieved with 5 convolutional layers with kernel sizes $3 \times 5 \times 5$, $2 \times 5 \times 5$, $1 \times 5 \times 5$, $1 \times 3 \times 3$ and $1 \times 3 \times 3$ respectively. Max pooling is performed after the first, second and fifth convolutional layers, and only on the image space with the kernel of size 2×2 (and not on the third time dimension). In our proposed architecture, the output of the last pooling layer is flattened to one dimensional vector of size 9680 and then is fully connected to the output layer of size 255 (5 frames $\times$ 17 joints $\times$ 3 dimensions). Complete 3D CNN architecture is shown in Fig. 2.

Fig. 2. Proposed 3D CNN Architecture. Legend: C stands for convolutional layer, P for pooling layer; kernel sizes are specified in parenthesis; second row shows the size of corresponding layer's output; images show slices of some 3D activation maps per layer.

Training. The network was trained using mini-batch (of size 10) stochastic gradient descent (with a learning rate of $10-5$ and Nestrov momentum [18] of 0.9). Xavier initialization method [19] was used to set the initial weights, while the biases in convolutional layers were set to zero. Due to the memory and time limitations, the maximum number of batches used was 20,000 for training, 2,000 for validation and 2,000 for testing (approximately half of the available data). The cost function to be minimized during training was chosen to be the mean per joint position error (MPJPE) [16], which is the mean euclidean distance between the true and predicted joint locations. This also serves as a good performance measure during testing. Early stopping technique was used to avoid overfitting, where the training was terminated when the performance on the validation set stopped improving for 15 consecutive epochs.

4.3   Post-processing

The shape of the network output contains estimated 3D joint positions for 5 consecutive frames. During inference time, this makes it possible to feed each video frames 5 times through the network at 5 different positions in the input sequence. This gives us 5 outputs for each frame. In order to get a more robust estimation, these overlapping outputs are averaged together.

5   Results

In Table 1 the best results are compared with state-of-the-art reported on the dataset website. All the numbers are MPJPEs in millimetres. It can be seen that network performs better on 11 actions and the MPJPE is 11 % smaller on average. However, the model performs worse on the actions where people are sitting on the chair or on the ground showing difficulties to deal with body part occlusions. Figure 3 shows some selected examples of pose estimation by the network. This could also be due to the fact that the temporal window of 5 frames is too short to capture these joint positions. Expanding the window or incorporating recurrent neural networks in this architecture could handle this better by capturing longer-term trajectories.

On further investigation, it was also found that the joint position of freely moving upper body joints like hands were relatively poorly predicted. Countering this, a further improvement in performance was obtained by training a separate network to estimate only the upper body joints, and merging the outputs together.

Unfortunately, the two most recent works in 3D pose estimation on the Human3.6M dataset by [11,15] fail to report their scores on the official test sets, thereby making it very hard to compare out works. However, they do report average MPJPE scores of 124 [11] and 113 [15] on two male subjects (S9 and S11, which are in our training set).

Additionally, a comparison was performed with a 2D convolution based model with an otherwise identical architecture and training. It was found that our

Fig. 3. Visualization of some good (left-half) and bad (right-half) 3D pose estimation results.

3D CNN architecture outperforms this 2D CNN based network even without the post-processing step, thereby suggesting that modelling temporal dynamics improves 3D human pose estimation, perhaps due to inherent body-joint trajectory tracking.

The average processing time per 5-frame sample during testing was about 1ms/13ms on a Nvidia GTX 1080 GPU/Intel Xeon E5 CPU, implying real-time frame rates.

Table 1. Results comparing with the state-of-the-art (s.o.t.a) on the Human3.6M test set. Legend: numbers denote MPJPE error in mm (less is better).

Action subset	KDE [16](s.o.t.a)	3DCNN (ours)	% Improvement (ours over s.o.t.a)
Directions	117	**91**	▲ 22%
Discussion	108	**89**	▲ 18%
Eating	**91**	94	▼ − 3%
Greeting	129	**102**	▲ 21%
Phoning	**104**	105	▼ − 1%
Posing	130	**99**	▲ 24%
Purchases	134	**112**	▲ 16%
Sitting	**135**	151	▼ − 12%
Sitting down	**200**	239	▼ − 20%
Smoking	117	**109**	▲ 7%
Taking Photo	195	**151**	▲ 23%
Waiting	132	**106**	▲ 20%
Walking	115	**101**	▲ 12%
Walking with Dog	162	**141**	▲ 13%
Walking together	156	**106**	▲ 32%
Average	133	**119**	▲ 11%

6   Conclusions

A discriminative 3D CNN model was implemented for the task of human pose estimation in 3D coordinate space using 2D RGB video data. To the best of our knowledge, this is the first attempt to utilize 3D convolutions for the formulated task. It was shown that such a model can cope with 3D human pose estimation in videos and outperform the existing methods on the Human3.6M dataset. Proposed model was officially tested on dataset provider's evaluation server and compared with other reported results, which it could outperform with real-time processing speeds. These results suggest that time can be successfully encoded as an additional convolutional dimension for the task of modelling real world objects from 2D sequence of images.

Future Work. There are a number of possible future work directions that can extend this work: More hyper-parameter tuning and utilizing higher computational resources could possibly lead to more accurate estimations; testing model's capabilities on other available datasets; expanding the temporal window and/or combining the proposed model with recurrent neural networks (known for their ability to process temporal information).

References

1. Jones, M.R.: Time, our lost dimension: toward a new theory of perception, attention, and memory. Psychol. Rev. **83**, 323–355 (1976)
2. Freyd, J.J.: Dynamic mental representations. Psychol. Rev. **94**(4), 427 (1987)
3. Tran, D., Bourdev, L., Fergus, R., Torresani, L., Paluri, M.: Learning spatiotemporal features with 3D convolutional networks. In: 2015 IEEE International Conference on Computer Vision (ICCV), pp. 4489–4497. IEEE (2015)
4. Grinciunaite, A.: Development of a deep learning model for 3D human pose estimation in monocular videos. Master's thesis, Vilniaus Gedimino Technikos Universitetas (2016)
5. Wang, C., Wang, Y., Lin, Z., Yuille, A., Gao, W.: Robust estimation of 3D human poses from a single image. In Proceedings of the IEEE Conference on Computer Vision and Pattern Recognition, pp. 2361–2368 (2014)
6. Oberweger, M., Wohlhart, P., Lepetit, V.: Hands deep in deep learning for hand pose estimation. arXiv preprint arXiv:1502.06807 (2015)
7. Du, Y., Huang, Y., Peng, J.: Full-body human pose estimation from monocular video sequence via multi-dimensional boosting regression. In: Jawahar, C.V., Shan, S. (eds.) ACCV 2014. LNCS, vol. 9010, pp. 531–544. Springer, Heidelberg (2015). doi:10.1007/978-3-319-16634-6_39
8. Toshev, A., Szegedy, C.: DeepPose: human pose estimation via deep neural networks. CoRR, abs/1312.4659 (2013)
9. Fan, X., Zheng, K., Lin, Y., Wang, S.: Combining local appearance, holistic view: dual-source deep neural networks for human pose estimation. CoRR, abs/1504.07159 (2015)
10. Zhou, F., De la Torre, F.: Spatio-temporal matching for human pose estimation in video (2016)

11. Zhou, X., Zhu, M., Leonardos, S., Derpanis, K., Daniilidis, K.: Sparseness meets deepness: 3D human pose estimation from monocular video. arXiv preprint 2015. arXiv:1511.09439
12. Tompson, J., Goroshin, R., Jain, A., LeCun, Y., Bregler, C.: Efficient object localization using convolutional networks. CoRR, abs/1411.4280 (2014)
13. Pfister, T., Simonyan, K., Charles, J., Zisserman, A.: Deep convolutional neural networks for efficient pose estimation in gesture videos. In: Cremers, D., Reid, I., Saito, H., Yang, M.-H. (eds.) ACCV 2014. LNCS, vol. 9003, pp. 538–552. Springer, Heidelberg (2015). doi:10.1007/978-3-319-16865-4_35
14. Ji, S., Wei, X., Yang, M., Kai, Y.: 3D convolutional neural networks for human action recognition. IEEE Trans. Pattern Anal. Mach. Intell. **35**(1), 221–231 (2013)
15. Tekin, B., Sun, X., Wang, X., Lepetit, V., Fua, P.: Predicting people's 3D poses from short sequences. arXiv preprint arXiv:1504.08200 (2015)
16. Ionescu, C., Papava, D., Olaru, V., Sminchisescu, C.: Human3.6M: large scale datasets and predictive methods for 3D human sensing in natural environments. IEEE Trans. Pattern Anal. Mach. Intell. **36**, 1325–1329 (2014)
17. He, K., Zhang, X., Ren, S., Sun, J.: Delving Deep into Rectifiers: Surpassing Human-Level performance on ImageNet classification. CoRR, abs/1502.01852 (2015)
18. Qian, N.: On the momentum term in gradient descent learning algorithms. Neural Netw. **12**(1), 145–151 (1999)
19. Glorot, X., Bengio, Y.: Understanding the difficulty of training deep feedforward neural networks. In: International Conference on Artificial Intelligence and Statistics, pp. 249–256 (2010)

Autonomous Driving Challenge: To Infer the Property of a Dynamic Object Based on Its Motion Pattern

Mona Fathollahi and Rangachar Kasturi[✉]

Department of Computer Science and Engineering,
University of South Florida, Tampa, USA
{mona2,r1k}@mail.usf.edu

Abstract. In autonomous driving applications a critical challenge is to identify the action to take to avoid an obstacle on a collision course. For example, when a heavy object is suddenly encountered it is critical to stop the vehicle or change the lane even if it causes other traffic disruptions. However, there are situations when it is preferable to collide with the object rather than take an action that would result in a much more serious accident than collision with the object. For example, a heavy object which falls from a truck should be avoided whereas a bouncing ball or a soft target such as a foam box need not be.

We present a novel method to discriminate between the motion characteristics of these types of objects based on their physical properties such as bounciness, elasticity, etc.

In this preliminary work, we use recurrent neural network with LSTM (Long Short Term Memory) cells to train a classifier to classify objects based on their motion trajectories. We test the algorithm on synthetic data, and, as a proof of concept, demonstrate its effectiveness on a limited set of real-world data.

1   Introduction

In recent years, the technology of self-driving cars has made dramatic progress. One of the critical challenges of this emerging technology is the safety of both car occupants and other road users. The current prototype of autonomous cars are equipped with advanced sensors such as ultrasonic, vision, radar and LIDAR. These sensors along with sophisticated data fusion algorithms are able to detect and track obstacles in real-time with very good resolution.

When an obstacle is detected in the planned path, either its planned route should be modified or the vehicle should come to stop. Depending on the traffic situation and vehicle speed, this policy could cause collision with other vehicles. Therefore, obstacle avoidance may not always be the safest action. Similar challenge has been discussed in [7].

The intuitive solution would be to recognize the object before taking an action. The intelligent unit should predict whether it is safe to pass over the object or it should inevitably follow avoiding policy.

© Springer International Publishing Switzerland 2016
G. Hua and H. Jégou (Eds.): ECCV 2016 Workshops, Part III, LNCS 9915, pp. 40–46, 2016.
DOI: 10.1007/978-3-319-49409-8_6

A sample video for each scenario is downloaded from Youtube and a few frames are shown in the Fig. 1. In the first video, an empty plastic container is bouncing in the road which is safe to pass. In the second video, a heavy object is falling out of the front car which should definitely be avoided.

(a)   (b)

Fig. 1. Selected frames of dynamic objects on the road. (a) A plastic container which is safe to collide, YouTube Link. (b) A heavy object that should be avoided, YouTube Link.

The immediate solution that one might consider is to formulate the problem as a regular image classification task and collect a dataset of collision safe and unsafe objects. While there is much progress in object detection/recognition methods [6], this approach has several challenges which makes it ineffective for this particular application.

First, collecting a dataset that contains different objects in different lighting conditions and viewpoints is a difficult task in itself. Second, it is almost impossible to infer the weight of an object by its visual cue; for example, two very similar boxes with one of them filled with metal pieces and the other one which is empty have similar images.

Finally, there is a high possibility of recognition failure because the image resolution is usually poor for far away objects. Also, the classifier should decide in a short period of time, where motion blur might make the problem even more challenging. For example, the white plastic container in the first column of Fig. 1 could be classified as a gas cylinder.

These challenges are easily resolved by a human by observing the trajectory of empty box versus heavy box (e.g. plastic container versus a gas cylinder). Therefore, assuming that the real-time trajectory of the dynamic object is available [2], we claim that motion pattern provides strong cue to infer the object dynamics accurately and to classify it as a "safe to pass over" or "must avoid" object.

2 Method

In this section, our goal is to design a classifier to infer object's bounciness characteristic based on its trajectory when it hits the ground. Our approach is based on the observation that the bouncing pattern of objects is directly affected by their mass.

2.1 Data

To collect data, we should throw different objects with different masses and shapes and record their trajectories. On the other hand, since the bounciness of the object is also related to initial velocity, we should collect a large amount of data to be able to learn the effect of mass on the trajectory. Therefore, dataset collection in this case is cumbersome and expensive.

Therefore, we generate synthetic videos with binary labels denoting heavy or light object trajectory. We utilized open source 3D creation suite, Blender [3], to generate motion data of bouncing objects. Blender uses "Bullet Physics Library" for collision detection, rigid body dynamic simulation and other Physics simulations tasks.

Each trajectory starts from random coordinates and Euler angles and the object has random initial linear and angular velocities. To generate random initial velocities, two key-frames are inserted at first and seventh frames. Also, the height of object at first frame and both linear and angular positions at seventh frame are randomized (Fig. 2). The physics engine takes over the object animation after seventh frame. The world coordinates of the object after the seventh frame are recorded as object trajectory time series.

In the initial phase of our project, we only consider two object categories; the first class is the trajectory of light objects that have a high tendency to bounce when they hit the ground, and the second class are the objects that are heavy and have more tendency to slide than bounce. To isolate the effect of shape on the bounciness, we kept the shape of the objects the same for all simulations. We generated 1000 training videos, and 1000 test videos for both categories.

Some randomly chosen examples of the generated trajectory data are shown in Fig. 3. Even though there is a clear distinction between Z dimension of the trajectories, we still see subtle difference in X and Y components. For example, for a light object (higher bounciness) it takes more time to come to a full stop and this is reflected in X and Y coordinates and this justify the superior performance of classification when 3D data is used (Table 1). Finally, although some statistical differences are detectable between the two categories, the plots in this figure suggests that no simple rule can be proposed based on, for example, the number of bounces or time series duration; therefore, a more involved classification algorithm is required.

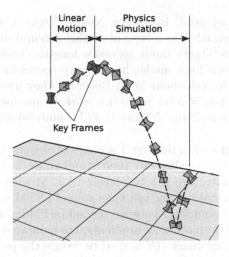

Fig. 2. Object trajectory synthesis in Blender. The first few frames are to generate initial velocity (Linear motion). The second part, physics simulation, is recorded as trajectory of the object.

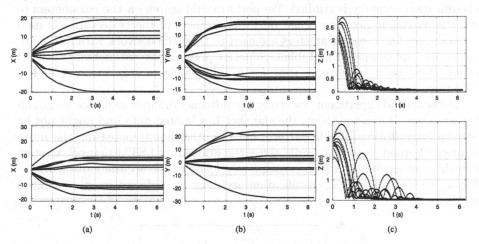

Fig. 3. Samples of synthesized trajectory data set. The figures shows time plots of (a) X, (b) Y, (c) Z coordinate of the (top) heavy, (bottom) light object.

Table 1. Best accuracy for 3D and 1D input sequence.

Trajectory dimension (s)	Best accuracy (%)
X, Y, Z	81
Only Z	78

2.2 Classifier

In this section, we assume that the trajectory of the object is given by a tracking algorithm. Therefore the problem is reduced to time series classification.

In this work, we adopted, Recurrent Neural Network models (RNN) for trajectory classification. RNN is a type of artificial neural network that is able to process data with arbitrary input sequence lengths. Their internal memory units and feedback loops have made them a very successful tool in sequential data prediction in various domains [4,5]. Recently, they have been used in the context of time series classification [9]. In this work we also use RNN architecture with peePhole Long Short-Term Memory (LSTM) units [8] for motion trajectory classification.

The input to the network is the first T seconds of objects' trajectory. Training and test time series are normalized by their standard deviations in each dimension. Our network architecture is a two-layered LSTM with 64 hidden units in each layer. The hidden state at the last time step of LSTM is fed into a softmax layer. We also add a dropout layer between second LSTM layer and softmax layer with rate 0.8. To compute parameter gradients, the truncated back-propagation-through-time (BPTT) approach [10] is used to reduce the probability of vanishing gradient problem for long input sequences. The entire implementation is done using Tensorflow [1] package.

In the first experiment, the impact of input dimension (XYZ vs Z) on the classification accuracy is studied. We perform grid search on the parameters to get the maximum accuracy when only z-coordinate of the trajectories is used for training. The same parameters are used to train the network with 3D input, the results are compared in Table 1. Superior performance was achieve with 3D inputs, because it takes more time for a light object to stop along X and Y direction.

In the second experiment, we study the influence of input sequence length on the accuracy. If it is too short, the classifier has limited data and might not be able to learn distinguishable pattern. On the other hand, increasing the input sequence beyond some limit could cause the gradient of LSTM network to start vanishing or exploding, which consequently leads to the accuracy drop. In the Fig. 4, we have shown the classification accuracy for different lengths of input sequence.

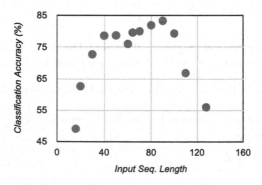

Fig. 4. Classification accuracy versus trajectory length.

2.3   Experiment on Real-World Data

In this section, we leverage the trained network on synthetic trajectories, to analyze the trajectory of real-world objects. One extreme example is chosen from each category: golf ball as an object with high bounciness, and wooden cube as an object with low bounciness. We throw them from different heights with different initial velocities and record the video, Fig. 6. The objects are marked with a distinct color to be able to use a simple color tracker. Lastly, when frames get blurred due to the fast motion of the object, missing part of the trajectory is reconstructed by a simple interpolation. The trajectories that are shorter than input sequence length get zero-padded. For each category we collected 20 videos and plotted the trajectories in Fig. 5. In this experiment, the trajectories are recorded with a single RGB camera and only trajectory along z direction is used for decision; therefore we used the trained network on z channel as well. We obtained an accuracy of 93 % on the ball and 100 % on the wooden cube.

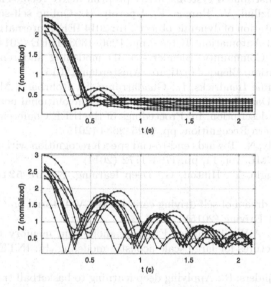

Fig. 5. Real-world trajectories: wooden cube (top), golf ball (bottom).

Fig. 6. Real-world experiment sample trajectories: (Left) golf ball (Right) wooden cube.

3 Conclusions and Future Work

In our preliminary experiments, we have found that motion pattern of an object provides strong cue on the object property. This has a potential application in the autonomous driving technology which reduces the number of dangerous stops or maneuvers when on object suddenly appears in front of the vehicle. Our preliminary experiments show promising results on synthetic and small set of real-world data. In the future, we are planning to collect more real-world examples to fully develop and test the concepts explored in this paper.

References

1. Abadi, M., Agarwal, A., Barham, P., Brevdo, E., Chen, Z., Citro, C., Corrado, G.S., Davis, A., Dean, J., Devin, M., et al.: Tensorflow: large-scale machine learning on heterogeneous distributed systems. arXiv preprint arXiv:1603.04467 (2016)
2. Bewley, A., Guizilini, V., Ramos, F., Upcroft, B.: Online self-supervised multi-instance segmentation of dynamic objects. In: 2014 IEEE International Conference on Robotics and Automation (ICRA), pp. 1296–1303. IEEE (2014)
3. Blender Online Community. Blender - a 3D modelling and rendering package. Blender Foundation, Blender Institute, Amsterdam (2015)
4. Donahue, J., Anne Hendricks, L., Guadarrama, S., Rohrbach, M., Venugopalan, S., Saenko, K., Darrell, T.: Long-term recurrent convolutional networks for visual recognition and description. In: Proceedings of the IEEE Conference on Computer Vision and Pattern Recognition, pp. 2625–2634 (2015)
5. Graves, A., Jaitly, N.: Towards end-to-end speech recognition with recurrent neural networks. In: ICML, vol. 14, pp. 1764–1772 (2014)
6. LeCun, Y., Bengio, Y., Hinton, G.: Deep learning. Nature 521(7553), 436–444 (2015)
7. Ramos, S.: The dream of self-driving cars. In: ICCV Tutorial on Computer Vision for Autonomous Driving (2015)
8. Sak, H., Senior, A.W., Beaufays, F.: Long short-term memory recurrent neural network architectures for large scale acoustic modeling. In: INTERSPEECH, pp. 338–342 (2014)
9. Shah, R., Romijnders, R.: Applying deep learning to basketball trajectories. arXiv preprint arXiv:1608.03793 (2016)
10. Williams, R.J., Peng, J.: An efficient gradient-based algorithm for on-line training of recurrent network trajectories. Neural Comput. 2(4), 490–501 (1990)

Temporal Convolutional Networks: A Unified Approach to Action Segmentation

Colin Lea[✉], René Vidal, Austin Reiter, and Gregory D. Hager

Johns Hopkins University, Baltimore, USA
clea1@jhu.edu, rvidal@cis.jhu.edu, {areiter,hager}@cs.jhu.edu

Abstract. The dominant paradigm for video-based action segmentation is composed of two steps: first, compute low-level features for each frame using Dense Trajectories or a Convolutional Neural Network to encode local spatiotemporal information, and second, input these features into a classifier such as a Recurrent Neural Network (RNN) that captures high-level temporal relationships. While often effective, this decoupling requires specifying two separate models, each with their own complexities, and prevents capturing more nuanced long-range spatiotemporal relationships. We propose a unified approach, as demonstrated by our Temporal Convolutional Network (TCN), that hierarchically captures relationships at low-, intermediate-, and high-level time-scales. Our model achieves superior or competitive performance using video or sensor data on three public action segmentation datasets and can be trained in a fraction of the time it takes to train an RNN.

1 Introduction

Action segmentation is crucial for numerous applications ranging from collaborative robotics to modeling activities of daily living. Given a video, the goal is to simultaneously segment every action in time and classify each constituent segment. While recent work has shown strong improvements on this task, models tend to decouple low-level feature representations from high-level temporal models. Within video analysis, these low-level features may be computed by pooling handcrafted features (e.g. Improved Dense Trajectories (IDT) [21]) or concatenating learned features (e.g. Spatiotemporal Convolutional Neural Networks (ST-CNN) [8,12]) over a short period of time. High-level temporal classifiers capture a local history of these low-level features. In a Conditional Random Field (CRF), the action prediction at one time step is are often a function of the prediction at the previous time step, and in a Recurrent Neural Network (RNN), the predictions are a function of a set of latent states at each time step, where the latent states are connected across time. This two-step paradigm has been around for decades (e.g., [6]) and typically goes unquestioned. However, we posit that valuable information is lost between steps.

In this work, we introduce a unified approach to action segmentation that uses a single set of computational mechanisms – 1D convolutions, pooling, and channel-wise normalization – to hierarchically capture low-, intermediate-, and

© Springer International Publishing Switzerland 2016
G. Hua and H. Jégou (Eds.): ECCV 2016 Workshops, Part III, LNCS 9915, pp. 47–54, 2016.
DOI: 10.1007/978-3-319-49409-8_7

high-level temporal information. For each layer, 1D convolutions capture how features at lower levels change over time, pooling enables efficient computation of long-range temporal patterns, and normalization improves robustness towards varying environmental conditions. In contrast with RNN-based models, which compute a set of latent activations that are updated sequentially per-frame, we compute a set of latent activations that are updated hierarchically per-layer. As a byproduct, our model takes much less time to train. Our model can be viewed as a generalization of the recent ST-CNN [8] and is more similar to recent models for semantic segmentation than it is to models for video-analysis. We show this approach is broadly applicable to video and other types of robot sensors.

Prior Work: Due to space limitations, here we will only briefly describe models for time-series and semantic segmentation. See [8] for related work on action segmentation or [20] for a broader overview on action recognition.

RNNs and CRFs are popular high-level temporal classifiers. RNN variations, including Long Short Term Memory (LSTM) and Gated Recurrent Units (GRU), model hidden temporal states via internal gating mechanisms. However, they are hard to introspect and difficult to correctly train [13]. It has been shown that in practice LSTM only keeps a memory of about 4 s on some video-based action segmentation datasets [15]. CRFs typically model pairwise transitions between the labels or latent states (e.g., [8]), which are easy to interpret, but over-simplify the temporal dynamics of complex actions. Both of these models suffer from the same fundamental issue: intermediate activations are typically a function of the low-level features at the current time step and the state at the previous time step. Our temporal convolutional filters are a function of raw data across a much longer period of time.

Until recently, the dominant paradigm for semantic was similar to that of action segmentation. Approaches typically combined low-level texture features (e.g., TextonBoost) with high-level spatial models (e.g., grid-based CRFs) that model the relationships between different regions of an image [7]. This is similar to action segmentation where low-level spatiotemporal features are used in tandem with high-level temporal models. Recently, with the introduction of Fully Convolutional Networks (FCNs), the dominant semantic segmentation paradigm has started to change. Long *et al.* [11] introduced the first FCN, which leverages typical classification CNNs like AlexNet, to compute per-pixel object labels. This is done by intelligently upsampling the intermediate activations in each region of an image. Our model is more similar to the recent encoder-decoder network by Badrinarayanan *et al.* [1]. Their encoder step uses the first half of a VGG-like network to capture patterns in different regions of an image and their decoder step takes the activations from the encoder, which are of a reduced image resolution, and uses convolutional filters to upsample back to the original image size. In subsequent sections we describe our temporal variation in detail.

2   Temporal Convolutional Networks (TCN)

The input to our Temporal Convolutional Network can be a sensor signal (e.g. accelerometers) or latent encoding of a spatial CNN applied to each frame.

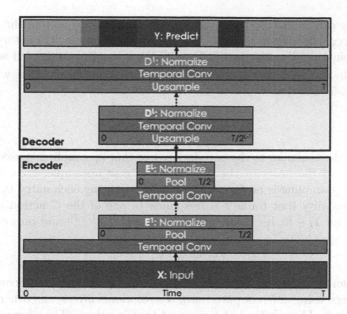

Fig. 1. Our temporal encoder-decoder network hierarchically models actions from video or other time-series data.

Let $X_t \in \mathbb{R}^{F_0}$ be the input feature vector of length F_0 for time step t for $1 < t \leq T$. Note that the time T may vary for each sequence, and we denote the number of time steps in each layer as T_l. The true action label for each frame is given by $y_t \in \{1, \ldots, C\}$, where C is the number of classes.

Our encoder-decoder framework, as depicted in Fig. 1, is composed of temporal convolutions, 1D pooling/upsampling, and channel-wise normalization layers.

For each of the L convolutional layers in the encoder, we apply a set of 1D filters that capture how the input signals evolve over the course of an action. The filters for each layer are parameterized by tensor $W^{(l)} \in \mathbb{R}^{F_l \times d \times F_{l-1}}$ and biases $b^{(l)} \in \mathbb{R}^{F_l}$, where $l \in \{1, \ldots, L\}$ is the layer index and d is the filter duration. For the l-th layer of the encoder, the i-th component of the (unnormalized) activation $\hat{E}_t^{(l)} \in \mathbb{R}^{F_l}$ is a function of the incoming (normalized) activation matrix $E^{(l-1)} \in \mathbb{R}^{F_{l-1} \times T_{l-1}}$ from the previous layer

$$\hat{E}_{i,t}^{(l)} = f(b_i^{(l)} + \sum_{t'=1}^{d} \langle W_{i,t',\cdot}^{(l)}, E_{\cdot, t+d-t'}^{(l-1)}\rangle) \tag{1}$$

for each time t where $f(\cdot)$ is a Leaky Rectified Linear Unit. The normalization process is described below.

Max pooling is applied with width 2 across time (in 1D) such that $T_l = \frac{1}{2}T_{l-1}$.[1] Pooling enables us to efficiently compute activations over a long period of time.

---

[1] In theory, this implies T must divisible by 2^L. In practice, we pad each sequence to be of an appropriate length, given the pooling operations, such that the input length of the whole sequence, T, and the length of the output predictions are the same.

We apply channel-wise normalization after each pooling step in the encoder. This has been effective in recent CNN methods including Trajectory-Pooled Deep-Convolutional Descriptors (TDD) [10]. We normalize the pooled activation vector $\hat{E}_t^{(l)}$ by the highest response at that time step, $m = \max_i \hat{E}_{i,t}^{(l)}$, with some small $\epsilon = 1\text{E-}5$ such that

$$E_t^{(l)} = \frac{1}{m + \epsilon} \hat{E}_t^{(l)}. \tag{2}$$

Our decoder is similar to the encoder, except that upsampling is used instead of pooling, and the order of the operations is now upsample, convolve, then normalize. Upsampling is performed by simply repeating each entry twice.

The probability that frame t corresponds to one of the C action classes is given by vector $\hat{Y}_t \in [0, 1]^C$ using weight matrix $U \in \mathbb{R}^{C \times F_0}$ and bias $c \in \mathbb{R}^C$

$$\hat{Y}_t = \text{softmax}(U D_t^{(1)} + c). \tag{3}$$

We explored many other mechanisms, such as adding skip connections between layers, using different patterns of convolutional layers, and other normalization schemes. These helped at times and hurt in others. The aforementioned solution was superior in aggregate.

Implementation Details: Each of the $L = 3$ layers has $F_l = \{32, 64, 96\}$ filters. Filter duration, d, is set as the mean segment duration for the shortest class from the training set. For example, $d = 10\,\text{s}$ for 50 Salads. Parameters of our model were learned using the cross entropy loss with Stochastic Gradient Descent and ADAM step updates. All models were implemented using Keras and TensorFlow.

For each frame in our video experiments, the input, X_t, is the first fully connected layer computed in a spatial CNN trained solely on each dataset. We trained the model of [8], except instead of using Motion History Images (MHI) as input to the CNN, we concatenate the following for image I_t at frame t: $[I_t, I_{t-d} - I_t, I_{t+d} - I_t, I_{t-2d} - I_t, I_{t+2d} - I_t]$ for $d = 0.5\,\text{s}$. In our experiments, these difference images – which can be viewed as a simple type of attention mechanism – tend to perform better than MHI or optical flow across these datasets. Furthermore, for each time step, we perform channel-wise normalization before feeding it into the TCN. This helps with large environmental fluctuations, such as changes in lighting.

3   Evaluation

We evaluate on three public datasets that contain action segmentation labels, video, and in two cases sensor data.

University of Dundee 50 Salads [18] contains 50 sequences of users making a salad. Each video is 5–10 min in duration and contains around 30 action instances such as cutting a tomato or peeling a cucumber. This dataset includes video and synchronized accelerometers attached to ten objects in the scene, such as the *bowl*, *knife*, and *plate*. We performed cross validation with 5 splits on the "eval" action granularity which includes 10 action classes. Our sensor results used the features from [9] which are the absolute values of accelerometer values. Previous results (e.g., [9,14]) were evaluated using different setups. For example, [9] smoothed out short interstitial background segments. We reran all results to be consistent with [14]. We also included an LSTM baseline for comparison which uses 64 hidden states.

JHU-ISI Gesture and Skill Assessment Working Set (JIGSAWS) [5] was introduced to improve quantitative evaluation of robotic surgery training tasks. We used Leave One User Out cross validation on the suturing activity, which consists of 39 sequences performed by 8 users about 5 times each. The dataset includes video and synchronized robot kinematics (position, velocity, and gripper angle) for each robot end effector as well as corresponding action labels with 10 action classes. Sequences are a few minutes long and typically contain around 20 action instances.

Georgia Tech Egocentric Activities (GTEA) [4] contains 28 videos of 7 kitchen activities including making a sandwich and making coffee. For each of the four subjects, there is one instance of each activity. The camera is mounted on the head of the user and is pointing at the area in front them. On average there are about 30 actions per video and videos are around a minute long. We used the 11 action classes defined in [3] and evaluated using leave one user out. We show results for user 2 to be consistent with [3] and [16].

Metrics: We evaluated using accuracy, which is simply the percent of correctly labeled frames, and segmental edit distance [9], which measures the correctness of the predicted temporal ordering of actions. This edit score is computed by applying the Levenshtein distance to the segmented predictions (e.g. $AAABBA \rightarrow ABA$). This is normalized to be in the range 0 to 100 such that higher is better.

4   Experiments and Discussion

Table 1 includes results for all datasets and corresponding sensing modalities. We include results from the spatial CNN which is input into the TCN, the Spatiotemporal CNN of Lea *et al.* [8] applied to the spatial features, and our TCN.

One of the most interesting findings is that some layers of convolutional filters appear to learn temporal shifts. There are certain actions in each dataset which are not easy to distinguish given the sensor data. By visualizing the activations for each layer, we found our model surmounts this issue by learning temporal offsets from activations in the previous layer. In addition, we find that despite the fact that we do not use a traditional temporal model, such as an RNN or CRF, our predictions do not suffer as heavily from issues like over-segmentation. This is highlighted by the large increase in edit score on most experiments.

Table 1. Results on 50 Salads, Georgia Tech Egocentric Activities, and JHU-ISI Gesture and Skill Assessment Working Set. Notes: (1) Results using VGG and Improved Dense Trajectories (IDT) were intentionally computed without a temporal component for ablative analysis, hence their low edit scores. (2) We re-computed [9] using the author's public code to be consistent with the setup of [14].

50 Salads ("eval" setup)

Sensor-based	Edit	Acc
LC-SC-CRF [9]	50.2	77.8
LSTM	54.5	73.3
TCN	**65.6**	**82.0**

Video-based	Edit	Acc
VGG [8]	7.6	38.3
IDT [8]	16.8	54.3
Seg-ST-CNN [8]	**62.0**	72.0
Spatial CNN	28.4	68.6
ST-CNN	55.5	74.2
TCN	61.1	**74.4**

GTEA

Video-based	Edit	Acc
Hand-crafted [3]	-	47.7
EgoNet [16]	-	57.6
TDD [16]	-	59.5
EgoNet+TDD [16]	-	**68.5**
Spatial CNN	36.6	56.1
ST-CNN	53.4	64.5
TCN	**58.8**	66.1

JIGSAWS

Sensor-based	Edit	Acc
LSTM [2]	75.3	80.5
LC-SC-CRF [9]	76.8	**83.4**
Bidir LSTM[2]	81.1	83.3
SD-SDL[17]	83.3	78.6
TCN	**85.8**	79.6

Vision-based	Edit	Acc
MsM-CRF [19]	-	71.7
IDT [8]	8.5	53.9
VGG [8]	24.3	45.9
Seg-ST-CNN [8]	66.6	74.7
Spatial CNN	37.7	74.0
ST-CNN	68.0	77.7
TCN	**83.1**	**81.4**

Richard et al. [14] evaluated their model on the mid-level action granularity of 50 Salads which has 17 action classes. Their model achieved 54.2% accuracy, 44.8% edit, 0.379 mAP IoU overlap with a threshold of 0.1, and 0.229 mAP with a threshold of 0.5.[2] Our model achieves 59.7% accuracy, 47.3% edit, 0.579 mAP at 0.1, and 0.378 mAP at 0.5.

On GTEA, Singh et al. [16] reported 64.4% accuracy by performing cross validation on users 1 through 3. We achieve 62.5% using this setup. We found performance of our model has high variance between different trials on GTEA– even with the same hyper parameters – thus, the difference in accuracy is not likely to be statistically significant. Our approach could be used in tandem with features from Singh et al.to achieve superior performance.

Our model can be trained much faster than an RNN-LSTM. Using an Nvidia Titan X, it takes on the order of a minute to train a TCN for each split, whereas it takes on the order of an hour to train an RNN-LSTM. The speedup comes from the fact that we compute one set of convolutions for each layer, whereas RNN-LSTM effectively computes one set of convolutions for each time step.

Conclusion: We introduced a model for action segmentation that learns a hierarchy of intermediate feature representations, which contrasts with the traditional low- versus high-level paradigm. This model achieves competitive or superior performance on several datasets and can be trained much more quickly than other models. A future version of this manuscript will include more comparisons and insights on the TCN.

---

[2] We computed our metrics using the predictions given by the authors.

References

1. Badrinarayanan, V., Handa, A., Cipolla, R.: SegNet: a deep convolutional encoder-decoder architecture for robust semantic pixel-wise labelling. arXiv preprint arXiv:1505.07293 (2015)
2. DiPietro, R., Lea, C., Malpani, A., Ahmidi, N., Vedula, S.S., Lee, G.I., Lee, M.R., Hager, G.D.: Recognizing surgical activities with recurrent neural networks. In: Ourselin, S., Joskowicz, L., Sabuncu, M.R., Unal, G., Wells, W. (eds.) MICCAI 2016. LNCS, vol. 9900, pp. 551–558. Springer, Heidelberg (2016). doi:10.1007/978-3-319-46720-7_64
3. Fathi, A., Farhadi, A., Rehg, J.M.: Understanding egocentric activities. In: ICCV (2011)
4. Fathi, A., Xiaofeng, R., Rehg, J.M.: Learning to recognize objects in egocentric activities. In: CVPR (2011)
5. Gao, Y., Vedula, S.S., Reiley, C.E., Ahmidi, N., Varadarajan, B., Lin, H.C., Tao, L., Zappella, L., Béjar, B., Yuh, D.D., et al.: JHU-ISI Gesture and Skill Assessment Working Set (JIGSAWS): a surgical activity dataset for human motion modeling. In: MICCAI Workshop: M2CAI (2014)
6. Hofmann, F.G., Heyer, P., Hommel, G.: Velocity profile based recognition of dynamic gestures with discrete hidden Markov models. In: International Workshop on Gesture and Sign Language in Human-Computer Interaction (1998)
7. Krähenbühl, P., Koltun, V.: Efficient inference in fully connected CRFs with Gaussian edge potentials. In: NIPS (2011)
8. Lea, C., Reiter, A., Vidal, R., Hager, G.D.: Segmental spatiotemporal CNNs for fine-grained action segmentation. In: Leibe, B., Matas, J., Sebe, N., Welling, M. (eds.) ECCV 2016. LNCS, vol. 9907, pp. 36–52. Springer, Heidelberg (2016). doi:10.1007/978-3-319-46487-9_3
9. Lea, C., Vidal, R., Hager, G.D.: Learning convolutional action primitives for fine-grained action recognition. In: ICRA (2016)
10. Limin Wang, Y.Q., Tang, X.: Action recognition with trajectory-pooled deep-convolutional descriptors. In: CVPR (2015)
11. Long, J., Shelhamer, E., Darrell, T.: Fully convolutional networks for semantic segmentation. In: CVPR (2015)
12. Ng, J.Y., Hausknecht, M.J., Vijayanarasimhan, S., Vinyals, O., Monga, R., Toderici, G.: Beyond short snippets: deep networks for video classification. In: CVPR (2015)
13. Pascanu, R., Mikolov, T., Bengio, Y.: On the difficulty of training recurrent neural networks. In: ICML (2013)
14. Richard, A., Gall, J.: Temporal action detection using a statistical language model. In: CVPR (2016)
15. Singh, B., Marks, T.K., Jones, M., Tuzel, O., Shao, M.: A multi-stream bi-directional recurrent neural network for fine-grained action detection. In: CVPR (2016)
16. Singh, S., Arora, C., Jawahar, C.V.: First person action recognition using deep learned descriptors. In: CVPR, June 2016
17. Stefati, S., Cowan, N., Vidal, R.: Learning shared, discriminative dictionaries for surgical gesture segmentation and classification. In: MICCAI Workshop: M2CAI (2015)
18. Stein, S., McKenna, S.J.: Combining embedded accelerometers with computer vision for recognizing food preparation activities. In: UbiComp (2013)

19. Tao, L., Zappella, L., Hager, G.D., Vidal, R.: Surgical gesture segmentation and recognition. In: Mori, K., Sakuma, I., Sato, Y., Barillot, C., Navab, N. (eds.) MIC-CAI 2013. LNCS, vol. 8151, pp. 339–346. Springer, Heidelberg (2013). doi:10.1007/978-3-642-40760-4_43
20. Vrigkas, M., Nikou, C., Kakadiaris, I.: A review of human activity recognition methods. Front. Robot. AI (2015)
21. Wang, H., Schmid, C.: Action recognition with improved trajectories. In: ICCV (2013)

Making a Case for Learning Motion Representations with Phase

S.L. Pintea$^{(\boxtimes)}$ and J.C. van Gemert

Computer Vision Lab, Delft University of Technology, Delft, Netherlands
{S.L.Pintea,J.C.vanGemert}@tudelft.nl

Abstract. This work advocates Eulerian motion representation learning over the current standard Lagrangian optical flow model. Eulerian motion is well captured by using phase, as obtained by decomposing the image through a complex-steerable pyramid. We discuss the gain of Eulerian motion in a set of practical use cases: (i) action recognition, (ii) motion prediction in static images, (iii) motion transfer in static images and, (iv) motion transfer in video. For each task we motivate the phase-based direction and provide a possible approach.

1 Introduction

We propose an Eulerian approach towards motion representation learning. The main difference between Lagrangian and Eulerian motion is that Lagrangian motion (optical flow) focuses on individual points and analyzes their change in location over time. Therefore, Lagrangian motion performs tracking of points over time and for this it requires a unique matching method between point or patches. On the other hand, Eulerian motion considers a set of locations in the image and analyzes the changes at these locations over time. Thus, Eulerian motion does not estimate where a given point moves to, instead, it measures flux properties. Figure 1 depicts this difference between Eulerian and Lagrangian motion. As a specific instance of the Eulerian model, we consider phase-based motion. The phase variations over time of the coefficients of the complex-steerable pyramid are indicatives of motion [9] and form the basis for learning motion representations.

The gain of an Eulerian motion approach is that it avoids the need for hand-crafted optical flow constructions. Phase is an innate property of the image, it does not need to be estimated from explicit patch correspondences. We propose a general-purpose phase-based motion description learning setup that can be used in any task relying on motion. Here we explore four use cases: (i) action recognition, (ii) motion prediction in static images, (iii) motion transfer in static images and, (iv) motion transfer in video. Note that phase-based motion representations are readily applicably to other motion-related task as well, including: human gait analysis, object tracking, action localization, etc.

© Springer International Publishing Switzerland 2016
G. Hua and H. Jégou (Eds.): ECCV 2016 Workshops, Part III, LNCS 9915, pp. 55–64, 2016.
DOI: 10.1007/978-3-319-49409-8_8

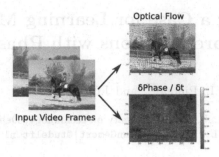

Fig. 1. While Lagrangian motion (optical flow) estimates the changes in position over time, it can miss correspondences or find mistaken correspondences. However, in the Eulerian approach (phase variations over time) the number of motion measurements stays constant between frames, as for each input image we analyze the phase variations over time at each image location over multiple orientations and scales.

2   Related Work

2.1   Eulerian Motion

Eulerian motion modeling has shown remarkable results for motion magnification [31] where a phase-based approach significantly improves the quality [28] and broadens its application [1,16]. A phase-based video interpolation is proposed in [18] and a phase-based optical flow estimation is proposed in [13]. Inspired by the these work, we advocate the use of the Eulerian model as exemplified by phase for learning motion representations.

2.2   Action Recognition

Optical flow-based motion features have been extensively employed for action recognition in works such as [14,19,26,30]. These works, use hand crafted features extracted from the optical flow. Instead, we propose to input phase-based motion measurements to a CNN to reap the benefits of deep feature representation learning methods.

A natural extension of going beyond a single frame in a deep net is by using $3D$ space-time convolutions [15,25]. $3D$ convolutions learn appearance and motion jointly. While elegant, it makes it difficult to add the wealth of information that is available for appearance-only datasets through pre-training. In our method, we keep the benefit of pre-training by separating the appearance and the phase-based motion streams.

Using pre-trained networks is possible in the two-stream network approaches proposed in [5,7,23]. This combines a multi-frame optical flow network stream with an appearance stream and obtains competitive results in practice. The appearance stream can employ a pretrained network. Similarly, we also consider the combination of appearance and motion in a two-stream fashion, but with innate phase information rather than using a hand-crafted optical flow.

The temporal frame ordering is exploited in [8], where the parameters of a ranking machine are used for video description. While in [6,17,24] recurrent neural networks are proposed for improving action recognition. In this paper we also model the temporal aspect, although we add the benefit of a two-stream approach by separating appearance and phase variation over time.

2.3   Motion Prediction

In [20], optical flow motion is learned from videos and predicted in static images in a structured regression formulation. In [29] the authors propose predicting optical flow in a CNN from input static images. Where these works predict optical flow, we propose to predict the motion through phase changes, which does not depend on pixel tracking.

Predicting the future RGB frame from the current RGB frame is proposed in [27] in the context of action prediction. Similar to this work, we also start from an input appearance and obtain an output appearance image, however in our case the learning part learns the mapping from input phase information to future phase.

2.4   Motion Transfer

Animating a static image by transferring the motion from an input video is related to the notion of artistic style transfer [11,12,21]. The style transfer aims at changing an input image or video such that the artistic style matches the one of a provided target image. Here, instead, we consider the motion transfer — given an input image, transfer the phase-based motion from the video to the image.

Additionally, we also consider video-to-video transfer where the style of performing a certain action is transferred from a target video to the input video. In [2] the authors allow the users to change the video by adding plausible object manipulations in the video. Similar to this work, we also want to change the video motion after the recording is done, by adjusting the style of the action being performed.

3   Learning Motion with Phase

The local phase and amplitude of an image are measured by complex oriented filters of the form: $G_\sigma^\theta + iH_\sigma^\theta$, where θ is the filter orientation and σ the filter scale [10],

$$(G_\sigma^\theta + iH_\sigma^\theta) \otimes I(x,y) = A_\sigma^\theta(x,y)e^{i\phi_\sigma^\theta(x,y)}, \tag{1}$$

where $\phi_\sigma^\theta(x,y)$ is the local phase at scale σ and orientation θ, and $A_\sigma^\theta(x,y,t_0)$ the amplitude, $I(x,y)$ is the image brightness/input channel, and $\otimes$ the convolution operator, and x,y are image coordinates. The filters have multiple scales and orientations, forming a complex steerable pyramid [22] which captures various levels of image resolution.

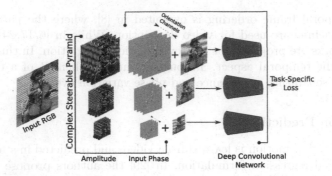

Fig. 2. Phase-based representation learning: from an input RGB image we extract phase information over multiple orientations and scales by employing complex steerable filters. For each scale, additional to the RGB input, we add the orientated phases as input to a network stream that optimizes a task-specific loss.

There is a direct relation between motion and the change measured in phase over time. The Fourier shift theorem makes the connection between the variation in phase of the subbands over time and the global image motion. Rather than estimating global motion, using a steerable pyramid we can decompose the image into localized subbands and thus, recover the local motion in the phase variations over time. From the above decomposition only the phase, not the amplitude, corresponds to motion. In [9] the authors show that the temporal gradient of phase computed from a spatially bandpassed video over time, directly relates to the motion field. Therefore, here, we focus on local phase at multiple scales and orientations to represent motion.

We propose using phase to learn motion representations for solving general motion-related tasks in a deep net. We add phase as an additional motion input channel to a standard appearance (RGB) convolutional deep neural network. Figure 2 shows our proposed general-purpose phase-based pipeline. The input video frame is decomposed using the complex steerable pyramid into amplitude and phase. Both phase and amplitude have multiple corresponding orientations and scales. Since the phase is an indicative of motion, we ignore the amplitude and we use the input phase for the motion representation learning. We treat the orientations as input channels while the scales represent different streams of the network, similar to [4] who use this setup for a different image pyramid.

4   Four Use Cases in Motion Learning

We explore phase-based motion representation learning in four practical use cases. While a thorough in-depth experimental investigation is out of scope, we detail the setup of motion representation learning for each use case.

4.1   Phase-Based Action Recognition

Separating appearance and motion in two-streams is effective for action recognition [23]. For the appearance stream we follow [23] and use the input

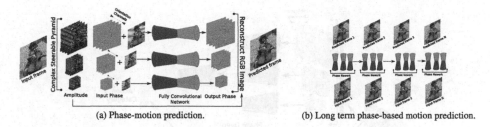

(a) Phase-motion prediction.   (b) Long term phase-based motion prediction.

Fig. 3. (a) Phase prediction in a Phase Network: from an input RGB image, we estimate the phase along multiple scales and orientations. For each scale we train a Fully
Convolutional Network that predicts oriented phase at a future time-step. From this
we recover the predicted future RGB image. (b) Long-term motion prediction in static
images: given the one step convolutional mapping from the input RGB image to the
future RGB image, defined in the 'Phase Network', combine multiple of these networks
in an Recurrent Neural Network to obtain plausible long-term phase predictions.

RGB frame, which offers the advantage of pre-training features on static images.
However, where [23] uses hand-crafted optical flow features, we propose to use
Eulerian motion for the second stream with oriented phase over multiple scales,
as depicted in Fig. 4.

For evaluating action recognition, a comparison of our two-stream phase-
based motion with the two-stream optical-flow approach of [23] on the two
datasets used in their paper — HMDB51 and UCF101 is needed. We expect
benefits from a phase-based motion representation because it does not depend
on a specific hand-crafted optical flow implementation and does not rely on pixel
tracking.

4.2   Phase-Based Motion Prediction in Static

The benefit of Eulerian motion for motion prediction is that the prediction locations are fixed over time. This contrasts sharply with Lagrangian motion, as
pixels tracked by optical flow may be lost as they move in or out of the frame,
or move to the same spatial location. Such lost pixels make it hard to recover
long-term relations beyond just the next frame. The fixed prediction locations
of a Eulerian motion representation do not suffer from this and offer long-term
relation predictions of several frames.

We propose to learn from a given input RGB the output future RGB, by
recovering from the RGB the phase scales and orientations, then predicting the
multi-scale future phase-orientations and transforming them back into future
RGB frames as in Fig. 3(a). For long-term motion prediction we propose an
RNN (Recurrent Neural Network) version of this phase-based frame prediction,
as depicted in Fig. 3(b). Thus, predicting motion N timesteps away from the
input.

For evaluating motion prediction we use the same datasets as in
[29] — HMDB51 and UCF101, where the authors aim at predicting optical-flow

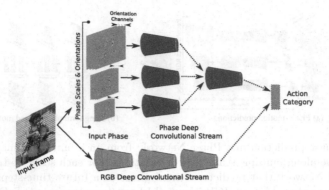

Fig. 4. Action recognition approach: two-stream CNN where the first stream receives input RGB frames, while the second stream receives input oriented phases of the video frame over multiple scales that are subsequently combined.

based motion in single images. To evaluate the difference between the predicted motion and the actual video motion, we use pixel accuracy, as in our method we recover the appearance of the future frame. For comparison with [29] which reports EPE (End Point Errors), we use their chosen optical flow estimation algorithm to recover optical flow from our predicted RGB.

4.3 Phase-Based Motion Transfer in Images

Similar to [12,21], where the style of a given target painting is transferred to another image, we propose to transfer the short motion of a given video sequence to an input static image. In [12] a combination of two losses is optimized: content loss which ensures that the objects present in the newly generated image remain recognizable and correspond to the ones in the input image, and a style loss which imposes that the artistic style of the new image is similar to the one of the provided target painting. For motion transfer we have an additional requirement, namely that parts of the image that are similar — e.g. horses, people, should move similar. For this we use two pretrained network streams, an RGB stream and a phase stream and consider certain convolutional layers along these streams for estimation RGB/phase responses. Therefore, we first estimate an element-wise correlation between the responses at a given convolutional network layer of the input RGB values of the static image and the target video frame:

$$\mathcal{K}_j^l = \frac{\sum_i^{N_l} C_{ij}^l D_{ij}^l}{\sqrt{\sum_i^{N_l} {C_{ij}^l}^2}\sqrt{\sum_i^{N_l} {D_{ij}^l}^2}}, \tag{2}$$

where N_l is the number of channels in the layer l, C^l and D^l the responses at layer l for the input image and video frame, respectively. Following [12], we subsequently define our motion-style loss by weighting the feature maps in the Gram matrix computation by the appearance correlation. The motion transfer is obtained by enforcing that the phase of objects over time in the input image, should be similar to the phase over time of the same objects present in the target video. The motion-style loss optimization is performed per phase-scale.

$$G_\sigma^l[ij] = \sum_k^{M_l} \mathcal{K}_k^l F_\sigma^l[ik] F_\sigma^l[kj], \; i,j \in \{1,..N_l\}, \tag{3}$$

$$A_\sigma^l[ij] = \sum_k^{M_l} \mathcal{K}_k^l P_\sigma^l[ik] P_\sigma^l[kj], \; i,j \in \{1,..N_l\}, \tag{4}$$

$$\mathcal{L}_l = \sum_\sigma \frac{1}{N_l^2 M_l^2} \sum_{i,j}^{N_l} \mathcal{K}_j^l (G_\sigma^l[ij] - A_\sigma^l[ij])^2, \tag{5}$$

where M_l is the number of elements in one channel of layer l, σ indicates the phase-scale, and G^l is the weighted Gram matrix of the phase-image to be generated, while A^l is the weighted Gram matrix of the current video frame and, F^l and P^l are the responses of the phase-image to be generated and the phase-image of the input video frame, respectively.

Because we want the find similar looking objects by using the element-wise correlations, we expect that the higher convolutional levels of the network will perform better. We additionally also add the content loss term of [12] to avoid large distortions of the image appearance. Due to the input being a static image, only short video motions can be transferred in this case.

For evaluating motion transfer, we perform a two-step evaluation. In the first step, we select an existing video frame and transfer the video motion to the selected frame and compare the transferred motion with the actual video motion. For this we use videos from HMDB51 and UCF101. The second evaluation is transferring the motion to actual static images. For this we select images from the static Willow dataset [3] and transfer the motion of corresponding videos from the HMDB51 and UCF101 datasets containing the same objects. For this we provide the static images animated with the transferred video motion.

4.4   Phase-Based Motion Transfer in Videos

We use as a starting point the work of [21], where artistic style is transferred to video. However in our case, the motion of one given video is transferred to another input video. The gain in so doing, is that we can transfer the style of performing a certain action. For example an amateur performing the moonwalk can be lifted to the expert level by transferring the motion of Michael Jackson himself.

The idea of transferring motion in videos is similar to the idea of transferring motion in static images, with the additional constraint that the motion must be temporally coherent. For this, similar to [21], we add a temporal loss term to the motion transfer loss discussed in Sect. 4.3.

For performing motion transfer between videos, we use a set of target videos: the walk of Charlie Chaplin, the moonwalk of Michael Jackson, and the walk of a runway model. We transfer these walking styles to a set of input videos of people walking, and provide the results as a qualitative form of evaluation.

4.5 Preliminary Proof of Concept

Here[1], we show a very simple proof of concept for phase-based motion transfer. We animate a static image by transfering the motion of another semantic related video. Correctly aligning the moving entities between the video frames and the static image is essential for this task. For this proof of concept the alignment was not very good and no learning was used whatsoever. Misalignment errors show up as artifacts in the results and we expect that adding (deep) learning will improve results.

5   Conclusions

We propose an Eulerian –phase-based– approach to motion representation learning. We argue for the intrinsic stability offered by the phase-based motion description. A phase-based approach does not require pixel tracking and directly encodes flux. Phase is an innate property of an image and does not rely on hand-crafted optical-flow algorithms. We explore a set of motion learning tasks in an Eulerian setting: (a) action recognition, (b) motion prediction in static images, (c) motion transfer from a video to a static image and (d) motion transfer in videos. For each one of these tasks we propose a phase-based approach and provide a small proof of concept. We do not offer in-depth experimental results but instead make a case for a brave new motion representation with phase.

Acknowledgments. This work is part of the research programme Technology in Motion (TIM [628.004.001]), financed by the Netherlands Organisation for Scientific Research (NWO).

References

1. Chen, J.G., Wadhwa, N., Cha, Y.J., Durand, F., Freeman, W.T., Buyukozturk, O.: Modal identification of simple structures with high-speed video using motion magnification. J. Sound Vib. **345**, 58–71 (2015)
2. Davis, A., Chen, J.G., Durand, F.: Image-space modal bases for plausible manipulation of objects in video. ACM-TOG **34**(6), 239:1–239:7 (2015)
3. Delaitre, V., Laptev, I., Sivic, J.: Recognizing human actions in still images: a study of bag-of-features and part-based representations. In: BMVC (2010)
4. Denton, E.L., Chintala, S., Fergus, R., et al.: Deep generative image models using a Laplacian pyramid of adversarial networks. In: NIPS, pp. 1486–1494 (2015)
5. Diba, A., Mohammad Pazandeh, A., Van Gool, L.: Efficient two-stream motion and appearance 3D CNNs for video classification. arXiv preprint arXiv:1608.08851 (2016)

---

[1] Demo: http://silvialaurapintea.github.io/motion_transfer/index.html.

6. Donahue, J., Hendricks, L.A., Guadarrama, S., Rohrbach, M., Venugopalan, S., Saenko, K., Darrell, T.: Long-term recurrent convolutional networks for visual recognition and description. In: CVPR, pp. 2625–2634 (2015)
7. Feichtenhofer, C., Pinz, A., Zisserman, A.: Convolutional two-stream network fusion for video action recognition. arXiv preprint arXiv:1604.06573 (2016)
8. Fernando, B., Gavves, E., Oramas, J.M., Ghodrati, A., Tuytelaars, T.: Modeling video evolution for action recognition. In: CVPR, pp. 5378–5387 (2015)
9. Fleet, D.J., Jepson, A.D.: Computation of component image velocity from local phase information. IJCV 5(1), 77–104 (1990)
10. Freeman, W.T., Adelson, E.H.: The design and use of steerable filters. PAMI 13(9), 891–906 (1991)
11. Gatys, L.A., Bethge, M., Hertzmann, A., Shechtman, E.: Preserving color in neural artistic style transfer. arXiv preprint arXiv:1606.05897 (2016)
12. Gatys, L.A., Ecker, A.S., Bethge, M.: A neural algorithm of artistic style. arXiv preprint arXiv:1508.06576 (2015)
13. Gautama, T., Van Hulle, M.: A phase-based approach to the estimation of the optical flow field using spatial filtering. TNN 13(5), 1127–1136 (2002)
14. Jain, M., Jegou, H., Bouthemy, P.: Better exploiting motion for better action recognition. In: CVPR, pp. 2555–2562 (2013)
15. Ji, S., Xu, W., Yang, M., Yu, K.: 3D convolutional neural networks for human action recognition. PAMI 35(1), 221–231 (2013)
16. Kooij, J.F.P., Gemert, J.C.: Depth-aware motion magnification. In: Leibe, B., Matas, J., Sebe, N., Welling, M. (eds.) ECCV 2016. LNCS, vol. 9912, pp. 467–482. Springer, Heidelberg (2016). doi:10.1007/978-3-319-46484-8_28
17. Li, Z., Gavves, E., Jain, M., Snoek, C.G.M.: Videolstm convolves, attends and flows for action recognition. arXiv preprint arXiv:1607.01794 (2016)
18. Meyer, S., Wang, O., Zimmer, H., Grosse, M., Sorkine-Hornung, A.: Phase-based frame interpolation for video. In: CVPR, pp. 1410–1418 (2015)
19. Oneata, D., Verbeek, J., Schmid, C.: Action and event recognition with fisher vectors on a compact feature set. In: ICCV, pp. 1817–1824 (2013)
20. Pintea, S.L., Gemert, J.C., Smeulders, A.W.M.: Déjà vu: motion prediction in static images. In: Fleet, D., Pajdla, T., Schiele, B., Tuytelaars, T. (eds.) ECCV 2014. LNCS, vol. 8691, pp. 172–187. Springer, Heidelberg (2014). doi:10.1007/978-3-319-10578-9_12
21. Ruder, M., Dosovitskiy, A., Brox, T.: Artistic style transfer for videos. arXiv preprint arXiv:1604.08610 (2016)
22. Simoncelli, E.P., Freeman, W.T., Adelson, E.H., Heeger, D.J.: Shiftable multiscale transforms. Trans. Inf. Theory 38(2), 587–607 (1992)
23. Simonyan, K., Zisserman, A.: Two-stream convolutional networks for action recognition in videos. In: NIPS, pp. 568–576 (2014)
24. Srivastava, N., Mansimov, E., Salakhutdinov, R.: Unsupervised learning of video representations using LSTMs. CoRR, abs/1502.04681, 2 (2015)
25. Tran, D., Bourdev, L., Fergus, R., Torresani, L., Paluri, M.: C3D: generic features for video analysis. CoRR, abs/1412.0767, 2:7 (2014)
26. van Gemert, J., Jain, M., Gati, E., Snoek, C.: APT: action localization proposals from dense trajectories. In: BMVC, vol. 2, p. 4 (2015)
27. Vondrick, C., Pirsiavash, H., Torralba, A.: Anticipating the future by watching unlabeled video. arXiv preprint arXiv:1504.08023 (2015)
28. Wadhwa, N., Rubinstein, M., Durand, F., Freeman, W.T.: Phase-based video motion processing. ACM-TOG 32(4), 80 (2013)

29. Walker, J., Gupta, A., Hebert, M.: Dense optical flow prediction from a static image. In: ICCV (2015)
30. Wang, L., Qiao, Y., Tang, X.: Action recognition with trajectory-pooled deep-convolutional descriptors. In: CVPR, pp. 4305–4314 (2015)
31. Wu, H.Y., Rubinstein, M., Shih, E., Guttag, J., Durand, F., Freeman, W.T.: Eulerian video magnification for revealing subtle changes in the world. SIGGRAPH 31(4), 1–8 (2012)

W06 – Geometry Meets Deep Learning

Preface

Welcome to the Proceedings for the 1st Workshop on Geometry Meets Deep Learning, held in conjunction with the European Conference on Computer Vision on October 9th 2016.

The goal of this workshop is to encourage the interplay between geometric vision and deep learning. Deep learning has emerged as a common approach to learning data-driven representations. While deep learning approaches have obtained remarkable performance improvements in most 2D vision problems such as image classification and object detection, they cannot be directly applied to geometric vision problems due to the fundamental differences between 2D and 3D vision problems such as the non-Euclidean nature of geometric objects, higher dimensionality, and the lack of large-scale annotated 3D datasets. Developing integrated geometric components to improve the performances of deep neural networks is also a promising direction worth further exploration. The workshop aims to bring together experts from both 3D vision and deep learning areas to summarize the recent advances, exchange ideas, and inspire new directions.

We received a total number of 21 full-paper submissions that covered a wide range of topics such as feature detection, 3D object/human pose estimation, shape reconstruction, scene understanding and 3D mapping. Each submission was sent to at least two independent reviewers who were senior researchers in the related area. According to the reviewers' suggestions and internal discussions among the workshop chairs, 16 papers were accepted to the workshop, five of which were accepted as oral presentations and the rest as poster presentations. The program additionally included a Best Paper Prize for the best contribution. The workshop chairs did not submit any paper to avoid conflicts in the review process.

We would like to thank all of the reviewers and authors for their hard work and professionalism. The 1st GMDL workshop could not have been a great success without them. Finally, we hope that all the attendees enjoyed the workshop and this was only the beginning of a series of exciting and effective events!

October 2016

Best regards
Xiaowei Zhou
Emanuele Rodol
Jonathan Masci
Pierre Vandergheynst
Sanja Fidler
Kostas Daniilidis

gvnn: Neural Network Library for Geometric Computer Vision

Ankur Handa[1(✉)], Michael Bloesch[3], Viorica Pătrăucean[2], Simon Stent[2],
John McCormac[1], and Andrew Davison[1]

[1] Dyson Robotics Laboratory, Department of Computing,
Imperial College London, London, UK
handa.ankur@gmail.com,
{brendon.mccormac13,ajd}@ic.ac.uk
[2] Department of Engineering, University of Cambridge, Cambridge, UK
{vp344,sais2}@cam.ac.uk
[3] Robotic Systems Lab, ETH Zurich, Zurich, Switzerland
bloeschm@ethz.ch

Abstract. We introduce **gvnn**, a neural network library in Torch aimed
towards bridging the gap between classic geometric computer vision and
deep learning. Inspired by the recent success of Spatial Transformer Networks, we propose several new layers which are often used as parametric
transformations on the data in geometric computer vision. These layers
can be inserted within a neural network much in the spirit of the original spatial transformers and allow backpropagation to enable end-to-
end learning of a network involving any domain knowledge in geometric
computer vision. This opens up applications in learning invariance to 3D
geometric transformation for place recognition, end-to-end visual odometry, depth estimation and unsupervised learning through warping with
a parametric transformation for image reconstruction error.

Keywords: Spatial transformer networks · Geometric vision · Unsupervised learning

1 Introduction

Spatial transformers [1] represent a class of differentiable layers that can be
inserted in a standard convolutional neural network architecture to enable invariance to certain geometric transformations on the input data and warping for
reconstruction error [2]. In this work, we build upon the 2D transformation layers
originally proposed in the spatial transformer networks [1] and provide various
novel extensions that perform geometric transformations which are often used
in geometric computer vision. These layers have mostly no internal parameters
that need learning but allow backpropagation and can be inserted in a neural
network for any fixed differentiable geometric operation to be performed on the
data. This opens up an exciting new path to blend ideas from geometric computer vision into deep learning architectural designs allowing the exploitation of
problem-specific domain knowledge.

© Springer International Publishing Switzerland 2016
G. Hua and H. Jégou (Eds.): ECCV 2016 Workshops, Part III, LNCS 9915, pp. 67–82, 2016.
DOI: 10.1007/978-3-319-49409-8_9

Geometric computer vision has heavily relied on generative parametric models of inverse computer graphics to enable reasoning and understanding of real physical environments that provide rich observations in the form of images or video streams. These fundamentals and principles have been very well understood and form the backbone of large-scale point cloud reconstruction from multi-view image data, visual odometry, and image registration. In this work, we provide a comprehensive library that allows implementation of various image registration and reconstruction methods using these geometric transformation modules within the framework of convolutional neural networks. This means that certain elements in the classic geometric vision based methods that are hand-engineered can be replaced by a module that can be learnt end-to-end within a neural network. Our library is implemented in Torch [3] and builds upon the open source implementation of spatial transformer networks [4].

2   gvnn: Geometric Vision with Neural Networks

We introduce **gvnn**, a Torch package dedicated to performing transformations that are often used in geometric computer vision applications within a neural network. These transformations are implemented as fixed differentiable computational blocks that can be inserted within a convolutional neural network and are useful for manipulating the input data as per the domain knowledge in geometric computer vision. We expand on various novel transformation layers below that form the core part of the library built on top of the open source implementation [4] of spatial transformer networks.

Let us assume that $\mathcal{C}$ represents the cost function being optimised by the neural network. For a regression network it can take the following form *e.g.* $\mathcal{C} = \frac{1}{2}||\mathbf{y}_{pred} - \mathbf{y}_{gt}||^2$ where $\mathbf{y}_{pred}$ is a prediction vector produced by the network and $\mathbf{y}_{gt}$ is the corresponding ground truth vector. This allows us to propagate derivatives from the loss function back to the input to any layer in the network.

2.1   Global Transformations

We begin by extending the 2D transformations introduced in the original spatial transformer networks (STN) to their 3D counterparts. These transformations encode the global movement of the whole image *i.e.* the same transformation is applied to every pixel in the image or any 3D point in the world.

SO3 Layer. Rotations in our network are represented by the so(3) vector (or $\mathfrak{so}(3)$ skew symmetric matrix), which is compact 3×1 vector representation, $\mathbf{v} = (v_1, v_2, v_3)^T$, and is turned into a rotation matrix via the SO3 exponential map, *i.e.* $\mathsf{R}(\mathbf{v}) = \exp([\mathbf{v}]_\times)$. The backpropagation derivatives for $\mathbf{v}$ can be conveniently written as [5]

$$\frac{\partial \mathcal{C}}{\partial \mathbf{v}} = \frac{\partial \mathcal{C}}{\partial \mathsf{R}(\mathbf{v})} \cdot \frac{\partial \mathsf{R}(\mathbf{v})}{\partial \mathbf{v}} \tag{1}$$

where

$$\frac{\partial R(\mathbf{v})}{\partial v_i} = \frac{v_i[\mathbf{v}]_\times + [\mathbf{v} \times (I - R)e_i]_\times}{||\mathbf{v}||^2} R \tag{2}$$

$[\ ]_\times$ turns a 3×1 vector to a skew-symmetric matrix and $\times$ is a cross product operation. I is the Identity matrix and e_i is the ith column of the Identity matrix. We have also implemented different parameterisations $e.g.$ quaternions and Euler-angles for rotations as additional layers. Below we show the code-snippet that performs backpropagation on this layer.

```
function RotationSO3:updateGradInput(_tranformParams, _gradParams)

    -- _transformParams are the input parameters i.e. so3 vector
    -- _gradParams is the derivative of the cost function
    -- with respect to the rotation matrix

    -- gradInput is the derivative of cost
    -- function with respect to so3 vector
    local tParams, gradParams
    tParams = _tranformParams
    gradParams = _gradParams:clone()

    local batchSize = tParams:size(1)
    self.gradInput:resizeAs(tParams)

    local rotDerv = torch.zeros(batchSize, 3, 3):typeAs(tParams)
    local gradInputRotationParams = self.gradInput:narrow(2,1,1)

    -- take the derivative with respect to v1
    rotDerv = dR_by_dvi(tParams,self.rotationOutput,1, self.threshold)
    local selectGradParams = gradParams:narrow(2,1,3):narrow(3,1,3)
    gradRotParams:copy(torch.cmul(rotDerv,selectGradParams):sum(2):sum(3))

    -- take the derivative with respect to v2
    rotDerv = dR_by_dvi(tParams,self.rotationOutput,2, self.threshold)
    gradRotParams = self.gradInput:narrow(2,2,1)
    gradRotParams:copy(torch.cmul(rotDerv,selectGradParams):sum(2):sum(3))

    -- take the derivative with respect to v3
    rotDerv = dR_by_dvi(tParams,self.rotationOutput,3, self.threshold)
    gradRotParams = self.gradInput:narrow(2,3,1)
    gradRotParams:copy(torch.cmul(rotDerv,selectGradParams):sum(2):sum(3))

    return self.gradInput

end
```

SE3 Layer. The SE3 layer adds translations on top of the SO3 layer where translations are represented by a 3×1 vector $\mathbf{t}$, and together they make up the 3×4 transformation, *i.e.* $\mathsf{T} = [\mathsf{R}|\mathbf{t}] \in \text{SE3}$.

Sim3 Layer. Sim3 layer builds on top of the SE3 layer and has an extra scale factor s to allow for any scale changes associated with the transformations $\mathsf{T} = \begin{bmatrix} s\mathsf{R} & \mathbf{t} \\ 0 & 1 \end{bmatrix}$.

3D Grid Generator. The 3D grid generator is an extension of the 2D grid generator proposed in the original STN. It takes additionally a depth map as input, to map the image pixels to corresponding 3D points in the world and transforms these points with T coming from the SE3 layer. Note that we have used a regular grid in this layer, but it is possible to extend this to the general case where the grid locations can also be learnt.

Projection Layer. Projection layer maps the transformed 3D points, $\mathbf{p} = (u, v, w)^T$, onto 2D image plane using the focal lengths and the camera centre location. *i.e.*

$$\pi \begin{pmatrix} u \\ v \\ w \end{pmatrix} = \begin{pmatrix} f_x \frac{u}{w} + p_x \\ f_y \frac{v}{w} + p_y \end{pmatrix} \tag{3}$$

where f_x and f_y represent the focal lengths of the camera along X and Y axes and p_x and p_y are the camera center locations. The backpropagation derivatives can be written as

$$\frac{\partial C}{\partial \mathbf{p}} = \frac{\partial C}{\partial \pi(\mathbf{p})} \cdot \frac{\partial \pi(\mathbf{p})}{\partial \mathbf{p}} \tag{4}$$

where

$$\frac{\partial \pi \begin{pmatrix} u \\ v \\ w \end{pmatrix}}{\partial \begin{pmatrix} u \\ v \\ w \end{pmatrix}} = \begin{pmatrix} f_x \frac{1}{w} & 0 & -f_x \frac{u}{w^2} \\ 0 & f_y \frac{1}{w} & -f_y \frac{v}{w^2} \end{pmatrix} \tag{5}$$

In fact, if focal lengths are also involved in the optimisation, it is straightforward to include them in the network for any geometric camera calibration style optimisations. Note that special care must be taken to ensure that w is not very small. Fortunately, in many geometric vision problems w corresponds to the z-coordinate of a 3D point and is measured in metres — when using Kinect or ASUS xtion cameras this happens to be always greater than $10\,\text{cm}$[1].

---

[1] We discovered that anything below than that the forward/backward gradient check fails.

2.2 Per-pixel Transformations

In many computer vision problems, particularly related to understanding dynamic scenes, it is often required to have per-pixel transformations to model the movements of the stimuli in the scene. In the following, we propose different layers for modelling per-pixel transformations for both RGB and RGB-D inputs.

RGB Based. In the context of RGB data, the classic optic flow problem is a case of per-pixel transformation to model the movement of pixels across time. We implement both the well-known minimal parameterisation in the form of translation as well as more recently studied over-parameterised formulations that encapsulate the knowledge of scene geometry into the flow movement.

Mimimal Parameterisation Optic Flow. In its minimal parameterisation, optic flow (t_x, t_y) models the movement of pixels in the 2D image plane *i.e.*

$$\begin{pmatrix} x' \\ y' \end{pmatrix} = \begin{pmatrix} x + t_x \\ y + t_y \end{pmatrix} \tag{6}$$

This is the most well-known and studied parameterisation of optic flow in the literature and needs only 2 parameters per-pixel. In general, an extra smoothness penalty is imposed to ensure that the gradient of the flow varies smoothly across a pixel neighbourhood. Patraucean *et al.* [2] implement exactly this to model the optic flow and use Huber penalty for smoothness. We include this as a part of our library together with recent extensions with over-parameterised formulations.

Over-Parameterised Optic Flow. Attempts to use the popular differential epipolar constraint [6] and the recent over-parameterised formulations of [7] and [8] have shown that if knowledge about the scene geometry and motion can be used, it can greatly improve the flow estimates per-pixel. For instance, if the pixel lies on a planar surface, the motion of the pixel can be modelled by an affine transformation. Although [8] use a 9-DoF per-pixel transformation that includes the knowledge about the homography, we describe the affine parameterisation used in [7].

$$\begin{pmatrix} x' \\ y' \end{pmatrix} = \begin{pmatrix} a_0 & a_1 & a_2 \\ a_3 & a_4 & a_5 \end{pmatrix} \begin{pmatrix} x \\ y \\ 1 \end{pmatrix} \tag{7}$$

It is interesting to note that popular 2-DoF translation optic flow describe earlier happens to be a special case of affine transformation.

$$\begin{pmatrix} x' \\ y' \end{pmatrix} = \begin{pmatrix} 1 & 0 & t_x \\ 0 & 1 & t_y \end{pmatrix} \begin{pmatrix} x \\ y \\ 1 \end{pmatrix} \tag{8}$$

We provide implementations of 6-DoF affine transformation as well as SE(2) transformation per-pixel but extensions to 9-DoF paramterisation [8] are straightforward.

```
function AffineOpticFlow:updateGradInput(_PerPixelAffineParams, _gradGrid)

    local batchsize = _PerPixelAffineParams:size(1)

    self.gradInput:resizeAs(_PerPixelAffineParams):zero()

    -- batchGrid is the regular 2D grid: B H W 2
    -- batches: B, height: H, width: W, channels: 2

    local Lx_x = torch.cmul(_gradGrid:select(4,1), self.batchGrid:select(4,1))
    local Lx_y = torch.cmul(_gradGrid:select(4,1), self.batchGrid:select(4,2))

    local Ly_x = torch.cmul(_gradGrid:select(4,2), self.batchGrid:select(4,1))
    local Ly_y = torch.cmul(_gradGrid:select(4,2), self.batchGrid:select(4,2))

    self.gradInput:select(4,1):copy(Lx_x)
    self.gradInput:select(4,2):copy(Lx_y)
    self.gradInput:select(4,3):copy(_gradGrid:select(4,1))

    self.gradInput:select(4,4):copy(Ly_x)
    self.gradInput:select(4,5):copy(Ly_y)
    self.gradInput:select(4,6):copy(_gradGrid:select(4,2))

    return self.gradInput

end
```

Slanted Plane Depth Disparity. Similar ideas have been used in [9] to obtain disparity of a stereo pair. They exploit the fact that scenes can be decomposed into piecewise slanted planes and consequently the disparity of a pixel can be expressed by the plane equation. This results in a over-paramterised 3-DoF formulation of disparity.

$$d = ax + by + c \tag{9}$$

Again, this over-parameterisation greatly improves the results. Note that this formulation can be easily generalised and lifted to higher dimensions in the spirit of Total Generalised Variation (TGV) [10], but we have only implemented the 3-DoF formulation.

We would like to stress that these layers are particularly tailored towards warping images which could be used as a direct signal for feedback loop in image reconstruction error in unsupervised training [2,11].

RGB-D Based. Our layers can be easily adapted to RGB-D to enable 3D point cloud registration and alignment via per-pixel rigid transformations. Such transformations have been used extensively in the computer graphics community for some time and exploited by [12–14] for non-rigid alignment. We extend similar ideas and implement 3D transformations for each pixel containing a 3D vector **x**, the 3D spatial coordinates coming from a depth-map. In principle, such alignment is general and not limited to just 3D spatial points *i.e.* any 3D feature per-pixel can be transformed. This is particularly useful when aligning feature maps as used in sketch and style transfer using deep learning [15].

Per-pixel Sim3 Transformation. We extend the global Sim3 transformation that models scale s, Rotation R, and translation t to a per-pixel Sim3 transformation *i.e.* $\mathsf{T}_i = \begin{bmatrix} s_i \mathsf{R}_i & t_i \\ 0 & 1 \end{bmatrix}$ where $\mathsf{R} \in SO3$.

$$\begin{pmatrix} x'_i \\ y'_i \\ z'_i \end{pmatrix} = \mathsf{T}_i \begin{pmatrix} x_i \\ y_i \\ z_i \\ 1 \end{pmatrix} \tag{10}$$

This allows for the attention like mechanism of [1] in 3D, as specific voxel areas can be cropped and zoomed, and also modelling any 3D registrations that require scale.

Per-pixel 10 DoF Transformation. In many non-rigid alignments the rotation need not happen around the origin but around an anchor point p_i which is also jointly estimated. In this case, the transformation extends to 10 degrees of freedom [12].

$$\mathbf{x}'_i = s_i(\mathsf{R}_i(\mathbf{x}_i - \mathbf{p}_i) + \mathbf{p}_i) + \mathbf{t}_i \tag{11}$$

Additionally, smoothness constraints can be added to ensure that transformations are locally smooth in just the same way as Huber penalty is imposed for smoothing 2D optic flow.

2.3   M-Estimators

The standard least-squares loss function often employed in parameter fitting greatly affects the quality of the solution obtained at convergence. Built on the assumption that noise in the data follows Gaussian distribution, the least-squares function treats both the inliers and outliers in the data uniformly. This is undesirable because even one bad sample in the data can sway the optimisation to an unexpected convergence point. Therefore, outlier samples should be culled or down-weighted accordingly to maintain the optimisation and estimation process from getting influenced by them. Fortunately, in computer vision this has been long studied since the early 90s by Black *et al.* [18–20] who pioneered the use of robust cost functions, often termed M-estimators for estimating a statistically robust mean of the data. We adapted the standard $\mathcal{L}_2^2$ loss function with various popular M-estimators. The table below shows various M-estimators, $\rho(\mathrm{x})$ and their corresponding derivatives, $\psi(\mathrm{x})$.

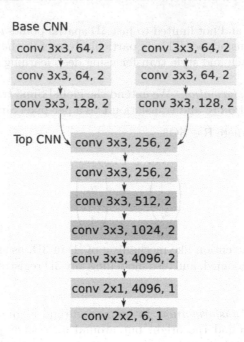

Fig. 1. Our Siamese network is inspired by the popular VGG-16 network [16] where 3×3 convolutions are used in most layers and works for 320×240 image resolution. Each convolution layer is followed by PReLU non-linearity [17]. We explicitly avoid any pooling and use a stride of 2 in every convolution layer for any downsampling.

M-estimator	$\rho(\mathrm{x})$	$\psi(\mathrm{x})$
Huber $\begin{cases} \text{if } |x| \leq \epsilon, \\ \text{otherwise.} \end{cases}$	$\begin{cases} \frac{x^2}{2}, \\ \epsilon(|x| - \frac{\epsilon}{2}) \end{cases}$	$\begin{cases} x, \\ \epsilon \frac{x}{|x|} \end{cases}$
Cauchy	$\frac{c^2}{2} \log(1 + (\frac{x}{c})^2)$	$\frac{x}{1+(\frac{x}{c})^2}$
Geman-McClure	$\frac{x^2/2}{1+x^2}$	$\frac{x}{(1+x^2)^2}$
Tukey $\begin{cases} \text{if} |x| \leq c \\ \text{otherwise.} \end{cases}$	$\begin{cases} \frac{c^2}{6}(1 - (1 - (\frac{x}{c})^2)^3) \\ \frac{c^2}{6} \end{cases}$	$\begin{cases} x(1 - (\frac{x}{c})^2)^2, \\ 0 \end{cases}$

The use of M-estimators has already started to trickle down in the deep learning community *e.g.* Patraucean *et al.* [2] use a Huber loss function in the smoothness term to regularise the optic flow. We believe our library will also continue to encourage people to use different loss functions that are more pertinent to the tasks where Gaussian noise assumptions fall apart.

3   Application: Training on RGB-D Visual Odometry

We perform early experiments on visual odometry for both SO3 as well as SE3 motion that involves depth based warping. We believe this is the first attempt towards end-to-end system for Visual Odometry with deep learning. Since we are aligning images à la dense image registration methods, this allows us to do sanity checks on different layers e.g. SE3 layer, 3D Grid Generator, and Projection layer all within the same network and optimisation scheme. Note that we could have also chosen to do minimisation on re-projection error of sparse keypoints as in classic Bundle Adjustment. However, this approach does not lend itself to generic iterative image alignment where each iteration provides a warped version of the reference image and can be fed back into the network for an end-to-end RNN based visual odometry system. Moreover, our approach is also naturally suited for unsupervised learning in the spirit of [2,11].

3.1   Network Architecture

Our architecture is composed of a siamese network that takes in a pair of consecutive frames, $\mathcal{I}_{ref}$ and $\mathcal{I}_{live}$, captured at time instances t and $t+1$ respectively, and returns a 6-DoF pose vector, δ_{pred} — where the first three elements correspond to rotation and the last three to translation — that transforms one image to the other. In case of pure rotation, the network predicts a 3×1 vector. It is assumed that the scene is mostly static and rigid, and the motion perceived in the image is induced only via the camera movement. However, instead of naïvely comparing the predicted 6-DoF vector, δ_{pred}, with the corresponding ground truth vector, δ_{gt}, we build upon the work of Patraucean et al. [2], to warp the images directly using our customised *3D Spatial Transformer* module, to compute the image alignment error as our cost function. This allows us to compare the transformations in the right space: naïve comparison of 6-DoF vectors would have involved a tunable parameter beforehand to weigh the translation and rotation errors appropriately to define the cost function since they are two different entities. Searching for the right weighting can quickly become tedious and may not generalise well. Although [21] are able to minimise a cost function by appropriately weighing the rotation and translation errors within optimal hand-eye coordination loop, this is not possible all the time. Discretising the poses as done in [22] may hamper the accuracy of pose estimation. On the other hand, computing pixel error via warping, as often done in classic dense image alignment methods [23,24], allows to compare the transformations in the space of pixel intensities without having to tune any external parameters. Moreover, dense alignment methods have an added advantage of accurately recovering the transformations by minimising sum of squared differences of pixel values at corresponding locations in the two images *i.e.*

$$\mathcal{C} = \frac{1}{2} \sum_{i=1}^{N} \left(\mathcal{I}_{ref}(\mathbf{x}) - \mathcal{I}_{live}(\pi(\mathsf{T}_{lr}\hat{\mathsf{p}}(\mathbf{x}))) \right)^2$$

where $\mathbf{x}$ is a homogenised 2D pixel location in the reference image, $\hat{p}(\mathbf{x})$ is the 4×1 corresponding homogenised 3D point obtained by projecting the ray from that given pixel location (x, y) into the 3D world via classic inverse camera projection and the depth, $d(x, y)$, at that pixel location.

$$\mathbf{x} = \begin{pmatrix} x \\ y \\ 1 \end{pmatrix}, \; \hat{p}(x, y) = \begin{pmatrix} \mathsf{K}^{-1}\mathbf{x} \cdot d(x, y) \\ 1 \end{pmatrix} \tag{12}$$

$$\mathsf{K} = \begin{bmatrix} f_x & 0 & p_x \\ 0 & f_y & p_y \\ 0 & 0 & 1 \end{bmatrix}, \; \pi \begin{pmatrix} u \\ v \\ w \end{pmatrix} = \begin{pmatrix} f_x \frac{u}{w} + p_x \\ f_y \frac{v}{w} + p_y \end{pmatrix} \tag{13}$$

K is the camera calibration matrix, f_x and f_y denote the focal lengths of the camera (in pixels) while p_x, p_y are the coordinates of the camera center location. π is the projection function that maps a 3D point to a 2D plane and T_{lr} (or T_{pred}) is a 3×4 matrix that transforms a 3D point in the reference frame to the live frame. In this work, we bridge the gap between learning and geometry based methods with our *3D Spatial Transformer* module which explicitly defines these operations as layers that act as computational blocks with no learning parameters but allow backpropagation from the cost function to the input layers.

Figure 2 shows an example of our customised STN for 3D transformation. The siamese network predicts a 6×1 vector that is turned into a 3×4 transformation matrix T_{pred} via SE3 layer. This matrix transforms the points generated by the 3D grid generator that additionally takes depth image as input and turns it into 3D points via inverse camera projection with K^{-1} as in Eq. 1. These transformed points are then projected back into the 2D image plane via the Projection layer (*i.e.* the π function) and further used to bilinearly interpolate the warped image as in the original STN [1].

Our siamese network is inspired from the popular VGG-16 network [16] and uses 3×3 convolutions in all but the last two layers where 2×1 and 2×2 convolutions are used to compensate for the 320×240 resolution used as input as opposed to the 224×224 used in original VGG-16. Figure 1 shows our siamese network where two heads are fused early to ensure that the relevant spatial information is not lost by the depth of the network. We also avoid any pooling operations throughout the network, again to ensure that the spatial information is preserved. All convolutional layers, with the exception of the last three, are followed by a non-linearity. We found PReLUs [17] to work better both in terms of convergence speed and accuracy than ReLUs for our network and therefore used them for all the experiments. We also experimented with recently introduced ELUs [25] but did not find any significant difference in the end to PReLUs. Weights of all convolution layers are initialised with MSRA initialisation proposed in [17]. However, the last layer has the weights all initialised to zero. This is to ensure that the relative pose between the consecutive frames is initialised with Identity transformation, as commonly used in many dense image alignment methods.

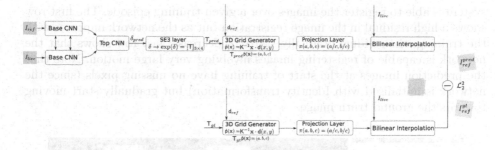

Fig. 2. We train a siamese network to regress to the relative pose vector between the two consecutive frames, I_{ref} and I_{live}. This pose vector is turned into a 3×4 transformation matrix that transforms 3D points coming from the 3D grid generator and further projected into a 2D plane via projection layer which are used to generate a warped image. Additionally, the 3D grid generator needs an explicit depth-map as input to generate 3D points for any 3D warping.

While one could use the pixel difference between the predicted live image, using the transformation returned by the siamese network, and the live image as the cost function, we chose instead to take the pixel difference between the predicted live image with the predicted transformation and the predicted live image with the ground truth transformation. This is because if there is significant motion between the input frames, warping may possibly lead to missing pixels in the predicted image which will get unnecessary penalised if compared against the live image directly since there is no explicit way to block out the corresponding pixels in the live image. However, if the predicted images from the predicted and ground truth transformations are compared, at optimal predicted transformations both should have the same missing pixels which would allow implicitly blocking out those pixels. Moreover, any external artefact in the images in the form of motion blur, intensity changes, or image noise would affect the registration since the cost function is a pixel-wise comparison. On the other hand, our way of comparing the pixels ensures that at convergence, the cost function is as close to zero as possible and is able to handle missing pixels appropriately. Ultimately, we only need a way to compare the predicted and ground truth transformations in the pixel space. We show early results of training on SO3 (pure rotation) and SE3 motion (involving rotation and translation).

SO3 Motion: Pure Rotation. To experiment with pure rotation motion, we gathered IMU readings of a camera undergoing rapid hand-held motion: we used [26] to capture an outdoor dataset but dropped the translation readings. This is only to ensure that the transformation in the images correspond to the real hand-held motion observed in real world. We use the rotation matrices to synthetically generate new images in the dataset and feed the corresponding pair through the network. We perform early experiments that serve as sanity checks for different layers working together in a network. Figure 3 shows how our system is able to register the images over a given training episode. The first row shows a high residual in the image registration but as the network improves with the training, the residual gradually starts to decrease: last row shows that the network is capable of registering images involving very large motion. Note that the prediction images at the start of training have no missing pixels (since the network is initialised with Identity transformation) but gradually start moving towards the ground truth image.

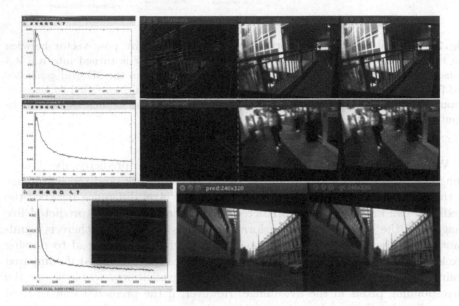

Fig. 3. Training results on pure rotation motion. The graphs show how the training error decreases as number of epochs increase. This serves as a sanity check for our network that includes many new layers that we propose in this library. The improvement in the training is qualitatively evident from the difference images: early stages in the optimisation show high residual in the registration but as more epochs are thrown to the optimisation, the residual error gracefully decreases.

SE3 Motion: Rotation and Translation. SE3 motion needs depth to enable registration of two images involving both rotation and translation. This is possible with our SE3 layer that additionally takes in depth-map as input and produces the interpolation coordinates to be further used by the bilinear interpolation layer. We use ICL-NUIM [27] and generate a long trajectory of 9.5K frames and use this as our training set. Figure 4 shows samples of generated frames in this new trajectory. Since we need per-pixel depth for this experiment we opted for synthetic dataset only for convenience. In future, we would like to test our approach on real world data.

Fig. 4. Sample frames from our new ICL-NUIM trajectory.

Similar to the pure rotation (SO3) motion, we show early results on SE3 motion involving rotation and translation. Figure 5 shows the network's ability to learn to align the predicted image with the ground truth image using depth that is given as an additional input to the 3D grid generator.

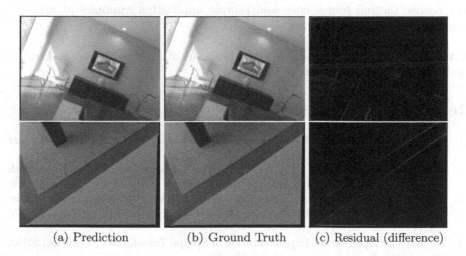

(a) Prediction   (b) Ground Truth   (c) Residual (difference)

Fig. 5. Sample results on the new trajectory generated with ICL-NUIM dataset. The SE3 layer allows warping image with 3D motion and this is evident in the registration error in the residual image. Note that the relative motion between consecutive frames is generally slow in the whole trajectory.

4 Future Work

We have only shown training on visual odometry as sanity checks of our layers and their ability to blend in with the standard convolution neural network.

In future, we would like to train both feed-forward as well as feedback connections based neural network on large training data. This data could either come from standard Structure from Motion [28], large scale synthetic datasets e.g. SceneNet [29] or large scale RGB or RGB-D videos for unsupervised learning.

5   Conclusions

We introduced a new library, **gvnn**, that allows implementation of various standard computer vision applications within a deep learning framework. In its current form, it allows end-to-end training for optic flow, disparity or depth estimation, visual odometry, small-scale bundle adjustment, super-resolution, place recognition with geometric invariance all with both supervised and unsupervised settings. In future, we plan to extend this library to include various different lens distortion models, camera projection models, IMU based transformation layers, sign distance functions, level-sets, and classic primal-dual methods [30] as RNN blocks to allow embedding higher order priors in the form of TGV [10]. We hope that our library will encourage researchers to use and contribute towards making this a comprehensive and complete resource for geometric computer vision with deep learning in the same way the popular **rnn** package [31] has fostered research in recurrent neural networks in the community. Upon publication, we will release the full source code and sample application examples at https:// github.com/ankurhanda/gvnn.

Acknowledgements. AH and AD would like to thank Dyson Technology Ltd. for kindly funding this research work.

References

1. Jaderberg, M., Simonyan, K., Zisserman, A., Kavukcuoglu, K.: Spatial transformer networks. In: NIPS (2015)
2. Patraucean, V., Handa, A., Cipolla, R.: Spatio-temporal video autoencoder with differentiable memory. CoRR abs/1511.06309 (2015)
3. Collobert, R., Kavukcuoglu, K., Farabet, C.: Torch7: a matlab-like environment for machine learning. In: BigLearn, NIPS Workshop. Number EPFL-CONF-192376 (2011)
4. Moodstocks: Open Source Implementation of Spatial Transformer Networks (2015). https://github.com/qassemoquab/stnbhwd
5. Gallego, G., Yezzi, A.J.: A compact formula for the derivative of a 3-D rotation in exponential coordinates (2013)
6. Brooks, M.J., Chojnacki, W., Baumela, L.: Determining the egomotion of an uncalibrated camera from instantaneous optical flow. JOSA A (1997)
7. Nir, T., Bruckstein, A.M., Kimmel, R.: Over-parameterized variational optical flow. Int. J. Comput. Vis. (IJCV) **76**(2), 205–216 (2008)
8. Hornáček, M., Besse, F., Kautz, J., Fitzgibbon, A., Rother, C.: Highly overparameterized optical flow using patchmatch belief propagation. In: Fleet, D., Pajdla, T., Schiele, B., Tuytelaars, T. (eds.) ECCV 2014. LNCS, vol. 8691, pp. 220–234. Springer, Heidelberg (2014). doi:10.1007/978-3-319-10578-9_15

9. Bleyer, M., Rhemann, C., Rother, C.: PatchMatch stereo – stereo matching with slanted support windows. In: Proceedings of the British Machine Vision Conference (BMVC) (2011)
10. Pock, T., Zebedin, L., Bischof, H.: TGV-fusion. In: Calude, C.S., Rozenberg, G., Salomaa, A. (eds.) Rainbow of Computer Science. LNCS, vol. 6570, pp. 245–258. Springer, Heidelberg (2011). doi:10.1007/978-3-642-19391-0_18
11. Garg, R., BG, V.K., Reid, I.D.: Unsupervised CNN for single view depth estimation: geometry to the rescue. CoRR abs/1603.04992 (2016)
12. Sumner, R.W., Schmid, J., Pauly, M.: Embedded deformation for shape manipulation. In: Proceedings of SIGGRAPH (2007)
13. Zollhöfer, M., Nießner, M., Izadi, S., Rehmann, C., Zach, C., Fisher, M., Wu, C., Fitzgibbon, A., Loop, C., Theobalt, C., et al.: Real-time non-rigid reconstruction using an RGB-D camera. ACM Trans. Graph. (TOG) (2014)
14. Newcombe, R.A., Fox, D., Seitz, S.M.: Dynamicfusion: reconstruction and tracking of non-rigid scenes in real-time. In: Proceedings of the IEEE Conference on Computer Vision and Pattern Recognition (CVPR) (2015)
15. Johnson, J., Alahi, A., Li, F.: Perceptual losses for real-time style transfer and super-resolution. CoRR abs/1603.08155 (2016)
16. Simonyan, K., Zisserman, A.: Very deep convolutional networks for large-scale image recognition. In: Proceedings of the International Conference on Learning Representations (ICLR) (2015)
17. He, K., Zhang, X., Ren, S., Sun, J.: Delving deep into rectifiers: surpassing human-level performance on imagenet classification. In: Proceedings of the International Conference on Computer Vision (ICCV) (2015)
18. Black, M.J., Anandan, P.: A framework for the robust estimation of optical flow. In: Proceedings of the International Conference on Computer Vision (ICCV) (1993)
19. Black, M., Anandan, P.: Robust dynamic motion estimation over time. In: Proceedings of the IEEE Conference on Computer Vision and Pattern Recognition (CVPR) (1991)
20. Black, M.J., Sapiro, G., Marimont, D.H., Heeger, D.: Robust anisotropic diffusion. IEEE Trans. Image Process. 7, 421–432 (1998)
21. Strobl, K.H., Hirzinger, G.: Optimal hand-eye calibration. In: 2006 IEEE/RSJ International Conference on Intelligent Robots and Systems. IEEE (2006)
22. Agrawal, P., Carreira, J., Malik, J.: Learning to see by moving. In: Proceedings of the IEEE International Conference on Computer Vision (2015)
23. Lucas, B.D., Kanade, T.: An iterative image registration technique with an application to stereo vision. In: Proceedings of the International Joint Conference on Artificial Intelligence (IJCAI) (1981)
24. Drummond, T., Cipolla, R.: Visual tracking and control using lie algebras. In: Proceedings of the IEEE Conference on Computer Vision and Pattern Recognition (CVPR) (1999)
25. Clevert, D.A., Unterthiner, T., Hochreiter, S.: Fast and accurate deep network learning by exponential linear units (elus). In: ICLR (2016)
26. Leutenegger, S., Lynen, S., Bosse, M., Siegwart, R., Furgale, P.: Keyframe-based visual-inertial odometry using nonlinear optimization. Int. J. Robot. Res. (2014)
27. Handa, A., Whelan, T., McDonald, J.B., Davison, A.J.: A benchmark for RGB-D visual odometry, 3D reconstruction and SLAM. In: Proceedings of the IEEE International Conference on Robotics and Automation (ICRA) (2014)
28. Wu, C.: VisualSfM : A visual structure from motion system. http://ccwu.me/vsfm/

29. Handa, A., Pătrăucean, V., Badrinarayanan, V., Stent, S., Cipolla, R.: SceneNet: understanding real world indoor scenes with synthetic data. arXiv preprint (2015). arXiv:1511.07041
30. Chambolle, A., Pock, T.: A first-order primal-dual algorithm for convex problems with applications to imaging. J. Math. Imaging Vis. 40(1), 120–145 (2011)
31. Léonard, N., Waghmare, S., Wang, Y., Kim, J.: RNN: recurrent library for torch. CoRR abs/1511.07889 (2015)

On-Line Large Scale Semantic Fusion

Tommaso Cavallari$^{(\boxtimes)}$ and Luigi Di Stefano

Department of Computer Science and Engineering,
University of Bologna, Bologna, Italy
{tommaso.cavallari,luigi.distefano}@unibo.it

Abstract. Recent research towards 3D reconstruction has delivered reliable and fast pipelines to obtain accurate volumetric maps of large environments. Alongside, we witness dramatic improvements in the field of semantic segmentation of images due to deployment of deep learning architectures. In this paper, we pursue bridging the semantic gap of purely geometric representations by leveraging on a SLAM pipeline and a deep neural network so to endow surface patches with category labels. In particular, we present the first system that, based on the input stream provided by a commodity RGB-D sensor, can deliver interactively and automatically a map of a large scale environment featuring both geometric as well as semantic information. We also show how the significant computational cost inherent to deployment of a state-of-the-art deep network for semantic labeling does not hinder interactivity thanks to suitable scheduling of the workload on an off-the-shelf PC platform equipped with two GPUs.

Keywords: SLAM · Deep learning · Semantic segmentation · Large scale reconstruction · Semantic fusion

1 Introduction

Most previous work on recovery the world from images has been concerned with 3D geometry only, the advent of commodity RGB-D sensors having made this task remarkably affordable and effective. On the other hand, Deep Learning is emerging as the state of the art approach to infer complex semantics from images. In this paper we bring together geometric reconstruction by RGB-D sensing and semantic perception by Deep Learning to create a novel Semantic SLAM pipeline. With the proposed system, the user can explore the environment interactively by a hand-held RGB-D sensor. As in most previous work, this allows to attain a dense, detailed 3D reconstruction of the scene; peculiarly to our system, though, the resulting map is also endowed *online* and *fully automatically* with semantic labels determining the likelihood of each surface patch to depict objects of specific categories. To achieve this objective, we build

Electronic supplementary material The online version of this chapter (doi:10.1007/978-3-319-49409-8_10) contains supplementary material, which is available to authorized users.

© Springer International Publishing Switzerland 2016
G. Hua and H. Jégou (Eds.): ECCV 2016 Workshops, Part III, LNCS 9915, pp. 83–99, 2016.
DOI: 10.1007/978-3-319-49409-8_10

upon a deep convolutional network for semantic image segmentation [11] and a real-time reconstruction approach suited to map large-scale environments [15]. Driving factor behind the development of this pipeline is the need for a system whereby an untrained user may reliably scan and acquire semantically annotated 3D reconstructions of large indoor environments. As highlighted in Sect. 2, previous work [18] would allow generation of similarly annotated 3D maps while requiring proper interaction with a trained user. Conversely, to minimize the effort by the user, we integrate seamlessly dense mapping and semantic labeling into a single pipeline that can output detailed reconstructions of large scale environments wherein each voxel stores a complete probability mass function over a set of semantic categories of interest. Hopefully, our accomplishment may foster research on topics such as indoor scene understanding, object discovery and/or recognition, human/robot interaction and navigation.

The paper is organised as follows: next section discusses previous work related to the proposed system, which will then be described in Sect. 3. Quantitative and qualitative results are provided in Sect. 4, while in Sect. 5 we will draw concluding remarks.

2   Related Work

One of the first breakthroughs in the field of real time 3D reconstruction is KinectFusion by Newcombe *et al.* [14]. Their system shows how the processing power of modern GPUs and the availability of affordable RGB-D sensors can be harnessed to accurately reconstruct the workspace in real time. KinectFusion, though, is bound to map small scale environments due to its reliance on a dense voxel grid as mapping data structure. Several subsequent works tackled this shortcoming, at first by moving the active reconstruction volume alongside with camera movements and downloading from GPU to CPU memory the map previously observed by the sensor [16,20]. More sophisticated data structures aimed at storing only those pieces of information required by the mapping task were then introduced, so to enlarge significantly the mappable volume and speed up the computation, either via hierarchical, octree-based methods [22], hash-based data-structures [9,15] or combinations of both techniques [10].

Thanks to the focus on deep learning in the last years, several semantic segmentation techniques were proposed that could process entire images in fractions of a second, providing pixel-wise category labels or probability mass functions over a set of such categories. Gupta *et al.* [8], process pairs of RGB and Depth images with multiple deep neural networks followed by an SVM classifier, providing a threefold output: bounding boxes for object detection, per-pixel confidences to segment such instances and a full-image semantic segmentation output. Long *et al.* [11] show how Fully Convolutional Networks can provide accurate per-pixel, per-category scores on entire images in a deterministic amount of time. Eigen and Fergus [6] demonstrate how a single deep network architecture can successfully be employed for three different tasks: predicting depth and normals from RGB images as well as performing semantic segmentation to infer, again, per-pixel category probabilities. Zheng *et al.* [23], then, join the strengths of Conditional Random fields and Convolutional Neural Networks within a unique framework trained end-to-end to obtain semantic segmentation.

Recently, works concerning semantic labeling of reconstructed environments have started appearing: Valentin *et al.* [18] show a system, based on the Infini-TAM 3D reconstruction pipeline [9], that, employing multi-modal user inter-action, can learn to classify user selected categories via random forests trained on-line. Miksik *et al.* [13] deploy a setup based on a head-mounted stereo camera together with the VoxelHashing 3D reconstruction pipeline [15]; by tracking the target of a portable laser pointer through the acquired frames, the user is able to mark areas of the scene as pertaining to a certain object category. Such labels are then fed to a densely connected Conditional Random Field that learns how to classify voxels online in the reconstructed scene. Differently from these recent works, the pipeline proposed in this paper does not require any user interaction to perform the labeling and train the classifier, and, therefore, an untrained user can proficiently reconstruct large scale environments just by moving around a hand-held RGB-D sensor.

The work by Cavallari and Di Stefano [5] shows integration of the semantic labels output by the Fully Convolutional Networks [11] into a dense reconstruc-tion obtained by the original KinectFusion [14]. While the approach described in [5] is similar to that proposed in this paper, their pipeline cannot map accurately large workspaces due to reliance on a dense voxel grid. Moreover, the structure of their pipeline makes it impossible to achieve interactive frame rates with current hardware. Hence, the system presented in this paper is the first ever to permit on-line fully automatic semantic reconstruction of large environments.

Finally, unlike all the above mentioned works addressing volumetric semantic reconstruction, the pipeline proposed in this paper yields at each voxel the full probability mass function across categories rather than estimating the most likely label only. Such a richer output enables not only generation of semantically labeled maps but also assessment of the likeliness of each and every category across the whole scene surface.

3   Description of the Method

The proposed pipeline is composed of two subsystems, each tailored to a spe-cific task, controlled by a main engine handling all input/output operations and dispatching work to both. The two subsystems are:

Labeling Subsystem: tasked with semantically labeling the RGB images gath-ered from the sensor.

SLAM Subsystem: dealing with camera tracking, map building and on-demand rendering of the reconstructed 3D scene from arbitrary viewpoints.

In the next paragraphs we will provide a detailed description of the above sub-systems and then show how the main engine ties them together to attain the overall system.

3.1   Labeling Subsystem

This subsystem represents the interface of our pipeline to an image-based semantic labeling algorithm: given an input RGB image and, optionally, a depth map, this block provides per pixel confidences for a set of categories of interest, thus providing us with a full probability mass function across categories for each pixel of the input image. More specifically, given input images of size $H \times W$ and a set of N categories of interest, C, the output is a "volume" of confidences, L, of size $N \times H \times W$ and wherein each element $L_{i,j,k}$ represents the confidence that the semantic labeling algorithm assigns to category i at pixel (j, k). Should a single label for a pixel become necessary, a simple argmax operation over the N confidences would provide the required output. In our system, though, we exploit the availability of multiple confidences at each image location to reconstruct a multi-label 3D map of the environment wherein each voxel is endowed with information about the likeliness of each category of interest.

The interface just described is sufficiently generic that any labeling algorithm may in principle be incorporated within our pipeline. For instance, algorithms returning rectangular or polygonal ROIs with associated labels can have their output post-processed to paint each ROI in the volume "slice" associated to the correct category. Overlapping ROIs of the same category may also be handled, e.g. by applying a max operator to the confidence stored in each pixel whereas overlapping regions of different categories can be drawn on the corresponding slices and a final per-pixel normalization can then turn the confidence values for each pixel in a proper probability mass function. Additionally, multiple labeling algorithms may be deployed, the only requirement being to run a normalization step independently on each pixel volume "column". Yet, to minimize the postprocessing necessary to obtain the labeled volume, those inherently more amenable to our pipeline are semantic labeling algorithms providing directly per-pixel confidences across categories, nowadays the most effective and efficient proposals in this space relying on Deep Learning [6,8,11,23]. As such, we found Deep Learning particularly conducive to on-line, fully-automatic semantic mapping.

Among deep networks for semantic labeling, our pipeline deploys the Fully Convolutional Network by Long et al. [11], as we found experimentally that, in our settings, this architecture can provide quite clearly the best trade-off between classification accuracy and speed. Given an input RGB image, the pre-trained networks[1] can yield per-pixel confidences for a large number of categories (20, 40 or 60, depending on the specific model) dealing with both indoor and outdoor objects. As the use case of our system concerns mapping indoor environments by a commodity RGB-D sensor, we reduce the number of categories of interest by dropping some unnecessary classes and applying per-pixel softmax normalization on the remaining raw scores to convert the output into a probability mass function.

---

[1] https://github.com/shelhamer/fcn.berkeleyvision.org.

3.2 SLAM Subsystem

The generation of a semantic map of the observed environment is a task left to the SLAM Subsystem. A typical Simultaneous Localization and Mapping pipeline consists of two main components: the first localizes the camera within the environment by tracking its movements over time (*localization* task); the second relies on the estimated camera pose to integrate the data provided by the sensor into the current representation of the scene (*mapping* task). Typically a third, optional, component is tasked with visualization of the reconstructed scene to provide feedback to the user.

In the system presented in this paper we add a fourth component to perform what we call the *semantic fusion* task, i.e. integration within the reconstructed scene of the semantic information provided by the Labeling Subsystem. This might also be seen as part of the standard *mapping* task but, as we will illustrate in Subsect. 3.3, we split the standard SLAM mapping operation (integrating data from the RGB-D sensor) and the semantic mapping operation (integrating the information provided by the labeler) in order to decouple them and allow for deferred integration of the per-pixel category probabilities into the scene representation. Indeed, this approach is mandatory to enable on-line operation of the overall semantic reconstruction pipeline.

The SLAM subsystem adopted in our system is built on top of the VoxelHashing reconstruction pipeline by Nießner et al. [15] that, unlike KinectFusion [14], permits mapping of large workspaces by storing the map as a hash-based data structure instead of a dense voxel grid. For a detailed description of VoxelHashing we refer the interested reader to the original paper. In the following, we highlight the main modifications required to store the semantic information peculiar to our approach.

Map Generation and Storage. VoxelHashing employs a hash-based data structure to efficiently index a heap of voxel data blocks. Each voxel block represents the map of a limited region of space. By storing into the GPU memory only such blocks conveying informations useful to the mapping task, and employing an efficient swapping technique to move unneeded blocks from GPU to CPU memory and vice-versa, the extent of the mappable environment can, in principle, be of arbitrary size. Each voxel in the map is endowed with three tokens of information:

TSDF Value: The truncated signed distance from the voxel to the closest surface; being a floating point value, it can be stored as a half precision number so to occupy 2 bytes of memory;

Weight: The confidence in the stored TSDF value; it is used in operations such as fusion of new depth measurements and raycasting of the map; typically is akin to a counter of the number of times the specific voxel has been observed, though other weighting strategies have been proposed [3,14]; again, a half-precision floating point number;

RGB Data: Colour of the surface patch associated with the voxel; typically encoded as a 4-tuple of unsigned chars to optimize memory alignment.

The memory occupancy for a single voxel amounts thus to 8 bytes. In our pipeline, we augment the standard voxel data structure by a histogram storing a probability mass function over a set of N categories. Each bin represents the probability that an item of a specific category is located in the surface area associated with the voxel. Each histogram bin should therefore be able to encode a floating point value in the interval $[0..1]$. To reduce memory occupancy, we encode such values into bytes by scaling the floating point number to the interval $[0..255]$. The final size of the voxel data structure thus increases by N bytes. The set of categories is application dependent and in our tests we employ 8 categories, thus having each voxel occupying 16 bytes, thereby doubling the memory footprint with respect to the standard data structure. Doubling the per-voxel memory occupancy would be worrying if we were using a dense data structure as deployed by KinectFusion. Conversely, thanks to the reduced memory pressure allowed by VoxelHashing, we can easily accommodate such informations onto the GPU memory and, if necessary, move it back and forth with the system RAM via swapping operations. When a new voxel is allocated by VoxelHashing, its histogram is set to the uniform probability, thus having each bin initialized to the value $255/N$, so to express maximum uncertainty on the type of object located within its boundaries.

Rendering. Visualization of the reconstructed scene is typically performed via raycasting. First, a synthetic range image is extracted: given a camera pose of interest, a ray is marched for each pixel of the output image from the camera center until a positive to negative zero-crossing of the TSDF function is encountered, this signaling the presence of a surface. Clearly, marching a ray from the camera centre is expensive since the hash table has to be queried for every step, therefore several optimizations are described in the VoxelHashing paper [15]. The InfiniTAM pipeline [9] also details more enhancements to the raycasting operation that can speed up sensibly the computation.

The raycasted range map can then be used to extract a coloured representation of the environment by trilinearly interpolating the RGB values of the 8 voxels closest to each zero crossing point. Point normals can also be computed by estimating the TSDF gradient in the location corresponding to the range map point.

Semantic labels for each rendered point can then be extracted. In order to determine the label of a single pixel, we apply an argmax operation over the N histogram bins associated to each raycasted 3D point and store the resulting label in an output category map and the associated confidence in an output probability map. While we could trilinearly interpolate between bins associated to the histograms of 8 neighboring voxels in order to obtain an interpolated histogram to subject the argmax operation, in practice we consider only the voxel whose center is closest to the candidate 3D point, on account that, typically, object categories are "large scale" scene attributes and the interpolation of neighboring voxel probabilities would not provide much additional information while notably slowing down the processing speed of the pipeline. The left picture in Fig. 1 provides an exemplar image obtained by raycasting into the current camera view the most likely label in each voxel provided by the argmax operation.

Fig. 1. Left: semantic labels assigned to the reconstruction of an office environment. Right: heat map showing the spatial distribution of "chair" objects. It can be seen how, even in presence of mislabeled areas (highlighted by the red ellipse), the "chair" confidence is not null and thus may help to segment out chairs. (Color figure online)

Our category representation scheme allows also to render the likeliness of a category in each voxel seen from the current camera view. Indeed, we can provide visualizations detailing the spatial distribution of a certain category of interest by selecting the histogram bin associated to that category in every voxel defined by the raycasted range image. For example, as shown in the right picture of Fig. 1, we might wish to render the "chairness" of the reconstructed scene. It is worth observing that, although some surface patches belonging to chairs are mislabeled in the left image of Fig. 1, the right image provides evidence that these indeed may possibly belong to chairs, this information may likely help performing an higher lever task such as segmenting out all the chairs present in the scene.

Once the range, normals, RGB, category and score maps are extracted, shading can be applied to obtain pleasant visualizations. While the described renderings may convey useful informations to the user, all but those dealing with the range and normal maps are optional in our pipeline and thus can be disabled to increase processing speed. The renderings of the range and normal maps, instead, are pivotal in the camera localization step that will be described next.

Camera Localization. Camera localization is an essential step of the SLAM pipeline: to integrate RGB-D frames coming from the sensor into the global map of the environment, one has to know the pose from which the camera captured such informations. Typically, thanks to the high processing rate of KinectFusion/VoxelHashing, this task can be simplified into the tracking of the camera movement from one frame to the following.

Several approaches to camera tracking task have been proposed in the literature related to KinectFusion, either relying on purely geometric clues, such as the projective ICP approach of the original paper [14] and the direct alignment methods described in [3,4], or aimed at deploying colour information to maximize the photo-consistency between pairs of consecutive frames [17,19] or between the current frame and the colour information stored into voxels [2].

In our system we employ the projective ICP approach described by Newcombe et al. [14] to estimate sensor pose. The method relies on the raycasted depth and normals map as seen from the previous camera pose and the current depth map. An iterative process performs a projective association between points in the current and in the raycasted range maps [1], computes an energy term at each pixel based on the point to plane metric [21], and finally minimizes the sum of all pixel energies by linearising such function in a neighborhood of the previous pose and computing an increment using the Lie algebra representation.

Semantic Fusion. The Semantic Fusion component integrates into the voxel-based map of the environment the per-pixel semantic labels extracted from an input RGB-D frame by the Labeling subsystem. As mentioned earlier, this task is kept disjoint from the canonical "fusion" operation performed by KinectFusion/VoxelHashing to allow the labeler to work asynchronously with respect to the SLAM process, thus not hindering the real-time nature of the latter due to the former being significantly slower.

Once a frame has been labeled, its associated pose, T_l, which was estimated by the camera localisation component, is retrieved and can be used to perform the actual fusion step. Likewise fusion of the RGB-D image, the process is applied to those voxels that fall into the camera frustum and are "close enough" to the surface described by the depth frame associated with the previously extracted labels (cached at the beginning of the labeling); purposely, we employ the same truncation distance as used by the depth integration step.

More precisely, as a first step, the location of each mapped voxel block in the world coordinate frame is transformed in the appropriate camera reference frame by the inverse transformation described by the camera pose. The transformed block center is then projected onto the image plane and, if the resulting coordinates lie inside the image, the block is marked as potentially visible and thus to be updated. Thanks to the GPU, this first step can be efficiently carried out in parallel by associating a thread to each voxel block. A *scan-and-compact* operation is then performed to gather the indexes of all the blocks to be updated in a single buffer, which in turn is used to launch an update thread for each voxel residing in such blocks.

Each voxel center is then projected onto the depth frame by applying the T_l^{-1} transformation and the depth camera intrinsics; its associated depth is then sampled: if the 3D point determined by such depth is sufficiently close to the voxel itself, then the label probabilities vector is subject to the update operation that will be described next.

To integrate the pixel category probabilities provided by the labeling algorithm into the probability histogram stored in each voxel, we perform an operation akin to the running average adopted for the depth integration step followed by a renormalization step to ensure attainment of a valid probability mass function. Denotes as $L \in \mathbb{R}^N$ the pixel p.m.f. and $H \in \mathbb{R}^N$ the corresponding voxel p.m.f., firstly we compute a weight w_p associated to the pixel (employing the same strategy used during the depth integration phase, i.e. we assign a unitary weight to the new labels; see also the description of the Weight field in Sect. 3.2); we then sample the weight stored in the voxel w_v. We compute the updated probability histogram H' as follows:

$$H'_i = \frac{H_i w_v + L_i w_p}{w_v + w_p} \qquad \text{with } i \in [1..N] \qquad (1)$$

We then normalize the histogram to obtain a valid probability mass function, H'', that is stored back into the voxel:

$$H''_i = \frac{H'_i}{\sum_i H'_i} \qquad \text{with } i \in [1..N] \qquad (2)$$

We do not update the associated voxel weight, leaving that task to the depth fusion component. While weights w_v depend on the number of times a specific voxel has been observed and that number typically differs from the number of times a voxel has been semantically labeled, we found no significant difference between using an ad-hoc semantic weight (that would need to be stored alongside the p.m.f.) and just piggy-backing on the already present TSDF weight. Hence, we exploit the w_v values to give an appropriate strength to the past probability values and prevent a single measurement from significantly changing the stored probabilities. Also, as typically the frame rate of the SLAM subsystem is constant and the time required by the labeling algorithm is also deterministic, the relationship between the depth weight (a counter of the number of integrated frames) and a "semantic weight" would be linear.

3.3   Main Engine

The Main Engine of our system interacts with the RGB-D sensor, dispatches the work to the SLAM and Labeling subsystems, and provides the user with feedback on the on-going operation by displaying rendered images.

One of the key novelties of our proposal is its ability to perform SLAM and semantic mapping fully automatically and on-line. This means that while the user moves around the RGB-D sensor she/he would see on the screen a semantic reconstruction of the workspace created incrementally at interactive frame-rate. In other words, while in KinectFusion/VoxelHashing the user would perceive incremental reconstruction of the geometry of the scene interactively, our system is aimed at providing, just as interactively, both geometry and semantics in the form of surfaces tagged with category labels. Processing speed is therefore of paramount importance to the pipeline as a whole. However, while the SLAM Subsystem can comfortably keep-up with the 30 Hz RGB-D stream delivered by the sensor, state-of-the-art deep networks for semantic labeling require hundreds of milliseconds or even seconds to process a single frame.

This state of affairs mandates the two subsystems to be decoupled so to execute their code in parallel and prioritize SLAM to provide interactive feedback

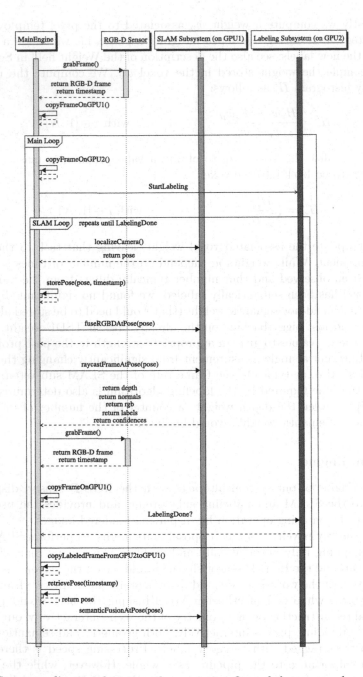

Fig. 2. Sequence diagram depicting the execution flow of the proposed system. The SLAM and Labeling subsystems are deployed on two different GPUs, here colour coded in red and blue. The main engine moves the data between the host memory and the two GPU memories as needed. (Color figure online)

to the user. The Labeling subsystem is thus run on the remaining CPU and GPU time and, by exploiting the deferred Semantic Fusion algorithm described in Sect. 3.2, its output is integrated into the voxel map as soon as it becomes available. To obtain an even higher throughput, we deploy the two subsystems onto two different GPUs, the Main Engine performing the appropriate copies or movements of the data to and from the different boards.

While all frames captured by the RGB-D sensor are used to perform the SLAM task (necessary to obtain an accurate map and a reliable camera localisation), only a minority of those are provided to the Labeling Subsystem. Choice of such candidate frames is left to the Main Engine and performed in a greedy fashion by ignoring all frames grabbed while the Labeling Subsystem is busy labeling a frame and marking for labeling the first new frame received after the labeler has finished its work on a previous frame. We elected not to use a queue-based system to privilege the labeling of several areas of the environment instead of filling the queue with similar frames acquired by nearby viewpoints and have the labeler unavailable to process newly explored areas of the environment.

Figure 2 shows a sequence diagram detailing the execution flow of the system. Once an RGB-D frame is grabbed by the sensor, its data is copied to both GPUs and the labeling thread is activated. At the same time, the camera pose from which the environment was observed is estimated by the SLAM Subsystem and stored in a pose database together with the frame timestamp, used to retrieve such pose at a later stage; subsequently, depth and colour information are fused into the hash-based TSDF structure. A raycasting operation is then performed to obtain the range and normals maps required by the ICP algorithm to localize the camera at the next iteration; if semantic visualization is desired, then colour, label and confidence maps are rendered as well.

The main engine then verifies if the labeling algorithm has terminated its computation; if not, another iteration of the SLAM pipeline is executed. Conversely, the labeling output (i.e. the $N \times H \times W$ volume storing per-pixel category probabilities described in Subsect. 3.1) is transferred from the labeler GPU to the SLAM GPU and the viewpoint from which the frame had been observed is retrieved from the pose database. The semantic labels are then fused via the algorithm described in Sect. 3.2. The process is repeated until the user wishes to terminate; at that point the entire map of the environment can be saved as a mesh via application of the marching cubes algorithm [12]. The mesh can be coloured using either the RGB values stored in the hash-based map or a colour mapped representation of category or confidence values.

4   Results

The system presented in this paper pursues interactive and fully automatic semantic mapping of large workspaces. In this section we will show quantitative and qualitative results provided by the system. Firstly, we present an evaluation of the computational requirements of the entire system, detailing the overall impact of the two main subsystems. Afterwards, we show qualitative results depicting the kind of semantic reconstructions that can be achieved by running the system. In the supplementary material we provide a video demonstrating interactive semantic mapping. From the video, one may perceive the effect of the deferred semantic fusion and how this approach does not hinder incremental interactive reconstruction while adding semantic information into the map over time.

4.1 Performance Evaluation

Our system relies on computation modules deployed on both the CPU and two graphics processors. Our testing setup consists in a PC with a Intel Core i7 4960X CPU and two GeForce Titan Black graphics cards (each with 6 GB of dedicated memory). The SLAM Subsystem is deployed on one card while the Labeling Subsytem based on the Fully Convolutional Network [11] is deployed on the other (the amount of GPU memory required by the neural network is ~5.5 GB).

Table 1 shows the average time spent in the main components of the pipeline. It is evident how the most computationally intensive component of the proposed system is that concerned with semantic labeling of input frames and how its decoupling and deployment on a separate GPU is necessary to maintain an interactive frame-rate (~17 Hz) that allows users to seamlessly deploy the system to semantically reconstruct a location. For comparison, in the last column we

Table 1. Processing time broken down by component. *Total time per frame does not include the exact time spent in executing the SemanticFusion step as this is performed only after the Labeling Subsystem terminates processing an input RGB-D image and therefore its execution time is amortized over a larger number of frames. The total time per frame is thus the average time spent to process a frame, yielding a frame-rate of 17.48 fps for the multi GPU system and of 5.4 fps for the single GPU setup.

Algorithm section	Times (ms.)		
	Multiple GPU		Single GPU
	GPU 1	GPU 2	
Frame Grabbing + Preprocessing	10.27	–	20.21
Camera Localisation	4.30	–	24.90
Depth + RGB Fusion	8.79	–	16.96
ICP Raycast (Depth + Normals)	5.16	–	13.35
RGB + Labels + Confidence Raycast	6.49	–	23.79
Shading + GUI update	11.32	–	71.64
Other processing	7.70	–	10.26
SemanticFusion*	9.59	–	10.44
Frame Labeling	–	284.09	438.91
Total time per frame*	57.20	284.09	186.55

■ Wall   ■ Monitor   ■ Keyboard   ▥ Table   ▥ Chair   ■ Cabinet   ■ Floor

Fig. 3. A semantically reconstructed office environment. The left image shows the coloured mesh generated by our system. The center image shows the most likely category label for each voxel, while the associated confidence values are displayed as a heat map on the right.

show the processing times that can be obtained by running the proposed pipeline on a single GPU accelerator. For this test, we employed a workstation with an Intel Core i7 4930K CPU and a Tesla K40, with 12 GB of memory. The availability of a single GPU, even with twice the memory as those deployed in the previous test, severely hinders the overall system speed due to the computation being bound by the number of available GPU cores rather than by memory availability, this bringing evidence towards the idea of deploying two separate GPUs to realize our system.

4.2   Qualitative Results

Our system enables the user to attain interactively a semantic reconstruction of the environment by employing a hand-held commodity RGB-D sensor such as the Kinect. In this section we show exemplar results obtained in different environments.

Several office sequences depicting a variety of indoor objects such as "monitors", "chairs", "tables", etc... were acquired and processed by our system. Figure 3 shows a view from one of such sequences where chairs, monitors, and the keyboard are labeled quite correctly. Wall and floor regions are also mostly correct while the "table" category shows a slightly lower segmentation accuracy, its labels bleeding into the "cabinet" located below. The Fully Convolutional Network model used to obtain the depicted results is "pascalcontext-fcn8s".

Using the same neural network as in Fig. 3, we have run our system also on sequences belonging to the Stanford 3D Scene Dataset [24,25]. In Figs. 4 and 5 we show the resulting reconstructions. It can be observed how the system can label correctly large objects, such as sofas and tables. Moreover, voxels pertaining to smaller objects, such as the stacked books in Fig. 4, are mostly correctly labeled alike. The two lamps in Fig. 4 (top row) are inevitably mislabeled because "lamp" does not belong to the set of categories handled by the neural network. As concerns the potted plant in Fig. 5, it is worth pointing out that labels tend to propagate into the wall due to the thin and partially reflective nature of the leaves which causes depth estimation by the RGB-D sensor to fail and prevent accurate 3D reconstruction of the object.

■ Wall ■ Floor ▨ Sofa ▢ Table ■ Books

Fig. 4. *ReadingRoom* sequence from the Stanford 3D Scene Dataset. Top row: ray-casted views acquired during the reconstruction. Bottom row: details from the final reconstruction. Columns as in Fig. 3.

Throughout our experiments, we observed that the boundaries between different objects are reasonably accurate for smaller items (*e.g.* books, keyboards, chairs, monitors,...) while the contours dealing with larger objects, such as tables, sofas and structural elements (*i.e.* walls, floors and ceilings) tend to be less accurately localized and "bleed" onto neighboring voxels. It is noteworthy, though, that the confidence associated to such incorrect boundary zones is typically significantly lower than that estimated within the internal portions of objects. This effect is especially evident if the object is observed from a significant distance and can be traced back to the 2D nature of the semantic labeling process: labeled pixels are reprojected onto the voxel-based map using the current depth image and thus a single (potentially mis-)labeled pixel affects a larger area of the reconstruction the farther away it is from the camera.

Overall, the experimental findings suggest that our system can label correctly both the main large-size scene structures such as floor, walls, tables, chairs as well as several smaller objects like monitors, books, keyboards. Moreover, the confidence maps turn out quite reliable, due to high confidence labels unlikely turning out wrong and mislabeled areas featuring low scores. Therefore, our semantic reconstructions and associated confidence maps may provide valuable cues to facilitate high-level reasoning pursuing indoor scene understanding.

■ Wall ■ Floor ▨ Sofa ■ Potted Plant ▨ Unknown

Fig. 5. Details of the reconstruction of the *Lounge* sequence from the Stanford 3D Scene Dataset. Columns as in Fig. 3.

5   Final Remarks

We have presented the first interactive system allowing an user to perform 3D reconstruction of a large scale environment while semantically labeling the observed surfaces seamlessly. To this purpose, we split the proposed pipeline in two subsystems, each relying on state-of-the-art approaches. The Labeling subsystem pursues per-pixel semantic segmentation of RGB images by a recently proposed deep neural network [11]. Indeed, our architecture is agnostic to the actual labeler and, thus, holds the potential to accommodate the advances in the field likely to be provided by the ever-increasing research efforts on deep learning architectures for semantic segmentation and object detection. The SLAM subsystem relies on the VoxelHashing approach [15] to handle reconstruction of large scenes. Nießner's pipeline, though, has been modified to achieve storage, deferred integration and visualization of semantic information. To provide the user with a fluid interactive experience we deploy the proposed system on a off-the-shelf Personal Computer endowed with two GPUs and suitably schedule the work-load on such platforms.

Among the shortcomings of our system is, *in primis*, reliance of the camera localization step on a purely geometric tracking approach (i.e. the standard projective ICP used by VoxelHashing and KinectFusion) which, while good enough to accurately estimate camera poses across frames, is not immune from a certain amount of drift that may become evident when the hand-held sensor is brought back to a previously observed area. Hence, we plan to deploy more recent approaches, such as [7], that may enable exploration of large-scale environments with negligible drift. Another issue worthy of further investigation concerns the accuracy of the semantically labeled 3D maps: sometimes labels bleed onto voxels belonging to neighboring objects due to the independence of category histograms computed at neighbouring voxels. Accordingly, the application of pairwise CRFs either at label integration or mesh generation time to ensure spatial consistency of neighboring labels is currently under investigation.

Acknowledgements. We gratefully acknowledge the support of NVIDIA Corporation with the donation of the Tesla K40 GPU used for this research.

References

1. Blais, G., Levine, M.: Registering multiview range data to create 3D computer objects. IEEE Trans. Pattern Anal. Mach. Intell. **17**(8), 820–824 (1995)
2. Bylow, E., Olsson, C.: Robust camera tracking by combining color and depth measurements. In: 2014 22nd International Conference on Pattern Recognition (ICPR) (2014)
3. Bylow, E., Sturm, J., Kerl, C., Kahl, F., Cremers, D.: Real-time camera tracking and 3D reconstruction using signed distance functions. In: Robotics: Science and Systems (RSS) (2013)
4. Canelhas, D.R., Stoyanov, T., Lilienthal, A.J.: SDF tracker: a parallel algorithm for on-line pose estimation and scene reconstruction from depth images. In: IEEE International Conference on Intelligent Robots and Systems, pp. 3671–3676 (2013)

5. Cavallari, T., Stefano, L.: Volume-based semantic labeling with signed distance functions. In: Bräunl, T., McCane, B., Rivera, M., Yu, X. (eds.) PSIVT 2015. LNCS, vol. 9431, pp. 544–556. Springer, Heidelberg (2016). doi:10.1007/978-3-319-29451-3_43
6. Eigen, D., Fergus, R.: Predicting Depth, Surface Normals and Semantic Labels with a Common Multi-Scale Convolutional Architecture. ICCV, November 2015
7. Fioraio, N., Taylor, J., Fitzgibbon, A., Di Stefano, L., Izadi, S.: Large-scale and drift-free surface reconstruction using online subvolume registration. In: 2015 IEEE Conference on Computer Vision and Pattern Recognition (CVPR), pp. 4475–4483. IEEE, June 2015
8. Gupta, S., Girshick, R., Arbeláez, P., Malik, J.: Learning rich features from RGB-D images for object detection and segmentation. In: Fleet, D., Pajdla, T., Schiele, B., Tuytelaars, T. (eds.) ECCV 2014. LNCS, vol. 8695, pp. 345–360. Springer, Heidelberg (2014). doi:10.1007/978-3-319-10584-0_23
9. Kahler, O., Prisacariu, V.A., Ren, C.Y., Sun, X., Torr, P., Murray, D.: Very high frame rate volumetric integration of depth images on mobile devices. IEEE Trans. Visual. Comput. Graph. 21(11), 1241–1250 (2015)
10. Kahler, O., Prisacariu, V., Valentin, J., Murray, D.: Hierarchical voxel block hashing for efficient integration of depth images. IEEE Rob. Autom. Lett. 3766(c), 1 (2015)
11. Long, J., Shelhamer, E., Darrell, T.: Fully convolutional networks for semantic segmentation. In: IEEE Conference on Computer Vision and Pattern Recognition (CVPR) (2015)
12. Lorensen, W.E., Cline, H.E.: Marching cubes: a high resolution 3D surface construction algorithm. In: Proceedings of the 14th Annual Conference on Computer Graphics and Interactive Techniques - SIGGRAPH 1987, vol. 21, issue 4, pp. 163–169 (1987)
13. Miksik, O., Torr, P.H., Vineet, V., Lidegaard, M., Prasaath, R., Nießner, M., Golodetz, S., Hicks, S.L., Pérez, P., Izadi, S.: The semantic paintbrush. In: Proceedings of the 33rd Annual ACM Conference on Human Factors in Computing Systems - CHI 2015, pp. 3317–3326. ACM, New York, April 2015
14. Newcombe, R.A., Davison, A.J., Izadi, S., Kohli, P., Hilliges, O., Shotton, J., Molyneaux, D., Hodges, S., Kim, D., Fitzgibbon, A.: KinectFusion: real-time dense surface mapping and tracking. In: 2011 10th IEEE International Symposium on Mixed and Augmented Reality, pp. 127–136. IEEE, October 2011
15. Nießner, M., Zollhöfer, M., Izadi, S., Stamminger, M.: Real-time 3D reconstruction at scale using voxel hashing. ACM Trans. Graph. 32(6), 1–11 (2013)
16. Roth, H., Marsette, V.: Moving volume KinectFusion. In: Proceedings of the British Machine Vision Conference, pp. 112.1–112.11 (2012)
17. Steinbrucker, F., Sturm, J., Cremers, D.: Real-time visual odometry from dense RGB-D images. In: 2011 IEEE International Conference on Computer Vision Workshops (ICCV Workshops), pp. 719–722. IEEE, November 2011
18. Valentin, J., Vineet, V., Cheng, M.M., Kim, D., Shotton, J., Kohli, P., Niessner, M., Criminisi, A., Izadi, S., Torr, P.: SemanticPaint: interactive 3D labeling and learning at your fingertips. ACM Trans. Graph. (TOG) (2015)
19. Whelan, T., Johannsson, H., Kaess, M., Leonard, J.J., McDonald, J.: Robust real-time visual odometry for dense RGB-D mapping. In: 2013 IEEE International Conference on Robotics and Automation, vol. 1, pp. 5724–5731. IEEE, May 2013
20. Whelan, T., Kaess, M., Fallon, M.: Kintinuous: spatially extended KinectFusion. In: Robotics Science and Systems (Workshop on RGB-D: Advanced Reasoning with Depth Cameras) (2012)

21. Yang, C., Medioni, G.: Object modelling by registration of multiple range images. Image Vis. Comput. **10**, 145–155 (1992). IEEE Computer Society Press
22. Zeng, M., Zhao, F., Zheng, J., Liu, X.: Octree-based fusion for realtime 3D reconstruction. Graph. Models **75**(3), 126–136 (2013)
23. Zheng, S., Jayasumana, S., Romera-Paredes, B., Vineet, V., Su, Z., Du, D., Huang, C., Torr, P.H.S.: Conditional random fields as recurrent neural networks. In: Proceedings of the IEEE International Conference on Computer Vision, pp. 1529–1537 (2015)
24. Zhou, Q.Y., Koltun, V.: Dense scene reconstruction with points of interest. ACM Trans. Graph. **32**(4), 112:1–112:8 (2013)
25. Zhou, Q.Y., Miller, S., Koltun, V.: Elastic fragments for dense scene reconstruction. In: 2013 IEEE International Conference on Computer Vision, pp. 473–480. IEEE, December 2013

Learning Covariant Feature Detectors

Karel Lenc[✉] and Andrea Vedaldi

Department of Engineering Science, University of Oxford, Oxford, UK
{karel,vedaldi}@robots.ox.ac.uk

Abstract. Local covariant feature detection, namely the problem of extracting viewpoint invariant features from images, has so far largely resisted the application of machine learning techniques. In this paper, we propose the first fully general formulation for learning local covariant feature detectors. We propose to cast detection as a regression problem, enabling the use of powerful regressors such as deep neural networks. We then derive a *covariance constraint* that can be used to automatically learn which visual structures provide stable anchors for local feature detection. We support these ideas theoretically, proposing a novel analysis of local features in term of geometric transformations, and we show that all common and many uncommon detectors can be derived in this framework. Finally, we present empirical results on translation and rotation covariant detectors on standard feature benchmarks, showing the power and flexibility of the framework.

1 Introduction

Image matching, i.e. the problem of establishing point correspondences between two images of the same scene, is central to computer vision. In the past two decades, this problem stimulated the creation of numerous *viewpoint invariant local feature detectors*. These were also adopted in problems such as large scale image retrieval and object category recognition, as a general-purpose image representations. More recently, however, deep learning has replaced local features as the preferred method to construct image representations; in fact, the most recent works on local feature descriptors are now based on deep learning [10,46].

Differently from *descriptors*, the problem of constructing local feature *detectors* has so far largely resisted machine learning. The goal of a detector is to extract stable local features from images, which is an essential step in any matching algorithm based on sparse features. It may be surprising that machine learning has not been very successful at this task given that it has proved very useful in many other detection problems. We believe that the reason is the difficulty of devising a learning formulation for viewpoint invariant features.

To clarify this difficulty, note that the fundamental aim of a local feature detector is to extract the same features from images regardless of effects such as viewpoint changes. In computer vision, this behavior is more formally called *covariant detection*. Handcrafted detectors achieve it by anchoring features to image structures, such as corners or blobs, that are preserved under a

© Springer International Publishing Switzerland 2016
G. Hua and H. Jégou (Eds.): ECCV 2016 Workshops, Part III, LNCS 9915, pp. 100–117, 2016.
DOI: 10.1007/978-3-319-49409-8_11

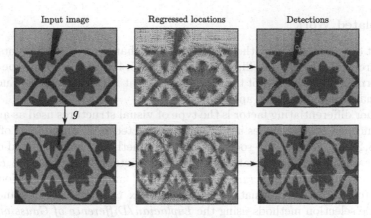

Fig. 1. *Detection by regression.* We train a neural network ϕ that, given a patch $\mathbf{x}|_p$ around each pixel p in an image, produces a displacement vector $h_p = \phi(\mathbf{x}|_p)$ pointing to the nearest feature location (middle column). Displacements from nearby pixels are then pooled to detect features (right column). The neural network is trained in order to be covariant with transformations g of the image (bottom row). Best viewed on screen. Image data from [4].

viewpoint change. However, there is no *a–priori* list of what visual structures constitute useful anchors. Thus, an algorithm must not only learn the appearance of the anchors, but needs to determine what anchors are in the first place. In other words, the challenge is to learn simultaneously a detector together with the detection targets.

In this paper we propose a method to address this challenge. Our first contribution is to introduce a novel *learning formulation for covariant detectors* (Sect. 2). This is based on two ideas: (i) defining an objective function in term of a *covariance constraint* which is anchor-agnostic (Sect. 2.1) and (ii) formulating detection as a *regression problem*, which allows to use powerful regressors such as deep networks for this task (Fig. 1).

Our second contribution is to support this approach theoretically. We show how covariant feature detectors are best understood and manipulated in term of image transformations (Sect. 2.2). Then, we show that, geometrically, different detector types can be characterized by which transformations they are covariant with and, among those, which ones they fix and which they leave undetermined (Sect. 2.3). We then show that this formulation encompasses all common and many uncommon detector types and allows to derive a covariance constraint for each one of them (Sect. 2.4).

Our last contribution is to validate this approach empirically. We do so by first discussing several important implementation details (Sect. 3), and then by training and assessing two different detector types, comparing them to off-the-shelf detectors (Sect. 4). Finally, we discuss future extensions (Sect. 5).

1.1   Related Work

Covariant detectors differ by the type of features that they extract: points [6, 11, 16, 36], circles [17, 19, 23], or ellipses [2, 18, 22, 24, 35, 42]. In turn, the type of feature determines which class of transformations that they can handle: Euclidean transformations, similarities, and affinities.

Another differentiating factor is the type of visual structures used as anchors. For instance, early approaches used corners extracted from an analysis of image edglets [8, 29, 34]. These were soon surpassed by methods that extracted corners and other anchors using operators of the image intensity such as the *Hessian of Gaussian* [3] or the *structure tensor* [7, 11, 47] and its generalizations [40]. In order to handle transformations more complex than translations and rotations, scale selection methods using the *Laplacian/Difference of Gaussian* operator (L/DoG) were introduced [19, 23], and further extended with *affine adaptation* [2, 24] to handle full affine transformations. While these are probably the best known detectors, several other approaches were explored as well, including parametric feature models [9, 28] and using self-dissimilarity [13, 38].

All detectors discussed so far are *handcrafted*. Learning has been mostly limited to the case in which detection anchors are defined *a-priori*, either by manual labelling [14] or as the output of a pre-existing handcrafted detector [5, 12, 31, 39], with the goal of accelerating detection. Closer to our aim, [32] use simulated annealing to optimise the parameters of their FAST detector for repeatability. To the best of our knowledge, the only line of work that attempted to learn repeatable anchors from scratch is the one of [25, 41], who did so using genetic programming; however, their approach is much more limited than ours, focusing only on the repeatability of corner points.

More recently, [44] learns to estimate the orientation of feature points using deep learning. Contrary to our approach, the loss function is defined on top of the local image feature descriptors and is limited to estimating the rotation of keypoints. The work of [27, 37, 45] also use Siamese deep learning architectures for local features, but for local image feature *description*, whereas we use them for feature *detection*.

2   Method

We first introduce our method in a special case, namely in learning a basic corner detector (Sect. 2.1), and then we extend it to general covariant features (Sects. 2.2 and 2.3). Finally, we show how the theory applies to concrete examples of detectors (Sect. 2.4).

2.1   The Covariance Constraint

Let $\mathbf{x}$ be an image and let $T\mathbf{x}$ be its version translated by $T \in \mathbb{R}^2$ pixels. A corner detector extracts from $\mathbf{x}$ a (small) collection of points $\mathbf{f} \in \mathbb{R}^2$. The detector is said to be covariant if, when applied to the translated image $T\mathbf{x}$, it returns the

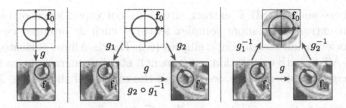

Fig. 2. Left: an oriented circular frame $\mathbf{f} = g\mathbf{f}_0$ is obtained as a unique similarity transformation $g \in G$ of the canonical frame $\mathbf{f}_0$, where the orientation is represented by the dot. Concretely, this could be the output of the SIFT detector after orientation assignment. **Middle:** the detector finds feature frames $\mathbf{f}_i = g_i\mathbf{f}_0, g_i = \phi(\mathbf{x}_i)$ in images $\mathbf{x}_1$ and $\mathbf{x}_2$ respectively due to covariance, matching the features allows to recover the underlying image transformation $\mathbf{x}_2 = g\mathbf{x}_1$ as $g = g_2 \circ g_1^{-1}$. **Right:** equivalently, then inverse transformations g_i^{-1} normalize the images, resulting in the same canonical view.

translated points $\mathbf{f} + T$. Most covariant detectors work by anchoring features to image structures that, such as corners, are preserved under transformation. A challenge in defining anchors is that these must be general enough to be found in most images and at the same time sufficiently distinctive to achieve covariance.

Anchor extraction is usually formulated as a *selection problem* by finding the features that maximize a handcrafted figure of merit such as Harris' cornerness, the Laplacian of Gaussian, or the Hessian of Gaussian. This indirect construction makes learning anchors difficult. As a solution, we propose to regard feature detection not as a selection problem but as a *regression one*. Thus the goal is to learn a function $\psi : \mathbf{x} \mapsto \mathbf{f}$ that directly maps an image (patch[1]) $\mathbf{x}$ to a corner $\mathbf{f}$. The key advantage is that this function can be implemented by any regression method, including a deep neural network.

This leaves the problem of defining a learning objective. This would be easy if we had example anchors annotated in the data; however, our aim is to discover useful anchors automatically. Thus, we propose to *use covariance itself as a learning objective*. This is formally captured by the *covariance constraint* $\psi(T\mathbf{x}) = T + \psi(\mathbf{x})$. A corresponding learning objective can be formulated as follows:

$$\min_\psi \frac{1}{n} \sum_{i=1}^n \|\psi(T_i\mathbf{x}_i) - \psi(\mathbf{x}_i) - T_i\|^2 \tag{1}$$

where $(\mathbf{x}_i, T_i)$ are example patches and transformations and the optimization is over the parameters of the regressor ψ (e.g. the filter weights in a deep neural network).

2.2 Beyond Corners

This section provides a first generalization of the construction above. While simple detectors such as Harris extract 2D points $\mathbf{f}$ in correspondence of

---

[1] As the function ψ needs to be location invariant it can be applied in a sliding window manner. Therefore x can be a single patch which represents its perception field.

corners, others such as SIFT extract circles in correspondence of blobs, and others again extract even more complex features such as oriented circles (e.g. SIFT with orientation assignment), ellipses (e.g. Harris-Affine), oriented ellipses (e.g. Harris-Affine with orientation assignment), etc. In general, due to their role in fixing image transformations, we will call the extracted shapes $\mathbf{f} \in \mathcal{F}$ *feature frames*.

The detector is thus a function $\psi : \mathcal{X} \to \mathcal{F}$, $\mathbf{x} \mapsto \mathbf{f}$ mapping an image patch $\mathbf{x}$ to a corresponding feature frame $\mathbf{f}$. We say that the detector is *covariant with a group of transformations*[2] $g \in G$ (e.g. similarity or affine) when

$$\forall \mathbf{x} \in \mathcal{X}, g \in G : \quad \psi(g\mathbf{x}) = g\psi(\mathbf{x}) \qquad (2)$$

where $g\mathbf{f}$ is the transformed frame and $g\mathbf{x}$ is the warped image.[3]

Working with feature frames is intuitive, but cumbersome and not very flexible. A much better approach is to drop frames altogether and replace them with corresponding transformations. For instance, in SIFT with orientation assignment all possible oriented circles $\mathbf{f}$ can be expressed uniquely as a similarity $g\mathbf{f}_0$ of a fixed oriented circle $\mathbf{f}_0$ (Fig. 2left). Hence, instead of talking about oriented circles $\mathbf{f}$, we can equivalently talk about similarities g. Likewise, in the case of the Harris' corner detector, all possible 2D points $\mathbf{f}$ can be expressed as translations $T + \mathbf{f}_0$ of the origin $\mathbf{f}_0$, and so we can talk about translations T instead of points $\mathbf{f}$.

To generalize this idea, we say that a class of frames $\mathcal{F}$ *resolves* a group of transformations G when, given a fixed *canonical frame* $\mathbf{f}_0 \in \mathcal{F}$, all frames are *uniquely generated* from it by the action of G:

$$\mathcal{F} = G\mathbf{f}_0 = \{g\mathbf{f}_0 : g \in G\} \quad \text{and} \quad \forall g, h \in G : \ g\mathbf{f}_0 = h\mathbf{f}_0 \Rightarrow g = h \text{ (uniqueness)}.$$

This bijective correspondence allows to "rename" frames with transformations. Using this renaming, the detector ψ can be rewritten as a function ϕ that outputs directly a transformation $\psi(\mathbf{x}) = \phi(\mathbf{x})\mathbf{f}_0$ instead of a frame.

With this substitution, the covariance constraint (2) becomes

$$\boxed{\phi(g\mathbf{x}) \circ \phi(\mathbf{x})^{-1} \circ g^{-1} = 1} \qquad (3)$$

Note that, for the group of translations $G = T(2)$, this constraint corresponds directly to the objective function (1). Figure 2 provides two intuitive visualizations of this constraint.

It is also useful to extend the learning objective (1) as follows. As training data, we consider n triplets $(\mathbf{x}_i, \hat{\mathbf{x}}_i, g_i), i = 1, \ldots, n$ comprising an image

---

[2] Here, a group of transformation $(G, \circ)$ is a set of functions $g, h : \mathbb{R}^2 \to \mathbb{R}^2$ together with composition $g \circ h \in G$ as group operation. Composition is associative; furthermore, G contains the identity transformation 1 and the inverse g^{-1} of each of its elements $g \in G$.

[3] The action $g\mathbf{x}$ of the transformation g on the image $\mathbf{x}$ is to warp it: $(g\mathbf{x})(u, v) = \mathbf{x}(g^{-1}(u, v))$.

(patch) $\mathbf{x}_i$, a transformation g_i, and the transformed and distorted image $\hat{\mathbf{x}}_i = g\mathbf{x}_i + \eta$. Here η represents additive noise or some other useful distortion such as a random rescaling of the intensity which allows to train a more robust detector. The learning problem is then given by:

$$\min_{\phi} \frac{1}{n} \sum_{i=1}^{n} d(r_i, 1)^2, \qquad r_i = \phi(\hat{\mathbf{x}}_i) \circ \phi(\mathbf{x}_i)^{-1} \circ g_i^{-1} \qquad (4)$$

where $d(r_i, 1)^2$ is the "distance" of the residual transformation r_i from the identity.

2.3 General Covariant Feature Extraction

The theory presented so far is insufficient to fully account for the properties of many common detectors. For this, we need to remove the assumptions that feature frames resolve (i.e. fix) completely the group of transformations G. Most detectors are in fact *covariant with transformation groups larger than the ones that they can resolve*. For example, the Harris's detector is covariant with rotation and translation (in the sense that the same corners are extracted after the image is roto-translated), but, by detecting 2D points, it only resolves translations. Likewise, SIFT without orientation assignment is covariant to full similarity transformations but, by detecting circles, only resolves dilations (i.e. rotations remains undetermined; Fig. 3).

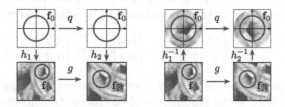

Fig. 3. Left: a (unoriented) circle identifies the translation and scale component of a similarity transformation $g \in G$, but leaves a residual rotation $q \in Q$ undetermined. Concretely, this could be the output of the SIFT detector prior orientation assignment. **Right:** normalization is achieved up to the residual transformation q.

Next, we explain how Eq. (3) must be modified to deal with detectors that (i) are covariant with a transformation group G but (ii) resolve only a subgroup $H \subset G$. In this case, the detector function $\phi(\mathbf{x}) \in H$ returns a transformation in the smaller group H, and the covariance constraint (3) is satisfied up to a complementary transformation $q \in Q$ that makes up for the part not resolved by the detector:

$$\exists q \in Q : \quad \phi(g\mathbf{x}) \circ q \circ \phi(\mathbf{x})^{-1} \circ g^{-1} = 1. \qquad (5)$$

This situation is illustrated graphically in Fig. 3.

For this construction to work, given $H \subset G$, the group $Q \subset G$ must be chosen appropriately. In Eq. (5), and following Fig. 3, call $h_1 = \phi(\mathbf{x})$ and $h_2 = \phi(g\mathbf{x})$. Rearranging the terms, we get that $h_2 q = h_1 g$, where $h_2 \in H, q \in Q$ and $h_1 g \in G$. This means that any element in G must be expressible as a composition hq, i.e. $G = HQ = \{hq : h \in H, q \in Q\}$. Formally (proofs in appendix):

Proposition 1. *If the group* $G = HQ$ *is the product of the subgroups* H *and* Q, *then, for any choice of* $g \in G$ *and* $h_1 \in H$, *there is always a decomposition*

$$h_2 q h_1^{-1} g^{-1} = 1, \quad such\ that \quad h_2 \in H, \ q \in Q. \tag{6}$$

In practice, given G and H, Q is usually easily found as the "missing transformation"; however, compared to (2), the transformation q in constraint (5) is an extra degree of freedom that complicates optimization. Fortunately, in many cases the following proposition shows that there is only one possible q:

Proposition 2. *If* $H \triangleleft G$ *is normal in* G *(i.e.* $\forall g \in G, h \in H : g^{-1}hg \in H$) *and* $H \cap Q = \{1\}$, *then, given* $g \in G$, *the choice of* q *in the decomposition* (5) *is unique.*

The next section works through several concrete examples to illustrate these concepts.

2.4   A Taxonomy of Detectors

This section applies the theory developed above to standard detectors. Concretely, we limit ourselves to transformations up to affine, and write:

$$h_i = \begin{bmatrix} M_i & P_i \\ 0 & 1 \end{bmatrix}, \ q = \begin{bmatrix} L & 0 \\ 0 & 1 \end{bmatrix}, \ g = \begin{bmatrix} A & T \\ 0 & 1 \end{bmatrix}.$$

Here P_i can be interpreted as the centre of the feature in image $\mathbf{x}_i$ and M_i as its affine shape, (A, T) as the parameters of the image transformation, and L as the parameter of the complementary transformation not fixed by the detector. The covariance constraint (5) can be written, after a short calculation, as

$$M_2 L M_1^{-1} = A, \qquad P_2 - A P_1 = T. \tag{7}$$

As a first example, consider a basic corner detector that resolves translations $H = G = T(2)$ with no (non-trivial) complementary transformation $Q = \{1\}$. Hence $M_1 = M_2 = L = A = I$ and (5) becomes:

$$P_2 - P_1 = T. \tag{8}$$

This is the same expression found in the simple example of Sect. 2.1 and requires the detected features to have the correct relative shift T.

The Harris corner detector is similar, but is covariant with rotations too. Formally, $H = T(2) \subset G = SE(2)$ (Euclidean transforms) and $Q = SO(2)$ (rotations). Since $T(2) \triangleleft SE(2)$ is a normal subgroup, we expect to find a unique choice for q. In fact, it must be $M_i = I$, $A = L = R$, and the constraint reduces to:

$$P_2 - RP_1 = T. \tag{9}$$

In SIFT, $G = S(2)$ is the group of similarities, so that $A = sR$ is the composition of a rotation $R \in SO(2)$ and an isotropic scaling $s \in \mathbb{R}_+$. SIFT prior to orientation assignment resolves the subgroup H of dilations (scaling and translation), so that $M_i = \sigma_i I$ (scaling) and the complement is a rotation $L \in SO(2)$. Once again $H \triangleleft G$, so the choice of q is unique, and in particular $L = R$. The constraint reduces to:

$$P_2 - sRP_1 = T, \qquad \sigma_2/\sigma_1 = s. \tag{10}$$

When orientation assignment is added to SIFT, the similarities are completely resolved $H = G = S(2)$, $M_i = \sigma_i R_i$ is a rotation and scaling, and the constraint becomes:

$$P_2 - sRP_1 = T, \qquad \sigma_2/\sigma_1 = s, \qquad R_2 R_1^\top = R. \tag{11}$$

Affine detectors such as Harris-Affine (without orientation assignment) are more complex. In this case $G = A(2)$ are affinities and $H = UA(2)$ are *upright affinities*, i.e. affinities where the linear map $M_i \in LT_+(2)$ is a lower-triangular matrix with positive diagonal (these affinities, which still form a group, leave the "up" direction unchanged). The residual $Q = SO(2)$ are rotations and $HQ = G$ is still satisfied. However, $UA(2)$ is *not* normal in $A(2)$, Proposition 2 does not apply, and the choice of Q is *not* unique.[4] The constraint has the form:

$$P_2 - AP_1 = T, \qquad M_2^{-1} A M_1 \in SO(2). \tag{12}$$

For affine detectors with orientation assignment, $H = G = A(2)$ and the constraint is:

$$P_2 - AP_1 = T, \qquad M_2 M_1^{-1} = A. \tag{13}$$

The generality of our formulation allows learning many new types of detectors. For example, by setting $H = T(2)$ and $G = A(2)$ it is possible to train a corner detector such as Harris which is covariant to full affine transformations. Furthermore, a benefit of working with transformations instead of feature frames is that we can train detectors that would be difficult to express in terms of geometric primitives. For instance, by setting $H = SO(2)$ and $G = SE(2)$, we can train a *orientation detector* which is covariant with *rotation and translation*. As for affine upright features, in this case H is not normal in G so the complementary translation $q = (I, T') \in Q$ is not uniquely fixed by $g = (R, T) \in G$; nevertheless, a short calculation shows that the only part of (5) that matters in this case is

$$R_2^\top R_1 = R \tag{14}$$

where $h_i = (R_i, 0)$ are the rotations estimated by the regressor.

---

[4] Concretely, from $M_2 L = A M_1$ the complement matrix L is given by the QR decomposition of the r.h.s. which is a function of M_1, i.e. not unique.

3 Implementation

This section discusses several implementation details of our method: the parametrization of transformations, example CNN architectures, multiple features detection, efficient dense detection, and preparing the training data.

Transformations: Parametrization and Loss. Implementing (4) requires parametrizing the transformation $\phi(\mathbf{x}) \in H$ predicted by the regressor. In the most general case of interest here, $H = A(2)$ are affine transformations and the simplest approach is to output the corresponding matrix of coefficients:

$$\phi(\mathbf{x}) = \begin{bmatrix} \mathbf{a} & \mathbf{b} & \mathbf{p} \\ 0 & 0 & 1 \end{bmatrix} = \begin{bmatrix} a_u & b_u & p_u \\ a_v & b_v & p_v \\ 0 & 0 & 1 \end{bmatrix}.$$

Here $\mathbf{p}$ can be interpreted as the feature center and $\mathbf{a}$ and $\mathbf{b}$ as the feature affine shape. By rearranging the terms in (2), the loss function in (4) takes the form

$$d^2(r, 1) = \min_{q \in Q} \| g\phi(\mathbf{x}) - \phi(g\mathbf{x})q \|_F^2, \tag{15}$$

where $\| \cdot \|_F$ is the Frobenius norm. As seen before, the complementary transformation q is often uniquely determined given g and the minimization can be removed by substituting this fixed value for q. In practice, g and q are also represented by matrices, as described in Sect. 2.4.

When the resolved transformations H are less general than affinities, the parametrization can be adjusted accordingly. For instance, for the basic detector of Sect. 2.1, where $H = T(2)$, on can fix $\mathbf{a} = (1, 0)$, $\mathbf{b} = (0, 1)$, $q = I$ and $g = (I, T)$, which reduces to Eq. (1). If, on the other hand, $H = SO(2)$ are rotation matrices as for the orientation detector (14),

$$\phi(\mathbf{x}) = \frac{1}{\sqrt{a_u^2 + a_v^2}} \begin{bmatrix} a_u & -a_v & 0 \\ a_v & a_u & 0 \\ 0 & 0 & 1 \end{bmatrix}. \tag{16}$$

Table 1. *Network architectures.* The DetNet-S and DetNet-L CNN architectures used which consist of a small number of convolutional layers applied densely and with no padding. The filter sizes and number is specified in the top part of each cell. Filters are followed by ReLU layers and, where indicated, by 2×2 max pooling and/or LRN.

Model	Conv1	Conv2	Conv3	Conv4	Conv5	Conv6	Conv7
DetNet-S	$5 \times 5 \times 40$	$5 \times 5 \times 100$	$4 \times 4 \times 300$	$1 \times 1 \times 500$	$1 \times 1 \times 500$	$1 \times 1 \times 2$	
	Pool ↓ 2	Pool ↓ 2					
DetNet-L	$5 \times 5 \times 60$	$5 \times 5 \times 150$	$4 \times 4 \times 450$	$1 \times 1 \times 600$	$1 \times 1 \times 600$	$1 \times 1 \times 600$	$1 \times 1 \times 2$
	Pool ↓ 2	Pool ↓ 2 + LRN					

Network Architectures. One of the benefits of our approach is that it allows to use deep neural networks in order to implement the feature regressor $\phi(\mathbf{x})$. Here we experiment with two such architectures, DetNet-S and DetNet-L, summarized in Table 1. For fast detection, these resemble the compact LeNet model of [15]. The main difference between the two is the number of layers and filters. The loss (15) is differentiable and easily implemented in a network loss layer. Note that the loss requires evaluating the network ϕ twice, once applied to image $\mathbf{x}$ and once to image $g\mathbf{x}$. Like in siamese architectures, these can be thought of as two networks with shared weights.

When implemented in a standard CNN toolbox (in our case in MatConvNet [43]), multiple patch pairs are processed in parallel by a single CNN execution in what is known as a minibatch. In practice, the operations in (15) can be implemented using off-the-shelf CNN components. For example, the multiplication by the affine transformation g in (15), which depends on which pair of images in the batch is considered, can be implemented by using convolution routines, 1×1 filters, and so called "filter groups".

From Local Regression to Global Detection. The formulation (4) learns a function ψ that maps an image patch $\mathbf{x}$ to a single detected feature $\mathbf{f} = \psi(\mathbf{x})$. In order to detect multiple features in a larger image, the function ψ is simply applied

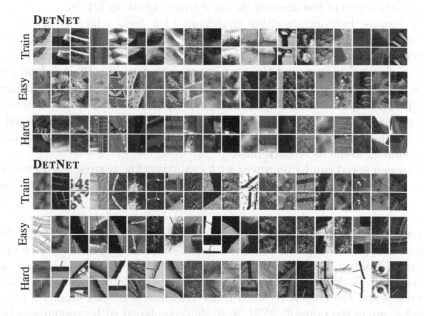

Fig. 4. *Training and validation patches.* Example of training triplets $(\mathbf{x}_1, \mathbf{x}_2, g)$ ($\mathbf{x}_1$ above and $\mathbf{x}_2 = g\mathbf{x}_1$ below) for different detectors. The figure also shows "easy" and "hard" patch pairs, extracted from the validation set based on the value of the loss (16). The crosses and bars represent respectively the detected translation and orientation, as learned by DetNet-L and RotNet-L.

convolutionally at all image locations (Fig. 1). Then, due to covariance, partially overlapping patches $\mathbf{x}$ that contain the same feature are mapped by ψ to the same detection $\mathbf{f}$. Such duplicate detections are collapsed and their number, which reflects the stability of the feature, is used as detection confidence.

For point features ($G = T(2)$), this voting process is implemented efficiently by accumulating votes in a map containing one bin for each pixel in the input image. Votes are accumulated using bilinear interpolation, after which non-maxima suppression is applied with a radius of two pixels. This scheme can be easily extended to more complex features, particularly under the reasonable assumption that only one feature is detected at each image location.

Note that some patches may in practice contain two or more clearly visible feature anchors. The detector ψ must then decide which one to select. This is not a significant limitation at test time (as the missed anchors would likely be selected by a translated application of ψ). Its effect at training time is discussed later.

Efficient Dense Evaluation. As most CNNs, architectures DetNet-S and DetNet-L rapidly downsample their input for efficiency. In order to perform dense feature detection, the easiest approach is to reapply the CNNs to slightly shifted versions of the image, filling the "holes" left in the downsampled output. An equivalent but much more efficient method, which reuses significant computations in the denser early layers of the network, is the *à trous* algorithm [21,26].

We propose here an algorithm equivalent to *à trous* which is just as efficient and more easily implemented. Given a CNN layer $\mathbf{x}_l = \phi_l(\mathbf{x}_{l-1})$ that downsamples the input tensor $\mathbf{x}_{l-1}$ by a factor of, say, two, the downsampling factor is changed to one, and the now larger output $\mathbf{x}_l$ is split into four parts $\mathbf{x}_l^{(k)}, k = 1, \ldots, 4$. Each part is obtained by downsampling $\mathbf{x}_l$ after shifting it by zero or one pixels in the horizontal and vertical directions (for a total of four combinations). Then the deeper layers of the networks are computed as usual on the four parts independently. The construction is repeated whenever downsampling needs to be performed.

Detection speed can be improved with evaluating the regressor with stride 2 (at every second pixel). We refer to these detector as DETNET*S2*. Source code and the DETNETmodels are freely available[5].

Training Data. Training images are obtained from the ImageNet ILSVRC 2012 training data [33], extracting twenty random 57×57 crops per image, for up to $6M$ crops. Uniform crops are discarded since they clearly cannot contain any useful anchor. To do so, the absolute response of a LoG filter of variance $\sigma = 2.5$ is averaged and the crop is retained if the response is greater than 1.5 (image intensities are in the range $[0, 255]$). Note that, combined with random selection, this operation *does not* center crops on blobs or any other pre-defined anchors, but simply discards uniform or very low contrast crops.

---

[5] https://github.com/lenck/ddet.

Recall that the formulation Sect. 2.2 requires triplets $(\mathbf{x}_1, \mathbf{x}_2, g)$. A triplet is generated by randomly picking a crop and then by extracting 28×28 patches $\mathbf{x}_1$ and $\mathbf{x}_2$ within 20 pixels of the crop center (Fig. 4). This samples two patches related by translation, corresponding to the translation sampled in g, while guaranteeing that patches overlap by least 27%. Then the linear part of g is sampled at random and used to warp $\mathbf{x}_2$ around its center. In order too achieve better robustness to photometric transformations, additive ($\pm 8\%$ of the intensity range) and multiplicative ($\pm 40\%$ of a pixel intensity) is added to the pixels.

Training uses batches of 64 patch pairs. An epoch contains $40 \cdot 10^3$ pairs, and the data is resampled after each epoch completes. The learning rate is set to $\lambda = 0.01$ and decreased tenfold when the validation error stops decreasing. Usually, training converges after 60 epochs, which, due to the small size of the network and input patches, takes no more than a couple of minutes on a GPU.

4   Experiments

We apply our framework to learn two complementary types of detectors in order to illustrate the flexibility of the approach: a corner detector (Sect. 4.1) and an orientation detector (Sect. 4.2).

Evaluation Benchmark and Metrics. We compare the learned detectors to standard ones: FAST [30, 31] (using OpenCV's implementation[6]), the Difference of Gaussian detector (DoG) or SIFT [20], the Harris corner point detector [11] and Hessian point detector [24] (all using VLFeat's implementation[7]). All experiments are performed at a single scale, but all detectors can be applied to a scale space pyramid if needed.

For evaluation of the corner detector, we use the standard VGG-Affine benchmark dataset [24], using both the *repeatability* and *matching score* criteria. For matching score, SIFT descriptors are extracted from a fixed region of 41×41 pixels around each corner. A second limitation in the original protocol of [24] is that repeatability can be made arbitrarily large simply by detecting enough features. Thus, in order to control for the number of features detected, we compute repeatability and matching score as the feature detection threshold is increased; we then plot the metrics as functions of the number of feature selected in the first image.

VGG-Affine contains scenes related by homography. We also consider the more recent DTU-Robots dataset [1] that contains 3D objects under changing viewpoint. Matches in DTU dataset are estimated using the known 3D shape of the objects and position of the camera. The data is divided in three "arcs", corresponding to three swipes of the robotic camera at different distances from the scene (0.5, 0.65, and 0.8 m respectively). Due to the large number of images in this dataset, only aggregated results for $n = 600$ are reported.

---

[6] opencv.org.
[7] www.vlfeat.org.

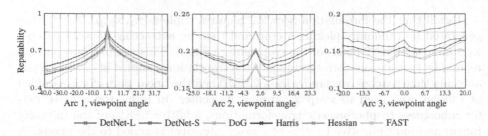

Fig. 5. *Repeatability on the DTU Dataset* averaged over all 60 scenes, divided by arc. Repeatability is computed over the top 600 detections for each detector.

4.1 Corner or Translation Detector

In this section we train a "corner detector" network DETNET. Using the formalism of Sect. 2, this is a detector which is covariant with translations $G = T(2)$, corresponding to the covariance constraint of Eq. (1). Figure 4 provides a few examples of the patches used for training, as well as of the anchors discovered by learning.

Figure 5 reports the performance of the two versions of DETNET, small and large, on the DTU data. As noted in [1], the Harris corner detector performs very well on the first arc; however, on the other two arcs DETNET-L clearly outperforms the other methods, whereas DETNET-S is on par or a little better than standard detectors.

Figure 6 evaluates the method on the VGG-Affine dataset. Here the learned networks perform generally well too, outperforming existing detectors in some scenarios and performing less well on others. Note that our current implementation is the simplest possible and the very first of its kind; in the future more refined setups may improve the learned detectors across the board (Sect. 5).

The speed of the tested detectors is shown in Table 2. While our goal is not to obtain the fastest detector but rather to demonstrate the possibility of learning detectors from scratch, we note that even an unoptimised MATLAB implementation can achieve reasonable performance on a GPU, especially with stride 2 with a slightly decreased performance compared to the dense evaluation (see Fig. 6).

Table 2. The detection speed (in FPS) for different image sizes of all tested detectors, computed as an average over 10 measurements. Please not that the DETNETdetectors run on a GPU, other detectors run on a CPU.

	DETNET-L	DETNET-L S2	DETNET-S	DETNET-S S2	Harris	DoG	Hessian	FAST
320×240	9.16	33.14	27.26	83.16	144.39	88.64	150.34	439.68
800×600	1.45	5.87	4.68	19.32	15.65	8.00	17.45	328.20
1024×768	0.39	1.56	2.78	11.68	12.21	6.05	11.17	206.96

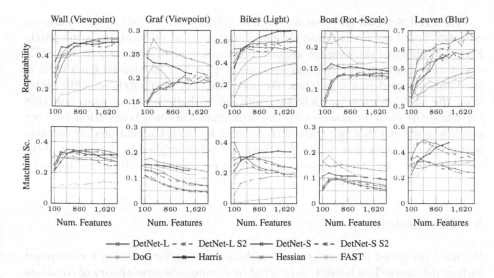

Fig. 6. *Repeatability and matching score on VGG dataset* comparing two versions of DetNet and standard detectors controlled for an increasing number of detected features. Dashed line values are for DetNet with stride 2. Scores are computed as an average over all 5 transformed images for each set (e.g. "wall").

4.2 Orientation Detector

This section evaluates a network, ROTNET, trained for orientation detection. This detector resolves $H = SO(2)$ rotations and is covariant to Euclidean transformations $G = SE(2)$, which means that translations $Q = T(2)$ are nuisance factor that the detector should ignore. The corresponding form of the covariance constraint is given by Eq. (14). Training proceeds as above, using 28×28 pixels patches and, for g, random 2π rotations composed with a maximum nuisance translation of 0, 3, or 6 pixels, resulting in three different versions of the network (Fig. 4).

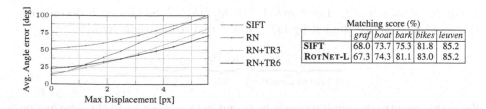

Fig. 7. *Orientation detector evaluation.* **Left:** versions of ROTNET(RN) and the SIFT orientation detector evaluated on recovering the relative rotation of random patch pairs. **Right:** matching score on the VGG-Affine benchmark when the native SIFT orientation estimation is replaced with ROTNET(percentage of correct matches using the DoG-Affine detector).

The SIFT detector [20] contains both a blob detector as well as an orientation detector, based on determining the dominant gradient orientation in the patch. Figure 7 compares the average angular registration error obtained by the SIFT orientation detector and different versions of RoTNeT, measured from pairs of randomly-sampled image patches. We note that: (1) RoTNeTis sensibly better than the SIFT orientation detector, with up to half the error rate, and that (2) while the error increases with the maximum nuisance translation between patches, networks that are trained to account for such translations are sensibly better than the ones that do not. Furthermore, when applied to the output of the SIFT blob detector, the improved orientation estimation results in an improved feature matching score, as measured on the VGG-Affine benchmark.

5   Discussion

We have presented the first general machine learning formulation for covariant feature detectors. The latter is supported by a comprehensive theory of covariant detectors, and builds on the idea of casting detection as a regression problem. We have shown that this method can successfully learn corner and orientation detectors that outperform in several cases off-the-shelf detectors. The potential is significant; for example, the framework can be used to learn scale selection and affine adaptation CNNs. Furthermore, many significant improvements to our basic implementation are possible, including explicitly modelling detection strength/confidence, predicting multiple features in a patch, and jointly training detectors and descriptors.

Acknowledgements. We would like to thank ERC 677195-IDIU for supporting this research.

A   Proofs

Proof (of Proposition 1). Due to group closure, $gh_1 \in G$. Since $HQ = G$, then there must be $h_2 \in H, q \in Q$ such that $h_2 q = gh_1$, and so $h_2 q h_1^{-1} g^{-1} = 1$.

Proof (of Proposition 2). Let $h_2 q(h_1)^{-1} = h_2' q'(h_1')^{-1}$ be two such decompositions and multiply to the left by $(q)^{-1}(h_2')^{-1}$ and to the right by h_1':

$$\underbrace{q^{-1} \left[(h_2')^{-1} h_2\right] q}_{\in H \text{ (due to normality)}} \underbrace{h_1^{-1} h_1'}_{\in H} = \underbrace{q^{-1} q'}_{\in Q}.$$

Since this quantity is simultaneously in H and in Q, it must be in the intersection $H \cap Q$, which by hypothesis contains only the identity. Hence $q^{-1} q' = 1$ and $q = q'$.

References

1. Aanæs, H., Dahl, A., Steenstrup Pedersen, K.: Interesting interest points. Int. J. Comput. Vis. **97**, 18–35 (2012)
2. Baumberg, A.M.: Reliable feature matching across widely separated views. In: Proceedings of the CVPR, pp. 774–781 (2000)
3. Beaudet, P.R.: Rotationally invariant image operators. In: International Joint Conference on Pattern Recognition, pp. 579–583 (1978)
4. Cordes, K., Rosenhahn, B., Ostermann, J.: Increasing the accuracy of feature evaluation benchmarks using differential evolution. In: IEEE Symposium on Differential Evolution (2011)
5. Dias, P., Kassim, A., Srinivasan, V.: A neural network based corner detection method. In: IEEE International Conference on Neural Networks (1995)
6. Dufournaud, Y., Schmid, C., Horaud, R.: Matching images with different resolutions. In: Proceedings of the CVPR (1999)
7. Förstner, W.: A feature based correspondence algorithm for image matching. Int. Arch. Photogrammetry Remote Sens. **26**(3), 150–166 (1986)
8. Freeman, H., Davis, L.S.: A corner-finding algorithm for chain-coded curves. IEEE Trans. Comput. **3**, 297–303 (1977)
9. Guiducci, A.: Corner characterization by differential geometry techniques. Pattern Recogn. Lett. **8**(5), 311–318 (1988)
10. Han, X., Leung, T., Jia, Y., Sukthankar, R., Berg, A.C.: Matchnet: Unifying feature and metric learning for patch-based matching. In: Proceedings of the CVPR (2015)
11. Harris, C., Stephens, M.: A combined corner and edge detector. In: Proceedings of the Fourth Alvey Vision Conference, pp. 147–151 (1988)
12. Holzer, S., Shotton, J., Kohli, P.: Learning to efficiently detect repeatable interest points in depth data. In: Fitzgibbon, A., Lazebnik, S., Perona, P., Sato, Y., Schmid, C. (eds.) ECCV 2012. LNCS, vol. 7572, pp. 200–213. Springer, Heidelberg (2012). doi:10.1007/978-3-642-33718-5_15
13. Kadir, T., Brady, M.: Saliency, scale and image description. Int. J. Comput. Vis. **45**, 83–105 (2001)
14. Kienzle, W., Wichmann, F.A., Schölkopf, B., Franz, M.O.: Learning an interest operator from human eye movements. In: CVPR Workshop (2006)
15. Lecun, Y., Bottou, L., Bengio, Y., Haffner, P.: Gradient-based learning applied to document recognition. In: Proceedings of the IEEE, November 1998
16. Lindeberg, T.: Scale-Space Theory in Computer Vision. Springer, Heidelberg (1994)
17. Lindeberg, T.: Feature detection with automatic scale selection. IJCV **30**(2), 77–116 (1998)
18. Lindeberg, T., Gårding, J.: Shape-adapted smoothing in estimation of 3-D depth cues from affine distortions of local 2-D brightness structure. In: Eklundh, J.-O. (ed.) ECCV 1994. LNCS, vol. 800, pp. 389–400. Springer, Heidelberg (1994). doi:10.1007/3-540-57956-7_42
19. Lowe, D.G.: Object recognition from local scale-invariant features. In: Proceedings of the ICCV (1999)
20. Lowe, D.G.: Distinctive image features from scale-invariant keypoints. IJCV **2**(60), 91–110 (2004)
21. Mallat, S.: A Wavelet Tour of Signal Processing. Academic Press, Cambridge (2008)

22. Matas, J., Obdržálek, S., Chum, O.: Local affine frames for wide-baseline stereo. In: International Conference on Pattern Recognition (2002)
23. Mikolajczyk, K., Schmid, C.: Indexing based on scale invariant interest points. In: Proceedings of the ICCV (2001)
24. Mikolajczyk, K., Schmid, C.: An affine invariant interest point detector. In: Heyden, A., Sparr, G., Nielsen, M., Johansen, P. (eds.) ECCV 2002. LNCS, vol. 2350, pp. 128–142. Springer, Heidelberg (2002). doi:10.1007/3-540-47969-4_9
25. Olague, G., Trujillo, L.: Evolutionary-computer-assisted design of image operators that detect interest points using genetic programming. Image Vis. Comput. **29**, 484–498 (2011)
26. Papandreou, G., Kokkinos, I., Savalle, P.-A.: Modeling local and global deformations in deep learning: epitomic convolution, multiple instance learning, and sliding window detection. In: Proceedings of the CVPR (2015)
27. Paulin, M., Douze, M., Harchaoui, Z., Mairal, J., Perronin, F., Schmid, C.: Local convolutional features with unsupervised training for image retrieval. In: ICCV (2015)
28. Rohr, K.: Recognizing corners by fitting parametric models. IJCV **9**(3), 213–230 (1992)
29. Rosenfeld, A., Johnston, E.: Angle detection on digital curves. IEEE Trans. Comput. **100**(9), 875–878 (1973)
30. Rosten, E., Drummond, T.: Fusing points and lines for high performance tracking. In: ICCV, vol. 2 (2005)
31. Rosten, E., Drummond, T.: Machine learning for high-speed corner detection. In: Leonardis, A., Bischof, H., Pinz, A. (eds.) ECCV 2006. LNCS, vol. 3951, pp. 430–443. Springer, Heidelberg (2006). doi:10.1007/11744023_34
32. Rosten, E., Porter, R., Drummond, T.: Faster and better: a machine learning approach to corner detection. In: PAMI, vol. 32 (2010)
33. Russakovsky, O., Deng, J., Su, H., Krause, J., Satheesh, S., Ma, S., Huang, Z., Karpathy, A., Khosla, A., Bernstein, M., Berg, A.C., Fei-Fei, L.: Imagenet large scale visual recognition challenge. IJCV **115**, 211–252 (2014)
34. Sankar, P., Sharma, C.: A parallel procedure for the detection of dominant points on a digital curve. Comput. Graph. Image Process. **7**(3), 403–412 (1978)
35. Schaffalitzky, F., Zisserman, A.: Viewpoint invariant texture matching and wide baseline stereo. In: Proceedings of the ICCV (2001)
36. Schmid, C., Mohr, R.: Local greyvalue invariants for image retrieval. IEEE Trans. Pattern Anal. Mach. Intell. **19**, 530–535 (1997)
37. Simo-Serra, E., Trulls, E., Ferraz, L., Kokkinos, I., Fua, P., Moreno-Noguer, F.: Discriminative learning of deep convolutional feature point descriptors. In: ICCV (2015)
38. Smith, S.M., Brady, J.M.: Susan - a new approach to low level image processing. Technical report, Oxford University (1995)
39. Sochman, J., Matas, J.: Learning fast emulators of binary decision processes. IJCV **83**, 149–163 (2009)
40. Triggs, B.: Detecting keypoints with stable position, orientation, and scale under illumination changes. In: Pajdla, T., Matas, J. (eds.) ECCV 2004. LNCS, vol. 3024, pp. 100–113. Springer, Heidelberg (2004). doi:10.1007/978-3-540-24673-2_9
41. Trujillo, L., Olague, G.: Synthesis of interest point detectors through genetic programming. In: Proceedings of the GECCO (2006)
42. Tuytelaars, T., Van Gool, L.: Wide baseline stereo matching based on local, affinely invariant regions. In: Proceedings of the BMVC, pp. 412–425 (2000)

43. Vedaldi, A., Lenc, K.: MatConvNet - convolutional neural networks for MATLAB. In: Proceedings of the ACM International Conference on Multimedia (2015)
44. Yi, K.M., Verdie, Y., Fua, P., Lepetit, V.: Learning to assign orientations to feature points. In: CVPR (2016)
45. Zagoruyko, S., Komodakis, N.: Learning to compare image patches via convolutional neural networks. In: CVPR (2015)
46. Zbontar, J., LeCun, Y.: Computing the stereo matching cost with a convolutional neural network. In: Proceedings of the CVPR (2015)
47. Zuliani, M., Kenney, C., Manjunath, B.S.: A mathematical comparison of point detectors. In: Proceedings of the CVPR (2005)

Scene Segmentation Driven by Deep Learning and Surface Fitting

Ludovico Minto, Giampaolo Pagnutti, and Pietro Zanuttigh[✉]

Department of Information Engineering, University of Padova, Padova, Italy
{mintolud,pagnutti,zanuttigh}@dei.unipd.it

Abstract. This paper proposes a joint color and depth segmentation scheme exploiting together geometrical clues and a learning stage. The approach starts from an initial over-segmentation based on spectral clustering. The input data is also fed to a Convolutional Neural Network (CNN) thus producing a per-pixel descriptor vector for each scene sample. An iterative merging procedure is then used to recombine the segments into the regions corresponding to the various objects and surfaces. The proposed algorithm starts by considering all the adjacent segments and computing a similarity metric according to the CNN features. The couples of segments with higher similarity are considered for merging. Finally the algorithm uses a NURBS surface fitting scheme on the segments in order to understand if the selected couples correspond to a single surface. The comparison with state-of-the-art methods shows how the proposed method provides an accurate and reliable scene segmentation.

Keywords: Segmentation · Depth · Color · Kinect · NURBS · Deep Learning · CNN

1 Introduction

The introduction of depth cameras in the consumer market has opened the way to novel algorithms able to exploit depth in order to tackle classical challenging computer vision problems. Among them segmentation has always been a critical issue despite a huge amount of research devoted to this problem since it is an ill-posed problem and the information content in color images is often not sufficient to completely solve the task. The 3D representation of the acquired scene contained in depth data is very useful for this task and recently various approaches combining it with color information have been proposed.

Among the various segmentation techniques, one of the best performing solutions is normalised cuts spectral clustering [25]. This approach can be easily extended to the joint segmentation of image and depth data by feeding to the clustering scheme multi-dimensional vectors containing both kinds of information [6]. In this way, a relatively reliable segmentation can be obtained but, since the approach has a bias towards segments of similar sizes, it is often difficult to properly segment all the objects and at the same time avoid an over-segmentation of the scene.

G. Hua and H. Jégou (Eds.): ECCV 2016 Workshops, Part III, LNCS 9915, pp. 118–132, 2016.
DOI: 10.1007/978-3-319-49409-8_12

The idea exploited in this work is to start from an over-segmentation performed with spectral clustering and then exploit an iterative region merging scheme in order to obtain the final segmentation. The key problem of deciding which segments must be merged is solved with the combined use of two clues. The first is a similarity index between segments computed by comparing the descriptors produced by a Convolutional Neural Network. The second has been derived from [22] and is based on the accuracy obtained by fitting a Non-Uniform Rational B-Spline (NURBS) model on the union of the two segments and comparing the accuracy of the fitting with the one obtained on each of the two merged regions alone. If the accuracy remains similar the segments are probably part of the same surface and the merging is accepted, otherwise it is discarded.

The paper is organized in the following way: a review of related works is presented in Sect. 2. Section 3 introduces the general architecture of the proposed algorithm. The over-segmentation step is described in Sect. 4 while Sect. 5 presents the similarity analysis based on deep learning. Then the employed region merging algorithm is presented in Sect. 7. The last two sections contain the results (Sect. 8) and the conclusions (Sect. 9).

2 Related Works

The idea of using also the information from an associated depth representation to improve segmentation algorithm performances has been exploited in various recent scene segmentation schemes, a review of this family of approaches is contained in [32]. Clustering techniques can easily be extended to joint depth and color segmentation by modifying the feature vectors as in [2,5,30]. A segmentation scheme based on spectral clustering able to automatically balance the relevance of color and depth clues has been proposed in [6].

Region splitting and growing approaches have also been considered. In [8] superpixels produced by an over-segmentation of the scene are combined together in regions corresponding to the planar surfaces using an approach based on Rao-Blackwellized Monte Carlo Markov Chain. The approach has been extended to the segmentation of multiple depth maps in [27]. The top down approach (region splitting) has been used in [21] where the segmentation is progressively refined in an iterative scheme by recursively splitting the segments that do not represent a single surface in the 3D space. Hierarchical segmentation based on the output of contour extraction has been used in [13], that also deals with object detection from the segmented data. Another combined approach for segmentation and object recognition has been presented in [26], that exploits an initial over-segmentation exploiting the watershed algorithm followed by a hierarchical scheme. A joint clustering method on the color, 3D position and normal information followed by a statistical planar region merging scheme has been presented in [17] and in the refined version of the approach of [16]. Finally dynamic programming has been used in [28] to extract the planar surfaces in indoor scenes.

Machine learning techniques have been used specially for the task of semantic segmentation where a label is also associated to each segment. In [24] a Markov

Random Fields superpixel segmentation is combined with a tree-structured approach for scene labeling. Conditional Random Fields have been employed in
[7] together with mutex constraints based on the geometric structure of the
scene. Deep learning techniques and in particular Convolutional Neural Networks
(CNN) have also been used for this task [4,19,20]. For example a multiscale CNN
has been used in [4] while the method of [20] is based on Fully Convolutional
Networks. Another approach based on deep learning is [14], that exploits a CNN
applied on features extracted from the geometry description.

3   General Overview

The proposed algorithm can be divided into three main steps as depicted in
Fig. 1. The color image and the depth map are firstly converted into a set of
9D vectors containing the 3D position, the orientation information and the color
coordinates in the CIELab color space of each sample. Then we perform an over-
segmentation of the scene based on the joint usage of the three sources of information inside a spectral clustering framework derived from [6] (see Sect. 4). In
parallel, the color and orientation data are also fed to a CNN classifier that computes a vector of descriptors for each pixel. The descriptors are then aggregated
inside each segment in order to produce a single descriptor for each segmented
region. The final step is an iterative region merging procedure. This stage starts
by analyzing the segmentation and computing an adjacency map for the segments, where two segments are considered adjacent if they touch each other and
their properties are similar on the common contour. The couples of adjacent

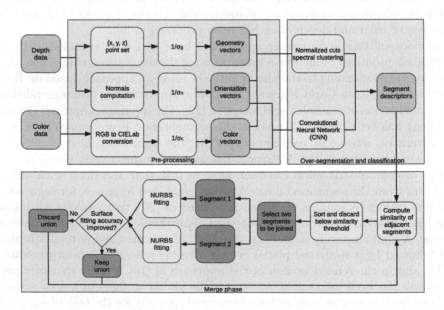

Fig. 1. Overview of the proposed approach

segments are sorted on the basis of the similarity of their descriptors computed by the CNN classifier and the couples with a similarity below a threshold are discarded. Starting from the most similar couple a parametric NURBS surface is fitted over each of the two segments. The same model is fitted also over the merged region obtained by fusing the two segments. Similarly to [22], the surface fitting error is computed and compared with the weighted average of the fitting error on the two merged pieces. If the error on the merged region is smaller (a hint that the two regions are part of the same surface) the merging operation is accepted, if it increases (i.e., they probably belong to two different surfaces), the merging is discarded. The procedure is repeated iteratively in a tree structure until no more merging operations are possible.

4   Over-Segmentation of Color and Depth Data

The proposed method takes as input a color image with its corresponding depth map. For each pixel with a valid depth value p_i, $i = 1, \ldots, N$ (where N is the number of valid pixels) it builds a 9-dimensional vector $\mathbf{p}_i^{9D}$ containing the color, spatial and orientation information. More in detail, the first three dimensions are the $L(p_i), a(p_i), b(p_i)$ components containing the color view information converted to the CIELab perceptually uniform space. The 3D coordinates $x(p_i), y(p_i), z(p_i)$ and the surface normals $n_x(p_i), n_y(p_i), n_z(p_i)$ associated to each sample are then computed exploiting the calibration information. The over-segmentation is performed by clustering the multi-dimensional vectors containing the color, the position in the 3D space and the orientation information associated to the samples [6,22].

The clustering algorithm must be insensitive to the scaling of the point-cloud geometry and needs geometry, color and orientation to be into consistent representations. For these reasons, the geometry components are normalized by the average σ_g of the standard deviations of the point coordinates, obtaining the vectors $[\bar{x}(p_i), \bar{y}(p_i), \bar{z}(p_i)]$. Following the same rationale, the normal vectors $[\bar{n}_x(p_i), \bar{n}_y(p_i), \bar{n}_z(p_i)]$ are computed by normalizing the three components of the orientation by the average σ_n of their standard deviations. Color information vectors $[\bar{L}(p_i), \bar{a}(p_i), \bar{b}(p_i)]$ are also obtained by normalizing color data with the average σ_c of the standard deviations of the L, a and b components. Finally, a 9D representation is built from the above normalized vectors, such that each point of the scene is represented as

$$\mathbf{p}_i^{9D} = [\bar{L}(p_i), \bar{a}(p_i), \bar{b}(p_i), \bar{x}(p_i), \bar{y}(p_i), \bar{z}(p_i), \bar{n}_x(p_i), \bar{n}_y(p_i), \bar{n}_z(p_i)], \quad i = 1, \ldots, N. \tag{1}$$

Normalized cuts spectral clustering [25] optimized with the Nyström method [11] is then applied to the 9D vectors in order to segment the acquired scene. Notice that the parameters of the clustering algorithm are set in order to produce a large number of segments that will later be merged in order to obtain the final solution by the method of Sect. 7.

5 Classification with Deep Learning

In order to be able to decide which segments from the over-segmentation need to be recombined we employed a machine learning stage based on a Convolutional Neural Network (CNN). The goal of this step is to obtain a fundamental clue to drive the merging operation described in Sect. 7 together with the NURBS surface fitting approach derived from [22]. The idea is to exploit the output of a CNN trained for a semantic segmentation task in order to produce a pixel-wise higher-level description of the input images, and use this information to compute a similarity measure between adjacent segments. The merging strategy described in Sect. 7 exploits the proposed similarity measure both in the selection of which adjacent segment pairs are going to be merged as well as in determining the order of the selection of the candidate pairs for the merging operations.

Both color and normal information is used as input to the CNN. Normalized color and normal components computed in Sect. 4 are first combined into 6D vectors representing each point of the scene as

$$\mathbf{p}_i^{cn} = [\bar{L}(p_i), \bar{a}(p_i), \bar{b}(p_i), \bar{n}_x(p_i), \bar{n}_y(p_i), \bar{n}_z(p_i)], \quad i = 1, \ldots, N. \quad (2)$$

Then, a six channel input image is produced for each scene in the dataset by arranging the vectors over the image pixels lattice.

A multi-scale architecture [9] is used to achieve a greater expressiveness without increasing the number of network parameters. Each input image is fed to the network at three different scales, both to account for the varying size at which similar objects may appear in the scene, and to take advantage of increasingly larger contexts. An overview of its structure is shown in Fig. 2.

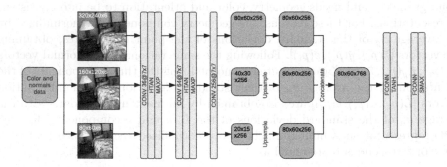

Fig. 2. Architecture of the Convolutional Neural Network

Similarly to [3,9], the network can be divided in two parts. In the first part a local representation of the input is extracted by applying a sequence of convolutional layers sharing their weights across the three scales. Specifically, the three input scales are feed-forwarded through three convolutional layers (denoted with CONV in Fig. 2). The first two convolutional layers are followed by a hyperbolic tangent activation function (TANH) and a max-pooling (MAXP) layer, while the third one is applied as a simple bank of linear filters, producing the three outputs corresponding to the three scales. The outputs are then upsampled and concatenated to provide for each pixel a vector of feature descriptors. The second part of the network is composed by two fully-connected layers (FCONN), with hyperbolic tangent and soft-max (SMAX) activation functions respectively.

Input images are fed to the network at three different scales, namely 320×240, 160×120 and 80×60, both to account for the varying size at which similar objects may appear in the scene, and to take advantage of increasingly larger contexts.

In our experiments the three convolutional layers have 36, 64 and 256 filters respectively, all filters being 7×7 pixels wide, while the fully-connected layers have 1024 and 15 units respectively. The filters in the first convolutional layer are divided into 6 groups and each group is connected to one of the 6 input channels separately. In order to ease the convergence of the first layer filter weights, local contrast normalization is applied to each channel independently.

The network is trained in order to assign one out of the 15 labels to each pixel in the input image. Specifically, we clustered the 894 categories from the ground truth provided by [12] into 15 classes similarly to [3,18,31]. As in [9] we split the training process into two separate steps. The filter weights of the three convolutional layers are first trained separately by applying a simple linear classifier to the output of the first part of the network, with soft-max activation and multi-class cross-entropy loss function. Next, the weights and biases of the last two fully-connected layers are trained while keeping the convolutional weights as calculated in the previous step fixed. Again, the multi-class cross-entropy loss function is minimized.

Rather than the final predicted labels, the output of the soft-max activation function in the last fully-convolutional layer is considered in order to compute the descriptors used for the similarity measure between any two segments. The output of the soft-max, a 3D array of size $80 \times 60 \times 15$, is linearly interpolated to the size of the input image so that a descriptor vector $\mathbf{c}_i = [c_i^1, \ldots, c_i^{15}]$ is associated to each pixel p_i. As each descriptor vector has non-negative elements summing up to one, it can be seen as a discrete probability distribution function (PDF) associated to the pixel. The PDF $\mathbf{s}_i = [s_i^1, \ldots, s_i^k]$ associated to a segment S_i can be computed simply as the average of the PDFs of the pixels belonging to the segment, i.e.,

$$\mathbf{s}_i = \frac{\sum_{j \in S_i} \mathbf{c}_j}{|S_i|}. \tag{3}$$

Given two segments S_i and S_j, their similarity can be estimated by comparing their descriptors $\mathbf{s}_i$ and $\mathbf{s}_j$, which are actually two PDFs. An effective approach in order to compare two PDFs is to use the Bhattacharrya coefficient

$$b_{i,j} = \sum_{t=1,\ldots,k} \sqrt{s_i^t s_j^t}. \tag{4}$$

An example of the output of this approach is shown in Fig. 3. The color of the boundary between each couple of segments in the figure is proportional to the

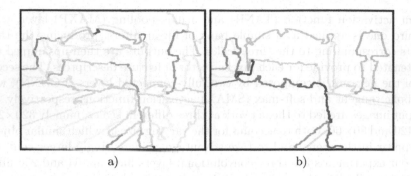

a)   b)

Fig. 3. Computation of $b_{i,j}$ on a sample scene (i.e., the one in the sixth row of Fig. 5):
(a) $b_{i,j}$ values on the initial over-segmentation; (b) $b_{i,j}$ values on the final result after
all the merging steps. The boundary of the segments have been colored proportionally
to the similarity between the two touching segments (black corresponds to low $b_{i,j}$
values and white to large ones)

corresponding $b_{i,j}$ value. Notice how in Fig. 3a the boundaries between different
objects correspond to low values of the coefficient, while boundaries between
parts of the same object that need to be merged correspond to high $b_{i,j}$ values.
In Fig. 3b it is possible to notice how the remaining boundaries at the end of the
procedure of Sect. 7 typically correspond to low similarity values.

6   Surface Fitting on the Segmented Data

In order to evaluate if each segment corresponds to a single scene object we
approximate it with a Non-Uniform Rational B-Spline (NURBS) surface [23].
By using this approach we are able to provide an appropriate geometric model
for quite complex shapes, unlike competing approaches [27,28] that are limited
to planar surfaces.

A parametric NURBS surface is defined as

$$\mathbf{S}(u,v) = \frac{\sum_{i=0}^{n} \sum_{j=0}^{m} N_{i,p}(u)N_{j,q}(v)w_{i,j}\mathbf{P}_{i,j}}{\sum_{i=0}^{n} \sum_{j=0}^{m} N_{i,p}(u)N_{j,q}(v)w_{i,j}}, \tag{5}$$

where $\mathbf{P}_{i,j}$ are the control points, $w_{i,j}$ the corresponding weights, $N_{i,p}$ the uni-
variate B-spline basis functions, and p, q the degrees in the u, v parametric directions respectively. We set the degrees in the u and v directions equal to 3 and the
weights all equal to one, thus our fitted surfaces are non-rational (i.e., splines).
The number of surface control points are the degrees of freedom in our model
and we adaptively set it depending on the number of input samples in the considered segment. This is necessary to prevent the fitting accuracy to be biased in
favor of smaller segments [22]. Finally, by using Eq. (5) evaluated at the depth
lattice points and equated to the points to fit (see [22] for details), we obtain an
over-determined system of linear equations and we solve it in the least-squares
sense thus obtaining the surface control points.

7   Region Merging Procedure

The final step of the proposed approach is the merging phase that recombines the large number of segments produced by the over-segmentation into a smaller number of segments representing the various structures in the scene. The procedure is summarized in the bottom part of Fig. 1 and in Algorithm 1.

Algorithm 1. Merge algorithm

Compute L_S (list of the segments)
For each segment S_i compute the set A_i of the adjacent segments.
Create list of couples of adjacent segments $A_{i,j}$
For each couple of adjacent segments i and j compute their similarity $b_{i,j}$ according to Equation (4)
Sort the list of adjacent couples $A_{i,j}$ according to $b_{i,j}$
Discard the couples with a score $b_{i,j} < T_{sim}$
for all the couples in $A_{i,j}$ **do**
   Compute the fitting error on the merged segment $S_{i \cup j}$
   Check if the threshold of Equation (9) is satisfied
   if Equation (9) is satisfied **then**
      Remove all the couples involving S_i and S_j from $A_{i,j}$
      Compute the adjacent segments S_k to $S_{i \cup j}$
      Compute $A_{i \cup j,k}$ for all the adjacent segments
      Insert the new segments in $A_{i,j}$ and sort
   end if
   Move to next entry in $A_{i,j}$
end for

Firstly the segments are analyzed in order to detect the couples of close segments that are candidate to be joined. For this task an approach similar to [22] is used in order to build an adjacency matrix storing for each couple of segments whether they are *adjacent* or not. Two segments are considered as *adjacent* if they satisfy the following conditions:

1. They must be connected on the lattice defined by the depth map.
2. The depth values on the shared boundary must be consistent. In order to perform this check, for each point P_i in the shared boundary C_C we compute the difference ΔZ_i between the depth values on the two sides of the edge. The difference must be smaller than a threshold T_d for at least half of the points in the shared boundary, i.e.:

$$\frac{|P_i : (P_i \in C_C) \wedge (\Delta Z_i \leq T_d)|}{|P_i : P_i \in C_C|} > 0.5 \tag{6}$$

3. The color values must also be similar on both sides of the common contour. The approach is the same used for depth data except that the color difference

in the CIELab space ΔC_i is used instead of the depth value. More in detail, being T_c the color threshold:

$$\frac{|P_i : (P_i \in C_C) \wedge (\Delta C_i \leq T_c)|}{|P_i : P_i \in C_C|} > 0.5 \tag{7}$$

4. Finally the same approach is used also for normal data. In this case the angle between the two normal vectors $\Delta \theta_i$ is compared to a threshold T_θ:

$$\frac{|P_i : (P_i \subset C_C) \wedge (\Delta \theta_i \leq T_\theta)|}{|P_i : P_i \in C_C|} > 0.5 \tag{8}$$

If all the conditions are satisfied the two segments are marked as adjacent (for the results we used $T_d = 0.2$ m, $T_c = 8$ and $T_\theta = 4°$). For more details on this step see [22]. Notice that the evaluation of the color, depth and orientation consistency on the couples of close segments can be skipped in order to simplify and speed-up the approach, but it allows to slightly improve the performances of the proposed method.

At this point the algorithm analyzes the couples of adjacent segments and computes the similarity between the two segments in each couple as described in Sect. 5.

The next step consists in sorting the couples of adjacent segments based on the $b_{i,j}$ values, that is, according to how the two segments were estimated to be similar during the machine learning stage. Furthermore the couples of segments with a similarity value $b_{i,j}$ below a threshold T_{sim} are discarded and they will not be considered for the merging operations (for the results we used $T_{sim} = 0.75$). The rationale behind this is to avoid merging segments with different properties since they probably belong to distinct objects and parts of the scene.

The algorithm then selects the couple with the highest similarity score. Let us denote with S_{i*} and S_{j*} the two segments in the couple and with $S_{i* \cup j*}$ the segment obtained by merging the two segments. A NURBS surface is fitted on each of the two regions i^* and j^* (see Sect. 6). The fitting error, i.e., the Mean Squared Error (MSE) between the actual surface and the fitted surface, is computed for both segments thus obtaining the values e_{i*} and e_{j*}. The fitting error $e_{i* \cup j*}$ on segment $S_{i* \cup j*}$ is also computed and compared to the weighted average of the errors on S_i^* and S_j^*:

$$e_{i*}|S_{i*}| + e_{j*}|S_{j*}| > e_{i* \cup j*}(|S_{i*}| + |S_{j*}|) \tag{9}$$

If the fitting accuracy is improved, i.e., the condition of Eq. (9) is satisfied, the two segments are merged together, otherwise the merging operation is discarded. If the two segments S_i^* and S_j^* are merged, all the couples involving them are removed from the list L_S. The adjacency information is then updated by considering the union $S_{i* \cup j*}$ as adjacent to all the segments that were previously adjacent to any of the two segments. The descriptor $s_{i* \cup j*}$ associated to $S_{i* \cup j*}$ is computed using Eq. (3) and the similarity score is computed for all the newly created couples involving the segment $S_{i* \cup j*}$ created by the merging operation.

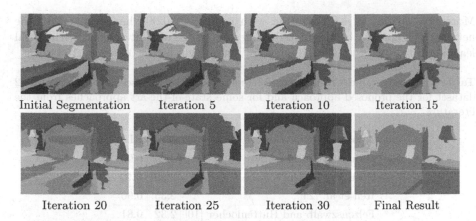

| Initial Segmentation | Iteration 5 | Iteration 10 | Iteration 15 |

| Iteration 20 | Iteration 25 | Iteration 30 | Final Result |

Fig. 4. Example of the merging procedure on the scene of Fig. 5, row 6. The images show the initial over-segmentation, the merging output after 5, 10, 15, 20, 25, 30 iterations and the final result (iteration 34). (Best viewed in the color version online)

Finally the new couples are inserted in the list L_S at the positions corresponding to their similarity score (provided their similarity is bigger than T_{sim}, otherwise they are discarded). The algorithm then selects the next couple in the sorted list and the procedure is repeated until no more segments can be considered for the merging operation. The procedure is summarized in Algorithm 1 and its progress on a sample scene is visualized in Fig. 4. The sequence of merging steps on some scenes is also shown in the videos available at http://lttm.dei.unipd.it/paper_data/deepnurbs.

8   Experimental Results

In order to evaluate the performances of the proposed method we tested it on the NYU-Depth V2 dataset (NYUDv2) [26]. This dataset has been acquired with the Kinect and contains 1449 depth and color frames from a variety of indoor scenes. The updated versions of the ground truth labels provided by the authors of [12] has been used.

The dataset has been split in two parts using the subdivision of [12]. In order to get the results on the full dataset we performed two independent tests. In the first test the CNN has been trained using the first part with the corresponding ground truth labels. The trained network has then been used to compute the descriptors for the scenes in the second part. In the second test we swapped the train and test sets and performed the same procedure. The semantic classification is not the main target of this work, however notice that the proposed deep learning architecture, if used for classification purposes, is able to obtain an average mean pixel accuracy on the dataset of 52.8 % that is similar to the results reported in [3]. To mitigate the effect of overfitting the dataset has been expanded by randomly rotating each sample by an angle between −6 and 6°.

Moreover, quadratic regularization with coefficient 0.001 has been used. The network weights have been updated using stochastic gradient descent, with initial learning rate equal to 0.01 and constant decay by a factor 0.5 every 15 epochs.

Table 1. Average values of the VoI and RI metrics on the 1449 scenes of the NYUDv2 dataset for the proposed approach and for some state-of-the-art approaches from the literature

Approach	VoI	RI
Hasnat et al. [17]	2.29	0.90
Hasnat et al. [16]	2.20	**0.91**
Ren et al. [24]	2.35	0.90
Felzenszwalb and Huttenlocher [10]	2.32	0.81
Taylor and Cowley [28]	3.15	0.85
Dal Mutto et al. [6]	3.09	0.84
Pagnutti and Zanuttigh [22]	2.23	0.88
Proposed method	**1.93**	**0.91**

Table 1 shows the comparison between our approach and some state-of-the-art approaches on this dataset (for the other approaches we collected the results from [17,22]). The compared approaches are the clustering and region merging method of [17], the MRF scene labeling scheme of [24], that exploits Kernel Descriptors and SVM for machine learning, a modified version of [10] that accounts also for geometry information, the dynamic programming scheme of [28], the clustering-based approach of [6] and the region merging scheme of [22]. Notice that the latter is also based on over-segmentation and NURBS fitting but it does not have a machine learning stage and it uses a different merging procedure. The comparison between the two approaches can be a hint of the improvement provided by the use of the CNN descriptors.

The results have been evaluated by comparing the results with ground truth data using two different metrics, i.e., the Variation of Information (VoI) and the Rand Index (RI). For a detailed description of these metrics see [1], notice that for the VoI metric a lower value is better while a higher one is better for RI. The average VoI score of our method is 1.93. According to this metric our approach is the best among the considered ones with a significant gap with respect of all the competing approaches. If the RI metric is employed the average score is 0.91. This value is better than the one of the schemes of [6,10,17,22,24,28] and is exactly the same of the best competing approach, i.e., [16]. Furthermore our approach does not assume the presence of planar surfaces thanks to the NURBS surface fitting scheme, while some competing ones (e.g., [16,17,28]) strongly rely on this clue that gives very good results on the NYUDv2 dataset where most of the surfaces are planar, but reduces the capability of the approaches to generalize to different kind of scenes with non-planar surfaces.

Some visual results for the proposed approach are shown in Fig. 5 while some videos showing the merging steps leading to the presented results are available

Scene   Initial Over-Segmentation   Final Result

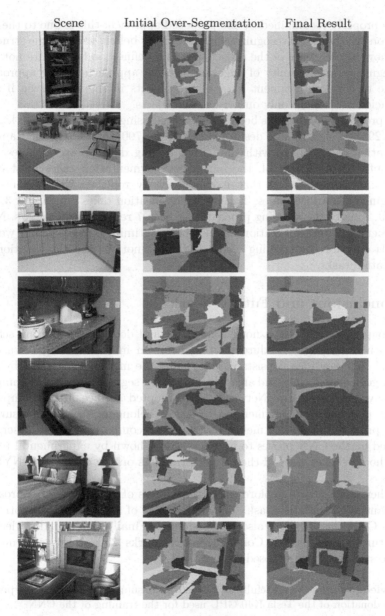

Fig. 5. Segmentation of some sample scenes from the NYUDv2 dataset. The figure shows the color images, the initial over-segmentation and the final result for scenes 72, 330, 450, 846, 1105, 1110 and 1313 (Color figure online)

at http://lttm.dei.unipd.it/paper_data/deepnurbs. By looking at the images it is possible to see how the approach is able to efficiently deal with different challenging situations and to various scene types. The initial over-segmentation typically divides the background and the large objects in several pieces but they are properly recombined by the proposed approach, this is due to the CNN descriptors that allow to recognize which segments belong to the same structure. Notice how the contours of the objects are well defined and there are not noisy small segments in proximity of edges as in other approaches. The approach is also able to correctly segment most of the objects in the scene even if a few inaccuracies are present only on very small objects.

The proposed method has been implemented using the Theano deep learning library [29]. On a standard desktop PC (an i7-4790 with 16 GB of Ram) the segmentation of an image with the corresponding depth map takes less than two minutes. More in detail, the initial over-segmentation takes most of the time (i.e., 87 s), but notice that it can be easily replaced with other super-pixel segmentation techniques. The CNN classification takes only about 3.7 s on the CPU. Finally the merging procedure of Sect. 7 requires around 20 s. Notice that the current implementation has not been optimized, in particular we used the GPU only for the training of the CNN but not for the classification and segmentation tasks.

9   Conclusions and Future Work

In this paper we proposed a novel joint color and depth segmentation scheme. An iterative merging procedure starting from an initial over-segmentation is employed. The key idea consists in controlling the merging operation by using together geometrical clues and an estimation of the segments similarity computed with Convolutional Neural Networks. The adopted surface fitting comparison makes it possible to avoid merging segments belonging to different surfaces, and the proposed similarity metric based on the comparison of the descriptors computed by the CNN proves to be reliable. As shown by experimental results, our method achieves state-of-the-art performances on the challenging NYUDv2 dataset.

Further research will explore the performances of the proposed approach in the semantic segmentation task. The exploitation of surface fitting information into the CNN classifier will also be considered. Finally different deep learning architectures including Fully Convolutional Networks [20] and hypercolumns [15] will be tested into the proposed framework.

Acknowledgments. We gratefully acknowledge the support of NVIDIA Corporation with the donation of the Tesla K40 GPU used for the training of the CNN.

References

1. Arbelaez, P., Maire, M., Fowlkes, C., Malik, J.: Contour detection and hierarchical image segmentation. IEEE Trans. Pattern Anal. Mach. Intell. **33**(5), 898–916 (2011)
2. Bleiweiss, A., Werman, M.: Fusing time-of-flight depth and color for real-time segmentation and tracking. In: Kolb, A., Koch, R. (eds.) Dyn3D 2009. LNCS, vol. 5742, pp. 58–69. Springer, Heidelberg (2009). doi:10.1007/978-3-642-03778-8_5

3. Couprie, C., Farabet, C., Najman, L., LeCun, Y.: Indoor semantic segmentation using depth information. In: International Conference on Learning Representations (2013)
4. Couprie, C., Farabet, C., Najman, L., Lecun, Y.: Convolutional nets and watershed cuts for real-time semantic labeling of RGBD videos. J. Mach. Learn. Res. **15**(1), 3489–3511 (2014)
5. Dal Mutto, C., Zanuttigh, P., Cortelazzo, G.: Scene segmentation assisted by stereo vision. In: Proceedings of 3DIMPVT 2011, Hangzhou, China, May 2011
6. Dal Mutto, D., Zanuttigh, P., Cortelazzo, G.: Fusion of geometry and color information for scene segmentation. IEEE J. Sel. Top. Sig. Process. **6**(5), 505–521 (2012)
7. Deng, Z., Todorovic, S., Jan Latecki, L.: Semantic segmentation of RGBD images with mutex constraints. In: Proceedings of International Conference on Computer Vision (ICCV), pp. 1733–1741 (2015)
8. Erdogan, C., Paluri, M., Dellaert, F.: Planar segmentation of RGBD images using fast linear fitting and Markov chain monte carlo. In: Proceedings of the CRV (2012)
9. Farabet, C., Couprie, C., Najman, L., LeCun, Y.: Learning hierarchical features for scene labeling. IEEE Trans. Pattern Anal. Mach. Intell. **35**(8), 1915–1929 (2013)
10. Felzenszwalb, P., Huttenlocher, D.: Efficient graph-based image segmentation. Int. J. Comput. Vis. **59**(2), 167–181 (2004)
11. Fowlkes, C., Belongie, S., Chung, F., Malik, J.: Spectral grouping using the nyström method. IEEE Trans. Pattern Anal. Mach. Intell. **26**(2), 214–225 (2004)
12. Gupta, S., Arbelaez, P., Malik, J.: Perceptual organization and recognition of indoor scenes from RGB-D images. In: Proceedings of IEEE Conference on Computer Vision and Pattern Recognition (CVPR) (2013)
13. Gupta, S., Arbeláez, P., Girshick, R., Malik, J.: Indoor scene understanding with RGB-D images: bottom-up segmentation, object detection and semantic segmentation. Int. J. Comput. Vis. **112**, 1–17 (2014)
14. Gupta, S., Girshick, R., Arbeláez, P., Malik, J.: Learning rich features from RGB-D images for object detection and segmentation. In: Fleet, D., Pajdla, T., Schiele, B., Tuytelaars, T. (eds.) ECCV 2014. LNCS, vol. 8695, pp. 345–360. Springer, Heidelberg (2014). doi:10.1007/978-3-319-10584-0_23
15. Hariharan, B., Arbeláez, P., Girshick, R., Malik, J.: Hypercolumns for object segmentation and fine-grained localization. In: Proceedings of the IEEE Conference on Computer Vision and Pattern Recognition, pp. 447–456 (2015)
16. Hasnat, M.A., Alata, O., Trémeau, A.: Joint color-spatial-directional clustering and region merging (JCSD-RM) for unsupervised RGB-D image segmentation. IEEE Trans. Pattern Anal. Mach. Intell. **38**(11) (2016)
17. Hasnat, M.A., Alata, O., Trémeau, A.: Unsupervised RGB-D image segmentation using joint clustering and region merging. In: Proceedings of British Machine Vision Conference (BMVC) (2014)
18. Hickson, S., Essa, I., Christensen, H.: Semantic instance labeling leveraging hierarchical segmentation. In: 2015 IEEE Winter Conference on Applications of Computer Vision, pp. 1068–1075. IEEE (2015)
19. Höft, N., Schulz, H., Behnke, S.: Fast semantic segmentation of RGB-D scenes with GPU-accelerated deep neural networks. In: Lutz, C., Thielscher, M. (eds.) KI 2014. LNCS (LNAI), vol. 8736, pp. 80–85. Springer, Heidelberg (2014). doi:10.1007/978-3-319-11206-0_9
20. Long, J., Shelhamer, E., Darrell, T.: Fully convolutional networks for semantic segmentation. In: Proceedings of IEEE Conference on Computer Vision and Pattern Recognition (CVPR), pp. 3431–3440 (2015)

21. Pagnutti, G., Zanuttigh, P.: Scene segmentation from depth and color data driven by surface fitting. In: Proceedings of IEEE International Conference on Image Processing (ICIP), pp. 4407–4411. IEEE (2014)
22. Pagnutti, G., Zanuttigh, P.: Joint color and depth segmentation based on region merging and surface fitting. In: Proceedings of the International Conference on Computer Vision Theory and Applications (VISAPP) (2016)
23. Piegl, L., Tiller, W.: The NURBS Book, 2nd edn. Springer, New York (1997)
24. Ren, X., Bo, L., Fox, D.: RGB-(D) scene labeling: features and algorithms. In: Proceedings of IEEE Conference on Computer Vision and Pattern Recognition (CVPR) (2012)
25. Shi, J., Malik, J.: Normalized cuts and image segmentation. IEEE Trans. Pattern Anal. Mach. Intell. **22**(8), 888–905 (2000)
26. Silberman, N., Hoiem, D., Kohli, P., Fergus, R.: Indoor segmentation and support inference from RGBD images. In: Fitzgibbon, A., Lazebnik, S., Perona, P., Sato, Y., Schmid, C. (eds.) ECCV 2012. LNCS, vol. 7576, pp. 746–760. Springer, Heidelberg (2012). doi:10.1007/978-3-642-33715-4_54
27. Srinivasan, N., Dellaert, F.: A Rao-Blackwellized MCMC algorithm for recovering piecewise planar 3D model from multiple view RGBD images. In: Proceedings of IEEE International Conference on Image Processing (ICIP) (2014)
28. Taylor, C.J., Cowley, A.: Parsing indoor scenes using RGB-D imagery. In: Robotics: Science and Systems. vol. 8, pp. 401–408 (2013)
29. Theano Development Team: Theano: a Python framework for fast computation of mathematical expressions. arXiv e-prints abs/1605.02688, May 2016. https://arxiv.org/abs/1605.02688
30. Wallenberg, M., Felsberg, M., Forssén, P.-E., Dellen, B.: Channel coding for joint colour and depth segmentation. In: Mester, R., Felsberg, M. (eds.) DAGM 2011. LNCS, vol. 6835, pp. 306–315. Springer, Heidelberg (2011). doi:10.1007/978-3-642-23123-0_31
31. Wang, A., Lu, J., Wang, G., Cai, J., Cham, T.-J.: Multi-modal unsupervised feature learning for RGB-D scene labeling. In: Fleet, D., Pajdla, T., Schiele, B., Tuytelaars, T. (eds.) ECCV 2014. LNCS, vol. 8693, pp. 453–467. Springer, Heidelberg (2014). doi:10.1007/978-3-319-10602-1_30
32. Zanuttigh, P., Marin, G., Dal Mutto, C., Dominio, F., Minto, L., Cortelazzo, G.M.: Time-of-Flight and Structured Light Depth Cameras. Springer, Heidelberg (2016)

Improving Constrained Bundle Adjustment Through Semantic Scene Labeling

Achkan Salehi[1]([✉]), Vincent Gay-Bellile[1], Steve Bourgeois[1],
and Frédéric Chausse[2]

[1] CEA LIST, Vision and Content Engineering Lab,
Point Courrier 94, 91191 Gif-sur-Yvette, France
{achkan.salehi,vincent.gay-bellile,steve.bourgeois}@cea.fr
[2] Institut Pascal, UMR 6602 CNRS, Clermont-Ferrand, France
frederic.chausse@univ-bpclermont.fr

Abstract. There is no doubt that SLAM and deep learning methods can benefit from each other. Most recent approaches to coupling those two subjects, however, either use SLAM to improve the learning process, or tend to ignore the geometric solutions that are currently used by SLAM systems. In this work, we focus on improving city-scale SLAM through the use of deep learning. More precisely, we propose to use CNN-based scene labeling to geometrically constrain bundle adjustment. Our experiments indicate a considerable increase in robustness and precision.

Keywords: SLAM · VSLAM · Bundle adjustment · Deep learning · Scene labeling

1 Introduction

The problem of the drift of monocular visual simultaneous localization and mapping (VSLAM) in seven degrees of freedom is well-known. Fusion of VSLAM, in particular key-frame bundle adjustment (BA) [1,2] with data from various sensors (*e.g.* GPS, IMU [3–5]) and databases (*e.g.* 3d textured or textureless 3d models, digital elevation models [6–8]) has proven to be a reliable solution to this problem. In this paper, we focus on fusion through constrained BA [2–4,6]. Among the available sensors and databases that can be used in constrained BA, textureless 3d building models are of particular interest, since the geometric constraints they impose on the reconstruction can prevent scale drift and also help in the estimation of camera yaw. Furthermore, they can be used to limit the impact of GPS bias on the reconstruction [9]. They are also, as opposed to textured models, widespread and easily (usually freely) available. However, methods that make use of such partial knowledge of the environment [6,8] face the problem of data association between 3d points and 3d building planes, that is, they must design a reliable method to segment the 3d point cloud and determine which points belong to buildings. In previous works [6,7], data association between 3d points and building models has been made by means of simple geometric constraints instead of photometric ones. This is due to the high cost of

© Springer International Publishing Switzerland 2016
G. Hua and H. Jégou (Eds.): ECCV 2016 Workshops, Part III, LNCS 9915, pp. 133–142, 2016.
DOI: 10.1007/978-3-319-49409-8_13

scene labeling algorithms. Unfortunately, these simple geometric criteria often introduce high amounts of noise, which can lead to failure even when used in conjunction with M-estimators or RANSAC-like algorithms. This is especially true when building facades are completely occluded by nearby objects on which an important number of interest points are detected (*e.g.* trees, advertising boards, etc.). Since these methods clearly reach their limits in such environments, we must investigate the alternative solution, namely scene labeling. While current state of the art scene labeling algorithms allow a highly accurate segmentation, their cost often remains prohibitive for real-time use, even on the GPU. However, some state of the art segmentation methods such as [10] operate in two steps: first, a (reasonably fast) convolutional neural network (CNN) provides a crude and often spatially incoherent segmentation, which is refined using graph-based methods in a second time consuming step. This observation leads to the idea that the raw outputs of a CNN can be used with key-frame bundle adjustment as an a priori in data association, without much overhead, and possibly in real-time.

In this paper, we propose the use of scene labeling for data association in bundle adjustment constrained to building models. We segment each key-frame using a CNN inspired by the first stage of [10]. In order to reduce time complexity, we do not refine the outputs of the CNN, which, as we mentioned previously, are tainted by high levels of uncertainty. Instead, we replace the compute-intensive regularizations by a fast likelihood computation, with respect to a density function that we have previously learned by modeling our particular CNN as a Dirichlet process.

Roadmap. The following section (Sect. 2) is dedicated to notations and preliminaries. We discuss related works in Sect. 3, and present our approach in Sect. 4. Experiments are presented in Sect. 5 and we conclude the paper in Sect. 6.

2   Notations and Preliminaries

2.1   Local Key-Frame Based Bundle Adjustment

Bundle adjustment (BA) refers to the minimization of the sum of reprojection errors, *i.e.* the minimization of:

$$B(x) = \sum_{i \in \mathcal{M}} \sum_{j \in \mathcal{C}_i} ||x_{ij} - \pi_j(X_i))||^2 \tag{1}$$

where $\mathcal{M}$ denotes the set of all 3d point indexes, and $\mathcal{C}_i$ the set of cameras from which the point i is observable. The function π_j maps each 3d point X_i to its normalized 2d coordinates in the image plane of camera j, where the observation of X_i is noted x_{ij}. Successive images in a sequence are often similar, therefore keeping every single camera pose, apart from being very inefficient, is redundant. Thus, it is usual to perform key-frame bundle adjustment [1], in which only frames that present a significant amount of new information are kept. We also distinguish between global BA, in which all the cameras and points are optimized, and local BA in which only the $n \in \mathbb{N}$ last camera poses and the points they observe are optimized. In this paper, the term bundle adjustment, unless otherwise stated, will refer to local key-frame based BA.

2.2 The Dirichlet Distribution

The Dirichlet distribution is a continuous distribution of discrete distributions, that can be seen as a generalization of the Beta distribution to higher dimensions. We will note

$$\mathfrak{D}(x_1, ...x_k, \alpha_1, ...\alpha_k) = \frac{1}{\beta(\alpha)} \prod_{s=1}^{k} x_s^{\alpha_s - 1} \qquad (2)$$

the Dirichlet probability density function of parameters $\alpha = \{\alpha_1, ..., \alpha_k\}$. Here, β is the multinomial Beta function.

3 Related Work

Our work is firstly related to those that combine deep learning methods with geometrical SLAM algorithms, and secondly to SLAM approaches that make use of 3d textured or texture-less building models. Works such as [11] are based on a pure machine learning approach, but can benefit from more precise datasets generated by VSLAM. Such methods can thus be considered as dual to approaches such as ours. In their work, Costante et al. [12] present a deep network architecture that learns to predict the relative motion between consecutive frames, based on the dense optical flow of input images. Their method and ours can be seen as complementary to each other, since theirs intervenes at a lower level and can be used as part of a more general framework (for example by replacing the PnP-solving methods in traditional key-frame based systems), while our work targets the optimization (BA) that refines the results of such pose computations. The loop closure detection of [13] is related to the present paper in the sense that it makes use of deep nets to improve visual SLAM, but also operates on a lower level that bundle adjustment.

In previous works, data association for city-scale SLAM, as far as we know, has been either carried out via simple geometric criteria [6–8], or left to outlier-elimination processes such as RANSAC (e.g. in [14]). In [6–8], a point p is associated to a building if the ray cast from the center of the camera that goes through p intersects a building plane. Although the time complexity of such an evaluation remains negligible, its results naturally tend to contain a considerable amount of noise. In [14], Google street view images with known poses are first back-projected on 3d building models in an off-line pre-processing step. In other terms, each pixel in the street view image is associated to a 3d position. The database obtained via this procedure is then used in an on-line localization algorithm, by matching SIFT features between each new image and the ones in the database. The resulting $2d \leftrightarrow 3d$ matches define a PnP problem that is solved using standard techniques. Poor matches and wrong 3d positions are eliminated by a RANSAC, But no explicit attempt at filtering points that do not belong to buildings are made during the back-projection step.

4   Proposed Method

We seek to correct the results of local key-frame based BA [1] by constraining the reconstruction using 3d building models. To this end, we minimize a cost function inspired by [3,4]. Intuitively, we seek to respect the geometric constraints provided by 3d building models, so long as the sum of squared reprojection errors $B(X)$ remains below a certain threshold t. More precisely, we solve:

$$\arg\min_{X} \frac{1}{t - B(X)} + \sum_{q \in Q} W_q d(q, N_q) \tag{3}$$

In the expression above, X is the vector that concatenates the parameters of all camera poses and the 3d positions of all 3d points. Q is the subset of 3D points from the map that have been classified as belonging to a building, $d(.)$ denotes the squared Euclidian distance, and N_q denotes the building plane closest to $q \in Q$. Each W_q is a weight, and its computation will be discussed at the end of section Sect. 4.2. This optimization problem has to be initialized with the minimizer of B. Thus, we first perform non-constrained BA and use its result as the initial value for X. We use the standard Levenberg-Marquardt algorithm to minimize the cost function of Eq. 3. We propose to use a fast CNN to determine the set Q.

4.1   Scene Labeling

The scene labeling algorithm we use is based on the first stage of the method presented in [10], but operates in a single scale, as opposed to the multiscale approach of the aforementioned paper. A Convolutional Neural Network (CNN) is trained on labeled data. The CNN assigns each pixel x in the input image I to a probability vector P_x of length 8. The $i - th$ component of P_x is the probability that x belongs to class i. The outputs of such of a CNN usually require post-processing in order to be regularized. Unfortunately, such methods are too time-consuming to be used in any BA system that runs in reasonable time. Thus, we are left with the raw outputs of the CNN, which more often than not lack spatial consistency.

To classify a pixel x mapped by the CNN to a distribution P_x, the most straight-forward approach would be to take the arg max of P_x. However, we think that a better approach is to take into account the general shape of the distribution. If a pixel x truly belongs to the class building, its distribution must have a specific form, and particular modes. Thus, by learning the expected form of this distribution, we can eliminate false positives, that is, distributions which reach their peak on the wrong label. To that end, we consider each distribution as a random variable, and given a set of labeled data, learn the Dirichlet distribution (defined in Sect. 1) from which the set

$$D_{\text{build}} = \{P_i \mid i \text{ belongs to a building in the image}\} \tag{4}$$

is a sample. Given a set of labeled data, the problem is to find the set of parameters $\alpha = \{\alpha_1, ..., \alpha_k\}$ for which the Dirichlet distribution fits best. This can be written as a maximum likelihood problem:

$$\arg\min_{\alpha} \prod_{X \in D_{\text{build}}} \mathfrak{D}(X|\alpha) \tag{5}$$

where $\mathfrak{D}$ is the Dirichlet density function of parameters α. To avoid underflow and also to simplify the notations, we solve the equivalent problem

$$\arg\min_{\alpha} \{-\ln(\prod_{X \in D_{\text{build}}} \mathfrak{D}(X|\alpha))\} \tag{6}$$

It can be shown using a few basic algebraic operations, that this can be written as

$$\arg\min_{\alpha} \{m \ln(\beta(\alpha)) + \sum_{i=1}^{k} (1 - \alpha_i) \ln(t_i)\} \tag{7}$$

where $t_i = \prod_{q \in D} \prod_{s=1}^{k} q(s)$ and k is the number of classes. We have $\alpha_i \geq 0$ for all i from the definition of the Dirichlet distribution. Therefore, we need to add k terms that will act as barriers, preventing the value of the α_i variables to become negative. The final cost function takes the form:

$$C(\alpha) = m \ln(\beta(\alpha)) + \sum_{i=1}^{k} (1 - \alpha_i) \ln(t_i) + \lambda \sum_{i=1}^{k} e^{-\alpha_i} \tag{8}$$

with $\lambda \in \mathbb{R}^+$ influencing the impact of the exponential terms. The Jacobian of this cost function is given by

$$\frac{\partial C}{\partial \alpha_l} = m(\psi_0(\alpha_l) - \psi_0(\sum_{i=1}^{k} \alpha_i)) - \ln(t_l) - \lambda e^{-\alpha_l} \tag{9}$$

where ψ_0 denotes the digamma function. We used the well known L-BFGS minimization algorithm [15] to learn the parameters α.

4.2 Integration in Constrained Bundle Adjustment

Each 3d point Z in the map has often more than one observation. Noting $\{I_0, I_1, .., I_n\}$ the key-frames in which Z is observed, and $\{z_0, ..., z_n\}$ its 2d observations, we seek to determine the class to which Z most likely belongs. As mentioned previously, our scene labeling algorithm runs once for each key-frame. This results in a set of probability distributions for each of the observations of Z, that we will note $M = \{P_0, P_1, ..., P_n\}$. In practice, this distributions can differ. We combine these distributions in the simplest possible manner, by computing a mean distribution

$$P_Z = \frac{1}{N_c} \sum_{i=1}^{n} P_i \tag{10}$$

Next, we compute $\mathfrak{D}(P_Z)$ and classify Z as belonging to Q if and only if $\mathfrak{D}(P_Z) > t_{\mathfrak{D}}$, where $t_{\mathfrak{D}}$ is a threshold. Finally, we set $W_q = \mathfrak{D}(P_Z)$ in Eq. 3.

5   Experimental Evaluation

We used a CNN implementation written in Torch 7 [16], based on the first stage of [10], but operating on only one scale, as opposed to the multiscale approach of the aforementioned paper. We used the following eight labels: {1: *sky*, 2: *tree*, 3: *road*, 4: *grass*, 5: *water*, 6: *building*, 7: *mountain*, 8: *object*}. The implementation was reasonably fast: the average segmentation time for a test image of size 640 × 480 was on average 0.6 s, when executed on a single core (on a single Intel(R) Core(TM) i7-4710HQ CPU @ 2.50 GHz) running at 1.6 GHz, under linux (Ubuntu 14.04). We used a subset of annotated images from the kitti dataset [17] to demonstrate the advantage of using the Dirichlet distribution $\mathfrak{D}$ to classify pixels compared to simply taking the arg max. On average, our method eliminated more than 71 % of false positives (*i.e.* points falsly classified as belonging to buildings by the CNN), while rejecting a small percentage (less than 5 %) of correctly classified building points. Examples are shown in Fig. 1. We conducted experiments on synthetic and real sequences in order to validate our bundle adjustment approach.

(a)   (b)

Fig. 1. Examples illustrating the advantage of using the Dirichlet distribution to filter out poor classification results. Row 1: images fed as input to the CNN. Row 2: the raw result of the CNN, determined by taking the arg max of the distribution for each pixel. Each color corresponds to a class, and red pixels are those that have been classified as belonging to buildings. Row 3: the results of our filtering (i.e. using $\mathfrak{D}$ instead of the arg max). This binary image shows pixels that present a higher than 80 % probability of being building pixels according to the Dirichlet distribution. It can be seen that most false positives (mostly, building detection on the road plane) have been eliminated, at the cost of discarding a small portion of correctly classified building points. (Color figure online)

5.1   Synthetic Sequence

We generated an urban scene with important levels of occlusion that was realistic enough to be segmented with good accuracy by scene labeling algorithms.

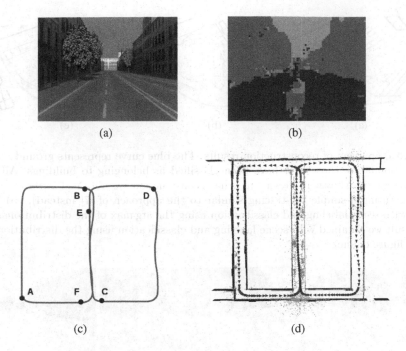

Fig. 2. (a) An example image of the synthetic sequence. (b) The result of the CNN (with the arg max taken) on the example image. Red pixels are those that correspond to the buildings. (c) The ground truth trajectory. The camera movement is given by A-B-C-D-E-F-A (d) the trajectory and the point cloud as refined by our method. The golden points are those that are classified as belonging to buildings. Other points are represented in green. (Color figure online)

The sequence was ~1200 m long and it included multiple loops. An example image from the sequence and its segmentation by the CNN is given in Fig. 2(a) and (b). The ground truth trajectory is given in Fig. 2(c). The trajectory and the point cloud as refined by our constrained BA approach is illustrated in Fig. 2(d). On this sequence, the mean translational error of our method was 1.3 cm, while the rotational error was 0.05 radians.

On this sequence, constrained BA without pixel-wise scene labeling fails. BA constrained to 3d building models with geometric segmentation of the point cloud (with ray-tracing and proximity criteria as in [6,8]) leads to a rapid deterioration of the geometric structure and ultimately to pose computation failure.

5.2 Real Data

In this section, we present BA results with and without scene labeling on a short but particularly challenging outdoors sequence[1], mainly because building

---

[1] We could not use the Kitti dataset, because it does not provide 3d building models.

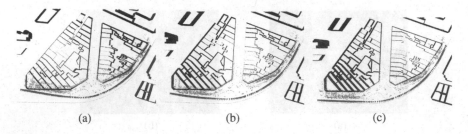

(a)   (b)   (c)

Fig. 3. Comparison of reconstruction results. The blue curve represents ground truth. Golden points are those that have been classified as belonging to buildings. All the other points are shown in green. (a) The reconstruction we obtained without scene labeling (using a simple ray-tracing similar to the approach of [7] instead). (b) The result with scene labeling and classification using the arg max of the distributions. (c) The result we obtained with scene labeling and classification using the distribution $\mathfrak{D}$. (Color figure online)

Fig. 4. Building model reprojections after bundle adjustment on the real sequence. This examples show that our solution is robust to occlusions, which are omnipresent on that sequence. Once again, note that the building models suffer from inaccurate heights.

facades are often almost completely occluded by trees, billboards, etc. The camera is approximately orthogonal to the trajectory. Additionally, the height of the 3d building models we used in this experiment were inaccurate. Unfortunately, we only had access to the in-plane positional ground truth (shown as a blue curve in Fig. 3) but did not have access to altitude or orientation ground truth. Instead, we used the proper alignment of building contours with the projection of 3d building models as a criteria for evaluating the precision of each solution. Figure 3 shows a comparison between the result we obtained without and with scene labeling. Additionally, this figure shows the trajectory that we obtained when classifying the pixels using the arg max of their distribution instead of the Dirichlet distribution $\mathfrak{D}$. It can be seen that in that case, as when scene labeling is not used, the high number of false correspondences between points and buildings causes an inacceptable error. Figure 4 shows building models reprojections after bundle adjustment with our method.

6   Conclusion and Future Directions

In this paper, we demonstrated that important accuracy gains can result from incorporating scene labeling into constrained bundle adjustment. We filtered out poor segmentation results by modeling our particular CNN as a Dirichlet process.

This method proved to be more efficient than simply taking the arg max. The computational complexity of the segmentation module prevented us from reaching real-time performance in a sequential implementation. However, it is possible to run the segmentation algorithm on a dedicated thread, and update the on-line reconstruction as soon as a result becomes available (similar approaches for combining real-time slam with high-latency solutions exist [18]). Thus, we will direct our future efforts toward developing such an architecture, while independently optimizing our CNN implementation.

References

1. Mouragnon, E., Lhuillier, M., Dhome, M., Dekeyser, F., Sayd, P.: Real time localization and 3D reconstruction. In: 2006 IEEE Computer Society Conference on Computer Vision and Pattern Recognition, vol. 1, pp. 363–370. IEEE (2006)
2. Triggs, B., McLauchlan, P.F., Hartley, R.I., Fitzgibbon, A.W.: Bundle adjustment — a modern synthesis. In: Triggs, B., Zisserman, A., Szeliski, R. (eds.) IWVA 1999. LNCS, vol. 1883, pp. 298–372. Springer, Heidelberg (2000). doi:10.1007/3-540-44480-7_21
3. Lhuillier, M.: Incremental fusion of structure-from-motion and GPS using constrained bundle adjustments. IEEE Trans. Pattern Anal. Mach. Intell. 34(12), 2489–2495 (2012)
4. Lhuillier, M.: Fusion of GPS and structure-from-motion using constrained bundle adjustments. In: 2011 IEEE Conference on Computer Vision and Pattern Recognition (CVPR), pp. 3025–3032. IEEE (2011)
5. Leutenegger, S., Furgale, P.T., Rabaud, V., Chli, M., Konolige, K., Siegwart, R.: Keyframe-based visual-inertial SLAM using nonlinear optimization. In: Robotics: Science and Systems (2013)
6. Larnaout, D., Bourgeois, S., Gay-Bellile, V., Dhome, M.: Towards bundle adjustment with GIS constraints for online geo-localization of a vehicle in urban center. In: 2012 Second International Conference on 3D Imaging, Modeling, Processing, Visualization and Transmission (3DIMPVT), pp. 348–355. IEEE (2012)
7. Lothe, P., Bourgeois, S., Dekeyser, F., Royer, E., Dhome, M.: Towards geographical referencing of monocular SLAM reconstruction using 3D city models: application to real-time accurate vision-based localization. In: IEEE Conference on Computer Vision and Pattern Recognition, CVPR 2009, pp. 2882–2889. IEEE (2009)
8. Tamaazousti, M., Gay-Bellile, V., Collette, S.N., Bourgeois, S., Dhome, M.: Nonlinear refinement of structure from motion reconstruction by taking advantage of a partial knowledge of the environment. In: 2011 IEEE Conference on Computer Vision and Pattern Recognition (CVPR), pp. 3073–3080. IEEE (2011)
9. Larnaout, D., Gay-Belllile, V., Bourgeois, S., Dhome, M.: Vision-based differential GPS: improving VSLAM/GPS fusion in urban environment with 3D building models. In: 2014 2nd International Conference on 3D Vision (3DV), vol. 1, pp. 432–439. IEEE (2014)
10. Farabet, C., Couprie, C., Najman, L., LeCun, Y.: Learning hierarchical features for scene labeling. IEEE Trans. Pattern Anal. Mach. Intell. 35(8), 1915–1929 (2013)
11. Kendall, A., Grimes, M., Cipolla, R.: PoseNet: a convolutional network for real-time 6-DOF camera relocalization. In: Proceedings of the IEEE International Conference on Computer Vision, pp. 2938–2946 (2015)

12. Costante, G., Mancini, M., Valigi, P., Ciarfuglia, T.A.: Exploring representation learning with CNNs for frame-to-frame ego-motion estimation. IEEE Robot. Autom. Lett. **1**(1), 18–25 (2016)
13. Gao, X., Zhang, T.: Loop closure detection for visual SLAM systems using deep neural networks. In: 2015 34th Chinese Control Conference (CCC), pp. 5851–5856. IEEE (2015)
14. Majdik, A.L., Verda, D., Albers-Schoenberg, Y., Scaramuzza, D.: Micro air vehicle localization and position tracking from textured 3D cadastral models. In: 2014 IEEE International Conference on Robotics and Automation (ICRA), pp. 920–927. IEEE (2014)
15. Liu, D.C., Nocedal, J.: On the limited memory BFGS method for large scale optimization. Math. Program. **45**(1–3), 503–528 (1989)
16. Collobert, R., Kavukcuoglu, K., Farabet, C.: Torch7: a matlab-like environment for machine learning. In: BigLearn, NIPS Workshop (2011)
17. Xu, P.: KITTI semantic segmentation. https://www.hds.utc.fr/xuphilip/dokuwiki/en/data
18. Oleynikova, H., Burri, M., Lynen, S., Siegwart, R.: Real-time visual-inertial localization for aerial and ground robots. In: 2015 IEEE/RSJ International Conference on Intelligent Robots and Systems (IROS), pp. 3079–3085. IEEE (2015)

A CNN Cascade for Landmark Guided Semantic Part Segmentation

Aaron S. Jackson$^{(\boxtimes)}$, Michel Valstar, and Georgios Tzimiropoulos

School of Computer Science, The University of Nottingham, Nottingham, UK
{aaron.jackson,michel.valstar,yorgos.tzimiropoulos}@nottingham.ac.uk

Abstract. This paper proposes a CNN cascade for semantic part segmentation guided by pose-specific information encoded in terms of a set
of landmarks (or keypoints). There is large amount of prior work on each
of these tasks separately, yet, to the best of our knowledge, this is the
first time in literature that the interplay between pose estimation and
semantic part segmentation is investigated. To address this limitation of
prior work, in this paper, we propose a CNN cascade of tasks that firstly
performs landmark localisation and then uses this information as input
for guiding semantic part segmentation. We applied our architecture to
the problem of facial part segmentation and report large performance
improvement over the standard unguided network on the most challenging face datasets. Testing code and models will be published online at
http://cs.nott.ac.uk/~psxasj/.

Keywords: Pose estimation · Landmark localisation · Semantic part
segmentation · Faces

1 Introduction

Pose estimation refers to the task of localising a set of landmarks (or keypoints)
on objects of interest like faces [1], the human body [2] or even birds [3]. Locating
these landmarks help establish correspondences between two or more different
instances of the same object class which in turn has been proven useful for fined-
grained recognition tasks like face and activity recognition. Part segmentation is
a special case of semantic image segmentation which is the task of assigning an
object class label to each pixel in the image. In part segmentation, the assigned
label corresponds to the part of the object that this pixel belongs to. In this
paper, we investigate whether pose estimation can guide contemporary CNN
architectures for semantic part segmentation. This seems to be natural yet to the
best of our knowledge this is the first paper that addresses this problem. To this
end, we propose a Convolutional Neural Network (CNN) cascade for landmark
guided part segmentation and report large performance improvement over a
standard CNN for semantic segmentation that was trained without guidance.

Although the ideas and methods presented in this paper can probably be
applied to any structured deformable object (e.g. faces, human body, cars, birds),

© Springer International Publishing Switzerland 2016
G. Hua and H. Jégou (Eds.): ECCV 2016 Workshops, Part III, LNCS 9915, pp. 143–155, 2016.
DOI: 10.1007/978-3-319-49409-8_14

we will confine ourselves to human faces. The main reason for this is the lack of annotated datasets. To the best of our knowledge, there are no datasets providing pixel-level annotation of parts and landmarks at the same time. While this is also true for the case of human faces, one can come up with pixel-level annotation of facial parts by just appropriately connecting a pseudo-dense set of facial landmarks for which many datasets and a very large number of annotated facial images exist, see for example [4]. Note that during testing we do not assume knowledge of the landmarks' location, and what we actually show is that a two-step process in which a CNN firstly predicts the landmarks and then uses this information to segment the face largely outperforms a CNN that was trained to directly perform facial part segmentation.

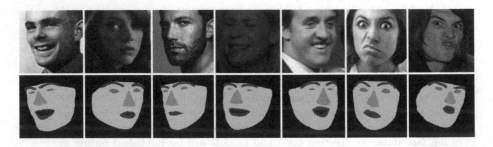

Fig. 1. Example faces and their corresponding output from the CNN cascade.

1.1 Main Contributions

In summary, this paper addresses the following research questions:

1. Is a CNN for facial part segmentation needed at all? One might argue that by just predicting the facial landmarks and then connecting them in the same way as we created the part labels, we could get high quality facial part segmentation thus completely by-passing the part segmentation task. Our first result in this paper is that indeed the latter method slightly outperforms a CNN trained for facial part segmentation (without guidance though).
2. Can facial landmarks be used for guiding facial part segmentation, thus reversing the result mentioned above? Indeed, we show that the proposed CNN cascade for landmark guided facial part segmentation largely outperforms both methods mentioned above without even requiring very accurate localisation of the landmarks. Some example output can be seen in Fig. 1.

2   Related Work

This section reviews related work on semantic segmentation, facial landmark localisation (also known as alignment) and facial part segmentation.

Face Alignment. State-of-the-art techniques in face alignment are based on the so-called cascaded regression [5]. Given a facial image, such methods estimate the landmarks' location by applying a sequence of regressors usually learnt from SIFT [6] or other hand-crafted features. The regressors are learnt in a cascaded manner such that the input to regressor k is the estimate of the landmarks' location provided by regressor $k - 1$, see also [7–11]. The first component in the proposed CNN cascade is a CNN landmark detector based on VGG-16 [12] converted to a fully convolutional network [13]. Although the main contribution of our paper is not to propose a method for landmark localisation, our CNN landmark localisation method performs comparably with all aforementioned methods. One advantage of our method over cascaded regression approaches is that it is not sensitive to initialisation and hence it does not rely on accurate face detection.

Semantic Segmentation. Thanks to its ability to integrate information from multiple CNN layers and its end-to-end training, the Fully Convolutional Network (FCN) of [13] has become the standard basic component for all contemporary semantic segmentation algorithms. The architecture of FCN is shown in Fig. 2. One of the limitations of the FCN is that prediction is performed in low-resolution, hence a number of methods have been recently proposed to compensate for this by usually applying a Conditional Random Field (CRF) on top of the FCN output. The work of [14] firstly upsamples the predicted scores using bilinear interpolation and then refines the output by applying a dense CRF. The method of [15] performs recurrent end-to-end training of the FCN and the dense CRF. Finally, the work in [16] employs learnt deconvolution layers, as opposed to fixing the parameters with an interpolation filter (as in FCN). These filters learn to reconstruct the object's shape, instead of just classifying each pixel. Although any of these methods could be incorporated within the proposed CNN cascade, for simplicity, we used the VGG-FCN [12]. Note that all the aforementioned methods perform unguided semantic segmentation, as opposed to the proposed landmark-guided segmentation which incorporates information about the pose of the object during both training and testing. To encode pose specific information we augment the input to our segmentation network with a multi-channel confidence map representation using Gaussians centred at the predicted landmarks' location, inspired by the human pose estimation method of [17]. Note that [17] is iterative an idea that could be also applied to our method, but currently we have not observed performance improvement by doing so.

Part Segmentation. There have been also a few works that extend semantic segmentation to part segmentation with perhaps the most well-known being the Shape Boltzman Machine [18,19]. This work has been recently extended to incorporate CNN refined by CRF features (as in [14]) in [20]. Note that this work aims to refine the CNN output by applying a Restricted Boltzmann Machine on top of it and does not make use of pose information as provided by landmarks. In contrast, we propose an enhanced CNN architecture which is landmark-guided, can be trained end-to-end and yields large performance improvement without the need of further refinement.

Face Segmentation. One of the first face segmentation methods prior to deep learning is known as LabelFaces [21] which is based on patch classification and further refinement via a hierarchical face model. Another hierarchical approach to face segmentation based on Restricted Boltzmann Machines was proposed in [22]. More recently, a multi-objective CNN has been shown to perform well for the task of face segmentation in [23]. The method is based on a CRF the unary and pairwise potentials of which are learnt via a CNN. Softmax loss is used for the segmentation masks, and a logistic loss is used to learn the edges. Additionally, the network makes use of a non-parametric segmentation prior which is obtained as follows: first facial landmarks on the test image are detected and then all training images with most similar shapes are used to calculate an average segmentation mask. This mask is finally used to augment RGB. This segmentation mask might be blurry, does not encode pose information and results in little performance improvement.

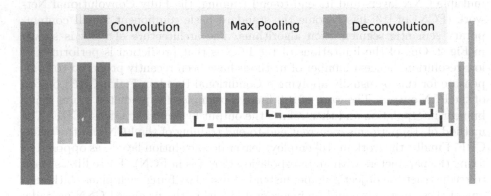

Fig. 2. Overview of the Fully Convolutional Network [13], low level information providing refinement are reintroduced into the network during deconvolution.

3   Datasets

There are a few datasets which provide annotations of pixel-level parts [24–26] but to the best of our knowledge there are no datasets containing both part and landmark annotations. Hence, in our paper we rely on datasets for facial landmarking. These datasets provide a pseudo-dense set of landmarks. Segmentation masks are constructed by joining the groundtruth landmarks together to fully enclose each facial component. The eyebrows are generated by a spline with a fixed width relative to the normalised face size, to cover the entire eyebrow. The selected classes are background, skin, eyebrows, eyes, nose, upper lip, inner mouth and lower lip. While this results in straight edges between landmarks, the network can learn a mean boundary for each class. The output from the network will be actually smoother than the groundtruth.

This process is illustrated in Fig. 3.

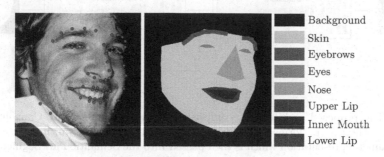

Fig. 3. Example groundtruth segmentation mask produced from the groundtruth landmarks.

For our experiments we used the 68-point landmark annotations provided by the 300W challenge [27]. In particular the training sets of LFPW [28], Helen [29], AFW [30] and iBUG [27] are all used for training while the 300W test set (600 images) is used for testing. Both training and test sets contain very challenging images in terms of appearance, pose, expression and occlusion.

This collection of images undergoes some pre-processing before they are used to train the network. The faces are normalised to be of equal size and cropped with some noise added to the position of the bounding box. Not all images are the same size, but their height is fixed at 350 pixels. With probability $p = 0.5$, a randomly sized black rectangle, large enough to occlude an entire component is layered over the input image. This assists the network in learning a robustness to partial occlusion.

4   Method

We propose a CNN cascade (shown in Fig. 4 and listed in Table 1) which performs landmark localisation followed by facial part segmentation. Our cascade was based on the VGG-FCN [12,13] using Caffe [31] and consists of two main components:

1. Firstly, an FCN is trained to detect facial landmarks using Sigmoid Cross Entropy Loss.
2. Secondly, inspired by the human pose estimation method of [17], the detected 68 landmarks are encoded as 68 separate channels each of which contains a 2D Gaussian centred at the corresponding landmark's location. The 68 channels are then stacked along with the original image and passed into our segmentation network. This is a second FCN trained for facial part segmentation using as input the stacked representation of 2D Gaussians and image, and a standard Softmax loss.

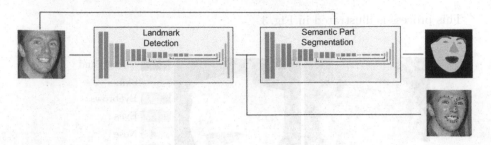

Fig. 4. The proposed architecture, comprising of two separate Fully Convolutional Networks. The first performs Landmark Detection, the output of which is encoded as multichannel representation which is then passed into the Semantic Part Segmentation network.

Overall we encode pose specific information by augmenting the input to our segmentation network with a multi-channel confidence map representation using Gaussians centred at the predicted landmarks' location. Hence, our FCN for semantic segmentation is trained to produce high quality, refined semantic masks by incorporating low level information with globally aware information. Each of the aforementioned components is now discussed in more detail:

Facial Landmark Detection. The training procedure for landmark detection is similar to training FCN for part segmentation. Landmarks are encoded as 2D Gaussians centred at the provided landmarks' location. Each landmark is allocated its own channel to prevent overlapping with other landmarks and allow the network to more easily distinguish between each point. The main difference with part segmentation is the loss function. Sigmoid Cross Entropy Loss [3] was chosen to regress the likelihood of a pixel containing a point. More concretely, given our groundtruth Gaussians $\hat{p}$ and predicted Gaussians p, each of equal dimensions $N \times W \times H$, we can define the Sigmoid Cross Entropy loss l as follows:

$$l = \frac{1}{N} \sum_{n=1}^{N} \sum_{i=1}^{W} \sum_{j=1}^{H} [p_{i,j}^n \log(\hat{p}_{i,j}^n) + (1 - p_{i,j}^n) \log(1 - \hat{p}_{i,j}^n)].$$

The loss was scaled by $1e^{-5}$ and a learning rate of 0.0001 was used. The network was trained in steps as previously described, for approximately 400,000 iterations, until convergence.

Guided Facial Part Segmentation. To train our guided FCN part segmentation network we followed [13]. Softmax Loss was also used. If N is the number of outputs (in our case, classes), $p_{i,j}$ is the predicted output for pixel (i,j), and n is the true label for pixel (i,j), then the Softmax loss l can be defined as:

$$l = \frac{-1}{N} \sum_{i=1}^{W} \sum_{j=1}^{H} \log(p_{i,j}^n).$$

We firstly trained an unguided FCN for facial part segmentation following [13]. Initially, the network was trained as 32 stride, where no information from the lower layers is used to refine the output. This followed by introducing information from pool4, followed by pool3. A learning rate of 0.0001 was chosen, and a momentum of 0.9. The network was trained for approximately 300,000 iterations until convergence.

Then, our guided FCN was initialised from the weights of the unguided one, by expanding the first layer to accommodate the additional 68 input channels. As mentioned earlier, each channel contains a 2D Gaussian centred at the corresponding landmark's location. A key aspect of our cascade is how the landmarks' location is determined during training. We cannot use the groundtruth landmark locations nor the prediction of our facial landmark detection network on our training set as those will be significantly more accurate than those observed during testing. Hence, we applied our facial landmark detection network on our validation set and recorded the landmark localisation error. We used this error to create a multivariate Gaussian noise model that was added to the groundtruth landmark locations of our training set. This way our guided segmentation network was initialised with much more realistic input in terms of landmarks' location. Furthermore, the same learning rate of 0.0001 was used. For the first 10,000 iterations, training was disabled on all layers except for the first. This allowed the network to warm up slightly, and prevent the parameters in other layers from getting destroyed by a high loss.

Table 1. The VGG-FCN [12, 13] architecture employed by our landmark detection and semantic part segmentation network.

Layer name	Kernel	Stride	Outputs	Layer name	Kernel	Stride	Outputs
conv1_1	3×3	1×1	64	pool4	2×2	2×2	–
conv1_2	3×3	1×1	64	conv5_1	3×3	1×1	512
pool1	2×2	2×2	–	conv5_2	3×3	1×1	512
conv2_1	3×3	1×1	128	conv5_3	3×3	1×1	512
conv2_2	3×3	1×1	128	pool5	2×2	2×2	–
pool2	2×2	2×2	–	fc6_conv	7×7	1×1	4096
conv3_1	3×3	1×1	256	fc7_conv	1×1	1×1	4096
conv3_2	3×3	1×1	256	fc8_conv	1×1	1×1	68 or 7
conv3_3	3×3	1×1	256	deconv_32	4×4	2×2	68 or 7
pool3	2×2	2×2	–	score_pool4	1×1	1×1	68 or 7
conv4_1	3×3	1×1	512	deconv_16	4×4	2×2	68 or 7
conv4_2	3×3	1×1	512	score_pool3	1×1	1×1	68 or 7
conv4_3	3×3	1×1	512	deconv_8	16×16	8×8	68 or 7

5 Experiments

5.1 Overview of Results

In all experiments we used the training and test sets detailed in Sect. 3. As a performance measure, we used the familiar intersection over union measure [13]. We report a comparison between the performance of four different methods of interest:

1. The first method is the VGG-FCN trained for facial part segmentation. We call this method **Unguided**.
2. The second method is the part segmentation result obtained by joining the landmarks obtained from VGG-FCN trained for facial landmark detection. We call this method **Connected Landmarks**.
3. The third method is the proposed landmark guided part segmentation network where the input is the groundtruth landmarks' location. We call this method **Guided by Groundtruth**.
4. Finally, the fourth method is the proposed landmark guided part segmentation network when input is detected landmarks' location. We call this method **Guided by Detected**.

The first two methods are the baselines in our experiments while the third one provides an upper bound in performance. The fourth method is the proposed CNN cascade.

5.2 Unguided Facial Part Segmentation

To establish a baseline, an unguided fully convolutional network was firstly trained. This was done as described in the FCN paper [13] and Sect. 4. Some visual results can be seen in Fig. 8. Additionally, a second baseline was obtained by simply connecting the landmarks of our facial landmark detection network also described in Sect. 4. The performance of both baselines can be seen in Fig. 5. We may observe that connecting the landmarks appears to offer slightly better performance than FCN for part segmentation alone. Nevertheless, we need to emphasise that the groundtruth masks were obtained by connecting the landmarks and hence there is some bias towards the connecting the landmarks approach.

5.3 Guided Facial Part Segmentation with Groundtruth

To establish an upper bounds to our performance, a fully convolutional network was trained to accept guidance from groundtruth landmarks. As described in Sect. 4, the guidance is provided in the form of landmarks encoded as 2D Gaussians. The performance difference between unguided and groundtruth guided part segmentation can be seen in Fig. 6. As we may observe the difference in performance between the two methods is huge. These results are not surprising given that the groundtruth semantic masks are generated from the landmarks guiding the network. Furthermore, landmark detection offers an advantage because, in

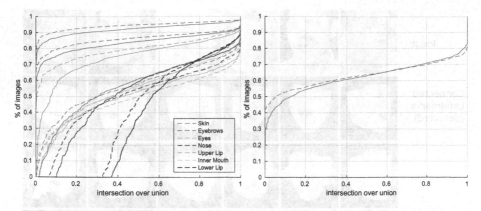

Fig. 5. Comparison of Unguided (—) and Connected Landmarks (- -). Per-class averages shown on the right.

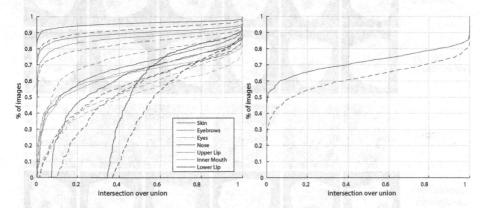

Fig. 6. Comparison of guided by groundtruth (—) and unguided (- -) facial part segmentation. Per-class averages shown on the right.

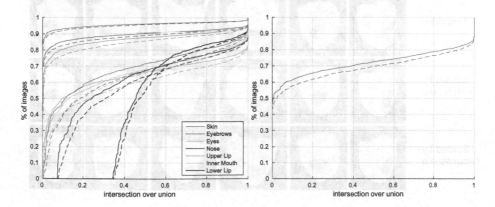

Fig. 7. Comparison of guidance from groundtruth landmarks (—) and guidance from detected landmarks (- -). Per-class averages shown on the right.

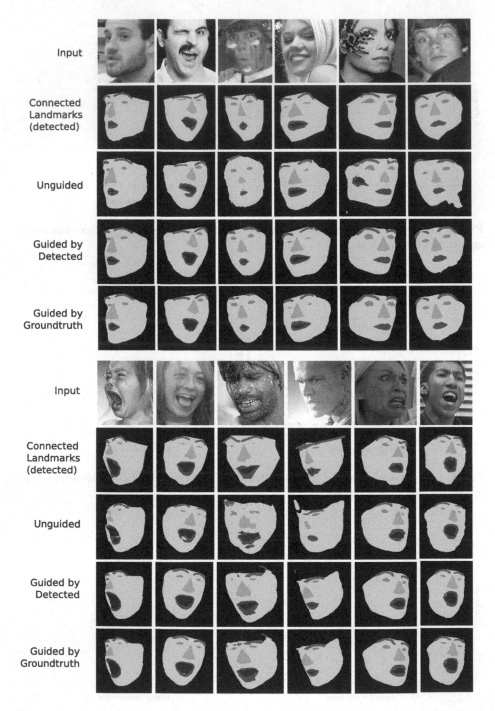

Fig. 8. Some visual results showing where the unguided network begins to fail, and where the guidance begins to pay off. Observe how visually close the results of the guided by groundtruth landmarks and the guided by detected landmarks networks are.

the case of faces, there can only be one tip of the nose, and one left side of the mouth. Giving some information to the network about where it is likely to be located can offer a significant advantage. Our next experiment shows that this is still the case when detected landmarks are used instead of groundtruth landmarks.

5.4   Guided Facial Part Segmentation with Detected Landmarks

With our upper bound and baselines defined, we can now see how much of an improvement we can achieve by guiding the network with our detected landmarks. The output of the landmark detection network is passed into the part segmentation network along with the original input image. We acknowledge that the performance of our landmark detector is far from groundtruth. We measure the performance as mean point to point Euclidean distance normalised by the outer interocular Euclidean distance, as in [27]. This results in an error of 0.0479. However, we show that the performance of the segmentation is improved significantly. The results of facial part segmentation guided by the detected landmarks, compared to the network guided by groundtruth landmarks can be seen in Fig. 7. Our main result is that performance of the guided by detected network is very close to the that of the guided by groundtruth illustrating that in practice accurate landmark localisation is not really required to guide segmentation. Some visual results can be seen in Fig. 8. Also, performance over all components for all methods is given in Fig. 9.

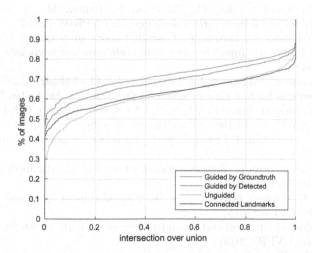

Fig. 9. Average performance of the four tested methods over all facial components: part segmentation guided by groundtruth landmarks, part segmentation guided by detected landmarks, unguided part segmentation, part segmentation by joining up the detected landmarks.

6 Conclusion

In this paper we proposed a CNN architecture to improve the performance of part segmentation by task delegation. In doing so, we provided both landmark localisation and semantic part segmentation on human faces. However, our method should be applicable to our objects as well. This is the focus of our ongoing work. We are also looking into how the segmentation masks can be further used to improve landmark localisation accuracy, thus leading to a recurrent architecture. Future work may also compare the performance of this method with a multitask architecture.

Acknowledgements. Aaron Jackson was funded by a PhD scholarship from the University of Nottingham. The work of Valstar is also funded by European Union Horizon 2020 research and innovation programme under grant agreement number 645378. Georgios Tzimiropoulos was supported in part by the EPSRC project EP/M02153X/1 Facial Deformable Models of Animals.

References

1. Cootes, T., Edwards, G., Taylor, C.: Active appearance models. TPAMI **23**(6), 681–685 (2001)
2. Yang, Y., Ramanan, D.: Articulated pose estimation with flexible mixtures-of-parts. In: CVPR (2011)
3. Zhang, N., Shelhamer, E., Gao, Y., Darrell, T.: Fine-grained pose prediction, normalization, and recognition. arXiv preprint arXiv:1511.07063 (2015)
4. Sagonas, C., Tzimiropoulos, G., Zafeiriou, S., Pantic, M.: A semi-automatic methodology for facial landmark annotation. In: CVPR-W (2013)
5. Dollár, P., Welinder, P., Perona, P.: Cascaded pose regression. In: CVPR (2010)
6. Lowe, D.G.: Distinctive image features from scale-invariant keypoints. IJCV **60**(2), 91–110 (2004)
7. Sánchez-Lozano, E., Martinez, B., Tzimiropoulos, G., Valstar, M.: Cascaded continuous regression for real-time incremental face tracking. In: Leibe, B., Matas, J., Sebe, N., Welling, M. (eds.) ECCV 2016. LNCS, vol. 9912, pp. 645–661. Springer, Heidelberg (2016). doi:10.1007/978-3-319-46484-8_39
8. Cao, X., Wei, Y., Wen, F., Sun, J.: Face alignment by explicit shape regression. In: CVPR (2012)
9. Xiong, X., De la Torre, F.: Supervised descent method and its applications to face alignment. In: CVPR (2013)
10. Zhu, S., Li, C., Change Loy, C., Tang, X.: Face alignment by coarse-to-fine shape searching. In: CVPR (2015)
11. Tzimiropoulos, G.: Project-out cascaded regression with an application to face alignment. In: CVPR (2015)
12. Simonyan, K., Zisserman, A.: Very deep convolutional networks for large-scale image recognition. arXiv preprint arXiv:1409.1556 (2014)
13. Long, J., Shelhamer, E., Darrell, T.: Fully convolutional networks for semantic segmentation. In: CVPR (2015)
14. Chen, L.C., Papandreou, G., Kokkinos, I., Murphy, K., Yuille, A.L.: Semantic image segmentation with deep convolutional nets and fully connected CRFs. In: ICLR (2015)

15. Zheng, S., Jayasumana, S., Romera-Paredes, B., Vineet, V., Su, Z., Du, D., Huang, C., Torr, P.H.: Conditional random fields as recurrent neural networks. In: CVPR (2015)
16. Noh, H., Hong, S., Han, B.: Learning deconvolution network for semantic segmentation. In: Proceedings of the IEEE International Conference on Computer Vision, pp. 1520–1528 (2015)
17. Carreira, J., Agrawal, P., Fragkiadaki, K., Malik, J.: Human pose estimation with iterative error feedback. In: CVPR (2016)
18. Eslami, S., Williams, C.: A generative model for parts-based object segmentation. In: NIPS (2012)
19. Eslami, S.A., Heess, N., Williams, C.K., Winn, J.: The shape boltzmann machine: a strong model of object shape. IJCV **107**(2), 155–176 (2014)
20. Tsogkas, S., Kokkinos, I., Papandreou, G., Vedaldi, A.: Deep learning for semantic part segmentation with high-level guidance. arXiv preprint arXiv:1505.02438 (2015)
21. Warrell, J., Prince, S.J.: Labelfaces: parsing facial features by multiclass labeling with an epitome prior. In: 2009 16th IEEE International Conference on Image Processing (ICIP), pp. 2481–2484. IEEE (2009)
22. Luo, P., Wang, X., Tang, X.: Hierarchical face parsing via deep learning. In: 2012 IEEE Conference on Computer Vision and Pattern Recognition (CVPR), pp. 2480–2487. IEEE (2012)
23. Liu, S., Yang, J., Huang, C., Yang, M.H.: Multi-objective convolutional learning for face labeling. In: Proceedings of the IEEE Conference on Computer Vision and Pattern Recognition, pp. 3451–3459 (2015)
24. Bo, Y., Fowlkes, C.C.: Shape-based pedestrian parsing. In: 2011 IEEE Conference on Computer Vision and Pattern Recognition (CVPR), pp. 2265–2272. IEEE (2011)
25. Kae, A., Sohn, K., Lee, H., Learned-Miller, E.: Augmenting CRFs with Boltzmann machine shape priors for image labeling. In: Proceedings of the IEEE Conference on Computer Vision and Pattern Recognition, pp. 2019–2026 (2013)
26. Chen, X., Mottaghi, R., Liu, X., Fidler, S., Urtasun, R., Yuille, A.: Detect what you can: detecting and representing objects using holistic models and body parts. In: CVPR (2014)
27. Sagonas, C., Tzimiropoulos, G., Zafeiriou, S., Pantic, M.: 300 faces in-the-wild challenge: the first facial landmark localization challenge. In: International Conference on Computer Vision, (ICCV-W), 300 Faces in-the-Wild Challenge (300-W), Sydney, Australia, 2013. IEEE (2013)
28. Belhumeur, P., Jacobs, D., Kriegman, D., Kumar, N.: Localizing parts of faces using a consensus of exemplars. In: CVPR (2011)
29. Le, V., Brandt, J., Lin, Z., Bourdev, L., Huang, T.S.: Interactive facial feature localization. In: Fitzgibbon, A., Lazebnik, S., Perona, P., Sato, Y., Schmid, C. (eds.) ECCV 2012. LNCS, vol. 7574, pp. 679–692. Springer, Heidelberg (2012). doi:10.1007/978-3-642-33712-3_49
30. Zhu, X., Ramanan, D.: Face detection, pose estimation, and landmark estimation in the wild. In: CVPR (2012)
31. Jia, Y., Shelhamer, E., Donahue, J., Karayev, S., Long, J., Girshick, R., Guadarrama, S., Darrell, T.: Caffe: Convolutional architecture for fast feature embedding. arXiv preprint arXiv:1408.5093 (2014)

3D Human Pose Estimation Using Convolutional Neural Networks with 2D Pose Information

Sungheon Park, Jihye Hwang, and Nojun Kwak[✉]

Graduate School of Convergence Science and Technology,
Seoul National University, Seoul, Korea
{sungheonpark,nojunk}@snu.ac.kr,
hjh881120@gmail.com

Abstract. While there has been a success in 2D human pose estimation with convolutional neural networks (CNNs), 3D human pose estimation has not been thoroughly studied. In this paper, we tackle the 3D human pose estimation task with end-to-end learning using CNNs. Relative 3D positions between one joint and the other joints are learned via CNNs. The proposed method improves the performance of CNN with two novel ideas. First, we added 2D pose information to estimate a 3D pose from an image by concatenating 2D pose estimation result with the features from an image. Second, we have found that more accurate 3D poses are obtained by combining information on relative positions with respect to multiple joints, instead of just one root joint. Experimental results show that the proposed method achieves comparable performance to the state-of-the-art methods on Human 3.6m dataset.

Keywords: Human pose estimation · Convolutional neural network · 2D-3D joint optimization

1 Introduction

Both 2D and 3D human pose recovery from images are important tasks since the retrieved pose information can be used to other applications such as action recognition, crowd behavior analysis, markerless motion capture and so on. However, human pose estimation is a challenging task due to the dynamic variations of a human body. Various skin colors and clothes also make the estimation difficult. Especially, pose estimation from a single image requires a model that is robust to occlusion and viewpoint variations.

Recently, 2D human pose estimation achieved a great success with convolutional neural networks (CNNs) [1–3]. Strong representation power and the ability to disentangle underlying factors of variation are characteristics of CNNs that enable learning discriminative features automatically [4] and show superior performance to the methods based on hand-crafted features. On the other hands, 3D human pose estimation using CNNs has not been studied thoroughly compared to the 2D cases. Estimating a 3D human pose from a single image is more

© Springer International Publishing Switzerland 2016
G. Hua and H. Jégou (Eds.): ECCV 2016 Workshops, Part III, LNCS 9915, pp. 156–169, 2016.
DOI: 10.1007/978-3-319-49409-8_15

challenging than 2D cases due to the lack of depth information. However, CNN can be a powerful framework for learning discriminative image features and estimating 3D poses from them. In the case where the target object is fixed such as human body, it is able to learn useful features directly from images without keypoint matching step in the typical 3D reconstruction tasks.

Though recent algorithms that are based on CNNs for 3D human pose estimation have been proposed [5–7], they do not make use of 2D pose information which can provide additional information for 3D pose estimation. From 2D pose information, undesirable 3D joint positions which generate unnatural human pose may be discarded. Therefore, if the information that contains the 2D position of each joint in the input image is used, the results of 3D pose estimation can be improved.

In this paper, we propose a simple yet powerful 3D human pose estimation framework based on the regression of joint positions using CNNs. We introduce two strategies to improve the regression results from the baseline CNNs. Firstly, not only the image features but also 2D joint classification results are used as input features for 3D pose estimation. This scheme successfully incorporates the correlation between 2D and 3D poses. Secondly, rather than estimating relative positions with respect to only one root joint, we estimated the relative 3D positions with respect to multiple joints. This scheme effectively reduces the error of the joints that are far from the root joint. Experimental results validate the proposed framework significantly improves the baseline method and achieves comparable performance to the state-of-the-art methods on Human 3.6m dataset [8] without utilizing the temporal information.

The rest of the paper is organized as follows. Related works are reviewed in Sect. 2. The structure of CNNs used in this paper and two key ideas of our method, (1) the integration of 2D joint classification results into 3D pose estimation and (2) multiple 3D pose regression from various root nodes, are explained in Sect. 3. Details of implementation and training procedures are explained in Sect. 4. Experimental results are illustrated in Sect. 5, and finally conclusions are made in Sect. 6.

2 Related Work

Human pose estimation has been a fundamental task since early computer vision literature, and numerous researches have been conducted on both 2D and 3D human pose estimation. In this section, we will cover both 2D and 3D human pose estimation methods focusing on the CNN-based methods.

Early works for 2D human pose estimation which are based on deformable parts model [9], pictorial structure [10–12], or poselets [13] train the relationship between body appearance and body joints using hand-crafted features. Recently proposed CNN based methods drastically improve the performance over the previous hand-crafted feature based methods. DeepPose [1] used CNN-based structure to regress joint locations with multiple iterations. Firstly, it predicts an initial pose using holistic view and refine the currently predicted pose using relevant parts of the image. Fan et al. [14] integrated both the local part appearance and the holistic view of an image using dual-source CNN. Convolutional pose machine [3] is a systematic approach to improve prediction of each stage. Each stage operates a CNN which accepts both the original image and confidence maps from preceding stages as an input. The performance is improved by combining the joint prediction results from the previous step with features from CNN. Carreira et al. [2] proposed a self-correcting method by a top-down feedback. It iteratively learns a human pose using a self-correcting CNN model which gradually improves the initial result by feeding back error predictions. Chu et al. [15] proposed an end-to-end learning system which captures the relationships among feature maps of joints. Geometrical transform kernels are introduced to learn features and their relationship jointly.

Similar to the 2D case, early stage of 3D human pose estimation is also based on the low-level features such as local shape context [16] or segmentation results [17]. With the extracted features, 3D pose estimation is formulated as a regression problem using relevance vector machines [16], structured SVMs [17], or random forest classifiers [18]. Recently, CNNs have drew a lot of attentions also for the 3D human pose estimation tasks. Since search space in 3D is much larger than 2D image space, 3D human pose estimation is often formulated as a regression problem rather than a classification task. Li and Chan [5] firstly used CNNs to learn 3D human pose directly from input images. Relative 3D position to the parent joint is learned by CNNs via regression. They also used 2D part detectors of each joints in a sliding window fashion. They found that loss function which combines 2D joint classification and 3D joint regression helps to improve the 3D pose estimation results. Li et al. [6] improved the performance of 3D pose estimation by integrating a structured learning framework into CNNs. Recently, Tekin et al. [7] proposed a structured prediction framework which learns 3D pose representations using an auto-encoder. Temporal information from video sequences also helps to predict more accurate pose estimation result. Zhou et al. [19] used the result of 2D pose estimation to reconstruct a 3D pose. They represented a 3D pose as a weighted sum of shape bases similar to typical non-rigid structure from motion, and they designed an EM-algorithm which formulates the 3D pose as a latent variable when 2D pose estimation results are available. The method achieved the state-of-the-art performance for 3D human pose estimation when combined with 2D pose predictions learned from CNN. Tekin et al. [20] used multiple consecutive frames to build a spatio-temporal features, and the features are fed to a deep neural network regressor to estimate the 3D pose.

The method proposed in this paper aims to provide an end-to-end learning framework to estimate 3D structure of a human body from a single image. Similar to [5], 3D and 2D pose information are jointly learned in a single CNN. Unlike the previous works, we directly propagate the 2D classification results to the 3D pose regressors inside the CNNs. Using additional information such as 2D classification results and the relative distance from multiple joints, we improve the performance of 3D human pose estimation over the baseline method.

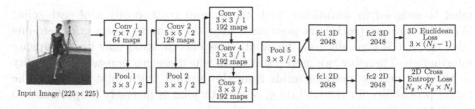

Fig. 1. The baseline structure of CNN used in this paper. Convolutional and pooling layers are shared for both 2D and 3D losses, and the losses are attached to different fully connected layers.

3 3D-2D Joint Estimation of Human Body Using CNN

The task of 3D human pose estimation is defined as predicting the 3D joint positions of a human body. Specifically, we estimate the relative 3D position of each joint with respect to the root joint. The number of joints N_j is set to 17 in this paper according to the dataset used in the experiment. The key idea of our method is to train CNN which performs 3D pose estimation using both image features from the input image and 2D pose information retrieved from the same CNN. In other words, the proposed CNN is trained for both 2D joint classification and 3D joint regression tasks simultaneously. Details of each part is explained in the following subsections.

3.1 Structure of the Baseline CNN

The CNN used in this experiment consists of five convolutional layers, three pooling layers, two parallel sets of two fully connected layers, and loss layers for 2D and 3D pose estimation tasks. The CNN accepts a 225×225 sized image as an input. The sizes and the numbers of filters as well as the strides are specified in Fig. 1. The filter sizes of convolutional and pooling layers are the same as those of ZFnet [21], but we reduced the number of feature maps to make the network smaller.

Joint optimization using both 3D and 2D information helps CNN to learn more meaningful features than the optimization using 3D regression alone. Li et al. [5] trained a CNN both for 2D joint detection task and for 3D pose regression task. Since both tasks share the same convolutional layers, features that are useful for estimating both 2D and 3D positions of joints in an image are learned in convolutional layers. Following the idea, we also used both 2D and 3D loss functions in the CNN. Convolutional layers are shared, and the feature maps after the last pooling layer are connected to two different fully connected layers, each of which is connected to 2D loss function and 3D loss function respectively (See Fig. 1).

We formulated 2D pose estimation as a classification problem. For the 2D classification task, we divided an input image into $N_g \times N_g$ grids and treat each grid as a separate class, which results in N_g^2 classes per joint. The ground truth label is assigned in accordance with the ground truth position of each joint. When the ground truth joint position is near the boundary of a grid, zero-one labeling that is typically used for multi-class classification may give unprecise information. Therefore, we used a soft label which assigns non-zero probability to the four nearest neighbor grids from the ground truth joint position. The target probability for the ith grid g_i of the jth joint is inversely proportional to the distance from the ground truth position, i.e.,

$$\hat{p}_j(g_i) = \frac{d^{-1}(\hat{\mathbf{y}}_j, \mathbf{c}_i)I(g_i)}{\sum_{k=1}^{N_g^2} d^{-1}(\hat{\mathbf{y}}_j, \mathbf{c}_k)I(g_k)}, \tag{1}$$

where $d^{-1}(\mathbf{x}, \mathbf{y})$ is the inverse of the Euclidean distance between the point $\mathbf{x}$ and $\mathbf{y}$ in the 2D pixel space, $\hat{\mathbf{y}}_j$ is the ground truth position of the jth joint in the image, and $\mathbf{c}_i$ is the center of the grid g_i. $I(g_i)$ is an indicator function that is equal to 1 if the grid g_i is one of the four nearest neighbors, i.e.,

$$\mathbf{I}(g_i) = \begin{cases} 1 & \text{if } d(\hat{\mathbf{y}}_j, \mathbf{c}_i) < w_g \\ 0 & \text{otherwise}, \end{cases} \tag{2}$$

where w_g is the width of a grid. Hence, higher probability is assigned to the grid closer to the ground truth joint position, and $\hat{p}_j(g_i)$ is normalized so that the sum of the class probabilities is equal to 1. Finally, the objective of the 2D classification task for the jth joint is to minimize the following cross entropy loss function.

$$\mathcal{L}_{2D}(j) = -\sum_{i=1}^{N_g^2} \hat{p}_j(g_i) \log p_j(g_i), \tag{3}$$

where $p_j(g_i)$ is the probability that comes from the softmax output of the CNN.

On the other hand, estimating 3D position of joints is formulated as a regression task. Since the search space is much larger than the 2D case, it is undesirable to solve 3D pose estimation as a classification task. The 3D loss function is designed as a square of the Euclidean distance between the prediction and the ground truth. We estimate 3D position of each joint relative to the root node. Hence, the loss function for the jth joint when the root node is the rth joint becomes

$$\mathcal{L}_{3D}(j, r) = \left\| \mathbf{R_j} - (\hat{\mathbf{J}}_\mathbf{j} - \hat{\mathbf{J}}_\mathbf{r}) \right\|^2, \tag{4}$$

where $\mathbf{R_j}$ is the predicted relative 3D position of the jth joint from the root node, $\hat{\mathbf{J}}_\mathbf{j}$ is the ground truth 3D position of the jth joint, and $\hat{\mathbf{J}}_\mathbf{r}$ is that of the root node. The overall cost function of the CNN combines (3) and (4) with weights, i.e.,

$$\mathcal{L}_{all} = \lambda_{2D} \sum_{j=1}^{N_j} \mathcal{L}_{2D}(j) + \lambda_{3D} \sum_{j \neq r}^{N_j} \mathcal{L}_{3D}(j, r). \tag{5}$$

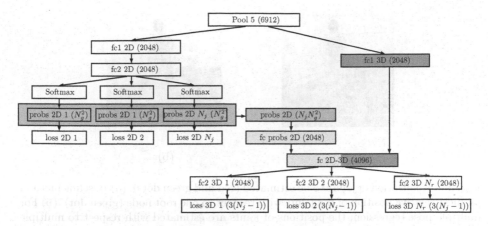

Fig. 2. Structure of fully connected layers and loss functions in the proposed CNN. The numbers in parentheses indicate the dimensions of the corresponding output feature vectors.

3.2 3D Joint Regression with 2D Classification Features

In the baseline architecture in Fig. 1, 2D and 3D losses are separated with different fully connected layers. Though convolutional layers learn features relevant to both 2D and 3D pose estimation thanks to the shared convolutional layers, the probability distribution that comes from 2D classification may give more stable and meaningful information in estimating 3D pose. The joint locations in an image are usually a strong cue for guessing 3D pose. To exploit 2D classification result as a feature for the 3D pose estimation, we concatenate the outputs of softmax in the 2D classification task with the outputs of the fully connected layers in the 3D loss part. The proposed structure after the last pooling layer is shown in Fig. 2. First, the 2D classification result is concatenated (*probs 2D* layer in Fig. 2) and passes the fully connected layer (*fc probs 2D*). Then, the feature vectors from 2D and 3D part are concatenated (*fc 2D-3D*), which is used for 3D pose estimation task. Note that the error from the *fc probs 2D* layer is not back-propagated to the *probs 2D* layer to ensure that layers used for the 2D classification are trained only by the 2D loss part. The idea of using 2D classification result as an input for another task is similar to [3], which repeatedly uses the 2D classification result as an input by concatenating it with feature maps from CNN. Unlike [3], we simply vectorized the softmax result to produce $N_g \times N_g \times N_j$ feature vector rather than convolving the probability map with features in the convolutional layers.

The proposed framework can be trained end-to-end via back-propagation algorithm. Because 2D classification will give an inaccurate prediction in the early stage of training, it is possible that 3D regression may be disturbed by the classification result. However, we empirically found that 3D loss converges successfully, and the performance of 3D pose estimation improves as well, as explained in Sect. 5.

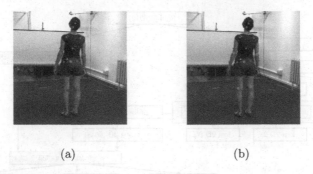

(a)   (b)

Fig. 3. Visualization of joints to be estimated (red and green dots). (a) Baseline method predicts relative position of the joints with respect to one root node (green dot). (b) For multiple pose regression, the positions of joints are estimated with respect to multiple root nodes (green dots) (Color figure online).

3.3   Multiple 3D Pose Regression from Different Root Nodes

In the baseline architecture, we predicted the relative 3D position of each joint with respect to only one root node which is around the position of the hip. When joints such as wrists or ankles are far from the root node, the accuracy of regression may be degraded. Li et al. [5] designed a 3D regression loss to estimate the relative position between each joint and its parent joint. However, errors may be accumulated when intermediate joint produces inaccurate result in this scheme. As an alternative solution, we estimate the relative position over multiple joints. We denote the number of selected root nodes as N_r. For the experiments in this paper, we set $N_r = 6$ and selected six joints so that most joints can either be the root node or their neighbor nodes. The selected joints are visualized in Fig. 3(b). Therefore, there are six 3D regression losses in the network, which is illustrated in Fig. 2. Then, the overall loss becomes

$$\mathcal{L}_{all} = \lambda_{2D} \sum_{j=1}^{N_j} \mathcal{L}_{2D}(j) + \lambda_{3D} \sum_{r \in \mathbf{R}} \sum_{j \neq r}^{N_j} \mathcal{L}_{3D}(j,r), \tag{6}$$

where $\mathbf{R}$ is the set containing the joint indices that are used as root nodes. When the 3D losses share the same fully connected layers, the trained model outputs the same pose estimation results across all joints. To break this symmetry, we put the fully connected layers for each 3D losses (*fc2 3D* layers in Fig. 2).

At the test time, all the pose estimation results are translated so that the mean of each pose becomes zero. Final prediction is generated by averaging the translated results. In other words, the 3D position of the jth joint $\mathbf{X}_j$ is calculated as

$$\mathbf{X}_j = \frac{\sum_{r \in \mathbf{R}} \mathbf{X}_j^{(r)}}{N_r}, \tag{7}$$

where $\mathbf{X}_j^{(r)}$ is the predicted 3D position of the jth joint when the rth joint is set to a root node.

4   Implementation Details

The proposed method is implemented using Caffe framework [22]. Batch normalization [23] is applied to all convolutional and fully connected layers. Also, drpoout [24] is applied to every fully connected layers with drop probability of 0.3. Stochastic gradient descent of batch size 128 is used for optimization. Initial learning rate is set to 0.01, and it is decreased by a factor of 0.5 for every 4 epochs. The optimization is finished after 28 epochs. The momentum and the weight decay parameters are set to 0.9 and 0.001 respectively. The weighting parameter λ_{2D} and λ_{3D} are initially set to 0.1 and 0.5 respectively. λ_{2D} is decreased to 0.01 after 16 epochs because we believe that 2D pose information plays an important role in learning informative features especially in the early stage of training.

Input images are cropped using the segmentation information provided with the dataset so that a person is located around the center of an image. The cropped image is resized to 250×250. We randomly cropped the resized image into an image of 225×225 size, then it is fed into the CNN as an input image. During the test time, only the center crop is evaluated for the pose prediction. Data augmentation based on the principal component analysis of training images [25] is also applied. N_g is set to 16, so the input image is divided into 256 square grids for 2D loss calculation. N_r is set to 6, and the position of the root nodes are illustrated in Fig. 3(b).

For the ground truth 3D pose that is used in the training step, we firstly translated the joints to make the shape to be zero mean. Then, we scaled the 3D shape so that the Frobenius norm of the 3D shape becomes 1. Since different person has different height and size, we believe that the normalization helps to reduce ambiguity of scale and to predict scale-invariant poses. During the testing phase, scale should be recovered to evaluate the performance of the algorithm. Similar to [19], we infer the scale using the training data. The lengths of all connected joints from the training set are averaged. The scale of the result from the test data is determined so that the length of connected joints in the estimated shape is equal to the pre-calculated average length. Since the lengths for arms and legs from the estimated shape often have a large variation, we only used the length of joints in the torso which is stable in most cases.

5   Experimental Results

We used Human 3.6m dataset [8] to evaluate our method and compared the proposed method with the other 3D human pose estimation algorithms. The dataset provides 3D human pose information acquired by a motion capture system with synchronized RGB images. It consists of 15 different sequences which contain specific actions such as discussion, eating, walking, and so on. There are 7 different persons who perform all 15 actions. We trained and tested each action individually. Following the previous works on the dataset [5,19], we used 5 subjects (S1, S5, S6, S7, S8) as a training set, and 2 subjects (S9, S11) as

Table 1. Quantitative results on Human 3.6m dataset. The best and the second best methods for each sequence are marked as (1) and (2) respectively.

	Directions	Discussion	Eating	Greeting	Phoning	Photo
LinKDE [8]	132.71	183.55	132.37	164.39	162.12	205.94
Li and Chan [5]	-	148.79	104.01	127.17	-	189.08
Li et al. [6]	-	136.88	96.94	124.74	-	168.68
Tekin et al. [7]	-	129.06	91.43	121.68	-	162.17
Tekin et al. [20]	102.41	147.72	**88.83**$^{(2)}$	125.28	118.02	182.73
Zhou et al. [19]	**87.36**$^{(1)}$	**109.31**$^{(1)}$	**87.05**$^{(1)}$	**103.16**$^{(1)}$	**116.18**$^{(2)}$	**143.32**$^{(1)}$
Our method	**100.34**$^{(2)}$	**116.19**$^{(2)}$	89.96	**116.49**$^{(2)}$	**115.34**$^{(1)}$	**149.55**$^{(2)}$
	Posing	Purchases	Sitting	Sitting down	Smoking	Waiting
LinKDE [8]	150.61	171.31	151.57	243.03	162.14	170.69
Li and Chan [5]	-	-	-	-	-	-
Li et al. [6]	-	-	-	-	-	-
Tekin et al. [7]	-	-	-	-	-	-
Tekin et al. [20]	**112.38**$^{(2)}$	129.17	138.89	224.90	118.42	138.75
Zhou et al. [19]	**106.88**$^{(1)}$	**99.78**$^{(1)}$	**124.52**$^{(1)}$	**199.23**$^{(2)}$	**107.42**$^{(2)}$	**118.09**$^{(1)}$
Our method	117.57	**106.94**$^{(2)}$	**137.21**$^{(2)}$	**190.82**$^{(1)}$	**105.78**$^{(1)}$	**125.12**$^{(2)}$
	Walk dog	Walking	Walk together	Average		
LinKDE [8]	177.13	96.60	127.88	162.14		
Li and Chan [5]	146.59	77.60	-	-		
Li et al. [6]	132.17	69.97	-	-		
Tekin et al. [7]	130.53	65.75	-	-		
Tekin et al. [20]	**126.29**$^{(2)}$	**55.07**$^{(1)}$	**65.76**$^{(1)}$	124.97		
Zhou et al. [19]	**114.23**$^{(1)}$	79.39	97.70	**113.01**$^{(1)}$		
Our method	131.90	**62.64**$^{(2)}$	**96.18**$^{(2)}$	**117.34**$^{(2)}$		

a test set. The training and the testing procedures are conducted on a single PC with a Titan X GPU. Training procedure takes 7–10 h for one action sequence depending on the number of training images. For the evaluation metric, we used the mean per joint position error (MPJPE).

First, we compared the performance of our method with the conventional methods on Human 3.6m dataset. Table 1 shows the MPJPE of our method and the previous works. The smallest and the second smallest errors for each sequence are marked. Our method achieves the best performance in 3 sequences and shows the second best performance in 9 sequences. Note that the methods of [20] and [19] make use of temporal information from multiple frames. Meanwhile, our method produce a 3D pose from a single image. Our method is also beneficial against [20] and [19] in terms of running time and the simplicity of the algorithm since the estimation is done by a forward pass of the CNN and simple averaging. Moreover, from Table 1, it is justified that our method outperforms the CNN based methods that predict 3D pose from a single image [5–7].

Table 2. Comparison of our method with the baseline.

	Discussion	Eating	Greeting	Phoning	Photo	Walking
Baseline CNN	125.45	95.21	120.69	119.66	153.76	72.55
Multi-reg	122.71	94.67	119.70	119.25	153.54	71.19
2D-cls	118.19	91.39	118.19	115.84	149.97	64.27
Multi-reg+2D-cls	**116.19**	**89.96**	**116.49**	**115.34**	**149.55**	**62.64**

Next, we measured the effect of our contribution, (1) the integration of 2D classification results and (2) regression from multiple root nodes, by comparing their performance with the baseline CNN. Note that the 2D classification loss is also used in the baseline CNN. The difference of the baseline CNN is that 2D classification results are not propagated to the 3D loss part, i.e., *probs 2D*, *fc probs 2D* and *fc 2D-3D* layers in Fig. 2 are deleted in the baseline CNN. The results are shown in Table 2. Multiple regression from different root nodes and the integration of 2D classification results are denoted as *Multi-reg* and *2D-cls* respectively. Both modifications improve the result over the baseline CNN in all tested sequences. 2D classification integration showed larger error reduction rate than the multiple regression strategy, which proves that the 2D classification information is indeed a useful feature for 3D pose estimation. Multiple regression can be considered as an ensemble of different estimation results, which improves the overall performance. It can be found that the error reduction rate for the case that both 2D classification result integration and multiple regression are applied is slightly bigger than the sum of the reduction rates when they are individually applied in most sequences. Since each 3D pose regressor takes advantage of 2D classification feature, there is a synergy effect between the two schemes.

We also analyzed the effect of integrating 2D classification result in terms of 3D losses. Training losses are measured every 50 iterations and testing losses are measured every 4 epochs. The results on the Walking sequence are illustrated in Fig. 4. For the training data, loss is slightly smaller when 2D classification

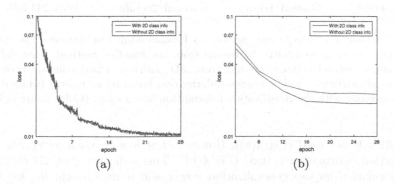

(a)   (b)

Fig. 4. The 3D losses of Walking sequence with and without 2D classification result integration. (a) Losses for training data. (b) Losses for test data.

Input Image   Ground Truth   Without 2D info   With 2D info

Fig. 5. Qualitative results of our method on Human 3.6m test dataset. The estimation results are compared with the results from the baseline method. First column: input images. Second column: ground truth 3D position. Third column: pose estimation result without 2D classification information integration. Fourth column: pose estimation result with 2D classification information integration. (Color figure online)

information is not used (Fig. 4(a)). However, test loss is much lower when 2D classification information is used (Fig. 4(b)). This indicates that 2D classification information impose generalization power and reduce overfitting for CNN regressor. Since the 2D joint probabilities provide more abstracted and subject-independent information compared to the features obtained from an image, the

CNN model is able to learn representations that are robust to variability of subjects in the image.

Finally, we illustrated qualitative results of our method in Fig. 5. Input images, ground truth poses, and the estimation results with and without 2D classification information are visualized. Different colors are used to distinguish the left and right sides of human bodies. It can be found that 2D pose estimation results help reducing the error of 3D pose estimation. While the CNN which does not use 2D classification information gives poor results, the estimated results are much more improved when 2D classification information is used for 3D pose estimation.

6 Conclusions

In this paper, we propose novel strategies which improve the performance of the CNN that estimates 3D human pose. By reusing 2D joint classification result, the relationship between 2D pose and 3D pose is implicitly learned during the training phase. Moreover, multiple regression results with different root nodes gives an effect of ensemble learning. When both strategies are combined, 3D pose estimation results are significantly improved and showed comparable performance to the state-of-the-art methods without exploiting any temporal information of video sequences.

We expect that the performance can be further improved by incorporating temporal information to the CNN by applying the concepts of recurrent neural network or 3D convolution [26]. Also, efficient aligning method for multiple regression results may boost the accuracy of pose estimation.

Acknowledgement. This work was supported by Ministry of Culture, Sports and Tourism (MCST) and Korea Creative Content Agency (KOCCA) in the Culture Technology (CT) Research & Development Program 2016.

References

1. Toshev, A., Szegedy, C.: Deeppose: human pose estimation via deep neural networks. In: Proceedings of the IEEE Conference on Computer Vision and Pattern Recognition, pp. 1653–1660 (2014)
2. Carreira, J., Agrawal, P., Fragkiadaki, K., Malik, J.: Human pose estimation with iterative error feedback. arXiv preprint arXiv:1507.06550 (2015)
3. Wei, S.E., Ramakrishna, V., Kanade, T., Sheikh, Y.: Convolutional pose machines. arXiv preprint arXiv:1602.00134 (2016)
4. Bengio, Y.: Learning deep architectures for AI. Found. Trends® Mach. Learn. **2**(1), 1–127 (2009)
5. Li, S., Chan, A.B.: 3D human pose estimation from monocular images with deep convolutional neural network. In: Cremers, D., Reid, I., Saito, H., Yang, M.-H. (eds.) ACCV 2014. LNCS, vol. 9004, pp. 332–347. Springer, Heidelberg (2015). doi:10.1007/978-3-319-16808-1_23

6. Li, S., Zhang, W., Chan, A.B.: Maximum-margin structured learning with deep networks for 3D human pose estimation. In: Proceedings of the IEEE International Conference on Computer Vision, pp. 2848–2856 (2015)
7. Tekin, B., Katircioglu, I., Salzmann, M., Lepetit, V., Fua, P.: Structured prediction of 3D human pose with deep neural networks. arXiv preprint arXiv:1605.05180 (2016)
8. Ionescu, C., Papava, D., Olaru, V., Sminchisescu, C.: Human3.6M: large scale datasets and predictive methods for 3D human sensing in natural environments. IEEE Trans. Pattern Anal. Mach. Intell. **36**(7), 1325–1339 (2014)
9. Felzenszwalb, P.F., Huttenlocher, D.P.: Pictorial structures for object recognition. Int. J. Comput. Vision **61**(1), 55–79 (2005)
10. Andriluka, M., Roth, S., Schiele, B.: Pictorial structures revisited: people detection and articulated pose estimation. In: IEEE Conference on Computer Vision and Pattern Recognition, CVPR 2009, pp. 1014–1021. IEEE (2009)
11. Dantone, M., Gall, J., Leistner, C., Van Gool, L.: Human pose estimation using body parts dependent joint regressors. In: Proceedings of the IEEE Conference on Computer Vision and Pattern Recognition, pp. 3041–3048 (2013)
12. Yang, Y., Ramanan, D.: Articulated pose estimation with flexible mixtures-of-parts. In: 2011 IEEE Conference on Computer Vision and Pattern Recognition (CVPR), pp. 1385–1392. IEEE (2011)
13. Bourdev, L., Malik, J.: Poselets: body part detectors trained using 3D human pose annotations. In: 2009 IEEE 12th International Conference on Computer Vision, pp. 1365–1372. IEEE (2009)
14. Fan, X., Zheng, K., Lin, Y., Wang, S.: Combining local appearance and holistic view: dual-source deep neural networks for human pose estimation. In: 2015 IEEE Conference on Computer Vision and Pattern Recognition (CVPR), pp. 1347–1355. IEEE (2015)
15. Chu, X., Ouyang, W., Li, H., Wang, X.: Structured feature learning for pose estimation, June 2016
16. Agarwal, A., Triggs, B.: Recovering 3D human pose from monocular images. IEEE Trans. Pattern Anal. Mach. Intell. **28**(1), 44–58 (2006)
17. Ionescu, C., Li, F., Sminchisescu, C.: Latent structured models for human pose estimation. In: 2011 International Conference on Computer Vision, pp. 2220–2227. IEEE (2011)
18. Shotton, J., Sharp, T., Kipman, A., Fitzgibbon, A., Finocchio, M., Blake, A., Cook, M., Moore, R.: Real-time human pose recognition in parts from single depth images. Commun. ACM **56**(1), 116–124 (2013)
19. Zhou, X., Zhu, M., Leonardos, S., Derpanis, K.G., Daniilidis, K.: Sparseness meets deepness: 3D human pose estimation from monocular video. In: The IEEE Conference on Computer Vision and Pattern Recognition (CVPR), June 2016
20. Tekin, B., Rozantsev, A., Lepetit, V., Fua, P.: Direct prediction of 3D body poses from motion compensated sequences. In: The IEEE Conference on Computer Vision and Pattern Recognition (CVPR), June 2016
21. Zeiler, M.D., Fergus, R.: Visualizing and understanding convolutional networks. In: Fleet, D., Pajdla, T., Schiele, B., Tuytelaars, T. (eds.) ECCV 2014. LNCS, vol. 8689, pp. 818–833. Springer, Heidelberg (2014). doi:10.1007/978-3-319-10590-1_53
22. Jia, Y., Shelhamer, E., Donahue, J., Karayev, S., Long, J., Girshick, R., Guadarrama, S., Darrell, T.: Caffe: convolutional architecture for fast feature embedding. arXiv preprint arXiv:1408.5093 (2014)

23. Ioffe, S., Szegedy, C.: Batch normalization: accelerating deep network training by reducing internal covariate shift. In: Proceedings of The 32nd International Conference on Machine Learning, pp. 448–456 (2015)
24. Srivastava, N., Hinton, G.E., Krizhevsky, A., Sutskever, I., Salakhutdinov, R.: Dropout: a simple way to prevent neural networks from overfitting. J. Mach. Learn. Res. **15**(1), 1929–1958 (2014)
25. Krizhevsky, A., Sutskever, I., Hinton, G.E.: Imagenet classification with deep convolutional neural networks. In: Advances in Neural Information Processing Systems, pp. 1097–1105 (2012)
26. Tran, D., Bourdev, L., Fergus, R., Torresani, L., Paluri, M.: Learning spatiotemporal features with 3D convolutional networks. In: 2015 IEEE International Conference on Computer Vision (ICCV), pp. 4489–4497. IEEE (2015)

Overcoming Occlusion with Inverse Graphics

Pol Moreno[1]([⊠]), Christopher K.I. Williams[1], Charlie Nash[1],
and Pushmeet Kohli[2]

[1] School of Informatics, University of Edinburgh, Edinburgh, Scotland
p.moreno-comellas@sms.ed.ac.uk, ckiw@inf.ed.ac.uk, charlie.nash@ed.ac.uk
[2] Microsoft Research, Redmond, USA
pkohli@microsoft.com

Abstract. Scene understanding tasks such as the prediction of object
pose, shape, appearance and illumination are hampered by the occlusions
often found in images. We propose a vision-as-inverse-graphics approach
to handle these occlusions by making use of a graphics renderer in combination with a robust generative model (GM). Since searching over scene
factors to obtain the best match for an image is very inefficient, we make
use of a *recognition model* (RM) trained on synthetic data to initialize
the search. This paper addresses two issues: (i) We study how the inferences are affected by the degree of occlusion of the foreground object,
and show that a robust GM which includes an outlier model to account
for occlusions works significantly better than a non-robust model. (ii) We
characterize the performance of the RM and the gains that can be made
by refining the search using the GM, using a new dataset that includes
background clutter and occlusions. We find that pose and shape are predicted very well by the RM, but appearance and especially illumination
less so. However, accuracy on these latter two factors can be clearly
improved with the generative model.

Keywords: Vision-as-inverse-graphics · Scene understanding ·
Occlusion

1 Introduction

Computer vision is fundamentally an ill-posed and extremely complex problem:
there are many different scene configurations that can produce a given image,
and many factors of variability. An old idea is to use a model of how images are
generated to solve the inverse process, which can also be seen as an instance of
analysis-by-synthesis, see e.g. [32]. In this work we make use of this idea, which
we call vision-as-inverse-graphics, in order to extract detailed descriptions of an
object in an indoor scene. Examples of these descriptions (or factors) include the
object's shape and appearance, pose, and the illumination of the scene. Stevens
and Beveridge [27] is an early example of combining vision and graphics.

Electronic supplementary material The online version of this chapter (doi:10.
1007/978-3-319-49409-8_16) contains supplementary material, which is available to
authorized users.

© Springer International Publishing Switzerland 2016
G. Hua and H. Jégou (Eds.): ECCV 2016 Workshops, Part III, LNCS 9915, pp. 170–185, 2016.
DOI: 10.1007/978-3-319-49409-8_16

Inverse-graphics is an elegant solution in which these factors are used as the variables that explain the generation of images. However, searching for the descriptions that best explain an image is a challenging task due to their high dimensionality, thus we make use of discriminative models, which we will call recognition models (RMs), as a way of cutting down the search (see e.g. Dayan et al. [6] and Williams et al. [28]). Combining the bottom-up and top-down information flows is a key aspect in the design of our solution, see Fig. 1. Our goal is to extract fine-grained descriptions that can be used for many different tasks, such as robotic systems that need to interact with the world.

Recent work (see e.g. Yildirim et al. [31]) has made some exploration of the combination of generative and recognition models for scene understanding. However, the experiments to date have typically been made on "clean" scenes which do not contain occluding objects and background clutter. Our contributions are:

- We study how the inferences are affected by the degree of occlusion of the foreground object, and show that a robust generative model which includes an outlier model to account for occlusions works significantly better than a non-robust Gaussian model.
- We characterize the performance of the recognition model and the gains that can be made by refining the search using a generative model. We find that pose and shape are predicted very well by the RM, but appearance and especially illumination less so. However, accuracy on these latter two factors can be clearly improved with the generative model.
- Production of a new synthetic dataset with which one can evaluate the performance of the models with variation across pose, shape, appearance, complex illumination (extracted from a collection of indoor environment maps), a diverse set of indoor scene backgrounds, and with the foreground object being partially occluded. This goes beyond prior work (e.g. [31]) which only explores shape, appearance and limited lighting variation.

The structure of the paper is as follows: we first describe the **generative model** as a differentiable renderer (see Sect. 2). The idea is to make use of approximate gradients that describe how the image intensities change with respect to the scene factors, leading to efficient search over these. The robust and Gaussian likelihood models are also explained here. The **recognition model** (see Sect. 3) is trained discriminatively to predict the scene factors of interest. In order to do this we have created a **synthetic dataset** of indoor scenes in which we can generate novel instantiations of object classes of interest, as explained in Sect. 4. The experimental setup and results are given in Sect. 5.

1.1 Related Work

Gradient Based Approaches. The problem of inferring the physical world that gave rise to a given image is a long-standing and fundamental problem in computer vision. One recent example of this reconstructive paradigm is the work of Barron and Malik [1] where depth maps, reflectance maps, and illumination

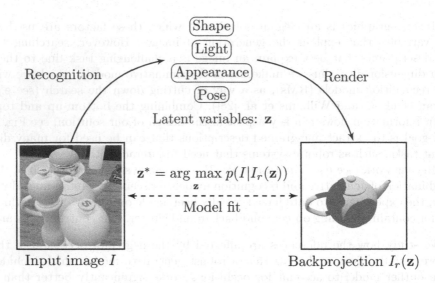

Fig. 1. Illustration of our inverse-graphics solution. Given an image, the recognition models of shape, lighting, appearance and pose initialize the latent variables. Then, the differentiable renderer generates an image which is fitted by optimizing over the latent variables $\mathbf{z}$ that best match the input image, i.e. $\mathbf{z}^* = \arg \max\limits_{\mathbf{z}} p(I_{GT}|I_r(\mathbf{z}))$. Detected occlusion mask is illustrated with red (Color figure online)

models are recovered from an input image by optimizing a data fit criterion and making use of prior distributions. Another nice example is the work of Loper and Black [21] as applied to the problem of fitting an articulated human body model to Kinect data.

Hybrid Generative-Discriminative Architectures. In the above papers the search over the latent factors of variation is made directly using gradient-based optimization methods. However, it is also possible to make use of a recognition model to predict these factors bottom-up. One example is the algorithm behind Kinect [26], which is shown to be a key component of efficiently estimating human pose.

The work of Jampani et al. [15] and Kulkarni et al. [18] makes use of bottom-up sampling probability distribution proposals to get an approximation of the posterior probability of the latent variables more efficiently for black-box renderers. Both papers show improved sampling performance using these data-driven proposals.

Krull et al. [17] work on estimating 6D pose from RGB-D images. Rather than explicitly modelling occlusions they learn an energy function that compares the rendered model and the input image (which may contain occlusions) using a convolutional neural network. At inference time a search is carried out in 6D pose space to minimize the energy function. Note that this work is restricted to inference of pose, while we also address object shape, appearance and illumination factors.

Perhaps the most closely related work to ours is that of Yildirim et al. [31] which makes use of both a recognition model and a generative model. They use the morphable face model [5] and explore variation in shape, texture, pose, and lighting direction. In our work we make use of more complex illumination (extracted from a collection of indoor environment maps), and also include scene backgrounds and foreground occlusions. We also analyze the performance of the recognition model with respect to the different factors. A further difference is that Yildirim et al. [31] make use of MCMC methods for inference, while we use local search using a differentiable renderer.

The Picture framework of [20] provides a general probabilistic programming framework for specifying scene understanding problems and general-purpose inference machinery, and applies it to a number of example problems. Rather than generating pixels it uses a "representation layer" of features to assess the match of an input image and the rendered scene, using a likelihood-free method. Note, however, that this means there is a choice of representation that needs to be made (by hand) in order to use the framework. Also, Picture does not explicitly handle occlusions, nor complex lighting.

Learning the Generative Model. Another piece of related work is to use a deep learning auto-encoder model for both the recognition model (encoder) and generative model (decoder), as in Kulkarni et al. [19]. This DC-IGN model does not make use of an explicit 3-d graphics model, but rather learns a mapping from the graphics code layer (hidden units) to images in the decoder. This gives a lot of freedom to the model as to how it wishes to represent variation in shape, illumination etc. However, it also means that the effect of e.g. pose variation has to be learned specifically for an object class, rather than being generic geometric knowledge. The ability of DC-IGN to generalize to novel images (e.g. under different rotations) seems to be limited if one looks at the visual quality of its renders. Experiments are again conducted wrt shape, texture, pose, and simple lighting direction variation, without scene backgrounds and foreground occlusions. Note also that the auto-encoder architecture means that there is no scope for refinement of the code predicted by the recognition model, in contrast to our work and that of [31].

The work of Dosovitskiy et al. [8] is somewhat similar to the DC-IGN model in that it learns a "decoder" network from variables representing shape class, pose and other transformations (e.g. in-plane rotation, colour transformations), although there is no corresponding encoder network. Their network shows impressive generalization over the chair class, but is not used to address issues of scene understanding.

2   Generative Models

We first describe how the foreground object is modelled, and then discuss the rendering process and our likelihood models.

2.1   Object Model

The factors that characterize a visual object are the pose, shape, appearance, and the incident illumination. The choice parametrization is a trade-off between its ability to model complex scenes and having a compact representation for efficient search over the latent variables. In this work we use the following:

Shape: We model the shape of a given object class using a deformable mesh characterized by Principal Component Analysis, as used e.g. by Blanz and Vetter [5] for modelling faces.

Pose (2D): We assume the camera is centered on the foreground object at a fixed distance with variable azimuth and elevation. Note that, to a large degree, the shape parameters can model the general scale of our object, thus including a distance variable for the position of the camera is not necessary.

Appearance (3D): A global RGB colour is used for all object vertices, which we also refer to as the albedo. The reflectance function is assumed to be Lambertian, as explained in more detail below.

Illumination (9D): Inverse illumination is known to be an ill-posed problem [22, Chap. 6], with the additional issue that real illumination can be very complex (thus modelled poorly by single directional light sources). We are interested in representations that are practical for our inverse-graphics framework. One of the most natural representations is to project lighting to basis functions such as Spherical Harmonics, see e.g. [23], a technique which is also widely used in computer graphics for efficient approximate rendering of lighting. Other representations include Haar wavelets [25], and so called basis images of the object class illuminated from different light conditions [3]. We use Spherical Harmonics (SH) due to its compact representation and the efficiency at which re-lighting is computed when rotating the light or changing the shape and pose of the modelled objects.

Spherical Harmonics form an orthogonal basis that can be used to approximate complex illumination. For Lambertian reflectance, it can be shown [2] that only 9 components can approximate images of a convex object by at least 99.22%. Lambertian reflectance is a diffuse surface property where the resulting RGB reflectance $\mathbf{r}(\mathbf{x}_i)$ of an incoming light a point $\mathbf{x}_i$ on the surface is given by

$$\mathbf{r}(\mathbf{x}_i) = \mathbf{a}_i \max(\mathbf{n}_i \cdot \mathbf{l_i}, 0), \tag{1}$$

where $\mathbf{a}_i$ is the RGB albedo, $\mathbf{l}_i$ is the incoming light direction and $\mathbf{n}_i$ is the vertex normal at point $\mathbf{x}_i$. Even though real world objects have cast shadows, specularities, and other non-Lambertian factors, our assumption is that a Lambertian approximation is sufficient for a large variety of tasks in inverse-graphics.

2.2   Renderer

We use a graphics renderer as a generative model that takes as input a set of object meshes (which include information of their vertex coordinates, normal vectors, textures and colors) and then generates the renders using OpenGL. Our renderer is based on OpenDR: Differentiable Renderer [21], which we have extended to make it capable of rendering multiple objects and textures, and also modernized its OpenGL back-end in order to support modern graphics features and hardware-accelerated rendering. The main advantage of OpenDR is that it provides approximate derivatives of the image with respect to the latent variables or any variable of interest. The approximation stems from the fact that the rendering function is non-differentiable due to self-occlusion and occlusion across objects. Having derivatives plays a key role in the efficiency of the optimization process as the dimensionality of our latent space increases.

We can think of the cost function of our generative process (i.e. the reconstruction error) in terms of a likelihood function. In this work we explore two possible models over the pixel intensities. Since we are modelling one foreground object, all the rendered pixels that lie outside the object mask are are considered as background and modelled by a uniform distribution. Given an image I, the likelihood of the foreground pixel (fg) intensities are modelled as follows:

- **Gaussian Model:** The simplest case is a Gaussian distribution on the pixel intensities:

$$p(\mathbf{c}_i|\mathbf{z}, fg) = \mathcal{N}(\mathbf{c}_i; \boldsymbol{\mu}_i(\mathbf{z}), \sigma^2 I) \qquad (2)$$

where $\mathbf{c}_i$ is the RGB color at pixel i, $\boldsymbol{\mu}_i(\mathbf{z})$ is the RGB color output of the renderer given scene latent variables $\mathbf{z}$, σ^2 is the spherical variance (assumed to be the same for all pixels), and $\mathcal{N}$ denotes the Gaussian distribution. In terms of the optimization landscape, this is equivalent to using a squared error cost function.

- **Robust Model:** We want our model to tolerate foreground occlusions by using outlier statistics as in Williams and Titsias [29]

$$p(\mathbf{c}_i|\mathbf{z}, fg) = \alpha\mathcal{N}(\mathbf{c}_i; \mu_i(\mathbf{z}), \sigma^2 I) + (1 - \alpha)\mathcal{U}(\mathbf{c}_i)), \qquad (3)$$

where α is the mixing probability of a pixel being unoccluded, and $\mathcal{U}$ is the uniform distribution. Note that we can learn α from our training set by e.g. taking the average of the proportion of unoccluded pixels. Thus, the overall log-likelihood of an image given the scene latent variables $\mathbf{z}$ is given by

$$L = \sum_{i \in fg} \log p(\mathbf{c}_i|\mathbf{z}, fg) + \sum_{j \in bg} \log \mathcal{U}(\mathbf{c}_j). \qquad (4)$$

The pixel-wise outlier model as used above does not impose spatial priors on regions of occlusion. One could enhance this e.g. using Markov random field models on the occlusion labels (see e.g. [11]), at the cost of greater complexity in inference. One could also consider more complex occlusion models that learn the structure of occlusions from data, see e.g. [12]. While Black and Rangarajan [4] propose robust statistical techniques for a number of vision tasks, the advantage of the latent variable formulation of our robust model is that it allows us to explain occlusions by using the posterior probabilities of the foreground/outlier pixel segmentation.

Estimating the latent variables of interest is obtained by initializing the OpenDR input with the estimates of the latent variables given by the recognition model, followed by locally improving its fit using the likelihood function, Eq. 4, subject to the constraint that the PCA coefficients of the shape model lie within ±3 standard deviations of the mean. This is why it is essential that the predictions of the recognition model should lie within the basin of attraction of the generative model.

3   Recognition Model

The choice of the recognition models architecture depends on the task domain and the scene factors we want to infer. For instance, the model can output a single point estimate or take a probabilistic approach; in this work we focus on the former case. Again, we want the estimates of the bottom-up predictions to lie within the basin of attraction of the generative model.

Using the right feature representation of the images is also key to good discriminative performance. After experimenting with a diverse set of features for each type of parameter (e.g. Histogram of Gradients for pose prediction, and different basis expansions for illumination) we found that learning the features from raw images gave the best prediction performance. Therefore, we make use of Convolutional Neural Networks (CNNs) to predict each of the latent variables as these have been key to the success for many computer vision tasks in recent years [16]. The architecture of choice is almost the same in all cases as it showed a good generalization capability: three convolutional layers (64 5 × 5 filters) with max-pooling and two dense hidden layer (with 256 and 32 hidden units each). In the case of pose and shape CNNs, the input is assumed to be grayscale. A dropout rate of 0.5 was used with Nesterov Accelerated Gradient descent with 0.9 momentum.

4   Synthetic Ground-Truth Dataset

Synthetic datasets have been used for a variety of computer vision tasks, see e.g. [26,33]. In order to generate synthetic data for training and evaluation of our method, we use an indoor scene generator based on the dataset of [10]. This consists of 10,000 CAD models they collected and stochastically arranged together in different plausible indoor scenes. Here, we use over 80 different indoor scenes.

In this work we focus on the teapot object class. The reason for choosing teapots is that they are a common object in indoor scenes and have a good degree of variability. However, our stochastic scene generation is not limited to only one type of object, and many different object models can be collected from sources such as the Princeton Modelnet [30] and easily embedded into the scenes.

10 PCA dimensions were chosen so as to capture 90 % of the variation in the training dataset of 23 3D teapot models.

To generate the scenes with complex and varied illumination settings, we collected over 70 complex indoor environment maps (also known as light probes) from different sources, see e.g. [7]. An environment map is the projection of the incident illumination on a point of a scene into e.g. an equirrectangular image. We use these environment maps to render illumination using Spherical Harmonics as in [24]. Since the Lambertian reflectance function acts as a low-pass filter, it effectively removes high-frequency information [2], hence the resulting illuminated objects are perceptually well approximated compared to using the actual environment maps.

The ground-truth of each sample in the dataset is generated by instantiating the teapot object in one of the indoor scenes. This involves sampling the shape parameters from the shape prior, as well as a uniformly sampled object rotation around the Z-axis (up axis). The camera's angles of azimuth and elevation are randomly sampled with a uniform distribution on the upper hemisphere and it is placed at a fixed distance from the object. The scene is then illuminated by one of the environment maps, rotated uniformly along the Z-axis. In total, we produced 10,000 training and 1,000 test images by the above process. We distinguish two different types of rendering methods: a non-photorealistic rendering which does not include global illumination and uses OpenGL, and a photorealistic rendering which uses the unbiased ray-tracer Cycles[1]. The OpenGL rendering is much quicker and we use it to generate the training data. Their width and height are set to 150 by 150 pixels. Figure 2 shows a few examples rendered with Cycles. Figure 2(c) shows the histogram of occlusion levels in our dataset, note how there are occlusions of all levels up to 90 % (it is not useful to have images with occlusions near 100 % for the purpose of training or evaluation). This scene generator and dataset will be made available upon the publication of this work.

5   Experiments

5.1   Experimental Setup

In the following experiment we use a test set which consists of 1000 test samples from our synthetic dataset with different levels of occlusions. These test images are rendered with the unbiased ray-tracer Cycles in order to assess our models using scenes with global illumination which simulate real images illumination. We are interested in understanding the performance of our models (recognition, gaussian and robustified) as the occlusion level is increased. As a reference evaluation, we provide a baseline prediction based on the mean values of the different factors on the training set (mean baseline). The evaluation metrics and optimization procedure for this experiment are explained below.

---

[1] http://www.blender.org/manual/render/cycles/introduction.html.

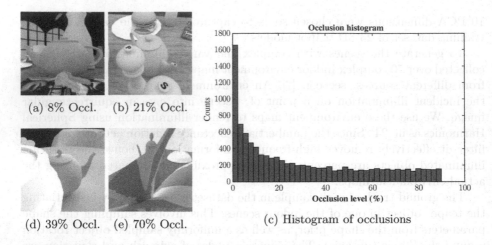

(a) 8% Occl.   (b) 21% Occl.

(d) 39% Occl.   (e) 70% Occl.

(c) Histogram of occlusions

Fig. 2. Examples of our synthetic data-set with different levels of occlusion

Evaluation Metrics. In general, evaluating predictions of the fine-grained scene latent variables (e.g. pose, shape, appearance, illumination) is difficult due to a lack of labelled datasets, but here we have the advantage of having a synthetic dataset in which all these factors are designed to have a rich variability. One way to evaluate the performance of our method is the log-likelihood on the test set. However, that does not give us an easily interpretable quantity. Instead, evaluation is carried out with respect to the predictive performance of the latent variables we are modelling, which have a more intuitive and physical interpretation. We also evaluate how well the unoccluded foreground pixels are predicted.

Choosing the evaluation metric for each of these factors in not necessarily straightforward. For pose azimuth and elevation, we define the errors to be the absolute angular difference for each angle (azimuth and elevation variables range 360 and 90 degrees respectively). Special care needs to be taken to measure the appearance and illumination attributes as they interact with each other multiplicatively, see Eq. 1. For the appearance error e_a^i, we convert the colour representation to Lab space[2] which is more perceptually uniform, and omit the luminance L to give

$$e_a^i = \sqrt{(a_{pred}^i - a_{gt}^i)^2 + (b_{pred}^i - b_{gt}^i)^2},\tag{5}$$

where a_{pred}^i and b_{pred}^i correspond to the predicted color dimensions of the Lab representation, and a_{gt}^i and b_{gt}^i to the ground-truth values for test image i.

For the illumination error we use the mean squared error (MSE) of the Spherical Harmonics coefficients. It is known that estimating the illumination from a single view can be potentially ill-conditioned [22, Chap. 6] so it is possible that

---

[2] https://en.wikipedia.org/wiki/Lab_color_space

the ground-truth illumination cannot be recovered exactly. It is easy to see that our metric is equivalent to the MSE of the incident SH illumination projected on a sphere. Furthermore, we use a scale-invariant version of this metric in order to account for the fact that appearance and illumination interact with each other multiplicatively. A similar evaluation metric is used in [1]. Finally, we evaluate shape reconstruction by using the mean Euclidean distance between the vertices of the ground-truth and predicted meshes, both aligned to a canonical pose.

The occlusion predictions from the robust model are evaluated thus: we obtain predicted un-occluded foreground pixels by evaluating the posterior probability at each pixel of belonging to the foreground or outlier component in Eq. 3, and thresholding at 0.5. These are then compared to the ground-truth un-occluded foreground pixels using the segmentation accuracy as defined e.g. in [9], where the number of true positives is divided by the sum of the true positives plus false positives plus false negatives. For the recognition model without iterative refinement, we assume that all of the predicted foreground pixels are unoccluded.

Optimization Procedure. For the robust model we explored different optimization strategies since convergence is sensitive to the choice of the likelihood variance. If we use a pixel variance that is too large, then occlusions and background clutter will affect the optimization negatively. On the other hand, if the variance is too small, the robust model tends to ignore large parts of the image including those which are important for a correct optimization. We jointly optimize the latent variables of pose, shape, appearance and illumination using a standard deviation of $\sigma = 0.03$ of the pixel likelihood. Note that the pixel color for each RGB channel ranges between 0 and 1. Also, we clamp shape parameters to be less than three standard deviations from the prior mean: it is much more likely that the optimization has gone wrong than it is having an input image with an unreasonably large (or small) deformation of the mesh.

We explored different minimization methods including gradient descent (with and without momentum and decay), nonlinear conjugate gradient (CG)[3], dogleg CG (as used in the OpenDR work), and BFGS. Nonlinear CG consistently converged to better minima in our tests hence we use it in our experiments. It is not surprising that these methods often converge differently since the optimization landscape is non-convex and the derivatives are approximate.

5.2   Results

Effect of Occlusion on Accuracy. Figure 3 shows the median cumulative predictive performance as a function of the percentage occlusion when evaluating on the photorealistic test images. (So, for example the performance at 75 % occlusion is obtained from all test cases with this much occlusion or less.) Note that in panels (a)–(e) lower error is better, while in panel (f) higher scores are better. Comparing the recognition network to the recognition network plus

---

[3] http://learning.eng.cam.ac.uk/carl/code/minimize/.

robust fitting, we see very similar performance for azimuth, elevation and shape factors, but marked improvements with fitting for appearance, illumination and occlusion. Pose and shape are predicted very well by the recognition model, which suggests that it is good at inferring latent variables for which there are clear and localized cues (e.g. for pose, the locations of tip of the spout, the handle, etc.), even under high levels of occlusion. Subsequent fitting of azimuth and shape factors on average shows little to no improvement, but we do see an improvement for elevation. We also see how the recognition model has not learned to predict the illumination and that occlusion has a strong effect on the prediction. This agrees with the intuition that the other factors can be more easily inferred by having a smaller portion of the object unoccluded.

Fitting Results. It is noticeable that the Gaussian model performs much worse than the robust model for elevation, appearance, and illumination. Indeed it sometimes performs worse after fitting than the recognition model itself, which is most likely explained by the fact that the Gaussian model does not handle occlusion and background clutter well. Plots of the mean performance rather than the median show similar trends to Fig. 3, except that the elevation angular error of the robust fit becomes worse than the recognition model over the occlusion range (increasing from 6 to 8 degrees). Analysis shows that this is due to some large errors that arise particularly at higher occlusion levels. A possible remedy we are investigating is to check if the fitting process has gone awry, and if so revert to the recognition model prediction. Table 1 summarizes the plots by showing the median prediction errors for the baseline, the recognition model prediction, and the Gaussian and robust fits for up to 75 % occlusion. For reference, we also show the results of the recognition and fitting when the test images are rendered with OpenGL, which is the method used for our differentiable renderer as well as to render the training images of the recognition models. We notice how the relative improvements when fitting is similar in both Cycles and OpenGL cases, but the OpenGL experiments have overall lower errors as is expected. Notice how robust fitting gives the best performance in all cases except for a slightly worse performance on elevation at high occlusion levels. We provide the median plots with both Cycles and OpenGL experiments in the supplementary materials along with some example videos of the fitting process.

Qualitative Evaluation. Figure 4 shows examples of how the robust model explains away the occlusion rather impressively for different levels occlusion, which is something difficult to achieve with purely bottom-up techniques. In Fig. 5 we show a few examples to illustrate how the environment map illumination is fitted to capture the main directional sources of illumination in a complex indoor illumination setting with multiple light sources. Note that all the scene latent variables were predicted and fitted in this experiment. Indeed, the robust model seems much more capable of capturing fine-grained descriptions such as illumination, appearance and occlusions than the recognition model.

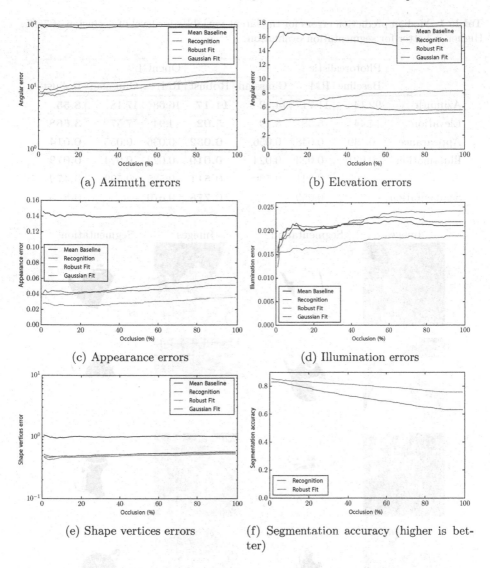

(a) Azimuth errors

(b) Elevation errors

(c) Appearance errors

(d) Illumination errors

(e) Shape vertices errors

(f) Segmentation accuracy (higher is better)

Fig. 3. Median errors for azimuth, elevation, appearance, illumination, shape; figure (e) is the segmentation accuracy

6 Discussion

Above we have investigated the use of vision-as-inverse-graphics with recognition models for a target object embedded in background clutter and subject to occlusions. A great advantage of using data generated by computer graphics is that it allows us complete access to the underlying scene parameters, and hence the ability to explore these systematically.

Table 1. Median prediction errors for the latent variables for level of occlusion of 75 %. Higher is better for segmentation evaluation

	Photorealistic				OpenGL		
	Baseline	RM	Gaussian	Robust	RM	Gaussian	Robust
Azimuth	92.14	11.71	14.52	**11.17**	10.68	17.18	**8.55**
Elevation	14.44	5.58	8.19	**5.02**	4.94	7.57	**3.668**
Appearance	0.140	0.048	0.056	**0.032**	0.036	0.055	**0.014**
Illumination	0.021	0.023	0.024	**0.019**	0.022	0.024	**0.019**
Shape	1.005	0.541	0.560	**0.511**	0.525	0.599	**0.479**
Segmentation	-	0.659	-	**0.778**	0.670	-	**0.828**

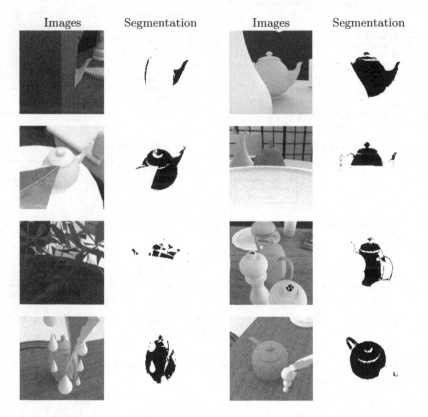

Fig. 4. Examples of occlusion inference using the posterior of the robust pixel probabilities

Our results show that some of the latent variables like pose and shape are well-predicted by the recognition network, while others such as illumination, appearance and occlusion benefit from subsequent refinement by fitting a robust generative model. Our results also show that the robustified model of Eq. 3

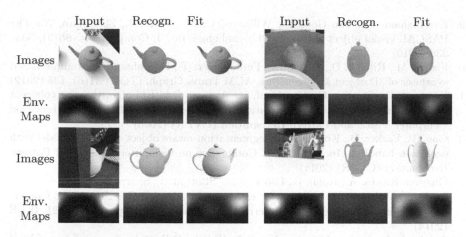

Fig. 5. Examples of how fitting with the robust model captures the correct illumination whereas RM is unable to do so

clearly outperforms a Gaussian likelihood, and provides a way to detect occlusions even in complicated cases.

Future directions for research include investigating: detecting if the fitting process has fallen into improbable basins of attraction, and the use of multimodal predictions in the recognition network (as per [14] or [13]).

References

1. Barron, J.T., Malik, J.: Shape, illumination, and reflectance from shading. IEEE Trans. Pattern Anal. Mach. Intell. **37**(8), 1670–1687 (2015)
2. Basri, R., Jacobs, D.W.: Lambertian reflectance and linear subspaces. IEEE Trans. Pattern Anal. Mach. Intell. **25**(2), 218–233 (2003)
3. Belhumeur, P.N., Kriegman, D.J.: What is the set of images of an object under all possible illumination conditions? Int. J. Comput. Vis. **28**(3), 245–260 (1998)
4. Black, M.J., Rangarajan, A.: On the unification of line processes, outlier rejection, and robust statistics with applications in early vision. Int. J. Comput. Vis. **19**(1), 57–91 (1996)
5. Blanz, V., Vetter, T.: A morphable model for the synthesis of 3D faces. In: Proceedings of the 26th Annual Conference on Computer graphics and Interactive Techniques, pp. 187–194 (1999)
6. Dayan, P., Hinton, G.E., Neal, R.M., Zemel, R.S.: The helmholtz machine. Neural Comput. **7**(5), 889–904 (1995)
7. Debevec, P.: Rendering synthetic objects into real scenes: bridging traditional and image-based graphics with global illumination and high dynamic range photography. In: Proceedings of the 25th Annual Conference on Computer Graphics and Interactive Techniques, SIGGRAPH 1998, New York, NY, USA, pp. 189–198 (1998)
8. Dosovitskiy, A., Springenberg, J.T., Brox, T.: Learning to generate chairs with convolutional neural networks. In: Proceedings of the IEEE Conference on Computer Vision and Pattern Recognition, pp. 1538–1546 (2015)

9. Everingham, M., Van Gool, L., Williams, C.K.I., Winn, J., Zisserman, A.: The PASCAL visual object classes (VOC) challenge. Int. J. Comput. Vis. **88**(2), 303–338 (2010)
10. Fisher, M., Ritchie, D., Savva, M., Funkhouser, T., Hanrahan, P.: Example-based synthesis of 3D object arrangements. ACM Trans. Graph. (TOG) **31**(6), 135 (2012)
11. Fransens, R., Strecha, C., Van Gool, L.: A mean field EM-algorithm for coherent occlusion handling in MAP-estimation problems. In: 2006 IEEE Conference on Computer Vision and Pattern Recognition (CVPR) (2006)
12. Gao, T., Packer, B., Koller, D.: A segmentation-aware object detection model with occlusion handling. In: 2011 IEEE Conference on Computer Vision and Pattern Recognition (CVPR) (2011)
13. Guzman-Rivera, A., Kohli, P., Glocker, B., Shotton, J., Sharp, T., Fitzgibbon, A., Izadi, S.: Multi-output learning for camera relocalization. In: 2014 IEEE Conference on Computer Vision and Pattern Recognition (CVPR), pp. 1114–1121. IEEE (2014)
14. Jacobs, R.A., Jordan, M.I., Nowlan, S.J., Hinton, G.E.: Adaptive mixtures of local experts. Neural Comput. **3**, 79–87 (1991)
15. Jampani, V., Nowozin, S., Loper, M., Gehler, P.V.: The informed sampler: a discriminative approach to Bayesian inference in generative computer vision models. Comput. Vis. Image Underst. **136**, 32–44 (2015)
16. Krizhevsky, A., Sutskever, I., Hinton, G.E.: ImageNet classification with deep convolutional neural networks. Adv. Neural Inf. Process. Syst. **25**, 1–9 (2012)
17. Krull, A., Brachmann, E., Michel, F., Ying Yang, M., Gumhold, S., Rother, C.: Learning analysis-by-synthesis for 6D pose estimation in RGB-D images. In: Proceedings of the IEEE International Conference on Computer Vision, pp. 954–962 (2015)
18. Kulkarni, T.D., Mansinghka, V.K., Kohli, P., Tenenbaum, J.B.: Inverse graphics with probabilistic CAD models. arXiv preprint arXiv:1407.1339 (2014)
19. Kulkarni, T.D., Whitney, W., Kohli, P., Tenenbaum, J.B.: Deep Convolutional Inverse Graphics Network. Neural Information Processing Systems (NIPS) (2015)
20. Kulkarni, T.D., Kohli, P., Tenenbaum, J.B., Mansinghka, V.K.: Picture: a probabilistic programming language for scene perception. In: IEEE Conference on Computer Vision and Pattern Recognition, CVPR 2015 (2015)
21. Loper, M.M., Black, M.J.: OpenDR: an approximate differentiable renderer. In: Fleet, D., Pajdla, T., Schiele, B., Tuytelaars, T. (eds.) ECCV 2014. LNCS, vol. 8695, pp. 154–169. Springer, Heidelberg (2014). doi:10.1007/978-3-319-10584-0_11
22. Ramamoorthi, R.: A signal-processing framework for forward and inverse rendering. Ph.D. thesis, Stanford University (2002)
23. Ramamoorthi, R.: Modeling illumination variation with spherical harmonics. In: Face Processing: Advanced Modeling Methods, pp. 385–424 (2006)
24. Ramamoorthi, R., Hanrahan, P.: An efficient representation for irradiance environment maps. In: Proceedings of the 28th Annual Conference on Computer Graphics and Interactive Techniques, pp. 497–500. ACM (2001)
25. Reinhard, E., Heidrich, W., Debevec, P., Pattanaik, S., Ward, G., Myszkowski, K.: High Dynamic Range Imaging: Acquisition, Display, and Image-based Lighting. Morgan Kaufmann, San Francisco (2010)
26. Shotton, J., Sharp, T., Kipman, A., Fitzgibbon, A., Finocchio, M., Blake, A., Cook, M., Moore, R.: Real-time human pose recognition in parts from single depth images. Commun. ACM **56**(1), 116–124 (2013)
27. Stevens, M.R., Beveridge, J.R.: Integrating Graphics and Vision for Object Recognition. Kluwer Academic Publishers, Boston (2001)

28. Williams, C.K.I., Revow, M., Hinton, G.E.: Instantiating deformable models with a neural net. Comput. Vis. Image Underst. **68**(1), 120–126 (1997)

29. Williams, C.K.I., Titsias, M.K.: Greedy learning of multiple objects in images using robust statistics and factorial learning. Neural Comput. **16**(5), 1039–1062 (2004)

30. Wu, Z., Song, S., Khosla, A., Yu, F., Zhang, L., Tang, X., Xiao, J.: 3D shapenets: a deep representation for volumetric shapes. In: Proceedings of the IEEE Conference on Computer Vision and Pattern Recognition, pp. 1912–1920 (2015)

31. Yildirim, I., Kulkarni, T.D., Freiwald, W.A., Tenenbaum, J.B.: Efficient analysis-by-synthesis in vision: a computational framework, behavioral tests, and comparison with neural representations. In: Proceedings of the Thirty-Seventh Annual Conference of the Cognitive Science Society (2015)

32. Yuille, A., Kersten, D.: Vision as Bayesian inference: analysis by synthesis? Trends in Cogn. Sci. **10**(7), 301–308 (2006)

33. Zia, M.Z., Stark, M., Schiele, B., Schindler, K.: Detailed 3D representations for object recognition and modeling. IEEE Trans. Pattern Anal. Mach. Intell. **35**(11), 2608–2623 (2013)

Deep Kinematic Pose Regression

Xingyi Zhou[1], Xiao Sun[2], Wei Zhang[1], Shuang Liang[3(✉)], and Yichen Wei[2]

[1] Shanghai Key Laboratory of Intelligent Information Processing,
School of Computer Science, Fudan University, Shanghai, China
{zhouxy13,weizh}@fudan.edu.cn
[2] Microsoft Research, Beijing, China
{xias,yichenw}@microsoft.com
[3] Tongji University, Shanghai, China
shuangliang@tongji.edu.cn

Abstract. Learning articulated object pose is inherently difficult because the pose is high dimensional but has many structural constraints. Most existing work do not model such constraints and does not guarantee the geometric validity of their pose estimation, therefore requiring a post-processing to recover the correct geometry if desired, which is cumbersome and sub-optimal. In this work, we propose to directly embed a kinematic object model into the deep neutral network learning for general articulated object pose estimation. The kinematic function is defined on the appropriately parameterized object motion variables. It is differentiable and can be used in the gradient descent based optimization in network training. The prior knowledge on the object geometric model is fully exploited and the structure is guaranteed to be valid. We show convincing experiment results on a toy example and the 3D human pose estimation problem. For the latter we achieve state-of-the-art result on Human3.6M dataset.

Keywords: Kinematic model · Human pose estimation · Deep learning

1   Introduction

Estimating the pose of objects is important for understanding the behavior of the object and relevant high level tasks, e.g., facial point localization for expression recognition, human pose estimation for action recognition. It is a fundamental problem in computer vision and has been heavily studied for decades. Yet, it remains challenging, especially when object pose and appearance is complex, e.g., human pose estimation from single view RGB images.

There is a vast range of definitions for object pose. In the simple case, the pose just refers to the global viewpoint of rigid objects, such as car [41] or head [18]. But more often, the pose refers to a set of semantically important points on the object (rigid or non-rigid). The points could be landmarks that can be easily distinguished from their appearances, e.g., eyes or nose on human face [15], and wings or tail on bird [37]. The points could further be the physical joints that

© Springer International Publishing Switzerland 2016
G. Hua and H. Jégou (Eds.): ECCV 2016 Workshops, Part III, LNCS 9915, pp. 186–201, 2016.
DOI: 10.1007/978-3-319-49409-8_17

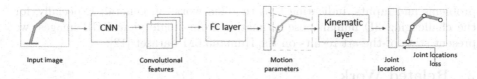

Fig. 1. Illustration of our framework. The input image undergoes a convolutional neutral network and a fully connected layer to output model motion parameters (global potision and rotation angles). The kinematic layer maps the motion parameters to joints. The joints are connected to ground truth joints to compute the joint loss that drives the network training.

defines the geometry of complex articulated objects, such as human hand [20, 40] and human body [16, 30, 39].

Arguably, the articulated object pose estimation is the most challenging. Such object pose is usually very high dimensional and inherently structured. How to effectively represent the pose and perform structure-preserving learning is hard and have been heavily studied. Some approaches represent the object pose in a non-parametric way (as a number of points) and directly learn the pose from data [5, 26, 27]. The inherent structure is implicitly learnt and modeled from data. Many other approaches use a low dimensional representation by using dimensionality reduction techniques such as PCA [12, 20], sparse coding [33, 38, 39] or auto-encoder [29]. The structure information is embedded in the low dimensional space. Yet, such embedding is mostly linear and cannot well preserve the complex articulated structural constraints.

In this work, we propose to directly incorporate the articulated object model into the deep neutral network learning, which is the dominant approach for object pose estimation nowadays, for hand [8, 20, 21, 28, 31, 40] or human body [10, 16, 17, 19, 29, 30, 32, 34, 39]. Our motivation is simple and intuitive. The kinematic model of such objects is well known as prior knowledge, such as the object bone lengths, bone connections and definition of joint rotations. From such knowledge, it is feasible to define a continuous and differentiable kinematic function with respect to the model motion parameters, which are the rotation angles. The kinematic function can be readily put into a neutral network as a special layer. The standard gradient descent based optimization can be performed in the same way for network training. The learning framework is exemplified in Fig. 1. In this way, the learning fully respects the model geometry and preserves the structural constraints. Such end-to-end learning is better than the previous approaches that rely on a separate post-processing step to recover the object geometry [31, 39].

This idea is firstly proposed in the recent work [40] for depth based hand pose estimation and is shown working well. However, estimating 3D structure from depth is a simple problem by nature. It is still unclear how well the idea can be generalized to other objects and RGB images. In this work, we apply the idea to more problems (a toy example and human pose estimation) and for the first time show that the idea works successfully on different articulated pose estimation problems and inputs, indicating that the idea works in general. Especially, for the challenging 3D human pose estimation from single view RGB images, we present state-of-the-art results on the Human3.6M dataset [12].

2   Related Work

The literature on pose estimation is comprehensive. We review previous work from two perspectives that are mostly related to our work: object pose representation and deep learning based human pose estimation.

2.1   Pose Representation

An object pose consists of a number of related points. The key for pose representation is how to represent the mutual relationship or structural constraints between these points. There are a few different previous approaches.

Pictorial Structure Model. Pictorial structure model [7] is one of the most popular methods in early age. It represents joints as vertexes and joint relations as edges in a non-circular graph. Pose estimation is formulated as inference problems on the graph and solved with certain optimization algorithms. Its extensions [14,23,35] achieve promising results in 2D human estimation, and has been extended to 3D human pose [2]. The main drawback is that the inference algorithm on the graph is usually complex and slow.

Linear Dictionary. A widely-used method is to denote the structural points as a linear combination of templates or basis [15,33,38,39]. [15] represent 3D face landmarks by a linear combination of shape bases [22] and expression bases [4]. It learns the shape, expression coefficients and camera view parameters alternatively. [33] express 3D human pose by an over-complex dictionary with a sparse prior, and solve the sparse coding problem with alternating direction method. [38] assign individual camera view parameters for each pose template. The sparse representation is then relaxed to be a convex problem that can be solved efficiently.

Linear Feature Embedding. Some approaches learn a low dimensional embedding [12,20,29] from the high dimensional pose. [12] applies PCA to the labeled 3D points of human pose. The pose estimation is then performed in the new orthogonal space. The similar idea is applied to 3D hand pose estimation [20]. It uses PCA to project the 3D hand joints to a lower space as a physical constraint prior for hand. [29] extend the linear PCA projector to a multi-layer anto-encoder. The decoder part is fine-tuned jointly with a convolutional neural network in an end-to-end manner. A common drawback in above linear representations is that the complex object pose is usually on a non-linear manifold in the high dimensional space that cannot be easily captured by a linear representation.

Implicit Representation by Retrieval. Many approaches [6,17,36] store massive examples in a database and perform pose estimation as retrieval, therefore avoiding the difficult pose representation problem. [6] uses a nearest neighbors search of local shape descriptors. [17] proposes a max-margin structured learning framework to jointly embed the image and pose into the same space, and then estimates the pose of a new image by nearest neighbor search in this space. [36] builds an image database with 3D and 2D annotations, and uses a KD-tree to retrieve 3D pose whose 2D projection is similar to the input image. The performance of these approaches highly depends on the quality of the database. The efficiency of nearest neighbor search could be an issue when the database is large.

Explicit Geometric Model. The most aggressive and thorough representation is to use an explicit and generative geometric model, including the motion and shape parameters of the object [3, 25]. Estimating the parameters of the model from the input image(s) is performed by heavy optimization algorithms. Such methods are rarely used in a learning based manner. The work in [40] firstly uses a generative kinematic model for hand pose estimation in the deep learning framework. Inspire by this work, we extend the idea to more object pose estimation problems and different inputs, showing its general applicability, especially for the challenging problem of 3D human pose estimation from single view RGB images.

2.2 Deep Learning on Human Pose Estimation

The human pose estimation problem has been significantly advanced using deep learning since the pioneer deep pose work [32]. All current leading methods are based on deep neutral networks. [34] shows that using 2D heat maps as intermediate supervision can dramatically improve the 2D human part detection results. [19] use an hourglass shaped network to capture both bottom-up and top-down cues for accurate pose detection. [10] shows that directly using a deep residual network (152 layers) [9] is sufficient for high performance part detection. To adopt these fully-convolutional based heat map regression method for 3D pose estimation, an additional model fitting step is used [39] as a post processing. Other approaches directly regress the 2D human pose [5,32] or 3D human pose [16,29,30]. These detection or regression based approaches ignore the prior knowledge of the human model and does not guarantee to preserve the object structure. They sometimes output geometrically invalid poses.

To our best knowledge, for the first time we show that integrating a kinematic object model into deep learning achieves state-of-the-art results in 3D human pose estimation from single view RGB images.

3   Deep Kinematic Pose Estimation

3.1   Kinematic Model

An articulated object is modeled as a kinematic model. A kinematic model is composed of several *bones* and *joints*. A bone is a segment of a fixed length, and a joint is the end point of a bone. One bone meets at another at a joint, forming a tree structure. Bones can rotate among a conjunct joint. Without

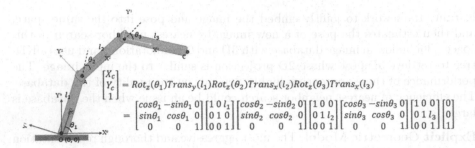

Fig. 2. A sample 2D kinematic model. It has 3 and 4 joints. The joint location is calculated by multiplying a series of transformation matrices.

loss generality, one joint is considered as the root joint (For example, wrist for human hand and pelvis for human body). The root defines the global position and global orientation of the object.

For a kinematic model of J joints, it has $J - 1$ bones. Let $\{l_i\}_{i=1}^{J-1}$ be the collection of bone lengths, they are fixed for a specific subject and provided as prior knowledge. For different subjects, we assume they only differ in a global scale, i.e. $\forall i, l_i' = s \times l_i$. The scale is also provided as prior knowledge, e.g. through a calibration process.

Let the rotation angle of the i-th joint be θ_i, the motion parameter Θ includes the global position $\mathbf{p}$, global orientation $\mathbf{o}$, and all the rotation angles, $\Theta = \{\mathbf{p}, \mathbf{o}\} \cup \{\theta_i\}_{i=1}^{J}$. The forward kinematic function is a mapping from motion parameter space to joint location space.

$$\mathcal{F} : \{\Theta\} \rightarrow \mathcal{Y} \tag{1}$$

where $\mathcal{Y}$ is the coordinate for all joints, $\mathcal{Y} \in \mathcal{R}^{3 \times J}$ for 3D object and $\mathcal{Y} \in \mathcal{R}^{2 \times J}$ for 2D object.

The kinematic function is defined on a kinematic tree. An example is shown in Fig. 2. Each joint is associated with a local coordinate transformation defined in the motion parameter, including a rotation from its rotation angles and a translation from its out-coming bones. The final coordinate of a joint is obtained by multiplying a series of transformation matrices along the path from the root joint to itself. Generally, the global position of joint u is

$$p_u = (\prod_{v \in Pa(u)} Rot(\theta_v) \times Trans(l_v)) \mathbf{O}^\top \tag{2}$$

where $Pa(u)$ is the set of its parents nodes at the kinematic tree, and $\mathbf{O}$ is the origin in homogenous coordinate, i.e., $\mathbf{O} = [0, 0, 1]^\top$ for 2D and $\mathbf{O} = [0, 0, 0, 1]^\top$ for 3D. For 3D kinematic model, each rotation is assigned with one of the $\{X, Y, Z\}$ axis, and at each joint there can be multiple rotations. The direction of translation is defined in the canonical local coordinate frame where the motion parameters are all zeros.

In [40], individual bounds for each angle can be set as additional prior knowledge for the objects. It is feasible for human hand since all the joints have at most 2 rotation angles and their physical meaning is clear. However, in the case of human body, angle constraint are not individual, it is conditioned on pose [1] and hard to formulate. We leave it as future work to explore more efficient and expressive constraints.

As shown in Fig. 2, the forward kinematic function is continuous with respect to the motion parameter. It is thus differentiable. As each parameter occurs in one matrix, this allows easy implementation of back-propagation. We simply replace the corresponding rotational matrix by its derivation matrix and keep other items unchanged. The kinematic model can be easily put in a neural network as a layer for gradient descent-based optimization.

3.2   Deep Learning with a Kinematic Layer

We discuss our proposed approach and the other two baseline methods to learn the pose of an articulated object. They are illustrated in Fig. 3. All three methods share the same basic convolutional neutral network and only differs in their ending parts, which is parameter-free. Therefore, we can make fair comparison between the three methods.

Now we elaborate on them. The first method is a baseline. It directly estimates the joint locations by a convolutional neural network, using Euclidean Loss on the joints. It is called **direct joint**. It has been used for human pose estimation [16,32] and hand pose estimation [20]. This approach does not consider the geometry constraints of the object. The output is less structured and could be invalid, geometrically.

Instead, we propose to use a kinematic layer at the top of the network. The network predicts the motion parameters of the object, while the learning is still guided by the joint location loss. We call this approach **kinematic joint**. The joint location loss with respect to model parameter Θ is Euclidean Loss

$$L(\Theta) = \frac{1}{2}||\mathcal{F}(\Theta) - Y||^2 \tag{3}$$

where $Y \in \mathcal{Y}$ is the ground truth joint location in the input image. Since this layer has no free parameters to learn and appears in the end of the network, we can think of the layer as coupled with the Euclidean loss Layer, serving as a geometrically more accurate loss layer.

Compared to direct joint approach, our proposed method fully incorporates prior geometric knowledge of the object, such as the bone lengths and spatial relations between the joints. The joint location is obtained by a generative process and guaranteed to be valid. The motion parameter space is more compact than the unconstrained joint space, that is, the degrees of freedom of motion parameters are smaller than that of joints, for example, in Sect. 4.2, the DOF is 27 for motion parameters but 51 for joints. Overall, our method can be considered as a better regularization on the output space.

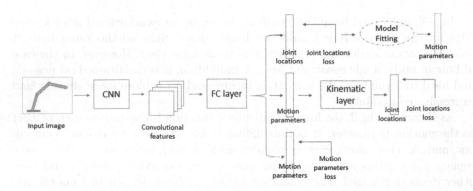

Fig. 3. Three methods for object pose estimation. Top (**Direct Joint**): the network directly outputs all the joints. Such estimated joints could be invalid geometrically. Optionally, they can be optimized via a model-fitting step to recover a correct model, referred to as **ModelFit** in the text. Middle (**Kinematic Joint**): our proposed approach. The network outputs motion parameters to the kinematic layer. The layer outputs joints. Bottom (**Direct Parameter**): the network directly outputs motion parameters.

Unlike dictionary-based representations [33,38] that require a heuristic sparse regularization, our approach has a clear geometrical interpretation and its optimization is feasible in deep neutral network training. Besides, it produces joint rotation angles that could be useful in certain applications.

The third method is a less obvious baseline. It directly estimates the motion parameters, using Euclidean loss on those parameters. It is called **direct parameter**. Intuitively, this approach cannot work well because the roles of different parameters are quite different and it is hard to balance the learning weights between those parameters. For example, the global rotation angles on the root joint affects all joints. It has much more impacts than those parameters on distal joints but it is hard to quantify this observation. Moreover, for complex articulated objects the joint locations to joint angles mapping is not one-to-one but ambiguous, e.g., when the entire arm is straight, roll angle on the shoulder joint can be arbitrary and it does not affect the location of elbow and wrist. It is hard to resolve such ambiguity in the network training. By contrast, the joint location loss in our kinematic approach is widely distributed over all object parts. It is well behaved and less ambiguous.

We note that it is possible to enforce the geometric constraints by fitting a kinematic model to some estimated joints as a post-processing [31,39]. For example, [31] recovers a 3D kinematic hand model using a PSO-based optimization, by fitting the model into the 2D hand joint heat maps. [39] obtains 3D human joints represented by a sparse dictionary using an EM optimization algorithm. In our case, we provide an additional **ModelFit** baseline that recovers a kinematic model from the output of direct joint baseline by minimizing the loss in Eq. 3.

4   Experiment

The work in [40] applies the kinematic pose regression approach for depth based 3D hand pose estimation and has shown good results. To verify the generality of the idea, we apply this approach for two more different problems. The first is a toy example for simple 2D articulated object on synthesized binary image. The second is 3D human pose estimation from single RGB images, which is very challenging.

4.1   A Toy Problem

In the toy problem, the object is 2D. The image is synthesized and binary. As shown in Fig. 4 top, the input image is generated from a 3 dimensional motion parameter $\Theta = \{x, y, \theta\}$, where x, y is the image coordinate (normalized between $0 - 1$) of the root joint, and θ indicates the angle between the each bone and the vertical line.

We use a 5 layer convolutional neutral network. The network structure and hyper-parameters are the same as [40]. The input image resolution is 128×128. The bone length is fixed as 45 pixels. We randomly synthesize $16k$ samples for training and $1k$ samples for testing. Each model is trained for 50 epoches.

As described in Fig. 3, we perform our **direct joint**, **kinematic joint** and **direct parameter** on this task. The joint location for **direct parameter** is computed by the kinematic layer as a post process in testing. It turns out all the 3 methods achieve low joint errors in this simple case. The mean joint errors for **direct joint**, **kinematic Joint**, **direct parameter** are 5.1 pixels, 4.9 pixels, and 4.8 pixels, respectively. **direct joint** is the worst, probably because the task is easy for all the setting and these two require to learn more parameters. When we evaluate the average length of the two bones for **direct joint** regression, we find it has a standard deviation of 5.3 pixels (11.8 % of the bone length 45 pixels), indicating that the geometry constraint is badly violated.

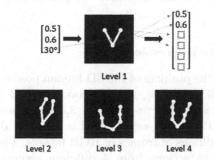

Fig. 4. Illustration of the toy problem. The input images are synthesized and binary. **Top**: Motion parameter and joint representation of a simple object with 3 motion parameters. **Bottom**: Example input images for 3 objects with different complexity levels. They have 6, 8, and 10 motion parameters, respectively.

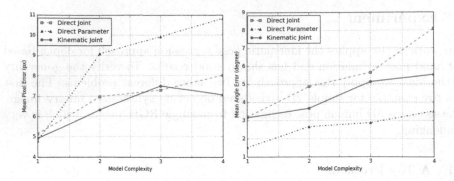

Fig. 5. Experimental results on mean joint locations error(**Left**) and mean angle error(**Right**) with respect to model complexity. It shows when as kinematic model becoming complex, our approach is stable in both metric.

Since it is hard to claim any other significant difference between the 3 method in such a simple case, we gradually increase the model complexity. Global orientation and more joint angles are added to the kinematic model. For each level of complexity, we add one more bone with one rotational angle on each distal bone. Example input image are illustrated in Fig. 4 bottom.

The joint location errors and angle errors with respect to the model complexity are shown in Fig. 5. Note that for **direct joint** regression, the angles are directly computed from the triangle. The results show that the task become more difficult for all methods. **Direct parameter** gets high joint location errors, probably because a low motion parameter error does not necessarily implies a low joint error. It is intuitive that it always get best performance on joint angle, since it is the desired learning target. **Direct joint** regression also has large error on its recovered joint angles, and the average length of each bone becomes more unstable. It shows that geometry structure is not easy to learn. Using a generative **kinematic joint** layer keeps a decent accuracy on both metric among all model complexity. This is important for complex objects in real applications, such as human body.

4.2 3D Human Pose Regression

We test our method on the problem of full 3D human pose estimation from single view RGB images. Following [16], the 3D coordinate of joints is represented by its offset to a root joint. We use Human 3.6M dataset [12]. Following the standard protocol in [12,16,38], we define J = 17 joints on the human body. The dataset contains millions of frames of RGB images. They are captured over 7 subjects performing 15 actions from 4 different camera views. Each frame is accurately annotated by a MoCap system. We treat the 4 cameras of the same subject separately. The training and testing data partition follows previous works [12,16,39]. All frames from 5 subjects(S1, S5, S6, S7, S8) are used for training. The remaining 2 subjects(S9, S11) are for testing.

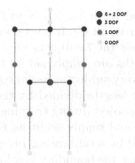

Fig. 6. Illustration of Human Model. It contains 17 joints and 27 motion parameters. See text for the detail kinematic structure.

Our kinematic human model is illustrated in Fig. 6. It defines 17 joints with 27 motion parameters. The pelvis is set as the root joint. Upside it is the neck, which can roll and yaw among the root. Torso is defined as the mid point of neck and pelvis. It has no motion parameter. Pelvis and neck orientation determine the positions of shoulders and hips by a fixed bone transform. Each shoulder/hip has full 3 rotational angles, and elbow/knee has 1 rotational angle. Neck also has 3 rotational angles for nose and head orientation. Note that there can be additional rotation angles on the model, for example shoulders can rotate among neck within a subtle degree and elbows can roll itself. Our rule of thumb is to simulate real human structure and keep the model simple.

Table 1. Results of Human3.6M Dataset. The numbers are mean Euclidean distance (mm) between the ground-truth 3D joints and the estimations of different methods.

	Directions	Discussion	Eating	Greeting	Phoning	Photo	Posing	Purchases
LinKDE [12]	132.71	183.55	132.37	164.39	162.12	205.94	150.61	171.31
Li et al. [16]	-	148.79	104.01	127.17	-	189.08	-	-
Li et al. [17]	-	136.88	96.94	124.74	-	168.68	-	-
Tekin et al. [29]	-	129.06	91.43	121.68	-	102.17	-	-
Tekin et al. [30]	132.71	158.52	87.95	126.83	118.37	185.02	114.69	107.61
Zhou et al. [39]	**87.36**	109.31	**87.05**	103.16	116.18	143.32	106.88	99.78
Ours(Direct)	106.38	104.68	104.28	107.80	115.44	**114.05**	103.80	109.03
Ours(ModelFit)	109.75	110.47	113.98	112.17	123.66	122.82	121.27	117.98
Ours(Kinematic)	91.83	**102.41**	96.95	**98.75**	**113.35**	125.22	**90.04**	**93.84**
	Sitting	SittingDown	Smoking	Waiting	WalkDog	Walking	WalkPair	Average
LinKDE [12]	151.57	243.03	162.14	170.69	177.13	96.60	127.88	162.14
Li et al. [16]	-	-	-	-	146.59	77.60	-	-
Li et al. [17]	-	-	-	-	132.17	69.97	-	-
Tekin et al. [29]	-	-	-	-	130.53	**65.75**	-	-
Tekin et al. [30]	136.15	205.65	118.21	146.66	128.11	65.86	**77.21**	125.28
Zhou et al. [39]	**124.52**	199.23	107.42	118.09	114.23	79.39	97.70	113.01
Ours(Direct)	125.87	**149.15**	112.64	105.37	**113.69**	98.19	110.17	112.03
Ours(ModelFit)	137.29	157.44	136.85	110.57	128.16	102.25	114.61	121.28
Ours(Kinematic)	132.16	158.97	**106.91**	**94.41**	126.04	79.02	98.96	**107.26**

We found that the ground truth 3D joints in the dataset has strictly the same length for each bone across all the frames on the same subject. Also, the lengths of the same bone across the 7 subjects are very close. Therefore, in our human model, the bone lengths are simply set as the average bone lengths of the 7 subjects. In addition, every subject is assigned a global scale. The scale is computed from the sum bone lengths divided by the average sum bone length. It is a fixed constant for each subject during training. During testing, we assume the subject scale is unknown and simply set it as 1. In practical scenarios, the subject scale can be estimated by a calibrating pre processing and then fixed.

Following [16,29], we assume the bounding box for the subject in known. The input images are resized to 224×224. Note that it is important not to change the aspect ratio for the kinematic based method, we use border padding to keep the real aspect ratio. The training target is also normalized by the bounding box size. Since our method is not action-dependent, we train our model using all the data from the 15 actions. By contrast, previous methods [12,17,39] use data for each action individually, as their local feature, retrieval database or pose dictionary may prefer more concrete templates.

We use the 50-layer Residual Network [9] that is pre-trained on ImageNet [24] as our initial model. It is then fine-tuned on our task. Totally available training data for the 5 subjects is about 1.5 million images. They are highly similar and redundant. We randomly sample 800 k frames for training. No data augmentation is used. We train our network for 70 epoches, with base learning rate 0.003 (dropped to 0.0003 after 50 epochs), batch size 52 (on 2 GPUs), weight decay 0.0002 and momentum 0.9. Batch-normalization [11] is used. Our implementation is based on Caffe [13].

The experimental results are shown in Table 1. The results for comparison methods [12,16,17,29,29,30,39] are from their published papers. Thanks to the powerful Residual Network [9], our **direct joint** regression base line is already

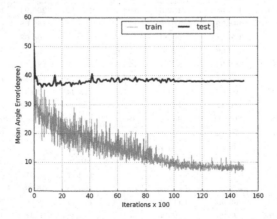

Fig. 7. Training curve of direct motion parameter regression. Although the training loss keeps dropping, the testing loss remains high.

Table 2. Qualitative results for direct joint regression and kinematic on Human3.6M dataset. They show some typical characters for these methods. The results are ploted at 3D space from the same viewpoint.

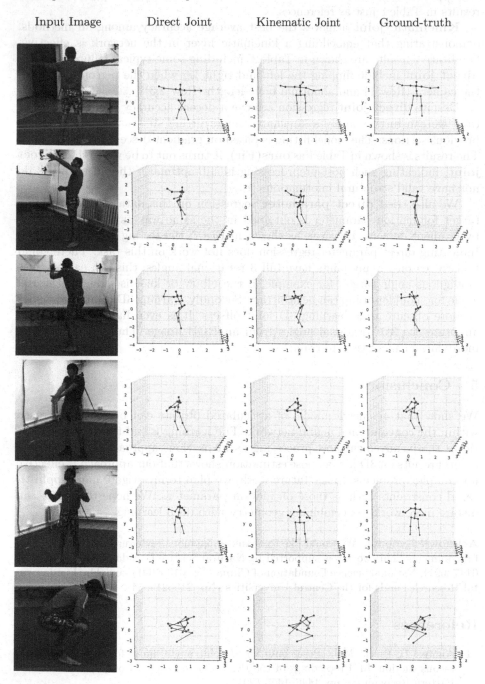

the state-of-the-art. Since we used additional training data from ImageNet, comparing our results to previous works is unfair, and the superior performance of our approach is not the contribution of this work. We include the previous works' results in Table 1 just as references.

Kinematic joint achieves the best average accuracy among all methods, demonstrating that embedding a kinematic layer in the network is effective. Qualitative results are shown in Table 2, including some typical failure cases for **direct joint** include flipping the left and right leg when the person is back to the camera (Row 1) and abnormal bone length (Row 2,3).

Despite **direct joint** regression achieve a decent accuracy for 3D joint location, we can further apply a kinematic model fitting step, as described in the previous sections. The model fitting is based on gradient-descent for each frame. The results is shown in Table 1 as **ours(Fit)**, it turns out to be worse than **direct joint**, indicating such post-preprocessing is sub-optimal if the initial poses do not have valid structural information.

We also tried **direct parameter** regression on this dataset. The training target for motion parameter is obtained in the same way as described above, by gradient descent. However, as shown in Fig. 7, the testing error keeps high. Indicating direct parameter regression does not work on this task. There could be two reasons: many joints have full 3 rotational angles, this can easily cause ambiguous angle target, for example, if the elbow or knee is straight, the roll angle for shoulder or hip can be arbitrary. Secondly, learning 3D rotational angles is more obscure than learning 3D joint offsets. It is even hard for human to annotate the 3D rotational angles from an RGB image. Thus it may require more data or more time to train.

5   Conclusions

We show that geometric model of articulated objects can be effectively used within the convolutional neural network. The learning is end-to-end and we get rid of the inconvenient post-processing as in previous approaches. The experimental results on 3D human pose estimation shows that our approach is effective for complex problems. In the future work, we plan to investigate more sophisticated constraints such as those on motion parameters. We hope this work can inspire more works on combining geometry with deep learning.

Acknowledgments. We would like to thank anonymous reviewers who gave us useful comments. This work was supported by Natural Science Foundation of China (No. 61473091), National Science Foundation of China (No. 61305091), and The Fundamental Research Funds for the Central Universities (No. 2100219054).

References

1. Akhter, I., Black, M.J.: Pose-conditioned joint angle limits for 3D human pose reconstruction. In: Proceedings of the IEEE Conference on Computer Vision and Pattern Recognition, pp. 1446–1455 (2015)

2. Belagiannis, V., Amin, S., Andriluka, M., Schiele, B., Navab, N., Ilic, S.: 3D pictorial structures for multiple human pose estimation. In: The IEEE Conference on Computer Vision and Pattern Recognition (CVPR), June 2014
3. Bogo, F., Kanazawa, A., Lassner, C., Gehler, P., Romero, J., Black, M.J.: http://arxiv.org/abs/1607.08128
4. Cao, C., Weng, Y., Zhou, S., Tong, Y., Zhou, K.: Facewarehouse: a 3D facial expression database for visual computing. IEEE Trans. Vis. Comput. Graph. **20**(3), 413–425 (2014)
5. Carreira, J., Agrawal, P., Fragkiadaki, K., Malik, J.: Human pose estimation with iterative error feedback. In: The IEEE Conference on Computer Vision and Pattern Recognition (CVPR), June 2016
6. Choi, C., Sinha, A., Hee Choi, J., Jang, S., Ramani, K.: A collaborative filtering approach to real-time hand pose estimation. In: The IEEE International Conference on Computer Vision (ICCV), December 2015
7. Felzenszwalb, P.F., Huttenlocher, D.P.: Pictorial structures for object recognition. Int. J. Comput. Vis. **61**(1), 55–79 (2005)
8. Ge, L., Liang, H., Yuan, J., Thalmann, D.: Robust 3D hand pose estimation in single depth images: from single-view CNN to multi-view CNNs. In: The IEEE Conference on Computer Vision and Pattern Recognition (CVPR), June 2016
9. He, K., Zhang, X., Ren, S., Sun, J.: Deep residual learning for image recognition. In: The IEEE Conference on Computer Vision and Pattern Recognition (CVPR), June 2016
10. Insafutdinov, E., Pishchulin, L., Andres, B., Andriluka, M., Schiele, B.: http://arxiv.org/abs/1605.03170
11. Ioffe, S., Szegedy, C.: Batch normalization: accelerating deep network training by reducing internal covariate shift. arXiv preprint arXiv:1502.03167 (2015)
12. Ionescu, C., Papava, D., Olaru, V., Sminchisescu, C.: Human3.6M: large scale datasets and predictive methods for 3D human sensing in natural environments. IEEE Trans. Pattern Anal. Mach. Intell. **36**(7), 1325–1339 (2014)
13. Jia, Y., Shelhamer, E., Donahue, J., Karayev, S., Long, J., Girshick, R., Guadarrama, S., Darrell, T.: Caffe: convolutional architecture for fast feature embedding. arXiv preprint arXiv:1408.5093 (2014)
14. Johnson, S., Everingham, M.: Learning effective human pose estimation from inaccurate annotation. In: 2011 IEEE Conference on Computer Vision and Pattern Recognition (CVPR), pp. 1465–1472. IEEE (2011)
15. Jourabloo, A., Liu, X.: Large-pose face alignment via CNN-based dense 3D model fitting. In: The IEEE Conference on Computer Vision and Pattern Recognition (CVPR), June 2016
16. Li, S., Chan, A.B.: 3D human pose estimation from monocular images with deep convolutional neural network. In: Cremers, D., Reid, I., Saito, H., Yang, M.-H. (eds.) ACCV 2014. LNCS, vol. 9004, pp. 332–347. Springer, Heidelberg (2015). doi:10.1007/978-3-319-16808-1_23
17. Li, S., Zhang, W., Chan, A.B.: Maximum-margin structured learning with deep networks for 3D human pose estimation. In: The IEEE International Conference on Computer Vision (ICCV), December 2015
18. Meyer, G.P., Gupta, S., Frosio, I., Reddy, D., Kautz, J.: Robust model-based 3D head pose estimation. In: The IEEE International Conference on Computer Vision (ICCV), December 2015
19. Newell, A., Yang, K., Deng, J.: Stacked hourglass networks for human pose estimation. CoRR abs/1603.06937 (2016). http://arxiv.org/abs/1603.06937

20. Oberweger, M., Wohlhart, P., Lepetit, V.: Hands deep in deep learning for hand pose estimation. arXiv preprint arXiv:1502.06807 (2015)
21. Oberweger, M., Wohlhart, P., Lepetit, V.: Training a feedback loop for hand pose estimation. In: Proceedings of the IEEE International Conference on Computer Vision, pp. 3316–3324 (2015)
22. Paysan, P., Knothe, R., Amberg, B., Romdhani, S., Vetter, T.: A 3D face model for pose and illumination invariant face recognition. In: Sixth IEEE International Conference on Advanced Video and Signal Based Surveillance, AVSS 2009, pp. 296–301. IEEE (2009)
23. Pishchulin, L., Andriluka, M., Gehler, P., Schiele, B.: Poselet conditioned pictorial structures. In: The IEEE Conference on Computer Vision and Pattern Recognition (CVPR), June 2013
24. Russakovsky, O., Deng, J., Su, H., Krause, J., Satheesh, S., Ma, S., Huang, Z., Karpathy, A., Khosla, A., Bernstein, M.S., Berg, A.C., Li, F.: Imagenet large scale visual recognition challenge. CoRR abs/1409.0575 (2014). http://arxiv.org/abs/1409.0575
25. Sharp, T., Keskin, C., Robertson, D., Taylor, J., Shotton, J., Kim, D., Rhemann, C., Leichter, I., Vinnikov, A., Wei, Y., Freedman, D., Kohli, P., Krupka, E., Fitzgibbon, A., Izadi, S.: Accurate, robust, and flexible realtime hand tracking. In: CHI (2015)
26. Shotton, J., Girshick, R., Fitzgibbon, A., Sharp, T., Cook, M., Finocchio, M., Moore, R., Kohli, P., Criminisi, A., Kipman, A., et al.: Efficient human pose estimation from single depth images. IEEE Trans. Pattern Anal. Mach. Intell. **35**(12), 2821–2840 (2013)
27. Sun, X., Wei, Y., Liang, S., Tang, X., Sun, J.: Cascaded hand pose regression. In: Proceedings of the IEEE Conference on Computer Vision and Pattern Recognition, pp. 824–832 (2015)
28. Supancic III., J.S., Rogez, G., Yang, Y., Shotton, J., Ramanan, D.: Depth-based hand pose estimation: methods, data, and challenges. arXiv preprint arXiv:1504.06378 (2015)
29. Tekin, B., Katircioglu, I., Salzmann, M., Lepetit, V., Fua, P.: Structured prediction of 3D human pose with deep neural networks. arXiv preprint arXiv:1605.05180 (2016)
30. Tekin, B., Rozantsev, A., Lepetit, V., Fua, P.: Direct prediction of 3D body poses from motion compensated sequences. In: The IEEE Conference on Computer Vision and Pattern Recognition (CVPR), June 2016
31. Tompson, J., Stein, M., Lecun, Y., Perlin, K.: Real-time continuous pose recovery of human hands using convolutional networks. ACM Trans. Graph. **33**, 169 (2014)
32. Toshev, A., Szegedy, C.: Deeppose: human pose estimation via deep neural networks. In: Proceedings of the IEEE Conference on Computer Vision and Pattern Recognition, pp. 1653–1660 (2014)
33. Wang, C., Wang, Y., Lin, Z., Yuille, A.L., Gao, W.: Robust estimation of 3D human poses from a single image. In: The IEEE Conference on Computer Vision and Pattern Recognition (CVPR), June 2014
34. Wei, S.E., Ramakrishna, V., Kanade, T., Sheikh, Y.: Convolutional pose machines. In: The IEEE Conference on Computer Vision and Pattern Recognition (CVPR), June 2016
35. Yang, Y., Ramanan, D.: Articulated pose estimation with flexible mixtures-of-parts. In: 2011 IEEE Conference on Computer Vision and Pattern Recognition (CVPR), pp. 1385–1392. IEEE (2011)

36. Yasin, H., Iqbal, U., Kruger, B., Weber, A., Gall, J.: A dual-source approach for 3D pose estimation from a single image. In: The IEEE Conference on Computer Vision and Pattern Recognition (CVPR), June 2016
37. Yu, X., Zhou, F., Chandraker, M.: Deep deformation network for object landmark localization. arXiv preprint arXiv:1605.01014 (2016)
38. Zhou, X., Leonardos, S., Hu, X., Daniilidis, K.: 3D shape estimation from 2D landmarks: a convex relaxation approach. In: The IEEE Conference on Computer Vision and Pattern Recognition (CVPR), June 2015
39. Zhou, X., Zhu, M., Leonardos, S., Derpanis, K.G., Daniilidis, K.: Sparseness meets deepness: 3D human pose estimation from monocular video. In: The IEEE Conference on Computer Vision and Pattern Recognition (CVPR), June 2016
40. Zhou, X., Wan, Q., Zhang, W., Xue, X., Wei, Y.: Model-based deep hand pose estimation. In: IJCAI (2016)
41. Zhu, M., Zhou, X., Daniilidis, K.: Single image pop-up from discriminatively learned parts. In: The IEEE International Conference on Computer Vision (ICCV), December 2015

How Useful Is Photo-Realistic Rendering for Visual Learning?

Yair Movshovitz-Attias[1](✉), Takeo Kanade[2], and Yaser Sheikh[2]

[1] Computer Science Department, Carnegie Mellon University, Pittsburgh, USA
yair@cs.cmu.edu
[2] The Robotics Institute, Carnegie Mellon University, Pittsburgh, USA
{Takeo.Kanade,yaser}@cs.cmu.edu

Abstract. Data seems cheap to get, and in many ways it is, but the process of creating a high quality labeled dataset from a mass of data is time-consuming and expensive.

With the advent of rich 3D repositories, photo-realistic rendering systems offer the opportunity to provide nearly limitless data. Yet, their primary value for visual learning may be the quality of the data they can provide rather than the quantity. Rendering engines offer the promise of perfect labels in addition to the data: what the precise camera pose is; what the precise lighting location, temperature, and distribution is; what the geometry of the object is.

In this work we focus on semi-automating dataset creation through use of synthetic data and apply this method to an important task – object viewpoint estimation. Using state-of-the-art rendering software we generate a large labeled dataset of cars rendered densely in viewpoint space. We investigate the effect of rendering parameters on estimation performance and show realism is important. We show that generalizing from synthetic data is not harder than the domain adaptation required between two real-image datasets and that combining synthetic images with a small amount of real data improves estimation accuracy.

1 Introduction

The computer vision community has been building datasets for decades, and as long as we have been building them, we have been fighting their biases. From the early days of COIL-100 [16] the Corel Stock Photos and 15 Scenes datasets [17] up to and including newer datasets such as PASCAL VOC [5] and Imagenet [4], we have experienced bias: every sample of the world is biased in some way – viewpoint, lighting, etc. Our task has been to build algorithms that perform well on these datasets. In effect, we have "hacked" each new dataset - exploring it, identifying weaknesses, and in sometimes flawlessly fitting to it.

For an in depth analysis of the evolution of datasets (and an enjoyable read) we refer the reader to [24]. In short, there are two main ways in which our community has addressed bias: making new datasets, and building bigger ones. By making new datasets we continuously get new samples of the visual world, and

© Springer International Publishing Switzerland 2016
G. Hua and H. Jégou (Eds.): ECCV 2016 Workshops, Part III, LNCS 9915, pp. 202–217, 2016.
DOI: 10.1007/978-3-319-49409-8_18

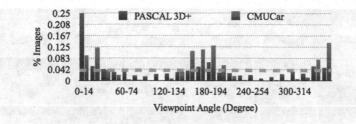

Fig. 1. Photographers tend to capture objects in *canonical* viewpoints. When real images are used as training data these viewpoints are oversampled. Here we show viewpoint distributions for two real image datasets. Note the oversampling of certain views, e.g. 0°, 180°. In comparison, an advantage of a synthetic dataset is that it is created to specification. A natural distribution to create is uniform (dashed line).

make sure our techniques handle more of its variability. By making our datasets larger we make it harder to over-fit to the dataset's individual idiosyncrasies.

This approach has been remarkably successful. It requires, however, a great amount of effort to generate new datasets and label them with ground truth annotations. Even when great care has been taken to minimize the sampling bias it has a way of creeping in. As an example, for the task of object viewpoint estimation, we can observe clear bias in the distribution viewpoint angles when exploring real image datasets. Figure 1 shows the distribution of azimuth angles for the training sets of the car class of PASCAL VOC, and the CMUCar dataset. There is clear oversampling of some angles, mainly around 0° and 180°.

In this work we explore the benefits of synthetically generated data for viewpoint estimation. 3D viewpoint estimation is an ideal task for the use of renders, as it requires high of accuracy in labeling. We utilize a large database of accurate, highly detailed, 3D models to create a large number of synthetic images. To diversify the generated data we vary many of the rendering parameters. We use the generated dataset to train a deep convolutional network using a loss function that is optimized for viewpoint estimation. Our experiments show that models trained on rendered data are as accurate as those trained on real images. We further show that synthetic data can be also be used successfully during validation, opening up opportunities for large scale evaluation of trained models.

With rendered data, we control for viewpoint bias, and can create a uniform distribution. We can also adequately sample lighting conditions and occlusions by other objects. Figure 2 shows renders created for a single object, an IKEA bed. Note how we can sample the different angles, lighting conditions, and occlusions. We will, of course, have other types of bias, and this a combined approach – augment real image datasets with rendered data. We explore this idea below.

We assert that a factor limiting the success of many computer vision algorithms is the *scarcity* of labeled data and the *precision* of the provided labels. For viewpoint estimation in particular the space of possible angles is immense, and collecting enough samples of every angle is hard. Furthermore, accurately labeling each image with the ground truth angle proves difficult for human

Fig. 2. Generating synthetic data allows us to control image properties, for example, by: sampling viewpoint angles (top row), sampling lighting conditions (middle), and sampling occlusions by controlling the placement of night stands and linens (bottom).

annotators. As a result, most current 3D viewpoint datasets resort to one of two methods for labeling data: (1) Provide coarse viewpoint information in the form of viewpoint classes (usually 8 to 16). (2) Use a two step process of labeling. First, ask annotators to locate about a dozen keypoints on the object (e.g., front-left most point on a car's bumper), then manually locate those same points in 3D space on a preselected model. Finally, perform PnP optimization [13] to learn a projection matrix from 3D points to 2D image coordinates, from which angle labels are calculated. Both methods are unsatisfying. For many downstream applications a coarse pose classification is not enough, and the complex point correspondence based process expensive to crowdsource. By generating synthetic images one can create large scale datasets, with desired label granularity level.

2   Related Work

The price of computational power and storage has decreased dramatically over the last decade. This decrease ushered in a new era in computer vision, one that makes use of highly distributed inference methods [3,23] and massive amounts of labeled data [7,15,19]. This shift was accompanied by a need for efficient ways to quickly and accurately label these large datasets. Older and smaller datasets were normally collected and labeled by researchers themselves. This ensured high quality labels but was not scalable. As computer vision entered the age of "Big Data" researchers began looking for better ways to annotate large datasets.

Online labor markets such as Amazon's Mechanical Turk have been used in the computer vision community to crowdsource simple tasks such as image level labeling, or bounding box annotation [12,19,26]. However, labor markets often lack expert knowledge, making some classes of tasks impossible to complete. Experts are rare in a population and when are not properly identified, their answers will be ignored when not consistent with other workers – exactly on the instances where their knowledge is most crucial [10].

The issues detailed above make for a compelling argument for automating the collection and labeling of datasets. The large increase in availability of 3D

CAD models, and the drop in the costs of obtaining them present an appealing avenue of exploration: Rendered images can be tailored for many computer vision applications. Sun and Saenko [22] used rendered images as a basis for creating object detectors, followed by an adaption approach based on decorrelated features. Stark et al. [20] used 3D models of cars as a source for labeled data. They learned spatial part layouts which were used for detection. However, their approach requires manual labeling of semantic part locations and it is not clear how easy this can scale up to the large number of objects now addresses in most systems. A set of highly detailed renders was used to train ensembles of exemplar detectors for vehicle viewpoint estimation in [14]. Their approach required no manual labeling but the joint discriminative optimization of the ensembles has a large computational footprint and will be hard to scale as well. Pepik et al. [18] showed that deep networks are not invariant to certain appearance changes, and use rendered data to augment the training data, and in [9, 25] rendered data is used to train pedestrian detectors.

Here, we show that detailed renders from a large set of high quality 3D models can be a key part of scaling up labeled data set curation. This was unfeasible just 10 years ago due to computational costs, but a single GPU today has three orders of magnitude more compute power than the server farm used by Pixar for their 1995 movie Toy Story [6]. The time is ripe for re-examining synthetic image generation as a tool for computer vision. Perhaps most similar to our work is [21] in which rendered images from a set of 3D models were employed for the task of viewpoint estimation. However, while they focus on creating an end-to-end system, our goal is to systematically examine the benefits of rendered data.

3 Data Generation Process

To highlight the benefits of synthetic data we opt to focus on the car object class. We use a database of 91 highly detailed 3D CAD models obtained from doschdesign.com and turbosquid.com.

For each model we perform the following procedure. We define a sphere of radius R centered at the model. We create virtual cameras evenly spaced on the sphere in one degree increments over rings at 5 elevations: $-5°, 0°, 10°, 20°, 30°$. Each camera is used to create a render of one viewpoint of the object. We explore the following rendering parameters:

Lighting Position. We uniformly sample the location of a directed light on a sphere, with elevation in $[10°, 80°]$.

Light Intensity. We uniformly sample the Luminous power (total emitted visible light power measured in lumens) between 1,400 and 10,000. A typical 100 W incandescent light bulb emits about 1500 lumens of light, and normal day light is between 5,000 and 10,000 lumens. The amount of power needed by the light source also depends on the size of the object, and the distance of the light source from it. As models were built at varying scales, the sampling of this parameter might require some adjustments between models.

Light Type	Candle	40W Tungsten	100W Tungsten	Halogen	Carbon	Noon Sun	Direct Sunlight	Overcast Sky	Clear Blue Sky
Temperature	1900	2600	2850	3200	5200	5400	6000	7000	20000
Color									

Fig. 3. Set of light source temperatures used in rendering process. We create each render with a randomly selected temperature.

Light Temperature. We randomly pick one of $K = 9$ light temperature profiles. Each profile is designed to mimic a real world light scenario, such as midday sun, tungsten light bulb, overcast sky, halogen light, etc. (see Fig. 3).

Camera F-stop. We sample the camera aperture F-stop uniformly between 2.7 and 8.3. This parameter controls both the amount of light entering the camera, and the depth of field in which the camera retains focus.

Camera Shutter Speed. We uniformly sample shutter speeds between $1/25$ and $1/200$ of a second. This controls the amount of light entering the camera.

Lens Vignetting. This parameter simulates the optical vignetting effect of real world cameras. Vignetting is a reduction of image brightness and saturation at the periphery compared to the image center. For 25 % of the images we add vignetting with a constant radius.

Background. Renders are layered with a natural image background patches that are randomly selected from PASCAL training images not from the "Car" class.

For rendering the images we use 3DS MAX, with the production quality VRAY rendering plug-in [8]. There has been considerable evidence that data augmentation methods can contribute to the accuracy of trained deep networks [27]. Therefore, we augment our rendered images by creating new images, as follows:

Compression Effects. Most of the images that the trained classifier will get to observe during test time are JPEG compressed images. Our renders are much cleaner, and are saved in lossless PNG format. In most cases JPEG compression is not destructive enough to be visually noticeable, but it was shown that it can influence classifier performance. We therefore JPEG compress all renders.

Color Cast. For each channel of the image, with probability $\frac{1}{2}$ we add a value sampled uniformly in $[-20, 20]$.

Channel Swap. With probability 50 % we randomly swap the color channels.

Image Degradation. Some ground truth bounding boxes are very small. The resulting object resolution is very different than our high resolution renders. In order for the model to learn to classify correctly lower resolution images, we estimate the bounding box area using the PASCAL training set, and 5 downsample 25 % of the renders to a size that falls in the lower 30 % of the distribution.

(a) Sample Images From RenderCar   (b) Fully Rendered Scene

Fig. 4. (a) Rendered training images with data augmentation. (b) To evaluate the use of renders as test data we create scenes in which an object is placed in a fully modeled environment. This is challenging for models trained on natural images (Table 1).

Occlusions. To get robustness to occlusions we randomly place rectangular patches either from the PASCAL training set, or of uniform color, on the renders. The size of the rectangle is sampled between 0.2 and 0.6 of the render size.

Finally, we perform a train/test split of the data such that images from 90 models are used for training, and one model is held out for testing. The resulting datasets have 819,000 and 1,800 images respectively. Figure 4(a) shows a number of rendered images after application of the data augmentation methods listed above. We name this dataset RenderCar.

With the steady increase in computational power, the lowered cost of rendering software, and the availability of 3D CAD models, for the first time it is now becoming possible to fully model not just the object of interest, but also its surrounding environment. Figure 4(b) shows a fully rendered images from one such scene. Rendering such a fully realistic image takes considerably more time

Table 1. Median angular error of car viewpoint estimation on ground truth bounding boxes. Note the distinct effect of dataset bias: the best model on each dataset is the one trained on the corresponding training set. On average, the model trained on rendered images performs similarly to that trained on PASCAL, and better than one that is trained on CMUCar. Combining rendered data with natural images produces lower error than when combining two natural-image datasets. Combining all three datasets provides lowest error. Last column shows average error on columns 1, 2, 5.

Training	Validation						
	PASCAL	CMUCar	RenderCar	Render full scene	P+C	Avg	Avg on natural
PASCAL (P)	16°	6°	18°	14°	8°	12.4°	10°
CMUCar (C)	29.5°	**2°**	27°	13°	5°	15.3°	12.17°
RenderCar (R)	18°	6°	**2°**	8°	8°	8.4°	10.67°
P+C	15°	3°	13°	9°	5°	9°	7.67°
P+R	**11°**	6°	4°	6°	6°	6.6°	7.67°
C+R	15°	**2°**	**2°**	**5°**	4°	5.6°	7°
P+C+R	12°	**2°**	**1°**	8°	**3°**	**5.2°**	**5.67°**

and computational resources than just the model. Note the interaction between the model and the scene – shadows, reflections, etc. While we can not, at the moment, produce a large enough dataset of such renders to be used for training purposes, we can utilize a smaller set of rendered scene images for *validation*. We create a dataset of fully rendered scenes which we term RenderScene. In Table 1 we show that such a set is useful for evaluating models trained on real images.

4   Network Architecture and Loss Function

Following the success of deep learning based approaches in object detection and classification, We base our network architecture on the widely used AlexNet model [11] with a number of modifications. The most important of those changes is our introduced loss function. Most previous work on viewpoint estimation task have simply reduced it to a regular classification problem. The continuous viewpoint space is discretized into a set of class labels, and a classification loss, most commonly SoftMax, is used to train the network. This approach has a number of appealing properties: (1) SoftMax is a well understood loss and one that has been used successfully in many computer vision tasks. (2) The predictions of a SoftMax are associated with probability values that indicate the model's confidence in the prediction. (3) The classification task is easier than a full regression to a real value angle which can reduce over-fitting.

There is one glaring problem with this reduction - it does not take into account the circular nature of angle values. The discretized angles are just treated as class labels, and any mistake the model makes is penalized in the same way. There is much information that is lost if the distance between the predicted angle and the ground truth is not taken into account when computing the error gradients. We use a generalization of the SoftMax loss function that allows us to take into account distance-on-a-ring between the angle class labels:

$$E = -\frac{1}{N} \sum_{n=1}^{N} \sum_{k=1}^{K} w_{l_n,k} \log(p_{n,k}), \tag{1}$$

where N is the number of images, K the number of classes, l_n the ground truth label of instance n, and $p_{n,k}$ the probability of the class k in example n. $w_{l_n,k}$ is a Von Mises kernel centered at l_n, with the width of the kernel controlled by σ:

$$w_{l_n,k} = \exp(-\frac{\min(|l_n - k|, K - |l_n - k|)}{\sigma^2}). \tag{2}$$

The Von Mises kernel implements a circular normal distribution centered at $0°$. This formulation penalizes predictions that are far, in angle space, more than smaller mistakes. By acknowledging the different types of mistakes, more information flows back through the gradients. An intuitive way to understand this loss, is as a matrix of class-to-class weights where the values indicate the weights w. A standard Softmax loss would have a weight of 1 on the diagonal of the matrix, and 0 elsewhere. In the angle-aware version, some weight is given to nearby classes, and there is a wrap-around such that weight is also given when the distance between the predicted and true class crosses the $0°$ boundary.

5 Evaluation

Our objective is to evaluate the usefulness of rendered data for training. First, we compare the result of the deep network architecture described in Sect. 4 on two fine-grained viewpoint estimation datasets:

CMU-Car. The MIT street scene data set [1] was augmented by Boddeti et al. [2] with landmark annotations for 3,433 cars. To allow for evaluation of precise viewpoint estimation Movshovitz-Attias et al. [14] further augmented this data set by providing camera matrices for 3,240 cars. They manually annotated a 3D CAD car model with the same landmark locations as the images and used the POSIT algorithm to align the model to the images.

PASCAL3D+. The dataset built by [28] augments 12 rigid categories of the PASCAL VOC 2012 with 3D annotations. Similar to above, the annotations were collected by manually matching correspondence points from CAD models to images. On top of those, more images are added for each category from the ImageNet dataset. PASCAL3D+ images exhibit much more variability compared to the existing 3D datasets, and on average there are more than 3,000 object instances per category. Most prior work however do not use the added ImageNet data and restrict themselves to only the images from PASCAL VOC 2012.

We also define two synthetic datasets, which consist the two types of rendered images described in Sect. 3 – **RenderCar** and **RenderScene**. The RenderCar dataset includes images from the entire set of 3D CAD models of vehicles. We use the various augmentation methods described above. For RenderScene we use a single car model placed in a fully modeled environment which depicts a fully realistic industrial scene as shown in Fig. 4(b), rendered over all 1800 angles as described in Sect. 3.

We focus our evaluation on the process of viewpoint prediction, and work directly on ground truth bounding boxes. Most recent work on detecting objects and estimating their viewpoint, first employ an RCNN style bounding box selection process [21] so we feel our approach is reasonable.

We split each dataset into train/validation sets and train a separate deep model on each one of the training sets. We then apply every model to the validation sets and report the results. We perform viewpoint estimation on ground truth bounding boxes for images of the car class. For PASCAL3D+ and CMU-Car these bounding boxes were obtained using annotators, and for the rendered images these were automatically created as the tightest rectangle that contains all pixels that belong to the rendered car.

Figure 5 shows the median angular azimuth error of 4 models when evaluated on the PASCAL validation set. While the model trained on PASCAL performs better than the one trained on rendered data it has an unfair advantage - the rendered model needs to overcome domain adaptation as well as the challenging task of viewpoint estimation. Note that the model trained on rendered data performs much better than the one trained on CMUCar. To us this indicates that some of the past concerns about generality of models trained from synthetic data may be unfounded. It seems that the adaptation task from synthetic data is not

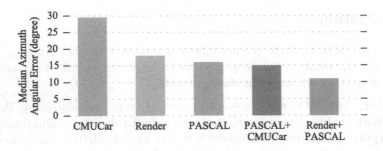

Fig. 5. Median angular error on the PASCAL test set for a number of models. The model trained on PASCAL is the best model trained on a single dataset, but it has the advantage of having access to PASCAL images during training. Combining PASCAL images with rendered training data performs better then combining them with additional natural images from CMUCar.

harder than from one real image set to another. Lastly note that best performance is achieved when combining real data with synthetic data. This model achieves better performance than when combining PASCAL data with images from CMUCar. CMUCar images are all street scene images taken from standing height. They have a strong bias, and add little to a model's generalization.

Figure 6 shows example results on the ground truth bounding boxes from the PASCAL3d+ test set. Successful predictions are shown in the top two rows, and failure cases in the bottom row. The test set is characterized by many cropped and occluded images, some of very poor image quality. Mostly the model is robust to these, but when it mostly fails due to these issues, or the 180° ambiguity.

Table 1 shows model error for azimuth estimation for all train/validation combinations. First, it is easy to spot dataset bias - the best performing model on each dataset is the one that was trained on a training set from that dataset. This is consistent with the findings of [24] that show strong dataset bias effects. It is also interesting to see how some datasets are better for generalizing. The two right most columns average prediction error across multiple datasets. The *Avg* column averages across all datasets, and *Avg On Natural* averages the results on the 3 columns that use natural images for testing. Notice that the model trained on PASCAL data performs better overall than the one trained on CMUcar. Also notice that the model trained on RenderCar performs almost as well as the one trained on PASCAL. When combining data from multiple datasets the overall error is reduced. Unsurprisingly, combining all datasets produces the best results. It is interesting to note, however, that adding rendered data to one of the natural image datasets produces better results than when combining the two real-image ones. We conclude that this is because the rendered data adds two forms of variation: (1) It provides access to regions of the label space that were not present in the small natural-image datasets. (2) The image statistics of rendered images are different than those of natural images and the learner is forced to generalize better in order to classify both types of images. We further examine the effect of combining real and synthetic data below.

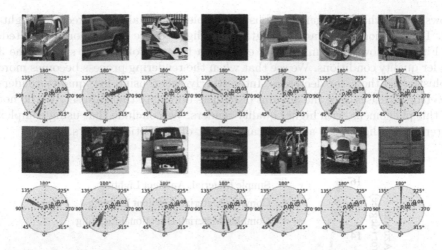

Fig. 6. Sample results of our proposed method from the test set of PASCAL3D+. Below each image we show viewpoint probabilities assigned by the model (blue), predictions (red), and ground truth (green). Right column shows failure cases. Strongly directional occluders and 180° ambiguity are the most common failures. (Color figure online)

Render Quality: Renders can be created in varying degrees of quality and realism. Simple, almost cartoon-like renders are fast to generate, while ones that realistically model the interplay of lighting and material can be quite computationally expensive. Are these higher quality renders worth the added cost?

Figure 7 shows 3 render conditions we use to evaluate the effect of render quality on system performance. The top row shows the basic condition, renders created using simplified model materials, and uniform ambient lighting. In the middle row are images created using a more complex rendering procedure – the materials used are complex. They more closely resemble the metallic surface of real vehicles. We still use ambient lighting when creating them. The bottom row

Fig. 7. We evaluate the effect of render quality under 3 conditions: simple object material, and ambient lighting (top row); complex material and ambient lighting (middle); and a sophisticated case using complex material, and directional lighting whose location, color, and strength are randomly selected (bottom).

shows images that were generated using complex materials and directional lighting. The location, color, and strength of the light source are randomly selected.

Figure 8 shows median angular error as a function of dataset size for the 3 render quality conditions. We see that when the rendering process becomes more sophisticated the error decreases. Interestingly, when using low quality renders the error increases once the amount of renders dominate the train set. We do not see this phenomena with higher quality renders. We conclude that using complex materials and lighting is an important aspect of synthetic datasets.

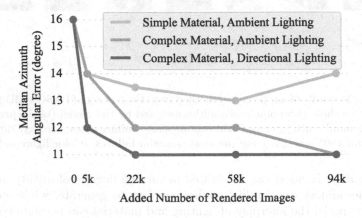

Fig. 8. Error as a function of dataset size for the 3 render quality conditions described in Fig. 7. All methods add rendered images to the PASCAL training set. There is a decrease in error when complex model materials are used, and a further decrease when we add random lighting conditions.

Balancing a Training Set Using Renders: So far we have seen that combining real images with synthetically generated ones improves performance. Intuitively this makes sense, the model is given more data, and thus learns a better representation. But is there something more than that going on? Consider a trained model. What are the properties we would want it to have? We would naturally want it to be as accurate as possible. We would also want it to be unbiased – to be accurate in all locations in feature/label space. But bias in the training set makes this goal hard to achieve. Renders can be useful for bias reduction.

In Fig. 9 we quantify this requirement. It shows the accuracy of 3 models as a function of the angle range in which they are applied. For example, a model trained on 5k PASCAL images (top row), has about 0.8 accuracy when it is applied on test images with a ground truth label in [0,9].

We want the shape of the accuracy distribution to be as close to uniform as possible. Instead, we see that the model performs much better on some angles, such as [0,30], than others, [80,100]. If the shape of the distribution seems familiar it is because it closely mirrors the training set distribution shown in Fig. 1. We calculate the models' entropy on the accuracy distribution entropy as a tool for

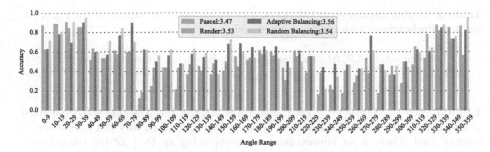

Fig. 9. Model accuracy as a function of ground truth angle. A model should perform uniformly well across all angles. The entropy of each distribution (legend) shows deviation from uniform. For the model trained on PASCAL images (blue), the accuracy mirrors the train set distribution (Fig. 1). The entropy of a model trained on rendered images is higher, but still not uniform (orange). This is due to biases in the test set. Brown and light blue bars show accuracy distribution of models for which rendered images were used to balance the training set. We see they have higher entropy with adaptive balancing having the highest. Models were tested on PASCAL test images. (Color figure online)

comparison. Higher entropy indicates a more uniform distribution. When using a fully balanced training set of rendered images (2nd row), the test entropy increases. This is encouraging, as the model contains less angle bias.

Rendered images can be used as a way to balance the training set to reduce bias while still getting the benefits of natural images. We experiment with two methods for balancing which we call adaptive balancing (3rd row), and random balancing (bottom row). In adaptive balancing we sample each angle reversely proportional to its frequency in the training set. This method transforms the training set to uniform using the least number of images. In random balancing the added synthetic images are sampled uniformly. As the ratio of rendered images in the training set increases, the set becomes more uniform. For this experiment both methods added 2,000 images to the PASCAL training set. Interestingly, the two balancing methods have a similar prediction entropy. However, no method's distribution is completely uniform. From that we can conclude that there are biases in the test data other than angle distribution, or that some angles are just naturally harder to predict than others.

These results raise an interesting question: how much of the performance gap we have seen between models trained on real PASCAL images, and those trained on rendered data stems from the angle bias of the test set? Table 2 shows the median errors of these models on a sample of the PASCAL test set in which all angles are equally represented. Once the test set is uniform we see that models based on a balanced training set perform best, and the model trained solely on PASCAL images has the worst accuracy.

Lastly, we hold constant the number of images used for training and vary the proportion of rendered images. Table 3 shows the error of models trained with varying proportions of real-to-rendered data. Models are trained using 5,000

Table 2. Median angular error (MAE) on a viewpoint-uniform sample of the PASCAL test set. Performance with rendered based training set is best.

Training set:	PASCAL	Render	Adaptive balancing	Random balancing
MAE:	26.5°	26.0°	**16.0°**	17.5°

Table 3. Median angular error (MAE) on PASCAL test set. Training set size is fixed at 5k images (the size of the PASCAL training set) and we modify the proportion of renders used. There is an improvement when replacing up to $\frac{1}{2}$ of the images with renders. The renders help balance the angle distribution and reduce bias.

Renders in train set:	0%	25%	50%	75%	100%
Median angular error:	16°	**14°**	**14°**	15°	22°

images – the size of the PASCAL training set. Notice that there is an improvement when replacing up to 50% of the images with rendered data. This is likely due to the balancing effect of the renders on the angle distribution which reduces bias. When most of the data is rendered, performance drops. This is likely because the image variability in renders is smaller than real images. More synthetic data is needed for models based purely on it to achieve the lowest error – 18°.

Size of Training Set: We examine the role of raw number of renders in performance. We keep the number of CAD models constant at 90, and uniformly sample renders from our pool of renders. Many of the cars in PASCAL are only partially visible, and we want the models to learn this, so in each set half the rendered images show full cars, and half contain random 60% crops Table 4 summarizes the results of this experiment. Better performance is achieved when increasing the number of renders, but there are diminishing returns. There is a limit to the variability a model can learn from a fixed set of CAD models, and one would need to increase the size of the model set to overcome this. Obtaining a large amount of 3D models can be expensive and so this motivates creation of large open source model datasets.

Loss Layer: When using Von Mises kernel-based SoftMax loss function is that it is impossible to obtain zero loss. In a regular SoftMax, if the model assigns prob-

Table 4. Effect of training set size and loss layer. We see a trend of better performance with increased size of training set, but the effect quickly diminishes. Clearly, more than just training set size influences performance. The Von Mises weighted SoftMax (wSM) performs better than regular SoftMax (SM) for all train sizes.

Train set size	10k		50k		330k		820k	
Loss layer	SM	wSM	SM	wSM	SM	wSM	SM	wSM
MAE	31°	27.5°	54.5°	21°	26°	21.5°	23°	**18°**

Table 5. Effect of kernel width (σ) of the Von Mises kernel. The loss function is not sensitive to the selection of kernel width.

σ	2	3	4	10	15
Effective width	6°	8°	12°	30°	50°
Median angular error	13°	14°	14°	**13°**	15°

Table 6. Effect of added occlusions to the training set. All models evaluated used datasets of 50,000 rendered images.

% Occluded images	0.0	0.1	0.35	0.4	0.5	1.0
MAE		25°	25°	**21°**	25°	28°	26°

ability 1.0 to the correct class it can achieve a loss of zero. In the weighted case, when there is some weight assigned to more than one class, a perfect prediction will actually result in infinite loss, as all other classes have probability values of zero, and the log-loss assigned to them will be infinite. Minimum loss will be reached when prediction probabilities are spread out across nearby classes. This is both a downside of this loss function, but also its strength. It does not let the model make wild guesses at the correct class. Nearby views are required to have similar probabilities. It trades angle resolution with added prediction stability.

Table 4 compares the results of SoftMax based models and models trained using the weighted SoftMax layer over a number of rendered dataset sizes. The weighted loss layer performs better for all sizes. This supports our hypothesis that viewpoint estimation is not a standard classification task. Most experiments in this section were performed using $\sigma = 2$ for the Von Mises kernel in Equation (2). This amounts to an effective width of 6°, meaning that predictions that are farther away from the ground truth will not be assigned any weight. Table 5 shows the effect of varying this value. Interestingly we see that the method is robust to this parameter, and performs well for a wide range of values. It appears that even a relatively weak correlation between angles provides benefits.

Occlusion: The PASCAL test set contains many instances of partially occluded cars. When augmenting synthetic data we add randomly sized occlusions to a subset of the rendered images. Table 6 shows that there is some benefit from generating occlusions, but when too many of the training images are occluded it becomes harder for the model to learn. What is the best way to generate occlusions? In our work we have experimented with simple, single color, rectangular occlusions, as well as occlusions based on random patches from PASCAL. We saw no difference in model performance. It would be interesting to examine the optimal spatial occlusion relationship. This is likely to be object class dependent.

6 Discussion

In this work we propose the use of rendered images as a way to automatically build datasets for viewpoint estimation. We show that models trained on renders are competitive with those trained on natural images – the gap in performance can be explained by domain adaptation. Moreover, models trained on a combination of synthetic/real data outperform ones trained on natural images.

The need for large scale datasets is growing with the increase in model size. Based on the results detailed here we believe that synthetic data should be an important part of dataset creation strategies. We feel that a combination a small set of carefully annotated images, combined with a larger number of synthetic renders, with automatically assigned labels, has the best cost-to-benefit ratio.

This strategy is not limited to viewpoint estimation, and can be employed for a range of computer vision tasks. Specifically we feel that future research should focus on human pose estimation, depth prediction, wide-baseline correspondence learning, and structure from motion.

References

1. Bileschi, S.M.: StreetScenes: towards scene understanding in still images. Ph.D. thesis, Massachusetts Institute of Technology (2006)
2. Boddeti, V.N., Kanade, T., Kumar, B.: Correlation filters for object alignment. In: Proceedings of the IEEE Conference on Computer Vision and Pattern Recognition (CVPR). IEEE (2013)
3. Dean, J., Corrado, G., Monga, R., Chen, K., Devin, M., Mao, M., Ranzato, M., Senior, A., Tucker, P., Yang, K., Le, Q.V., Ng, A.Y.: Large scale distributed deep networks. In: Advances in Neural Information Processing Systems (NIPS), pp. 1223–1231 (2012)
4. Deng, J., Dong, W., Socher, R., Li, L.J., Li, K., Fei-Fei, L.: Imagenet: a large-scale hierarchical image database. In: Proceedings of the IEEE Conference on Computer Vision and Pattern Recognition (CVPR) (2009)
5. Everingham, M., Van Gool, L., Williams, C., Winn, J., Zisserman, A.: The pascal visual object classes challenge 2011 (VOC2011) results (2011)
6. Fatahalian, K.: Enolving the real-time graphics pipeline for micropolygon rendering. Ph.D. thesis, Stanford University (2011)
7. Goodfellow, I.J., Bulatov, Y., Ibarz, J., Arnoud, S., Shet, V.: Multi-digit number recognition from street view imagery using deep convolutional neural networks. arXiv preprint arXiv:1312.6082 (2013)
8. Group, C: Vray rendering engine (2015). http://www.chaosgroup.com
9. Hattori, H., Naresh Boddeti, V., Kitani, K.M., Kanade, T.: Learning scene-specific pedestrian detectors without real data. In: Proceedings of the IEEE Conference on Computer Vision and Pattern Recognition (CVPR) (2015)
10. Heimerl, K., Gawalt, B., Chen, K., Parikh, T., Hartmann, B.: CommunitySourcing: engaging local crowds to perform expert work via physical kiosks. In: Proceedings of the SIGCHI Conference on Human Factors in Computing Systems. ACM (2012)
11. Krizhevsky, A., Sutskever, I., Hinton, G.E.: Imagenet classification with deep convolutional neural networks. In: NIPS (2012)
12. Law, E., Settles, B., Snook, A., Surana, H., Von Ahn, L., Mitchell, T.: Human computation for attribute and attribute value acquisition. In: Proceedings of the First Workshop on Fine-Grained Visual Categorization (FGVC) (2011)
13. Lepetit, V., Moreno-Noguer, F., Fua, P.: EPnP: an accurate $O(n)$ solution to the PnP problem. International Journal Computer Vision **81**, 155–166 (2009)
14. Movshovitz-Attias, Y., Naresh Boddeti, V., Wei, Z., Sheikh, Y.: 3D pose-by-detection of vehicles via discriminatively reduced ensembles of correlation filters. In: Proceedings of the British Machine Vision Conference (BMVC), Nottingham, UK, September 2014

15. Movshovitz-Attias, Y., Yu, Q., Stumpe, M., Shet, V., Arnoud, S., Yatziv, L.: Ontological supervision for fine grained classification of street view storefronts. In: Proceedings of the IEEE Conference on Computer Vision and Pattern Recognition (CVPR) (2015)
16. Nene, S.A., Nayar, S.K., Murase, H., et al.: Columbia object image library (coil-20). Technical report CUCS-005-96 (1996)
17. Oliva, A., Torralba, A.: Modeling the shape of the scene: a holistic representation of the spatial envelope. Int. J. Comput. Vis. **42**(3), 145–175 (2001)
18. Pepik, B., Benenson, R., Ritschel, T., Schiele, B.: What is holding back convnets for detection? CoRR (2015). http://arxiv.org/abs/1508.02844
19. Russakovsky, O., Deng, J., Su, H., Krause, J., Satheesh, S., Ma, S., Huang, Z., Karpathy, A., Khosla, A., Bernstein, M., Berg, A.C., Fei-Fei, L.: Imagenet large scale visual recognition challenge. Int. J. Comput. Vis. **115**, 211–252 (2014)
20. Stark, M., Goesele, M., Schiele, B.: Back to the future: learning shape models from 3D cad data. In: Proceedings of the British Machine Vision Conference (BMVC) (2010)
21. Su, H., Qi, C.R., Li, Y., Guibas, L.J.: Render for CNN: viewpoint estimation in images using CNNs trained with rendered 3D model views. In: Proceedings of the IEEE International Conference on Computer Vision (ICCV) (2015)
22. Sun, B., Saenko, K.: From virtual to reality: fast adaptation of virtual object detectors to real domains. In: Proceedings of the British Machine Vision Conference (BMVC) (2014)
23. Szegedy, C., Liu, W., Jia, Y., Sermanet, P., Reed, S., Anguelov, D., Erhan, D., Vanhoucke, V., Rabinovich, A.: Going deeper with convolutions. arXiv:1409.4842 [cs], September 2014
24. Torralba, A., Efros, A.: Unbiased look at dataset bias. In: Proceedings of the IEEE Conference on Computer Vision and Pattern Recognition (CVPR). IEEE (2011)
25. Vazquez, D., Lopez, A.M., Marin, J., Ponsa, D., Geronimo, D.: Virtual and real world adaptation for pedestrian detection. IEEE Trans. Pattern Anal. Mach. Intell. **36**, 797–809 (2014)
26. Von Ahn, L., Dabbish, L.: Labeling images with a computer game. In: Proceedings of the SIGCHI Conference on Human Factors in Computing Systems. ACM (2004)
27. Wu, R., Yan, S., Shan, Y., Dang, Q., Sun, G.: Deep image: scaling up image recognition. arXiv preprint arXiv:1501.02876 (2015). http://arxiv.org/abs/1501.02876
28. Xiang, Y., Mottaghi, R., Savarese, S.: Beyond pascal: a benchmark for 3D object detection in the wild. In: Winter Conference on Applications of Computer Vision (WACV) (2014)

Learning the Structure of Objects from Web Supervision

David Novotny[1,2(✉)], Diane Larlus[2], and Andrea Vedaldi[1]

[1] Visual Geometry Group, University of Oxford, Oxford, UK
{david,vedaldi}@robots.ox.ac.uk
[2] Computer Vision Group, Xerox Research Centre Europe, Meylan, France
diane.larlus@xrce.xerox.com

Abstract. While recent research in image understanding has often focused on recognizing *more types of objects*, understanding *more about the objects* is just as important. Learning about object parts and their geometric relationships has been extensively studied before, yet learning large space of such concepts remains elusive due to the high cost of collecting detailed object annotations for supervision. The key contribution of this paper is an algorithm to learn geometric and semantic structure of objects and their semantic parts automatically, from images obtained by querying the Web. We propose a novel embedding space where geometric relationships are induced in a soft manner by a rich set of non-semantic mid-level anchors, bridging the gap between semantic and non-semantic parts. We also show that the resulting embedding provides a visually-intuitive mechanism to navigate the learned concepts and their corresponding images.

Keywords: Object part detection · Web supervision · Mid-level patches

1 Introduction

Modern deep learning methods have dramatically improved the performance of computer vision algorithms, from image classification [1] to image captioning [2,3] and activity recognition [4]. Even so, image understanding remains rather crude, oblivious to most of the nuances of real world images. Consider for example the notion of *object category*, which is a basic unit of understanding in computer vision. Modern benchmarks consider an increasingly large number of such categories, from thousands in the ILSVRC challenge [5] to hundred thousands in the full ImageNet [6]. Despite this ontological richness, there is only limited understanding of the internal geometric structure and semantics of these categories.

Electronic supplementary material The online version of this chapter (doi:10. 1007/978-3-319-49409-8_19) contains supplementary material, which is available to authorized users.

G. Hua and H. Jégou (Eds.): ECCV 2016 Workshops, Part III, LNCS 9915, pp. 218–235, 2016.
DOI: 10.1007/978-3-319-49409-8_19

Fig. 1. Our goal is to learn the semantic structure of objects automatically using Web supervision. For example, given noisy images obtained by querying an Internet search engine for "car wheel" and for "cars", we aim at learning the "car wheel" concept, and its dual nature: as an object in its own right, and as a component of another object.

Fig. 2. Top images retrieved from an Internet search engine for some example queries. Note that part results are more noisy than full object results (the remaining collected images get even noisier, not shown here).

In this paper we aim at learning the internal details of object categories by jointly *learning about objects, their semantic parts, and their geometric relationships*. Learning about semantic *nameable* parts plays a crucial role in visual understanding. However, standard supervised approaches are difficult to apply to this problem due to the cost of collecting large quantities of annotated example images. A scalable approach needs to discover this information with *minimal or no supervision*.

As a scalable source of data, we look at Web supervision to learn the structure of objects from thousands of images obtained automatically by querying search engines (*crf.* Fig. 1). This poses two significant challenges: identifying images of the semantic parts in very noisy Web results (crf. Fig. 2) while, at the same time, discovering their geometric relationships. The latter is particularly difficult due to the drastic scale changes of parts when they are imaged in the context of the whole object or in isolation.

If parts are looked at independently, noise and scale changes can easily confuse image recognition models. Instead, one needs to account for the fact that object classes have a well-defined geometric structure which constraints how different parts fit together. Thus, we need to introduce a *geometric frame* that can, for any view of an object class, constrain and regularize the location of the visible semantic parts, establishing better correspondences between views.

Traditional representations such as spring models were found to be too fragile to work in our Webly-supervised setting. To solve this issue, we introduce a novel vector embedding that encodes the geometry of parts relatively to a robust reference frame. This reference frame builds on non-semantic anchor parts which are learned automatically using a new method for non-semantic part discovery (Sect. 2.2); we show that this method is significantly better than alternative and more complex techniques for part discovery. The new geometric embedding is further combined with appearance cues and used to improve the performance in semantic part detection and matching.

A byproduct of our method is a large collection of images annotated with objects, semantic parts, and their geometric relationships, that we refer to as a *visual semantic atlas* (Sect. 4). This atlas allows to *visually navigate* images based on conceptual and geometric relations. It also emphasizes the dual nature of parts, as components of an object and as semantic categories, by naturally bridging images that zooms on a part or that contain the object as a whole.

1.1 Related Work

Our work touches on several active research areas: localizing objects with weak supervision, learning with Web images, and discovering or learning mid-level features and object parts.

Localizing Objects with Weak Supervision. When training models to localize objects or parts, it is impractical to expect large quantities of bounding box annotations. Recent works have tackled the localization problem with only image-level annotations. Among them, *weakly supervised object localization* methods [7–13] assume for each image a list of every object type it contains. In the *co-detection* [14–17] and *co-segmentation* [18–21] problems, the algorithm is given a set of images that all contain at least one instance of a particular object. They differ in their output: co-detection predicts bounding boxes, while segmentation predicts pixel-level masks. Yet, co-detection, co-segmentation and weakly-supervised object localization (WSOL) are different flavors of the localization problem with weak supervision. For co-detection and WSOL, the task is nearly always formulated as a multiple instance learning (MIL) problem [7,8,16,22,23]. The formulation in [11,12] departs from MIL by leveraging the strong annotations for some categories to transfer knowledge to the remaining categories. A few approaches model images using topic models [10,17].

Recently, CNN architectures were also proved to work well in weakly supervised scenarios [24]. We will compare with [24] in the experiments section. None of these works have considered semantic parts. Closer to our work, the method of [25] proposes unsupervised discovery of dominant objects using part-based region matching. Because of its unsupervised process, this method is not suited to name the discovered objects or matched regions, and hence lack semantics. Yet we also compare with this approach in our experiments.

Learning from Web Supervision. Most previous works [26–29] that learn from noisy Web images have focused on image classification. Usually, they adopt an iterative approach that jointly learns models and finds clean examples of a target concept. Only few works have looked at the problem of localization. Some approaches [21,30] discover common segments within a large set of Web images, but they do not quantitatively evaluate localization. The recent method of [31] localizes objects with bounding boxes, and evaluate the learnt models, but as the previous two, it does not consider object parts.

Closer to our work, [32] aims at discovering common sense knowledge relations between object categories from Web images, some of which correspond to the "part-of" relation. In the process of organizing the different appearance variations of Webly mined concepts, [33] uses a "vocabulary of variance" that may include part names, but those are not associated to any geometry.

Unsupervised Parts, Mid-level Features, and Semantic Parts. Objects are modeled using the notion of *parts* since the early work on pictorial structure [34], in the constellation [35] and ISM [36] models, and more recently the DPM [37]. Parts are most commonly defined as localized components with consistent appearance and geometry in an object. All these works have in common to discover object parts without naming them. In practice, only some of these parts have an actual semantic interpretation. *Mid-level features* [38–43] are discriminative [41,44] or rare [38] blocks, which are leveraged for object recognition. Again, these parts lack semantic. The non-semantic anchors that we use share similarities with [45] and [42], that we discuss in Sect. 2.2. *Semantic* parts have triggered recent interest [46–48]. These works require strong annotations in the form of bounding boxes [46] or segmentation masks [47,48] at the part level. Here we depart from existing work and aim at mining semantic nameable parts with as little supervision as possible.

2 Method

This section introduces our method to learn semantic parts using weak supervision from Web sources. The key challenge is that search engines, when queried for object parts, return many outliers containing other parts as well, the whole object, or entirely unrelated things (Fig. 2). In this setting, standard weakly-supervised detection approaches fail (Sect. 3). Our solution is a novel, robust, and flexible representation of object parts (Sect. 2.1) that uses the output of a simple but very effective non-semantic part discovery algorithm (Sect. 2.2).

2.1 Learning Semantic Parts Using Non-semantic Anchors

In this section, we first flesh out our method for weakly-supervised part learning and then dive into the theoretical justification of our choices.

MIL: Baseline, Context, and Geometry-Aware. As standard in weakly-supervised object detection, our method starts from the *Multiple Instance Learning* (MIL) [49] algorithm. Let $\mathbf{x}_i$ be an image and let $\mathcal{R}(\mathbf{x}_i)$ be a shortlist of image regions R that are likely to contain objects or parts, obtained for instance using selective search [50]. Each image $\mathbf{x}_i$ can be either positive $y_i = +1$ if it is deemed to contain a certain part or negative $y_i = -1$ if not. MIL fits to this data a (linear) scoring function $\langle \phi(\mathbf{x}_i|R), \mathbf{w} \rangle$, where $\mathbf{w}$ is a vector of parameters and $\phi(\mathbf{x}_i|R) \in \mathbb{R}^d$ is a descriptor of the region R of image $\mathbf{x}_i$, by minimizing:

$$\min_{\mathbf{w} \in \mathbb{R}^d} \frac{\lambda}{2} \|\mathbf{w}\|^2 + \frac{1}{n} \sum_{i=1}^{n} \max\{0, 1 - y_i \max_{R \in \mathcal{R}(\mathbf{x}_i)} \langle \phi(\mathbf{x}_i|R), \mathbf{w} \rangle\} \qquad (1)$$

In practice, Eq. (1) is optimized by alternatively selecting the maximum scoring region for each image (also known as "re-localization") and optimizing $\mathbf{w}$ for a fixed selection of the regions. In this manner, MIL should automatically discover regions that are most predictive of a given label, and which therefore should correspond to the sought visual entity (object or semantic part). However, this process may fail if descriptors are not sufficiently strong.

For **baseline MIL** the descriptor $\phi(\mathbf{x}|R) = \phi^a(\mathbf{x}|R) \in \mathbb{R}^{d_a}$ captures the region's appearance. A common improvement is to extend this descriptor with *context information* by appending a descriptor of a region $R' = \mu(R)$ surrounding R, where $\mu(R)$ isotropically enlarges R; thus in **context-aware MIL**, $\phi(\mathbf{x}|R) = \text{stack}(\phi^a(\mathbf{x}|R), \phi^a(\mathbf{x}|\mu(R)))$.

Neither baseline or context-aware MIL leverage the fact that objects have a well-defined geometric structure, which significantly constrains the search space for parts. DPM uses such constraints, but as a fixed set of geometric relationships between part pairs that are difficult to learn when examples are extremely noisy. Furthermore, DPM-like approaches learn the most visually-stable parts, which often are *not* the semantic ones.

We propose here an alternative method that captures geometry indirectly, on top of a rich set of unsupervised mid-level non-semantic parts $\{p_1, \ldots, p_K\}$, which we call *anchors* (Fig. 3). Let us assume that, given an image $\mathbf{x}$, we can locate the (selective search) regions $R_{p_k, \mathbf{x}}$ containing each anchor p_k. We define the following geometric embedding ϕ^g of a region R with respect to the anchors:

$$\phi^g(\mathbf{x}|R) = \begin{bmatrix} \rho(R, R_{p_1, \mathbf{x}}) \\ \vdots \\ \rho(R, R_{p_K, \mathbf{x}}) \end{bmatrix}. \qquad (2)$$

Here ρ is a measure such as intersection-over-union (IoU) that tells whether two regions overlap. By choosing a function ρ such as IoU which is invariant to

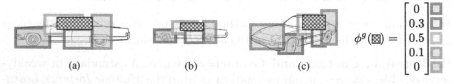

(a)   (b)   (c)

$$\phi^g(\boxtimes) = \begin{bmatrix} 0 \\ 0.3 \\ 0.5 \\ 0.1 \\ 0 \end{bmatrix}$$

Fig. 3. Anchor-induced geometry. (a) A set of anchors (light boxes) are obtained from a large number of unsupervised non-semantic part detectors. The geometry of a semantic part or object is then expressed as a vector ϕ^g of anchor overlaps. (b) The representation is scale and translation invariant. (c) The representation implicitly codes for multiple aspects.

scaling, rotation, and translation of the regions, so is the embedding ϕ^g. Hence, as long as anchors stay attached to the object, $\phi^g(\mathbf{x}|R)$ encodes the location of R relative to an object-centric frame. This representation is robust because, even if some anchors are missing or misplaced, the vector $\phi^g(\mathbf{x}|R)$ is not greatly affected. The geometric encoding $\phi^g(\mathbf{x}|R)$ is combined with the appearance descriptor $\phi^a(\mathbf{x}|R)$ in a joint appearance-geometric embedding

$$\phi^{ag}(\mathbf{x}|R) = \phi^a(\mathbf{x}|R) \otimes \phi^g(\mathbf{x}|R) \tag{3}$$

where $\otimes$ is the Kronecker product. After vectorization, this vector is used as a descriptor $\phi(\mathbf{x}|R) = \phi^{ag}(\mathbf{x}|R)$ of region R in **geometry-aware MIL**. The next few paragraphs discuss its properties.

Modeling Multiple Parts. Plugging ϕ^{ag} of Eq. (3) into Eq. (1) of MIL results in the scoring function $\langle \mathbf{w}, \phi^{ag}(\mathbf{x}|R)\rangle = \sum_{k=1}^{K}\langle \mathbf{w}_k, \phi^a(\mathbf{x}|R)\rangle \rho(R, R_{p_k}, \mathbf{x})$ which interpolates between K appearance models *based on how the region R is geometrically related to the anchors* $R_{p_k}, \mathbf{x}$. In particular, by selecting different anchors this model may capture simultaneously the appearance of all parts of an object. In order to control the capacity of the model, the smoothness of the interpolator can be increased by replacing IoU with a softer version, which we do next.

Smoother Overlap Measure. The IoU measure is a special case of the following family of PD kernels:

Theorem 1. *Let R and Q be vectors in a Hilbert $\mathcal{H}$ space such that $\langle R, R\rangle + \langle Q, Q\rangle - \langle R, Q\rangle > 0$. Then the function $\rho(R, Q) = \frac{\langle R, Q\rangle}{\langle R, R\rangle + \langle Q, Q\rangle - \langle R, Q\rangle}$ is a positive definite kernel.*

The IoU is obtained when R and Q are indicator functions of the respective regions (because $\langle R, Q\rangle = \int R(x, y)Q(x, y)\, dx\, dy = |R \cap Q|$). This suggests a simple modification to construct a Soft IoU (SIoU) version of the latter. For a region $R = [x_1, x_2] \times [y_1, y_2]$, the indicator can be written as $R(x, y) = H(x - x_1)H(x_2 - x)H(y - y_1)H(y_2 - y)$ where $H(z) = [z \geq 0]$ is the Heaviside step function. SIoU is obtained by replacing the indicator by the smoother function $H_\alpha(z) = \exp(\alpha z)/(1 + \exp(\alpha z))$ instead. Note that SIoU is non-zero even when regions do not intersect.

Theorem 1 provides also an interpretation of the geometric embedding ϕ^g of Eq. (2) as a vector of region coordinates relative to the anchors. In fact, its entries can be written as $\rho(R, R_{p_k}, \mathbf{x}) = \langle \psi_{\mathrm{SIoU}}(R), \psi_{\mathrm{SIoU}}(R_{p_k}, \mathbf{x})\rangle$ where $\psi_{\mathrm{SIoU}}(R) \in \mathcal{H}_{\mathrm{SIoU}}$ is the linear embedding (feature map) induced by the kernel ρ^1.

Modeling Multiple Aspects. So far, we have assumed that all parts are always visible; however, anchors also provide a mechanism to deal with the multiple aspects of 3D objects. As depicted in Fig. 3c, as the object rotates out of plane, anchors naturally appear and disappear, therefore activating and de-activating

---

[1] The anchor vectors $\psi_{\mathrm{SIoU}}(R_{p_k}, \mathbf{x})$ are not necessarily orthonormal (they are if anchors do not overlap), but this can be restored up to a linear transformation of the coordinates.

aspect-specific components in the model. In turn, this allows to model viewpoint-specific parts or appearances. In practice, we extract the L highest scoring detections R_l of the same anchor p_k, and keep the one closest to R.

In order to allow anchors to turn off in the model, the geometric embedding is modified as follows. Let $s_k(R_l|\mathbf{x})$ be the detection score of anchor k in correspondence of the region R_l; then

$$\rho(R, R_{p_k, \mathbf{x}}) = \max_{l \in \{1, \ldots, L\}} \text{SIoU}(R, R_l) \times \max\{0, s_k(R_l|\mathbf{x})\}. \tag{4}$$

If the anchor is never detected ($s_k(R_l|\mathbf{x}) \leq 0$ for all R_l) then $\rho(R, R_{p_k, \mathbf{x}}) = 0$. Furthermore, this expression also disambiguates ambiguous anchor detections by picking the one closest to R. Note that in Eq. (4) one can still interpret the factors $\text{SIoU}(R, R_l)$ as projections $\langle \psi_{\text{SIoU}}(R), \psi_{\text{SIoU}}(R_l) \rangle$.

Relation to DPM. DPM is also a MIL method using a joint embedding $\phi^{\text{DPM}}(\mathbf{x}|R_1, \ldots, R_K)$ that codes simultaneously for the appearance of K parts and their pairwise geometric relationships. Our Webly-supervised learning problem requires a representation that can bridge object-focused images (where several parts are visible together as components) and part-focused images (where parts are regarded as objects in their own right). This is afforded by our embedding $\phi^{ag}(\mathbf{x}|R)$ but not by the DPM one. Besides bridging parts as components and parts as objects, our embedding is very robust (important in order to deal with very noisy training labels), automatically codes for multiple object aspects, and bridges unsupervised non-semantic parts (the anchors) with semantic ones.

2.2 Anchors: Weakly-Supervised Non-semantic Parts

The geometric embedding in the previous section leverages the power of an intermediate representation: a collection of anchors $\{p_k\}_{k=1}^K$, learned automatically using weak supervision. While there are many methods to discover discriminative non-semantic mid-level parts from image collections (Sect. 1.1), here we propose a simple alternative that, empirically, works better in our context.

We learn the anchors using a formulation similar to the MIL objective (Eq. (1)):

$$\min_{\boldsymbol{\omega}_1, \ldots, \boldsymbol{\omega}_K} \sum_{k=1}^K \left[\frac{\lambda}{2} \|\boldsymbol{\omega}_k\|^2 - \frac{1}{n} \sum_{i=1}^n y_i \left[\max_{R \in \mathcal{R}(\mathbf{x}_i)} \langle \phi^a(\mathbf{x}_i|R), \boldsymbol{\omega}_k \rangle \right]_+ \right] + \gamma \sum_{k \neq q} \left\langle \frac{\boldsymbol{\omega}_k}{\|\boldsymbol{\omega}_k\|}, \frac{\boldsymbol{\omega}_q}{\|\boldsymbol{\omega}_q\|} \right\rangle^2, \tag{5}$$

where $[z]_+ = \max\{0, z\}$. Intuitively, anchors are learnt as discriminative mid-level parts using weak supervision. Anchor scores $s_k(R|\mathbf{x}) = \langle \phi^a(\mathbf{x}|R), \boldsymbol{\omega}_k \rangle$ are parametrized by vectors $\boldsymbol{\omega}_1, \ldots, \boldsymbol{\omega}_K$; the first term in Eq. (5) is akin to the baseline MIL formulation of Sect. 2.1 and encourages each anchor p_k to score highly in images $\mathbf{x}_i$ that contain the object ($y_i = +1$) and to be inactive otherwise ($y_i = -1$). The last term is very important and encourages the learned models $\{\boldsymbol{\omega}_k\}_{k=1}^K$ to be mutually orthogonal, enforcing *diversity*. Note that anchors use the pure appearance-based region descriptor $\phi^a(\mathbf{x})$ since the geometric-aware descriptor $\phi^{ag}(\mathbf{x})$ can be computed only once anchors are available. Optimization uses stochastic gradient descent with momentum.

This formulation is similar to the MIL approach of [45] which, however, does not contain the orthogonality term. When this term is removed, we observed that the solution degenerates to detecting the most prominent object in an image. [39] uses instead a significantly more complex formulation inspired by mode seeking; in practice we opted for our approach due to its simplicity and effectiveness.

2.3   Incorporating Strong Annotations in MIL

While we are primarily interested in understanding whether semantic object parts can be learned from Web sources alone, in some cases the precise definition of the extent of a part is inherently ambiguous (e.g. what is the extent of a "human nose"?). Different benchmark datasets may use somewhat different definition of these concepts, making evaluation difficult. In order to remove or at least reduce this dataset-dependent ambiguity, we also explore the idea of using a single strongly annotated example to fix this degree of freedom.

Denote by $(\mathbf{x}_a, R_a)$ the single strongly-annotated example of the target part. This is incorporated in the MIL formulation, Eq. (1), by augmenting the score with a factor that compares the appearance of a region to that of R_a:

$$\langle \phi(\mathbf{x}_i|R), \mathbf{w} \rangle \times \begin{cases} \frac{1}{C} \exp \beta \langle \phi^a(\mathbf{x}_i|R), \phi^a(\mathbf{x}_a|R_a) \rangle, & y_i = +1, \\ 1, & y_i = -1. \end{cases} \tag{6}$$

where $C = \mathrm{avg}_{i:y_i=+1} \exp \beta \langle \phi^a(\mathbf{x}_i|R), \phi^a(\mathbf{x}_a|R_a) \rangle$ is a normalizing constant. In practice, this is used only during re-localization rounds of the training phase to guide spatial selection; at test time, bounding boxes are scored solely by the model of Eq. (1) without the additional term. Other formulations, that may use a mixture of strongly and Webly supervised examples, are also possible. However, this is besides our focus, which is to see whether parts are learnable from the Web automatically, and the single supervision is only meant to reduce the ambiguity in the task for evaluation.

3   Experiments

This section thoroughly evaluates the proposed method. Our main evaluation is a comparison with existing state-of-the-art techniques on the task of Webly-supervised semantic part learning. In Sect. 3.1 we show that our method is substantially more accurate than existing alternatives and, in some cases, close to fully-supervised part learning.

Having established that, we then evaluate the weakly-supervised mid-level part learning (Sect. 2.2) that is an essential part of our approach. It compares favorably in terms of simplicity, scalability, and accuracy against existing alternatives for discriminability as well as spatial matching of object categories (Sect. 3.2).

Datasets. The Labeled Face Parts in the Wild (LFPW) dataset [51] contains about 1200 face images annotated with outlines for landmarks. Outlines are converted into bounding box annotations and images with missing annotations are removed from the test set. These test images are used to locate the following entities: *face, eye, eyebrow, nose,* and *mouth.*

The PascalParts dataset [47] augments the PASCAL VOC 2010 dataset with segmentation masks for object parts. Segmentation masks are converted into bounding boxes for evaluation. Parts of the same type (*e.g.* left and right wheels) are merged in a single entity (*wheel*). Objects marked as truncated or difficult are not considered for evaluation. The evaluation focuses on the bus and car categories with 18 entity types overall: *car, bus,* and their *door, front, headlight, mirror, rear, side, wheel,* and *window* parts. This dataset is more challenging, as entities have large intra-class appearance and pose variations. The evaluation is performed on images from the validation set that contain at least one object instance. Furthermore, following [48], object occurrences are roughly localized before detecting the parts using their localization procedure. Finally, objects whose bounding box larger side is smaller than 80 pixels are removed as several parts are nearly invisible below that scale.

The training sets from both datasets are utilized solely for training the fully supervised baselines (Sect. 3.1), and they are not used by MIL approaches.

Experimental Details. Regions are extracted using selective search [50], and described using ℓ_2-normalized Decaf [52] fc6 features to compute the appearance embedding $\phi^a(\mathbf{x}|R)$. The context descriptor $\mu(R)$ is extracted from a region triple the size of R. The joint appearance-geometric embedding $\phi^{ag}(\mathbf{x}|R)$ is obtained by first extracting the top $L = 5$ non-overlapping detections of each anchor and then applying Eqs. (3) and (4).

A separate mid-level anchor dictionary $\{p_1, \ldots, p_K\}$ is learnt for each object class using the Web images for all the semantic parts for the target object (including images of the object as a whole) as positive images and the background clutter images of [53] as negative ones. Equation (5) is optimized using stochastic gradient descend (SGD) with momentum for 40k iterations, alternating between positive and negative images. We train 150 anchor detectors per object class.

MIL semantic part detectors are trained solely on the Web images and the background class of [53] is used as negative bag for all the objects. The first five relocalization rounds are performed using the appearance only and the following five use the joint appearance-geometry descriptor (the joint embedding performs better with these two distinct steps). The MIL λ hyperparameter is set by performing leave-one-category-out cross-validation.

Web images for parts are acquired by querying the BING image search engine. For car and bus parts, the query concatenates the object and the part names (e.g. "car door"). For face parts, we do not use the object name. We retrieve 500 images of the class corresponding to the object itself and 100 images of all other semantic part classes.

3.1 Webly Supervised Localization of Objects and Semantic Parts

This section evaluates the detection performance of our approach. We gradually incorporate the proposed improvements, *i.e.* the context descriptor (C) and the geometrical embedding (G) to the basic MIL baseline (B) as defined in Sect. 2.1 and monitor their impact.

We compare our method to the state-of-the-art co-localization algorithm of Cho *et al.* [25] and the state-of-the-art weakly supervised detection method from Bilen and Vedaldi [24]. To detect a given part with [25], we run their code on all images that contain that part (*e.g.* for co-localizing eyes we consider *face* and *eye* images). As reference, we also report a fully supervised detector, trained using bounding-boxes from the training set, for all objects and parts (F). For this, we use the R-CNN method of [54] on top of the same features used in MIL.

We mainly report the Average Precision (AP) per part/object class and its average (mAP) over all parts in each class. We also report the CorLoc (for correct localization) measure, as it is often used in the co-localization literature [14,55]. As most parts in both datasets are relatively small, following [47], the IoU threshold for correct detection is set to 0.4.

Table 1. Part detection results averaged for the face, car, and bus parent classes. mAP and average CorLoc for the MIL baseline (B), our improved versions that use context (C), geometrical embedding (G) compared to the fully supervised R-CNN (F).

Measure	mAP			averageCorLoc		
Parent class	{Face}	{Car}	{Bus}	{Face}	{Car}	{Bus}
Cho *et al.* [25]	16.6	16.9	12.4	31.4	29.9	15.5
Bilen and Vedaldi [24]	2.7	12.0	4.7	7.2	15.3	6.7
B	20.6	29.1	22.7	22.0	38.1	29.4
B+C	22.4	27.3	21.4	29.1	37.6	28.4
B+G	29.0	34.1	**23.3**	33.1	45.5	**31.5**
B+C+G	**44.9**	**34.4**	23.0	**52.5**	**47.8**	29.6
F	53.7	51.2	48.2	60.5	62.9	63.8
F+C+G	**61.4**	**60.3**	**54.1**	**67.8**	**71.8**	**66.0**

Results. Table 1 reports the average AP and CorLoc over all parts of a given object class for all these methods. First, we observe that even the MIL baseline (B) outperforms off-the-shelf methods such as [24,25]. For [24], we have observed that the part detectors degrade to detecting subparts of semantic parts, suggesting that [24] lacks robustness to drastic scale variations and to the large amount of noise present in our dataset. Second, we see that using the geometric embedding (+G) always improves the baseline results by $1 - 10$ mAP points. On top of geometry, using context (+C) helps for face and car parts, but not for buses. Overall the unified embedding brings a large improvement for faces (+24.3 mAP) and for cars (+5.3 mAP) and more contained for buses (+0.6 mAP). Importantly, these improvements significantly reduce the gap between using noisy Web supervision and the fully supervised R-CNN (F); overall, Webly supervision achieves respectively 84%, 67%, and 48% of the performance of (F).

Last but not least, we also experimented extending the fully supervised R-CNN method with the joint appearance-geometry embedding and context descriptor (F+C+G), which improves part detections by +7.7, +9.1, +5.9 mAP points respectively. This suggests that our representation may be applicable well beyond weakly supervised learning.

Table 2. **Individual part detection results for car**: APs for the MIL baseline (B), our improved versions that use context (C), geometrical embedding (G) and the different flavors of the fully supervised R-CNN (F).

Class		Door	Rear	Wheel	Wind	Side	Car	Front	Headl	Mirror	Mean{car}
Web	B	0.4	10.8	34.9	3.6	63.1	92.6	**55.2**	0.7	**0.3**	29.1
	B+C	0.8	11.4	31.3	4.9	58.8	83.0	54.0	**1.0**	0.2	27.3
	B+G	0.7	11.8	**47.9**	**22.7**	71.3	**97.8**	54.5	0.2	0.2	34.1
	B+C+G	**5.1**	**14.7**	43.6	22.6	**72.3**	95.7	54.7	0.3	0.2	**34.4**
Full	F	17.0	**39.0**	66.3	53.3	83.2	95.1	75.9	25.3	5.5	51.2
	F+C+G	**31.1**	30.7	**72.3**	**67.3**	**90.1**	**98.7**	**82.9**	**48.1**	**21.3**	**60.3**

Table 2 shows per-part detection results for the car parts. We see that geometry helps for 6 parts out of 9. Out of the three remaining parts, two are cases where the MIL baseline failed. In the less ambiguous fully-supervised scenario, the geometric embedding improves the performance in 8 out of 9 cases.

Leveraging a Single Annotation. As noted in Sect. 2.3, one issue with weakly supervised part learning is the inherent ambiguity in the part extent, that may differ from dataset to dataset. Here we address the ambiguity by adding a single strong annotation to the mix using the method described in Sect. 2.3. We asked an annotator to select 25 representative part annotations per part class from the training sets of each dataset. We retrain every part detector for each of the annotations and report mean and standard deviation of mAP. As a baseline, we also consider an exemplar detector trained using the single annotated example (A).

Results are reported in Table 3. Compared to pure Web supervision (B+C+G) in Table 1, the single annotation (A+B+C+G) does not help for faces, for which the proposed method was already working very well, but there is a +2 mAP point improvement for cars and +6.8 mAP for buses, which are more challenging. We also note that the complete method (A+B+C+G) is substantially superior to the exemplar detector (A).

Table 3. Part detection results using a single strong annotation (A): mAP and average CorLoc for the MIL baseline (B), our improved versions that use context (C), geometrical embedding (G). Mean and standard deviation over 25 random annotations.

Measure	mAP			averageCorLoc		
Parent class	{Face}	{Car}	{Bus}	{Face}	{Car}	{Bus}
A	29.4 ± 2.6	25.1 ± 2.7	24.5 ± 2.7	38.2 ± 2.5	39.8 ± 3.2	39.6 ± 3.2
A+B	27.3 ± 3.1	33.3 ± 1.1	26.9 ± 1.3	34.6 ± 3.7	46.6 ± 1.5	40.0 ± 2.3
A+B+C	38.2 ± 3.1	32.4 ± 1.2	26.6 ± 1.6	51.7 ± 3.2	49.4 ± 1.5	4 3.9 ± 3.0
A+B+G	34.5 ± 4.3	35.7 ± 1.1	28.1 ± 1.2	43.5 ± 4.8	48.8 ± 1.6	42.2 ± 2.2
A+B+C+G	**43.0 ± 3.6**	**36.4 ± 1.0**	**30.1 ± 1.8**	**54.7 ± 3.2**	**51.6 ± 1.6**	**45.9 ± 2.8**

3.2 Validation of Weakly-Supervised Mid-level Anchors

This section validates the mid-level anchors (Sect. 2.2) against alternatives in terms of discriminative information content and its ability of establishing meaningful matches between images, which is a key requirement in our application.

Discriminative Power of Anchors. Since most of the existing methods for learning mid-level patches are evaluated in terms of discriminative content in a classification setting, we adopt the same protocol here. In particular, we evaluate the anchors as mid-level patches on the MIT Scene 67 indoor scene classification task [56]. The pipeline first learns 50 mid-level anchors for each of the 67 scene classes. Then, similar to [43], images are split into spatial grids (2×2 and 1×1) and described by concatenating the maximum scores attained by each anchor detector inside each bin of the grid. All the grid descriptors are then concatenated to form a global image descriptor which is ℓ_2 normalized. 67 one-vs-rest SVM classifiers are trained on top of these descriptors. To be comparable with other methods, we consider both Decaf fc6 and VGG-VD fc7 [57] descriptors.

Table 4 contains the results of the classification experiment. Our weakly-supervised anchors clearly outperform other mid-level element approaches that are not based on CNN features [39,40,44,45]. Among CNN based approaches, our method outperforms the state-of-the-art mid-level feature based method from [43] on both VGG-VD and Decaf features. Remarkably, using our part detectors

Table 4. Classification results on MIT scenes [56]. Methods using mid-level elements are marked with [†]. For CNN-based approaches, features rely on Decaf or VGG-VD.

Method	BoP[†] [40]	DMS[†] [39]	Jian *et al.* [†] [45]	RFDC[†] [44]	FC *Decaf* [52]	FC *VGG-VD* [57]
Accuracy (%)	46.1	64.0	58.1	54.4	57.7	68.9
Method	BoE[†] *Decaf* [43]	ours[†] *Decaf*	FV-CNN *Decaf* [58]	BoE[†] *VGG-VD* [43]	ours[†] *VGG-VD*	FV-CNN *VGG-VD* [58]
Accuracy (%)	69.7	**71.5**	69.7	77.6	77.8	**81.6**

improves over the baseline which uses the global image CNN descriptor (FC) by 13.8 and 8.7 average accuracy points for Decaf and VGG-VD features respectively. Compared to other methods which are not based on detecting mid-level elements, our pipeline outperforms state-of-the-art FV-CNN for Decaf features and is inferior for VGG-VD.

Ability of Anchors to Establish Semantic Matches. The previous experiment assessed favorably the mid-level parts in terms of discriminative content; however, in the embedding ϕ^g, these are used as *geometric anchors*. Hence, here we validate the ability of the mid-level anchors to induce good semantic matches between pairs of images (before learning the semantic part models).

To perform semantic matching between a source image x_S and a target image x_T, we consider each part annotation R_S in the source and predict its best match $\hat{R}_T$ in the target. The quality of the match is evaluated by measuring the IoU between the predicted $\hat{R}_T$ and ground-truth R_T part. When a part appears more than once (*e.g.* eyes often appear twice), we choose the most overlaping pair. Performance is reported by averaging the match IoU for all part occurrences and pairs of images in the test set, reporting the results for each object category.

Given a source part R_S, the joint appearance-geometry embedding (*anchor-ag*) is extracted for the source part $\phi^{ag}(x_S|R_S)$ and the target region $\hat{R}_T$ that maximizes the inner product $\langle \phi^{ag}(x_S|R_S), \phi^{ag}(x_T|\hat{R}_T) \rangle$ is returned as the predicted match. We also compare *anchor-g* that uses only the geometric embedding $\phi^g(x|R)$ and the baseline a that uses only the appearance embedding $\phi^a(x|R)$.

We also compare two strong off-the-shelf baselines: DSP [59], state-of-the-art pairwise semantic matching method, and the method of [60], state-of-the-art for joint alignment. To perform box matching with [59] and [60] we fit an affine transformation to the disparity map contained inside a given source bounding box and apply this transform to move this box to the target image. Due to

Table 5. Semantic matching. For every parent class, we report average overlap (IoU) over all semantic parts. The face class results are obtained on the LFPW dataset while bus and car results come from the PascalParts dataset.

Set	Parent class	Matching method				
		Anchor-ag	Anchor-g	a	Flowweb [60]	DSP [59]
50 images	{Car}	**0.36**	**0.36**	0.31	0.34	0.23
	{Bus}	**0.37**	0.36	0.31	0.31	0.22
	{Face}	0.41	0.39	0.33	**0.43**	0.19
Full	{Car}	**0.36**	**0.36**	0.30	-	0.22
	{Bus}	**0.35**	**0.35**	0.29	-	0.21
	{Face}	**0.41**	0.39	0.34	-	0.21

scalability issues, we were unable to apply [60] to the full dataset[2], so we perform this comparison on a random subset of 50 images.

Table 5 presents the results of our benchmark. On the small subset of 50 images the costly approach of [60] performs better than our embedding only on the LFPW faces, where the viewpoint variation is limited. On the car and bus categories our method outperforms [60] by 10 % and 16 % average IoU respec-

Fig. 4. Navigating the *visual semantic atlas*. Each pair of solid bounding boxes connected by an arrow denotes a preselected part bounding box (near the starting point of an arrow) as *detected by our algorithm* and the most similar semantic match (the endpoint of the arrow). The best matching bounding box is the detection with highest appearance-geometry descriptor similarity among *all the detections in our database* of web images. The dashed boxes denote anchors that contributed the most to the similarity. Please note that the matching gracefully occurs across scales.

---

[2] More precisely, we were not able to apply [60] on a dataset with more than 60 128×68 pixel images on a server with 120 GB of RAM.

tively. Our method is also consistently better than DSP [59], on both the small and full test set.

We also note that the matching using geometric embeddings alone (*anchor-g*) achieves similar performance than the appearance-geometry matching (*anchor-ag*) which validates our intuition that the local geometry of an object is well-captured by the anchors.

4   An Atlas for Visual Semantic

As a byproduct of Webly-supervised learning, our method annotates the Web images with semantic parts. By endowing an image dataset with such concepts, we show here that it is possible to browse these annotated images. All of this composes our visual semantic atlas (see a subset of the atlas in Fig. 4) that allows to navigate from one image to another, even between an image of a full object and a zoomed-in image of one of its parts.

5   Conclusions

We have proposed a novel method for learning about objects, their semantic parts, and their geometric relationships, from noisy Web supervision. This is achieved by first learning a weakly supervised dictionary of mid-level visual elements which define a robust object-centric coordinate frame. Such property theoretically motivates our approach. The geometric projections are then used in a novel appearance-geometry embedding that improves learning of semantic object parts from noisy Web data. We showed improved performance over co-localization [25], deep weakly supervised approach [24] and a MIL baseline on all benchmarked datasets. Extensive evaluation of our proposed mid-level elements shows comparable results to state-of-the-art in terms of their discriminative power and superior results in terms of the ability to establish semantic matches between images. Finally, our method also provides a visually intuitive way to navigate Web images and predicted annotations.

Acknowledgments. We would like to thank Xerox Research Center Europe and ERC 677195-IDIU for supporting this research.

References

1. Krizhevsky, A., Sutskever, I., Hinton, G.E.: Imagenet classification with deep convolutional neural networks. In: Proceeding of NIPS (2012)
2. Frome, A., Corrado, G.S., Shlens, J., Bengio, S., Dean, J., Ranzato, M.A., Mikolov, T.: Devise: a deep visual-semantic embedding model. In: Proceeding of NIPS (2013)
3. Karpathy, A., Joulin, A., Fei-Fei, L.: Deep fragment embeddings for bidirectional image-sentence mapping. In: Proceeding of NIPS (2014)
4. Simonyan, K., Zisserman, A.: Two-stream convolutional networks for action recognition in videos. In: Proceeding of NIPS (2014)

5. Russakovsky, O., et al.: Imagenet large scale visual recognition challenge. Int. J. Comput. Vis. 115(3), 211–252 (2015)
6. Deng, J., Dong, W., Socher, R., Li, L.J., Li, K., Fei-Fei, L.: ImageNet: a large-scale hierarchical image database. In: Proceeding of CVPR (2009)
7. Nguyen, M.H., Torresani, L., de la Torre, F., Rother, C.: Weakly supervised discriminative localization and classification: a joint learning process. In: Proceeding of ICCV (2009)
8. Pandey, M., Lazebnik, S.: Scene recognition and weakly supervised object localization with deformable part-based models. In: Proceeding of ICCV (2011)
9. Deselaers, T., Alexe, B., Ferrari, V.: Weakly supervised localization and learning with generic knowledge. Int. J. Comput. Vis. 100(3), 275–293 (2012)
10. Wang, C., Ren, W., Huang, K., Tan, T.: Weakly supervised object localization with latent category learning. In: Fleet, D., Pajdla, T., Schiele, B., Tuytelaars, T. (eds.) ECCV 2014. LNCS, vol. 8694, pp. 431–445. Springer, Heidelberg (2014). doi:10.1007/978-3-319-10599-4_28
11. Hoffman, J., Guadarrama, S., Tzeng, E.S., Hu, R., Donahue, J., Girshick, R., Darrell, T., Saenko, K.: LSDA: large scale detection through adaptation. In: Ghahramani, Z., Welling, M., Cortes, C., Lawrence, N., Weinberger, K., eds.: Proceeding of NIPS (2014)
12. Hoffman, J., Pathak, D., Darrell, T., Saenko, K.: Detector discovery in the wild: joint multiple instance and representation learning. In: Proceeding of CVPR (2015)
13. Cinbis, R.G., Verbeek, J., Schmid, C.: Weakly supervised object localization with multi-fold multiple instance learning. In: PAMI, September 2015
14. Joulin, A., Tang, K., Fei-Fei, L.: Efficient image and video co-localization with Frank-Wolfe algorithm. In: Fleet, D., Pajdla, T., Schiele, B., Tuytelaars, T. (eds.) ECCV 2014. LNCS, vol. 8694, pp. 253–268. Springer, Heidelberg (2014). doi:10.1007/978-3-319-10599-4_17
15. Tang, K., Joulin, A., Li, L.J., Fei-Fei, L.: Co-localization in real-world images. In: Proceeding of CVPR (2014)
16. Ali, K., Saenko, K.: Confidence-rated multiple instance boosting for object detection. In: Proceeding of CVPR (2014)
17. Shi, Z., Hospedales, T., Xiang, T.: Bayesian joint modelling for object localisation in weakly labelled images. PAMI 37(10), 1959–1972 (2015)
18. Joulin, A., Bach, F., Ponce, J.: Efficient optimization for discriminative latent class models. In: Proceeding of NIPS (2010)
19. Vicente, S., Rother, C., Kolmogorov, V.: Object cosegmentation. In: Proceeding of CVPR (2011)
20. Joulin, A., Bach, F., Ponce, J.: Multi-class cosegmentation. In: Proceeding of CVPR (2012)
21. Rubinstein, M., Joulin, A., Kopf, J., Liu, C.: Unsupervised joint object discovery and segmentation in internet images. In: Proceeding of CVPR (2013)
22. Song, H.O., Girshick, R., Jegelka, S., Mairal, J., Harchaoui, Z., Darrell, T.: On learning to localize objects with minimal supervision. In: Proceeding of ICML (2014)
23. Li, Q., Wu, J., Tu, Z.: Harvesting mid-level visual concepts from large-scale internet images. In: Proceeding of CVPR (2013)
24. Bilen, H., Vedaldi, A.: Weakly supervised deep detection networks. arXiv preprint (2015). arXiv:1511.02853
25. Cho, M., Kwak, S., Schmid, C., Ponce, J.: Unsupervised object discovery and localization in the wild: part-based matching with bottom-up region proposals. In: Proceeding of CVPR (2015)

26. Fergus, R., Fei-Fei, L., Perona, P., Zisserman, A.: Learning object categories from google's image search. In: Proceeding of ICCV, pp. 1816–1823 (2005)
27. Parkhi, O.M., Vedaldi, A., Zisserman, A.: On-the-fly specific person retrieval. In: International Workshop on Image Analysis for Multimedia Interactive Services. IEEE (2012)
28. Schroff, F., Criminisi, A., Zisserman, A.: Harvesting image databases from the web. In: Proceeding of ICCV (2007)
29. Tsai, D., Jing, Y., Liu, Y., Rowley, H., Ioffe, S., Rehg, J.: Large-scale image annotation using visual synset. In: Proceeding of ICCV, pp. 611–618 (2011)
30. Kim, G., Xing, E.P.: On Multiple Foreground cosegmentation. In: Proceeding of CVPR (2012)
31. Chen, X., Gupta, A.: Webly supervised learning of convolutional networks. In: Proceeding of ICCV (2015)
32. Chen, X., Shrivastava, A., Gupta, A.: Neil: extracting visual knowledge from web data. In: Proceeding of ICCV (2013)
33. Divvala, S.K., Farhadi, A., Guestrin, C.: Learning everything about anything: webly-supervised visual concept learning. In: Proceeding of CVPR (2014)
34. Felzenszwalb, P.F., Huttenlocher, D.P.: Pictorial structures for object recognition. IJCV **61**, 55–79 (2005)
35. Fergus, R., Perona, P., Zisserman, A.: Object class recognition by unsupervised scale-invariant learning. Proc. CVPR **2**, 264–271 (2003)
36. Leibe, B., Leonardis, A., Schiele, B.: Robust object detection with interleaved categorization and segmentation. IJCV **77**(1–3), 259–289 (2008)
37. Felzenszwalb, P.F., Girshick, R.B., McAllester, D., Ramanan, D.: Object detection with discriminatively trained part based models. PAMI **32**(9), 1627–1645 (2010)
38. Singh, S., Gupta, A., Efros, A.A.: Unsupervised discovery of mid-level discriminative patches. In: Fitzgibbon, A., Lazebnik, S., Perona, P., Sato, S., Schmid, C. (eds.) ECCV 2012. LNCS, vol. 7573, pp. 73–86. Springer, Heidelberg (2012)
39. Doersch, C., Gupta, A., Efros, A.A.: Mid-level visual element discovery as discriminative mode seeking. In: Proceeding of NIPS (2013)
40. Juneja, M., Vedaldi, A., Jawahar, C.V., Zisserman, A.: Blocks that shout: distinctive parts for scene classification. In: Proceeding of CVPR (2013)
41. Endres, I., Shih, K.J., Jiaa, J., Hoiem, D.: Learning collections of part models for object recognition. In: Proceeding of CVPR (2013)
42. Doersch, C., Gupta, A., Efros, A.A.: Unsupervised visual representation learning by context prediction. In: Proceeding of ICCV (2015)
43. Li, Y., Liu, L., Shen, C., van den Hengel, A.: Mid-level deep pattern mining. In: 2015 IEEE Conference on Computer Vision and Pattern Recognition (CVPR), pp. 971–980. IEEE (2015)
44. Bossard, L., Guillaumin, M., Gool, L.: Food-101 – mining discriminative components with random forests. In: Fleet, D., Pajdla, T., Schiele, B., Tuytelaars, T. (eds.) ECCV 2014. LNCS, vol. 8694, pp. 446–461. Springer, Heidelberg (2014). doi:10.1007/978-3-319-10599-4_29
45. Sun, J., Ponce, J.: Learning dictionary of discriminative part detectors for image categorization and cosegmentation. Submitted to International Journal of Computer Vision, under minor revision (2015)
46. Zhang, N., Donahue, J., Girshick, R., Darrell, T.: Part-based R-CNNs for fine-grained category detection. In: Fleet, D., Pajdla, T., Schiele, B., Tuytelaars, T. (eds.) ECCV 2014. LNCS, vol. 8689, pp. 834–849. Springer, Heidelberg (2014). doi:10.1007/978-3-319-10590-1_54

47. Chen, X., Mottaghi, R., Liu, X., Fidler, S., Urtasun, R., Yuille, A.: Detect what you can: detecting and representing objects using holistic models and body parts. In: Proceeding of CVPR (2014)
48. Wang, P., Shen, X., Lin, Z.L., Cohen, S., Price, B.L., Yuille, A.L.: Joint object and part segmentation using deep learned potentials. In: Proceeding of ICCV (2015)
49. Dietterich, T.G., Lathrop, R.H., Lozano-Pérez, T.: Solving the multiple instance problem with axis-parallel rectangles. Artif. Intell. **89**(1–2), 31–71 (1997)
50. Uijlings, J.R.R., et al.: Selective search for object recognition. Int. J. Comput. Vis. **104**(2), 154–171 (2013)
51. Belhumeur, P.N., et al.: Localizing parts of faces using a consensus of exemplars. IEEE Trans. Pattern Anal. Mach. Intell. **35**(12), 2930–2940 (2013)
52. Jia, Y., Shelhamer, E., Donahue, J., Karayev, S., Long, J., Girshick, R., Guadarrama, S., Darrell, T.: Caffe: convolutional architecture for fast feature embedding. arXiv preprint (2014). arXiv:1408.5093
53. Fei-Fei, L., Fergus, R., Perona, P.: Learning generative visual models from few training examples: an incremental bayesian approach tested on 101 object categories. Comput. Visi. Image Underst. **106**(1), 59–70 (2007)
54. Girshick, R., Donahue, J., Darrell, T., Malik, J.: Rich feature hierarchies for accurate object detection and semantic segmentation. In: Proceeding of CVPR (2014)
55. Deselaers, T., Alexe, B., Ferrari, V.: Localizing objects while learning their appearance. In: Daniilidis, K., Maragos, P., Paragios, N. (eds.) ECCV 2010. LNCS, vol. 6314, pp. 452–466. Springer, Heidelberg (2010). doi:10.1007/978-3-642-15561-1_33
56. Quattoni, A., Torralba, A.: Recognizing indoor scenes. In: Proceeding of CVPR (2009)
57. Simonyan, K., Zisserman, A.: Very deep convolutional networks for large-scale image recognition (2014). arXiv:1409.1556
58. Cimpoi, M., Maji, S., Vedaldi, A.: Deep filter banks for texture recognition and segmentation. In: Proceeding of CVPR (2015)
59. Kim, J., Liu, C., Sha, F., Grauman, K.: Deformable spatial pyramid matching for fast dense correspondences. In: Proceeding of CVPR (2013)
60. Zhou, T., Jae Lee, Y., Yu, S.X., Efros, A.A.: Flowweb: Joint image set alignment by weaving consistent, pixel-wise correspondences. In: Proceeding of CVPR (2015)

VConv-DAE: Deep Volumetric Shape Learning Without Object Labels

Abhishek Sharma[1]([⊠]), Oliver Grau[2], and Mario Fritz[3]

[1] Intel Visual Computing Institute, Saarbrücken, Germany
asharma@mpi-inf.mpg.de
[2] Intel, Saarbrücken, Germany
[3] Max Planck Institute for Informatics, Saarbrücken, Germany

Abstract. With the advent of affordable depth sensors, 3D capture becomes more and more ubiquitous and already has made its way into commercial products. Yet, capturing the geometry or complete shapes of everyday objects using scanning devices (e.g. Kinect) still comes with several challenges that result in noise or even incomplete shapes.

Recent success in deep learning has shown how to learn complex shape distributions in a data-driven way from large scale 3D CAD Model collections and to utilize them for 3D processing on volumetric representations and thereby circumventing problems of topology and tessellation. Prior work has shown encouraging results on problems ranging from shape completion to recognition. We provide an analysis of such approaches and discover that training as well as the resulting representation are strongly and unnecessarily tied to the notion of object labels. Thus, we propose a full convolutional volumetric auto encoder that learns volumetric representation from noisy data by estimating the voxel occupancy grids. The proposed method outperforms prior work on challenging tasks like denoising and shape completion. We also show that the obtained deep embedding gives competitive performance when used for classification and promising results for shape interpolation.

Keywords: Denoising auto-encoder · 3D deep learning · Shape completion · Shape blending

1 Introduction

Despite the recent advances in 3D scanning technology, acquiring 3D geometry or shape of an object is a challenging task. Scanning devices such as Kinect are very useful but suffer from problems such as sensor noise, occlusion, complete failure modes (e.g. dark surfaces and gracing angles). Incomplete geometry poses severe challenges for a range of application such as interaction with the environment in Virtual Reality or Augmented Reality scenarios, planning for robotic interaction or 3D print and manufacturing.

To overcome some of these difficulties, there is a large body of work on fusing multiple scans into a single 3D model [1]. While the surface reconstruction is

© Springer International Publishing Switzerland 2016
G. Hua and H. Jégou (Eds.): ECCV 2016 Workshops, Part III, LNCS 9915, pp. 236–250, 2016.
DOI: 10.1007/978-3-319-49409-8_20

impressive in many scenarios, acquiring geometry from multiple viewpoint can be infeasible in some situations. For example, failure modes of the sensor will not be resolved and some viewing angles might simply be not easily accessible e.g. for a bed or cupboard placed against a wall or chairs occluded by tables.

There also has been significant research on analyzing 3D CAD model collections of everyday objects. Most of this work [2,3] use an assembly-based approach to build part based models of shapes. Thus, these methods rely on part annotations and can not model variations of large scale shape collections across classes. Contrary to this approach, Wu et al. (Shapenet [4]) propose a first attempt to apply deep learning to this task and learn the complex shape distributions in a data driven way from raw 3D data. It achieves generative capability by formulating a probabilistic model over the voxel grid and labels. Despite the impressive and promising results of such Deep belief nets [5,6], these models can be challenging to train. While they show encouraging results on challenging task of shape completion, there is no quantitative evaluation. Furthermore, it requires costly sampling techniques for test time inference, which severely limits the range of future 3D Deep Learning applications.

While deep learning has made remarkable progress in computer vision problems with powerful hierarchical feature learning, unsupervised feature learning remains a future challenge that is only slowly getting more traction. Labels are even more expensive to obtain for 3D data such as point cloud. Recently, Lai et al. [7] propose a sparse coding method for learning hierarchical feature representations over point cloud data. However, their approach is based on dictionary learning which is generally slower and less scalable than convolution based models. Our work also falls in this line of work and aims at bringing the success of deep and unsupervised feature learning to 3D representations.

To this end, we make the following contributions:

- We propose a fully convolutional volumetric auto-encoder which, to our knowledge, is the first attempt to learn a deep embedding of object shapes in an unsupervised fashion.
- Our method outperforms previous supervised approach of shapenet [4] on denoising and shape completion task while it obtains competitive results on shape classification. Furthermore, shape interpolation on the learned embedding space shows promising results.
- We provide an extensive quantitative evaluation protocol for task of shape completion that is essential to compare and evaluate the generative capabilities of deep learning when obtaining ground truth of real world data is challenging.
- Our method is trained from scratch and end to end thus circumventing the training issues of previous work, shapenet [4], such as layer wise pre-training. At test time, our method is at least two orders of magnitude faster than shapenet.

2   Related Work

Part and Symmetry Based Shape Synthesis. Prior work [2,3] uses an assembly-based approach to build deformable part-based models based on CAD models.

There is also work that detect the symmetry in point cloud data and use it to complete the partial or noisy reconstruction. A comprehensive survey of such techniques is covered in Mitra *et al.* [8]. Huang *et al.* [19] learns to predict procedural model parameters for shape synthesis given a 2D sketch using CNN. However, part and symmetry based methods are typically class specific and require part annotations which are expensive. In contrast, our work does not require additional supervision in the form of parts, symmetry, multi-view images or their correspondence to 3D data.

Deep Learning for 3D Data. ShapeNet [4] is the first work that applied deep learning to learn the 3D representation on large scale CAD model database. Apart from recognition, it also desires capability of shape completion. It builds a generative model with convolutional RBM [5,6] by learning a probability distribution over class labels and voxel grid. The learned model is then fine tuned for the task of shape completion. Following the success of Shapenet, there have been recent work that improves the recognition results on 3D data [10], uses 3D-2D(multi-view images) correspondence to improve shape completion (repairing) results [9,31] propose intrinsic CNN [17,18] for 3D data or learn correspondence between two surfaces(depth map) [20]. Our work is mainly inspired by Shapenet in the functionality but differs in methodology. In particular, our network is trained completely unsupervised and discovers useful visual representations without the use of explicitly curated labels. By learning to predict missing voxels from input voxels, our model ends up learning an embedding that is useful for both classification as well as interpolation.

Denoising Auto-encoders. Our network architecture is inspired by DAE [11, 12] main principle that predicting any subset of variables from the rest is a sufficient condition for completely capturing the joint distribution between a set of variables. In order to share weights for stationary distributions such as they occur in images, convolutional auto-encoders have been proposed [13]. Our model differs with such architecture as it is not stacked and learned end to end without any layer fine-tuning or pre-taining. Furthermore, we use learnable upsampling unit (deconvolutional layers) to reconstruct back the encoded input.

Learnable Upsampling Layer. The concept of upsampling layer was first introduced by Zeiler and Fergus [14] to visualize the filters of internal layer in a 2D ConvNet. However, they simply transpose the weights and do not learn the filter for upsampling. Instead, Long *et al.* [15] and Dosovitskiy *et al.* [21] first introduced the idea of deconvolution (up-sampling) as a trainable layer although for different applications. Recently, using up-sampling to produce spatial output [29,30,32] - has also seen first applications for computer graphics. Note that a few concurrent works [16,28] also propose a decoder based on volumetric upsampling that outputs 3D reconstruction. In particular, Yumer and Mitra [28] uses a similar architecture for predicting deformed version of the input shape. In contrast, we propose a denoising volumetric auto encoder for shape classification and completion that learns an embedding of shapes in an unsupervised manner.

Rest of the paper is organized as follows: In the next section, we first formulate the problem and describe our deep network and training details. We then move on to the experiment section where we first show the experiments for classification on ModelNet database and the qualitative results for shape interpolation on the learned embedding. We then formulate the protocol for evaluating current techniques for the task of shape completion and show our quantitative results. We conclude with qualitative results for shape completion and denoising.

3 Unsupervised Learning of Volumetric Representation by Completion

Given a collection of shapes of various objects and their different poses, our aim is to learn the shape distributions of various classes by predicting the missing voxels from the rest. Later, we want to leverage the learnt embedding for shape recognition and interpolation tasks as well as use the generative capabilities of the auto encoder architectures for predicting enhanced version of corrupted representations. These corruptions can range from noise like missing voxels to more severe structured noise patterns.

3.1 VConv-DAE: Fully Convolutional Denoising Auto Encoder

Voxel Grid Representation. Following Shapenet [4], we adopt the same input representation of a geometric shape: a voxel cube of resolution 24^3. Thereafter, each mesh is first converted to a voxel representation with 3 extra cells of padding in both directions to reduce the convolution border artifacts and stored as binary tensor where 1 indicates the voxel is inside the mesh surface and 0 indicates the voxel is outside the mesh. This results in the overall dimensions of voxel cube of size $30 \times 30 \times 30$.

Overview of Architecture. To this end, we learn an end to end, voxel to voxel mapping by phrasing it as two class (1–0) auto encoder formulation from a whole voxel grid to a whole voxel grid. An overview of our VConv-DAE architecture is shown in Fig. 1. Labels in our training corresponds to the voxel occupancy and not class label. Our architecture starts with a dropout layer directly connected to the input layer. The left half of our network can be seen as an encoder stage that results in a condensed representation (bottom of figure) which is connected to a fully connected layer in between. In the second stage (right half), the network reconstructs back the input from this intermediate representation by deconvolutional (Deconv) layers which acts as a learnable local up-sampling unit. We will now explain the key components of the architecture in more detail.

Data Augmentation Layer. While data augmentation has been used a lot to build deep invariant features for images [22], it is relatively little explored on volumetric data. We put a dropout [23] layer on the input. This serves the purpose of input data augmentation and an implicit training on a virtually infinite amount of data and has shown in our experiments to greatly avoid over-fitting.

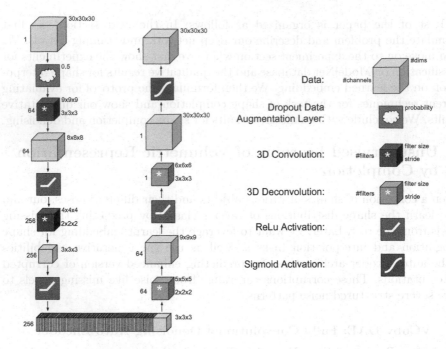

Fig. 1. VConv-DAE: convolutional denoising auto encoder for volumetric representations

Encoding Layers: 3D Convolutions. The first convolutional layer has 64 filters of size 9 and stride 3. The second convolutional layer has 256 filters of size 4 and stride 2 meaning each filter has $64 \times 4 \times 4 \times 4$ parameters. This results into 256 channels of size $3 \times 3 \times 3$. These feature maps are later flattened into one dimensional vector of length $6912(= 256 \times 3 \times 3 \times 3)$ which is followed by a fully connected layer of same length (6912). This bottleneck layer later acts as a shape embedding for classification and interpolation experiments later. The fixed size encoded input is now reconstructed back with two deconv layers. First Deconv layer contains 64 filters of size 5 and stride 2 while the last deconv layer finally merges all 64 feature cubes back to the original voxel grid. It contains a filter of size 6 and stride 3.

Decoding Layers: 3D Deconvolutions. While CNN architecture based on convolution operator have been very powerful and effective in a range of vision problems, Deconvolutional (also called convolutional transpose) based architecture are gaining traction recently. Deconvolution (Deconv) is basically convolution transpose which takes one value from the input, multiplies the value by the weights in the filter, and place the result in the output channel. Thus, if the 2D filter has size f × f, it generates a f × f output matrix for each pixel input. The output is generally stored with a overlap (stride) in the output channel.

Thus, for input x, filter size f, and stride d, the output is of dims $(x - i) * d + f$. Upsampling is performed until the original size of the input has been regained.

We did not extensively experiment with different network configurations. However, small variations in network depth and width did not seem to have significant effect on the performance. Some of the design choice also take into account the input voxel resolution. We chose two convolutional layers for encoder to extract robust features at multiple scales. Learning a robust shape representation essentially means capturing the correlation between different voxels. Thus, receptive field of convolutional filter plays a major role and we observe the best performance with large conv filters in the first layer and large deconv filter in the last layer. We experimented with two types of loss functions: mean square loss and cross entropy loss. Since we have only two classes, there is not much variation in performance with cross entropy being slightly better.

3.2 Dataset and Training

Dataset. Wu et al. [4] use Modelnet, a large scale 3D CAD model dataset for their experiments. It contains 151,128 3D CAD models belonging to 660 unique object categories. They provide two subset of this large scale dataset for the experiments. The first subset contains 10 classes that overlaps with the NYU dataset [24] and contains indoor scene classes such as sofa, table, chair, bed etc. The second subset of the dataset contains 40 classes where each class has at least 100 unique CAD models. Following the protocol of [4], we use both 10 and 40 subset for classification while completion is restricted to subset of 10 that mostly corresponds to indoor scene objects.

Training Details. We train our network end-to-end from scratch. We experiment with different levels of dropout noise and observe that training with more noisy data helps in generalising well for the task of denoising and shape completion. Thus, we set a noise level of $p = 0.5$ for our Dropout data augmentation layer which eliminates half of the input at random and therefore the network is trained for reconstruction by only observing 50 % of the input voxels. We train our network with pure stochastic gradient descent and a learning rate of 0.1 for 500 epochs. We use momentum with a value of 0.9. We use the open source library Torch for implementing our network and will make our code public at the time of publication.

4 Experiments

We conduct a series of experiments in particular to establish a comparison to the related work of Shapenet [4]. First, we evaluate the representation that our approach acquires in an unsupervised way on a classification task and thereby directly comparing to Shapenet. We then support the empirical performance of feature learning with qualitative results obtained by linear interpolation on the embedding space of various shapes. Thereafter, we propose two settings to evaluate quantitatively the generative performance of 3D deep learning approach on a denoising and shape completion task – on which we also benchmark against Shapenet and baselines related to our own setup. We conclude the experiments with qualitative results.

4.1   Evaluating the Unsupervised Embedding Space

Features learned from deep networks are state-of-the-art in various computer vision problems. However, unsupervised volumetric feature learning is a less explored area. Our architecture is primarily designed for shape completion and denoising task. However, we are also interested in evaluating how the features learned in unsupervised manner compare with fully supervised state-of-the-art 3D classification only architecture.

Classification Setup. We conduct 3D classification experiments to evaluate our features. Following shapenet, we use the same train/test split by taking the first 80 models for training and first 20 examples for test. Each CAD model is rotated along gravity direction every 30 degree which results in total 38,400 CAD models for training and 9,600 for testing. We propose following two methods to evaluate our network for the task of classification:

1. Ours-UnSup: We feed forward the test set to the network and simply take the fixed length bottleneck layer of dimensions 6912 and use this as a feature vector for a linear SVM. Note that the representation is trained completely unsupervised.
2. Ours-Fine Tuned (FT): We follow the set up of Shapenet [4] which puts a layer with class labels on the top most feature layer and fine tunes the network. In our network, we take the bottleneck layer which is of 6912 dimensions and put another layer in between bottleneck and softmax layer. So, the resulting classifier has an intermediate fully connected layer 6912-512-40.

For comparison, we also report performance for Light Field descriptor (LFD [25], 4,700 dimensions) and Spherical Harmonic descriptor (SPH [26], 544 dimensions). We also report the overall best performance achieved so far on this dataset [10,27] (Table 1).

Table 1. Shape classification results

10 classes	SPH [26]	LFD [25]	SN [4]	Ours-UnSup	Ours-FT	VoxNet	MvCnn [27]
AP	79.79	79.87	83.54	80.50	**84.14**	92	
40 classes	SPH [26]	LFD [25]	SN [4]	Ours-UnSup	Ours-FT	VoxNet	MvCnn [27]
AP	68.23	75.47	77.32	75.50	**79.84**	83.00	**90.10**

Discussion. Our representation, Ours-UnSup, achieves 75 % accuracy on the 40 classes while trained completely unsupervised. When compared to the setup of fine tuned shapenet, our fine tuned representation, Ours-FT, compares favorably and outperforms shapenet on both 10 and 40 classes.

Comparison with the State-of-the-Art. Our architecture is designed for shape completion and denoising while Voxnet and MvCnn is for recognition only. We demonstrate that it also lends to recognition and shows promising performance. MvCnn [27] outperforms other methods by a large margin. However, unlike the rest of the methods, it works in the image domain. For each model, MvCnn [27] first renders it in different views and then aggregates the scores of all rendered images obtained by CNN. Compared to the fully supervised classification network of Voxnet, our accuracy is only 3 % less on 40 classes. This is because Voxnet architecture is shallow and contains pooling layers that help classification but are not suitable for reconstruction purpose, as also noted in 3D Shapenet [4].

4.2   Linear Interpolation in the Embedding Space

Encouraged by the unsupervised volumetric feature learning performance, we analyze the representation further to understand the embedding space learned by our auto-encoder. To this end, we randomly choose two different instances of a class in the same pose as input and then, feed it to the encoder part of our trained model which transforms any shape into a fixed length encoding vector of length 6912. We call these two instances Source and Target in Table 2. On a scale from 1 to 10, where 1 corresponds to source instance and 10 to target, we then linearly interpolate the eight intermediate encoded vectors. These interpolated vectors are then fed to the second (decoder) part of the model which decodes the encoded vector into volumes. Note that we chose linear interpolation over non-linear partially because of the simplicity and the fact that the feature space already achieves linear separability on 10 classes with an accuracy of 80 %. In Table 2, we show the interpolated volumes between source and target at each alternative step. We observe that in most cases new, connected shapes are inferred as intermediate steps and a plausible transition is produced even for highly non-convex shapes.

5   Denoising and Shape Completion

In this section, we show experiments that evaluate our network on the task of denoising and shape completion. This is very relevant in the scenario where geometry is captured with depth sensors that often comes with holes and noise due to sensor and surface properties. Ideally, this task should be evaluated on real world depth or volumetric data but obtaining ground truth for real world data is very challenging and to the best of our knowledge, there exists no dataset that contains the ground truth for missing parts and holes of Kinect data. Kinect fusion type approach still suffer from sensor failure modes and large objects like furnitures often cannot be scanned from all sides in their typical location.

Table 2. Shape interpolation results

Source(t=1)	t= 3	t=5	t=7	t = 9	Target(t= 10)

We thus rely on CAD model dataset where complete geometry of various objects is available and we simulate different noise characteristics to test our network. We use the 10-class subset of ModelNet database for experiments. In order to remain comparable to Shapenet, we use their pretrained generative model for comparison and train our model on the first 80 (before rotation) CAD models for each class accordingly. This results in 9600 training models for the following experiments.

5.1 Denoising Experiments

We first evaluate our network on the same random noise characteristics with which we train the network. This is challenging since the test set contains different instances than training set. We also vary the amount of random noise injected during test time for evaluation. Training is same as that for classification and we use the same model trained on the first 80 CAD models. At test time, we use all the test models available for these 10 classes for evaluation.

Baseline and Metric. To better understand the network performance for reconstruction at test time, we study following methods:

Table 3. Average error for denoising

Class	30 % noise				50 % noise			
	CAE	SN-2	SN-1	Ours	CAE	SN-2	SN-1	Ours
Bed	2.88	6.88	6.76	**0.83**	6.56	9.87	7.25	**1.68**
Sofa	2.60	7.48	7.97	**0.74**	6.09	9.51	8.67	**1.81**
Chair	2.51	6.73	11.76	**1.62**	4.98	7.82	11.97	**2.45**
Desk	2.26	7.94	10.76	**1.05**	5.38	9.35	11.04	**1.99**
Toilet	4.25	16.05	17.92	**1.57**	9.94	17.95	18.42	**3.36**
Monitor	3.01	11.30	14.75	**1.26**	7.01	12.42	14.95	**2.37**
Table	1.17	3.47	5.77	**0.53**	2.79	4.65	5.88	**0.80**
Night-stand	5.07	20.00	17.90	**1.20**	13.57	25.15	20.49	**2.50**
Bathtub	2.56	6.71	10.11	**0.97**	5.30	8.26	10.51	**1.77**
Dresser	5.56	20.07	18.00	**0.70**	15.11	27.74	20.00	**1.95**
Mean error	3.18	10.66	12.10	**1.04**	7.67	13.27	12.91	**2.06**

1. Convolutional Auto Encoder (CAE): We train the same network without any noise meaning without any dropout layer. This baseline tells us the importance of data augmentation or injecting noise during training.
2. Shapenet (SN): We use pretrained generative model for 10 class subset made public by Shapenet and their code for completion. We use the same hyperparameters as given in the their source code for completion. Therefore, we set number of epochs to 50, number of Gibbs iteration to 1 and threshold parameter to 0.1. Their method assumes that an object mask is available for the task of completion at test time. Our model does not make such assumption since this is difficult to obtain at test time. Thus, we evaluate shapenet with two different scenario for such a mask: first, SN-1, by setting the whole voxel grid as mask and second, SN-2, by setting the occupied voxels in test input as mask. Given the range of hyper-parameters, we report performance for the best hyperparameters (Table 3).

Metric : We count the number of voxels which differs from the actual input. So, we take the absolute difference between the reconstructed version of noisy input and original (no-noise) version. We then normalise reconstruction error by total number of voxels in the grid ($13824 = 24 \times 24 \times 24$)). Note that the voxel resolution of $30 \times 30 \times 30$ is obtained by padding 3 voxels on each side thus network never sees a input with voxel in those padding. This gives us the resulting reconstruction or denoising error in %.

5.2 Slicing Noise and Shape Completion

In this section, we evaluate our network for a structured version of noise that is motivated by occlusions in real world scenario failure modes of the sensor which

Table 4. Shape denoising results for random noise (50 %)

	Reference Model	Noisy input	Our Reconstruction	3DShapeNet Reconstruction
Chair				
Night Stand				
Desk				
Table				
Sofa				
Monitor				
Bed				
Dresser				

generates "holes" in the data. To simulate such scenarios, we inject slicing noise in the test set as follows: For each instance, we first randomly choose n slices of volumetric cube and remove them. We then evaluate our network on three amount of slicing noise depending upon how many slices are removed. Injected slicing noise is challenging on two counts: First, our network is not trained for this noise. Secondly, injecting 30 % of slicing noise leads to significant removal of object with large portion of object missing. hus, evaluating on this noise relates

Table 5. Average error for completion

Class	10%			20%			30%		
	SN-1	SN-2	Ours	SN-1	SN-2	Ours	SN-1	SN-2	Ours
Bed	7.09	4.71	**1.11**	7.25	5.70	**1.63**	7.53	6.89	**2.40**
Sofa	8.05	5.51	**0.97**	8.32	6.39	**1.51**	8.66	7.23	**2.33**
Chair	12.22	5.66	**1.64**	12.22	6.13	**2.02**	12.40	6.51	**2.37**
Desk	11.00	6.86	**1.25**	11.00	7.25	**1.70**	11.26	7.83	**2.44**
Toilet	17.34	13.46	**1.81**	17.78	14.55	**2.78**	18.25	15.50	**4.18**
Monitor	14.55	9.45	**1.45**	14.72	10.21	**2.05**	14.85	14.85	**3.01**
Table	5.95	2.63	**0.66**	6.00	2.98	**0.89**	6.10	3.41	**1.21**
Night-stand	15.01	12.63	**1.76**	16.20	16.26	**3.15**	17.74	19.38	**5.19**
Bathtub	10.18	5.39	**1.09**	10.25	5.93	**1.56**	13.22	6.53	**2.16**
Dresser	14.65	14.47	**1.41**	15.69	18.33	**2.77**	17.57	21.52	**5.29**
Mean error	11.44	8.77	**1.31**	11.94	9.37	**2.00**	12.75	10.96	**3.05**

to the task of shape completion. For comparison, we again use Shapenet with the same parameters as described in the previous section. In the Table below, 10, 20, 30 indicates the % of slicing noise. So, 30% means that we randomly remove all voxels lying on 9 (30%) faces of the cube. We use the same metric as described in the previous section to arrive at the following numbers in % (Table 5).

Discussion. Our network performance is significantly better than the CAE as well as Shapenet. This is also shown in the qualitative results shown later in Table 4. Our network superior performance over no noise network (CAE) justifies learning voxel occupancy from noisy shape data. The performance on different noise also suggest that our network finds completing slicing noise (completion) more challenging than denoising random noise. 30% of slicing noise removes significant chunk of the object.

6   Qualitative Comparison

In Tables 4 and 6, each row contains 4 images where the first one corresponds to the ground truth, second one is obtained by injecting noise (random and slicing) and acts as a input to our network. Third image is the reconstruction obtained by our network while fourth image is the outcome of shapenet. As shown in the qualitative results, our network can fill in significant missing portion of objects when compared to shapenet. All images shown in Table 6 are for 30% slicing noise scenario whereas the Table 4 corresponds to inputs with 50% random noise. Judging by our quantitative evaluation, our model finds slicing noise to be the most challenging scenario. This is also evident in the qualitative results and partially explained by the fact that network is not trained for slicing noise. Edges and boundaries are smoothed out to some extent in some cases.

Table 6. Shape completion results for slicing noise

	Reference Model	Noisy input	Our Reconstruction	3DShapeNet Reconstruction

Chair

Night Stand

Desk

Bathtub

Table

Monitor

Bed

Runtime Comparison with Shapenet. We compare our runtime during train and test with Shapenet. All runtime reported here are obtained by running the code on Nvidia K40 GPU. Training time for Shapenet is quoted from their paper where it is mentioned that pre-training as well as fine tuning each takes 2 days and test time of 600 ms is calculated by estimating the time it takes for one test completion. In contrast, our model trains in only 1 day. We observe strongest improvements in runtime at test time, where our model only takes 3 ms which is 200x faster than Shapenet – *an improvement of two orders of magnitude.* This is in part due to our network not requiring sampling at test time.

7   Conclusion and Future Work

We have presented a simple and novel unsupervised approach that learns volumetric representation by completion. The learned embedding delivers comparable results on recognition and promising results for shape interpolation. Furthermore, we obtain stronger results on denoising and shape completion while being trained without labels. We believe that the transition from RBM to feed forward models, first evaluation-qualitative results for shape completion, promising recognition performance and shape interpolation results will stimulate further work on deep learning for 3D geometry. In future, we plan to extend our work to deal with deformable objects and larger scenes.

Acknowledgement. This work was supported by funding from the European Union's Horizon 2020 research and innovation program under the Marie Sklodowska-Curie grant agreement No. 642841.

References

1. Newcombe, R.A., Izadi, S., Hilliges, O., Molyneaux, D., Kim, D., Davison, A.J., Kohi, P., Shotton, J., Hodges, S., Fitzgibbon, A.: Kinectfusion: real-time dense surface mapping and tracking. In: 10th IEEE International Symposium on Mixed and Augmented Reality (ISMAR) (2011)
2. Chaudhuri, S., Kalogerakis, E., Guibas, L., Koltun, V.: Probabilistic reasoning for assembly-based 3D modeling. In: SIGGRAPH (2011)
3. Kalogerakis, E., Chaudhuri, S., Koller, D., Koltun, V.: A Probabilistic model of component-based shape synthesis. In: SIGGRAPH (2012)
4. Wu, Z., Song, S., Khosla, A., Yu, F., Zhang, L., Tang, X., Xiao, J.: 3D shapenets: a deep representation for volumetric shapes. In: CVPR (2015)
5. Hinton, G.E., Osindero, S., Teh, Y.W.: A fast learning algorithm for deep belief nets. Neural Comput. **18**(7), 1527–1554 (2006)
6. Lee, H., Grosse, R., Ranganath, R., Ng, A.Y.: Unsupervised learning of hierarchical representations with convolutional deep belief networks. Commun. ACM **54**(10), 95–103 (2011)
7. Lai, K., Bo, L., Fox, D.: Unsupervised feature learning for 3D scene labeling. In: ICRA (2014)
8. Mitra, N.J., Pauly, M., Wand, M., Ceylan, D.: Symmetry in 3D geometry: extraction and applications. In: Computer Graphics Forum, vol. 32, pp. 1–23. Wiley Online Library (2013)
9. Thanh Nguyen, D., Hua, B.S., Tran, K., Pham, Q.H., Yeung, S.K.: A field model for repairing 3D shapes. In: The IEEE Conference on Computer Vision and Pattern Recognition (CVPR), June 2016
10. Maturana, D., Scherer, S.: 3D convolutional neural networks for landing zone detection from lidar. In: ICRA (2015)
11. Vincent, P., Larochelle, H., Bengio, Y., Manzagol, P.A.: Extracting and composing robust features with denoising autoencoders. In: ICML (2008)
12. Vincent, P., Larochelle, H., Lajoie, I., Bengio, Y., Manzagol, P.A.: Stacked denoising autoencoders: learning useful representations in a deep network with a local denoising criterion. JMLR **11**, 3371–3408 (2010)

13. Masci, J., Meier, U., Cireşan, D., Schmidhuber, J.: Stacked convolutional auto-encoders for hierarchical feature extraction. In: Honkela, T., Duch, W., Girolami, M., Kaski, S. (eds.) ICANN 2011. LNCS, vol. 6791, pp. 52–59. Springer, Heidelberg (2011). doi:10.1007/978-3-642-21735-7_7
14. Zeiler, M.D., Fergus, R.: Visualizing and understanding convolutional networks. In: Fleet, D., Pajdla, T., Schiele, B., Tuytelaars, T. (eds.) ECCV 2014. LNCS, vol. 8689, pp. 818–833. Springer, Heidelberg (2014). doi:10.1007/978-3-319-10590-1_53
15. Long, J., Shelhamer, E., Darrell, T.: Fully convolutional networks for semantic segmentation. In: CVPR (2015)
16. Choy, C.B., Xu, D., Gwak, J., Chen, K., Savarese, S.: 3D-R2N2: a unified approach for single and multi-view 3D object reconstruction (2015). arXiv.1604.00449
17. Boscaini, D., Masci, J., Rodolà, E., Bronstein, M.M.: Learning shape correspondence with anisotropic convolutional neural networks (2016). arXiv:1605.06437
18. Boscaini, D., Masci, J., Rodolà, E., Bronstein, M.M., Cremers, D.: Anisotropic diffusion descriptors. In: Computer Graphics Forum (2016)
19. Huang, H., Kalogerakis, E., Yumer, M. E., Mech, R.: Shape synthesis from sketches via procedural models, convolutional networks. In: IEEE Transactions on Visualization and Computer Graphics (2016)
20. Wei, L., Huang, Q., Ceylan, D., Etienne, V., Li, H.: Dense human body correspondences using convolutional networks. In: CVPR (2016)
21. Dosovitskiy, A., Springenberg, J.T., Brox, T.: Learning to generate chairs with convolutional neural networks. In: CVPR (2015)
22. Krizhevsky, A., Sutskever, I., Hinton, G.E.: Imagenet classification with deep convolutional neural networks. In: NIPS (2012)
23. Srivastava, N., Hinton, G., Krizhevsky, A., Sutskever, I., Salakhutdinov, R.: Dropout: a simple way to prevent neural networks from overfitting. JMLR **15**, 1929–1958 (2014)
24. Silberman, N., Hoiem, D., Kohli, P., Fergus, R.: Indoor segmentation and support inference from RGBD images. In: Fitzgibbon, A., Lazebnik, S., Perona, P., Sato, Y., Schmid, C. (eds.) ECCV 2012. LNCS, vol. 7576, pp. 746–760. Springer, Heidelberg (2012). doi:10.1007/978-3-642-33715-4_54
25. Chen, D.Y., Tian, X.P., Shen, Y.T., Ouhyoung, M.: On visual similarity based 3D model retrieval. In: Computer Graphics Forum, vol. 22, pp. 223–232. Wiley Online Library (2003)
26. Kazhdan, M., Funkhouser, T., Rusinkiewicz, S.: Rotation invariant spherical harmonic representation of 3D shape descriptors. In: Symposium on geometry processing, vol. 6, pp. 156–164 (2003)
27. Su, H., Maji, S., Kalogerakis, E., Learned-Miller, E.G.: Multi-view convolutional neural networks for 3D shape recognition. In: Proceedings of ICCV (2015)
28. Yumer, M.E., Mitra, N.J.: Learning semantic deformation flows with 3D convolutional networks. In: Leibe, B., Matas, J., Sebe, N., Welling, M. (eds.) ECCV 2016. LNCS, vol. 9910, pp. 294–311. Springer, Heidelberg (2016). doi:10.1007/978-3-319-46466-4_18
29. Georgoulis, S., Rematas, K., Ritschel, T., Fritz, M., Gool, L.V., Tuytelaars, T.: Deep reflectance maps. In: CVPR (2016)
30. Rematas, K., Ritschel, T., Fritz, M., Gavves, E., Tuytelaars, T.: DeLight-Net: decomposing reflectance maps into specular materials and natural illumination (2016). arXiv:1602.00328
31. Rezende, D.J., Eslami, S.M., Mohamed, S., Battaglia, P., Jaderberg, M., Heess, N.: Unsupervised learning of 3D structure from images (2016). arXiv:1607.00662
32. Nalbach, O., Arabadzhiyska, E., Mehta, D., Seidel, H.P., Ritschel, T.: Deep shading: convolutional neural networks for screen-space shading (2016). arXiv:1603.06078

Deep Shape from a Low Number of Silhouettes

Xinhan Di[(✉)], Rozenn Dahyot, and Mukta Prasad

School of Computer Science and Statistics, Trinity College Dublin, Dublin, Ireland
{dixi,Rozenn.Dahyot,prasadm}@tcd.ie

Abstract. Despite strong progress in the field of 3D reconstruction from multiple views, holes on objects, transparency of objects and textureless scenes, continue to be open challenges. On the other hand, silhouette based reconstruction techniques ease the dependency of 3d reconstruction on image pixels but need a large number of silhouettes to be available from multiple views. In this paper, a novel end to end pipeline is proposed to produce high quality reconstruction from a low number of silhouettes, the core of which is a deep shape reconstruction architecture. Evaluations on ShapeNet [1] show good quality of reconstruction compared with ground truth.

Keywords: Deep 3D reconstruction · End to end architecture · Silhouettes

1 Introduction

3D geometry reconstruction techniques have made significant progress during this two decades from theoretical development to software implementation. The aim of both contributions are to build high-quality 3D reconstruction of scenes and objects from 2D or 2.5D source information in terms of image pixels, depth and other source data. Current progress in this filed involves wider application of 3D reconstruction towards real world application including video data application, large-scale scene reconstruction, light field reconstruction and other applications. However, several open questions remain challenging for 3D reconstruction such as holes, wrinkles, coarse region and other unwanted artifacts in the 3D rebuilt world for the reconstruction of transparent objects, textureless scenes and other challenging objects and scenes (Fig. 1).

Among the two most popular 3D reconstruction technique groups including the increment multiview reconstruction and volume-based reconstruction, the first technique framework is based on 2D image source information. Lots of techniques and theories have been developed to produce high-quality 3D reconstruction. Furthermore, for the 3D reconstruction of challenging objects such as transparent objects and objects containing textureless parts, lots of priors including surface normals, object-specific shape priors and other priors are applied and integrated in the reconstruction systems. These priors are demonstrated to improve the quality of 3D reconstruction in order to avoid of holes, wrinkles, and other artifacts.

G. Hua and H. Jégou (Eds.): ECCV 2016 Workshops, Part III, LNCS 9915, pp. 251–265, 2016.
DOI: 10.1007/978-3-319-49409-8_21

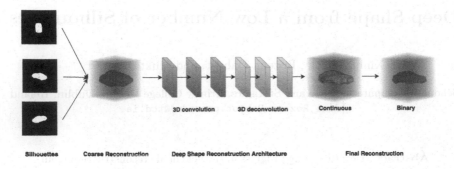

Fig. 1. Two stage direct 3D reconstruction pipeline

The second technique groups build the 3D real world in the grid space consists of voxels. Priors such as connectivity priors, surface orientation priors are represented as data constraint terms. These terms are calculated in a mathematical framework such as multiple label convex framework or MRF pipelines to provide solutions to the opening challenges. Besides, sufficient information of viewpoints including camera parameter matrix of each viewpoint, a large number of silhouettes and 2D image pixels are the base of quality of 3D reconstruction in the grid space.

The proposed pipeline is a deep reconstruction pipeline consisting of two reconstruction stages. The first stage is shape coarse reconstruction stage. It takes a small number of silhouettes as input with known camera parameters of the associated viewpoints, and produces a coarse visual hull. The second stage is deep shape reconstruction stage, it works based on a deep shape reconstruction architecture. This proposed 3D convolution networks (3D-CNNs) architecture reconstructs good quality shapes from coarse shapes. The currently proposed pipeline is designed for reconstructing category-specific object shapes.

Two contributions are made. First, this pipeline produces high quality of 3D reconstruction based on a low number of silhouettes. It is not dependent on images pixels, depth data and et al. Therefore, this silhouettes based technique is considered as a potential solution for 3D reconstruction of transparent objects or objects with textureless parts. Second, compared with techniques relying on a large number of images taken in different viewpoints, the proposed pipeline reduces the number of views.

This paper is organized as follows. We review related work in Sect. 2. We formulate the problem in Sect. 3. Both the solution to the formulated problem and the proposed reconstruction pipeline is presented in Sect. 4. Evaluation details including the dataset, traning, test and results are shown in Sect. 5. Finally, conclusion and future work for our pipeline is discussed in Sect. 6.

2   Related Work

End to end deep learning architectures have been applied successfully to a variety of vision problems such as segmentation [2–5], edge prediction [6], classification [7], optical flow prediction [8], depth prediction [9], keypoint prediction [4] and feature learning [10, 11]. Also, fully convolutional networks prove their efficiency in one dimensional input strings [12] extended from LeNet [13], two dimensional detection [14, 15] with learning and inference, three dimensional representation [16], volumetric 3D shapes classification and interpolation [17].

Convolutional Neural Networks(CNNs) have been proven their efficiency in improving 3D reconstruction. For example, CNNs is developed for the task of prediction of surface normals from a single image [18]. A combined framework for viewpoint estimation and local keypoint prediction is proposed through application of a convolutional neural network architectures [19]. A convolutional neural network is built to perform extremely well for stereo matching [20].

Unlike the above methods, end to end deep architectures are built for 3D reconstruction. For example, convolution network is applied to build 3D models from single images [21], 3D recurrent reconstruction neural network (3D-R2N2) is built to unify both single and multi-view 3D object reconstruction [22], Semantic deformation flows are learned with 3D convolution networks for improving 3D reconstruction [23], 3D volumetric reconstruction is learned from single-view with projective transformations [24]. However, these 3D reconstruction deep architectures are dependent on image pixels, transformation and etc. In contrast, a novel reconstruction pipeline is proposed directly from a small number of silhouettes input end to 3D reconstruction end.

3   Problem Formulation

We aim at building a function V of Visual Hull H_k (inferred from k silhouettes [25]) that reconstructs a shape as close as possible to the Ground Truth (GT) shape:

$$V(H_k) \simeq GT \tag{1}$$

It is commonly understood that the visual hull improves as the number k of silhouettes increases such that:

$$\lim_{k \to \infty} H_k = H \tag{2}$$

where the limit visual hull H is the best approximation possible of the object shape estimated from silhouettes. H itself is often far away from the true shape GT as concave areas fail to be recovered from Shape-from-Silhouettes techniques [26].

To avoid these artifacts, we propose an improvement on visual hull inferred by shape-from-silhouettes techniques using a Bayesian like framework where we aim at using prior information about the object category to design a function $V(H_k) = V_k$ that is as close as possible to GT. The function V is designed using deep neural network and is trained using ShapeNets dataset [1]. Our formulation is tested for $k = 2, 3, 4, 5$ silhouettes available as input of the pipeline.

4   Two-Stage Deep Shape Reconstruction Pipeline

An end to end deep shape reconstruction pipeline is proposed. The input end is a small number of silhouettes with known camera parameters and the output end is reconstructed 3D shape in the form of volume. The volume grid consists of voxels whose values are binary. 0 represents the empty space and 1 represents the occupied space of the shape. To be noted, both space on the surface of the shape and inside the shape are represented as 1. The proposed shape reconstruction pipeline is split in two stages including coarse shape reconstruction stage and deep shape reconstruction stage. The first stage is to produce a 3D shape of object H_k with known silhouettes and corresponding camera parameters. The second stage is to reconstruct a good quality of 3D shape V_k with known H_k through a deep shape reconstruction architecture. This architecture works as a solver to the formulated problem. H_k is produced through a common method of intersection of known silhouette cones [25]. And the architecture of the second stage is represented as follows.

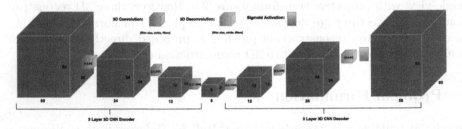

Fig. 2. Deep shape reconstruction architecture. Details of the deep shape reconstruction architecture are represented including the number of 3D convolution layers and 3D deconvolution layers, size of filters, the umber of filters and parameters of the stride

4.1   Architecture

Both the input end H_k and the output end V_k are in the forms of volume space consisting of voxels. The values of the voxels are binary. The key components of the deep learning architecture we built for the deep shape reconstruction are the convolutional encoding layers(recognition network) and convolutional decoding layers(generative network). As shown in Fig. 2, there are three 3D convolutional layers and three 3D deconvolutional layers in our deep shape reconstruction architectures. From the input end to the output end of the deep shape architecture, we use different size of filters. From the beginning layer of the recognition network, the filter size changes from $4 \times 4 \times 4$ to $2 \times 2 \times 2$, the number of filters increase from 64 to 1024. In contrast, from the beginning layer of the generative network, the filter size changes from $2 \times 2 \times 2$ to $4 \times 4 \times 4$, and the number of filters reduces from 1024 to 64.

4.2 Convolution and Deconvolution

CNNs are good at extracting high-level abstract information of data by inter-leaving convolutional and deconvolutional layers, pooling and spatially shrinking. For both convolutional and deconvolutional layers, learnable filters are important components for the stronger learning ability of these layers. A filter of a trainable convolutional layer acts as a learnable local down-sampling unit and the filter of a trainable deconvolutional layer acts as a learnable local up-sampling unit. In 3D convolution, 3D input signals are convolved by the kernel filter and the values are placed on the output 3D grid. Conversely, 3D deconvolution takes the values of the input 3D grid and the result values are got through multiplying the values by weights in the filters. If one 3D filter has size $s \times s \times s$, it generates a $s \times s \times s$ output matrix for each voxel input. The output matrices can be stored overlapping and the amount of the output overlap depends on the output stride. If the amount of output stride of the convolution filter is bigger than 1, then the convolution layer produces an output with size smaller than the input and works as down-sampler. While, if the amount of input stride of the deconvolution filter is bigger than 1, the deconvolution layer produces an output with size bigger than the input and works as up-sampler.

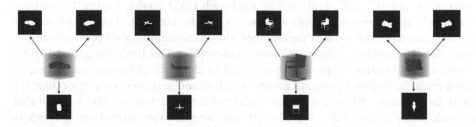

Fig. 3. Triple silhouettes and viewpoints for training deep 3D reconstruction model. For the training of 4 object categories including cars, planes, motorbikes and chairs, both silhouettes and views used to produce coarse shapes are represented

5 Evaluation

Evaluation are conducted for the proposed pipeline. First, training of a deep shape model is conducted through usage of the ShapeNet [1] dataset. Second, test is carried on to reconstruct 3D shapes from a low number of silhouettes. Finally, comparison between the reconstructed 3D shapes and the ground truth shape is made and the reconstruction errors are calculated. We did 4 experiments. The goal of each experiment is to reconstruct the 3D shape of instances of a specific object category. For conducting each experiment, category-specific deep shape model is trained and then the evaluation on the reconstruction accuracy is calculated.

5.1   Dataset

ShapeNet is presented as a richly-annotated, large-scale repository of shapes containing 3D CAD models of objects for a rich number of object categories. ShapeNets contains more than $3,000,000$ models, and $220,000$ models of which are classified into $3,135$ categories. And ShapeNets has been used in a range of deep 3D shape research work [27–29]. Here, we use a subset of ShapeNets to train our category-specific deep shape reconstruction model. For example, we use 372 car CAD models for training our car deep shape reconstruction network, and then use 110 car CAD models for testing the performance of our pipeline. The number of CAD models used in the training for other three categories including planes, motorbikes and chairs are 372, 277, 315 respectively. The number of CAD models for testing are 107, 164 and 62 respectively.

5.2   Training

In the training, both the ground truth shape and the coarse shape of each CAD model are used. The coarse shapes for training a category-specific deep shape reconstruction model are produced through applying triple silhouettes. These silhouettes are taken from three different views around each CAD model. The three views are $0°$, $120°$, and $240°$ around each CAD model. Figure 3 visualizes the fixed three views and triple silhouettes for the training. Then, with known triple silhouettes and camera parameters, the coarse shapes are produced simply from the intersection of three silhouette cones [25]. And both the ground truth shape and the coarse shape are represented in the form of volume consisting of binary voxels. Figure 4 presents ground truth shape and their corresponding H_3 used for training. To be noted, for both training and testing, the volume size of each shape is $50 \times 50 \times 50$. The category-specific reconstruction network is trained end to end from scratch and with pure stochastic gradient decent. And the learning rate is $1e^{-5}$ for 200 epoches. The value of momentum is 0.9 and the implementation is based on the open source library Torch.

5.3   Testing

In the testing, the category-specific 3D shape reconstruction pipeline is evaluated for 4 object categories including cars, planes, chairs and motorbikes. For each object category, we test the 3D deep shape reconstruction pipeline for 4 different number of views. First, we test the 3D deep shape reconstruction pipeline with input of 2 silhouettes. These 2 silhouettes are produced from 2 fixed views, $0°$ and $180°$ around a ground truth CAD model. The other three tests evaluate the performance of the deep shape reconstruction pipeline for 3 fixed views, 4 fixed views and 5 fixed views respectively. Also, the views chosen for these three tests are $[0°, 120°, 240°]$, $[0°, 90°, 180°, 270°]$ and $[0°, 72°, 144°, 216°, 288°]$ respectively. Figure 5 visualizes the four arrangements of views for the test.

GT H_3 GT H_3 GT H_3 GT H_3

Fig. 4. Sample shapes for training deep shape reconstruction architecture. Both ground truth (GT) shapes and coarse shapes H_3 are alternatively presented from the left to right columns. Both two kinds of shapes are used for training category-specific deep shape reconstruction architecture. Samples of the shapes for training 4 object categories are all represented

Fig. 5. Four view arrangements of silhouettes for test. The view arrangements for the test of the car object category are shown

5.4   Results

The reconstructed shape in the two stages of our deep 3D reconstruction pipeline are represented. For the test of the 4 view arrangements and 4 object categories, both the coarse shapes and final shapes are shown qualitatively and quantitatively. Both the qualitative and quantitative results show that the deep 3D reconstruction pipeline is capable of reconstructing category-specific 3D shapes with a small number of silhouettes as input. It also demonstrates that the network improves the reconstruction after coarse shape stage. The reconstruction error between V_k and GT is shown to be smaller than the reconstruction error between H_k and GT, proving that the deep shape reconstruction architecture reconstructs v_k which is better than H_k.

Qualitative Results. Figures 6, 7, 8, 9 visualize the shape reconstruction of four object categories including cars, planes, motorbikes and chairs. Ground truth shapes, shapes reconstructed in both the coarse shape reconstruction stage and the deep shape reconstruction stage are all represented in the figures.

Quantitative Results. In order to get quantitative measures of the reconstructed shape, we evaluate the 3D reconstruction in two ways. The first evaluation is the mean square error between a 3D voxel reconstruction before thresholding and its ground truth voxelized model. The second evaluation is the voxel Intersection-over-Union(IoU) between the 3D voxel reconstruction and the ground truth model. More formally,

$$Reconstruction\ Error = \frac{\sum_{i=1}^{n} |vp_i - Gvp_i|^2}{n} \tag{3}$$

where vp_i represents the final output at voxel i in a grid space before thresholding, $vp_i \in [0,1]$. And let the corresponding ground truth occupancy be Gvp_i, $Gvp_i \in \{0,1\}$. Lower error indicates better reconstruction. To be noted, we train and test in a $50 \times 50 \times 50$ grid space so the total number of voxels is determined as $n = 50 \times 50 \times 50$.

$$Voxel\ IoU = \frac{\sum_{i=1}^{n} [I(vp_i > t)\ I(Gvp_i)]}{\sum_{i=1}^{n} I(I(vp_i > t) + I(Gvp_i))} \tag{4}$$

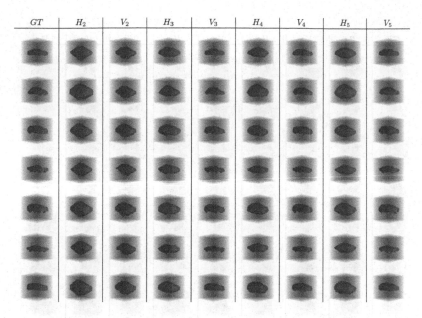

Fig. 6. Qualitative car reconstruction results. Samples of reconstructed car shapes are represented, the *GT* column represents the ground truth shapes, the other eight columns represent reconstructed shapes from the coarse stage and the 3D deep reconstruction stage. H_2 column represents coarse reconstructed shapes in the 2-view arrangement. V_2 column represents final reconstructed shapes in the 2-view arrangement. Shapes in other columns are represented in a similar way

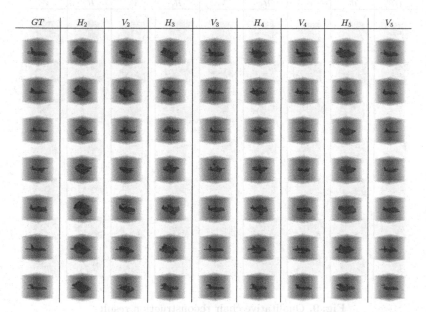

Fig. 7. Qualitative plane reconstruction results

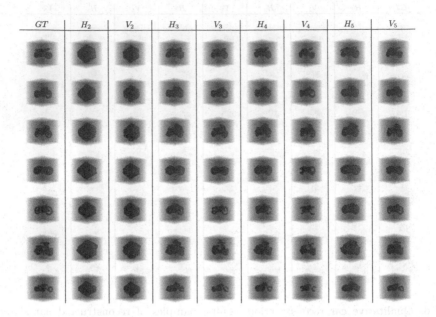

Fig. 8. Qualitative motorbike reconstruction results

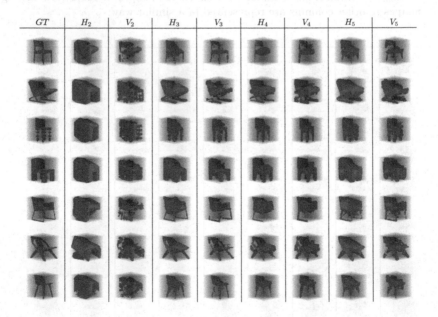

Fig. 9. Qualitative chair reconstruction results

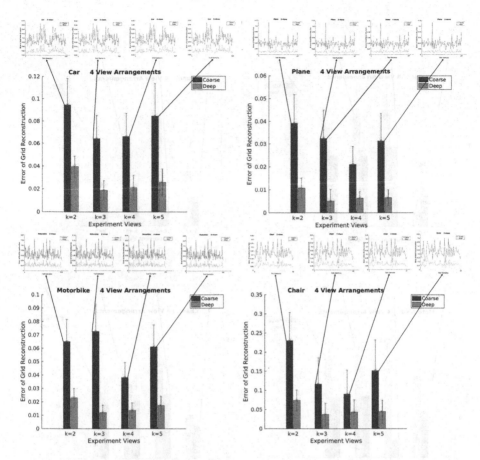

Fig. 10. Reconstruction errors for four object categories. For each object category, reconstruction errors of reconstructed shapes from both the 2 stages including coarse stage (in blue curves/bars) and the deep stage (in yellow curves/bars) are shown. The errors of each test sample of 4 view arrangements are shown on the top 4 sub-figures, the average error for each view arrangement is shown in the bar figures. Variance of errors is plot in red lines (Color figure online)

where $I(.)$ is an indicator function and $t \in [0, 1]$ is a voxelization threshold. Higher IoU values indicates better reconstruction. In the test, the value of threshold is set to $t = 0.5$ for cars, planes and motorbikes. $t = 0.3$ is chosen for chairs.

Figure 10 visualizes the reconstruction errors of all tests. Error of each test sample, the average error and variance of error for each object ategory and each view arrangement are all shown. Figure 11 visualizes the voxel IoU of all tests. Voxel IoU of each test sample, the average voxel IoU and variance of voxel IoU for each object category and each view arrangement are all shown.

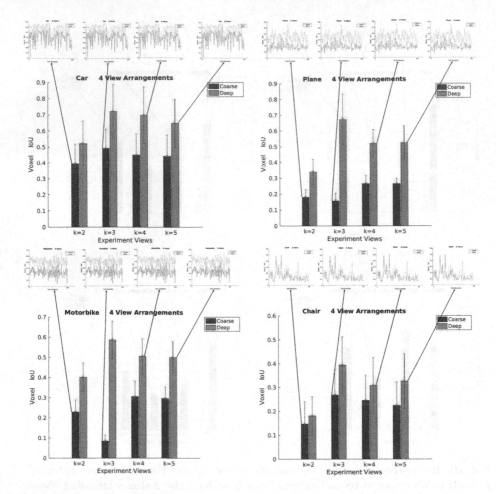

Fig. 11. Voxel IoU for four object categories. For each object category, voxel IoU of reconstructed shapes from both the 2 stages including coarse stage (in blue curves/bars) and the deep stage (in yellow curves/bars) are shown. Voxel IoU of each test sample of 4 view arrangements are shown on the top 4 sub-figures, the average Voxel IoU for each view arrangement is shown in the bar figures. Variance of each voxel IoU is plot in red lines (Color figure online)

6   Conclusion and Future Work

Our 3D reconstruction pipeline using 3D CNNs networks has been trained end to end. The input of the pipeline are a small number of silhouettes with corresponding camera parameter matrix and the output is the reconstruction of category-specific 3D shapes. Our approach proves its efficiency in tackling the complexity of the shapes considered where the object categories contain instances with large non-linear shape variations. The proposed pipeline works in two stages including coarse shape reconstruction stage and deep shape reconstruction stage.

Our 3D reconstruction pipeline works from a low number of silhouettes given as inputs, to reconstruct good-quality 3D category-specific shapes. This reconstruction pipeline is independent on pixel values, feature matches and other forms of data. It provides a potential solution to opening challenges in current 3D reconstruction field including reconstruction failures for objects containing textureless, transparent parts and low-quality reconstruction due to insufficient dense feature correspondences. Furthermore, this pipeline is practical to use because it depends on a low number of silhouettes inputs as opposed to providing a large number of images/silhouettes from multiple views as needed for reconstruction.

However, some limitations of the reconstruction pipeline exists. First, the proposed pipeline is not capable of reconstructing good shapes from two silhouettes or a single silhouette. Second, the proposed pipeline is demonstrated to produce reconstruction for a range of selected view arrangements: the selected silhouettes were taken from evenly spaced locations on a circle around the object. Third, the reconstruction pipeline relies on camera parameters matrix to be available. Finally, quality of the final reconstruction is not very good for chairs that have legs broken. Moreover, our current shape resolution is only $50 \times 50 \times 50$ (inputs, and outputs) and this is an open computational challenge to address high resolution volumetric shape in 3D reconstruction.

Therefore, our future work will improve the reconstruction quality of our pipeline in four aspects. First, we will explore to produce good reconstruction from two silhouettes or a single silhouette. Second, more work is planed to produce good reconstruction from random views. Third, in order to let our pipeline to work more automatically, we will improve our pipeline to reduce the input to only silhouettes without the knowledge of their camera parameter matrix. Finally, the improvement on both higher resolution of final reconstruction and less failure such as broken legs will also be made.

Acknowledgments. This work has been supported by a scholarship from Trinity College Dublin (Ireland), and partially supported by EU FP7-PEOPLE-2013-IAPP GRAISearch grant (612334).

References

1. Chang, A.X., Funkhouser, T., Guibas, L., Hanrahan, P., Huang, Q., Li, Z., Savarese, S., Savva, M., Song, S., Su, H., Xiao, J., Yi, L., Yu, F.: ShapeNet: an information-rich 3D model repository. Technical report [cs.GR], Stanford University – Princeton University – Toyota Technological Institute at Chicago (2015). arXiv:1512.03012
2. Farabet, C., Couprie, C., Najman, L., LeCun, Y.: Learning hierarchical features for scene labeling. IEEE Trans. Pattern Anal. Mach. Intell. **35**(8), 1915–1929 (2013)
3. Girshick, R., Donahue, J., Darrell, T., Malik, J.: Rich feature hierarchies for accurate object detection and semantic segmentation. In: Proceedings of the IEEE Conference on Computer Vision and Pattern Recognition, pp. 580–587 (2014)

4. Hariharan, B., Arbeláez, P., Girshick, R., Malik, J.: Hypercolumns for object segmentation and fine-grained localization. In: Proceedings of the IEEE Conference on Computer Vision and Pattern Recognition, pp. 447–456 (2015)
5. Long, J., Shelhamer, E., Darrell, T.: Fully convolutional networks for semantic segmentation. In: Proceedings of the IEEE Conference on Computer Vision and Pattern Recognition, pp. 3431–3440 (2015)
6. Ganin, Y., Lempitsky, V.: N^4-fields: neural network nearest neighbor fields for image transforms. In: Cremers, D., Reid, I., Saito, H., Yang, M.-H. (eds.) ACCV 2014. LNCS, vol. 9004, pp. 536–551. Springer, Heidelberg (2015). doi:10.1007/978-3-319-16808-1_36
7. Karpathy, A., Toderici, G., Shetty, S., Leung, T., Sukthankar, R., Fei-Fei, L.: Large-scale video classification with convolutional neural networks. In: Proceedings of the IEEE Conference on Computer Vision and Pattern Recognition, pp. 1725–1732 (2014)
8. Dosovitskiy, A., Fischery, P., Ilg, E., Hazirbas, C., Golkov, V., van der Smagt, P., Cremers, D., Brox, T., et al.: Flownet: learning optical flow with convolutional networks. In: 2015 IEEE International Conference on Computer Vision (ICCV), pp. 2758–2766. IEEE (2015)
9. Eigen, D., Puhrsch, C., Fergus, R.: Depth map prediction from a single image using a multi-scale deep network. In: Advances in Neural Information Processing Systems, pp. 2366–2374 (2014)
10. Szegedy, C., Liu, W., Jia, Y., Sermanet, P., Reed, S., Anguelov, D., Erhan, D., Vanhoucke, V., Rabinovich, A.: Going deeper with convolutions. In: Proceedings of the IEEE Conference on Computer Vision and Pattern Recognition, pp. 1–9 (2015)
11. Tran, D., Bourdev, L., Fergus, R., Torresani, L., Paluri, M.: Learning spatiotemporal features with 3D convolutional networks. In: 2015 IEEE International Conference on Computer Vision (ICCV), pp. 4489–4497. IEEE (2015)
12. Matan, O., Burges, C.J., LeCun, Y., Denker, J.S.: Multi-digit recognition using a space displacement neural network. In: NIPS, pp. 488–495 (1991)
13. LeCun, Y., Boser, B., Denker, J.S., Henderson, D., Howard, R.E., Hubbard, W., Jackel, L.D.: Backpropagation applied to handwritten zip code recognition. Neural Comput. 1(4), 541–551 (1989)
14. Wolf, R., Platt, J.C.: Postal address block location using a convolutional locator network. In: Advances in Neural Information Processing Systems, p. 745 (1994)
15. Ning, F., Delhomme, D., LeCun, Y., Piano, F., Bottou, L., Barbano, P.E.: Toward automatic phenotyping of developing embryos from videos. IEEE Trans. Image Process. 14(9), 1360–1371 (2005)
16. Dosovitskiy, A., Tobias Springenberg, J., Brox, T.: Learning to generate chairs with convolutional neural networks. In: Proceedings of the IEEE Conference on Computer Vision and Pattern Recognition, pp. 1538–1546 (2015)
17. Sharma, A., Grau, O., Fritz, M.: VConv-DAE: deep volumetric shape learning without object labels. arXiv preprint (2016). arXiv:1604.03755
18. Wang, X., Fouhey, D., Gupta, A.: Designing deep networks for surface normal estimation. In: Proceedings of the IEEE Conference on Computer Vision and Pattern Recognition, pp. 539–547 (2015)
19. Tulsiani, S., Malik, J.: Viewpoints and keypoints. In: 2015 IEEE Conference on Computer Vision and Pattern Recognition (CVPR), pp. 1510–1519. IEEE (2015)
20. Luo, W., Schwing, A.G., Urtasun, R.: Efficient deep learning for stereo matching. In: Proceedings of the IEEE Conference on Computer Vision and Pattern Recognition, pp. 5695–5703 (2016)

21. Tatarchenko, M., Dosovitskiy, A., Brox, T.: Multi-view 3D models from single images with a convolutional network. In: Leibe, B., Matas, J., Sebe, N., Welling, M. (eds.) ECCV 2016. LNCS, vol. 9911, pp. 322–337. Springer, Heidelberg (2016). doi:10.1007/978-3-319-46478-7_20

22. Choy, C.B., Xu, D., Gwak, J., Chen, K., Savarese, S.: 3D–R2N2: a unified approach for single and multi-view 3D object reconstruction. arXiv preprint (2016). arXiv:1604.00449

23. Yumer, M.E., Mitra, N.J.: Learning semantic deformation flows with 3D convolutional networks. In: Leibe, B., Matas, J., Sebe, N., Welling, M. (eds.) ECCV 2016. LNCS, vol. 9910, pp. 294–311. Springer, Heidelberg (2016). doi:10.1007/978-3-319-46466-4_18

24. Yan, X., Yang, J., Yumer, E., Guo, Y., Lee, H.: Learning volumetric 3D object reconstruction from single-view with projective transformations. In: Neural Information Processing Systems (NIPS 2016) (2016)

25. Laurentini, A.: The visual hull concept for silhouette-based image understanding. IEEE Trans. Pattern Anal. Mach. Intell. **16**(2), 150–162 (1994)

26. Kim, D., Ruttle, J., Dahyot, R.: Bayesian 3D shape from silhouettes. Digit. Signal Proc. **23**(6), 1844–1855 (2013)

27. Su, H., Qi, C.R., Li, Y., Guibas, L.J.: Render for CNN: viewpoint estimation in images using CNNs trained with rendered 3D model views. In: Proceedings of the IEEE International Conference on Computer Vision, pp. 2686–2694 (2015)

28. Maturana, D., Scherer, S.: Voxnet: a 3D convolutional neural network for real-time object recognition. In: 2015 IEEE/RSJ International Conference on Intelligent Robots and Systems (IROS), pp. 922–928. IEEE (2015)

29. Wu, Z., Song, S., Khosla, A., Yu, F., Zhang, L., Tang, X., Xiao, J.: 3D shapenets: a deep representation for volumetric shapes. In: Proceedings of the IEEE Conference on Computer Vision and Pattern Recognition, pp. 1912–1920 (2015)

Deep Disentangled Representations for Volumetric Reconstruction

Edward Grant[1(✉)], Pushmeet Kohli[2], and Marcel van Gerven[1]

[1] Radboud University, Nijmegen, The Netherlands
edward339@gmail.com, m.vangerven@donders.ru.nl
[2] Microsoft Research, Cambridge, UK
pkohli@microsoft.com

Abstract. We introduce a convolutional neural network for inferring a compact disentangled graphical description of objects from 2D images that can be used for volumetric reconstruction. The network comprises an encoder and a twin-tailed decoder. The encoder generates a disentangled *graphics code*. The first decoder generates a volume, and the second decoder reconstructs the input image using a novel training regime that allows the *graphics code* to learn a separate representation of the 3D object and a description of its lighting and pose conditions. We demonstrate this method by generating volumes and disentangled graphical descriptions from images and videos of faces and chairs.

1 Introduction

Images depicting natural objects are 2D representations of an underlying 3D structure from a specific viewpoint in specific lighting conditions.

This work demonstrates a method for recovering the underlying 3D geometry of an object depicted in a single 2D image or video. To accomplish this we first encode the image as a separate description of the shape and transformation properties of the input such as lighting and pose. The shape description is used to generate a volumetric representation that is interpretable by modern rendering software.

State of the art computer vision models perform recognition by learning hierarchical layers of feature detectors across overlapping sub-regions of the input space. Invariance to small transformations to the input is created by sub-sampling the image at various stages in the hierarchy.

In contrast, computer graphics models represent visual entities in a canonical form that is disentangled with respect to various realistic transformations in 3D, such as pose, scale and lighting conditions. 2D images can be rendered from the graphics code with the desired transformation properties.

A long standing hypothesis in computer vision is that vision is better accomplished by inferring such a disentangled graphical representation from 2D images. This process is known as 'de-rendering' and the field is known as 'vision as inverse graphics' [1].

© Springer International Publishing Switzerland 2016
G. Hua and H. Jégou (Eds.): ECCV 2016 Workshops, Part III, LNCS 9915, pp. 266–279, 2016.
DOI: 10.1007/978-3-319-49409-8_22

One obstacle to realising this aim is that the de-rendering problem is ill-posed. The same 2D image can be rendered from a variety of 3D objects. This uncertainty means that there is normally no analytical solution to de-rendering. There are however, solutions that are more or less likely, given an object class or the class of all natural objects.

Recent work in the field of vision as inverse graphics has produced a number of convolutional neural network models that accomplish de-rendering [2–4]. Typically these models follow an encoding/decoding architecture. The encoder predicts a compact 3D graphical representation of the input. A control signal is applied corresponding with a known transformation to the input and a decoder renders the transformed image. We use a similar architecture. However, rather than rendering an image from the graphics code, we generate a full volumetric representation.

Unlike the disentangled graphics code generated by existing models, which is only renderable using a custom trained decoder, the volumetric representation generated by our model is easily converted to a polygon mesh or other professional quality 3D graphical format. This allows the object to be rendered at any scale and with other rendering techniques available in modern rendering software.

2   Related Work

Several models have been developed that generate an disentangled representation given a 2D input, and output a new image subject to a transformation.

Kulkarni et al. proposed the Deep Convolutional Inverse Graphics Network (DC-IGN) trained using Stochastic Gradient Variational Bayes [2]. This model encodes a factored latent representation of the input that is disentangled with respect to changes in azimuth, elevation and light source. A decoder renders the graphics code subject to the desired transformation as a 2D image. Training is performed with batches in which only a single transformation or the shape of the object are different. The activations of the graphics code layer chosen to represent the static parameters are clamped as the mean of the activations for that batch on the forward pass. On the backward pass the gradients for the corresponding nodes are set to their difference from this mean. The method is demonstrated by generating chairs and face images transformed with respect to azimuth, elevation and light source.

Tatarchenko et al. proposed a similar model that is trained in a fully supervised manner [3]. The encoder takes a 2D image as input and generates a graphics code representing a canonical 3D object form. A signal is added to the code corresponding with a known transformation in 3D and the decoder renders a new image corresponding with that transformation. This method is also demonstrated by generating rotated images of cars and chairs.

Yang et al. demonstrated an encoder/decoder model similar to the above but utilize a recurrent structure to account for long-term dependencies in a sequence of transformations, allowing for realistic re-rendering of real face images from different azimuth angles [4].

Spatial Transformer Networks (STN) allow for the spatial manipulation of images and data within a convolutional neural network [5]. The STN first generates a transformation matrix given an input, creates a grid of sampling points based on the transformation and outputs samples from the grid. The module is trained using back-propagation and transforms the input with an input dependent affine transformation. Since the output sample can be of arbitrary size, these modules have been used as an efficient down-sampling method in classification networks. STNs transform existing data by sampling but they are not generative, so cannot make predictions about occluded data, which is necessary when predicting 3D structure.

Girdhar *et al.* and Rezende *et al.* present methods for volumetric reconstructing from 2D images but do not generate disentangled representations [6,7].

The contribution of this work is an encoding/decoding model that generates a compact graphics code from 2D images and videos that is disentangled with respect to shape and the transformation parameters of the input, and that can also be used for volumetric reconstruction. To our knowledge this is the first work that generates a disentanlged graphical representation that can be used to reconstruct volumes from 2D images. In addition, we show that Spatial Transformer Networks can be used to replace max-pooling in the encoder as an efficient sampling method. We demonstrate this approach by generating a compact disentangled graphical representation from single 2D images and videos of faces and chairs in a variety of viewpoint and lighting conditions. This code is used to generate volumetric representations which are rendered from a variety of viewpoints to show their 3D structure.

3   Model

3.1   Architecture

As shown in Fig. 1, the network has one encoder, a *graphics code* layer and two decoders. The *graphics code* layer is separated into a *shape code* and a *transformation code*. The encoder takes as input an 80×80 pixel color image and generates the *graphics code* following a series of convolutions, point-wise randomized rectified linear units (RReLU) [8], down-sampling Spatial Transformer Networks and max pooling. Batch normalization layers are used after each convolutional layer to speed up training and avoid problems with exploding and vanishing gradients [9].

The two decoders are connected to the *graphics code* by switches so that the message from the *graphics code* is passed to either one of the decoders. The first decoder is the volume decoder. The volume decoder takes the *shape code* as input and generates an $80 \times 80 \times 80$ voxel volumetric prediction of the encoded shape. This is accomplished by a series of volumetric convolutions, point-wise RReLU and volumetric up-sampling. A parametric rectified linear unit (PReLU) [10] is substituted for the RReLU in the output layer. This is done to avoid the saturation problems with rectified linear units early in training but

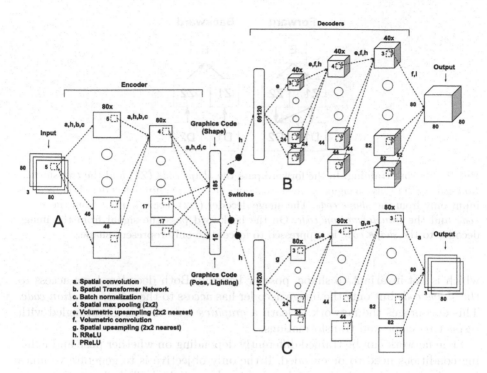

Fig. 1. Network architecture: The network consists of an encoder (A), a volume decoder (B) and an image decoder (C). The encoder takes as input a 2D image and generates a 3D *graphics code* through a series of spatial convolutions, down-sampling Spatial Transformer Networks and max pooling layers. This code is split into a *shape code* and a *transformation code*. The volume decoder takes the *shape code* as input and generates a prediction of the volumetric contents of the input. The image decoder takes the *shape code* and the *transformation code* as input and reconstructs the input image.

allows for learning an activation threshold later in training, corresponding with the positive-valued output targets.

The second decoder reconstructs the input image with the correct pose and lighting, showing that pose and lighting parameters of the input are contained in the *graphics code*. The image decoder takes as input both the *shape code* and the *transformation code*, and generates a reconstruction of the original input image. This is accomplished by a series of spatial convolutions, point-wise RReLU, spatial up-sampling and point-wise PReLU in the final layer. During training, the backward pass from the image decoder to the *shape code* is blocked (see Fig. 2). This encourages the *shape code* to only represent shape, as it only receives an error signal from the volume decoder.

The volume decoder only requires knowledge about the shape of the input since it generates binary volumes that are invariant to pose and lighting. However, the image decoder must generate a reconstruction of the original image

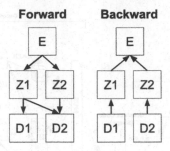

Fig. 2. Network training: In the forward pass the *shape code* (Z1) and the *transformation code* (Z2) receive a signal from the encoder (E). The volume decoder (D1) receives input only from the *shape code*. The image decoder (D2) receives input from the *shape code* and the *transformation code*. On the backward pass the signal from the image decoder to the *shape code* is suppressed to force it to only represent shape.

which is not invariant to shape, pose or lighting. Both decoders have access to the *shape code* but only the image decoder has access to the *transformation code*. This encourages the network to learn a *graphics code* that is disentangled with respect to shape and transformations.

The network can be trained differently depending on whether pose and lighting conditions need to be encoded. If the only objective is to generate volumes from the input then the image decoder can be switched off during training. In this case the *graphics code* will learn to be invariant to viewpoint and lighting. If the volume decoder and image decoder are both used during training the *graphics code* learns a disentangled representation of shape and transformations.

3.2   Spatial Transformer Networks

Spatial Transformer Networks (STNs) perform input dependent geometric transformations on images or sets of feature maps [5]. There are two STNs in our model (see Fig. 1).

Each STN comprises a localisation network, a grid generator and sampling grid. The localisation network takes the activations of the previous layer as input and regresses the parameters of an affine transformation matrix. The grid generator generates a sampling grid of (x, y) coordinates corresponding with the desired height and width of the output. The sampling grid is obtained by multiplying the generated grid with the transformation matrix. In our model this takes the form:

$$\begin{pmatrix} x_i^s \\ y_i^s \end{pmatrix} = \mathcal{T}_\theta(G_i) = \begin{bmatrix} \theta_{11} & \theta_{12} & \theta_{13} \\ \theta_{21} & \theta_{22} & \theta_{23} \end{bmatrix} \begin{pmatrix} x_i^t \\ y_i^t \\ 1 \end{pmatrix} \tag{1}$$

where (x_i^t, y_i^t) are the generated grid coordinates and (x_i^s, y_i^s) define the sample points. The transformation matrix $\mathcal{T}_\theta$ allows for cropping, scale, translation, scale, rotation and skew. Cropping and scale, in particular allow the STN to focus on the most important region in a feature map.

STNs have been shown to improve performance in convolutional network classifiers by modelling attention and transforming feature maps. Our model uses STNs in a generative setting to perform efficient down-sampling and assist the network in learning invariance to pose and lighting.

The first STN in our model is positioned after the first convolutional layer. It uses a convolutional neural network to regress the transformation coefficients. This localisation network consists of four 5×5 convolutional layers, each followed by batch normalization and the first three also followed by 2×2 max pooling.

The second STN in our model is positioned after the second convolutional layer and regresses the transformation parameters with a convolutional network consisting of two 5×5 an one 6×6 convolutional layers each followed by batch normalization and the last two also by 2×2 max pooling.

3.3 Data

The model was trained using $16,000$ image-volume pairs generated from the Basel Face Model [11]. Images of size 80×80 were rendered in RGB from five different azimuth angles and three ambient lighting settings. Volumes of size $80 \times 80 \times 80$ were created by discretizing the triangular mesh generated by the Basel Face Model.

4 Experimental Results

4.1 Training

We evaluated the model's volume prediction capacity by training it on $16,000$ image-volume pairs. Each example pair was shown to the network only once to discourage memorization of the training data.

Training was performed using the Torch framework on a single NVIDIA Tesla K80 GPU. Batches of size 10 were given as input to the encoder and forward propagated through the network. The mean-squared error of the predicted and target volumes was calculated and back-propagated using the Adam learning algorithm [12]. The initial learning rate was set to 0.001.

4.2 Volume Predictions from Images of Faces

In this experiment we used the network to generate volumes from a single 2D images. The network was presented with unseen face images as input and generated 3D volume predictions. The image decoder was not used in this experiment.

The predicted volumes were binarized with a threshold of 0.01. A triangular mesh was generated from the coordinates of active voxels using Delaunay triangulation. The patch was smoothed and the resulting image rendered using OpenGL and Matlab's `trimesh` function.

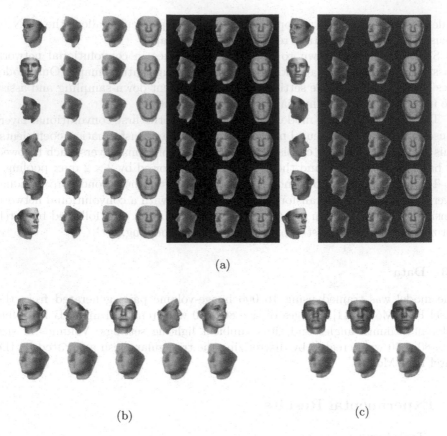

(a)

(b)   (c)

Fig. 3. Generated volumes: Qualitative results showing the volume predicting capacity of the network on unseen data. (a) First column: network inputs. Columns 2–4 (white): network predictions shown from three viewpoints. Columns 5–7 (black): ground truth from the same viewpoints. Column 8: nearest neighbour image. Columns 9–11 (blue): nearest neighbour image ground truth. (b) Each column is an input/output pair. The inputs are in the first row. Each input is the same face viewed from a different position. The generated volumes in the second row are shown from the same viewpoint for comparison. (c) Each column is an input/output pair. The inputs are in the first row. Each input is the same face in different lighting conditions. (Color figure online)

Figure 3(a) shows the input image, network predictions, ground truth, nearest neighour in the input space and the ground truth of the nearest neighour. The nearest neighbour was determined by searching the training images for the image with the smallest pixel-wise distance to the input. The generated volumes are visibly different depending on the shape of the input.

Figure 3(b) shows the network output for the same input presented from different viewpoints. The images in the first row are the inputs to the network and the second row contains the volumes generated from each input. These are shown from the same viewpoint for comparison. The generated volumes are visually very similar, showing that the network generated volumes that are invariant to the pose of the input.

Figure 3(c) shows the network output for the same face presented in different lighting conditions. The first row images are the inputs and the second row are the generated volumes also shown from the same viewpoint for comparison. These volumes are also visually very similar to each other showing that the network output appears invariant to lighting conditions in the input.

4.3   Nearest Neighbour Comparison

The network's quantitative performance was benchmarked using a nearest neighbour test. A test set of 200 image/volume pairs was generated using the Basel Face Model (ground truth). The nearest neighbour to each test image in the training set was identified by searching for the training set image with the smallest pixel-wise Euclidean distance to the test set image (nearest neighbour). The network generated a volume for each test set input (prediction).

Nearest neighbour error was determined by measuring the mean voxel-wise Euclidean distance between the ground truth and nearest neighbour volumes. Prediction error was determined by measuring the mean voxel-wise Euclidean distance between the ground truth volumes and the predicted volumes.

A paired-samples t-test was conducted to compare error score in predicted and nearest neighbour volumes. There was a significant difference in the error score for predictions ($M = 0.0096$, $SD = 0.0013$) and nearest neighbours ($M = 0.017$, $SD = 0.0038$) conditions; $t(199) = -21.5945, p = 4.7022e - 54$.

These results show that network is better at predicting volumes than using the nearest neighbour.

4.4   Internal Representations

In this experiment we tested the ability of the encoder to generate a *graphics code* that can be used to generate a volume that is invariant to pose and lighting. Since the volume encoder doesn't need pose and lighting information we didn't use the image decoder in this experiment.

To test the invariance of the encoder with respect to pose, lighting and shape we re-trained the model without using batch normalization. Three sets of 100 image batches were prepared where two of these parameters were clamped and the target parameter was different. This makes it possible to measure the variance of activations for changes in pose, lighting and shape. The set-wise mean of the mean variance of activations in each batch was compared for all layers in the network.

Figure 4(a) shows that the network's heightened sensitivity to shape relative to pose and lighting begins in the second convolutional layer. There is a sharp increase in sensitivity to shape in the *graphics code*, which is much more sensitive to shape than pose or lighting, and more sensitive to pose than lighting. This relative invariance to pose and lighting is retained in the volume decoder.

Figure 4(b) shows a visual representation of the activations for the same face with different poses. The effect of the first STN can be seen in the second

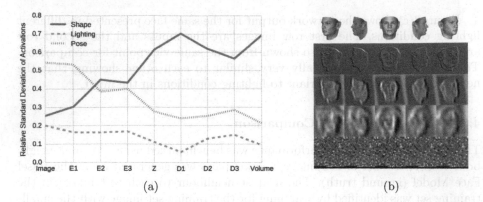

(a)   (b)

Fig. 4. Invariance to pose and lighting: (a) The relative mean standard deviation (SD) of activations in each network layer is compared for changes in shape, pose and lighting. Image is the input image, E1-E3 are the convolutional encoder layers, Z is the *graphics code*, D1-D3 are the convolutional decoder layers and Volume is the generated volume. In the input, changes to pose account for the highest SD. By the second convolutional layer the network is more sensitive to changes in shape than pose or lighting. The *graphics code* is much more sensitive to shape than pose or lighting. (b) The first row is five images of the same face from different viewpoints. Rows 2–4 show sampled encoder activations for the input image at the top of each column. The last row shows sampled *graphics code* activations reshaped into a square.

convolutional layer activations which are visibly warped. The difference in the warp depending on the pose of the face suggests that the STNs may be helping to create invariance to pose later in the network. The example input images have a light source which is directed from the left of the camera. The second convolutional layer activations show a dark area on the right side of each face which is less evident in the first convolutional layer, suggesting that shadowing is an important feature for predicting the 3D shape of the face.

4.5   Disentangled Representations

In this experiment we tested the network's ability to generate a compact 3D description of the input that is disentangled with respect to the shape of the object and transformations such as pose and lighting.

In order to generate this description we used the same network as in the volume generation experiment but with an additional fully connected RReLU layer of size 3,000 in the encoder to compensate for the increased difficulty of the task.

During training, images were given as input to the encoder which generated an activity vector of 200 scalar values. These were divided in the *shape code* comprising 185 values and the *transformation code* comprising 15 values. The network was trained on 16,000 image/volumes pairs with batches of size 10.

The switches connecting the encoder to the decoders were adjusted after every three training batches to allow the volume decoder and the image decoder to see the same number of examples. The volume decoder only received the *shape code*, whereas the image decoder received both the *shape code* and the *transformation code*.

To test if the *shape code* and the *transformation code* learned the desired invariance we measured the mean standard deviation of activations for batches where only one of shape, pose or lighting conditions were changed. The same batches as in the invariance experiment were used.

Figure 5(a) shows the relative mean standard deviation of activations of each layer in the encoder, *graphics code* and image decoder. The bifurcation at point Z on the plot shows that the two codes learned to respond differently to the same input. The *shape code* learned to be more sensitive to changes in shape than pose or lighting, and the *transformation code* learned to be more sensitive to changes in pose and lighting than shape.

To make sure the image decoder used the shape code to reconstruct the input we compared the output of the image decoder with input only from the *shape code*, the *transformation code* and both together. Figure 5(b) shows the output of the volume decoder and image decoder on a number of unseen images. The first column shows the input to the network. The second column shows the output of the image decoder with input only from the *shape code*. The third column shows the same for the output of the *transformation code*. The fourth column shows the combined output of the *shape code* and the *transformation code*. The fifth column shows the output of the volume decoder.

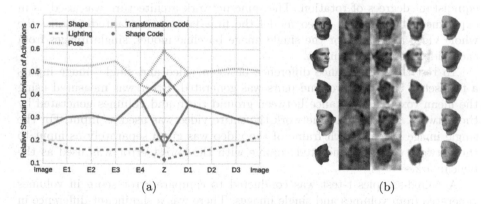

(a)   (b)

Fig. 5. Disentangled representations: (a) The relative mean standard deviation (SD) of activations in the encoder, *shape code*, *transformation code* and image decoder is compared for changes in shape, pose and lighting. The *shape code* is most sensitive to changes in shape. The *transformation code* is most sensitive to changes in pose and lighting. Error bars show standard deviation. (b) The output of the volume decoder and image decoder on a number of unseen images. The first column is the input image. The second column is the image decoded from the *shape code* only. The third column is the image decoded from the *transformation code* only. The fourth column is the image decoded from the *shape code* and the *transformation code*. The fifth column is the output of the volume decoder shown from the same viewpoint for comparison.

4.6   Face Recognition in Novel Pose and Lighting Conditions

To measure the invariance and representational quality of the *shape code* we tested it on a face recognition task.

The point-wise Euclidean distance between the *shape code* generated by an image was measured for a batch of 150 random images including one image that was the same face with a different pose (target). The random images were ordered from the smallest to greatest distance and the rank of the target was recorded. This was repeated 100 times and an identical experiment was performed for pose. The mean rank for the same face with a different pose was 11.08. The mean rank of the same face with different lighting was 1.02. This demonstrates that the *shape code* can be used as a pose and lighting invariant face classifier.

To test if the *shape code* was more invariant to pose and lighting than the full *graphics code* we repeated this experiment using the full *graphics code*. The mean rank for the same face with a different pose was 26.86. The mean rank of the same face with different lighting was 1.14. This shows that the *shape code* was relatively more invariant to pose and lighting than the full *graphics code*.

4.7   Volume Predictions from Videos of Faces

To test if video input improved the quality of the generated volumes we adapted the encoder to take video as input and compared to a single image baseline. 10,000 video/volume pairs of faces were created. Each video consisted of five RGB frames of a face rotating from left facing profile to right facing profile in equidistant degrees of rotation. The same network architecture was used as in experiment 4.5. For the video model the first layer was adapted to take the whole video as input. For the single image baseline model, single images from each video were used as input.

To test the performance difference between video and single image inputs a test set of 500 video/volume pairs was generated. Error was measured using the mean voxel-wise distance between ground truth and volumes generated by the network. For the video network the entire video was used as input. For the single image baseline each frame of the video was given separately as input to the network and the generated volume with the lowest error was used as the benchmark.

A paired-samples t-test was conducted to compare error score in volumes generated from volumes and single images. There was a significant difference in the error score for video based volume predictions ($M = 0.0073$, $SD = 0.0009$) and single image based predictions ($M = 0.0089$, $SD = 0.0014$) conditions; $t(199) = -13.7522, 1.0947e{-}30$.

These results show that video input results in superior volume reconstruction performance compared with single images.

4.8   Volume Predictions from Images of Chairs

In this experiment we tested the capacity of the network to generate volume predictions from objects with more variable geometry. 5000 Volume/image pairs of chairs were created from the ModelNet dataset [13]. The images were 80×80 RGB images and the volumes were $30 \times 30 \times 30$ binary volumes. The predicted volumes were binarized with a threshold of 0.2. Both decoders were used in this experiment. The *shape code* consisted of 599 activations and the *transformation code* consisted of one activation. The *shape code* was used to reconstruct the volumes. Both the *shape code* and *transformation code* were used to reconstruct the input.

Figure 6 demonstrates the network's capacity to generate volumetric predictions of chairs from novel images.

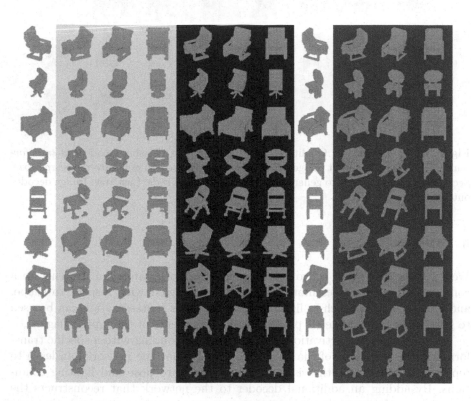

Fig. 6. Generated chair volumes: Qualitative results showing the volume predicting capacity of the network on unseen data. First column: network inputs. Columns 2–4 (Yellow): network predictions shown from three viewpoints. Columns 5–7 (black): ground truth from the same viewpoints. Column 8: nearest neighbour image in the training set. Columns 9–11 (blue): nearest neighbour image ground truth. (Color figure online)

4.9 Interpolating the Graphics Code

In order to qualitatively demonstrate that the *graphics code* in experiment 4.8 was disentangled with respect to shape and pose, we swapped the *shape code* and *transformation code* of a number of images and generated new images from the interpolated code using the image decoder. Figure 7 shows the output of the image decoder using the interpolated code. The shape of the chairs in the generated images is most similar to the shape of the chairs in the images used to generate the *shape code*. The pose of each chair is most similar to the pose of the chairs in the images used to generate the *transformation code*. This demonstrates that the *graphics code* is disentangled with respect to shape and pose.

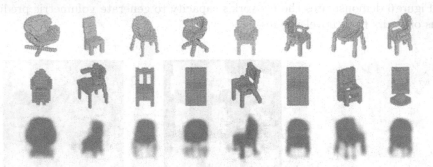

Fig. 7. Interpolated code: Qualitative results combining the shape code and *transformation code* from different images. First row: images used to generate the *shape code*. Second row: images used to generate the *transformation code*. Last row: Image decoder output.

5   Discussion

We have shown that a convolutional neural network can learn to generate a compact graphical representation that is disentangled with respect to shape, and transformations such as lighting and pose. This representation can be used to generate a full volumetric prediction of the contents of the input image.

By comparing the activations of batches corresponding with a specific transformation or the shape of the image, we showed that the network can learn to represent a *shape code* that is relatively invariant to pose and lighting conditions. By adding an additional decoder to the network that reconstructs the input image, the network can learn to represent a *transformation code* that represents the pose and lighting conditions of the input.

Extending the approach to real world scenes requires consideration of the viewpoint of the generated volume. Although the volume is invariant in the sense that it contains all the information necessary to render the generated object from any viewpoint, a canonical viewpoint was used for all volumes so that they were generated from a frontal perspective. Natural scenes do not always have a canonical viewpoint for reference. One possible solution is to generate a volume from the same viewpoint as the input. Experiments show that this approach is promising but further work is needed.

In order to learn, the network requires image-volume pairs. This limits the type of data that can be used as volumetric datasets of sufficient size, or models that generate them are limited in number. A promising avenue for future work is incorporating a professional quality renderer into the decoder structure. This theoretically allows for 3D graphical representations to be learned, provided that the rendering process is approximately differentiable.

Acknowledgements. Thanks to Thomas Vetter for access to the Basel Face Model.

References

1. Yuille, A., Kersten, D.: Vision as Bayesian inference: analysis by synthesis? Trends Cogn. Sci. **10**(7), 301–308 (2006)
2. Kulkarni, T.D., Whitney, W.F., Kohli, P., Tenenbaum, J.: Deep convolutional inverse graphics network. In: Advances in Neural Information Processing Systems, pp. 2530–2538 (2015)
3. Tatarchenko, M., Dosovitskiy, A., Brox, T.: Single-view to multi-view: reconstructing unseen views with a convolutional network arXiv preprint (2015). arXiv:1511.06702
4. Yang, J., Reed, S.E., Yang, M.H., Lee, H.: Weakly-supervised disentangling with recurrent transformations for 3D view synthesis. In: Advances in Neural Information Processing Systems, pp. 1099–1107 (2015)
5. Jaderberg, M., Simonyan, K., Zisserman, A., et al.: Spatial Transformer Networks. In: Advances in Neural Information Processing Systems, pp. 2008–2016 (2015)
6. Girdhar, R., Fouhey, D.F., Rodriguez, M., Gupta, A.: Learning a predictable and generative vector representation for objects arXiv preprint (2016). arXiv:1603.08637
7. Rezende, D.J., Eslami, S., Mohamed, S., Battaglia, P., Jaderberg, M., Heess, N.: Unsupervised learning of 3d structure from images arXiv preprint (2016). arXiv:1607.00662
8. Xu, B., Wang, N., Chen, T., Li, M.: Empirical evaluation of rectified activations in convolutional network arXiv preprint (2015). arXiv:1505.00853
9. Ioffe, S., Szegedy, C.: Batch normalization: accelerating deep network training by reducing internal covariate shift. In: Proceedings of The 32nd International Conference on Machine Learning, pp. 448–456 (2015)
10. He, K., Zhang, X., Ren, S., Sun, J.: Delving deep into rectifiers: surpassing human-level performance on ImageNet classification. In: Proceedings of the IEEE International Conference on Computer Vision, pp. 1026–1034 (2015)
11. Paysan, P., Knothe, R., Amberg, B., Romdhani, S., Vetter, T.: A 3D face model for pose and illumination invariant face recognition. In: Sixth IEEE International Conference on Advanced Video and Signal Based Surveillance AVSS 2009, pp. 296–301. IEEE (2009)
12. Kingma, D., Ba, J.: Adam: a method for stochastic optimization. arXiv preprint (2014). arXiv:1412.6980
13. Wu, Z., Song, S., Khosla, A., Yu, F., Zhang, L., Tang, X., Xiao, J.: 3D shapenets: a deep representation for volumetric shapes. In: Proceedings of the IEEE Conference on Computer Vision and Pattern Recognition, pp. 1912–1920 (2015)

Class-Specific Object Pose Estimation and Reconstruction Using 3D Part Geometry

Arun C.S. Kumar[1(✉)], András Bódis-Szomorú[2], Suchendra Bhandarkar[1],
and Mukta Prasad[3]

[1] University of Georgia, Athens, USA
aruncs@uga.edu, suchi@cs.uga.edu
[2] ETH Zürich, Zürich, Switzerland
bodis@vision.ee.ethz.ch
[3] Trinity College Dublin, Dublin, Ireland
prasadm@tcd.ie

Abstract. We propose a novel approach for detecting and reconstructing class-specific objects from 2D images. Reconstruction and detection, despite major advances, are still wanting in performance. Hence, approaches that try to solve them jointly, so that one can be used to resolve the ambiguities of the other, especially while employing data-driven class-specific learning, are increasingly popular. In this paper, we learn a deformable, fine-grained, part-based model from real world, class-specific, image sequences, so that given a new image, we can simultaneously estimate the 3D shape, viewpoint and the subsequent 2D detection results. This is a step beyond existing approaches, which are usually limited to 3D CAD shapes, regression based pose estimation, template based deformation modelling etc. We employ Structure from Motion (SfM) and part based models in our learning process, and estimate a 3D deformable object instance and a projection matrix that explains the image information. We demonstrate our approach with high quality qualitative and quantitative results on our real world RealCar dataset, as well as the EPFL car dataset.

1 Introduction

Despite big advances, core computer vision problems in the area of detection and reconstruction are far from perfectly solved. It is increasingly recognized that to combat the problems faced by these areas of vision, effective solutions must tackle them jointly, modelling the physics of image formation, learn from data, expert-knowledge and allow one problem to handle the ambiguities of the other. Although 3D geometric reasoning has become increasingly common in several computer vision applications, it is still some way off from becoming a standard consumer-level technique.

In this paper, we propose a framework that, given a 2D image, simultaneously detects an object category instance, estimates the object pose and shape in 3D, reasons about its part appearance and occlusion, thus performing object

© Springer International Publishing Switzerland 2016
G. Hua and H. Jégou (Eds.): ECCV 2016 Workshops, Part III, LNCS 9915, pp. 280–295, 2016.
DOI: 10.1007/978-3-319-49409-8_23

reconstruction in 3D and detection in 2D, jointly. The problem is ambitious because the proposed framework learns a class-specific, deformable fine-grained, part-based model from image sequences, learning both appearance and geometry. Note that the ill-posed nature of the problem results in a complex solution landscape with several local minima. In order to enable reasonable solutions, we solve the problem by tackling the complexity in a gradual, incremental way. We start from a constrained setup for which the solution can be found reliably and then gradually increase the flexibility in the model to handle more variables in the problem.

The idea of tackling vision problems jointly, has been gaining traction recently [10,12,13,15,23,24]. But the modern approaches, while making strides in tackling this problem, have often resorted to using high quality CAD models (which are expensive, painstaking to design, and/or limited in their capability to capture the object shape, appearance, especially the surface texture). Another tendency, is to model camera viewpoint using regression rather than modelling the physical projection process. Also, shape variation has been often been modelled using a bank of representations/templates. In our proposed approach, we learn SfM based class-specific shape and appearance models from real image sequences as faithfully as possible. Some supervised input is acquired through minimal, intuitive input for fine-grained part understanding. At test time, we formulate the detection and reconstruction problem in terms of the actual reprojection error (this models the scene physics more accurate than regression) and use a variety of RANSAC-based techniques in order to make estimation efficient and effective. We will expand on the related work in the next section.

2 Related Work

As mentioned above, the problem of joint detection, reconstruction and pose estimation of object classes from images has received considerable attention within the computer vision research community in recent years [10,12,24]. Existing approaches to solve this problem can be broadly categorized into two main subclasses, i.e., distinctive view-based techniques and 3D geometry-based techniques. Distinctive view-based techniques exploit robust but less descriptive 2D features for view-specific models for detection and recognition [2,3,5]. The proven usefulness and robustness of statistical 2D feature based methods from the computer vision research literature inspired the development of most distinctive view-based techniques. Existing techniques [4,6,8] treat viewpoint estimation as a classification problem by dividing the viewpoint range into discrete bins. Ghodrati et al. [6] train multiple Support Vector Machine (SVM) classifiers, one for each discrete viewpoint, treating each classifier independently of the others. He et al. [8] use a two-step process, wherein a viewpoint-parametrized classifier is first used to estimate a coarse viewpoint followed by fine-tuning step. Fenzi et al. [4] treat continuous viewpoint estimation as a regression problem which is solved using a Radial Basis Function Neural Network (RBF-NN). The RBF-NN is trained to predict the appearance features as a function of the viewpoint. Tulsiani et al. [15] train a Convolutional Neural Network (CNN) that can jointly predict the viewpoints for all classes using a shared feature representation. The CNN is used to estimate the coarse viewpoint which is subsequently leveraged for keypoint prediction. Though these view-based methods have been effective, one would expect that accurately modelling the physical projection process would be beneficial.

In recent years, due to the wide availability of affordable depth sensors, 3D shape repositories and 3D CAD models, coupled with the fact that it makes more sense to reason in terms of the underlying 3D structure of the object, the research focus has shifted towards 3D geometry-based techniques for solving the 3D object pose estimation and reconstruction problem. With improved optimization techniques and processing power, we are able to learn these, more powerful models. Pepik et al. [12,13] extended the Deformable Parts Model (DPM) [3] to represent the part locations and deformations in 3D. Yu et al. [17] on the other hand, propose an approach for learning a shape appearance and pose (SAP) model for both 2D and 3D cases, where the training instances with unknown pose are used to learn a probabilistic object part-based model. The class label and the pose of the object are inferred simultaneously by joint discovery of parts and alignment to a canonical pose. Xiao et al. [16] and Kim et al. [11], exploit synthetic 3D models to incorporate 3D geometric information into the DPM framework [3] for pose estimation. More recently, Choy et al. [1] use Non-Zero Whitened Histogram-of-Gradients (NZ-WHO) features [7] to synthesize, on the fly, discriminative appearance templates from 3D CAD models, for several poses, scales on multiple CAD model instances of the object, to jointly estimate the viewpoint and the instance associated with the object. In particular, Pepik et al. [12,13] rephrase the DPM framework [3] to formulate a structured learning output predictor to estimate the 2D bounding box of the object along with its viewpoint by enriching the object appearance model using 3D CAD data. The combination of robust DPM matching with the representational power of 3D CAD models is shown to result in a boost in performance across several datasets. We aim to extend this work by learning from real, SfM shapes and associated image appearance models and also treat viewpoint using a full projection model instead of regression.

There has been progress in this regard. Hejrati and Ramanan [9] learned the 3D geometry and shape of the object from 2D part annotations using a non-rigid SFM technique. In particular, Hejrati and Ramanan [10] represent 2D object part appearances using a Gaussian mixture model (GMM) that captures the appearance variations due to variations in the viewing angle. Zia et al. [18] use a 3D shape representation scheme to jointly model multiple objects allowing them to reason about inter-dependencies between the objects, such as occlusion, in a more deterministic and systematic manner.

Our proposed method departs from the beaten path described above, through the following means: (i) employing automatically estimated, real world 3D shapes to learn deformable models (manually generated 3D CAD models are often lacking in appearance details (such as surface texture) and make simplifying approximations about the actual 3D geometry that undermine the challenges underlying the 3D object pose estimation and reconstruction problem), (ii) modelling the projection process for geometric reasoning instead of relying on regression models, (iii) solving the shape recovery and view estimation problems using an effective RANSAC based scheme (as opposed to the computationally intensive generative process of [10]) and (iv) using a fine-grained part representation, learnt from real data, to model the shape to a high resolution and accuracy for more complex analysis in the future. The pipeline of the proposed RANSAC based scheme for shape recovery and viewpoint estimation is shown in Fig. 1

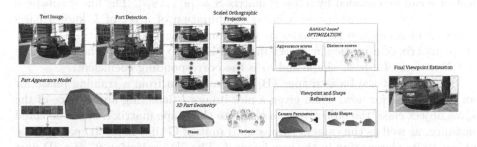

Fig. 1. The proposed object shape and pose (or viewpoint) estimation pipeline. Given a test image, we perform part candidate detection using the learned mixture-model-based part appearance model, followed by viewpoint (scaled orthographic cameras) estimation using a RANSAC-based scheme. The optimization gradually fits more deformation to the shape to recover a realistic reconstruction with a refined camera estimate.

3   The Proposed Method

3.1   Problem Statement

Given a set of image sequences of the same object class, *e.g.* cars, each sequence being taken around a single object instance, our objective is to reconstruct the shape and pose of a new instance observed in a new input image. More precisely, we aim to learn a deformable shape model for the particular object class, which then allows us to estimate both the best deformed shape and the 3D object pose in a new image such that visible semantic, salient parts of the object project to their 2D observations in the image. The latter also involves an occlusion reasoning for the new viewpoint and object instance.

To formulate this, we will use the following notation. Each of the K uncalibrated image sequences given in the training set, indexed by $k \in \{1 \ldots K\}$, contains N_k images taken around an object instance. Let us denote the n-th image in the k-th sequence by I_{nk}, and its associated 3×4 camera (projection) matrix by $\mathbf{C}_{nk}$, which encodes the relative object pose and the camera intrinsics. The estimation task is to predict the full projection model $\mathbf{C}$ and the 3D shape S of the object in a new uncalibrated input image I. For simplicity, we define the 2D object detection mask in I as projection of the fitted shape instance through the estimated camera.

3.2 A Class-Specific Deformable Model

There are different ways to represent the shape of an object instance that is of a particular object class. Due to its simplicity and elegance, we have chosen to use a semantic part-based construction in combination with a linear subspace deformation model.

We define the shape S of any object instance via the 3D positions of its P semantic parts in space. The set of parts is predefined per object class. If $\mathbf{s}_p$ is the position of the p-th part of an object instance, then the shape of this instance can be encoded by a $3 \times P$ matrix $\mathbf{S} = [\mathbf{s}_1 \dots \mathbf{s}_P]$. The linear subspace model describes any shape as a linear combination of a set of L known basis shapes which capture the modes of variation in the training data. Thus, the shape matrix of a particular object instance is $\mathbf{S} = \sum_{l=1}^{L} \alpha_l \mathbf{B}_l$, where $\mathbf{B}_l$ is the $3 \times P$ matrix of a basis shape and α_l is the corresponding coefficient.

Assume that the basis shapes $\{\mathbf{B}_l\}_{l=1}^{L}$ are known from a training phase for an object class for now. Then given a new image I depicting an instance of the same object class, the objective is to compute the shape matrix $\mathbf{S}$ of the depicted instance, as well as the camera (projection) matrix $\mathbf{C}$ that maps 3D parts of the object to its observation in the new image I. The 2D projection $\hat{\mathbf{x}}_p$ of a 3D part location $\mathbf{s}_p$ can be formulated as

$$\hat{\mathbf{x}}_p = \rho(\mathbf{C} \cdot \mathbf{s}_p) = \rho\left(\mathbf{C} \sum_{l=1}^{L} \alpha_l . \mathbf{b}_{lp}\right) \tag{1}$$

where $\mathbf{b}_{lp}$ is the p-th column of basis shape matrix $\mathbf{B}_l$, $\rho(.)$ is a mapping that maps any vector (u, v, w) with $h \neq 0$ to $(u/w, v/w)$. The camera matrix $\mathbf{C}$ can describe a perspective or an orthographic projection. However, not all points on the surface of an object are visible in an image. The binary visibility state of a 3D point $\mathbf{s}$ in an image I of camera matrix $\mathbf{C}$ is modeled by a boolean variable $v(\mathbf{s}, \mathbf{C}) \in \{0, 1\}$, where 0 stands for *occluded* and 1 for *visible*.

Given the matrices of the basis shapes $\{\mathbf{B}_l\}$, the shape of an object instance is fully determined by its deformation parameters $\{\alpha_l\}$. The loss function for computing the shape matrix $\mathbf{S}$ and the camera matrix $\mathbf{C}$ of an object instance depicted in a query image I can be defined as the sum-of-squared Euclidean distances between the projections and the observations $\mathbf{x}_p$ of the visible object parts in image I:

$$L(\{\alpha_l\}, \mathbf{C}) = \sum_{p=1}^{P} v(\mathbf{s}_p, \mathbf{C}) \cdot \|\mathbf{x}_p - \rho(\mathbf{C} \cdot \mathbf{s}_p)\|^2, \quad \mathbf{s}_p = \sum_{l=1}^{L} \alpha_l \mathbf{b}_{lp}, \tag{2}$$

where the vectors $\mathbf{b}_{lp}$ are known from the training phase. The joint shape-pose problem for an input image I can be solved by a minimization of L with respect to the shape coefficients $\{\alpha_l\}$ and projection parameters $\mathbf{C}$.

The loss function for the training phase can be obtained in a similar fashion. There, the squared projection errors of K object instances needs to be measured over all images of the training set. The loss function for training can be written as

$$L_T = \sum_{k=1}^{K} \sum_{n=1}^{N_k} \sum_{p=1}^{P} v(\mathbf{s}_{kp}, \mathbf{C}_{nk}) \cdot ||\mathbf{x}_{klp} - \rho(\mathbf{C}_{nk} \cdot \mathbf{s}_{kp})||^2, \quad \mathbf{s}_{kp} = \sum_{l=1}^{L} \alpha_{kl} \mathbf{b}_{lp}, \quad (3)$$

where $\mathbf{s}_{kp}$ is the 3D location of the p-th part of the k-th object instance, and $\mathbf{C}_{nk}$ is the camera matrix corresponding to the training image I_{nk} as introduced in Sect. 3.1.

In the followings, we present our approach for learning the basis shapes and part appearance from multi-view 3D mesh reconstructions of our input sequences.

3.3 From Dense 3D Reconstructions to Part-Based Shape Models

In order to learn the 3D basis shapes, a 3D surface model of each object instance of the training set is needed. Moreover, we will augment the shape model with an image-based appearance model per object part (Sect. 3.5). This requires the additional knowledge of all camera matrices $\mathbf{C}_{nk}$ for the training images I_{nk}. We now discuss how these prerequisites are obtained and postpone the learning algorithms to Sects. 3.4 and 3.5.

Prior to training, we first apply a state-of-the-art 3D reconstruction pipeline to each sequence, separately. A Structure-from-Motion (SfM) procedure computes the camera matrices $\mathbf{C}_{nk}$, while a dense Multi-View Stereo (MVS) and surface reconstruction algorithm computes a triangle mesh surface of the visible surface areas of the scene, given the camera models. We use 123DCatch that integrates all these steps, but note that other similar tools are also possible here. As a result, each 3D object instance in the training set is reconstructed as a mesh with an arbitrary number of vertices and triangles (see Fig. 2). Intra-class variations and the varying vertex counts make meshes difficult to relate, not to mention that most vertices may not correspond to any salient entity on the object surface or its corresponding images.

Fig. 2. Training set examples for 'car': 3D meshes obtained from real-world 2D image sequences from 123DCatch. These models are used for data-driven 3D geometric reasoning throughout the paper. Note the intra-class shape variability.

In a subsequent step, we annotate each 3D mesh (Fig. 2) with a fixed set of parts (up to the closest vertex location), where each part is a repeatable and semantically meaningful region of the object, *e.g.* (center of) *front-left-wheel* or *rear-licence-plate*. The 3D part annotations are obtained via an intuitive user interface by performing a multi-view triangulation of part annotations from two or more images observing the same object instance. As a result, each object instance (indexed by $k \in \{1 \ldots K\}$) yields an ordered set of 3D object part locations $\{\mathbf{s}_{kp}\}_{p=1}^{P}$.

Once the 3D meshes are annotated, the coordinate frames can be aligned using the part annotations. Due to the shape variations, this gives a more accurate alignment than simply applying the Iterated-Closest-Point (ICP) algorithm in our experience. Figure 3 shows the scatter of object part locations (across training instances), as well as the covariance ellipsoids (corresponding to 1σ) to visualize intra-class shape variations in our example training set.

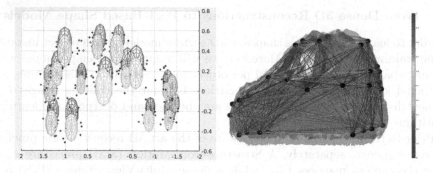

Fig. 3. 3D Part Geometry. *Left:* The standard deviation of part location is plotted in spheres (yellow on car's right, blue on the left). Interestingly, the front door handles vary considerably in location, while the bumpers and lights, not so much. *Right:* Variances in the mutual distance between each pair of parts are overlaid on a sample graph (*red* corresponds to higher variation, *blue* corresponds to lower variation). (Color figure online)

3.4   Learning a Class-Specific Object Shape

Based on the 3D shape model discussed in Sect. 3.2, we perform a Principal Component Analysis (PCA) on the object part positions and retrieve the top M modes of deformation ($M = 4$ in all our experiments), which gives us a set of $L = M + 1$ basis shapes (where $\mathbf{B}_1$ is explicitly defined as the mean shape) for an effective and compact linear subspace model to describe the subspace of possible intra-class shapes.

3.5   Learning the Appearance of Object Parts

The shape bases define a subspace of possible shapes for a particular object class. However, we also need to understand the appearance of the class in order to efficiently relate the shape model to new images. For each object part in the 3D shape representation, we construct an appearance model.

For the training sequences, by estimating visibility and projection, an appearance model for each part is learnt from the ground truth image sequences under real illumination, projection *etc.* For every part, CNN features (*conv5* layer) are extracted from the input images at their projections (when visible), using publicly available network weights [14]. These weights are obtained via training on the ImageNet Challenge 2014 (ILSVRC) dataset based on the part annotations. A mixture model [3,10] over these CNN features is then used to represent the variation in appearance, viewpoint *etc.* We learn a binary SVM classifier for each mixture component of each part of the class, to act as a part detector in images.

3.6 Detecting an Object Shape and Pose in a Query Image

Given a new query image I, and the learnt shape subspace spanned by basis shapes $\{\mathbf{B}_l\}$, and given the appearance-based object part detectors based on deep features and on SVM classifiers, our goal is to jointly fit the deformable shape model and compute the camera matrix $\mathbf{C}$ for this image such that 3D part locations of the fitted 3D shape model project to corresponding part observations in the image. The corresponding loss function is formulated in Eq. 2. The proposed pipeline is outlined in Algorithm 1 (which also invokes Algorithm 2) (Fig. 4).

Algorithm 1. Shape recovery, pose estimation and detection

1: **Part Detection.** Possible candidates for part detections are collected by convolving the trained SVM weight filters on conv5 feature pyramids [25]. Filter responses across multiple scales are combined using Non-Maxima Supression followed by Platt's Scaling [22] to obtain the probabilities of positive responses, such that the responses of different SVM classifiers are comparable. Responses stronger than a certain probability (p=0.35) are considered plausible candidates for the next step.

2: **Viewpoint Estimation.** We find the best camera parameters to project the mean shape to the test image by performing a RANSAC-based view estimation routine explained in Algorithm 2. In this case, the minimal set needs to be size 3 and the unknown parameters correspond to those of scaled orthographic projection.

3: **Viewpoint and Shape Refinement.** We perform a subsequent pass of viewpoint refinement allowing for shape deformation. This is equivalent to optimizing Eq. 2, with respect to the deformation parameters $\{\alpha_l\}_{l=1}^{L}$ in addition to the scaled-orthographic camera parameters. The RANSAC-based procedure can be repeated, but in each pass, one more mode of shape deformation is considered for a stable, incremental optimization. Finally, the a minimal set of 5 2D part candidates is needed for estimation of the extra $L - 1 = 4$ basis shape weights. The optimization of the loss function in Eq. 2, is modified to reflect the new parameters.

4: **Object Mask.** The estimated deformable shape and camera parameters represent the best reconstruction estimate for this image. When projected to the image, this gives us an object detection silhouette for this image.

Algorithm 2. RANSAC-based Viewpoint Estimation Algorithm

1: Perform part detection using the trained part appearance classifiers to obtain *Filter Response* $\mathcal{F}$, on the test image. Threshold these to obtain a set of possible candidates.
2: **for** N iterations **do**
3:     Assemble a minimal set of randomly-sampled unique parts from the candidates (constraint: they must be simultaneously visible in at least one view).
4:     Fit the unknown parameters minimizing the projection loss between the mean 3D shape parts corresponding to the 2D minimal set selected above.
5:     Check for inliers, based on whether candidate detections are within threshold τ_1 for the remaining visible parts projected according to the above derived projection.
6:     If the number of inliers are greater than τ_2 then store this minimal set and the estimated parameters.
7: For the set with maximum inliers, re-estimate the parameters minimizing the projection loss, through least-squares fitting on all the inliers, instead of only the minimal set. This is the best parameter estimate.

Fig. 4. Examples of 2D image sequences from the EPFL Multi-view Cars dataset (*Left*) and our RealCar dataset (*Right*).

4 Evaluation

4.1 Dataset

Our RealCar dataset consists of 35 image sequences taken around unique and distinct instances of cars, captured in real world conditions with challenging variations in scale, orientation, illumination with instances of occlusion. The total number of images per sequence varies between 30 and 115, across the dataset. When an SfM method like 123DCatch is used to estimate the car shapes and camera matrices, we get full mesh shapes along with full projection matrices (see Fig. 2). We use 29 of these sequences (and associated SfM results) for training and reserve 6 for testing.

The EPFL Multi-view cars dataset [20] contains image sequences of car instances on a turntable. Such sequences do not respond well to SfM pre-processing like RealCar dataset as the scene is not rigid, so this provide images to test on, but no ground truth 3D meshes or part annotations. This dataset is used purely as a second test set of images.

4.2   Experimental Setup

In this section, we evaluate the performance of our approach based on two tasks, (1) Viewpoint Estimation, to measure the accuracy of the estimated camera projection and, (2) Reconstruction, to measure how well the shape of the object in the test image is recovered.

Viewpoint Estimation: In order to evaluate the viewpoint estimation performance of the proposed approach, we run Algorithm 1 and report the Mean Precision of Pose Estimation [19] and Mean Angular Error [21], on individual images from the 6 test sequences of our RealCar dataset as well as from all 20 sequences of the EPFL Multi-view Cars dataset [20], where each car is imaged over a complete 360 degrees, with approximately one image for every 3–4 degrees. To measure viewpoint estimation accuracy we report our results using two standard metrics, Mean Precision of Pose Estimation (MPPE) [19] and Mean Angular Error (MAE) [21]. To report MPPE, we discretize azimuth angles (ϕ) into k number of bins where $k \in \{8, 12, 16, 18, 36\}$ and compute the precision of the viewpoint estimation for different number of bins. Table 1 shows the MPPE obtained using our approach on both images from our RealCar dataset and the EPFL dataset, and compares with Pepik et al. [13] and Ozuysal et al. [20], on EPFL dataset. Similarly, the Mean Angular Error [21], to evaluate the continuous viewpoint estimation performance of the proposed system, on both datasets is shown in Table 2 in comparison with Pepik et al. [13] and Glasner et al. [21] on the EPFL Multi-view cars dataset. In addition to estimating the Mean Angular Error for predicting the azimuth angle, we also estimate MAE for predicting all *3 Euler angles* [15], to provide a more accurate measure of performance of the proposed approach, for continuous viewpoint estimation. Table 3 shows MAE (Mean Angular Error) computed by estimating all *3 Euler angles*.

Table 1. Viewpoint Classification Accuracy using MPPE [19] on our RealCar dataset *(left)*, and on EPFL Multi-view Cars dataset [20] *(right)*. For our dataset, in addition to the test set, pose estimation experiments are also conducted on a subset of the training set to demonstrate the performance of the proposed approach in estimating viewpoint &recovering shape, on images, where the part detection accuracy is quite high.

θ	RealCar dataset		EPFL-Multiview cars dataset [20]		
	(Ours) Training set	(Ours) Test set	(Ours)	3D²PM-D [13]	Ozuysal et al. [20]
$\pi/4$	93.79	86.09	59.86	78.5	-
$\pi/6$	89.44	79.13	50.06	75.5	-
$\pi/8$	83.85	71.30	40.47	69.8	41.6
$\pi/9$	78.26	65.22	36.67	71.8	-
$\pi/18$	46.58	43.48	19.22	45.8	-

Table 2. Continous/Fine-Grained Viewpoint Estimation error using MAE [21] on our dataset *(left)* and on EPFL Multi-view Cars dataset [20] *(right)*.

θ	RealCar Dataset		EPFL-Multiview Cars Dataset [20]		
	(Ours) Training set	(Ours) Test set	(Ours)	3D^{2}PM-D [13]	Glasner et al. [21]
$\pi/4$	13.02	14.13	17.35	12.9	24.8
$\pi/6$	11.88	12.35	13.58	9.0	-
$\pi/8$	11.05	10.87	10.68	7.2	-
$\pi/9$	10.32	9.92	9.58	6.2	-
$\pi/18$	5.47	6.2	4.81	5.2	-

Table 3. Continous/Fine-Grained Viewpoint Estimation using our Ransac-based viewpoint estimation technique, MAE [21] on EPFL Cars dataset [20] by computing all *3 Euler angles*.

θ	Our dataset		EPFL-Multiview cars dataset [20]
	Training set	Test set	(Ours)
$\pi/4$	16.08	18.28	31.48
$\pi/6$	14.92	16.31	22.71
$\pi/8$	13.15	14.45	17.27
$\pi/9$	12.32	13.54	15.06
$\pi/18$	6.92	6.59	8.05

The result tables show that our method performs very well on our dataset and competes well with the state of the art on the EPFL dataset, despite training on a smaller dataset appearance-wise. We report the viewpoint estimation accuracy on our dataset as well as on EPFL Multi-view cars dataset, we used our dataset (barely 29 3D object instances) to learn part appearances and 3D part geometry, and test it on EPFL Multi-view cars dataset. The performance of our approach relies heavily on the part detection performance generating inliers for at least a few parts. If part detections are even reasonable, the viewpoint/shape estimation is generally accurate, and so the accuracy on the RealCar dataset tends to be high (running our approach on the data that it has been trained on, shows best case results and an upper bound on how well our algorithm can do, due to the familiarity with appearance, though projection must still be figured out). The experiments show that, most of the bad viewpoint estimations are mainly due to bad part detection performance as shown in shown in Fig. 6 or mistakes due to symmetry of the car class.

Another important factor that affects the viewpoint estimation performance of our approach is the lack of a strong global appearance prior or a root filter. Unlike other regression based methods, we solely rely on detected 2D part locations for reasoning the 3D shape of the object, where slight anomalies with one or more part detections can cause a considerable error in the estimated final

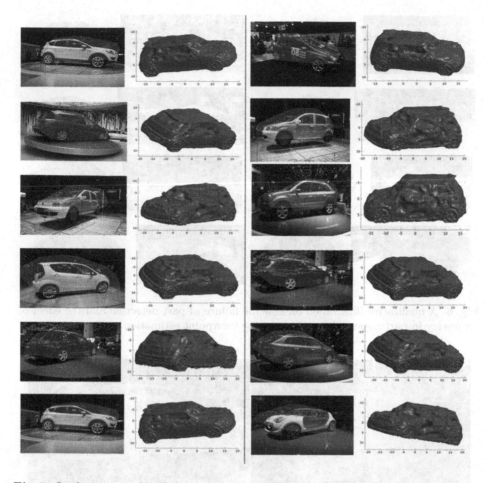

Fig. 5. Qualitative results of the proposed *RANSAC*-based Viewpoint Estimation and Shape Recovery, on EPFL Multi-view Car dataset. Odd columns illustrate the test image with corresponding Viewpoint/Shape estimations overlayed on it. Even columns illustrate the Viewpoint Estimation of their corresponding test image (on its left), using a sample mesh (from our dataset) for better visualization. (*note:* meshes (in even columns) are not generated/reconstructed by our viewpoint estimation approach, and are used only for the purpose of better visualization in all our qualitative results).

viewpoint. In the future, we will train robust part appearance classifiers over more appearance data with hard-mined data negatives, along with strong root filters, to try improving part detection accuracy and performance.

Figure 5 shows qualitative results on the EPFL dataset. Figure 6 demonstrates the challenges of part detection and appearance symmetry in viewpoint estimation success. Figure 7 shows the viewpoint/shape recovery results on our dataset. Also Fig. 8 compares the shape recovery results before and after the viewpoint and shape refinement step.

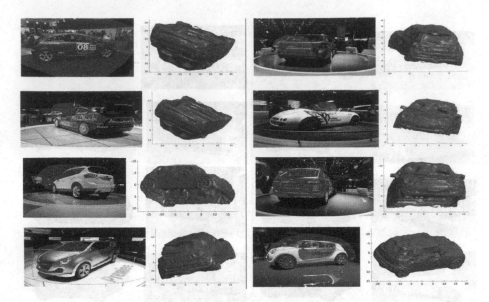

Fig. 6. A qualitative illustration on how the failure of part detection and the effect of symmetry in part appearances affect the the viewpoint estimation performance.

Fig. 7. Qualitative results of the proposed *RANSAC*-based viewpoint estimation on *our* dataset, with Viewpoint/Shape estimations overlayed on the object.

Fig. 8. An illustration on the improvement in Viewpoint and Shape Estimation due to the *Viewpoint and Shape refinement* step. Each pair of the image represents the Viewpoint and Shape estimations before *(left)* and after *(right)* the *Viewpoint and Shape refinement* step. The shapes on the right (of each pair) tend to be more compact and has a better viewpoint estimate, than the ones on the left.

Reconstruction. Unlike EPFL dataset, the RealCar dataset has the ground truth 3D parts annotated, so we can qualitatively compare the estimated 3D part based model with its actual ground truth, to evaluate shape accuracy. To report the shape recovery performance of our approach, we computed the average sum of squared distances between the estimated and ground truth 3D part locations of the object in the test image, for the 3D parts normalized to unit scale. The reconstruction/shape recovery error is 0.07 on the training set and 0.082 on test set of the RealCar dataset.

5   Conclusion and Future Work

We have shown qualitatively that our method for class-specific shape detection, recovery and pose estimation can yield good results on unseen state-of-the-art data as well as the original training data. We expect our RANSAC based process to be faster, while still efficient, than brute force exhaustive search and also models the projection process more accurately than regression. The fine-grained part representation and linear subspace representation allows us to model deformation effectively, but work with far fewer vertices than an SfM mesh with thousands of vertices. Importantly, we aim to learn such a part representation automatically, and automatically warp and improve the full mesh reconstructions also. As mentioned, better training and engineering should help perform even better. Going forward, using more image evidence (edges, contours, textures *etc.*) to fit the camera projection and reconstruction parameters, should allow for more accurate estimation. We could also perform GraphCut based segmentations for improved detection outlines.

References

1. Choy, C.B., Stark, M., Corbett-Davies, S., Savarese, S.: Enriching object detection with 2D–3D registration and continuous viewpoint estimation. In: Proceedings of IEEE CVPR (2015)
2. Felzenszwalb, P.F., Huttenlocher, D.P.: Pictorial structures for object recognition. IJCV **61**(1), 55–79 (2005)

3. Felzenszwalb, P.F., Girshick, R., McAllester, D., Ramanan, D.: Object detection with discriminatively trained part based models. IEEE T-PAMI (2009)
4. Fenzi, M., Leal-Taix, L., Ostermann, J., Tuytelaars, T.: Continuous pose estimation with a spatial ensemble of Fisher regressors. In: Proceedings of ICCV (2015)
5. Fergus, R., Perona, P., Zisserman, A.: Object class recognition by unsupervised scale-invariant learning. In: Proceedings of IEEE CVPR (2003)
6. Ghodrati, A., Pedersoli, M., Tuytelaars, T.: Is 2D information enough for viewpoint estimation? In: Proceedings of BMVC (2014)
7. Hariharan, B., Malik, J., Ramanan, D.: Discriminative decorrelation for clustering and classification. In: Fitzgibbon, A., Lazebnik, S., Perona, P., Sato, Y., Schmid, C. (eds.) ECCV 2012. LNCS, vol. 7575, pp. 459–472. Springer, Heidelberg (2012). doi:10.1007/978-3-642-33765-9_33
8. He, K., Sigal, L., Sclaroff, S.: Parameterizing object detectors in the continuous pose space. In: Fleet, D., Pajdla, T., Schiele, B., Tuytelaars, T. (eds.) ECCV 2014. LNCS, vol. 8692, pp. 450–465. Springer, Heidelberg (2014). doi:10.1007/978-3-319-10593-2_30
9. Hejrati, M., Ramanan, D.: Analyzing 3D objects in cluttered images. In: Proceedings of NIPS (2012)
10. Hejrati, M., Ramanan, D.: Analysis by synthesis: 3D object recognition by object reconstruction. In: Proceedings of IEEE CVPR (2014)
11. Lim, J.J., Khosla, A., Torralba, A.: FPM: fine pose parts-based model with 3D CAD models. In: Fleet, D., Pajdla, T., Schiele, B., Tuytelaars, T. (eds.) ECCV 2014. LNCS, vol. 8694, pp. 478–493. Springer, Heidelberg (2014). doi:10.1007/978-3-319-10599-4_31
12. Pepik, B., Gehler, P., Stark, M., Schiele, B.: $3D^2PM$ - 3D deformable part models. In: Proceedings of ECCV (2012)
13. Pepik, B., Stark, M., Gehler, P., Schiele, B.: Teaching 3D geometry to deformable part models. In: Proceedings of IEEE CVPR (2012)
14. Simonyan, K., Zisserman, A.: Very deep convolutional networks for large-scale image recognition arXiv preprint 2014. arXiv:1409.1556
15. Tulsiani, S., Malik, J.: Viewpoints and keypoints. In: Proceedings of IEEE CVPR (2015)
16. Xiao, J., Russell, B., Torralba, A.: Localizing 3D cuboids in single-view images. In: Proceedings of NIPS (2012)
17. Yu, T.-H.: Classification and pose estimation of 3D shapes and human actions. Ph.D. thesis, University of Cambridge (2013)
18. Zia, M.Z., Stark, M., Schindler, K.: Are cars just 3D boxes? Jointly estimating the 3D shape of multiple objects. In: Proceedings of IEEE CVPR (2014)
19. LÃspez-Sastre, R.J., Tuytelaars, T., Savarese, S.: Deformable part models revisited: a performance evaluation for object category pose estimation. In: Proceedings of IEEE ICCVW (2011)
20. Ozuysal, M., Lepetit, V., Fua, P.: Pose estimation for category specific multiview object localization. In: Proceedings of IEEE CVPR (2009)
21. Glasner, D., Galun, M., Alpert, S., Basri, R., Shakhnarovich, G.: Viewpoint-aware object detection and pose estimation. In: Proceedings of IEEE ICCV (2011)
22. Platt, J.: Probabilistic outputs for support vector machines and comparisons to regularized likelihood methods. In: Advances in large margin classifiers (1999)
23. Zia, M.Z., Stark, M., Schiele, B., Schindler, K.: Detailed 3d representations for object recognition and modeling. In: IEEE Transactions on PAMI (2013)
24. Kar, A., Tulsiani, S., Carreira, J., Malik, J.: Category-specific object reconstruction from a single image. In: IEEE CVPR (2015)

25. Girshick, R., Iandola, F., Darrell, T., Malik, J.: Deformable part models are convolutional neural networks. IEEE CVPR (2015)
26. Yingze Bao, S., Chandraker, M., Lin, Y., Savarese, S.: Dense object reconstruction with semantic priors. In: IEEE CVPR (2013)
27. Khosla, A., Zhou, T., Malisiewicz, T., Efros, A.A., Torralba, A.: Undoing the damage of dataset bias. In: Fitzgibbon, A., Lazebnik, S., Perona, P., Sato, Y., Schmid, C. (eds.) ECCV 2012. LNCS, vol. 7572, pp. 158–171. Springer, Heidelberg (2012). doi:10.1007/978-3-642-33718-5_12

Monocular Surface Reconstruction Using 3D Deformable Part Models

Stefan Kinauer[✉], Maxim Berman, and Iasonas Kokkinos

Center for Visual Computing, CentraleSupélec, Inria, Université Paris-Saclay,
Paris, France
{stefan.kinauer,maxim.berman,iasonas.kokkinos}@centralesupelec.fr

Abstract. Our goal in this work is to recover an estimate of an object's surface from a single image. We address this severely ill-posed problem by employing a discriminatively-trained graphical model: we incorporate prior information about the 3D shape of an object category in terms of pairwise terms among parts, while using powerful CNN features to construct unary terms that dictate the part placement in the image. Our contributions are three-fold: firstly, we extend the Deformable Part Model (DPM) paradigm to operate in a three-dimensional pose space that encodes the putative real-world coordinates of object parts. Secondly, we use branch-and-bound to perform efficient inference with DPMs, resulting in accelerations by two orders of magnitude over linear-time algorithms. Thirdly, we use Structured SVM training to properly penalize deviations between the model predictions and the 3D ground truth information during learning.

Our inference requires a fraction of a second at test time and our results outperform those published recently in [17] on the PASCAL 3D+ dataset.

1 Introduction

The advent of deep learning has led to dramatic progress in object detection [11,12] and also in tasks that can lead to 3D object perception, such as viewpoint estimation [25]. Even though Convolutional Networks seem to be the method of choice for such problems, they may not be yet appropriate for structured prediction tasks that are 'beyond detection' and involve multiple, real-valued and interrelated variables that need to be estimated with high precision. The scarcity of data for many of these tasks, as well as the rich structure inherent in the problems advocate a more explicit, modelling-based method.

Our work addresses in particular the problem of estimating the three-dimensional shape of an object from a single RGB image. Apart from the inherent interest of the problem, this can lead to applications in graphics (rendering, augmented reality), robotics (grasping, navigation) and object detection (dataset augmentation, 3D-based classification). This severely ill-posed problem requires

---

S. Kinauer and M. Berman – Both authors contributed equally.

G. Hua and H. Jégou (Eds.): ECCV 2016 Workshops, Part III, LNCS 9915, pp. 296–308, 2016.
DOI: 10.1007/978-3-319-49409-8_24

somehow introducing knowledge about the 3D geometry of an object through a model-based approach.

A model-based approach to solving such a problem typically involves (a) using multiple images during training to construct a three-dimensional surface model, and (b) interpreting a single image at test time by adapting the model to it. It is clear that restricting the surface reconstruction task to a specific category simplifies the generic surface reconstruction problem [1,14,21], since we now have a more specific, model-based prior knowledge about the anticipated solution. The main question is which model is best suited for this task.

Our approach builds on the recent advances of [17] where it was shown that accurate surface reconstructions can be obtained from RGB images for a wide variety of categories in the PASCAL VOC dataset. We use the same procedure for recovering the 3D geometry of categories from 2D datasets, but change entirely their modelling approach, which leads to different learning and optimization tasks. The work of [17] was using iterative optimization algorithms that can get stuck at local minima, while the cost function driving the optimization was hand-crafted, making it hard to profit from rich features or large datasets. We propose instead an approach that comes with guarantees of obtaining a globally optimal solution, and develop an associated Structured SVM training algorithm that can optimally design the cost function for the task at hand.

For this, we introduce a graphical model inspired from the Deformable Part Model paradigm [8,10], treating part positions as nodes of a graph and incorporating geometrical constraints within graph cliques. In particular, we lift Deformable Part Models [8] to 3D, allowing the object parts to live in a 3D pose space, reflecting the 'real-world' part coordinates. We represent prior information about the 3D shape of an object category in terms of viewpoint-conditioned pairwise terms among parts, and use rich CNN features to construct unary terms that dictate the part placement in the image. In order to make this three-dimensional model practically exploitable we develop customized optimization and learning techniques.

Regarding optimization, our method is guaranteed to deliver the optimal solution when using a loop-free graph, like a star or a tree. Even though inference would in principle be possible using generic efficient message-passing algorithms, such as Generalized Distance Transforms [9], the 3D nature of our task makes such techniques memory- and time- inefficient: the complexity scales linearly in the depth resolution, so one would need to trade off accuracy for speed. Instead, in Sect. 4 we extend Dual-Tree Branch-and-Bound [19] to 3D, keeping the memory complexity constant and the computational complexity logarithmic in the depth resolution - this allows us to use a fine-grained depth resolution with negligible computational overhead.

Regarding learning, we use discriminative training which allows us to design the cost function so as to place the model predictions as close as possible to the ground-truth surface. In particular we use Structured SVM training with a loss function that penalizes the deviation between the estimated 3D position of the parts and the ground-truth position of the associated object landmarks.

We jointly learn how to score the CNN features that are used for the construction of our unary terms and the displacement features that are used for our pairwise terms, while it would be also possible to backpropagate on the CNN that delivers the CNN features.

We demonstrate the merit of our contributions through systematic comparisons on the PASCAL 3D+ dataset, obtaining better results than the current state-of-the-art method of [17] on most categories.

2   Related Work

There are several problems pertaining to our task, including (i) the acquisition of 3D geometry from RGB images, (ii) the modelling of 3D deformations, and (iii) the interpretation of a test image in terms of a learned 3D deformation model. We start by presenting the techniques underlying the current state-of-the-art method of [17] and then turn to techniques that are closer to our own work.

Regarding (i), several techniques have recently tackled the problem of establishing 3D geometric models from RGB images [5,16,18], while a closely related task aims at establishing non-rigid correspondences across unstructured sets of images [4,29]. We follow the work of [17,26] where a minimal annotation, in terms of a few landmarks per object instance, is combined with non-rigid structure from motion algorithms to lift the PASCAL dataset to 3D and estimate surface models for 10 categories.

Turning to (ii), the modeling of shape variability, the deformable model paradigm used in [17] relies on a linear, low-dimensional subspace to parameterize the possible surface variation that a category can have with respect to the mean, nominal surface. A particular shape instance can thus be expressed in terms of a low-dimensional coefficient vector.

Turning to (iii), adapting a deformable shape model to a novel image, the authors of [17] estimate the coefficients of the surface model so that the projection of the estimated 3D surface on the 2D camera plane is aligned with the object silhouette, while some designated mesh points project close to two-dimensional landmark positions; segmentation and landmarks are provided either by humans or by external modules [17]. While exploiting several acceleration techniques that are particular to the cost function being used, the optimization time is in the order of seconds and the gradient descent procedure used by the authors is prone to getting stuck in local minima.

Turning to works that rely on DPMs, as we do, several works have recently aimed at coupling DPMs with three-dimensional modelling, e.g. [22,23,28,30,31]. However, none of the existing works treats the 3D positions of the parts as variables that are being optimized over. We note that in our case we have $M = 100$ landmarks in $3D$ while in most of these works the three-dimensional variable being optimized corresponds to the relative angle of the camera to the object [13,22,23,28,30,31] and potentially also the visibility of points [28,30]. Several works go beyond this and search also over CAD models, typically represented as exemplars, e.g. [22], while certain other works, e.g. [23,30], also search over part positions in 2D.

In our case we actually consider that the viewpoint is provided by an external module or by ground-truth annotations. Our modelling part is fairly similar to that of [23], but the major difference lies in the solution space: to the best of our knowledge we are the first work that achieves efficient and guaranteed optimal placement of object parts in 3D. Our focus is on the solution of the combinatorial optimization problem obtained by trying to jointly position all 3D parts of an object in a mutually consistent configuration. For this we have built on fast techniques for inference with 2D DPMs, [2,19], and adapted them to operate in 3D.

3   3D Deformable Part Models for Category Surface Estimation

Given an image I and a viewpoint v, our task is to estimate the 3D coordinates of P mesh nodes $\mathbf{X} = \{\mathbf{x}_1, \ldots, \mathbf{x}_P\}$, where every node is a 3D position vector $\mathbf{x}_i = (h_i, v_i, d_i)$. We will be denoting vectors with boldface letters and will alternate between the vector notation $\mathbf{x}$ and the horizontal/vertical/depth notation (h, v, d) based on convenience.

For this we use Deformable Part Models [8] (DPMs) which provide a rigorous, energy-based approach to modelling and detecting deformable object categories. As we describe below, DPMs can also be adapted to our problem. We break the problem into three steps; firstly in Sect. 3.1 we determine the 3D model, defining the graph nodes and relationships between them. Secondly, in Sect. 3.2 we determine how the surface would look like when projected in 2D. Finally, in Sect. 3.3 we describe how to use the image so as to indicate which of the possible 3D surfaces projects in a way that matches with the image observations.

3.1   Model Graph Construction

We start by describing how we obtain the nodes of the DPM graph, which requires having access to 3D geometry related to an object category. As in [17], we rely on the work of [26] to recover 3D geometry from a 2D dataset, such as the PASCAL VOC dataset; given a set of images of an object category and K category-specific keypoint annotations, Non-Rigid Structure-from-Motion (NRSfM)[3] delivers a joint estimation of (1) the 3D position of the K category-specific keypoints (including occluded keypoints) and (2) a camera viewpoint estimate for each training instance. Given the viewpoint estimates, a class-specific triangulated 3D mesh is obtained from ground-truth segmentation masks by constructing a visual hull from the training instance.

This 3D mesh and the K 3D-lifted keypoints are associated by projecting every keypoint to the 3D mesh point that is closest to it on average over the training set. This provides us with the first K nodes of our model. A denser sampling of the mesh allows our model to more thoroughly capture the object's shape; we obtain $P = 100$ nodes using Geodesic Surface Remeshing [24], which ensures that the K keypoints are selected, while the remaining points are roughly

Fig. 1. Our approach models a three-dimensional object in terms of a graphical model, where the nodes correspond to 3D part positions and the edges encode geometric constraints between part positions. Given an input image and a viewpoint estimate the cost function of our energy model dictates the optimal placement of the parts in *three dimensional space*, obtaining a reconstruction of the object's surface from a monocular image.

equidistant. In Fig. 1(a) we illustrate an example of the input and the downsampled mesh for the car category.

We obtain a Deformable Part Model by treating each of those mesh points as a graph node. Edges between nodes capture geometric constraints; each edge $e_{i,j}$ is associated with a 3D nominal displacement vector $\mu_{i,j}$ equalling the average displacement between nodes i and j, and a spherical precision matrix $C_{i,j}$ indicating the typical inverse variance around that displacement. We note that the edges do not coincide with the ones in the mesh triangulation described above. In particular, we use edges that connect potentially opposite surface points, as these may better capture volume constraints.

3.2   Viewpoint-Adapted 3D DPMs

Having defined the model's 3D geometry, we now turn to accounting for the effects of camera pose, so as to connect our model to the 2D images that will be available at test time. This includes 6 degrees of freedom, 3 for translation, and 3 for rotation.

We consider momentarily that the object is at a fixed depth, which amounts to working with images that are scale-normalized, where scale is indicated either by an object detection module, or by a ground-truth bounding box. As our experiments show, searching around this originally estimated scale can yield some improvements, but we ignore it from the following discussion. Regarding horizontal and vertical translation, our algorithm effectively does an efficient, exhaustive search.

The remaining degrees of variation include the camera's azimuth, elevation and rotation with respect to the object's canonical coordinate system in 3D. For this we introduce an additional viewpoint variable, v, which can either be provided by the output of NRSfM (which requires multiple images and landmark annotations), or by a bottom-up viewpoint estimator, as e.g. in [25]. In all of our experiments we use the NRSfM-based viewpoint estimate, and compare to results of systems that use the same viewpoint estimate. One can actually search for the viewpoint through the optimization of our model's objective, but we leave this for future work.

This viewpoint variable influences the model in two ways. Firstly, the 3D nominal displacements are rotated in 3D by multiplying with R_v, the rotation matrix corresponding to v; we denote this by adding a viewpoint superscript to the nominal displacement vector: $\mu_{i,j}^v \doteq R_v\mu_{i,j}$. The precision matrix, being spherical, is unaffected by viewpoint; dealing with elliptical matrices is equally easy, but the induced coupling of coordinates would pose challenges when we turn to optimization in Sect. 4. Secondly, the variable v is discretized into V distinct viewpoints, obtained by uniformly quantizing the 360 azimuth degrees; we denote by $\lfloor v \rfloor$ the discretized value. This is used to determine in a viewpoint-dependent manner the image-to-part affinities, as detailed below.

3.3 Cost Function

Having identified the model variables and the 3D-to-2D transformation, we can now describe how we go from 2D to 3D, when presented with an image. The image provides us with 'bottom-up' evidence about the 2D positions where each visible landmark is likely to be seen. This expressed in terms of a landmark-specific unary term of the form:

$$\mathcal{U}_{I,v,i}(\mathbf{x}_i) = \langle \mathbf{u}_i^{\lfloor v \rfloor}, f_I(h_i, v_i) \rangle, \tag{1}$$

where $\mathbf{u}_i^{\lfloor v \rfloor}$ is a viewpoint-specific weight vector for node i and f_I are dense image features. We use orthographic projection, assuming that the 3D landmark $\mathbf{x}_i = (h_i, v_i, d_i)$ projects to the 2D image point (h_i, v_i). We note also that the argument of the unary term, $\mathbf{x}_i$ is three-dimensional, while the underlying information is two-dimensional.

The geometric arrangement between two landmarks i, j is controlled by a function of two 3D arguments that prescribes preferences for the arrangement of landmark pairs in 3D:

$$\mathcal{V}_{i,j,v}(\mathbf{x}_i, \mathbf{x}_j) = -\left(\mathbf{x}_j - \mathbf{x}_i - \mu_{i,j}^v\right)^T C_{i,j} \left(\mathbf{x}_j - \mathbf{x}_i - \mu_{i,j}^v\right), (i,j) \in \mathcal{E}. \tag{2}$$

In Eq. 2 $\mu_{i,j}^v = R_v\mu_{i,j}$ is the viewpoint-adapted nominal displacement and $C_{i,j}$ is the viewpoint-invariant precision matrix described in the previous subsection. Since $C_{i,j}$ is a spherical precision matrix, we can write $\mathcal{V}_{i,j,v}(\mathbf{x}_i, \mathbf{x}_j) = \gamma_{i,j}\|\mathbf{x}_j - \mathbf{x}_i - \mu_{i,j}^v\|^2$, showing that our model penalizes the ℓ_2 norm of the deviations of the 3D part displacements from their rotated nominal value.

Putting things together, given an image I and a viewpoint v, we score a landmark configuration $\mathbf{X}$ with a merit function S formed as the sum of unary and pairwise terms:

$$S_{I,v}(\mathbf{X}) = \sum_{i=1}^{P} \mathcal{U}_{I,\lfloor v \rfloor,i}(\mathbf{x}_i) + \sum_{(i,j)\in\mathcal{E}} \mathcal{V}_{i,j,v}(\mathbf{x}_i, \mathbf{x}_j), \tag{3}$$

where $\mathcal{E}$ is the set of edges on the graph. The unary terms introduce image-based evidence, and the pairwise terms enforce model-based priors. The minimization of this objective will result in an optimal placement of K landmarks in 3D while having a 2D input.

4   Efficient Optimization for 3D DPMs

Having developed our cost function in 3D we now turn to its optimization. We consider a star-shaped graph, where a single node ('root') is connected to all remaining nodes ('leaves'). The logarithm of the root node's max-marginals for a star-shaped graph equal:

$$S(\mathbf{x}_r) = \max_{\mathbf{X}:\mathbf{X}_r=\mathbf{x}_r} S(\mathbf{X}) = \sum_i \max_{\mathbf{x}_i} \left[\mathcal{U}_i(\mathbf{x}_i) + \mathcal{V}_{i,r}(\mathbf{x}_i, \mathbf{x}_r) \right], \tag{4}$$

effectively scoring a candidate root position $\mathbf{x}_r$ by optimizing over all possible part positions that may support it. In order to simplify notation we have removed the image and viewpoint dependence and introduced $\mathcal{V}_{i,r}(\mathbf{x}_i, \mathbf{x}_r)$ which is defined to be zero when $\mathbf{x}_i = \mathbf{x}_r$ and infinity otherwise.

For the particular form of the pairwise term used here one can use the Generalized Distance Transform (GDT) of [9], reducing the computational complexity of message-passing from $O(N^2)$ to $O(N)$ in the number of voxels. This can be fast in 2D, but in 3D we face a linear increase of complexity and memory in the depth resolution - so we will need to eventually tradeoff speed for accuracy.

However, we realize that the Dual-Tree Branch-and-Bound (DTBB) algorithm of [19] directly applies to this problem. In particular, in DTBB rather than first exhaustively computing Eq. 4 for all values of $\mathbf{x}_r$ and then picking the maximum, one instead performs prioritized search for the maximum - which can replace a complexity of $O(N)$ with one of $\omega(\log N)$, i.e. logarithmic in the best-case, which is typically orders of magnitude faster. Furthermore, since for our case the unary terms are depth-independent, one never needs to occupy memory to represent $U_r(\mathbf{x}_r)$, as would be required by GDT - instead our algorithm's memory complexity is *constant* in depth resolution.

In a bit more detail, the DTBB algorithm performs prioritized search over intervals of root positions, denoted by X, using as priority an upper bound to the score in the interval. For this one bounds the right side of Eq. 4 over a root interval X, using the following series of inequalities:

$$\begin{aligned}
\max_{\mathbf{x}_r \in X} S(\mathbf{x}_r) &\leq \sum_i \max_{\mathbf{x}_r \in X, \mathbf{x}_i} \mathcal{U}_i(\mathbf{x}_i) + \mathcal{V}_{i,r}(\mathbf{x}_i, \mathbf{x}_r) \\
&\leq \sum_i \max_{\mathbf{x}_i} \mathcal{U}_i(\mathbf{x}_i) + \sum_i \max_{\mathbf{x}_r \in X, \mathbf{x}_i} \mathcal{V}_{i,r}(\mathbf{x}_i, \mathbf{x}_r),
\end{aligned} \tag{5}$$

where both inequalities follow from $\max_x f(x) + g(x) \leq \max_x f(x) + \max_x g(x)$. Intuitively, the first inequality opportunistically uses contributions from different nodes, even if they do not agree on the particular $\mathbf{x}_r \in X$ that they support, and the second inequality opportunistically uses contributions from the unary and pairwise terms of a single node, even if they do not agree on the value of $\mathbf{x}_i$ that lends the support.

Two facts prove useful in computing Eq. 5 efficiently: firstly, the maximization $\max_{\mathbf{x}_i} U_i(\mathbf{x}_i)$ can be computed in 2D, since $U_i(\mathbf{x}_i)$ is independent of the d_i component of $\mathbf{x}_i$. As such, we never need to explicitly allocate memory to store the unary term in 3D, as would be required by GDTs. Secondly, the maximization over the combinations of $\mathbf{x}_i, \mathbf{x}_r$ can be computed *analytically*, with a cost that is constant, and independent of the cardinality of the two sets; all one needs to do is extend the 2D bounding schemes of [20] to 3D, and the complexity increases from 4 summation and multiplication operations (in [20]) to 6. Other than these two observations, we use the exact same algorithm as in [19,20]; for lack of space we refer the interested reader to those references for a more thorough presentation of DTBB.

Another substantial accelaration can be obtained by noting that the pairwise term is invariant to depth translations. Combining this with the depth-independent nature of our unary terms, means that we have a one-dimensional family of equally good solutions. Intuitively, the only constraint imposed by our model consists in properly 'unfolding' the object in 3D space, while the particular depth value around which this happens is irrelevant. As illustrated in our experimental results in Fig. 2, Branch-and-Bound would waste time on exploring evenly all those equivalent solutions; instead we fix the model's root node at a fixed depth, and use it as an anchor point for the leaf nodes.

5   Model Learning

Having outlined our cost function and our optimization algorithm we now turn to parameter estimation. Given a candidate configuration $\mathbf{X} = (\mathbf{x}_1, \ldots, \mathbf{x}_P)$ of P parts, we treat our cost function in 3 as the inner product between an image-specific feature vector $\mathbf{F}(\mathbf{X})$ and a model-specific weight vector $\mathbf{w}$, $S(\mathbf{X}) = \langle \mathbf{w}, \mathbf{F}(\mathbf{X}) \rangle$.

The feature vector comprises the P D-dimensional vectors extracted from the part positions $\mathbf{f}(\mathbf{x}_p), p = 1, \ldots, P$, and the model deformations with respect to the nominal displacements from the leaves to the root node $(x_p - x_l - \mu_{r,p}^v)^2, p = 2, \ldots, P$ for each of the 3 dimensions. This accounts for a total size of $PD + 3$ $(P-1)$, which is also the dimension of the learned weight vector. We do not estimate $\mu_{r,p}^v$ discriminatively, as this would impede the viewpoint-based coupling of these parameters described in Sect. 3.2. We do however estimate the relative weight of the above ℓ_2 distance and use the average displacement to define μ, which combined with the viewpoint v yields $\mu_{r,p}^v$. The unary terms of graph nodes that do not correspond to one of the human-annotated keypoints are set to 0, meaning that the image evidence does not affect their position - while for a given viewpoint we set to zero the features of points that are not visible.

In order to learn the corresponding parameter weights, we use Structured Support Vector Machine (SSVM) training a cutting-plane optimizer [15], as done in the context of Deformable Part Models e.g. in [2,23]. In particular we measure the performance of a particular weight vector in terms of a loss function $\Delta(\mathbf{X}_{I_i}^*, \hat{\mathbf{X}}_i)$ which represents the cost incurred by labelling image i as $\mathbf{X}_{I_i}^*$ when the ground truth is $\hat{\mathbf{X}}_i$. We choose to use the Mean Euclidean Distance, $\Delta(\hat{\mathbf{X}}, \mathbf{X}) = \frac{1}{P} \sum_{p=1}^{P} \|\mathbf{x}_p - \hat{\mathbf{x}}_p\|_2$ as a loss for our learning task, penalizing the 3D displacement of our estimated landmarks from their ground truth positions.

This loss decomposes over each node of the graph. This allows us to leverage the tractability of the inference in the learning procedure, as is common in Structured SVMs.

More specifically, each iteration of the cutting plane algorithm requires the computation of the most violated constraint given the current estimate of the joint weight vector w^i, finding a configuration $\mathbf{X}_{cp}^i$ that is consistent with the model, yet incurs a high loss. This subroutine corresponds to the optimization problem:

$$\mathbf{X}_{cp}^i = \arg\max_{\hat{\mathbf{X}}} S_{I,v}(\hat{\mathbf{X}}) + \Delta(\hat{\mathbf{X}}, \mathbf{X}) \tag{6}$$

for each instance $(I, \mathbf{X})$ of the labelled training set. By incorporating the loss in the expression of our model's configuration score , this problem is cast as an equivalent inference problem with modified unaries, scoring a configuration as:

$$\tilde{S}_{I,v}(\hat{\mathbf{X}}) = \sum_{i=1}^{P} \left(\mathcal{U}_{I,\lfloor v \rfloor,i}(\mathbf{x}_i) + \delta(\hat{\mathbf{x}}_i, \mathbf{x}_i) \right) + \sum_{(i,j)\in\mathcal{E}} \mathcal{V}_{i,j,v}(\mathbf{x}_i, \mathbf{x}_j) \tag{7}$$

where $\delta(\hat{\mathbf{x}}_i, \mathbf{x}_i) = 1/P\|\hat{\mathbf{x}}_i - \mathbf{x}_i\|$. The complexity of the subroutine is therefore equivalent to the complexity of our inference algorithm. This framework allows to learn the joint weight vectors in a tractable time of the order of a few hours per view and category.

6   Results

We use the Pascal 3D+ dataset for all of our experiments [27], comprising 1408 images over 10 object categories. The ground truth 3D objects are given by the dataset via rotated and positioned CAD models. We use these CAD models solely for the evaluation of our method.

For feature computation we extract dense image features using the Deeplab network of [6], which is a fully convolutional neural network (FCNN) trained for semantic segmentation. We use the intermediate-level layer activations from layers 3 and 5 yielding a position-dependent feature vector of dimension $D = 769$. Using both lower- and mid-level features gives our unary terms the option of achieve both good localization results (low-level), and good invariance to intra-class appearance variability (high-level).

We evaluate our models in terms of inference acceleration and model performance. Firstly we benchmark the runtime of Branch-and-Bound in 3D and compare it to message-passing with Generalized Distance Transforms [9], commonly used in Deformable Part Models. Secondly we demonstrate that our method outperform the previous state of the art of [17] on 7 out of 10 categories using multi-scale of the Pascal 3D+ dataset. The single-scale version doesn't decisively outperform [17] (5/10), but yields comparable results in much faster runtime.

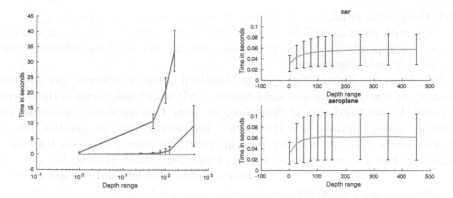

Fig. 2. Left: acceleration of branch-and-bound versus Generalized Distance Transforms as a function of depth resolution. The yellow curve shows the runtime of inference with our Branch-and-Bound algorithm in 3D. The red curve reveals the effect of not anchoring the model in depth, whereas the blue curve represents the implementation with GDTs. Branch-and-Bound is orders of magnitude faster than the GDT based implementation even on moderate depth ranges. Right: Branch-and-Bound performance on two indicative categories, car and aeroplane. The runtime of our algorithm is hardly affected when increasing the number of depth layers. (Color figure online)

6.1 Branch-and-Bound in 3D

To benchmark the acceleration delivered by Branch-and-Bound in 3D we test our algorithm with a varying number of depth layers n_d; Our algorithm has a logarithmic best-case complexity, while inference with the Generalized Distance Transform (GDT) [9] scales linearly in n_d.

Figure 2 on the left empirically demonstrates that this is the case, showing the runtime of Branch-and-Bound on a varying number of depth layers (yellow graph). We set it against a Generalized Distance Transform (GDT) based implementation (blue graph). The timings have been obtained by averaging over the individual contributions of 100 images, 10 from each category, the average standard deviation has been annotated in the graph. The GDT-based inference is about two orders of magnitude slower than the inference with Branch-and-Bound if we set $n_d = 100$. The red graph displays the runtime of Branch-and-Bound when the model is not anchored in depth to distinguish between otherwise equivalent solutions. We note that above a certain size of depth range the computation times increases sharply, indicating that the number of equivalent solutions increases and Branch-and-Bound explores these solutions. By contrast the anchored Branch-and-Bound only increases logarithmically in n_d, being able to perform inference in less than 0.2 s.

6.2 Surface Estimation

Following the methodology of Kar *et al.* [17], we measure the performance of our method by using the Hausdorff distance d_H to compare the system's output with the ground truth, $d_H(X,Y) = \max\{\sup_{x \in X} \inf_{y \in Y} d(x,y), \sup_{y \in Y} \inf_{x \in X} d(x,y)\}$, with points $x \in X$ being the points on the surface of the ground truth shape X and points $y \in Y$ being the points on the surface of the inferred shape Y following rigid alignment.

We display in Table 1 the average Hausdorff distance between the inferred mesh of our star-graph model, and reference CAD model associated to the object instance. In the third row of this table, we show that applying the model on different scales improves the Hausdorff error, which hints at possible future improvements of our method incorporating viewpoint estimation in the inference. Moreover, Fig. 3 shows some examples of inferred placed models. We observe that despite the simplicity of star-shaped graphical models and the speed of the inference, we are competitive to [17], obtaining a better accuracy [17] in most categories.

Table 1. Mesh errors computed using the Hausdorff error with respect to the centered ground-truth CAD models provided in Pascal VOC 3D+ (lower is better).

	Plane	Bike	Boat	Bus	Car	Chair	Sofa	Train	Tv	Mbike	Mean
Kar *et al.* [17]	**2.2**	4.4	6.0	3.9	3.2	**2.6**	8.8	6.6	4.5	**2.9**	4.5
1 star	2.4	4.1	6.1	4.1	**3.1**	3.2	**5.3**	6.3	3.4	3.0	4.1
1 star multiscale	2.4	**4.0**	**5.7**	**3.8**	**3.1**	3.0	5.5	**6.0**	**3.3**	3.0	**4.0**

Fig. 3. Some reconstructed surfaces in 5 categories.

7   Conclusion and Future Work

In this work we present an energy-based 3D DPM framework to learn 3D models from 2D prior information. The method is both expressive and captures the 3D shapes of object, while maintaining tractability during inference. To this end, we present a 3D Branch-and-Bound algorithm that provides a logarithmic scalability. The framework includes a tractable structured learning from 2D keypoint and viewpoint annotations. The method is simple, but outperforms the model of Kar *et al.* [17] in some categories by a significant margin, yielding an 11 % smaller Hausdorff error on average.

From our results, we see that 3D DPMs can be suitable for 3D shape reconstruction, the tractability being provided by Branch-and-Bound for rapid inference.

Our future investigations will aim at extending Branch-and-Bound to more general energies (for example loopy graph structures) and other types of potentials. Using an energy-based model also leaves open the potential of coupling structured prediction techniques with CNN training [7] for the task of surface estimation. We consider this a promising research direction opened up by our energy-based DPM approach.

Acknowledgement. This research has been supported by the FP7-RECONFIG and H2020–I-SUPPORT projects of the European Union.

References

1. Barron, J.T., Malik, J.: Shape, illumination, and reflectance from shading. IEEE Trans. Pattern Anal. Mach. Intell. **37**(8), 1670–1687 (2015)
2. Boussaid, H., Kokkinos, I.: Fast and exact: ADMM-based discriminative shape segmentation with loopy part models. In: Proceedings of the IEEE Conference on Computer Vision and Pattern Recognition, pp. 4058–4065 (2014)
3. Bregler, C., Hertzmann, A., Biermann, H.: Recovering non-rigid 3d shape from image streams. In: 2000 Proceedings of IEEE Conference on Computer Vision and Pattern Recognition, vol. 2, pp. 690–696. IEEE (2000)
4. Carreira, J., Kar, A., Tulsiani, S., Malik, J.: Virtual view networks for object reconstruction. In: IEEE Conference on Computer Vision and Pattern Recognition, CVPR 2015, Boston, MA, USA, 7–12 June 2015, pp. 2937–2946 (2015)
5. Cashman, T.J., Fitzgibbon, A.W.: What shape are dolphins? Building 3d morphable models from 2d images. IEEE Trans. Pattern Anal. Mach. Intell. **35**(1), 232–244 (2013)
6. Chen, L.-C., Papandreou,I. Kokkinos, Murphy, K., Yuille, A.L.: Semantic image segmentation with deep convolutional nets and fully connected CRFs. In: ICLR (2015)
7. Chen, L.-C., Schwing, A.G., Yuille, A.L., Urtasun, R.: Learning Deep Structured models. In: Proceedings of ICML (2015)
8. Felzenszwalb, P.F., Girshick, R.B., McAllester, D., Ramanan, D.: Object detection with discriminatively trained part based models. IEEE Trans. Pattern Anal. Mach. Intell. **32**(9), 1627–1645 (2010)
9. Felzenszwalb, P.F., Huttenlocher, D.P.: Distance transforms of sampled functions. Technical report, Cornell CS (2004)
10. Fischler, M., Erschlanger, R.: The Representation and Matching of Pictorial Structures. IEEE Trans. Comput. **22**(1), 67–92 (1973)
11. Girshick, R.B., Iandola, F.N., Darrell, T., Malik, J.: Deformable part models are convolutional neural networks. In: IEEE Conference on Computer Vision and Pattern Recognition, CVPR 2015, Boston, MA, USA, 7–12 June 2015, pp. 437–446 (2015)
12. He, K., Zhang, X., Ren, S., Sun, J.: Deep residual learning for image recognition. CoRR, abs/1512.03385 (2015)
13. Hejrati, M., Ramanan, D.: Analysis by synthesis: 3d object recognition by object reconstruction. In: 2014 IEEE Conference on Computer Vision and Pattern Recognition (CVPR), pp. 2449–2456. IEEE (2014)
14. Horn, B.K.P., Brooks, M.J.: Shape from Shading. MIT Press, Cambridge (1989)

15. Joachims, T., Finley, T., Yu, C.-N.J.: Cutting-plane training of structural svms. Mach. Learn. **77**(1), 27–59 (2009)
16. Kanazawa, D., Jacobs, M.C.: WarpNet: weakly supervised matching for single-view reconstruction. In: CVPR (2016)
17. Kar, A., Tulsiani, S., Carreira, J., Malik, J.: Category-specific object reconstruction from a single image. In: 2015 IEEE Conference on Computer Vision and Pattern Recognition (CVPR), pp. 1966–1974. IEEE (2015)
18. Kemelmacher-Shlizerman, I.: Internet based morphable model. In: IEEE International Conference on Computer Vision, ICCV 2013, Sydney, Australia, 1–8 December 2013, pp. 3256–3263 (2013)
19. Kokkinos, I.: Rapid deformable object detection using dual-tree branch-and-bound. In: NIPS (2011)
20. Kokkinos, I.: Bounding part scores for rapid detection with deformable part models. In: Fusiello, A., Murino, V., Cucchiara, R. (eds.) ECCV 2012. LNCS, vol. 7585, pp. 41–50. Springer, Heidelberg (2012). doi:10.1007/978-3-642-33885-4_5
21. Kulkarni, T.D., Kohli, P., Tenenbaum, J.B., Mansinghka, V.K.: Picture: a probabilistic programming language for scene perception. In: IEEE Conference on Computer Vision and Pattern Recognition, CVPR 2015, Boston, MA, USA, 7–12 June 2015, pp. 4390–4399 (2015)
22. Lim, J.J., Khosla, A., Torralba, A.: FPM: fine pose parts-based model with3D CAD models. In: Fleet, D., Pajdla, T., Schiele, B., Tuytelaars, T. (eds.) ECCV 2014. LNCS, vol. 8694, pp. 478–493. Springer, Heidelberg (2014). doi:10.1007/978-3-319-10599-4_31
23. Pepik, B., Stark, M., Gehler, P.V., Schiele, B.: Multi-view and 3d deformable part models. IEEE Trans. Pattern Anal. Mach. Intell. **37**(11), 2232–2245 (2015)
24. Peyré, G., Cohen, L.D.: Geodesic remeshing using front propagation. Int. J. Comput. Vis. **69**(1), 145–156 (2006)
25. Tulsiani, S., Malik,J.: Viewpoints and keypoints. In: IEEE Conference on Computer Vision and Pattern Recognition, CVPR 2015, Boston, MA, USA, 7–12 June 2015, pp. 1510–1519 (2015)
26. Vicente, S., Carreira, J., de Agapito, L., Batista, J.: Reconstructing PASCAL VOC. In: 2014 IEEE Conference on Computer Vision and Pattern Recognition, CVPR 2014, Columbus, OH, USA, 23–28 June 2014, pp. 41–48 (2014)
27. Xiang, Y., Mottaghi, R., Savarese, S.: Beyond PASCAL: a benchmark for 3d object detection in the wild. In: IEEE Winter Conference on Applications of Computer Vision (WACV) (2014)
28. Yoruk, E., Vidal, R.: Efficient object localization and pose estimation with 3d wireframe models. In: 2013 IEEE International Conference on Computer Vision Workshops (ICCVW), pp. 538–545. IEEE (2013)
29. Zhou, T., Lee, Y.J., Yu, S.X., Efros, A.A.: Flowweb: Joint image set alignment by weaving consistent, pixel-wise correspondences. In: IEEE Conference on Computer Vision and Pattern Recognition, CVPR 2015, Boston, MA, USA, 7–12 June 2015, pp. 1191–1200 (2015)
30. Zhu, M., Zhou, X., Daniilidis, K.: Single image pop-up from discriminatively learned parts. In: 2015 IEEE International Conference on Computer Vision, ICCV 2015, Santiago, Chile, 7–13 December 2015, pp. 927–935 (2015)
31. Zia, M.Z. , Stark, M., Schindler,K.: Are cars just 3d boxes? Jointly estimating the 3d shape of multiple objects. In: 2014 IEEE Conference on Computer Vision and Pattern Recognition, CVPR 2014, Columbus, OH, USA, 23–28 June 2014, pp. 3678–3685 (2014)

W09 – ChaLearn Looking at People Workshop on Apparent Personality Analysis and First Impressions Challenge

Preface

Welcome to the Proceedings for the ChaLearn Looking at People Workshop on Apparent Personality Analysis and First Impressions Challenge @ ECCV2016, held in conjunction with the European Conference on Computer Vision on October 9th 2016.

Automatic analysis of videos and any other kind of input data to characterize human behavior has become an area of active research with applications in affective computing, human-machine interfaces, gaming, security, marketing, health, and other domains. Research advances in multimedia information processing, computer vision and pattern recognition have lead to established methodologies that are able to successfully recognize consciously executed actions, or intended movements (e.g., gestures, actions, interactions with objects and other people). However, recently there has been much progress in terms of computational approaches to characterize sub-conscious behaviors, which may be revealing aptitudes or competence, hidden intentions, and personality traits.

The ChaLearn Looking at People Workshop on Apparent Personality Analysis and First Impressions Challenge aimed at compiling the latest research advances on apparent personality analysis and related topics. Collocated with the workshop we organized an academic competition on first impressions, where the goal was to develop methods for recognizing apparent personality traits of people from very short videos.

Overall, we accepted a total of 9 relevant submissions, some of them describing the solutions developed by the top ranked participants of the challenge. The competition attracted a total of 88 participants, 14 of which continued until the final test phase. A second round of the challenge has been recently organized at ICPR16. Our workshop also included invited talks by prestigious researchers in the field: Björn W. Schuller, Maja Pantic, Michael Valstar, Daniel Gatica-Perez, and Roland Goecke. This first edition of the workshop paved the way for a series of events in the topic of personality analysis that will surely advance the state of the art in this pretty much exciting field of research.

Many thanks to sponsors, reviewers, authors, participants and invited speakers for your support, we are looking forward seeing you in future events organized by ChaLearn Looking at people, please stay tuned: *gesture.chalearn.org*.

October 2016

Hugo Jair Escalante
Sergio Escalera
Xavier Baró
Isabelle Guyon
Víctor Ponce López

Deep Bimodal Regression for Apparent Personality Analysis

Chen-Lin Zhang, Hao Zhang, Xiu-Shen Wei, and Jianxin Wu$^{(\boxtimes)}$

National Key Laboratory for Novel Software Technology,
Nanjing University, Nanjing, China
{zhangcl,zhangh,weixs,wujx}@lamda.nju.edu.cn

Abstract. Apparent personality analysis from short video sequences is a challenging problem in computer vision and multimedia research. In order to capture rich information from both the visual and audio modality of videos, we propose the Deep Bimodal Regression (DBR) framework. In DBR, for the visual modality, we modify the traditional convolutional neural networks for exploiting important visual cues. In addition, taking into account the model efficiency, we extract audio representations and build the linear regressor for the audio modality. For combining the complementary information from the two modalities, we ensemble these predicted regression scores by both early fusion and late fusion. Finally, based on the proposed framework, we come up with a solution for the Apparent Personality Analysis competition track in the ChaLearn Looking at People challenge in association with ECCV 2016. Our DBR is the winner (first place) of this challenge with 86 registered teams.

Keywords: Apparent personality analysis · Deep regression learning · Bimodal learning · Convolutional neural networks

1 Introduction

Video analysis is one of the key tasks in computer vision and multimedia research, especially human-centered video analysis. In recent years, human-centered videos have become ubiquitous on the internet, which has encouraged the development of algorithms that can analyze their semantic contents for various applications, including first-person video analyses [14, 19, 21], activity recognition [1, 4], gesture and pose recognition [8, 11, 22] and many more [13, 15, 20, 23].

Moreover, apparent personality analysis (APA) is an important problem of human-centered video analysis. The goal of APA is to develop algorithms for recognizing personality traits of users in short video sequences. Personality traits are usually decomposed into components called the *Big Five Traits*, including

This work was supported by the Collaborative Innovation Center of Novel Software Technology and Industrialization. X.-S. Wei is the team director of the APA competition, and J. Wu is the corresponding author.

© Springer International Publishing Switzerland 2016
G. Hua and H. Jégou (Eds.): ECCV 2016 Workshops, Part III, LNCS 9915, pp. 311–324, 2016.
DOI: 10.1007/978-3-319-49409-8_25

openness to experience, conscientiousness, extraversion, agreeableness, and *neuroticism.* Effective apparent personality analysis is challenging due to several factors: cultural and individual differences in tempos and styles of articulation, variable observation conditions, the small size of faces in images taken in typical scenarios, noise in camera channels, infinitely many kinds of out-of-vocabulary motion, and real-time performance constraints.

In this paper, we propose the Deep Bimodal Regression (DBR) framework for APA. As shown in Fig. 1, DBR treats human-centered videos as having with two modalities, i.e., the visual and the audio modality. Then, in these two modalities, deep visual regression networks and audio regression models are built for capturing both visual and audio information for the final personality analysis.

In the visual modality, we firstly extract frames from each original video. Then, deep convolutional neural networks are adopted to learn deep regressors for predicting the Big Five Traits values. Inspired by our previous work [17,18], in these visual deep regression networks, we modify the traditional CNN architecture by discarding the fully connected layers. And then, the deep descriptors of the last convolutional layer are both averaged and max pooled into 512-d feature vectors. After that, the standard ℓ_2-normalization is followed. Finally, the feature vectors are concatenated into the final 1024-d image representations, and a regression (fc+sigmoid) layer is added for end-to-end training. The modified CNN model is called Descriptor Aggregation Network (DAN). Furthermore, the ensemble of multiple layers is used for boosting the regression performance of the visual modality, which is DAN$^+$. Beyond DAN and DAN$^+$, Residual Networks [5] is also utilized in our visual modality of DBR. As discussed in Sect. 4.3, the epoch fusion is used as the early fusion to boost the visual regression performance.

For the audio modality, the log filter bank (logfbank) [3] features are extracted from the original audio of each video. Based on the logfbank features, we train the linear regressor to obtain the Big Five Traits values. Finally, the two modalities are lately fused by averaging the scores of these deep visual models and the audio model. Thus, the final predicted Big Five Traits values are returned.

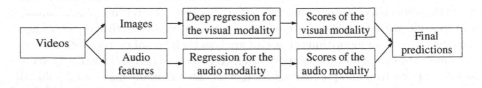

Fig. 1. Framework of the proposed Deep Bimodal Regression method. In DBR, the original videos are treated as having two natural modalities, i.e., the visual modality for images and the audio modality for speeches. After learning the (deep) regressors on these two modalites, the final predicted personality traits are obtained by late fusion.

In consequence, based on the proposed DBR framework, we come up with a solution for the Apparent Personality Analysis track in the ChaLearn Looking at People (LAP) challenge in association with ECCV 2016. In the challenge, we are given a large newly collected video data set, which contains 10,000 videos of about 15 s each collected from YouTube, and annotated with the Big Five Traits by Amazon Mechanical Turk workers. In the Final Evaluation phase, our DBR framework achieved the best regression accuracy (0.9130 mean accuracy), which ranked *the first place* in this challenge.

2   Related Work

In this section, we will briefly review the related work for visual-based deep learning, audio representations and apparent personality analysis.

2.1   Visual-Based Deep Learning

Deep learning refers to a class of machine learning techniques, in which many information processing layers organized in a sequential structure are exploited for pattern classification and for feature or representation learning.

Recently, for image-related tasks, Convolutional Neural Networks (CNNs) [7] allow computational models that are composed of multiple processing layers to learn representations of images with multiple levels of abstraction, which have been demonstrated as an effective class of models for understanding image content, giving state-of-the-art results on image recognition, segmentation, detection and retrieval. Specifically, the CNN model consists of several convolutional layers and pooling layers, which are stacked up with one on top of another. The convolution layer shares many weights, and the pooling layer sub-samples the output of the convolution layer and reduces the data rate from the layer below. The weight sharing in the convolutional layer, together with appropriately chosen pooling schemes, endows the CNN with some invariance properties (e.g., translation invariance).

In our DBR framework, we employ and modify multiple CNNs to learn the image representations for the visual modality, and then obtain the Big Five Traits predictions by end-to-end training.

2.2   Audio Representations

In the past few years, many representations for audio have been proposed: some of them are time domain features, and others are frequency domain features. Among them, there are several famous and effective audio features, to name a few, Mel Frequency Cepstral Coefficients (MFCC) [3], Linear Prediction Cepstral Coefficient (LPCC) [9] and Bark Frequency Cepstral Coefficient (BFCC) [9].

Particularly, the Mel Frequency Cepstral Coefficients (MFCC) [3] features have been widely used in the speech recognition community. MFCC refers to a kind of short-term spectral-based features of a sound, which is derived from spectrum-of-a-spectrum of an audio clip. MFCC can be derived in four steps. During the four steps, the log filter bank (logfbank) features can be also obtained.

In the proposed DBR framework, we extract the MFCC and logfbank features from the audios of each original human-centered video for APA. In our experiments, the results of logfbank are slightly better than the ones of MFCC. Thus, the logfbank features are used as the audio representations in DBR.

2.3   Apparent Personality Analysis

Personality analysis is a task that is specific to the psychology domain. Previous researches in personality analysis usually need psychology scientists to figure out the results, or need participants to do specific tests containing large number of questions which can reflect their personalities. However, such process will cost a lot of time and funds.

A similar task to personality analysis in computer vision is the emotion analysis tasks, e.g., [2,6]. Emotion analysis can be regarded as a multiple class classification problem, where usually four emotions (*sadness, happiness, anger* and *neutral state*) are recognized by the algorithms. However, in apparent personality analysis, it needs to predict the Big Five Traits (*openness to experience, conscientiousness, extraversion, agreeableness,* and *neuroticism*) which are independent with each other and whose scores are continuous values in the range of $[0, 1]$. Thus, it is obvious to see the apparent personality analysis tasks is more realistic but difficult than emotion analysis.

3   The Proposed DBR Framework

In this section, we will introduce the proposed Deep Bimodal Regression (DBR) framework for the apparent personality analysis task. As shown in Fig. 1, DBR has three main parts: the first part is the visual modality regression, the second part is the audio one, and the last part is the ensemble process for fusing information of the two modalities.

3.1   Deep Regression for the Visual Modality

The deep regression part contains three subparts: image extraction, deep regression network training and regression score prediction.

Image Extraction. The inputs of traditional convolutional neural networks are single images. But for the APA task, the original inputs are the human-centered videos. In order to utilize powerful CNNs to capture the visual information, it is necessary to extract images from these videos. For example, for a fifteen seconds length video whose frame rate is 30fps, there are 450 images/frames from each original video. However, if all the images/frames are extracted, the computational cost and memory cost will be quite large. Besides, in fact, nearby frames look extremely similar. Therefore, we downsample these images/frames to 100 images per video. That is to say, in each second, we extract 6 images from a video. After that, the extracted images/frames are labeled with the same personality traits values as the ones of their corresponding video. In consequence, based on the images, we can train the deep regressors by CNNs for APA.

Deep Regression Network Training. In the visual modality of DBR, the main deep CNN models are modified based on our previous work [17,18], which are called Descriptor Aggregation Networks (DANs). What distinguishes DAN from the traditional CNN is: the fully connected layers are discarded, and replaced by both average- and max-pooling following the last convolutional layers ($Pool_5$). Meanwhile, each pooling operation is followed by the standard ℓ_2-normalization. After that, the obtained two 512-d feature vectors are concatenated as the final image representation. Thus, in DAN, the deep descriptors of the last convolutional layers are aggregated as a single visual feature. Finally, because APA is a regression problem, a regression (fc+sigmoid) layer is added for end-to-end training. The architecture of DAN is illustrated in Fig. 2.

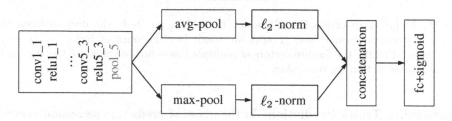

Fig. 2. Architecture of the Descriptor Aggregation Network (DAN) model. Note that we removed the fully connected layers. The deep descriptors of the last convolutional layer ($Pool_5$) are firstly aggregated by both average- and max-pooling, and then concatenated into the final image representation for regression.

Because DAN has no fully connected layers, it will bring several benefits, such as reducing the model size, reducing the dimensionality of the final feature, and accelerating the model training. Moreover, the model performance of DAN is better than traditional CNNs with the fully connected layers, cf. Table 1 and also the experimental results in [18]. In the experiments of the proposed DBR framework, we adopt the pre-trained VGG-Face model [10] as the initialization of the convolutional layers in our DANs.

For further improving the regression performance of DAN, the ensemble of multiple layers is employed. Specifically, the deep convolutional descriptors of $ReLU_{5\_2}$ are also incorporated in the similar aforementioned aggregation approach, which is shown in Fig. 3. Thus, the final image feature is a 2048-d vector. We call this end-to-end deep regression network as "DAN$^+$".

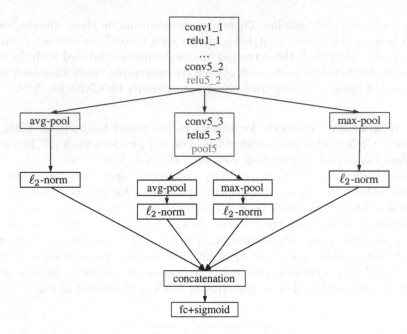

Fig. 3. Architecture of the DAN$^+$ model. In DAN$^+$, not only the deep descriptors of the last convolutional layer (Pool$_5$) are used, but the ones of ReLU$_{5\_2}$ are also aggregated. Finally, the feature vectors of multiple layers are concatenated as the final image representation for regression.

Personality Traits Prediction. In the phase of predicting regression values, images are also extracted from each testing video. Then, the predicted regression scores of images are returned based on the trained visual models. After that, we average the scores of images from a video as the predicted scores of that video.

3.2   Regression for the Audio Modality

As aforementioned, in the audio modality, we choose the log filter bank (logf-bank) features as the audio representations. The logfbank features can be extracted directly from the original audios from videos. After that, we use a model composed of a fully-connected layer followed by a sigmoid function layer to train the audio regressor. The ℓ_2 distance is used as the loss function to cal-culate the regression loss. The whole pipeline of the audio modality can be seen in Fig. 4.

3.3   Modality Ensemble

After the training of both the visual and the audio modalities, modality ensem-ble is used as the late fusion approach for getting the final regression scores.

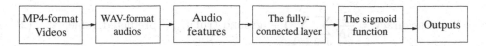

Fig. 4. Pipeline of the regresssion for the audio modality. The log filter bank features are used as the audio representations/features. Based on the audio features, a linear regressor is trained for predictions.

The ensemble method we used in DBR is the simple yet effective simple averaging method. In APA, the predicted result of a trained regressor is a five-dimensional vector which represents the Big Five Traits values, i.e., $s_i = (s_{i1}, s_{i2}, s_{i3}, s_{i4}, s_{i5})^T$. We treat each predicted result of these two modalities equally. For example, the predicted results of the visual modality are s_1, s_2 and s_3, and the results of the audio one are s_4 and s_5. The final ensemble results are calculated as follows:

$$\text{Final score} = \frac{\sum_{i=1}^{5} s_i}{5}. \tag{1}$$

4 Experiments

In this section, we first describe the dataset of apparent personality analysis at the ECCV ChaLearn LAP 2016 competition. Then, we give a detailed description about the implementation details of the proposed DBR framework. Finally, we present and analyze the experimental results of the proposed framework on the competition dataset.

4.1 Datasets and Evaluation Criteria

The apparent personality analysis at the ECCV ChaLearn LAP 2016 competition is the first version for this track. In total, 10,000 videos are labeled to perform automatic apparent personality analysis. For each video sample, it has about fifteen seconds length. In addition, the RGB and audio information are provided, as well as continuous ground-truth values for each of the 5 Big Five Traits annotated by Amazon Mechanical Turk workers.

The dataset is divided into three parts: the training set (6,000 videos), the validation set (2,000 videos) and the evaluation set (2,000 videos). During the Development phase, we train the visual and audio models of DBR on the training set, and verify its performance on the validation set. In the Final Evaluation phase, we use the optimal models in the Development phase to return the predicted regression scores on the final evaluation set.

For evaluation, given a video and the corresponding traits values, the accuracy is computed simply as one minus the absolute distance among the predicted values and the ground truth values. The mean accuracy among all the Big Five traits values is calculated as the principal quantitative measure:

$$\text{Mean accuracy} = \frac{1}{5N} \sum_{j=1}^{5} \sum_{i=1}^{N} 1 - \left| \text{ground\_truth}_{i,j} - \text{predicted\_value}_{i,j} \right|, \quad (2)$$

where N is the number of predicted videos.

4.2   Implementation Details

In this section, we describe the implementation details of the proposed DBR framework on the APA competition dataset.

Details of the Visual Modality. As aforementioned, in the visual modality, we firstly extract about 100 images from each video. Specifically, for most videos, 92 images are extracted (about 6.1fps). After that, we resize these images into the 224×224 image resolution. In consequence, there are 560,393 images extracted from the training videos, 188,561 images from the validation ones, and 188,575 images from testing. Figure 5 illustrates three examples of extracting image from videos.

Fig. 5. Examples of extracting images from videos. For each video, we extract about 100 images.

In our experiments, the visual DAN models in the proposed DBR framework are implemented using the open-source library MatConvNet [16]. Beyond the DAN models, we also employ a popular deep convolutional network, i.e., Residual Network [5], as another regression network for boosting the visual regression performance. In the training stage, the learning rate is 10^{-3}. The weight decay is 5×10^{-4}, and the momentum is 0.9 for all the visual models.

Details of the Audio Modality. In the audio modality, we firstly extract the audio features from the original videos, and then learn a linear regressor based on these audio features. In the APA competition, the open-source library FFmpeg[1] is employed for extracting audios from the original videos. Regarding the parameters of FFmpeg, we choose two channels for the WAV format audio outputs, 44,100 Hz for the sampling frequency, and 320 kbps for the audio quality. The average memory cost of each audio file is about 2.7 MB in Disk. Figure 6 presents the wave forms of one sampled audio from its corresponding video. Based on the extracted audios, we use the Python open source library to extract the MFCC and logfbank features.[2]

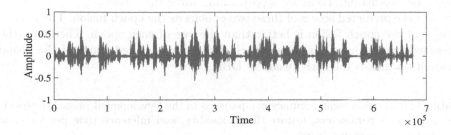

Fig. 6. The wave forms of a sampled audio. The horizontal axis stands for the time. Because we set the sampling frequency as 44,100 Hz, the unit of the horizontal axis is 1/44100 s. The vertical axis is the amplitude.

For the regression model training, we use the Torch platform.[3] Thus, the GPUs can be used for accelerating the model training. The linear regressor is composed of a fully-connected layer and a sigmoid function layer to regress the values of the Big Five Traits' ground truth (in the range of $[0, 1]$). For optimization, the traditional stochastic gradient descent (SGD) method is used, and the momentum is set as 0.9. The batch-size of the audio features is 128. The learning rate of SGD is 8.3×10^{-4}. The weight decay is 6.5, and the learning rate decay is 1.01×10^{-6}.

All the experiments above were conducted on a Ubuntu 14.04 Server with 512 GB memory and K80 Nvidia GPUs support.

4.3 Experimental Results

In this section, we first present the experimental results of the Development phase and analyze our proposed DBR framework. Then, we present the qualitative evaluation of the deep visual regression networks in DBR. Finally, we show the Final Evaluation results of this apparent personality analysis competition.

---

[1] http://ffmpeg.org/.
[2] https://github.com/jameslyons/python_speech_features.
[3] http://torch.ch/.

Development. In Table 1, we present the main results of both the visual and audio modality in the Development phase.

For the visual modality, we also fine-tune the available VGG-Face [10] model on the competition data for comparison. As shown in Table 1, the regression accuracy of DAN (0.9100) is better than VGG-Face (0.9072) with the traditional VGG-16 [12] architecture, and even better than Residual Networks (0.9080). Meanwhile, because DAN has no traditional fully connected layers, the number of the DAN parameters is only 14.71M, which is much less than 134.28M of VGG-16 and 58.31M of ResNet. It will bring storage efficiency.

In addition, from the results of the first and second epoch, we can find the regression accuracy becomes lower when the training epochs increase, which might be overfitting. Thus, we stop training after the second epoch. Then, we average the predicted scores of these two epochs as the epoch fusion. The performance of the epoch fusion is better than the one of each epoch. Therefore, the averaged regression scores of the epoch fusion are the predictions of the visual modality, which is the early fusion in DBR.

Table 1. Regression mean accuracy comparisons in the Development phase. Moreover, the number of parameters, feature dimensionality, and inference time per video of different models are also listed.

Modality	Model	♯ Para.	Dim.	*Epoch 1*	*Epoch 2*	*Epoch Fusion*
Visual	VGG-Face	134.28M	4,096	0.9065	0.9060	0.9072
	ResNet	58.31M	512	0.9072	0.9063	0.9080
	DAN	14.71M	1,024	0.9082	0.9080	0.9100
	DAN$^+$	14.72M	2,048	0.9100	0.9103	0.9111
Audio	Linear regressor	0.40M	79,534	0.8900	–	0.8900

For the audio modality, MFCC and logfbank are extracted. In the experiments of the competition, we extract 3,059 frames per audio. MFCC of one frame is a 13-d feature vector, and logfbank is 26-d. Then, we directly concatenate these frames' feature vectors into a single feature vector of 39,767-d for MFCC and 79,534-d for logfbank.

Because the audio features of this competition are in large scale, we simply train a linear regressor by Torch on GPUs. In order to choose the optimal audio representation of the audio modality, we randomly split the training set (6,000) into two parts: one has 5,000 samples, and the other has 1,000 samples. On the MFCC and logfbank features, we separately learn two linear regressors on the 5,000 samples. Then the rest 1,000 samples are used to validate the performance of different audio features. Figure 7(a) and (b) shows the learning curves of MFCC and logfbank, respectively. The vertical axis is the regression error. It can be seen from these figures that, logfbank could outperform MFCC by 0.75 %. Therefore, the logfbank features are chosen as the optimal audio representation.

After the model training of both two modalities, we obtain three deep visual regression networks (i.e., ResNet, DAN and DAN$^+$) and one audio regression

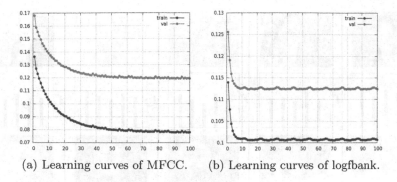

(a) Learning curves of MFCC.   (b) Learning curves of logfbank.

Fig. 7. Learning curves of two different audio features, i.e., MFCC and logfbank. The horizontal axis is the training epoch, and the vertical axis is the regression error.

Table 2. Comparison of performances of the proposed DBR framework with that of the top five teams in the Final Evaluation phase. The results in the "extra.", "agree.", "consc.", "neuro." and "open." columns stand for the separate Big Five Traits regression accuracy, respectively. ("NJU-LAMDA" is our team.)

Rank	Team name	Mean Acc.	Extra.	Agree.	Consc.	Neuro.	Open.
1	**NJU-LAMDA**	**0.9130**	0.9133	**0.9126**	**0.9166**	**0.9100**	**0.9123**
2	evolgen	0.9121	0.9150	0.9119	0.9119	0.9099	0.9117
3	DCC	0.9109	0.9107	0.9102	0.9138	0.9089	0.9111
4	ucas	0.9098	0.9129	0.9091	0.9107	0.9064	0.9099
5	BU-NKU	0.9094	**0.9161**	0.9070	0.9133	0.9021	0.9084

model (a linear regressor). As described in Sect. 3.3, we average all the four predicted Big Five Traits scores, and get the final APA predictions. Finally, we can get 0.9141 mean accuracy in the Development phase.

Qualitative Evaluation of the Deep Visual Regression Networks. In order to further justify the effectiveness of the deep visual regression networks of DBR, we visualize the feature maps of these three networks (i.e., ResNet, DAN and DAN$^+$) in Fig. 8. In that figure, we randomly sample five extracted images from different APA videos, and show the Pool$_5$ feature maps. As shown in those figures, the strongest responses in the corresponding feature maps of these deep networks are quite different from each other, especially the ones of ResNet vs. the ones of DAN/DAN$^+$. It seems that ResNet could pay its attention on the human beings, while DAN/DAN$^+$ will focus on not only the human, but also the environments/backgrounds of these videos. Apparently, different deep visual regression networks could extract complementary information for images in apparent personality analysis.

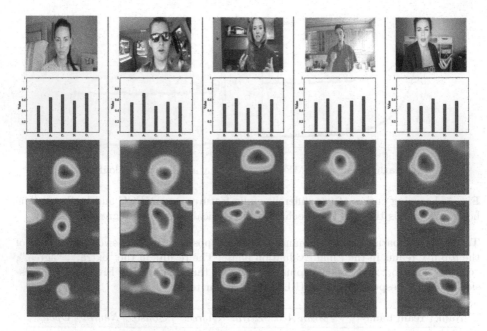

Fig. 8. Feature maps of five sampled images in the visual modality of DBR. The first row shows the images, and the second row presents their corresponding Big Five Traits values. The third, fourth and fifth rows show the featmaps of ResNet, DAN and DAN$^+$, respectively. For each feature map, we sum the responses values of all the channels in the final pooling layer for each deep network. These figures are best viewed in color. (Color figure online)

Final Evaluation. In the Final Evaluation phase, we directly employ the optimal models in the Development phase to predict the Big Five Traits values on the testing set. The final challenge results are shown in Table 2. Our final result (0.9130) ranked the first place, which significantly outperformed the other participants. Moreover, for the regression accuracy of each Big Five Trait value, our proposed DBR framework achieved the best result in four traits.

Since we just use the simple average method to do the late fusion, for further improving regression performance of the proposed method, advanced ensemble methods, e.g., stacking, can be used to learn the appropriate weights for the late fusion. Additionally, the deep audio networks should be tried to learn the more discriminative audio representations. The ensemble of multiple audio models can be also applied into our DBR framework to achieve better apparent personality analysis performance.

5   Conclusions

Apparent personality analysis from videos is an important and challenging problem in computer vision and multimedia research. In order to exploit and capture important cues from both the visual and audio modality, this paper has proposed the Deep Bimodal Regression (DBR) framework. Also, in DBR, we modified the traditional CNNs as Descriptor Aggregation Networks (DANs) for improving the visual regression performance. Finally, we utilized the proposed DBR framework and DANs for the track of apparent personality analysis at the ChaLearn LAP challenge in association with ECCV 2016, and achieved the 1st place in the Final Evaluation phase.

In the future, we will introduce advanced ensemble methods into our framework and incorporating more discriminative deep audio representations for apparent personality analysis.

References

1. Amer, M.R., Lei, P., Todorovic, S.: HiRF: hierarchical random field for collective activity recognition in videos. In: Fleet, D., Pajdla, T., Schiele, B., Tuytelaars, T. (eds.) ECCV 2014. LNCS, vol. 8694, pp. 572–585. Springer, Heidelberg (2014). doi:10.1007/978-3-319-10599-4_37
2. Busso, C., Deng, Z., Yildirim, S., Bulut, M., Lee, C.M., Kazemzadeh, A., Lee, S., Neumann, U., Narayanan, S.: Analysis of emotion recognition using facial expressions, speech and multimodal information. In: Proceedings of the International Conference on Multimodal Interfaces, pp. 205–211 (2004)
3. Davis, S., Mermelstein, P.: Comparison of parametric representations for monosyllabic word recognition in continuously spoken sentences. IEEE Trans. Acoust. Speech Signal Process. **28**(4), 357–366 (1980)
4. Hasan, M., Roy-Chowdhury, A.K.: Continuous learning of human activity models using deep nets. In: Fleet, D., Pajdla, T., Schiele, B., Tuytelaars, T. (eds.) ECCV 2014. LNCS, vol. 8691, pp. 705–720. Springer, Heidelberg (2014). doi:10.1007/978-3-319-10578-9_46
5. He, K., Zhang, X., Ren, S., Sun, J.: Deep residual learning for image recognition. In: Proceedings of IEEE Conference on Computer Vision and Pattern Recognition, pp. 770–778 (2016)
6. Koelstra, S., Muhl, C., Soleymani, M., Lee, J.S., Yazdani, A., Ebrahimi, T., Pun, T., Nijholt, A., Patras, I.: DEAP: a database for emotion analysis using physiological signals. IEEE Trans. Affect. Comput. **3**(1), 18–31 (2012)
7. Krizhevsky, A., Sutskever, I., Hinton, G.E.: ImageNet classification with deep convolutional neural networks. In: Advances in Neural Information Processing Systems, pp. 1097–1105 (2012)
8. Ma, S., Sigal, L., Sclaroff, S.: Learning activity progression in LSTMs for activity detection and early detection. In: Proceedings of the IEEE Conference on Computer Vision and Pattern Recognition, pp. 1942–1950 (2016)
9. Makhoul, J.: Linear prediction: a tutorial review. Proc. IEEE **63**(4), 561–580 (1975)
10. Parkhi, O.M., Vedaldi, A., Zisserman, A.: Deep face recognition. In: British Machine Vision Conference, pp. 1–12 (2015)
11. Pfister, T., Charles, J., Zisserman, A.: Flowing convNets for human pose estimation in videos. In: Proceedings of the IEEE International Conference on Computer Vision, pp. 1913–1921 (2015)
12. Simonyan, K., Zisserman, A.: Very deep convolutional networks for large-scale image recognition. In: International Conference on Learning Representations, pp. 1–14 (2015)

13. Song, Y., Bao, L., Yang, Q., Yang, M.-H.: Real-time exemplar-based face sketch synthesis. In: Fleet, D., Pajdla, T., Schiele, B., Tuytelaars, T. (eds.) ECCV 2014. LNCS, vol. 8694, pp. 800–813. Springer, Heidelberg (2014). doi:10.1007/978-3-319-10599-4_51

14. Soo Park, H., Hwang, J.J., Shi, J.: Force from motion: decoding physical sensation in a first person video. In: Proceedings of the IEEE Conference on Computer Vision and Pattern Recognition, pp. 3834–3842 (2016)

15. Thies, J., Zollhofer, M., Stamminger, M., Theobalt, C., Niessner, M.: Face2Face: real-time face capture and reenactment of RGB videos. In: Proceedings of the IEEE Conference on Computer Vision and Pattern Recognition, pp. 2387–2395 (2016)

16. Vedaldi, A., Lenc, K.: MatConvNet - convolutional neural networks for MATLAB. In: Proceeding of ACM International Conference on Multimedia, pp. 689–692 (2015). http://www.vlfeat.org/matconvnet/

17. Wei, X.S., Luo, J.H., Wu, J.: Selective convolutional descriptor aggregation for fine-grained image retrieval. arXiv preprint arXiv:1604.04994 (2016)

18. Wei, X.S., Xie, C.W., Wu, J.: Mask-CNN: localizing parts and selecting descriptors for fine-grained image recognition. arXiv preprint arXiv:1605.06878 (2016)

19. Xiong, B., Grauman, K.: Detecting snap points in egocentric video with a web photo prior. In: Fleet, D., Pajdla, T., Schiele, B., Tuytelaars, T. (eds.) ECCV 2014. LNCS, vol. 8693, pp. 282–298. Springer, Heidelberg (2014). doi:10.1007/978-3-319-10602-1_19

20. Yan, X., Chang, H., Shan, S., Chen, X.: Modeling video dynamics with deep dynencoder. In: Fleet, D., Pajdla, T., Schiele, B., Tuytelaars, T. (eds.) ECCV 2014. LNCS, vol. 8692, pp. 215–230. Springer, Heidelberg (2014). doi:10.1007/978-3-319-10593-2_15

21. Yonetani, R., Kitani, K.M., Sato, Y.: Recognizing micro-actions and reactions from paired egocentric videos. In: Proceedings of the IEEE Conference on Computer Vision and Pattern Recognition, pp. 2629–2638 (2016)

22. Zhang, D., Shah, M.: Human pose estimation in videos. In: Proceedings of the IEEE International Conference on Computer Vision, pp. 2012–2020 (2015)

23. Zhu, Y., Jiang, C., Zhao, Y., Terzopoulos, D., Zhu, S.C.: Inferring forces and learning human utilities from videos. In: Proceedings of the IEEE Conference on Computer Vision and Pattern Recognition, pp. 3823–3833 (2016)

SASE: RGB-Depth Database for Human Head Pose Estimation

Iiris Lüsi[1], Sergio Escarela[2], and Gholamreza Anbarjafari[1(✉)]

[1] iCV Research Group, Institute of Technology,
University of Tartu, Tartu, Estonia
{iiris,shb}@icv.tuit.ut.ee
[2] Computer Vision Center, Universitat de Barcelona, Barcelona, Spain
sergio@maia.ub.es

Abstract. Head pose estimation has become very important in relation to facial and emotional recognition, as well as in human-computer interaction. There is an ultimate need for a 3D head pose database in order to develop head pose estimation methods using RGB and depth information. There are a few available datasets, such as Biwi Kinect head pose database, which is composed using Kinect 1, but it offers low-quality depth information. In this paper, a new 3D head database, SASE, is introduced. The data in SASE is acquired with Microsoft Kinect 2 camera, including RGB and depth information. The SASE database is composed by a total of 30000 frames with annotated markers. The samples include 32 male and 18 female subjects. For each person a large sample of head poses are included, within the bounds of yaw from -45 to 45, pitch -75 to 75 and roll -45 to 45° of rotation around each axis. The details of acquiring the database and its characteristics are explained in detail.

Keywords: Head-pose database · Head-pose estimation · Microsoft Kinect 2 · Facial database

1 Introduction

The visualisation and animation of human movements [1–3] has recently been garnering the attention of numerous researchers. In order to improve the computer-human interactions it is necessary to develop algorithms that can interpret the behavioural movements made by humans and also mimic these actions in a natural way.

Over the years it has become quite common to use large databases to train and test active appearance models (AAM) that pinpoint and track the locations of landmark points in a human face [4–6]. One of the fresher approaches presented in [7] mixed Lucas-Kanade optical flow with and active appearance model that utilizes gradient descent. As a different approach, the correlation between appearance and shape was used in [8]. This type of models follow and find the necessary facial features easily when the head orientation is near-frontal, with

© Springer International Publishing Switzerland 2016
G. Hua and H. Jégou (Eds.): ECCV 2016 Workshops, Part III, LNCS 9915, pp. 325–336, 2016.
DOI: 10.1007/978-3-319-49409-8_26

only slight changes in angle, but tend to go awry when the proportions of the face change due to rotation.

To prevent that, in [9] a method using auxiliary attributes was proposed. The authors added traits such as gender, whether the person was wearing glasses, or whether the person was looking to left, right or front. This extra info was included in their deep convolutional network. It was shown that this approach gives more accurate results, as the AAM could be aligned based on samples more similar to each other, rather than using a model without any data stratification.

There have been several techniques proposed on robust tracking by incorporating geometric constraints to corrclate the position of facial landmarks [10,11]. Even though single step face alignment methods have been proposed [12,13], the most common and recent approach for face alignment is to model the relationship between texture and geometry with a cascade of regression functions [14,15]. Many methods used RGB-D cameras to conduct real-time depth-based facial tracking and tried to register dynamic expression model with observed depth data [16–18].

However, the aforementioned method of head pose estimation relies heavily on the lighting conditions. To have accurate head orientation recognition in real-life, the method would have to be trained with a large variety of poses in a all kinds of different lighting conditions. On the other hand training with highly disperse data could make the classification less reliable and produce false detection of angle or facial landmarks. To cross that gap, in [19] the depth-data and RGB data from Kinect were used. As a preliminary step the authors constructed a 3D head shape-model. After which they took three RGB images of the subject, from the left, the right and the front. These images were fitted onto the 3D AAM. Later the 3D AAM was aligned to the input 3D frame by benefiting from using the RGB data as constraining parameters.

Fanelli et al. [20] proposed a head pose estimation purely based on depth data. Fanelli et al. [21] also tried using their method with data from the Microsoft Kinect 1, but the sensor at that time gave fairly inaccurate results due to the low quality of available depth information. With this work a depth database, BIWI, was also provided. However adding different AAM type algorithms on top of Fanelli's framework has produced fairly accurate real-time facial landmark tracking applications [22,23]. Now that the Kinect 2 is available with much more accurate depth information and higher resolution RGB images, the results of depth-based head pose estimation algorithms could be improved upon and further analysed to achieve faster and smoother facial landmark detection and tracking [24].

Another application for depth information is face-recognition that does not depend on lighting conditions. In [25] such real-time identification was proposed. The face was segmented out based on the depth discontinuity and disregarded those with a resolution lower than 60×60. Then a suitable number of canonical faces were formed, and consequentially iterative closest point (ICP) algorithm [26] was used to align gallery faces to the standardised faces. In the recognition stage, the ICP algorithm was used to align the probed face to the canonical ones, and then the gallery face with most similar aligned faces was picked as the match. This proved to be a robust and computationally cheap method.

One of the most important concepts to understand about the 3D sensors and algorithms trained on the data acquired by them, is that the RGB-D data provided by a sensor is unique, as some outputs are denser, while others produce a lesser error. Due to this fact, a method trained on a set of data from one sensor is incompatible with data from other sensors. The necessity for a head pose database for Microsoft Kinect 2 rises from the fact that nowadays this is one of the most accurate and easily available RGB-D sensors. Additionally, for further development of depth-based recognition methods, a variety of databases with heads in different poses is needed; thus, in this paper, we present the SASE database, which is gathered with Kinect 2 and can contribute to future research within the depth-related facial recognition field.

The SASE database is composed of depth and RGB frames of 50 subjects performing different head poses in front of the sensor. The head poses have high variations in yaw, pitch and roll angles, resulting in a myriad of poses. For each subjects 600+ frames were captured and most of them are labelled with location and rotation angles.

The rest of the paper is organized as follows: in Sect. 2 a short overview of available 3D face databases is presented. In Sect. 3 the acquisition of the SASE database, in quintessence and method of calculating ground truth values are described in detail. Also images of the setup, the process and necessary formula are provided, after which a conclusion is drawn in the last section.

2   Brief Overview of Existing 3D Head Databases

The number of available depth databases is quite insignificant, and most of them have been captured with sophisticated scanners that require lots of time for data collection. These types of devices have very few real-time applications, which reduces the overall fruitfulness of datasets captured with them. Databases that capture high definition laser scanners are: ND-2004 [27], BJUT-3D [28] and UMD-DB [29]. High-quality stereo-imaging systems were used for capturing the BU-3DFE [30], XM2VTSDB [31] and the Texas 3D-FRD [32].

Some databases were captured using a system of structured lights instead of a depth camera, like the 3D-RMA database [33] and the Bosphorus [34] database. While Bosphorus contains high quality data, only 4000 points are provided for the depth in 3D-RMA. By using synchronised cameras, the Spacetime faces [35], which contains face meshes made up of 23000 vertices, was captured. There is not RGB nor grayscale information provided along with the previously mentioned datasets.

Databases captured using Kinect 1 include the Biwi Kinect Database [20] and the KinecFaceDB [36]. Facewarehouse [37] contains raw depth RGB-D data and also reconstructed faces using Kinect Fusion. There are also two online 3D databases where the sensor is not specified: the University of York 3D Face Database [38] and the 3dMD [39] database, which as a project also contains 3D reconstruction of heads and entire human bodies. Samples from nine databases that had both 2D and 3D samples available are shown in Fig. 1. The detailed comparison of the aforementioned nine head pose databases is summarized in Table 1.

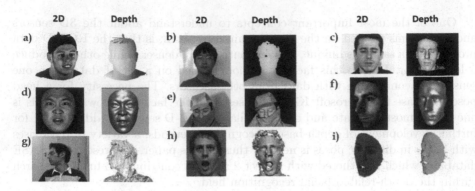

Fig. 1. 3D and depth samples from databases: (a) BJUT-3D, (b) Kinect FDB, (d) BU-3DFE, (e) TEXAS 3DFDB, (f) York, (g) BIWI, (h) Warehouse and (i) Bosphorus.

Table 1. Summarized comparison of nine head pose databases.

Name	Year	Modality	Sensor	Different poses	Pose variation	Size of database	nr of subjects	Age
ND-2004	2006	RGB-D	Minota Vivid 910	No	-	13450	888	NA
BJUT-3D	2005	3D model	CyberWare 3030RGB/PS	Yes	Yaw	NA	500	NA
UMD-DB	2011	RGB-D	Minolta Vivid 900	No	-	1473	143	NA
BU-3DFE	2006	RGB, 3D model	3DMD digitizer	Yes	Yaw: ±45	2500	100	18–70
XM2VTSDB	1999	Audio, video, 3D model	Stereo camera	Yes	Yaw, pitch separately	1180	295	NA
Texas 3D-FRD	2010	RGB-D	Mu-2 stereo imaging system	No	-	1149	118	NA
3D-RMA	1998	3D point cloud	Structured lights	Yes	3 yaw poses	360	120	20–60
Bosphorus	2007	RGB-D	Structured lights	Yes	13 yaw and pitch rotations	4666	105	NA
Spacetime faces	2004	3D mesh	Synchronised- cameras structured-lights	-	-	384	-	-
Biwi Kinect Database	2011	RGB-D	Kinect1	Yes	Yaw: ±75; pitch: ±60	15000	20	NA
KinecFaceDB	2014	RGB-D	Kinect1	Yes	Yaw: ±90; pitch: ±45	NA	52	27–40
Facewarehouse	2014	RGB-D	Kinect1	No	-	3000	150	7–80
York 3D Face Database	NA	RGB-D	NA	Yes	5 poses	5250	350	NA
SASE Database	2016	RGB-D	Kinect2	Yes	pitch: ±75; yaw, roll: ±45	30000	50	7–35

These databases are available for testing 3D facial recognition or head pose estimation algorithms. Regretfully, not all of them include varying head poses and one of them is missing 2D data (3D-RMA), while in the case of the others (captured with laser scanners), the RGB data was not well-aligned with the 3D data.

Another issue with the available databases is that even though they can be used for the testing of 3D face recognition and head pose estimation, the fitted models are sensor dependent. It makes sense that a classifier trained on one type of input data would fail with the test data acquired using a different scanning device.

Given that there exist various methods for RGB-D head-pose estimation, but all require a database captured with the same type of scanner and there is a lack of such publicly avalible collections, in the next section we present the novel SASE database, captured with Kinect 2, that attempts to address the aforementioned issues.

3   SASE Database Description

3.1   Overall Description

The database introduced in this paper contains RGB-D information (424×512 16-bit depth frames and 1080×1920 RGB frames) obtained using the Microsoft Kinect 2 sensor of different head poses of 50 subjects, including 32 male and 18 female in the age range of 7–35 years old. The subjects were asked to move their heads slowly in front of the device to achieve different combinations of yaw, pitch and roll rotation. Altogether around 600+ frames of each subject were recorded. For those frames where the nose tip location was attainable, the ground truth of the 3D nose tip location and head orientation described by yaw, roll, pitch angles is provided by using the formulae shown in Sect. 3.4. The rest of the samples were retained as more sophisticated methods like ICP can be used in the future to label them. The depth information (scaled for display purposes) and corresponding RGB data can be seen in part (a) in Fig. 2.

3.2   Kinect 2

The Microsoft Kinect 2 consists of 3 main components, namely, RGB camera, IR emitter and IR sensor. The RGB resolution of this new sensor is 1080×1920 which is the resolution of a full HD image, in comparison to the Kinect 1's 480×640. The IR is used to employ time of flight technology to calculate the distance of each point. Which results in 1 mm depth accuracy at around 1 m distance. Even though this version also gives false information at very abrupt edges (70+ degrees), the failure angles are steeper than the ones with Kinect 1 [40].

3.3   Acquisition Details

In this section details of the setup and recording process are explained thoroughly. Overall the recording process elapsed about a month as the subjects were recorded during a number of sessions, which differed in the number of people captured.

The software used for the capture was a python script written using the Kinect 2 python library and OpenCV. The laptop used for the capturing process has an i5-4200u processor with an integrated graphics card and 8GB of RAM. It also carried an SSD to speed up the frame rate. However, due to restrictions of the processor of the laptop, the frame rate was measured to be at 5fps.

The head poses in the database are with values of yaw varying from −75 to 75, pitch and roll varying from −45 to 45. These constrains were chosen because they represent the maximum angles that can be achieved under normal conditions by a human sitting in front of a camera, and only moving the head while not changing their body position. The aforementioned restrictions were achieved experimentally and are not necessarily applied to all humans but rather seem to be an average trend.

The angle limitations are different for each subject. This is due to the fact that not all people can rotate their head the same exact amount. In order to avoid this problem, all the people were trained in advance, so that they did not rotate their heads too much during the capturing process. Also participants were free to perform different facial expressions in the different poses when capturing the data in order to have a more natural database. This resulted in a collection of mostly neutral faces with some happy expressions mixed in. It is important to note that this data base is not focusing on representing various emotions and thus can not be used for emotion recognition applications.

The sketch and the actual experimental setup can be seen in Fig. 3(a) and (b), respectively. The Kinect 2 was placed on a stand, and the subject sat approximately 1 m distance away from the camera. A white canvas screen was used as background.

In order to label the database, five (in case of facial hair sometimes six) light blue stickers were stuck onto each participants face: one on the forehead/between eyebrows, one on the chin, one on the tip of the nose and two on the cheekbones/cheeks as can be seen in part (b) in Fig. 2.

These locations were picked as they are visible from various angles by the camera. However, the exact placement and even symmetry of the markers are unimportant as the markers remained unchanged throughout the whole recording process of each subject. Only the marker on the nose tip was placed exactly at the same spot for each person. Due to the fact that the 3D coordinates of the nose tip are considered to be the location of the head provided in the database labels.

The illumination condition was kept low in order not to over illuminate the light blue markers and make them undetectable. The color of the marker was chosen as it is easily distinguishable from the human face. The thickness of the stickers is negligible, thus they do not cause notable occlusions to the depth information.

3.4 Optimisation and Ground Truth Values

In order to calculate head poses, the initial pose of the person was taken as the reference pose. The initial pose has a frontal orientation, in which the subject is looking at the camera. Considering the noise of the sensor, 20 frames of this pose were captured to average a good starting value for further calculations.

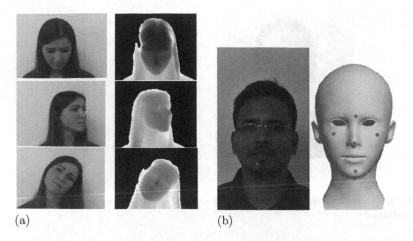

(a)   (b)

Fig. 2. (a) Cutouts from the database, for rows as (pitch, yaw, roll): (−32, 0, 3), (2, −49, 2) and (3, −1, −39), respectively and (b) the placement of coloured stickers.

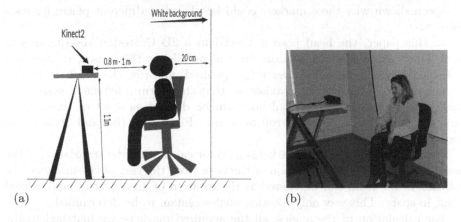

(a)   (b)

Fig. 3. The (a) sketck and (b) real scene of the setup of acquiring data for the database.

After which markers were used to calculate the pairwise difference between an averaged initial pose and the current pose.

The detection of these markers has been done by using their colour information. As the poses are changing, not all of these markers are visible to the acquisition device all the time. In order to be able to calculate the orientation of the head pose, we need at least three of the markers to be visible. Their real-world coordinates and the vectors between them were calculated. Then the rotation matrix between the initial and current vectors was found, which was used to obtain the orientation of the head. These vectors are illustrated in Fig. 4, part (a). The central point of the head is considered to be the nose tip because this is easy to locate using depth information and fits the application of the database.

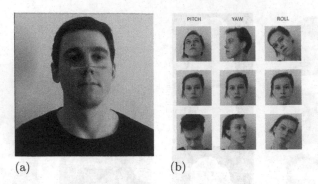

Fig. 4. In (a) vectors used for calculation and in (b) rotation angles yaw, pitch and roll, explained

The following optimisation process and calculation of rotation angles is described in fine detail in order to illustrate how the markers were used. Also it has been shown why these markers could be placed at different places for each subject.

In this paper, the head pose is viewed in a 3D Cartesian coordinate system. The x-axis is defined horizontally and parallel to the sensor, right-side is positive, the y-axis is defined vertically, pointed upwards, the z-axis is defined perpendicular to both of these axises, so that they form a left-hand system. In this coordinate system, the head pose can be defined as a set of six parameters, angles for pitch, yaw and roll as seen in Fig. 4 part (b), and 3D location coordinates x, y, z.

In this database the nose marker is used for calculating the translation of the head. By subtracting the location of the nose from the rest of the markers, the rotation of the head can be viewed as the rotation of an object around a fixed point in space. This way only rotation angles remain to be determined.

For calculation of the angles, all the acquired markers are matched to the original positions. For the first few frames, the average vectors starting from the nose are calculated. For next steps, all the vectors from the nose to all existing vertices (visible markers) are used to determine the angles from simple optimisation problem.

From Euler's fixed point rotation theorem [41], it follows that any $3D$ rotation can be described as the product of 3 separate rotations around each axis. The pitch describes the rotation angle around the x axis, yaw around the y-axis and roll around the z-axis. Thus using the Euler fixed point rotations, the matrix that describes the rotation for pitch angle, α, is:

$$R_\alpha = \begin{pmatrix} 1 & 0 & 0 \\ 0 & cos(\alpha) & -sin(\alpha) \\ 0 & sin(\alpha) & cos(\alpha) \end{pmatrix} \tag{1}$$

Similarly, matrices R_β and R_γ for yaw and roll are defined, respectively.

By using matrix multiplication, the overall rotation matrix $R(\alpha\beta\gamma) = (r_{ij}^{\alpha\beta\gamma})$ can be achieved by:

$$R(\alpha, \beta, \gamma) = R_\alpha R_\beta R_\gamma \tag{2}$$

So when the initial vectors are in the matrix $X = (x_{ij})$ and the new vectors are in the matrix $\tilde{X} = (\tilde{x}_{ij})$, then the rotation can be written as:

$$\tilde{X} = R(\alpha, \beta, \gamma)X \tag{3}$$

In the case of more than three equations, a linear system may not be uniquely solvable. It is an overdetermined linear equation system [42], which can be solved as a least-squares optimisation problem:

$$\operatorname*{argmin}_{\alpha,\beta,\gamma} \left[\sum_i \sum_j \left(x_{ij} - \sum_k r_{ik}^{\alpha\beta\gamma} \tilde{x}_{kj} \right)^2 \right] \tag{4}$$

The optimisation was performed by the default constrained optimisation process [43] provided by $SciPy$ [44]. The minimum and maximum angle restrictions explained to the subjects were also fed into the optimisation process. In Fig. 5 various head poses of one of the subject in the SASE database are illustrated with the respective rotated bases vectors. Blue vector is the rotated y-axis, red vector is the rotated x-axis and the green vector is the rotated z-axis. For the purpose of easier illustration, they were all projected onto the original xy-plane.

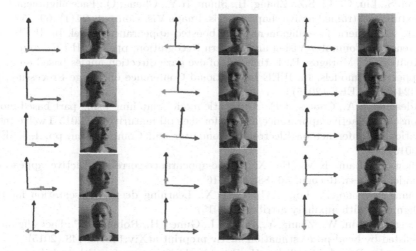

Fig. 5. Various head poses of a subject from proposed SASE database.

4 Conclusion

We presented a 3D head pose database using the Kinect 2 camera, which can be used in a variety of relevant contexts, such as testing the performance of 3D head pose estimation algorithms. Due to the exhaustiveness of the data provided by the Kinect camera, which involves color and depth, the foregoing database can be considered a useful resource for producing training sets. In fact, the main motivation for creating the database has been the fact that no 3D head pose database has been offered through the existing literature by means of the second generation of the Kinect camera. For creating the database, 50 subjects where recorded while taking different head poses in front of the camera, which resulted in more than 600 sample frames in total per person, and a total size of the database of more than 30000 multi-modal head pose annotated frames.

Acknowledgement. This work has been partially supported by Estonian Research Grand (PUT638) and Spanish project TIN2013-43478-P.

References

1. Cao, C., Wu, H., Weng, Y., Shao, T., Zhou, K.: Real-time facial animation with image-based dynamic avatars. ACM Trans. Graph. **35**(4), 126 (2016)
2. Shuster, G.S., Shuster, B.M.: Avatar eye control in a multi-user animation environment. US Patent Ap. 14/961,744, 7 Dec 2015
3. Demirel, H., Anbarjafari, G.: Data fusion boosted face recognition based on probability distribution functions in different colour channels. EURASIP J. Adv. Signal Process. **2009**, 25 (2009)
4. Yan, S., Liu, C., Li, S.Z., Zhang, H., Shum, H.Y., Cheng, Q.: Face alignment using texture-constrained active shape models. Image Vis. Comput. **21**(1), 69–75 (2003)
5. Liu, X.: Generic face alignment using boosted appearance model. In: IEEE Conference on Computer Vision and Pattern Recognition, pp. 1–8. IEEE (2007)
6. Koutras, P., Maragos, P.: Estimation of eye gaze direction angles based on active appearance models. In: IEEE International Conference on Image Processing, pp. 2424–2428. IEEE (2015)
7. Adeshina, S.A., Cootes, T.F.: Automatic model matching using part based model constrained active appearance models for skeletal maturity. In: 2015 Twelve International Conference on Electronics Computer and Computation, pp. 1–5. IEEE (2015)
8. Zhou, H., Lam, K.M., He, X.: Shape-appearance-correlated active appearance model. Pattern Recogn. **56**, 88–99 (2016)
9. Zhang, Z., Luo, P., Loy, C.C., Tang, X.: Learning deep representation for face alignment with auxiliary attributes (2015)
10. Yang, H., Mou, W., Zhang, Y., Patras, I., Gunes, H., Robinson, P.: Face alignment assisted by head pose estimation. arXiv preprint arXiv:1507.03148 (2015)
11. Vlasic, D., Brand, M., Pfister, H., Popović, J.: Face transfer with multilinear models. ACM Trans. Graph. **24**, 426–433 (2005). ACM
12. Sun, Y., Wang, X., Tang, X.: Deep convolutional network cascade for facial point detection. In: IEEE Conference on Computer Vision and Pattern Recognition, pp. 3476–3483. IEEE (2013)
13. Zhang, J., Shan, S., Kan, M., Chen, X.: Coarse-to-fine auto-encoder networks (CFAN) for real-time face alignment. In: Fleet, D., Pajdla, T., Schiele, B., Tuytelaars, T. (eds.) ECCV 2014. LNCS, vol. 8690, pp. 1–16. Springer, Heidelberg (2014). doi:10.1007/978-3-319-10605-2_1

14. Cao, X., Wei, Y., Wen, F., Sun, J.: Face alignment by explicit shape regression. Int. J. Comput. Vis. **107**(2), 177–190 (2014)

15. Xiong, X., De la Torre, F.: Supervised descent method and its applications to face alignment. In: IEEE Conference on Computer Vision and Pattern Recognition, pp. 532–539. IEEE (2013)

16. Weise, T., Bouaziz, S., Li, H., Pauly, M.: Realtime performance-based facial animation. ACM Trans. Graph. **30**, 77 (2011). ACM

17. Kazemi, V., Sullivan, J.: One millisecond face alignment with an ensemble of regression trees. In: IEEE Conference on Computer Vision and Pattern Recognition, pp. 1867–1874. IEEE (2014)

18. Traumann, A., Daneshmand, M., Escalera, S., Anbarjafari, G.: Accurate 3D measurement using optical depth information. Electron. Lett. **51**(18), 1420–1422 (2015)

19. Wang, H.H., Dopfer, A., Wang, C.C.: 3D AAM based face alignment under wide angular variations using 2D and 3D data. In: IEEE International Conference on Robotics and Automation, pp. 4450–4455. IEEE (2012)

20. Fanelli, G., Gall, J., Van Gool, L.: Real time head pose estimation with random regression forests. In: IEEE Conference on Computer Vision and Pattern Recognition, pp. 17–624. IEEE (2011)

21. Fanelli, G., Weise, T., Gall, J., Gool, L.: Real time head pose estimation from consumer depth cameras. In: Mester, R., Felsberg, M. (eds.) DAGM 2011. LNCS, vol. 6835, pp. 101–110. Springer, Heidelberg (2011). doi:10.1007/978-3-642-23123-0_11

22. Yang, F., Huang, J., Yu, X., Cui, X., Metaxas, D.: Robust face tracking with a consumer depth camera. In: IEEE International Conference on Image Processing, pp. 561–564. IEEE (2012)

23. Fanelli, G., Dantone, M., Van Gool, L.: Real time 3D face alignment with random forests-based active appearance models. In: IEEE International Conference and Workshops on Automatic Face and Gesture Recognition, pp. 1–8. IEEE (2013)

24. Lusi, I., Anbarjafari, G., Meister, E.: Real-time mimicking of Estonian speaker's mouth movements on a 3D avatar using kinect 2. In: International Conference on Information and Communication Technology Convergence, pp. 141–143. IEEE (2015)

25. Min, R., Choi, J., Medioni, G., Dugelay, J.L.: Real-time 3D face identification from a depth camera. In: International Conference on Pattern Recognition, pp. 1739–1742. IEEE (2012)

26. Chetverikov, D., Svirko, D., Stepanov, D., Krsek, P.: The trimmed iterative closest point algorithm. In: 16th International Conference on Pattern Recognition, 2002. Proceedings, vol. 3, pp. 545–548. IEEE (2002)

27. Faltemier, T.C., Bowyer, K.W., Flynn, P.J.: Using a multi-instance enrollment representation to improve 3D face recognition. In: IEEE International Conference on Biometrics: Theory, Applications, and Systems, pp. 1–6. IEEE (2007)

28. Baocai, Y., Yanfeng, S., Chengzhang, W., Yun, G.: BJUT-3D large scale 3D face database and information processing. J. Comput. Res. Dev. **6**, 020 (2009)

29. Colombo, A., Cusano, C., Schettini, R.: UMB-DB: a database of partially occluded 3D faces. In: IEEE International Conference on Computer Vision Workshops, pp. 2113–2119. IEEE (2011)

30. Yin, L., Wei, X., Sun, Y., Wang, J., Rosato, M.J.: A 3D facial expression database for facial behavior research. In: International Conference on Automatic Face and Gesture Recognition, pp. 211–216. IEEE (2006)

31. Messer, K., Matas, J., Kittler, J., Luettin, J., Maitre, G.: XM2VTSDB: the extended M2VTS database. In: Second International Conference on Audio and Video-based Biometric Person Authentication, vol. 964, pp. 965–966. Citeseer (1999)
32. Gupta, S., Castleman, K.R., Markey, M.K., Bovik, A.C.: Texas 3D face recognition database. In: IEEE Southwest Symposium on Image Analysis & Interpretation, pp. 97–100. IEEE (2010)
33. 3D RMA: 3D database. http://www.sic.rma.ac.be/~beumier/DB/3d_rma.html. Accessed 15 Apr 2016
34. Savran, A., Alyüz, N., Dibeklioğlu, H., Çeliktutan, O., Gökberk, B., Sankur, B., Akarun, L.: Bosphorus database for 3D face analysis. In: Schouten, B., Juul, N.C., Drygajlo, A., Tistarelli, M. (eds.) BioID 2008. LNCS, vol. 5372, pp. 47–56. Springer, Heidelberg (2008). doi:10.1007/978-3-540-89991-4_6
35. Zhang, L., Snavely, N., Curless, B., Seitz, S.M.: Spacetime faces: high-resolution capture for ~ modeling and animation. In: Deng, Z., Neumann, U. (eds.) Data-Driven 3D Facial Animation, pp. 248–276. Springer, London (2008)
36. Min, R., Kose, N., Dugelay, J.L.: KinectFaceDB: a kinect database for face recognition. IEEE Trans. Syst. Man Cybern.: Syst. 44(11), 1534–1548 (2014)
37. Cao, C., Weng, Y., Zhou, S., Tong, Y., Zhou, K.: FaceWarehouse: a 3D facial expression database for visual computing. IEEE Trans. Vis. Comput. Graph. 20(3), 413–425 (2014)
38. University of york 3D face database. https://www-users.cs.york.ac.uk/nep/research/3Dface/tomh/3DFaceDatabase.html. Accessed 15 Apr 2016
39. 3DMD head database. http://www.3dmd.com/. Accessed 15 Apr 2016
40. Smisek, J., Jancosek, M., Pajdla, T.: 3D with kinect. In: Fossati, A., Gall, J., Grabner, H., Ren, X., Konolige, K. (eds.) Consumer Depth Cameras for Computer Vision. Advances in Computer Vision and Pattern Recognition, pp. 3–25. Springer, London (2013)
41. Palais, B., Palais, R.: Euler's fixed point theorem: the axis of a rotation. J. Fixed Point Theory Appl. 2(2), 215–220 (2007)
42. Trefethen, L.N., Bau III, D.: Numerical Linear Algebra, vol. 50. SIAM, Philadelphia (1997)
43. Zhu, C., Byrd, R.H., Lu, P., Nocedal, J.: Algorithm 778: L-BFGS-B: fortran subroutines for large-scale bound-constrained optimization. ACM Trans. Math. Softw. 23(4), 550–560 (1997)
44. SciPY: Scientific python. http://docs.scipy.org/doc/scipy/reference/index.html. Accessed 18 July 2016

Bi-modal First Impressions Recognition Using Temporally Ordered Deep Audio and Stochastic Visual Features

Arulkumar Subramaniam[(✉)], Vismay Patel, Ashish Mishra, Prashanth Balasubramanian, and Anurag Mittal

Department of Computer Science and Engineering,
Indian Institute of Technology Madras, Chennai, India
{aruls,vismay,mishra,bprash,amittal}@cse.iitm.ac.in

Abstract. We propose a novel approach for First Impressions Recognition in terms of the Big Five personality-traits from short videos. The Big Five personality traits is a model to describe human personality using five broad categories: Extraversion, Agreeableness, Conscientiousness, Neuroticism and Openness. We train two bi-modal end-to-end deep neural network architectures using temporally ordered audio and novel stochastic visual features from few frames, without over-fitting. We empirically show that the trained models perform exceptionally well, even after training from a small sub-portions of inputs. Our method is evaluated in ChaLearn LAP 2016 Apparent Personality Analysis (APA) competition using ChaLearn LAP APA2016 dataset and achieved excellent performance.

Keywords: Deep learning · Bi-modal neural networks · First impressions analysis · Apparent personality analysis

1 Introduction

A "First Impression" is the event when a person encounters another person and forms a mental image about the person [1]. Here the mental image can be based on lot of characteristics such as facial expressions, action, physical appearance, the way of interaction, body language, etc. According to research in Psychology [2], the first impressions are formed even with a limited exposure (as less as 100 ms) to unfamiliar faces. Forming a first impression is usually done in terms of Personality-traits recognition. Determining Personality-traits automatically will be helpful in human resourcing, recruitment process. An automatic analysis of Personality-traits will help people to train themselves.

The problem can be represented as in Table 1. A short video with a person's interview is given as input and the output is expected to be 5 fractional values in the range [0, 1] representing Extraversion, Agreeableness, Conscientiousness, Neuroticism, Openness. These five are collectively known as the "Big-Five personality-traits".

A. Subramaniam, V. Patel—Authors contributed equally.

© Springer International Publishing Switzerland 2016
G. Hua and H. Jégou (Eds.): ECCV 2016 Workshops, Part III, LNCS 9915, pp. 337–348, 2016.
DOI: 10.1007/978-3-319-49409-8_27

Table 1. Example of input and target. Input is the raw video containing a person's interview & output will be the predicted personality-traits values.

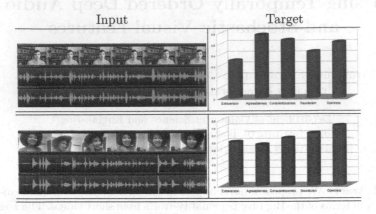

There has not been much work in literature for First-impressions recognition, though the researchers have explored Emotion recognition [3–8], a related area in terms of the type of problem and features (hand-crafted features as well as deep features) used. There are many ways, people express their emotions, among which facial expressions are the most useful [3–6]. Cohen et al. [4] used HMM based models to categorize the emotions in a video into six types: (1) happy, (2) angry, (3) surprise, (4) disgust, (5) fear, (6) sad. Their extended work [5] in multilevel HMM performed automatic segmentation and recognition from a continuous signal. Zhao et al. [8] proposed iterative Multi-Output Random Forests for face analysis in images using a combination of three tasks namely Facial landmark detection, Head pose estimation and Facial expression recognition. Deep features have also been used for facial analysis. Razuri et al. [9] have extracted features from regions around eyes and mouth for recognizing the human emotions. Their idea was that information related to emotions could be captured by tracking the expressions around eyes and mouth region. The extracted features are then input into a feed-forward neural network trained by back-propagation for classification of emotions.

Although, facial expressions form an important cue, they alone are not sufficient to recognize emotions effectively. Loic et al. [7] used facial expressions, gestures and acoustic analysis of speech based features. In their work, they have used a Bayesian classifier to recognize one of the eight types of emotions (Anger, Despair, Interest, Pleasure, Sadness, Irritation, Joy and Pride). They presented uni-modal (trained separately with all three types of features), bi-modal (combine two modes together) and multi-modal (combine all three modes together). Among all combinations, they observed that multi-modal based classification yielded the best performance.

We propose two end-to-end trained deep learning models that use audio features and face images for recognizing first impressions. In the first model, we propose a Volumetric (3D) convolution based deep neural network for determining personality-traits. 3D convolution was also used by Ji et al. [10], although for the task of action recognition from videos of unconstrained settings. In the second model, we formulate an LSTM (Long Short Term Memory) based deep neural network for learning temporal patterns in the audio and visual features. Both the models concatenate the features extracted from audio and visual data in a later stage. This is in spirit of the observations made in some studies [7] that multi-modal classification yields superior performance.

Our contribution in this paper is two-fold. First, mining temporal patterns in audio and visual features is an important cue for recognizing first impressions effectively. Secondly, such patterns can be mined from a few frames selected in a stochastic manner rather than the complete video, and still predict the first impressions with good accuracy. The proposed methods have been ranked second on the ChaLearn LAP APA2016 challenge (first round) [11].

This paper is organized as follows. In Sect. 2, we describe the two models in detail and the steps followed to prepare the input data and features for the models. Section 3 describes the novel stochastic method of training and testing the networks. In Sect. 4, we discuss the Apparent Personality Analysis 2016: First Impressions Dataset, the evaluation protocol, the implementation details and the experimental results obtained in two phases of the competition. Section 5 concludes the paper providing future direction for the work.

2   Methodology

We propose two bi-modal deep neural network architectures that have two branches, one for encoding audio features and the other for visual features.

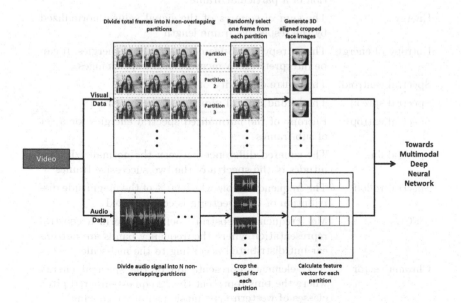

Fig. 1. Data pre-processing pipeline, where the face aligned images are extracted from image frames and spectral audio features are extracted from audio data.

Inputs to both the audio and visual branches of the model are generated after pre-processing the raw video data. Features extracted from both the branches are fused in a later stage of the model, while the complete network is trained end-to-end. In this section, we describe the pre-processing that was performed on the data and the architecture of models in detail.

2.1 Audio Data Pre-processing

Given a video, we extract its audio component and split the audio component into N non-overlapping partitions as shown in Fig. 1. From each individual partition, we extract "mean and standard deviation" of certain properties (Table 2) of audio signal. We use an open-source python based audio processing library called pyAudioAnalysis [12,13] for this purpose. The hand-crafted features are of 68 dimensions, which includes the mean and standard deviation of the following attributes:

2.2 Visual Data Pre-processing

The visual processing branch of the model takes as input, a set of 'N' 3D aligned segmented face images. We segment the face images to prevent the background

Table 2. Audio features extracted using pyAudioAnalysis [14]

Attribute name	Description
Zero crossing rate	The rate of sign-changes of the signal during the duration of a particular frame
Energy	The sum of squares of the signal values, normalized by the respective frame length
Entropy of energy	The entropy of sub-frames' normalized energies. It can be interpreted as a measure of abrupt changes
Spectral centroid	The centre of gravity of the spectrum
Spectral spread	The second central moment of the spectrum
Spectral entropy	Entropy of the normalized spectral energies for a set of sub-frames
Spectral flux	The squared difference between the normalized magnitudes of the spectra of the two successive frames
Spectral rolloff	The frequency below which 90 % of the magnitude distribution of the spectrum is concentrated
MFCCs	Mel Frequency Cepstral Coefficients form a cepstral representation where the frequency bands are not linear but distributed according to the mel-scale
Chroma vector	A 12-element representation of the spectral energy where the bins represent the 12 equal-tempered pitch classes of western-type music (semitone spacing)
Chroma deviation	The standard deviation of the 12 chroma coefficients

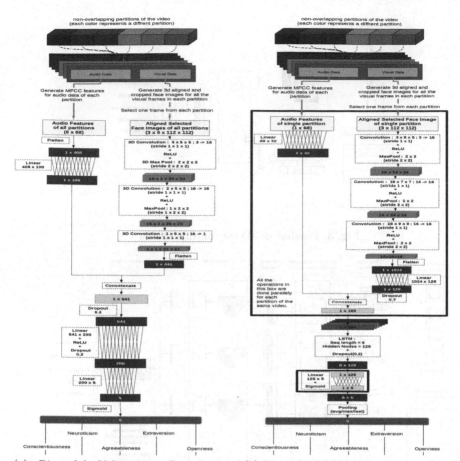

(a) Bi-modal Volumetric Convolutional Neural Network architecture

(b) Bi-modal LSTM Neural Network architecture

Fig. 2. Model architecture diagram

from affecting the predictions, which should rather depend only on the features of the face (gaze direction, movements of eye, lips, etc.). We use facial landmark detection and tracking to segment the faces. The landmark points are then aligned to fixed locations, which give us segmented face images that have also been aligned. We use an open-sourced C++ library OpenFace [15,16] for all the visual pre-processing tasks.

2.3 Model Architecture

We propose two models in our work. The models are shown in Fig. 2a and b respectively. We divide each video into N non-overlapping partitions. From each

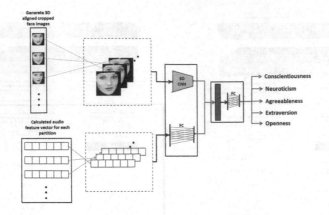

Fig. 3. Pipeline of 3D-convolution model

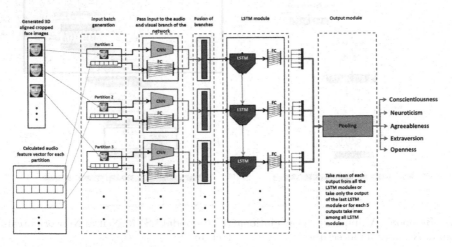

Fig. 4. Pipeline of LSTM model

of the N partitions, both audio and visual features are extracted (Fig. 1) and used as inputs to the models. Here, only the inter-partition variations are learned as temporal patterns, while the intra-partition variations are ignored. We do so, to handle redundancy in consecutive frames especially in high fps videos. As we can see in Figs. 3 and 4, the audio and visual features from each block are passed through consecutive layers of neural network. Now, in our first model, the temporal patterns across the N sequential partitions are learned using a 3D convolution module. While in the second model, we use an LSTM to learn the temporal patterns across the partitions. The kernel sizes and stride information are available in the Fig. 2. By empirical analysis, we fixed N as 6.

Volumetric (3D) Convolution Model: Our first model is inspired from the work of Ji et al. [10]. The architecture is shown in Fig. 2a and the pipeline is demonstrated in Fig. 3. The visual data processing branch learns the change in facial expressions from face aligned images using 3D convolution. At first, the 6 face aligned temporally ordered images of size $3 \times 112 \times 112$ are passed through a 3D convolution layer, followed by a ReLU and a 3D max-pooling layer. The 3D convolution as well as max-pooling are done in a volume comprised of X, Y and t dimensions. The resulting feature maps are in-turn passed through a second set of similar layers of 3D convolution, ReLU and 3D max-pooling but with different kernel sizes (refer to Fig. 2a for details about parameters). This is followed by another layer of 3D convolution, which result in a single feature map of size $1 \times 21 \times 21$ which is flattened to a 441 dimensional feature vector. Simultaneously, the audio-data processing branch gets a 6×68 dimensional feature vector which is reduced to a 100 dimensional vector using a fully connected layer. The feature vectors from audio and visual branches are concatenated and yields a 541 (100 from audio + 441 from visual data) dimensional feature vector, which is then input to a fully connected (FC) layer of 200 nodes and a ReLU layer, followed by another FC layer of 5 nodes which has the activation function as sigmoid. These 5 nodes represent the predicted values of the Big-Five Personality traits.

LSTM Based Model: We designed our second model to learn the task based on temporal relationship within the input. The architecture and pipeline of the model are shown in Figs. 2b and 4 respectively. We propose LSTM units to capture the temporal patterns of the input data to predict the personality traits. Each aligned face image is passed through a series of spatial convolution, ReLU and spatial max-pooling layers of varying kernel sizes (refer to Fig. 2b for details about parameters). The generated feature maps are flattened to get 1024 dimensional feature vector and it is connected to a fully connected layer of 128 nodes. Simultaneously, the audio-data (6 feature vectors of 68 dimension) is passed through a 32-node fully connected layer and reduced to 32-dimension. After these steps, the output feature vectors from audio and visual data processing branches are concatenated to yield 6 feature vectors of 160 dimension (32 dim of audio + 128 dim of visual data for each 6 partition) which are still maintained in temporal order. The extracted temporally ordered 6 feature vectors are then passed through an LSTM with output dimension of 128. The LSTM takes 6×160 dimensional input and outputs a sequence of 6 128-dimensional feature vector. The LSTM generates output for each time step and then, each output is passed through 5 dimensional fully-connected layer with sigmoid activation function. Thus, we get 6 outputs of predicted 5 personality traits. For each personality trait, we average the predicted value, output by all 6 LSTM output units. Thus we get a single prediction value for each of the Big Five personality traits.

3   Stochastic Training and Testing

According to Psychology research [2], it is observed that first impressions of unfamiliar faces can be formed even with exposure times as small as 100-ms. Their results suggest that predictions made with a 100-ms exposure correlated highly with judgments made in the absence of time constraints, suggesting that small exposure times were sufficient for participants to form an impression. On similar lines, we also hypothesize that deep models can learn effective representations for recognizing first impressions from a few randomly selected frames.

3.1 Stochastic Training

Training of the two proposed models is carried out using Stochastic Gradient Optimization (SGD) method. The parameters used for SGD are: learning rate $- 0.05$, weight decay $= 5 \times e^{-4}$, momentum $= 0.9$, batch size $= 128$, learning rate decay $= 1 \times e^{-4}$.

As mentioned earlier (Fig. 1), each raw video file is split into non-overlapping 6 partitions and the audio as well as visual features are extracted from each partition individually. We propose to train the models by using a combined feature set such that we take single face aligned image from each partition, as well as the pre-processed audio features from each partition. Particularly, in video data, since we are only using 1 frame from whole partition, there are multiple combinations of frames from each partition possible for training. Consider there are N partitions & F frames per partition and we intend to take a single frame from each partition, hence F^N combinations of frames are possible per video. We assume N as 6 and typically, F is in the range of ~ 75 (considering 30 fps and each video of 15 s). Training the model with 75^6 combinations of frames is an overkill. Empirically, we found that training only on several hundreds of combinations (typically ~ 500) is enough for the model to generalize for whole dataset.

Going with the above explanation, the 6 input frames (single frame from each partition) for model training is selected randomly by keeping temporal ordering in mind. At every epoch, the random selection will yield new input combination for each video. This stochastic way of training produces new sample at every epoch and "regularizes" the learning effectively, thus increasing the generalization of the model.

3.2 Testing

Testing the model also faces the same issue of exponential combination of frames per video. Empirically, we choose to use only a random subset (10 combinations) from total possible combinations and use the average of 10 evaluations as the Personality-traits recognition results. The validation and test results suggest that the model and evaluation method performs significantly better than the other submissions and the LSTM model stood at second place in the Final evaluation phase of competition.

4   Experiments and Results

In this section, we first briefly describe about the dataset and the evaluation protocol from our experiments. Then we provide the implementation details for our method and discuss the results.

4.1 Dataset: Apparent Personality Analysis (APA) - First Impressions

In our validation experiment, we use the ChaLearn LAP 2016 APA dataset provided by the challenge organizers [11]. This dataset has 6000 videos for training with ground truth Personality-traits, 2000 videos for validation without ground truth (performance is revealed on submission of predictions) and 2000 videos for test (Ground truth is not available until the competition is finished). Each video is of length 15 s and generally has 30 frames/second. The ground truth consists of fractional scores in the range between 0 to 1 for each of Big-Five Personality traits: Extraversion, Agreeableness, Conscientiousness, Neuroticism, Openness.

4.2 Evaluation Protocol

The evaluation is done in terms of Mean Average Accuracy.
The individual personality traits Average Accuracy is calculated as,

$$\text{Average Accuracy}_j = \frac{1}{N} \sum_{i=1}^{N} (1 - |Target_{ij} - y_{ij}|) \tag{1}$$

where $j = 1 \ldots 5$, N is the number of total videos, $Target_{ij}$ is the ground truth value for i^{th} video and j^{th} personality-trait, y_{ij} is the predicted value for i^{th} video and j^{th} personality-trait.

The Mean Average Accuracy between the predictions and the ground truth personality-traits values:

$$\text{Mean Average Accuracy} = \frac{1}{m} \sum_{j=1}^{m} (\text{Average accuracy}_j) \tag{2}$$

where m = 5 (the number of Personality Traits).

Note, that the maximum value of the Mean Average Accuracy, as well as Average Accuracy is equal to 1, which represents the best result and the minimum is equal to 0 representing the worst match.

4.3 Implementation Details

Both of the deep learning models are implemented using Torch [17] scientific computing framework. The training of 3D convolution based model takes 30 s per epoch and LSTM based model takes 3 min per epoch on a GeForce GTX Titan Black graphics card. The training of each individual model is done for up-to whole 1 day. We used only the ChaLearn LAP 2016 APA dataset [11] for training. The comparison of mean squared error(MSE) of both models during training is shown in Fig. 5. The source code files of both the training and final proposed prediction method are available in github[1] repository.

---

[1] Refer https://github.com/InnovArul/first-impressions for more information.

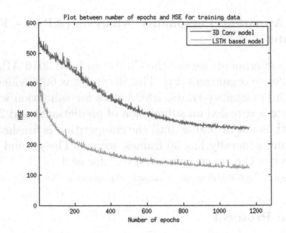

Fig. 5. Number of epochs vs. mean squared error (MSE) for individual models during training phase

Table 3. Evaluation during learning phase on ChaLearn LAP 2016 APA: first impressions challenge

	LSTM model	3D conv. based model
Accuracy	**0.913355**	0.912473
Extraversion	0.914548	0.915650
Agreeableness	0.915749	0.916123
Conscientiousness	0.913594	0.908370
Neuroticism	0.909814	0.909931
Openness	0.913069	0.912292

4.4 Development Phase

In the development phase of the APA2016 competition [11], only the training set ground truths were released and the methods were evaluated online by submitting the predictions on the validation videos to a server. The best performance of our models during development phase is shown in Table 3.

4.5 Test Phase

In the test phase of the APA2016 competition [11], the testing videos were released. The testing ground truths were kept secret and the teams were invited to submit their results on the testing videos. The organizers announced the final ranking after the test phase. The results are summarized in Table 4. The proposed LSTM model secured the second place in the leader-board and shown in bold font.

Table 4. Leaderboard of test-phase on ChaLearn LAP 2016 APA: first impressions challenge. Our entry is with **bold**

Rank	Team	Accuracy
1	NJU-LAMDA	0.912968
2	**evolgen (*LSTM model)**	**0.912063**
3	DCC	0.910933
4	ucas	0.909824
5	BU-NKU	0.909387
6	pandora	0.906275
7	Pilab	0.893602
8	Kaizoku	0.882571

4.6   Results and Discussion

The performance of CNN (3D convolution) based model and LSTM model can be seen from learning phase evaluation shown in Table 3:

The test phase leader-board standings is shown in the Table 4.

As we noticed from the Table 3, during learning phase, LSTM based model performs superior to 3D convolution based model. It maybe due to the fact that, LSTM is able to learn better temporal relationships than 3D convolution based approach. Also, the audio-features were not used to define temporal relationship in 3D convolution based model (only 3D face aligned images are used), but LSTM model used both audio and visual features to learn the temporal correspondences, which could have made it perform better. Because of these reasons, we chose LSTM model to be used for test phase: Our method secured second place in ChaLearn LAP 2016: APA challenge [11].

5   Conclusions and Future Works

In this work, we proposed two deep neural network based models that use audio and visual features for the task of First Impressions Recognition. These networks mine the temporal patterns that exist in a sequence of frames. It was also shown that such sequences can be small and selected in a stochastic manner respecting the temporal order. The proposed methods have been shown to yield excellent performance on the ChaLearn LAP APA2016 Challenge [11]. As deep neural networks are known for their representation and feature extracting ability, they can be used to learn the optimal representations without having to pre-process the data. Appearance and Pose features can also be explored to see if they improve the performance given by the proposed audio and visual features.

References

1. Wikipedia. Definition of psychological term First impression. https://en.wikipedia. org/wiki/First_impression_(psychology)
2. Willis, J., Todorov, A.: First impressions making up your mind after a 100-ms exposure to a face. Psychol. Sci. **17**(7), 592–598 (2006)
3. Cowie, R., Douglas-Cowie, E., Tsapatsoulis, N., Votsis, G., Kollias, S., Fellenz, W., Taylor, J.G.: Emotion recognition in human-computer interaction. IEEE Signal Process. Mag. **18**(1), 32–80 (2001)
4. Cohen, I., Garg, A., Huang, T.S., et al.: Emotion recognition from facial expressions using multilevel HMM. In: Neural Information Processing Systems, vol. 2. Citeseer (2000)
5. Cohen, I., Sebe, N., Garg, A., Chen, L.S., Huang, T.S.: Facial expression recognition from video sequences: temporal and static modeling. Comput. Vis. Image Underst. **91**(1), 160–187 (2003)
6. Kim, Y., Lee, H., Provost, E.M.: Deep learning for robust feature generation in audiovisual emotion recognition. In: 2013 IEEE International Conference on Acoustics, Speech and Signal Processing, pp. 3687–3691. IEEE (2013)
7. Kessous, L., Castellano, G., Caridakis, G.: Multimodal emotion recognition in speech-based interaction using facial expression, body gesture and acoustic analysis. J. Multimodal User Interfaces **3**(1), 33–48 (2010)
8. Zhao, X., Kim, T.K., Luo, W.: Unified face analysis by iterative multi-output random forests (2014)
9. Razuri, J.G., Sundgren, D., Rahmani, R., Moran Cardenas, A.: Automatic emotion recognition through facial expression analysis in merged images based on an artificial neural network (2013)
10. Ji, S., Xu, W., Yang, M., Yu, K.: 3D convolutional neural networks for human action recognition. IEEE Trans. Pattern Anal. Mach. Intell. **35**(1), 221–231 (2013)
11. Lopez, V.P., Chen, B., Places, A., Oliu, M., Corneanu, C., Baro, X., Escalante, H.J., Guyon, I., Escalera, S.: ChaLearn lap. 2016: first round challenge on first impressions - dataset and results. ChaLearn looking at people workshop on apparent personality analysis. In: ECCV Workshop Proceedings (2016)
12. Giannakopoulos, T.: pyAudioanAlysis: an open-source python library for audio signal analysis. PloS one **10**(12), e0144610 (2015)
13. Giannakopoulos, T.: pyAudioAnalysis. An open Python library that provides a wide range of audio-related functionalities. https://github.com/tyiannak/pyAudioAnalysis
14. Giannakopoulos, T.: pyAudioAnalysis. Features extracted using pyAudioAnalysis. https://github.com/tyiannak/pyAudioAnalysis/wiki/3.-Feature-Extraction
15. Baltru, T., Robinson, P., Morency, L.P., et al.: OpenFace: an open source facial behavior analysis toolkit. In: 2016 IEEE Winter Conference on Applications of Computer Vision (WACV), pp. 1–10. IEEE (2016)
16. Baltru, T., Robinson, P., Morency, L.P., et al.: OpenFace. A state-of-the art open source tool intended for facial landmark detection, head pose estimation, facial action unit recognition, and eye-gaze estimation. https://github.com/TadasBaltrusaitis/OpenFace
17. Collobert, R., Kavukcuoglu, K., Farabet, C.: Torch7: a matlab-like environment for machine learning. In: BigLearn, NIPS Workshop. Number EPFL-CONF-192376 (2011)

Deep Impression: Audiovisual Deep Residual Networks for Multimodal Apparent Personality Trait Recognition

Yağmur Güçlütürk[✉], Umut Güçlü, Marcel A.J. van Gerven,
and Rob van Lier

Donders Institute for Brain, Cognition and Behaviour, Radboud University,
Nijmegen, The Netherlands
{y.gucluturk,u.guclu,m.vangerven,r.vanlier}@donders.ru.nl

Abstract. Here, we develop an audiovisual deep residual network for multimodal apparent personality trait recognition. The network is trained end-to-end for predicting the Big Five personality traits of people from their videos. That is, the network does not require any feature engineering or visual analysis such as face detection, face landmark alignment or facial expression recognition. Recently, the network won the third place in the ChaLearn First Impressions Challenge with a test accuracy of 0.9109.

Keywords: Big five personality traits · Audiovisual · Deep neural network · Deep residual network · Multimodal

1 Introduction

Appearances influence what people think about the personality of other people, even without having any interaction with them. These judgments can be made very quickly - already after 100 ms [35]. Although some studies have shown that people are good at forming accurate first impressions about the personality traits of people after viewing their photographs or videos [4,21], it has also been shown that simply relying on the appearance does not always result in correct first impression judgments [22].

Several characteristics of people varying from clothing to facial expressions, contribute to the first impression judgments about personality [29]. For example, [30] has shown that the photographs of the same person taken with a different facial expression changes the judgments about the person's personality traits such as trustworthiness and extravertedness as well as other perceived characteristics such as attractiveness and intelligence. Furthermore, people are better at guessing other's personality traits if they find them attractive after short encounters with them [18]. The same study also showed that people form more positive first impressions about more attractive people.

Studies of personality prediction generally either deal with correctly recognizing the actual personality traits of people, which can be measured as

© Springer International Publishing Switzerland 2016
G. Hua and H. Jégou (Eds.): ECCV 2016 Workshops, Part III, LNCS 9915, pp. 349–358, 2016.
DOI: 10.1007/978-3-319-49409-8_28

self- or acquaintance-reports or apparent personality traits, which are the impressions about the personality of an unfamiliar individual [34]. Below we review the recent work in apparent personality prediction.

Most of the previous work on apparent personality modeling and prediction have been in the domain of paralanguage, i.e. speech, text, prosody, other vocalizations and fillers [34]. Conversations (both text and audio) [19] and speech clips [20,23] were the materials that were most commonly analyzed. In this domain, INTERSPEECH 2012 Speaker Trait Challenge [25] enabled a systematic comparison of computational methods by providing a dataset comprising audio data and extracted features. The competition had three sub-challenges for predicting the Big Five personality traits, likability and pathology of speakers.

Recently, prediction of apparent personality traits from social media content has become a challenge that attracted much attention in the field. For example [6,26] demonstrated that the images that the users "favorite" on Flickr enabled the prediction of both apparent and actual (self-assessed) personality traits of Flickr users. [32] looked at the influence of a large number of physical attributes (e.g. chin length, head size, posture) on people's impressions regarding approachability, youthful-attractiveness and dominance of them. They studied these influences based on people's impressions formed after looking at face photographs. They performed factor analysis to quantify the contribution of physical attributes and used these factors as inputs to a linear neural network to predict impressions. Their predictions were significantly correlated to the actual impression data.

Given that the exact facial expression [30] and the posture [32] of the person in a photograph influences the first impression judgments about that person, as well as the importance of paralinguistic information in impression formation [19], continuous audio-visual data seems to be a suitable medium to study first impressions. In a series of studies using YouTube video blogs (vlogs) [1–3,29], researchers showed that this is indeed the case. Furthermore, [5] showed that audiovisual annotations along with audiovisual cues enabled the best prediction performance for their regression models compared to either using only either one of them.

At the same time, deep neural networks [16,24] in general and deep residual networks [11] in particular have achieved state-of-the-art results in many computer vision tasks. For example, [11] won the first places in the object detection task and the object localization task at the ImageNet Large Scale Visual Recognition Challenge 2015[1] with their seminal work that introduced deep residual networks. Furthermore, deep residual networks have been successfully used in a variety of other computer vision tasks ranging from style transfer [14] and image super-resolution [14] to semantic segmentation [7] and face hallucination [9].

Recently, [33] suggested that deep neural networks can be used for personality trait recognition because of the hierarchical organization of the personality traits [36]. Following this line of reasoning as well as the recent success of deep residual networks, we develop an audiovisual deep residual network for multimodal

---

[1] http://image-net.org/.

personality trait recognition. The network is trained end-to-end for predicting the apparent Big Five personality traits of people from their videos. That is, the network does not require any feature engineering or visual analysis such as face detection, face landmark alignment or facial expression recognition.

2   Methods

2.1   Architecture

Figure 1 shows an illustration of the network architecture. The network comprises an auditory stream of a 17 layer deep residual network, a visual stream of another 17 layer deep residual network and an audiovisual stream of a fully-connected layer.

The auditory stream and the visual stream are similar to the first 17 layers of the 18 layer deep residual network in [11]. That is, each stream comprises one convolutional layer and eight residual blocks of two convolutional layers. The convolutional layers are followed by batch normalization [13] (all layers), rectified linear units (all layers), max pooling (first layer) and global average pooling (last layer). In the residual blocks that do not change the dimensionality of their inputs, identity shortcut connections are used. In the remaining residual blocks, convolutional shortcut connections are used. In contrast to [11], the number of convolutional kernels are halved.

Similar to [8], the difference between the auditory stream and the visual stream is that inputs, convolutional/pooling kernels and strides of the auditory stream are one-dimensional whereas those of the visual stream are two-dimensional if the number of channels are ignored. That is:

- An $n^2 \times 1 \times 1$ input of the auditory stream corresponds to an $n \times n \times m$ input of the visual stream.
- An $n^2 \times 1 \times m/n^2 \times 1$ convolutional/pooling kernel of the auditory stream corresponds to an $n \times n \times m/n \times n$ convolutional/pooling kernel of the visual stream.
- An $n^2 \times 1$ stride of the auditory stream corresponds to an $n \times n$ stride of the visual stream.

where m is the number of channels.

Outputs of the auditory stream and the visual stream are merged in an audiovisual stream. The audiovisual stream comprises a fully-connected layer. The fully-connected layer is followed by hyperbolic tangent units. Outputs of the audiovisual stream are scaled to $[0, 1]$.

2.2   Training

We used Adam [15] with initial $\alpha = 0.0002$, $\beta_1 = 0.5$, $\beta_2 = 0.999$, $\epsilon = 10^{-8}$ and mini-batch size $= 32$ to train the network by iteratively minimizing the mean absolute error loss function between the target traits and the predicted traits

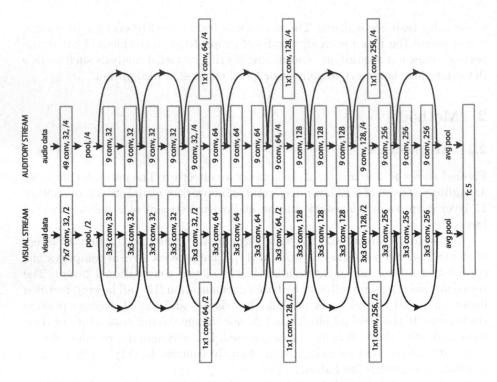

Fig. 1. Illustration of the network architecture.

for 900 epochs. We initialized the biases/weights as in [10] and reduced α by a factor of 10 after every 300 epochs. Each training video clip was processed as follows:

- The audio data and the visual data of the video clip are extracted.
- A random 50176 sample temporal crop of the audio data is fed into the auditory stream. The activities of the penultimate layer of the auditory stream are temporally pooled.
- A random 224 pixels × 224 pixels spatial crop of a random frame of the visual data is randomly flipped in the left/right direction and fed into the visual stream. The activities of the penultimate layer of the visual stream are spatially pooled.
- The pooled activities of the auditory stream and the visual stream are concatenated and fed into the fully-connected layer.
- The fully-connected layer outputs five continuous prediction values between the range [0, 1] corresponding to each trait for the video clip.

2.3   Validation/Test

Each validation/test video clip was processed as follows:

- The audio data and the visual data of the video clip are extracted.

- The entire audio data are fed into the auditory stream. The activities of the penultimate layer of the auditory stream are temporally pooled (see below note).
- The entire visual data are fed into the visual stream one frame at a time. The activities of the penultimate layer of the visual stream are spatiotemporally pooled (see below note).
- The pooled activities of the auditory stream and the visual stream are concatenated and fed into the fully-connected layer.
- The fully-connected layer outputs five continuous prediction values between the range [0, 1] corresponding to each trait for the video clip.

It should be noted that the network can process video clips of arbitrary sizes since the penultimate layers of the auditory stream and the visual stream are followed by global average pooling.

3   Results

We evaluated the network on the dataset that was released as part of the ChaLearn First Impressions Challenge[2] [17]. The dataset consists of 10000 15-second-long video clips that were drawn from YouTube[3], of which 6000 were used for training, 2000 were used for validation and 2000 were used for test. The video clips were annotated with the Big Five personality traits (i.e. openness to experience, conscientiousness, extraversion, agreeableness, and neuroticism) by Amazon Mechanical Turk[4] workers. Each trait was represented with a value between the range [0, 1].

The video clips were preprocessed by temporally resampling the audio data to 16000 Hz as well as spatiotemporally the video data to 456 pixels × 256 pixels and 25 frames per second.

We implemented the network in Chainer [31] with CUDA and cuDNN. Most of the processing took place on a single chip of an Nvidia Tesla K80 GPU accelerator[5]. Processing took approximately 50 ms per training example and 2.7 s per validation/test example on a single chip of an Nvidia Tesla K80 GPU accelerator. Figure 2 shows five validation examples and the corresponding predictions.

Accuracy was defined as 1 - mean absolute error. We report the validation accuracy of the network after 300, 600 and 900 epochs of training (Table 1). Average validation accuracy of the network increased as a function of number of epochs of training with the highest average validation accuracy of 0.9121. We report also the test accuracy of the network after 900 epochs of training, which won the third place in the challenge, and compare it with those of the models that won the first two places in the challenge (Table 2).

---

[2] http://gesture.chalearn.org.
[3] http://www.youtube.com/.
[4] http://www.mturk.com/.
[5] The implementation is available at https://github.com/yagguc/deep_impression.

Table 1. Validation accuracies of the challenge model after 300, 600 and 900 epochs of training.

Epoch	Validation accuracy					
	Average	Openness	Agreeableness	Conscientiousness	Neuroticism	Extraversion
300	0.906461	0.905451	0.911128	0.902121	0.907886	0.905721
600	0.911929	0.911924	**0.915610**	0.911717	**0.909891**	**0.910503**
900	**0.912132**	**0.911983**	0.915466	**0.913077**	0.909705	0.910429

Table 2. Test accuracies of the models that won the first three places in the challenge.

Rank	Test accuracy					
	Average	Openness	Agreeableness	Conscientiousness	Neuroticism	Extraversion
1 [37]	**0.912968037541**	**0.91237757**	**0.91257098**	**0.91663743**	**0.9099631**	0.91329111
2 [28]	0.912062557634	0.91167725	0.91186694	0.91185413	0.90991703	**0.91499745**
3 (ours)	0.910932616931	0.91108539	0.91019226	0.91377735	0.90890031	0.91070778
			. . .			
10	0.875888740066	0.87026111	0.88423626	0.87270874	0.87526563	0.87697196

Fig. 2. Example thumbnails of the videos of five people and the corresponding predicted personality traits. Each trait takes a value between [0, 1]. Each color represents a trait. From left to right: Openness, agreeableness, conscientiousness, neuroticism and extraversion.

4   Post Challenge Models

For completeness, we briefly report our preliminary work on two models that we have evaluated after the end of the challenge.

First, we separately fine-tuned the original DNN after 300 epochs of training for each trait. Everything about the fine-tuned DNNs (i.e. architecture, training and validation/test) were the same with the original DNN except for their fully-connected layers that output one value rather than five values.

Table 3. Validation accuracies of the challenge model and the post challenge models.

Model	Validation accuracy					
	Average	Openness	Agreeableness	Conscientiousness	Neuroticism	Extraversion
DNN	0.912132	**0.911983**	0.915466	0.913077	**0.909705**	0.910429
5 × DNN	0.911987	0.911522	0.915413	0.913211	0.909062	0.910727
DNN + RNN	**0.912158**	0.911676	**0.915761**	**0.913300**	0.909056	**0.910996**

Second, we trained a recurrent neural network (RNN) on top of the original network. The RNN comprised two layers of 512 long short-term memory units [12] and one layer of five linear units. At each time point, the RNN took as input the layer 5 features of a second-long video clip and the output of the RNN was the predicted traits. Dropout [27] was used to regularize the hidden layers.

We used Adam to train the model by iteratively minimizing the mean absolute error loss function between the target traits and the predicted traits at each time point. Backpropagation was truncated after every 15 time points. Once the model was trained, the predicted traits were averaged over the entire video clip.

Table 3 shows the validation accuracy of the post challenge models. While the post challenge models failed to outperform the challenge model to a large extent, we strongly believe that variants thereof have the potential to do so and will be the subject matter of future work.

5   Conclusion

In this study, we presented our approach and results that won the third place in the ChaLearn First Impressions Challenge. Summarizing, we developed and trained an audiovisual deep residual network for predicting the apparent personality traits of people in an end-to-end manner. This approach enabled us to obtain very high performance for all traits while exploiting the similarities between the organization of the personality traits and the deep neural networks in terms of the hierarchical organization and circumventing extensive analyses for identifying/designing relevant features for the task of apparent personality traits prediction. Our results demonstrate the potential of deep neural networks in the field of automatic (perceived) personality prediction. Future work will focus on the extensions of the current work with recurrent neural networks and language models as well as identifying the factors that drive first impressions.

References

1. Biel, J.I., Aran, O., Gatica-Pere, D.: You are known by how you vlog: personality impressions and nonverbal behavior in youtube. In: International Conference on Weblogs and Social Media (2011)
2. Biel, J.I., Gatica-Perez, D.: The youtube lens: crowdsourced personality impressions and audiovisual analysis of vlogs. IEEE Trans. Multimed. **15**(1), 41–55 (2013). http://dx.doi.org/10.1109/TMM.2012.2225032

3. Biel, J.I., Teijeiro-Mosquera, L., Gatica-Perez, D.: FaceTube. In: Proceedings of the 14th ACM International Conference on Multimodal Interaction. Association for Computing Machinery (ACM) (2012). http://dx.doi.org/10.1145/2388676.2388689

4. Borkenau, P., Liebler, A.: Trait inferences: surces of validity at zero acquaintance. J. Pers. Soci. Psychol. **62**(4), 645–657 (1992). http://dx.doi.org/10.1037/0022-3514.62.4.645

5. Celiktutan, O., Gunes, H.: Automatic prediction of impressions in time and across varying context: personality, attractiveness and likeability. In: IEEE Transaction on Affective Computing, p. 1 (2016). http://dx.doi.org/10.1109/TAFFC.2015.2513401

6. Cristani, M., Vinciarelli, A., Segalin, C., Perina, A.: Unveiling the multimedia unconscious. In: Proceedings of the 21st ACM International Conference on Multimedia. Association for Computing Machinery (ACM) (2013). http://dx.doi.org/10.1145/2502081.2502280

7. Dai, J., He, K., Sun, J.: Instance-aware semantic segmentation via multi-task network cascades. CoRR abs/1512.04412 (2015)

8. Güçlü, U., Thielen, J., Hanke, M., van Gerven, M.A.J.: Brains on beats. CoRR abs/1606.02627 (2016)

9. Güçlütürk, Y., Güçlü, U., van Lier, R., van Gerven, M.A.J.: Convolutional sketch inversion. CoRR abs/1606.03073 (2016)

10. He, K., Zhang, X., Ren, S., Sun, J.: Spatial pyramid pooling in deep convolutional networks for visual recognition. CoRR abs/1406.4729 (2014)

11. He, K., Zhang, X., Ren, S., Sun, J.: Deep residual learning for image recognition. CoRR abs/1512.03385 (2015)

12. Hochreiter, S., Schmidhuber, J.: Long short-term memory. Neural Comput. **9**(8), 1735–1780 (1997). http://dx.doi.org/10.1162/neco.1997.9.8.1735

13. Ioffe, S., Szegedy, C.: Batch normalization: accelerating deep network training by reducing internal covariate shift. CoRR abs/1502.03167 (2015)

14. Johnson, J., Alahi, A., Fei-Fei, L.: Perceptual losses for real-time style transfer and super-resolution. CoRR abs/1603.08155 (2016)

15. Kingma, D., Ba, J.: Adam: a method for stochastic optimization. CoRR abs/1412.6980 (2014)

16. LeCun, Y., Bengio, Y., Hinton, G.: Deep learning. Nature **521**(7553), 436–444 (2015). http://dx.doi.org/10.1038/nature14539

17. Lopez, V.P., Chen, B., Places, A., Oliu, M., Corneanu, C., Baro, X., Escalante, H.J., Guyon, I., Escalera, S.: ChaLearn LaP 2016: first round challenge on first impressions - dataset and results. In: ChaLearn Looking at People Workshop on Apparent Personality Analysis, ECCV Workshop proceedings. Springer Science + Business Media, Berlin (2016, in press)

18. Lorenzo, G.L., Biesanz, J.C., Human, L.J.: What is beautiful is good and more accurately understood: physical attractiveness and accuracy in first impressions of personality. Psychol. Sci. **21**(12), 1777–1782 (2010). http://dx.doi.org/10.1177/0956797610388048

19. Mairesse, F., Walker, M.A., Mehl, M.R., Moore, R.K.: Using linguistic cues for the automatic recognition of personality in conversation and text. J. Artif. Intell. Res. **30**(1), 457–500 (2007). http://dl.acm.org/citation.cfm?id=1622637.1622649

20. Mohammadi, G., Vinciarelli, A.: Automatic personality perception: prediction of trait attribution based on prosodic features extended abstract. In: 2015 International Conference on Affective Computing and Intelligent Interaction (ACII). Institute of Electrical & Electronics Engineers (IEEE), September 2015. http://dx.doi.org/10.1109/ACII.2015.7344614

21. Naumann, L.P., Vazire, S., Rentfrow, P.J., Gosling, S.D.: Personality judgments based on physical appearance. Pers. Soc. Psychol. Bull. **35**(12), 1661–1671 (2009). http://dx.doi.org/10.1177/0146167209346309
22. Olivola, C.Y., Todorov, A.: Fooled by first impressions? Reexamining the diagnostic value of appearance-based inferences. J. Exp. Soc. Psychol. **46**(2), 315–324 (2010). http://dx.doi.org/10.1016/j.jesp.2009.12.002
23. Polzehl, T., Moller, S., Metze, F.: Automatically assessing personality from speech. In: 2010 IEEE Fourth International Conference on Semantic Computing. Institute of Electrical & Electronics Engineers (IEEE), September 2010. http://dx.doi.org/10.1109/ICSC.2010.41
24. Schmidhuber, J.: Deep learning in neural networks: an overview. Neural Netw. **61**, 85–117 (2015). http://dx.doi.org/10.1016/j.neunet.2014.09.003
25. Schuller, B., Steidl, S., Batliner, A., Nöth, E., Vinciarelli, A., Burkhardt, F., van Son, R., Weninger, F., Eyben, F., Bocklet, T., Mohammadi, G., Weiss, B.: A survey on perceived speaker traits: personality, likability, pathology, and the first challenge. Comput. Speech Lang. **29**(1), 100–131 (2015). http://dx.doi.org/10.1016/j.csl.2014.08.003
26. Segalin, C., Perina, A., Cristani, M., Vinciarelli, A.: The pictures we like are our image: continuous mapping of favorite pictures into self-assessed and attributed personality traits. In: IEEE Transactions on Affective Computing, p. 1 (2016). http://dx.doi.org/10.1109/TAFFC.2016.2516994
27. Srivastava, N., Hinton, G., Krizhevsky, A., Sutskever, I., Salakhutdinov, R.: Dropout: a simple way to prevent neural networks from overfitting. J. Mach. Learn. Res. **15**, 1929–1958 (2014)
28. Subramaniam, A., Patel, V., Mishra, A., Balasubramanian, P., Mittal, A.: Bimodal first impressions recognition using temporally ordered deep audio and stochastic visual features. In: ChaLearn Looking at People Workshop on Apparent Personality Analysis, ECCV Workshop proceedings. Springer Science + Business Media, Berlin (2016, in press)
29. Teijeiro-Mosquera, L., Biel, J.I., Alba-Castro, J.L., Gatica-Perez, D.: What your face vlogs about: expressions of emotion and big-five traits impressions in YouTube. IEEE Trans. Affective Comput. **6**(2), 193–205 (2015). http://dx.doi.org/10.1109/TAFFC.2014.2370044
30. Todorov, A., Porter, J.M.: Misleading first impressions: different for different facial images of the same person. Psychol. Sci. **25**(7), 1404–1417 (2014). http://dx.doi.org/10.1177/0956797614532474
31. Tokui, S., Oono, K., Hido, S., Clayton, J.: Chainer: a next-generation open source framework for deep learning. In: Workshop on Machine Learning Systems at Neural Information Processing Systems (2015)
32. Vernon, R.J.W., Sutherland, C.A.M., Young, A.W., Hartley, T.: Modeling first impressions from highly variable facial images. Proc. Natl. Acad. Sci. **111**(32), E3353–E3361 (2014). http://dx.doi.org/10.1073/pnas.1409860111
33. Vinciarelli, A., Mohammadi, G.: More personality in personality computing. IEEE Trans. Affect. Comput. **5**(3), 297–300 (2014). http://dx.doi.org/10.1109/TAFFC.2014.2341252
34. Vinciarelli, A., Mohammadi, G.: A survey of personality computing. IEEE Trans. Affect. Comput. **5**(3), 273–291 (2014). http://dx.doi.org/10.1109/TAFFC.2014.2330816
35. Willis, J., Todorov, A.: First impressions: making up your mind after a 100-ms exposure to a face. Psychol. Sci. **17**(7), 592–598 (2006). http://dx.doi.org/10.1111/j.1467-9280.2006.01750.x

36. Wright, A.G.: Current directions in personality science and the potential for advances through computing. IEEE Trans. Affect. Comput. 5(3), 292–296 (2014). http://dx.doi.org/10.1109/TAFFC.2014.2332331
37. Zhang, C.L., Zhang, H., Wei, X.S., Wu, J.: Deep bimodal regression for apparent personality analysis. In: ChaLearn Looking at People Workshop on Apparent Personality Analysis, ECCV Workshop proceedings. Springer Science + Business Media (2016, in press)

Deep Learning for Facial Action Unit Detection Under Large Head Poses

Zoltán Tősér[1], László A. Jeni[2(✉)], András Lőrincz[1], and Jeffrey F. Cohn[2,3]

[1] Faculty of Informatics, Eötvös Loránd University, Budapest, Hungary
{toserzoltan,lorincz}@inf.elte.hu
[2] Robotics Institute, Carnegie Mellon University, Pittsburgh, PA, USA
laszlojeni@cmu.edu
[3] Department of Psychology, The University of Pittsburgh, Pittsburgh, PA, USA
jeffcohn@pitt.edu

Abstract. Facial expression communicates emotion, intention, and physical state, and regulates interpersonal behavior. Automated face analysis (AFA) for the detection, synthesis, and understanding of facial expression is a vital focus of basic research with applications in behavioral science, mental and physical health and treatment, marketing, and human-robot interaction among other domains. In previous work, facial action unit (AU) detection becomes seriously degraded when head orientation exceeds 15° to 20°. To achieve reliable AU detection over a wider range of head pose, we used 3D information to augment video data and a deep learning approach to feature selection and AU detection. Source video were from the BP4D database (n = 41) and the FERA test set of BP4D-extended (n = 20). Both consist of naturally occurring facial expression in response to a variety of emotion inductions. In augmented video, pose ranged between −18° and 90° for yaw and between −54° and 54° for pitch angles. Obtained results for action unit detection exceeded state-of-the-art, with as much as a 10 % increase in F_1 measures.

Keywords: Deep learning · Facial action unit detection · Pose dependence

1 Introduction

The face is one of the most powerful channels of nonverbal communication [3,5]. Facial expression provides cues about emotion, intention, alertness, pain, personality, regulates interpersonal behavior [4], and communicates psychiatric [8] and biomedical status [10] among other functions.

There has been increasing interest in automated facial expression analysis within the computer vision and machine learning communities. Several applications for related technologies exist: distracted driver detection [27], emotional response measurement for advertising [23,25], and human-robot collaboration [2] are just some possibilities.

© Springer International Publishing Switzerland 2016
G. Hua and H. Jégou (Eds.): ECCV 2016 Workshops, Part III, LNCS 9915, pp. 359–371, 2016.
DOI: 10.1007/978-3-319-49409-8_29

Given the time-consuming nature of manual facial expression coding and the alluring possibilities of the aforementioned applications, recent research has pursued computerized systems capable of automatically analyzing facial expressions. The dominant approach adopted by these researchers has been to identify a number of fiduciary points on the face, extract hand-crafted or learned features that can characterize the appearance of the skin, and train classifiers in a supervised manner to detect the absence or presence of expressions.

Recently, deep learning based solutions have been proposed for coding holistic facial expressions and facial actions units. Li et al. [21] used a convolutional neural network (CNN) based deep representation of facial 3D geometric and 2D photometric attributes for recognizing holistic facial expressions. Liu et al. [22] proposed an Action Unit aware deep architecture to learn local appearance variations on the face and constructed a group-wise sub-network to code facial expressions. Xu et al. [28] explored transfer learning of high-level features from face identification data to holistic facial expression recognition. Only recently did Jaiswal and Valstar [12] propose a deep learning approach for recognizing facial action units under uncontrolled conditions. Action Units were coded using a memory network that jointly learns shape, appearance and dynamics in a deep manner.

Even though significant progress has been made [7], the current state-of-the-art science is still limited in several key respects. Stimuli to elicit spontaneous facial actions have been highly controlled and camera orientation has been frontal with little or no variation in head pose. Head motion and orientation to the camera are important if AU detection is to be accomplished in social settings where facial expressions often co-occur with head motion [1,17]. As the head pose moves away from frontal, parts of the face may become self-occluded and the classifier's ability to measure expressions degrades. Here, we study the efficiency of a novel deep learning method for AU detection under large head poses.

This paper advances two main novelties:

AU Detection under Large Head Poses with 3D Augmentation. In our work we use the BP4D spontaneous dataset and its extension detailed in Sect. 2.2. An augmented dataset has been created using the 3D information and renderings of the faces with broad range of yaw and pitch rotations. We show that performance is high for the networks trained around different pose directions opening the door for a number of useful applications.

Selective Gradient Descent Optimization. Threshold performance metrics (such as the F_1 score) are piecewise-constant functions and including them directly in the CNN cost function would degrade the convergence of the optimization method. In our algorithm, we combined gradient descent with selective methods to overcome this issue. This approach results in a small but highly effective network that outperforms the more complex state-of-the-art systems.

The paper is organized as follows. The method section (Sect. 2) contains the overview of the architecture (Sect. 2.1), the descriptions about database (Sect. 2.2), its extension (Sect. 2.3), the facial landmark tracking method

(Sect. 2.4) and the deep learning components (Sect. 2.5). These descriptions are followed by our results (Sect. 3) and the related discussion (Sect. 4). We conclude in the last section (Sect. 5).

2   Methods

2.1   Architecture

The main steps of pre-processing, such as face detection, mesh fitting, pose estimation are depicted in Fig. 1. Details are to follow below.

2.2   BP4D-Spontaneous Dataset

We used the BP4D-Spontaneous dataset [31] from the FERA 2015 Challenge [26]. This database includes digital video of 41 participants (56.1 % female, 49.1 % white, ages 18–29). These individuals were recruited from the departments of psychology and computer science and from the school of engineering at Binghamton University. All participants gave informed consent to the procedures and permissible uses of their data. Participants sat approximately 51 in. in front of a Di3D dynamic face capturing system during a series of eight emotion elicitation tasks. Target emotional expressions include anxiety, surprise, embarrassment, fear, pain, anger, and disgust. Example tasks include being surprised by a loud sound, submerging a hand in ice water, and smelling rotten meat. For each task, the 20-second segment with the highest AU density was identified; this segment then was coded for AU onset (start) and offset (end) by certified and reliable FACS coders.

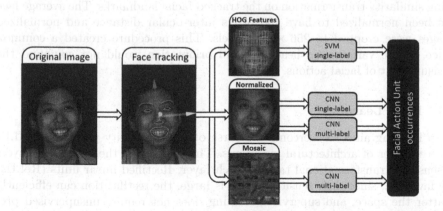

Fig. 1. Overview of the system. The original image underwent face tracking and was pre-processed in three different ways; Histogram of Gradients (HoG), similarity normalized (scaled and cropped), and cut and put together from patches around landmark positions (Mosaic). Training methods included Support Vector Machine (SVM), Convolutional Neural Networks (CNN) in single and multi-label versions.

The FERA 2015 Challenge [26] employed the 41 subjects from BP4D - Spontaneous dataset [31] as a training set. In this paper we refer this subset as "Train" set. Additional videos from 20 subjects were collected using the same setup and were used for testing in the challenge [26]. In this paper we refer this subset as "Test" set.

2.3 Database Extension

The subjects in the BP4D-Spontaneous dataset exhibit only a moderate level of head movements in the video sequences. The dataset [31] comes with frame-level high-resolution 3D models. To validate the proposed method on larger viewpoint angles, an augmented dataset has been created using the 3D information and renderings of the faces with different yaw and pitch rotations. We used all the FACS coded data to synthesize the rotated views.

2.4 Facial Landmark Tracking and Face Normalization

The first step in automatically detecting AUs was to locate the face and facial landmarks. Landmarks refer to points that define the shape of permanent facial features, such as the eyes and lips. This step was accomplished using the ZFace tracker [14,15], which is a generic tracker that requires no individualized training to track facial landmarks of persons it has never seen before. It locates the two- and three-dimensional coordinates of main fiducial landmarks in each image. These landmarks correspond to important facial points such as the eye and mouth corners, the tip of the nose, and the eyebrows. The moderate level of rigid head motion exhibited by the subjects in the BP4D-Spontaneous dataset was minimized as follows: facial images were warped to the average pose and face using similarity transformation on the tracked facial landmarks. The average face has been normalized to have 100 pixels inter-ocular distance and normalized images were cropped to 256 × 256 pixels. This procedure created a common space, where variation in head size and orientation would not confound the measurement of facial actions.

2.5 Deep Learning

Deep learning aims to overcome the curse of dimensionality problem of MLPs via a number of architectural inventions. The increase of the number of layers lessens the transformational tasks of each layer. Rectified linear units (ReLUs) are favoured, since their sensitive range is large, the rectification can efficiently shatter the space, and supervised training does not require unsupervised pre-training (see [9] and the references therein).

Layers of the Network. Convolutional layers make another efficient innovation. They are particularly useful for images. One can view each layer as a set of trainable template matchings [6]. It has the following attractive properties:

(a) The templates (also called filters) can be matched at each pixel of the image relatively quickly due to the convolution operation itself [20]. The result for each filter is called the feature map. (b) While the number of neurons can be large, still the number of variables, the weights, is kept low, saving in memory requirements and decreasing the curse of dimensionality problem. (c) Each convolutional layer may be followed by a subsampling layer. The role of this step is to decrease the number of units that scale as the product of the dimension of the input of that layer and the number of filters. Max-pooling that solicits the largest response in each pooling region is one of the preferred methods. The effective result of pooling is that the precision of the feature map degrades, which is nicely compensated by the number of feature maps and the option of further convolutional processing steps without explosion in the number of units. Subsampling also reduces overfitting. For more details, see [19] and the references therein.

Convolutional networks typically add densely connected layers after the convolutional layers, often made of ReLUs. Our architecture is sketched in Fig. 2.

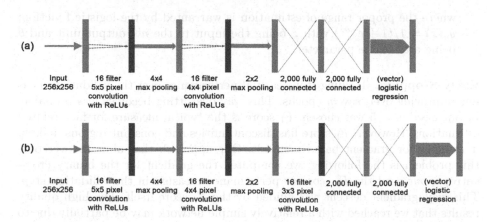

Fig. 2. Deep neural network, main components: convolutional layers with ReLUs (CL), pooling layers (PL), fully connected layers (FC), output layer with logistic regression (OL). There are two versions. (a): CL-PL-CL-PL-FC-FC-OL, (b): additional CL between the second PL and the first FC layer.

We used typical regularization, stabilization, early stopping, and local minima avoiding procedures [24] with a reasonably small network and we found that larger networks would not improve performance considerably. The parameters and some procedures of the architecture are as follows:

(a) The dimension of the input layer is 256×256. The original three channel color images were converted to a single grayscale channel and the values were scaled between 0 and 1.
(b) The first and second convolutional cascades have 16 filters each, with 5×5 in the first and 4×4 pixels in the second cascade. The stride was 1 in both cases. Max pooling was 4×4 and 2×2 applied with a stride of 4 and 2,

respectively. Occasionally a third convolutional layer with 16 filters of 3×3 pixels each was added when the representation power of the architecture was questioned (Fig. 2).

(c) There are two densely connected layers of 2,000 ReLU units in each.

(d) The output is a sigmoid layer for the action units. Special procedures include dropout before the two dense and the sigmoid layers with 50 % rate. Gradient training is controlled by Adamax (see later). Minibatch size is 500.

(e) The cost function to be minimized has two components, the sum of two terms, a regularizing ℓ_2 norm for the weights and the binary cross-entropy cost on the outputs of the network. This latter takes the average of all cross entropies in the sample: assume that we have $1 \leq n \leq N$ samples with binary labels $y_n \in \{-1, +1\}$ and network responses $\hat{y}_n$ for all n. The loss function is

$$J(\hat{y}_1, \ldots, \hat{y}_n) = \frac{1}{N} \sum_{n=1}^{N} y_n \log \hat{y}_n + (1 - y_n) \log(1 - \hat{y}_n). \tag{1}$$

where the proper range of estimation is warranted by the logistic function: $\hat{y}_n(z) = 1/(1 + e^{-\theta z})$ with z being the input to the nth output unit and θ being a trainable parameter.

Early Stopping. Training stops early if performance over the validation set is not improving over, say m epochs. This way overfitting becomes less probable. In our case, $m = 5$ was chosen. F_1 score is the typical measure for face related estimations. However, F_1 score has discontinuities and constant regions making it dubious for gradient based methods. Our approach that aims to overcome this problem is the following: we computed the gradient for the binary cross-entropy, *but* used the F_1 score as performance measure in the validation step. This way, gradient descent was guided by the F_1 score itself. The high quality results that we reached with a relatively simple network may be partially due to this procedure.

Cross-Validation. All the results and methods reported on the "Train" set have been validated with a 10-fold, subject-independent cross-validation. In the other experiments we trained on the "Train" set and reported performance measures on the "Test" set, following the challenge protocol [26].

Details of the Backpropagation Algorithm. Beyond the advances of GPU technology and deep learning architectures, error backpropagation also underwent fast and efficient changes. We used one of the most recent methods called Adamax [18]. It is a version of the Adam algorithm, a first-order gradient-based optimization, designed for stochastic objective functions exploiting adaptive estimates of lower-order moments. Adam estimates the ℓ_2 norm of the current and past gradients. If the gradients are small, the step size is made larger; inverse proportionality is applied. Adamax generalizes the ℓ_2 norm to ℓ_p norm and suggests to take the $p \to \infty$ limit. For more details, see [18].

Applied Software. There are many implementations of deep learning, mostly based on Python or C++. For a comprehensive list of software tools, today, the link http://deeplearning.net/software_links/ is a good starting point. We used Lasagne, a lightweight library built on top of Theano. Theano (http://deeplearning.net/software/theano) has been developed by the Montreal Institute for Learning Algorithms. It is a symbolic expression compiler that works both on CPU and on GPU and it is written in Python.

3 Results

First, we evaluated the performance on the FERA Train set, employing a 10-fold, subject independent CV. According to Table 1, HoG based SVM is the best for AU14 and AU15, and performance is superior for AU15. The representation at around the decision surface seems superior for these AUs. For the other AUs, SNI based CNNs with single AU classification are better. Multi-label classification is somewhat worse for almost all AUs, but let us note that these evaluations are faster, time scales linearly with the number of AUs for the single AU case.

In the next experiment we trained the system on the FERA 2015 Train set, and tested it on the Test set. The AU base-rates are significantly different on these subsets [26] and F_1 score is attenuated by skewed distributions [13]. For this reason we report the degree of skew, F_1 score, its skew normalized version ($F_1^{s.n.}$) [13], and area under the receiver operating characteristic (ROC) curves. The AUC values are shown in Table 2 for the FERA BP4D test set, where skew parameters range between 1 and 20.

Head pose has three main angles, roll, yaw and pitch. Roll can be compensated in the frontal view by the normalization step. The case is more complex for non-frontal views. We studied yaw and pitch angles around the frontal view. Yaw is symmetric in this case and we show data for $(-18°, +18°)$ ranges around head poses 0, 18, 36, 54 and 72 degrees that covers the full frontal–to–profile view range. Angle dependence is relatively large for AU4, AU15, and AU23, but the mean F_1 score is a weak function of the head pose angle (Fig. 3).

We studied the asymmetric pitch around the frontal view for $(-18°, +18°)$ ranges around -36, -18, $+18$, and $+36$ degrees. The mean F_1 score is also a

Table 1. F_1 measures on the FERA BP4D Train set with different classifiers (C), input features (IF) and output label (OL) structures. The input features are Histogram of Gradients (HOG), mosaic images (MI), and similarity normalized images (SNI). The output structures are either single- (S) or multi-label (M).

C	IF	OL	Action units											
			1	2	4	6	7	10	12	14	15	17	23	Mean
SVM	HOG	S	0.44	0.29	0.45	0.77	0.75	0.81	0.87	**0.62**	**0.39**	0.58	0.41	0.58
CNN	MI	M	0.22	0.01	0.43	0.76	0.64	0.77	0.85	0.47	0.00	0.27	0.00	0.40
	SNI	S	**0.63**	**0.44**	**0.54**	**0.82**	**0.80**	**0.85**	**0.90**	0.58	0.27	**0.60**	**0.45**	**0.63**
		M	0.55	0.38	0.53	0.80	0.75	0.83	**0.90**	0.55	0.23	0.59	0.37	0.59

Table 2. Results on the FERA BP4D Test set with multi-label CNN and SNI. Performance measures include F_1 score, its skew normalized version ($F_1^{s.n.}$) [13], and area under ROC curve (AUC). The table shows the degree of skew (ratio of negative and positive labels) for each AU.

	Action units											
	1	2	4	6	7	10	12	14	15	17	23	Mean
skew	15.31	20.02	12.23	2.11	0.66	1.01	1.37	0.98	11.78	6.81	6.78	7.19
F_1	0.26	0.23	0.27	0.76	0.75	0.8	0.8	0.64	0.26	0.38	0.3	0.50
$F_1^{s.n.}$	0.74	0.67	0.69	0.84	0.7	0.8	0.83	0.64	0.43	0.68	0.38	0.67
AUC	0.84	0.79	0.76	0.92	0.77	0.88	0.92	0.72	0.75	0.77	0.74	0.81

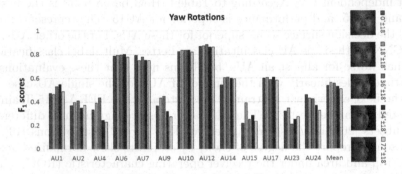

Fig. 3. F_1 measures as a function of yaw rotation on the augmented BP4D Train set, using the single-label classifier.

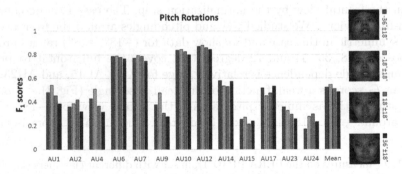

Fig. 4. F_1 measures as a function of pitch rotation on the augmented BP4D Train set, using the single-label classifier.

weak function of the pitch angle. AU1, AU4, and AU23 are affected by this angle more strongly than the other AUs (AU2, AU6, AU7, AU10, AU12, AU14, AU15, and AU17), see, Fig. 4.

Occlusion sensitivity maps [30] were generated for the different action units. We used 200 images for each subject, giving 8,200 images for the map generations. At around certain pixels, the pixels of the 21×21 sized patches were set to 0.5, the middle of the normalized range, $[0, 1]$. Central pixels were laid uniformly on each image at $32 \times 32 = 1,024$ positions. The modified images, more than 8 million, were then tried on the trained network for each AU and the binary cross-entropy measure was computed. Results are shown in condensed form, the value is color coded on a 32×32 occlusion sensitivity map in Fig. 5.

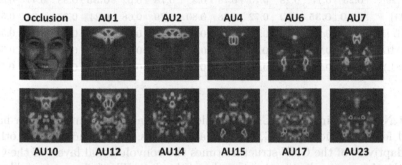

Fig. 5. Occlusion Sensitivity Maps [30]. (a): cropped 256×256 pixel images are covered by uniform grey 21×21 pixel patches at around pixels of a 32×32 pixel grid uniformly placed over the image. (b)-(n): the modified images are evaluated for binary cross-entropy performance. Performance is color coded at the central pixel of the patch and the 32×32 image is depicted for the different AUs.

We end the result section by comparing our results with the most recent ones reported in the literature (Table 3), the Local Gabor Binary Pattern (LGBP) [26], the geometric feature based deep network (GDNN) [12], the Discriminant Laplacian Embedding (DLE) [29], Deep Learning with Global Contrast Normalization (DL) [11], and the Convolutional and Bi-directional Memory Neural Networks (CRML) [12] methods. DLE wins for AU15, CMLR is the best for AU10, and AU 14, and DL performs the best for AU1 and AU2. Our architecture comes first for the other AUs, with one exception, the single label case wins. Since the multi-label case is considerably harder, we suspect that better training can improve the results further, e.g., by adding noise to the input on top of the dropout and/or increasing the database.

The single label case produced the best mean value. A special difference between the CMRL method and ours is that we can work on single images, whereas CMRL requires frame series. Furthermore, the inclusion of temporal information should improve performance for our case, too.

4 Discussion

Recent progress in convolutional neural networks (e.g., [12, 22, 28, 30] and see also the general review [24] and the cited references therein) shows that Deep

Table 3. Comparison of the single-label (SL) and multi-label (ML) version with other methods in the literature.

	Action units											
	1	2	4	6	7	10	12	14	15	17	23	Mean
LGBP [26]	0.18	0.16	0.22	0.67	0.75	0.8	0.79	0.67	0.14	0.24	0.24	0.44
GDNN [12]	0.33	0.25	0.21	0.64	0.79	0.8	0.78	0.68	0.19	0.28	0.33	0.48
DLE [29]	0.25	0.17	0.28	0.73	0.78	0.8	0.78	0.62	**0.35**	0.38	0.44	0.51
DL [11]	**0.40**	**0.35**	0.32	0.72	0.78	0.80	0.79	0.68	0.24	0.37	0.31	0.52
CRML [12]	0.28	0.28	0.34	0.7	0.78	**0.81**	0.78	**0.75**	0.2	0.36	0.41	0.52
this (ML)	0.26	0.23	0.27	**0.76**	0.75	0.8	0.8	0.64	0.26	0.38	0.3	0.50
this (SL)	0.34	0.21	**0.40**	0.74	**0.82**	**0.81**	**0.83**	0.73	0.25	**0.44**	**0.47**	**0.55**

Neural Networks, including CNNs are flexible enough to compete with hand-crafted features, such as HoG, SIFT, Gabor filters, LBP, among many others. The adaptivity of the CNN structure tunes the convolutional layers of the CNN to the database according to the statistics of the data. The fully connected layers, on the other hand, serve to collect, combine and exclude certain portions of the image.

The big progress is due to the tricks of avoiding local minima during the training procedure and the collection of such methods keeps increasing. We used high dropout rates, early stopping, and rectified linear units to overcome the danger of falling into one of the local minima too early during training. We have no doubt that this quickly developing field will come up superior solutions and performance will increase further. The maturation of deep learning neural network technologies offer great promises in the field of facial expression estimations.

The success of our relatively small network is most probably due to another additional trick; we combined gradient descent with selective methods. Although the contribution of this trick that we detail below is hard to grab quantitatively, we should note that we used no binary mask [12], no temporal extensions [12,16], known to have a considerable impact on performance.

The problem of optimization lies in the dubious F_1 score, which is not a good cost function, due to its discontinuities and flat, constant regions. Instead, a closely related quantity, the binary cross-entropy is preferred for gradient computations. Selection does not require well behaving, smooth costs and it can be introduced into the procedure at the validation step that guides early stopping. If performance is not improving on the validation set for a number of steps, in spite of the fact that it still does on the training set, then the gradient procedure should be stopped, since a local minimum of the training set is approached. Upon early stopping a new minibatch can be used for improving the performance.

This validation step can serve the selective process if gradient descent is stopped according to a different measure instead of the cost function. In our case, this measure was the F_1 score. It should be noted that the ideal values for the F_1 score and the binary cross entropy are the same, although they are rarely reached for real problems.

Clearly, special procedures, such as binary masks and temporal information should improve our results further, alike to performance increases in the studies mentioned previously.

Our main finding is that performance is a weak function of the head pose for CNNs and it remains high for a broad variety of angles. This opens the possibility of many real-life applications from cyber-physical systems with human in the loop, including smart factories, medical cyber-physical systems, independent living situation among many others. Furthermore, insights, sometimes of diagnostic value can be gained for affective disorders, addiction, and social relations. The progress of GPU technology will provide further gains in evaluation time that will decrease training time and evaluation frequency, too. The single-label version of our system runs at 58 FPS, while the multi-label version reaches over 600 FPS on a Titan X GPU.

Real life applications may require "in the wild" databases. This point remains to be seen.

5   Conclusions

Recent progress in deep learning technology and the availability of high quality databases enabled powerful learning methods to enter the field of face processing. We used these deep learning methods and the BP4D database for training an architecture for action unit recognition. Our results surpassed the state-of-the-art for images and could be further improved if temporal information is available. The main result is that angle dependence is minor, a large yaw and pitch range can be covered without considerable deterioration in performance. In turn, relevant applications from human-computer interaction to psychiatric interviews may gain momentum by applying such tools.

Acknowledgements. This work was supported in part by US National Institutes of Health grant MH096951 to the University of Pittsburgh and by US National Science Foundation grants CNS-1205664 and CNS-1205195 to the University of Pittsburgh and the University of Binghamton. Neither agency was involved in the planning or writing of the work.

References

1. Ambadar, Z., Cohn, J.F., Reed, L.I.: All smiles are not created equal: morphology and timing of smiles perceived as amused, polite, and embarrassed/nervous. J. Nonverbal Behav. **33**(1), 17–34 (2009)
2. Bauer, A., Wollherr, D., Buss, M.: Human-robot collaboration: a survey. Int. J. Humanoid Rob. **5**(01), 47–66 (2008)
3. Ekman, P., Rosenberg, E.L.: What the Face Reveals: Basic and Applied Studies of Spontaneous Expression Using the Facial Action Coding System (FACS), 2nd edn. Oxford University Press, New York (2005)

4. Fairbairn, C.E., Sayette, M.A., Levine, J.M., Cohn, J.F., Creswell, K.G.: The effects of alcohol on the emotional displays of whites in interracial groups. Emotion **13**(3), 468–477 (2013)
5. Fridlund, A.J.: Human Facial Expression: An Evolutionary View. Academic Press, Cambridge (1994)
6. Fukushima, K.: Neocognitron: a self-organizing neural network model for a mechanism of pattern recognition unaffected by shift in position. Biol. Cybern. **36**(4), 193–202 (1980)
7. Girard, J.M., Cohn, J.F., Jeni, L.A., Sayette, M.A., De La Torre, F.: Spontaneous facial expression in unscripted social interactions can be measured automatically. Beh. Res. Methods **47**, 1 12 (2014). articles/Girard14BRM.pdf
8. Girard, J.M., Cohn, J.F., Mahoor, M.H., Mavadati, S.M., Hammal, Z., Rosenwald, D.P.: Nonverbal social withdrawal in depression: evidence from manual and automatic analyses. Image Vis. Comput. **32**(10), 641–647 (2014)
9. Glorot, X., Bordes, A., Bengio, Y.: Deep sparse rectifier neural networks. In: International Conference on Artificial Intelligence and Statistics, pp. 315–323 (2011)
10. Griffin, K.M., Sayette, M.A.: Facial reactions to smoking cues relate to ambivalence about smoking. Psychol. Addict. Behav. **22**(4), 551 (2008)
11. Gudi, A., Tasli, H.E., den Uyl, T.M., Maroulis, A.: Deep learning based FACS action unit occurrence and intensity estimation. In: 2015 11th IEEE International Conference and Workshops on Automatic Face and Gesture Recognition (FG), vol. 6, pp. 1–5. IEEE (2015)
12. Jaiswal, S., Valstar, M.F.: Deep learning the dynamic appearance and shape of facial action units. In: Winter Conference on Applications of Computer Vision, (WACV). IEEE, March 2015
13. Jeni, L.A., Cohn, J.F., De La Torre, F.: Facing imbalanced data-recommendations for the use of performance metrics. In: 2013 Humaine Association Conference on Affective Computing and Intelligent Interaction (ACII) (2013)
14. Jeni, L.A., Cohn, J.F., Kanade, T.: Dense 3D face alignment from 2D videos in real-time. In: 2015 11th IEEE International Conference and Workshops on Automatic Face and Gesture Recognition (FG) (2015). http://zface.org
15. Jeni, L.A., Cohn, J.F., Kanade, T.: Dense 3D face alignment from 2D video for real-time use. Image and Vis. Comput. (2016). doi:10.1016/j.imavis.2016.05.009
16. Jeni, L.A., Lőrincz, A., Szabó, Z., Cohn, J.F., Kanade, T.: Spatio-temporal event classification using time-series kernel based structured sparsity. In: Fleet, D., Pajdla, T., Schiele, B., Tuytelaars, T. (eds.) ECCV 2014. LNCS, vol. 8692, pp. 135–150. Springer, Heidelberg (2014). doi:10.1007/978-3-319-10593-2_10
17. Keltner, D., MOffitt, T.E., Stouthamer-Loeber, M.: Facial expressions of emotion and psychopathology in adolescent boys. J. Abnorm. Psychol. **104**(4), 644 (1995)
18. Kingma, D., Ba, J.: Adam: a method for stochastic optimization. arXiv preprint arxiv:1412.6980 (2014)
19. LeCun, Y., Bengio, Y., Hinton, G.: Deep learning. Nature **521**(7553), 436–444 (2015)
20. LeCun, Y., Bottou, L., Bengio, Y., Haffner, P.: Gradient-based learning applied to document recognition. Proc. IEEE **86**(11), 2278–2324 (1998)
21. Li, H., Sun, J., Wang, D., Xu, Z., Chen, L.: Deep representation of facial geometric and photometric attributes for automatic 3D facial expression recognition. arXiv preprint arxiv:1511.03015 (2015)
22. Liu, M., Li, S., Shan, S., Chen, X.: Au-inspired deep networks for facial expression feature learning. Neurocomputing **159**, 126–136 (2015)

23. McDuff, D., el Kaliouby, R., Demirdjian, D., Picard, R.: Predicting online media effectiveness based on smile responses gathered over the internet. In: International Conference on Automatic Face and Gesture Recognition (2013)
24. Schmidhuber, J.: Deep learning in neural networks: an overview. Neural Netw. **61**, 85–117 (2015)
25. Szirtes, G., Szolgay, D., Utasi, A.: Facing reality: an industrial view on large scale use of facial expression analysis. In: Proceedings of the Emotion Recognition in the Wild Challenge and Workshop, pp. 1–8 (2013)
26. Valstar, M.F., Almaev, T., Girard, J.M., McKeown, G., Mehu, M., Yin, L., Pantic, M., Cohn, J.F.: Fera 2015-second facial expression recognition and analysis challenge. In: 2015 11th IEEE International Conference and Workshops on Automatic Face and Gesture Recognition (FG), vol. 6, pp. 1–8. IEEE (2015)
27. Vicente, F., Huang, Z., Xiong, X., De la Torre, F., Zhang, W., Levi, D.: Driver gaze tracking and eyes off the road detection system. IEEE Trans. Intell. Transp. Syst. **16**(4), 2014–2027 (2015)
28. Xu, M., Cheng, W., Zhao, Q., Ma, L., Xu, F.: Facial expression recognition based on transfer learning from deep convolutional networks. In: 2015 11th International Conference on Natural Computation (ICNC), pp. 702–708. IEEE (2015)
29. Yuce, A., Gao, H., Thiran, J.P.: Discriminant multi-label manifold embedding for facial action unit detection. In: 2015 11th IEEE International Conference and Workshops on Automatic Face and Gesture Recognition (FG), vol. 6, pp. 1–6 (2015)
30. Zeiler, M.D., Fergus, R.: Visualizing and understanding convolutional networks. In: Fleet, D., Pajdla, T., Schiele, B., Tuytelaars, T. (eds.) ECCV 2014. LNCS, vol. 8689, pp. 818–833. Springer, Heidelberg (2014). doi:10.1007/978-3-319-10590-1_53
31. Zhang, X., Yin, L., Cohn, J.F., Canavan, S., Reale, M., Horowitz, A., Liu, P., Girard, J.M.: BP4D-spontaneous: a high-resolution spontaneous 3D dynamic facial expression database. Image Vis. Comput. **32**(10), 692–706 (2014)

Combining Deep Facial and Ambient Features for First Impression Estimation

Furkan Gürpınar[1], Heysem Kaya[2](✉), and Albert Ali Salah[3]

[1] Program of Computational Science and Engineering, Boğaziçi University,
Bebek, Istanbul, Turkey
furkan.gurpinar@boun.edu.tr
[2] Department of Computer Engineering, Namık Kemal University,
Çorlu, Tekirdağ, Turkey
hkaya@nku.edu.tr
[3] Department of Computer Engineering, Boğaziçi University,
Bebek, Istanbul, Turkey
salah@boun.edu.tr

Abstract. First impressions influence the behavior of people towards a newly encountered person or a human-like agent. Apart from the physical characteristics of the encountered face, the emotional expressions displayed on it, as well as ambient information affect these impressions. In this work, we propose an approach to predict the first impressions people will have for a given video depicting a face within a context. We employ pre-trained Deep Convolutional Neural Networks to extract facial expressions, as well as ambient information. After video modeling, visual features that represent facial expression and scene are combined and fed to a Kernel Extreme Learning Machine regressor. The proposed system is evaluated on the ChaLearn Challenge Dataset on First Impression Recognition, where the classification target is the "Big Five" personality trait labels for each video. Our system achieved an accuracy of 90.94 % on the sequestered test set, 0.36 % points below the top system in the competition.

Keywords: Personality traits · First impression · Deep learning · ELM

1 Introduction and Related Work

It is not possible to judge the personality of a person by a mere glimpse of the face, but people attribute apparent personality traits for a face they newly encounter, in a stereotypical way, and with remarkable consistency [1]. In this work, we tackle the problem of predicting the apparent personality using the data and protocol from the ChaLearn Looking at People 2016 First Impression Challenge [2].

It is not surprising that emotional expressions influence the attribution of personality traits. It is more likely for a smiling person to be perceived as more

G. Hua and H. Jégou (Eds.): ECCV 2016 Workshops, Part III, LNCS 9915, pp. 372–385, 2016.
DOI: 10.1007/978-3-319-49409-8_30

trustworthy, and friendly. Todorov et al. convincingly argued that rapid, unreflective trait inferences from faces can influence consequential decisions [3]. This is why people do not typically use frowning or angry pictures in their resumés. Also the context of the image can affect the perception of the face. In our proposed approach, we estimate emotional facial expressions, as well as cues from the context of the face to predict first impressions.

Before describing the followed approach, we provide a brief literature review on automatic personality trait recognition. In the past, various approaches have been used for recognizing apparent personality traits from different modalities such as audio [4,5], text [6–8] and visual information [9,10]. As in other recognition problems, multimodal systems are also investigated to improve robustness of prediction [11–14]. These works aim to estimate personality traits from given input. In psychology, personality is often assessed by running a "Big Five" questionnaire that measures Openness, Conscientiousness, Extraversion, Agreeableness, and Neuroticism (OCEAN) [15]. Apparent personality is also frequently assessed in these five dimensions.

In their work, Borkenau and Liebler used the Brunswik's lens model and categorized the particular cues that may communicate a certain personality [16]. They included a large number of indicators such as overall impression variables (e.g. estimated age, masculinity, attractiveness), acoustic variables (e.g. softness of voice, pleasantness, clarity), static visual variables (e.g. appearance, make-up, garments, thin lips, hair style, facial expression), and dynamic visual variables (e.g. movement speed, hand movements, walking style). In order to assess the personality trait attributions, they measured "validity," which indicates the correlation between self-ratings of personality and ratings by strangers or acquaintances. The Brunswik's lens model looks at cues used for perceived traits, and links some of these cues to actual traits by assessing their ecological validity [17]. It is a useful conceptualization, also used in approaches to personality computing [18].

According to the literature, faces are a rich source of cues for apparent personality attribution, related to stereotype judgments. For an automatic analysis system, the first steps of a visual face analysis pipeline are face detection [19,20] and facial landmark localization [21–23]. Face alignment (or registration) is an important step, as all further processing depends on its accuracy. Recent deep neural network approaches are known to be more resistant to registration errors.

Face alignment is followed by visual feature extraction, which can include image-level appearance descriptors such as Local Binary Patterns (LBP) [24], Histogram of Oriented Gradients (HOG) [25], Scale-invariant Feature Transform (SIFT) [26], video-level descriptors such as Local Gabor Binary Patterns from Three Orthogonal Planes (LGBP-TOP) [27] and Local Phase Quantization (LPQ)-TOP [28], or geometric information [9,10].

Deep learning based approaches have achieved state-of-the-art results in human behavior analysis. These approaches, when trained with large datasets, can provide representations that are very robust to variations exhibited in the data. Deep learning has been successfully applied to many tasks related to computer vision such as object recognition [29,30], face recognition [31], emotion recognition [32] and age estimation [33–37]. Moreover, deep representations of images are often usable for multiple tasks, enabling transfer learning from pre-trained models. The disadvantages are the relatively high computational requirements for training such systems, the large amount of training data required, and (relatively) poor temporal extension to video processing.

In recent approaches to personality impressions classification, Support Vector Machines (SVM) [38] have been widely used [5, 8, 12, 14]. Recently, a learning approach called Extreme Learning Machines (ELM) that is similar to SVMs but providing faster learning schemes has become popular [39]. The use of ELM's name is debated in the literature, because of its strong resemblance to earlier methods. We continue to use it in this work for convenience. The approach has been shown to provide good performance in a number of applications including face recognition [40, 41], emotion recognition [42, 43], and smile detection [44].

Given the success of deep learning approaches and the speed of ELM, we propose to use a fusion of deep face and scene features, followed by regularized regression with a kernel ELM classifier. The main contribution of this work is the effective combination of emotion related and ambient features that are efficiently extracted from pre-trained/fine-tuned Deep Convolutional Neural Network (DCNN) models. Our method is illustrated in a simplified flowchart in Fig. 1.

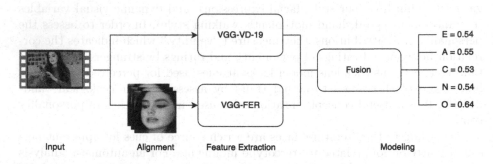

Fig. 1. Flowchart of the proposed method.

The remainder of this paper is organized as follows. In the next section we provide background and details on the methodology. Then in Sect. 3, we present the experimental results, followed by implementation details in Sect. 4. Finally, Sect. 5 concludes with future directions.

2   Methodology

Our proposed approach evaluates a short video clip that contains a single person, and outputs an estimate of apparent personality traits in the five dimensions mentioned earlier. In this section, we describe the three main steps of our pipeline, namely, face alignment, feature extraction, and modeling.

2.1   Face Alignment

For detecting and aligning faces from the videos, we use Xiong and de la Torre's Supervised Descent Method (SDM), also known as IntraFace [21]. This approach locates 49 landmarks on the face. After the landmarks are located, we estimate the roll angle of the face from the eye corner locations and rotate the image to rectify the face. We then add a margin of 20 % interocular distance around the outer landmarks to compute a loose bounding box from which we crop facial images. After the face is cropped, it is resized to 64 × 64 pixels, and registered as a new frame. Frames from a sample input video and the corresponding aligned face images are shown in Fig. 2.

Input video

Aligned video

Fig. 2. Face alignment example.

2.2   Feature Extraction

We extract facial features that are summarized over an entire video segment, and scene features from the first image of each video. The assumption is that videos do not stretch over multiple shots.

Face Features: After aligning the faces, we extract image-level deep features from a network that is trained for facial emotion recognition. The training of this network is explained in more detail in Sect. 2.3. For comparison, we also extract features from the original VGG-Face network that was trained for face recognition [31]. For both networks, we use the response of the 33rd layer of the 37-layer architecture, which is the lowest-level 4096-dimensional descriptor.

We compare deep features with traditional appearance descriptors and geometric information that is shown to be effective in emotion recognition [45]. We report the cross validation accuracy of each approach in Sect. 3.2.

Video Features: After extracting frame-level features from each registered face, we summarize the videos by computing functional statistics of each dimension over time. The functionals include mean, standard deviation, offset, slope, and curvature. Offset and slope are calculated from the first order polynomial fit to each feature contour, while curvature is the leading coefficient of the second order polynomial. An empirical comparison of the individual functionals is given in Sect. 3.2.

Scene Features: In order to use ambient information in the images to our advantage, we extract features using the VGG-19 network [30], which is trained for an object recognition task on the ILSVRC 2012 dataset. Similar to face features, we use the 4096-dimensional feature from the 39th layer of the 43-layer architecture, hence we obtain a description of the overall image that contains both the face and the scene, which we combine with face features using feature-level fusion.

2.3 CNN Fine Tuning

We start with the VGG-Face network [31], changing the final layer (originally a 2622-dimensional recognition layer), to a 7-dimensional emotion recognition layer, where the weights are initialized randomly. We fine-tune this network with the softmax loss function using around 30,000 training images from the FER-2013 dataset [46]. We choose an initial learning rate of 0.0001, a momentum of 0.9 and a batch size of 64. We train the model for 5 epochs, and we show the validation set performance for each epoch in Fig. 3.

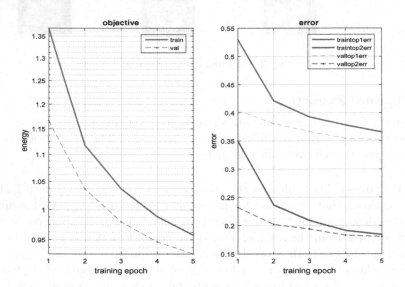

Fig. 3. Fine tuning the VGG-Face network on the FER-2013 public test set. The figure on the left shows the softmax loss, whereas the figure on the right shows the top-1 and top-2 classification errors.

2.4 Regression with Kernel ELM

In order to model personality traits from visual features, we used kernel ELM, due to the learning speed and accuracy of the algorithm. In the following paragraphs, we briefly explain the learning strategy of ELM.

ELM proposes a simple and robust learning algorithm for single-hidden layer feedforward networks. The input layer's bias and weights are initialized randomly to obtain the output of the second (hidden) layer. The bias and weights of the second layer are calculated by a simple generalized inverse operation of the hidden layer output matrix.

ELM tries to find the mapping between the hidden node output matrix $\mathbf{H} \in \mathbb{R}^{N \times h}$ and the label vector $\mathbf{T} \in \mathbb{R}^{N \times 1}$ where N and h denote the number of samples and the hidden neurons, respectively. The set of output weights $\beta \in \mathbb{R}^{h \times 1}$ is calculated by the least squares solution of the set of linear equations $\mathbf{H}\beta = \mathbf{T}$, as:

$$\beta = \mathbf{H}^{\dagger}\mathbf{T}, \tag{1}$$

where $\mathbf{H}^{\dagger}$ denotes the Moore-Penrose generalized inverse [47] that minimizes the L_2 norms of $||\mathbf{H}\beta - \mathbf{T}||$ and $||\beta||$ simultaneously.

To increase the robustness and the generalization capability of ELM, a regularization coefficient $\mathbf{C}$ is included in the optimization procedure. Therefore, given a kernel $\mathbf{K}$, the set of weights is learned as follows:

$$\beta = (\frac{\mathbf{I}}{C} + \mathbf{K})^{-1}\mathbf{T}. \tag{2}$$

In order to prevent parameter overfitting, we use the linear kernel $\mathbf{K}(x, y) = x^T y$, where x and y are the original feature vectors after min-max normalization of each dimension among the training samples. With this approach, the only parameter of our model is the regularization coefficient C, which we optimize with a 5-fold subject independent cross-validation on the training set. In Sect. 3.2, we report the average score of each fold with the selected parameter.

3   Experiments

3.1   Challenge and Corpus

The "ChaLearn LAP Apparent Personality Analysis: First Impressions" challenge consists of 10,000 clips collected from 5,563 YouTube videos, where the poses are more or less frontal, but the resolution, lighting and background conditions are not controlled, hence providing a dataset with in-the-wild conditions. Each clip in the training set is labeled for the Big Five personality traits. Basic statistics of the dataset partitions are provided in Table 1. The detailed information on the challenge and corpus can be found in [2].

Performance Evaluation: The performance score in this challenge is the Mean Absolute Error subtracted from 1, which is formulated as follows:

$$1 - \sum_{i}^{N} \frac{|\hat{y}_i - y_i|}{N}, \tag{3}$$

where N is the number of samples, $\hat{y}$ is the predicted label and y is the true label ($0 \leq y \leq 1$). This score is then averaged over five tasks. This means the final score varies between 0 (worst case) and 1 (best case).

Table 1. Dataset summary

	Train	Val	Test
#Clips	6,000	2,000	2,000
#YouTube videos	2,624	1,484	1,455
#Given frames	2.56 M	0.86 M	0.86 M
#Detected frames	2.45 M	0.82 M	0.82 M

3.2 Experimental Results

In this section, we report the regression performance of various visual descriptors. Tables 2 and 3 summarize the performances of the different systems with 5-fold subject-independent cross-validation on the training set.

We first look at the performance of individual functionals, which are described in Sect. 2.2. As can be seen in Table 2, the combination of mean, standard deviation, and offset features works well, and the mean by itself is the most informative functional.

Table 2. Functional statistics with deep face features.

Feature	Mean	Extr.	Agre.	Cons.	Neur.	Open.
Mean	0.900	0.906	0.902	0.897	0.894	0.902
Std	0.883	0.891	0.881	0.876	0.880	0.886
Curvature	0.880	0.876	0.891	0.874	0.876	0.882
Slope	0.880	0.876	0.892	0.874	0.876	0.882
Offset	0.899	0.904	0.901	0.895	0.893	0.901
Fusion of all 5	0.902	0.908	0.903	0.898	**0.898**	0.904
Mean+Std+Offset	**0.902**	**0.909**	**0.903**	**0.899**	0.897	**0.904**

We evaluate a set of features with different dimensionalities individually. Geometric features (GEO), LPQ-TOP, LBP-TOP, and different deep neural network features were individually tested. Table 3 summarizes the results, and gives the dimensionality of each selected feature set. We observe that features from the deep face model fine tuned on the FER emotion corpus provide higher performances compared to both original deep features and hand-crafted visual features. Combining these features with ambient (scene) information further improves the prediction performance.

The best fusion system (ID 9 in Table 3) gives a test set mean accuracy of 0.9094, which ranks the fifth in the official competition. Considering the obtained test set performance in comparison to other competitors' accuracies (see Table 4),

Table 3. Regression performance with various visual descriptors

ID	Feature	Dim.	Mean	Extr.	Agre.	Cons.	Neur.	Open.
1	GEO	115	0.892	0.896	0.896	0.883	0.888	0.896
2	LPQ-TOP	12288	0.901	0.904	0.901	0.898	0.899	0.903
3	LBP-TOP	5568	0.900	0.903	0.900	0.895	0.897	0.902
4	LGBP-TOP	100224	0.903	0.907	0.902	0.900	**0.901**	0.905
5	VGG-19	4096	0.890	0.886	0.895	0.892	0.884	0.894
6	Caffe-Alex	4096	0.890	0.887	0.895	0.890	0.885	0.894
7	VGGFace	12288	0.901	0.907	0.901	0.898	0.896	0.903
8	VGGFace+FER	12288	0.902	0.909	0.903	0.899	0.897	0.904
9	Fusion (5 & 8)	16384	**0.904**	**0.909**	**0.904**	**0.902**	0.899	**0.907**

Table 4. Final ranking on the test set

Rank	Team	Accuracy
1	NJU-LAMDA	0.9130
2	evolgen	0.9121
3	DCC	0.9109
4	ucas	0.9098
5	**BU-NKU (ours)**	0.9094
6	pandora	0.9063
7	Pilab	0.8936
8	Kaizoku	0.8826
9	ITU_SiMiT	0.8815
10	sp	0.8759

we observe that the performances are around 0.90–0.91 in general. The top accuracy is 0.9130, while the top six teams' accuracies are higher than 0.9.

We show the estimations of our system during cross validation in Figs. 4 and 5. The results in Fig. 4 show how precisely our system can estimate the personality traits under various imaging conditions. Figure 5 shows that examples with labels very close to 0 or 1 tend to have higher error, which might be due to the approximately normal distribution of training labels with mean values around 0.5.

Fig. 4. Six examples from the training set where our approach produced good estimations for the traits. For each example, the first column shows the ground truth (True), and the second column shows the estimation of the model (Pred.)

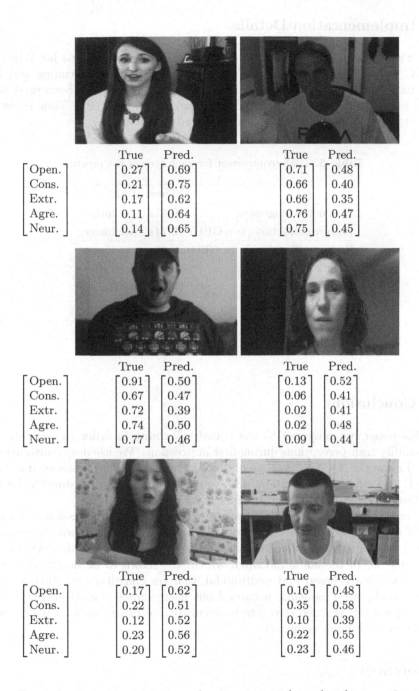

Fig. 5. Examples from the training set where our approach produced poor estimations for the traits. For each example, the first column shows the ground truth (True), and the second column shows the estimation of the model (Pred.)

4   Implementation Details

The whole system is implemented in MATLAB R2015b on a 64-bit Windows 10 PC with 32 GB RAM and an Intel i7-6700 CPU. For fine-tuning and feature extraction with CNNs, the MatConvNet library [48] has been used with GPU parallelization, using an NVidia GeForce GTX 970 GPU. Time spent on important parts of the pipeline is summarized in Table 5.

Table 5. Time requirement for each step of the pipeline

Task	Time	Unit
Face det. & alignment	0.17 s	per image
Feature extraction (w/o GPU)	0.24 s	per image
Feature extraction (with GPU)	0.03 s	per image
Functional encoding	3 s	per video
Kernel ELM training	0.37 s	for train set
Kernel ELM testing	10^{-5} s	per video
Total	98 s	per video

5   Conclusions

In this paper, we proposed to use transfer learning in order to estimate the personality trait perceptions during first impressions. We use deep convolutional neural networks (DCNN) that are originally trained for other tasks such as face, object, and emotion recognition, and we employ their features directly. Hence, we show the feasibility of deep transfer learning for this task.

Combining two sets of DCNN features that carry facial expression and ambient information, we achieve better results compared to each of these approaches, as well as compared to other hand-crafted visual features. In this work, we did not make use of the audio modality, which was shown to be beneficial in earlier works. Audio-based and multimodal analyses constitute our future work. In this work, video modeling is carried out using simple statistical functionals. This approach is fast and shown to be accurate. For future works, a wider set of functionals will be investigated.

References

1. Cuddy, A.J., Fiske, S.T., Glick, P.: Warmth and competence as universal dimensions of social perception: the stereotype content model and the bias map. Adv. Exp. Soc. Psychol. **40**, 61–149 (2008)

2. Lopez, V.P., Chen, B., Places, A., Oliu, M., Corneanu, C., Baro, X., Escalante, H.J., Guyon, I., Escalera, S.: ChaLearn LAP 2016: first round challenge on first impressions - dataset and results. In: ChaLearn Looking at People Workshop on Apparent Personality Analysis, ECCV Workshop Proceedings (2016)
3. Todorov, A., Mandisodza, A.N., Goren, A., Hall, C.C.: Inferences of competence from faces predict election outcomes. Science **308**(5728), 1623–1626 (2005)
4. Valente, F., Kim, S., Motlicek, P.: Annotation and recognition of personality traits in spoken conversations from the AMI meetings corpus. In: INTERSPEECH, pp. 1183–1186 (2012)
5. Madzlan, N., Han, J., Bonin, F., Campbell, N.: Towards automatic recognition of attitudes: prosodic analysis of video blogs. In: Speech Prosody, Dublin, Ireland, pp. 91–94 (2014)
6. Alam, F., Stepanov, E.A., Riccardi, G.: Personality traits recognition on social network-Facebook. In: WCPR (ICWSM-2013), Cambridge, MA, USA (2013)
7. Nowson, S., Gill, A.J.: Look! who's talking? Projection of extraversion across different social contexts. In: Proceedings of the 2014 ACM Multimedia Workshop on Computational Personality Recognition, pp. 23–26. ACM (2014)
8. Gievska, S., Koroveshovski, K.: The impact of affective verbal content on predicting personality impressions in Youtube videos. In: Proceedings of the 2014 ACM Multimedia Workshop on Computational Personality Recognition, pp. 19–22. ACM (2014)
9. Fernando, T., et al.: Persons' personality traits recognition using machine learning algorithms and image processing techniques. Adv. Comput. Sci.: Int. J. **5**(1), 40–44 (2016)
10. Qin, R., Gao, W., Xu, H., Hu, Z.: Modern physiognomy: an investigation on predicting personality traits and intelligence from the human face. arXiv preprint arXiv:1604.07499 (2016)
11. Sarkar, C., Bhatia, S., Agarwal, A., Li, J.: Feature analysis for computational personality recognition using Youtube personality data set. In: Proceedings of the 2014 ACM Multimedia Workshop on Computational Personality Recognition, pp. 11–14. ACM (2014)
12. Alam, F., Riccardi, G.: Predicting personality traits using multimodal information. In: Proceedings of the 2014 ACM Multimedia Workshop on Computational Personality Recognition, pp. 15–18. ACM (2014)
13. Farnadi, G., Sushmita, S., Sitaraman, G., Ton, N., De Cock, M., Davalos, S.: A multivariate regression approach to personality impression recognition of vloggers. In: Proceedings of the 2014 ACM Multimedia Workshop on Computational Personality Recognition, pp. 1–6. ACM (2014)
14. Sidorov, M., Ultes, S., Schmitt, A.: Automatic recognition of personality traits: a multimodal approach. In: Proceedings of the 2014 Workshop on Mapping Personality Traits Challenge, pp. 11–15. ACM (2014)
15. Gosling, S.D., Rentfrow, P.J., Swann, W.B.: A very brief measure of the big-five personality domains. J. Res. Pers. **37**(6), 504–528 (2003)
16. Borkenau, P., Liebler, A.: Trait inferences: sources of validity at zero acquaintance. J. Pers. Soc. Psychol. **62**(4), 645 (1992)
17. Zebrowitz, L.A., Collins, M.A.: Accurate social perception at zero acquaintance: the affordances of a gibsonian approach. Pers. Soc. Psychol. Rev. **1**(3), 204–223 (1997)
18. Vinciarelli, A., Mohammadi, G.: A survey of personality computing. IEEE Trans. Affect. Comput. **5**(3), 273–291 (2014)

19. Viola, P., Jones, M.J.: Robust real-time face detection. Int. J. Comput. Vis. **57**(2), 137–154 (2004)
20. Mathias, M., Benenson, R., Pedersoli, M., Gool, L.: Face detection without bells and whistles. In: Fleet, D., Pajdla, T., Schiele, B., Tuytelaars, T. (eds.) ECCV 2014. LNCS, vol. 8692, pp. 720–735. Springer, Heidelberg (2014). doi:10.1007/978-3-319-10593-2_47
21. Xiong, X., De la Torre, F.: Supervised descent method and its application to face alignment. In: IEEE Conference on Computer Vision and Pattern Recognition, pp. 532–539(2013)
22. Ren, S., Cao, X., Wei, Y., Sun, J.: Face alignment at 3000 FPS via regressing local binary features. In: Proceedings of the IEEE Conference on Computer Vision and Pattern Recognition, pp. 1685–1692 (2014)
23. Xiong, X., De la Torre, F.: Global supervised descent method. In: Proceedings of the IEEE Conference on Computer Vision and Pattern Recognition, pp. 2664–2673 (2015)
24. Ojala, T., Pietikainen, M., Maenpaa, T.: Multiresolution gray-scale and rotation invariant texture classification with local binary patterns. IEEE Trans. Pattern Anal. Mach. Intell. **24**(7), 971–987 (2002)
25. Dalal, N., Triggs, B.: Histograms of oriented gradients for human detection. In: IEEE Conference on Computer Vision and Pattern Recognition, vol. 1, pp. 886–893. IEEE (2005)
26. Lowe, D.G.: Distinctive image features from scale-invariant keypoints. Int. J. Comput. Vis. **60**(2), 91–110 (2004)
27. Almaev, T.R., Valstar, M.F.: Local Gabor binary patterns from three orthogonal planes for automatic facial expression recognition. In: Humaine Association Conference on Affective Computing and Intelligent Interaction, pp. 356–361. IEEE (2013)
28. Jiang, B., Valstar, M.F., Pantic, M.: Action unit detection using sparse appearance descriptors in space-time video volumes. In: 2011 IEEE International Conference on Automatic Face and Gesture Recognition and Workshops (FG 2011), pp. 314–321. IEEE (2011)
29. Krizhevsky, A., Sutskever, I., Hinton, G.E.: Imagenet classification with deep convolutional neural networks. In: Advances in neural information processing systems, pp. 1097–1105 (2012)
30. Simonyan, K., Zisserman, A.: Very deep convolutional networks for large-scale image recognition. CoRR abs/1409.1556 (2014)
31. Parkhi, O.M., Vedaldi, A., Zisserman, A.: Deep face recognition. In: British Machine Vision Conference (2015)
32. Kim, B.K., Lee, H., Roh, J., Lee, S.Y.: Hierarchical committee of deep CNNs with exponentially-weighted decision fusion for static facial expression recognition. In: Proceedings of the 2015 ACM on International Conference on Multimodal Interaction, pp. 427–434. ACM (2015)
33. Rothe, R., Timofte, R., Gool, L.: Dex: deep expectation of apparent age from a single image. In: Proceedings of the IEEE International Conference on Computer Vision Workshops, pp. 10–15 (2015)
34. Liu, X., Li, S., Kan, M., Zhang, J., Wu, S., Liu, W., Han, H., Shan, S., Chen, X.: Agenet: deeply learned regressor and classifier for robust apparent age estimation. In: Proceedings of the IEEE International Conference on Computer Vision Workshops, pp. 16–24 (2015)

35. Zhu, Y., Li, Y., Mu, G., Guo, G.: A study on apparent age estimation. In: Proceedings of the IEEE International Conference on Computer Vision Workshops, pp. 25–31 (2015)
36. Escalera, S., Torres, M., Martinez, B., Baro, X., Jair Escalante, H., Guyon, I., Tzimiropoulos, G., Corneou, C., Oliu, M., Bagheri, M.A., Valstar, M.: Chalearn looking at people and faces of the world: Face analysis workshop and challenge 2016. In: The IEEE Conference on Computer Vision and Pattern Recognition (CVPR) Workshops, pp. 1–8, June 2016
37. Gürpınar, F., Kaya, H., Dibeklioğlu, H., Salah, A.A.: Kernel ELM and CNN based facial age estimation. In: The IEEE Conference on Computer Vision and Pattern Recognition (CVPR) Workshops, Las Vegas, Nevada, USA, pp. 80–86, June 2016
38. Cortes, C., Vapnik, V.: Support-vector networks. Mach. Learn. **20**(3), 273–297 (1995)
39. Huang, G.B., Zhou, H., Ding, X., Zhang, R.: Extreme learning machine for regression and multiclass classification. IEEE Trans. Syst. Man Cybern. Part B: Cybern. **42**(2), 513–529 (2012)
40. Zong, W., Huang, G.B.: Face recognition based on extreme learning machine. Neurocomputing **74**(16), 2541–2551 (2011)
41. Mohammed, A.A., Minhas, R., Wu, Q.J., Sid-Ahmed, M.A.: Human face recognition based on multidimensional PCA and extreme learning machine. Pattern Recogn. **44**(10), 2588–2597 (2011)
42. Utama, P., Ajie, H., et al.: A framework of human emotion recognition using extreme learning machine. In: 2014 International Conference of Advanced Informatics: Concept, Theory and Application (ICAICTA), pp. 315–320. IEEE (2014)
43. Kaya, H., Karpov, A.A., Salah, A.A.: Robust acoustic emotion recognition based on cascaded normalization and extreme learning machines. In: Cheng, L., Liu, Q., Ronzhin, A. (eds.) ISNN 2016. LNCS, vol. 9719, pp. 115–123. Springer, Heidelberg (2016). doi:10.1007/978-3-319-40663-3_14
44. An, L., Yang, S., Bhanu, B.: Efficient smile detection by extreme learning machine. Neurocomputing **149**, 354–363 (2015)
45. Kaya, H., Gürpınar, F., Afshar, S., Salah, A.A.: Contrasting and combining least squares based learners for emotion recognition in the wild. In: Proceedings of the 2015 ACM on International Conference on Multimodal Interaction, pp. 459–466. ACM (2015)
46. Goodfellow, I.J., et al.: Challenges in representation learning: a report on three machine learning contests. In: Lee, M., Hirose, A., Hou, Z.-G., Kil, R.M. (eds.) ICONIP 2013. LNCS, vol. 8228, pp. 117–124. Springer, Heidelberg (2013). doi:10.1007/978-3-642-42051-1_16
47. Rao, C.R., Mitra, S.K.: Generalized Inverse of Matrices and Its Applications, vol. 7. Wiley, New York (1971)
48. Vedaldi, A., Lenc, K.: MatConvNet - convolutional neural networks for MATLAB. (2015)

The Static Multimodal Dyadic Behavior Dataset for Engagement Prediction

P. Daphne Tsatsoulis[1]([⊠]), Paige Kordas[1], Michael Marshall[1], David Forsyth[1], and Agata Rozga[2]

[1] University of Illinois at Urbana-Champaign, Champaign, USA
{tsatsou2,pkordas2,mtmarsh2,daf}@illinois.edu
[2] Georgia Institute of Technology, Atlanta, Georgia
agata@gatech.edu

Abstract. The Rapid-Attention, Back and Forth, and Communication (Rapid ABC) assessment is a semi-structured play interaction during which an examiner engages a child in five activities intended to elicit social-communication behaviors and turn taking. The examiner scores the frequency and quality of the child's social behavior in each activity, generating a total score that reflects the child's social engagement with her during the assessment. The standard Rapid ABC dataset contains a daunting amount of detail. We have produced a static version that captures the action-reaction dynamic of the assessment as frames. We have conducted a user study on our dataset to see if subjects can predict the engagement of a child in the video. We presented subjects both frames from our staticMMDB dataset and the full video of the original MMDB dataset and found little difference in their performance. In this paper we show that computer vision methods can predict children's engagement. We automatically identify the ease-of-engagement of a child and provide evaluation baselines for the task.

1 Introduction

A child's early developmental period is crucial and being able to capture characteristic differences between children's behaviors is important. The Rapid ABC assessment is a standardized play assessment for eliciting early social-interactive behaviors in toddlers [1]. Such assessments are common in developmental psychology research, where they are used both to understand typical behavior and to identify children who may be experiencing delays, such as autism. The Rapid ABC scores children on how they participated in the assessment by checking for specific behaviors and the overall ease of engagement. During this assessment an examiner prompts a child and measures the child's response. The examiner then scores the child.

We use the Multimodal Dyadic Behavior Dataset (MMDB), a dataset with videos of children undergoing the Rapid ABC assessment [2]. This dataset contains hours of videos in which examiners and children are interacting. The dataset has annotations of behavior, speech, and the child's engagement in tasks. It is

© Springer International Publishing Switzerland 2016
G. Hua and H. Jégou (Eds.): ECCV 2016 Workshops, Part III, LNCS 9915, pp. 386–399, 2016.
DOI: 10.1007/978-3-319-49409-8_31

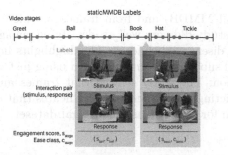

Fig. 1. The original MMDB dataset contains videos of scripted interactions with children that are broken into five stages. During each stage, the examiner scores the engagement of the child. We have created the staticMMDB dataset by capturing the most important interactions during the assessment. We extracted frames to represent the stimulus-response pairings of each interaction.

a rich resource for structured examiner prompts and spontaneous child reactions. An examiner follows a script and will prompt a child identically in every Rapid ABC assessment making the examiner actions across assessments equivalent. The reactions from children however, are unscripted and varied.

Our goal is to summarize the MMDB Dataset (visualized in Fig. 1) so that visually important interactions are highlighted. We label the videos in the MMDB dataset so that every important visual interaction (when an examiner prompts a child) is represented by a stimulus and a response. Our resulting dataset, the staticMMDB dataset, supplements the original dataset and is comprised of time-stamps that identify important interaction frames. Our dataset gives indices into the data that correspond to the most interesting visual events. The staticMMDB dataset gives the opportunity to explore very hard questions, like how engaged a child is during interactions and what is the appropriate response to a stimulus.

Our labelling supplements the original dataset. It is comprised of time-stamps that identify important interaction frames and gives the vision community indices into the dataset that correspond to the most interesting visual events. Our dataset still encapsulates the hard aspects of the data and removes distractions. Even though we select frames to represent the video we still retain the ability to compute video features. It is easy to extract video data surrounding those frames to use for experimentation.

We automatically identify the engagement of children from the frames in the staticMMDB dataset. Our predictions agree with those of the examiner. We can predict the engagement of children not present in the training set, and most importantly, we can identify disengaged children. Our dataset and the evaluation task serve as baselines for future work to build on.

In order to verify that the staticMMDB dataset is as informative as the original MMDB dataset we conducted a user study. The user study tested whether subjects could accurately predict a child's engagement in an activity from clips of video (the original MMDB) and from frames of video (our staticMMDB). The subjects in our study did very well at identifying engaged children but had difficulty identifying disengaged children. This highlights how difficult this task is. We also compared subject performance when using just videos or just frames to make their decision. The study showed that frames and video are equally informative for predicting engagement. This indicates that our dataset contains the same information for this task as the original dataset.

Contributions:

1. We have summarized an extensive video dataset, the MMDB, to provide a series of standard interactions that emphasize visual events. Our summary, called the staticMMDB dataset, provides time stamps of frames and is a structured annotation for the MMDB dataset.
2. We have conducted a user-study that demonstrates the difficulty of the task and validates our claim that the staticMMDB dataset is as informative for engagement prediction as the original MMDB dataset.
3. We demonstrate a method that is able to identify the engagement of children and beat baseline evaluations for the task.

2   Background

2.1   The Multimodal Dyadic Behavior Dataset

The Multimodal Dyadic Behavior (MMDB) dataset presents a unique opportunity to investigate real interactions between two people. It is different from existing behavior datasets because the actions that we see are not drawn from a curated collection like the internet. Children's responses are open-ended and do not fall naturally into categories of behavior.

Engagement. For every child's video there exist a fixed number of important interactions when the examiner prompts the child and the child reacts. The examiner scores the child's engagement based upon that reaction. The examiner tries to engage the child during five substages: greeting, ball play, book, putting on a hat, and tickling. Each substage is identically structured and contains many interactions that occur in the same order in each video. The examiner scores the level of engagement of the child during each substage. An example of the evaluation script an examiner uses is shown in Fig. 2.

2.2   Engagement Prediction

There is little work on the Multimodal Dyadic Behavior dataset and in engagement prediction. We are aware of three works, Rehg et al. [2], Presti et al. [3], and Gupta et al. [4] that predict engagement on this data. The three works address the question of ease-of-engagement classification and approach the problem as a binary ([2,3]) or three-class [4] classification problem.

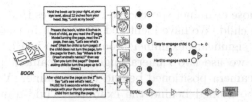

Fig. 2. A portion of the scoring form an examiner completed during a Rapid ABC assessment. The assessment is broken into five stages, one of which is the Book stage. An examiner scores explicit actions of the child during the assessment and also the overall ease with which she engaged the child. These two values are summed to produce the engagement score of the stage. In this example the ease class is 1 and the engagement score is 6. In this work we predict the ease-of-engagement of the child as a binary task. Engaged children have an ease-of-engagement score of 0 and disengaged children have a score of 1 or 2.

Rehg et al. [2] introduce the MMDB dataset. They detect gaze direction, smiles, and predict the ease-of-engagement in the videos. When using vision-features, they predict whether a child is engaged (binary task) in two substages ('ball' and 'book') on 14 test videos. After incorporating speech features, they are able to predict whether a child is engaged during all five substages for those 14 videos. Gupta et al. [4] perform a 3-way classification task on the ease of engagement (0 - easy to engage, 1 - moderately easy, 2 - hard to engage) using prosodic speech cues. They report their performance on 74 test videos using a stage-wise per-class recall. Presti et al. [3] predict a binary ease-of-engagement class using vision features. They propose a Hidden Markov Model for predicting the engagement class on 33 test videos. They also classify the stage (greeting, ball, book, hat, tickle) of each video clip.

None of the existing work is comparable. Each work uses different subsets of the original dataset that each contain a different distribution of disengaged children. The dataset we have created solves this problem. Our dataset summarizes the original MMDB dataset in a way that allows for comparisons between different methods and between various time points in the exam.

3   The staticMMDB Dataset

The original MMDB dataset contains a lot of extraneous video, and our summarization removes unnecessary noise while preserving the structure of the assessment. The reduced dataset we create is still a very hard dataset. We labeled the original dataset to create a more concise representation of the two-person interactions occurring in the videos. For each video we selected frames to represent key interactions between the examiner and child. The staticMMDB dataset summarizes every video and creates a more tightly defined task to which future work can compare.

We summarize the dataset so that every important interaction (when an examiner prompts a child) is represented by a stimulus and a response. The decisions we made when selecting interactions were based on the original dataset's annotations. We chose examiner speech and motion cues that would elicit visual responses from the child. We have identified 22 stimuli in the examination that represent the most significant examiner prompts (seen in Fig. 4).

For each video we use two camera angles: the camera positioned behind the child and the camera positioned behind the examiner. We will call frames from the camera positioned behind the examiner 'child-frames' because they are focused on the child. In a child-frame, the child and the adult holding the child are in the middle of the frame. The back of the examiner is also visible in the child-frame so that the frame captures the whole interaction. An 'examiner-frame' is focused on the examiner with part of the child's back visible.

The examiner-frame was extracted at the start of a stimulus and the child-frame was selected to capture the child's response to the examiner's prompt. To find an accurate portrayal of the child's interaction around a time-slot, we sampled a number of frames for 10 s after the examiner-frame. We then looked at the subset of frames and chose the one we thought best described the child's interaction.

The dataset frames were selected by a labeler who was shown a subset of frames for every interaction and asked to select the best child-response frame. They selected 22 child and 22 examiner frames for each subject. We used 98 subjects and their corresponding engagement scores for our experiments.

3.1   Stimulus Selection

When making the staticMMDB dataset, we wanted the examiner's speech and actions to be identical across the videos we used. Every video in the original MMDB dataset has been annotated with 11 elements (seen in Fig. 3) [2]. The

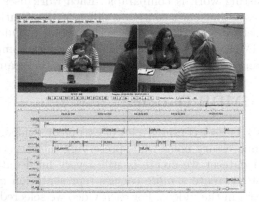

Fig. 3. A screenshot to show both the child and examiner video along with the annotation provided with each video in the MMDB dataset. The annotations are rich and many overlap making it unnecessary for us to use all of them in our dataset. For example, 'ball present', 'look at my ball' and 'let's play ball' all occur at about the same time. We chose to represent all three by using the single stimulus 'look at my ball'.

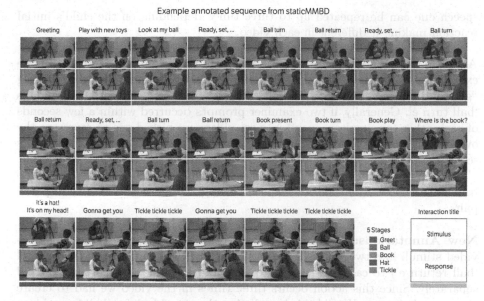

Fig. 4. This is an example of one annotated video in the staticMMDB dataset. Each stimulus-response pair represents one interaction. The color of the line under the interaction represents the stage in which the interaction occurred. The title of the interaction is the action of the examiner or the speech of the examiner that serves as the stimulus. The examiner-frame chosen to represent a stimulus is the first frame in the video labeled as a specific stimulus. The child-frame was selected within 10 s of the examiner's stimulus. (Color figure online)

figure shows each element as a row in which a professional annotator has indicated if a specific type of action is occurring. We are interested in visually interesting actions like the child's gestures (reaching, pointing) and the child's gaze direction (at the examiner, the book, the ball). Of the videos given to us we chose the 98 videos with identical speech cues. For example, we excluded videos that used 'one, two, three' instead of 'ready, set, go' in the ball phase. We also chose to use videos for which the cannon cameras had been annotated. This was to ensure the same view direction and resolution between subjects.

The MMDB dataset contains a plethora of annotations that do not all correspond to visually interesting events. In order to create the staticMMDB dataset we selected key interactions by dropping some annotations, consolidating others, and creating new annotations to capture important instances.

Dropping Annotations: We used the five stages listed in the engagement evaluation form excluding 'name_s' and 'name_f'. We used the annotations in speech_e_cv, ball_book_cv, and present_play_cv as stimuli since these are scripted and identical across videos. Speech and actions that were not the same across videos were not used. For example, 'can you turn the page?', occurs during the book stage and the examiner asks the child to turn the page of the book. This speech cue can be repeated up to three times depending on the child's initial reaction making it different in each video.

Annotation Consolidation: We do not include all speech and actions of the examiner because they may fall immediately after each other; for example, saying "go!" and passing the ball to the child have been consolidated into the stimulus 'ball turn e'. Generally, if two examiner prompts occurred within a few seconds of each other (or simultaneously) in most videos we picked one to represent the overlapping group. We tried to pick the first stimulus in the group though this sometimes varied slightly between videos and so we selected to the best of our ability. By grouping overlapping stimuli we avoided having too few response frames to choose from and we avoided having very similar stimulus-response pairs.

New Annotations: We also created three new stimuli by breaking the provided stimuli into two. We split 'ball turn e' into two stimuli ('ball turn e' and 'ball return e') to capture the pass to the child and the return from the child separately. Since this action occurs three times in the video we had to create three new instances. We did this by splitting the time block for 'ball turn e' into two equally sized time blocks.

Some stimuli (such as 'ready set ...' and 'tickle tickle tickle') occur multiple times throughout the video. It is important to distinguish between each instance of the same stimulus because children will react differently every time. For example, 'tickle tickle tickle' is repeated three times and children's reactions escalate throughout the video because they know what to expect after the first instance. Similarly, 'ready set ...' is followed by 'ball turn e' (which represents the phrase 'go!' and 'ball turn e') three times. On the last 'ready set ...' the examiner waits a few seconds before releasing the ball to the child. In this case both the stimulus and reaction are different highlighting the need for stimuli with the same speech to be unique.

3.2   Response Selection

After selecting the 22 stimuli we extracted the examiner frame at the start of the stimulus to represent the response. The original MMDB dataset provides timestamps corresponding to the start of each of the stimuli. We then showed a labeler child-frames that occurred in the 10 s after the examiner's stimulus. If a new stimulus started before 10 s had elapsed we truncated the 10 s so that the child's response would not overlap with a new stimulus.

Labeler: During labeling we showed 15 frames from the first 5 s and 5 frames from the second 5 s for each response. The labeler then picked the child frame that best captured the child's response to the stimulus. Many of the labelling decisions made were motivated by the data itself. For example, if the examiner asked "look at my ball" and 10 of the 11 frames showed the child looking down, and only 1 frame where the child looked up, the labeler chose a frame with the child looking down.

The labeler also made the decision to be consistent among videos for which frames he chose to represent certain scenes. For example, if the examiner said, "catch the ball!", resulting frames showed a child looking in anticipation, reaching their hands out, and finally holding the ball. In these scenarios, the labeler chose a specific frame for each child that behaved in the same way. For example, in the case of the ball being passed, he chose the frame with the child holding the ball. This made sure that children that performed the same interactions were indeed represented in the same way in our resulting frames.

3.3 Contributions and Challenges

The staticMMDB supports a wide variety of studies. In Sect. 4 we explore the task of engagement prediction in both the video and frames of children interacting. This task is very hard to perform on this dataset. A number of sometimes subtle actions are used to score a child. There is no single clear indicator for predicting engagement. Children of varying engagement will sit close to an adult, will look at the examiner, and will react to the presence of an object. Furthermore, for each stage there are very few examples of low-engagement children making the dataset very biased as seen in Fig. 5.

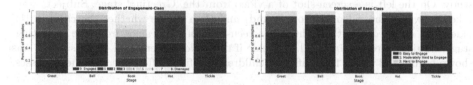

Fig. 5. The staticMMDB dataset has engagement scores and ease classes for every interaction. We have plotted the scores for each of the five stages in the 98 videos. The datasets are strongly biased towards high-engagement children (low-scoring) making the tasks of predicting engagement and ease class very challenging.

The staticMMDB dataset gives the opportunity to explore pairing stimuli and responses. Very hard questions, like what the best response to a stimulus is, can be explored using this data.

4 User Study

The purpose of this study was to test whether subjects can predict a child's engagement in an activity from clips of video and from frames of video. Since engagement is not a concrete action (as is smiling or gaze direction) it is difficult to define and predict. Our user study indicates how well a user can match the gold-standard engagement scores provided by expert examiners.

Our goal was also to compare the performance of the two sources (clips and frames) in order to confirm which is more informative or if they are equally informative. We have introduced the staticMMDB dataset, a summary of the MMDB dataset. We claim that our dataset is a cleaner version of the original dataset and captures the information of the original MMDB dataset with less noise. By showing that frames and video are equally informative for predicting engagement we have shown that our dataset contains the same information for this task as did the original dataset.

4.1   Method

We collected examples of disengaged and engaged children for each of the five stages. We then had users look at example videos (from the original MMDB dataset) and example frames (from our staticMMDB dataset) during each stage. Please see Fig. 6 for an example of the interface subjects used.

Fig. 6. Examples of the screens that would be shown to a subject during our user study. On the left is a screen-shot of a video from the 'Greeting' stage. Subjects were asked to watch the video (without sound) and then decide whether the child in the video was engaged. On the right is a screen-shot of the frames from the 'Greeting' stage. Subjects were again asked to decide if the child was engaged. Each subject was shown frames and videos from different children and from different engagement classes.

We recruited 23 users for our study. The subjects were randomly split into three groups; each group was shown the same data to annotate. For every stage a subject was shown 9 video examples and 9 frame examples. Six of the nine examples were children who scored a '0' (engaged), two of them scored a '1' (disengaged) and one child who scored a '2' (disengaged). Subjects were given examples of dis/engaged frames and videos before making their own predictions in order to train them on the task. They were told that engagement is determined by a number of factors including eye gaze direction, gestures, and reciprocity.

The study was divided across five days: one day for every stage (greet, ball, book, hat, tickle). The dataset contains 98 children with very few disengaged children. We spread the study across multiple days in order to prevent subjects remembering the behavior of a child across stages since they could potentially see the same child twice.

4.2   Results

Engagement Prediction: Subjects were very good at correctly identifying engaged children as shown in the class confusion matrices in Fig. 7. They did

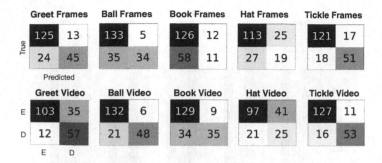

Fig. 7. Class-confusion matrices for the frame (top row) and video (bottom row) predictions for all examples. Subjects were very good at identifying engaged children (E) using both frames and videos for all stages. They were not as precise when identifying disengaged children (D) especially in the Book and Hat stages.

not do as well when predicting disengaged children. Engagement can represent itself subtly and can vary greatly between children. For certain activities, like greeting a person, it is much more obvious what cues to look for when making the decision (waving, eye contact). When engaging in a book however, it can be much more difficult to see if the child is interested and participating. Another particularly difficult stage for subjects was the Hat stage since very few children are disengaged (see Fig. 5 for statistics). All children in our dataset made eye-contact with the examiner during the Hat stage but it was not enough to decisively determine that the child was engaged.

Video vs. Frames: Correctly identifying disengaged children is critical when using this dataset. Since disengagement is a strong indicator of developmental delays such as autism it is most important to identify low-engagement children. We use the F1 score to report our results. The F1 score $\in [0,1]$ captures the method's performance using both precision and recall $F1 = 2 \times \frac{p\,r}{p+r}$. The scores for every stage, divided by performance on the engaged children (class 0) and disengaged children (class 1), can be seen in Fig. 1.

There is little performance difference when seeing videos (the original MMDB dataset) and our selected frames (the staticMMDB dataset). This supports our claim that the staticMMDB dataset is a useful summary of the MMDB dataset since it captures the important engagement information with far less data. We report the Kolmogorov-Smirnov test's p-value above every frame-video comparison. This test assumes that the data (frame predictions and video predictions) are sampled from the same distribution. The hypothesis is true for all our comparisons (Fig. 8).

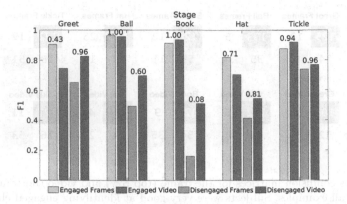

Fig. 8. For every stage we compare the F1 score of subjects when predicting the engagement for engaged children (green) and disengaged children (red). There is very little performance difference when seeing videos and frames (with the exception of disengaged children in the book stage). This supports the fact that the staticMMDB dataset captures the important information for predicting engagement in a much smaller dataset. We report the Kolmogorov-Smirnov test's p-value above every frame-video comparison. (Color figure online)

5   Engagement Prediction

5.1   Method

In our work we focus on representing the child's face because facial expressions, vocalizations, and gaze direction are of particular interest to examiners as outlined in their evaluation form.

Face Detection: Before extracting faces from the frames we cropped out a region around the child's face. We did this because our face detector either failed to detect faces in the full frame or only succeeded at detecting the parent's face.

For each child, we ran the frontal and profile Viola-Jones face detectors in MATLAB on each of the 22 annotated child-frames in the staticMMDB. If the algorithm detected more than one face we filtered out detections that were too low in the frame (since the children sit at a table), that had significant overlap with other detections, or that had very small bounding boxes. If two unique faces remained in the image, we selected the lowest face to represent the child (since the higher face is that of the adult). Face detections were manually checked and corrected to ensure that a child face had been identified.

We then expanded the face detection in the 22 frames to a larger box around the child's face. We applied the same box to surrounding frames. For frames located between two annotated face-box frames we applied a weighted (based upon temporal distance) average of the crop locations. This way we had a crop containing a child-face for every frame in the video. A visualization of our pipeline can be seen in Fig. 9. We passed the crop from every frame through the dlib face detector provided by [5].

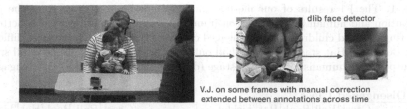

Fig. 9. Our method's pipeline. Frames are reduced to crops around the child's face using 22 corrected Viola-Jones face detections in each video. A face detector is run over the crops of all frames in the videos. We extract VGG Face features for every face and train a SVM to predict engagement.

Train - Test Split: We split our data into train and test sets based upon children. Since the scores of children across frames and stages are correlated we could not include the same child in training and testing. We split the children into 10 groups - eight of which contained 10 children and two of which contained 9 children. The groups were split so that every stage would contain at least one disengaged child. This allowed us to perform a 10-fold cross validation on the data. For each fold we randomly chose 8 groups of children to use in training and 1 to use in validation. The last group was reserved for testing.

VGG Face and SVM: Face identification networks extract features that describe the face and could be useful in predicting engagement. We chose the VGG Face network because of its state-of-the-art performance on face identification. The VGG-Face descriptors are computed using an implementation based on the VGG-Very-Deep-16 CNN architecture as described in [6]. We passed our detected child faces through the VGG Face network and extracted the features from the second-to-last layer. We normalize the feature representation and train a SVM to predict the engagement of the child in each frame. The SVM has a uniform prior as to not over-predict engagement.

Prediction: Children were given five ease-of-engagement scores, one score per stage. We report our method's performance based upon votes over the predictions for a child in every stage. For each stage the staticMMDB contains a set number of annotated frames (the Book stage has 3 frames for example). The annotated frames vote to predict the ease-of-engagement for the child in that stage and the final decision is what we use in evaluation.

5.2 Results

Baselines: We present two baselines for comparison. All results are computed and reported per-stage.

Prior: The prior performance on the dataset is analogous to what would happen if we drew a label (engaged or disengaged) from the training data's distribution (think of flipping a weighted coin). This strongly favors the engaged class.

Table 1. The F1 results of our method and two baselines: a draw from the prior distribution and human performance on frames. All methods perform much better at predicting engaged children than disengaged children. Humans have the most difficulty in the Book and Hat stages. Our method outperforms the Prior baseline in all stages and outperforms humans in the Book stage (disengaged) and the Hat stage (engaged).

F1 Disengaged Class

	Greet	Ball	Book	Hat	Tickle
Prior	31	17	30	8	22
Human	71	63	24	42	74
VGG Face	45	17	31	15	32

F1 Engaged Class

	Greet	Ball	Book	Hat	Tickle
Prior	65	79	66	89	75
Human	87	87	78	82	87
VGG Face	80	82	76	94	84

Human: We compare our method's performance to that of human prediction. It is not our goal to outperform humans at this task but rather to understand how much potential we have for improvement.

VGG Face Results: Our method performs strongly when predicting engaged children. It clearly outperforms the prior in all stages and outperforms humans in the Hat stage. Our method and humans perform worse when considering disengaged children. Our method beats human performance on the book stage and beats the prior baseline in all stages. Table 1 lists the F1 results on engaged and disengaged children for the baselines and our method.

Greeting Results: Our method performs strongly on the Greeting stage. The Greeting stage is a short and clear stage in which the child is expected to make eye-contact with the examiner, smile, or wave. This type of engagement is easily captured by our face features.

Ball Results: Our method struggles to rank disengaged children in the Ball stage. The ball stage is strongly determined by the child's interaction with the ball itself, an interaction that is difficult to capture using face features.

Book Results: Our method performs well at this stage and outperforms humans on the disengaged class. Humans struggle with the Book stage because of its subtlety and because of the stark contrast in a child's behavior between the ball and book stages. The Book stage's evaluation also depends on physical interactions with the book not visible in the face.

Hat Results: The hat stage is a difficult stage as reflected by the human performance on engaged children. We are able to predict engaged children more accurately than humans but do not perform as well as humans on disengaged children. The hat stage is evaluated using two prompts: "Where is the book?" and "It's a hat! It's on my head!". The examiner then looks to see if the child looked at her and if the child laughed. In the data, all children (including disengaged children) looked at the examiner. This stage also has the smallest number of disengaged children making it a difficult stage to predict engagement.

Tickle Results: We perform well on this stage. Children are most likely to hide their faces and move a lot in this stage but we are able to predict their engagement regardless. Humans still strongly outperform our method on disengaged children leaving room for improvement.

Conclusions: We have created a dataset that summarizes the very complex MMDB dataset. Our static version captures the action-reaction dynamic of the original assessment by highlighting the most important interactions. Our user study shows that our dataset preserves the information needed for predicting engagement while being much simpler than the original dataset. Our dataset provides the opportunity to work on the important task of engagement prediction and we have provided a baseline for future work to compare to.

Acknowledgements. This material is based in part upon work supported by the National Science Foundation under Grant Numbers IRI-1029035. Any opinions, findings, and conclusions or recommendations expressed in this material are those of the author(s) and do not necessarily reflect the views of the National Science Foundation.

References

1. Ousley, O.Y., Arriage, R.I., Morrier, M.J., Mathys, J.B., Allen, M.D., Abowd, G.D.: Beyond parental report: findings from the rapid-abc, a new 4-minute interactive autism. Technical report, Georgia Institute of Technology, September 2013
2. Rehg, J.M., Abowd, G.D., Rozga, A., Romero, M., Clements, M.A., Sclaroff, S., Essa, I.A., Ousley, O.Y., Li, Y., Kim, C., Rao, H., Kim, J.C., Presti, L.L., Zhang, J., Lantsman, D., Bidwell, J., Ye, Z.: Decoding children's social behavior. In: CVPR, pp. 3414–3421. IEEE (2013)
3. Lo Presti, L., Sclaroff, S., Rozga, A.: Joint alignment and modeling of correlated behavior streams. In: The IEEE International Conference on Computer Vision (ICCV) Workshops, December 2013
4. Gupta, R., Bone, D., Lee, S., Narayanan, S.: Analysis of engagement behavior in children during dyadic interactions using prosodic cues. Comput. Speech Lang. **37**, 47–66 (2015)
5. Amos, B., Ludwiczuk, B., Satyanarayanan, M.: Openface: a general-purpose face recognition library with mobile applications. Technical report, CMU-CS-16-118, CMU School of Computer Science (2016)
6. Parkhi, O.M., Vedaldi, A., Zisserman, A.: Deep face recognition. In: Proceedings of the British Machine Vision Conference (BMVC) (2015)

ChaLearn LAP 2016: First Round Challenge on First Impressions - Dataset and Results

Víctor Ponce-López[1,2,6], Baiyu Chen[4], Marc Oliu[6], Ciprian Corneanu[1,2(✉)], Albert Clapés[2], Isabelle Guyon[3,5], Xavier Baró[1,6], Hugo Jair Escalante[3,7], and Sergio Escalera[1,2,3]

[1] Computer Vision Center, Campus UAB, Barcelona, Spain
[2] Department of Mathematics, University of Barcelona, Barcelona, Spain
cipriancorneanu@gmail.com
[3] ChaLearn, Berkeley, CA, USA
[4] UC Berkeley, Berkeley, CA, USA
[5] University of Paris-Saclay, Paris, France
[6] EIMT/IN3 at the Open University of Catalonia, Barcelona, Spain
[7] INAOE, Puebla, Mexico

Abstract. This paper summarizes the ChaLearn Looking at People 2016 First Impressions challenge data and results obtained by the teams in the first round of the competition. The goal of the competition was to automatically evaluate five "apparent" personality traits (the so-called "Big Five") from videos of subjects speaking in front of a camera, by using human judgment. In this edition of the ChaLearn challenge, a novel data set consisting of 10,000 shorts clips from YouTube videos has been made publicly available. The ground truth for personality traits was obtained from workers of Amazon Mechanical Turk (AMT). To alleviate calibration problems between workers, we used pairwise comparisons between videos, and variable levels were reconstructed by fitting a Bradley-Terry-Luce model with maximum likelihood. The CodaLab open source platform was used for submission of predictions and scoring. The competition attracted, over a period of 2 months, 84 participants who are grouped in several teams. Nine teams entered the final phase. Despite the difficulty of the task, the teams made great advances in this round of the challenge.

Keywords: Behavior analysis · Personality traits · First impressions

1 Introduction

"You don't get a second chance to make a first impression", a saying famously goes. First impressions are rapid judgments of personality traits and complex social characteristics like dominance, hierarchy, warmth, and threat [1–3]. Accurate first impressions of personality traits have been shown to be possible when observers were exposed to relatively short intervals (4 to 10 min) of ongoing streams of individuals behavior [1,4], and even to static photographs present for 10 s [2]. Most extraordinarily, trait assignment among human observers has been shown to be as fast as 100 ms [5].

© Springer International Publishing Switzerland 2016
G. Hua and H. Jégou (Eds.): ECCV 2016 Workshops, Part III, LNCS 9915, pp. 400–418, 2016.
DOI: 10.1007/978-3-319-49409-8_32

Personality is a strong predictor of important life outcomes like happiness and longevity, quality of relationships with peers, family, occupational choice, satisfaction, and performance, community involvement, criminal activity, and political ideology [6,7]. Personality plays an important role in the way people manage the images they convey in self-presentations and employment interviews, trying to affect the audience first impressions and increase effectiveness. Among the many other factors influencing employment interview outcomes like social factors, interviewer-applicant similarity, application fit, information exchange, preinterview impressions, applicant characteristics (appearance, age, gender), disabilities and training [8], personality traits are one of the most influential [9].

The key-assumption of personality psychology is that stable individual characteristics result into stable behavioral patterns that people tend to display independently of the situation [10]. The Five Factor Model (or the Big Five) is currently the dominant paradigm in personality research. It models the human personality along five dimensions: Extraversion, Agreeableness, Conscientiousness, Neuroticism and Openness. Many studies have confirmed consistency and universality of this model.

In the field of Computer Science, Personality Computing studies how machines could automatically recognize or synthesize human personality [10]. The literature in Personality Computing is considerable. Methods were proposed for recognizing personality from nonverbal aspects of verbal communication [11,12], multimodal combinations of speaking style (prosody, intonation, etc.) and body movements [13–18], facial expressions [19,20], combining acoustic with visual cues or physiological with visual cues [19,21–23]. Visual cues can refer to eye gaze [14], frowning, head orientation [22,23], mouth fidgeting [14], primary facial expressions [19,20] or characteristics of primary facial expressions like presence, frequency or duration [19].

As far as we know, there is no consistent data corpus in personality computing and no bench-marking effort has yet been organized. It is a great impediment in the further advancement of this line of research and the main motivator of this challenge. This challenge is part of a larger project which studies outcomes of job interviews. We have designed a dataset collected from publicly available YouTube videos where people talk to the camera in a self-presentation context. The setting is similar to video-conference interviews. Consistent to research in psychology and the related literature in automatic personality computing we have labeled the data based on the Big Five model using the Amazon Mechanical Turk (see Sect. 3). We are running a second round for the ICPR 2016 conference. It will take the form of a coopetition in which participants both compete and collaborate by sharing their code.

This challenge belongs to a series of events organized by ChaLearn since 2011[1]: the 2011–2012, user dependent One-shot-learning Gesture Recognition challenge [24,25], the 2013–2014 user independent Multi-modal Gesture Recognition challenge, the 2014–2015 human pose recovery and action recognition [26,27], and the 2015–2016 cultural event recognition [28] and apparent age estimation

---

[1] http://gesture.chalearn.org/.

[29, 30]. In this 2016 edition, it is the first time we organize the First Impression challenge on automatic personality recognition.

The rest of this paper is organized as follows: in Sect. 2 we present the schedule of the competition and the evaluation procedures, in Sect. 3 we describe the data we have collected, Sect. 4 is dedicated to presenting, comparing and discussing the methods submitted in the competition. Section 5 concludes the paper with an extended discussion and suggestions about future work.

2   Challenge Protocol, Evaluation Procedure, and Schedule

The ECCV ChaLearn LAP 2016 challenge consisted in a single track competition to quantitatively evaluate the recognition of the apparent Big Five personality traits on multi-modal audio+RGB data from YouTube videos. The challenge was managed using the CodaLab open source platform of Microsoft[2]. The participants had to submit prediction results during the challenge. The winners had to publicly release their source code.

The competition had two phases:

– A development phase during which the participants had access to 6,000 manually labeled continuous video sequences of 15 s each. Thus, 60 % of the videos used for training are randomly grouped in 75 training batches. They could get immediate feedback on their prediction performance by submitting results on an unlabeled validation set of 2000 videos. These 2,000 videos used in validation represent 20 % over the total set of videos and are also randomly grouped in 25 validation batches.
– A final phase during which the competitors could submit their predictions on 2,000 new test videos (the remainder 20 % over the total set of videos, also grouped in 25 test batches). The prediction scores on test data were not revealed until the end of the challenge.

2.1   Evaluation Metrics

The participants of the different teams trained their models to imitate human judgments consisting in continuous target values in the range $[0, 1]$ for each trait. Thus, their goal was to produce for each video in the validation set or the test set, 5 continuous prediction values in the range $[0, 1]$, one for each trait.

For this task (similar in spirit to a regression) the evaluation consisted in computing the **mean accuracy** over all traits and videos. Accuracy for each trait is defined as:

$$A = 1 - \frac{1}{N_t} \sum_{i=1}^{Nt} |t_i - p_i| / \sum_{i=1}^{Nt} |t_i - \bar{t}| \tag{1}$$

---

[2] https://competitions.codalab.org/.

where p_i are the predicted scores, t_i are the ground truth scores, with the sum running over the N_t test videos, and $\bar{t}$ is the average ground truth score over all videos[3]. Additionally, we also computed (but did not use to rank the participants) the coefficient of determination:

$$R^2 = 1 - \sum_{i=1}^{Nt}(t_i - p_i)^2 / \sum_{i=1}^{Nt}(t_i - \bar{t})^2. \qquad (2)$$

We also turned the problems into classification problems by thresholding the target values at 0.5. This way we obtained 5 binary classification problems (one for each trait). We used the Area under the ROC curve (AUC) to estimate the classification accuracy[4].

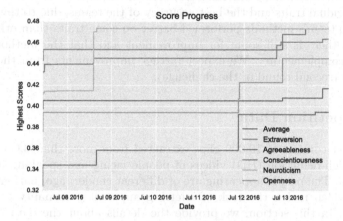

Fig. 1. Progress of validation set leaderboard highest scores of all teams for each trait and progress of the highest ranking score (mean accuracy over all traits). The score used is the accuracy, normalized as in Eq. 1.

2.2 Schedule

The competition lasted two months and attracted 84 participants, who were grouped into several teams. The schedule was the following:

May 15, 2016: Beginning of the quantitative competition, release of the development data (with labels) and validation data (without labels).

June 30, 2016: Release of encrypted final evaluation data (without labels). Participants can start training their methods with the whole data set.

July 2, 2016: Deadline for code submission.

---

[3] This definition is slightly different from what we used on the leaderboard. The leaderboard accuracy is not normalized $A = 1 - \frac{1}{N_t}\sum_{i=1}^{Nt}|t_i - p_i|$. This change does not affect the ranking.

[4] See e.g. https://en.wikipedia.org/wiki/Receiver_operating_characteristic.

July 3, 2016: Release of final evaluation data decryption key. Participants start predicting the results on the final evaluation data.

July 13, 2016: End of the quantitative competition. Deadline for submitting the predictions over the final evaluation data. The organizers started the code verification by running it on the final evaluation data.

July 15, 2016: Deadline for submitting the fact sheets. Release of the verification results to the participants for review. Participants of the top ranked teams are invited to follow the workshop submission guide for inclusion at ECCV 2016 ChaLearn LAP 2016 Workshop on Apparent Personality Analysis.

As can be seen in Fig. 1 progresses were made throughout the challenge and improvements were made until the very end. At the date the challenge ended, there was still a noticeable difference between the average of the best accuracies on the individual traits and the best accuracy of the teams, due to the fact that some of the team's methods performed better on some traits than others. This shows that there is still room for improvement and that the methods of the teams are complementary. We expect further improvements from the ongoing coopetition (second round of the challenge).

3   Competition Data

The data set consists of 10,000 clips extracted from more than 3,000 different YouTube high-definition (HD) videos of people facing and speaking in English to a camera. The people appearing are of different gender, age, nationality, and ethnicity, which makes the task of inferring apparent personality traits more challenging. In this section, we provide the details about the data collection, preparation, and the final data set[5].

3.1   Video Data

We collected a large pool of HD (720p) videos from YouTube. After visioning a large number of videos, we found Q&A videos to be particularly suitable and abundant talking-to-the-camera videos. These are generally videos with fewer people appearing, little moving background, and clear voice. Since YouTube videos are organized in channels, which can contain a variable number of videos, we limited the number of videos per YouTube channel (author) to 3 in order to keep a balance of unique subjects.

After having downloaded an initial pool of 13,951 YouTube videos using pytube Python's API[6], we manually filtered out unsuitable footage (too short sequences or non English speakers). From the remaining 8,581 videos, we automatically generated a set of 32,139 clips of 15 s each. The clip generation was automatically done by searching continuous 15-second video segments in which

---

[5] Data set is available at http://gesture.chalearn.org/2016-looking-at-people-eccv-work shop-challenge/data-and-description.

[6] PyTube API: https://github.com/nficano/pytube.

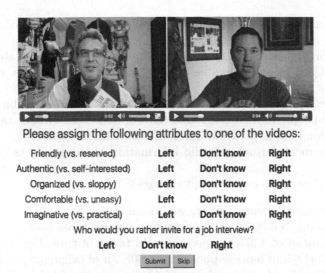

Please assign the following attributes to one of the videos:

Friendly (vs. reserved)	**Left**	**Don't know**	**Right**
Authentic (vs. self-interested)	**Left**	**Don't know**	**Right**
Organized (vs. sloppy)	**Left**	**Don't know**	**Right**
Comfortable (vs. uneasy)	**Left**	**Don't know**	**Right**
Imaginative (vs. practical)	**Left**	**Don't know**	**Right**

Who would you rather invite for a job interview?

Left   Don't know   Right

Submit | Skip

Fig. 2. Data collection web page. Comparing pairs of videos, the AMT workers had to indicate their preference for five attributes representing the "Big Five" personality traits, following these instructions: *"You have been hired as a Human Resource (HR) specialist in a company, which is rapidly growing. Your job is to help screening potential candidates for interviews. The company is using two criteria: (A) competence, and (B) personality traits. The candidates have already been pre-selected for their competence for diverse positions in the company. Now you need to evaluate their personality traits from video clips found on the Internet and decide to invite them or not for an interview. Your tasks are the following. (1) First, you will compare pairs of people with respect to five traits: Extraversion = Friendly (vs. reserved); Agreeableness = Authentic (vs. self-interested); Conscientiousness = Organized (vs. sloppy); Neuroticism = Comfortable (vs. uneasy); Openness = Imaginative (vs. practical). (2) Then, you will decide who of the 2 people you would rather interview for the job posted."* In this challenge we did not use the answers to the last question.

one and only one face appeared. Faces were detected using Viola-Jones from OpenCV [31]. We retained only faces with at least one visible eye – with eyes being also detected using Viola-Jones. To increase robustness, we kept only those clips meeting both criteria ("one and only one face bounding box containing at least one eye") in 75 % of the frames. Videos were of various duration, hence we limited the number of clips per video to at most 6.

We then performed a second fine-grained manual filtering – this time considering clips, instead of whole videos – using a custom web interface to filter out those clips not meeting the following criteria:

– One unique person as foreground at a safe distance from the camera.
– Good quality of audio and images.
– Only English speaking.
– People above 13–15 years old. Non-identified babies appearing with the parents might be allowed.

- Not too much camera movement (changing background allowed, but avoid foreground constantly blurred).
- No adult or violent contents (except people casually talking about sex or answering Q&A in an acceptable manner). Discard any libelous, doubtful or problematic contents.
- No nude (except if only parts above shoulders and neck are visible).
- Might have people in the background (crowd, audience, without talking, with low resolution of faces to avoid any confusion with the speaker).
- No advertisement (visual or audio information about products or company names).
- Avoid visual or audio cuts (abrupt changes).

From this second manual filter, we obtained the final set of 10,000 clips. These correspond to 3,060 unique originating videos. From those, we were able to generate a mean of 3.27 clips per video. In terms of time duration, the clips correspond to 41.6 h of footage pooled from 608.7 h of originating videos.

On the other hand, the originating videos were provided by 2,764 unique YouTube channels. Note, however, that the number of channels do not correspond to number of people (a youtuber can have different channels or participate in other youtubers' channels), but it provides an estimation of the diversity of people appearing in the data set. The originating videos are also quite diverse in both their number of views and their 5-star ratings, which also helped to alleviate bias towards any particular kind of videos. This information is summarized in Table 1 together with other statistics computed from videos' meta-data. The table is completed with the 20 most common keywords (or tags) associated to the originating videos. As we stated before, we focused on Q&A videos, often related to other video content such as vlogging, HOW TOs, and beauty tips (mostly makeup).

3.2 Ground-Truth Estimation

Obtaining ground truth for Personality Traits can be challenging. Before deciding to use human labeling of videos, we considered using self-administered personality tests on subjects we interviewed. We concluded that such test results are biased and variable. Additionally, performing our own interviews did not allow us to collect massive amounts of data. Therefore, for this dataset, we resorted to use the perception of human subjects visioning the videos. This is a different task than evaluating real personality traits, but equally useful in the context of human interaction (e.g. job interviews, dating, etc.).

To rapidly obtain a large number of labels, we used Amazon Mechanical Turk (AMT), as is now common in computer vision [32]. Our budget allowed us to get multiple votes per video, in an effort to reduce variance. However, because each worker (aka voter) contributes only a few labels in a large dataset, this raises the problem of bias and the need for calibrating the labels. Biases, which can be traced for example to harshness, prejudices for race, age, or gender, and cultural prejudices, are very hard to measure.

We addressed this problem by using pairwise comparisons. We designed a custom interface (see Fig. 2).

Each AMT worker labeled small batches of pairs of videos. To ensure a good coverage and some overlap in the labeling of pairs of videos across workers, we generated pairs with a small-world algorithm [33]. Small-world graphs provide high connectivity, avoid disconnected regions in the graph, have a well distributed edges, and minimum distance between nodes [34] (Fig. 3).

Cardinal scores were obtained by fitting a BTL model [35]. This is a probabilistic model such that the probability that an object j is judged to have more

Table 1. Video data preparation and final data set statistics.

Preparation	Downloaded videos	13,951* (HD 720p @ 30 FPS)
	Remaining videos (supervised from*)	8,581**
	Sampled videos per channel	3 (at most)
	Sampled clips per video	6 (at most)
	Clip length	15 s
	Candidate clips (sampled from**)	32,139†
Final data set	**Final set of clips** (supervised from †)	**10,000‡**
	Total duration of clips	41.6 h (4.5M frames)
	Unique channels (originating‡)	2,764; {1: 2,584, 2: 161, 3: 19}§
	Unique videos (originating‡)	3,060; {1: 721, 2: 533, 3: 464, 4: 398, 5: 435, 6: 509}¶
	Mean no. clips per video	3.27
	Duration of originating videos	608.7 h
	Total no. views of originating videos	More than 115M; {0–100: 27.64 %, 100–1K: 34.15 %, 1K–10K: 22.68 %, 10K–100K: 11.44 %, >100K : 4.08 %}$^\parallel$
	Originating videos' avg. rating	4.6/5.0; {1: 8, 2: 11, 3: 43, 4: 1340, 5: 1,395}
	Originating videos' keywords (top 20)	'Q&A', 'q&a', 'vlog', 'questions', 'makeup', 'beauty', 'answers', 'funny', 'Video Blog (Website Category)', 'question and answer', 'answer', 'question', 'fashion', 'Vlog', 'Questions', 'vlogger', 'how to', 'tutorial', 'q and a', 'Answers'

§ is a frequency count, i.e. how many channels contribute to the final set of 10,000 clips with 1, 2, or 3 clips respectively;
¶ analogously to ($\S$), that is how many videos contribute to the 10,000 clips with $1, 2, \ldots, 6$ clips;
$^\parallel$ is a relative frequency count of videos with a number of views ranging in different intervals (0 to 100, 100 to 1K, etc.).

Fig. 3. Screenshot of sample videos voted to clearly perceive the traits, on either end of the spectrum.

of an attribute than object i is a sigmoid function of the difference between cardinal scores. Maximum Likelihood estimation was used to fit the model. Deeper details and explanations of the procedure to convert from pairwise scores to cardinal scores are provided in a companion paper [36], where a study is conducted to evaluate how many videos we could label with the constraints of our financial budget. We ended up affording 321,684 pairs to label 10,000 videos.

4   Challenge Results and Methods

In this section we summarize the methods proposed by the teams and provide a detailed description of the winning methods. The teams submitted their code and predictions for the test sets; the source code is available from the challenge website.[7] Then, we provide a statistical analysis of the results and highlight overall aspects of the competition.

4.1   Summary of Methods Used

In Table 2 we summarize the various approaches of the teams who participated in the final phase, uploaded their models, and returned a survey about methods we asked them to answer (so-called "fact sheets").

The vast majority of approaches, including the best performing methods, used both audio and video modalities. Most of the teams represented the audio with handcrafted spectral features, a notable exception being the method proposed by team *DCC*, where a residual network [37] was used instead. For the video modality the dominant approach was to learn the representations through convolutional neural networks [38]. The modalities were late-fused in most methods before being fed to different regression methods like fully connected neural networks or Support Vector Regressors. A notable exception is the method proposed by team *evolgen*, which includes temporal structure by partitioning the video sequences and sequentially feeding the learned audio-video representation to a recurrent Long Short Term Memory layer [39].

Most teams made semantic assumptions about the data by separating face from background. Usually, this was achieved by preprocessing such as face frontalisation. However, it is important to notice that the winning method of team *NJU-LAMDA* does not make any kind of semantic separation of the content.

Finally, a common approach was to use pre-trained deep models fine-tuned on the dataset provided for this challenge. The readers are referred to Table 2 for a synthesis of the main characteristics of the methods that have been submitted to this challenge and to Table 3 for the achieved results. Next, we provide a more detailed description of the three winning methods.

First place: The *NJU-LAMDA* team proposed two separate models for still images and audio, processing multiple frames from the video and employing a two-step late fusion of the frame and audio predictions [40]. For the video modality, it proposed DAN+, an extension to Descriptor Aggregation Networks [43] which applies max and average pooling at two different layers of the CNN, normalizing and concatenating the outputs before feeding them to a fully connected layers. A pretrained VGG-face model [44] is used, replacing the fully-connected layers and fine-tuning the model with the First Impressions dataset. For the

---

[7] http://gesture.chalearn.org/2016-looking-at-people-eccv-workshop-challenge/winner_code.

Table 2. Overview of the team methods comparing pretraining (topology and data), preprocessing if performed, representation, learning strategy per modality and fusion.

	Pretraining	Preprocessing	Modality				Fusion
			Audio		Video		
			R[a]	L[b]	R[a]	L[b]	
NJU-LAMDA [40]	VGG-face	-	Logfbank[c]	NN	CNN	CNN	Late
Evolgen [41]	-	Face alignment	Spectral	RCNN[j]	RCNN[j]	RCNN[j]	Early
DCC [42]	-	-	ResNet	ResNet+FC	ResNet	ResNet+FC	Late
ucas	VGG, AlexNet, ResNet	Face alignment	Spectral	PSLR[d], SVR[e]	CNN(face/scene)	PSLR[d], SVR[e]	Late
BU-NKU	VGG-face, FER2013	Face alignment	-	-	CNN(face/scene)	KELM[f]	Early
Pandora	-	Face alignment	LLD[h]	Bagged regressor	CNN(face/scene)	CNN	Early
Pilab	-	-	Spectral	RF regressor	-	-	-
Kaizoku	-	-	MFCC[i]/CNN	CNN	CNN	CNN	Late
ITU-SiMiT	VGG-face, VGG-16	Face detection	-	-	CNN(face/scene)	SVR[e]	Late

[a]R = Representation, [b]L = Learning Strategy, [c]logfbank = Logarithm Filterbank Energies, [d]PSLR = Partial Least Square Regressor, [e]SVR = Support Vector Regression, [f]KELM = Kernel Extreme Learning Machine, [g]FER = Facial Expression Recognition Dataset, [h]LLD = Low Level Descriptor, [i]MFCC = Mel Frequency Cepstral Coefficient, [j]RCNN = Recurrent Convolutional Neural Networks.

audio modality it employs log filter bank (logfbank) features and a single fully-connected layer with sigmoid activations. At test time, a predefined number of frames are fed to the visual network and the predictions averaged. The final visual predictions are averaged again with the output of the audio predictor.

Second place: The *evolgen* team proposed a multimodal LSTM architecture for predicting the personality traits [41]. In order to maintain the temporal structure, the input video sequences are split in six non-overlapping partitions. From each of the partitions the audio representation is extracted using classical spectral features and statistical measurements, forming a 68-dimensional feature vector. The video representation is extracted by randomly selecting a frame from the partition, extracting the face and centering it through face alignment. The preprocessed data is passed to a Recurrent CNN, trained end-to-end, which uses a separate pipeline for audio and video. Each partition frame is processed with convolutional layers, afterwards applying a linear transform to reduce the dimensionality. The audio features of a given partition go through a linear transform and are concatenated with the frame features. The Recurrent layer is sequentially fed with the features extracted from each partition. In this way, the recurrent network captures variations in audio and facial expressions for personality trait prediction.

Third place: The DCC team proposed a multimodal personality trait recognition model comprising of two separate auditory and visual streams (deep residual networks, 17 layers each), followed by an audiovisual stream (one fully-connected layer with hyperbolic tangent activation) that is trained end-to-end to predict the big five personality traits [42]. There is no pretraining, but a simple preprocessing is performed where a random frame and crop of the audio are selected as inputs. During test, the whole audio and video sequences are fed into the auditory and visual streams, applying average pooling before being fed to the fully-connected layer.

The approaches of all three winning methods use separate streams for audio and video, applying neural networks for both streams. The first and second places both use some kind of data preprocessing, with the NJU-LAMDA team using logfbank features for the audio and the evolgen team using face cropping and spectral audio features. The second and third methods both use end-to-end training, fusing the audio and video streams with fully-connected layers.

4.2   Statistical Analysis of the Results

Table 3 lists the results on test data using different metrics. One can also observe very close and competitive results among the top five teams. The results of the top ranking teams are within the error bar.

For comparison, we indicated the results obtained by using the median predictions of all ranked teams. No improvement is gained by using this voting scheme. We also show "random guess", which corresponds to randomly permuting these random predictions.

We treated the problem either as a regression problem or as a classification problem:

– **As a regression problem.** The metric that was used in the challenge to rank teams is the mean (normalized) accuracy (Eq. 1). We normalized it in such a way that making constant predictions of the average target values yields a score of 0. The best score is 1. During the challenge we did not normalize the accuracy; however this normalization does not affect the ranking. Normalizing makes the Accuracy more comparable to the R^2 and results are easier to interpret. The results obtained with the R^2 metric (Eq. 2) are indeed similar, except that the third and fourth ranking teams are swapped. The advantage of using the Accuracy over the R^2 is that it is less sensitive to outliers.
– **As a classification problem.** The AUC metric (for which random guesses yield a score of 0.5, and exact predictions a score of 1) yields slightly different results. The fourth ranking team performs best according to that metric. Classification is generally an easier problem than regression. We see that classification results are quite good compared to regression results.

For the regression analysis, we graphically represented the Accuracy results (the official ranking score) as a box plot (Fig. 4) showing the distribution of scores for each trait and the overall accuracy. For the classification analysis,

Table 3. Results of the first round of the Personality Trait challenge. Top: the Accuracy score used to rank the teams (Eq. 1). Middle: R^2 score (Eq. 2). Bottom: Area under the ROC Curve (AUC) evaluating predictions by turning the problem into a classification problem. The error bars are the standard deviations computed with the bootstrap method. The best results are indicated in bold.

Rank	Team Name	Extraversion	Agreeableness	Conscientiousness	Neuroticism	Openness	Average
	Accuracy score (normalized)						
	Median Pred.	0.4188 ± 0.0132	0.3179 ± 0.0148	0.4193 ± 0.0097	0.3892 ± 0.0121	0.3749 ± 0.0116	0.3840 ± 0.0123
1	NJU-LAMDA	0.4215 ± 0.0146	**0.3450** ± 0.0210	**0.4497** ± 0.0145	0.4087 ± 0.0171	0.3876 ± 0.0171	**0.4025** ± 0.0169
2	evolgen	0.4358 ± 0.0164	0.3318 ± 0.0178	0.4295 ± 0.0126	0.4069 ± 0.0238	**0.3920** ± 0.0181	0.3992 ± 0.0178
3	DCC	0.3987 ± 0.0217	0.3236 ± 0.0157	0.4310 ± 0.0153	**0.4091** ± 0.0116	0.3740 ± 0.0184	0.3873 ± 0.0165
4	ucas	0.4180 ± 0.0129	0.3123 ± 0.0111	0.4128 ± 0.0168	0.3891 ± 0.0134	0.3811 ± 0.0118	0.3827 + 0.0132
5	BU-NKU	**0.4416** ± 0.0188	0.2990 ± 0.0175	0.4324 ± 0.0217	0.3586 ± 0.0156	0.3651 ± 0.0162	0.3794 ± 0.0180
6	pandora	0.3771 ± 0.0150	0.3008 ± 0.0187	0.3770 ± 0.0156	0.3767 ± 0.0211	0.3670 ± 0.0200	0.3597 ± 0.0181
7	Pilab	0.2825 ± 0.0142	0.2464 ± 0.0214	0.2581 ± 0.0124	0.2897 ± 0.0142	0.2977 ± 0.0166	0.2749 ± 0.0158
8	Kaizoku	0.1620 ± 0.0314	0.1848 ± 0.0242	0.2183 ± 0.0299	0.1885 ± 0.0313	0.2353 ± 0.0179	0.1978 ± 0.0270
9	ITU-SiMiT	0.1847 ± 0.0067	0.1953 ± 0.0106	0.1750 ± 0.0082	0.1990 ± 0.0099	0.1915 ± 0.0091	0.1891 ± 0.0089
	Random Guess	0.0697 ± 0.0423	0.1253 ± 0.0456	0.0865 ± 0.0512	0.1039 ± 0.0383	0.0799 ± 0.0490	0.0931 ± 0.0453

Rank	Team Name	Extraversion	Agreeableness	Conscientiousness	Neuroticism	Openness	Average
	R^2 score						
	Median Pred.	0.5048 ± 0.0307	0.2972 ± 0.0361	0.5239 ± 0.0301	0.4565 ± 0.0284	0.4144 ± 0.0353	0.4394 ± 0.0321
1	NJU-LAMDA	0.4808 ± 0.0367	**0.3381** ± 0.0247	0.4883 ± 0.0298	**0.4745** ± 0.0318	0.4370 ± 0.0276	**0.4548** ± 0.0800
2	evolgen	**0.5151** ± 0.0812	0.3289 ± 0.0366	0.4883 ± 0.0298	0.4554 ± 0.0287	0.4141 ± 0.0391	0.4404 ± 0.0331
3	DCC	0.4312 ± 0.0405	0.2961 ± 0.0293	0.4781 ± 0.0360	0.4484 ± 0.0322	0.4026 ± 0.0249	0.4113 ± 0.0326
4	ucas	0.4890 ± 0.0394	0.2921 ± 0.0242	0.5195 ± 0.0330	0.4573 ± 0.0369	0.4391 ± 0.0295	0.4394 ± 0.0326
5	BU-NKU	0.5143 ± 0.0318	0.2339 ± 0.0313	0.4866 ± 0.0318	0.3634 ± 0.0325	0.3721 ± 0.0279	0.3941 ± 0.0311
6	pandora	0.4141 ± 0.0316	0.2440 ± 0.0290	0.4020 ± 0.0375	0.3772 ± 0.0406	0.3675 ± 0.0255	0.3610 ± 0.0328
7	Pilab	0.2204 ± 0.0343	0.1208 ± 0.0349	0.1554 ± 0.0342	0.2292 ± 0.0237	0.2266 ± 0.0288	0.1905 ± 0.0312
8	Kaizoku	0.2260 ± 0.0324	0.1098 ± 0.0210	0.2248 ± 0.0326	0.2246 ± 0.0248	0.2269 ± 0.0346	0.2024 ± 0.0291
9	ITU-SiMiT	0.0074 ± 0.0082	0.0020 ± 0.0035	0.0061 ± 0.0059	0.0015 ± 0.0015	0.0033 ± 0.0047	0.0040 ± 0.0048
	Random Guess	0.0024 ± 0.0025	0.0020 ± 0.0023	0.0017 ± 0.0016	0.0019 ± 0.0036	0.0015 ± 0.0026	0.0019 ± 0.0025

Rank	Team Name	Extraversion	Agreeableness	Conscientiousness	Neuroticism	Openness	Average
	AUC score						
	Median Pred.	0.8333 ± 0.0138	0.7625 ± 0.0255	0.8504 ± 0.0196	0.8112 ± 0.0196	0.8179 ± 0.0170	0.8241 ± 0.0181
1	NJU-LAMDA	0.8391 ± 0.0247	0.7634 ± 0.0239	**0.8696** ± 0.0147	0.8199 ± 0.0147	0.8217 ± 0.0173	0.8227 ± 0.0191
2	evolgen	0.8376 ± 0.0160	**0.7771** ± 0.0210	0.8492 ± 0.0165	0.8260 ± 0.0184	0.8135 ± 0.0156	0.8207 ± 0.0175
3	DCC	0.8178 ± 0.0187	0.7528 ± 0.0227	0.8579 ± 0.0160	0.8131 ± 0.0239	0.8138 ± 0.0233	0.8111 ± 0.0209
4	ucas	0.8421 ± 0.0193	0.7767 ± 0.0253	0.8569 ± 0.0166	**0.8338** ± 0.0181	**0.8290** ± 0.0159	**0.8277** ± 0.0190
5	BU-KNU	**0.8438** ± 0.0201	0.7372 ± 0.0299	0.8586 ± 0.0154	0.7854 ± 0.0255	0.7991 ± 0.0172	0.8048 ± 0.0212
6	pandora	0.8097 ± 0.0173	0.7435 ± 0.0239	0.8074 ± 0.0161	0.7987 ± 0.0169	0.8026 ± 0.0150	0.7924 ± 0.0178
7	Pilab	0.7139 ± 0.0277	0.6608 ± 0.0229	0.6870 ± 0.0254	0.7321 ± 0.0199	0.7195 ± 0.0278	0.7026 ± 0.0247
8	Kaizoku	0.7286 ± 0.0198	0.6603 ± 0.0241	0.7393 ± 0.0263	0.7277 ± 0.0179	0.7051 ± 0.0218	0.7122 ± 0.0220
9	ITU-SiMiT	0.4410 ± 0.0255	0.4669 ± 0.0216	0.4778 ± 0.0212	0.4863 ± 0.0193	0.4706 ± 0.0154	0.4685 ± 0.0206
	Random Guess	0.4988 ± 0.0272	0.5129 ± 0.0214	0.5161 ± 0.0255	0.5010 ± 0.0264	0.5193 ± 0.0252	0.5096 ± 0.0252

we show ROC curves in Fig. 5. In both cases Agreeableness seems significantly harder to predict than other traits, while Conscientiousness is the easiest (albeit with a large variance). We also see that all top ranking teams have similar ROC curves.

An analysis of the correlation between the five personality traits for both the ground truth and the median predictions (Fig. 6) shows some correlation between labels, particularly the group Extraversion, Neurotism, and Openness.

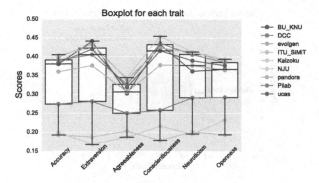

Fig. 4. Distribution of final scores for each trait and performance of the individual teams. We see that "Agreeableness" is consistently harder to predict by the top ranking teams.

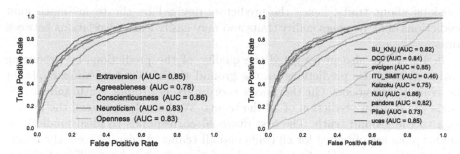

Fig. 5. Receiver operating characteristic curve of the median prediction of each trait, the median taken over all ranked teams predictions (left) and averaged over all traits for each team (right)

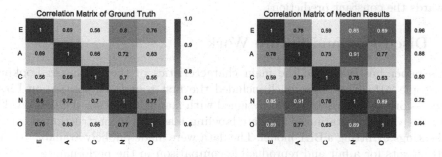

Fig. 6. Correlation matrices. Correlation for all videos between ground truth labels (left), and between the median predictions of the teams (right).

This remains true for the team' predictions; Agreeableness is also significantly correlated to that group. For the predictions the correlation between any given pair of traits is 25–35 % higher for the team' predictions than for the ground truth. Nothing in the challenge setting encourages methods to "orthogonalize"

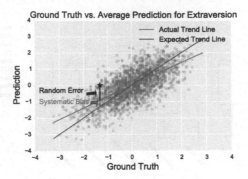

Fig. 7. Ground truth vs. average prediction for extraversion. Each dot represents a video. The average is taken over all final submissions.

decisions about traits, hence the predictors devised by the teams make joint predictions of all five personality traits and may easily learn correlations between traits.

In Fig. 7, we also investigated the quality of the predictions by producing scatter plots of the predictions vs. the ground truth. We show an example for the trait Extraversion. On the x-axis coordinate is ground truth and on the y-axis the median prediction of all the teams. We linearly regressed the predictions to the ground truth. The first diagonal corresponds to ideal predictions. Similar plots are obtained for all traits and all teams. As can be seen, the points do not gather around the first diagonal and the two lines have different slopes. We interpret this as follows: there are two sources of error, a systematic error corresponding to a bias in prediction towards the average ground truth value, and a random error. Essentially the models are under-fitting (they are biased towards the constant prediction).

5   Discussion and Future Work

This paper has described the main characteristics of the ChaLearn Looking at People 2016 Challenge which included the first round competition on First Impressions. A large dataset was designed with manual selection of videos, AMT pairwise video annotation to alleviate labeling bias, and reconstruction of cardinal ratings by fitting a BLT model. The data were made publicly available to the participants for a fair and reproducible comparison in the performance results. Analyzing the methods used by 9 teams that participated in the final evaluation and uploaded their models (out of a total of 84 participants), several conclusions can be drawn:

– There was a lot of emulation during the challenge and the final results are close to one another even though the methods are quite diverse.
– Feature learning (via deep learning methods) dominates the analysis, but pretrained models are widely used (perhaps due to the limited amount of available training data).

- Late fusion is generally applied, though additional layers fusing higher level representations from separate video and audio streams are often used.
- Video is usually analyzed at a per-frame basis, pooling the video features or fusing the predictions. The second place winner is an exception, using an LSTM to integrate the temporal information.
- Many teams used contextual cues and extracted faces, but some top ranking teams did not.

Even though performances are already quite good, from the above analysis it is still difficult to ensure the achievement of human level performance. Since there is a wide variety of complementary approaches, to push participants to improve their performances by joining forces, we are organizing a first coopetition (combination of competition and collaboration) for ICPR 2016. In this first edition of coopetition, we reward people for sharing their code by combining the traditional accuracy score with the number of downloads of their code. With this setting, the methods are not only evaluated by the organizers, but also by the other participants.

We are preparing a more sophisticated coopetition that will include more interactive characteristics, such as the possibility for teams to share modules of their overall system. To that end, we will exploit CodaLab worksheets (http://worksheets.codalab.org), a new feature resembling iPython notebooks, which allow user to share code (not limited to Python) intermixed with text, data, and results. We are working on integrating into CodaLab worksheets a system of reward mechanisms suitable to keep challenge participants engaged.

As mentioned in the introduction, the First Impressions challenge is part of a larger project on Speed Interviews for job hiring purposes. Some of our next steps will consist in including more modalities that can be used together with audio-RGB data as part of a multimedia CV. Examples of such modalities include handwritten letters and/or traditional CVs.

Acknowledgments. We are very grateful for the funding provided by Microsoft Research without which this work would not have been possible, and for the kind support provided by Evelyne Viegas, director of the Microsoft AI Outreach project, since the inception of this project. We also thank the Microsoft CodaLab support team for their responsiveness and particularly Flavio Zhingri. We sincerely thank all the teams who participated in ChaLearn LAP 2016 for their interest and for having contributed to improve the challenge with their comments and suggestions. Special thanks to Marc Pomar for preparing the annotation interface for Amazon Mechanical Turk (AMT). The researchers who joined the program committee and reviewed for the ChaLearn LAP 2016 workshop are gratefully acknowledged. We are very grateful to our challenge sponsors: Facebook, NVIDIA and INAOE, whose support was critical for awarding prizes and travel grants. This work was also partially supported by Spanish projects TIN2015-66951-C2-2-R, TIN2012-39051, and TIN2013-43478-P, the European Comission Horizon 2020 granted project SEE.4C under call H2020-ICT-2015 and received additional support from the Laboratoire d'Informatique Fondamentale (LIF, UMR CNRS 7279) of the University of Aix Marseille, France, via the LabeX Archimede program, the Laboratoire de Recherche en Informatique of Paris Sud

University, INRIA-Saclay and the Paris-Saclay Center for Data Science (CDS). We thank our colleagues from the speed interview project for their contribution, and particularly Stephane Ayache, Cecile Capponi, Pascale Gerbail, Sonia Shah, Michele Sebag, Carlos Andujar, Jeffrey Cohn, and Erick Watson.

References

1. Ambady, N., Bernieri, F.J., Richeson, J.A.: Toward a histology of social behavior: judgmental accuracy from thin slices of the behavioral stream. Adv. Exp. Soc. Psychol. **32**, 201–271 (2000)
2. Berry, D.S.: Taking people at face value: evidence for the kernel of truth hypothesis. Soc. Cogn. **8**(4), 343 (1990)
3. Hassin, R., Trope, Y.: Facing faces: studies on the cognitive aspects of physiognomy. JPSP **78**(5), 837 (2000)
4. Ambady, N., Rosenthal, R.: Thin slices of expressive behavior as predictors of interpersonal consequences: a meta-analysis. Psychol. Bull. **111**(2), 256 (1992)
5. Willis, J., Todorov, A.: First impressions making up your mind after a 100-ms exposure to a face. PSS **17**(7), 592–598 (2006)
6. Ozer, D.J., Benet-Martinez, V.: Personality and the prediction of consequential outcomes. Annu. Rev. Psychol. **57**, 401–421 (2006)
7. Roberts, B.W., Kuncel, N.R., Shiner, R., Caspi, A., Goldberg, L.R.: The power of personality: the comparative validity of personality traits, socioeconomic status, and cognitive ability for predicting important life outcomes. PPS **2**(4), 313–345 (2007)
8. Posthuma, R.A., Morgeson, F.P., Campion, M.A.: Beyond employment interview validity: a comprehensive narrative review of recent research and trends over time. Pers. Psychol. **55**(1), 1–81 (2002)
9. Huffcutt, A.I., Conway, J.M., Roth, P.L., Stone, N.J.: Identification and meta-analytic assessment of psychological constructs measured in employment interviews. JAP **86**(5), 897 (2001)
10. Vinciarelli, A., Mohammadi, G.: A survey of personality computing. TAC **5**(3), 273–291 (2014)
11. Mairesse, F., Walker, M.A., Mehl, M.R., Moore, R.K.: Using linguistic cues for the automatic recognition of personality in conversation and text. JAIR **30**, 457–500 (2007)
12. Ivanov, A.V., Riccardi, G., Sporka, A.J., Franc, J.: Recognition of personality traits from human spoken conversations. In: INTERSPEECH, pp. 1549–1552 (2011)
13. Pianesi, F., Mana, N., Cappelletti, A., Lepri, B., Zancanaro, M.: Multimodal recognition of personality traits in social interactions. In: ICMI, pp. 53–60. ACM (2008)
14. Batrinca, L.M., Mana, N., Lepri, B., Pianesi, F., Sebe, N.: Please, tell me about yourself: automatic personality assessment using short self-presentations. In: ICMI, pp. 255–262. ACM (2011)
15. Batrinca, L., Lepri, B., Mana, N., Pianesi, F.: Multimodal recognition of personality traits in human-computer collaborative tasks. In: ICMI, pp. 39–46. ACM, New York (2012)
16. Mana, N., Lepri, B., Chippendale, P., Cappelletti, A., Pianesi, F., Svaizer, P., Zancanaro, M.: Multimodal corpus of multi-party meetings for automatic social behavior analysis and personality traits detection. In: ICMI Workshop, pp. 9–14. ACM (2007)

17. Lepri, B., Subramanian, R., Kalimeri, K., Staiano, J., Pianesi, F., Sebe, N.: Connecting meeting behavior with extraversion - a systematic study. TAC **3**(4), 443–455 (2012)
18. Polzehl, T., Moller, S., Metze, F.: Automatically assessing personality from speech. In: ICSC, pp. 134–140. IEEE (2010)
19. Biel, J.I., Teijeiro-Mosquera, L., Gatica-Perez, D.: Facetube: predicting personality from facial expressions of emotion in online conversational video. In: ICMI, pp. 53–56. ACM (2012)
20. Sanchez-Cortes, D., Biel, J.I., Kumano, S., Yamato, J., Otsuka, K., Gatica-Perez, D.: Inferring mood in ubiquitous conversational video. In: MUM, p. 22. ACM (2013)
21. Abadi, M.K., Correa, J.A.M., Wache, J., Yang, H., Patras, I., Sebe, N.: Inference of personality traits and affect schedule by analysis of spontaneous reactions to affective videos. FG (2015)
22. Ponce-López, V., Escalera, S., Baró, X.: Multi-modal social signal analysis for predicting agreement in conversation settings. In: ICMI. ICMI 2013, pp. 495–502. ACM, New York (2013)
23. Ponce-López, V., Escalera, S., Pérez, M., Janés, O., Baró, X.: Non-verbal communication analysis in victim-offender mediations. PRL 67, Part 1, pp. 19–27. Cognitive Systems for Knowledge Discovery (2015)
24. Guyon, I., Athitsos, V., Jangyodsuk, P., Escalante, H.J., Hamner, B.: Results and analysis of the ChaLearn gesture challenge 2012. In: Jiang, X., Bellon, O.R.P., Goldgof, D., Oishi, T. (eds.) WDIA 2012. LNCS, vol. 7854, pp. 186–204. Springer, Heidelberg (2013). doi:10.1007/978-3-642-40303-3_19
25. Guyon, I., Athitsos, V., Jangyodsuk, P., Escalante, H.J.: The ChaLearn gesture dataset (CGD 2011). Mach. Vis. Appl. **25**(8), 1929–1951 (2014)
26. Escalera, S., Gonzàlez, J., Baró, X., Reyes, M., Lopes, O., Guyon, I., Athitsos, V., Escalante, H.J.: Multi-modal gesture recognition challenge 2013: dataset and results. ICMI Workshop, pp. 445–452 (2013)
27. Escalera, S., et al.: ChaLearn looking at people challenge 2014: dataset and results. In: Agapito, L., Bronstein, M.M., Rother, C. (eds.) ECCV 2014. LNCS, vol. 8927, pp. 459–473. Springer, Heidelberg (2015). doi:10.1007/978-3-319-16178-5_32
28. Baró, X., Gonzalez, J., Fabian, J., Bautista, M.A., Oliu, M., Escalante, H.J., Guyon, I., Escalera, S.: ChaLearn looking at people 2015 challenges: action spotting and cultural event recognition. In: CVPR Workshop, pp. 1–9. IEEE (2015)
29. Escalera, S., Fabian, J., Pardo, P., Baró, X., Gonzalez, J., Escalante, H.J., Misevic, D., Steiner, U., Guyon, I.: ChaLearn looking at people 2015: apparent age and cultural event recognition datasets and results. In: ICCV Workshop, pp. 1–9 (2015)
30. Escalera, S., Torres, M., Martinez, B., Baró, X., Escalante, H.J., et al.: ChaLearn looking at people and faces of the world: face analysis workshop and challenge 2016. In: CVPR Workshop (2016)
31. Viola, P., Jones, M.J.: Robust real-time face detection. IJCV **57**(2), 137–154 (2004)
32. Lang, A., Rio-Ross, J.: Using Amazon mechanical Turk to transcribe historical handwritten documents (2011)
33. Watts, D.J., Strogatz, S.H.: Collective dynamics of 'small-world' networks. Nature **393**(6684), 409–410 (1998)
34. Humphries, M., Gurney, K., Prescott, T.: The brainstem reticular formation is a small-world, not scale-free, network. PRSL-B **273**(1585), 503–511 (2006)
35. Bradley, R., Terry, M.: Rank analysis of incomplete block designs: the method of paired comparisons. Biometrika **39**, 324–345 (1952)

36. Chen, B., Escalera, S., Guyon, I., Ponce-López, V., Shah, N., Oliu, M.: Overcoming calibration problems in pattern labeling with pairwise ratings: application to personality traits. In: ECCV LAP Challenge Workshop (2016, submitted)
37. He, K., Zhang, X., Ren, S., Sun, J.: Deep residual learning for image recognition. arXiv (2015)
38. LeCun, Y., Bottou, L., Bengio, Y., Haffner, P.: Gradient-based learning applied to document recognition. Proc. IEEE **86**(11), 2278–2324 (1998)
39. Hochreiter, S., Schmidhuber, J.: Long short-term memory. Neural Comput. **9**(8), 1735–1780 (1997)
40. Zhang, C.L., Zhang, H., Wei, X.S., Wu, J.: Deep bimodal regression for apparent personality analysis. In: ECCV Workshop Proceedings (2016)
41. Subramaniam, A., Patel, V., Mishra, A., Balasubramanian, P., Mittal, A.: Bimodal first impressions recognition using temporally ordered deep audio and stochastic visual features. In: ECCV Workshop Proceedings (2016)
42. Güçlütürk, Y., Güçlü, U., van Gerven, M., van Lier, R.: Deep impression: audiovisual deep residual networks for multimodal apparent personality trait recognition. In: ECCV Workshop Proceedings (2016)
43. Wei, X.S., Luo, J.H., Wu, J.: Selective convolutional descriptor aggregation for fine-grained image retrieval. arXiv (2016)
44. Parkhi, O.M., Vedaldi, A., Zisserman, A.: Deep face recognition. BMVC **1**, 6 (2015)

Overcoming Calibration Problems in Pattern Labeling with Pairwise Ratings: Application to Personality Traits

Baiyu Chen[4]($\boxtimes$), Sergio Escalera[1,2,3], Isabelle Guyon[3,5],
Víctor Ponce-López[1,2,6], Nihar Shah[4], and Marc Oliu Simón[6]

[1] Computer Vision Center, Campus UAB, Barcelona, Spain
[2] Department of Mathematics and Computer Science, University of Barcelona,
Barcelona, Spain
[3] ChaLearn, Berkeley, California, USA
[4] University of California Berkeley, Berkeley, California, USA
andrewcby@gmail.com
[5] University of Paris-Saclay, Paris, France
[6] EIMT at the Open University of Catalonia, Barcelona, Spain

Abstract. We address the problem of calibration of workers whose task is to label patterns with continuous variables, which arises for instance in labeling images of videos of humans with continuous traits. Worker bias is particularly difficult to evaluate and correct when many workers contribute just a few labels, a situation arising typically when labeling is crowd-sourced. In the scenario of labeling short videos of people facing a camera with personality traits, we evaluate the feasibility of the pairwise ranking method to alleviate bias problems. Workers are exposed to pairs of videos at a time and must order by preference. The variable levels are reconstructed by fitting a Bradley-Terry-Luce model with maximum likelihood. This method may at first sight, seem prohibitively expensive because for N videos, $p = N(N-1)/2$ pairs must be potentially processed by workers rather that N videos. However, by performing extensive simulations, we determine an empirical law for the scaling of the number of pairs needed as a function of the number of videos in order to achieve a given accuracy of score reconstruction and show that the pairwise method is affordable. We apply the method to the labeling of a large scale dataset of 10,000 videos used in the ChaLearn Apparent Personality Trait challenge.

Keywords: Calibration of labels · Label bias · Ordinal labeling · Variance models · Bradley-Terry-Luce model · Continuous labels · Regression · Personality traits · Crowd-sourced labels

1 Introduction

Computer vision problems often involve labeled data with continuous values (regression problems). This includes, job interview assessments [1], personality

© Springer International Publishing Switzerland 2016
G. Hua and H. Jégou (Eds.): ECCV 2016 Workshops, Part III, LNCS 9915, pp. 419–432, 2016.
DOI: 10.1007/978-3-319-49409-8_33

analysis [2,3], or age estimation [4], among others. To acquire continuous labeled data, it is often necessary to hire professionals that have had training on the task of visually examining image or video patterns. For example, the data collection that motivated this study requires the labeling of 10,000 short videos with personality traits on a scale of -5 to 5. Because of the limited availability of trained professionals, one often resorts to the "wisdom of crowds" and hire a large number of untrained workers whose proposed labels are averaged to reduce variance. A typical service frequently used for crowd-sourcing labeling is Amazon Mechanical Turk[1] (AMT). In this paper, we work on the problem of obtaining accurate labeling for continuous target variables, with time and budgetary constraints.

The variance between labels obtained by crowd-sourcing stems from several factors, including the **intrinsic** variability of labeling of a single worker (who, due to fatigue and concentration may be inconsistent with his/her own assessments), and the **bias** that a worker may have (his/her propensity to over-rate or under-rate, e.g. a given personality trait). Intrinsic variability is often referred to as "random error" while "bias" is referred to as "systematic error". The problem of intrinsic variability can be alleviated by pre-selecting workers for their consistency and by shortening labeling sessions to reduce worker fatigue. The problem of **bias reduction** is the central subjet of this paper.

Reducing bias has been tackled in various ways in the literature. Beyond simple averaging, aggregation models using confusion matrices have been considered for classification problems with binary or categorical labels (e.g [5]). Aggregating continuous labels is reminiscent of Analysis of Variance (ANOVA) models and factor analysis (see, e.g. [6]) and has been generalized with the use of factor graphs [5]. Such methods are referred to in the literature as "cardinal" methods to distinguish them from "ordinal methods", which we consider in this paper.

Ordinal methods require that workers rank patterns as opposed to rating them. Typically, a pair of patterns A and B is presented to a worker and he/she is asked to judge whether $value(A) < value(B)$, for instance $extroverted(A) < extroverted(B)$. Ordinal methods are by design immune to additive biases (at least global biases, not discriminative biases, such as gender or race bias). Because of their built-in insensitivity to global biases ordinal methods are well suited when many workers contribute each only a few labels [7]. In addition, there is a large body of literature [8–13] showing evidence that ordinal feed-back is easier to provide than cardinal feed-back from untrained workers. In preliminary experiments we conducted ourselves, workers were also more engaged and less easily bored if they had to make comparisons rather than rating single items.

In the applications we consider, however, the end goal is to obtain for every pattern a cardinal rating (such as the level of friendliness). To that end, pairwise comparisons must be converted to cardinal ratings such as to obtain the desired labels. Various models have been proposed in the literature, including the Bradley-Terry-Luce (BTL) model [14], the Thurstone class of models [15], and non-parametric models based on stochastic transitivity assumptions [16].

---

[1] https://www.mturk.com/.

Such methods are commonly used, for instance, to convert tournament wins in chess to ratings and in online video games such as Microsoft's Xbox [17]. In this paper, we present experiments performed with the Bradley-Terry-Luce (BTL) model [14], which provided us with satisfactory results. By performing simulations, we demonstrate the viability of the method within the time and budget constraints of our data collection.

Contribution. For a given target accuracy of cardinal rating reconstruction, we determine the practical economical feasibility of running such a data labeling and the practical computational feasibility by running extensive numerical experiments with artificial and real sample data from the problem at hand. We investigate the advantage of our proposed method from the scalability, noise resistance, and stability points of view. We derive an empirical scaling law of the number of pairs necessary to achieve a given level of accuracy of cardinal rating reconstruction from a given number of pairs. We provide a fast implementation of the method using Newton's conjugate gradient algorithm that we make publicly available on Github. We propose a novel design for the choice of pairs based on small-world graph connectivity and experimentally prove its superiority over random selection of pairs.

2   Problem Formulation

2.1   Application Setting: The Design of a Challenge

The main focus of this research is the organization of a pattern recognition challenge in the ChaLearn Looking at People (LAP) series [18–25], which is being run for ECCV 2016 [3] and ICPR 2016. This paper provides a methodology, which we are using in our challenge on automatic personality trait analysis from video data [26]. The automatic analysis of videos to characterize human behavior has become an area of active research with a wide range of applications [1,2,27,28]. Research advances in computer vision and pattern recognition have lead to methodologies that can successfully recognize consciously executed actions, or intended movements, for instance, gestures, actions, interactions with objects and other people [29]. However, much remains to be done in characterizing sub-conscious behaviors [30], which may be exploited to reveal aptitudes or competence, hidden intentions, and personality traits. Our present research focuses on a quantitative evaluation of personality traits represented by a numerical score for a number of well established psychological traits known as the "big five" [31]: Extraversion, agreableness, conscientiousness, neurotism, and openness to experience.

Personality refers to individual differences in characteristic patterns of thinking, feeling and behaving. Characterizing personality automatically from video analysis is far from being a trivial task because perceiving personality traits is difficult even to professionally trained psychologists and recruiting specialists. Additionally, quantitatively assessing personality traits is also challenging due to the subjectivity of assessors and lack of precise metrics. We are organizing a challenge on "first impressions", in which participants will develop solutions for recognizing personality traits of subjects from a short video sequence of the person facing the camera. This work could become very relevant to training young people to present themselves better by changing their behavior in simple ways, as the first impression made is very important in many contexts, such as job interviews.

We made available a large newly collected data set sponsored by Microsoft Research of 10,000 15-s videos collected from YouTube, annotated with the "big-five" personality traits by AMT workers. See the data collection interface in Fig. 1.

We budgeted 20,000 USD for labeling the 10,000 videos. We originally estimated that by paying 10 cents per rating of video pair (a conservative estimate of cost per task), we could afford rating 200,000 pairs. This paper presents the methodology we used to evaluate whether this budget would allows us to accurately estimate the cardinal ratings, which we support by numerical experiments on artificial data. Furthermore, we investigated the computational feasibility of running maximum likelihood estimation of the BTL model for such a large number of videos. Since this methodology is general, it could be used in other contexts.

Fig. 1. Data collection interface. The AMT workers must indicate their preference for five attributes representing the "big five" personality traits.

2.2   Model Definition

Our problem is parameterized as follows. Given a collection of N videos, each video has a trait with value in $[-5, 5]$ (this range is arbitrary, other ranges can be chosen). We treat each trait separately; in what follows, we consider a single trait. We require that only p pairs will be labeled by the AMT workers out of the $P = N(N-1)/2$ possible pairs. For scaling reasons that we explain later, p is normalized by $N \log N$ to obtain parameter $\alpha = p/(N \log N)$. We consider a model in which the ideal ranking may be corrupted by "noise", the noise representing errors made by the AMT workers (a certain parameter σ). The three parameters α, N, and σ fully characterize our experimental setting depicted in Fig. 2 that we now describe.

Let $\mathbf{w}^*$ be the N dimensional vector of "true" (unknown) cardinal ratings (e.g. of videos) and $\tilde{\mathbf{w}}$ be the N dimensional vector of estimated ratings obtained from the votes of workers after applying our reconstruction method based on pairwise ratings. We consider that i is the index of a *pair* of videos $\{j, k\}$, $i = 1 : p$ and that $y_i \in \{-1, 1\}$ represents the ideal ordinal rating ($+1$ if $w_j^* > w_k^*$ and -1 otherwise, ignoring ties). We use the notation $\mathbf{x_i}$ to represent a special kind of indicator vector, which has value $+1$ at position j, -1 at position k and zero otherwise, such that $< \mathbf{x_i}, \mathbf{w}^* > = w_j^* - w_k^*$.

We formulate the problem as estimating the cardinal rating values of all videos based on p independent samples of ordinal ratings $y_i \in \{-1, 1\}$ coming from the distribution:

$$P[y_i = 1 | \mathbf{x_i}, \mathbf{w}^*] = \mathbf{F}(\frac{< \mathbf{x_i}, \mathbf{w}^* >}{\sigma}),$$

where F is a known function that has value in $[0, 1]$ and σ is the noise parameter. We use Bradley-Terry-Luce model, which is a special case where F is logistic function, $F(t) = 1/(1 + exp(-t))$.

In our simulated experiments, we first draw the w_j^* cardinal ratings uniformly in $[-5, 5]$, then we draw p pairs randomly as training data and apply noise to get the ordinal ratings y_i. As test data, we draw another set of p pairs from the remaining data.

It can be verified that the likelihood function of the BTL model is log-concave. We simply use the maximum likelihood method to estimate the cardinal rating values and get our estimation $\tilde{\mathbf{w}}$. This method should lead to a single global optimum for such a convex optimization problem.

2.3   Evaluation

To evaluate the accuracy of our cardinal rating reconstruction, we use two different scores (computed on test data):

Coefficient of Determination (R^2). We use the coefficient of determination to measure how well $\tilde{\mathbf{w}}$ reconstructs $\mathbf{w}^*$. The residual residual sum of squares is defined as $SS_{res} = \sum_i (w_i^* - \tilde{w}_i)^2$. The total sum of squares SS_{var} is defined as: $SS_{var} = \sum_i (w_i^* - \overline{w^*})^2$, where $\overline{w^*}$ denotes the average rating. The coefficient of Determination is defined as $R^2 = 1 - SS_{res}/SS_{var}$. Note that since the w_i^* are on an arbitrary scale $[-5, +5]$, we must normalize the $\tilde{w}_i$ before computing the R^2. This is achieved by finding the optimum shift and scale to maximize the R^2.

Test-Accuracy. We define test Accuracy as the fraction of pairs correctly re-oriented using $\tilde{\mathbf{w}}$ from the test data pairs, i.e. those pairs not used for evaluating $\tilde{\mathbf{w}}$.

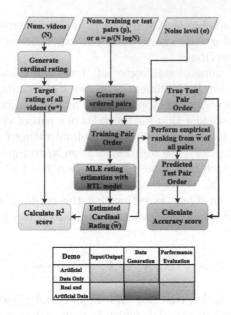

Fig. 2. Work flow diagram

2.4   Experiment Design

In our simulations, we follow the workflow of Fig. 2. We first generate a score vector $\mathbf{w}^*$ using a uniform distribution in $[-5,5]^N$. Once $\mathbf{w}^*$ is chosen, we select training and test pairs.

One original contribution of our paper is the choice of pairs. We propose to use a small-world graph construction method to generate the pairs [32]. Small-world graphs provide high connectivity, avoid disconnected regions in the graph, have a well distributed edges, and minimum distance between nodes [33]. An edge is selected at random from the underlying graph, and the chosen edge determines the pair of items compared. We compare the small-world strategy to draw pairs with drawing pairs at random from a uniform distribution, which according to [7] yield near-optimal results.

The ordinal rating of the pairs is generated with the BTL model using the chosen $\mathbf{w}^*$ as the underlying cardinal rating, flipping pairs according to the noise level. Finally, the maximum likelihood estimator for the BTL model is employed to estimate $\tilde{\mathbf{w}}$.

We are interested in the effect of three variables: total number of pairs available, p; total number of videos, N; noise level, σ. First we experiment on performance progress (as measured by R^2 and Accuracy on test data) for fixed values of N and σ, by varying the number of pairs p. According to [14] with no noise and error, the minimum number of pairs needed for exactly recovering of original ordering of data is $N log N$. This prompted us to vary p as a multiple of $N log N$. We define the parameter $\alpha = p/(N \log N)$. The results are shown in

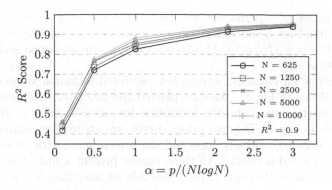

Fig. 3. Evolution of R^2 for different α with noise level $\sigma = 1$.

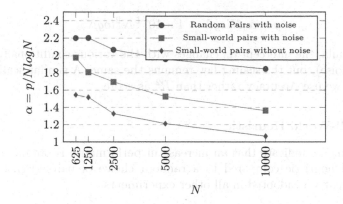

Fig. 4. Evolution of α^* : α at $R^2 = 0.9$ for with and without noise, with $\sigma = 1$. (Color figure online)

Figs. 3 and 7. This allows us, for a given level of reconstruction accuracy (e.g. 0.95) or R^2 (e.g. 0.9) to determine the number of pairs needed. We then fix p and σ and observe how performance progress with N (Figs. 6 and 8).

3   Results and Discussion

In this section, we examine performances in terms of test set R^2 and Accuracy for reconstructing the cardinal scores and recovering the correct pairwise ratings when noise is applied at various levels in the BTL model.

3.1   Number of Pairs Needed

We recall that one of the goals of our experiments was to figure out scaling laws for the number of pairs p as a function of N for various levels of noise. From theoretical analyses, we expected that p would scale with $NlogN$ rather than

N^2. In a first set of experiments, we fixed the noise level at $\sigma = 1$. We were pleased to see in Figs. 3 and 7 that our two scores (the R^2 and Accuracy) in fact *increase* with $\alpha = p/(NlogN)$. This indicates that our presumed scaling law is, in fact, pessimistic.

To determine an empirical scaling law, we fixed a desired value of R^2 (0.9, see horizontal line in Fig. 3). We then plotted the five points resulting from the intersection of the curves and the horizontal line as a function of N to obtain the red curve in Fig. 4. The two other curves are shown for comparison: The blue curve is obtained without noise and the brown curve with an initialisation with the small-world heuristic. All three curves present a quasi-linear decrease of *alpha* with N with the same slope. From this we infer that $\alpha = p/(NlogN) \simeq \alpha_0 - 4 \times 10^{-5}N$. And thus we obtain the following empirical scaling law of p as a function of N:

$$p = \alpha_0 NlogN - 4 \times 10^{-5}N^2logN.$$

In this formula, the intercept α_0 changes with the various conditions (choices of pairs and noise), but the scaling law remains the same. A similar scaling law is obtained if we use Accuracy rather than R^2 as score.

3.2   Small-World Heuristic

Our experiments indicate that an increase in performance is obtained with the small-world heuristic compared to a random choice of pairs (Fig. 4). This is therefore what was adopted in all other experiments.

3.3   Experiment Budget

In the introduction, we indicated that our budget to pay AMT workers would cover at least $p = 200,000$ pairs. However, the efficiency of our data collection setting reduced the cost per elementary task and we ended up labeling $p = 321,684$ pairs within our budget. For our $N = 10,000$ videos, this corresponds to $\alpha = p/(NlogN) = 3.49$. We see in Fig. 4 that, for $N = 10,000$ videos, in all cases examined, the α required to attain $R^2 = 0.9$ is lower than 2.17, and therefore, our budget was sufficient to obtain this level of accuracy.

Furthermore, we varied the noise level in Figs. 6 and 8. In these plots, we selected a smaller value of α than what our monetary budget could afford ($\alpha = 1.56$). Even at that level, we can see that we have a sufficient number of pairs to achieve $R^2 = 0.9$ for all levels of noise considered and all values of N considered. We also achieve an accuracy near 0.95 for $N = 10,000$ for all levels of noise considered. As expected, a larger σ requires a larger number of pairs to achieve the same level of R^2 or Accuracy.

3.4   Computational Time

One of the feasibility aspect of using ordinal ranking concerns computational time. Given that collecting and annotating data takes months of work, any computational time ranging from a few hours to a few days would be reasonnable. However, to be able to run systematic experiments, we optimized our algorithm sufficiently that any experiment we performed took less than three hours. Our implementation, which uses Newton's conjugate gradient algorithm [34], was made publicly available on Github[2]. In Fig. 5 we see that the log of running time increases quite rapidly with α at the beginning and then almost linearly. We also see that the log of the running time increases linearly with N for any fixed value of α. In the case of our data collection, we were interested in $\alpha = 2.17$ (see the previous section), which corresponds to using 200,000 pairs for 10,000 videos (our original estimate). For this value of α, we were pleased to see that the calculation of the cardinal labels would take less than three hours. This comforted us on the feasibility of using this method for out particular application.

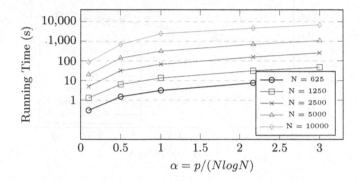

Fig. 5. Evolution of running time for different α and N with noise and $\sigma = 1$ on log scale.

3.5   Experiments on Real Data

The data collection process included collecting labels from AMT workers. Each worker followed the protocol we described in Sect. 2 (see Fig. 1). We obtained 321,684 pairs of real human votes for each trait, which were divided into 300,000 pairs for training and used the remainder 21,684 pairs for testing. This corresponds to $\alpha = 3.26$ for training.[3]

---

[2] https://github.com/andrewcby/Speed-Interview.

[3] These experiments concern only cardinal label reconstruction, they have nothing to do with the pattern recognition task from the videos, for which a different split between training/validation/test sets was done for the challenge.

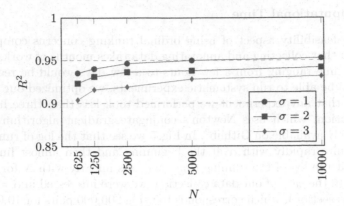

Fig. 6. Evolution of R^2 for different σ with $\alpha = 1.56$, a value that guarantees $R^2 \geq 0.9$ when $\sigma = 1$.

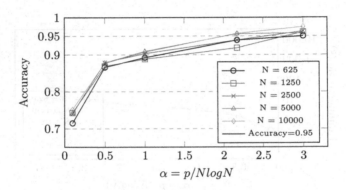

Fig. 7. Evolution of Accuracy for different α with noise with $\sigma = 1$.

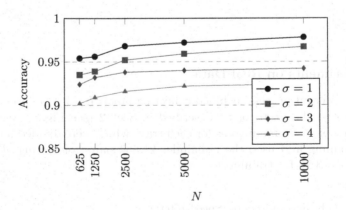

Fig. 8. Evolution of accuracy for different σ with $\alpha = 1.56$, a value that guarantees accuracy ≥ 0.9 when $\sigma = 1$.

Table 1. Estimation accuracy of 10,000 videos and 321,684 pairs ($3.49 \times NlogN$).

Trait	BTL model		Averaging ordinal ratings	
	Accuracy	STD	Accuracy	STD
Extraversion	0.692	±0.027	0.575	±0.095
Agreeableness	0.720	±0.025	0.533	±0.087
Conscientiousness	0.669	±0.032	0.559	±0.092
Neuroticism	0.706	±0.022	0.549	±0.084
Openness	0.735	±0.021	0.542	±0.089

We ran our cardinal score reconstruction algorithm on these data set and computed test accuracy. The results, shown in Table 1, give test accuracies between 0.66 and 0.73 for the various traits. Such reconstruction accuracies are significantly worse than those predicted by our simulated experiments. Looking at Fig. 7, the accuracies for $\alpha > 3$ are larger than 0.95.

Several factors can explain such lower accuracies of reconstruction:

1. **Use of "noisy" ground truth** estimation in real data to compute the target ranking in the accuracy calculation. The overly optimistic estimation of the accuracy in simulations stems in part from using exact ground truth, not available in real data. In real data, we compared the human ranking and the BTL model reconstructed ranking in test data. This may account for at least doubling the variance, one source of error being introduced when estimating the cardinal scores, and the other when estimating the accuracy using pair reconstruction with "noisy" real data.

2. **Departure of the real label distribution** from the uniform distribution. We carried out complementary simulations with a Gaussian distribution instead of a uniform distribution of labels (closer to a natural distribution) and observed a decrease of 6 % in accuracy and a decrease of 7 % in R^2.

3. **Departure of the real noise distribution from the BTL model.** We evaluated the validity of the BTL model by comparing the results to those produced with a simple baseline method introduced in [35]. This method consists in averaging the ordinal ratings for each video (counting +1 if it is rated higher than another video an −1 if it is rated lower). The performances of the BTL model are consistently better across all traits, based on the one sigma error bar calculated with 30 repeat experiments. Therefore, even though the baseline method is considerably simpler and faster, it is worth running the BTL model for the estimation of cardinal ratings. Unfortunately, there is no way to quantitatively estimate the effect of the third reason.

4. **Under-estimation of the intrinsic noise level** (random inconsistencies in rating the same video pair by the same worker). We evaluated the σ in the BTL model using bootstrap re-sampling of the video pairs. With an increasing level of σ, the results are consistently decreasing, as shown in Fig. 8. Therefore the parameters we chose for the simulation model proved to be optimistic and underestimated the intrinsic noise level.

5. **Sources of bias not accounted for** (we only took into account a global source of bias, not stratified sources of bias such as gender bias and racial bias. This is a voter-specific factor that we did not take into consideration when setting up the simulation. As this kind of bias is hard to measure, especially quantitatively, it can negatively influence the accuracy of the prediction.

4 Discussion and Conclusion

In this paper we evaluated the viability of an ordinal rating method based on labeling pairs of videos, a method intrinsically insensitive to (global) worker bias.

Using simulations, we showed that it is in principle possible to accurately produce a cardinal rating by fitting the BTL model with maximum likelihood, using artificial data generated with this model. We calculated that it was possible to remain within our financial budget of 200,000 pairs and incur a reasonable computational time (under 3 h).

However, although in simulations we pushed the model to levels of noise that we thought were realistic, the performance we attained with simulations ($R^2 = 0.9$ of Accuracy $= 0.95$ on test data) turned out to be optimistic. Reconstruction of cardinal ratings from ordinal ratings on real data lead to a lower level of accuracy (in the range 69 % and 73 %), showing that there are still other types of noise that are not reducible by the model. Future work can focus on methods to reduce this noise.

Our financial budget and time constraints also did not allow us to conduct a comparison with direct cardinal rating. An ideal, but expensive, experiment could be to duplicate the ground truth estimation by using AMT workers to directly estimate cardinal ratings, within the same financial budget. Future work includes validating our labeling technique in this way on real data.

Acknowledgments. This work was supported in part by donations of Microsoft Research to prepare the personality trait challenge, and Spanish Projects TIN2012-38187-C03-02, TIN2013-43478-P and the European Comission Horizon 2020 granted project SEE.4C under call H2020-ICT-2015. We are grateful to Evelyne Viegas, Albert Clapés i Sintes, Hugo Jair Escalante, Ciprian Corneanu, Xavier Baró Solé, Cécile Capponi, and Stéphane Ayache for stimulating discussions. We are thankful for Prof. Alyosha Efros for his support and guidance.

References

1. Marcos-Ramiro, A., Pizarro-Perez, D., Marron-Romera, M., Nguyen, L., Gatica-Perez, D.: Body communicative cue extraction for conversational analysis. In: 2013 10th IEEE International Conference and Workshops on Automatic Face and Gesture Recognition (FG), pp. 1–8, April 2013
2. Aran, O., Gatica-Perez, D.: One of a kind: inferring personality impressions in meetings. In: Proceedings of the 15th ACM on International Conference on Multimodal Interaction, ICMI, pp. 11–18. ACM, New York (2013)
3. Chalearn lap 2016: First round challenge on first impressions - dataset and results

4. Escalera, S., Gonzlez, J., Bar, X., Pardo, P., Fabian, J., Oliu, M., Escalante, H.J., Huerta, I., Guyon, I.: Chalearn looking at people 2015 new competitions: age estimation and cultural event recognition. In: 2015 International Joint Conference on Neural Networks (IJCNN), pp. 1–8, July 2015
5. Venanzi, M., Guiver, J., Kazai, G., Kohli, P., Shokouhi, M.: Community-based Bayesian aggregation models for crowdsourcing. In: Proceedings of the 23rd International Conference on World Wide Web, WWW 2014, pp. 155–164. ACM, New York (2014)
6. Miller, J., Haden, P.: Statistical Analysis with The General Linear Model (2006)
7. Shah, N., Balakrishnan, S., Bradley, J., Parekh, A., Ramchandran, K., Wainwright, M.: Estimation from pairwise comparisons: sharp minimax bounds with topology dependence. CoRR abs/1505.01462 (2015)
8. Whitehill, J., Wu, T.J., Bergsma, J., Movellan, J.R., Ruvolo, P.L.: Whose vote should count more: optimal integration of labels from labelers of unknown expertise. In: Bengio, Y., Schuurmans, D., Lafferty, J.D., Williams, C.K.I., Culotta, A. (eds.) Advances in Neural Information Processing Systems 22, pp. 2035–2043. Curran Associates, Inc. (2009)
9. Welinder, P., Branson, S., Perona, P., Belongie, S.J.: The multidimensional wisdom of crowds. In: Lafferty, J., Williams, C., Shawe-taylor, J., Zemel, R., Culotta, A. (eds.) Advances in Neural Information Processing Systems 23, pp. 2424–2432 (2010)
10. Welinder, P., Perona, P.: Online crowdsourcing: rating annotators and obtaining cost-effective labels. In: Workshops on Advancing Computer Vision with Humans in the Loop (2010)
11. Raykar, V.C., Yu, S., Zhao, L.H., Valadez, G.H., Florin, C., Bogoni, L., Moy, L.: Learning from crowds. J. Mach. Learn. Res. 11, 1297–1322 (2010)
12. Kamar, E., Hacker, S., Horvitz, E.: Combining human and machine intelligence in large-scale crowdsourcing. In: Proceedings of the 11th International Conference on Autonomous Agents and Multiagent Systems - Volume 1, AAMAS 2012, Richland, SC, pp. 467–474. International Foundation for Autonomous Agents and Multiagent Systems (2012)
13. Bachrach, Y., Graepel, T., Minka, T., Guiver, J.: How to grade a test without knowing the answers – a Bayesian graphical model for adaptive crowdsourcing and aptitude testing. ArXiv e-prints (2012)
14. Bradley, R., Terry, M.: Rank analysis of incomplete block designs: the method of paired comparisons. Biometrika 39, 324–345 (1952)
15. Thurstone, L.L.: A law of comparative judgment. Psychol. Rev. 34(4), 273 (1927)
16. Shah, N.B., Balakrishnan, S., Guntuboyina, A., Wainwright, M.J.: Stochastically transitive models for pairwise comparisons: statistical and computational issues. arXiv preprint (2015). arXiv:1510.05610
17. Herbrich, R., Minka, T., Graepel, T.: Trueskill: a Bayesian skill rating system. Adv. Neural Inf. Process. Syst. 19, 569 (2007)
18. Escalera, S., Gonzàlez, J., Baró, X., Reyes, M., Lopés, O., Guyon, I., Athitsos, V., Escalante, H.J.: Multi-modal gesture recognition challenge 2013: dataset and results. In: ChaLearn Multi-modal Gesture Recognition Workshop, ICMI (2013)
19. Escalera, S., Gonzàlez, J., Baro, X., Reyes, M., Guyon, I., Athitsos, V., Escalante, H., Argyros, A., Sminchisescu, C., Bowden, R., Sclarof, S.: Chalearn multi-modal gesture recognition 2013: grand challenge and workshop summary. In: ICMI, pp. 365–368 (2013)

20. Escalera, S., Baro, X., Gonzàlez, J., Bautista, M., Madadi, M., Reyes, M., Ponce-López, V., Escalante, H., Shotton, J., Guyon, I.: Chalearn looking at people challenge 2014: dataset and results (2014)
21. Escalera, S., Gonzàlez, J., Baro, X., Pardo, P., Fabian, J., Oliu, M., Escalante, H.J., Huerta, I., Guyon, I.: Chalearn looking at people 2015 new competitions: age estimation and cultural event recognition. In: IJCNN (2015)
22. Baro, X., Gonzàlez, J., Fabian, J., Bautista, M., Oliu, M., Escalante, H., Guyon, I., Escalera, S.: Chalearn looking at people 2015 challenges: action spotting and cultural event recognition. In: ChaLearn LAP Workshop, CVPR (2015)
23. Escalera, S., Fabian, J., Pardo, P., Baró, X., Gonzàlez, J., Escalante, H., Misevic, D., Steiner, U., Guyon, I.: Chalearn looking at people 2015: apparent age and cultural event recognition datasets and results. In: International Conference in Computer Vision, ICCVW (2015)
24. Escalera, S., Athitsos, V., Guyon, I.: Challenges in multimodal gesture recognition. J. Mach. Learn. Res. (2016)
25. Escalera, S., Gonzàlez, J., Baró, X., Shotton, J.: Special issue on multimodal human pose recovery and behavior analysis. IEEE Trans. Pattern Anal. Mach. Intell. (2016)
26. Park, G., Schwartz, H., Eichstaedt, J., Kern, M., Stillwell, D., Kosinski, M., Ungar, L., Seligman, M.: Automatic personality assessment through social media language. J. Pers. Soc. Psychol. **108**, 934–952 (2014)
27. Ponce-López, V., Escalera, S., Baró, X.: Multi-modal social signal analysis for predicting agreement in conversation settings. In: Proceedings of the 15th ACM on International Conference on Multimodal Interaction, ICMI, pp. 495–502. ACM, New York (2013)
28. Ponce-López, V., Escalera, S., Pérez, M., Janés, O., Baró, X.: Non-verbal communication analysis in victim-offender mediations. Pattern Recogn. Lett. **67**(Part 1), 19–27 (2015). Cognitive Systems for Knowledge Discovery
29. Laptev, I., Marszalek, M., Schmid, C., Rozenfeld, B.: Learning realistic human actions from movies. In: IEEE Conference on Computer Vision and Pattern Recognition, CVPR 2008, pp. 1–8, June 2008
30. Pentland, A.: Honest Signals: How They Shape Our World. The MIT Press, Cambridge (2008)
31. Goldberg, L.: The structure of phenotypic personality traits (1993)
32. Watts, D.J., Strogatz, S.H.: Collective dynamics of 'small-world' networks. Nature **393**(6684), 409–410 (1998)
33. Humphries, M., Gurney, K., Prescott, T.: The brainstem reticular formation is a small-world, not scale-free, network. Proc. R. Soc. London B: Biol. Sci. **273**(1585), 503–511 (2006)
34. Knoll, D.A., Keyes, D.E.: Jacobian-free Newton-Krylov methods: a survey of approaches and applications. J. Comput. Phys. **193**, 357–397 (2004)
35. Shah, N.B., Wainwright, M.J.: Simple, robust and optimal ranking from pairwise comparisons. arXiv preprint (2015). arXiv:1512.08949

W13 – Transferring and Adapting Source Knowledge in Computer Vision

Preface

The workshop on Transferring and Adapting Source Knowledge in Computer Vision (TASK-CV) aims at bringing together computer vision and multimedia researchers interested in domain adaptation and knowledge transfer techniques, which are receiving increasing attention in computer vision research.

During the first decade of the XXI century, progress in machine learning has had an enormous impact in computer vision. The ability to learn models from data has been a fundamental paradigm in image classification, object detection, semantic segmentation or tracking.

A key ingredient of such a success has been the availability of visual data with annotations, both for training and testing, and well-established protocols for evaluating the results.

However, most of the time, annotating visual information is a tiresome human activity prone to errors. This represents a limitation for addressing new tasks and/or operating in new domains. In order to scale to such situations, it is worth finding mechanisms to reuse the available annotations or the models learned from them.

This also challenges the traditional machine learning theory, which usually assumes that there are sufficient labeled data of each task, and the training data distribution matches the test distribution.

Therefore, transferring and adapting source knowledge (in the form of annotated data or learned models) to perform new tasks and/or operating in new domains has recently emerged as a challenge to develop computer vision methods that are reliable across domains and tasks.

This is the 3rd Edition of TASK-CV workshop, in conjunction to ECCV 2016. The workshop has gained a lot of attentions starting from the submission period. We have received twice more submission than expectation. Finally, a half of them are accepted after peer-review and extensive discussions by the chairs. We hope those papers will be appreciated by the readers. Thank all the programm committee members for their contributions in providing valuable comments to the submissions.

October 2016

Wen Li
Tatiana Tommasi
Francesco Orabona
David Vázquez
Antonio M. López
Jiaolong Xu
Hugo Larochelle

Best Practices for Fine-Tuning Visual Classifiers to New Domains

Brian Chu$^{(\boxtimes)}$, Vashisht Madhavan$^{(\boxtimes)}$, Oscar Beijbom, Judy Hoffman, and Trevor Darrell

University of California, Berkeley, Berkeley, USA
{brian.c,vashisht.madhavan}@berkeley.edu,
{obeijbom,jhoffman,trevor}@eecs.berkeley.edu

Abstract. Recent studies have shown that features from deep convolutional neural networks learned using large labeled datasets, like ImageNet, provide effective representations for a variety of visual recognition tasks. They achieve strong performance as generic features and are even more effective when fine-tuned to target datasets. However, details of the fine-tuning procedure across datasets and with different amount of labeled data are not well-studied and choosing the best fine-tuning method is often left to trial and error. In this work we systematically explore the design-space for fine-tuning and give recommendations based on two key characteristics of the target dataset: visual distance from source dataset and the amount of available training data. Through a comprehensive experimental analysis, we conclude, with a few exceptions, that it is best to copy as many layers of a pre-trained network as possible, and then adjust the level of fine-tuning based on the visual distance from source.

1 Introduction

One of the key factors which contributes to the impact of convolutional neural networks (CNNs) is the transferability of their internal deep representations for a variety of visual recognition tasks. Such deep representations, or 'features,' are empirically superior [1,2] to traditional features when classifying datasets such as Caltech-101, Caltech-256, and SUN397 [3–5]. Recently, methods of fine-tuning pre-trained networks towards new target datasets have become very popular, as they are usually more effective than training deep networks from scratch. With fine-tuning, the first n layers from a pre-trained network are copied to the target network, while other layers are randomly initialized and trained towards the target dataset. One can either choose to adapt, or fine-tune, the copied layers or leave them unchanged (frozen) during training [6,7]. Past work has even shown

---

B. Chu and V. Madhavan—These authors contributed equally to this work.

Electronic supplementary material The online version of this chapter (doi:10.1007/978-3-319-49409-8_34) contains supplementary material, which is available to authorized users.

© Springer International Publishing Switzerland 2016
G. Hua and H. Jégou (Eds.): ECCV 2016 Workshops, Part III, LNCS 9915, pp. 435–442, 2016.
DOI: 10.1007/978-3-319-49409-8_34

the superiority of fine-tuning over using generic CNN features for different visual tasks like detection [7–9].

When faced with a new dataset, however, there is little guidance on how many layers to copy and whether to fine-tune or freeze these layers. We argue that the best practice may vary depending upon a few key factors of the transfer setup. As a result, we choose to analyze the performance of fine-tuning methods across seven target datasets, comparing these methods among two intrinsic properties of the datasets: difference from source dataset and the amount of available target training data. Through our analysis, we uncover the best training methods in each scenario and use the results to provide two main recommendations:

1. **Copy all layers except the classification layer.** This is often standard practice, though we are the first to provide comprehensive evidence across a variety of datasets and many different operating points of the amount of labeled data available in the target dataset.
2. **Fine-tune the copied layers.** We find that even with very few examples, fine-tuning is possible and beneficial. The exception being if the dataset distance is small and there is only a small amount of training data. In this case, freeze the copied layers.

2   Related Work

Although networks have been shown to increase in class and representation specificity from lower to higher layers [6,8], for many datasets the best performance of generic AlexNet [10] features occurs at the third-to-last (fc6) [2], or second-to-last (fc7) fully-connected layer [1]. Moreover, Girshick et al.'s ablation studies found it is best to copy all layers from a network pre-trained on ImageNet and fine-tune these layers towards the PASCAL VOC detection task [7].

Yosinski et al. [6] varied the number of pre-trained layers copied and examined the target dataset accuracy for networks that were fine-tuned and frozen (unchanged). With the source dataset as one half of ImageNet's classes and the target dataset as the remaining half, Yosinski et al. found that fine-tuning was the optimal technique, with performance slightly improving as more layers were copied. When layers were frozen, they saw performance degrade as more layers were copied. However, Yosinski et al.'s work studied a target dataset that was virtually identical to the source dataset and had an extremely large number of samples (approximately 645,000). This directly motivates our broader analysis of target datasets of varying distances to the source dataset, and datasets with scarce and plentiful training data.

The need to characterize distance between source and target is further motivated by Azizpour et al. and Zhou et al., who both demonstrated substantial variation in the performance of generic features depending on the source dataset and qualitative characteristics of the target dataset [9,11]. Zhou et al. specifically demonstrated that a CNN pre-trained on a scene dataset is superior to an ImageNet model when fine-tuned towards other scene datasets.

3   Experiments

We follow the experimental setup used by Yosinski et al. [6]. Specifically we use the 8-layer Caffe implementation of AlexNet (CaffeNet), pre-trained on the entire ImageNet training set [12].

We evaluate the performance of fine-tuning and freezing when adapting the pre-trained model to 6 target datasets. For each dataset, we define 3–4 dataset splits with a varying number of images per class, for a total of 23 dataset splits. We also define fixed validation and test sets which, due to different amounts of training data, differ in size between datasets. The splits are outlined in Table 1.

For each dataset split, we randomly initialize the top 1, 3, or 5 layers in the pre-trained model while copying the rest of the layers. Additionally, we either freeze the copied layers, setting the learning rate to 0, or fine-tune them, setting the learning rate to 0.2 times that of random initialization. We follow this procedure for all target datasets, resulting in 138 experiments. For notation, $T(a\text{-}b)$ denotes that layers a-b are copied and fine-tuned, whereas $F(a\text{-}b)$ denotes that layers a-b are copied and frozen. $R(a\text{-}b)$ denotes that layers a-b are randomly initialized. For example, $T(1\text{-}7)R(8)$ denotes the experiment where we copy and fine-tune layers 1–7 and randomly initialize the final fully-connected layer, fc8.

Table 1. Properties of datasets and dataset splits. * indicates we used the dataset's provided validation or test set as our test set.

Dataset	# categories	Classification task	# Images per class		
			Val	Test	Train
Caltech256	256	Object	2	25	1, 10, 25, 53
SUN397	397	Scene	2	25	1, 10, 50, 70
MITIndoor	67	Scene	2	*	1, 10, 25, 75
CUB-200	200	Object (fine-grained)	2	*	5, 20, 35
Coral	9	Coral	50	300	10, 50, 200, 450
Plankton	103	Plankton	50	85	1, 10, 300, 550
Yosinski	500	Object	20	*	1, 10, 25, 53, 120

We evaluated our experiments on 6 datasets: Caltech256, SUN397, MIT Indoor Scene Recognition (MITIndoor) [13], Caltech-UCSD-Birds-200 (CUB) [14], Moorea Labeled Corals (Coral) [15], and Imaging Flow Cytobot Data Plankton (Plankton) [16]. Properties of these datasets are summarized in Table 1. We only used 8 of the Coral categories and 34 of the Plankton categories in our experiments due to insufficient training data per class.

In addition to these 138 experiments, we chose to include an additional artificial dataset from Yosinksi et al. [6], denoted as Yosinski in Table 1. In their experiments, ImageNet is randomly split into two disjoint 500-category datasets (dataset 500 A and dataset 500B) of roughly equal size (approximately 645,000 images). CaffeNet is pre-trained on dataset 500A, with the target as dataset 500B. We use this setup to analyze the case when datasets are essentially identical and also compare our results to theirs. We use the same experiment setups as before for an additional 40 experiments.

3.1 Difference from Source

To measure the difference between the source and target datasets, we compute the cosine distance, $1 - \frac{\mu_s^T \mu_t}{||\mu_s||_2 ||\mu_t||_2}$, between the mean fc7 responses of the source, μ_s, and target, μ_t, datasets. Although not a formal distance measure due to its violation of the triangle inequality, cosine distance effectively measures the similarity of two vectors, which in our case measures the similarity of two datasets. In Table 2, we compare the cosine distance to other metrics such as MMD between source and target dataset in fc7 feature space which, when using a linear kernel, is equivalent to the Euclidean distance between the means of the fc7 responses. We also consider the accuracy of two classifiers trained to distinguish between datasets: a linear SVM in fc7 feature space and a small CNN model used by Krizhevsky for CIFAR-10 classification in pixel space [17]. This approach was recently used to minimize domain difference for adaptation [18–20]. When generating fc7 responses, we use CaffeNet pre-trained on the source dataset: this source dataset is ImageNet for all datasets setups except Yosinski, where source is 500A.

Table 2. Distance between source and target dataset. For Yosinski, source is dataset 500 A and target is dataset 500 B. For others, source is ImageNet and target is listed.

Dataset	Cosine distance	MMD	Linear SVM	CNN
Yosinski	0.003	2.3	57.3 %	51.0 %
Caltech-256	0.071	10.6	71.4 %	69.0 %
SUN397	0.194	17.8	81.5 %	76.4 %
MIT-Indoor	0.307	23.9	90.0 %	84.5 %
CUB-200	0.358	37.2	92.9 %	86.5 %
Coral	0.455	38.7	97.3 %	99.4 %
Plankton	0.534	39.1	97.2 %	99.7 %

Although these metrics differ in the distances between entries, they yield the same ordering. This suggests that the other metrics are viable substitutes for cosine distance, yet we settle on cosine distance because its computation does not require training a classifier and because it is bounded between 0 and 1.

4   Results

In this analysis we will refer to a *low* source-target distance as a cosine distance of between 0–0.2, a *medium* distance as 0.2–0.4, and a *high* distance as 0.4–1.

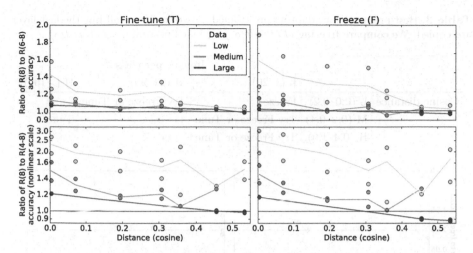

Fig. 1. Top: Ratio between accuracy for $R(8)$ and accuracy for $R(6\text{-}8)$. **Bottom:** Ratio between $R(8)$ and $R(4\text{-}8)$. Each point represents a pair of experiments with other conditions fixed. At **Left** are fine-tune (T) experiments only, at Right are freeze (F) experiments only. Values above 1.0 imply copying is better than random initialization. Values below 1.0 imply copying is worse. Trend lines are averages.

We will refer to a *low* amount of target data as 1–20 images per class, a *medium* amount as 21–99 images per class, and a *large* amount as 100 or more images per class. All raw experimental results can be found in Fig. 3 in the Appendix.

We begin by studying whether random initialization or initializing with copied parameters yields higher performance across a variety of dataset shifts. To do this, we hold all parameters of a particular experiment fixed except for whether certain layers are randomly initialized or copied. The results across all experiments are shown in Fig. 1, where the ratio of performance between copying and randomly initializing layers is indicated. Here, we found that randomly initializing layers beyond the necessary fc8 layer almost always degrades performance (all numbers across experiments are >1). The notable exception being when source and target datasets have high difference and there are a large number of labeled target examples available for fine-tuning. In this setting randomly initializing offers a stronger benefit when the lowest layers are frozen during the final training step, but marginal or no improvement over copying when all layers are fine-tuned. Therefore, we conclude that copying all but the last layer of the network is generally the best practice for fine-tuning to a new dataset.

Our finding of copying all but the last layer is in direct contrast with Yosinski et al., who showed that copying fewer layers is better when freezing [6]. The contrasting results are easily explained by the much larger amounts of data used in that study, whereas we seek to analyze scenarios in which large amounts of data are not available: the largest amount of data we use for the Yosinski target dataset is 120 images/class (60,000 images). Clearly, there is an inflection point between 60,000 and approximately 645,000 training examples where it no longer becomes beneficial to copy more layers when freezing. For the remainder of our

Table 3. Best practices for adapting pre-trained networks where all but the last layer are copied. We compare freezing $(F(1\text{-}7)R(8))$ against fine-tuning $(T(1\text{-}7)R(8))$.

		Images per class		
		L (1–20)	M (21–99)	H ($\geq$100)
Cosine distance	L (0.0–0.2)	Freeze	Try Freeze or Tune	Tune
	M (0.2–0.4)	Try Freeze or Tune	Tune	Tune
	H (0.4–1.0)	Try Freeze or Tune	Tune	Tune

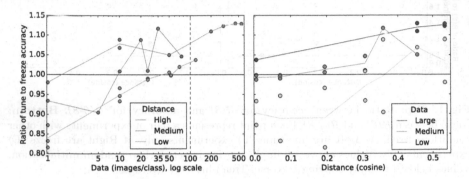

Fig. 2. Ratio between accuracy when fine-tuning and accuracy when freezing, measured across pairs of experiments with other conditions fixed. Only showing $R(8)$ experiments. Values above 1.0 imply fine-tuning is better. Values below 1.0 imply freezing is better. **Left** examines the effect of data on this ratio. The dotted line denotes large amounts of data. **Right** examines the effect of source-target distance on this ratio. Trend lines are averages.

analysis, we follow our first finding to copy all parameters from the initial source network and therefore choose between $F(1\text{-}7)R(8)$ and $T(1\text{-}7)R(8)$. We present our recommendations in Table 3 and discuss evidence from our experiments next.

Figure 2 (left) shows that with a large amount of target data, fine-tuning is always best, fitting our intuition that more data reduces overfitting. But Fig. 2 (right) shows that when there is a low or medium amount of training data, the distance between source and target plays a more important role. Broadly, as distance increases, fine-tuning improves relative to freezing, supporting the notion that learned features are less transferable to distant datasets. At one end, in the low data and low distance setting, freezing outperforms fine-tuning. At the other end, in the medium data and medium-to-high distance setting, fine-tuning outperforms freezing.

The inflection point occurs in settings where (1) target data is low and distance is medium or high, or (2) target data is moderate and distance is low. Here there is no consistent winner between fine-tuning and freezing. In these situations we recommend trying both fine-tuned and frozen networks. An additional consideration, though not shown in the figure, is that fine-tuned models generally take more time to train - one might choose a preferred training technique based on preference towards training speed or accuracy.

References

1. Zeiler, M.D., Fergus, R.: Visualizing and understanding convolutional networks. In: Fleet, D., Pajdla, T., Schiele, B., Tuytelaars, T. (eds.) ECCV 2014. LNCS, vol. 8693, pp. 818–833. Springer, Heidelberg (2014). doi:10.1007/978-3-319-10590-1_53
2. Donahue, J., Jia, Y., Vinyals, O., Hoffman, J., Zhang, N., Tzeng, E., Darrell, T.: DeCAF: a deep convolutional activation feature for generic visual recognition. In: International Conference in Machine Learning (ICML) (2014)
3. Fei-Fei, L., Fergus, R., Perona, P.: Learning generative visual models from few training examples: an incremental Bayesian approach tested on 101 object categories. Comput. Vis. Image Underst. (2007)
4. Griffin, G., Holub, A., Perona, P.: Caltech-256 object category dataset. Technical report 7694, California Institute of Technology (2007)
5. Xiao, J., Hays, J., Ehinger, K.A., Oliva, A., Torralba, A.: Sun database: large-scale scene recognition from abbey to zoo. In: Proceedings of the IEEE Conference on Computer Vision and Pattern Recognition (CVPR) (2010)
6. Yosinski, J., Clune, J., Bengio, Y., Lipson, H.: How transferable are features in deep neural networks? In: Advances in Neural Information Processing Systems (NIPS) (2014)
7. Girshick, R., Donahue, J., Darrell, T., Malik, J.: Rich feature hierarchies for accurate object detection and semantic segmentation. In: Proceedings of the IEEE Conference on Computer Vision and Pattern Recognition (CVPR) (2014)
8. Agrawal, P., Girshick, R., Malik, J.: Analyzing the performance of multilayer neural networks for object recognition. In: Fleet, D., Pajdla, T., Schiele, B., Tuytelaars, T. (eds.) ECCV 2014. LNCS, vol. 8693, pp. 329–344. Springer, Heidelberg (2014). doi:10.1007/978-3-319-10584-0_22
9. Zhou, B., Lapedriza, A., Xiao, J., Torralba, A., Oliva, A.: Learning deep features for scene recognition using places database. In: Advances in Neural Information Processing Systems (NIPS) (2014)
10. Krizhevsky, A., Sutskever, I., Hinton, G.E.: Imagenet classification with deep convolutional neural networks. In: Advances in Neural Information Processing Systems (NIPS) (2012)
11. Azizpour, H., Razavian, A., Sullivan, J., Maki, A., Carlsson, S.: Factors of transferability for a generic convnet representation. IEEE Trans. Pattern Anal. Mach. Intell. (2015)
12. Jia, Y., Shelhamer, E., Donahue, J., Karayev, S., Long, J., Girshick, R., Guadarrama, S., Darrell, T.: Caffe: convolutional architecture for fast feature embedding. arXiv preprint (2014). arXiv:1408.5093
13. Quattoni, A., Torralba, A.: Recognizing indoor scenes. In: Proceedings of the IEEE Conference on Computer Vision and Pattern Recognition (CVPR) (2009)
14. Wah, C., Branson, S., Welinder, P., Perona, P., Belongie, S.: The Caltech-UCSD Birds-200-2011 dataset. Technical report CNS-TR-2011-001, California Institute of Technology (2011)
15. Beijbom, O., Edmunds, P.J., Kline, D.I., Mitchell, B.G., Kriegman, D.: Automated annotation of coral reef survey images. In: Proceedings of the IEEE Conference on Computer Vision and Pattern Recognition (CVPR) (2012)
16. Orenstein, E.C., Beijbom, O., Peacock, E.E., Sosik, H.M.: Whoi-Plankton- a large scale fine grained visual recognition benchmark dataset for Plankton classification. CoRR abs/1510.00745 (2015)

17. Krizhevsky, A.: Learning multiple layers of features from tiny images. Technical report (2009)
18. Tzeng, E., Hoffman, J., Darrell, T., Saenko, K.: Simultaneous deep transfer across domains and tasks. In: International Conference in Computer Vision (ICCV) (2015)
19. Ganin, Y., Lempitsky, V.: Unsupervised domain adaptation by backpropagation. In: ICML (2015)
20. Long, M., Wang, J.: Learning transferable features with deep adaptation networks. In: ICML (2015)

Deep CORAL: Correlation Alignment for Deep Domain Adaptation

Baochen Sun[1(✉)] and Kate Saenko[2]

[1] University of Massachusetts Lowell, Lowell, USA
bsun@cs.uml.edu
[2] Boston University, Boston, USA
saenko@bu.edu

Abstract. Deep neural networks are able to learn powerful representations from large quantities of labeled input data, however they cannot always generalize well across changes in input distributions. Domain adaptation algorithms have been proposed to compensate for the degradation in performance due to domain shift. In this paper, we address the case when the target domain is unlabeled, requiring unsupervised adaptation. CORAL [18] is a simple unsupervised domain adaptation method that aligns the second-order statistics of the source and target distributions with a linear transformation. Here, we extend CORAL to learn a nonlinear transformation that aligns correlations of layer activations in deep neural networks (Deep CORAL). Experiments on standard benchmark datasets show state-of-the-art performance. Our code is available at: https://github.com/VisionLearningGroup/CORAL.

1 Introduction

Many machine learning algorithms assume that the training and test data are independent and identically distributed (i.i.d.). However, this assumption rarely holds in practice as the data is likely to change over time and space. Even though state-of-the-art Deep Convolutional Neural Network features are invariant to low level cues to some degree [15,16,19], Donahue et al. [3] showed that they still are susceptible to domain shift. Instead of collecting labeled data and training a new classifier for every possible scenario, unsupervised domain adaptation methods [4,6,17,18,20,21] try to compensate for the degradation in performance by transferring knowledge from labeled source domains to unlabeled target domains. A recently proposed CORAL method [18] aligns the second-order statistics of the source and target distributions with a linear transformation. Even though it is easy to implement, it works well for unsupervised domain adaptation. However, it relies on a linear transformation and is not end-to-end trainable: it needs to first extract features, apply the transformation, and then train an SVM classifier in a separate step.

In this work, we extend CORAL to incorporate it directly into deep networks by constructing a differentiable loss function that minimizes the difference between source and target correlations–the CORAL loss. Compared to CORAL,

© Springer International Publishing Switzerland 2016
G. Hua and H. Jégou (Eds.): ECCV 2016 Workshops, Part III, LNCS 9915, pp. 443–450, 2016.
DOI: 10.1007/978-3-319-49409-8_35

our proposed Deep CORAL approach learns a non-linear transformation that is more powerful and also works seamlessly with deep CNNs. We evaluate our method on standard benchmark datasets and show state-of-the-art performance.

2   Related Work

Previous techniques for unsupervised adaptation consisted of re-weighting the training point losses to more closely reflect those in the test distribution [9, 11] or finding a transformation in a lower-dimensional manifold that brings the source and target subspaces closer together [4, 6–8]. Re-weighting based approaches often assume a restricted form of domain shift–selection bias–and are thus not applicable to more general scenarios. Geodesic methods [6, 7] bridge the source and target domains by projecting them onto points along a geodesic path [7], or finding a closed-form linear map that transforms source points to target [6]. [4, 8] align the subspaces by computing the linear map that minimizes the Frobenius norm of the difference between the top n eigenvectors. In contrast, CORAL [18] minimizes domain shift by aligning the second-order statistics of source and target distributions.

Adaptive deep neural networks have recently been explored for unsupervised adaptation. DLID [1] trains a joint source and target CNN architecture with two adaptation layers. DDC [23] applies a single linear kernel to one layer to minimize Maximum Mean Discrepancy (MMD) while DAN [13] minimizes MMD with multiple kernels applied to multiple layers. ReverseGrad [5] and Domain-Confusion [22] add a binary classifier to explicitly confuse the two domains.

Our proposed Deep CORAL approach is similar to DDC, DAN, and ReverseGrad in the sense that a new loss (CORAL loss) is added to minimize the difference in learned feature covariances across domains, which is similar to minimizing MMD with a polynomial kernel. However, it is more powerful than DDC (which aligns sample means only), much simpler to optimize than DAN and ReverseGrad, and can be integrated into different layers or architectures seamlessly.

3   Deep CORAL

We address the unsupervised domain adaptation scenario where there are no labeled training data in the target domain, and propose to leverage both the deep features pre-trained on a large generic domain (*e.g.*, ImageNet [2]) and the labeled source data. In the meantime, we also want the final learned features to work well on the target domain. The first goal can be achieved by initializing the network parameters from the generic pre-trained network and fine-tuning it on the labeled source data. For the second goal, we propose to minimize the difference in second-order statistics between the source and target feature activations–the CORAL loss. Figure 1 shows a sample Deep CORAL architecture using our proposed correlation alignment layer for deep domain adaptation. We refer to Deep CORAL as any deep network incorporating the CORAL loss for domain adaptation.

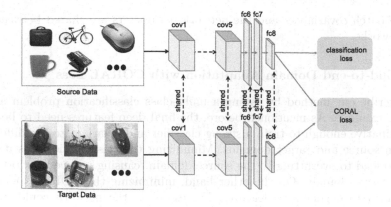

Fig. 1. Sample Deep CORAL architecture based on a CNN with a classifier layer. For generalization and simplicity, here we apply the CORAL loss to the $fc8$ layer of AlexNet [12]. Integrating it into other layers or network architectures is also possible.

3.1 CORAL Loss

We first describe the CORAL loss between two domains for a single feature layer. Suppose we are given source-domain training examples $D_S = \{\mathbf{x}_i\}, \mathbf{x} \in \mathbb{R}^d$ with labels $L_S = \{y_i\}, i \in \{1, ..., L\}$, and unlabeled target data $D_T = \{\mathbf{u}_i\}, \mathbf{u} \in \mathbb{R}^d$. Suppose the numbers of source and target data are n_S and n_T respectively. Here both $\mathbf{x}$ and $\mathbf{u}$ are the d-dimensional deep layer activations $\phi(I)$ of input I that we are trying to learn. Suppose D_S^{ij} (D_T^{ij}) indicates the j-th dimension of the i-th source (target) data example and C_S (C_T) denote the feature covariance matrices.

We define the CORAL loss as the distance between the second-order statistics (covariances) of the source and target features:

$$\mathcal{L}_{CORAL} = \frac{1}{4d^2}\|C_S - C_T\|_F^2 \tag{1}$$

where $\|\cdot\|_F^2$ denotes the squared matrix Frobenius norm. The covariance matrices of the source and target data are given by:

$$C_S = \frac{1}{n_S - 1}(D_S^\top D_S - \frac{1}{n_S}(\mathbf{1}^\top D_S)^\top(\mathbf{1}^\top D_S)) \tag{2}$$

$$C_T = \frac{1}{n_T - 1}(D_T^\top D_T - \frac{1}{n_T}(\mathbf{1}^\top D_T)^\top(\mathbf{1}^\top D_T)) \tag{3}$$

where $\mathbf{1}$ is a column vector with all elements equal to 1.

The gradient with respect to the input features can be calculated using the chain rule:

$$\frac{\partial \mathcal{L}_{CORAL}}{\partial D_S^{ij}} = \frac{1}{d^2(n_S - 1)}((D_S^\top - \frac{1}{n_S}(\mathbf{1}^\top D_S)^\top \mathbf{1}^\top)^\top(C_S - C_T))^{ij} \tag{4}$$

$$\frac{\partial \mathcal{L}_{CORAL}}{\partial D_T^{ij}} = -\frac{1}{d^2(n_T - 1)}((D_T^\top - \frac{1}{n_T}(\mathbf{1}^\top D_T)^\top \mathbf{1}^\top)^\top(C_S - C_T))^{ij} \tag{5}$$

We use batch covariances and the network parameters are shared between the two networks.

3.2   End-to-end Domain Adaptation with CORAL Loss

We describe our method by taking a multi-class classification problem as the running example. As mentioned before, the final deep features need to be both discriminative enough to train a strong classifier and invariant to the difference between source and target domains. Minimizing the classification loss itself is likely to lead to overfitting to the source domain, causing reduced performance on the target domain. On the other hand, minimizing the CORAL loss alone might lead to degenerated features. For example, the network could project all of the source and target data to a single point, making the CORAL loss trivially zero. However, no strong classifier can be constructed on these features. Joint training with both the classification loss and CORAL loss is likely to learn features that work well on the target domain:

$$\mathcal{L} = \mathcal{L}_{CLASS} + \sum_{i=1}^{t} \lambda_i \mathcal{L}_{CORAL} \qquad (6)$$

where t denotes the number of CORAL loss layers in a deep network and λ is a weight that trades off the adaptation with classification accuracy on the source domain. As we show below, these two losses play counterparts and reach an *equilibrium* at the end of training, where the final features are discriminative and generalize well to the target domain.

4   Experiments

We evaluate our method on a standard domain adaptation benchmark–the Office dataset [17]. The Office dataset contains 31 object categories from an office environment in 3 image domains: *Amazon, DSLR*, and *Webcam*.

We follow the standard protocol of [3,5,6,13,23] and use all the labeled source data and all the target data without labels. Since there are 3 domains, we conduct experiments on all 6 shifts (5 runs per shift), taking one domain as the source and another as the target.

In this experiment, we apply the CORAL loss to the last classification layer as it is the most general case–most deep classifier architectures (*e.g.*, convolutional neural networks, recurrent neural networks) contain a fully connected layer for classification. Applying the CORAL loss to other layers or other network architectures is also possible.

The dimension of the last fully connected layer ($fc8$) was set to the number of categories (31) and initialized with $\mathcal{N}(0, 0.005)$. The learning rate of $fc8$ was set to 10 times the other layers as it was training from scratch. We initialized the other layers with the parameters pre-trained on ImageNet [2] and kept the original layer-wise parameter settings. In the training phase, we set the batch size to 128, base learning rate to 10^{-3}, weight decay to 5×10^{-4}, and momentum to 0.9. The weight of the CORAL loss (λ) is set in such way that at the end of training the classification loss and CORAL loss are roughly the same. It seems be a reasonable choice as we want to have a feature representation that is both discriminative and also minimizes the distance between the source and target domains. We used Caffe [10] and BVLC Reference CaffeNet for all of our experiments.

We compare to 7 recently published methods: CNN [12] (no adaptation), GFK [6], SA [4], TCA [14], CORAL [18], DDC [23], DAN [13]. GFK, SA, and TCA are manifold based methods that project the source and target distributions into a lower-dimensional manifold and are not end-to-end deep methods. DDC adds a domain confusion loss to AlexNet [12] and fine-tunes it on both the source and target domain. DAN is similar to DDC but utilizes a multi-kernel selection method for better mean embedding matching and adapts in multiple layers. For direct comparison, DAN in this paper uses the hidden layer $fc8$. For GFK, SA, TCA, and CORAL, we use the $fc7$ feature fine-tuned on the source domain ($FT7$ in [18]) as it achieves better performance than generic pre-trained features, and train a linear SVM [4,18]. To have a fair comparison, we use accuracies reported by other authors with exactly the same setting or conduct experiments using the source code provided by the authors.

From Table 1 we can see that Deep CORAL (D-CORAL) achieves better average performance than CORAL and the other 6 baseline methods. In 3 out of 6 shifts, it achieves the highest accuracy. For the other 3 shifts, the margin between D-CORAL and the best baseline method is very small ($\leqslant 0.7$).

Table 1. Object recognition accuracies for all 6 domain shifts on the standard Office dataset with deep features, following the standard unsupervised adaptation protocol.

	A→D	A→W	D→A	D→W	W→A	W→D	AVG
GFK	52.4±0.0	54.7±0.0	43.2±0.0	92.1±0.0	41.8±0.0	96.2±0.0	63.4
SA	50.6±0.0	47.4±0.0	39.5±0.0	89.1±0.0	37.6±0.0	93.8±0.0	59.7
TCA	46.8±0.0	45.5±0.0	36.4±0.0	81.1±0.0	39.5±0.0	92.2±0.0	56.9
CORAL	65.7±0.0	64.3±0.0	48.5±0.0	**96.1**±0.0	48.2±0.0	**99.8**±0.0	70.4
CNN	63.8±0.5	61.6±0.5	51.1±0.6	95.4±0.3	49.8±0.4	99.0±0.2	70.1
DDC	64.4±0.3	61.8±0.4	52.1±0.8	95.0±0.5	**52.2**±0.4	98.5±0.4	70.6
DAN	65.8±0.4	63.8±0.4	**52.8**±0.4	94.6±0.5	51.9±0.5	98.8±0.6	71.3
D-CORAL	**66.8**±0.6	**66.4**±0.4	**52.8**±0.2	95.7±0.3	51.5±0.3	99.2±0.1	**72.1**

To get a better understanding of Deep CORAL, we generate three plots for domain shift A→W. In Fig. 2(a) we show the training (source) and testing (target) accuracies for training with v.s. without CORAL loss. We can clearly see that adding the CORAL loss helps achieve much better performance on the

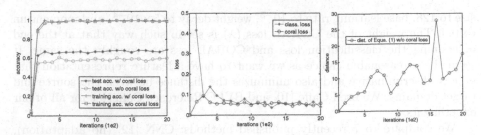

Fig. 2. Detailed analysis of shift A→W for training w/ v.s. w/o CORAL loss. (a): training and test accuracies for training w/ v.s. w/o CORAL loss. We can see that adding CORAL loss helps achieve much better performance on the target domain while maintaining strong classification accuracy on the source domain. (b): classification loss and CORAL loss for training w/ CORAL loss. As the last fully connected layer is randomly initialized with $\mathcal{N}(0, 0.005)$, CORAL loss is very small while classification loss is very large at the beginning. After training for a few hundred iterations, these two losses are about the same. (c): CORAL distance for training w/o CORAL loss (setting the weight to 0). The distance is getting much larger ($\geqslant 100$ times larger compared to training w/ CORAL loss).

target domain while maintaining strong classification accuracy on the source domain.

In Fig. 2(b) we visualize both the classification loss and the CORAL loss for training w/ CORAL loss. As the last fully connected layer is randomly initialized with $\mathcal{N}(0, 0.005)$, in the beginning the CORAL loss is very small while the classification loss is very large. After training for a few hundred iterations, these two losses are about the same and reach an *equilibrium*. In Fig. 2(c) we show the CORAL distance between the domains for training w/o CORAL loss (setting the weight to 0). We can see that the distance is getting much larger ($\geqslant 100$ times larger compared to training w/ CORAL loss). Comparing Fig. 2(b) and (c), we can see that even though the CORAL loss is not always decreasing during training, if we set its weight to 0, the distance between source and target domains becomes much larger. This is reasonable as fine-tuning without domain adaptation is likely to overfit the features to the source domain. Our CORAL loss constrains the distance between source and target domain during the fine-tuning process and helps to maintain an *equilibrium* where the final features work well on the target domain.

5   Conclusion

In this work, we extended CORAL, a simple yet effective unsupervised domain adaptation method, to perform end-to-end adaptation in deep neural networks. Experiments on standard benchmark datasets show state-of-the-art performance. Deep CORAL works seamlessly with deep networks and can be easily integrated into different layers or network architectures.

Acknowledgments. This research was supported by NSF awards IIS-1451244 and IIS-1212928. The Tesla K40 and Titan X GPUs used for this research were donated by the NVIDIA Corporation.

References

1. Chopra, S., Balakrishnan, S., Gopalan, R.: DLID: deep learning for domain adaptation by interpolating between domains. In: ICML Workshop (2013)
2. Deng, J., Dong, W., Socher, R., Li, L.J., Li, K., Fei-Fei, L.: ImageNet: a large-scale hierarchical image database. In: CVPR (2009)
3. Donahue, J., Jia, Y., Vinyals, O., Hoffman, J., Zhang, N., Tzeng, E., Darrell, T.: Decaf: a deep convolutional activation feature for generic visual recognition. In: ICML (2014)
4. Fernando, B., Habrard, A., Sebban, M., Tuytelaars, T.: Unsupervised visual domain adaptation using subspace alignment. In: ICCV (2013)
5. Ganin, Y., Lempitsky, V.: Unsupervised domain adaptation by backpropagation. In: ICML (2015)
6. Gong, B., Shi, Y., Sha, F., Grauman, K.: Geodesic flow kernel for unsupervised domain adaptation. In: CVPR (2012)
7. Gopalan, R., Li, R., Chellappa, R.: Domain adaptation for object recognition: an unsupervised approach. In: ICCV (2011)
8. Harel, M., Mannor, S.: Learning from multiple outlooks. In: ICML (2011)
9. Huang, J., Smola, A.J., Gretton, A., Borgwardt, K.M., Schölkopf, B.: Correcting sample selection bias by unlabeled data. In: NIPS (2006)
10. Jia, Y., Shelhamer, E., Donahue, J., Karayev, S., Long, J., Girshick, R., Guadarrama, S., Darrell, T.: Caffe: convolutional architecture for fast feature embedding. arXiv preprint arXiv:1408.5093 (2014)
11. Jiang, J., Zhai, C.: Instance weighting for domain adaptation in NLP. In: ACL (2007)
12. Krizhevsky, A., Sutskever, I., Hinton, G.E.: Imagenet classification with deep convolutional neural networks. In: NIPS (2012)
13. Long, M., Cao, Y., Wang, J., Jordan, M.I.: Learning transferable features with deep adaptation networks. In: ICML (2015)
14. Pan, S.J., Tsang, I.W., Kwok, J.T., Yang, Q.: Domain adaptation via transfer component analysis. In: IJCAI (2009)
15. Peng, X., Sun, B., Ali, K., Saenko, K.: Learning deep object detectors from 3D models. In: ICCV (2015)
16. Peng, X., Sun, B., Ali, K., Saenko, K.: What do deep CNNs learn about objects? In: ICLR Workshop Track (2015)
17. Saenko, K., Kulis, B., Fritz, M., Darrell, T.: Adapting visual category models to new domains. In: Daniilidis, K., Maragos, P., Paragios, N. (eds.) ECCV 2010. LNCS, vol. 6316, pp. 213–226. Springer, Heidelberg (2010). doi:10.1007/978-3-642-15561-1_16
18. Sun, B., Feng, J., Saenko, K.: Return of frustratingly easy domain adaptation. In: AAAI (2016)
19. Sun, B., Peng, X., Saenko, K.: Generating large scale image datasets from 3D CAD models. In: CVPR 2015 Workshop on The Future of Datasets in Vision (2015)
20. Sun, B., Saenko, K.: From virtual to reality: fast adaptation of virtual object detectors to real domains. In: BMVC (2014)

21. Sun, B., Saenko, K.: Subspace distribution alignment for unsupervised domain adaptation. In: BMVC (2015)
22. Tzeng, E., Hoffman, J., Darrell, T., Saenko, K.: Simultaneous deep transfer across domains and tasks. In: International Conference in Computer Vision (ICCV) (2015)
23. Tzeng, E., Hoffman, J., Zhang, N., Saenko, K., Darrell, T.: Deep domain confusion: maximizing for domain invariance. CoRR abs/1412.3474 (2014). http://arxiv.org/abs/1412.3474

Nonlinear Embedding Transform for Unsupervised Domain Adaptation

Hemanth Venkateswara[✉], Shayok Chakraborty,
and Sethuraman Panchanathan

Center for Cognitive Ubiquitous Computing,
Arizona State University, Tempe, AZ, USA
{hemanthv,schakr10,panch}@asu.edu

Abstract. The problem of domain adaptation (DA) deals with adapting classifier models trained on one data distribution to different data distributions. In this paper, we introduce the Nonlinear Embedding Transform (NET) for unsupervised DA by combining domain alignment along with similarity-based embedding. We also introduce a validation procedure to estimate the model parameters for the NET algorithm using the source data. Comprehensive evaluations on multiple vision datasets demonstrate that the NET algorithm outperforms existing competitive procedures for unsupervised DA.

Keywords: Unsupervised · MMD · Nonlinear embedding · Validation

1 Introduction

Classification models trained on labeled datasets are ineffective over data from different distributions owing to data-shift [14]. The problem of domain adaptation (DA) deals with adapting models trained on one data distribution (source domain) to different data distributions (target domains). For the purpose of this paper, we organize unsupervised DA procedures under two categories: *linear* and *nonlinear*, based on feature representations used in the model. *Linear* techniques determine linear transformations of the source (target) data and align it with the target (source), or learn a linear classifier with the source data and adapt it to the target data [2,13,15]. *Nonlinear* procedures on the other hand, apply nonlinear transformations to reduce cross-domain disparity [6,11].

In this work we present the Nonlinear Embedding Transform (NET) procedure for unsupervised DA. The NET consists of two steps, (i) Nonlinear domain alignment using Maximum Mean Discrepancy (MMD) [9], (ii) similarity-based embedding to cluster the data for enhanced classification. In addition, we introduce a procedure to sample source data in order to generate a validation set for model selection. We study the performance of the NET algorithm with popular DA datasets for computer vision. Our results showcase significant improvement in the classification accuracies compared to competitive DA procedures.

© Springer International Publishing Switzerland 2016
G. Hua and H. Jégou (Eds.): ECCV 2016 Workshops, Part III, LNCS 9915, pp. 451–457, 2016.
DOI: 10.1007/978-3-319-49409-8_36

2   Related Work

In this section we provide a concise review of some of the unsupervised DA procedures closely related to the NET. Under *linear* methods, Burzzone et al. [2], proposed the DASVM algorithm to iteratively adapt a SVM trained on the source data, to the unlabeled target data. The state-of-the-art linear DA procedures are Subspace Alignment (SA), by Fernando et al. [5], and the CORAL algorithm, by Sun et al. [13]. The SA aligns the subspaces of the source and the target with a linear transformation and the CORAL transforms the source data such that the covariance matrices of the source and target are aligned.

Nonlinear procedures generally project the data to a high-dimensional space and align the source and target distributions in that space. The popular GFK algorithm by Gong et al. [6], projects the two distributions onto a manifold and learns a transformation to align them. The Transfer Component Analysis (TCA) [11], Transfer Joint Matching (TJM) [8], and Joint Distribution Adaptation (JDA) [9], algorithms, apply MMD-based projection to nonlinearly align the domains. In addition, the TJM implements instance selection using $\ell_{2,1}$-norm regularization and the JDA performs a joint distribution alignment of the source and target domains. The NET implements nonlinear alignment of the domains along with a similarity preserving projection, which ensures that the projected data is clustered based on category. We compare the NET with only kernel-based nonlinear methods and do not include deep learning based DA procedures.

3   DA with Nonlinear Embedding

In this section we outline the problem of unsupervised DA and develop the NET algorithm. Let $\mathbf{X}_S = [\mathbf{x}_1^s, \ldots, \mathbf{x}_{n_s}^s] \in \mathbb{R}^{d \times n_s}$ and $\mathbf{X}_T = [\mathbf{x}_1^t, \ldots, \mathbf{x}_{n_t}^t] \in \mathbb{R}^{d \times n_t}$ be the source and target data points respectively. Let $Y_S = [y_1^s, \ldots, y_{n_s}^s]$ and $Y_T = [y_1^t, \ldots, y_{n_t}^t]$ be the source and target labels respectively. Here, $\mathbf{x}_i^s$ and $\mathbf{x}_i^t \in \mathbb{R}^d$ are data points and y_i^s and $y_i^t \in \{1, \ldots, C\}$ are the associated labels. We define $\mathbf{X} := [\mathbf{x}_1, \ldots, \mathbf{x}_n] = [\mathbf{X}_S, \mathbf{X}_T]$, where $n = n_s + n_t$. In the case of unsupervised DA, the labels Y_T are missing and the joint distributions for the two domains are different, i.e. $P_S(X, Y) \neq P_T(X, Y)$. The task lies in learning a classifier $f(\mathbf{x}) = p(y|\mathbf{x})$, that predicts the labels of the target data points.

3.1   Nonlinear Embedding for DA

One of the techniques to reduce domain disparity is to project the source and target data to a common subspace. KPCA is a popular nonlinear projection algorithm where data is first mapped to a high-dimensional (possibly infinite-dimensional) space given by $\Phi(\mathbf{X}) = [\phi(\mathbf{x}_1), \ldots, \phi(\mathbf{x}_n)]$. $\phi : \mathbb{R}^d \to \mathcal{H}$ defines the mapping and $\mathcal{H}$ is a RKHS with a psd kernel $k(\mathbf{x}, \mathbf{y}) = \phi(\mathbf{x})^\top \phi(\mathbf{y})$. The kernel matrix for $\mathbf{X}$ is given by $\mathbf{K} = \Phi(\mathbf{X})^\top \Phi(\mathbf{X}) \in \mathbb{R}^{n \times n}$. The mapped data is then projected onto a subspace of eigen-vectors (directions of maximum nonlinear variance in the RKHS). The top k eigen-vectors in the RKHS are obtained using the representer theorem, $\mathbf{U} = \Phi(\mathbf{X})\mathbf{A}$, where $\mathbf{A} \in \mathbb{R}^{n \times k}$ is the matrix of coefficients that needs to be determined. The nonlinearly projected data is then given by, $\mathbf{Z} = [\mathbf{z}_1, \ldots, \mathbf{z}_n] = \mathbf{A}^\top \mathbf{K} \in \mathbb{R}^{k \times n}$, where $\mathbf{z}_i \in \mathbb{R}^k$, $i = 1, \ldots, n$, are the projected data points.

In order to reduce the domain discrepancy in the projected space, we implement the joint distribution adaptation (JDA), as outlined in [9]. The JDA seeks to align the marginal and conditional probability distributions of the projected data $(\mathbf{Z})$, by estimating the coefficient matrix $\mathbf{A}$, which minimizes:

$$\min_{\mathbf{A}} \sum_{c=0}^{C} \text{tr}(\mathbf{A}^\top \mathbf{K} \mathbf{M}_c \mathbf{K}^\top \mathbf{A}). \tag{1}$$

$\text{tr}(.)$ refers to trace and $\mathbf{M}_c$, where $c = 0, \ldots, C$, are $n \times n$ matrices given by,

$$(M_c)_{ij} = \begin{cases} \frac{1}{n_s^{(c)} n_s^{(c)}}, & \mathbf{x}_i, \mathbf{x}_j \in \mathcal{D}_s^{(c)} \\ \frac{1}{n_t^{(c)} n_t^{(c)}}, & \mathbf{x}_i, \mathbf{x}_j \in \mathcal{D}_t^{(c)} \\ \frac{-1}{n_s^{(c)} n_t^{(c)}}, & \begin{cases} \mathbf{x}_i \in \mathcal{D}_s^{(c)}, \mathbf{x}_j \in \mathcal{D}_t^{(c)} \\ \mathbf{x}_j \in \mathcal{D}_s^{(c)}, \mathbf{x}_i \in \mathcal{D}_t^{(c)} \end{cases} \\ 0, & \text{otherwise}, \end{cases} \tag{2}$$

$$(M_0)_{ij} = \begin{cases} \frac{1}{n_s n_s}, & \mathbf{x}_i, \mathbf{x}_j \in \mathcal{D}_s \\ \frac{1}{n_t n_t}, & \mathbf{x}_i, \mathbf{x}_j \in \mathcal{D}_t \\ \frac{-1}{n_s n_t}, & \text{otherwise}, \end{cases} \tag{3}$$

where $\mathcal{D}_s$ and $\mathcal{D}_t$ are the sets of source and target data points respectively. $\mathcal{D}_s^{(c)}$ is the set of source data points belonging to class c and $n_s^{(c)} = |\mathcal{D}_s^{(c)}|$. Likewise, $\mathcal{D}_t^{(c)}$ is the set of target data points belonging to class c and $n_t^{(c)} = |\mathcal{D}_t^{(c)}|$. Since the target labels are unknown, we use predicted labels for the target data points. We begin with predicting the target labels using a classifier trained on the source data and refine these labels over iterations, to arrive at the final prediction. For more details please refer to [9].

In addition to domain alignment, we would like the projected data $\mathbf{Z}$, to be classification friendly (easily classifiable). To this end, we introduce Laplacian eigenmaps to ensure a similarity-preserving projection such that data points with the same class label are clustered together. The similarity relations are captured by the $(n \times n)$ adjacency matrix $\mathbf{W}$, and the optimization problem estimates the projected data $\mathbf{Z}$;

$$\mathbf{W}_{ij} := \begin{cases} 1 & y_i^s = y_j^s \text{ or } i = j \\ 0 & y_i^s \neq y_j^s \text{ or labels unknown}, \end{cases} \tag{4}$$

$$\min_{\mathbf{Z}} \frac{1}{2} \sum_{ij} \left\| \frac{\mathbf{z}_i}{\sqrt{d_i}} - \frac{\mathbf{z}_j}{\sqrt{d_j}} \right\|^2 \mathbf{W}_{ij} = \text{tr}(\mathbf{Z}\mathbf{L}\mathbf{Z}^\top). \tag{5}$$

$\mathbf{D} = diag(d_1, \ldots, d_n)$ is the $(n \times n)$ diagonal matrix where, $d_i = \sum_j \mathbf{W}_{ij}$ and $\mathbf{L}$ is the normalized graph laplacian matrix that is symmetric positive semidefinite and is given by $\mathbf{L} = \mathbf{I} - \mathbf{D}^{-1/2}\mathbf{W}\mathbf{D}^{-1/2}$, where $\mathbf{I}$ is an identity matrix. When $\mathbf{W}_{ij} = 1$, the projected data points $\mathbf{z}_i$ and $\mathbf{z}_j$ are close together (as they belong to the same category). The normalized distance between the vectors $||\mathbf{z}_i/\sqrt{d_i} - \mathbf{z}_j/\sqrt{d_j}||^2$, captures a more robust measure of data point clustering compared to the un-normalized distance $||\mathbf{z}_i - \mathbf{z}_j||^2$, [4].

3.2   Optimization Problem

The optimization problem for NET is obtained from (1) and (5) by substituting, $\mathbf{Z} = \mathbf{A}^\top\mathbf{K}$. Along with regularization and a constraint, we get,

$$\min_{\mathbf{A}^\top\mathbf{K}\mathbf{D}\mathbf{K}^\top\mathbf{A}=\mathbf{I}} \alpha.\mathrm{tr}(\mathbf{A}^\top\mathbf{K}\sum_{c=0}^{C}\mathbf{M}_c\mathbf{K}^\top\mathbf{A}) + \beta.\mathrm{tr}(\mathbf{A}^\top\mathbf{K}\mathbf{L}\mathbf{K}^\top\mathbf{A}) + \gamma||\mathbf{A}||_F^2. \quad (6)$$

$\mathbf{A} \in \mathbb{R}^{n \times k}$ is the projection matrix. The regularization term $||\mathbf{A}||_F^2$ (Frobenius norm), controls the smoothness of projection and the magnitudes of (α, β, γ), denote the importance of the individual terms in (6). The constraint prevents the data points from collapsing onto a subspace of dimensionality less than k, [1]. Equation (6) can be solved by constructing the Lagrangian $L(\mathbf{A}, \boldsymbol{\Lambda})$, where, $\boldsymbol{\Lambda} = diag(\lambda_1, \ldots, \lambda_k)$, is the diagonal matrix of Lagrangian constants (see [8]). Setting the derivative $\frac{\partial L}{\partial \mathbf{A}} = 0$, yields the generalized eigen-value problem,

$$(\alpha\mathbf{K}\sum_{c=0}^{C}\mathbf{M}_c\mathbf{K}^\top + \beta\mathbf{K}\mathbf{L}\mathbf{K}^\top + \gamma\mathbf{I})\mathbf{A} = \mathbf{K}\mathbf{D}\mathbf{K}^\top\mathbf{A}\boldsymbol{\Lambda}. \quad (7)$$

$\mathbf{A}$ is the matrix of the k-smallest eigen-vectors of (7) and $\boldsymbol{\Lambda}$ is the diagonal matrix of eigen-values. The projected data points are given by, $\mathbf{Z} = \mathbf{A}^\top\mathbf{K}$.

3.3   Model Selection

Current DA methods use the target data to validate the optimum parameters for their models [8,9]. We introduce a new technique to evaluate $(\alpha, \beta, \gamma, k)$, using a subset of the source data as a validation set. The subset is selected by weighting the source data points using Kernel Mean Matching (KMM). The KMM computes source instance weights w_i, by minimizing, $||\frac{1}{n_s}\sum_{i=1}^{n_s} w_i\phi(\mathbf{x}_i^s) - \frac{1}{n_t}\sum_{j=1}^{n_t}\phi(\mathbf{x}_j^t)||_{\mathcal{H}}^2$. Defining $\kappa_i := \frac{n_s}{n_t}\sum_{j=1}^{n_t} k(\mathbf{x}_i^s, \mathbf{x}_j^t)$, $i = 1, \ldots, n_s$ and $\mathbf{K}_{S_{ij}} = k(\mathbf{x}_i^s, \mathbf{x}_j^s)$, the minimization can be written in terms of quadratic programming:

$$\min_{\mathbf{w}} = \frac{1}{2}\mathbf{w}^\top\mathbf{K}_S\mathbf{w} - \kappa^\top\mathbf{w}, \quad \mathrm{s.t.}\ w_i \in [0, B], \quad \left|\sum_{i=1}^{n_s} w_i - n_s\right| \le n_s\epsilon. \quad (8)$$

The first constraint limits the scope of discrepancy between source and target distributions with $B \to 1$, leading to an unweighted solution. The second constraint ensures the measure $w(x)P_S(x)$, is a probability distribution [7]. In our experiments, the validation set is 30 % of the source data with the largest weights. This validation set is used to estimate the best values for $(\alpha, \beta, \gamma, k)$.

4   Experiments

We compare the NET algorithm with the following baseline and state-of-the-art methods. NA (No Adaptation - classifier trained on the source and tested on the target), SA (Subspace Alignment [5]), CA (Correlation Alignment (CORAL) [13]), GFK (Geodesic Flow Kernel [6]), TCA (Transfer Component Analysis [11]), JDA (Joint Distribution Adaptation [9]). NET_v is a special case of the NET algorithm where parameters $(\alpha, \beta, \gamma, k)$, have been estimated using (8) (see Sect. 3.3). For NET*, the optimum values for $(\alpha, \beta, \gamma, k)$ are estimated using the target data for cross validation.

4.1   Datasets

Office-Caltech **Datasets**: This object recognition dataset [6], consists of images of everyday objects categorized into 4 domains; Amazon, Caltech, Dslr and Webcam. It has 10 categories of objects and a total of 2533 images. We experiment with two kinds of features (i) SURF features obtained from [6], (ii) Deep features. To extract deep features, we use an 'off-the-shelf' deep convolutional neural network (VGG-F model [3]). We use the 4096-dimensional features from the $fc8$ layer and apply PCA to reduce the feature dimension to 500.

MNIST-USPS **Datasets**: We use a subset of the popular handwritten digit (0–9) recognition datasets (2000 images from MNIST and 1800 images from USPS based on [8]). The images are resized to 16×16 pixels and represented as 256-dimensional vectors.

CKPlus-MMI **Datasets**: The CKPlus [10], and MMI [12], datasets consist of facial expression videos. From these videos, we select the frames with the most-intense expression to create the domains CKPlus and MMI, with around 1500 images each and 6 categories viz., *anger, disgust, fear, happy, sad, surprise*. We use a pre-trained deep neural network to extract features (see *Office-Caltech*).

4.2   Results and Discussion

For k, we explore optimum values in the set $\{10, 20, \ldots, 100, 200\}$. For (α, β, γ), we select from $\{0, 0.0001, 0.0005, 0.001, 0.005, 0.01, 0.05, 0.1, 0.5, 1, 5, 10\}$. For the sake of brevity, we evaluate and present one set of parameters $(\alpha, \beta, \gamma, k)$, for all the DA experiments in a dataset. For all the experiments, we choose 10 iterations to converge to the predicted test/validation labels when estimating M_c. Figure 1, depicts the variation in validation set accuracies for each of the parameters. We select the parameter value with the highest validation set accuracy as the optimal value in the NET_v experiments.

For fair comparison with existing methods, we follow the same experimental protocol as in [6,8]. We train a nearest neighbor (NN) classifier on the projected source data and test on the projected target data. Table 1, captures the results for the digit and face datasets. Table 2, outlines the results for the *Office-Caltech* dataset. The accuracies reflect the percentage of correctly classified target data

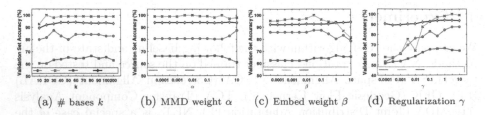

(a) # bases k (b) MMD weight α (c) Embed weight β (d) Regularization γ

Fig. 1. Each figure depicts the accuracies over the validation set for a range of values. When studying a parameter (say k), the remaining parameters (α, β, γ) are fixed at the optimum value.

Table 1. Recognition accuracies (%) for DA experiments on the digit and face datasets. {MNIST(M), USPS(U), CKPlus(CK), MMI(MM)}. M→U implies M is source domain and U is target domain. The best and second best results are in **bold** and *italic*.

Expt.	NA	SA	CA	GFK	TCA	JDA	NET$_v$	NET*	Expt.	NA	SA	CA	GFK	TCA	JDA	NET$_v$	NET*
M→ U	65.94	67.39	59.33	66.06	60.17	67.28	*72.72*	**75.39**	CK→ MM	29.90	31.12	31.89	28.75	32.72	29.78	**30.54**	*29.97*
U→ M	44.70	51.85	50.80	47.40	39.85	*59.65*	61.35	**62.60**	MM→ CK	41.48	39.75	37.74	37.94	31.33	28.39	*40.08*	**45.83**
Avg.	55.32	59.62	55.07	56.73	50.01	63.46	*67.04*	**68.99**	Avg.	35.69	35.43	34.81	33.35	32.02	29.08	*35.31*	**37.90**

points. The accuracies obtained with NET$_v$, demonstrate that the validation set generated from the source data is a good option for validating model parameters in unsupervised DA. The parameters for the NET* experiment are estimated using the target datset; $(\alpha = 1, \beta = 1, \gamma = 1, k = 20)$ for the object recognition datasets, $(\alpha = 1, \beta = 0.01, \gamma = 1, k = 20)$ for the digit dataset and $(\alpha = 0.01, \beta = 0.01, \gamma = 1, k = 20)$ for the face dataset. The accuracies obtained with the NET algorithm are consistently better than existing methods, demonstrating the role of nonlinear embedding along with domain alignment.

Table 2. Recognition accuracies (%) for DA experiments on the *Office-Caltech* dataset with SURF and Deep features. {Amazon(A), Webcam(W), Dslr(D), Caltech(C)}. A→W implies A is source and W is target. The best and second best results are in **bold** and *italic*.

Expt.	SURF Features								Deep Features							
	NA	SA	CA	GFK	TCA	JDA	NET$_v$	NET*	NA	SA	CA	GFK	TCA	JDA	NET$_v$	NET*
A→ C	34.19	38.56	33.84	39.27	39.89	39.36	*43.10*	**43.54**	**83.01**	80.55	*82.47*	81.00	75.53	**83.01**	82.28	**83.01**
A→ D	35.67	37.58	36.94	34.40	33.76	*39.49*	36.31	**40.76**	84.08	82.17	87.90	82.80	82.17	*89.81*	80.89	**91.08**
A→ W	31.19	37.29	31.19	*41.70*	33.90	37.97	35.25	**44.41**	79.32	82.37	80.34	84.41	76.61	87.12	*87.46*	**90.85**
C→ A	36.01	43.11	36.33	*45.72*	44.47	44.78	46.24	**46.45**	90.70	88.82	*91.12*	90.60	89.13	90.07	90.70	**92.48**
C→ D	38.22	43.95	38.22	43.31	36.94	*45.22*	36.31	**45.86**	83.44	80.89	82.80	77.07	75.80	89.17	*90.45*	**92.36**
C→ W	29.15	36.27	29.49	35.59	32.88	*41.69*	33.56	**44.41**	76.61	77.29	79.32	78.64	78.31	*85.76*	84.07	**90.85**
D→ A	28.29	29.65	28.39	26.10	31.63	33.09	*35.60*	**39.67**	88.51	84.33	86.63	88.40	88.19	91.22	*91.43*	**91.54**
D→ C	29.56	31.88	29.56	30.45	30.99	31.52	*34.11*	**35.71**	77.53	76.26	75.98	78.63	74.43	80.09	**83.38**	*82.10*
D→ W	83.73	87.80	83.39	79.66	85.42	*89.49*	**90.51**	87.80	*99.32*	98.98	*99.32*	98.31	97.97	98.98	**99.66**	**99.66**
W→ A	31.63	32.36	31.42	27.77	29.44	32.78	*39.46*	**41.65**	82.34	84.01	82.76	88.61	86.21	91.43	*91.95*	**92.58**
W→ C	28.76	29.92	28.76	28.41	32.15	31.17	*32.77*	**35.89**	76.53	78.90	74.98	76.80	76.71	**82.74**	82.28	*82.56*
W→ D	84.71	90.45	85.35	82.17	85.35	*89.17*	**91.72**	89.81	*99.36*	**100.00**	**100.00**	**100.00**	**100.00**	**100.00**	**100.00**	*99.36*
Avg.	40.93	44.90	41.07	42.88	43.07	*46.31*	46.24	**49.66**	85.06	84.55	85.30	85.44	83.42	*89.12*	88.71	**90.70**

5 Conclusions and Acknowledgments

We have proposed the NET algorithm for unsupervised DA along with a procedure for generating a validation set for model selection using the source data. Both the validation procedure and NET have better recognition accuracies than competitive visual DA methods across multiple vision based datasets. This material is based upon work supported by the National Science Foundation (NSF) under Grant No:1116360. Any opinions, findings, and conclusions or recommendations expressed in this material are those of the authors and do not necessarily reflect the views of the NSF.

References

1. Belkin, M., Niyogi, P.: Laplacian eigenmaps for dimensionality reduction and data representation. Neural Comput. **15**(6), 1373–1396 (2003)
2. Bruzzone, L., Marconcini, M.: Domain adaptation problems: a DASVM classification technique and a circular validation strategy. IEEE, PAMI **32**(5), 770–787 (2010)
3. Chatfield, K., Simonyan, K., Vedaldi, A., Zisserman, A.: Return of the devil in the details: Delving deep into convolutional nets. In: BMVC (2014)
4. Chung, F.R.: Spectral Graph Theory. American Mathematical Society, Providence (1997)
5. Fernando, B., Habrard, A., Sebban, M., Tuytelaars, T.: Unsupervised visual domain adaptation using subspace alignment. In: CVPR, pp. 2960–2967 (2013)
6. Gong, B., Shi, Y., Sha, F., Grauman, K.: Geodesic flow kernel for unsupervised domain adaptation. In: IEEE CVPR (2012)
7. Gretton, A., Smola, A., Huang, J., Schmittfull, M., Borgwardt, K., Schölkopf, B.: Covariate shift by kernel mean matching. Dataset Shift Mach. Learn. **3**(4), 5 (2009)
8. Long, M., Wang, J., Ding, G., Sun, J., Yu, P.: Transfer joint matching for unsupervised domain adaptation. In: CVPR, pp. 1410–1417 (2014)
9. Long, M., Wang, J., Ding, G., Sun, J., Yu, P.S.: Transfer feature learning with joint distribution adaptation. In: Proceedings of the IEEE International Conference on Computer Vision, pp. 2200–2207 (2013)
10. Lucey, P., Cohn, J.F., Kanade, T., Saragih, J., Ambadar, Z., Matthews, I.: The extended cohn-kanade dataset (CK+): a complete dataset for action unit and emotion-specified expression. In: CVPR, pp. 94–101. IEEE (2010)
11. Pan, S.J., Tsang, I.W., Kwok, J.T., Yang, Q.: Domain adaptation via transfer component analysis. IEEE Trans. Neural Netw. **22**(2), 199–210 (2011)
12. Pantic, M., Valstar, M., Rademaker, R., Maat, L.: Web-based database for facial expression analysis. In: ICME, IEEE (2005)
13. Sun, B., Feng, J., Saenko, K.: Return of frustratingly easy domain adaptation. In: ICCV, TASK-CV (2015)
14. Torralba, A., Efros, A.A.: Unbiased look at dataset bias. In: 2011 IEEE Conference on Computer Vision and Pattern Recognition (CVPR), pp. 1521–1528. IEEE (2011)
15. Venkateswara, H., Lade, P., Ye, J., Panchanathan, S.: Coupled support vector machines for supervised domain adaptation. In: ACM MM, pp. 1295–1298 (2015)

Unsupervised Domain Adaptation
with Regularized Domain Instance Denoising

Gabriela Csurka$^{(\boxtimes)}$, Boris Chidlowskii, Stéphane Clinchant, and Sophia Michel

Xerox Research Center Europe, 6 Chemin de Maupertuis, 38240 Meylan, France
{Gabriela.Csurka,Boris.Chidlowskii,Stephane.Clinchant,
Sophia.Michel}@xrce.xerox.com

Abstract. We propose to extend the marginalized denoising autoencoder (MDA) framework with a domain regularization whose aim is
to denoise both the source and target data in such a way that the
features become domain invariant and the adaptation gets easier. The
domain regularization, based either on the maximum mean discrepancy
(MMD) measure or on the domain prediction, aims to reduce the distance between the source and the target data. We also exploit the source
class labels as another way to regularize the loss, by using a domain
classifier regularizer. We show that in these cases, the noise marginalization gets reduced to solving either the linear matrix system $\mathbf{AX} = \mathbf{B}$,
for which there exists a closed-form solution, or to a Sylvester linear
matrix equation $\mathbf{AX} + \mathbf{XB} = \mathbf{C}$ that can be solved efficiently using
the Bartels-Stewart algorithm. We did an extensive study on how these
regularization terms improve the baseline performance and we present
experiments on three image benchmark datasets, conventionally used for
domain adaptation methods. We report our findings and comparisons
with state-of-the-art methods.

Keywords: Unsupervised domain adaptation · Marginalized Denoising
Autoencoder · Sylvester equation · Domain regularization

1 Introduction

Domain Adaptation problems arise each time we need to leverage labeled data
in one or more related *source* domains, to learn a classifier for unseen or unlabeled data in a *target* domain. The domains are assumed to be related, but
not identical. The underlying *domain shift* occurs in multiple real-world applications. Numerous approaches have been proposed in the last years to address tex-
tual and visual domain adaptation (we refer the reader to [23,32,36] for recent
surveys on transfer learning and domain adaptation methods). For text data,
the domain shift is frequent in named entity recognition, statistical machine
translation, opinion mining, speech tagging and document ranking [3,11,33,41].
Domain adaptation has equally received a lot of attention in computer vision
[1,13–15,17,20–22,29,34,35] where domain shift is a consequence of changing
conditions, such as background, location or pose, or considering different image
types, such as photos, paintings, sketches [4,9,25].

© Springer International Publishing Switzerland 2016
G. Hua and H. Jégou (Eds.): ECCV 2016 Workshops, Part III, LNCS 9915, pp. 458–466, 2016.
DOI: 10.1007/978-3-319-49409-8_37

In this paper, we build on an approach to domain adaptation based on noise marginalization [5]. In deep learning, a denoising autoencoder (DA) learns a robust feature representation from training examples. In the case of domain adaptation, it takes the unlabeled instances of both source and target data and learns a new feature representation by reconstructing the original features from their noised counterparts. A *marginalized denoising autoencoder* (MDA) is a technique to marginalize the noise at training time; it avoids the explicit data corruption and does not require an optimization procedure for learning the model parameters but computes the model in a closed form. This makes MDAs scalable and computationally faster than the regular denoising autoencoders. The principle of noise marginalization has been successfully extended to learning with corrupted features [30], link prediction and multi-label learning [6], relational learning [7], collaborative filtering [26] and heterogeneous cross-domain learning [27,40].

The *marginalized domain adaptation* refers to such a denoising of source and target instances that explicitly makes their features *domain invariant*. To achieve this goal, we extend the MDA with a domain regularization term. We explore three ways of such a regularization. The first way uses the *maximum mean discrepancy* (MMD) measure [24]. The second way is inspired by the adversarial learning of deep neural networks [19]. The third regularization term is based on preserving accurate classification of the denoised source instances. In all cases, the regularization term belongs to the class of squared loss functions. This guarantees the noise marginalization and the computational efficiency, either as a closed form solution or as a solution of Sylvester linear matrix equation $\mathbf{AX} + \mathbf{XB} = \mathbf{C}$.

2   Feature Denoising for Domain Adaptation

Let $\mathbf{X}^s = [\mathbf{X}_1, \ldots, \mathbf{X}_{n_S}]$ denote a set of n_S source domains, with the corresponding labels $\mathbf{Y}^s = [\mathbf{Y}_1, \ldots \mathbf{Y}_{n_S}]$, and let $\mathbf{X}^t$ denote the unlabeled target domain data. The *Marginalized Denoising Autoencoder* (MDA) approach [5] is to reconstruct the input data from partial random corruption [39] with a marginalization that yields optimal reconstruction weights $\mathbf{W}$ in a closed form. The MDA minimizes the loss written as:

$$\mathcal{L}(\mathbf{W}, \mathbf{X}) = \frac{1}{K} \sum_{k=1}^{K} \|\mathbf{X} - \tilde{\mathbf{X}}_k \mathbf{W}\|^2 + \omega \|\mathbf{W}\|^2, \tag{1}$$

where $\tilde{\mathbf{X}}_k \in \mathbb{R}^{N \times d}$ is the k-th corrupted version of $\mathbf{X} = [\mathbf{X}^s, \mathbf{X}^t]$ by random feature dropout with a probability p, $\mathbf{W} \in \mathbb{R}^{d \times d}$, and $\omega \|\mathbf{W}\|^2$ is a regularization term. To avoid the explicit feature corruption and an iterative optimization, Chen et al. [5] has shown that in the limiting case $K \to \infty$, the weak law of large numbers allows to rewrite $\mathcal{L}(\mathbf{W}, \mathbf{X})$ as its expectation. The optimal solution $\mathbf{W}$ can be written as $\mathbf{W} = (\mathbf{Q} + \omega \mathbf{I}_d)^{-1} \mathbf{P}$, where $\mathbf{P} = \mathbb{E}[\mathbf{X}^\top \tilde{\mathbf{X}}]$ and $\mathbf{Q} = \mathbb{E}[\tilde{\mathbf{X}}^\top \tilde{\mathbf{X}}]$

depend only on the covariance matrix $\mathbf{S}$ of the uncorrupted data, $\mathbf{S} = \mathbf{X}^\top \mathbf{X}$, and the noise level p:

$$\mathbf{P} = (1-p)\mathbf{S} \quad \text{and} \quad \mathbf{Q}_{ij} = \begin{bmatrix} \mathbf{S}_{ij}(1-p)^2, \text{ if } & i \neq j, \\ \mathbf{S}_{ij}(1-p), \text{ if } & i = j. \end{bmatrix} \tag{2}$$

2.1 Domain Regularization

To better address the domain adaptation, we extend the feature denoising with a *domain regularization* in order to favor the learning of domain invariant features. We explore three versions of the domain regularization. We combine them with the loss (1) and show how to marginalize the noise for each version and to keep $\mathbf{W}$ as a solution of a linear matrix equation. The three versions of the domain regularization are as follows:

Regularization $\mathcal{R}_m$ Based on the Maximum Mean Discrepancy (MMD) with the Linear Kernel; It aims at reducing the gap between the denoised domain means. The MMD was already used for domain adaptation with feature transformation learning [2,31] and as a regularizer for the cross-domain classifier learning [13,28,38]. In this paper, in contrast to these papers where the distributions are approximated with MMD using multiple nonlinear kernels we use MMD with the linear kernel[1], the only one allowing us to keep the solution for $\mathbf{W}$ closed form.

The regularization term for K corrupted versions of $\mathbf{X}$ is given by:

$$\mathcal{R}_m = \frac{1}{K} \sum_{k=1}^{K} Tr(\mathbf{W}^\top \tilde{\mathbf{X}}_k^\top \mathbf{N} \tilde{\mathbf{X}}_k \mathbf{W}), \quad \text{where} \quad \mathbf{N} = \begin{bmatrix} \frac{1}{N_s^2} \mathbf{1}^{s,s} & \frac{1}{N_s N_t} \mathbf{1}^{s,t} \\ \frac{1}{N_s N_t} \mathbf{1}^{s,t} & \frac{1}{N_t^2} \mathbf{1}^{t,t} \end{bmatrix},$$

$\mathbf{1}^{a,b}$ is a constant matrix of size $N_a \times N_b$ with all elements being equal to 1 and N_s, N_t are the number of source and target examples. After the noise marginalization, we obtain $\mathbb{E}[\mathcal{R}_m] = Tr(\mathbf{W}^\top \mathbf{M} \mathbf{W})$, where $\mathbf{M} = \mathbb{E}[\tilde{\mathbf{X}}^\top \mathbf{N} \tilde{\mathbf{X}}]$ is computed similarly to $\mathbf{Q}$ in (2), by using $\mathbf{S}_m = \mathbf{X}^\top \mathbf{N} \mathbf{X}$ instead of the correlation matrix $\mathbf{S}$.

Regularization $\mathcal{R}_d$ Based on Domain Prediction; It explicitly pushes the denoised source examples toward target instances. The domain regularizer $\mathcal{R}_d$, proposed in [8], is inspired by [18] where intermediate layers in a deep learning model are regularized using a domain prediction task. The main idea is to learn the denoising while pushing the source towards the target (or *vice versa*) and hence allowing the source classifier to perform better on the target. The regularization term $\mathcal{R}_d$ can be written as follows:

$$\mathcal{R}_d = \frac{1}{K} \sum_{k=1}^{K} \|\mathbf{Y}_\mathcal{T} - \tilde{\mathbf{X}}_k \mathbf{W} \mathbf{Z}_\mathcal{D}\|^2, \tag{3}$$

where $\mathbf{Z}_\mathcal{D} \in \mathbb{R}^d$ is a domain classifier trained on the uncorrupted data to distinguish the target from the source and $\mathbf{Y}_\mathcal{T} = \mathbf{1}^N$ is a vector containing only ones,

---

[1] Minimizing the distance between the corresponding domain centroids.

Table 1. A summary of our models and corresponding notations.

Method	Loss	$\mathbf{W}$ closed form solution
M1	$\mathcal{L}$	$(\mathbf{Q} + \omega\mathbf{I}_d)^{-1}\mathbf{P}$
MRm	$\mathcal{L} + \gamma_m\mathcal{R}_m$	$(\mathbf{Q} + \omega\mathbf{I}_d + \gamma_m\mathbf{M})^{-1}\mathbf{P}$
	Loss	$\mathbf{W}$ solution of $\mathbf{AW} + \mathbf{WB} = \mathbf{C}$
MRd	$\mathcal{L} + \gamma_d\mathcal{R}_d$	$\mathbf{A} = \omega\mathbf{Q}^{-1},\ \mathbf{B} = (\mathbf{I}_d + \gamma_d\mathbf{Z}_{\mathcal{D}}\mathbf{Z}_{\mathcal{D}}^{\top})$
		$\mathbf{C} = \mathbf{Q}^{-1}(\mathbf{P} + \gamma_d(1-p)\mathbf{X}^{\top}\mathbf{Y}_{\mathcal{T}}\mathbf{Z}_{\mathcal{D}}^{\top})$
MRl	$\mathcal{L} + \gamma_l\mathcal{R}_l$	$\mathbf{A} = \mathbf{Q}_l^{-1}(\mathbf{Q} + \omega\mathbf{I}_d),\ \ \mathbf{B} = \gamma_l\mathbf{Z}_l\mathbf{Z}_l^{\top}$
		$\mathbf{C} = \mathbf{Q}_l^{-1}(\mathbf{P} + \gamma_l(1-p)\mathbf{X}_l^{\top}\mathbf{Y}_l\mathbf{Z}_l^{\top})$

as all denoised instances should look like the target[2]. After the noise marginalization, the partial derivatives on $\mathbf{W}$ of this term expectation are the following:

$$\frac{\partial\,\mathbb{E}[\mathcal{R}_d]}{\partial\mathbf{W}} = -2(1-p)\mathbf{X}^{\top}\mathbf{Y}_{\mathcal{T}}\mathbf{Z}_{\mathcal{D}} + 2\mathbf{QWZ}_{\mathcal{D}}\mathbf{Z}_{\mathcal{D}}^{\top}.$$

Classification Regularization $\mathcal{R}_l$; It encourages the denoised source data to remain well classified by the classifier pre-trained on source data. The regularizer $\mathcal{R}_l$ is similar to $\mathcal{R}_d$, except that $\mathbf{Z}_l$ is trained on the uncorrupted source $\mathbf{X}^s$ and acts only on the labeled source data. Also, instead of $\mathbf{Y}_{\mathcal{T}}$, the groundtruth source labels $\mathbf{Y}_l = \mathbf{Y}^s$ are used[3]. In the marginalized version of $\mathcal{R}_l$, The partial derivatives on $\mathbf{W}$ can be written as

$$\frac{\partial\,\mathbb{E}[\mathcal{R}_l]}{\partial\mathbf{W}} = -2(1-p)\mathbf{X}_l^{\top}\mathbf{Y}_l\mathbf{Z}_l + 2\mathbf{Q}_l\mathbf{WZ}_l\mathbf{Z}_l^{\top},$$

where $\mathbf{X}_l = \mathbf{X}^s$ and $\mathbf{Q}_l$ is computed similarly to $\mathbf{Q}$, with $\mathbf{S}_l = \mathbf{X}_l^{\top}\mathbf{X}_l$.

2.2 Minimizing the Regularized Loss

We extend the noise marginalization framework for optimizing the data reconstruction loss (1) and minimize the expected loss $\mathbb{E}[\mathcal{L} + \gamma_\phi\mathcal{R}_\phi]$, denoted $\mathbb{E}[\mathcal{L}_\phi]$, where in the regularization term $\mathcal{R}_\phi$, ϕ refers to m, d or l version. From the marginalized terms presented in the previous sections, it is easy to show that when minimizing these regularized losses, the optimal solution for $\mathbf{W}$ given by $\partial\,\mathbb{E}[\mathcal{L}_\phi]/\partial\mathbf{W} = \mathbf{0}$ can be reduced to solving the linear matrix system $\mathbf{AW} = \mathbf{B}$, for which there exists a closed-form solution, or to a Sylvester linear matrix equation $\mathbf{AW} + \mathbf{WB} = \mathbf{C}$ that can be solved efficiently using the Bartels-Stewart algorithm. Due to the limited space, we report all the details in the full version

---

[2] In the multi source case, $\mathbf{Z}_{\mathcal{D}} \in \mathbb{R}^{d\times(n_S+1)}$, with the columns corresponding n_S sources and 1 target domain classifiers, and $\mathbf{Y}_{\mathcal{T}} \in \mathbb{R}^{N\times(n_S+1)}$, with $y_{ns} = 1$ if $s = n_S + 1$ and -1 otherwise. N is the total number of instances (source and target).

[3] $\mathbf{Y}_l \in \mathbb{R}^{N_s\times C}$, where $y_{nc} = 1$ if $\mathbf{x}_n$ belongs to the class c and -1 otherwise. In the multi source case, we concatenate n_S multi-class $\mathbf{Z}_l^a$ linear classifiers and the corresponding $\mathbf{Y}_l^a$ label matrices, where $\mathbf{Z}_l^a$ was trained on the source $\mathcal{D}^{s_a}$.

and summarize the baseline, three extensions and the corresponding solutions in Table 1.

Similarly to the stacked MDAs, we can stack several layers together with only forward learning, where the denoised features of the previous layer serve as the input to the next layer and nonlinear functions such as tangent hyperbolic or rectified linear units can be applied between the layers.

3   Experimental Results

Datasets. We run experiments on the popular **OFF31** [34] and **OC10** [22] datasets, both with the *full training* protocol [21] where all source data is used for training and with the *sampling* protocol [22,34]. We evaluated our models both with the provided SURFBOV and the DECAF6 [12] features. In addition we run experiments with the full training protocol on the Testbed Cross-Dataset [37] (**TB**) using both the provided SIFTBOV and the DECAF7 features.

Parameter Setting. To compare different models we run all experiments with the same preprocessing and parameter values[4]. Features are L2 normalized and the feature dimensionality is PCA reduced to 200 (BOV features are in addition power normalized). Parameter values are $\omega = 0.01$, $\gamma_\phi = 1$ and $p = 0.1$. Between layers we apply tangent hyperbolic nonlinearities and we concatenate the outputs of all layers with the original features (as in [5]).

We evaluate how the optimal denoising matrix $\mathbf{W}$ influences three different classification methods, a regularized multi-class ridge classifier trained on the

Table 2. Single source domain adaptation with a single ($r = 1$) and 3 stacked layers ($r = 3$). Bold indicates the best result per column, underline refers to best single layer results.

DECAF	OC10			OFF31			TB		
	NN	DSCM	Ridge	NN	DSCM	Ridge	NN	DSCM	Ridge
BL (full)	84.5	78.7	82.6	65.2	61.6	62.8	39.8	42.6	37.2
BL (PCA)	84.1	81.8	82.5	65.4	63.7	62.4	40.9	42.7	39.7
M1 ($r = 1$)	84.1	82.0	83.6	65.3	63.6	64.4	41.0	42.8	40.6
MRm ($r = 1$)	84.1	82.1	83.6	65.4	63.6	64.4	41.0	42.8	40.6
MRd ($r = 1$)	84.4	<u>82.9</u>	<u>83.7</u>	65.7	64.0	64.7	41.1	43.2	40.6
MRl ($r = 1$)	<u>84.5</u>	82.2	82.2	<u>66.9</u>	<u>65.6</u>	<u>65.6</u>	<u>41.3</u>	<u>43.3</u>	<u>40.9</u>
M1 ($r = 3$)	84.3	82.4	84.0	64.7	63.6	65.6	41.2	42.6	41.3
MRm ($r = 3$)	84.3	82.4	84.0	64.7	63.6	65.6	41.2	42.6	41.3
MRd ($r = 3$)	**84.8**	**83.9**	**84.9**	66.0	64.7	66.0	41.4	43.8	41.2
MRl ($r = 3$)	84.1	82.2	81.8	**67.7**	**65.9**	**66.5**	**41.8**	**43.9**	**41.5**

---

[4] Cross validation on the source was only helpful for some of the configurations, for others it yielded performance decrease.

source ($\mathbf{Z} = (\mathbf{X}_l^\top \mathbf{X}_l + \delta \mathbf{I}_d)^{-1} \mathbf{X}_l^\top \mathbf{Y}_l$), the nearest neighbor classifier (NN) and the Domain Specific Class Means (DSCM) classifier [10] where a target test example is assigned to a class based on a soft-max distance to the domain specific class means. Two last classifiers are selected for their non-linearity. Also the NN is related to retrieval and DSCM to clustering, so the impact of $\mathbf{W}$ on these two extra tasks is indirectly assessed.

Table 2 shows the domain adaptation results with a single source and Table 3 shows multi source results, both under the full training protocol. For each dataset, we consider all possible source-target pairs for the domain adaptation tasks. Hence we average over 9 tasks on **OFF31** (with 3 domains A,D,W), and over 12 tasks on **OC10** (4 domains (A,C,D,W) and **TB** (4 domains B,C,I,S).

Table 2 shows the results on L2 normalized DECAF features. It compares the domain regularization extensions to the baselines (BL) obtained with the L2 normalized features (full) and with the PCA reduced features as well as with MDA. As the table shows, the best results are often obtained with **MRl**, except in the OC10 case where **MRd** performs better. On the other hand, the $\mathcal{R}_m$ regularizer (**MRm**) does not improve the M1 performance. Stacking several layers can further improve the results. When comparing these results to the literature we can see that on **OC10** we perform comparably to DAM [14] (84 %) and DDC [38] (84.6 %) but worse than more complex methods such as JDA [29] (87.5 %), TTM [16] (87.5 %) or DAN [28] (87.3 %). On **OFF31**, the deep adaptation method DAN [28] (72.9 %) significantly outperforms our results. On the **TD** dataset, in order to compare our results on DECAF6 to CORAL+SVM [35] (40.2 %) we average six source-task pairs (without the domain B) and obtain 43.6 % with **MRd+DSCM** and 43.1 % with **MRl+DSCM**. We also outperform[5] CORAL+SVM [35] (64 %) with our **MRd+Ridge** (65.2 %) when using the sampling protocol on **OFF31**.

Concerning the BOV features, the best results (using 3 layers) with the full training protocol on **OFF31** are with **MRl+NN** (29.7 %) and on **OC10** with **MRd+Ridge**(48.2 %). The latter is comparable to CORAL+SVM [35] (48.8 %),

Table 3. Multi-source adaptation results without stacking. Bold indicates best result per column.

BOV	OC10			OFF31			TB		
	NN	DSCM	Ridge	NN	DSCM	Ridge	NN	DSCN	Ridge
BL	50.4	54.6	51.9	39.7	33.3	25.4	16.5	17.6	21
M1	50.8	**54.7**	52.1	39.9	33.8	25.6	16.6	17.7	21
MRd	50.8	54.1	51.5	**40.1**	33.5	26.9	16.6	17.7	**21.1**
MRl	**53.8**	53.3	**52.5**	39	**36.5**	**28.5**	**17.1**	19.6	20.9

---

[5] Their best results (68.5 % and 69.4 %) obtained with fine-tuned features are not directly comparable as our results can also be boosted when using these fine-tuned features.

but is below LSSA [1] (52.3 %) that first selects landmarks before learning the transformation. The landmark selection is complementary to our approach and can boost our results as well.

In Table 3, we report the averaged results for the multi-source cases, obtained with BOV features, under the full training protocol. For each dataset, all the configurations with at least 2 source domains are considered. It yields 6 such configurations for **OFF31** and 16 configurations for **OC10** and **TB**. The results indicate clearly that taking into account the domain regularization improves the performance.

4 Conclusion

In this paper we extended the marginalized denoising autoencoder (MDA) framework with a domain regularization to enforce domain invariance. We studied three versions of regularization, based on the maximum mean discrepancy measure, the domain prediction and the class predictions on source. We showed that in all these cases, the noise marginalization is reduced to closed form solution or to a Sylvester linear matrix system, for which there exist efficient and scalable solutions. This allows furthermore to easily stack several layers with low cost. We studied the effect of these domain regularizations and run single source and multi-source experiments on three benchmark datasets showing that adding the new regularization terms allow to outperform the baselines. Compared to the state-of-the-art, our method performs better than classical feature transformation methods but it is outperformed by more complex deep domain adaptation methods. Compared to the latter methods, the main advantage of the proposed approach, beyond its low computational cost, is that as we learn an unsupervised feature transformation, we can boost the performance of other tasks such as retrieval or clustering in the target space.

References

1. Aljundi, R., Emonet, R., Muselet, D., Sebban, M.: Landmarks-based kernelized subspace alignment for unsupervised domain adaptation. In: Proceedings of CVPR, pp. 56–63. IEEE (2015)
2. Baktashmotlagh, M., Harandi, M., Lovell, B., Salzmann, M.: Unsupervised domain adaptation by domain invariant projection. In: Proceedings of ICCV, pp. 769–776. IEEE (2013)
3. Blitzer, J., Kakade, S., Foster, D.P.: Domain adaptation with coupled subspaces. In: Proceedings of AISTATS, pp. 173–181 (2011)
4. Castrejón, L., Aytar, Y., Vondrick, C., Pirsiavash, H., Torralba, A.: Learning aligned cross-modal representations from weakly aligned data. In: Proceedings of CVPR, IEEE (2016)
5. Chen, M., Xu, Z., Weinberger, K.Q., Sha, F.: Marginalized denoising autoencoders for domain adaptation. In: Proceedings of ICML, pp. 767–774 (2012)
6. Chen, Z., Chen, M., Weinberger, K.Q., Zhang, W.: Marginalized denoising for link prediction and multi-label learning. In: Proceedings of AAAI (2015)

7. Chen, Z., Zhang, W.: A marginalized denoising method for link prediction in relational data. In: Proceedings of ICDM (2014)
8. Clinchant, S., Csurka, G., Chidlovskii, B.: A domain adaptation regularization for denoising autoencoders. In: Proceedings of ACL (2016)
9. Crowley, E.J., Zisserman, A.: In search of art. In: Agapito, L., Bronstein, M.M., Rother, C. (eds.) ECCV 2014. LNCS, vol. 8927, pp. 54–70. Springer, Heidelberg (2015). doi:10.1007/978-3-319-16178-5_4
10. Csurka, G., Chidlovskii, B., Perronnin, F.: Domain adaptation with a domain specific class means classifier. In: Agapito, L., Bronstein, M.M., Rother, C. (eds.) ECCV 2014. LNCS, vol. 8927, pp. 32–46. Springer, Heidelberg (2015). doi:10.1007/978-3-319-16199-0_3
11. Daume, H., Marcu, D.: Domain adaptation for statistical classifiers. J. Artif. Intell. Res. 26(1), 101–126 (2006)
12. Donahue, J., Jia, Y., Vinyals, O., Hoffman, J., Zhang, N., Tzeng, E., Darrell, T.: Decaf: a deep convolutional activation feature for generic visual recognition. CoRR (2013). arXiv:1310.1531
13. Duan, L., Tsang, I.W., Xu, D.: Domain transfer multiple kernel learning. Trans. Pattern Recogn. Mach. Anal. (PAMI) 34(3), 465–479 (2012)
14. Duan, L., Tsang, I.W., Xu, D., Chua, T.S.: Domain adaptation from multiple sources via auxiliary classifiers. In: Proceedings of ICML, pp. 289–296 (2009)
15. Farajidavar, N., deCampos, T., Kittler, J.: Adaptive transductive transfer machines. In: Proceedings of BMVC (2014)
16. Farajidavar, N., Campos, T., Kittler, J.: Transductive transfer machine. In: Cremers, D., Reid, I., Saito, H., Yang, M.-H. (eds.) ACCV 2014. LNCS, vol. 9005, pp. 623–639. Springer, Heidelberg (2015). doi:10.1007/978-3-319-16811-1_41
17. Fernando, B., Habrard, A., Sebban, M., Tuytelaars, T.: Unsupervised visual domain adaptation using subspace alignment. In: Proceedings of ICCV, pp. 2960–2967. IEEE (2013)
18. Ganin, Y., Lempitsky, V.: Unsupervised domain adaptation by backpropagation, CoRR (2014). arXiv:1409.7495
19. Ganin, Y., Lempitsky, V.: Unsupervised domain adaptation by backpropagation. In: Proceedings of ICML, pp. 1180–1189 (2015)
20. Glorot, X., Bordes, A., Bengio, Y.: Domain adaptation for large-scale sentiment classification: a deep learning approach. In: Proceedings of ICML, pp. 513–520 (2011)
21. Gong, B., Grauman, K., Sha, F.: Connecting the dots with landmarks: Discriminatively learning domain invariant features for unsupervised domain adaptation. In: Proceedings of ICML, pp. 222–230 (2013)
22. Gong, B., Shi, Y., Sha, F., Grauman, K.: Geodesic flow kernel for unsupervised domain adaptation. In: Proceedings of CVPR, pp. 2066–2073. IEEE (2012)
23. Gopalan, R., Li, R., Patel, V.M., Chellappa, R.: Domain adaptation for visual recognition. Found. Trends Comput. Graph. Vis. 8(4), 285–378 (2015)
24. Huang, J., Smola, A., Gretton, A., Borgwardt, K., Schölkopf, B.: Correcting sample selection bias by unlabeled data. In: Proceedings of NIPS, (Curran Associates) (2007)
25. Klare, B.F., Bucak, S.S., Jain, A.K., Akgul, T.: Towards automated caricature recognition. In: Proceedings of ICB (2012)
26. Li, S., Kawale, J., Fu, Y.: Deep collaborative filtering via marginalized denoising auto-encode. In: Proceedings of CIKM, pp. 811–820. ACM (2015)
27. Li, Y., Yang, M., Xu, Z., Zhang, Z.: Learning with marginalized corrupted features and labels together. In: Proceedings of AAAI (2016). arXiv:1602:07332

28. Long, M., Cao, Y., Wang, J., Jordan, M.I.: Learning transferable features with deep adaptation networks. In: Proceedings of ICML (2015)
29. Long, M., Wang, J., Ding, G., Sun, J., Yu, P.S.: Transfer feature learning with joint distribution adaptation. In: Proceedings of ICCV, pp. 2200–2207. IEEE (2013)
30. Maaten, L.V.D., Chen, M., Tyree, S., Weinberger, K.: Learning with marginalized corrupted features. In: Proceedings of ICML (2013)
31. Pan, S.J., Tsang, I.W., Kwok, J.T., Yang, Q.: Domain adaptation via transfer component analysis. Trans. Neural Netw. **22**(2), 199–210 (2011)
32. Pan, S.J., Yang, Q.: A survey on transfer learning. Trans. Knowl. Data Eng. **22**(10), 1345–1359 (2010)
33. Pan, S.J., Ni, X., Sun, J.T., Yang, Q., Chen, Z.: Cross-domain sentiment classification via spectral feature alignment. In: Proceedings of WWW (2010)
34. Saenko, K., Kulis, B., Fritz, M., Darrell, T.: Adapting visual category models to new domains. In: Daniilidis, K., Maragos, P., Paragios, N. (eds.) ECCV 2010. LNCS, vol. 6316, pp. 213–226. Springer, Heidelberg (2010). doi:10.1007/978-3-642-15561-1_16
35. Sun, B., Feng, J., Saenko, K.: Return of frustratingly easy domain adaptation. In: Proceedings of AAAI (2016)
36. Sun, S.S., Shi, H., Wu, Y.: A survey of multi-source domain adaptation. Inf. Fusion **24**, 84–92 (2015)
37. Tommasi, T., Tuytelaars, T.: A testbed for cross-dataset analysis. In: Agapito, L., Bronstein, M.M., Rother, C. (eds.) ECCV 2014. LNCS, vol. 8927, pp. 18–31. Springer, Heidelberg (2015). doi:10.1007/978-3-319-16199-0_2
38. Tzeng, E., Hoffman, J., Zhang, N., Saenko, K., Darrell, T.: Deep domain confusion: Maximizing for domain invariance. CoRR (2014). arXiv:1412.3474
39. Vincent, P., Larochelle, H., Bengio, Y., Manzagol, P.A.: Extracting and composing robust features with denoising autoencoders. In: Proceedings of ICML (2008)
40. Zhou, J.T., Pan, S.J., Tsang, I.W., Yan, Y.: Hybrid heterogeneous transfer learning through deep learning. In: Proceedings of AAAI (2014)
41. Zhou, M., Chang, K.C.: Unifying learning to rank and domain adaptation: enabling cross-task document scoring. In: Proceedings of SIGKDD (ACM), pp. 781–790 (2014)

Online Heterogeneous Transfer Learning by Weighted Offline and Online Classifiers

Yuguang Yan, Qingyao Wu$^{(\boxtimes)}$, Mingkui Tan$^{(\boxtimes)}$, and Huaqing Min

School of Software Engineering, South China University of Technology,
Guangzhou, China
qyw@scut.edu.cn, mingkuitan@scut.edu.cn

Abstract. In this paper, we study online heterogeneous transfer learning (HTL) problems where offline labeled data from a source domain is transferred to enhance the online classification performance in a target domain. The main idea of our proposed algorithm is to build an offline classifier based on heterogeneous similarity constructed by using labeled data from a source domain and unlabeled co-occurrence data which can be easily collected from web pages and social networks. We also construct an online classifier based on data from a target domain, and combine the offline and online classifiers by using the Hedge weighting strategy to update their weights for ensemble prediction. The theoretical analysis of error bound of the proposed algorithm is provided. Experiments on a real-world data set demonstrate the effectiveness of the proposed algorithm.

1 Introduction

Heterogeneous Transfer Learning (HTL) aims to transfer knowledge from a source domain with sufficient labeled data to enhance learning performance on a target domain where the source and target data are from different feature spaces [10,12,17,18]. It has been shown that the learning performance of HTL tasks can be significantly enhanced if co-occurrence data is considered [5,9,12,13,15–18,21]. Co-occurrence data is cheap and easily collected from web pages or social networks. For example, the target learning task is image classification, a set of labeled text documents is given as auxiliary data in a source domain, and we can easily collect some text and image co-occurrence data (such as image annotations or documents around images) for text-to-image heterogeneous transfer learning.

Most existing studies of HTL work on offline/batch learning fashion, in which all the training instances from a target domain are assumed to be given in advance. However, this assumption may not be valid in practice where target instances are received one by one in an online/sequential manner. Unlike the previous studies, we investigate HTL under an online setting [1,8]. For instance, we consider an image classification task for user generated content on some social computing applications. The social network users usually post pictures and attach some text comments for the pictures. The text data is given as a source

© Springer International Publishing Switzerland 2016
G. Hua and H. Jégou (Eds.): ECCV 2016 Workshops, Part III, LNCS 9915, pp. 467–474, 2016.
DOI: 10.1007/978-3-319-49409-8_38

domain data and text-image pairs are considered as co-occurrence information, and the task is to classify new image instances sequentially in a target domain. The crucial issue is how to effectively use offline text data and text-image pairs to improve the online image classification performance.

There are only a few research works that address online transfer learning problems. In [7,14,19,20], researchers studied online homogenerous transfer learning problems where source and target instances are represented in the same feature space. For online heterogeneous setting, existing methods are based on the assumption that the feature space of the source domain is a subset of that of the target domain [19,20].

Motivated by recent research in transfer learning and online learning, in this paper, we study online heterogeneous transfer learning (HTL) problems where labeled data from a source domain and unlabeled co-occurrence data from auxiliary information are under offline mode and data from a target domain is under online mode. We propose a novel method called *Online Heterogeneous Transfer with Weighted Classifiers* (OHTWC) to deal with this learning problem (see Fig. 1). In OHTWC, we build an offline classifier based on heterogeneous similarity constructed by using labeled data from a source domain and unlabeled co-occurrence data from auxiliary information, and construct an online classifier based on data from a target domain. The offline and online classifiers are then combined by using the **Hedge** (β) method [6] to make ensemble prediction dynamically. The theoretical analysis of the error bound of the proposed method is also provided.

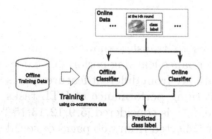

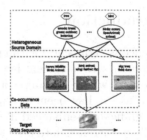

Fig. 1. Overall heterogeneous transfer learning system using offline and online classifiers.

Fig. 2. Heterogeneous knowledge transfer based on co-occurrence data.

2   The Proposed Method

We study online heterogeneous transfer learning (HTL) problems where labeled instances $\{(\mathbf{x}_i^s, y_i^s)\}_{i=1}^{n^s} \in \mathcal{X}^s \times \mathcal{Y}^s$ from a source domain and unlabeled co-occurred pairs $\{(\mathbf{u}_i^c, \mathbf{v}_i^c)\}_{i=1}^{n^c} \in \mathcal{X}^c$ from an auxiliary information are under offline mode and instances $\{(\mathbf{x}_i, y_i)\}_{i=1}^{n} \in \mathcal{X} \times \mathcal{Y}$ from a target domain is under online mode. Here n^s and n^c refer to the number of labeled instances in the source domain and the number of co-occurred pairs. The feature space $\mathcal{X}^s$ of the source domain is different from the feature space $\mathcal{X}$ of the target domain. The class labels are the same as in both source and target domains, i.e., $\mathcal{Y}^s = \mathcal{Y} = \{+1, -1\}$. There are two components $\mathbf{u}_i^c$ and $\mathbf{v}_i^c$ in the co-occurred pair where $\mathbf{u}_i^c$ belongs to $\mathcal{X}^s$ and $\mathbf{v}_i^c$ belongs to $\mathcal{X}$. The objective of online HTL is to learn an online classifier $f(\mathbf{x}_i)$ to generate a predicted class label $\hat{y}_i$ where the instance $\mathbf{x}_i$ arrives at the i-th trial. The classifier then receives the correct class label y_i and update itself according to their difference to obtain a better classification ability.

2.1 The Offline Classifier

The offline classifier is based on the similarity relationship between the instances in the source and target domains via the co-occurrence data. The idea of similarity calculation is given in a text-image classification example in Fig. 2. In this example, we have target image instances which arrive in an online manner, labeled text data in the heterogeneous source domain under an offline setting, and unlabeled co-occurred pairs which provide information between text data in the source domain and image data in the target domain.

When the j-th instance $\mathbf{x}_j$ arrives in the target domain, we make use of the Pearson correlation to measure the similarity $a_j(i)$ between $\mathbf{x}_j$ and $\mathbf{v}_i^c$: $a_j(i) = \frac{(\mathbf{x}_j - \bar{\mathbf{x}}_j)^\top (\mathbf{v}_i^c - \bar{\mathbf{v}}_i^c)}{\|\mathbf{x}_j - \bar{\mathbf{x}}_j\| \|\mathbf{v}_i^c - \bar{\mathbf{v}}_i^c\|}, 1 \leq i \leq n^c$, where $\bar{\mathbf{z}}$ is a vector whose all elements are equal to mean$(\mathbf{z})$ (i.e., the mean value of all elements of vector $\mathbf{z}$), and $\|\cdot\|$ is the Euclidean distance. Similarly, we construct the similarity $b_l(i)$ between $\mathbf{x}_l^s$ and $\mathbf{u}_i^c$: $b_l(i) = \frac{(\mathbf{x}_l^s - \bar{\mathbf{x}}_l^s)^\top (\mathbf{u}_i^c - \bar{\mathbf{u}}_i^c)}{\|\mathbf{x}_l^s - \bar{\mathbf{x}}_l^s\| \|\mathbf{u}_i^c - \bar{\mathbf{u}}_i^c\|}, 1 \leq i \leq n^c$, Therefore, we compute the similarity $r_j(l)$ between $\mathbf{x}_j$ and $\mathbf{x}_l^s$ via co-occurred pairs as follows: $r_j(l) = \sum_{i=1}^{n^c} a_j(i) b_l(i), 1 \leq l \leq n^s$. According to $r_j(l)$, we can make a prediction $h^s(\mathbf{x}_j)$ for the given instance $\mathbf{x}_j$ by computing the weighted sum of the labels of its k nearest neighbors from the source domain:

$$h^s(\mathbf{x}_j) = \Big(\sum_{k \in N} r_j(k) y_k^s\Big) \Big/ \Big(\sum_{k \in N} r_j(k)\Big), \tag{1}$$

where the set N includes indices of $\mathbf{x}_j$'s k nearest neighbors that are found in the source domain.

2.2 The Online Classifier

Besides the classifier $h^s(\mathbf{x}_i)$ obtained from the heterogeneous source domain, we construct another classifier $h_i(\mathbf{x}_i) = \mathbf{w}_i^\top \mathbf{x}_i$ by using target instances based on online learning algorithm (PA) [4,11]. The PA algorithm models online learning as a constrained convex optimization problem, and updates the classifier as follows

$$\mathbf{w}_{i+1} = \mathbf{w}_i + \tau_i y_i \mathbf{x}_i, \tag{2}$$

where $\tau_i = \min\left\{c, \frac{\ell^*(\mathbf{x}_i, y_i; \mathbf{w}_i)}{||\mathbf{x}_i||^2}\right\}$, c is a positive regularization parameter, and $\ell^*(\mathbf{x}, y; \mathbf{w}) = \max\{1 - y(\mathbf{w}^\top \mathbf{x}), 0\}$ is the hinge loss.

2.3   Hedge(β) Strategy for Weighted Classifers

We propose to combine the offline and online classifiers suitably such that the resulting classification performance can be enhanced. In this paper, we make use of the **Hedge**(β) strategy [6] to update the weights of offline and online classifiers dynamically. Let ℓ_i^s and ℓ_i be the loss values that are generated by $h^s(\mathbf{x}_i)$ and $h_i(\mathbf{x}_i)$, respectively. The **Hedge**(β) stragtey is used to generate the positive weights θ_i^s and θ_i for $h^s(\mathbf{x}_i)$ and $h_i(\mathbf{x}_i)$ such that the resulting prediction is given by

$$\hat{y}_i = \text{sign}\left(\theta_i^s \phi(h^s(\mathbf{x}_i)) + \theta_i \phi(h_i(\mathbf{x}_i)) - \frac{1}{2}\right), \tag{3}$$

where $\theta_i^s + \theta_i = 1$, and ϕ is a predefined function that maps the predicted value into range $[0, 1]$ The two weights (i.e., θ_i^s and θ_i) are updated by using the following rules:

$$\theta_{i+1}^s = \theta_i^s \beta^{\psi(y_i h^s(\mathbf{x}_i))}, \quad \theta_{i+1} = \theta_i \beta^{\psi(y_i h_i(\mathbf{x}_i))}, \tag{4}$$

where $\beta \in (0, 1)$ and ψ is also a predefined loss function for controlling the update of the weights. We see in (4) that a larger loss will result in a larger decay, thus the better classifier will relatively obtain a larger weight value.

For simplicity, let h be the predicted value (i.e., $h_i(\mathbf{x}_i)$ or $h^s(\mathbf{x}_i)$), We design the following mapping function

$$\phi(h) = \frac{1}{1 + \exp\{-h\}}; \quad \psi(yh) = \frac{1}{1 + \exp\{yh\}}. \tag{5}$$

The loss value is dependent on the predicted result and the confidence we have on the predicted value. The absolute value $|h|$ measures the confidence we have on the predicted result. On the other hand, $\psi(yh)$ maps the margin value yh into range $[0, 1]$, leading the decay of the weights of classifiers. In general, when we get a margin with a large absolute value, if our prediction is correct, we will obtain a small loss. However, if our prediction is incorrect, we have to suffer a large loss because of our wrong guess.

2.4   Theoretical Analysis

Theorem 1. Define $\ell_i^s = \psi(y_i h^s(\mathbf{x}_i))$, $\ell_i = \psi(y_i h_i(\mathbf{x}_i))$, and $\beta \in (0, 1)$ is the decay factor. Given $\theta_1 = \theta_1^s = \frac{1}{2}$. Let M be the number of mistakes made by the OHTWC algorithm after receiving a sequence of T instances, then we have

$$M \leq \frac{2}{1 - \beta} \min\{\Delta^s, \Delta\}, \tag{6}$$

where $\Delta^s = \ln 2 + (\ln \frac{1}{\beta}) \sum_{i=1}^{T} \ell_i^s$ and $\Delta = \ln 2 + (\ln \frac{1}{\beta}) \sum_{i=1}^{T} \ell_i$.

Remark. Theorem 1 states that the entire number of mistakes, which sums up the error at all T trials, is not much larger than the loss value made by the better single classifier.

3 Experiments

3.1 Data Set and Baseline Methods

We use the NUS-WIDE data set [3] as text-to-image online heterogeneous transfer learning data set. We refer the images as the data in the target domain, and the text instances as the auxiliary data in the heterogeneous source domain. Images and their corresponding tag data are used as the co-occurrence data. We randomly select 10 classes to build $\binom{10}{2} = 45$ binary image classification tasks. For each binary classification task, we randomly pick up 600 image instances, 1,200 text instances, and 1,600 co-occurred image-text pairs.

We compare our proposed algorithms with the PA [4], SVM [2], HTLIC [21] and HET algorithms. PA is used as a baseline method without knowledge transfer. To fit the online setting, we periodically train the SVM classifier when $\frac{T}{20}$ new target instances arrive, and use the trained classifier to make predictions for the next $\frac{T}{20}$ coming instances, where T is the total number of the target data. And HTLIC is adjusted to online learning problems. Specifically, PA algorithm is conducted on new features constructed by the approach in HTLIC. HET finds the nearest neighbors of each target instance in the co-occurrence data, and uses the heterogeneous views of the neighbors as the new representation of the target instance; then PA algorithm is performed on these heterogeneous new features.

We set the regularization parameter $c = 1$ for all the algorithms, $\beta = \frac{\sqrt{T}}{\sqrt{T}+\sqrt{2\ln 2}}$ for OHTWC, and the number of the nearest neighbors to $k = \frac{n^c}{10}$, where n^c is the number of co-occurrence data. In order to obtain stable results, we draw 20 times of random permutation of the data set and evaluate the performance of learning algorithms based on average rate of mistakes.

3.2 Results and Discussion

In Table 1, we present numerical results of all adopted algorithms on several representative tasks and the average results over all 45 tasks. We see that on average, SVM and HTLIC achieve comparable results, while OHTWC achieves the best results. Batch learning algorithm SVM does not have much superiority compared with other online learning algorithms. Remind that in order to fit the online setting, we periodically perform SVM algorithm to train the classifier after receiving $\frac{T}{20}$ instances. SVM algorithm does not have any prior training instances to learn the classifier for the first coming data, which could be the principal reason that SVM does not achieve the lower error rates.

Figure 3 shows detailed learning processes of all used algorithms on several representative classification tasks, and the dotted lines indicate the standard deviations. We see that as the number of target data increases, all the algorithms usually obtain lower error rates. And our proposed OHTWC algorithm

Table 1. Average rate of mistakes on example tasks of text-image data set.

Task	PA	HET	SVM	HTLIC	OHTWC
4	0.3604 ± 0.0163	0.3776 ± 0.0141	0.3395 ± 0.0133	0.3218 ± 0.0103	**0.3075 ± 0.0090**
10	0.3668 ± 0.0143	0.4113 ± 0.0210	0.3475 ± 0.0115	0.3514 ± 0.0099	**0.3291 ± 0.0114**
11	0.2622 ± 0.0119	0.2947 ± 0.0138	0.2480 ± 0.0138	0.2515 ± 0.0090	**0.2328 ± 0.0087**
17	0.2706 ± 0.0100	0.3018 ± 0.0162	0.2462 ± 0.0132	0.2476 ± 0.0166	**0.2235 ± 0.0089**
20	0.3015 ± 0.0102	0.3301 ± 0.0134	0.2918 ± 0.0146	0.2907 ± 0.0109	**0.2776 ± 0.0132**
22	0.2321 ± 0.0145	0.2635 ± 0.0193	0.2384 ± 0.0136	**0.2043 ± 0.0095**	0.2123 ± 0.0110
31	0.4243 ± 0.0132	0.4412 ± 0.0182	0.4316 ± 0.0119	0.4381 ± 0.0184	**0.3547 ± 0.0102**
35	0.2298 ± 0.0124	0.2686 ± 0.0102	0.2110 ± 0.0112	0.2421 ± 0.0152	**0.1922 ± 0.0088**
41	0.2707 ± 0.0116	0.2838 ± 0.0116	0.2601 ± 0.0126	0.2815 ± 0.0149	**0.2493 ± 0.0069**
Average	0.2997	0.3363	0.2844	0.2834	**0.2608**

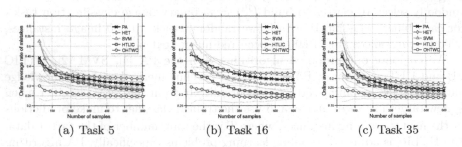

(a) Task 5   (b) Task 16   (c) Task 35

Fig. 3. Online average rate of mistakes on example tasks of text-image data set.

consistently achieves the best or at least highly competitive results compared with the baseline methods. In addition, OHTWC algorithm usually obtains low mistake rates at the beginning stage, which verifies our approach of heterogeneous transfer does take advantage of useful knowledge from the source domain. Because of the lack of training data, SVM usually gets higher mistake rates, while is able to achieve comparable results by using more training data. Similar results can be observed in other learning tasks.

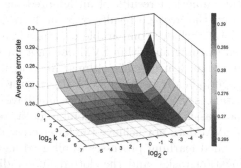

Fig. 4. Results of OHTWC on varying values of parameters c and k.

Parameter Sensitivity. We also investigate how different values of parameters affect the mistake rates of the proposed algorithm. It can be seen that using more nearest neighbors to build an offline classifier can improve the performance of OHTWC algorithm. Nevertheless, the average results do not change too much with respect to parameter c or k. Small numbers of neighbors can also achieve low error rates.

4 Conclusion

In this paper, we propose a novel online heterogeneous transfer learning method, called OHTWC, by leveraging the co-occurrence data of heterogeneous domains. In OHTWC, a heterogeneous similarity via the co-occurrence data is constructed to seek k nearest neighbors (kNN) in the source domain. An offline classifier is built on the source data, while an online classifier is built by using the target data, and we use the Hedge weighting strategy to dynamically combine these two classifiers to make ensemble classification. The theoretical analysis of the proposed OHTWC algorithm is also provided. Experimental results on a real-world data set demonstrate the effectiveness our proposed method.

References

1. Cesa-Bianchi, N., Lugosi, G.: Prediction, Learning, and Games. Cambridge University Press, Cambridge (2006)
2. Chang, C.C., Lin, C.J.: LIBSVM: a library for support vector machines. ACM Trans. Intell. Syst. Technol. **2**(3), 27 (2011)
3. Chua, T.S., Tang, J., Hong, R., Li, H., Luo, Z., Zheng, Y.T.: NUS-WIDE: a real-world web image database from National University of Singapore. In: CIVR (2009)
4. Crammer, K., Dekel, O., Keshet, J., Shalev-Shwartz, S., Singer, Y.: Online passive-aggressive algorithms. J. Mach. Learn. Res. **7**, 551–585 (2006)
5. Dai, W., Chen, Y., Xue, G.R., Yang, Q., Yu, Y.: Translated learning: transfer learning across different feature spaces. In: NIPS (2008)
6. Freund, Y., Schapire, R.E.: A decision-theoretic generalization of on-line learning and an application to boosting. J. Comput. Syst. Sci. **55**(1), 119–139 (1997)
7. Ge, L., Gao, J., Zhang, A.: OMS-TL: a framework of online multiple source transfer learning. In: CIKM, pp. 2423–2428 (2013)
8. Hoi, S.C., Wang, J., Zhao, P.: LIBOL: a library for online learning algorithms. J. Mach. Learn. Res. **15**(1), 495–499 (2014)
9. Ng, M.K., Wu, Q., Ye, Y.: Co-transfer learning via joint transition probability graph based method. In: The First International Workshop on Cross Domain Knowledge Discovery in Web and Social Network Mining, KDD (2012)
10. Pan, S.J., Yang, Q.: A survey on transfer learning. IEEE Trans. Knowl. Data Eng. **22**(10), 1345–1359 (2010)
11. Shalev-Shwartz, S., Crammer, K., Dekel, O., Singer, Y.: Online passive-aggressive algorithms. In: NIPS (2004)
12. Tan, B., Song, Y., Zhong, E., Yang, Q.: Transitive transfer learning. In: KDD, pp. 1155–1164 (2015)

13. Tan, B., Zhong, E., Ng, M.K., Yang, Q.: Mixed-transfer: transfer learning over mixed graphs. In: SDM (2014)
14. Wang, B., Pineau, J.: Online boosting algorithms for anytime transfer and multi-task learning. In: AAAI (2015)
15. Wang, G., Hoiem, D., Forsyth, D.: Building text features for object image classification. In: CVPR (2009)
16. Wu, Q., Ng, M.K., Ye, Y.: Cotransfer learning using coupled markov chains with restart. IEEE Intell. Syst. **29**(4), 26–33 (2014)
17. Yang, L., Jing, L., Ng, M.K.: Robust and non-negative collective matrix factorization for text-to-image transfer learning. IEEE Trans. Image Process. **24**(12), 4701–4714 (2015)
18. Yang, L., Jing, L., Yu, J., Ng, M.K.: Learning transferred weights from co-occurrence data for heterogeneous transfer learning. In: IEEE Transactions on Neural Networks and Learning Systems (2015)
19. Zhao, P., Hoi, S.C.: OTL: a framework of online transfer learning. In: ICML (2010)
20. Zhao, P., Hoi, S.C., Wang, J., Li, B.: Online transfer learning. Artif. Intell. **216**, 76–102 (2014)
21. Zhu, Y., Chen, Y., Lu, Z., Pan, S.J., Xue, G.R., Yu, Y., Yang, Q.: Heterogeneous transfer learning for image classification. In: AAAI (2011)

Learning the Roots of Visual Domain Shift

Tatiana Tommasi[1](✉), Martina Lanzi[2], Paolo Russo[2], and Barbara Caputo[2]

[1] University of North Carolina at Chapel Hill, Chapel Hill, NC, USA
ttommasi@cs.unc.edu
[2] Department of Computer, Control and Management Engineering,
University of Rome La Sapienza, Rome, Italy
{lanzi,russo,caputo}@dis.uniroma1.it

Abstract. In this paper we focus on the spatial nature of visual domain shift, attempting to learn *where* domain adaptation originates in each given image of the source and target set. We borrow concepts and techniques from the CNN visualization literature, and learn *domainness maps* able to localize the degree of domain specificity in images. We derive from these maps features related to different domainness levels, and we show that by considering them as a preprocessing step for a domain adaptation algorithm, the final classification performance is strongly improved. Combined with the whole image representation, these features provide state of the art results on the Office dataset.

Keywords: Domain adaptation · CNN visualization

1 Introduction

In 2010 Saenko et al. imported the notion of domain adaptation from natural language processing to visual recognition [17]. They showed how training visual classifiers on data acquired in a given setting, and testing them in different scenarios, leads to poor performance because the training and test data belong to different visual domains. Since then, domain adaptation has become a widely researched topic. The vastly dominant trend is to summarize images into global features (being them handcrafted BoWs or the most modern CNN-activation values) and remove the domain shift through an optimization problem over feature data points distributions. This strategy is theoretically sound and effective, as it has been largely demonstrated over the years. To give a quantitative estimate of the progress in the field, one might look at the accuracy values obtained over the Office-31 dataset, a data collection presented in [17] and quickly become the domain adaptation reference benchmark: performance has increased on average from 27.8 % [8] to 72.9 % in only three years [16]. While such progress is certainly impressive, it is not fully clear that it is coupled with an equally deepened knowledge of the roots of domain shift.

We believe the time is ripe for gaining a better understanding of how visual concepts such as illumination conditions, image resolution or background give

© Springer International Publishing Switzerland 2016
G. Hua and H. Jégou (Eds.): ECCV 2016 Workshops, Part III, LNCS 9915, pp. 475–482, 2016.
DOI: 10.1007/978-3-319-49409-8_39

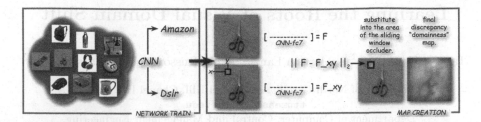

Fig. 1. A CNN network is initially trained for domain classification. The obtained model is used as feature extractor both for the original and the occluded images. The difference among the obtained representation is saved and visualized in the image area, creating the domainnes map. Yellow/Blue indicate areas at high/low domainnnes. Best viewed in color. (Color figure online)

rise to the domain shift. As these visual concepts often have a spatial connotation – more or less illuminated parts of images, informative object parts that are more or less visible, etc. – our goal is to localize the domain shift in the source and target data, or at least to spatially ground it. Is it doable? and if yes, what do we learn from it? Could it be used to improve the effectiveness of *any* domain adaptation algorithm?

This paper attempts to answer these questions. We first show that by learning to classify visual domains (binary classification on source-target domain pairs), it is possible to obtain domain localization maps as a byproduct, where high/low map values indicate high/low domain specificity (Fig. 1, Sect. 3). We dub the score used to define the map *domainness*. By analyzing the domainnes map we are able to evaluate the correlation between domain-specificity and object-specificity. Depending on the domain-pairs we can identify when the domain shift come mostly from the background and when instead it involves the objects (Sect. 4). Armed with this knowledge, we create 3 different features from each image: a low-domainness feature, a mid-domainness feature and a high-domainness feature (Fig. 3, Sect. 5). With this strategy each domain-pair becomes a set of 9 pairs. We show that by applying domain adaptation over each pair and then recombining the results through high level integration, we systematically achieve a substantial increase in performance as opposed to previously reported results obtained by the same methods on the whole images. This approach enables us to obtain the new state of the art on the Office-31 dataset for unsupervised domain adaptation.

2   Related Work

Domain Adaptation. The goal of domain adaptation is to compensate the variation among two data distributions, allowing to reuse information acquired from a source domain on a new, different but related, target domain. Some techniques perform this by simply re-weighting or selecting the samples in the source domain [6,15], or clustering them to search for visually coherent sub-domains

[7,10]. Other approaches modify existing source classifiers to make them suitable for the target task [1,2], or search for transformations that map the source distribution into the target one [3,9]. Different strategies propose to learn both a classification model and a feature transformation jointly. Few of them rely on SVM-like risk minimization objectives and shallow representation models [4,11], while more recent approaches leverage over deep learning [16,19,20].

Despite their specific differences, all these methods consider the whole image as a data unit, corresponding to a sample drawn from a given domain distribution. Some work has been recently done for dealing directly with image patches within the NBNN framework [14,18] with promising results. Here we push research further in the direction of relating domain adaptation and spatial localities in images: we study how the domain information is distributed inside each image, and how to deal with domain-specific and domain-generic image patches.

CNN Visual Analysis. A number of works have focused on understanding the representation learned by CNNs. A visualization technique which reveals the input stimuli that excite individual feature maps was introduced in [22]. Girshick et al. [5] visualized which patches within a dataset are the most responsible for strong activations at higher layers in the model. Simonyan et al. [13] demonstrated how saliency maps can be obtained from CNN by projecting back from the fully connected layers of the network. Zhou et al. [23] focused on scene images, and by visualizing the representation learned by each unit of the network, they showed that object detectors are implicitly learned.

Inspired by these works we introduce an image mask-out procedure to visualize what a domain classification network learns and how the domain information is spatially distributed. We are not aware of previous work attempting to learn what part of images are more or less responsible for the domain shift.

3   Domainness Prediction

Given the images of a source/target domain pair we resize them to 256×256, and we randomly split them into a training and test set. On the training set we learn a CNN for domain recognition: specifically we initialize the parameters of conv1-fc7 using the released CaffeNet [12] weights and we then further fine-tuned the network for binary classification on the domain labels. The test set is extended by replicating each image many times with small random occluders at different locations: we use 16×16 image patches positioned on a dense grid with stride 8. This results in about 1000 occluded images per original image. Finally we feed both the original and the occluded test images into the defined network and we record the difference between their respective fc7 activation values (4096-dimensional output of the seventh fully connected layer after ReLu). The L_2-norm of this difference is spatially saved in the image inside the occluder area and the obtained value for overlapping occluders is averaged defining a smooth discrepancy map with values rescaled in $\{0, 1\}$ (see Fig. 1). We call it *domainness* map: an area of high domainness corresponds to a region that highly influences

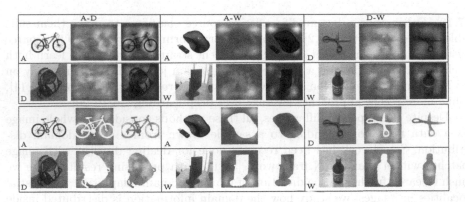

Fig. 2. Top: each table element shows the original image (left), the domainness map (center) and the map-image overlap (right - low domainness regions occluded). Column titles indicate the domain-pairs. Bottom: original image (left), the background part of domainness map (center) and the foreground part of the map (right) when using the segmentation masks. Best viewed in color. (Color figure online)

the final domain choice for the image, and thus it can be considered as domain-specific. On the other hand, an area of low domainness appears to be less relevant for domain recognition, hence more domain-generic. Note that the procedure we propose is unsupervised with respect to the object classes depicted in the source and target images.

4   Domainness Analysis

To have a better understanding of the information captured by the domainness maps we analyze here how the domainness distribution in each image relates with image foreground and background areas.

We use the standard Office-31 dataset [17] which collects images from three distinct domains, Amazon (A), Dslr (D) and Webcam (W). The first contains images downloaded from online merchants and mainly present white background, while the second and the third are acquired respectively with a high resolution DSL camera and with a low resolution webcam in real settings with background and lighting variations. The 31 categories in the dataset consist of objects commonly encountered in office settings, such as keyboards, scissors, monitors and telephones. We define train/test split of respectively 3000/612, 3000/315 and 1000/293 images for the A-W, A-D and W-D pairs and we follow the procedure described in the Sect. 3 to generate a map for each test image. Some of the obtained maps are shown in Fig. 2 - top.

By using object image masks obtained by manual segmentation we evaluated the average domainness value inside and outside the objects. Specifically, we focus on the central 227×227 area of the image to avoid artifacts that might be due to the CNN architecture used. Our evaluation reveals that for A-D and

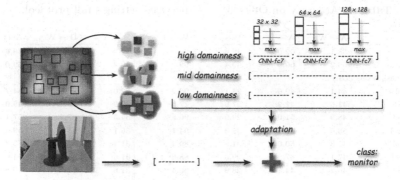

Fig. 3. Patches of three different dimensions are cropped from an image and organized according to their domainness score. CNN-fc7 features are extracted from the patches, max pooled and stacked. Classifiers are trained and tested using the obtained representation and the whole image. Confidence scores are combined for the final prediction.

D-W pairs the average domainness value is actually higher inside the objects (respectively 0.48 and 0.44) than outside (0.43, 0.41). This indicates that most of the domain specific information tend to appear within the foreground rather than in the background part of the image. On the other way round, for A-W the background is the main responsible of domain shift, with an average domainness value of 0.24 against 0.27 obtained for the object area (see Fig. 2 - bottom).

5   Exploiting Domainness Levels for Adaptation

Finally we use the domainness maps to guide domain adaptation (see Fig. 3). Information from the images at three domainness levels (DL) are collected through local feature extraction. We start by sampling 100 patches of sizes 32×32 randomly from each image and associating to each one its average domainness. We then treat the patches as samples of the domainness distribution and identify its 33th and 66th percentiles. This allows to divide the patches into three groups with low- (L), mid- (M) and high-domainness (H). We follow [21] and used the CNN Caffe implementation pre-trained on Imagenet to collect fc7 features for each patch. Maximum pooling (element-wise maximum) is applied separately over the patches collected at different domainness levels. The procedure is repeated separately over other two image scales using patches of dimension 64×64 and 128×128. As a result, each image is represented by three feature vectors, each with 12288 elements, obtained by stacking the max pooled features at scale 32, 64 and 128. Besides these per-domainness-level descriptors we extracted fc7 features on the whole image as global representation both with (G-FT) and without (G) fine tuning on the source.

How good are the descriptors? We perform object classification with linear SVM on all the domain pairs of the Office-31 dataset when using each DL descriptor

Table 1. Accuracy on Office-31, unsupervised setting - full protocol.

	A → W	A → D	W → A	W → D	D → A	D → W	Average
G	58.1	62.0	48.6	99.4	47.9	95.8	68.6
G-FT	60.2	60.0	49.4	99.2	49.2	95.9	69.0
Domainness levels (DL)							
L-L level	44.1	49.0	28.1	90.2	32.0	84.8	54.7
L-H level	41.6	42.2	27.9	77.8	30.9	73.6	49.0
L-M level	48.9	51.0	29.9	90.8	34.5	87.4	57.1
M-M level	53.0	52.1	33.3	94.1	35.1	88.6	59.4
M-L level	45.3	50.0	31.8	89.4	31.4	84.0	55.3
M-H level	47.1	47.9	29.3	88.8	31.6	83.1	54.6
H-H level	46.2	44.1	28.9	90.4	31.6	81.6	53.8
H-L level	44.1	42.6	31.0	83.3	30.3	76.5	51.3
H-M level	52.4	47.4	33.1	92.5	35.1	85.7	57.7
Applying domain adaptation machine on domainness levels (DAM-DL)							
L-L level	40.8	50.0	28.4	99.9	32.9	88.9	55.7
L-H level	42.8	44.5	28.6	82.5	32.2	81.0	51.9
L-M level	48.3	50.6	31.5	92.8	34.5	91.7	58.3
M-M level	51.5	51.9	35.1	96.9	38.2	92.2	60.9
M-L level	41.8	48.8	33.7	93.8	33.8	87.5	56.6
M-H level	47.8	48.3	31.4	93.2	35.5	87.3	57.3
H-H level	42.7	45.8	31.2	93.2	34.3	84.3	55.2
H-L level	40.2	42.7	32.9	85.5	31.8	77.8	51.8
H-M level	47.8	50.6	34.9	94.3	36.4	87.9	58.7
Combining domainness levels and whole image classification							
G + DL	70.6 ± 0.9	74.9 ± 1.1	53.5 ± 0.3	100.0 ± 0.1	54.5 ± 0.5	98.3 ± 0.1	75.3
G + DAM-DL	70.6 ± 1.3	**76.9 ± 0.4**	54.5 ± 0.2	100.0 ± 0.1	**56.6 ± 0.5**	**99.5 ± 0.1**	**76.3**
G-FT + DL	**71.5 ± 0.6**	74.8 ± 1.2	54.0 ± 0.1	100.0 ± 0.1	55.8 ± 0.8	97.9 ± 0.3	75.7
G-FT + DAM-DL	71.3 ± 1.1	75.3 ± 1.0	**55.4 ± 0.3**	100.0 ± 0.1	55.2 ± 0.7	98.9 ± 0.3	**76.3**
DDC [20]	61.8 ± 0.4	64.4 ± 0.3	52.2 ± 0.4	98.5 ± 0.4	52.1 ± 0.8	95.0 ± 0.5	70.6
DAN [16]	68.5 ± 0.4	67.0 ± 0.4	53.1 ± 0.3	99.0 ± 0.2	54.0 ± 0.4	96.0 ± 0.3	72.9

to represent the images. We consider all the source labeled data as training samples and all the unlabeled target images define our test set (full protocol). The results are reported in the top part of Table 1, together with the performance obtained using the whole image representation. The obtained classification accuracies indicate M as the most informative level. Although by construction L is the level which capture the most domain-generic cues, we speculate that M works best at balancing domain-generic and object-specific information.

Can we adapt across DLs? We use the Domain Adaptation Machine (DAM, [1]) to reduce the discrepancy across domainness levels. The results in the central part of Table 1 show an average accuracy improvement which ranges in 0.5–3 % with respect to the previous results, confirming that adaptive techniques are beneficial.

Are DLs complementary to the whole image? We believe that different domainness levels provide complementary knowledge useful to solve domain adaptation. To test this hypothesis we integrate the per-class confidence score provided by the classifiers trained over DLs with that obtained when training on the whole image.

Let's indicate with $j = 1 \ldots 9$ the different DL pairs and with $c = 1 \ldots C$ the object classes. Once we have all the margins D_c^j obtained by separate-level classification and the margin D_c^G obtained from the whole image we perform the final prediction with $c^* = argmax_c \{\frac{1}{9} \sum_{j=1}^{9} D_c^j + D_c^G\}$. The obtained results (Table 1 – bottom part) compare favorably against the current state of the art CNN-architectures [16,20] created on purpose to overcome visual domain shift.

6 Conclusion

The goal of this paper is to identify the spatial roots of visual domain shift. To this end we learned domainness maps from source and target data which are able to localize the image parts more or less responsible for the domain shift. We proved experimentally that generating features from image regions with different degrees of domainness and feeding them to a domain adaptation algorithm leads to a significant boost in performance. Moreover, in combination with whole image features, they allow to obtain state of the art results on the Office dataset.

References

1. Duan, L., Tsang, I.W., Xu, D., Chua, T.S.: Domain adaptation from multiple sources via auxiliary classifiers. In: International Conference on Machine Learning - ICML (2009)
2. Duan, L., Tsang, I.W., Xu, D., Maybank, S.J.: Domain transfer svm for video concept detection. In: IEEE International Conference on Computer Vision and Pattern Recognition - CVPR (2009)
3. Fernando, B., Habrard, A., Sebban, M., Tuytelaars, T.: Unsupervised visual domain adaptation using subspace alignment. In: International Conference in Computer Vision - ICCV (2013)
4. Fernando, B., Tommasi, T., Tuytelaars, T.: Joint cross-domain classification and subspace learning for unsupervised adaptation. Pattern Recogn. Lett. **65**, 60–66 (2015)
5. Girshick, R., Donahue, J., Darrell, T., Malik, J.: Rich feature hierarchies for accurate object detection and semantic segmentation. In: IEEE Conference on Computer Vision and Pattern Recognition - CVPR (2014)
6. Gong, B., Grauman, K., Sha, F.: Connecting the dots with landmarks: discriminatively learning domain-invariant features for unsupervised domain adaptation. In: International Conference on Machine Learning - ICML (2013)
7. Gong, B., Grauman, K., Sha, F.: Reshaping visual datasets for domain adaptation. In: Advances in Neural Information Processing Systems - NIPS (2013)
8. Gong, B., Shi, Y., Sha, F., Grauman, K.: Geodesic flow kernel for unsupervised domain adaptation. In: IEEE Conference on Computer Vision and Pattern Recognition - CVPR (2012)
9. Gretton, A., Borgwardt, K.M., Rasch, M.J., Schölkopf, B., Smola, A.: A kernel two-sample test. J. Mach. Learn. Res. **13**(1), 723–773 (2012)

10. Hoffman, J., Kulis, B., Darrell, T., Saenko, K.: Discovering latent domains for multisource domain adaptation. In: Fitzgibbon, A., Lazebnik, S., Perona, P., Sato, Y., Schmid, C. (eds.) ECCV 2012. LNCS, vol. 7578, pp. 702–715. Springer, Heidelberg (2012). doi:10.1007/978-3-642-33709-3_50

11. Hoffman, J., Rodner, E., Donahue, J., Saenko, K., Darrell, T.: Efficient learning of domain-invariant image representations. In: International Conference on Learning Representations - ICLR (2013)

12. Jia, Y., Shelhamer, E., Donahue, J., Karayev, S., Long, J., Girshick, R., Guadarrama, S., Darrell, T.: Caffe: convolutional architecture for fast feature embedding. arXiv preprint abs/1408.5093 (2014)

13. Simonyan, K., Vedaldi, A., Zisserman, A.: Deep inside convolutional networks: visualising image classification models and saliency maps. In: ICLR Workshop (2014)

14. Kuzborskij, I., Carlucci, F.M., Caputo, B.: When naïve bayes nearest neighbours meet convolutional neural networks. In: IEEE Conference on Computer Vision and Pattern Recognition - CVPR (2016)

15. Lim, J.J., Salakhutdinov, R., Torralba, A.: Transfer learning by borrowing examples for multiclass object detection. In: Neural Information Processing Systems - NIPS (2011)

16. Long, M., Cao, Y., Wang, J., Jordan, M.: Learning transferable features with deep adaptation networks. In: International Conference on Machine Learning - ICML (2015)

17. Saenko, K., Kulis, B., Fritz, M., Darrell, T.: Adapting visual category models to new domains. In: Daniilidis, K., Maragos, P., Paragios, N. (eds.) ECCV 2010. LNCS, vol. 6316, pp. 213–226. Springer, Heidelberg (2010). doi:10.1007/978-3-642-15561-1_16

18. Tommasi, T., Caputo, B.: Frustratingly easy NBNN domain adaptation. In: International Conference on Computer Vision - ICCV (2013)

19. Tzeng, E., Hoffman, J., Darrell, T., Saenko, K.: Simultaneous deep transfer across domains and tasks. In: International Conference in Computer Vision - ICCV (2015)

20. Tzeng, E., Hoffman, J., Zhang, N., Saenko, K., Darrell, T.: Deep domain confusion: maximizing for domain invariance. arXiv preprint abs/1412.3474 (2014)

21. Gong, Y., Wang, L., Guo, R., Lazebnik, S.: Multi-scale orderless pooling of deep convolutional activation features. In: Fleet, D., Pajdla, T., Schiele, B., Tuytelaars, T. (eds.) ECCV 2014. LNCS, vol. 8693, pp. 392–407. Springer, Heidelberg (2014). doi:10.1007/978-3-319-10584-0_26

22. Zeiler, M.D., Fergus, R.: Visualizing and understanding convolutional networks. In: Fleet, D., Pajdla, T., Schiele, B., Tuytelaars, T. (eds.) ECCV 2014. LNCS, vol. 8693, pp. 818–833. Springer, Heidelberg (2014). doi:10.1007/978-3-319-10590-1_53

23. Zhou, B., Khosla, A., Lapedriza, A., Oliva, A., Torralba, A.: Object detectors emerge in deep scene CNNs. In: International Conference on Learning Representations - ICLR (2015)

Heterogeneous Face Recognition with CNNs

Shreyas Saxena[⊠] and Jakob Verbeek

INRIA Grenoble, Laboratoire Jean Kuntzmann, Grenoble, France
{shreyas.saxena,jakob.verbeek}@inria.fr

Abstract. Heterogeneous face recognition aims to recognize faces across different sensor modalities. Typically, gallery images are normal visible spectrum images, and probe images are infrared images or sketches. Recently significant improvements in visible spectrum face recognition have been obtained by CNNs learned from very large training datasets. In this paper, we are interested in the question to what extent the features from a CNN pre-trained on visible spectrum face images can be used to perform heterogeneous face recognition. We explore different metric learning strategies to reduce the discrepancies between the different modalities. Experimental results show that we can use CNNs trained on visible spectrum images to obtain results that are on par or improve over the state-of-the-art for heterogeneous recognition with near-infrared images and sketches.

Keywords: Domain adaptation · Face recognition

1 Introduction

Heterogeneous face recognition aims to recognize faces across different modalities. In most cases gallery of known individuals consists of normal visible spectrum images. Probe images may be forensic or composite sketches, which are useful in the absence of photos in a forensic context [8,14]. In comparison to the visible spectrum (VIS) images, near-infrared (NIR) and shortwave-infrared images are less sensitive to illumination variation. Midwave-infrared and longwave-infrared (LWIR), also referred to as "thermal infrared", is suitable for non-intrusive and covert low-light and nighttime acquisition for surveillance [9]. Differences between the gallery and probe modality, make heterogeneous face recognition more challenging than traditional face recognition, see Fig. 1 for an examples of VIS and NIR images, as well as sketches.

Visible spectrum face recognition has been extensively studied, and recently much progress has been made using deep convolutional neural networks (CNN) [18,21,23,25]. In part, this progress is due to much larger training datasets. For example, Schroff *et al.* [21] report an error of 0.37 % on Labeled

Electronic supplementary material The online version of this chapter (doi:10.1007/978-3-319-49409-8_40) contains supplementary material, which is available to authorized users.

G. Hua and H. Jégou (Eds.): ECCV 2016 Workshops, Part III, LNCS 9915, pp. 483–491, 2016.
DOI: 10.1007/978-3-319-49409-8_40

Fig. 1. Top: Example images of an individual in the CASIA NIR-VIS dataset (NIR left, VIS right). Bottom: Examples from e-PRIP: (left to right) photo, FACES sketch, and IdentiKit sketch.

Faces in the Wild (LFW) dataset [5], using a CNN trained on a proprietary dataset of 200 million face images. Earlier state-of-the-art work [22] used only 10 thousand train images, yielding an error in the order of 7%.

Large visible spectrum datasets can be constructed from internet resources, such as *e.g.* IMDb [25], or social media websites. This is, however, not possible for IR images or sketches. For the same reason, it is even harder to establish large cross-modal datasets where we have individuals with images in both modalities. The question we address in this paper is how we can leverage the success of CNN models for visible spectrum face recognition to improve heterogeneous face recognition. We evaluate a number of strategies to use deep CNNs learned from large visible spectrum datasets to solve heterogeneous face recognition tasks. We obtain results that are on par or better than the state of the art for both VIS-NIR and VIS-sketch heterogeneous face recognition.

2   Related Work

Most heterogeneous face recognition work falls in one of two families discussed below.

Reconstruction Based Methods. These methods, see *e.g.* [7,20], learn a mapping from one modality (typically that of the probe) to the other. Once this mapping has been performed, standard homogeneous face recognition approaches can be applied. Sarfraz and Stiefelhagen [20] learn a deep fully-connected neural network to regress densely sampled local SIFT descriptors in the VIS domain from corresponding descriptors in the LWIR domain. Once the local descriptors in a probe image are mapped to the gallery domain, face descriptors are matched using the cosine similarity. Juefei-Xu *et al.* [7] learn a dictionary for both VIS and NIR domains while forcing the same sparse coefficients for corresponding VIS and NIR images, so that the coefficients of the NIR image can be used to reconstruct the VIS image and vice-versa. The advantage of reconstruction-based methods is that allow re-use of existing VIS face recognition systems. On the

Layer	C11	C12	P1	C21	C22	P2	C31	C32	P3	C41	C42	P4	C51	C52	P5	S
Filters	32	64	64	64	128	128	96	192	192	128	256	256	160	320	320	10,575

Fig. 2. CNN architecture: convolutions (C) use 3×3 filters and stride 1, max-pooling (P) act on 2×2 regions and use stride 2. The final soft-max classification layer is denoted as S.

other hand, the problem of cross-modality reconstruction may prove a harder problem than cross-modality face recognition in itself.

Common Subspace Methods. These methods learn a mapping from both the probe and the gallery modality to a common subspace, where matching and retrieval among images across the domains can be performed. Mignon and Jurie [14] adapt the metric learning objective function of PCCA [15] to only take into account cross-domain pairs. We explore similar metric learning approaches, but explicitly investigate the relative importance of using intra and inter domain pairs, and separate projection matrices. Crowley et al. [2] use a triplet-loss similar to LMNN [24] to learn projections to map photos and paintings to a common subspace. Using CNN face descriptors [18] they obtain better performance, but do not observe improvements by subspace learning. We also use of CNN features, but instead of simply using the penultimate network layer, we also investigate the effectiveness of different layers and find these to be more effective.

Domain Adaptation. Heterogeneous face recognition is also related to domain adaptation, we refer the reader to [19] for a general review thereof. We do highlight the unsupervised domain adaptation approach of Fernando et al. [3], which aligns PCA bases of both domains. Despite its simplicity, this approach was shown to be a state-of-the-art domain adaptation method. We use it as a baseline in our experiments.

3   Cross-Modal Recognition Approach

We describe our CNN model and how we use metric learning to align modalities.

Learning a Deep CNN Model. We use the CASIA Webface dataset [25] which contains 500 K images of 10,575 individuals collected from IMDb. The images display a wide range of variability in pose, expression, and illumination. We use 100×100 input images to train a CNN with an architecture, detailed in Fig. 2, similar to [25]. The only difference with the network of [25] is that we use gray-scale images as input to the network to ensure compatibility with NIR and sketch images. We use the trained CNN to extract image features at layers ranging from P3 to the soft-max layer. Representations from other layers are very high-dimensional and do not improve performance.

We explore fine-tuning the network to adapt to the target domain. We keep the weights fixed throughout the network, except for the topmost soft-max layer, and possibly several more preceding layers. When fine-tuning the model we use images from subjects for which we have images in both modalities. In this manner images of the same subject in the two domains are mapped to similar outputs in the last layer.

Metric Learning to Align Modalities. Nuisance factors such as pose, illumination, and expression, make face recognition a challenging problem. The problem is further complicated in heterogeneous face recognition, since images in different modalities differ even if they were acquired at the same moment under the same viewpoint. In single-modality face verification, metric learning has been used extensively used to deal with these difficulties [4,10,18,22,25]. Most methods learn a Mahalanobis distance, which is equivalent to the ℓ_2 distance after a linear projection of the data. In our work we use LDML [4] to learn Mahalanobis metrics from pairwise supervision.

Shared vs. Separate Projection Matrices. In the multi-modal case we can treat the acquisition modality as another nuisance factor. This naive approach requires the use of the same features for both modalities. Alternatively, we can learn a separate projection matrix for each domain which allows us to learn a common subspace in cases where domain-specific features of different dimensionality are extracted in each domain. For *e.g.* features at different layers of the CNN for the two modalities.

Inter-domain and Intra-domain Pairs. Another design choice in the metric learning concerns the pairs that are used for training. We make a distinction between intra-domain pairs, which are pairs of images that are both from the same domain, and inter-domain pairs, which consist of one image from each domain. Our goal is to match a probe in one modality with a gallery image of the other modality, the inter-domain pairs directly reflect this. Intra-domain pairs are not related to the multi-modal nature of our task, but as we show in experiments they provide a form of regularization.

4   Experimental Evaluation

We present the datasets and evaluation protocols and image pre-processing used in our experiments in Sect. 4.1, followed by evaluation results in Sects. 4.2 and 4.3.

4.1   Dataset, Protocols, and Pre-processing

Labeled Faces in the Wild. This dataset [5] consists of 13,233 images of 5,749 subjects and is the most widely used benchmark for uncontrolled face verification. We use the standard "un-restricted" training protocol to validate our baseline CNN model. We experimented with features extracted from different CNN layers and present the results in supplementary material. The most important observation is that while using only gray scale images instead of color ones, our network (96.9%) performs comparable to that of Yi *et al.* [25] (97.7%).

CASIA NIR-VIS. This is the largest heterogeneous NIR-VIS face recognition dataset [11] and contains 17,580 visible spectrum and near-infrared images of 725 subjects. The images present variations in pose, age, resolution, and illumination conditions. See Fig. 1 for example face images. We follow the standard evaluation protocol, and report the report the rank-1 recognition rate, *i.e.* for which fraction of probes the right identity is reported first, and the verification rate (VR) at 0.1 % false accept rate (FAR).

ePRIP VIS-Sketch. This dataset [16] contains composite sketches for the 123 subjects from AR dataset [13]. There are two types of composite sketches released for evaluation, see Fig. 1 for example faces and corresponding sketches. We use the standard evaluation protocol and report the mean identification accuracy at Rank-10.

Face Alignment and Normalization. We align the images in all datasets using a similarity transform, based on facial landmarks. We also apply an additive and multiplicative normalization, so as to match the per-pixel mean and variance of the CASIA Webface images. This normalization step gives a significant boost in performance by correcting for differences in these first and second order statistics of the signal.

Table 1. Evaluation on the CASIA NIR-VIS dataset of features from different layers of the CNN (columns) and different metric learning configurations (rows).

		S	P5	C52	C51	P4	C42	C41	P3
Inter+Intra	Shared	72.6	75.3	**80.6**	**82.9**	**85.9**	**84.8**	**83.5**	**79.5**
	Separate	66.6	70.4	78.6	80.0	82.4	80.7	76.6	69.2
Inter	Shared	70.0	74.3	79.8	81.7	83.6	82.0	78.6	72.3
	Separate	**73.0**	**75.7**	77.9	76.8	76.91	74.7	63.1	52.9

4.2 Results on the CASIA NIR-VIS Dataset

Metric Learning Configurations. In Table 1 we consider the effect of (a) using intra-domain pairs in addition to inter-domain pairs for metric learning, and (b) learning a shared projection matrix for both domains, or learning separate projection matrices.

The results show that learning a shared projection matrix using both inter+intra domain pairs is the most effective, except when using S or P5 features. The overall best results are obtained using P4 features. Unless stated otherwise, below we will used shared projection matrices below, as well as both intra and inter domain pairs.

Combining Different Features. The optimal features might be different depending on the modality. Therefore, we experiment with using a different CNN feature for each modality. We learn separate projection matrices, since the feature dimensionalities may differ across the domains. Experimental results for the evaluation are reported in the supplementary material. The best results are obtained by using P4 features in both domains. Therefore, we will use the same feature in both domains in further experiments.

Fine-Tuning. In the supplementary material we evaluate the effect of fine-tuning the pre-trained CNN using the training data of the CASIA NIR-VIS dataset. The results show that fine-tuning improves the S, P5, and C52 features. Fine-tuning layers deeper than that results in overfitting and inferior results. The best results, however, are obtained with the P4 features extracted from the pre-trained net (85.9). In the remainder of the experiments we do not use any fine-tuning.

Table 2. Comparison on CASIA NIR-VIS of our approach, using raw CNN features, and unsupervised domain adaptation. For the latter, projection dimensions are set on the validation set.

	S	P5	C52	C51	P4	C42	C41	P3
Raw features	63.1	62.7	63.8	51.0	29.4	26.8	18.8	14.8
Domain adapt. [3]	63.1	62.7	64.2	51.8	31.8	28.6	19.1	13.7
Our approach	72.6	75.3	80.6	82.9	**85.9**	84.8	83.5	79.5

Comparison to the State of the Art. In Table 2, we compare our results of the (Shared, Inter+Intra) setting to the state-of-the-art unsupervised domain-adaptation approach of Fernando *et al.* [3], and a ℓ_2 distance baseline that uses the raw CNN features without any projection. From the results we can observe that our supervised metric learning results compare favorably to the results obtained with unsupervised domain adaptation. Moreover, we find that for this problem unsupervised domain adaptation improves only marginally over the raw features. This shows the importance of using supervised metric learning to adapt features of the pre-trained CNN model to the heterogeneous face recognition task.

Table 3. Comparison of our results with the state of the art on CASIA-NIR dataset.

	Rank-1	VR at 0.1 % FR
Jin *et al.* [6]	75.7 ± 2.5	55.9
Juefei-Xu *et al.* [7]	78.5 ± 1.7	**85.8**
Lu *et al.* [12]	81.8 ± 2.3	47.3
Yi *et al.* [26]	**86.2 ± 1.0**	81.3
Ours	85.9 ± 0.9	78.0

In Table 3 we compare our results to the state of the art. For the identification experiments, we obtain (85.9 ± 0.9) rank-1 identification rate which is comparable to the state of the art reported by Yi *et al.* [26] (86.2 ± 1.2). Yi *et al.* [26] extract Gabor features at some localized facial landmarks and then use a restricted Boltzman machine to learn a shared representation locally for each facial point. Our approach is quite different from them, since we do not learn our feature representations on CASIA-NIR dataset rather we only learn a metric on top of features from a pre-trained CNN. For the verification experiments, our result (78.0%) is below the state of the art performance of Juefei-Xu *et al.* [7] (85.8%), their Rank-1 accuracy however (78.5%) is far below ours (85.9%).

4.3   Results on the ePRIP VIS-Sketch Dataset

For this dataset we found the P3 features to be best, in contrast to the CASIA NIR-VIS dataset where *Pool4* was better. The fact that here deeper CNN features are better may be related to the fact that in this dataset, the domain shift is relatively large compared to CASIA NIR-VIS dataset. Detailed results are given in supplementary material.

	Faces(In)	IdentiKit(As)
Bhatt et al. [1]	24.0 ± 3.4	15.4 ± 3.1
Mittal et al. [16]	53.3 ± 1.4	45.3 ± 1.5
Mittal et al. [17]	60.2 ± 2.9	$\mathbf{52.0 \pm 2.4}$
Ours	$\mathbf{65.6 \pm 3.7}$	51.5 ± 4.0

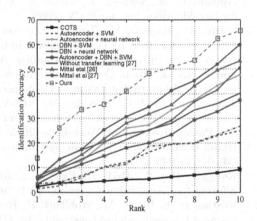

Fig. 3. Rank-10 identification accuracy on the e-PRIP composite sketch database (left), and CMC curve for the Faces(In) database (right) for our result reported in the table.

In Fig. 3 (left panel) we compare our results to the state of the art on the e-PRIP dataset. We obtain the best performance on the Faces(In) sketches, outperforming the previous state-of-the-art result of Mittal *et al.* [17] by 5 %. For the IdentiKit(As) sketches our results are on par with those reported by Mittal *et al.* [17]. In Fig. 3 (right panel) we plot the CMC curve for our method compared to the existing approaches on Faces(In) dataset, curves for other methods are taken from [17]. The figure shows that we obtain significant gain at all ranks compared to the state of the art.

5   Conclusion

We studied different aspects of leveraging a CNN pre-trained on visible spectrum images for heterogenous face recognition, including extracting features from different CNN layers, finetuning the CNN, and using various forms of metric learning. We evaluate the impact of these design choices via means of extensive benchmark results on different heterogenous datasets. The results we obtained are competitive with the state of the art for CASIA-NIR, and improve the state of the art on e-PRIP.

References

1. Bhatt, H.S., Bharadwaj, S., Singh, R., Vatsa, M.: Memetically optimized MCWLD for matching sketches with digital face images. Trans. Inf. Forensics Secur. **7**(5), 1522–1535 (2012)
2. Crowley, E., Parkhi, O., Zisserman, A.: Face painting: querying art with photos. In: BMVC (2015)
3. Fernando, B., Habrard, A., Sebban, M., Tuytelaars, T.: Unsupervised visual domain adaptation using subspace alignment. In: ICCV (2013)
4. Guillaumin, M., Verbeek, J., Schmid, C.: Is that you? Metric learning approaches for face identification. In: ICCV (2009)
5. Huang, G., Ramesh, M., Berg, T., Learned-Miller, E.: Labeled faces in the wild: a database for studying face recognition in unconstrained environments. Technical report 07-49, University of Massachusetts, Amherst (2007)
6. Jin, Y., Lu, J., Ruan, Q.: Large margin coupled feature learning for cross-modal face recognition. In: International Conference on Biometrics (2015)
7. Juefei-Xu, F., Pal, D., Savvides, M.: NIR-VIS heterogeneous face recognition via cross-spectral joint dictionary learning and reconstruction. In: Computer Vision and Pattern Recognition Workshops (2015)
8. Klare, B., Li, Z., Jain, A.: Matching forensic sketches to mug shot photos. PAMI **33**(3), 639–646 (2011)
9. Kong, S., Heo, J., Abidi, B., Paik, J., Abidi, M.: Recent advances in visual and infrared face recognition - a review. CVIU **97**(1), 103–135 (2005)
10. Köstinger, M., Hirzer, M., Wohlhart, P., Roth, P., Bischof, H.: Large scale metric learning from equivalence constraints. In: CVPR (2012)
11. Li, S., Yi, D., Lei, Z., Liao, S.: The CASIA NIR-VIS 2.0 face database. In: Computer Vision and Pattern Recognition Workshops (2013)
12. Lu, J., Liong, V., Zhou, X., Zhou, J.: Learning compact binary face descriptor for face recognition. PAMI **37**, 2041–2056 (2015)
13. Martinez, A., Benavente, R.: The AR face database. Technical report (1998)
14. Mignon, A., Jurie, F.: CMML: a new metric learning approach for cross modal matching. In: ACCV (2012)
15. Mignon, A., Jurie, F.: PCCA: a new approach for distance learning from sparse pairwise constraints. In: CVPR (2012)
16. Mittal, P., Jain, A., Goswami, G., Singh, R., Vatsa, M.: Recognizing composite sketches with digital face images via SSD dictionary. In: International Joint Conference on Biometrics (2014)
17. Mittal, P., Vatsa, M., Singh, R.: Composite sketch recognition via deep network-a transfer learning approach. In: International Conference on Biometrics (2015)

18. Parkhi, O., Vedaldi, A., Zisserman, A.: Deep face recognition. In: BMVC (2015)
19. Patel, V., Gopalan, R., Li, R., Chellappa, R.: Visual domain adaptation: a survey of recent advances. IEEE Sig. Process. Mag. **32**(3), 53–69 (2015)
20. Sarfraz, M., Stiefelhagen, R.: Deep perceptual mapping for thermal to visible face recognition. In: BMVC (2015)
21. Schroff, F., Kalenichenko, D., Philbin, J.: FaceNet: a unified embedding for face recognition and clustering. In: CVPR (2015)
22. Simonyan, K., Parkhi, O., Vedaldi, A., Zisserman, A.: Fisher vector faces in the wild. In: BMVC (2013)
23. Taigman, Y., Yang, M., Ranzato, M., Wolf, L.: DeepFace: closing the gap to human-level performance in face verification. In: CVPR (2014)
24. Weinberger, K., Saul, L.: Distance metric learning for large margin nearest neighbor classification. JMLR **10**, 207–244 (2009)
25. Yi, D., Lei, Z., Liao, S., Li, S.: Learning face representation from scratch. Arxiv preprint (2014)
26. Yi, D., Lei, Z., Li, S.Z.: Shared representation learning for heterogeneous face recognition. In: International Conference on Automatic Face and Gesture Recognition (2015)

VLAD Is not Necessary for CNN

Dan Yu$^{(\boxtimes)}$ and Xiao-Jun Wu

School of IoT Engineering, Jiangnan University,
1800 Lihu Avenue, Wuxi, China
xiaojun_wu_jnu@163.com, wu_xiaojun@jiangnan.edu.cn

Abstract. Global convolutional neural networks (CNNs) activations lack geometric invariance, and in order to address this problem, Gong et al. proposed multi-scale orderless pooling(MOP-CNN), which extracts CNN activations for local patches at multiple scale levels, and performs orderless VLAD pooling to extract features. However, we find that this method can improve the performance mainly because it extracts global and local representation simultaneously, and VLAD pooling is not necessary as the representations extracted by CNN is good enough for classification. In this paper, we propose a new method to extract multi-scale features of CNNs, leading to a new structure of deep learning. The method extracts CNN representations for local patches at multiple scale levels, then concatenates all the representations at each level separately, finally, concatenates the results of all levels. The CNN is trained on the ImageNet dataset to extract features and it is then transferred to other datasets. The experimental results obtained on the databases MITIndoor and Caltech-101 show that the performance of our proposed method is superior to the MOP-CNN.

Keywords: CNN · Multi-scale · Deep learning · VLAD · Transfer learning

1 Introduction

Image classification [1–5] is one of the most important research tasks in computer vision and pattern recognition. To choose the right features plays the key role in a recognition system. There are many feature descriptors such as SIFT [6] and HOG [7], but they need to be designed by handcraft carefully, which is time-consuming and may not get the best feature sometimes. Many researches show that the features of the best performing recognition models are learned unsupervisedly from raw data.

Recently, deep convolutional neural networks (CNNs) have been considered as a powerful class of models for image recognition problems [8–11]. The feature representation learned by these networks achieves state-of-the-art performance not only on the task for which the network was trained, but also on various other classification tasks. A lot of recent works [12–14] showed that the feature representation trained on a large dataset can be successfully transferred to other visual tasks. For example: classification on Catech-101 [15], Catech-256 [5]; scene recognition on the Pascal VOC 2007 and 2012 [12] databases and so on.

However, global CNN activations lack geometric invariance, which limit their performance for the task of high variable scenes. Gong et al. [16] proposed a simple

© Springer International Publishing Switzerland 2016
G. Hua and H. Jégou (Eds.): ECCV 2016 Workshops, Part III, LNCS 9915, pp. 492–499, 2016.
DOI: 10.1007/978-3-319-49409-8_41

scheme called multi-scale orderless pooling CNN (MOP-CNN) to solve this problem, which combining activations extracted at multiple local image windows. The main idea of MOP-CNN is extracting features from the local patches via CNN at multiple scales, then adopting Vectors of Locally Aggregated Descriptors (VLAD) [17, 18] to encode those local features for each level separately, finally, concatenating the encoded features for all levels.

It is well known that the feature representation of CNN is very good, so is the VLAD really necessary? To explore this question, in this paper, we propose a method of MOP-CNN without the VLAD encoding. First, we extract local features via CNN at multiple scales, then we concatenate all the features at each level and PCA is adopted to reduce the dimensions of the concatenated features. Finally, we concatenate the features after PCA for all levels. We compare our proposed method with MOP-CNN on three datasets MITIndoor and Caltech-101 and evaluate their performances in accuracy and efficiency using strategy of transfer learning.

The rest of the paper is organized as follows. In Sect. 2, we introduce the proposed method in detail. Section 3 shows the experimental and compared results on the datasets MITIndoor and Caltech-101 respectively. We conclude the paper in Sect. 4.

2 The Proposed Method

We take the activation for the entire 256 × 256 image as the feature representation of the first level. For the second level, we extract activations for all 128 × 128 patches sampled with a stride of 32 pixels. Then we simply concatenate the activations for all

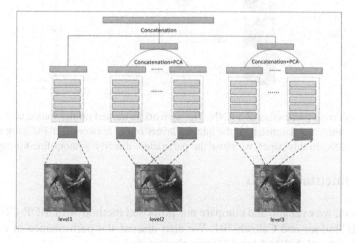

Fig. 1. Illustration of how the proposed method extracts features from an image through multi-scale concatenation for CNN activations. There are also three levels in our method: Level 1 extracts the 4096-dimension feature of the last connected layer of CNN for the entire 256 × 256 image. Level 2 extracts 4096-dimension representation for each 128 × 128 patch and concatenates all representations of all patches from the image, which is then reduced to 4096-dimension via PCA. Level 3 formed in the same way as level 2 but replaces the patch size 128 × 128 with 64 × 64. Finally, we concatenate all the features of three levels.

patches, which results in quite high dimensional vector, so we use PCA to reduce them to 4096, finally, the reduced feature vectors are normalized as the final feature representation of the second level. The third level is the same as the second level but replacing the patches size 128 × 128 with 64 × 64, which can extract more local information intuitively (but we found it does not work well, which we will discuss in Sect. 3). Finally, we concatenate the original 4096-dimensional feature representation from the first level and the two PCA-reduced 4096-dimensional feature representations from the second and third levels to form the final feature representation of an image (shown as Fig. 1).

A direct transfer learning strategy is adopted for visual classification. The CNN is trained on the ImageNet to extract features and it is then transferred to other datasets. In order to indicate the ability to learn rich image representations of CNN, we reuse layers trained on the ImageNet without fine-tuning. The main idea is shown in Fig. 2. A CNN representation trained on the Imagenet dataset used on other dataset is a standard practice now, but it is a transfer procedure.

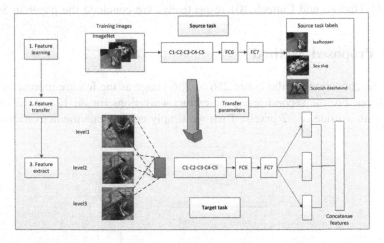

Fig. 2. Transferring parameters of a CNN. The network is trained on the source task (ImageNet classification), then the parameters of the internal layers of the network (C1-FC7) are transferred to the target tasks. In this paper, we reuse the parameters directly without fine-tuning.

3   Experimental Results

In this section, we evaluate and compare our proposed method with MOP-CNN on two datasets: MITIndoor and Caltech-101. We also discuss the performance of each level, which means the global and local information of an image.

3.1   DataSets

MITIndoor [20] contains 67 categories, and a total of 15620 images. There is a standard training/test split, which contains 80 training and 20 test images per category.

Caltech-101 [21] contains 101 categories, and about 40 to 800 images per category, most categories have about 50 images. We follow the procedure of [22] and randomly select 5,10,15,20,25 images per class for training and test on up to 20 images per class, repeat 5 times and report the average of the per-class accuracy.

3.2 Results

In all the experiments of this paper, we adopt the SVM [23–25] implementation from the libsvm [26, 27] as the classifier.

The results on MITIndoor is shown in Table 1. From Table 1, one can see that simply concatenating the features of all patches is better than VLAD pooling, which implies that we can extract pretty good features for classification just via CNN and without VLAD encoding. And the training time and test time of our proposed method are shorter than that of VLAD encoding. One can also see that the concatenation of level 1 and level 2 achieves best recognition accuracy, which may because level 1 can extract the global feature and level 2 can extract the local feature, and concatenating level 1 and level 2 can obtain the local and global information simultaneously to improve the recognition accuracy. That means that the multi-scale information is useful to improve the performance of CNN. However, concatenating all the three scale levels is not very good, it may because the patch size of level 3 is too small, which could not extract the main discriminative information and may introduce some noises.

Table 1. Performance on MITIndoor

Pooling method	Scale	Training time (1.0e+04 *) (s)	Test time (s)	Acc (%)
VLAD pooling	level1	1.06	1.36	59.68
	level2	1.75	2.52	54.80
	level3	2.51	3.95	51.88
	level1+level2	2.19	3.38	63.29
	level1+level3	2.98	4.86	63.81
	level2+level3	3.65	5.88	57.88
	level1+level2+level3 (MOP-CNN)	4.12	6.86	64.34
Concatenation+PCA	level1	0.52	0.95	59.68
	level2	1.17	2.10	58.41
	level3	1.96	3.49	52.85
	level1+level2 (Our method)	1.69	2.99	**64.34**
	level1+level3	2.47	4.40	63.44
	level2+level3	3.11	5.51	58.33
	level1+level2+level3	3.68	6.37	63.81

We implement the experiments of MOP-CNN using the same experimental conditions as Gong et al. First, we extract multi-scale features on different patches size via CNN, then use VLAD to encode the features, the parameters of VLAD is the same as

Gong et al. But the results is worse than that reported in the MOP-CNN paper from Gong et al., which may come from two implementation details: one possible reason is that we use the CNN trained on the ImageNet directly without fine-tuning on the target datasets. However, fine-tuning was not reported in [16] explicitly. Another reason may be from different implementations of SVM classifier. We adopt the SVM implementation from the libsvm [26, 27] rather than the linear SVM implementation from the INRIA JSGD package on [16].

Table 2 shows the results on Caltech-101 of 20 images per class for training and up to 20 images per class for test. Figure 3 shows the results of different training images. From Table 2, we can see that the trends are consistent with those on MITIndoor, which implies that our proposed method is superior to MOP-CNN, which means VLAD is not necessary. There is one interesting difference from Table 1, the concatenation of level 1 and level 2 performs much better than level 1 or level 2 alone on MITIndoor, while the advantage is not very significant on Caltech-101. The possible reason is that indoor scenes are better described by the concatenation of local and global discriminative information. From Fig. 3 we can see that the performance increases as more training images are used, and our method is better than MOP-CNN no matter how training images are used.

Table 2. Performance on Caltech-101

Pooling method	Scale	Training time (1.0e+04 *) (s)	Test time (s)	Acc (%)
VLAD pooling	level1	0.26	1.17	86.44
	level2	0.48	2.25	69.42
	level3	0.78	3.75	50.53
	level1+level2	0.65	3.08	85.36
	level1+level3	0.95	4.53	85.06
	level2+level3	1.17	5.61	68.21
	level1+level2+level3 (MOP-CNN)	1.34	6.44	83.98
Concatenation +PCA	level1	0.19	0.86	86.44
	level2	0.41	1.94	82.71
	level3	0.70	3.39	64.88
	level1+level2 (Our method)	0.58	2.77	**88.31**
	level1+level3	0.87	4.27	86.68
	level2+level3	1.09	5.30	78.78
	level1+level2+level3	1.26	6.12	87.06

From the experimental results on the two datasets, we can conclude that: (a) The features extracted via CNN is good enough for the recognition tasks and the simple concatenation of the features of level 1 and level 2 is better than the features via VLAD encoding no matter in performance or time consumption, and no matter how training

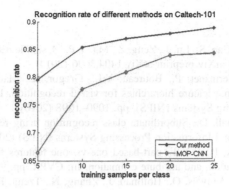

Fig. 3. Recognition rates of different methods on Caltech-101

images are used, which means VLAD is not necessary. (b) The concatenation of level 1 and level 2 is superior to level 1 or level 2 alone shows that the multi-scale information is useful to improve the performance of CNN, while the features of level 3 is not as good as level 1 and level 2, that probably because the patch size of level 3 is too small to capture discriminative information and may introduce noise. (c) The contribution of the local information varies from datasets, indoor scenes are better described by local patches that have highly distinctive appearance but can vary greatly in terms of location.

4 Conclusion

In this paper, we propose a new simple method to extract multi-scale feature representation of CNN, which concatenates the features of all patches on each level simply, rather than using VLAD encoding. The experimental results on two datasets: MITIndoor and Caltech-101 show that the features extracted by CNN are good enough for classification tasks and VLAD encoding is not necessary. From the experimental results, we can also learn that the multi-scale information is helpful but the patch size is important for the extraction of local information, while it may not be helpful if the patch is too small. Furthermore, we can see that the contribution of the local information is specific to datasets depending on the visual content of images.

In this paper, we only discuss the classification task, and there are many other tasks in computer vision and pattern recognition. In the future, we will study the influence of the multi-scale features to other tasks, such as detection task, localization task and so on.

Acknowledgments. The paper is supported by the National Natural Science Foundation of China (Grant No. 61373055, 61672265), Industry Project of Provincial Department of Education of Jiangsu Province (Grant No. JH10-28), and Industry oriented project of Jiangsu Provincial Department of Technology (Grant No. BY2012059).

References

1. Chan, T.H., Jia, K., Gao, S., Lu, J., Zeng, Z., Ma, Y.P.: A simple deep learning baseline for image classification? arXiv preprint arXiv:1404.3606 (2014)
2. Kavukcuoglu, K., Sermanet, P., Boureau, Y.L., Gregor, K., Mathieu, M., Cun, Y. L.: Learning convolutional feature hierarchies for visual recognition. In: Advances in Neural Information Processing Systems (NIPS), pp. 1090–1098 (2010)
3. Hillel, A.B., Weinshall, D.: Subordinate class recognition using relational object models. In: Advances in Neural Information Processing Systems (NIPS) (2007)
4. Berg, T., Belhumeur, P.: POOF: part-based one-vs.-one features for fine-grained categorization, face verification, and attribute estimation. In: CVPR, pp. 955–962 (2013)
5. Donahue, J., Jia, Y., Vinyals, O., Hoffman, J., Zhang, N., Tzeng, E., Darrell, T.: Decaf: a deep convolutional activation feature for generic visual recognition. arXiv preprint arXiv: 1310.1531 (2013)
6. Lowe, D.G.: Distinctive image features from scale-invariant keypoints. Int. J. Comput. Vis. (IJCV) **60**, 91–110 (2004)
7. Dalal, N., Triggs, B.: Histograms of oriented gradients for human detection. In: CVPR, pp. 886–893 (2005)
8. Huang, F.J., LeCun, Y.: Large-scale learning with SVM and convolutional netw for generic object recognition. In: CVPR (2006)
9. Krizhevsky, A., Sutskever, I., Hinton, G. E.: Imagenet classification with deep convolutional neural networks. In: Advances in Neural Information Processing Systems (NIPS), pp. 1097–1105 (2012)
10. Chen, Y.N., Han, C.C., Wang, C.T., Jeng, B.S., Fan, K.C.: The application of a convolution neural network on face and license plate detection. In: ICPR, pp. 552–555 (2006)
11. Karpathy, A., Toderici, G., Shetty, S., Leung, T., Sukthankar, R., Fei-Fei, L.: Large-scale video classification with convolutional neural networks. In: CVPR, pp. 1725–1732 (2014)
12. Oquab, M., Bottou, L., Laptev, I., Sivic, J.: Learning and transferring mid-level image representations using convolutional neural networks. In: CVPR, pp. 1717–1724 (2014)
13. Sermanet, P., Eigen, D., Zhang, X., Mathieu, M., Fergus, R., LeCun, Y.: Overfeat: integrated recognition, localization and detection using convolutional networks. arXiv preprint arXiv:1312.6229 (2013)
14. Simonyan, K., Zisserman, A.: Very deep convolutional networks for large-scale image recognition. arXiv preprint arXiv:1409.1556 (2014)
15. Zeiler, M.D., Fergus, R.: Visualizing and understanding convolutional networks. In: Fleet, D., Pajdla, T., Schiele, B., Tuytelaars, T. (eds.) ECCV 2014. LNCS, vol. 8689, pp. 818–833. Springer, Heidelberg (2014). doi:10.1007/978-3-319-10590-1_53
16. Gong, Y., Wang, L., Guo, R., Lazebnik, S.: Multi-scale orderless pooling of deep convolutional activation features. In: Fleet, D., Pajdla, T., Schiele, B., Tuytelaars, T. (eds.) ECCV 2014. LNCS, vol. 8695, pp. 392–407. Springer, Heidelberg (2014). doi:10.1007/978-3-319-10584-0_26
17. Jégou, H., Douze, M., Schmid, C., Pérez, P.: Aggregating local descriptors into a compact image representation. In: CVPR, pp. 3304–3311 (2010)
18. Perronnin, F., Dance, C.: Fisher kernels on visual vocabularies for image categorization. In: CVPR, pp. 1–8 (2007)
19. Krizhevsky, A., Sutskever, I., Hinton, G.E.: Imagenet classification with deep convolutional neural networks. In: Advances in Neural Information Processing Systems (NIPS), pp. 1097–1105 (2012)
20. Quattoni, A., Torralba, A.: Recognizing indoor scenes. In: CVPR, pp. 413–420 (2009)

21. Fei-Fei, L., Fergus, R., Perona, P.: Learning generative visual models from few training examples: an incremental bayesian approach tested on 101 object categories. Comput. Vis. Image Underst. **106**, 59–70 (2007)
22. Fei-Fei, L., Fergus, R., Perona, P.: One-shot learning of object categories. IEEE Trans. Pattern Anal. Mach. Intell. **28**, 594–611 (2006)
23. Burges, C.J.: A tutorial on support vector machines for pattern recognition. Data Min. Knowl. Discov. **2**, 121–167 (1998)
24. Cristianini, N., Shawe-Taylor, J.: An Introduction to Support Vector Machines and Other Kernel-Based Learning Methods. Cambridge University Press, Cambridge (2000)
25. Smola, A.J., Schölkopf, B.: A tutorial on support vector regression. Stat. Comput. **14**, 199–222 (2004)
26. Hsu, C.W., Chang, C.C., Lin, C.J.: A practical guide to support vector classification (2003)
27. Chang, C.C., Lin, C.J.: LIBSVM: a library for support vector machines. ACM Trans. Intell. Syst. Technol. (TIST) (2011)

Training a Mentee Network by Transferring Knowledge from a Mentor Network

Elnaz Jahani Heravi[(✉)], Hamed Habibi Aghdam, and Domenec Puig

Department of Computer Engineering and Mathematics,
University Rovira i Virgili, Tarragona, Spain
{elnaz.jahani,hamed.habibi,domenec.puig}@urv.cat

Abstract. Automatic classification of foods is a challenging problem. Results on ImageNet dataset shows that ConvNets are very powerful in modeling natural objects. Nonetheless, it is not trivial to train a ConvNet from scratch for classification of foods. This is due to the fact that ConvNets require large datasets and to our knowledge there is not a large public dataset of foods for this purpose. An alternative solution is to transfer knowledge from already trained ConvNets. In this work, we study how transferable are state-of-art ConvNets to classification of foods. We also propose a method for transferring knowledge from a bigger ConvNet to a smaller ConvNet without decreasing the accuracy. Our experiments on UECFood256 dataset show that state-of-art networks produce comparable results if we start transferring knowledge from an appropriate layer. In addition, we show that our method is able to effectively transfer knowledge to a smaller ConvNet using unlabeled samples.

Keywords: Food classification · Convolutional neural network · Deep learning · Transfer learning

1   Introduction

Obesity is known as a disease in developed countries and it can be controlled by monitoring the food intake. However, accurate calculation of calorie intake is not trivial and patients tend to calculate it quickly and conveniently. Automatic estimation of calorie intake can be done using the image of a food. To this end, first the system recognizes foods in the classification stage and, then, it estimates calorie based on the category of food.

Early attempts on food recognition focused on the traditional approached which extracts features using hand-crafted methods and then applies a classifier

Electronic supplementary material The online version of this chapter (doi:10.1007/978-3-319-49409-8_42) contains supplementary material, which is available to authorized users.

G. Hua and H. Jégou (Eds.): ECCV 2016 Workshops, Part III, LNCS 9915, pp. 500–507, 2016.
DOI: 10.1007/978-3-319-49409-8_42

for recognizing foods. Kong and Tan [7] classified foods using multiple viewpoints. They compute SIFT and Gaussian region detector as the feature vector. Also, Kawano and Yanai [5] proposed a system which asks the user to draw a bounding box around food regions. Then, SURF based bag of features and color histograms are extracted and classified using a linear SVM. Matsuda *et al.* [9] proposed a method which takes into account the co-occurrence statistics of 100 food items. Similar to previous methods they applied Multiple Kernel Learning SVM on the image feature vectors such as color, SIFT, CSIFT, HOG and Gabor. Also, they utilized deformable part model, circle detector and JSEG methods for detecting candidate regions. Similarly, Hoashi *et al.* [4] classified 85 food classes by fusing BoF, color histogram, Gabor and HOG using Multiple Kernel Learning. In contrast to the previous methods, Yang *et al.* [13] classified food images with considering spatial relationship between food items. In this work, each image is represented by a pairwise feature distribution.

Lately, researchers have started to utilize Convolutional Neural Networks (ConvNets) in the task of food recognition. For instance, Christodoulidis *et al.* [1] proposed a 6 layer ConvNet to classify 7 items of food. They applied the ConvNet on the already segmented food images and used a voting method for determining the class of each food item. Also, Yanai and Kawano [12] fused Fisher Vector (FV) with pre-trained Deep Convolutional Neural Network features trained on 2000 ImageNet categories. Taking into account that food recognition systems might be implemented on mobile devices, we need a ConvNet with low memory and power consumption. Besides, time-to-completion of the ConvNet must be low in order to have a better user experience. To our knowledge, there are a few public food datasets such as UEC-Food100, UEC-Food256, and Pittsburgh Food Image Dataset. The problem of these datasets is that the number of samples in each class is scarce and highly imbalanced which makes them inapplicable for training a deep ConvNet with millions of parameters from scratch.

Contribution: In this paper, we partially address this problem by transferring knowledge of ConvNets trained on ImageNet dataset to a *smaller* ConvNet and fine-tune it using the dataset of food images. To be more specific, we first transfer knowledge of GoogleNet [11], AlexNet [8], VGGNet [10] and Microsoft Residual Net [2] on the UECFood 256 dataset. Our experiments show that if the knowledge of these ConvNet are transferred appropriately, they are able to outperform the state of art methods applied on this dataset. More importantly, we propose a method to transfer knowledge of the these ConvNets to a smaller ConvNet with less time-to-completion, less memory and similar accuracy.

2 Knowledge Transfer

One of the major barriers in utilizing ConvNets on the task of food recognition is that public food datasets are usually small. For this reason, it is not practical to train a ConvNet from scratch for this task. One alternative solution for solving this problem is to use the pre-trained ConvNets as a generic feature extraction method. For a ConvNet with L layers, we use

$\Phi_l(x; W_1 \ldots W_l)$ to represent the vector function in the lth layer parametrized by $\{W_1 \ldots W_l\}$. With this formulation, $\Phi_L(x)$ represents the classification layer. Utilizing a ConvNet as a generic feature extractor means that we collect set $\mathcal{X} = \{(\Phi_{L-1}(x_1), y_1), \ldots, (\Phi_{L-1}(x_N), y_N)\}$ where x_i is the image of food and y_i is its actual label. Then, we train a classifier (linear or non-linear) using the samples in $\mathcal{X}$.

As we show and explain in Sect. 3, this method does not produce accurate results with a linear classifier. For this reason, it is better to adjust the parameters of the ConvNet using the current dataset. By this way, the pre-trained ConvNets classify foods more accurately. As we mentioned earlier, we need an accurate ConvNet with lower time-to-completion and less memory requirement. Hence, we must find a way to compress these pre-trained ConvNet. To this end, we propose a method that transfers the knowledge of a large pre-trained ConvNets to a smaller ConvNet by keeping the accuracy high. Our method is inspired by the recently proposed method by Hinton et al. [3] called *Knowledge Distillation*. Given a pre-trained network $\mathbf{z}^{source} = \Phi^{source}(x; W_1 \ldots W_{L_s})$, the aim of this method is to train $\mathbf{z}^{distilled} = \Phi_{distilled}(x; W_1 \ldots W_{L_d})$ so that:

$$\left\| \frac{e^{z_i^{distill}}}{\sum_j e^{z_j^{distilled}}} - \frac{e^{\frac{z_i^{source}}{T}}}{\sum_j e^{\frac{z_j^{source}}{T}}} \right\| \tag{1}$$

is minimum for all sample in training set. In this equation, z_i indicates the ith output and T is a parameter to soften the output of source network. One property of this method is that the classification score of the source ConvNet could be significantly different from the distilled ConvNet. This is due to the fact that there could be infinite combinations of classification score $z^{distill}$ to produce the same $softmax(z^{source})$ where $\|z^{distill} - z^{source}\|$ might be very large. For example, suppose that $softmax(z^{source}) = [0.99, 0.01]$ for a network with two outputs. Then, $z^{distill} = [10, 5.4049]^1$ and $z^{distill} = [100, 95.4049]^2$ will be the same $softmax(z^{distill})$. In other words, $\Phi_{distilled}(x)$ found by minimizing (1) may not accurately approximate $\Phi^{source}(x)$. Instead, it may mimic the normalized output of this function.

The advantage of this property is on distilled networks which are shallower than the source network. To be more specific, shallower networks *might* not be able to accurately approximate the z^{source} if they are not adequately wide. However, they might be able to produce $z^{distill}$ such that (1) is minimized. A drawback of this property is on networks that are deeper than or as deep as the source network. These networks might be able to accurately approximate z^{source}. However, training the distilled network by minimizing (1) is likely not to accurately approximate z^{source}. Besides, two different initialization might end up with two different distilled network where their $z^{distill}$ are significantly different from each other.

---

[1] [10,5.4048801498654111] to be exact.
[2] [100, 95.404880149865406] to be exact.

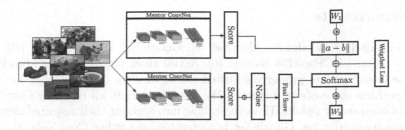

Fig. 1. Our proposed method for transferring knowledge from a larger network called Mentor to a smaller network called Mentee.

2.1 Proposed Method

We formulate knowledge transfer from one network to another network in terms of *function approximation*. Our proposed method is illustrated in Fig. 1. It consists of a Mentor ConvNet which is a pre-trained network and a Mentee ConvNet which is smaller and faster than the Mentor. Our aim is that Mentee performs similar to Mentor. Representing the Mentor with $\Phi_{mentor}(x)$ and the Mentee with $\Phi_{mentee}(x)$, we want to train $\Phi_{mentee}(x)$ such that $\forall_{x \in \mathcal{X}} \Phi_{mentor}(x) = \Phi_{mentee}(x)$ where $\mathcal{X}$ is a set consists of many *unlabelled* images. In other words, we formulate the knowledge transfer from Mentor to Mentee as a function approximation problem. By this way, the Mentee ConvNet is trained to approximate *un-normalized* Mentor ConvNet. Formally, our objective function is defined as *sum of square error*:

$$E = \sum_{i}^{N} \| \Phi^{mentor}(x) - \Phi^{mentee}(x) \|^2. \tag{2}$$

Theoretically, we do not need labelled images to transfer knowledge from Mentor to Mentee since the above loss function does not depend on labels of image. Consequently, we can use any large dataset of unlabelled images to approximate $\Phi_{mentor}(x)$ using $\Phi_{mentee}(x)$. By this way, Mentee is trained with non-food images. Notwithstanding, $\Phi_{mentee}(x)$ requires a large dataset of unlabelled images to be generalized. Since collecting this dataset is not tedious, we modified the above loss function as a weighted average of sum of square error and log likelihood:

$$E = \sum_{i}^{N} \alpha_1 \| \Phi^{mentor}(x) - \Phi^{mentee}(x) \|^2 - \alpha_2 \sum_{\forall \{i | y_i > 0\}} \log(softmax(\Phi^{mentee}(x_i))). \tag{3}$$

During the first iterations, we set $alpha_2 = \epsilon$ so Mentee is mainly trained using sum of square error. Eventually, $alpha_2$ is increased in order to take into account the information coming from labelled images. In the next section, we explain the architecture of Mentor as well as Mentee networks.

3 Experiments

We transferred knowledge of AlextNet [8], GoogleNet [11], VGGNet [10] and ResNet [2] on UECFood256 dataset [6]. As we show shortly, if the knowledge of these ConvNets are properly adjusted to the domain of foods, they are able to outperform state-of-art methods. We also show that all of these ConvNets produce comparable results. However, taking into account their required memory and time-to-completion, GoogleNet is preferable over other ConvNets. For this reason, we use GoogleNet as the Mentor in Fig. 1.

Our aim is to train Mentee so it approximates Mentor as accurate as possible. For this reason, we choose the architecture of Mentee to be exactly similar to GoogleNet. However, we reduce the width of Mentee by reducing the number of filters in each inception module to 90 % of the original size. We use a combination of the ImageNet and the Caltech 256 datasets by ignoring their labels and use them as the set of unlabelled samples. Besides, we use UECFood256 dataset in order to compute the second term in (3) using labelled samples.

Results: In order to adapt knowledge of the ConvNets we mentioned earlier, we conducted the following procedure. First, all the layers are frozen except the last fully connected layer. Freezing a layer means that we set the learning rate of that particular later to zero so it does not change during backpropagation. Then, the last layer is trained on the food dataset. Second, we unfreeze the last two layers and keep the rest of the layers frozen. Third, the last three layers are unfrozen and the rest of the layers are kept frozen. Table 1 shows the top-1 and top-5 accuracies of the ConvNets in these settings.

Table 1. Adapting knowledge of ConvNets trained on ImageNet dataset to UECFood-256 dataset in different settings.

	Last layer		2nd last layer		3rd last layer	
	top-1 (%)	top-5 (%)	top-1 (%)	top-5 (%)	top-1 (%)	top-5 (%)
Alexnet	49	76	56	81	59	83
Googlenet	55	81	61	86	62	86
Vggnet	51	78	60	84	62	86
Resnet	60	83	62	86	NA	NA

The results suggest that adapting knowledge of the ConvNets must start from the two last layers. When we only adapt the knowledge of the last layer on UECFood-256 dataset, this means that the weights of the linear classifier are adapted. However, because these ConvNets are trained on ImageNet dataset their domain are different from UECFood-256 dataset. In other words, these ConvNets have been basically trained to distinguish the objects in ImageNet dataset. So, when they are applied on UECFood-256 dataset, foods might not be linearly separable in the last 2nd layer. Nonetheless, when the ConvNets are adapted starting from the last two layers, they learn to transform the feature vectors produced in the last 3rd layer to be linearly separable in the last 2nd layer. Therefore, foods become linearly separable in the last layer. Besides, we observe that adapting the ConvNets starting from the last 3rd layer does not change the results. This might be due to the size of UECFood-256 dataset being small. Since the number of parameters starting from the last 3rd layer are high, they are not able to generalize properly provided by a small dataset.

Next, we use the GoogleNet adapted from the last three layers as the Mentor and trained the Mentee network. The architecture of the Mentee network has been explained in the beginning of this section. Table 2 illustrates the accuracy of Mentee for different valued of k. Comparing the plot with Table 1 shows that Mentee has accurately approximated the Mentor network and yet it is smaller and faster than Mentor.

We also compared our Mentee with the best results reported on UECFood-256 dataset. It is worth mentioning that [12] have used AlexNet as feature extractor and trained a classifier on top of it. Also, they have not augmented the original dataset. For this reason, their result is different from our result. In addition, DCNN-Food is modified version (number of neuron in the fully connected layer has been increased to 6144) of AlexNet which is specifically trained on the food images from ImageNet dataset. We observe that our Mentee has produced comparable results with respect to FV+DCNN-Food method with a much smaller network. Also, the top-5 accuracy of both of these methods are equal. Moreover, FV+DCNN-Food needs much more computations since it must compute Spatial Pyramid Fisher Vectors and apply a large network on the image. However,

Table 2. Accuracy of Mentee computed for different k

top (%)									
1	2	3	4	5	6	7	8	9	10
62	74	80	83	86	88	89	90	91	92

Table 3. Comparing our Mentee network with other methods reported in [12]

Method	top-1 (%)	top-5 (%)
Color FV	42	64
RootHOG FV	36	59
FV (Color+HOG)	53	76
DCNN	44	71
DCNN-Food	59	83
FV+DCNN	59	82
FV+DCNN-Food	64	86
Our Mentee	62	86

because we have trained our Mentor network properly (we trained the last three layers), the Mentee network is also able to predict classes, accurately (Table 3).

We have also computed the precision and recall of each class separately. You can find these results in the supplementary materials.

4 Conclusion

In this paper, we proposed a method for transferring knowledge from a bigger network called Mentor to a smaller network called Mentee in two phases. In the first phase Mentee uses unlabelled images to approximate the score produced by Mentor. In the second, phase, a dataset of labelled images are used to further tune the knowledge of small network in a supervised fashion. Our experiments on UECFood-256 dataset shows that pretrained ConvNet produce more accurate results when their knowledge is adapted starting from the last 2nd or 3rd layer. Using this information, we used GoogleNet as the Mentor and its compressed version as Mentee and transferred knowledge of the Mentor to Mentee. We showed that the Mentee network is as accurate as Mentor network and, yet, it is faster and consume less memory since its widths is less than the Mentor network.

References

1. Christodoulidis, S., Anthimopoulos, M., Mougiakakou, S.: Food recognition for dietary assessment using deep convolutional neural networks. In: Murino, V., Puppo, E., Sona, D., Cristani, M., Sansone, C. (eds.) ICIAP 2015. LNCS, vol. 9281, pp. 458–465. Springer, Heidelberg (2015). doi:10.1007/978-3-319-23222-5_56
2. He, K., Zhang, X., Ren, S., Sun, J.: Deep residual learning for image recognition. arXiv preprint arXiv:1506.01497 (2015)
3. Hinton, G., Vinyals, O., Dean, J.: Distilling the knowledge in a neural network. In: NIPS 2014 Deep Learning Workshop, pp. 1–9 (2015)
4. Hoashi, H., Joutou, T., Yanai, K.: Image recognition of 85 food categories by feature fusion. In: Proceedings - 2010 IEEE International Symposium on Multimedia, ISM 2010, pp. 296–301 (2010)
5. Kawano, Y., Yanai, K.: Real-time mobile food recognition system. In: 2013 IEEE Conference on Computer Vision and Pattern Recognition Workshops (CVPRW), pp. 1–7 (2013)
6. Kawano, Y., Yanai, K.: Automatic expansion of a food image dataset leveraging existing categories with domain adaptation. In: Agapito, L., Bronstein, M.M., Rother, C. (eds.) ECCV 2014. LNCS, vol. 8927, pp. 3–17. Springer, Heidelberg (2015). doi:10.1007/978-3-319-16199-0_1
7. Kong, F., Tan, J.: DietCam: regular shape food recognition with a camera phone. In: Proceedings - 2011 International Conference on Body Sensor Networks, BSN 2011, pp. 127–132 (2011)
8. Krizhevsky, A., Sutskever, I., Hinton, G.: Imagenet classification with deep convolutional neural networks. In: Advances in neural information processing systems, pp. 1097–1105. Curran Associates Inc. (2012)

9. Matsuda, Y., Hoashi, H., Yanai, K.: Multiple-food recognition considering co-occurrence employing manifold ranking. In: 2012 21st International Conference on Pattern Recognition (ICPR), pp. 2017–2020 (2012)
10. Simonyan, K., Zisserman, A.: Very deep convolutional networks for large-scale image recognition. In: International Conference on Learning Representation (ICLR), pp. 1–13 (2015)
11. Szegedy, C., Reed, S., Sermanet, P., Vanhoucke, V., Rabinovich, A.: Going deeper with convolutions. arXiv preprint arXiv:1409.4842, pp. 1–12 (2014)
12. Yanai, K., Kawano, Y.: Food image recognition using deep convolutional network with pre-training and fine-tuning. In: 2015 IEEE International Conference on Multimedia Expo Workshops (ICMEW), pp. 1–6, June 2015
13. Yang, S., Chen, M., Pomerleau, D., Sukthankar, R.: Food recognition using statistics of pairwise local features. In: Proceedings of the IEEE Computer Society Conference on Computer Vision and Pattern Recognition, pp. 2249–2256 (2010)

Lightweight Unsupervised Domain Adaptation by Convolutional Filter Reconstruction

Rahaf Aljundi[✉] and Tinne Tuytelaars

ESAT-PSI - iMinds, KU Leuven, Leuven, Belgium
Rahaf.aljundi@esat.kuleuven.be

Abstract. Recently proposed domain adaptation methods retrain the network parameters and overcome the domain shift issue to a large extent. However, this requires access to all (labeled) source data, a large amount of (unlabeled) target data, and plenty of computational resources. In this work, we propose a lightweight alternative, that allows adapting to the target domain based on a limited number of target samples in a matter of minutes. To this end, we first analyze the output of each convolutional layer from a domain adaptation perspective. Surprisingly, we find that already at the very first layer, domain shift effects pop up. We then propose a new domain adaptation method, where first layer convolutional filters that are badly affected by the domain shift are reconstructed based on less affected ones.

1 Introduction

In recent years, great advances have been realized towards image understanding in general and object recognition in particular, thanks to end-to-end learning of convolutional neural networks, seeking the optimal representation for the task at hand. Unfortunately, performance remarkably decreases when taking the trained algorithms and systems out of the lab and into the real world of practical applications. This is known in the literature as the domain shift problem. The default solution is to retrain or finetune the system using additional training data, mimicking as close as possible the conditions during testing. However, such large labeled data is not always available.

Overcoming this domain shift problem without additional annotated data is the main goal of unsupervised domain adaptation. State-of-the-art methods for unsupervised domain adaptation of deep neural network architectures such as Domain Adversarial Training of Neural Networks(DANN) [1] and Learning Transferable Features with Deep Adaptation Networks (DAN) [2] proceed by adding new layers to the deep network or learning a joint architecture in order to come up with representations that are more general and informative across the source and target domains.

However, in spite of their good results on various benchmarks, these methods seem to be of limited value in a practical application. Indeed, deep adaptation methods require access to all the source data, a lot of computation time, a lot of resources, and a lot of unlabeled target data. This is in contrast to the typical

© Springer International Publishing Switzerland 2016
G. Hua and H. Jégou (Eds.): ECCV 2016 Workshops, Part III, LNCS 9915, pp. 508–515, 2016.
DOI: 10.1007/978-3-319-49409-8_43

domain adaptation setting, where we want networks trained on big datasets such as Imagenet to be readily usable by different users and in a variety of settings.

So instead, we advocate the need for *light-weight domain adaptation schemes*, that require only a small number of target samples and can be applied quickly without heavy requirements on available resources, in an *on-the-fly* spirit. Using only a few samples, such a system could adapt to new conditions at regular time intervals, making sure the models are well adapted to the current conditions. The simpler sub-space based domain adaptation methods developed earlier for shallow architectures [3–5] seem good candidates for this setting. Unfortunately, when applied to the last fully connected layer of a standard convolutional neural network, they yield minimal improvement [6, 7]. However, the last layer might not be the best place to perform domain adaptation (DA). In this work, we start by analyzing the different layers of a deep network from a domain adaptation perspective. First, we show that *domain shift does not only affect the last layers of the network*, but can already manifest itself as early as the very first layer. Second, we show that the *filters exhibit different behavior in terms of domain shift*: while some filters result in a largely domain invariant representation, others lead to very different filter responce distributions for the source and target data. Based on this analysis, we propose a new light-weight domain adaptation method, focusing just on the first layer of the network.

2 Analysis of Domain Shift in the Context of Deep Learning

Deep adaptation methods typically assume that the first layers are generic and need no adaptation, while the last layers are more specific to the dataset used for training and thus sensitive to the shift between the two domains. Therefore, most adaptation methods tend to adapt only the last layers and freeze the first layers [2, 8]. This assumption is based on the fact that the first layers mainly detect colors, edges, textures, etc. - features that are generic to all domains. On the other hand, in the last layers we can see high level information about the objects, which might be domain-specific. However, *even if the feature extraction method is generic, the features may still convey information about the domain*. This is indeed what one would expect for features that are not trained to be domain invariant. To understand how the domain shift evolves through the different layers, we perform an analysis of the output of each layer using Alexnet [9]. We use the standard adaptation benchmark, the Office dataset [10], specifically the two sets Amazon (A) and Webcam (W). This setup resembles the typical case of domain adaptation where the datasets are gathered from different resources. In addition, to study the low level shift, we created a gray scale set that contains the same images as in the Amazon dataset but converted to gray scale. We call it Amazon-Gray (AG). We consider two adaptation cases: A→AG and A→W. We start by fine-tuning AlexNet on the Amazon dataset (the source). Then, we consider each convolutional layer as an independent feature extraction step. Each layer is composed of a set of filter maps. We consider one filter from one

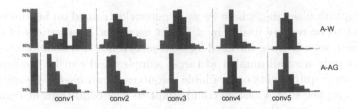

Fig. 1. The histograms of the filters' H-divergences for different layers.

layer at a time, and consider, for this analysis, the corresponding filter map as our feature space. Each instance (image) is a point in that space. For example, the first convolutional layer is composed of 96 filter maps, each of size [55 × 55]. We reshape each [55 × 55] filter map into a feature vector of length 3025 and consider this the feature representation of the image.

To quantify the domain shift, we study the H-divergence [11] w.r.t. each layer/filter and using linear SVM as our hypothesis. In Fig. 1, we show the histograms of the filters' H-divergences w.r.t. each layer regarding the two study cases A→W and A→AG. We encode the value of the H-divergence by the color where blue indicates a low H-divergence (= "good" filters) while red indicates a high H-divergence (= "bad" filters).

Discussion. From Fig. 1, we can conclude that, in contrast to common belief, the *first layers are susceptible to domain shift even more than the later layers* (i.e., the distributions of the source and target filter outputs show bigger differences in feature space, resulting in larger H-divergence scores). Indeed, the filters of the first layers are similar to HOG, SURF or SIFT (edge detectors, color detectors, texture, etc.); they are generic w.r.t. different datasets, i.e. they give representative information regardless of the dataset. However, this information also conveys the specific characteristics of the dataset and thus the dataset bias. As a result, when the rest of the network processes this output, it will be affected by the shown bias, causing a degradation in performance.

Especially in the first layer of the convolutional neural network, we see large differences between different filters while in later layers the H-divergence of the filters follows a normal distribution as their input is affected by the domain shift in some of the first layer filters and thus it is harder to find non affected filters in later layers. Based on this analysis of the domain bias over different layers, we believe that *a good solution of the domain adaptation problem should start from the first layers* in order to correct each shift at the right level rather than waiting till the last layer and then trying to match the two feature spaces.

Our DA Strategy. Based on these findings we suggest: (1) to compute the divergence of the two datasets with respect to each filter as a measure for how good each filter is, and (2) since the filters of a convolutional layer are often correlated, to re-estimate the response map of the filters that are affected by the domain shift using those filters that are not. Here the goal is to obtain a new response map that resembles more the response of a source image for the affected filters. Instead of applying a threshold to decide on a set of good filters and bad filters and use the former set to re-estimate the later which might not be correlated and thus not optimal, we decide which filters to reconstruct and which to use for their reconstruction in one step using a Lasso based optimization problem. Below, we first explain the divergence measure and then proceed to the core of the proposed method.

Divergence Measure. Instead of using the H-divergence that will add an extra cost due the need to train a domain classifier and also the need to have access to sufficient amount of data, we use the KL-divergence [12,13] which is a measure of the difference between two probability distributions, in our case the source distribution P_S and the target distribution P_T. We estimate the probability distribution of the filter response given a small subset of the source data as input and likewise for the target data.

Filter Selection. As we explained before, we want to find the affected filters and the ones to be used in their reconstruction in one step. For that purpose we put each filter under a sanity check where we try to select the set of filters to be used in a regression function that predicts its output. Here, we do not consider the entire filter map, but rather the filter response at each point of the filter map separately, where, given the response of the other filters at this point we want to predict the current response. We use (a subset of) the source data as our training set. Going back to the literature, feature selection for regression has been studied widely. Lasso [14] and Elastic net [15] have shown good performance. We favor Lasso as it introduces the sparsity which is essential in our case to select as few and effective filters as possible. Having the response f_y and the set of predictors f_x, the main equation of Lasso can be written as follows:

$$B^* = argmin_B\{\sum_{i=1}^{n}(f_{y_i} - \beta_0 - \sum_{j=1}^{p} f_{j_{x_i}}\beta_j)^2 + \lambda \sum_{j=1}^{p} |\beta_j|\} \quad (1)$$

where β_0 is the residual, $B = \{\beta_j\}$ the estimated coefficients, n the number of source samples, p the number of filters, and λ a tuning parameter to control the amount of shrinkage needed. Clearly, if we have the response itself as a choice in the filters set, it will be directly selected as it is the most correlated with the output (i.e. itself). What we need to do next is to insert our additional selection criterion, i.e. the KL-divergence, where for each filter f_j, we have computed a KL divergence value, Δ_j^{KL}. We will use this divergence value to guide the selection procedure. This can be achieved by simply plugging the Δ_j^{KL} value in the L_1 norm regularization as follows:

$$B^* = argmin_B\{\sum_{i=1}^{n}(f_{y_i} - \beta_0 - \sum_{j=1}^{p} f_{j_{x_i}}\beta_j)^2 + \lambda \sum_{j=1}^{p} |\Delta_j^{KL} \cdot \beta_j|\} \quad (2)$$

Solving this optimization problem, we obtain the weights vector B^*, with a weight β_j^* for each filter f_j, including the filter we try to reconstruct. If the filter in hand has a non-zero weight, that means it is considered a good filter and we will keep its value. On the other hand, if the filter has zero weight then it will be marked for reconstruction and its set of filters with non-zero weights are used for this purpose.

Reconstruction. After selecting the set of filters to be used for reconstruction $\{f_b\}$, we use the linear regression method to predict the filter output f_{b_y} given the responses of the selected filters. The linear regression is in its turn simple and efficient to compute. As a result, we obtain the final set of coefficients B_b for each bad filter f_b.

Prediction. At test time we receive a target sample x_t. We pass it through the first layer and obtain the response of each filter map. Then, for each bad filter f_b, we use the responses of the selected set of filters to predict a source like response given the coefficients B_b. After that, we pass the reconstructed data to the next layer up to prediction.

3   Experiments

3.1   Setup and Datasets

Office Benchmark [10]: we use three sets of samples: Webcam (W), DSLR (D) and Amazon (A). In addition, we use the gray scale version of the Amazon data (AG). The main task is object recognition. We use Alexnet [9] pretrained on Imagenet and fine-tuned on the Amazon data. We deal with three adaptation problems: A → AG, A → W and A → D. We do not consider D↔W, as with deep features the shift between the two sets is minimal.

Synthetic Traffic Signs → Dark Illumination (Syn→Dark): to imitate the real life condition, we train a traffic signs recognition network [16] on synthetic traffic signs [17] and test it on extreme dark cases that we extract from GSTRB [18]. In all experiments we used 10 % of the target dataset as our available target samples and retain only 1 % of the source for the adaptation purpose.

Baselines: We compare with the following baselines: **No adaptation(NA)** by testing the network fine-tuned on the source dataset directly on the target set without adaptation. **DDC** [8] adapts the last layer of AlexNet. **Subspace Alignment(SA)**[3] is a simple method, yet shows good performance. To make a fair comparison, we take the activations of the last fully connected layer before the classification layer and use them as features for this baseline. We perform the subspace alignment and retrain an SVM with a linear kernel on the aligned source data, then use the learned classifier to predict the labels of the target data. We also show the result of the SVM classifier trained on the source features before alignment(**SVM-fc**). We don't compare with deep DA methods such as DAN and DANN as they are not lightweight and don't fir our specifications.

3.2 Results and Discussion

Table 1 shows the results achieved by different methods. In spite of the method's simplicity and the fact that it is just active on the first layer, we systematically improve over the raw performance obtained without domain adaptation. In the case of low level shift (Syn-Dark and in Amazon-Gray), the method adapts by anticipating the color information of the target dataset, i.e. reconstructing the color filters. In the case of Amazon-Webcam and Amazon-DSLR, the method tries to ignore the background of Webcam and DSLR datasets that is different from the white background in Amazon dataset. Of course in this case there is also a high level shift that can be corrected by adapting the last layer features. In Fig. 2 we show a filter reconstruction example from Amazon-Gray target set where we have the original color image from Amazon and also each filter output which serves as a reference. The method also outperforms the DDC [8] which is dedicated to correct the shift at the last layer only as well as SA [3] where the method improvement was moderate.

Table 1. Recognition accuracies of our method and the baselines

Method	A→W	A→D	A→AG	Syn→Dark
CNN(NA)	60.5	65.8	94.8	75.0
DDC [8]	61.8	64.4	-	-
SVM-fc(NA)	60.5	61.5	95.0	74.0
SA	61.8	61.5	95.2	76.1
Filter reconstruction (Our)	**62.0**	**67.2**	**97.0**	**80.0**

Fig. 2. From left to right: a sample image from Amazon, the corresponding gray image, the output of a bad filter w.r.t. the color image, the output of the same bad filter w.r.t. the gray image and the reconstructed output. (Color figure online)

4   Conclusion

In this work, we aim to push the limits of unsupervised domain adaptation methods to settings where we have few samples and limited resources to adapt, both in terms of memory and time. To this end, we perform an analysis of the output of a deep network from a domain adaptation point of view. We deduce that even though filters of the first layer seem relatively generic, domain shift issues already manifest themselves at this early stage. Therefore, we advocate that the adaptation process should start from the early layers rather than just adapting the last layer features, as is often done in the literature. Guided by this analysis, we propose a new method that corrects the low level shift without retraining the network. The proposed method is suitable when moving a system to a new environment and can be seen as a preprocessing step that requires just a few images to be functional.

Acknowledgment. This work was supported by the FWO project "Representations of and algorithms for the captation, visualization and manipulation of moving 3D objects, subjects and scenes". The first author PhD is funded by the FWO scholarship.

References

1. Ganin, Y., Ustinova, E., Ajakan, H., Germain, P., Larochelle, H., Laviolette, F., Marchand, M., Lempitsky, V.: Domain-adversarial training of neural networks. J. Mach. Learn. Res. **17**(59), 1–35 (2016)
2. Long, M., Wang, J.: Learning transferable features with deep adaptation networks. CoRR abs/1502.02791, **1**, 2 (2015)
3. Fernando, B., Habrard, A., Sebban, M., Tuytelaars, T.: Unsupervised visual domain adaptation using subspace alignment. In: Proceedings of the IEEE International Conference on Computer Vision, pp. 2960–2967 (2013)
4. Gong, B., Grauman, K., Sha, F.: Connecting the dots with landmarks: discriminatively learning domain-invariant features for unsupervised domain adaptation. In: Proceedings of The 30th International Conference on Machine Learning, pp. 222–230 (2013)
5. Gopalan, R., Li, R., Chellappa, R.: Domain adaptation for object recognition: an unsupervised approach. In: 2011 IEEE International Conference on Computer Vision (ICCV), pp. 999–1006. IEEE (2011)
6. Tommasi, T., Patricia, N., Caputo, B., Tuytelaars, T.: A deeper look at dataset bias. In: Gall, J., Gehler, P., Leibe, B. (eds.) GCPR 2015. LNCS, vol. 9358, pp. 504–516. Springer, Heidelberg (2015). doi:10.1007/978-3-319-24947-6_42
7. Donahue, J., Jia, Y., Vinyals, O., Hoffman, J., Zhang, N., Tzeng, E., Darrell, T.: DeCAF: a deep convolutional activation feature for generic visual recognition. arXiv preprint arXiv:1310.1531 (2013)
8. Tzeng, E., Hoffman, J., Zhang, N., Saenko, K., Darrell, T.: Deep domain confusion: maximizing for domain invariance. arXiv preprint arXiv:1412.3474 (2014)
9. Krizhevsky, A., Sutskever, I., Hinton, G.E.: Imagenet classification with deep convolutional neural networks. In: Advances in neural information processing systems, pp. 1097–1105 (2012)
10. Saenko, K., Kulis, B., Fritz, M., Darrell, T.: Adapting visual category models to new domains. In: Daniilidis, K., Maragos, P., Paragios, N. (eds.) ECCV 2010. LNCS, vol. 6314, pp. 213–226. Springer, Heidelberg (2010). doi:10.1007/978-3-642-15561-1_16
11. Ben-David, S., Blitzer, J., Crammer, K., Pereira, F., et al.: Analysis of representations for domain adaptation. Adv. Neural Inf. Process. Syst. **19**, 137 (2007)
12. Kullback, S., Leibler, R.A.: On information and sufficiency. Ann. Math. Statist. **22**(1), 79–86 (1951)

13. Kullback, S.: Letter to the editor: the kullback-leibler distance (1987)
14. Tibshirani, R.: Regression shrinkage and selection via the lasso. J. Roy. Stat. Soc.: Ser. B (Methodol.) **58**, 267–288 (1996)
15. Zou, H., Hastie, T.: Regularization and variable selection via the elastic net. J. Roy. Stat. Soc.: Ser. B (Stat. Methodol.) **67**(2), 301–320 (2005)
16. Cireşan, D., Meier, U., Masci, J., Schmidhuber, J.: Multi-column deep neural network for traffic sign classification. Neural Netw. **32**, 333–338 (2012)
17. Moiseev, B., Konev, A., Chigorin, A., Konushin, A.: Evaluation of traffic sign recognition methods trained on synthetically generated data. In: Blanc-Talon, J., Kasinski, A., Philips, W., Popescu, D., Scheunders, P. (eds.) ACIVS 2013. LNCS, vol. 8192, pp. 576–583. Springer, Heidelberg (2013). doi:10.1007/978-3-319-02895-8_52
18. Sermanet, P., LeCun, Y.: Traffic sign recognition with multi-scale convolutional networks. In: The 2011 International Joint Conference on Neural Networks (IJCNN), pp. 2809–2813. IEEE (2011)

Deep Attributes for One-Shot Face Recognition

Aishwarya Jadhav[1,3]($\boxtimes$), Vinay P. Namboodiri[2], and K.S. Venkatesh[3]

[1] Xerox Research Center India, Bengaluru, India
aishwaryauj@gmail.com
[2] Department of Computer Science, IIT Kanpur, Kanpur, India
vinaypn@iitk.ac.in
[3] Department of Electrical Engineering, IIT Kanpur, Kanpur, India
venkats@iitk.ac.in

Abstract. We address the problem of one-shot unconstrained face recognition. This is addressed by using a deep attribute representation of faces. While face recognition has considered the use of attribute based representations, for one-shot face recognition, the methods proposed so far have been using different features that represent the limited example available. We postulate that by using an intermediate attribute representation, it is possible to outperform purely face based feature representation for one-shot recognition. We use two one-shot face recognition techniques based on exemplar SVM and one-shot similarity kernel to compare face based deep feature representations against deep attribute based representation. The evaluation on standard dataset of 'Labeled faces in the wild' suggests that deep attribute based representations can outperform deep feature based face representations for this problem of one-shot face recognition.

Keywords: Face recognition · Attributes · One-shot classification

1 Introduction

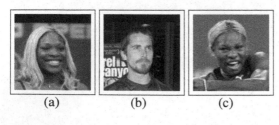

(a)   (b)   (c)

Fig. 1. Given a query image (a), the task is to determine if it resembles (b) or (c)

Consider that we have seen a face. How would we go about recognizing the face that we have seen only once? The problem of recognizing examples from a single training example is termed one shot recognition. The task becomes especially challenging for unconstrained pose with variable illumination setting ("in the wild"). While, the problem of face recognition has been widely studied in computer vision [2], that of one shot face recognition has not yet been as well studied. In this paper, we focus on this scenario.

© Springer International Publishing Switzerland 2016
G. Hua and H. Jégou (Eds.): ECCV 2016 Workshops, Part III, LNCS 9915, pp. 516–523, 2016.
DOI: 10.1007/978-3-319-49409-8_44

Our approach towards solving this problem is based on a deep attribute based description of a face. While, this approach was prevalent some time back [4], lately this approach has been overshadowed. Current computer vision related research has shown great progress in describing faces using deep neural network based approaches [11,16]. These have shown remarkable performance for unconstrained face recognition in real world settings. However, these make use of a large number of training data for training for face recognition. One commonly used option is that of pre-training these deep neural networks using large amount of training data, and then using them as a means to obtain high-level features, which are then matched for face recognition.

The task of one shot recognition differs from the general datasets in that we have at least one sample of the test class. We can make use of the limited information in training in order to obtain a better representation of the class. To solve the problem, we evaluate two classes of methods, one that is based on the deep learned face feature and the other that is based on attribute based features. Our evaluation suggests that for one shot recognition, attribute based one-shot methods outperforms the deep learned face features. We further analyse this performance in different settings.

Table 1 shows importance of attribute based representation in face recognition where the list of attribute scores predicted by CNN suggest that person (a) must resemble person (c) which is evident in Fig. 1.

Through this paper we make the following contributions:

(1) We show that attribute based deep feature representation outperforms deep learned face features in one-shot face recognition.
(2) We observe that a one-shot recognition system that uses the attribute based deep representation from the pre-final layer output of a convolutional neural network is more suited for various one-shot face recognition settings.

2   Related Work

Table 1. L: labels of groundtruth '0': absence '1': presence of attribute. P: probability score of attribute predicted by our CNN. Score clearly shows that face (a) is more closer to (c) than (b). Thus concatenating these attribute scores gives a good representation of face. Our attribute representation is of higher dimension and these outputs are shown for illustration of the concept

Attribute	L (a)	P (a)	L (b)	P (b)	L (c)	P (c)
Male	0	0.0333	1	1.0000	0	0.1097
Blond hair	1	0.9990	0	0.0000	1	0.8589
Mustache	0	0.0083	1	0.9998	0	0.0035
Black hair	0	0.0000	0	0.4984	0	0.0000
Oval face	0	0.0722	0	0.0014	0	0.0439
Cheekbones	1	1.0000	0	0.0000	1	0.9913
Pointy nose	0	0.0005	1	0.5039	0	0.0007
Chubby	0	0.0019	0	0.0146	0	0.0727

There have been a number of techniques that address one-shot recognition. One such set of methods make use of Bayesian formulation to categorise objects [7,13].

Another stream in one-shot learning focuses on building generative models to build extra examples [5]. These methods rely on elaborate feature vector representations. There have also been a number of interesting discriminative methods like [18] and [9] that explicitly make use of the one-shot recognition setting. In this paper, we evaluate both these methods for one-shot recognition.

All the models described above do not explore ways to generalise concepts learnt from one or few examples. Generalization of semantic concepts based on attributes has been widely studied in the problem of zero shot learning [6, 10, 14]. However, these ideas have not been explored in the context of one-shot learning. There has been several works that address the task of obtaining attribute based representations for faces [4, 8, 19]. We compare our attribute prediction results with the results in [8].

3 Method

3.1 Deep Attribute Representation

We first obtain attribute vectors of face images using convolutional neural networks (CNN). The architecture of our CNN (Fig. 2) is similar to VGG-Face CNN [11]. The filters in CNN are initialised with pre-trained parameters from VGG-Face CNN. For each attribute a separate CNN is trained in binary classification setting.

3.2 Exemplar-SVM

In Exemplar-SVM [9] a separate linear SVM is trained for each face in positive training set using negative faces. A set of negative faces does not contain any face from positive training identities. The final identity of the query face is then predicted by comparing calibrated scores of all SVMs. If x is input and f(x) is decision value given by SVM, the calibrated score is given by

$$p(x) = \frac{1}{e^{Af(x)+B}} \tag{1}$$

where A and B are estimated independently for each Exemplar-SVM. Calculating calibrated scores generalises output of all SVM and makes them comparable. Higher score indicates the query face is closer to the positive face on which corresponding SVM is trained.

3.3 One-Shot Similarity

In this approach we use one-shot similarity (OSS) kernel to train SVM. In this, similarity between two faces is calculated by first learning a model for each face with a set of negatives and then these models are used to predict similarity between the two faces [17]. Wolf et al. [18] show that for free-scale Linear Discriminant Analysis (LDA), one shot similarity score and its exponent can be used as kernels in one versus all SVM.

Let A be set of negatives of size n_A containing feature vectors a_i. m_A and S are mean and covariance of vectors in A. S is given by

$$S = \frac{1}{n_A} \sum_{i=1}^{n_A} (a_i - m_A)(a_i - m_A)^T \tag{2}$$

In case of binary classification, consider two positive faces are represented by feature vectors x and y. Their one-shot similarity with free-scale LDA (Linear Discriminant Analysis) is given by

$$OSS(x,y) = (x - m_A)^T S^+ \left(y - \frac{x + m_A}{2} \right) (y - m_A)^T S^+ \left(x - \frac{y + m_A}{2} \right) \quad (3)$$

where S^+ is pseudo-inverse of S. Using above formula, similarity score between two training faces is calculated which is then used to train SVM classifier.

4 Experiment

4.1 Dataset

We use Large-scale CelebFaces Attributes (CelebA) dataset [15] (202599 face images and 40 binary attributes) to train CNN for attribute classification. The test dataset is LFW dataset [3].

4.2 Deep Attribute Representation

For all the attributes, we fine tuned CNN (Fig. 2) using randomly chosen 10000 images from CelebA dataset. Randomly cropped and horizontally flipped with probability 0.5 patches of 224×224 size of rescaled images are fed to the network. We do not apply any alignment to input images. Learning rate is varied from 10e-4 to 10e-6.

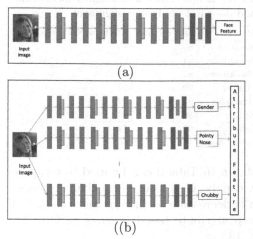

(a)

((b))

Fig. 2. Architecture of VGG-CNN shown in figure (a). Each colour block represents a specific layer given by Blue: Convolutional Layer +ReLu, Green: Max pooling, purple: Fully Connected and Brown: ReLu. Figure (b) shows collection of CNN from figure (a) (Color figure online)

The performance of fine tuned CNNs is evaluated on LFW dataset for attribute prediction. The results are given in the Table 2. It can be seen that even though our CNNs are fine tuned with limited number of training images, they predict attributes with good accuracy compared to LNets+ANet.

While choosing 8 attributes to represent face for one-shot recognition, we have considered several points [4]:

(1) Attributes which are related to accessories or facial expression are not considered for selection. (2) From Eq. 3, complexity to calculate one-shot similarity kernel per pair is $O(d^2)$ where d = 4096*n and n

is number of attributes. (3) More accurate classifier is more likely to extract true attribute features. (4) An attribute which is specific to a region of face is more likely to help in recognition. We use five local attributes Pointy Nose, High Cheekbone, Black Hair, Blond Hair, Mustache and remaining three are global.

The output of the pre-final fully connected layer is used as descriptor of that attribute while binary output of CNN is used for attribute prediction. A single vector of size 8*4096 is then formed by concatenating descriptors of 8 attributes for each face image and used as its deep attribute based representation.

4.3   One-Shot Face Recognition

To evaluate performance of one-shot face recognition, we follow experiments given in [18]. We use positive set as subset of 6733 images of 610 identities from LFW dataset such that each has at least 4 images. Negative examples are images of identities having only one image each from LFW. Negative set is formed by randomly choosing 1000 negative examples.

To compare performance of one-shot face recognition with [18], we vary number of identities by 5, 10, 20 and 50. For each identity we randomly select two probe images and two gallery images from positive set. Then we compare performance of two one-shot methods by training Exemplar-SVMs and OSS-SVM with deep attribute descriptors of gallery images and negative images. We use Libsvm [1] to train all SVMs. Calibration score is calculated in Libsvm by using improved Platt method [12].

For each number of identities, 20 repetitions are performed by randomly choosing different identities in each iteration. The result of test accuracy in terms of mean and standard deviation is shown in Table 3. As per our knowledge, there are no experimental results available for one-shot face recognition on LFW dataset

Table 2. Percentage accuracy of attribute classification on LFW. LNets+Anet uses aligned faces while our method does not apply any alignment

Attribute	Our method	LNets+ANet [8]
Black hair	86	90
Blond hair	94	97
Cheekbones	81	88
Chubby	90	73
Mustache	93	92
Gender	96	94
Oval face	69	74
Pointy nose	73	80

more recent than [18]. So accuracies shown in Table 3 can be used to compare any future work on this task. Also it can be seen that as number of classes increase to 50, accuracy of recognition is decreasing as there is more chance of misclassification. Also as expected, deep attribute based features perform far better than bag of features taken from [18].

4.4   Face Representation vs Deep Attribute Representation

In this experiment, we select 10 identities randomly from positive set and repeat exactly same steps as above experiment in Sect. 4.3 using attribute based representation of faces. These experiments are further repeated when images are

Table 3. Results of one-shot face recognition for different classes using Bag of features (BoF) representation (first row) and deep attribute representation (last two rows) with Exemplar-SVM (E-SVM) and OSS-SVM

Class	5	10	20	50
OSS (BoF) [18]	0.7550 ± 0.1432	0.7300 ± 0.0768	0.7000 ± 0.0782	0.5855 ± 0.0365
E-SVM	0.9600 ± 0.0730	0.9375 ± 0.0521	0.8887 ± 0.0539	0.8407 ± 0.0366
OSS	0.9600 ± 0.0940	0.9450 ± 0.0473	0.8887 ± 0.0573	0.8613 ± 0.0413

represented as VGG-Face descriptors. The results are shown in Table 4. It can be seen that, deep attribute features give more accurate recognition results than using just deep learned face features for each of the three methods. Also exponential OSS-SVM trained with deep attribute features gives most accurate performance.

Table 4. Comparisons of accuracy and standard deviation for 10 identities represented by VGG-face and attribute descriptors with Exemplar-SVM (E-SVM), SVM with free-scale LDA OSS kernel and exponential of OSS kernel. Attribute features perform better than face features

Input	ESVM	OSS	Exponential OSS
VGG-Face	0.9075 ± 0.0638	0.9000 ± 0.0725	0.9100 ± 0.0815
Attribute	0.9250 ± 0.0829	0.9250 ± 0.0512	0.9300 ± 0.068

Figure 3 shows comparison of accuracies during testing with VGG-Face and deep attribute descriptors when the experiment is repeated 20 times. For most of the experiments, attribute features perform better than face features.

In OSS based SVM, positive faces are first compared with each other using similarity scores. These scores are then used determine decision boundaries in the similarity space. In Exemplar-SVM, one compares a positive sample with a fixed set of negatives and the scores of other positive samples are not considered. As a result of these differences, it can be seen that Exponential OSS-SVM performs better than Exemplar-SVM.

In these experiments the deep attribute based feature vectors are observed to perform better. These encode both the characteristics of faces as well as specific attribute characteristics. As explained earlier, in one-shot recognition knowledge from negative examples is used to generalise concepts learnt from one or few positive examples. Attributes provide better generalisation than face features over negative and positive identities. Attribute feature space has higher dimension than face feature space. Also, since each attribute is represented by 4096 vector, we believe that it contains much higher level description of that attribute for a person.

Due to all these advantages of attribute features over face features, attribute space enables one-shot methods to characterise entire positive identity from one example using knowledge acquired from other identities. Hence the attributes aid in face recognition and therefore as expected, we observe the performance of attribute based feature vectors to be better.

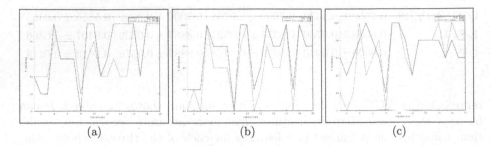

(a)   (b)   (c)

Fig. 3. Accuracy for 20 repetitions of experiment using VGG-Face and attribute descriptors with classifiers (a) Exemplar-SVM (b) OSS kernel (c) Exponential of OSS

5   Conclusion

In this paper we have proposed the use of deep attribute based representation for one-shot face recognition. The deep attribute representations are obtained by fine-tuning a deep CNN for face recognition on data for specific attributes such as gender and shape of face. While, specific face information is challenging, it is far more easier to obtain attribute related information. We observed that the face features when further adapted by various attributes yield consistent improvement in accuracy for one-shot recognition. This was observed for two different methods, one-shot recognition using Exemplar-SVM based and one-shot similarity kernel based techniques. In future we would be interested in exploring the kind of attributes that are useful for improving face recognition.

References

1. Chang, C., Lin, C.: LIBSVM: a library for support vector machines. ACM Trans. Intelli. Syst. Technol. (TIST) **2**(3), 27 (2011)
2. Ding, C., Tao, D.: A comprehensive survey on pose-invariant face recognition. ACM Trans. Intell. Syst. Technol. **7**(3), 37:1–37:42 (2016)
3. Huang, G.B., Ramesh, M., Berg, T., Learned-Miller, E.: Labeled faces in the wild: a database for studying face recognition in unconstrained environments. Technical report 07–49, University of Massachusetts, Amherst (2007)
4. Kumar, N., Berg, A.C., Belhumeur, P.N., Nayar, S.K.: Describable visual attributes for face verification and image search. IEEE Trans. Pattern Anal. Mach. Intell. **33**(10), 1962–1977 (2011)
5. Lake, B.M., Salakhutdinov, R., Gross, J., Tenenbaum, J.B.: One shot learning of simple visual concepts. In: Proceedings of the 33rd Annual Conference of the Cognitive Science Society, vol. 172, p. 2 (2011)

6. Lampert, C.H., Nickisch, H., Harmeling, S.: Attribute-based classification for zero-shot visual object categorization. IEEE Trans. Pattern Anal. Mach. Intell. **36**(3), 453–465 (2014)
7. Li, F.F., Fergus, R., Perona, P.: One-shot learning of object categories. IEEE Trans. Pattern Anal. Mach. Intell. **28**(4), 594–611 (2006)
8. Liu, Z., Luo, P., Wang, X., Tang, X.: Deep learning face attributes in the wild. In: Proceedings of the IEEE International Conference on Computer Vision, pp. 3730–3738 (2015)
9. Malisiewicz, T., Gupta, A., Efros, A.A.: Ensemble of exemplar-svms for object detection and beyond. In: 2011 IEEE International Conference on Computer Vision (ICCV), pp. 89–96. IEEE (2011)
10. Palatucci, M., Pomerleau, D., Hinton, G.E., Mitchell, T.M.: Zero-shot learning with semantic output codes. In: Advances in neural information processing systems. pp. 1410–1418 (2009)
11. Parkhi, O.M., Vedaldi, A., Zisserman, A.: Deep face recognition. Proc. Br. Mach. Vis. **1**(3), 6 (2015)
12. Platt, J., et al.: Probabilistic outputs for support vector machines and comparisons to regularized likelihood methods. Adv. Large Margin Classif. **10**(3), 61–74 (1999)
13. Salakhutdinov, R., Tenenbaum, J., Torralba, A.: One-shot learning with a hierarchical nonparametric Bayesian model (2010)
14. Socher, R., Ganjoo, M., Manning, C.D., Ng, A.: Zero-shot learning through cross-modal transfer. In: Advances in Neural Information Processing Systems, pp. 935–943 (2013)
15. Sun, Y., Chen, Y., Wang, X., Tang, X.: Deep learning face representation by joint identification-verification. In: Advances in Neural Information Processing Systems, pp. 1988–1996 (2014)
16. Taigman, Y., Yang, M., Ranzato, M., Wolf, L.: Deepface: closing the gap to human-level performance in face verification. In: Proceedings of the IEEE Conference on Computer Vision and Pattern Recognition, pp. 1701–1708 (2014)
17. Wolf, L., Hassner, T., Taigman, Y.: Descriptor based methods in the wild. In: Workshop on Faces in 'Real-Life' Images: Detection, Alignment, and Recognition (2008)
18. Wolf, L., Hassner, T., Taigman, Y.: The one-shot similarity kernel. In: 2009 IEEE 12th International Conference on Computer Vision, pp. 897–902. IEEE (2009)
19. Zhang, N., Paluri, M., Ranzato, M., Darrell, T., Bourdev, L.: Panda: pose aligned networks for deep attribute modeling. In: Proceedings of the IEEE Conference on Computer Vision and Pattern Recognition, pp. 1637–1644 (2014)

Hard Negative Mining for Metric Learning Based Zero-Shot Classification

Maxime Bucher[1,2], Stéphane Herbin[1(✉)], and Frédéric Jurie[2]

[1] ONERA - The French Aerospace Lab, Palaiseau, France
stephane.herbin@onera.fr
[2] Normandie Univ, UNICAEN, ENSICAEN, CNRS, Caen, France

Abstract. Zero-Shot learning has been shown to be an efficient strategy
for domain adaptation. In this context, this paper builds on the recent
work of Bucher *et al.* [1], which proposed an approach to solve Zero-
Shot classification problems (ZSC) by introducing a novel metric learning based objective function. This objective function allows to learn an
optimal embedding of the attributes jointly with a measure of similarity between images and attributes. This paper extends their approach
by proposing several schemes to control the generation of the negative
pairs, resulting in a significant improvement of the performance and giving above state-of-the-art results on three challenging ZSC datasets.

Keywords: Domain adaptation · Zero-shot learning · Hard negative
mining · Bootstrapping

1 Introduction

Among the different image interpretation methods exploiting some kind of
knowledge transfer in their design, Zero Shot Classification (ZSC) can be considered as a domain adaptation problem where the new target domain is defined
using an intermediate level of representation made of human understandable
semantic attributes. The source domain is defined by an annotated image database expected to capture the relation between data and attribute based representation of classes.

Most of the recent approaches addressing ZSC [2–8] rely on the computation
of a similarity function in the semantic space. They learn the semantic embedding, either from data or from class description, and compare the embedded data
using standard distance.

Recently, [1] proposed to add a metric learning (ML) step to adapt empirically the similarity distance in the embedding space, leading to a multi-objective
criterion optimizing both the metric and the embedding. The metric is learned
using an empirical optimized criterion on random but equally sampled pairs of
similar (positive) and dissimilar (negative) data.

In this paper, following observations from the active learning community (see
e.g., [9]), we show that a careful choice of the negative pairs combined with the
multi-objective criterion proposed in [1] leads to above state of the art results.

© Springer International Publishing Switzerland 2016
G. Hua and H. Jégou (Eds.): ECCV 2016 Workshops, Part III, LNCS 9915, pp. 524–531, 2016.
DOI: 10.1007/978-3-319-49409-8_45

2   Improved ZSL by Efficient Hard Negative Mining

In a recent work, Bucher *et al.* [1] introduced a metric learning step in their zero-shot classification pipeline. Their model is trained from pairs of data, where positive (resp. negative) pairs are obtained by taking the training images associated with their own provided attribute vector (resp. by randomly assigning attribute vector of another image) and are assigned to the class label '1' (resp. '−1'). The set of positive pairs are denoted $\mathbf{D}_+$ in the following, and $\mathbf{D}_-$ for the negatives. This paper investigates improved ways to select negative pairs.

2.1   Bucher *et al.* Metric Learning Framework for Zero-Shot Classification

This section summarizes Bucher *et al.* [1] paper, to which the reader should refer for more details. Zero-shot classification problem is cast into an optimal framework of the form:

$$\mathbf{Y}^* = \arg\min_{\mathbf{Y} \in \mathcal{Y}} S(\mathbf{X}, \mathbf{Y}),$$

where $\mathbf{X}$ is an image, $\mathbf{Y}$ a vector of attributes and S a parametric similarity measure. A metric matrix denoted as $\mathbf{W}_A$ transforms the attribute embedding space into a space where the Euclidean distance can be used. The similarity between images and attributes is computed as:

$$S(\mathbf{X}, \mathbf{Y}) = \left\| (\hat{\mathbf{A}}_X(\mathbf{X}) - \mathbf{Y})^T \mathbf{W}_A \right\|_2 \tag{1}$$

where $\hat{\mathbf{A}}_X$ embeds the $\mathbf{X}$ modality into the space of $\mathbf{Y}$ using a linear transformation combined with a ReLU type transfer function:

$$\hat{\mathbf{A}}_X(\mathbf{X}) = \max(0, \mathbf{X}^T \mathbf{W}_X + \mathbf{b}_X). \tag{2}$$

The role of learning is to estimate jointly the two matrices $\mathbf{W}_X$ and $\mathbf{W}_A$. The empirical learning criterion used is the sum of 3 terms:

(i) a term for the metric $\mathbf{W}_A$:

$$l_H(\mathbf{X}_i, \mathbf{Y}_i, Z_i, \tau) = \max\left(0, 1 - Z_i(\tau - S(\mathbf{X}_i, \mathbf{Y}_i)^2)\right). \tag{3}$$

where Z_i states that the two modalities are consistent ($Z_i = 1$) or not ($Z_i = -1$). τ is the threshold separating similar and dissimilar examples.

(ii) a quadratic loss for the linear attribute prediction $\mathbf{W}_X$ (only applied to positive pairs):

$$l_A(\mathbf{X}_i, \mathbf{Y}_i, Z_i) = \max(0, Z_i) . \left\| \mathbf{Y}_i - \hat{\mathbf{A}}_X(\mathbf{X}_i) \right\|_2^2 . \tag{4}$$

(iii) a quadratic penalization to prevent overfitting:

$$R(\mathbf{W}_A, \mathbf{W}_X, \mathbf{b}_X) = \|\mathbf{W}_X\|_F^2 + \|\mathbf{b}_X\|_2^2 + \|\mathbf{W}_A\|_F^2 \tag{5}$$

The overall objective function can then now be written as the sum of the previously defined terms:

$$\mathcal{L}(\mathbf{W}_A, \mathbf{W}_X, \mathbf{b}_X, \tau) = \sum_i l_H(\mathbf{X}_i, \mathbf{Y}_i, Z_i, \tau) + \lambda \sum_i l_A(\mathbf{X}_i, \mathbf{Y}_i, Z_i)$$
$$+ \mu R(\mathbf{W}_A, \mathbf{W}_X, \mathbf{b}_X) \tag{6}$$

In this context, ZSC is achieved by finding the most consistent attribute description from a set of exclusive attribute class descriptors $\{\mathbf{Y}_k^*\}_{k=1}^C$ given the image where k, is the index of a class:

$$k^* = \arg \min_{k \in \{1...C\}} S(\mathbf{X}, \mathbf{Y}_k^*) \tag{7}$$

2.2 Hard Negative Mining

In a metric learning problem, while the set of positive pairs $\mathbf{D}_+$ is fixed and given by the training set with one pair per positive image, the set of negative pairs $\mathbf{D}_-$ can be chosen more freely; indeed, as there are many more ways of being different than being equal, the number of negative and positive pairs may not be identical. Moreover, we will see that increasing the size of $\mathbf{D}_-$ compared to that of $\mathbf{D}_+$ by some factor n leads to better overall results.

In the following, we explore three different strategies to sample the distribution of negative pairs using several learning epochs: we first present a variant of the method of [1] and then describe two iterative greedy schemes.

Random. In [1], negative pairs are obtained by associating a training image with an attribute vector chosen randomly among those of other seen classes, with one negative pair for each positive one. As a variant, we propose to generate randomly n negative pairs (instead of one) for each positive pair, chosen as in [1], *i.e.*, by randomly sampling the set of attribute vectors from the other classes. We include in the objective function a penalization to compensate for the unbalance between positive and negative pairs (see Sect. 2.3).

Uncertainty. This strategy is inspired by hard mining for object detection [9–12] and consists in selecting the most informative negative pairs and iteratively updating the scoring function given by Eq. (1). We denote by $S_t(\mathbf{X}, \mathbf{Y})$ this score at time t. During training, each time step t corresponds to a learning epoch. At the first epoch, $S_1(\mathbf{X}, \mathbf{Y})$ is learned using the random negative pairs of [1]. At each time t each pair of training image $\mathbf{X}_i$ and candidate annotation $\mathbf{Y}$ coming from different (but seen) classes is ranked according to the uncertainty score:

$$u_t(\mathbf{Y}|\mathbf{X}_i) = \exp(-(S_t(\mathbf{X}_i, \mathbf{Y}) - S_t(\mathbf{X}_i, \mathbf{Y}^*))) \tag{8}$$

where $\mathbf{Y}^*$ is the true vector of attributes of $\mathbf{X}_i$. The vector of attributes which are most similar to the actual one while coming from different classes are the most relevant for improving the model. We define a probability of generating the pair based on this similarity score and sample this distribution.

Uncertainty/Correlation. We propose to improve the previous approach by taking into account the intra-class correlation. The underlying principle governing the selection is that the most correlated vectors of attribute, in a given class, are the most useful ones to consider. The correlation can be measured by:

$$q(\mathbf{Y}) = \exp \left(\frac{-1}{|\mathcal{Y}_k|} \sum_{\mathbf{Y}' \in \mathcal{Y}_k} \|\mathbf{Y} - \mathbf{Y}'\|_2 \right) \tag{9}$$

where k is the true class index of $\mathbf{Y}$ and $\mathcal{Y}_k$ is the set of attribute vector representations.

A trade-off between uncertainty and correlation is obtained globally by using the following scoring function:

$$p_t(\mathbf{Y}|\mathbf{X}_i) = u_t(\mathbf{Y}|\mathbf{X}_i) * q(\mathbf{Y}) \tag{10}$$

where each image attribute vector $\mathbf{Y}$ at epoch t has a score of p_t to be associated with $\mathbf{X}_i$. The current set of negative pairs $\mathbf{D}_-$ at epoch t is obtained by iteratively increasing the set with new data sampled according to Eq. (10).

2.3   Adaptation of the Objective Function

The original learning criterion (6), such as defined in [1], assumes that negative and positive pairs are evenly distributed. This is not the case in the proposed approach: the criterion must be adapted to compensate for the imbalance between positive and negative pairs, by weighting the positive and negative pairs according to their frequencies:

$$\mathcal{L}(\mathbf{W}_A, \mathbf{W}_X, \mathbf{b}_X, \tau) = \frac{1}{|\mathbf{D}_+|} \left(\sum_{i \in \mathbf{D}_+} l_H(\mathbf{X_i}, \mathbf{Y_i}, Z_i, \tau) + \lambda l_A(\mathbf{X_i}, \mathbf{Y_i}, Z_i) \right)$$
$$+ \frac{1}{|\mathbf{D}_-|} \left(\sum_{j \in \mathbf{D}_-} l_H(\mathbf{X_j}, \mathbf{Y_j}, Z_j, \tau) \right) + \mu R(\mathbf{W}_A, \mathbf{W}_X, \mathbf{b}_X) \tag{11}$$

This criterion is updated at each new epoch when learning the model.

3   Experiments

Datasets. In this section we evaluate the proposed hard mining strategy on different challenging zero-shot learning tasks, by doing experiments on the 4 following public datasets: aPascal&aYahoo (aP&Y) [13], Animals with Attributes

Table 1. Zero-shot classification accuracy (mean ± std) on 5 runs. We report results with VGG-verydeep-19 [18] features. unc./cor. = *Uncertainty/Correlation* method. The unc./cor. method can't be apply to the AwA dataset since all images of the same class have the same attributes, contrarily to the aP&Y, CUB and SUN datasets.

Feat.	Method	aP&Y	AwA	CUB	SUN
VGG-VeryDeep [18]	Lampert *et al.* [2]	38.16	57.23	-	72.00
	Romera-Paredes and Torr [4]	24.22 ± 2.89	75.32 ± 2.28	-	82.10 ± 0.32
	Zhang and Saligrama [5]	46.23 ± 0.53	76.33 ± 0.83	30.41 ± 0.20	82.50±1.32
	Zhang and Saligrama [6]	50.35 ± 2.97	80.46 ± 0.53	42.11 ± 0.55	83.83±0.29
	Wang and Chen [7]	-	78.3	48.6 ± 0.8	-
	Bucher *et al.* [1]	53.15 ± 0.88	77.32 ± 1.03	43.29 ± 0.38	84.41 ± 0.71
	Ours 'random'	54.41 ± 1.47	83.48 ± 0.99	43.79 ± 0.68	85.98 ± 1.14
	Ours 'uncertainty'	56.01 ± 0.58	**86.55 ± 1.07**	45.41 ± 0.10	**86.21 ± 0.88**
	Ours 'unc./cor.'	**56.77 ± 0.75**	-	45.87 ± 0.34	86.10 ± 1.09

(AwA) [14], CUB-200-2011 (CUB) [15] and SUN attribute (SUN) [16] datasets. They have been designed to evaluate ZSC methods and contain a large number of categories (indoor and outdoor scenes, objects, person, animals, *etc.*) described using various semantic attributes (shape, material, color, part name *etc.*). To make comparisons with previous works possible, we used the same training/testing splits as [13] (aP&Y), [14] (AwA), [3] CUB and [17] (SUN).

Image Features. For each dataset, we used the VGG-VeryDeep-19 [18] CNN models, pre-trained on imageNet (without fine tuning) and extract the fully connected layer (*e.g.*, FC7 4096-d) for representing the images.

Hyper-parameters. To estimate the three hyper-parameters (λ, the dimensionality of the metric space (m) and μ) we apply a grid search validation procedure by randomly keeping 20 % of the training classes. $\mathbf{W}_A$ and $\mathbf{W}_X$ are randomly initialized with normal distribution and optimized with stochastic gradient descent.

3.1   Zero-Shot Classification

The experiments follow the standard ZSC protocol: during training, a set of images from known classes is available for learning the model parameters. At test time, images from unseen classes have to be assigned to one of the possible classes. Classes are described by a vector of attributes. Performance is measured by mean accuracy and std over the classes.

Tables 1 and 2 show the performance given by our hard-mining approach, which outperforms previous methods on 3 of the 4 datasets by more than 3 % on average (+9 % on AwA). The smart selection of negative pairs plays a role on the decision boundaries especially where classes have close attribute descriptions. We did not compare our results with [3] or [8] as they use different

Table 2. Zero-shot classification accuracy (mean ± std) on aP&Y dataset as a function of the ratio of positive/negative pairs.

Method/#neg. pair	1	10	50	100
Random	53.15 ± 0.88	53.98 ± 0.79	54.41 ± 1.47	54.37 ± 1.05
Uncertainty	55.47 ± 1.00	55.84 ± 1.09	55.48 ± 1.37	56.01 ± 0.58
Uncertainty/correlation	**56.08 ± 0.41**	**56.05 ± 0.54**	**56.69 ± 1.78**	**56.77 ± 0.75**

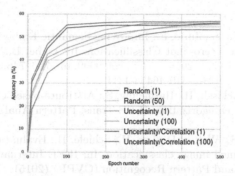

Fig. 1. Evolution of the performance as a function of the number of epochs, on the aP&Y dataset, with a neg/pos ratio of 1 and 100.

image features. The 2 alternatives explored in the paper (*Uncertainty* vs *Uncertainty/Correlation*) give similar performance, but, as shown in the next section *Uncertainty/Correlation* is faster.

3.2 Performance as a Function of the Ratio of Positive/Negative Pair

Table 2 give accuracy performances on aP&Y dataset for the three methods in function of the number of negative examples for each positive pair. Bucher *et al.* [1] configuration corresponds to random method with one negative example per positive one. Our new negative pair selection method have a strong impact on the performance with a noticeable mean improvement of 3%. Augmenting the ratio of negative pairs over positive ones has a positive influence on the accuracy.

3.3 Convergence

We also made experiments to evaluate the impact of the hard mining selection on the convergence during training. Figure 1 shows that *Uncertainty/Correlation* converges around 4 times faster than the *Uncertainty* and *Random* methods. This confirms the fact that more informative (negative) pairs are selected with this strategy. The negative/positive ratio has a (small) positive impact on the convergence.

4   Conclusions

This paper extended the original work of Bucher *et al.* [1] by proposing a novel hard negative mining approach used during training. The proposed selection strategy gives close or above state-of-the-art performance on four standard benchmarks and has a positive impact on convergence.

References

1. Bucher, M., Herbin, S., Jurie, F.: Improving Semantic Embedding Consistency by Metric Learning for Zero-Shot Classiffication. In: Leibe, B., Matas, J., Sebe, N., Welling, M. (eds.) ECCV 2016. LNCS, vol. 9909, pp. 730–746. Springer, Heidelberg (2016). doi:10.1007/978-3-319-46454-1_44
2. Lampert, C.H., Nickisch, H., Harmeling, S.: Attribute-based classification for zero-shot visual object categorization. IEEE Trans. Pattern Anal. Mach. Intell. **36**(3), 453–465 (2014)
3. Akata, Z., Reed, S., Walter, D., Lee, H., Schiele, B.: Evaluation of output embeddings for fine-grained image classification. In: IEEE International Conference on Computer Vision and Pattern Recognition (CVPR) (2015)
4. Romera-Paredes, B., Torr, P.H.: An embarrassingly simple approach to zero-shot learning. In: ICML, pp. 2152–2161(2015)
5. Zhang, Z., Saligrama, V.: Zero-shot learning via semantic similarity embedding. In: IEEE International Conference on Computer Vision (ICCV) (2015)
6. Zhang, Z., Saligrama, V.: Zero-shot learning via joint latent similarity embedding. In: Proceedings of the IEEE Conference on Computer Vision and Pattern Recognition, pp. 6034–6042 (2016)
7. Wang, Q., Chen, K.: Zero-shot visual recognition via bidirectional latent embedding. arXiv preprint arXiv:1607.02104 (2016)
8. Xian, Y., Akata, Z., Sharma, G., Nguyen, Q., Hein, M., Schiele, B.: Latent embeddings for zero-shot classification. arXiv preprint arXiv:1603.08895 (2016)
9. Fu, Y., Zhu, X., Li, B.: A survey on instance selection for active learning. Knowl. Inf. Syst. **35**(2), 249–283 (2013)
10. Shrivastava, A., Gupta, A., Girshick, R.: Training region-based object detectors with online hard example mining. arXiv preprint arXiv:1604.03540 (2016)
11. Li, X., Snoek, C.M., Worring, M., Koelma, D., Smeulders, A.W.: Bootstrapping visual categorization with relevant negatives. IEEE Trans. Multimed. **15**(4), 933–945 (2013)
12. Canévet, O., Fleuret, F.: Efficient sample mining for object detection. In: ACML (2014)
13. Farhadi, A., Endres, I., Hoiem, D., Forsyth, D.: Describing objects by their attributes. In: IEEE International Conference on Computer Vision and Pattern Recognition (CVPR) (2009)
14. Lampert, C.H., Nickisch, H., Harmeling, S.: Learning to detect unseen object classes by between-class attribute transfer. In: IEEE International Conference on Computer Vision and Pattern Recognition (CVPR) (2009)
15. Wah, C., Branson, S., Welinder, P., Perona, P., Belongie, S.: The Caltech-UCSD Birds-200-2011 dataset. Technical report, July 2011

16. Patterson, G., Xu, C., Su, H., Hays, J.: The SUN attribute database: beyond categories for deeper scene understanding. Int. J. Comput. Vis. **108**(1–2), 59–81 (2014)
17. Jayaraman, D., Grauman, K.: Zero-shot recognition with unreliable attributes. In: Conference on Neural Information Processing Systems (NIPS) (2014)
18. Simonyan, K., Zisserman, A.: Very deep convolutional networks for large-scale image recognition. In: ICLR (2014)

Transfer Learning for Cell Nuclei Classification in Histopathology Images

Neslihan Bayramoglu[(✉)] and Janne Heikkilä

Center for Machine Vision and Signal Analysis, University of Oulu, Oulu, Finland
{nyalcinb,jth}@ee.oulu.fi

Abstract. In histopathological image assessment, there is a high demand to obtain fast and precise quantification automatically. Such automation could be beneficial to find clinical assessment clues to produce correct diagnoses, to reduce observer variability, and to increase objectivity. Due to its success in other areas, deep learning could be the key method to obtain clinical acceptance. However, the major bottleneck is how to train a deep CNN model with a limited amount of training data. There is one important question of critical importance: Could it be possible to use transfer learning and fine-tuning in biomedical image analysis to reduce the effort of manual data labeling and still obtain a full deep representation for the target task? In this study, we address this question quantitatively by comparing the performances of transfer learning and learning from scratch for cell nuclei classification. We evaluate four different CNN architectures trained on natural images and facial images.

1 Introduction

There are two key concepts that makes neural networks powerful in various applications. First, unlike conventional machine learning techniques, deep convolutional neural networks (CNNs) extract features automatically only by using the training data. Second, deep learning methods discover image features at multiple levels (layers) which is called "feature hierarchies". Features at each layer are computed from the previous layer representations and it was shown that features are learned gradually from low-level to high-level. Multi-level abstraction enables deep learning networks to handle very complex functions and high dimensional data.

While deep learning algorithms achieves state-of-the-art results in different machine learning applications, there are several challenges in their application in biomedical domain. First, training deep CNN requires large amount of annotated images to learn millions of parameters. Although large-scale annotated databases are available for generic object recognition task (e.g. ImageNet), it is currently lacking in biomedical domain. Annotating biomedical data requires expertise therefore it is expensive, time consuming, and subject to observer variability. Second, limited amount of training data leads "overfitting" and features can not generalize well on data. Overfitting becomes more serious when the data contain

© Springer International Publishing Switzerland 2016
G. Hua and H. Jégou (Eds.): ECCV 2016 Workshops, Part III, LNCS 9915, pp. 532–539, 2016.
DOI: 10.1007/978-3-319-49409-8_46

high variability in the image appearance which is usually the case in biomedical domain. Third, training deep CNNs from scratch requires high computational power, extensive memory resources, and time. Such approaches have practical limitations in biomedical field.

In generic object recognition tasks, "transfer learning" and "fine-tuning" methods are proposed to overcome these challenges [13]. Transfer learning and fine-tuning aims at reusing image representations learned from a source task and a dataset with large amount of labeled data on a second target dataset and a task [20]. It is shown to be an effective tool to overcome overfitting when the target dataset has limited amount of labeled data [13,20]. However, transferability of deep networks across unrelated domains have been found to be limited due to data bias [8,13,20]. In this study, we exploit the transfer learning properties of CNNs for cell nuclei classification in histopathological images. Although, there are significant differences in image statistics between biomedical image datasets and natural images, this study evaluates whether the features learned from deep CNNs trained on generic recognition tasks could generalize to biomedical tasks with limited training data. We evaluate four different CNN architectures trained on natural images (ImageNet [6]) and facial images [7]. We compare the performances of CNN models learned from scratch and fine-tuned from pre-trained models for cell nuclei classification. We present an empirical validation that initializing the network parameters with transferred features can improve the classification performance for any model and learning from pre-trained network model requires less training time than learning from scratch.

2   Related Work and Method

2.1   Nuclei Classification in Histopathology Images

Although there has been a progress in the development of image analysis algorithms in histopathological image assessment [4,10,19], there is a still high demand to obtain fast and precise quantification automatically. Such techniques could be beneficial to find clinical assessment clues to produce correct diagnoses, to reduce observer variability, and to increase objectivity. Due to its success in other fields, deep learning could be the key method to obtain clinical acceptance. However, the major bottleneck is how to train a deep CNN model with a limited amount of training data. There is one important question of critical importance: Could it be possible to use transfer learning and fine-tuning in biomedical image analysis to reduce the effort of manual data labeling and still obtain a full deep representation for the target task? In this study, we address this question quantitatively by comparing the performances of transfer learning and learning from scratch for nuclei classification using unrelated source tasks and datasets from different distributions.

Cancer is still one of the top leading cause of death worldwide. In order to develop better cancer treatments, it is important to analyse tumors at cellular level to understand disease development and progression. In cancer histopathology image analysis, convolutional neural networks are used for region of interest

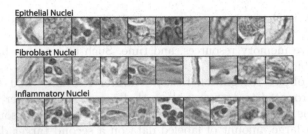

Fig. 1. Examples of different classes of cell nuclei in routine hematoxylin and eosin (H&E) stained histopathology images of colorectal adenocarcinoma. *(From top to bottom)* Epithelial nuclei, Fibroblasts, and Inflammatory nuclei.

detection, segmentation, and also for mitosis detection [2]. On the other hand, there is a relatively little work on cell nuclei classification for histopathology images. However, the analysis of nuclei types provides deeper understanding about the state of the disease [4] which has a critical importance for treatment strategies. Hand-crafted (morphological and intensity) features are often employed for classification purposes [4,11]. They include complex preprocessing pipeline including stain normalization, nucleus detection, and region of interest segmentation. This is mainly due to the heterogeneous structure of histopathology images. In this study, we evaluate performances of convolutional neural network models to classify cell nuclei in hematoxylin and eosin (H&E) stained histopathology images of colorectal adenocarcinoma. We used a dataset of H&E stained histology images of size 500 × 500 cropped from non-overlapping areas of whole slide images from 9 patients. The database (HistoPhenotypes) is published recently by Sirinukunwattana *et al.* in [16] where they also follow a CNN approach for detection and classification purposes. Example patches of different classes of cell nuclei in the dataset are shown in Fig. 1.

2.2 Transfer Learning, Fine Tuning, and Full Training

Transfer learning has been explored in many problems including character recognition [3], generic object recognition [13], computer aided diagnosis of lymph node detection and interstitial lung disease classification [14], polyp detection and image quality assessment in colonoscopy videos, human epithelial type 2 cell classification in indirect immunofluorescence images [1], embolism detection [18], and segmentation [12,18]. Earlier works in deep convolutional neural networks studied 'learning from related tasks' whereas recent studies follow domain adaptation by learning shallow representation models to minimize the negative effects of domain discrepancy [9]. Yosinski *et al.* [20] show that the feature transferability drops significantly when the domain discrepancy increases. They also confirm that modern deep neural networks learn *general* features on the first layers and features learned on the last layers depend greatly on the data and therefore, they are *specific*. While *shallower* networks suppress domain specific features and reduce domain discrepancy they have limited capacity to explore and learn more complex features. On the other hand, there is a high feature variability in the domain of biomedical imaging which requires *deeper* architectures to obtain full representation for the target data. In this study, we used CNN architectures with different depths and structures to explore their effects on transfer learning and fine-tuning. We investigate four different CNN architectures: AlexNet [6], GenderNet [7], GoogLeNet [17], and VGG-16 [15].

AlexNet [6] is the winner of ImageNet 2012 challenge that popularized CNNs. It contains five convolutional and pooling layers and three fully connected layers including local response normalization (ReLU) layers and dropouts. It operates on $227 \times 227 \times 3$ input images which are cropped randomly from 256×256 images.

GoogLeNet [17] architecture achieved the state-of-the art results in ImageNet challenge in 2014. It has 22 layers with 9 inception units and finally a fully connected layer before the output. The inception module has two layers and 6 convolutional blocks which is an intrinsic component of GoogLeNet. The main contribution of this architecture is reducing the number of parameters of neural networks. Although GoogLeNet is very deep, it has $12\times$ fewer parameters than AlexNet which makes it computationally efficient to train.

VGG-16 [15] has a similar architecture with AlexNet with more convolutional layers. It has 13 convolutional layers followed by rectification and pooling layers, and 3 fully connected layers. All convolutional layers use small 3×3 filters and the network performs only 2×2 pooling. VGG-16 has a receptive field of size 224×224. Although VGG-16 performs better than AlexNet and has a simpler architectural design, it has $3\times$ more parameters which requires more computation.

GenderNet [7], this small network contains three convolutional layers followed by rectified linear operation and pooling layers, and two fully connected layers. GenderNet is used for both age and gender classification from real-world, unconstrained facial images which comes from a much smaller dataset than ImageNet.

There are basically two techniques in transfer learning: fine-tuned features and frozen features [20]. When the layers are frozen and initialized from a pretrained network model, there is no need to back-propagate through them during training and they behave as fixed features without changing on the new task. Fine-tuning involves back-propagating the errors from the new tasks into the copied layers [20]. In this study, we adopt a different strategy by choosing different learning rates for the layers coming from the source network and the new layers in the target network. We allow layers copied from the source network change slowly whereas we learn features at higher layers (last fully connected layers) with higher learning rates (fine-tuning). We propose to utilize this to train the network data specific features while tuning the well learned features from the source task without overfitting. On the other hand, full training requires learning from scratch with all the network layers initialized randomly.

3   Experiments and Results

HistoPhenotypes dataset involves 29,756 manually marked cell nuclei from 100 H&E stained images. Out of these, 22,444 nuclei are classified into four labels: epithelial, inflammatory, fibroblast, and miscellaneous. Miscellaneous category consists of mixed cell nuclei therefore, we have excluded it from this study. There are 7,772 epithelial, 5,712 fibroblast, and 6,971 inflammatory cell nuclei. In our experiments, a total number of 20,405 cell nuclei are divided randomly into training (17,004 nuclei) and testing (3,401 nuclei) set. We cropped small patches of sizes 32 × 32 around the cell nuclei centers which is large enough to contain whole nucleus. However, the network models we use in our experiments have larger receptive fields (∼256 × 256). Therefore, we upsampled cell nuclei patches to 256 × 256 images. Raw images are then used without any other preprocessing or data augmentation. During training, mean intensity subtraction is employed to normalize illumination changes.

In our experiments, all networks are trained using the minibatch stochastic gradient descent with a momentum factor of 0.9. We initialize the base learning rate (lr) as 0.001 and decrease the learning rate as follows: $lr_{new} = lr_{base} \times (1 + \gamma \times iteration\_number)^{power}$ with power = 0.75 and $\gamma = 0.001$. All network models are trained for 10 epochs either learned from scratch or fine-tuned from pre-trained models. We utilize a batch size of 100 images for AlexNet and GenderNet, whereas GoogLeNet and VGG-16 operates on a minibatch of 50 images due to memory constraints. Our implementation is based on the *Caffe* library [5].

When we learn models from scratch, the network parameters are initialized randomly either from Gaussian distributions (AlexNet and GenderNet) or with Xavier algorithm (GoogLeNet and VGG-16) which is provided in Caffe. For transfer learning, we used models pre-trained on ImageNet database for generic object recognition except GenderNet architecture which is trained on a much smaller facial dataset [7] for gender classification. For all the network architectures we experimented, firstly we copied all the layers from source models to our target networks except the last fully connected layer. Then we modified the last fully connected layers for adapting models to our nuclei classification task in which the output is fed into a 3-way softmax, initialized randomly and trained from scratch.

Figure 2 shows classification accuracies of test set for AlexNet (Fig. 2a), GenderNet (Fig. 2b), GoogLeNet (Fig. 2c), and VGG-16 (Fig. 2d). For simplicity and to avoid clutter we present only test set accuracies. In each figure, we plot the performance of transfer learning and fine-tuning, and full training against the number of iterations. Because the batch sizes are smaller in GoogLeNet and VGG-16, required number of iterations are higher to train them for 10 epochs. First, we can observe from the comparisons that the transfer learning outperforms full training. In the GenderNet model, the classification accuracy of the test set for transfer learning and full training are comparable. This difference could be due to the size of the feature space of the source task and the depth of the network. Second, we also observed that fine-tuned models converges much earlier than their fully trained counterparts which concludes that transfer learning requires

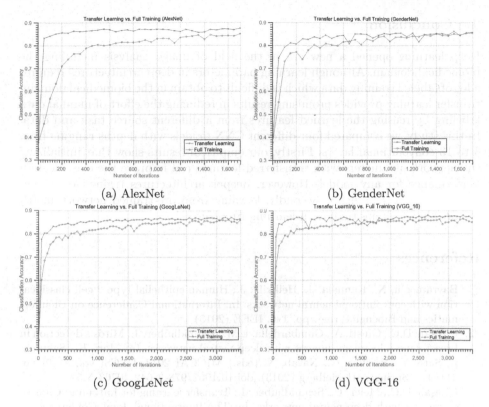

Fig. 2. Comparison of transfer learning with fine tuning and full training for networks (a) AlexNet, (b) GenderNer, (c) GoogLeNet, and (d)VGG-16.

less training time to achieve the maximum performance. After the first epoch, the classification accuracies for fine-tuned AlexNet, GenderNet, GoogLeNet and VGG-16 are 85.68 %, 80.62 %, 84.03 %, and 87.27 % respectively. Accuracies at the same time for full training are 71.13 %, 77.18 %, 77.42 %, and 82.18 % in the same order. Deeper architectures AlexNet and VGG-16 convergence faster in the fine-tuned settings which is an indication that they can handle more complex features. A maximum of 88.03 % accuracy is achieved with fine-tuned VGG-16 model.

Although there is a great difference between natural/facial images and biomedical images, transfer learning and fine tuning provides much better results than learning from scratch. We confirm that the feature transferability is affected by the depth of the network, source task, and the diversity of the source data. Experimental results are promising that the features learned from deep CNN networks trained on generic recognition tasks could generalize to biomedical tasks and they could be used to fine-tune new tasks having small datasets.

4   Conclusion

Deep learning opened a new era in the field of image analysis including the biomedical domain. Although learning parameters in deep architectures requires a lot of labeled training data which is difficult to obtain in the biomedical domain, transfer learning provides promising results in reducing the effort of manual data labeling by reusing the learned features from a different source task and data. In this study, we compared four different CNN models with depths ranging from 3 to 13 convolutional layers. Firstly, our empirical results show that initializing the network parameters with transferred features can improve the classification performance for any model. However, deeper architectures trained on bigger datasets converges quickly. Secondly, learning from pre-trained network model requires less training time than learning from scratch.

References

1. Bayramoglu, N., Kannala, J., Heikkilä, J.: Human epithelial type 2 cell classification with convolutional neural networks. In: International Conference on Bioinformatics and Bioengineering, pp. 1–6. IEEE (2015)
2. Cireşan, D.C., Giusti, A., Gambardella, L.M., Schmidhuber, J.: Mitosis detection in breast cancer histology images with deep neural networks. In: Mori, K., Sakuma, I., Sato, Y., Barillot, C., Navab, N. (eds.) MICCAI 2013. LNCS, vol. 8149, pp. 411–418. Springer, Heidelberg (2013). doi:10.1007/978-3-642-40763-5_51
3. Cireşan, D.C., Meier, U., Schmidhuber, J.: Transfer learning for Latin and Chinese characters with deep neural networks. In: The International Joint Conference on Neural Networks, pp. 1–6. IEEE (2012)
4. Irshad, H., Veillard, A., Roux, L., Racoceanu, D.: Methods for nuclei detection, segmentation, and classification in digital histopathology: a review-current status and future potential. IEEE Rev. Biomed. Eng. **7**, 97–114 (2014)
5. Jia, Y., Shelhamer, E., Donahue, J., Karayev, S., Long, J., Girshick, R., Guadarrama, S., Darrell, T.: Caffe: convolutional architecture for fast feature embedding. arXiv preprint arXiv:1408.5093 (2014)
6. Krizhevsky, A., Sutskever, I., Hinton, G.E.: ImageNet classification with deep convolutional neural networks. In: Advances in Neural Information Processing Systems, pp. 1097–1105 (2012)
7. Levi, G., Hassner, T.: Age and gender classification using convolutional neural networks. In: Proceedings of the IEEE Conference on Computer Vision and Pattern Recognition Workshops, pp. 34–42 (2015)
8. Long, M., Wang, J.: Learning transferable features with deep adaptation networks. arXiv preprint arXiv:1502.02791 (2015)
9. Long, M., Wang, J., Jordan, M.I.: Deep transfer learning with joint adaptation networks. arXiv preprint arXiv:1605.06636 (2016)
10. McCann, M.T., Ozolek, J.A., Castro, C.A., Parvin, B., Kovacevic, J.: Automated histology analysis: opportunities for signal processing. IEEE Sig. Process. Mag. **32**(1), 78 (2015)
11. Nguyen, K., Bredno, J., Knowles, D.A.: Using contextual information to classify nuclei in histology images. In: IEEE 12th International Symposium on Biomedical Imaging (ISBI), pp. 995–998. IEEE (2015)

12. van Opbroek, A., Ikram, M.A., Vernooij, M.W., De Bruijne, M.: Transfer learning improves supervised image segmentation across imaging protocols. IEEE TMI **34**(5), 1018–1030 (2015)
13. Oquab, M., Bottou, L., Laptev, I., Sivic, J.: Learning and transferring mid-level image representations using convolutional neural networks. In: CVPR, pp. 1717–1724. IEEE (2014)
14. Shin, H.C., Roth, H.R., Gao, M., Lu, L., Xu, Z., Nogues, I., Yao, J., Mollura, D., Summers, R.M.: Deep convolutional neural networks for computer-aided detection: CNN architectures, dataset characteristics and transfer learning. IEEE Trans. Med. Imaging **35**(5), 1285–1298 (2016)
15. Simonyan, K., Zisserman, A.: Very deep convolutional networks for large-scale image recognition. arXiv preprint arXiv:1409.1556 (2014)
16. Sirinukunwattana, K., Raza, S.E.A., Tsang, Y.W., Snead, D.R., Cree, I.A., Rajpoot, N.M.: Locality sensitive deep learning for detection and classification of nuclei in routine colon cancer histology images. IEEE Trans. Med. Imaging **35**(5), 1196–1206 (2016)
17. Szegedy, C., Liu, W., Jia, Y., Sermanet, P., Reed, S., Anguelov, D., Erhan, D., Vanhoucke, V., Rabinovich, A.: Going deeper with convolutions. In: CVPR, pp. 1–9. IEEE (2015)
18. Tajbakhsh, N., Shin, J.Y., Gurudu, S.R., Hurst, R.T., Kendall, C.B., Gotway, M.B., Liang, J.: Convolutional neural networks for medical image analysis: full training or fine tuning? IEEE Trans. Med. Imaging **35**(5), 1299–1312 (2016)
19. Veta, M., Pluim, J.P., van Diest, P.J., Viergever, M.A.: Breast cancer histopathology image analysis: a review. IEEE Trans. Biomed. Eng. **61**(5), 1400–1411 (2014)
20. Yosinski, J., Clune, J., Bengio, Y., Lipson, H.: How transferable are features in deep neural networks? In: Advances in Neural Information Processing Systems, pp. 3320–3328 (2014)

Visual Analogies: A Framework for Defining Aspect Categorization

P. Daphne Tsatsoulis$^{(\boxtimes)}$, Bryan A. Plummer, and David Forsyth

University of Illinois at Urbana-Champaign, Champaign, USA
{tsatsou2,bplumme2,daf}@illinois.edu

Abstract. Analogies are common simple word problems (calf is to cow as x is to sheep?) and we use them to identify analogies between images. Let $\mathcal{I}[\mathcal{A}, \theta]$ be an image of object $\mathcal{A}$ at view θ. We show how to learn to choose an image $\mathcal{I}$ such that $\mathcal{I}[\mathcal{A}, \phi]$ is to $\mathcal{I}[\mathcal{A}, \theta]$ as $\mathcal{I}$ is to $\mathcal{I}[\mathcal{B}, \theta]$. We introduce a framework to identify an image of a familiar object at an unfamiliar angle and extend our method to treat unfamiliar objects. By doing so, we identify pairs of objects that are good at finding new views of one another. This yields an operational notion of aspectual equivalence: objects are equivalent if they can predict each other's appearance well.

1 Introduction

Objects look different when looked at from different directions, an effect known as aspect. In this paper we attack a problem with little history: how do we decide which objects share aspectual properties? We do this based on a predictive notion of aspect without using geometric or appearance information.

We propose the analogy task (visualized in Fig. 1(i)) to model the relationship between different objects and aspects in a category-independent manner. Our experiments show we can transfer the knowledge from an analogy to recognize an object from an unseen aspect. By doing so we implicitly capture 3D structure through a learning-based approach without explicit models. We introduce the idea of Aspectual Categories, equivalence classes between objects that capture shared aspectual properties. We use analogies to define three problems:

(I) Aspect Transfer. A system should take the views it has of an object and use them to identify the same object in new views. This is difficult since we cannot expect to have images of an object at all angles.

(II) Aspect Transfer across Objects. A system should be able to take many views of one particular object and use them to predict the changes that occur when the viewpoint changes for images of a *different object*.

(III) Aspect Categorization. We cannot expect a successful aspect transfer across all pairs of objects. For example, two views of a box are unlikely to make it easier to predict a second view of a hedgehog. We would like to know which pairs of objects support aspect transfer.

G. Hua and H. Jégou (Eds.): ECCV 2016 Workshops, Part III, LNCS 9915, pp. 540–547, 2016.
DOI: 10.1007/978-3-319-49409-8_47

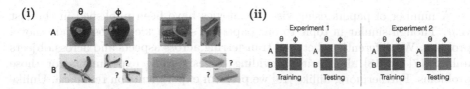

Fig. 1. (i) Given images of object A at angles θ and ϕ, with an image of object B at angle θ, we can correctly predict which image of object B completes the visual analogy. (ii) Two unique sets (red, blue) of angles (left) or objects (right) are defined for each experiment. The angle (ϕ) or object ($\mathcal{B}$) of the fourth element in the 4-tuple has not been seen in training. (Color figure online)

The results of our Aspect Transfer across Objects experiments are used to create Aspect Categories. These categories summarize which objects share aspectual properties. Objects are equivalent if they correctly predict views of each other during the Aspect Transfer across Objects experiment.

Contributions: 1. Our method can identify a particular new view of a known object by analogy. **2.** This method can be used to decompose a set of objects into aspectual equivalence classes. Two objects are equivalent if one can use views of one object to predict views of the other. **3.** We evaluate our framework on the three problems presented and develop baselines to which future work can compare using the RGBD-3D Dataset.

2 Related Work

Aspect in Object Recognition: There are three main strategies for handling aspect. One is to build a **comprehensive representation of aspectual phenomena** (an **aspect graph**; review in [1], critique in [2], summary of results in [3]). This usually results in complex representations and has fallen into disuse.

Another, to represent an object using **aspect-enriched models**. In the extreme, rather than build a "car" recognizer, one might build "frontal-car", "lateral-car" and "overhead-car" recognizers. Usually, these multiple classes are compacted into a single model, assembled from local patches, tied together by observation [4], with geometric reasoning [5], with statistical reasoning [6,7], or with a combination [8–10]. This strategy is expensive in data. However, one may interpolate missing aspects [11], or interpolate models corresponding to missing aspects [12].

Generally, there is little direct study of aspect transfer across objects. The models of Xiang and Savarese [9,10] decompose objects into salient parts from different views, and record when each is visible. It is likely that numerous objects could be encoded by a single part decomposition of this form, but using distinct appearance models (for example, matchboxes and omnibuses). An alternative is to build **aspect invariant features** which are known only from distinct special constructions (e.g. [13] for specialized cases; ([14,15]) for human activities; [16] for ASL). A disadvantage of this is it handles categories independently.

A number of papers using visual analogies have been published in the last year. Though similar in topic to our paper we still tackle a substantially novel problem. We differentiate between transferring across aspects and across objects unlike [17] or [18] along with providing corresponding experiments for those problems. Furthermore, unlike [18] we preform experiments on real data. Unlike [19] and [20] we formulate the problem as an analogy problem.

3   Task

Given two pairs (A, A') and (B, B'), an analogy exists if the relation between A and A' is equivalent to the one between B and B'. We apply this concept to the image domain and predict the equivalence.

We write objects as $\{\mathcal{A}, \mathcal{B}\}$, and view angles as $\{\theta, \phi\}$; write $\mathcal{I}([\mathcal{A}, \theta])$ for an image of object $\mathcal{A}$ at view angle θ. We can operationalize this analogical reasoning by choosing a function F that accepts four images such that,

$$F(\mathcal{I}[\mathcal{A}, \theta], \mathcal{I}[\mathcal{A}, \phi], \mathcal{I}[\mathcal{B}, \theta], \mathcal{I}[\mathcal{B}, \phi]) > F(\mathcal{I}[\mathcal{A}, \theta], \mathcal{I}[\mathcal{A}, \phi], \mathcal{I}[\mathcal{B}, \theta], \mathcal{J})$$

where $\mathcal{J}$ is any image other than $\mathcal{I}[\mathcal{B}, \phi]$. We require that this property be true for all $\mathcal{A}$, $\mathcal{B}$, θ, ϕ. Given F with this property, it is straightforward to identify a view of object $\mathcal{B}$ at view ϕ. We search for the image $\mathcal{I}$ such that $F(\mathcal{I}[\mathcal{A}, \theta], \mathcal{I}[\mathcal{A}, \phi], \mathcal{I}[\mathcal{B}, \theta], \mathcal{I})$ is largest. We conduct three experiments to answer the following questions:

I Aspect Transfer: Can our method generalize over angle? Can it correctly select $\mathcal{I}[\mathcal{B}, \phi]$ if trained with object $\mathcal{B}$ but not angle ϕ.

II Aspect transfer Across Objects: Can our method generalize over objects? Can it correctly select $\mathcal{I}[\mathcal{B}, \phi]$ if trained with angle ϕ but not object $\mathcal{B}$.

III Aspect Categorization: Which object-pairs are easy to generalize over?

3.1   Experimental Design

Experimental design matters a lot for this problem, particularly the test-train split. It is easy to confuse train and test data when creating 4-tuples by including a prediction image in a training 4-tuple and in a testing 4-tuple. It is also easy to make too-easy examples by setting $\theta = \phi$. Similarly, the task can also be made too difficult by using disjoint sets of objects and angles in test and train.

I: Transfer Across Aspect. The method learns how an image can change from angle θ to ϕ_{train} and needs to predict if the change from θ to ϕ_{test} is correct. To do so, all angles are split into two sets, test and train, with 4 angles in each. These were used to create a train set $\{\mathcal{I}[\cdot, \theta], \mathcal{I}[\cdot, \phi_{\text{train}}], \mathcal{I}[\cdot, \theta], \mathcal{I}[\cdot, \phi_{\text{train}}]\}_{\text{train}}$ and a test set $\{\mathcal{I}[\cdot, \theta], \mathcal{I}[\cdot, \phi_{\text{test}}], \mathcal{I}[\cdot, \theta], \mathcal{I}[\cdot, \phi_{\text{test}}]\}_{\text{test}}$. The training set was used to define θ and ϕ_{train}. The testing set was used to define ϕ_{test}. Please see Fig. 1(i) for a visualization.

II: Aspect Transfer Across Objects. In this experiment, the method learns how an object $\mathcal{A}$ changes angles and needs to predict whether a new object $\mathcal{B}_{\text{test}}$ changed in the same way. To do so, we took all objects and split them into two sets. These created a training set $\{\mathcal{I}[\mathcal{A},\cdot],\mathcal{I}[\mathcal{A},\cdot],\mathcal{I}[\mathcal{B}_{\text{train}},\cdot],\mathcal{I}[\mathcal{B}_{\text{train}},\cdot]\}_{\text{train}}$ and a testing set $\{\mathcal{I}[\mathcal{A},\cdot],\mathcal{I}[\mathcal{A},\cdot],\mathcal{I}[\mathcal{B}_{\text{test}},\cdot],\mathcal{I}[\mathcal{B}_{\text{test}},\cdot]\}_{\text{test}}$. The training set was used to define $\mathcal{A}$ and $\mathcal{B}_{\text{train}}$. The testing set was used to define $\mathcal{B}_{\text{test}}$.

Evaluation Metrics for Experiments I and II. For experiments I and II we wanted to evaluate the method over many angle- (or object-) pairs. To do so, we used a pooled AUC. We regarded each tuple $\{\mathcal{I}[\mathcal{A},\theta],\mathcal{I}[\mathcal{A},\phi],\mathcal{I}[\mathcal{B},\theta],\mathcal{I}[\mathcal{B},\phi]\}$ as positive (whatever $\mathcal{A},\mathcal{B},\theta,\phi$) and all others as negative. We then computed the AUC. By doing so, we obtained a summary of performance for each case.

III: Aspect Categorization. In this experiment we address question III posed above: Can our method generate categories with similar aspect? In this Experiment we use the results from Experiment II to create our aspect categories. We regard objects $\mathcal{A}$ and $\mathcal{B}$ as aspectually similar if, for many angle pairs θ,ϕ, our method accurately finds $\mathcal{I}([\mathcal{B},\phi])$. We can capture this notion by computing the AUC over angles for pairs of objects. The result is the AUC when using object $\mathcal{A}$ to predict object $\mathcal{B}$ for all pairs of objects.

We cluster on the AUC using an agglomerative clustering with complete-link distance. Objects that share a cluster are better at predicting one another.

4   Method

4.1   Gradient Tree Boost

We use Gradient Boosting [21] to predict which 4-tuples are analogies. Gradient boosting constructs an ensemble of learners: in our case, regression trees. Each iteration, $1 \ldots m$, learns a new tree, h_m, from the residuals of the previous iteration's forest, $F_{m-1}(\mathbf{x})$. More specifically, it regresses the input features, $\mathbf{x}$, against the negative gradient of the loss function evaluated at the predicted output $f(\mathbf{x})$. It also learns a weight for each tree. The forest is grown for a number of iterations, m, and evaluated using a loss function and its gradient.

Exponential Loss. The exponential loss, $\mathscr{L}(y, f(\mathbf{x})) = e^{-yf(\mathbf{x})}$, with derivative, $\frac{\partial}{\partial f(\mathbf{x})} = -ye^{-yf(\mathbf{x})}$, penalizes examples $\mathbf{x}$ for which $f(\mathbf{x})$ is incorrectly predicted.

AUC Loss. The Area Under the Receiver-Operating-Characteristic (AUC) is a cost function that cannot be directly applied as a per-example loss function. However, because we are trying to find the best fit for a visual analogy, it makes sense to define a loss that relates prediction $f(\mathbf{x})$ to all other predictions in the way a ranker would. We want positive examples, f_i, to score higher than all negative examples, f_j, which is captured by the AUC. A high AUC reflects a method in which there are a low number of false positives and a high number of true positives. We modify the AUC cost function to define a loss as [22],

$$\mathscr{L}(\mathbf{y}, f(\mathbf{x})) = 1 - \mathrm{AUC}(\mathbf{y}, f(\mathbf{x})) = 1 - \frac{1}{|S_+||S_-|} \sum_{i \in S_+} \sum_{j \in S_-} \mathbb{1}(f_i - f_j > 0)$$

Where S_+ are examples with a true positive label and S_- are examples with a true negative label. The indicator function $\mathbb{1}(f_i - f_j > 0)$ is not differentiable and needs to be approximated with the sigmoid function, $\sigma(f_i - f_j) = \frac{1}{1+e^{-\beta(f_i-f_j)}}$. As $\beta \to \infty$ this approximates the indicator function's step-like behavior. The partial derivative of the loss function with respect to a single point is:

$$\frac{\partial}{\partial f_{a \in S_+}} = \frac{-\beta}{|S_+||S_-|} \sum_{j \in S_-} \frac{e^{\beta(f_a-f_j)}}{(1 + e^{\beta(f_a-f_j)})^2}, \quad \frac{\partial}{\partial f_{a \in S_-}} = \frac{\beta}{|S_+||S_-|} \sum_{i \in S_+} \frac{e^{\beta(f_i-f_a)}}{(1 + e^{\beta(f_i-f_a)})^2}$$

4.2 Data and Features

We used the training set of the RGBD-3D Dataset [23] that contains 51 types of objects at 360 angles. We used the crops of the first example in each class and angles $\{0, 45, 90, 135, 180, 225, 270, 315\}$. We extracted features, $h(x_{a,t})$, for every item, a, at angle, t, using a Deep Residual Network described in [24]; a 152 layer network pre-trained on imagenet.We used the activations before the last fully connected layer (res5c). We used a combination of per-image features for a set of images: $f(x_{A,\theta}, x_{A,\phi}, x_{B,\theta}, x_{B,\psi}) = [\Delta h_{A,\{\theta,\phi\}}, \Delta h_{\{A,B\},\theta}, \Delta h_{B,\{\theta,\phi\}}, \Delta h_{\{A,B\},\phi}, \Delta h_{A,\{\theta,\phi\}} - \Delta h_{B,\{\theta,\phi\}}, \Delta h_{\{A,B\},\theta} - \Delta h_{\{A,B\},\phi}]$. Feature $f(x_{A,\theta}, x_{A,\phi}, x_{B,\theta}, x_{B,\psi})$ is a positive example, $+1$, if $\phi = \psi$ and a negative example, -1, if $\phi \neq \psi$.

4.3 The Model

We use Gradient Boosting [21] to model visual analogies. Each regression tree was grown using the entire training set. We ran the method for a maximum of 100 iterations (for a maximum of 100 trees per forest). Each tree was grown until a minimum leaf size of 10, 50, or 100 was reached. We used both Exponential and AUC loss methods and varied the AUC loss parameter β to be 100 or 1000.

5 Results

We evaluate predictions using the area under the ROC curve (AUC). This metric best captures the results in a biased dataset. There are almost an order-of-magnitude more negative than positive examples (for each correct angle there are seven incorrect angles). The AUC simulates a forced-choice test in which the system must pick between a positive and negative example. For the aspect transfer and aspect transfer across object experiments we report AUC where

Table 1. Results of the **angle-split** (left) and object-split (right) experiments for two losses and varying minimum leaf size (MLS). Chance performance is 0.5.

Loss	MLS = 10	50	100	MLS = 10	50	100
AUC, $\beta = 100$	0.6728	0.6925	**0.6950**	0.5676	0.5717	**0.5726**
= 1000	0.6563	0.6904	0.6910	0.5676	0.5717	**0.5726**
Exponential	0.5980	0.6534	0.6393	0.5543	0.5415	0.5595

we computed the AUC over all examples. For the aspect category experiment we report a per-object-pair $\text{AUC}_{\text{obj-pair}}$ which was pooled over angles for each pairing of objects. This AUC captures how well two objects predict each other (Table 1).

(I) Aspect Transfer: We identify $\mathcal{I}([\mathcal{B}, \phi])$ given $\{\mathcal{I}([\mathcal{A}, \theta]), \mathcal{I}([\mathcal{A}, \phi]), \mathcal{I}([\mathcal{B}, \theta])\}$ with no instance of angle ϕ in the training set. We correctly identify $\mathcal{I}([\mathcal{B}, \phi])$ with a pooled AUC of 0.6950 when using the AUC loss function with a β parameter equal to 100 and a minimum leaf size of 100. Using the exponential loss with the same minimum leaf size gave an AUC of 0.6393 suggesting gains were made by penalizing based on the AUC loss.

(II) Aspect Transfer Across Objects: We identify $\mathcal{I}([\mathcal{B}, \phi])$ given $\{\mathcal{I}([\mathcal{A}, \theta]), \mathcal{I}([\mathcal{A}, \phi]), \mathcal{I}([\mathcal{B}, \theta])\}$ with no instance of object $\mathcal{B}$ in the training set. We correctly identify $\mathcal{I}([\mathcal{B}, \phi])$ with a pooled AUC of 0.5726 when using the AUC loss with a β parameter equal to 100 and a minimum leaf size of 100.

Transfer across objects (II) is more difficult than the transfer across aspect (I) because the model only used comparisons between *other* object pairs when training. Predicting a rotation to an unseen viewpoint is not as extreme a task as predicting the viewpoint changes of unseen objects.

(III) Aspect Categorization: We clustered objects that had high AUC when used together in an analogy. Figure 2 provides is an illustration of groups of

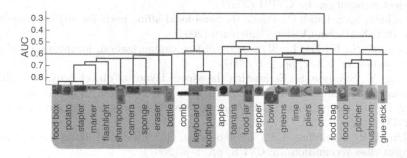

Fig. 2. The complete-clustering over two-object AUCs. Objects that quickly cluster together predict each other's rotation with high AUC. For a chosen AUC of 0.6 (red line) clusters are formed that depend on the shape of the objects. There are boxy clusters (green), round clusters (orange), and one cluster (blue) is a mix of shapes. (Color figure online)

objects that best predict each other's orientations. Neighboring objects have better AUC performance when used to predict each other. For example, it would be better to compare a toothpaste with a keyboard than a water-bottle because the toothpaste-keyboard analogies had an AUC ≈ 0.75 and the toothpaste-bottle analogies had an AUC ≈ 0.52. The lower the bar that connects two objects (the higher the AUC) the better they are at predicting each other. The clustering shows how the method picks up on strong coordinated behavior between objects.

The clusters formed respect general geometric descriptions of the objects. The {food stapler, marker, sponge,...} and {keyboard, toothpaste} clusters are made of boxy objects that have clear differences between most of their orientations. Our features are able to pick up on strong coordinated behavior such as the boxy structure in the previous cluster and the curves in circular objects or objects labels in the {food-cup,pitcher, pitcher, mushroom} cluster. Since we have clustered based on the two-object AUC we can tell which observed object {$\mathcal{A}$} will best predict object {$\mathcal{B}$}. For a tolerable predictive AUC we have defined the cluster of objects with which to make predictions.

References

1. Bowyer, K., Dyer, C.: Aspect graphs: an introduction and survey of recent results. Int. J. Imaging Syst. Technol. **2**, 315–328 (1990)
2. Faugeras, O., Mundy, J., Ahuja, N., Dyer, C., Pentland, A., Jain, R., Ikeuchi, K., Bowyer, K.: Why aspect graphs are not (yet) practical for computer vision. CVGIP **55**(2), 212–218 (1992)
3. Forsyth, D., Ponce, J.: Computer Vision: A Modern Approach. Prentice-Hall, Upper Saddle River (2002)
4. Thomas, A., Ferrari, V., Leibe, B., Tuytelaars, T., Schiele, B., Gool, L.V.: Towards multi-view object class detection. In: CVPR, pp. 1589–1596 (2006)
5. Huang, C.Y., Camps, O., Kanungo, T.: Object recognition using appearance-based parts and relations. In: CVPR, pp. 877–83 (1997)
6. Kushal, A., Schmid, C., Ponce, J.: Flexible object models for category level 3D object recognition. In: CVPR (2007)
7. Lazebnik, S., Schmid, C., Ponce, J.: Semi-local affine parts for object recognition. In: British Machine Vision Conference (2004)
8. Savarese., S., Fei-Fei, L.: 3D generic object categorization, localization and pose estimation. In: ICCV, pp. 1–8 (2007)
9. Xiang, Y., Savarese, S.: Estimating the aspect layout of object categories (2012)
10. Xiang, Y., Savarese, S.: Object detection by 3D aspectlets and occlusion reasoning. In: 4th International IEEE Workshop on 3D Representation and Recognition (2013)
11. Chiu, H.P., Kaelbling, L.P., Lozano-Perez, T.: Virtual training for multi-view object class recognition. In: CVPR, pp. 1–8 (2007)
12. Savarese, S., Fei-Fei, L.: View synthesis for recognizing unseen poses of object classes. In: Forsyth, D., Torr, P., Zisserman, A. (eds.) ECCV 2008. LNCS, vol. 5305, pp. 602–615. Springer, Heidelberg (2008). doi:10.1007/978-3-540-88690-7_45
13. Forsyth, D., Mundy, J., Zisserman, A., Coelho, C., Heller, A., Rothwell, C.: Invariant descriptors for 3D object recognition and pose. PAMI **13**(10), 971–991 (1991)

14. Junejo, I., Dexter, E., Laptev, I., Perez, P.: Cross-view action recognition from temporal self-similarities. Technical report, Irisa, Rennes (2008). Publication interne N 1895, ISSN 1166–8687
15. Farhadi, A., Tabrizi, M.K.: Learning to recognize activities from the wrong view point. In: Forsyth, D., Torr, P., Zisserman, A. (eds.) ECCV 2008. LNCS, vol. 5305, pp. 154–166. Springer, Heidelberg (2008). doi:10.1007/978-3-540-88682-2_13
16. Farhadi, A., Forsyth, D., White, R.: Transfer learning in sign language. In: CVPR (2007)
17. Sadeghi, F., Zitnick, C.L., Farhadi, A.: Visalogy: answering visual analogy questions. In: Cortes, C., Lawrence, N.D., Lee, D.D., Sugiyama, M., Garnett, R. (eds.) Advances in Neural Information Processing Systems 28, pp. 1882–1890. Curran Associates, Inc. (2015)
18. Reed, S.E., Zhang, Y., Zhang, Y., Lee, H.: Deep visual analogy-making. In: Cortes, C., Lawrence, N.D., Lee, D.D., Sugiyama, M., Garnett, R. (eds.) Advances in Neural Information Processing Systems 28, pp. 1252–1260. Curran Associates, Inc. (2015)
19. Ghifary, M., Bastiaan Kleijn, W., Zhang, M., Balduzzi, D.: Domain generalization for object recognition with multi-task autoencoders. In: The IEEE International Conference on Computer Vision (ICCV), December 2015
20. Tulsiani, S., Carreira, J., Malik, J.: Pose induction for novel object categories. In: The IEEE International Conference on Computer Vision (ICCV), December 2015
21. Friedman, J.H.: Stochastic gradient boosting. Comput. Stat. Data Anal. **38**, 367–378 (1999)
22. Ma, S., Huang, J.: Regularized ROC method for disease classification and biomarker selection with microarray data. Bioinformatics **21**(24), 4356–4362 (2005)
23. Lai, K., Bo, L., Ren, X., Fox, D.: A large-scale hierarchical multi-view RGB-D object dataset. In: IEEE International Conference on on Robotics and Automation (2011)
24. He, K., Zhang, X., Ren, S., Sun, J.: Deep residual learning for image recognition. CoRR abs/1512.03385 (2015)

W14 – Recovering 6D Object Pose

Preface

Welcome to the Proceedings for the 2nd Workshop on Recovering 6D Object Pose, held in conjunction with the European Conference on Computer Vision on October 9th, 2016.

The proposed workshop is the second attempt at gathering researchers working on 6 DoF object pose estimation, 3D object detection and registration problems. The concerned topic is re-emerging in the field of computer vision and robotics after the development of RGB-D sensors and high GPU computing that have opened the door to a whole new range of technologies and applications which require detecting and estimating object poses in 3D environments for a variety of scenarios, e.g. picking and placing for logistics. The workshop (a) gathers people from both industry and academia who work on this topic, (b) help share knowledge and up-to-date advances, and (c) discuss benchmarks, baselines and evaluation metrics in the community. A majority of existing data sets and methods are limited on a certain degree of background clutters and foreground occlusions, and scenarios of a single target instance per image. The community needs to make one step forward and, thus our goal is to evaluate more challenging and realistic scenarios, where multiple target objects appear interacting and occluding each other or cases of articulated objects. We also aim at comparing new and established methods based on RGB and/or RGBD for object pose estimation on varied datasets covering multiple scenarios and settings.

Our program features oral and poster presentations of papers as well as several high-quality invited talk and challenge results, to identify key research questions and highlight future research directions. We have received a good number of high-quality original paper submissions, and among them, have accepted 9 papers in total (4 oral and 5 poster papers). The topics include, but not limited to: 3D object detection, object detection in depth images, joint registration of multiple 3D objects, 6 DoF object pose under heavy occlusions and background clutters, occlusion-aware segmentation, bin-picking, 3D object tracking, surface representation and fitting, non-rigid object registration, 3D object modelling, multiple object instance detection, object class (category) detection.

We would like to thank the authors, invited speakers and the technical program committee for the involvement and attendance at our R6D workshop event. Their participation has made our workshop a very successful event.

November 2016

Kind regards,
Tae-Kyun Kim
Jiri Matas
Vincent Lepetit
Carsten Rother
Ales Leonardis
Krzysztof Wallas
Carsten Steger
Rigas Kouskouridas

Organization

Workshop Chairs

Tae-Kyun Kim	Imperial College London
Jiri Matas	Chech Technical University
Vincent Lepetit	Technical University Graz
Carsten Rother	Technical University Dresden
Ales Leonardis	University of Birmingham
Krzysztof Wallas	Poznan University of Technology
Carsten Steger	MVTec GmbH
Rigas Kouskouridas	Imperial College London

Challenge Chairs

Frank Michel	Technical University Dresden
Alexander Krull	Technical University Dresden
Andreas Doumanoglou	Imperial College London
Tomas Hodan	Chech Technical University
Krzysztof Wallas	Poznan University of Technology
Alberto Crivellaro	EPFL

Technical Program Committee

A. Argyros	H. Fujiyoshi	Y. Konishi	D. Tan
U. Bonde	S. Hinterstoisser	V. Lempitsky	D. Teney
E. Brachman	S. Ilic	J.J. Lim	U. Thomas
A.D. Bue	E. Johns	J. Piater	
B. Drost	H. Kasaei	C. Rennie	
O. Erkent	W. Kehl	C. Sahin	

A Direct Method for Robust Model-Based 3D Object Tracking from a Monocular RGB Image

Byung-Kuk Seo$^{(\boxtimes)}$ and Harald Wuest

Fraunhofer IGD, Darmstadt, Germany
byung-kuk.seo@igd-extern.fraunhofer.de, harald.wuest@igd.fraunhofer.de

Abstract. This paper proposes a novel method for robust 3D object tracking from a monocular RGB image when an object model is available. The proposed method is based on direct image alignment between consecutive frames over a 3D target object. Unlike conventional direct methods that only rely on image intensity, we newly model intensity variations using the surface normal of the object under the Lambertian assumption. From the prediction about image intensity in this model, we also employ a constrained objective function, which significantly alleviates degradation of the tracking performance. In experiments, we evaluate our method using datasets that consist of test sequences under challenging conditions, and demonstrate its benefits compared to other methods.

Keywords: Pose estimation · Object tracking · Model-based · Direct image alignment · Motion model

1 Introduction

3D tracking (or 6D pose estimation) of target objects is a crucial issue in computer vision, robotics, and augmented reality. Over the last decade, numerous methods have been proposed and successfully demonstrated for 3D object tracking. Despite that, achieving accurate, robust, and fast tracking is still challenging in everyday environments where there exists a large range of 3D objects under various backgrounds, illuminations, occlusions, and motions.

In early methods, feature points have prominently been used to handle pose estimation problems of 2D/3D objects [27,30], but such feature-based methods require that the objects have sufficient texture on their surfaces. For poorly textured 3D objects, strong edges have been popular and are still promising in many industrial applications [7,11]. However, they are often troublesome against heavy background clutter due to the nature of edge property. As recent RGBD cameras enable to obtain more dense information about 3D scenes including objects,

---

Electronic supplementary material The online version of this chapter (doi:10.1007/978-3-319-49409-8_48) contains supplementary material, which is available to authorized users.

G. Hua and H. Jégou (Eds.): ECCV 2016 Workshops, Part III, LNCS 9915, pp. 551–562, 2016.
DOI: 10.1007/978-3-319-49409-8_48

Fig. 1. Tracking results using the proposed method under challenging conditions (green lines visualize object models projected on images with estimated poses). (Color figure online)

RGBD-based methods have been boosted to tackle challenging pose estimation problems [15,18,29]. Nevertheless, RGBD cameras have several issues need to be considered: depth information is quite noisy and only available within limited ranges with material difficulties (such as specular and transparent materials). Moreover, they are not commonly supported yet in real application domains, compared to RGB cameras.

On the other hand, direct methods have been attractive because they allow that rich information in an image can be contributed to pose estimation, instead of being limited by local features [1,4,5,8,12]. In direct methods, the brightness (intensity) constancy is commonly assumed, but it is often violated by intensity variations, which are induced by illumination changes, surface reflectance properties, or even changes in camera gain. In this paper, we propose a direct method for robust 3D object tracking from a monocular RGB image when an object model is available. In our method, we model intensity variations by deriving differential entities from image formation under the Lambertian assumption, and define a compensation parameter using the surface normal of a 3D target object. From the prediction about image intensity in this model, we also employ a constrained objective function, resulting in suppressing the error accumulation and converging with less iteration. In addition, we provide new datasets that comprise challenging conditions such as partial occlusions, background clutters, and illumination changes (see Fig. 3), in order to evaluate our method in an intensive manner and explicitly demonstrate its advantages.

Our main contribution is a novel direct method based on an elaborate motion model between consecutive frames over a 3D target object, leading to robust 3D object tracking as shown in Fig. 1. Here, we clarify that this paper focuses on robust frame-to-frame pose estimation when an initial pose is only given without preparing or training a set of reference images; thus, the initialization (or reinitialization) issue is out of scope in this paper, and if available, its relevant methods can be combined with the proposed method.

2   Related Work

In the literature, lots of methods have been proposed for dealing with 6D pose estimation problems. As more relevant works in our interest, we briefly highlight model-based approaches for 3D object tracking in a monocular RGB view where 3D knowledge of a target object, such as a 3D model or a set of registered patches, is known as *a prior*.[1]

In a typical way of model-based approaches, the pose estimation is performed by establishing 3D-2D correspondences between 3D knowledge and 2D observation in an image (such as feature points [27,30] or edges [7,11]); thus, most of methods in this manner highly depend on how to extract and match distinctive local features, which are not trivial tasks under challenging conditions.

Region-based methods have been of interest in terms of 6D pose estimation. In particular, level set based segmentation methods have successfully been demonstrated for 3D object tracking [9,24]. These methods follow a general statistical representation of a level set function and evolve a contour of a 3D model over a camera pose, without considering the correspondence problem. In principle, however, such region segmentation requires intensive tasks because the contour is evolved in an infinite-dimensional space, and it is also difficult to guarantee good segmentation results according to scene complexity, even though these issues have been improved [22,26].

To date, direct methods have actively been adopted for 2D object tracking. Similar to region-based methods, direct methods exploit rich information in an image instead of local features, but they directly align image intensity with one of registered templates. As a pioneer work, the Lucas and Kanade framework [19] has played a prominent role and has brought about many variants with improvements; for example, efficient optimization algorithms [1,4] or robust similarity measures [10,16,23,25]. With the availability of 3D knowledge of a target object, direct methods have also successfully been applied for 3D object tracking [5,8].

Even though direct methods have been promising for pose estimation, its underlying assumption (i.e., brightness constancy) is often violated by intensity variations. To tackle such errors, intensity variations have been modeled not only in a typical form, represented by a multiplicative term [32], an additive term [6], or both terms [2,17,20], but also in a more generalized framework, described by complex physical processes [14]. In an alternative way, direct methods have also employed learning-based approaches to handle 3D objects with complex shapes as well as challenging conditions such as illumination changes and occlusions [21,28], but they require computationally demanding training stages with a significant number of data, which are quite cumbersome in practice.

---

[1] In model-based approaches, simultaneous localization and mapping-based methods can be considered for pose estimation in unknown 3D environments, but they are not suitable for 3D object tracking that aims at estimating poses relative to target objects; thus, we do not detail methods in this category.

3   Proposed Method

We start by briefly defining fundamental relations between consecutive frames over a 3D target object under a camera motion in Sect. 3.1. The proposed method is then detailed in Sect. 3.2 (modeling intensity variations) through Sect. 3.3 (objective function and optimization).

3.1   Motion Model Between Consecutive Frames

Consider a camera is moving relative to a 3D target object as shown in Fig. 2. Under the perspective projection Π, the 3D point on the object surface in the camera coordinate system $\mathbf{s}^C = (X^C, Y^C, Z^C)^\top$ is mapped to the 2D point on the image plane $\mathbf{u} = (u, v)^\top$:

$$\mathbf{u} = \Pi(\mathbf{s}^C) = \left(\frac{X^C f_u}{Z^C} + u_0, \frac{Y^C f_v}{Z^C} + v_0 \right)^\top, \tag{1}$$

where (f_u, f_v) are the focal lengths of the camera, and (u_0, v_0) are the principal points of the camera. Under the rigid body transformation $\mathcal{G} \in \mathrm{SE}(3)$, the $\mathbf{s}^C$ is transformed from the 3D point on the object surface in the world coordinate system $\mathbf{s}^O$:

$$\mathbf{u} = \Pi(\mathcal{G}(\mathbf{s}^O; \boldsymbol{\xi})) \quad \text{with} \quad \boldsymbol{\xi} = (\boldsymbol{\omega}^\top, \boldsymbol{\tau}^\top)^\top, \tag{2}$$

where $\boldsymbol{\xi}$ is the parameter associated with the Lie algebra se(3)[2], described by the translational velocity $\boldsymbol{\omega}$ and the rotational velocity $\boldsymbol{\tau}$. In a monocular RGB view, the $\mathbf{s}^O$ is in general unknown, but it can be determined when the object model $\mathbf{m}^O$ is given; thus, Eq. (2) can be rewritten as

$$\mathbf{u} = \Pi(\mathcal{G}(\mathbf{s}^O \to \mathbf{m}^O(\mathbf{u}); \boldsymbol{\xi})) \quad \text{with} \quad \mathbf{m}^O(\mathbf{u}) = \mathcal{G}^{-1}(\Pi^{-1}(\mathbf{u}, d^C); \boldsymbol{\xi}), \tag{3}$$

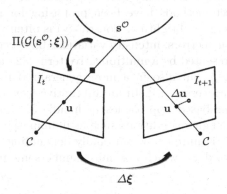

Fig. 2. Illustration and notations of image information between consecutive frames over a 3D target object under a camera motion.

---

[2] Since the relation of the $\mathcal{G}$ to the camera pose is straightforward, this paper retains the same notation $\boldsymbol{\xi}$ for the camera pose or motion.

where $d^{\mathcal{C}}$ is the depth buffer to be rendered using the object model with respect to the $\boldsymbol{\xi}$.

Under the camera motion between consecutive frames $\Delta\boldsymbol{\xi}$, on the other hand, the 2D point on the image plane at time t is mapped to the corresponding 2D point on the image plane at time $t+1$, and it can be defined as the following consistency constraint (under the brightness constancy assumption):

$$I_{t+1}(\mathbf{u} + \Delta\mathbf{u}) = I_t(\mathbf{u}), \tag{4}$$

where $I_t(\mathbf{u})$ is the image intensity of the 2D point $\mathbf{u}$ at time t, and $\Delta\mathbf{u}$ is the displacement of the point on the image plane. Since the $\Delta\mathbf{u}$ can be represented by the $\Delta\boldsymbol{\xi}$ from Eq. (2), it can also be redefined as a consistency constraint with respect to the $\Delta\boldsymbol{\xi}$ by coupling both of relations (Eqs. (3) and (4)):

$$I_{t+1}(\Pi(\mathcal{G}(\mathbf{m}^{\mathcal{O}}(\mathbf{u}); \boldsymbol{\xi} + \Delta\boldsymbol{\xi}))) = I_t(\mathbf{u}). \tag{5}$$

3.2   Modeling Intensity Variations

Assuming that a 3D target object is rigid and has a Lambertian surface; the object is illuminated by a distant point light; and a camera undergoes a rigid motion relative to the target object, the observed image intensity at a 2D point $\mathbf{u}$ on the image plane is given by

$$I(\mathbf{u}) = \sigma(\mathbf{s})\mathbf{n}(\mathbf{s})^{\top}\mathbf{l}, \tag{6}$$

where σ is the surface albedo, $\mathbf{n}$ is the unit surface normal, $\mathbf{l}$ is the unknown scaled light vector representing the light direction and intensity, and $\mathbf{s}$ is the surface point corresponding to the $\mathbf{u}$. For the differential change of the intensity, we take the total derivative of the intensity with respect to t:

$$\frac{dI}{dt} = (\mathbf{n}^{\top}\mathbf{l})\frac{d\sigma}{dt} + \sigma\frac{d}{dt}(\mathbf{n}^{\top}\mathbf{l}). \tag{7}$$

Since the $\frac{d\sigma}{dt}$ is an entity on the surface, it is constant over time, and the differential change of the intensity is then simplified to $dI = \sigma d(\mathbf{n}^{\top}\mathbf{l})$. Therefore, the intensity variations between consecutive frames ΔI_t^{t+1} can be described by

$$\begin{aligned}\Delta I_t^{t+1} &= \sigma\Delta(\mathbf{n}^{\top}\mathbf{l})_t^{t+1} = \sigma(\mathbf{n}_{t+1}^{\top}\mathbf{l}_{t+1} - \mathbf{n}_t^{\top}\mathbf{l}_t) \\ &= \sigma(\mathbf{n}_t^{\top}\mathbf{l}_t)(\kappa - 1) = I_t(\kappa - 1),\end{aligned} \tag{8}$$

where κ is the compensation parameter, given by $\kappa = \mathbf{n}_t^{\top}\mathbf{l}_{t+1}/\mathbf{n}_t^{\top}\mathbf{l}_t$ under the given object rigidity assumption ($\mathbf{n}_{t+1} = \mathbf{n}_t$). Here the conventional brightness constancy assumption is satisfied when $\kappa = 1$.

In general, the illumination is unknown, and its complete modeling is nearly impossible. In this model, however, the κ can be estimated using the surface normal of the object:

$$\kappa = \frac{\mathbf{n}_t^{\top}\mathbf{l}_{t+1}}{\mathbf{n}_t^{\top}\mathbf{l}_t} \approx \frac{\mathcal{E}[I_{t+1}|\mathbf{n}_t]}{\mathcal{E}[I_t|\mathbf{n}_t]}, \tag{9}$$

where $\mathcal{E}[I|\mathbf{n}]$ is the conditional expectation of I given $\mathbf{n}$, modeled by the first-order approximation of the radiance model from any Lambertian object under the general distant light distribution [3]: $I \approx \mathcal{E}[I|\mathbf{n}] = \sigma(l_0 + n_x l_x + n_y l_y + n_z l_z)$, where $\mathbf{n} = (n_x, n_y, n_z)^\top$ and $\mathbf{l} = (l_x, l_y, l_z)^\top$ are the surface normal and illumination vectors, and l_0 is the additional offset. Here, the conditional expectation is computed using the multivariate linear regression when the surface normal of the object is given.

3.3 Objective Function and Optimization

In the proposed method, the 6D pose estimation is formulated by the minimization of an objective function, including an error term and a stability term. By combining Eqs. (5) and (8), the error term $e_{\mathcal{I}}(\mathbf{u}; \boldsymbol{\xi})$ is defined as

$$e_{\mathcal{I}}(\mathbf{u}; \boldsymbol{\xi}) = I_{t+1}(\Pi(\mathcal{G}(\mathbf{m}^{\mathcal{O}}(\mathbf{u}); \boldsymbol{\xi}))) - \kappa I_t(\mathbf{u}). \tag{10}$$

From the prediction about image intensity in Eq. (9), on the other hand, it follows that, for any function Θ of $\mathbf{n}$,

$$\begin{aligned}
\mathcal{E}[(I - \Theta(\mathbf{n}))^2] &= \mathcal{E}[(I - \mathcal{E}[I|\mathbf{n}] + \mathcal{E}[I|\mathbf{n}] - \Theta(\mathbf{n}))^2] \\
&= \mathcal{E}[(I - \mathcal{E}[I|\mathbf{n}])^2] + \mathcal{E}[(\mathcal{E}[I|\mathbf{n}] - \Theta(\mathbf{n}))^2] \\
&\geq \mathcal{E}[(I - \mathcal{E}[I|\mathbf{n}])^2],
\end{aligned} \tag{11}$$

where the cross term is zero, so that we define the stability term $e_{\mathcal{S}}(\mathbf{u}; \boldsymbol{\xi})$ as follows:

$$e_{\mathcal{S}}(\mathbf{u}; \boldsymbol{\xi}) = I_{t+1}(\Pi(\mathcal{G}(\mathbf{m}^{\mathcal{O}}(\mathbf{u}); \boldsymbol{\xi}))) - \mathcal{E}[I_t|\mathbf{n}](\mathbf{u}). \tag{12}$$

Therefore, the minimization becomes

$$\min_{\boldsymbol{\xi}} \sum_{\mathbf{u} \in \mathcal{R}} \psi\big(e_{\mathcal{I}}(\mathbf{u}; \boldsymbol{\xi})^2 + \gamma(\kappa) e_{\mathcal{S}}(\mathbf{u}; \boldsymbol{\xi})^2\big), \tag{13}$$

where $\Psi(\cdot)$ is the robust estimator to penalize outliers, $\gamma(\kappa)$ is the weight function to balance both of terms, and $\mathcal{R}$ is the object region where the depth information is available. For robust estimation, we adopt the Charbonnier penalty function: $\psi(e) = (e^2 + \epsilon^2)^{0.5}$. For balancing the weight, we define an exponential decay function: $\gamma(\kappa) = \exp(-\lambda|\kappa - 1|)$, where λ is the constant.

For optimization, the minimization can be linearized using the first-order Taylor series expansion under a small camera motion $\delta\boldsymbol{\xi}$. In the form of Eqs. (10) and (12), moreover, efficient optimization algorithms [1] can be applied with less modification because the $\Pi(\mathcal{G}(\cdot))$ can be considered as a family of warps (i.e., a warp between image planes over a 3D object). In the proposed method, we adopt the forward compositional (FC) algorithm, which is efficiently compatible with our objective function, and then the minimization is written as (under the assumption that $\Pi(\mathcal{G}(\mathbf{m}^{\mathcal{O}}(\mathbf{u}); 0)) = \mathbf{u}$)

$$\min_{\delta\boldsymbol{\xi}} \sum_{\mathbf{u} \subseteq \mathcal{R}} \psi\Big(||e_{\mathcal{I}}(\mathbf{u}; \boldsymbol{\xi}) + \mathbf{J}_{\mathcal{I}}\delta\boldsymbol{\xi}||^2 + \gamma(\kappa)||e_{\mathcal{S}}(\mathbf{u}; \boldsymbol{\xi}) + \mathbf{J}_{\mathcal{I}}\delta\boldsymbol{\xi}||^2\Big), \tag{14}$$

where $\mathbf{J}_{\mathcal{T}}$ is the chain of the Jacobian matrices, detailed by

$$\nabla I_{t+1}(\Pi(\mathcal{G}(\mathbf{m}^{\mathcal{O}}(\mathbf{u});\boldsymbol{\xi})))\frac{\partial\Pi(\mathcal{G}(\mathbf{m}^{\mathcal{O}}(\mathbf{u});\boldsymbol{\xi}))}{\partial\boldsymbol{\xi}}\bigg|_{\boldsymbol{\xi}=0}. \tag{15}$$

Here, pixels with small gradient are filtered out because they do not much contribute to the optimization, and then remaining pixels are regularly sampled with a grid ($\mathbf{u} \subseteq \mathcal{R}$). The final pose is therefore determined by iteratively updating the latest pose with the estimated motion until the norm of the estimated parameters is small or the maximum number of iterations is reached.

4 Experiments

4.1 Details on Implementation

To handle large motions, we adopted a multiscale strategy. In our implementation, we used four levels (the image resolution at the finest level was 640×480), and each level was downsampled by a factor of two with a Gaussian smoothing (5×5 kernel) and a bilinear interpolation. The depth and surface normal information were not scaled down to avoid interpolation across boundaries, but they were directly interpolated from ones at the finest level. The optimization was started at the coarsest level, and the estimated pose was used as the initial pose for the next fine level. The pixel filtering and sampling were only performed at the finest level. For all evaluations, several parameters were set: $\lambda = 1.0, \epsilon = 0.001$, the minimum magnitude of the gradient $= 0.1$, the grid interval $= 4$ pixels, the minimum norm of the estimated parameters $= 10e\text{-}6$, and the maximum number of iterations $= 200$. Here, the grid interval was adaptively set (with an increment or decrement of one pixel) relative to the object area, which is changed according to the distance between the camera and object. In addition, several steps to acquire information, such as depth, surface normal, object silhouette, and image gradient, were implemented using the rendering pipeline of a GPU.

4.2 Datasets

For intensive evaluations, we created new datasets that provide test sequences (RGB images), ground truth poses, camera intrinsic parameters, and 3D object models. As target objects, we chose two 3D objects (**Gear** and **Wheel**) that have complex shapes and no texture, rather than other objects that have common shapes (like a box or cup) and/or sufficient texture. For their 3D models, wireframe models were prepared without texture maps. Test sequences were captured with various camera motions under three different conditions such as controlled scene (**Seq1**), partial occlusions and background clutters (**Seq2**), and illumination changes (**Seq3**). For obtaining ground truth poses, each object was manually registered on multiple ARUCO markers [13]. Prior to capturing test sequences, the camera (standard USB RGB camera) was calibrated once. Automatic camera settings related to exposure time, gain, and white balance were not controlled during the capturing, except for an automatic focus. Figure 3 shows examples of test sequences in our datasets.

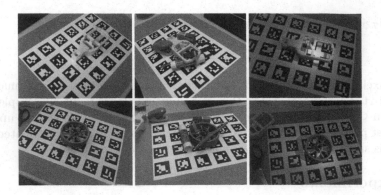

Fig. 3. Examples of test sequences in our datasets: (Top-Row) Gear-Seq1, Seq2, Seq3, (Bottom-Row) Wheel-Seq1, Seq2, Seq3.

4.3 Evaluations and Comparisons

We evaluated our method with several different methods, which can be derived from both terms in our objective function, in order to validate its benefits:

- BCC ($\kappa = 1$ and $\gamma(\kappa) = 0$): An objective function has a single error term based on the brightness consistency constraint.
- BCC+S ($\kappa = 1$ and $\gamma(\kappa) = 1$): An objective function has an error term based on the brightness consistency constraint and a stability term, where both terms are equally weighted.
- Ours (κ and $\gamma(\kappa)$ are estimated): An objective function has an error term, compensated by the κ and a stability term, weighted by the $\gamma(\kappa)$.

Here, these methods were tested in combination with the FC algorithm and the efficient second order minimization (ESM) algorithm [4] as well, wheter a better convergence rate can be expected. We also compared our method with edge-based tracking using a Gaussian mixture model (EBT-GM) [31], which is one of promising approaches in model-based 3D object tracking. Note that, in all tests, the initial poses were set with the ground truth poses.

For evaluations, we computed the average distance (AD) of all model points transformed with the estimated pose and the ground truth pose, which was defined in [15]. In this metric, we decided that the estimated pose was correct when the average distance was below 10 % of the object model diameter and calculated the success rate. To detail error profiles, we also computed the distances of rotation and translation parameters between the estimated pose and the ground truth pose. In addition, we computed the average processing times and the average iteration numbers in each case to examine the runtime performance and computational efficiency.

Table 1 summarizes results of our evaluations. Overall, the proposed method consistently performed well in every case. In particular, it outperformed other methods on challenging scenes (Seq2 and Seq3). The BCCs were often drifted and unstable due to the error accumulation (some details are shown by error

Table 1. Evaluation results: (First Rows) success rates based on the AD criterion [15] and (Second Rows) average processing times (ms) (the highest scores in the success rates are bold; asterisks denote that the tracking totally failed from certain sequences; and numbers in parentheses indicate the total numbers of test sequences).

Method	Gear			Wheel			Average
	Seq1 (850)	Seq2 (934)	Seq3 (1046)	Seq1 (811)	Seq2 (981)	Seq3 (941)	
$BCC_{(FC)}$	0.701	0.320	0.165	0.459	0.235	0.180*	0.344
	32.74	32.49	34.77	32.49	32.51	33.51	33.08
$BCC_{(ESM)}$	0.611	0.338	0.079	0.859	0.411	0.054	0.392
	33.43	30.41	32.86	32.73	32.42	37.07	33.15
$BCC+S_{(FC)}$	0.961	0.916	0.155*	**1.000**	0.919	0.410*	0.727
	30.86	29.06	34.10	30.55	30.27	31.98	31.14
$Ours_{(FC)}$	0.962	0.919	0.992	**1.000**	0.920	**1.000**	**0.966**
	46.28	41.00	49.11	44.20	44.44	46.43	45.24
$Ours_{(ESM)}$	0.974	**0.941**	**0.999**	1.000	**0.955**	0.868	0.956
	41.90	38.07	45.09	39.88	37.30	42.71	40.83
EBT-GM [31]	**0.981**	0.027*	0.770*	0.352*	0.004*	0.191*	0.388
	23.23	44.02	22.05	44.00	61.13	40.15	39.10

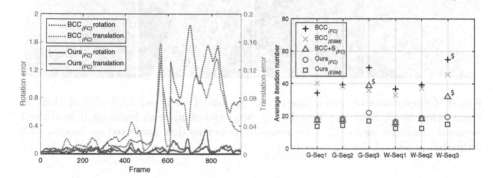

Fig. 4. (Left) Error profiles of $BCC_{(FC)}$ and $Ours_{(FC)}$ in Gear-Seq2, (Right) Average iteration numbers (asterisks denote that the tracking totally failed from certain sequences).

profiles in Fig. 4-(Left)). The EBT-GM was very sensitive to partial occlusions, background clutters, and even object clutters (e.g., which are caused by near edges in thin parts of the objects), so that in most of cases, it totally failed from certain sequences. From results of the BCC+S, it was verified that both of terms in our objective function contributed not only to significantly alleviate degradation of the tracking performance, but also to provide a better convergence rate (see Fig. 4-(Right)). Figures 5 and 6 show several comparison results in Seq2 and Seq3, and more results are shown in a supplementary video. On the

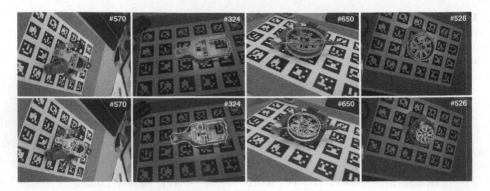

Fig. 5. Comparisons of (green lines) Ours$_{(FC)}$ and (yellow lines) BCC$_{(FC)}$ in (Left to Right) Gear-Seq2, Seq3 and Wheel-Seq2, Seq3 (numbers with hashtags indicate test sequence numbers, and color lines visualize object models projected on images with estimated poses). (Color figure online)

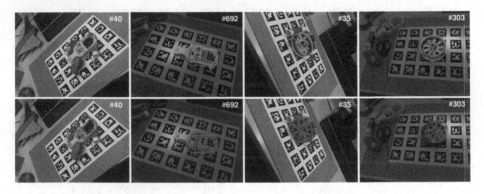

Fig. 6. Comparisons of (green lines) Ours$_{(FC)}$ and (red lines) EBT-GM in (Left to Right) Gear-Seq2, Seq3 and Wheel-Seq2, Seq3 (numbers with hashtags indicate test sequence numbers, and color lines visualize object models projected on images with estimated poses). (Color figure online)

other hand, the proposed method relatively needed more computations, but the average processing times were fairly acceptable for real-time applications (about 20–24 fps on a desktop with a 2.93 GHz CPU). Moreover, our implementation was not fully optimized and can be improved for more speed-up; for example, pixel-wise computations can obviously be parallelized using a GPU.

5   Conclusion

This paper proposed a new direct method for robust 3D object tracking. In our method, the image alignment was newly formulated by modeling intensity variations using surface normal information of an object and defining a stability term based on the prediction model about image intensity. Experimental results showed that our method successfully performed even on challenging scenes.

In this paper, we focused on 6D pose estimation of a single 3D object instance in a monocular RGB view, but it would be very interesting to explore further improvements and extensions of our method.

Acknowledgements. This work was carried out during the tenure of an ERCIM 'Alain Bensoussan' Fellowship Programme.

References

1. Baker, S., Matthews, I.: Lucas-Kanade 20 years on: a unifying framework. Int. J. Comput. Vis. **56**(3), 221–255 (2004)
2. Bartoli, A.: Groupwise geometric and photometric direct image registration. IEEE Trans. Pattern Anal. Mach. Intell. **30**(12), 2098–2108 (2008)
3. Basri, R., Jacobs, D.W.: Lambertian reflectance and linear subspaces. IEEE Trans. Pattern Anal. Mach. Intell. **25**(2), 218–233 (2003)
4. Benhimane, S., Malis, E.: Real-time image-based tracking of planes using efficient second-order minimization. In: International Conference on Robotics and Automation, pp. 943–948 (2004)
5. Caron, G., Dame, A., Marchand, E.: Direct model based visual tracking and pose estimation using mutual information. Image Vis. Comput. **32**(1), 54–63 (2014)
6. Chambolle, A., Pock, T.: A first-order primal-dual algorithm for convex problems with applications to imaging. J. Math. Imaging Vis. **40**(1), 120–145 (2010)
7. Comport, A.I., Marchand, E., Pressigout, M., Chaumette, F.: Real-time markerless tracking for augmented reality: the virtual visual servoing framework. IEEE Trans. Visual Comput. Graph. **12**(4), 615–628 (2006)
8. Crivellaro, A., Lepetit, V.: Robust 3D tracking with descriptor fields. In: International Conference on Computer Vision and Pattern Recognition, pp. 3414–3421 (2014)
9. Dambreville, S., Sandhu, R., Yezzi, A., Tannenbaum, A.: Robust 3D pose estimation and efficient 2D region-based segmentation from a 3D shape prior. In: Forsyth, D., Torr, P., Zisserman, A. (eds.) ECCV 2008. LNCS, vol. 5303, pp. 169–182. Springer, Heidelberg (2008). doi:10.1007/978-3-540-88688-4_13
10. Dame, A., Marchand, E.: Second-order optimization of mutual information for real-time image registration. IEEE Trans. Image Process. **21**(9), 4190–4203 (2012)
11. Drummond, T., Cipolla, R.: Real-time visual tracking of complex structures. IEEE Trans. Pattern Anal. Mach. Intell. **24**(7), 932–946 (2002)
12. Engel, J., Schöps, T., Cremers, D.: LSD-SLAM: large-scale direct monocular SLAM. In: Fleet, D., Pajdla, T., Schiele, B., Tuytelaars, T. (eds.) ECCV 2014. LNCS, vol. 8690, pp. 834–849. Springer, Heidelberg (2014). doi:10.1007/978-3-319-10605-2_54
13. Garrido-Jurado, S., Muñoz Salinas, R., Madrid-Cuevas, F.J., Marín-Jiménez, M.J.: Automatic generation and detection of highly reliable fiducial markers under occlusion. Pattern Recogn. **47**(6), 2280–2292 (2014)
14. Haussecker, H.W., Fleet, D.J.: Computing optical flow with physical models of brightness variation. IEEE Trans. Pattern Anal. Mach. Intell. **23**(6), 661–673 (2001)
15. Hinterstoisser, S., Lepetit, V., Ilic, S., Holzer, S., Bradski, G., Konolige, K., Navab, N.: Model based training, detection and pose estimation of texture-less 3D objects in heavily cluttered scenes. In: Lee, K.M., Matsushita, Y., Rehg, J.M., Hu, Z. (eds.) ACCV 2012. LNCS, vol. 7724, pp. 548–562. Springer, Heidelberg (2013). doi:10.1007/978-3-642-37331-2_42

16. Irani, M., Anandan, P.: Robust multi-sensor image alignment. In: International Conference on Computer Vision, pp. 959–966 (1998)
17. Jin, H., Favaro, P., Soatto, S.: Real-time feature tracking and outlier rejection with changes in illumination. In: International Conference on Computer Vision, pp. 684–689 (2001)
18. Krull, A., Brachmann, E., Michel, F., Ying Yang, M., Gumhold, S., Rother, C.: Learning analysis-by-synthesis for 6D pose estimation in RGB-D images. In: International Conference on Computer Vision, pp. 954–962 (2015)
19. Lucas, B.D., Kanade, T.: An iterative image registration technique with an application to stereo vision. In: International Joint Conference on Artificial Intelligence, pp. 674–679 (1981)
20. Negahdaripour, S.: Revised definition of optical flow: integration of radiometric and geometric cues for dynamic scene analysis. IEEE Trans. Pattern Anal. Mach. Intell. **20**(9), 961–979 (1998)
21. Nguyen, M.H., de la Torre, F.: Metric learning for image alignment. Int. J. Comput. Vis. **88**(1), 69–84 (2010)
22. Prisacariu, V.A., Reid, I.D.: PWP3D: real-time segmentation and tracking of 3D objects. Int. J. Comput. Vis. **98**(3), 335–354 (2012)
23. Richa, R., Sznitman, R., Taylor, R., Hager, G.: Visual tracking using the sum of conditional variance. In: International Conference on Intelligent Robots and Systems, pp. 2953–2958 (2011)
24. Rosenhahn, B., Brox, T., Weickert, J.: Three-dimensional shape knowledge for joint image segmentation and pose tracking. Int. J. Comput. Vis. **73**(3), 243–262 (2007)
25. Scandaroli, G.G., Meilland, M., Richa, R.: Improving NCC-based direct visual tracking. In: Fitzgibbon, A., Lazebnik, S., Perona, P., Sato, Y., Schmid, C. (eds.) ECCV 2012. LNCS, vol. 7577, pp. 442–455. Springer, Heidelberg (2012). doi:10.1007/978-3-642-33783-3_32
26. Schmaltz, C., Rosenhahn, B., Brox, T., Weickert, J.: Region-based pose tracking with occlusions using 3D models. Mach. Vis. Appl. **23**(3), 557–577 (2012)
27. Skrypnyk, I., Lowe, D.G.: Scene modelling, recognition and tracking with invariant image features. In: International Symposium on Mixed and Augmented Reality, pp. 110–119 (2004)
28. Tan, D.J., Ilic, S.: Multi-forest tracker: a chameleon in tracking. In: International Conference on Computer Vision and Pattern Recognition, pp. 1202–1209 (2014)
29. Tejani, A., Tang, D., Kouskouridas, R., Kim, T.-K.: Latent-class hough forests for 3D object detection and pose estimation. In: Fleet, D., Pajdla, T., Schiele, B., Tuytelaars, T. (eds.) ECCV 2014. LNCS, vol. 8694, pp. 462–477. Springer, Heidelberg (2014). doi:10.1007/978-3-319-10599-4_30
30. Vacchetti, L., Lepetit, V., Fua, P.: Stable real-time 3D tracking using online and offline information. IEEE Trans. Pattern Anal. Mach. Intell. **26**(10), 1385–1391 (2004)
31. Wuest, H., Wientapper, F., Stricker, D.: Adaptable model-based tracking using analysis-by-synthesis techniques. In: International Conference on Computer Analysis of Images and Patterns, pp. 20–27 (2007)
32. Zhang, L., Curless, B., Hertzmann, A., Seitz, S.M.: Shape and motion under varying illumination: unifying structure from motion, photometric stereo, and multiview stereo. In: International Conference on Computer Vision, pp. 618–625 (2003)

A Radial Search Method for Fast Nearest Neighbor Search on Range Images

Federico Tombari[1], Samuele Salti[1], Luca Puglia[2(✉)], Giancarlo Raiconi[3], and Luigi Di Stefano[1]

[1] Dipartimento di Informatica - Scienza e Ingegneria,
University of Bologna, Bologna, Italy
{federico.tombari,samuele.salti,luigi.distefano}@unibo.it

[2] Dipartimento di Informatica, University of Salerno, Salerno, Italy
lpuglia@unisa.it

[3] D.I.E.M., University of Salerno, Salerno, Italy
gianni@unisa.it

Abstract. In this paper, we propose an efficient method for the problem of Nearest Neighbor Search (NNS) on 3D data provided in the form of range images. The proposed method exploits the organized structure of range images to speed up the neighborhood exploration by operating radially from the query point and terminating the search by evaluating adaptive stop conditions. Despite performing an approximate search, our method is able to yield results comparable to the exhaustive search in terms of accuracy of the retrieved neighbors. When tested against open source implementations of state-of-the-art NNS algorithms, radial search obtains better performance than the other algorithms in terms of speedup, while yielding the same level of accuracy. Additional experiments show how our algorithm improves the overall efficiency of a highly computational demanding application such as 3D keypoint detection and description.

1 Introduction and Related Work

In the past few years there has been a growing interest in processing 3D data for computer vision tasks such as 3D keypoint detection and description, surface matching and segmentation, 3D object recognition and categorization. The relevance of such applications has been fostered by the availability, in the consumer market, of new low-cost RGB-D cameras, which can simultaneously capture RGB and range images at a high frame rate. Such devices are either based on structured light (e.g. Microsoft Kinect, Asus Xtion) or Time-of-Flight (TOF) technology (e.g., Kinect II), and belong to the class of active acquisition methods. On the other hand, low-cost RGB-D sensors belonging to the class of passive acquisition technologies are mostly based on stereo cameras [13] or Structure-from-Motion.

Independently from the specific technology being used, each sensor acquires 3D data in the form of range images, a type of 3D representation that stores

G. Hua and H. Jégou (Eds.): ECCV 2016 Workshops, Part III, LNCS 9915, pp. 563–577, 2016.
DOI: 10.1007/978-3-319-49409-8_49

depth measurements obtained from a specific point in 3D space (i.e., sensor viewpoint) — for this reason, it is sometimes referred to as 2.5D data. Such representation is *organized*, in the sense that each depth value is logically stored in a 2D array, so that spatially correlated points can be accessed by looking at nearby positions on such grid. By estimating the intrinsic parameters of the sensors, usually available via calibration, the (x, y, z) coordinates associated to each depth value can be directly obtained. Conversely, point clouds are *unorganized* 3D representation that simply stores 3D coordinates in an unordered list.

Arguably the most ubiquitous task performed on 3D data for the aforementioned computer vision applications is represented by the Nearest Neighbors Search (NNS), i.e. given a query 3D point, find its k nearest neighbors (*kNN Search*), or, alternatively, all its neighbors falling within a sphere of radius r (*Radius Search*). This is for example necessary for computing standard surface differential operators such as normals and curvatures. In addition, NNS is a required step also for keypoint detection and description on 3D data, which are deployed, in turn, for 3D object recognition and segmentation. Another relevant example (among many others) of the use of NNS is the Iterative Closest Point (ICP) [5] algorithm, a key step for most 3D registration, 3D reconstruction and SLAM applications.

When NNS has to be solved on a point cloud, being it an unorganized type of 3D data representation, efficient indexing scheme are typically employed to speed up the otherwise mandatory linear search. Nevertheless, despite such schemes are particularly efficient, the NNS on point clouds can still be extremely time consuming, since the complexity grows with the size of the point cloud. In particular, over the years several methods have been proposed to solve optimally the NNS problem in the fastest way possible based on heuristic strategy [6], clustering techniques (e.g. hierarchical k-means, [8]) or hashing techniques [2]. Currently, the most popular approach is the kd-tree approach [7], or its 3D-specific counterpart known as octree.

In addition to exact algorithms, also approximated methods have been proposed, which trade-off a non optimal search accuracy with a higher speed-up with respect to the linear search. In [4], a modified kd-tree approach known as Best Bin First (BBF) is presented, where a priority queue with a maximum size is deployed to limit the maximum number of subtrees visited while traversing the tree bottom up, i.e. from the leaf node to the root. In [3] a similar approach is proposed, where the stop criteria is imposed as a bound on the precision of the result. More recently, [15] proposed the use of an ensemble of trees where the split on each dimension is computed randomly and that rely on an unified priority queue: such approach is known as multiple randomized kd-trees, or randomized kd-forest. In [12], a library including several approximated NNS algorithms is proposed, including multiple randomized kd-trees [15], BBF kd-tree [4] and hierarchical k-means [8]. In addition, [12] also proposes a method to automatically determine the best algorithm and its parameters given the current dataset. Such, library, known as Fast Library for Approximate Nearest Neighbors (FLANN), is one of the most used libraries for NNS on point clouds: for example, it is the default choice for NNS within the Point Cloud Library (PCL) [1], the reference library for 3D computer vision and robotic perception.

Although all the aforementioned methods for approximated NNS on points clouds can be used also on range images simply by turning this 3D data representation into a point cloud, it is possible to leverage on the organized trait of such data representation to speed up the search. Nevertheless, exploiting the 2D grid available when dealing with range images is not trivial, since nearest neighbor on the 2D grid are not guaranteed to be nearest neighbors also in 3D space (think about two points lying nearby on the image plane but on two different sides of a depth border). Furthermore, and especially for the Radius Search case, it is not trivial to turn a metric radius into a pixel-wise radius in the general case, when calibration data are not available.

In literature, the specialization of NNS to the case of range images is almost unexplored. One of the most relevant techniques is the one implemented in the PCL library for both the Radius Search and the kNN Search, where the main idea is to adaptively define the extent in pixels of the search area on the image based on the 3D data as well as the camera parameters. In particular, in the kNN Search case, the query point is first projected onto the range image by explicitly taking into account the intrinsic camera parameters and the camera pose. In case the projected point lays outside the range image, the nearest element in the image is used as start position. Then, the first k nearest neighbors are sought for by looking in the nearby positions on the image plane. The search area in pixel is then defined based on the distance, projected on the image plane, of the query to the farthest point among the found k neighbors, which is finally searched exhaustively to refine the list of retrieved neighbors. Instead, in the Radius Search case, the intrinsic parameters and the camera pose are used also to translate the input metric radius into the pixel-wise radius of the search area on the image plane, by projecting the estimated 3D spherical neighborhood onto the image plane of the sensor. Additionally, each neighbor on the range image 2D grid is also checked with respect to its 3D distance from the query before being added to the list of neighbors. Notably, this radius search algorithm is similar to the one presented in [10], where NNS is applied to the specific task of normal estimation on range images.

In this work we present a method, dubbed *Radial Search Method* (RSM), which can be used as an alternative to the methods available in PCL [1] for fast approximate NNS on range images. The idea of our approach is, starting from the query point, to incrementally look for neighbors on the 2D grid along radial regions of increasing radius. Specific stop conditions are employed to terminate the search when the candidates obtained are estimated to approximate well enough the real set of neighbors. In particular, we propose two variants of such approach, derived for both the kNN Search and the Radius Search problems. Notably, and advantageously with respect to [1, 10], our method does not require to know neither the intrinsic parameters of the sensor nor the sensor pose. By means of experimental results on 3D data obtained with a consumer RGB-D camera, we evaluate the performance of our approach against the NNS methods in PCL and against the FLANN randomized kd-forest approach in terms of both accuracy as well as efficiency. In addition, we also show how RSM can help improving the performance of a typical 3D computer vision application of NNS such as 3D keypoint detection and description.

2   RSM Algorithm

Our approach is based on the incremental exploration of the neighborhood starting from the query point, along concentric frames. While in the NNS search for range images available in PCL [1], hereinafter referred to as *organized*, the search is carried out over an image sub-region row after row (*raster scan*), in our method the search is made in radial order as depicted in Fig. 1. This allows our algorithm to evaluate less points in the neighborhood of the query point to obtain a similar level of approximation in the search result. Another important characteristic of our exploration strategy is that it is adaptive, i.e. the size of the 2D neighborhood that is considered changes at each query point by evaluating a stop condition that depends on the improvements of the search at each step.

Let q be the query index and e an element of the range image. If the query point is only available as a point in 3D space, it is projected onto the image and the nearest element to the projection is used as starting point q. We define a non-euclidean distance $\hat{D}(q,e)$ on a range image I as the minimum number of horizontal, vertical or diagonal moves to reach e from q. We also use the classic euclidean distance $D(q,e)$ to measure the distance in 3D space between the (x,y,z) points corresponding to q and e. Furthermore, we define $\mathcal{Q}$ as a min-priority queue of (e,p) pairs in which e is the index of a range image element and $p = D(q,e)$ is the priority key. Finally, we define the frame at distance h from a query point q as:

$$f_h(q) = \{e \mid \hat{D}(q,e) = h\}. \tag{1}$$

Figure 2 shows the elements belonging to the sets of the first 3 frames, i.e. $f_1(q)$, $f_2(q)$ and $f_3(q)$, of a query point q.

The key idea is to explore, at every iteration, the space of 3D point candidates defined by one full frame of pixels around the query point, and to stop the search

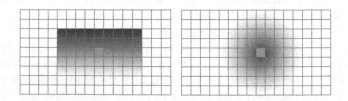

Fig. 1. Depiction of *Organized* (left) and RSM (right) search strategies: the light-colored square in the middle is the query point, while the darker a cell is the earlier it is explored. (Color figure online)

				3	3	3	3	3	3	3						
				3	2	2	2	2	2	3						
				3	2	1	1	1	2	3						
				3	2	1	q	1	2	3						
				3	2	1	1	1	2	3						
				3	2	2	2	2	2	3						
				3	3	3	3	3	3	3						

Fig. 2. Elements in the set of frames $f_1(q)$, $f_2(q)$ and $f_3(q)$.

whencver the number of *inliers* (e.g., found nearest neighbors) in the currently explored frame is too low. It is also important to make the exploration robust with respect to the presence of invalid points in the range image. In fact in many practical cases the acquired range images contains several invalid points, due to limitations in the sensing range or in dealing with specific surfaces, such as dark and reflective surfaces for active sensors, non-Lambertian surfaces and low-textured regions for passive sensors. Figure 3 shows how the algorithm has to work in the presence of invalid points. Even if an invalid point is encountered along the exploration of a frame, the search must continue beyond it. In the extreme case of one or more frames of invalid points, the stop condition should offer a setup that allows to continue the search in the next valid frames to be able to find other valid neighbors.

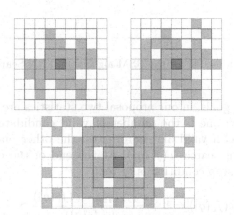

Fig. 3. The solution is represented by yellow points, while in gray we denote invalid elements. On the left, an example of the solution in the absence of invalid points; on the right, an example of the same neighborhood where some of the points are invalid, e.g. due to a change in viewpoint. Bottom: a case where an entire frame is composed of invalid points. The valid points in the neighborhood should still be evaluated and inserted in the solution.

```
function RSM_KNN(K, q, δ̃)
    i ← 1
    Q ← (q, 0)
    while fᵢ(q) ∈ image do
        ι ← 0
        ν ← 0
        for all e ∈ fᵢ(q) do
            if is_valid(e) then
                ν ← ν + 1
                if Q.size() < K then
                    Q.push(e, D(e, q))
                    ι ← ι + 1
                else if Q.top > D(e, q) then
                    Q.pop()
                    Q.push(e, D(e, q))
                    ι ← ι + 1
                end if
            end if
        end for
        if ν > 0 then
            δ ← δ + (ν−ι)/ν
        else
            δ ← δ + 1
        end if
        if δ > δ̃ then break
        if ι > 0 then δ ← 0
        i ← i + 1
    end while
    return Q
end function
```

Fig. 4. Pseudo-code for the RSM algorithm, kNN Search mode.

To meet all these goals, in our proposal two statistics are accumulated while exploring each frame: one is the number of valid candidates $\nu\left(f_i\left(q\right)\right)$, i.e. all neighboring points with valid 3D coordinates, the other one is the number of inliers for the current search, $\iota\left(f_i\left(q\right)\right)$. At the end of the exploration of each frame, the following stop condition is tested:

$$\delta\left(f_i\left(q\right)\right) = 1 - \frac{\nu\left(f_i\left(q\right)\right) - \iota\left(f_i\left(q\right)\right)}{\nu\left(f_i\left(q\right)\right)} > \tilde{\delta} \qquad (2)$$

where $\tilde{\delta}$ is a user defined parameter. Intuitively, if the percentage of outliers (i.e., 1 minus the percentage of inliers) for the current frame is greater than a pre-defined threshold, the search is terminated.

To take into account the possibility that multiple frames are entirely composed of invalid points or outliers we allow the parameter $\tilde{\delta}$ to take integer values greater than 1. In this case, the parameter counts the number of frames entirely

```
function RSM_RADIUS(Radius, q, δ̃)
    i ← 1
    L ← (q, 0)
    while fᵢ(q) ∈ image do
        ι ← 0
        ν ← 0
        for all e ∈ fᵢ(q) do
            if is_valid(e) then
                ν ← ν + 1
                if D(q, e) < Radius then
                    L.push(e, D(e, q))
                    ι ← ι + 1
                end if
            end if
        end for
        if ν > 0 then
            δ ← δ + (ν−ι)/ν
        else
            δ ← δ + 1
        end if
        if δ > δ̃ then break
        if ι > 0 then δ ← 0
        i ← i + 1
    end while
    return L.sort()
end function
```

Fig. 5. Pseudo-code for the RSM algorithm, Radius Search mode.

composed of invalid points or outliers to be consecutively met before stopping the search. Every time such kind of frames are met, we set

$$\delta (f_i (q)) = \delta (f_{i-1} (q)) + 1 \tag{3}$$

and then check the stop condition.

The pseudo-code of the kNN Search can be found in Fig. 4. For each query point, the algorithm keeps the discovered neighbors in a priority queue $\mathcal{Q}$, which holds the sorted result at the end of the search. $\mathcal{Q}$ is a min-priority queue in which the order is based on the distance between the query point and the element. Starting form the query point, we evaluate the frames in order of increasing distance, push each valid element of the frame in the priority queue if needed, and check if the termination criterion is met after processing every frame. After initialization of the data structures, the search starts from the first frame and continues until the stop criterion is met. In particular, the algorithm accumulates for each frame the number of valid examined candidates ν, as well as the number of those currently included in the nearest neighbor set, i.e. the inliers ι. With this value, it updates the percentage of outliers in the explored frames, δ, taking

Fig. 6. Examples showing one object view of each of the four datasets used in our experiments.

into account the previously exposed rules in case of fully invalid frames. When such percentage exceeds the user provided parameter $\tilde{\delta}$, the search ends.

The pseudo-code of the Radius Search can be found in Fig. 5. For each query point, the algorithm keeps all the elements that have distance less than the radius parameter R. All the points are successively stored in a list $\mathcal{L}$, which is sorted at the end of the search to return the points in distance order. The overall structure of the algorithm is similar to the kNN Search, but due to the nature of the radius search, if a point is pushed into the list it is never removed because it surely belongs to the final solution. For the same reason, the list is not kept sorted during the exploration, and is just sorted at the end, to save computation time.

The only step that may introduce approximations in the result in both algorithms is the stop criterion, the results being identical to the linear search one in the case of exploration of the whole range image. Therefore, the parameter $\tilde{\delta}$ trades off search accuracy for efficiency: since an unnecessary high accuracy negatively affects run-time performance, it is important to choose the right value of such parameter. In the Experimental results section we will analyze the sensitivity of the RSM algorithm to this parameter and provide guidelines on how to choose it appropriately.

3   Experimental Results

In this section, we provide an experimental evaluation of the RSM method. The method has been implemented in C++, and it is here compared with the randomized kd-tree forest algorithm available in FLANN [12], as a representative of the state of the art for approximated NNS on point clouds, as well as with the *organized* NNS algorithm available in PCL [1], as a representative of approximated NNS algorithms for range images. The comparison has been done on a PC equipped with an Intel Xeon E312xx 2.00 GHz (4 cores) processor with 8 Gb of RAM. We have compiled our framework under Visual Studio 2013 with optimization O2, and inline function expansion level set to Ob2. No evaluated algorithm includes any kind of parallelization, so the tests are always run on a single core.

The experiments were performed on four datasets composed of RGB-D images acquired with a Kinect dataset, recently proposed in literature and publicly available[1]. These datasets were originally proposed for the task of point cloud registration, and each of them includes different views of an object without the background: they are denoted here as *Frog*, *Mario*, *Squirrel* and *Duck*. A sample view for each dataset is shown in Fig. 6. The measured average distance of each point from its nearest neighbor on this data is approximately 1 mm. Each dataset includes at least 13 range images. On each range image, 1000 query points have been randomly extracted from the available valid 3D point set, and the results averaged over this set.

We evaluate both the execution times and the accuracy achieved by the tested algorithms. To measure the accuracy, the NNS for each query point has been also carried out by a brute force algorithm performing an exhaustive investigation, and used as ground truth in order to count the number of correctly retrieved neighbors by each approximated NNS algorithm.

3.1 Parameter Sensitivity Analysis

The first experimental analysis we carried out is a sensitivity analysis with the goal of choosing a good value for parameter $\tilde{\delta}$, which is the main parameter the RSM algorithm relies on, in both kNN and Radius versions. In particular, as anticipated, such parameter trades-off accuracy for efficiency: the higher it is, the more precise the outcome of the search will be compared to that of an exhaustive search, but also the longer the whole process will take.

Figure 7 reports the charts relatively to the results, in terms of accuracy and efficiency, on the evaluated datasets where each curve is associated to different values of parameter $\tilde{\delta}$. The two top charts report results in the kNN Search case, while the two bottom charts are relative to the Radius Search case. In each case, the left chart measures the relative search accuracy with respect to the exhaustive search (number of correct neighbors found), while the right chart reports the average time to process 1000 query points in a range image. In the kNN Search case, the x axis reports increasing values of k, while in the Radius Search case, it reports increasing values of the radius (in meters), with values typically used in most applications of such 3D NNS algorithms. In particular, the tests were performed using, for the k parameter, a range of values between 2 and 150, while for the Radius parameter we have chosen a range from 0.005 to 0.030 m.

From the charts related to the accuracy, RSM shows to be equivalent to the exhaustive search if the value of $\tilde{\delta}$ is greater than or equal to 1. Yet, the drop in performance is limited even if $\tilde{\delta}$ is set to low values: the worst result we get is to retrive 92 % of the real neighbors when using $\tilde{\delta} = 0.5$ in the radius search. This result confirms the intution that a radial search can be a good exploration pattern for NNS and shows that the statistics used to define the stop condition are able to limit the explored neighbors to the most interesting

---

[1] http://www.vision.deis.unibo.it/lrf.

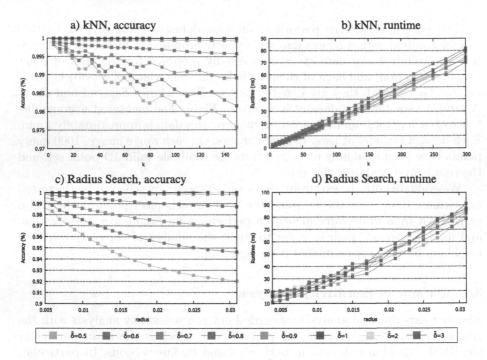

Fig. 7. Sensitivity analysis for the parameter $\tilde{\delta}$. The accuracy is reported on the left charts, the runtime on the right ones. Top charts: kNN Search; bottom charts: Radius Search. The scale of the y axis in (a) and (c) has been expanded for better visualization of the results.

ones. At the same time, looking at the reported runtime, as expected the lower the value of the parameter, the faster the overall efficiency. The gap between different approximation levels increases the larger k or radius get. As the gap in runtime is limited between the different choices of $\tilde{\delta}$, in the remainder of the experimental Section, we will employ the value of $\tilde{\delta} = 1$, given that it yields the highest efficiency among those reporting perfect accuracy.

3.2 Comparison with the State of the Art

Figure 8 shows the results in term of accuracy and runtime reported by the evaluated methods (RSM, FLANN and *Organized*) on the test dataset. As before, the top charts report the kNN Search case, while the bottom charts are relative to the Radius Search case, each chart showing the results at increasing values of the k and the radius parameter. In each case, the left chart measures the relative search accuracy with respect to the exhaustive search (number of correct neighbors found), while the right chart reports the average runtime over all the images of the datasets when processing 1000 query points on each range image.

Interestingly, in terms of accuracy all methods report, in both Search cases, a negligible loss of accuracy with respect to the exhaustive investigation. As far

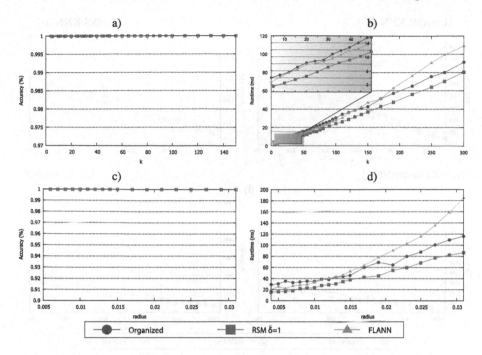

Fig. 8. Accuracy (a, c) and runtime (b, d) reported by RSM, FLANN and *Organized* methods on the evaluated dataset. The scale of the y axis in (a) and (c) has been expanded for better visualization of the results.

as the runtime is concerned, FLANN shows to scale worse than the other methods when k or the radius increases. Nevertheless, when just a few neighbors are sought, it turns out faster than *Organized*, which is surprising given that *Organized* has been specifically conceived for range images. RSM is consistently the fastest for all k and radii. This confirms that taking advantage of the structure inherent to range images can improve NNS efficiency with respect to using a general purpose solution like FLANN, and that a more natural exploration pattern like the radial one deployed by RSM can explore more promising areas of the image first and terminate the search earlier than the raster-scan search deployed by *Organized*.

3.3 Relevance of NNS in Keypoint Detection

To complement previous results, we have compared FLANN, *Organized* and RSM when used within a real and widely deployed application of the NNS problem such as 3D keypoint detection. As for the datasets, we have used the same data used in the previous experiments. In this case, results have been measured in terms of overall runtime of the whole detection process, so to measure out how much the computational advantage brought in by RSM impact in terms of the whole application. In addition, we have also measured the accuracy of the NNS

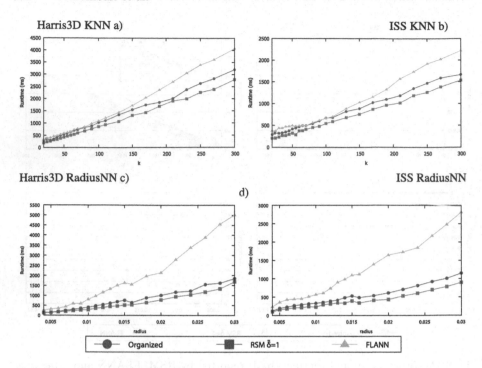

Fig. 9. Runtime reported, respectively, by the Harris3D detector (a, c) and the ISS detector (b, d) when employing, respectively, RSM, FLANN and *Organized* methods for the NNS.

in terms of the final application, i.e. by computing the relative repeatability [17] between the extracted 3D keypoints on pairs of overlapping views. To perform the repeatability evaluation, we have exploited the registration ground truth available with the dataset, that provides the 3D translation and 3D rotation registering each view into all other overlapping ones.

As for the choice of the 3D detectors, based on the analysis in [17] we have selected the Intrinsic Shape Signatures (ISS) detector [18], which provides a good trade-off between repeatability, distinctiveness and computational efficiency. In addition, we have also included in the comparison the Harris3D detector [1], which is an extension of the Harris corner detector [9] to the 3D case. For both detectors, we have used the available implementation in PCL [1]. As typically done by most 3D keypoint detectors [17], both methods rely on a NNS at each point of the range image to compute a local saliency: the extrema of such saliency are then used to localize distinctive keypoints. We have appropriately modified the code so to use, for the NNS, one method among RSM, *Organized* and FLANN, which have been tested both in the kNN Search as well as in the Radius Search version.

Figure 9 shows the results in terms of overall detection time for Harris3D (left charts) and ISS (right charts), both in the kNN Search (top charts) and in the

Radius Search (bottom charts) case. These charts show that by deploying RSM, we can clearly reduce the overall time required to perform keypoints detection, especially when analyzing structures at larger scales, i.e. those defined by larger k or radii, and confirm the practical importance of designing efficient methods to solve the NNS in 3D data.

3.4 Relevance of NNS in Descriptor Computation

In Fig. 10 are shown the results relative to the descriptors tests. On the vertical axis are shown the perfomances relative to the mean time for a descriptor computation. As in the previous tests on the detectors the runtime is evaluated on the Kinect datasets (Fig. 6), the keypoints used are obtained using ISS detectors. Since PCL implements only radius searchability for each descriptor algorithm only the RadiusNN search is compared in the tests. In the figures is possible to see how much the performances are influenced by the neighborhood search. First of all using Fast Point Feature Histograms (FPFH) [14] both RSM and Organized are faster than FLANN (Fig. 10a), but since the main computation is spent around the non-search part (the runtime axis is expressed in thousands of milliseconds) they are very close in the diagram, more explicative results were obtained using Signature of Histograms of OrienTations (SHOT) [16] and Spin Images [11] (respectively Fig. 10b, c), looking closer is possible to see the improvement given by RSM over both Organized and FLANN methods. Furthermore, comparing descriptors results is impossible to notice differences between a description obtained using FLANN algorithm compared to one obtained using RSM or Organized.

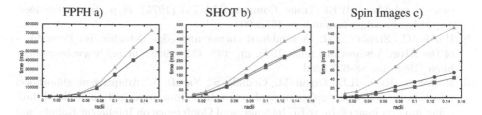

Fig. 10. Mean runtime reported for each keypoint descriptor evaluation, respectively we have FPFH (a), SHOT (b) and Spin Images (c), every descriptor was evaluated with RadiusNN search on a ISS type keypoint.

4 Concluding Remarks

In this paper, we have proposed a new method for NNS on range images, dubbed RSM, which proves to be faster than available algorithms for NNS on this kind of organized data, while preserving the same level of accuracy as the currently employed NNS methods for points clouds and range images. In particular, RSM is

able to leverage on the organized structure of range images and on effective stop
conditions applied while exploring the neighborhood radially from the query
point to terminate the search process as soon as the currently probed locations
do not seem to contain additional nearest neighbors. RSM proved to provide
computational savings both in the Radius Search as well as in the kNN Search
case. Furthermore, the method proved to be particularly effective for speeding
up 3D keypoint detection and description without reducing the quality of the
results in terms of repeatability and distinctiveness.

References

1. Point cloud library. http://pointclouds.org/
2. Andoni, A., Indyk, P.: Near-optimal hashing algorithms for approximate nearest
   neighbor in high dimensions. In: Proceedings - Annual IEEE Symposium on Foundations of Computer Science, FOCS, pp. 459–468 (2006)
3. Arya, S., Mount, D.M., Netanyahu, N.S., Silverman, R., Wu, A.Y.: An optimal
   algorithm for approximate nearest neighbor searching fixed dimensions. J. ACM
   45(212), 891–923 (1998)
4. Beis, J., Lowe, D.: Shape indexing using approximate nearest-neighbour search in
   high-dimensional spaces. In: Proceedings of IEEE Computer Society Conference
   on Computer Vision and Pattern Recognition (1997)
5. Besl, P., McKay, N.D.: A method for registration of 3-D shapes. IEEE Trans.
   Pattern Anal. Mach. Intell. **14**(2), 239–256 (1992)
6. Burkhard, W.A., Keller, R.M.: Some approaches to best-match file searching. Commun. ACM **16**(4), 230–236 (1973)
7. Freidman, J.H., Bentley, J.L., Finkel, R.A.: An algorithm for finding best matches
   in logarithmic expected time. ACM Trans. Math. Softw. **3**(3), 209–226 (1977)
8. Fukunaga, K., Narendra, P.: A branch and bound algorithm for computing k-
   nearest neighbors. IEEE Trans. Comput. 750–753 (1975). http://ieeexplore.ieee.
   org/xpls/abs_all.jsp?arnumber=1672890
9. Harris, C., Stephens, M.: A combined corner and edge detector. In: Procedings
   of the Alvey Vision Conference 1988, pp. 147–151 (1988). http://www.bmva.org/
   bmvc/1988/avc-88-023.html
10. Holzer, S., Rusu, R.B., Dixon, M., Gedikli, S., Navab, N.: Adaptive neighborhood
    selection for real-time surface normal estimation from organized point cloud data
    using integral images. In: IEEE International Conference on Intelligent Robots and
    Systems, pp. 2684–2689 (2012)
11. Johnson, A., Hebert, M.: Surface matching for object recognition in complex 3D
    scenes. Image Vis. Comput. **16**, 635–651 (1998)
12. Muja, M., Lowe, D.G.: Fast approximate nearest neighbors with auto-
    matic algorithm configuration. In: International Conference on Com-
    puter Vision Theory and Applications (VISAPP 2009), pp. 1–10 (2009).
    papers2://publication/uuid/3C5A483A-ADCA-4121-A768-8E31BB293A4D
13. Puglia, L., Vigliar, M., Raiconi, G.: SASCr3: a real time hardware coprocessor for
    stereo correspondence. In: Campilho, A., Kamel, M. (eds.) ICIAR 2014. LNCS, vol.
    8815, pp. 383–391. Springer, Heidelberg (2014). doi:10.1007/978-3-319-11755-3_43
14. Rusu, R., Blodow, N., Beetz, M.: Fast point feature histograms (FPFH) for 3D
    registration. In: Proceedings of the IEEE International Conference on Robotics
    and Automation (ICRA), Kobe, Japan (2009)

15. Silpa-Anan, C., Hartley, R.: Optimised KD-trees for fast image descriptor matching. In: 26th IEEE Conference on Computer Vision and Pattern Recognition, CVPR (2008)
16. Tombari, F., Salti, S., Stefano, L.: Unique signatures of histograms for local surface description. In: Daniilidis, K., Maragos, P., Paragios, N. (eds.) ECCV 2010. LNCS, vol. 6316, pp. 356–369. Springer, Heidelberg (2010). doi:10.1007/978-3-642-15558-1_26
17. Tombari, F., Salti, S., Di Stefano, L.: Performance evaluation of 3D keypoint detectors. Int. J. Comput. Vis. **102**, 198–220 (2013)
18. Yu, Z.: Intrinsic shape signatures: a shape descriptor for 3D object recognition. In: 2009 IEEE 12th International Conference on Computer Vision Workshops, ICCV Workshops 2009, pp. 689–696 (2009)

Direct-from-Video: Unsupervised NRS*f*M

Karel Lebeda[(✉)], Simon Hadfield, and Richard Bowden

Centre for Vision, Speech and Signal Processing, University of Surrey, Guildford, UK
{k.lebeda,s.hadfield,r.bowden}@surrey.ac.uk

Abstract. In this work we describe a novel approach to online dense non-rigid structure from motion. The problem is reformulated, incorporating ideas from visual object tracking, to provide a more general and unified technique, with feedback between the reconstruction and point-tracking algorithms. The resulting algorithm overcomes the limitations of many conventional techniques, such as the need for a reference image/template or precomputed trajectories. The technique can also be applied in traditionally challenging scenarios, such as modelling objects with strong self-occlusions or from an extreme range of viewpoints. The proposed algorithm needs no offline pre-learning and does not assume the modelled object stays rigid at the beginning of the video sequence. Our experiments show that in traditional scenarios, the proposed method can achieve better accuracy than the current state of the art while using less supervision. Additionally we perform reconstructions in challenging new scenarios where state-of-the-art approaches break down and where our method improves performance by up to an order of magnitude.

Keywords: Non-rigid SfM · Structure from motion · Visual tracking · Template-free · Gaussian process

1 Introduction

Non-Rigid Structure-from-Motion (NRS*f*M) is a problem which has attracted considerable interest in recent years, from application areas such as medical imaging and the special effects industry. The problem is usually formulated as the estimation of camera motion and of a time-varying 3D shape for an *a priori* unknown object, using only a set of 2D point trajectories [1–4]. We propose a modified formulation, where the task is completely unsupervised (with the only input being a selection of what object to model). In other words, our task is to estimate the camera motion and time-varying 3D shape of an *a priori* unknown object from a previously unseen video-sequence, using only a bounding box in the first frame. As far as the authors are aware, there is no previous work addressing simultaneous tracking and non-rigid modelling from a monocular camera.

Electronic supplementary material The online version of this chapter (doi:10.1007/978-3-319-49409-8_50) contains supplementary material, which is available to authorized users.

© Springer International Publishing Switzerland 2016
G. Hua and H. Jégou (Eds.): ECCV 2016 Workshops, Part III, LNCS 9915, pp. 578–594, 2016.
DOI: 10.1007/978-3-319-49409-8_50

The NRS*f*M problem is very challenging, due to the ambiguous separation of 2D observations into rigid camera motion and non-rigid object deformation. This is exacerbated in the unsupervised scenario, where the observations are noisy, contain outliers (due to matching failure) and may even belong to background clutter. Despite these issues, we are able to successfully address the problem by adapting techniques from 3D visual tracking. Online estimates of camera trajectory and object shape can be fed back, to improve the accuracy of the point tracking as the sequence progresses.

Another major contribution of this paper is that the traditional 3D object model (defined as a 3D point cloud) is upgraded to a continuous 3D surface using Gaussian Process shape modelling [5]. This makes it possible to segment the object from the background, to reason about self-occlusions, and to intelligently sample points in regions of low confidence (due to the probabilistic nature of the model).

To the best of our knowledge, all state-of-the-art NRS*f*M techniques use 2D point tracks as their input (with varying levels of density). In this publication, we present a unified framework which jointly addresses the problems of 2D point tracking and NRS*f*M directly on video frames. The additional 3D information improves the 2D tracking far beyond what is possible from a generic stand-alone system. In turn these more accurate point tracks help to refine future NRS*f*M estimates.

The 2D tracks required by state-of-the-art techniques are often precomputed (or taken from known annotations). For this precomputation, it is common to work with a reference template or video frame, against which all other frames are registered. This is important as the concatenation of frame-to-frame correspondences (*e.g.* from optical flow) inevitably leads to an accumulation of errors (drift). However, reference frames limit the possible applications of the technique. In contrast, we address the problem of track drift explicitly, using multiple overlapping (both spatially and temporally) sets of dense trajectories, in addition to easily localised sparse trajectories for long-term consistency. This obviates the need for a reference frame, and makes it possible to process a wider range of scenarios. These include strong rotations and self-occlusions, where there may be zero overlap between the first frame and some frames later in the video.

Even though the proposed technique does not require any supervision (beyond a single target bounding box), it extends easily to the more traditional supervised scenarios using precomputed 2D tracks. Additional point correspondences (such as tracks of SIFT features, regressed facial landmarks, *etc.*) can be exploited within the framework to further improve performance.

One major issue in NRS*f*M research is the regularisation of non-rigid object deformations. With unconstrained deformation, there is a trivial solution for any set of observations, where the camera does not move and observations are explained by complicated object deformations. To prevent this, the shape deformation is usually defined as arising from a weighted combination of basis shapes. In this paper we employ a novel set of constraints and regularisation, which ensure that every basis shape represents an extreme (but feasible) pose of the target object. Shape deformations are then constrained to lie within the *feasible* manifold (a convex subspace) formed by these basis shapes. This regularisation renders the method very robust to overfitting.

To summarise, the primary contributions of this paper are: (1) a unified framework to jointly solve the online (although not real-time), direct, template-free NRSfM and point tracking tasks, (2) the use of Gaussian Process shape model and (3) novel constraints to regularise the basis shape selection. The source code of the method will be made available online.

2   Related Work

Most approaches to NRSfM are factorisation-based [6], as introduced by Bregler et al. [7]. To simplify the problem, the orthographic camera model is used [3,4,8,9]. This way, the 2D point locations (per frame) can be expressed as an affine function of the 3D locations, which are in turn a linear combination of *basis shapes*. The set of projection equations (for each 3D point and video frame where it is visible) is then rewritten as a matrix-matrix multiplication. The projection multiplication is decomposed (usually using SVD) back to the factors, yielding the camera parameters (translation and rotation, for each frame), basis shape mixing parameters (i.e. coefficients of the linear combination, for each frame) and basis shape locations (for each point).

This problem is inherently ill-posed, having significantly more unknowns than equations. To render it solvable, additional constraints are applied. In the original paper [7], the low-rank constraint was applied, effectively setting/limiting the number of basis shapes. All following approaches use this constraint and apply additional constraints, priors, heuristics and regularisations. These include spatial smoothness of shape [3,10–12] (the points lying close to each other in 2D tend to lie close to each other in 3D); temporal smoothness of shape [1,3,9,10] (the shape changes smoothly over time); temporal smoothness of camera poses [1,3] (the camera trajectory is smooth in time); and inextensibility [11,12] and other physics-based priors [1,13]. In this paper we propose an additional constraint, that each basis shape must relate to a feasible target pose, greatly improving the stability of the optimisation.

One limitation of the factorisation-based formulation is that it is conditional on all 2D tracks spanning the length of the video. This condition is removed by either estimating the missing data [14] or using methods based on Bundle Adjustment (BA) [1,10], such as the proposed method. In this case, matrix factorisation is replaced with global optimisation of the model parameters (basis shapes, mixing coefficients and camera trajectory). Another reason for the use of Bundle Adjustment is its ability to solve for more complicated camera models. Finally, BA-based techniques also scale well in terms of memory and computation time.

Table 1 compares the properties of selected state-of-the-art NRSfM approaches. Although there are many more works, this comparison captures general trends which can be observed in the field. All current techniques use either a template, a precomputed set of 2D trajectories, or an RGBD camera to address the task. To the best of the authors' knowledge, there has been no prior

Table 1. Comparison of state-of-the-art approaches for dynamic shapes reconstruction.

Property	Zollhofer [15]	Newcombe [16]	Garg [17]	Yu [18]	Proposed
Template-free		✓	✓		✓
Direct	✓	✓		✓	✓
Monocular RGB			✓	✓	✓
Online	✓	✓		✓	✓

approach to solve NRS*f*M which would be at the same time direct, template-free and using only a single RGB camera.

3   Method

In this section, we present our novel formulation of the NRS*f*M problem. See Fig. 2 for an overview of the proposed algorithm. Its input is a video-sequence and optionally additional (independently estimated) trajectories. Its outputs are the camera trajectory, reconstructed basis shapes (point clouds) and the mixing parameters for each frame. From these, the time-varying shape can be reconstructed at any frame (*i.e.* the *instantaneous shape*). Optionally, the shape can be extracted in the form of an explicit polygonal mesh, parametrisable by the coefficients.

As the first step (line 1 in Fig. 2) for the first frame, a bounding box is used to specify the target. Within this boundary, sparse and dense 2D features are extracted (lines 2 and 3) as detailed in Sect. 3.1. Optionally, further supervision points can be supplied (line 4) from another source (such as regressed landmarks in the case of a face sequence). These 2D points are backprojected to the dense object model (see Sect. 3.3 for details) and then duplicated K times to form the initial basis shapes (line 5). The mixing coefficients are initialised to $1/K$. For more details on how the (time-varying) point clouds are represented, see Sect. 3.2.

On every subsequent frame, we first track the existing 2D features in the new image frame, as specified in Sect. 3.1 (lines 7 and 8). Using these 2D tracks and their 3D correspondences, we estimate the current camera parameters (line 10). Unless the camera has undergone significant motion (line 11 in Fig. 2), the algorithm continues processing the next frame.

In the case where the camera has moved far enough since the last Bundle Adjustment to provide a sufficient baseline for depth estimation, we jointly optimise (line 13) all the variables in the system: basis shapes, their per-frame mixing coefficients up to the current time and the camera trajectory to the current frame. Bundle Adjustment is preferred over filtering and other methods since it provides better performance given the same inputs [19]. Due to the novel regularisation, the obtained basis shapes are well constrained and extremely stable, which helps avoid difficulties with the *basis ambiguity issue* [8].

After the 3D point clouds have been optimised, the implicit model is retrained (line 14). This model then provides the object/background segmentation, needed for creation of new points to be tracked. New dense tracks are initialised in the whole image region containing the target object (line 16), while new sparse tracks are initialised only where low confidence in the 3D shape renders them beneficial (line 15). This directed sampling is the main advantage of tackling tracking and reconstruction simultaneously. The corresponding 3D point clouds are initialised by back-projecting the points locations to the model. See Sects. 3.1 and 3.3 for details.

3.1   Obtaining Point Trajectories

Estimation of dense point tracks within a video sequence is inherently burdened by the drift problem: concatenation of frame-to-frame point correspondences leads to error accumulation, rendering long term dense trajectories unreliable. This is traditionally countered by having a reference frame, to which all other frames are registered, instead of concatenation. While this removes drift caused by accumulation of errors, it adds the requirement to have a single frame which overlaps all other frames. This in turn prevents application to sequences with strong rotation and self-occlusion. We instead address this problem directly, by limiting the temporal span of dense tracks to a fixed number of frames. Multiple sets of these tracks are then created, overlapping in both time and space. These are combined during the optimisation, being reconstructed in the common 3D world. Additionally, for long-term consistency, sparse features are used, which are easily localisable and can be tracked frame-to-frame more robustly. Furthermore, the visibility of these sparse points is maintained based on the dense model (*i.e.* due to self-occlusion) and the points may be redetected when they become visible again, facilitating *loop closures*.

The dense features $\mathcal{D}^t$ are sampled on a regular grid within the initial bounding box (in the first frame), or within the area of the estimated object boundary found by projecting the model into the current frame $P(\mathbf{M}|\mathbf{C}^t)$. The density of these points is set by the user to control the trade-off between processing time and level of model detail. After each BA, new dense features are created, spanning the entire area of the projected model, to ensure overlap between the subsets of dense trajectories within $\mathcal{D}^t$. The dense frame-to-frame tracks are obtained by registering feature images obtained through deep-learning [20].

For the sparse tracks $\mathcal{S}^t$, we extract SIFT and Hessian-Affine feature points, which are specifically chosen to be robustly localisable over long timescales. These are then tracked using pyramidal Lucas-Kanade. Unlike the dense features, the temporal span of the sparse tracks is unlimited. This means that we do not need to ensure spatial overlap between consecutive "batches" of tracks, as for the dense points. Indeed, it is counterproductive to sample too many sparse points within any particular region of the target object, as this results in wasted computation. To prevent this, we employ the probabilistic nature of our model which is based on Gaussian Processes and extract new features only in areas with high uncertainty of the shape (*i.e.* where the new features will be the most beneficial; see Sect. 3.3 for details).

For both sparse and dense tracks, background features may become included in either the initial bounding box or later segmentation. For this reason, feature filtering takes place, based on their reconstructed 3D location relative to the model. Features inconsistent with the model are considered outliers and are not used in further computations.

3.2   Non-rigid 3D Reconstruction

Along with the majority of state-of-the-art approaches, we express the instantaneous 3D shape B^t as a linear combination of basis shapes B:

$$B^t = B\alpha^t. \tag{1}$$

This instantaneous shape can be projected to find the equivalent 2D observations:

$$\hat{u}^t = P\left(B^t | C^t\right), \tag{2}$$

i.e. every 3D point in B^t is projected by a camera with parameters C^t to create the concatenated 2D point matrix $\hat{u}^t$. The camera model used in our experiments is full projective, however the approach generalises to any other camera model (*e.g.* orthographic, spherical, *etc.*) as long as it provides a unique back-projection (a 2D point to a 3D ray) for any 2D image location. This way we separate (for every frame) the rigid motion as the camera motion (captured by C^t) and the non-rigid motion as the shape deformation (captured by α^t).

The common $3K$-rank constraint used extensively throughout the NRSfM literature, is equivalent to fixing the number of basis shapes to K. In this paper we introduce a novel regularisation which forces the basis shapes to be meaningful modes, or linearly independent "extremes", of the target's shape. This is done via the following constraints:

$$1_K^\top \alpha = 1 \quad \text{and} \quad \alpha_j \in [0;1], \tag{3}$$

where α_j is the j-th element of α. This effectively limits the targets shape to a *convex* combination of the basis shapes (*i.e.* a finite $K-1$ dimensional manifold in the full shape space, *e.g.* a triangle on a 2D hyperplane for $K = 3$). This is important during the optimisation process (see below) and is also useful for modelling and visualisation.

The projection equation provides a simple geometric error to be minimised during the rigid camera pose estimation:

$$C^t = \arg\min_C \left\| \rho \left(u^t - P\left(B^t|C\right)\right) \right\| \tag{4}$$

where u^t comprises the 2D sparse, dense and supervision points, and ρ is an element-wise robust cost function, to provide outlier tolerance (similar to [21]). This is minimised using the conditional gradient method.

There are two ways in which the instantaneous 3D shape for each frame could be estimated. Firstly, the unknown set of coefficients α^t could be included as parameters to Eq. (4) and estimated for each frame, jointly with the camera pose. The second approach is to postpone the estimation of the mixing coefficients

($\alpha^t \leftarrow \alpha^{t-1}$) until the next bundle adjustment. Empirically we find that the latter approach is more stable as it allows more observations and additional regularisation to be used to constrain the non-rigid deformations.

Theoretically, there is nothing preventing BA from being executed on every frame, however that would be excessively time-demanding (BA is the most time-consuming stage of the algorithm even with sparse execution, see Table 3). Requiring a baseline of sufficient width (non-negligible camera motion) between two consecutive BA runs creates well-timed on-request executions on keyframes characterised by equidistant camera poses.

The cost function optimised in BA is similar to (4), with several major differences:

$$
\min_{B, \mathcal{C}^t, \mathcal{A}^t} \sum_{\tau=1}^{t} \| \rho \left(\mathbf{u}^\tau - P \left(B\alpha^\tau | \mathbf{C}^\tau \right) \right) \| + \Lambda_\alpha(\mathcal{A}^t) + \Lambda_B(B) + \Lambda_C(\mathcal{C}^t)
\tag{5}
$$
$$
\text{s.t.} \quad \mathbf{1}_K^\top \alpha^\tau = 1 \quad \text{and} \quad \alpha_j^\tau \in [0; 1] \quad \forall j, \tau,
$$

where $\mathcal{A}^t$ includes all mixing vectors up to frame t and $\mathcal{C}^t$ contains all cameras up to frame t. Since it is vital to update the mixing coefficients α during BA, the combination of basis shapes needs to be expressed explicitly. The projection errors are summed across all the frames seen thus far (a windowed version, limited to a recent history may be considered if speed is an issue). The robust cost function ρ employed here is the Cauchy loss, as provided by the Ceres Solver [22]. Finally, there are additional priors and regularisations employed. Significant effort is given to these throughout the literature, and sometimes they constitute the major novelty of an article [10,23].

We employ the *temporal smoothness of shape* prior. This means the shape cannot change suddenly over time. This is achieved by penalising fast changes in the mixing coefficients:

$$
\Lambda_\alpha(\mathcal{A}^t) = w_\alpha \sum_{\tau=2}^{t} \| \alpha^{\tau-1} - \alpha^\tau \|^2
\tag{6}
$$

where w_α is an appropriate weighting.

In the proposed method, we want the basis shapes to be extremes (rare, but feasible instances) of the shape variation. In other words, the instantaneous shapes are required to span a (convex) subspace, tightly bounded by the basis shapes. This renders the method very robust to overfitting. The first requirement, that the instantaneous shapes span a limited space, is achieved by limiting the α coefficients (Eq. (3)). The second requirement, that the bounding subspace is tight around the observed poses, stems from the need to decouple the rigid and non-rigid motions. Therefore we introduce the final regularisation term:

$$
\Lambda_B(B) = w_B \sum_{i=2}^{K} \sum_{j=1}^{i-1} \| B_i - B_j \|^2
\tag{7}
$$

where w_B is an appropriate weighting.

Finally, to enforce the prior of *temporal smoothness of camera trajectory*, a different cost is chosen. It is desirable to penalise sudden changes in camera parameters without creating an energy inhibiting free camera motion in the world. Therefore the following is used:

$$\Lambda_{\mathbf{C}}(\mathcal{C}^t) = w_{\mathbf{C}} \sum_{\tau=2}^{t} \begin{cases} 1 & \text{if} \|\mathbf{C}^{\tau-1} - \mathbf{C}^\tau\| \geq \theta_{\mathbf{C}} \\ 0 & \text{if} \|\mathbf{C}^{\tau-1} - \mathbf{C}^\tau\| < \theta_{\mathbf{C}} \end{cases}, \tag{8}$$

where $\theta_{\mathbf{C}}$ is a chosen threshold and $w_{\mathbf{C}}$ is a large (relative to the other costs) constant.

3.3   Object-Background Segmentation

For successful 2D tracking in the presence of background clutter, it is necessary to segment the object of interest from the background. The reconstructed 3D points can give a rough idea where the object is located, however they are not sufficient for segmentation. For this reason, we keep a dense model of the object. It is modelled as a Gaussian Process (GP) in polar coordinates, similarly to [24], where the distance of the surface from the object centre is a function of its bearing angles (azimuth and elevation).

The Gaussian Process is trained on the reconstructed 3D points, and is retrained after every bundle adjustment as follows. Firstly, the 3D points in a *canonical shape* (combined from the basis shapes B using α' averaged over the history thus far) are expressed as vectors in polar coordinates, *i.e.* as a radius r and a pair of angles (θ, ϕ) per point. All the points are then used as training data, regressing the radius from the angles: $r = \text{GP}(\theta, \phi | \kappa)$, where κ is the *kernel* of the GP (in this work we use a combination of exponential, white-noise and bias kernel; its parameters are optimised to maximise the observation likelihood on the training data).

The model can be queried in any direction (θ, ϕ), yielding the local radius. As a result, the model densifies the point cloud, fitting a continuous surface to the sparse points. This way, it tells us where the object is; both in the 3D space (reasoning about occupancy, intersections and self-occlusion) and in the 2D image plane (the aforementioned object-background segmentation). Hence when initialising new point tracks, these can be filtered to occupy only the target area. The depth of the 3D features can then be initialised using the intersection between rays from the camera centre and the shape model.

3.4   Final Model Extraction

This section deals with creation of an explicit 3D model, which is the final product of any SfM algorithm. The GP model described above is *implicit* and non-parameteric, *i.e.* while the object's presence/absence can be queried at any point, it has no discrete set of parameters or elements (*e.g.* vertices or edges), and therefore cannot be simply stored for later use, without also storing the entire state of the system. Furthermore, it tends to oversmooth in both interpolated and extrapolated regions. Finally, the canonical GP model cannot be warped according to the mixing coefficients α. For these reasons, we produce another model, which is a standard watertight triangular mesh. This model can be provided online, *i.e.* after processing every new frame, however that is usually not required. The triangular model is created using Poisson reconstruction [25, 26] on the canonical shape B'. To achieve this, a set of surface normals $\mathcal{N}$ is estimated from the GP model (by sampling points in a very close neighbourhood and fitting a tangent plane), corresponding to every point in B'. The Poisson equation is solved to find the hidden function H, whose gradient approximates these normals

$$\Delta H = \nabla \mathcal{N}. \tag{9}$$

A collection of smoothed model vertices may then be selected from the H_0 isosurface.

Since the task in NRSfM is reconstruction of *time-varying* shape, the model needs to be non-rigid as well. The transfer of the deformation is achieved as follows. Firstly, a rigid model is created using the canonical shape B', analogously to the GP model training. Every vertex of the mesh model is assigned a fixed set of features in the cloud, determined as its k nearest neighbours (set to 3 in our experiments). Since for each 3D feature the offset of basis poses (from the canonical shape) is known, the offset of basis poses of each vertex can be computed as a mean of offsets of its k nearest neighbours. Since the topology of the model does not change when performing the warp, its basis shapes differ only by the vertex coordinates: these are computed by applying the offsets to the canonical model.

Finally, the texture of the model is extracted from the image sequence. As we only provide the model at the end, the sequence is processed again in the second pass. The model is warped into the appropriate shape for each frame using previously estimated mixing coefficients, and the texture of visible mesh faces is updated. For every pixel of the texture, we keep a full-covariance normal distribution in the RGB space and the mean is used as the resulting colour. The observer "samples" are weighted according to the observation angle.

4   Experimental Results

4.1   Synthetic Experiments

We perform an initial quantitative evaluation on the synthetic CubicGlobe dataset. This sequence contains a rotating globe which repeatedly warps into cubic shape and then back to sphere. We report performance of the proposed algorithm with a number of quantitative measures, comparing against several state-of-the-art template-free NRSfM techniques which have source code available online. These include BALM [27], using Augmented Lagrange multipliers to solve for the bilinear factorisation problem in the presence of missing data, LIIP [28], using isometric deformation instead of basis shape combination and

SoftInex [12] which employs the material inextensibility prior as a soft constrain in its energy function. These tests measure three important properties of a successful NRS*f*M technique. Firstly its accuracy of modelling: the fit of the basis shapes to a perfect cube/sphere (the error is expressed relative to the model size, *i.e.* the sphere radius and half of the cube side). The second measured quantity is the accuracy of camera tracking: camera rotation error measured in the angle-axis representation as angular error of both the axis and the rotation angle (since the global coordinate frame is not fixed, the rotation is measured as relative to the first frame). Finally, we measure the depth error of the instantaneous point locations, as Spearman correlation (to overcome the inherent scale ambiguity of the 3D reconstruction) between the measured and ground-truth depth. The sequence will be made available online including all ground truth information, such as shape, trajectory, depth, *etc.*.

It is important to note that all three state-of-the-art comparison methods use the orthographic camera model to simplify computation. This makes it more challenging to evaluate the camera trajectory and depth correlations against the ground truth. To resolve this issue a state of the art Perspective-n-Point algorithm [29] with outlier rejection was used to find the optimal projective camera pose, given the reconstructed 3D point clouds.

Since there are no ground-truth point tracks for this sequence, we provided the state-of-the-art techniques with tracks obtained by our technique. LIIP and SoftInex do not handle occlusions; therefore we run them only on a limited portion of the sequence (the first 50 frames), with only those tracks, which are visible in all 50 frames. Furthermore, the competing approaches do not directly provide meaningful basis shapes. Therefore we use the instantaneous shape from frames 30, 90 and 150 for cube, and 1, 60, 120 and 180 for sphere (where the ground truth shape is pure). The table contains the best possible performance for each of these.

See Table 2 for results. It is clearly visible that BALM failed completely on this sequence, producing large reconstruction and camera rotation errors. Similarly, the depth reported by BALM is not correlated to the GT depth. The results of LIIP are significantly better, with much lower reconstruction errors and rotation error reduced by an order of magnitude, compared to BALM. The average depth correlation is 0.5. SoftInex produces even better 3D reconstructions, with error comparable to the proposed method (although of only one side of the object since it does not handle occlusions). The camera pose is less accurate than that

Table 2. Reconstruction results on the CUBICGLOBE sequence.

	Cube (%)	Sphere (%)	Axis (°)	Angle (°)	Depth (%)
BALM	51 ± 54	14 ± 12	52.6 ± 28.0	56.9 ± 39.7	5 ± 26
LIIP	29 ± 20	5 ± 5	12.9 ± 20.4	8.1 ± 4.4	50 ± 29
SoftInex	4 ± 3	3 ± 2	22.3 ± 8.5	11.8 ± 8.1	79 ± 13
Proposed	3 ± 3	3 ± 3	0.4 ± 0.8	3.5 ± 1.4	95 ± 3

of LIIP, the reported depth is nevertheless strongly correlated with the ground truth.

The results of SoftInex demonstrate an interesting phenomenon. While the per-frame point depth, returned by the algorithm (and used to infer the non-rigid shape) is realistic, it is "flipped" in the z-direction for some frames (*i.e.* the object side is turned inside out; this is probably due to the lack of temporal smoothness constraint). For a fair comparison, we had to detect and correct this during our experiments. Without this, the results of SoftInex are significantly worse, *e.g.* the depth correlation drops to 16 %. When using the proposed method, the reconstructed models cover the whole object (as visualised in Fig. 1) with very low errors. The camera rotation demonstrates even better performance, with error reduced by an order of magnitude due to its inherent ability to perform tracking and modelling simultaneously. The depth estimated by the proposed method is nearly perfect, reaching 95 % correlation with the observed depth.

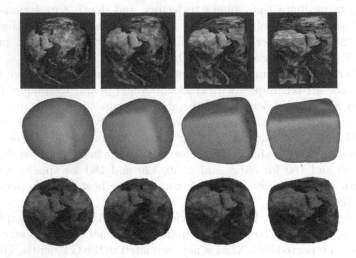

Fig. 1. Example of input sequence and models output by our method: frames #60, 70, 80 and 90 of the sequence CubicGlobe.

See Fig. 3 for visualisation of the obtained mixing coefficients α^t in the first 180 frames of the CubicGlobe sequence. The shape is changing from spherical to cubic linearly, which was closely captured by the coefficient change. Notice the "cropped" peaks, a typical artefact of the proposed method. This is caused by the compactness prior, forcing the basis shapes (spherical and cubical in this case) to lie close to each other and hence being unable to truly capture the very extremes. It, however, does not significantly affect the overall performance, as can be seen in both the qualitative (Fig. 1 and the supplementary material) and quantitative (Table 2) results.

Table 3 shows a breakdown of the execution speed for the different algorithms. It should be reiterated that the competing state-of-the-art techniques use point

1: request bounding box from user
2: $\mathcal{S}^1 \leftarrow$ detect initial sparse features
3: $\mathcal{D}^1 \leftarrow$ initialise dense features
4: *$\mathcal{L}^1 \leftarrow$ load any supervision features
5: B $\leftarrow$ initialise 3D point basis $(\mathcal{S}^1, \mathcal{D}^1, \mathcal{L}^1)$
6: **for** $t = 2 \rightarrow T$ **do**
7:     $\mathcal{S}^t \leftarrow$ track by Lucas-Kanade $(\mathcal{S}^{t-1})$
8:     $\mathcal{D}^t \leftarrow$ track by dense image registration $(\mathcal{D}^{t-1})$
9:     *$\mathcal{L}^t \leftarrow$ load any supervision features
10:     $\mathbf{C}^t \leftarrow$ estimate camera pose $(\mathbf{B}, \mathcal{S}^t, \mathcal{D}^t, \mathcal{L}^t)$
11:     **if** $||\mathbf{C}' - \mathbf{C}^t|| > \theta_{\mathbf{C}}$ **then**
12:         $\mathbf{C}' \leftarrow \mathbf{C}^t$
13:         Optimise B, $\mathbf{C}^1 ... \mathbf{C}^t$, $\boldsymbol{\alpha}^1 ... \boldsymbol{\alpha}^t$ by BA
14:         M $\leftarrow$ retrain shape model $(\mathbf{B}, \boldsymbol{\alpha}^1 ... \boldsymbol{\alpha}^t)$
15:         $\mathcal{S}_{\text{new}}^t \leftarrow \mathcal{S}^t \cup$ detect sparse features (M)
16:         $\mathcal{D}_{\text{new}}^t \leftarrow \mathcal{D}^t \cup$ detect dense features (M)
17:     **end if**
18:     *Create and output explicit mesh model.
19: **end for**

Fig. 2. The proposed algorithm overview. Lines marked with * are optional.

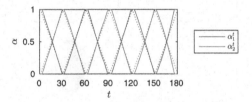

Fig. 3. Mixing coefficients $\boldsymbol{\alpha}^t$ in the CUBICGLOBE sequence (GT shown dotted).

Table 3. Times of processing the first 180 frames of the CUBICGLOBE sequence. The last row does not sum up to 100 % due to various overhead computations, visualisation, I/O wait, *etc.*

	Tracking	Reconstruction	Modelling
BALM (s)	1 357	248	372
LIIP (s)	1 357	18 768	372
SoftInex (s)	1 357	5 416	372
Proposed (s)	1 357	3 234	372
	22 %	52 %	6 %

tracks provided by the proposed method. Therefore the times for point tracking and model training (necessary for tracking) should be included in their timings for a fair comparison. These are marked in grey. It is also worth noting, that the time for LIIP and SoftInex was consumed in computing reconstruction from only 260 tracks in 50 frames, while the others from nearly 20 000 tracks in 180 frames.

BALM also has scaling issues in terms of memory usage. Operating on the same point tracks used in the proposed approach, BALM consumed more than 200 GB of RAM, two orders of magnitude more than the proposed algorithm.

4.2   Real Data Experiments

To show the performance of the proposed algorithm on real data, we firstly use the recently published 300VW dataset [30–32]. In Fig. 4 we compare the performance of the proposed technique against BALM on the 300VW:002 sequence. When given only the sparse facial landmarks, BALM performs similarly to the proposed technique. However, it has difficulties integrating noisier observations; when BALM is provided with the denser internal trajectories generated by the proposed method, it fails to produce a reasonable reconstruction. In contrast the proposed technique is able to fuse these, to produce a far more detailed reconstruction than from the landmarks alone. Figure 5 shows the resulting

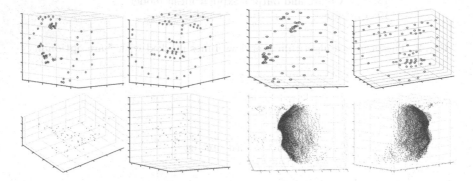

Fig. 4. Comparison of BALM (left two columns) against the proposed technique (right two columns) on the 300VW:002 sequence. Results are shown using only the sparse supervision (top row), and using the sparse supervision with additional densely estimated trajectories (bottom row).

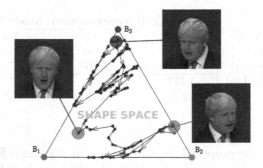

Fig. 5. Reconstructed model overlaid over frames from the 300VW:002 sequence. The shape space visualises the weighted combination of the independent basis shapes. See the supplementary material for an animated version of this figure.

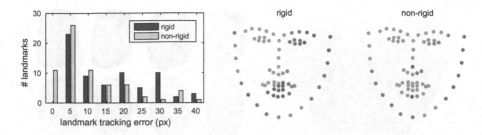

Fig. 6. Landmark tracking error on the 300VW:002 sequence, when using rigid and non-rigid tracking and reconstruction. Left: error histogram, right: landmark error from low (green) to high (red). (Color figure online)

reconstruction of our technique and the trajectory of the model in the shape space defined by B.

It is not only the reconstruction which benefits from the proposed joint approach. Using a non-rigid model can significantly improve tracking results as well. This is demonstrated in Fig. 6, where results are compared between rigid and non-rigid 3D tracking. For non-rigid objects, a "centre" is ill defined. Therefore, a face-tracking scenario is used and the accuracy of landmark tracking is measured. The error is defined as the distance between the GT and the landmarks tracked using the non-rigid 3D model. For each landmark, the error is averaged over all frames. It can be seen that the proposed method has a fraction of landmarks tracked with near-zero error, while the rigid case has no "perfectly tracked" landmarks. Additionally, the rigid variant has a significant portion of landmarks tracked with errors around 20–30 px (mostly near the mouth where the non-rigid deformation is the most pronounced). On average, the tracking error is reduced from 17.4±14.1 to 10.8±10.5 px by using a non-rigid model.

In Fig. 7 we explore the performance of the proposed technique in the fully unsupervised scenario, on the FACE [17] and T-SHIRT [33] sequences. See the

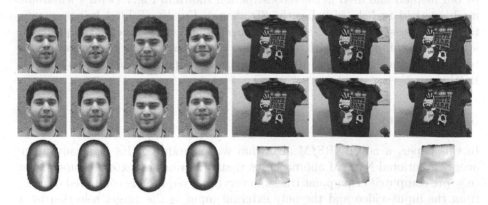

Fig. 7. Example of modelling results on FACE [17] (left) and T-SHIRT [33] (right). From top to bottom: original video frames; video frames overlaid with the instantaneous models; the instantaneous model on its own (untextured).

(a)   (b)

Fig. 8. (a) Details of the model obtained (directly) from the T-SHIRT sequence [33]. (b) Basis shapes obtained from the FACE sequence [17].

Table 4. Quantitative results on the T-SHIRT sequence.

	PCA [33]	Uncon. LVM [33]	CLVM [33]	DDD [18]	Proposed
Error (mm)	18.44	15.50±1.78	14.79±0.90	7.05	17.82±4.72

supplementary material for resulting videos. The models generated by our approach are similar to the results generated by state-of-the-art NRSƒM techniques. However, it should be re-emphasised that we solve a much more challenging problem: the fully unsupervised online scenario. As can be seen, all estimated target poses are feasible and the estimated shapes model the deformations well despite the lack of supervision. It is also obvious from the second row that estimates of the rigid motion (*i.e.* the camera pose) are extremely accurate. In Fig. 8a, the canonical T-SHIRT model (before cropping to contain only the region of interest) is shown in detail. Notice the creases near the top of the model, caused by the way the t-shirt is held. Figure 8b shows the basis shapes automatically identified by our method and used in the reconstruction shown in Fig. 7 (with a wireframe mesh overlaid to help visualise the 3D shape). Finally, Table 4 brings quantitative comparison on the T-SHIRT sequence. The results indicate the proposed approach is competitive with state of the art, even though it does not use a template or another kind of prior knowledge and operates directly on the raw RGB images.

5 Summary

In this paper, a novel NRSƒM algorithm was introduced. Its main advantage over conventional NRSƒM approaches is that it requires no external supervision (e.g. pre-computed clean point tracks): everything required is computed directly from the input video and the only external input is the target selection by a bounding box in the first frame. It is able to autonomously create 3D models from unseen video-sequences. The proposed algorithm is more generic than state-of-the-art methods, with trivial extension to different camera models and additional priors, constraints and regularisations. In addition, it removes several important limitations of conventional methods, most importantly it provides robustness against strong target rotation and self-occlusion.

One of the limitations of the approach is the assumption that the object is roughly compact. Therefore the model is unable to capture more complicated shapes such as walking humans. This is however a limitation of virtually all current model-free approaches.

Acknowledgements. This work was supported by the EPSRC project EP/I011811/1: "Learning to Recognise Dynamic Visual Content from Broadcast Footage" and the SNSF Sinergia project "Scalable Multimodal Sign Language Technology for Sign Language Learning and Assessment" (SMILE) grant agreement number CRSII2 160811.

References

1. Agudo, A., Agapito, L., Calvo, B., Montiel, J.: Good vibrations: a modal analysis approach for sequential non-rigid structure from motion. In: CVPR (2014)
2. Agudo, A., Montiel, J., Agapito, L., Calvo, B.: Online dense non-rigid 3D shape and camera motion recovery. In: BMVC (2014)
3. Paladini, M., Bartoli, A., Agapito, L.: Sequential non-rigid structure-from-motion with the 3d-implicit low-rank shape model. In: Daniilidis, K., Maragos, P., Paragios, N. (eds.) ECCV 2010. LNCS, vol. 6312, pp. 15–28. Springer, Heidelberg (2010). doi:10.1007/978-3-642-15552-9_2
4. Tao, L., Matuszewski, B.J.: Non-rigid structure from motion with diffusion maps prior. In: CVPR (2013)
5. Lebeda, K., Hadfield, S., Bowden, R.: 2D or Not 2D: bridging the gap between tracking and structure from motion. In: Cremers, D., Reid, I., Saito, H., Yang, M.-H. (eds.) ACCV 2014. LNCS, vol. 9006, pp. 642–658. Springer, Heidelberg (2015). doi:10.1007/978-3-319-16817-3_42
6. Tomasi, C., Kanade, T.: Shape and motion from image streams under orthography: a factorization method. Int. J. Comput. Vis. **9**, 137–154 (1992)
7. Bregler, C., Hertzmann, A., Biermann, H.: Recovering non-rigid 3D shape from image streams. In: CVPR (2000)
8. Dai, Y., Li, H., He, M.: A simple prior-free method for non-rigid structure-from-motion factorization. In: CVPR (2012)
9. Rabaud, V., Belongie, S.: Linear embeddings in non-rigid structure from motion. In: CVPR (2009)
10. Bartoli, A., Gay-Bellile, V., Castellani, U., Peyras, J., Olsen, S., Sayd, P.: Coarse-to-fine low-rank structure-from-motion. In: CVPR (2008)
11. Perriollat, M., Hartley, R., Bartoli, A.: Monocular template-based reconstruction of inextensible surfaces. Int. J. Comput. Vis. **95**, 124–137 (2011)
12. Vicente, S., Agapito, L.: Soft inextensibility constraints for template-free non-rigid reconstruction. In: Fitzgibbon, A., Lazebnik, S., Perona, P., Sato, Y., Schmid, C. (eds.) ECCV 2012. LNCS, vol. 7574, pp. 426–440. Springer, Heidelberg (2012). doi:10.1007/978-3-642-33712-3_31
13. Agudo, A., Calvo, B., Montiel, J.: Finite element based sequential bayesian non-rigid structure from motion. In: CVPR (2012)

14. Eriksson, A., van den Hengel, A.: Efficient computation of robust low-rank matrix approximations in the presence of missing data using the L1 norm. In: Proceedings of the IEEE Conference on Computer Vision and Pattern Recognition (2010)

15. Zollhofer, M., Niessner, M., Izadi, S., Rehmann, C., Zach, C., Fisher, M., Wu, C., Fitzgibbon, A., Loop, C., Theobalt, C., Stamminger, M.: Real-time non-rigid reconstruction using an RGB-D camera. ACM Trans. Graph. (TOG) **33**, 156 (2014)

16. Newcombe, R., Fox, D., Seitz, S.: DynamicFusion: reconstruction and tracking of non-rigid scenes in real-time. In: CVPR (2015)

17. Garg, R., Roussos, A., Agapito, L.: A variational approach to video registration with subspace constraints. Int. J. Comput. Vis. **104**, 286–314 (2013)

18. Yu, R., Russell, C., Campbell, N.D.F., Agapito, L.: Direct, dense, and deformable: template-based non-rigid 3D reconstruction from RGB video. In: ICCV (2015)

19. Strasdat, H., Montiel, J., Davison, A.: Real-time monocular SLAM: why filter? In: ICRA (2010)

20. Weinzaepfel, P., Revaud, J., Harchaoui, Z., Schmid, C.: DeepFlow: large displacement optical flow with deep matching. In: ICCV (2013)

21. Torr, P., Zisserman, A.: MLESAC: a new robust estimator with application to estimating image geometry. Comput. Vis. Image Underst. **78**, 138–156 (2000)

22. Agarwal, S., Mierle, K., et al.: Ceres solver. http://ceres-solver.org

23. Paladini, M., Del Bue, A., Stosic, M., Dodig, M., Xavier, J., Agapito, L.: Factorization for non-rigid and articulated structure using metric projections. In: CVPR (2009)

24. Lebeda, K., Hadfield, S., Bowden, R.: Dense rigid reconstruction from unstructured discontinuous video. In: ICCV 3DRR (2015)

25. Kazhdan, M., Bolitho, M., Hoppe, H.: Poisson surface reconstruction. In: SGP (2006)

26. Kazhdan, M., Hoppe, H.: Screened poisson surface reconstruction. ACM Trans. Graph. (TOG) **32**, 29 (2013)

27. Del Bue, A., Xavier, J., Agapito, L., Paladini, M.: Bilinear modeling via augmented lagrange multipliers (BALM). TPAMI (2012)

28. Chhatkuli, A., Pizarro, D., Bartoli, A.: Non-rigid shape-from-motion for isometric surfaces using infinitesimal planarity. In: BMVC (2014)

29. Ferraz, L., Binefa, X., Moreno-Noguer, F.: Very fast solution to the PnP problem with algebraic outlier rejection. In: CVPR (2014)

30. Chrysos, G., Antonakos, E., Zafeiriou, S., Snape, P.: Offline deformable face tracking in arbitrary videos. In: ICCVW (2015)

31. Shen, J., Zafeiriou, S., Chrysos, G., Kossaifi, J., Tzimiropoulos, G., Pantic, M.: The first facial landmark tracking in-the-wild challenge: Benchmark and results. In: ICCVW (2015)

32. Tzimiropoulos, G.: Project-out cascaded regression with an application to face alignment. In: CVPR (2015)

33. Varol, A., Salzmann, P., Urtasun, R.: A constrained latent variable model. In: CVPR (2012)

Physical Reasoning for 3D Object Recognition Using Global Hypothesis Verification

Shuichi Akizuki[✉] and Manabu Hashimoto

Graduate School of Information Science and Technology,
Chukyo University, Nagoya, Japan
{akizuki,mana}@isl.sist.chukyo-u.ac.jp

Abstract. In this paper, we propose a method to recognize the 6DoF pose of multiple objects simultaneously. One good solution to recognize them is applying a Hypothesis Verification (HV) algorithm. This type of algorithm evaluates consistency between an input scene and scene hypotheses represented by combinations of object candidates generated from the model based matching. Its use achieves reliable recognition because it maximizes the fitting score between the input scene and the scene hypotheses instead of maximizing the fitting score of an object candidate. We have developed a more reliable HV algorithm that uses a novel cue, the naturalness of an object's layout (its physical reasoning). This cue evaluates whether the object's layout in a scene hypothesis can actually be achieved by using simple collision detection. Experimental results show that using the physical reasoning have improved recognition reliability.

Keywords: Hypothesis Verification · 3D object recognition · Collision detection · Point cloud

1   Introduction

3D object recognition and 6DoF pose estimation from depth data is one of the fundamental techniques for scene understanding, bin-picking for industrial robots, and semantic grasping for partner robots.

A Model-based Matching (MM) method is generally used to recognize 6DoF of target objects. The MM detects 6DoF pose parameters having high fitting score exceeding a predefined threshold.

However, this method sometimes detects false positives on surfaces having a high fitting score. The reasons are the occurrence of a pseudo surface shared by multiple objects and the presence of objects having parts similar to those of the target object. This is the essential problem of the MM approaches because they detect objects on basis of local consistency such as the surface of object model and the partial regions of the input scene data.

One good solution to solve this problem is applying the Hypothesis Verification (HV) algorithm shown in Fig. 1. HV is an algorithm for scene understanding that uses the MM algorithm as a module for generating object candidates.

© Springer International Publishing Switzerland 2016
G. Hua and H. Jégou (Eds.): ECCV 2016 Workshops, Part III, LNCS 9915, pp. 595–605, 2016.
DOI: 10.1007/978-3-319-49409-8_51

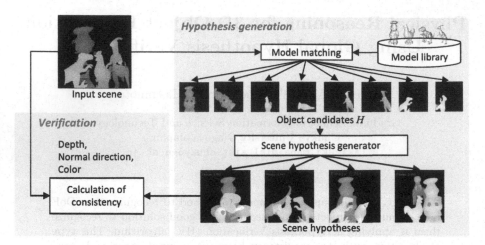

Fig. 1. The overview of the HV algorithm for multiple object recognition.

This algorithm simultaneously recognizes the 6DoF poses of multiple objects by matching an input scene and the scene hypotheses represented by combinations of object candidates generated by the MM with low thresholds. Using this algorithm enables reliable recognition. This is because it maximizes the consistency calculated from global information, such as consistency between the input scene and the scene hypothesis, instead of maximizing the local consistency.

Using the HV algorithm helps to achieve reliable recognition; however, it sometimes detects spatially overlapping objects. This is because it evaluates 2.5D consistency, the similarity of scene point cloud and rendered scene hypothesis (2.5D point cloud or depth image), but it does not consider volumetric information behind point cloud data.

In this research, we have enhanced the reliability of the HV algorithm by using a novel cue, the naturalness of an object's layout (its physical reasoning). This cue evaluates whether the object's layout in the scene hypothesis can actually be achieved. Our HV algorithm evaluates not only the shape consistency between an input scene and a scene hypothesis but also the physical reasoning of the scene hypothesis.

The contributions of this work are the following.

1. We developed a method to detect multiple 3D objects in highly cluttered scenes using the HV algorithm, which uses two types of cues, the physical reasoning of the object's layout and the shape consistency.
2. We developed and propose a simple and fast collision detector using the Sphere Set Approximation method [16].
3. We demonstrated that, when using a well-known dataset, our method outperforms the state-of-the-art HV method from the viewpoint of recognition performance and processing time.

2   Related Work

In this section, we will introduce the algorithm of the HV method and various kinds of model matching methods as an object hypothesis generator of the HV method.

Model matching: This method detects the 6DoF parameter (object candidate) of each object in the scene by matching features obtained from each object model. The model matching role in HV is to detect object candidate with no undetected positives, but where false positives are allowed. The HV method does this by using various model matching approaches as the object candidate generator [1].

There are various kind of features for 6DoF estimation. 3D feature generated from local point cloud around a keypoint [6,14] is generally used. SHOT [14] feature encodes the distribution of surface normal. RoPS [6] feature encodes the statistics (central moments and Shannon entropy) of projected local point clouds onto 2D planes. When the shape of target object is smooth or flat, it is effective extending the region for feature description. OUR-CVFH [2] feature encodes the semi-global surface structures, such as smooth segments. Using RGB information helps to enhance the uniqueness of the feature. The methods [5,15] use such multimodal information. Recently, learned features such as those using decision forest [4] and deep learning [8] have been proposed, and they can deliver robust detection result.

HV method: This approach simultaneously recognize multiple objects by calculating consistency between the scene hypotheses and the input scene. The scene hypothesis is generated by combining object candidates obtained by the model matching method. The HV method regards the multiple object recognition problem as a combinatorial optimization problem of object candidates. The important thing here is what kind of information is suitable for calculating scene consistency. Methods [7,10,13] used depth data in order to evaluate shape consistency. Papazov and Burschka [11] and Aldoma et al. [3] minimizes the number of scene points described by multiple object candidates. Aldoma et al. [3] also used similarity of normal vector direction in addition to the depth similarity. The method [1] have used not only shape information but also color information if it is available.

3   Proposal of HV Method Using Shape Consistency and Physical Reasoning

3.1   Overview

The proposed method consists of main two modules: a hypothesis generation module and a verification module. It's same as general HV algorithm described by Fig. 1.

First of all, in the hypothesis generation module, object hypotheses $H = \{h_i, \ldots, h_n\}$ are generated by using the model matching module. All object

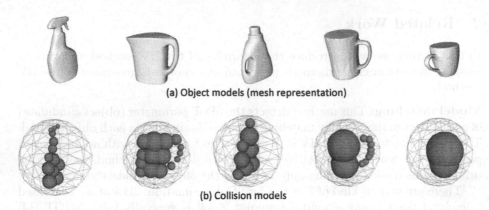

(a) Object models (mesh representation)

(b) Collision models

Fig. 2. Examples of the collision model for the object model. (a) Object models. (b) Collision models of (a). The red spheres are circumscribed spheres of (a). The gray spheres approximate the object shapes. (Color figure online)

models $M = \{M_i, \ldots, M_m\}$ stored in the library are matched to the input point cloud data S. Object hypothesis h_i is given by the pair (M_i, T_i), where T_i represents the 6DoF parameter of object M_i in the scene S. The scene hypothesis generator generates scene hypothesis $hs(X)$ by combining a number of object candidates. X is a bit string with length of n. The bit indicating 1 means a corresponding object candidate is selected as the scene hypothesis.

In the verification module, the similarity between S and $hs(X)$ is calculated. The proposed method solves the combinatorial optimization problem, which explores the scene hypothesis with the highest similarity value by selecting arbitrary bits from X. Therefore, the size of the solution space is 2^n. The proposed method optimizes a fitness function consisting of the physical reasoning and the shape consistency. Each component is explained in the following subsections.

3.2   Physical Reasoning: $f_P(X)$

This term, shown in Eq. 1, evaluates the physical reasoning of scene hypothesis $hs(X)$. In particular, this term evaluates whether an intersection occurs in the object hypotheses of $hs(X)$.

$$f_P(X) = 1 - \frac{1}{R} \sum_{i,j \in R} C(hi, hj) \qquad (1)$$

In this equation, function $C(h_i, h_j)$ is a collision detector. If an intersection occurs between the object hypotheses h_i and h_j, this function returns 1. The term R indicates all combinations of valid object hypotheses (without any identical pairs occurring) in $hs(X)$.

In order to evaluate intersections occurring in object hypotheses, we used collision models for each object. Figure 2 shows the proposed collision models.

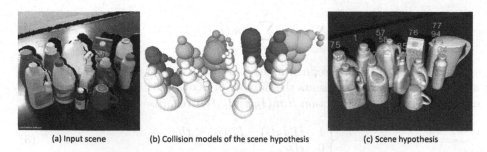

(a) Input scene   (b) Collision models of the scene hypothesis   (c) Scene hypothesis

Fig. 3. Example of the collision detection. (a) Input scene. (b) Collision models of the scene hypothesis. Spatial intersection did not occur with white models, but it did occur with colored models. (c) Scene hypothesis of (b). (color figure online)

They comprise two types of spheres, outer spheres (red) and inner spheres (gray). The outer spheres represent circumscribed spheres of the object shapes; inner spheres represent sets of spheres approximating object shapes.

Using these models enables fast collision detection, because a sphere is the simplest primitive for computing collisions. If two spheres intersect, the following condition (the distance between the centers of two spheres) < (sum of sphere radii) is satisfied.

Collisions in paired object candidates are detected by carrying out the following two sequential steps.

Step 1. Detecting collisions in outer spheres
Step 2. Detecting collisions in the inner spheres of h_i and h_j

Step 2 is skipped if no intersections occur in the outer spheres, but is executed otherwise. Using such a two-stage decision enables fast calculation to be achieved even if scene hypotheses include many object candidates. If intersections occur in spheres, the paired object candidates are regarded as *unnatural*. This means that the paired object candidates h_i and h_j are spatially overlapped.

Figure 3 shows the result of collision detection. (a) shows the overview of the input scene. (b) shows the collision models of a scene hypothesis with 13 object candidates. Spatial intersection did not occur with the white models, but it did occur with the colored models. In this case, this scene hypothesis has the low physical reasoning value $f_P(X)$. (c) shows the actual object candidates of this scene hypothesis. Green numbers indicates the index of each candidate.

In order to generate inner spheres, applying the method proposed in [16] is one practical solution. However, the inner spheres used in the work reported in this paper are manually generated.

3.3   Shape Consistency: $f_S(X)$

This term, shown in Eq. 2, evaluates the shape consistency of the hypothesis scene $hs(X)$. In particular, an image similarity between the depth image of input scene S and that of $hs(X)$ is calculated.

$$f_S(X) = \frac{1}{N} \sum_{i=1}^{N} Sim(I_S(i), I_{hs}(i)) \tag{2}$$

Here, $I_S(i)$ and $I_{hs}(i)$ represent the i th pixel value of the depth image of S and $hs(X)$. Value N represents the number of pixels that have a depth value of either $I_S(i)$ or $I_{hs}(i)$. Function $Sim(I_S(i), I_{hs}(i))$ returns

$$\begin{cases} 1 & if |I_S(i) - I_{hs}(i)| < th_d \\ 0 & else. \end{cases} \tag{3}$$

where th_d is the depth similarity threshold. This value is adjusted by considering the quality of input depth data.

3.4   Optimization

The proposed method solves the combinatorial optimization that maximizes function $F(X)$ by modifying bit string X. The cost function is defined as Eq. 4.

$$\tilde{X} = \arg\max\{F(X) = wf_P(X) + (1 - w)f_S(X)\} \tag{4}$$

where w means the weighting value of two terms. The effect of value w on recognition performance is described in Sect. 4.2. We solved this optimization by using the Genetic Algorithm (GA). The chromosome is defined as the bit string X and the fitness value is the value of cost function $F(X)$.

The GA parameters we used in experiments are as follows: The number of population was 200, Crossover rate was 97 %, Mutation rate was 3 %. When crossover occurred, then two individuals are generated by swapping randomly chosen bits of the parent. When mutation occurred, then a new individual is generated by switching a randomly chosen bit of a randomly chosen chromosome. Initial individuals are generated by turning on randomly chosen bits (valid bits). The optimal number of valid bits are experimentally decided (see Sect. 4.2).

4   Experiments

4.1   Dataset

We evaluated the recognition performance of the proposed HV algorithm. In order to evaluate the method's versatility, two kinds of datasets (Laser Scanner and Kinect) with different data quality are used.

Laser Scanner [9]: This dataset consists of 50 scenes, which are captured by a laser scanner, and five object models. Each object in the scene has ground truth data as the transformation matrix.

Kinect Dataset [3]: This dataset consists of 50 scenes, which are captured by a Kinect sensor, and 35 CAD models of household objects. This dataset also has ground truth data as the transformation matrix.

In order to evaluate the HV performance while ignoring the performance of the model matching method as the object candidate generator, we used artificially generated object candidates (test data elements). Test data elements were prepared by combining ground truth and automatically generated object candidates that represent randomly chosen object models and ground truth transformations which are affected by noise for the translation in the range of ±10 [mm] and ±5 [cm] for Laser scanner dataset and Kinect dataset). As for the Laser scanner dataset, we selected 38 scene which do not include model "rhino" for generating test data elements. Because full 3D surface model of it is not provided. We generate one test data element per scene. As for the Kinect dataset, we selected especially complicated scene data including 12 closely placed objects (see Fig. 3). We prepared 30 test data elements for this scene.

4.2 Parameters

There are some parameters that affect recognition performance. In this section, we discuss the optimal value of each parameter.

Weighted value w: This is the most significant parameter for recognition performance. In the experiment we conducted for this, we explored the optimal w value by iterating a recognition test while changing the value w in the range [0,1]. The recognition performance for the Kinect dataset is shown in Fig. 4. This figure shows recall/precision values and the number of undetected/false positives for each value w. In our experiment, recall is computed by (# of detected true positive) / (# of all true positive), precision rate is computed by (# of detected true positive) / (# of detected object candidate).

$w = 0$: In this case, the proposed HV algorithm does not take into account the physical reasoning of the object's layout. As a result, many false positives were detected. Specifically, about 15.5 objects per scene were detected. (Each scene contained 12 objects.)

$w > 0$: In this case, the proposed HV algorithm takes the physical reasoning into account. The number of false positives per scene was less than 1. However, when the value w was larger than 0.4, the recall rate was decreased. A typical recognition result for this case is shown in Fig. 5.

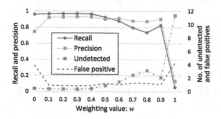

Fig. 4. Relationship between recognition performance and the value w.

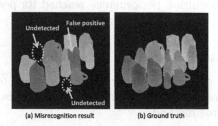

Fig. 5. Typical example of misrecognition when the value w was too large.

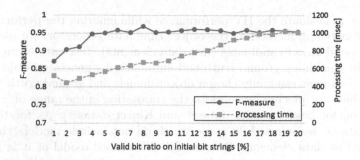

Fig. 6. Relationship between the recognition performance and the valid bit ratio.

In this figure, (a) shows the recognition result obtained using $w = 0.7$, and (b) shows the ground truth (the correct scene hypothesis). In this case, there were two objects that were not detected. The common point these objects share is that they appear small in a depth image, which means that the image similarity would not be improved much if they were detected. As a result, they were frequently not detected.

The result shown in Fig. 4 seems to indicate that $w = 0.3$ is the optimal value.

Depth threshold th_d: This parameter is used for calculating the shape consistency $f_S(X)$. This parameter should be adjusted by taking into account the accuracy of the depth data acquired from the sensor. In the experiment we conducted for this, the parameters we used were 1.0 mm for the Laser Scanner dataset and 1.5 mm for the Kinect dataset.

Valid bits for initial bit strings: One important parameter is the number of valid bits on the initial bit string. In the experiment we conducted for this, we investigated the recognition performance (F-measure and Processing time) while changing the valid bit ratio (indicated as 1) on the initial bit strings. F-measure is computed by $(2 \cdot \text{precision} \cdot \text{recall})/(\text{precision} + \text{recall})$. Results are shown in Fig. 6.

The figure results confirm that the processing time lineally increased when the valid bit ratio was increased. When the valid bit ratio is larger than 5 %, the recognition performance reached its peak. Therefore, we used 5 % as the ratio for the experiments described below.

4.3   Recognition Performance

In order to evaluate the performance of the proposed method, we carried out a recognition experiment for two datasets. In these we compared the following three methods.

1. GHV [3]
2. Proposed HV (S)
3. Proposed HV (S+P)

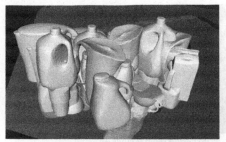

(a) Initial object candidates (100 objects)   (b) Recognition result

Fig. 7. Recognition results. (a) Initial object candidates. Each of them are represented as the surface model. (b) Recognition result.

Table 1. Recognition performance for Laser Scanner dataset. (T: processing time)

Method	Recall	Precision	F-measure	T [msec]
GHV [3]	0.48	0.89	0.62	2471
HV (S)	0.97	0.92	0.94	**742**
HV (S+P)	**0.99**	**0.99**	**0.99**	977

To describe these methods specifically, GHV is the HV algorithm proposed by Aldoma et al. at ECCV2012, HV (S) is the proposed HV algorithm using only shape consistency for evaluating the effectiveness of the proposed physical reasoning, and HV (S+P) is the proposed HV algorithm using shape consistency and physical reasoning with $w = 0.3$. All three methods were implemented by using the Point Cloud Library [12]. All experiments were performed on a desktop computer with an Intel Core i7-6700 3.40 GHz CPU and 16 GB RAM.

Example recognition results obtained with the proposed method are shown in Fig. 7. Initial object candidates are shown in (a). In (a), 100 objects rendered as a surface are illustrated; the red points represent input point clouds. (b) shows recognition result. A scene hypotheses having maximum score are shown. Overview of the input scene is shown in Fig. 3(a).

Table 1 shows the recognition performance for the Laser Scanner dataset. For the method HV(S), its precision rate is lower than its recall rate because some object hypotheses are falsely detected. Such object hypotheses are spatially overlapped (see Fig. 8(a)). This problem has been solved by taking physical reasoning into account. As a result, the precision rate of HV(S+P) was higher than that of HV(S).

Table 2 shows the recognition performance for the Kinect dataset. This dataset poses greater problems than the Laser Scanner dataset because of its noise, point cloud sparseness, the number of objects in the scene (12 objects), and the size of the model library (35 objects). The best precision rate obtained was that for the GHV method, but the proposed method showed almost the same performance. In terms of processing time, however, the proposed method's performance was four times faster than that of the GHV method.

(a) False positive result for HV(S)   (b) Correct result for HV(S+P)

Fig. 8. False positive result for HV(S) and correct result for HV(S+P).

Table 2. Recognition performance for Kinect dataset. (T: processing time)

Method	Recall	Precision	F-measure	T [msec]
GHV [3]	0.91	**0.94**	0.93	2559
HV (S)	0.96	0.75	0.84	713
HV (S+P)	**0.97**	0.93	**0.95**	**613**

5   Conclusion

We have developed and in this paper proposed a novel Hypothesis Verification (HV) algorithm that can recognize the 6 DoF parameters of multiple objects. Our method optimizes the layout of the objects in the scene by using two cues. One is the shape consistency for evaluating similarity between the input scene and the scene hypothesis representing a candidate for the object's layout. The other is a novel cue, the layout's physical reasoning. It evaluates the physical naturalness of the object's layout by using simple and fast collision detection. We have demonstrated that using the physical reasoning is an effective way to improve precision rate. We also confirmed that the proposed method shows higher reliability than that of the state-of-the-art method.

Acknowledgements. This work was partially supported by Grant-in-Aid for Scientific Research (C) 26420398.

References

1. Aldoma, A., Tombari, F., Prankl, J., Richtsfeld, A., di Stefano, L., Vincze, M.: Multimodal cue integration through hypotheses verification for RGB-D object recognition and 6DOF pose estimation. In: IEEE International Conference on Robotics and Automation (ICRA), pp. 2104–2111 (2013)

2. Aldoma, A., Tombari, F., Rusu, R.B., Vincze, M.: OUR-CVFH – oriented, unique and repeatable clustered viewpoint feature histogram for object recognition and 6DOF pose estimation. In: Pinz, A., Pock, T., Bischof, H., Leberl, F. (eds.) DAGM/OAGM 2012. LNCS, vol. 7476, pp. 113–122. Springer, Heidelberg (2012). doi:10.1007/978-3-642-32717-9_12

3. Aldoma, A., Tombari, F., Stefano, L., Vincze, M.: A global hypotheses verification method for 3D object recognition. In: Fitzgibbon, A., Lazebnik, S., Perona, P., Sato, Y., Schmid, C. (eds.) ECCV 2012. LNCS, vol. 7574, pp. 511–524. Springer, Heidelberg (2012). doi:10.1007/978-3-642-33712-3_37

4. Tejani, A., Tang, D., Kouskouridas, R., Kim, T.-K.: Latent-class hough forests for 3D object detection and pose estimation. In: Fleet, D., Pajdla, T., Schiele, B., Tuytelaars, T. (eds.) ECCV 2014. LNCS, vol. 8694, pp. 462–477. Springer, Heidelberg (2014). doi:10.1007/978-3-319-10599-4_30

5. Drost, B., Ilic, S.: 3D object detection and localization using multimodal point pair features. In: Second International Conference on 3D Imaging, Modeling, Processing, Visualization and Transmission (3DIMPVT), pp. 9–16 (2012)

6. Guo, Y., Sohel, F.A., Bennamoun, M., Lu, M., Wan, J.: Rotational projection statistics for 3D local surface description and object recognition. Int. J. Comput. Vis. **105**(1), 63–86 (2013)

7. Hashimoto, M., Sumi, K., Usami, T.: Recognition of multiple objects based on global image consistency. In: Proceedings of the British Machine Vision Conference (BMVC), pp. 1–10 (1999)

8. Kehl, W., Milletari, F., Tombari, F., Ilic, S., Navab, N.: Deep learning of local RGB-D patches for 3D object detection and 6D pose estimation. In: Leibe, B., Matas, J., Sebe, N., Welling, M. (eds.) ECCV 2016. LNCS, vol. 9907, pp. 205–220. Springer, Heidelberg (2016). doi:10.1007/978-3-319-46487-9_13

9. Mian, A.S., Bennamoun, M., Owens, R.: Three-dimensional model-based object recognition and segmentation in cluttered scenes. IEEE Trans. Pattern Anal. Mach. Intell. **28**(10), 1584–1601 (2006)

10. Narayanan, V., Likhachev, M.: PERCH: perception via search for multi-object recognition and localization. In: IEEE International Conference on Robotics and Automation (ICRA), pp. 5052–5059 (2016)

11. Papazov, C., Burschka, D.: An efficient RANSAC for 3D object recognition in noisy and occluded scenes. In: Kimmel, R., Klette, R., Sugimoto, A. (eds.) ACCV 2010. LNCS, vol. 6492, pp. 135–148. Springer, Heidelberg (2011). doi:10.1007/978-3-642-19315-6_11

12. Rusu, R.B., Cousins, S.: 3D is here: Point cloud library (PCL). In: IEEE International Conference on Robotics and Automation (ICRA), pp. 1–4 (2011)

13. Sui, Z., Jenkins, O.C., Desingh, K.: Axiomatic particle filtering for goal-directed robotic manipulation. In: IEEE/RSJ International Conference on Intelligent Robots and Systems (IROS), pp. 4429–4436 (2015)

14. Tombari, F., Salti, S., Stefano, L.: Unique signatures of histograms for local surface description. In: Daniilidis, K., Maragos, P., Paragios, N. (eds.) ECCV 2010. LNCS, vol. 6313, pp. 356–369. Springer, Heidelberg (2010). doi:10.1007/978-3-642-15558-1_26

15. Tombari, F., Salti, S., di Stefano, L.: A combined texture-shape descriptor for enhanced 3D feature matching. In: 18th IEEE International Conference on Image Processing (ICIP), pp. 809–812 (2011)

16. Wang, R., Zhou, K., Snyder, J., Liu, X., Bao, H., Peng, Q., Guo, B.: Variational sphere set approximation for solid objects. Vis. Comput. **22**(9–11), 612–621 (2006)

On Evaluation of 6D Object Pose Estimation

Tomáš Hodaň[✉], Jiří Matas, and Štěpán Obdržálek

Center for Machine Perception, Czech Technical University in Prague,
Prague, Czech Republic
hodantom@cmp.felk.cvut.cz

Abstract. A pose of a rigid object has 6 degrees of freedom and its full
knowledge is required in many robotic and scene understanding applications. Evaluation of 6D object pose estimates is not straightforward.
Object pose may be ambiguous due to object symmetries and occlusions, *i.e.* there can be multiple object poses that are indistinguishable
in the given image and should be therefore treated as equivalent. The
paper defines 6D object pose estimation problems, proposes an evaluation methodology and introduces three new pose error functions that
deal with pose ambiguity. The new error functions are compared with
functions commonly used in the literature and shown to remove certain types of non-intuitive outcomes. Evaluation tools are provided at:
https://github.com/thodan/obj_pose_eval.

1   Introduction

Object localization and detection are among the core problems of computer
vision. Traditional methods work with 2D images and typically describe pose of
the detected object by a bounding box, which encodes 2D translation and scale
[1,2]. There is no information about the object orientation and only a rough
notion of the object distance. A pose of a rigid object has 6 degrees of freedom,
3 in translation and 3 in rotation, and its full knowledge is required in many
robotic and scene understanding applications.

Although methods trying to extract a richer pose description from 2D images
exist [3,4], the task can be simplified if depth images are used as additional input
data. RGB-D – aligned color and depth – images which concurrently capture
appearance and geometry of the scene can be obtained by *e.g.* Kinect-like sensors
that are common in robotic applications.

Evaluation of 6D object pose estimates is not straightforward. Object pose
can be ambiguous due to object symmetries and occlusions, *i.e.* there can be
multiple object poses that are indistinguishable in the given image and should
be therefore treated as equivalent (Fig. 1). This issue has been out of focus in the
work on 6D object pose estimation. In evaluation of pose estimates described
by 2D bounding boxes, the indistinguishable poses are treated as equivalent
implicitly since all are described by the same bounding box.

The main contribution of this paper are three new functions to measure error
of an estimated 6D object pose w.r.t. the ground truth 6D object pose. All three

© Springer International Publishing Switzerland 2016
G. Hua and H. Jégou (Eds.): ECCV 2016 Workshops, Part III, LNCS 9915, pp. 606–619, 2016.
DOI: 10.1007/978-3-319-49409-8_52

(a)   (b)   (c)   (d)   (e)

Fig. 1. Different poses of the cup (a–b) cannot be distinguished if the handle is not visible due to self-occlusion (c). Pose of the pen (d) is ambiguous if its discriminative ends are occluded by another objects (e).

are invariant under pose ambiguity, *i.e.* they treat the indistinguishable poses as approximately equivalent. The Visible Surface Discrepancy (e_{VSD}) measures misalignment over the visible surface of the object model and is thus inherently invariant under pose ambiguity. The Average and the Maximum Corresponding Point Distance (e_{ACPD}, e_{MCPD}) measure misalignment over the entire model surface when considering all indistinguishable poses, which are assumed known.

We define two 6D object pose estimation problems in Sect. 2, propose an evaluation methodology in Sect. 3, review the commonly used pose error functions and introduce the new functions in Sect. 4, present experimental comparison of the pose error functions in Sect. 5, and conclude in Sect. 6.

2   6D Object Pose Estimation Problems

A 6D object pose estimator is assumed to report its predictions on the basis of two sources of information. First, at training time, it is provided with a training set $T = \{T_1, T_2, \dots, T_n\}$ for a set of rigid objects represented by identifiers $O = \{1, 2, \dots, n\}$. The training data T_i may have different forms, *e.g.* a 3D object model or a set of RGB or RGB-D images, where each image shows one object instance in a known 6D pose. Second, at test time, it is provided with a single test RGB or RGB-D image I, which might be accompanied with information about objects that are visible in the image. The goal is to estimate a single 6D pose for each visible object instance.

Prior information about the object presence in I distinguishes two problems:

6D Localization Problem

Training input: A training set T, as described above.

    Test input: An image I and a multiset $L_I = \{o_1, o_2, \dots, o_k\}$, where $o_i \in O$ are identifiers of the objects present in I. Note: Multiple instances of an object may be present in I, *i.e.* the same identifier may be multiple times in L_I.

Test output: A sequence $E_I = ((o_1, \hat{\mathbf{P}}_1, s_1), (o_2, \hat{\mathbf{P}}_2, s_2), \dots, (o_k, \hat{\mathbf{P}}_k, s_k))$, where $\hat{\mathbf{P}}_i$ is an estimated 6D pose of an instance of object $o_i \in O$ with confidence $s_i \in (0, 1]$. Note: $|E_I| = |L_I|$, the size of the output is fixed by the input.

6D Detection Problem

Training input: A training set T, as described above.

Test input: An image I. No prior information about the object presence is provided, there may be $j \geq 0$ instances of each object $o \in O$.

Test output: A sequence $E_I = ((o_1, \hat{\mathbf{P}}_1, s_1), (o_2, \hat{\mathbf{P}}_2, s_2), \ldots, (o_m, \hat{\mathbf{P}}_m, s_m))$, where $\hat{\mathbf{P}}_i$ is an estimated 6D pose of an instance of object $o_i \in O$ with confidence $s_i \in (0, 1]$. Note: The size of the output $|E_I|$ depends on the estimator.

The 6D localization problem is a generalization of the problem defined by Hinterstoisser et al. [5], where the goal is to detect a single instance of a given object per image, *i.e.* $|L_I| = 1$.

In evaluation of the 6D localization problem, if there are for some object more estimated poses than the specified number j of instances, which is given by L_I, only j estimated poses with the highest confidence s are considered.

3   Evaluation Methodology

We propose the following methodology to evaluate performance of a 6D object pose estimator in the problems defined above. It includes an algorithm that determines the estimated poses that are considered correct (Sect. 3.1), a definition of pose error functions (described later in Sect. 4), and a definition of performance scores (Sect. 3.2).

In this paper, a pose of a rigid 3D object is represented by a 4×4 matrix $\mathbf{P} = [\mathbf{R}, \mathbf{t}; 0, 1]$, where $\mathbf{R}$ is a 3×3 rotation matrix, and $\mathbf{t}$ is a 3×1 translation vector. An object is represented by a model $\mathcal{M}$, which is typically a mesh given by a set of points in $\mathbb{R}^3$ and a set of triangles. Matrix $\mathbf{P}$ transforms a 3D point $\mathbf{x}_m$ in the model coordinate system to a 3D point $\mathbf{x}_c$ in the camera coordinate system: $\mathbf{x}_c = \mathbf{P}\mathbf{x}_m$. The 3D points are represented in homogeneous coordinates.

3.1   Determination of Pose Correctness

For each test image I, there is a ground truth set $G_I = \{(o_1, \bar{\mathbf{P}}_1), (o_2, \bar{\mathbf{P}}_2), \ldots, (o_k, \bar{\mathbf{P}}_k)\}$, where $\bar{\mathbf{P}}_i$ is the ground truth pose of an instance of object $o_i \in O$. Determination of estimated poses that are considered correct is formulated as finding a maximal matching in a bipartite graph $B = ((E_I, G_I), F)$, where F is a set of edges that connect the ground truth poses G_I with matchable estimated poses E_I.

An estimated pose $(o, \hat{\mathbf{P}}, s) \in E_I$ is considered matchable with a ground truth pose $(o', \bar{\mathbf{P}}) \in G_I$, if it satisfies the necessary matching condition: $o = o' \wedge e(\hat{\mathbf{P}}, \bar{\mathbf{P}}; \mathcal{M}, I) < t$, where t is a threshold of a pose error function e (Sect. 4). As in the PASCAL VOC challenge [6], estimated poses E_I are greedily assigned to the matchable ground truth poses G_I in the order of decreasing confidence s. This results in the maximal matching $M = \{(\hat{x}_1, \bar{x}_1), (\hat{x}_2, \bar{x}_2), \ldots, (\hat{x}_l, \bar{x}_l)\} \subseteq F$, where $\hat{x}_i \in E_I$ and $\bar{x}_i \in G_I$, and no two edges share an endpoint. The set of correct poses is defined as $E_I^c = \{\hat{x} \in E_I : \exists \bar{x} \in G_I : (\hat{x}, \bar{x}) \in M\}$, *i.e.* an estimated pose is considered correct if it is matched to some ground truth pose.

Alternatively, one may not prioritize matchable pairs based on the confidence s, since they all satisfy the necessary matching condition, and maximize the number of matches instead. This would correspond to finding a maximum cardinality matching in the bipartite graph B, which can be done using *e.g.* the Hopcroft-Karp algorithm [7]. However, if the threshold t is set judiciously, the two matching approaches lead to nearly identical results and thus we prefer the simpler greedy approach.

3.2   Performance Score

Following Hinterstoisser et al. [5], we suggest to measure performance in the 6D localization problem by the Mean Recall (MR), calculated as the mean of the per-object recall rates:

$$\text{MR} = \underset{o \in O}{\text{avg}} \frac{\sum_I |\{(o', \hat{\mathbf{P}}, s) \in E_I^c : o' = o\}|}{\sum_I |\{(o', \bar{\mathbf{P}}) \in G_I : o' = o\}|}, \qquad (1)$$

where $I \in \mathcal{I}$ and $\mathcal{I}$ is a set of test images.

In the 6D detection problem, we suggest to measure performance by the Mean Average Precision (MAP), calculated as the mean of the per-object Average Precision (AP) rates:

$$\text{MAP} = \underset{o \in O}{\text{avg}} \ \underset{r \in S_o}{\text{avg}} \frac{\sum_I |\{(o', \hat{\mathbf{P}}, s) \in E_I^c : o' = o, s \geq r\}|}{\sum_I |\{(o', \hat{\mathbf{P}}, s) \in E_I : o' = o, s \geq r\}|}, \qquad (2)$$

where $S_o = \bigcup_I \{s : (o, \hat{\mathbf{P}}, s) \in E_I^c\}$ is a set of confidence values of estimated poses that are considered correct. The AP rate effectively summarizes the shape of the Precision-Recall curve and we suggest to calculate it as in the PASCAL VOC challenge from 2010 onwards [1] – by the average of the precision observed each time a new positive sample is recalled, *i.e.* a correct pose is estimated.

Both scores, MR and MAP, depend on parameters of the necessary matching condition, which include the threshold t, the pose error function e and parameters of e. The scores can be calculated for several interesting parameter settings or integrated over a reasonable range of settings. Section 4.5 discusses the parameters in more detail.

4   Measuring Error of Estimated Pose

This section introduces the notion of indistinguishable poses (Sect. 4.1) and the requirement on the pose error functions to be invariant under pose ambiguity (Sect. 4.2). It reviews the common pose error functions (Sect. 4.3), proposes new functions that are invariant under pose ambiguity (Sect. 4.4), and discusses the condition for matching of an estimated pose to the ground truth pose (Sect. 4.5).

4.1   Indistinguishable Poses

The set of poses of model $\mathcal{M}$ that are ε-indistinguishable from pose $\mathbf{P}$ in image I is defined as: $[\mathbf{P}]_{\mathcal{M},I,\varepsilon} = \{\mathbf{P}' : d(v_I[\mathbf{P}\mathcal{M}], v_I[\mathbf{P}'\mathcal{M}]) \leq \varepsilon\}$, where $v_I[\mathcal{M}] \subseteq \mathcal{M}$ is the part of model surface that is visible in I (*i.e.* the part that is not self-occluded or occluded by some other object), d is a distance between surfaces, and ε is a tolerance that controls the level of detail to be distinguished. A possible choice for d is the Hausdorff distance [8], which measures distance of surface shapes (appearance could be also considered if $\mathcal{M}$ is colored).

When object pose is ambiguous due to object symmetries or occlusions, the set of ε-indistinguishable poses $[\mathbf{P}]_{\mathcal{M},I,\varepsilon}$ contains various object poses, not only the poses that are nearly identical to $\mathbf{P}$. Note that $[\mathbf{P}]_{\mathcal{M},I,\varepsilon}$ is an equivalence class of $\mathbf{P}$ iff $\varepsilon = 0$ (for $\varepsilon > 0$, the binary relation defining the set is not transitive).

An object pose $\mathbf{P}' \in [\mathbf{P}]_{\mathcal{M},I,\varepsilon}$ is related to $\mathbf{P}$ by a transformation $\mathbf{T} \in T_{\mathbf{P},\mathcal{M},I,\varepsilon} : \mathbf{P}' = \mathbf{TP}$, which consists of a translation and a rotation. The set $T_{\mathbf{P},\mathcal{M},I,\varepsilon}$ represents partial ε-symmetries [8], which describe repetitions of the visible surface part $v_I[\mathbf{P}\mathcal{M}]$ on the entire surface of $\mathbf{P}\mathcal{M}$. It is allowed that $v_I[\mathbf{P}\mathcal{M}] \cap v_I[\mathbf{P}'\mathcal{M}] \neq \emptyset$, *i.e.* the matching surface patches can overlap. The partial ε-symmetries can be found by *e.g.* the method of Mitra et al. [9].

4.2   Invariance to Pose Ambiguity

The error $e(\hat{\mathbf{P}}, \bar{\mathbf{P}}; \mathcal{M}, I) \in \mathbb{R}_0^+$ of an estimated 6D object pose $\hat{\mathbf{P}}$ w.r.t. the ground truth pose $\bar{\mathbf{P}}$ of object model $\mathcal{M}$ in image I is required to be invariant under pose ambiguity, *i.e.* $\forall \hat{\mathbf{P}}' \in [\hat{\mathbf{P}}]_{\mathcal{M},I,\varepsilon}, \forall \bar{\mathbf{P}}' \in [\bar{\mathbf{P}}]_{\mathcal{M},I,\varepsilon} : e(\hat{\mathbf{P}}', \bar{\mathbf{P}}') \approx e(\hat{\mathbf{P}}, \bar{\mathbf{P}})$, where the equality is approximate due to the tolerance ε. A pose error function e that satisfies this property is said to be *ambiguity-invariant*. Note: This property is required because a 6D object pose estimator makes predictions only from a single input image. There is no tracking or any other source of information which the estimator could use to remove the pose ambiguity.

4.3   Common Pose Error Functions

This section reviews the common pose error functions and discusses their properties. None of these functions that operate in 3D space are ambiguity-invariant.

Average Distance of Model Points. The most widely used pose error function is the one proposed by Hinterstoisser et al. [5]. It is used for evaluation in *e.g.* [10–16]. The error of the estimated pose $\hat{\mathbf{P}}$ w.r.t. the ground truth pose $\bar{\mathbf{P}}$ of object model $\mathcal{M}$ that has no indistinguishable views is calculated as the average distance to the corresponding model point:

$$e_{\mathrm{ADD}}(\hat{\mathbf{P}}, \bar{\mathbf{P}}; \mathcal{M}) = \operatorname*{avg}_{\mathbf{x} \in \mathcal{M}} \left\| \bar{\mathbf{P}}\mathbf{x} - \hat{\mathbf{P}}\mathbf{x} \right\|_2 . \tag{3}$$

If the model $\mathcal{M}$ has indistinguishable views, the error is calculated as the average distance to the closest model point:

$$e_{\text{ADI}}(\hat{\mathbf{P}}, \bar{\mathbf{P}}; \mathcal{M}) = \underset{x_1 \in \mathcal{M}}{\text{avg}} \, \underset{x_2 \in \mathcal{M}}{\min} \left\| \bar{\mathbf{P}}\mathbf{x}_1 - \hat{\mathbf{P}}\mathbf{x}_2 \right\|_2. \tag{4}$$

Object model $\mathcal{M}$ is considered to have indistinguishable views if $\exists \mathbf{P}, \exists \mathbf{P}'$, $\exists C : d(v_C[\mathbf{P}\mathcal{M}], v_C[\mathbf{P}'\mathcal{M}]) \leq \varepsilon \wedge f(\mathbf{P}, \mathbf{P}') \geq \rho$, where $v_C[\mathcal{M}] \subseteq \mathcal{M}$ is the part of model surface that is visible from camera C (*i.e.* the part that is not self-occluded), the function d measures a distance between two surfaces (as in Sect. 4.1), and ρ is the minimum required distance f between the poses (this is required because there are many nearly identical poses for which the surface distance is below ε).

Although it became a common practise, values of e_{ADD} and e_{ADI} should not be directly compared. This is because e_{ADI} yields relatively small errors even for views that are distinguishable, and is thus more permissive than e_{ADD} (e_{ADI} is in fact the lower bound of e_{ADD}). The objects evaluated with e_{ADI} are therefore advantaged. Moreover, neither e_{ADD} or e_{ADI} is ambiguity-invariant (see Sect. 5).

Translational and Rotational Error. Model-independent pose error functions are used in [16–18]. The error of the estimated pose $\hat{\mathbf{P}} = (\hat{\mathbf{R}}, \hat{\mathbf{t}})$ w.r.t. the ground truth pose $\bar{\mathbf{P}} = (\bar{\mathbf{R}}, \bar{\mathbf{t}})$ is measured by the translational (e_{TE}) and the rotational error (e_{RE}):

$$e_{\text{TE}}(\hat{\mathbf{t}}, \bar{\mathbf{t}}) = \left\| \bar{\mathbf{t}} - \hat{\mathbf{t}} \right\|_2, \tag{5}$$

$$e_{\text{RE}}(\hat{\mathbf{R}}, \bar{\mathbf{R}}) = \arccos\left((\text{Tr}(\hat{\mathbf{R}}\bar{\mathbf{R}}^{-1}) - 1) / 2 \right). \tag{6}$$

The error e_{RE} is given by the angle from the axis–angle representation of rotation [19] (*p.* 23). Neither e_{TE} nor e_{RE} is ambiguity-invariant. As discussed in Sect. 4.5, fitness of object surface alignment is the main indicator of object pose quality, model-dependent pose error functions should be therefore preferred.

Complement over Union. A popular way how to measure accuracy of detection and segmentation methods in 2D domain is to calculate the Intersection over Union score [1]:

$$s_{\text{IOU}}(\hat{B}, \bar{B}) = area(\hat{B} \cap \bar{B}) \, / \, area(\hat{B} \cup \bar{B}), \tag{7}$$

where $\hat{B}$ and $\bar{B}$ is the estimated and the ground truth 2D region respectively. The related cost function is the Complement over Union:

$$e_{\text{COU}}(\hat{B}, \bar{B}) = 1 - area(\hat{B} \cap \bar{B}) \, / \, area(\hat{B} \cup \bar{B}). \tag{8}$$

Depending on the task, $\hat{B}$ and $\bar{B}$ can be rectangular regions (given by bounding boxes) or segmentation masks. For evaluation of 6D object pose estimates, the 2D regions can be obtained by projection of the object model $\mathcal{M}$ in the estimated pose $\hat{\mathbf{P}}$ and the ground truth pose $\bar{\mathbf{P}}$. Such pose error function is ambiguity-invariant, but since it operates in the projective space, it provides only a weak information about fitness of the object surface alignment. Another possibility is to extend e_{COU} to work with 3D volumes. Such function can be made ambiguity-invariant (by *e.g.* taking the minimum over the sets of ε-indistinguishable poses), but requires well-defined 3D models with hole-free surfaces. We define a more practical extension of e_{COU} in Sect. 4.4.

4.4 Ambiguity-Invariant Pose Error Functions

We propose three pose error functions that are ambiguity-invariant. The Visible Surface Discrepancy is of the highest practical relevance since it is inherently ambiguity-invariant.

Errors Based on Corresponding Point Distance. If the sets $[\hat{\mathbf{P}}]_{\mathcal{M},I,\varepsilon}$ and $[\bar{\mathbf{P}}]_{\mathcal{M},I,\varepsilon}$ are available, we propose to calculate the average or the maximum of distances between corresponding points of model $\mathcal{M}$ for each pose pair $(\hat{\mathbf{P}}',\bar{\mathbf{P}}') \in Q = [\hat{\mathbf{P}}]_{\mathcal{M},I,\varepsilon} \times [\bar{\mathbf{P}}]_{\mathcal{M},I,\varepsilon}$, and take the minimum as the pose error:

$$e_{\text{ACPD}}(\hat{\mathbf{P}},\bar{\mathbf{P}};\mathcal{M},I,\varepsilon) = \min_{(\hat{\mathbf{P}}',\bar{\mathbf{P}}')\in Q} \operatorname*{avg}_{\mathbf{x}\in\mathcal{M}} \left\| \bar{\mathbf{P}}'\mathbf{x} - \hat{\mathbf{P}}'\mathbf{x} \right\|_2, \tag{9}$$

$$e_{\text{MCPD}}(\hat{\mathbf{P}},\bar{\mathbf{P}};\mathcal{M},I,\varepsilon) = \min_{(\hat{\mathbf{P}}',\bar{\mathbf{P}}')\in Q} \max_{\mathbf{x}\in\mathcal{M}} \left\| \bar{\mathbf{P}}'\mathbf{x} - \hat{\mathbf{P}}'\mathbf{x} \right\|_2. \tag{10}$$

The pose error e_{ACPD} is an extension of e_{ADD}. It can be used to evaluate results for objects with or without indistinguishable views, and thus allows their impartial comparison, which is not the case of e_{ADD} and e_{ADI} (Sect. 4.3). The pose error e_{MCPD} might be more relevant for robotic manipulation, in which the maximum surface deviation strongly indicates the chance of a successful grasp.

Determination of the sets $[\hat{\mathbf{P}}]_{\mathcal{M},I,\varepsilon}$ and $[\bar{\mathbf{P}}]_{\mathcal{M},I,\varepsilon}$ complicates the evaluation process, especially because $[\hat{\mathbf{P}}]_{\mathcal{M},I,\varepsilon}$ needs to be determined during evaluation. Hence, we suggest to prefer the Visible Surface Discrepancy in general. However, e_{ACPD} and e_{MCPD} can be still useful when the sets are easy to obtain, *i.e.* when object symmetries can be enumerated and occlusions (including self-occlusions) do not cause any ambiguity.

Visible Surface Discrepancy. To achieve the ambiguity-invariance while avoiding the need to determine the sets $[\hat{\mathbf{P}}]_{\mathcal{M},I,\varepsilon}$ and $[\bar{\mathbf{P}}]_{\mathcal{M},I,\varepsilon}$, we propose to calculate the error only over the visible part of the model surface. The Visible Surface Discrepancy is defined as follows:

$$e_{\text{VSD}}(\hat{\mathbf{P}},\bar{\mathbf{P}};\mathcal{M},I,\delta,\tau) = \operatorname*{avg}_{p\in\hat{V}\cup\bar{V}} c(p,\hat{D},\bar{D},\tau), \tag{11}$$

where $\hat{V}$ and $\bar{V}$ is a 2D mask of the visible surface of $\hat{\mathcal{M}} = \hat{\mathbf{P}}\mathcal{M}$ and $\bar{\mathcal{M}} = \bar{\mathbf{P}}\mathcal{M}$ respectively (Fig. 2). $\hat{D}$ and $\bar{D}$ are distance images obtained by rendering of $\hat{\mathcal{M}}$

and $\bar{\mathcal{M}}$. A distance image stores at each pixel p the distance from the camera center to the closest 3D point $\mathbf{x}_p$ on the model surface that projects to p^1. δ is a tolerance used for estimation of the visibility masks, and $c(p, \hat{D}, \bar{D}, \tau) \in [0, 1]$ is the matching cost at pixel p:

$$c(p, \hat{D}, \bar{D}, \tau) = \begin{cases} d / \tau & \text{if } p \in \hat{V} \cap \bar{V} \wedge d < \tau \\ 1 & \text{otherwise,} \end{cases} \tag{12}$$

where $d = |\hat{D}(p) - \bar{D}(p)|$ is the distance between the surfaces of $\hat{\mathcal{M}}$ and $\bar{\mathcal{M}}$ at pixel p, and τ is the misalignment tolerance that limits the allowed range of d. The cost c linearly increases from 0 to 1 as d increases to τ. This allows to distinguish well aligned surfaces from surfaces whose distance is close to the tolerance τ. For pixels with $d \geq \tau$ or pixels which are not in the intersection of the visibility masks, the matching cost is set to the maximum value of 1.

Since pixels from both visibility masks are considered, the estimated pose $\hat{\mathbf{P}}$ is penalized for the non-explained parts of the visible surface of $\bar{\mathcal{M}}$ and also for hallucinating its non-present parts. The function e_{VSD} can be seen as an extension of the Complement over Union (Sect. 4.3) calculated on the visibility masks, where pixels in the intersection of the masks can have a non-zero cost.

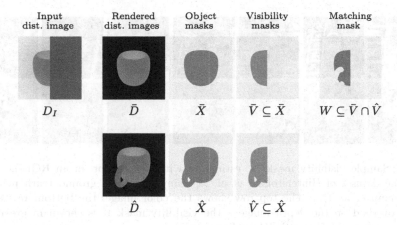

Fig. 2. Example of distance images and masks that are employed in calculation of the Visible Surface Discrepancy (e_{VSD}). The smaller the distance, the darker the pixel intensity in the distance image (pixels with unknown distances are black). Input distance image D_I captures a cup whose right part is occluded. The pose of the cup is ambiguous – from the given view it is impossible to determine the position of the handle. The matching mask W includes pixels at which the difference of the visible surface distance is smaller than τ.

---

[1] The distance image can be readily computed from a depth image, which at each pixel stores the Z coordinate of the closest scene surface.

Visibility Masks. The visibility mask $\bar{V}$ is defined as a set of pixels where the surface of $\bar{\mathcal{M}}$ is in front of the scene surface, or at most by a tolerance δ behind:

$$\bar{V} = \{p : p \in X_I \cap \bar{X} \wedge \bar{D}(p) - D_I(p) \leq \delta\}, \tag{13}$$

where D_I is the distance image of the test scene, $X_I = \{p : D_I(p) > 0\}$ and $\bar{X} = \{p : \bar{D}(p) > 0\}$ is a set of valid scene pixels and a set of valid object pixels respectively. $D(p) = 0$ if the distance at pixel p in distance image D is unknown.

Similar visibility condition as in (13) is applied to obtain the visibility mask $\hat{V}$ of $\hat{\mathcal{M}}$. In addition to that, to ensure that the visible surface of the sought object captured in D_I does not occlude the surface of $\hat{\mathcal{M}}$, all object pixels $p \in \hat{X} = \{p : \hat{D}(p) > 0\}$ which are included in $\bar{V}$ are added to $\hat{V}$, regardless of the surface distance at these pixels. The visibility mask $\hat{V}$ is defined as follows:

$$\hat{V} = \{p : (p \in X_I \cap \hat{X} \wedge \hat{D}(p) - D_I(p) \leq \delta) \vee p \in \bar{V} \cap \hat{X}\}. \tag{14}$$

The tolerance δ should reflect accuracy of the ground truth poses and also the noise characteristics of the used depth sensor, *i.e.* it should increase with depth, as the measurement error typically does [20]. However, in our experiments we obtained satisfactory results even with δ fixed to 1.5 cm. Sample visibility masks are shown in Fig. 3.

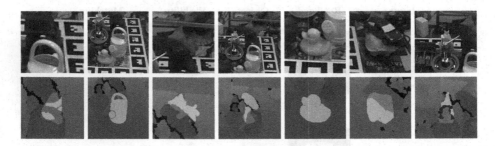

Fig. 3. Sample visibility masks $\bar{V}$ estimated with $\delta = 1.5$ cm in an RGB-D image from the dataset of Hinterstoisser et al. [5] using additional ground truth poses by Brachmann et al. [13]. The top row shows the color image, the bottom row shows masks overlaid on the depth image – the visibility mask $\bar{V}$ is shown in green, the occlusion mask $\bar{X} \setminus \bar{V}$ in red. (Color figure online)

4.5   Discussion on the Necessary Matching Condition

An estimated 6D object pose $\hat{\mathbf{P}}$ is considered matchable with the ground truth pose $\bar{\mathbf{P}}$, if $e(\hat{\mathbf{P}}, \bar{\mathbf{P}}; \mathcal{M}, I) < t$ (Sect. 3.1). The choice of both the pose error function e and the threshold t largely depends on the target application. We discuss two areas in which the 6D object pose estimation is of great importance and which have different requirements on quality of the estimated pose – robotic manipulation and augmented reality.

In robotic manipulation, where a robotic arm operates in the 3D space, the absolute error of the estimated pose is important – especially in terms of misalignment of the object surface. The requirements are different for augmented reality applications, where the perceivable error is more relevant. This error depends on perspective projection and thus the closer the object to the camera, the more accurate the pose should be. Additionally, accuracy of the object position in the X and Y axis of the camera coordinate system is more important than accuracy in the Z axis, which represents the viewing direction of the camera.

Hinterstoisser et al. [5] adapt the threshold to the object size by requiring e_{ADD} or e_{ADI} to be below 10 % of the object diameter. Others use fixed thresholds. Shotton et al. [18] require e_{TE} to be below 5 cm and e_{RE} below 5°. Everingham et al. [1] require the e_{IOU} score to be above 0.5.

The adaptive threshold of Hinterstoisser et al. [5] makes a little sense. This is because the task is actually easier for larger objects since there are more pixels available to estimate the pose. It is more reasonable to adapt the threshold to the object distance from the camera (*e.g.* to the average distance of the visible surface of the model in the ground truth pose). This reflects the noise characteristics of the current RGB-D sensors (the depth measurement error increases quadratically with depth [20]), and also allows to control the perceivable error which is important for the augmented reality applications. On the other hand, for robotic manipulation, it is more appropriate to keep the threshold fixed.

For e_{VSD} (Sect. 4.4), we propose to keep the threshold of the error fixed. Depending on the target application, the misalignment tolerance τ, which is used in calculation of e_{VSD}, can be either fixed or adapted to the object distance from the camera.

5   Comparison of Pose Error Functions

The discussed pose error functions were evaluated on a synthetic sequence $(\mathbf{P}_0, \mathbf{P}_1, \ldots, \mathbf{P}_{359})$ of 6D poses of a rotating cup (Fig. 4). Each pose $\mathbf{P}_i$ represents a rotation by $i°$ around axis perpendicular to the bottom of the cup. The poses were evaluated against the ground truth pose $\bar{\mathbf{P}}$, which was set to be the rotation by 90°. The handle of the cup is not visible in $\bar{\mathbf{P}}$ and thus its pose

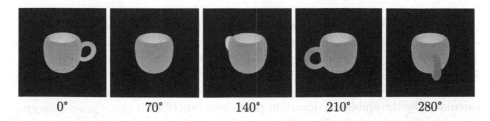

| 0° | 70° | 140° | 210° | 280° |

Fig. 4. Sample rendered depth images of a rotating cup (the rotation axis is perpendicular to the bottom of the cup).

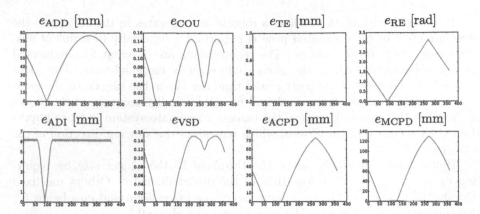

Fig. 5. Comparison of the pose error functions on the rotating cup. X axis shows rotation of the cup (from $0°$ to $359°$). Y axis shows the calculated error.

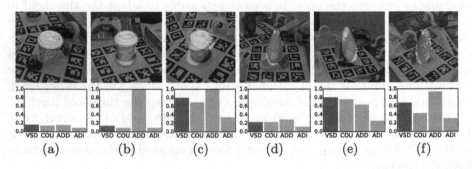

Fig. 6. Comparison of pose error functions on sample images from the dataset of Tejani et al. [12]. The visualized errors were normalized by the threshold t and thus all ranges from 0 to 1. The top row shows renderings of the object model in the estimated poses (blue), which are overlaid on the cropped color component of the input RGB-D image. (a,d) All errors are low for pose estimates that are close to the ground truth. (c,e) e_{VSD} and e_{COU} are sensitive to misalignment of object silhouettes, encouraging low perceivable error. (f) Unlike e_{COU}, which operates only in the 2D space, e_{VSD} penalizes also inconsistency in depth – the estimated pose is too close to the camera in this case. As expected, e_{ADD} produces non-intuitive values for these symmetric objects. (Color figure online)

is ambiguous. $[\bar{\mathbf{P}}]_{\mathcal{M},I,\varepsilon}$ was set to contain rotations from the range $[55°, 125°]$, which represent all poses from the sequence in which the handle is not visible. The set $[\mathbf{P}_i]_{\mathcal{M},I,\varepsilon}$ of the evaluated pose $\mathbf{P}_i$ was set to be the same as $[\bar{\mathbf{P}}]_{\mathcal{M},I,\varepsilon}$ if $55 \leq i \leq 125$, and to $\{\mathbf{P}_i\}$ otherwise.

The calculated errors are shown in Fig. 5. Note that the error $e(\mathbf{P}_i, \bar{\mathbf{P}}; \mathcal{M}, I)$ calculated by the ambiguity-invariant pose error functions (e_{VSD}, e_{ACPD}, e_{MCPD}, e_{COU}) is close to zero for $\mathbf{P}_i \in [\bar{\mathbf{P}}]_{\mathcal{M},I,\varepsilon}$, which is the intuitive behavior.

Besides the synthetic sequence, we analyzed the pose error functions on the dataset of Tejani et al. [12]. The estimated poses produced by a method of the same authors were evaluated against the ground truth poses provided with the dataset. For e_{VSD}, the tolerances δ and τ were set to 1.5 cm and 10 cm respectively. The threshold t was set to 0.5 for both e_{VSD} and e_{COU}, and to 15 % of the object diameter for e_{ADD} and e_{ADI}. Figure 6 discusses several examples of the calculated errors.

6   Conclusion

We defined two 6D object pose estimation problems – the 6D localization, in which prior information about presence of known objects in a test image is provided, and the 6D detection, in which no prior information is provided.

To measure error of an estimated 6D object pose w.r.t. the ground truth pose, we proposed to use the Visible Surface Discrepancy (e_{VSD}), which calculates the error over the visible surface of the object model. It is inherently ambiguity-invariant, $i.e.$ it treats the ε-indistinguishable poses as approximately equivalent. Alternatively, if the sets of ε-indistinguishable poses are available, we proposed to use the Average or the Maximum Corresponding Point Distance (e_{ACPD}, e_{MCPD}), which measure misalignment over the entire surface of the object model.

Determination of which estimated poses are correct is formulated as finding a maximal matching in a bipartite graph, where edges connect the ground truth poses with matchable estimated poses. The estimated poses are greedily assigned to the matchable ground truth poses in the order of decreasing confidence. An estimated pose is considered correct if the resulting matching includes an edge connecting the pose with some ground truth pose.

We proposed to apply a fixed threshold t on the value of e_{VSD} to decide if an estimated object pose is matchable with the ground truth pose. The misalignment tolerance τ, which is a parameter of e_{VSD}, can be either fixed or adapted to the object distance from the camera. For e_{ACPD} or e_{MCPD}, we proposed to keep the threshold t fixed or to adapt it to the object distance.

We suggested to measure performance of a 6D object pose estimator by the Mean Recall (MR) in the 6D localization problem, and by the Mean Average Precision (MAP) in the 6D detection problem.

The ongoing work is focused on a thorough validation of the proposed evaluation methodology, its application to data represented by sparse point clouds, and on extension of the Visible Surface Discrepancy to a multi-camera setting.

Implementation of the discussed pose error functions and the performance score functions is provided at: https://github.com/thodan/obj_pose_eval.

Acknowledgements. We thank Caner Sahin, Rigas Kouskouridas and Tae-Kyun Kim from Imperial College London for providing results of the method by Tejani et al. [12], and Eric Brachmann from TU Dresden for discussion about the matching condition.

We thank the anonymous reviewer for pointing out the issue with data represented by sparse point clouds and the issue of extending the Visible Surface Discrepancy to a multi-camera setting. We are interested in a further discussion.

This work was supported by CTU student grant SGS15/155/OHK3/2T/13 and by the Technology Agency of the Czech Republic research program (V3C – Visual Computing Competence Center) TE01020415.

References

1. Everingham, M., Eslami, S.A., Van Gool, L., Williams, C.K., Winn, J., Zisserman, A.: The PASCAL visual object classes challenge: a retrospective. Int. J. Comput. Vis. **111**(1), 98–136 (2015)
2. Russakovsky, O., Deng, J., Su, H., Krause, J., Satheesh, S., Ma, S., Huang, Z., Karpathy, A., Khosla, A., Bernstein, M., et al.: Imagenet large scale visual recognition challenge. Int. J. Comput. Vis. **115**(3), 211–252 (2015)
3. Xiang, Y., Mottaghi, R., Savarese, S.: Beyond PASCAL: a benchmark for 3D object detection in the wild. In: IEEE Winter Conference on Applications of Computer Vision, pp. 75–82. IEEE (2014)
4. Tulsiani, S., Malik, J.: Viewpoints and keypoints. In: 2015 IEEE Conference on Computer Vision and Pattern Recognition (CVPR), pp. 1510–1519. IEEE (2015)
5. Hinterstoisser, S., Lepetit, V., Ilic, S., Holzer, S., Bradski, G., Konolige, K., Navab, N.: Model based training, detection and pose estimation of texture-less 3D objects in heavily cluttered scenes. In: Lee, K.M., Matsushita, Y., Rehg, J.M., Hu, Z. (eds.) ACCV 2012. LNCS, vol. 7727, pp. 548–562. Springer, Heidelberg (2013). doi:10.1007/978-3-642-37331-2_42
6. Everingham, M., Van Gool, L., Williams, C.K., Winn, J., Zisserman, A.: The PASCAL visual object classes (VOC) challenge. Int. J. Comput. Vis. **88**(2), 303–338 (2010)
7. Ahuja, R.K., Magnanti, T.L., Orlin, J.B.: Network flows. Technical report, DTIC Document (1988)
8. Mitra, N.J., Pauly, M., Wand, M., Ceylan, D.: Symmetry in 3D geometry: extraction and applications. In: Computer Graphics Forum, vol. 32, pp. 1–23. Wiley Online Library (2013)
9. Mitra, N.J., Guibas, L.J., Pauly, M.: Partial and approximate symmetry detection for 3D geometry. ACM Trans. Graph. (TOG) **25**(3), 560–568 (2006)
10. Hodaň, T., Zabulis, X., Lourakis, M., Obdržálek, Š., Matas, J.: Detection and fine 3D pose estimation of texture-less objects in RGB-D images. In: 2015 IEEE/RSJ International Conference on Intelligent Robots and Systems (IROS)
11. Rios-Cabrera, R., Tuytelaars, T.: Discriminatively trained templates for 3D object detection: a real time scalable approach. In: ICCV, pp. 2048–2055(2013)
12. Tejani, A., Tang, D., Kouskouridas, R., Kim, T.-K.: Latent-class hough forests for 3D object detection and pose estimation. In: Fleet, D., Pajdla, T., Schiele, B., Tuytelaars, T. (eds.) ECCV 2014. LNCS, vol. 8693, pp. 462–477. Springer, Heidelberg (2014). doi:10.1007/978-3-319-10599-4_30
13. Brachmann, E., Krull, A., Michel, F., Gumhold, S., Shotton, J., Rother, C.: Learning 6D object pose estimation using 3D object coordinates. In: Fleet, D., Pajdla, T., Schiele, B., Tuytelaars, T. (eds.) ECCV 2014. LNCS, vol. 8693, pp. 536–551. Springer, Heidelberg (2014). doi:10.1007/978-3-319-10605-2_35

14. Krull, A., Brachmann, E., Michel, F., Yang, M.Y., Gumhold, S., Rother, C.: Learning analysis-by-synthesis for 6D pose estimation in RGB-D images. arXiv preprint (2015). arXiv:1508.04546
15. Wohlhart, P., Lepetit, V.: Learning descriptors for object recognition and 3D pose estimation. arXiv preprint (2015). arXiv:1502.05908
16. Drost, B., Ulrich, M., Navab, N., Ilic, S.: Model globally, match locally: efficient and robust 3D object recognition. In: CVPR, pp. 998–1005 (2010)
17. Choi, C., Christensen, H.: 3D pose estimation of daily objects using an RGB-D camera. In: IROS, pp. 3342–3349 (2012)
18. Shotton, J., Glocker, B., Zach, C., Izadi, S., Criminisi, A., Fitzgibbon, A.: Scene coordinate regression forests for camera relocalization in RGB-D images. In: CVPR, pp. 2930–2937 (2013)
19. Morawiec, A.: Orientations and Rotations: Computations in Crystallographic Textures. Springer Science & Business Media, Berlin (2004)
20. Khoshelham, K.: Accuracy analysis of kinect depth data. In: ISPRS Workshop Laser Scanning, vol. 38 (2011)

Reconstructing Articulated Rigged Models from RGB-D Videos

Dimitrios Tzionas[1,2] and Juergen Gall[1(✉)]

[1] University of Bonn, Bonn, Germany
{tzionas,gall}@iai.uni-bonn.de
[2] MPI for Intelligent Systems, Tübingen, Germany

Abstract. Although commercial and open-source software exist to reconstruct a static object from a sequence recorded with an RGB-D sensor, there is a lack of tools that build rigged models of articulated objects that deform realistically and can be used for tracking or animation. In this work, we fill this gap and propose a method that creates a fully rigged model of an articulated object from depth data of a single sensor. To this end, we combine deformable mesh tracking, motion segmentation based on spectral clustering and skeletonization based on mean curvature flow. The fully rigged model then consists of a watertight mesh, embedded skeleton, and skinning weights.

Keywords: Kinematic model learning · Skeletonization · Rigged model acquisition · Deformable tracking · Spectral clustering · Mean curvature flow

1 Introduction

With the increasing popularity of depth cameras, the reconstruction of rigid scenes or objects at home has become affordable for any user [1] and together with 3D printers allows novel applications [2]. Many objects, however, are non-rigid and their motion can be modeled by an articulated skeleton. Although articulated models are highly relevant for computer graphic applications [3] including virtual or augmented reality and robotic applications [4], there is no approach that builds from a sequence of depth data a fully rigged 3D mesh with a skeleton structure that describes the articulated deformation model.

In the context of computer graphics, methods for automatic rigging have been proposed. In [3], for instance, the geometric shape of a static mesh is used to fit a predefined skeleton into the mesh. More detailed human characters including cloth simulation have been reconstructed from multi-camera video data in [5]. Both approaches, however, assume that the skeleton structure is given. On the contrary, the skeleton structure can be estimated from high-quality mesh animations [6]. The approach, however, cannot be applied to depth data. At the end, we have a typical chicken-and-egg problem. If a rigged model with predefined skeleton is given the mesh deformations can be estimated accurately [7] and if the mesh deformations are known the skeleton structure can be estimated [6].

© Springer International Publishing Switzerland 2016
G. Hua and H. Jégou (Eds.): ECCV 2016 Workshops, Part III, LNCS 9915, pp. 620–633, 2016.
DOI: 10.1007/978-3-319-49409-8_53

In this paper, we propose an approach to address this dilemma and create a fully rigged model from depth data of a single sensor. To this end, we first create a static mesh model of the object. We then reconstruct the motion of the mesh in a sequence captured with a depth sensor by deformable mesh tracking. Standard tracking, however, fails since it maps the entire mesh to the visible point cloud. As a result, the object is squeezed as shown in Fig. 4. We therefore reduce the thinning artifacts by a strong regularizer that prefers smooth mesh deformations. Although the regularizer also introduces artifacts by oversmoothing the captured motion, in particular at joint positions as shown for the pipe sequence in Fig. 1, the mesh can be segmented into meaningful parts by spectral clustering based on the captured mesh motion as shown in Fig. 5. The skeleton structure consisting of joints and bones is then estimated based on the mesh segments and mean curvature flow.

As a result, our approach is the first method that creates a fully rigged model of an articulated object consisting of a watertight mesh, embedded skeleton, and skinning weights from depth data. Such models can be used for animation, virtual or augmented reality, or in the context of robot-object manipulation. We perform a quantitative evaluation with five objects of varying size and deformation characteristics and provide a thorough analysis of the parameters.

2 Related Work

Reconstructing articulated objects has attracted a lot of interest during the past decade. Due to the popularity of different image sensors over the years, research focus has gradually shifted from reconstructing 2D skeletons from RGB data [8–11] to 3D skeletons from RGB [12–15] or RGB-D data [4,16,17].

A popular method for extracting 2D skeletons from videos uses a factorization-based approach for motion segmentation. In [8,9] articulated motion is modeled by a set of independent motion subspaces and the joint locations are obtained from the intersections of connected motion segments. A probabilistic graphical model has been proposed in [10]. The skeleton structure is inferred from 2D feature trajectories by maximum likelihood estimation and the joints are located in the center of the motion segments. Recently, [11] combine a fine-to-coarse motion segmentation based on iterative randomized voting with a distance function based on contour-pruned skeletonization. The kinematic model is inferred with a minimum spanning tree approach.

In order to obtain 3D skeletons from RGB videos, structure-from-motion (SfM) approaches can be used. [12] perform simultaneous segmentation and sparse 3D reconstruction of articulated motion with a cost function minimizing the re-projection error of sparse 2D features, while a spatial prior favors smooth segmentation. The method is able to compute the number of joints and recover from local minima, while occlusions are handled by incorporating partial sequences into the optimization. In contrast to [18], it is able to reconstruct complex articulated structures. [15] use ray-space optimization to estimate 3D trajectories from 2D trajectories. The approach, however, assumes that the number of parts is known. In [13,14] markers are attached to the objects to get precise

3D pose estimations of object parts. They use a probabilistic approach with a mixture of parametrized and parameter-free representations based on Gaussian processes. The skeleton structure is inferred by computing the minimum spanning tree over all connected parts.

The recent advances in RGB-D sensors allow to work fully in 3D. An early approach [16] uses sparse KLT and SIFT features and groups consistent 3D trajectories with a greedy approach. The kinematic model is inferred by sequentially fitting a prismatic and a rotational joint with RANSAC. In [4] the 3D trajectories are clustered by density-based spatial clustering. For each cluster, the 3D pose is estimated and the approach [14] is applied to infer the skeleton structure. Recently, [17] presented a method that combines shape reconstruction with the estimation of the skeleton structure. While these approaches operate only with point clouds, our approach generates fully rigged models consisting of a watertight mesh, embedded skeleton, and skinning weights.

3 Mesh Motion

Our approach consists of three steps. We first create a watertight mesh of the object using a depth sensor that is moved around the object while the object is not moving. Creating meshes from static objects can be done with standard software. In our experiments, we use Skanect [19] with optional automatic mesh cleaning using MeshLab [20]. In the second step, we record a sequence where the object is deformed by hand-object interaction and track the mesh to obtain the mesh motion. In the third step, we estimate the skeleton structure and rig the model. The third step will be described in Sect. 4.

3.1 Preprocessing

For tracking, we preprocess each frame of the RGB-D sensor. We first discard points that are far away and only keep points that are within a 3D volume. This is actually not necessary but it avoids unnecessary processing like normal computation for irrelevant points. Since the objects are manipulated by hands, we discard the hands by skin color segmentation on the RGB image using a Gaussian mixtures model (GMM) [21]. The remaining points are then smoothed by a bilateral filter [22] and normals are computed as in [23].

3.2 Mesh Tracking

For mesh tracking, we capitalize on a Laplacian deformation framework similar to [24]. While in [7,25] a Laplacian deformation framework was combined with skeleton-based tracking in the context of a multi-camera setup, we use the Laplacian deformation framework directly for obtaining the mesh motion of an object with unknown skeleton structure. Since we use only one camera and not an expensive multi-camera setup, we observe only a portion of the object and the regularizer will be very important as we will show in the experiments.

For mesh tracking, we align the mesh $\mathcal{M}$ with the preprocessed depth data D by minimizing the objective function

$$E(\mathcal{M}, D) = \mathcal{E}_{smooth}(\mathcal{M}) + \gamma_{def}\Big(\mathcal{E}_{model \to data}(\mathcal{M}, D) + \mathcal{E}_{data \to model}(\mathcal{M}, D)\Big).$$
(1)

with respect to the vertex positions of the mesh $\mathcal{M}$. The objective function consists of a smoothness term $\mathcal{E}_{smooth}$ that preserves geometry by penalizing changes in surface curvature, as well as two data terms $\mathcal{E}_{model \to data}$ and $\mathcal{E}_{data \to model}$ that align the mesh model to the observed data and the data to the model, respectively. The impact of the smoothness term and the data terms is steered by the parameter γ_{def}.

For the data terms, we use the same terms that are used for articulated hand tracking in [26]. For the first term

$$\mathcal{E}_{model \to data}(\mathcal{M}, D) = \sum_i \|\mathbf{V}_i - \mathbf{X}_i\|_2^2$$
(2)

we establish correspondences between the visible vertices $\mathbf{V}_i$ of the mesh $\mathcal{M}$ and the closest points $\mathbf{X}_i$ of the point cloud D and minimize the distance. We discard correspondences for which the angle between the normals of the vertex and the closest point is larger than $45°$ or the distance between the points is larger than $10\,\mathrm{mm}$.

The second data term

$$\mathcal{E}_{data \to model}(\mathcal{M}, D) = \sum_i \|\mathbf{V}_i \times \mathbf{d}_i - \mathbf{m}_i\|_2^2$$
(3)

minimizes the distance between a vertex $\mathbf{V}_i$ and the projection ray of a depth discontinuity observed in the depth image. To compute the distance, the projection ray of a 2D point is expressed by a Plücker line [27] with direction $\mathbf{d}_i$ and moment $\mathbf{m}_i$. The depth discontinuities are obtained as in [26] by an edge detector applied to the depth data and the correspondence between a depth discontinuity and a vertex are obtained by searching the closest projected vertex for each depth discontinuity.

Due to the partial view of the object, the data terms are highly underconstrained. This is compensated by the smoothness term that penalizes changes of the surface curvature [24]. The term can be written as

$$\mathcal{E}_{smooth}(\mathcal{M}) = \sum_i \|\mathbf{LV}_i - \mathbf{LV}_{i,t-1}\|_2^2$$
(4)

where $\mathbf{V}_{i,t-1}$ is the previous vertex position. In order to model the surface curvature, we employ the cotangent Laplacian [24] matrix $\mathbf{L}$ given by

$$L_{ij} = \begin{cases} \sum_{\mathbf{V}_k \in \mathcal{N}_1(\mathbf{V}_i)} w_{ik}, & i = j \\ -w_{ij}, & \mathbf{V}_j \in \mathcal{N}_1(\mathbf{V}_i) \\ 0, & \text{otherwise}, \end{cases} \quad \text{where } w_{ij} = \frac{1}{2|A_i|}(\cot \alpha_{ij} + \cot \beta_{ij})$$
(5)

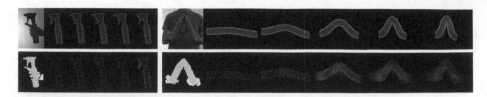

Fig. 1. Tracked mesh with the deformable tracker presented in Sect. 3.2 and the corresponding 3D vertex trajectories. We present images for the sequences "spray" and "pipe 1/2" showing the temporal evolution at 20%, 40%, 60%, 80% and 100% of the sequence.

where $\mathcal{N}_1(\mathbf{V}_i)$ denotes the set of one-ring neighbor vertices of vertex $\mathbf{V}_i$. The weight w_{ij} for an edge in the triangular mesh between two vertices $\mathbf{V}_i$ and $\mathbf{V}_j$ depends on the cotangents of the two angles α_{ij} and β_{ij} opposite of the edge (i,j) and the size of the Voronoi cell $|A_i|$ that is efficiently approximated by half of the sum of the triangle areas defined by $\mathcal{N}_1(\mathbf{V}_i)$.

We minimize the least squares problem (1) by solving a large but highly sparse linear system using sparse Cholesky decomposition. For each frame, we use the estimate of the previous frame for initialization and iterate between computing correspondences and optimizing (1) 15 times.

4   Kinematic Model Acquisition

After having estimated the mesh motion as described in Sect. 3, we have for each vertex the trajectory $\mathcal{T}_i$. We use the trajectories together with the shape of the mesh $\mathcal{M}$ to reconstruct the underlying skeleton. To this end, we first segment the trajectories as described in Sect. 4.1 and then infer the skeleton structure, which will be explained in Sect. 4.2.

4.1   Motion Segmentation

In contrast to feature based trajectories, the mesh motion provides trajectories of the same length and a trajectory for each vertex, even if the vertex has never been observed in the sequence due to occlusions. This means that clustering the trajectories also segments the mesh into rigid parts.

Similar to 2D motion segmentation approaches for RGB videos [28], we define an affinity matrix based on the 3D trajectories and use spectral clustering for motion segmentation. The affinity matrix

$$\Phi_{ij} = \exp\left(-\lambda d(\mathcal{T}_i, \mathcal{T}_j)\right) \tag{6}$$

is based on the pairwise distance between two trajectories $\mathcal{T}_i$ and $\mathcal{T}_j$. $\Phi_{ij} = 1$ if the trajectories are the same and close to zero if the trajectories are very dissimilar. As in [28], we use $\lambda = 0.1$.

To measure the distance between two trajectories $\mathcal{T}_i$ and $\mathcal{T}_j$, we measure the distance change of two vertex positions $\mathbf{V}_i$ and $\mathbf{V}_j$ within a fixed time interval. We set the length of the time interval proportional to the observed maximum displacement, i.e.

$$dt = 2 \max_{i,t} \| \mathbf{V}_{i,t} - \mathbf{V}_{i,t-1} \|_2. \tag{7}$$

Since the trajectories are smooth due to the mesh tracking as described in Sect. 3.2, we do not have to deal with outliers and we can take the maximum displacement over all vertices. The object, however, might be deformed only at a certain time interval of the entire sequence. We are therefore only interested in the maximum distance change over all time intervals, i.e.

$$d^v(\mathcal{T}_i, \mathcal{T}_j) = \max_t \left| \| \mathbf{V}_{i,t} - \mathbf{V}_{j,t} \|_2 - \| \mathbf{V}_{i,t-dt} - \mathbf{V}_{j,t-dt} \|_2 \right|. \tag{8}$$

This means that if two vertices belong to the same rigid part, the distance between them should not change much over time. In addition, we take the change of the angle between the vertex normals $\mathbf{N}$ into account. This is measured in the same way as maximum over the intervals

$$d^n(\mathcal{T}_i, \mathcal{T}_j) = \max_t \left| \arccos \left(\mathbf{N}_{i,t}^T \mathbf{N}_{j,t} \right) - \arccos \left(\mathbf{N}_{i,t-dt}^T \mathbf{N}_{j,t-dt} \right) \right|. \tag{9}$$

The two distance measures are combined by

$$d(\mathcal{T}_i, \mathcal{T}_j) = (1 + d^n(\mathcal{T}_i, \mathcal{T}_j)) \, d^v(\mathcal{T}_i, \mathcal{T}_j). \tag{10}$$

The distances are measured in mm and the angles in rad. Adding 1 to d^n was necessary since d^n can be close to zero despite of large displacement changes.

Based on (6), we build the normalized Laplacian graph [29]

$$\mathcal{L} = D^{-\frac{1}{2}}(D - \Phi)D^{-\frac{1}{2}} \tag{11}$$

where D is an $n \times n$ diagonal matrix with

$$D_{ii} = \sum_j \Phi_{ij} \tag{12}$$

and perform eigenvalue decomposition of $\mathcal{L}$ to get the eigenvalues $\lambda_1, \ldots, \lambda_n$, ($\lambda_1 \leq \cdots \leq \lambda_n$), as well as the corresponding eigenvectors $\mathbf{v}_1, \ldots, \mathbf{v}_n$. The number of clusters k is determined by the number of eigenvalues below a threshold λ_{thresh} and the final clustering of the trajectories is then obtained by k-means clustering [29] on the rows of the $n \times k$ matrix $\mathcal{F} = [\mathbf{v}_1 \ \ldots \ \mathbf{v}_k]$.

In practice, we sample uniformly 1000 vertices from the mesh to compute the affinity matrix. This turned out to be sufficient while reducing the time to compute the matrix. For each vertex that has not been sampled, we compute the closest sampled vertex on the mesh and assign it to the same cluster. This results in a motion segmentation of the entire mesh as shown in Fig. 2b.

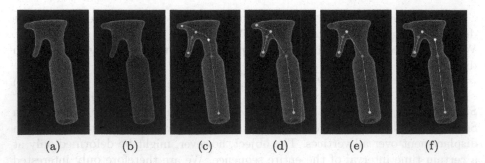

(a) (b) (c) (d) (e) (f)

Fig. 2. The steps of our pipeline. (a) *Initial mesh* (b) *Motion segments* (c) *Mean curvature skeleton* where the endpoints are shown with cyan, the junction points with yellow, the virtual point due to collision with white and the motion joints with magenta (d) *Initial skeleton* (e) *Refined skeleton* after removal of redundant bone (f) *Final skeleton* after replacement of the colliding bone with two non-colliding ones and a virtual joint.

Algorithm 1. Overview of the steps of our algorithm.

Deformable motion capture
 └ - Perform *deformable* tracking of the object   Sect. 3.2 - Eq. (1)

Motion segmentation of the object
 ├ - Generate dense vertex *trajectories* from tracking result   Sect. 4.1
 ├ - Sample 1000 trajectories for tractability   Sect. 4.1
 ├ - Build an *affinity matrix* of vertex trajectories   Sect. 4.1 - Eq. (6–10)
 └ - Segment mesh by *spectral clustering*   Sect. 4.1 - Eq. (11)

Kinematic model acquisition for the object
 ├ - Infer *joints* at intersections of mesh segments   Sect. 4.2
 ├ - Infer *skeleton topology*   Sect. 4.2
 └ - Compute *skinning weights*   Sect. 4.2

4.2 Kinematic Topology

Given the segmented mesh, it remains to determine the joint positions and topology of the skeleton. To obtain a bone structure, we first skeletonize the mesh by extracting the mean curvature skeleton (MCS) based on the mean curvature flow [30] that captures effectively the topology of the mesh by iteratively contracting the triangulated surface. The red 3D curve in Fig. 2c shows the mean curvature skeleton for an object. In order to localize the joints, we compute the intersecting boundary of two connected mesh segments using a half-edge representation. For each intersecting pair of segments, we compute the centroid of the boundary vertices and find its closest 3D point on the mean curvature skeleton. In this way, the joints are guaranteed to lie inside the mesh. In order to create the skeleton structure with bones, we first create auxiliary joints without any degree of freedom at the points where the mean curvature skeleton branches or ends as shown in Fig. 2c. After all 3D joints on the skeleton are determined, we follow the mean curvature skeleton and connect the detected joints accordingly to build a hierarchy of bones that defines the topology of a skeleton structure.

Although the number of auxiliary joints usually does not matter, we reduce the number of auxiliary joints and irrelevant bones by removing bones that link an endpoint with another auxiliary joint if they belong to the same motion segment. The corresponding motion segment for each joint can be directly computed from the mean curvature flow [30]. We finally ensure that each bone is inside the mesh. To this end, we detect bones colliding with the mesh with a collision detection approach based on bounding volume hierarchies. We then subdivide each colliding bone in two bones by adding an additional auxiliary joint at the middle of the mean curvature skeleton that connects the endpoints of the colliding bone. The process is repeated until all bones are inside the mesh. In our experiments, however, one iteration was enough. This procedure defines the refined topology of the skeleton that is already embedded in the mesh. The skinning weights are then computed as in [3].

As a result, we obtain a fully rigged model consisting of a watertight mesh, an embedded skeleton structure, and skinning weights. The entire steps of the approach are summarized in Algorithm 1. Results for a few objects are shown in Fig. 5.

5   Experiments

We quantitatively evaluate our approach for five different objects shown in Table 1: the "spray", the "donkey", the "lamp", as well as the "pipe 1/2" and "pipe 3/4" which have a joint at 1/2 and 3/4 of their length, respectively. We acquire a 3D template mesh using the commercial software *skanect* [19] for the first three objects, while for the pipe we use the publicly available template model used in [26]. All objects have the same number of triangles, so the average triangle size varies from $3.7\,mm^2$ for the "spray", 13.8 for the "donkey", 24.8 for the "lamp" and 4.4 for the "pipe" models. We captured sequences of the objects while deforming them using a Primesense Carmine 1.09 RGB-D sensor. The recorded sequences, calibration data, scanned 3D models, deformable motion data, as well as the resulting models and respective videos for the proposed parameters are available online[1].

We perform deformable tracking (Sect. 3.2) to get 3D dense vertex trajectories as depicted in Fig. 1. Deformable tracking depends on the weight γ_{def} in the objective function (1) that steers the influence of the smoothness and data terms. As depicted in Fig. 4, a very low γ_{def} gives too much weight to the smoothness term and prevents an accurate fitting to the input data, while a big γ_{def} results in over-fitting to the partial visible data and a strong thinning effect can be observed. The thinning gets more intense for an increasing γ_{def}.

Despite of γ_{def}, our approach also depends on the eigenvalue threshold λ_{thr} for spectral clustering. To study the effect of the parameters, we created a test dataset. For each object, we scanned the objects in four different poses. To this end, we fixed the object in a pose with adhesive tape and reconstructed it by moving the camera around the object. The target poses of the objects are shown

---

[1] http://files.is.tue.mpg.de/dtzionas/Skeleton-Reconstruction.

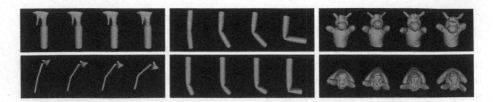

Fig. 3. Each object is scanned in four target poses with increasing difficulty and pose estimation from an initial state is performed for evaluation while spanning the parameter space of $(\gamma_{def}, \lambda_{thresh})$. For the "donkey" object both a front and a top view are presented.

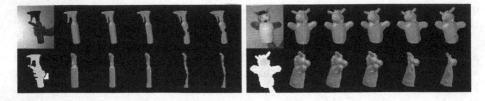

Fig. 4. Deformable tracking for $\gamma_{def} = 0.001, 0.005, 0.01, 0.05, 0.1$ (from left to right) that steers the influence of the smoothness and data terms in Eq. (1). We depict the front (top) and side view (bottom) for the last frame of the sequences "spray" and "donkey".

in Fig. 3. To measure the quality of a rigged model for a parameter setting, we align the model $\mathcal{M}(\theta)$ parametrized by the rotations of the joints and the global rigid transformation to the reconstructed object $\mathcal{O}$ from an initial pose. For the alignment, we use only the inferred articulated model, i.e. we estimate the rigid transformation and the rotations of the joints of the inferred skeleton. As data term, we use

$$\frac{1}{|\mathcal{M}(\theta)| + |\mathcal{O}|} \left(\sum_{\mathbf{V}(\theta) \in \mathcal{M}(\theta)} \|\mathbf{V}(\theta) - \mathbf{V}_{\mathcal{O}}\|_2^2 + \sum_{\mathbf{V}_{\mathcal{O}} \in \mathcal{O}} \|\mathbf{V}_{\mathcal{O}} - \mathbf{V}(\theta)\|_2^2 \right) \qquad (13)$$

based on the closest vertices from mesh $\mathcal{M}(\theta)$ to $\mathcal{O}$ and vice versa. This measure is also used to measure the 3D error in mm after alignment.

Table 1 summarizes the average 3D vertex error for various parameter settings, with the highlighted values indicating the best qualitative results for each object, while Fig. 5 shows the motion segments and the acquired skeletons for the best configuration. The optimal parameter γ_{def} seems to depend on the triangle size since the smoothness term is influenced by the areas of the Voronoi cells $|A_i|$ (5) and therefore by the areas of the triangles. The objects "Donkey" and "Lamp" have *large triangles* ($>10\,\text{mm}^2$) and prefer $\gamma_{def} = 0.05$, while the objects with small triangles ($<10\,\text{mm}^2$) perform better for $\gamma_{def} = 0.005$. Spectral clustering on the other hand works well for $\lambda_{thr} = 0.7$ when *reasonably sized parts undergo a pronounced movement*, however, a higher value of $\lambda_{thr} = 0.98$ is better

Table 1. Evaluation of our approach using the target poses shown in Fig. 3. We create a rigged model while spanning the parameter space for the deformable tracking weight γ_{def} and the spectral clustering threshold λ_{thr}. The rigged model is aligned to the target poses by articulated pose estimation. We report the average vertex error in mm.

	γ_{def} \ λ_{thr}	0.40	0.50	0.60	0.70	0.80	0.90	0.95	0.98
Spray	0.001	1.9	1.9	1.9	1.9	1.9	1.9	1.9	1.9
	0.005	1.9	1.9	1.9	1.9	1.9	1.9	1.9	1.4
	0.01	1.9	1.9	1.9	1.9	1.9	1.9	1.9	1.4
	0.05	1.9	1.9	1.9	1.9	1.9	1.9	1.5	1.5
	0.1	1.9	1.9	1.9	1.9	1.9	1.9	1.9	1.9
Pipe 1/2	0.001	10.0	2.4	2.4	2.4	4.5	3.4	3.3	3.6
	0.005	2.4	2.4	2.4	2.4	2.4	4.6	3.8	2.6
	0.01	2.7	2.7	2.7	4.7	3.4	3.7	4.3	4.4
	0.05	2.6	2.6	3.5	2.7	3.6	3.6	3.6	3.6
	0.1	10.0	10.0	10.0	10.0	10.0	10.0	10.0	10.0
Pipe 3/4	0.001	8.3	5.1	5.1	5.1	2.5	3.0	2.8	2.4
	0.005	2.4	2.4	2.4	2.4	3.6	2.5	2.6	2.4
	0.01	2.4	2.4	2.4	2.4	2.8	2.4	2.4	2.4
	0.05	8.3	8.3	8.3	8.3	8.3	8.3	8.3	8.3
	0.1	8.3	8.3	8.3	8.3	8.3	8.3	8.3	8.3
Donkey	0.001	6.7	6.7	6.7	6.7	6.7	6.7	6.7	6.7
	0.005	6.7	6.7	6.7	6.7	6.7	6.7	6.7	5.7
	0.01	6.7	6.7	6.7	6.7	5.8	5.8	4.8	4.1
	0.05	4.6	5.1	5.0	4.5	4.4	3.9	3.6	3.6
	0.1	6.3	5.1	5.0	5.1	3.8	4.0	4.0	4.0
Lamp	0.001	12.9	12.9	12.9	12.9	12.9	12.9	11.8	11.8
	0.005	8.2	6.1	6.0	4.7	5.1	4.9	4.6	4.6
	0.01	6.0	6.0	4.6	5.0	5.0	4.7	4.7	4.6
	0.05	11.8	4.7	4.7	4.7	4.7	4.7	5.2	4.8
	0.1	12.6	12.8	5.2	5.3	4.7	4.7	4.6	4.6

for *small parts* undergoing a *small motion* compared to the size of the object like the handle of the "spray". As shown in Fig. 6, a high threshold results in an over-segmentation and increases the number of joints. An over-segmentation is often acceptable as we see for example in Fig. 2b or in Fig. 5 for the "spray" and the "lamp". In general, a slight over-segmentation is not problematic for many applications since joints can be disabled or ignored for instance for animation.

(0.005, 0.98)   (0.005, 0.70)   (0.050, 0.70)   (0.050, 0.70)

(0.005, 0.70)

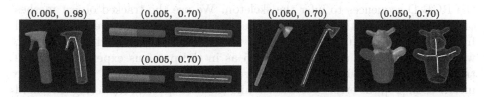

Fig. 5. Results for the best configuration $(\gamma_{def}, \lambda_{thr})$ for each object. The images show the motion segments and the inferred 3D skeleton, where the joints with DoF are depicted with red color. (Color figure online)

(0.005, 0.70)   (0.05, 0.70)   (0.005, 0.98)   (0.05, 0.98)

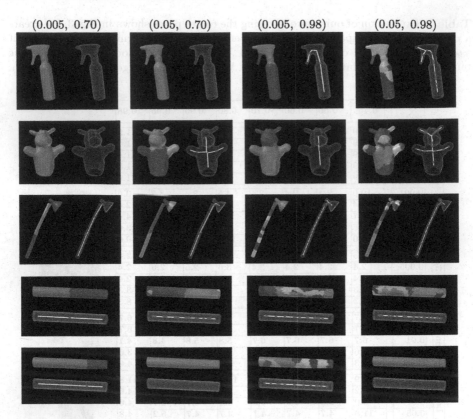

Fig. 6. Results for the four configurations (γ_{def}, λ_{thr}) that arise from the proposed parameters. The images show for each object the motion segments and the inferred 3D skeleton, where the joints with DoF are depicted with red color. (Color figure online)

A slight increase of the degrees of freedom also does not slow down articulated pose estimation, it even yields sometimes a lower alignment error as shown in Table 1.

We also evaluated our method on the public sequences *"Bending a Pipe"* and *"Bending a Rope"* of [26], in which the skeleton was manually modeled with 1 and 35 joints, respectively. As input we use the provided mesh of each object and the RGB-D sequences to infer the skeleton. We use the tracked object meshes of [26] as ground-truth and measure the error as in (13), but averaged over all frames. We first evaluate the accuracy of the deformable tracking in Table 2, which performs best with $\gamma_{def} = 0.005$ as in the previous experiments. If we track the sequence with the inferred articulated model using a point-to-plane metric as in [26], the error decreases. While the best spectral clustering threshold λ_{thr} for the pipe is again 0.70, the rope performs best for 0.98 due to the small size of the motion segments and the smaller motion differences of neighboring segments. We also report the error when the affinity matrix is computed only based on d^v without d^n (10). This slightly increases the error for the pipe with

Table 2. Evaluation of our method and resulting kinematic models for the public sequences "Bending a Pipe" and "Bending a Rope" of [26]. We report the average vertex error in mm.

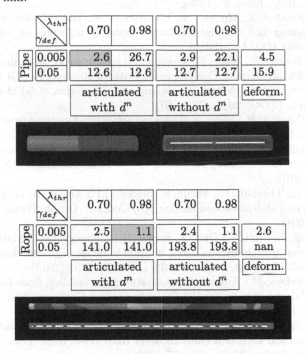

λ_{thr} $\backslash$ γ_{def}	0.70	0.98	0.70	0.98	
0.005	2.6	26.7	2.9	22.1	4.5
0.05	12.6	12.6	12.7	12.7	15.9
	articulated with d^n		articulated without d^n		deform.

λ_{thr} $\backslash$ γ_{def}	0.70	0.98	0.70	0.98	
0.005	2.5	1.1	2.4	1.1	2.6
0.05	141.0	141.0	193.8	193.8	nan
	articulated with d^n		articulated without d^n		deform.

optimal parameters. The motion segments and the acquired skeletons for the best configurations are also depicted in Table 2.

6   Conclusion

We presented an approach that generates fully rigged models consisting of a watertight mesh, an embedded skeleton and skinning weights that can be used out of the box for articulated tracking or animation. In that respect we operate fully in 3D capitalizing on deformable tracking, spectral clustering and skeletonization based on mean curvature flow. The thorough evaluation of the parameters provides a valuable intuition about the important factors and opens up possibilities for further generalization in future work. For instance, a regularizer that is adaptive to the areas of the triangles can be used for deformable tracking to compensate seamlessly for the varying triangle sizes across different objects. Furthermore, we have shown in our experiments that the proposed approach generates nicely working rigged models and has prospects for future practical applications.

Acknowledgements. The authors acknowledge financial support by the DFG Emmy Noether program (GA 1927/1-1).

References

1. Newcombe, R.A., Izadi, S., Hilliges, O., Molyneaux, D., Kim, D., Davison, A.J., Kohli, P., Shotton, J., Hodges, S., Fitzgibbon, A.: Kinectfusion: real-time dense surface mapping and tracking. In: International Symposium on Mixed and Augmented Reality (ISMAR) (2011)
2. Sturm, J., Bylow, E., Kahl, F., Cremers, D.: Copyme3d: Scanning and printing persons in 3d. In: German Conference on Pattern Recognition (GCPR) (2013)
3. Baran, I., Popović, J.: Automatic rigging and animation of 3d characters. ACM Trans. Graph. (TOG) 26(3), 72 (2007)
4. Pillai, S., Walter, M.R., Teller, S.: Learning articulated motions from visual demonstration. In: Robotics: Science and Systems (RSS) (2014)
5. Stoll, C., Gall, J., de Aguiar, E., Thrun, S., Theobalt, C.: Video-based reconstruction of animatable human characters. ACM Trans. Graph. (TOG) 29(6), 139: 1–139: 10 (2010)
6. De Aguiar, E., Theobalt, C., Thrun, S., Seidel, H.P.: Automatic conversion of mesh animations into skeleton-based animations. Comput. Graph. Forum (CGF) 27(2), 389–397 (2008)
7. Liu, Y., Gall, J., Stoll, C., Dai, Q., Seidel, H.P., Theobalt, C.: Markerless motion capture of multiple characters using multiview image segmentation. IEEE Trans. Pattern Anal. Mach. Intell. (PAMI) 35(11), 2720–2735 (2013)
8. Yan, J., Pollefeys, M.: Automatic kinematic chain building from feature trajectories of articulated objects. In: IEEE Conference on Computer Vision and Pattern Recognition (CVPR) (2006)
9. Yan, J., Pollefeys, M.: A factorization-based approach for articulated nonrigid shape, motion and kinematic chain recovery from video. IEEE Trans. Pattern Anal. Mach. Intell. (PAMI) 30(5), 865–877 (2008)
10. Ross, D.A., Tarlow, D., Zemel, R.S.: Learning articulated structure and motion. Int. J. Comput. Vis. (IJCV) 88(2), 214–237 (2010)
11. Chang, H.J., Demiris, Y.: Unsupervised learning of complex articulated kinematic structures combining motion and skeleton information. In: IEEE Conference on Computer Vision and Pattern Recognition (CVPR) (2015)
12. Fayad, J., Russell, C., Agapito, L.: Automated articulated structure and 3d shape recovery from point correspondences. In: International Conference on Computer Vision (ICCV) (2011)
13. Sturm, J., Pradeep, V., Stachniss, C., Plagemann, C., Konolige, K., Burgard, W.: Learning kinematic models for articulated objects. In: International Joint Conference on Artificial Intelligence (IJCAI) (2009)
14. Sturm, J., Stachniss, C., Burgard, W.: A probabilistic framework for learning kinematic models of articulated objects. J. Artif. Intell. Res. (JAIR) 41(2), 477–626 (2011)
15. Yücer, K., Wang, O., Sorkine-Hornung, A., Sorkine-Hornung, O.: Reconstruction of articulated objects from a moving camera. In: ICCVW (2015)
16. Katz, D., Kazemi, M., Bagnell, A.J., Stentz, A.: Interactive segmentation, tracking, and kinematic modeling of unknown 3d articulated objects. In: IEEE International Conference on Robotics and Automation (ICRA) (2013)
17. Martín-Martín, R., Höfer, S., Brock, O.: An integrated approach to visual perception of articulated objects. In: IEEE International Conference on Robotics and Automation (ICRA) (2016)

18. Tresadern, P., Reid, I.: Articulated structure from motion by factorization. In: IEEE Conference on Computer Vision and Pattern Recognition (CVPR) (2005)
19. Skanect: http://skanect.occipital.com. Accessed 19 Aug 2016
20. MeshLab: http://meshlab.sourceforge.net. Accessed 19 Aug 2016
21. Jones, M.J., Rehg, J.M.: Statistical color models with application to skin detection. Int. J. Comput. Vis. (IJCV) **46**(1), 81–96 (2002)
22. Paris, S., Durand, F.: A fast approximation of the bilateral filter using a signal processing approach. Int. J. Comput. Vis. (IJCV) **81**(1), 24–52 (2009)
23. Holzer, S., Rusu, R.B., Dixon, M., Gedikli, S., Navab, N.: Adaptive neighborhood selection for real-time surface normal estimation from organized point cloud data using integral images. In: IEEE/RSJ International Conference on Intelligent Robots and Systems (IROS) (2012)
24. Botsch, M., Sorkine, O.: On linear variational surface deformation methods. IEEE Trans. Vis. Comput. Graph. (TVCG) **14**(1), 213–230 (2008)
25. Gall, J., Stoll, C., De Aguiar, E., Theobalt, C., Rosenhahn, B., Seidel, H.P.: Motion capture using joint skeleton tracking and surface estimation. In: IEEE Conference on Computer Vision and Pattern Recognition (CVPR) (2009)
26. Tzionas, D., Ballan, L., Srikantha, A., Aponte, P., Pollefeys, M., Gall, J.: Capturing hands in action using discriminative salient points and physics simulation. Int. J. Comput. Vis. (IJCV) **118**, 172–193 (2016)
27. Pons-Moll, G., Rosenhahn, B.: Model-based pose estimation. In: Moeslund, T.B., Hilton, A., Krüger, V., Sigal, L. (eds.) Visual Analysis of Humans: Looking at People, pp. 139–170. Springer, London (2011). doi:10.1007/978-0-85729-997-0_9
28. Brox, T., Malik, J.: Object segmentation by long term analysis of point trajectories. In: Daniilidis, K., Maragos, P., Paragios, N. (eds.) ECCV 2010. LNCS, vol. 6315, pp. 282–295. Springer, Heidelberg (2010). doi:10.1007/978-3-642-15555-0_21
29. Ng, A.Y., Jordan, M.I., Weiss, Y.: On spectral clustering: analysis and an algorithm. In: Advances in Neural Information Processing Systems NIPS (2002)
30. Tagliasacchi, A., Alhashim, I., Olson, M., Zhang, H.: Mean curvature skeletons. Comput. Graph. Forum (CGF) **31**, 1735–1744 (2012)

RobotFusion: Grasping with a Robotic Manipulator via Multi-view Reconstruction

Daniele De Gregorio$^{(\boxtimes)}$, Federico Tombari, and Luigi Di Stefano

DISI, University of Bologna, Bologna, Italy
{daniele.degregorio3,federico.tombari,luigi.distefano}@unibo.it

Abstract. We propose a complete system for 3D object reconstruction and grasping based on an articulated robotic manipulator. We deploy an RGB-D sensor as an end effector placed directly on the robotic arm, and process the acquired data to perform multi-view 3D reconstruction and object grasping. We leverage the high repeatability of the robotic arm to estimate 3D camera poses with millimeter accuracy and control each of the six sensor's DOF in a dexterous workspace. Thereby, we can estimate camera poses directly by robot kinematics and deploy a Truncated Signed Distance Function (TSDF) to accurately fuse multiple views into a unified 3D reconstruction of the scene. Then, we propose an efficient approach to segment the sought objects out of a planar workbench as well as a novel algorithm to automatically estimate grasping points.

Keywords: Grasp · Manipulation · Reconstruction

1 Introduction

Object recognition and 3D pose estimation are key tasks in industrial applications requiring autonomous robots to understand the surroundings and pursue grasping and manipulation [14]. Indeed, manipulation mandates estimation of the 6 Degree-Of-Freedom (6DOF) pose (position and orientation) of the objects with respect to the base coordinate system of the robot. This pose estimation should be not only robust to clutter, occlusion and sensor noise, but also efficient to avoid slowing down the manipulation process.

Most object recognition and pose estimation algorithms rely on matching 2D or 3D features between off-line 3D models (either sets of 3D scans or CAD models) and scene measurements in the form of depth or RGB-D images. In particular, exploitation of color and depth cues from RGB-D images through suitable integration of texture-based and 3D features can yield quite remarkable performance across a variety of benchmark RGB-D datasets [1,24].

Although providing compelling results on standard benchmarks, the above mentioned multi-stage, multi-modal, feature-based pipelines turn out unsuited

Electronic supplementary material The online version of this chapter (doi:10.1007/978-3-319-49409-8_54) contains supplementary material, which is available to authorized users.

© Springer International Publishing Switzerland 2016
G. Hua and H. Jégou (Eds.): ECCV 2016 Workshops, Part III, LNCS 9915, pp. 634–647, 2016.
DOI: 10.1007/978-3-319-49409-8_54

to practical real-time industrial applications due to exceedingly slow execution times. Furthermore, due to reliance on a single vantage point, these approaches may fail when the sought objects are captured under high levels of occlusion [2] and/or their shape and texture do not appear distinctive enough in the chosen view. Finally, an additional nuisance that may hinder the performance of such approaches is represented by the high sensor noise affecting the depth frame provided as as input to the algorithms, which tends to distort significantly the 3D surfaces and often cause holes and artifacts [13].

In this paper, we investigate on the use of an RGB-D sensor mounted on top of a robotic arm to explore the surrounding environment in order to gather and process together RGB-D frames taken from different vantage points. This approach holds the potential to tackle the aforementioned issues inherent to perception from a single viewpoint, as also highlighted by the recent multi-view object recognition approach of Faulhammer et al. [7], who show how multi-view information can increase recognition accuracy and robustness by the integration of features from different viewpoints. In our work, we aim at 3D object reconstruction and grasping within a typical industrial robotics environment, namely a robotic arm performing *pick-and-place* operations on objects laying on planar surfaces such as workbenches, conveyor belts or positioners. The only working assumptions underpinning our approach consist in the robot being endowed with a highly accurate and repeatable encoder system (as it is typically the case of industrial robotic arms) and in objects laying on a plane. In these settings, we leverage on the high accuracy of robot encoders to automatically fuse together different views. First, at each vantage point we collect and fuse together multiple frames within a voxelized 3D representation, so to smooth out 3D data without distorting the underlying object geometries. Then, the views taken from different vantage points are merged together into a Truncated Signed Distance Function (TSDF) representation: we dub our approach *Robot Fusion* on account of its affinity to the well-known Kinect Fusion system [12]. Successively, we introduce a segmentation approach based on the planar assumption that allows for quick computation of grasping points without the need to carry out object recognition. Finally, the obtained grasping points are deployed to perform grasping via the robotic gripper mounted on the arm.

The novel contributions of our paper thus concern: (i) the *Robot Fusion* approach to reconstruct 3D objects by leveraging on robot encoders and TSDF representations, (ii) an algorithm to segment objects out of a planar surface, (iii) an algorithm to compute grasping points from surfaces without requiring any previous object recognition step. We report experimental results that demonstrate the effectiveness and accuracy of the proposed object reconstruction and segmentation stages, as well as the ability to attain good grasping points that enable to perform grasping successfully in cluttered scenes comprising several objects of diverse shapes.

2   Related Work

On-line fusion of the range images gathered by a moving sensor to achieve 3D reconstruction of the environment is a key task for RGB-D SLAM (Simultaneous

Localization and Mapping) frameworks. Among prominent approaches, Kinect Fusion [12,23] attains a highly accurate 3D reconstruction of the environment by fusing the depth measurements taken from different viewpoints alongside with camera movement into an occupancy map, i.e. a discrete voxel grid where each cell may either be void or contain the distance from the nearest surface via a Truncated Signed Distance Function (TSDF).

Besides mapping, the other key task in SLAM frameworks consists in sensor localization. Purposely, the Iterative Closest Point (ICP) algorithm is widely deployed to align the current depth image with respect to either the previous one or the global map. However, due to the algorithm allowing to estimate successfully small motions only, ICP is prone to failure when the incoming frames get processed at a pace that turns out too slow compared to sensor movements. To overcome this issue, sparse matching of 2D/3D features or dense, direct matching of image intensities may be deployed to coarsely align the current depth image prior to running ICP [5]. Several other methods, such as e.g. [10], rely on optimization of a global cost function to estimate all sensor poses coherently. Although very effective, these approaches are unsuited to real-time industrial robotics due to excessive running times, such as e.g. several minutes [10].

Differently, we address the SLAM localization task by relying on the high accuracy and repeatability of the robot encoders as well as on forward kinematics, as explained in details in Sect. 3.2. This leads to a fast and highly accurate 3D reconstruction step which is conducive to estimate a reliable set of grasping points on the reconstructed surfaces in absence of any information concerning the types of objects present in the scene. Indeed, estimating a set of contact point providing a stable grasp [11] based only on 3D geometry mandates very accurate 3D reconstruction of surfaces.

As for approaches aimed at grasping and manipulation based on grasp point detection, methods that try to estimate grasp points on unknown objects from a single range image have been proposed in [16,25]. These works are based on edge analysis and estimate the approach position of the gripper with respect to the target object (i.e., no estimation of the individual grasp points). Unfortunately, these methods can deal with thin objects or thin object parts only in scenes with low occlusion levels, both constraint due to the inherent limitations of relying on a single viewpoint already described in Sect. 1. Another issue with these approaches is that the grasp configuration is computed for grippers with a simple geometry, like parallel grippers. Indeed, as in [16], using a complex gripper, like a five fingered anthropomorphic hand, requires shaping it as a parallel gripper to achieve successful grasp.

Another possible approach consists in estimating directly the grasp points on the object surface and compute, via inverse kinematics, the position and orientation of the gripper. Saut et al. [20] describes how it can be hard to achieve a grasp configuration for a multi-finger anthropomorphic hand in real-time, and similar conclusions are drawn in [8]. Thus, these methods are suitable to autonomous grasping based on offline estimation of grasp points on known objects, an object recognition stage to detect object instances and associated poses, a final strategy to choose automatically the optimal grasp configuration between a pre-defined list.

3   Proposed Method

This Section describes in detail the main stages of the proposed system. As already mentioned, our approach relies on typical assumptions for industrial manipulation and *pick-and-place*, i.e. the presence of a high precision industrial robotic arm and a planar workbench holding objects.

In Subsect. 3.1 we illustrate how forward and inverse kinematics can be employed to accurately compute the camera 6DOF pose with respect to the robot main coordinate system regardless of the mounting point used on the robotic arm, this effectively replacing the visual data-based localization necessary to perform SLAM reconstruction of the scene. Then, we show how to attain accurate multi-view 3D reconstruction by fusing together range images within a voxelized TSDF representation. In Subsect. 3.2, we propose a segmentation approach based on a novel plane extraction method, dubbed *HeightMap*, which estimates all scene planes orthogonal to a given *gravity vector*. This results in a small and predictable computational time, which compares favorably to RANSAC-based plane fitting and allows for segmenting effectively the individual objects from the previously obtained 3D reconstruction. Finally, in Subsect. 3.3, we describe our proposed method for grasp points extraction from the 3D surface of segmented objects, which does not require an explicit object recognition stage. In particular, grasp points and grasp approach position are computed by leveraging on the object *Canonical Reference Frame* and so to avoid collisions between the robotic arm and the environment.

3.1   Multi-view Reconstruction via RobotFusion

We assume to deploy an industrial robot with high accuracy and repeatability (i.e. $\approx 0.05\,mm$ [9]). High accuracy means that we can impose a 6-DOF end effector pose $^{0}\mathbf{T_{EE}}$ with high precision in a dexterous workspace:

$$^{0}T_{EE} = \begin{bmatrix} ^{0}R_{EE} & ^{0}\mathbf{p}_{EE} \\ 0 & 1 \end{bmatrix}$$

In our system, the end effector is an RGB-D camera (i.e. an Asus Xtion) with a 3D-printed housing, this yielding an unknown transformation between the robot wrist and the 3D coordinate system attached to the camera (i.e. the camera coordinate system):

$$^{0}T_{EE} =^{0} T_{W} \cdot^{W} T_{EE}$$

While $^{0}\mathbf{T_{W}}$ is the result of a simple application of forward kinematic equations on the target robot, $^{W}\mathbf{T_{EE}}$ is estimated during an offline calibration stage by means of a fiducial marker having a known 3D pose, $^{0}\mathbf{T_{M}}$, in the main robot coordinate system. To accomplish this, we use an Augmented Reality Framework [18] to estimate the pose of the fiducial marker w.r.t. the camera coordinate system: $^{Cam}\mathbf{T_{M}} = {}^{EE}\mathbf{T_{M}}$, thereby closing the loop in the equation

$$^{0}T_{W} \cdot^{W} T_{EE} \cdot^{EE} T_{M} =^{0} T_{M}$$

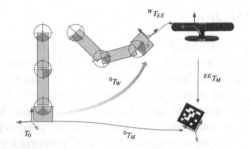

Fig. 1. Kinematics chain to compute the transformation between the wrist and the camera ($^W T_{EE}$).

in order to estimate the unknown transformation between the wrist and the camera

$$^W T_{EE} =^W T_0 \cdot^0 T_M \cdot^M T_{EE}$$

Now, each point, p_i, belonging to the point cloud $\mathcal{P} = \{p_1, ..., p_n\}$ acquired by the RGB-D sensor can be expressed as:

$$^0 p_i =^0 T_{EE} \cdot^{EE} p_i$$

Hence, for each new view gathered alongside robot movement, we can directly obtain a point cloud registered into the main robot coordinate system without the need to estimate any alignment transformation with respect to the previously acquired clouds (Fig. 1).

A 3D object reconstruction algorithm needs multiple *range images* from different viewpoints to build an unified representation of the surface of the target object. State-of-the-art SLAM techniques pursuing accurate and dense scene reconstruction, such as e.g. [4,12], first localize the camera and then merge each newly acquired range image into a global representation of the environment based on a *Truncated Signed Distance Function* (TSDF) defined on a voxel grid. Therein, each voxel either is void or stores the signed distance from its center to the nearest surface.

We adopt the same TSDF representation. However, as described, we do not need to carry out an explicit camera localization step as we can seamlessly integrate depth measurements into a global voxel grid by deploying robot kinematics. It is worthwhile pointing out that the use of a TSDF-based representation allows our system to fuse together seamlessly not only acquisitions from diverse viewpoints, but multiple range images taken from the same vantage point alike. The latter process turns out highly effective to counteract the significant amount of noise that typically affects the RGB-D data acquired by consumer depth cameras.

To minimize the amount of calculations, we update only the voxels visible from the current vantage point (view frustum) rather than the entire grid[1].

---

[1] https://github.com/sdmiller/cpu_tsdf.

Moreover, we rely on an *octree* representation of the voxel grid, this decreasing memory requirements significantly [21]. Thanks to the reduced computational complexity, and unlike most previous works on dense volumetric mapping that leverage on GP-GPU acceleration, we can run efficiently our reconstruction system on the CPU, this being a beneficial trait as regards its potential implementation on the compact embedded platforms often deployed in industrial environments.

To assess quantitatively the accuracy provided by the proposed RobotFusion approach based on fusing depth measurements into a TSDF within a viewpoint and across viewpoints, we created a synthetic setup in the Gazebo simulator integrated in the ROS framework. In particular, we simulated an industrial robot equipped with an RGB-D sensor and a table-top scene. As the simulation environment provides noiseless RGB-D data, we implemented a noise model similar to that proposed by Nguyen *et al.* [13]. In the experiments, we compared the reconstructions provided by RobotFusion to those that one would achieve by simply stitching together the point clouds from the different vantage points into the global coordinate system of the robot, which is also straightforwardly attainable by deploying robot kinematics. Figure 2a shows that the proposed approach can achieve smooth and accurate 3D reconstructions as well as how the devised fusion process provides a significantly higher accuracy with respect to simple stitching of the point clouds. Figure 2c pertains a reconstruction experiment carried out with real data: while RobotFusion can recover the object's surface accurately, the reconstruction created by stitching together the points clouds shows many gross errors due to sensor noise. Eventually, Fig. 2b concerns en experiment aimed at evaluating the benefits brought in by fusing together multiple depth images at each viewpoint: the reconstruction error tends to decrease and then stabilize as more and more depth images get fused at a single viewing position. As such, it turns out beneficial to deploy a sufficient number of images (e.g. 10–15) to effectively smooth out noise and minimize the reconstruction error.

3.2   Plane-Based Segmentation

Industrial robots can be mounted only in three standard positions: *floor, wall, ceiling* (seldom at *45 degrees*). Thus, we can always calculate the relation between the *gravity vector* and the *z-axis* of the robot in the robot (or world) coordinate system. For example, in a *floor-mounted* robot the gravity vector is parallel and opposite to the *z-axis*: $\mathbf{g} = (0, 0, -\mathbf{z}) = (0, 0, -1)$.

Hence, given a point cloud $\mathcal{P} = \{\mathbf{p_1}, ..., \mathbf{p_n}\}$ and the associated set of normals $\mathcal{N} = \{\mathbf{n_1}, ..., \mathbf{n_n}\}$, we extract the points belonging to planes orthogonal to the *gravity vector* by creating a *1-D* histogram $\mathcal{H} = \{S_1, .., S_k\}$ where each bin represents a subset (or *slice*) of points belonging approximately to the same plane. More precisely, assuming a *floor-mounted* robot and denoting the *slice-size (histogram bin-size)* as λ:

$$\mathbf{p_i} \in S_j \iff \mathbf{n_i} \cdot (-\mathbf{g}) < cos(\alpha), j = \lfloor p_{\mathbf{z},i}/\lambda \rfloor \tag{1}$$

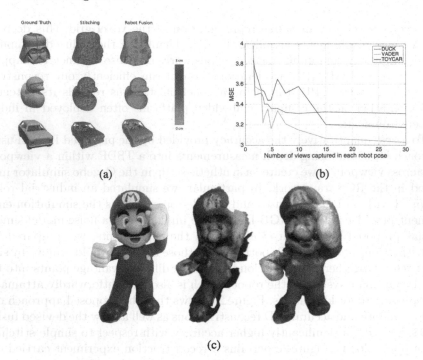

Fig. 2. (a) *Synthetic data.* Left: original 3D CAD model used as ground truth. Center: reconstruction by stitching point clouds. Right: TSDF-based reconstruction by Robot-Fusion. Colors encode the metric error w.r.t. the ground truth at reconstructed surface points. (b) Mean square error in function of the number of views for the 3 different models of Fig. 2c. The proposed TSDF-based approach obtains an increasing accuracy with a higher number of frames captured in each robot poses (in this case 12 robot poses around object). (c) *Real data.* Left: original 3D object. Center: reconstruction by stitching point clouds. Right: TSDF-based reconstruction by RobotFusion.

α being an arbitrary angular threshold used to define the maximum allowed plane inclination w.r.t the gravity vector and to withstand the presence of noise on the computed normals.

As illustrated in Fig. 3a, for a *floor-mounted* robot histogram $\mathcal{H}$ highlights the position along the *gravity axis* of possible horizontal planes. By defining $S_{z_{\min},j}, S_{z_{\max},j}$ as, respectively, the minimum and maximum z coordinates in slice S_j, we can extract planes by selecting subsets of points belonging to those histogram bins that report a value over a pre-defined threshold. We call this approach as *HeightMap* segmentation.

Remarkably, plane extraction methods such as those based on *RANSAC* have no predictable execution time [17] due to their intrinsic randomized iterative nature. This is also the case of the *1-Point RANSAC* approach [22], which enables to estimate dominant planes by means of a 1-point (rather than 3) RANSAC plane fitting by exploiting the normal associated to each point. Conversely, the proposed *HeightMap* approach enjoys a deterministic and fast execution time, due to its complexity being linear in the size of the point cloud.

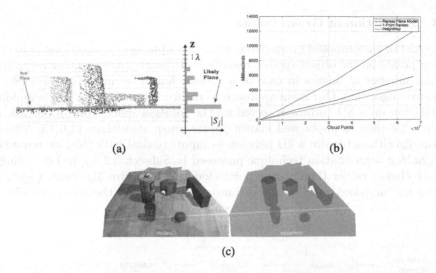

Fig. 3. (a) Side view of a point cloud representing a table-top scene, with four objects. Accordingly, the bin of the histogram reported on the right hand-side corresponding to the table is the highest one, while object surfaces tend to report much smaller bin values. (b) Execution times of plane extraction algorithms while increasing the point cloud size. (c) Example of horizontal planes extracted by a single run of the proposed *HeightMap* segmentation algorithm.

Figure 3b reports the running times yielded by different plane extraction methods, namely *HeightMap*, standard RANSAC and 1-point RANSAC, in experiments carried out in the simulated working environment already described in Subsect. 3.1. As we can see, *HeightMap* is the fastest approach and features a linear growth of the measured execution time with respect to the point cloud size. Figure 3c shows an example of the horizontal planes extracted by the *HeightMap* method from a point cloud. It is worth pointing out that a single run of the method allows to extract all the sought parallel planes, while getting an equivalent result by RANSAC-based approaches would require multiple iterations.

On a broader level, we wish to point out that *HeightMap* may be applied to extract planes orthogonal to any arbitrarily oriented *gravity-vector*. Purposely, the point cloud may require a rotation to align one axis (e.g. the *z-axis*) to the considered *gravity-vector*.

Under the previously highlighted assumption of objects placed on a planar support, plane extraction provides a strong cue to segment the individual objects. Indeed, the largest plane extracted by *HeightMap* can be quite safely assumemed to represent the workbench and thus simply removed from the point cloud. Thereby, the objects become disconnected one to another and the points belonging to each object's surface can be identified straightforwardly by standard tools such as Euclidean Clustering[2].

---

[2] http://www.pointclouds.org/documentation/tutorials/cluster_extraction.php.

3.3   Extraction of Grasp Points

The goal of the proposed grasp point extraction approach is to estimate directly grasp points on the object surface regardless of the gripper shape (or regardless of the number of fingers in case of a robotic hand) by means of an efficient iterative algorithm. Our main approach to reduce the complexity of grasp point estimation on a 3D surface is to reduce the solution space from 3D to 2D, so to be able then to apply well known *planar grasp* algorithms [3,6,15]. Planar grasp algorithms require a 2D polygon as input: to deal with this, we reuse the *HeightMap* segmentation technique proposed in Subsect. 3.2 applied on a single object cluster rather than on the point cloud of the entire 3D scene. Figure 4a shows the proposed pipeline to compute grasp points in the robot coordinate system, which is described in the following.

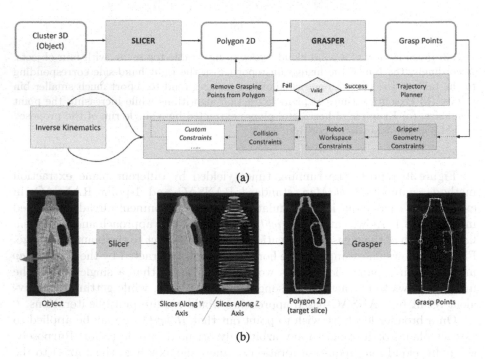

Fig. 4. (a) Proposed pipeline for grasp points extraction. Each subset of the polygon points (defined as Grasping Points) will be validated through N validation stages. In addition to fixed constraints, the user can choose custom constraints for a specific task. (b) Graphical representation of a 3D object passing through the previous pipeline until it reaches a valid grasp point configuration.

Principal Axes. To begin with, each 3D object cluster is sliced along its principal axes. To obtain these stable axes, we compute the EigenValue Decomposition (EVD) of the covariance matrix of each object cluster [19], which yields three repeatable directions.

Slicer. The algorithm selects a slice and projects the points onto a plane orthogonal to the slicing axis. To simplify the obtained shape, the system computes the concave hull of the slice, this yielding a 2D polygon suitable to the next stages.

Grasp Point Extraction. At this stage, N points are randomly extracted from the polygon boundary (in practice, only the first points are randomly extracted, the remaining ones are chosen so to avoid useless point subsets, e.g. adjacent points).

Validation. The extracted grasp points are then evaluated through several stages. The first stage checks for geometrical constraints: if the detected grasp points lie outside of the gripper (or robotic hand) workspace, the grasp points are removed. This can be carried out, e.g., by checking if the distance between 2 grasp points is larger than the maximum opening of a parallel gripper. The second stage checks for robot workspace constraints, by evaluating whether grasp points can be reached in a dexterous portion of the workspace. The third stage evaluates collision constraints, by checking if the gripper, with the 6-DOF pose relative to the grasp points, would collide with environment. In addition, *custom* constraints can also be further added to refine grasp points in case of specific tasks or manipulators, by adding additional validation stages.

Grasp Point Removal. If one of the validation stages fails, the set of grasp points is removed for the current 2D polygon. Conversely, if no validation stage fails, since the grasp points are already in the robot coordinate system , the system can directly compute the full inverse kinematic chain from the grasp points to the robot base, so that a trajectory planner can be instructed to easily allow the robot approach the object and carry out the grasp.

Of course, given the greedy and iterative nature of this algorithm, the determined solution may not be the optimal one, and the system may also fail to find a feasible solution if the required iterations exceed the maximum number of allowed iterations.

4   Grasping Experiments

The entire pipeline comprising 3D reconstruction, plane-based segmentation and extraction of grasp points was tested in real grasping experiments dealing with 8 scenes created by placing several objects (between a set of 8) on a planar support, as illustrated in Fig. 5b. The experimental setup consists of an Industrial Robot, i.e. a *Comau Smart Six* with six degrees of freedom and an accuracy and repeatability lesser than *0.05 mm*. The end effector, shown in Fig. 5a, is a dualuse tool: the first part of the tool is an Asus Xtion RGB-D sensor, the second part a two finger Robotic Hand with three contact point providing a more stable grasp compared to a simple parallel gripper with only two contact points.

Each scene was tested 5 times and in each experiment the robot had to grasp all the objects present in the scene. Accordingly, a binary outcome (*Success* or

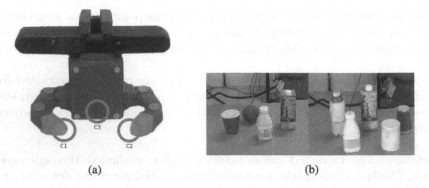

(a)   (b)

Fig. 5. (a) End Effector used during the experiments. The top part is an Asus Xtion RGB-D Sensor, the bottom part is the Gripper: a two finger robotic hand with three contacts points $(C1, C2, C3)$. (b) Two sample scenes of our grasping experiments.

Table 1. Grasping results

Object Type	Grasp carried by the robot and corresponding grasp configuration	Possible Trials	Success (%)
Ball		20	100
Bottle		20	100
Box		20	100
Cup		30	95
Cylinder		20	100
Milk		30	100
Showergel		20	75
Winepack		30	100

Failure) was reported for each possible grasp depending on whether or not the robot succeeds in grasping the object and placing it into a bin. Thus, *Success* requires all the stages in our pipeline to work effectively, while a *Failure* may be ascribed to a variety of causes, such as missing an object because of a wrong segmentation or an unstable grasp (e.g. the robot does not picks up the object or the object falls while being moved towards the bin) due imprecise extraction of the grasping points.

Table 1 summarizes the results of our grasping experiments. In particular, for each of the 8 objects, the last two columns report the number of possible grasps within the 40 experiments (5 tests for each of the 8 scenes) as well as the percentage of successful ones. Each row depicts also two examples of grasps performed by the robot together with the associated contact points computed by the algorithm described in Subsect. 3.3. It is worth highlighting that, as each object was placed in the different scenes according to different poses (see the pictures in Table 1), those automatically determined by our algorithm are not simple caging grasps but, indeed, stable predetermined grasp configurations. The overall success rate over all the grasping experiments turned out to be *96,56 %*, with the failures mainly due to imprecise localization of the grasping points.

Additional results are provided in the supplementary material, which includes a video recorded during the grasping experiments.

5   Conclusions

We have described a practical and effective approach to 3D reconstruction and object grasping whereby, instead of registering the depth data acquired from different viewpoints with greedy algorithms, such as Iterative Closest Point (ICP), we deploy the high accuracy an repeatability of industrial robots to compute sensor poses directly by robot kinematics. To accomplish accurate 3D reconstruction, we rely on the TSDF representation popularized by KinectFusion and then propose original algorithms to both segment the objects out of a planar support as well as estimate automatically grasping points from the object surfaces. We have reported results aimed at highlighting the advantages brought in by each stage of the proposed pipeline as well as demonstrated the effectiveness of the overall system in real grasping experiments carried out in our Lab by an industrial robot equipped with an RGB-D camera and a two finger gripper.

References

1. Aldoma, A., Tombari, F., Prankl, J., Richtsfeld, A., Stefano, L.D., Vincze, M.: Multimodal cue integration through hypotheses verification for RGB-D object recognition and 6DOF pose estimation. In: 2013 IEEE International Conference on Robotics and Automation (ICRA), pp. 2104–2111, May 2013
2. Aldoma, A., Vincze, M., Blodow, N., Gossow, D., Gedikli, S., Rusu, R.B., Bradski, G.: CAD-model recognition and 6DOF pose estimation using 3d cues. In: 2011 IEEE International Conference on Computer Vision Workshops (ICCV Workshops), pp. 585–592, November 2011

3. Bicchi, A., Kumar, V.: Robotic grasping and contact: a review. In: 2000 Proceedings of IEEE International Conference on Robotics and Automation, ICRA 2000, vol. 1, pp. 348–353 (2000)
4. Bylow, E., Sturm, J., Kerl, C., Kahl, F., Cremers, D.: Real-time camera tracking and 3d reconstruction using signed distance functions. In: Robotics: Science and Systems (RSS), Online Proceedings (2013)
5. Engel, J., Schöps, T., Cremers, D.: LSD-SLAM: large-scale direct monocular SLAM. In: Fleet, D., Pajdla, T., Schiele, B., Tuytelaars, T. (eds.) ECCV 2014. LNCS, vol. 8693, pp. 834–849. Springer, Heidelberg (2014). doi:10.1007/978-3-319-10605-2_54
6. Ferrari, C., Canny, J.: Planning optimal grasps. In: Proceedings of 1992 IEEE International Conference on Robotics and Automation, vol. 3, pp. 2290–2295, May 1992
7. Fulhammer, T., Aldoma, A., Zillich, M., Vincze, M.: Temporal integration of feature correspondences for enhanced recognition in cluttered and dynamic environments. In: International Conferenec on Robotics and Automation (ICRA), pp. 3003–3009, May 2015
8. Hang, K., Stork, J., Kragic, D.: Hierarchical fingertip space for multi-fingered precision grasping. In: 2014 IEEE/RSJ International Conference on Intelligent Robots and Systems (IROS 2014), pp. 1641–1648, September 2014
9. ISO TC 184SC 2 Robots, robotic devices: ISO 9283. Manipulating industrial robots- Performance criteria and related test methods. International Organization for Standardization, Geneva, Switzerland (2015). http://www.iso.org
10. Kehl, W., Navab, N., Ilic, S.: Coloured signed distance fields for full 3d object reconstruction. In: Proceedings of the British Machine Vision Conference. BMVA Press (2014)
11. Montana, D.: The condition for contact grasp stability. In: IEEE International Conference on Robotics and Automation (1991)
12. Newcombe, R.A., Davison, A.J., Izadi, S., Kohli, P., Hilliges, O., Shotton, J., Molyneaux, D., Hodges, S., Kim, D., Fitzgibbon, A.: KinectFusion: real-time dense surface mapping and tracking. In: 10th IEEE International Symposium on Mixed and Augmented Reality, pp. 127–136, October 2011. http://ieeexplore.ieee.org/lpdocs/epic03/wrapper.htm?arnumber=6162880
13. Nguyen, C., Izadi, S., Lovell, D.: Modeling kinect sensor noise for improved 3d reconstruction and tracking. In: 2012 Second International Conference on 3D Imaging, Modeling, Processing, Visualization and Transmission (3DIMPVT), pp. 524–530, October 2012
14. Papazov, H., Parusel, K., Krieger, B.: Rigid 3d geometry matching for grasping of known objects in cluttered scenes. Int. J. Robot. Res. **31**, 538–553 (2012)
15. Ponce, J., Faverjon, B.: On computing three-finger force-closure grasps of polygonal objects. In: Fifth International Conference on Advanced Robotics, Robots in Unstructured Environments, ICAR 1991, vol. 2, pp. 1018–1023, June 1991
16. Popovi, M., Kraft, D., Bodenhagen, L., Baeski, E., Pugeault, N., Kragic, D., Asfour, T., Krger, N.: A strategy for grasping unknown objects based on coplanarity and colour information. Robot. Auton. Syst. **58**(5), 551–565 (2010)
17. Raguram, R., Frahm, J.-M., Pollefeys, M.: A comparative analysis of RANSAC techniques leading to adaptive real-time random sample consensus. In: Forsyth, D., Torr, P., Zisserman, A. (eds.) ECCV 2008. LNCS, vol. 5303, pp. 500–513. Springer, Heidelberg (2008). doi:10.1007/978-3-540-88688-4_37

18. Garrido-Jurado, S., Muoz-Salinas, R., Madrid-Cuevas, F.J., Marn-Jimnez, M.J.: Automatic generation and detection of highly reliable fiducial markers under occlusion. Pattern Recogn. **47**(6), 2280–2292 (2014)
19. Salti, S., Tombari, F., Stefano, L.D.: Shot: unique signatures of histograms for surface and texture description. Comput., Vis. Image Underst. **125**, 251–264 (2014). http://www.sciencedirect.com/science/article/pii/S1077314214000988
20. Saut, J.P., Sidobre, D.: Efficient models for grasp planning with a multi-fingered hand. Robot. Autonom. Syst. **60**(3), 347–357 (2012). http://www.sciencedirect.com/science/article/pii/S0921889011001515, Autonomous Grasping
21. Steinbrucker, F., Kerl, C., Cremers, D.: Large-scale multi-resolution surface reconstruction from RGB-D sequences. In: The IEEE International Conference on Computer Vision (ICCV), December 2013
22. Tombari, F., Fioraio, N., Cavallari, T., Salti, S., Petrelli, A., Stefano, L.D.: Automatic detection of pole-like structures in 3d urban environments. In: 2014 IEEE/RSJ International Conference on Intelligent Robots and Systems (IROS 2014), pp. 4922–4929, September 2014
23. Whelan, T., Kaess, M., Johannsson, H., Fallon, M., Leonard, J.J., Mcdonald, J.: Real-time large scale dense RGB-D SLAM with volumetric fusion. Int. J. Robot. Res. IJRR **34**, 598–626 (2014)
24. Xie, Z., Singh, A., Uang, J., Narayan, K.S., Abbeel, P.: Multimodal blending for high-accuracy instance recognition. In: 2013 IEEE/RSJ International Conference on Intelligent Robots and Systems (IROS), pp. 2214–2221, November 2013
25. Jiang, Y., Moseson, S., Saxena, A.: Efficient grasping from RGBD images: learning using a new rectangle representation. In: 2011 IEEE International Conference on Robotics and Automation (ICRA) (2011)

SemanticFusion:
Joint Labeling, Tracking and Mapping

Tommaso Cavallari[✉] and Luigi Di Stefano

Department of Computer Science and Engineering,
University of Bologna, Bologna, Italy
{tommaso.cavallari,luigi.distefano}@unibo.it

Abstract. Kick-started by deployment of the well-known KinectFusion, recent research on the task of RGBD-based dense volume reconstruction has focused on improving different shortcomings of the original algorithm. In this paper we tackle two of them: drift in the camera trajectory caused by the accumulation of small per-frame tracking errors and lack of semantic information within the output of the algorithm. Accordingly, we present an extended KinectFusion pipeline which takes into account per-pixel semantic labels gathered from the input frames. By such clues, we extend the memory structure holding the reconstructed environment so to store per-voxel information on the kinds of object likely to appear in each spatial location. We then take such information into account during the camera localization step to increase the accuracy in the estimated camera trajectory. Thus, we realize a SemanticFusion loop whereby per-frame labels help better track the camera and successful tracking enables to consolidate instantaneous semantic observations into a coherent volumetric map.

Keywords: SLAM · Deep learning · Semantic segmentation · Semantic fusion · Semantic camera tracking

1 Introduction

Since the publication of the KinectFusion paper by Newcombe and colleagues [1], significant interest has spurred on the topic of dense surface mapping and tracking by means of a handheld RGB-D sensor, this resulting in a multitude of proposals focused on extending and/or improving the original algorithm from a variety of diverse perspectives. Thus, for example, attention has been devoted to extend KinectFusion to reconstruct either large scale [2] or non-rigid [3] scenes, to improve the tracking module [4] or also to achieve detection of known object instances [5].

Electronic supplementary material The online version of this chapter (doi:10. 1007/978-3-319-49409-8_55) contains supplementary material, which is available to authorized users.

© Springer International Publishing Switzerland 2016
G. Hua and H. Jégou (Eds.): ECCV 2016 Workshops, Part III, LNCS 9915, pp. 648–664, 2016.
DOI: 10.1007/978-3-319-49409-8_55

Picture
Chair
Wall
Floor

Fig. 1. Advantages of the proposed technique. Left: scene reconstruction provided by the geometry-based KinectFusion tracker shows gross errors due to the flat wall, while deployment of semantic cues enables correct handling of planar surfaces. Right: while KinectFusion is concerned with surface information only, our method can provide a semantically labeled volumetric reconstruction of the workspace.

Differently, the work described in this paper is concerned with endowing KinectFusion with the ability to create a semantically labeled dense reconstruction of the environment as well as with deploying per-frame semantic information to improve camera tracking, the two processes carried out jointly and synergistically. Indeed, on one hand we track the camera by relying also on per-pixel semantic labeling of the current RGB-D frame, so that a likely camera pose should explain not only the geometry of the scene but also its semantics: *e.g.*, a pixel labeled as *picture* should preferably project onto a voxel tagged as *picture* than as *wall*. On the other hand, upon successful camera tracking we fuse the category map associated with the current frame into a volumetric representation, so that the final labeling results from suitable integration over time of the many fragile instantaneous observations delivered by the per-frame labeler. Thereby, semantic labeling ameliorates camera tracking, especially while acquiring scene elements – such as walls or windows – that may not provide distinctive geometric cues. Camera tracking then robustifies semantic labeling by allowing for identification of observations dealing with the same surface patch at different times so to assess their likelihood and confidence. The two key advantages brought in by our proposal are exemplified in Fig. 1.

Previous work has demonstrated how deployment of additional cues, such as color [6] or contours [4], can significantly improve the accuracy of the original KinectFusion tracker, which relies on geometrical information only. Unlike previous work, in this paper we advocate reliance on higher-level observations, such as per-pixel object category tags, to improve the tracking module and present a method that can also output automatically a fully labeled dense reconstruction of the environment with confidence scores for multiple object categories stored into each voxel of the mapped space. This kind of semantically rich output may vastly facilitate difficult tasks related to 3D indoor scene understanding, object discovery, object recognition and grasping, path planning and human/robot navigation.

2   Related Work

Newcombe's work [1], well-favored in its simplicity and effective in its core task – mapping of small/medium size environments rich in geometric structure – suffers from the four main shortcomings highlighted as follows. (a) Reliance on a memory-demanding data structure located on the GPU, such as a dense fixed-size voxel grid, makes it impossible to map large scale scenes. (b) The drift error inherently accumulated during the tracking process may cause gross reconstruction errors when observing smooth/flat surfaces or closing camera path loops. (c) The requirement for static and rigid scenes hampers usability outside controlled settings, which severely limits the breadth of practical applications. (d) Finally, KinectFusion outputs a purely geometric map of the environment, thus providing no semantic hints to support higher level reasoning about sensor surroundings.

In the remainder of this section we will mention some works tackling each of the aforementioned issues and describe how our proposed technique addresses two of them originally.

(a) Different approaches can be taken to extend the mapped workspace: the reference frame for the volume can be moved alongside with sensor movements, possibly downloading parts of the voxel grid from GPU to CPU memory [7,8]; alternatively, sparse voxel grids indexed as hierarchical structures or Hash tables can be stored in memory to diminish occupancy and increase the bounds of the mappable space [2,9].

(b) Some works have proposed to rely on additional clues with respect to the purely-geometric KinectFusion tracker to attempt reducing the inherent drift error. In particular, Bylow and Olsson [6] show that injecting per-pixel color measurements within the cost function optimized by the tracker does improve accuracy, especially when dealing with flat or smooth surfaces that present distinctive color features. Conversely, Zhou and Koltun [4] posit to deploy occluding contours rather than color and demonstrate the effectiveness of their proposal in experiments focused on scanning individual objects featuring smooth and evenly colored surfaces. Other approaches concern tackling drift by a global optimization step on a pose graph, which may better counteract misalignments showing up at loop closures. The pose optimization step may be run either off-line, after the capture process is terminated, or on-line, by continuously optimizing the poses of partial volumes, possibly deforming the surfaces contained therein [10–13].

(c) Lightly dynamic scenes are allowed by the original KinectFusion algorithm, though only due to the volume update step behaving as a low-pass filter that forgets old measurements after a certain number of frames. However, scene motion is not explicitly considered, sudden movements of relatively large-size objects inevitably causing tracking failures. Recent works, instead, have demonstrated impressive results in non-rigid and dynamic settings by modeling motion as a fundamental property of the captured scene [3,14].

(d) The work by Fioraio et al. [5] attempts to gather semantic knowledge while tracking and mapping by KinectFusion. In particular, deployment of their Semantic Bundle Adjustment framework [15] together with KinectFusion enables to detect known object instances, estimate their 6 DOF poses and embed objects into a globally optimized pose graph which helps counteracting drift. Although pursuing a diverse graph-based mapping strategy, the SLAM++ system by Salas-Moreno et al. [16] relies on the detection of known object instances to perform camera tracking by an approach akin to Kinect-Fusion. On the other hand, Valentin *et al.* [17] show compelling results in the task of interactively labeling a scene already reconstructed via Kinect-Fusion. Their approach combines user interaction with on-line learning by *streaming random forests* to obtain per-voxel semantic labels representing personalized categories of the objects present in the environment. Eventually, the very recent paper by Cavallari and Di Stefano [18] describes the first attempt to obtain automatically a labeled volumetric reconstruction. Here, the authors track the camera by a standard geometric KinectFusion approach and, upon successful tracking, fuse the labels delivered by a per-frame semantic segmentation algorithm into the voxel grid by means of a simple evidence counting scheme that allows storing information concerning a single category per voxel only.

Therefore, the first contribution provided by this paper deals with the issue of the inherent drift that may be accumulated by a purely geometric tracker. Unlike previous work, we propose to rely on semantic observations such as category labels rather than low-level cues like color [6] or occluding contours [4]. The second contribution concerns gathering not only structure but also semantics, our proposal delivering a densely labeled volumetric reconstruction of the workspace. While previous work [17] has addressed interactive scenarios and shown how to obtain a similar output by placing the user in the loop, in this paper we propose a fully automatic approach. With respect to the automatic labeling method recently reported in [18], our proposal is not constrained to keeping track of only one label per voxel but instead can gather evidence concerning all categories across the whole voxel grid. As it will be discussed in Subsect. 3.2, besides providing a semantically richer output, mantaining information about all categories in each voxel is instrumental to the realization of a semantic tracker. Moreover, while the works in [17,18] assume surface reconstruction to be achieved by standard KinecFusion, we realize a closed loop between the semantic labeling and the dense mapping and tracking processes, so to allow one process to beneficially influence the other. In this respect, our approach is more similar in spirit to previous works aimed at creating synergistic interactions between object detection and SLAM [5,15,16].

3 Description of the Method

A TSDF (Truncated Signed Distance Function) volume employed during the execution of a KinectFusion-like tracking and mapping pipeline typically contains the following information in each voxel:

1. Truncated signed distance of the voxel from the closest world surface.
2. Weight used to compute the running average during the voxel update step.
3. (Optional) RGB values representing the color of the surface and associated weights.

To obtain a semantically labeled voxel, we store also the category labels as a histogram wherein the value stored in each bin is as higher as the corresponding label is observed more frequently and with higher confidence scores. As such, a bin value becomes correlated to the probability that an object of a certain category is located at the voxel's 3D position. This representation allows us to both compare the evidence about the diverse categories gathered within each voxel as well as to rank the labeling confidence between different voxels.

Without loss of generality, we assume to employ a semantic labeling algorithm capable to output a per-pixel category label for each input frame together with an associated score map representing the degree of belief in the predicted pixel labels. Indeed, this is the most typical kind of output delivered by semantic segmentation algorithms working with either RGB or RGB-D images. Should the labeler at hand provide a more comprehensive output, such as a full *pmf* across categories at each pixel position, we would easily remap it into the format currently accepted by our method. In the following subsections we will describe in detail how to augment the standard KinectFusion volume update technique to account also for per-pixel labels and how to deploy such semantic information to robustify the tracking process.

3.1   Volume Update Process

The update process allows for integration of a new measurement into the volume capturing the structure of the world as previously seen by the sensor. We denote with $T = (R, \mathbf{t}) \in \mathbb{SE}_3$ the affine transformation mapping points in the camera reference frame to world coordinates and $\mathbf{u} = (u, v)^T$ the coordinates of a pixel in the input frame. We also assume the intrinsic parameters of the camera (f_x, f_y, c_x, c_y) to be known, so to be able to perform perspective projection of 3D points into pixels and vice-versa. We will indicate the projection operation as $\pi(\mathbf{p}) : \mathbb{R}^3 \rightarrow \mathbb{R}^2$ and reprojection as $\pi^{-1}(\mathbf{u}, z) : (\mathbb{R}^2, \mathbb{R}) \rightarrow \mathbb{R}^3$. Thus, as soon as a new input frame has been tracked, we wish to integrate into the volume the depth image, $d(\mathbf{u})$, the RGB image, $i(\mathbf{u})$, as well as the pair of maps, $l(\mathbf{u})$ and $s(\mathbf{u})$, representing, respectively, the per-pixel labels and scores yielded by the semantic labeler.

The original KinectFusion algorithm [1] updates the volume by visiting each voxel and projecting the 3D location of its center, $\mathbf{p_v}$, onto the image plane according to the tracked pose and the projection function:

$$\mathbf{u_v} = \pi(T^{-1}\mathbf{p_v}) \tag{1}$$

Then, if the projected location falls within the bounds of the input image, the data contained in the voxel get updated. The signed distance from the voxel center to the surface described by the depth image is computed by considering the z coordinate of the voxel center in the camera reference frame:

$$SDF_v = (T^{-1}\mathbf{p_v})_z - d(\mathbf{u_v}) \tag{2}$$

A truncation distance, δ, is then considered, so that only voxels within the sensor view frustum and whose $SDF_v \geq -\delta$ are updated. The voxel TSDF value, D, and associated weight, W_d, are modified as follows:

$$TSDF_v = \begin{cases} 1 \text{ for } SDF_v \geq \delta \\ \frac{SDF_v}{\delta} \text{ for } -\delta \leq SDF_v \leq \delta \end{cases} \tag{3}$$

$$D^{t+1}(\mathbf{p_v}) = \frac{D^t(\mathbf{p_v})W_d^t(\mathbf{p_v}) + TSDF_v}{W_d^t(\mathbf{p_v}) + 1} \tag{4}$$

$$W_d^{t+1}(\mathbf{p_v}) = \min(W_d^t(\mathbf{p_v}) + 1, \text{MaxWeight}) \tag{5}$$

with superscripts t and $t + 1$ denoting the current and updated values, respectively. Thus, the quantity stored in a voxel amounts to a running average over time of the measured TSDF values. The saturation of the weight (Eq. 5) allows for forgetting old values, which, in turn, enables mapping of slightly dynamic scenes. Other weighting schemes aimed at possibly improving the volume update process have been shown in literature [1, 6, 19]. Then, as for integration of the color data acquired from the RGB image, $i(\mathbf{u})$, we follow the approach presented in the paper by Bylow and colleagues [6].

In principle, updating the bins of the label histogram associated with a voxel may be performed similarly to the just described TSDF and color updating processes. However, as already mentioned, we assume the semantic segmentation algorithm to provide a single label and associated confidence score at each pixel position of the input frame. When integrating a new frame then, at each voxel we would be able to update only the bin associated with the label observed at the corresponding pixel and we are faced with the issue of whether and how to update the other bins. Updating only the observed bin would inevitably result in the *plateauing* of the histogram at relatively high values in case several highly confidently and incoherent labels get integrated into a voxel. Instead, we devised a suitable updating technique that tackles this issue by both increasing the value of the bin associated with the observed label as well as decreasing those of all other bins. In particular, the increment is proportional to the confidence score provided by the labeler while the decrement factor takes also into account the evidence hitherto gathered into the histogram to penalize less higher bins.

Formally, denoting the category histogram stored in each voxel as $L \in \mathbb{R}^N$, with N the number of categories of interest, we define the weight update factor for each label i based on the label assigned to the pixel, $l(\mathbf{u})$, and the corresponding score $s(\mathbf{u})$:

$$w_{l_i} = \begin{cases} s(\mathbf{u}) \text{ for } i = l(\mathbf{u}) \\ L_i^t(\mathbf{p_v})(1 - s(\mathbf{u})) \text{ for } i \neq l(\mathbf{u}) \end{cases} \tag{6}$$

Then, we update each histogram bin as follows:

$$L_i^{t+1}(\mathbf{p_v}) = \frac{L_i^t(\mathbf{p_v})W_d^t(\mathbf{p_v}) + w_{l_i}}{W_d^t(\mathbf{p_v}) + 1} \tag{7}$$

It worth observing that, analogously to TSDF and color, the label update step is tantamount to a running average over the number of observations for a voxel.

3.2 Tracking Algorithm

To update the information stored into the volume by integrating new measurements, we need to track the RGB-D sensor as it moves within the environment. In KinectFusion [1] camera tracking is performed by ICP-based alignment between the surface associated with the current depth image and that extracted from the TSDF. Later, Bylow et al. [19] and Canelhas et al. [20] proposed to track the camera by direct alignment of the current depth image to the mapped environment encoded into the TSDF as the zero-level isosurface. This approach has been proven to be faster and more accurate than the original KinectFusion tracker.

Camera tracking by direct alignment of the acquired depth image with respect to the TSDF volume relies on the following consideration: assuming that the estimated pose of the camera is correct and noise does not affect the current and previous depth measurements, then each depth pixel should correspond to the projection of a 3D world point that, given the content of the TSDF grid, features a null distance function (i.e. lies on the surface). Clearly, noiseless depth images and perfectly accurate camera pose estimations cannot be obtained in real settings. However, Bylow et al. [19] show that for small camera movements (as it is the case during real-time tracking) iteratively minimizing the sum of the squared distances between the 3D points corresponding to depth pixels and their corresponding TSDF values allows for accurate estimation of camera poses.

In this paper, we propose to consider also the category labels assigned to pixels within the objective function minimized by the tracker. Indeed, a shortcoming of both the standard KinectFusion ICP tracking algorithm and the tracker based on direct alignment of depth images consists in the difficulty to localize the camera when the acquired frames depict scenes poor in geometry such as smooth or flat surfaces. We argue that exploiting the inherent structure determined by the boundaries between labeled objects can improve tracking accuracy when the scene features insufficient geometric clues.

Camera pose estimation is thus performed by finding the affine transformation, T, that minimizes a cost function consisting of two separate terms. One term measures the geometric alignment of the depth frame to the surface implicitly encoded into the TSDF, while the other term captures the coherence between the per-pixel labeling proposed by the semantic segmentation algorithm with respect to the label histograms already stored into voxel grid. We define $\mathbf{p_u}$ as the 3D location of the point determined by a pixel $\mathbf{u}$ having a valid value in the depth image:

$$\mathbf{p_u} = \pi^{-1}(\mathbf{u}, d(\mathbf{u})) \tag{8}$$

The geometric error term is then given by the truncated signed distance from a voxel to the closest surface:

$$E_d(T, \mathbf{u}) = D(T\mathbf{p_u}) \tag{9}$$

We define the semantic error term based on both the confidence of the labeler in the predicted pixel label and the amount of evidence already gathered on that label within the corresponding voxel:

$$E_l(T, \mathbf{u}) = s(\mathbf{u}) \left(1 - L_{l(\mathbf{u})}(T\mathbf{p_u})\right) \tag{10}$$

Thereby, the error term turns out high when the per-pixel labeler confidently predicts a category for which the degree of previous evidence is small.

The final objective function to be minimized by the tracker takes the following form:

$$E(T) = \sum_{\mathbf{u}} \left(E_d(T, \mathbf{u})^2 + \alpha E_l(T, \mathbf{u})^2\right) \tag{11}$$

Given a candidate pose, the first term of the sum quantifies the geometric misalignment between the current frame and the surface embedded into the TSDF. The second, instead, penalizes those poses where the labels assigned to pixels turn out incoherent with respect to the category histograms stored into the corresponding voxels. As such, the second term of the sum may be thought of as quantifying the semantic misalignment between the current frame and the volumetric map. The blending parameter, α, enables to weigh properly the contribution of the two error terms.

By employing a minimal parametrization $\xi = (v_x, v_y, v_z, \omega_x, \omega_y, \omega_z) \in \mathbb{R}^6$ of the $T = (R, \mathbf{t}) \in \mathbb{SE}(3)$ transformation, and knowing that the Lie algebra allows expressing $T = e^{\xi}$ and $\xi = \ln(T)$ via the exponential and logarithm map operations [21], we can define:

$$E_{d\mathbf{u}}(\xi) = D(e^{\xi}\mathbf{p_u}) \tag{12}$$

and

$$E_{l\mathbf{u}}(\xi) = s_{\mathbf{u}} \left(1 - L_{l\mathbf{u}}(e^{\xi}\mathbf{p_u})\right) \tag{13}$$

so to rewrite Eq. 11 as:

$$E(\xi) = \sum_{\mathbf{u}} \left(E_{d\mathbf{u}}(\xi)^2 + \alpha E_{l\mathbf{u}}(\xi)^2\right) \tag{14}$$

Using Eq. 14 we can finally express the camera tracking cost function as:

$$\xi = \underset{\xi}{\mathrm{argmin}} \sum_{\mathbf{u}} \left(E_{d\mathbf{u}}(\xi)^2 + \alpha E_{l\mathbf{u}}(\xi)^2\right) \tag{15}$$

By linearizing the function around an initial pose $\hat{\xi}$ (such as the estimated camera pose for the previously tracked frame) and assuming a small movement between the two acquisitions (as mentioned before, a reasonable assumption in the hand-held tracking scenario), it is possible to perform an iterative nonlinear minimization using a method such as Levemberg-Marquardt in order to estimate the camera pose, ξ, that optimally aligns the current frame to the current volumetric reconstruction both geometrically and semantically.

The gradient of the cost function required by the iterative minimization to compute the increment applied to ξ is attained independently for the two terms. As for the gradient of the geometric term, in each pixel $\mathbf{u}$, we trilinearly interpolate the values of the TSDF in the 8 voxels closest to point $e^{\xi}\mathbf{p_u}$. The gradient for the semantic error term is also computed by trilinear interpolation, though, in this case, of the values $1 - L_{l(\mathbf{u})}(\mathbf{x})$, with $\mathbf{x}$ representing voxel coordinates. Thereby, for each pixel we consider the category histogram bin associated to the label assigned to the pixel itself. It is worthwhile observing that optimization of the semantic error mandates maintaining in each voxel an histogram concerning the likeliness of all categories, as we propose in this paper, whilst storing the evidence gathered for the most likely label only, as described in [18], would make it impossible to compute the gradient of the semantic error due to voxels lacking the information on whether moving along a certain direction would either increase of decrease the likeliness of the sensed pixel label.

4   Experimental Evaluation

In this section we present quantitative (Subsect. 4.1) and qualitative (Subsect. 4.2) results showing how the proposed camera localization algorithm based on both geometry and semantics can successfully reduce the trajectory error in several challenging sequences. Purposely, we employ the well-known RGB-D SLAM Dataset by Sturm *et al.* [22] and the ICL NUIM Dataset by Handa and colleagues [23]. We also show reconstructed environments obtained from sequences part of the Sun3D Dataset [24] together with a sequence depicting a household environment.

As mentioned in Sect. 3, to successfully track the camera pose and update the volume, we assume to be provided in each frame with per-pixel labels and confidence scores by a semantic segmentation algorithm. In our tests, we employed the Fully Convolutional Networks recently proposed by Long and colleagues [25]. Such technique, based on a Convolutional Neural Network, performs an image labeling suitable to our needs by computing, for each pixel in the input image, a complete probability distribution over all the categories of interest. We then select the label having the maximum probability and use such values to populate the $l(\mathbf{u})$ and $s(\mathbf{u})$ matrices given as input to our algorithm. The authors provide several pretrained networks[1] based on different sets of object categories and input features. We considered two such networks, one based on the 59 categories of the Pascal Context dataset [26] (FCN-8s PASCAL-Context, as the authors name it in their paper) and another trained on 40 categories of the NYUDv2 dataset [27] (FCN-16s NYUDv2). While the FCN-8s network process only the input RGB frame to obtain the categories, the network trained on the NYUD dataset requires also computation of the HHA depth embedding [28]. The deployment of either network requires a vast amount of GPU computing power and memory but the latter, relying on processing both an RGB and HHA image,

---

[1] https://github.com/BVLC/caffe/wiki/Model-Zoo#fcn.

needs twice the GPU RAM as the former (about 8.8 GB), which reduces significantly the GPU memory available to store the proposed voxel grid containing category histograms. Eventually we decided to privilege the FCN-8s PASCAL-Context network in our experimental evaluation. We point out, though, that our proposed semantic tracking technique does not rely on a specific image labeling algorithm but merely expects to be provided with per-pixel labels and scores.

As between the 59 categories detected by the aforementioned labeling algorithm we are interested only in a subset comprising indoor objects (e.g. "tables", "chairs", "walls", "tv monitors" and not categories such as "sheep" or "mountain"), we filter the network output at each pixel so to keep the most likely label within the subset of categories of interest. All the performed tests consider 12 categories. Each voxel has the following layout in memory:

TSDF Value Half precision float, 2 bytes
TSDF Weight Half precision float, 2 bytes
Color R,G,B and weight channels stored each as unsigned char, 4 bytes
Category histogram Each bin as a floating point value in the interval $[0..1]$, mapped as $[0..255]$ into an unsigned char, 12 bytes

The total occupancy for a 512^3 voxel grid is therefore $\sim$2.5 GB of GPU memory, well within the possibilities of modern graphic cards.

We would like to point out that, with a dense volume-based mapping approach, the memory footprint of the system exhibits a cubic dependence on both the voxel and workspace sizes. Comparatively, increasing the amount of bytes stored in each voxel increases memory occupancy only linearly. Thus, storing 12 more bytes in each voxel, as we do for labels, does not change the working constraints of the system dramatically. To clarify this claim, let us assume the extent of the environment to be 8^3 m^3: by employing a quite standard 512^3 voxel grid we would be able to map the environment with a resolution of $\sim$1.6 cm, this requiring 1 GB of GPU memory without storing per voxel-labels and, as mentioned before, $\sim$2.5 GB when also storing an histogram with 12 label scores in each voxel. Conversely, should we wish to map the same environment with a voxel resolution of 0.5 cm, a grid of 1600^3 voxels would be necessary, this requiring 32GB of GPU memory without per voxel-labels and $\sim$80 GB in case of the semantic voxel grid. Both cases are intractable with the current graphics hardware thus, in practice, with the proposed system we are able to handle workspaces of similar size as KinectFusion.

4.1   Quantitative Results

As mentioned, we evaluate the performances of the proposed label-aware tracking method on RGB-D sequences part of the TUM [22] and ICL_NUIM [23] datasets. As customary in the evaluation of SLAM algorithms, we deploy the RMS Absolute Trajectory Error performance metric described by Sturm *et al.* [22]. We compare our approach to a standard geometry-based tracker based on direct alignment of the depth image as well as to the improved tracker that employs also color information [6]. As the article describing the color-based tracker did not consider the ICL_NUIM dataset in the evaluation, we implemented their tracking algorithm and show here the RMS ATE also for our implementation.

As for the runtime configuration of our algorithm, we employ a voxel grid spanning 8^3 m^3 of space. The truncation distance has been set to 0.3 m and the α blending coefficient applied to our semantic error term to 0.085, after a grid search over the parameter space.

Figure 2 shows the accuracy of different tracking approaches in several sequences of the RGBD-SLAM Dataset. Overall, we observe that most TUM sequences can be tracked quite successfully by a purely geometric approach, so that both semantics and color have got no chances to bring in notable improvements in accuracy. Nor they cause any harm, though. Instead, in those sequences, like "floor" and "room", turning more challenging for a purely geometric tracker, employment of additional clues, such as semantic labels – or color – does help reducing the tracking error quite significantly. Indeed, the improvement achievable by our semantic tracker versus a purely geometric approach is much higher in "room" than in "floor", as the former sequence is characterized by a richer semantic content (i.e. presence of several object categories) while in the latter the sensor continuously observes the floor of a room, which renders color cues more distinctive than semantics.

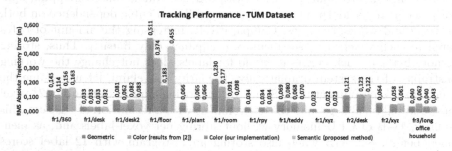

Fig. 2. Tracking performances in sequences part of the TUM [22] dataset. *Geometric* represents the purely geometric KinectFusion tracker. For the *Color*-based approach we show both the results reported by Bylow in [6] ($\alpha = 0.1$), as well as those achieved by our own implementation of Bylow's approach. *Semantic* denotes our proposal.

Figure 3 shows the tracking error on the sequences of the ICL_NUIM dataset. Handa *et al.* [23] provide two sets of four RGBD sequences obtained by rendering views from a synthetically generated model of two environments: a living room and an office. One set contains noiseless images while the depth frames in the other have been corrupted by noise akin to that present in the images acquired by a real Kinect sensor. In our tests we consider the latter, noisy, set. Once again, it can be observed how, in those sequences where the geometric tracker has more difficulties in estimating the correct camera trajectory, deployment of semantic labels can ameliorate tracking accuracy notably. Moreover, unlike

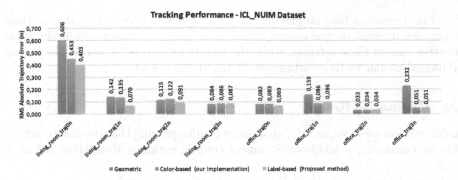

Fig. 3. Tracking performances in sequences part of the ICL_NUIM [23] dataset. Series as in Fig. 2.

the TUM dataset, it turns out here that, more often than not, semantic labels compare favorably with respect to color cues, possibly due to the richer semantic content of the scenes.

Finally, Zhou and Koltun [4] evaluate their contour-based tracking method on a small subset of the TUM dataset, *i.e.* four sequences, each focused on scanning a single object featuring smooth and evenly colored surfaces. In Fig. 4 we report the trajectory errors for the considered tracking methods, including Zhou's, on the four sequences used for the evaluation in [4]. Clearly, scanning a single object is neither the typical operating mode nor particularly suitable a scenario to our method, which, instead, is aimed at automatic reconstruction and volumetric labeling of relatively large workspaces featuring a number of diverse categories of interest (indeed, we set the volume size to $2.5^3\,\mathrm{m}^3$ in these four sequences).

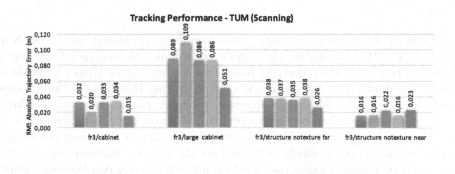

Fig. 4. Tracking performances in the object scanning sequences considered in [4]. The method proposed in [4] is referred to as *Contour*. As for the original color based tracker, we show here the results reported in [4], which were obtained by the authors running Bylow's code. As usual, we also show the results attained by our own implementation of Bylow's tracker.

Yet, Fig. 4 vouches how employing semantic labels in object scanning settings is not detrimental to the overall tracking accuracy. Contours seem the most effective cues in these settings, while the results yielded by semantic labels may be judged on par to those attainable by deploying colors.

4.2 Qualitative Results

In this section we show, at first, qualitative results proving the advantages attainable by employing a label-aware camera tracker within a KinectFusion framework.

Figure 5 concerns an RGB-D sequence that we captured via a Kinect sensor in a corridor within a household environment. While the flatness of the wall prevents successful tracking based solely on the geometry of the surfaces, the low confidence of the "wall" label associated with the paintings provides enough distinctive cues to enable correct reconstruction of the environment.

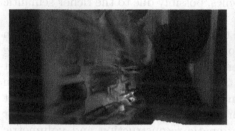

Fig. 5. Household scene captured with a kinect sensor. Left: a purely geometric tracker cannot estimate camera poses accurately due to the flatness of the wall. Right: deployment of semantic labels enable to map the environment correctly.

Figure 6 deals with the hotel room sequence contained in the SUN3D dataset [24]. When mapping the hotel's bathroom, the camera briefly lingers on the mirror above the faucet. An RGBD sensor such as the Kinect is unable to detect the mirror as a flat surface, instead *mirroring* the shape of the reflected environment as a window on a different room. A purely geometric tracking, thus, is unable to estimate the correct camera trajectory, resulting in a very bad reconstruction such as that shown by the left picture. However, the correct and coherent semantic labels associated to the surfaces surrounding the mirror deployed in our tracking cost function allow for better constraining camera poses and obtain an accurate reconstruction. The mirror still appears as a hole in the wall showing the rest of the hotel room because depth measurements in that spatial location are farther away than the mirror itself, but the rest of the bathroom is correctly reconstructed.

Finally, we provide qualitative results to demonstrate the capability of our method to output semantically labeled volumes. Additional results are available in the supplementary material. Figure 7 shows details of the "room" sequence

Fig. 6. Fatal tracking failure prevented. Left: the mirror causes a purely geometric approach to fail, the reconstructed volume turning out unrecognizable. Right: tracking succeeds and the bathroom is correctly mapped thanks to semantic labels.

(TUM dataset, top row) and the aforementioned household sequence (also depicted in Fig. 5, bottom row), with each voxel labeled according to the tag exhibiting the highest score in the category histogram and the corresponding confidence shown as a heat map. It can be observed that most voxels are labeled correctly and confidence heat maps are quite reliable, due to high confidence labels unlikely turning out wrong and mislabeled areas featuring low scores. Moreover, the maps provide evidence on the presence of both large scene structures as well as smaller objects. It is worth highlighting that with the "room" sequence the quality of the 3D reconstruction is equivalent to that achievable by deploying color cues (see Fig. 2) however, by our method, one can also gather high level information concerning which types of objects are present in the environment and where they are located in space.

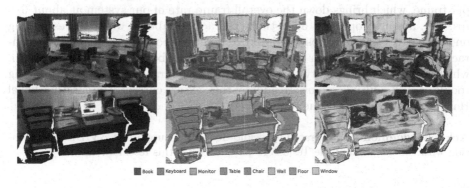

Fig. 7. Details of the reconstruction from the "room" sequence (TUM Dataset, Top) and household sequence (Fig. 5, Bottom). Left: RGB mesh. Center: labels associated to the reconstructed volume. Right: confidence scores assigned to the labels (blue: low – red: high). (Color figure online)

5 Concluding Remarks

We have shown how high-level observations, such as per-pixel object category tags, can improve the dense mapping and tracking process popularized by KinectFusion when dealing with surfaces featuring scarce geometric cues. Quantitative experiments on standard benchmark datasets suggest that, overall, reliance on semantic labels for tracking yields results comparable to deployment of color. However, we believe that semantic information holds the potential to enable more reliable tracking as category tags are less affected by nuisances such as light changes, shadows, reflections, blur. For example, a labeler working only on depths would allow to semantically track the camera in very low-light conditions or even in the dark. More generally, we expect the performance of semantic tracking to improve alongside advances in labeling algorithms, our framework allowing for accommodating such foreseeable advances seamlessly. Also, peculiarly with respect to previous work aimed at robustifying the KinectFusion tracker, our proposal automatically outputs a semantically labeled volume wherein each voxel is endowed with the likeliness of the whole set of categories of interest. The semantic map attainable by our method seems to provide valuable cues to facilitate indoor scene understanding, as it would typically detect and coarsely localize major large-size scene structures such as floor, walls, tables, windows, chairs as well as several smaller objects like monitors, books, keyboards. Such information comes together with a reliable confidence map that may be deployed effectively within the high-level reasoning process.

The first major limitation of our approach concerns speed. Indeed, while the semantic tracker can run comfortably at about 50–60 fps, the Fully Convolutional Network we currently rely upon for semantic labeling takes about 250 ms per frame, which brings down the overall frame rate of our system at about 3–4 fps. Yet, as our proposal is agnostic to the actual labeler, we are investigating on alternatives that may possibly improve speed without overly penalizing accuracy. The second limitation deals with our current fixed-size volume approach, which hinders the possibility to semantically map large workspaces such as big rooms or even multiple rooms. To address this, we are currently integrating Voxel Hashing [2] within our framework.

Acknowledgements. We gratefully acknowledge the support of NVIDIA Corporation with the donation of the Tesla K40 GPU used for this research.

References

1. Newcombe, R.A., Davison, A.J., Izadi, S., Kohli, P., Hilliges, O., Shotton, J., Molyneaux, D., Hodges, S., Kim, D., Fitzgibbon, A.: KinectFusion: real-time dense surface mapping and tracking. In: 2011 10th IEEE International Symposium on Mixed and Augmented Reality, pp. 127–136. IEEE, October 2011
2. Nießner, M., Zollhöfer, M., Izadi, S., Stamminger, M.: Real-time 3D reconstruction at scale using voxel hashing. ACM Trans. Graph. **32**(6), 1–11 (2013)

3. Newcombe, R.A., Fox, D., Seitz, S.M.: DynamicFusion: reconstruction and tracking of non-rigid scenes in real-time. In: 2015 IEEE Conference on Computer Vision and Pattern Recognition (CVPR), pp. 343–352. IEEE, June 2015
4. Zhou, Q.-Y., Koltun, V.: Depth camera tracking with contour cues. In: 2015 IEEE Conference on Computer Vision and Pattern Recognition (CVPR), pp. 632–638. IEEE, June 2015
5. Fioraio, N., Cerri, G., Di Stefano, L.: Towards semantic kinectfusion. In: Petrosino, A. (ed.) ICIAP 2013. LNCS, vol. 8157, pp. 299–308. Springer, Heidelberg (2013). doi:10.1007/978-3-642-41184-7_31
6. Bylow, E., Olsson, C.: Robust camera tracking by combining color and depth measurements. In: 2014 22nd International Conference on Pattern Recognition (ICPR) (2014)
7. Roth, H., Marsette, V.: Moving volume kinectfusion. Proc. Br. Mach. Vis. Conf. **112**(1–112), 11 (2012)
8. Whelan, T., Kaess, M., Fallon, M.: Kintinuous: spatially extended kinectfusion. In: Robotics Science and Systems (Workshop on RGB-D: Advanced Reasoning with Depth Cameras) (2012)
9. Chen, J., Bautembach, D., Izadi, S.: Scalable real-time volumetric surface reconstruction. ACM Trans. Graph. **32**(4) (2013)
10. Henry, P., Fox, D., Bhowmik, A., Mongia, R.: Patch volumes: segmentation-based consistent mapping with RGB-D cameras. In: 2013 International Conference on 3D Vision, pp. 398–405 (2013)
11. Zhou, Q.Y., Miller, S., Koltun, V.: Elastic fragments for dense scene reconstruction. In: 2013 IEEE International Conference on Computer Vision, pp. 473–480. IEEE, December 2013
12. Zhou, Q.Y., Koltun, V.: Dense scene reconstruction with points of interest. ACM Trans. Graph. **32**(4), 112:1–112:8 (2013)
13. Fioraio, N., Taylor, J., Fitzgibbon, A., Di Stefano, L., Izadi, S.: Large-scale and drift-free surface reconstruction using online subvolume registration. In: 2015 IEEE Conference on Computer Vision and Pattern Recognition (CVPR), pp. 4475–4483. IEEE, June 2015
14. Dou, M., Taylor, J., Fuchs, H., Fitzgibbon, A., Izadi, S.: 3D scanning deformable objects with a single RGBD sensor. In: 2015 IEEE Conference on Computer Vision and Pattern Recognition (CVPR), pp. 493–501. IEEE, June 2015
15. Fioraio, N., Di Stefano, L.: Joint detection, tracking and mapping by semantic bundle adjustment. In: Proceedings of the IEEE Computer Society Conference on Computer Vision and Pattern Recognition, pp. 1538–1545, June 2013
16. Salas-Moreno, R.F., Newcombe, R.A., Strasdat, H., Kelly, P.H., Davison, A.J.: SLAM++: simultaneous localisation and mapping at the level of objects. In: 2013 IEEE Conference on Computer Vision and Pattern Recognition, pp. 1352–1359, June 2013
17. Valentin, J., Vineet, V., Cheng, M.M., Kim, D., Shotton, J., Kohli, P., Niessner, M., Criminisi, A., Izadi, S., Torr, P.: SemanticPaint: interactive 3D labeling and learning at your fingertips. ACM Trans. Graph. (TOG) (2015)
18. Cavallari, T., Di Stefano, L.: Volume-based semantic labeling with signed distance functions. In: Pacific Rim Symposium on Image and Video Technology (2015)
19. Bylow, E., Sturm, J., Kerl, C., Kahl, F., Cremers, D.: Real-time camera tracking and 3D reconstruction using signed distance functions. In: Robotics: Science and Systems (RSS) (2013)

20. Canelhas, D.R., Stoyanov, T., Lilienthal, A.J.: SDF Tracker: a parallel algorithm for on-line pose estimation and scene reconstruction from depth images. In: IEEE International Conference on Intelligent Robots and Systems, pp. 3671–3676 (2013)
21. Blanco, J.: A tutorial on SE(3) transformation parameterizations and on-manifold optimization. University of Malaga. Technical Report (3) (2010)
22. Sturm, J., Engelhard, N., Endres, F., Burgard, W., Cremers, D.: A benchmark for the evaluation of RGB-D SLAM systems. In: 2012 IEEE/RSJ International Conference on Intelligent Robots and Systems, pp. 573–580, October 2012
23. Handa, A., Whelan, T., McDonald, J., Davison, A.J.: A benchmark for RGB-D visual odometry, 3D reconstruction and SLAM. In: 2014 IEEE International Conference on Robotics and Automation (ICRA), pp. 1524–1531, May 2014
24. Xiao, J., Owens, A., Torralba, A.: SUN3D: a database of big spaces reconstructed using SfM and object labels. In: Proceedings of the IEEE International Conference on Computer Vision, pp. 1625–1632, December 2013
25. Long, J., Shelhamer, E., Darrell, T.: Fully convolutional networks for semantic segmentation. In: IEEE Conference on Computer Vision and Pattern Recognition (CVPR) (2015)
26. Mottaghi, R., Chen, X., Liu, X., Cho, N.G., Lee, S.W., Fidler, S., Urtasun, R., Yuille, A.: The role of context for object detection and semantic segmentation in the wild. In: 2014 IEEE Conference on Computer Vision and Pattern Recognition, pp. 891–898 (2014)
27. Silberman, N., Hoiem, D., Kohli, P., Fergus, R.: Indoor segmentation and support inference from RGBD images. In: Fitzgibbon, A., Lazebnik, S., Perona, P., Sato, Y., Schmid, C. (eds.) ECCV 2012. LNCS, vol. 7578, pp. 746–760. Springer, Heidelberg (2012). doi:10.1007/978-3-642-33715-4_54
28. Gupta, S., Girshick, R., Arbeláez, P., Malik, J.: Learning rich features from RGB-D images for object detection and segmentation. In: Fleet, D., Pajdla, T., Schiele, B., Tuytelaars, T. (eds.) ECCV 2014. LNCS, vol. 8693, pp. 345–360. Springer, Heidelberg (2014). doi:10.1007/978-3-319-10584-0_23

Towards Categorization and Pose Estimation of Sets of Occluded Objects in Cluttered Scenes from Depth Data and Generic Object Models Using Joint Parsing

Hector Basevi[✉] and Aleš Leonardis

School of Computer Science, University of Birmingham, Birmingham, UK
{H.R.A.Basevi,A.Leonardis}@cs.bham.ac.uk

Abstract. This work addresses the task of categorizing and estimating the six-dimensional poses of all visible and partly occluded objects present in a scene from depth image information, in the absence of ground truth training examples and exact geometrical models of objects. A novel multi-stage algorithm is proposed to perform this task by first estimating object category probabilities for each depth pixel using local depth features computed from multiple viewpoints. It then generates a large set of object category and pose pairs, and reduces this set via joint parsing to best match the observed scene depth and per-pixel object category probabilities, while minimizing the physical overlap between objects within the subset. A decision forest is trained on synthetic data and used to estimate pixel category probabilities which are then used to generate a set of pose estimates for all categories. Finally a combinatorial optimization algorithm is used to perform joint parsing to find a best subset of poses. The algorithm is applied to the challenging Heavily Occluded Object Challenge data set which contains depth data of sets of objects placed on a table and generic object models for each category, but does not include registered RGB data or human annotations for training. It is tested on difficult scenes containing 10 or 20 objects and successfully categorizes and localizes 29 % of objects. The joint parsing algorithm successfully categorizes and localizes 56 % of objects when ground truth poses are added to the set of pose estimates.

Keywords: Joint parsing · Categorization · Object recognition · Pose estimation · Scene understanding · Robotic vision

1 Introduction

Computer vision algorithms use a wide range of features to locate, categorize, and estimate the poses of objects in depth, RGB, and RGB-D images [1–3]. Many recent works use machine learning algorithms, which learn features from training rather than using hand-designed features [4–6], and popular examples include convolutional neural networks (CNNs) [5,7–11] and decision forests [4], which

© Springer International Publishing Switzerland 2016
G. Hua and H. Jégou (Eds.): ECCV 2016 Workshops, Part III, LNCS 9915, pp. 665–681, 2016.
DOI: 10.1007/978-3-319-49409-8_56

were famously used in Microsoft's Kinect human pose estimation algorithms [12]. Machine learning techniques rely on data sets of annotated examples in order to learn features via supervised learning and generally require large data sets to learn robust features [7,13]. However, these are not always available.

For example, take the case of a mobile robot navigating an unknown office environment. Assume that the robot is using a Lidar system for vision and has a low bandwidth cellular network connection for communication. The robot has been told by its operator to find and retrieve a teacup, but the robot has not previously learned to recognize teacups. It would not be practical to send a data set of annotated images of teacups to the robot over the low bandwidth connection (and in the case of some categories of object, such a data set may not yet exist), but it is possible to send a model of the geometry of a generic teacup, which may not precisely match any of the actual teacups in the scene. It is also not sufficient to be able to recognize the presence of a teacup in the scene as the robot needs to estimate its 6D pose in order to manipulate the teacup.

If this is taking place in a typical office environment then there are also other challenges that cannot be avoided. The scene may contain a number of different categories of object. The robot's ability to move within the environment may be limited, and it may only able to image the scene from a few viewpoints. The teacup may or may not be in the scene and it may be partially occluded by other objects. The robot may need to categorize and estimate pose for these objects as well in case that these must be manipulated in order to gain access to the teacup.

A variety of approaches have been used for categorizing and estimating the pose of objects in RGB images, including the use of image gradient-based part templates and deformable part models [1,14], and complete 3D CAD models which are either aligned to 2D RGB images [15] or are used to train detectors with task-dependent performance [6]. Recent growth in the availability of RGB-D sensors has enabled the generation of a large number of RGB-D data sets, and the creation of many algorithms that perform object detection [5,11] and pose estimation [4,10,16,17] on RGB-D images. Some algorithms that operate on RGB-D data sets deliberately discard RGB cues to remove the influences of illumination and texture, and operate purely on depth data [18], and some augment or replace parts of RGB-D data sets with synthetic data using CAD objects [10]. An alternative goal is scene completion, where the categories of the objects in a scene are not important but a geometric representation of occluded parts of the scene are desired [19].

Some algorithms detect individual objects of specific categories in depth images [18] or RGB-D images [11]. Others detect individual objects and estimate object 6D poses in RGB-D images [4,10,17]. Certain approaches fit for a number of objects jointly on RGB-D images, but do not attempt to categorize the objects [19]. This work presents a method for categorizing and estimating 6D pose for all objects in a scene simultaneously, including those that are partially occluded, from single or sparse multiple-view depth data. It does not require annotated depth data for training and generates its own synthetic labelled training data using generic object models.

The proposed algorithm generates random synthetic images of scenes using generic object models and learns decision forests on local depth features incorporating all available camera views, adapting the approach of Brachmann *et al.* [4]. These decision forests estimate the probability that each pixel belongs to one of the object categories or to the background. For each category, sampling a random pixel from one of the views proportional to its category probability enables a bounding box to be placed on each of the available views to extract a 3D object fragment from the depth images. The generic category model is then matched to the 3D object fragment to estimate a 6D pose. Many such object fragments and resulting poses are generated for each category, and the best fitting poses for each category are then processed by a joint parsing algorithm. This algorithm finds a subset of categories and poses that fits well with the depth data and pixel category probabilities while minimising the physical overlap between objects. Unlike Brachmann *et al.*, we generate features from multiple camera views in the absence of exact object instance information, and search for all objects of classes of interest rather than searching for a single instance of a specific object.

The contributions of this work lie in the use of local depth features incorporating multiple views to categorize objects and estimate their poses combined with the use of global properties of the scene to refine the set of all categories and poses simultaneously. Unlike Brachmann *et al.* [4], the use of multiple views to form a feature allows full 3D features to be learnt. The use of local depth features enables the algorithm to detect occluded objects but inevitably produces spurious categories and poses due to ambiguous object fragments and the use of generic models that could not be expected to match object fragments exactly. Global depth, pixel category probabilities, and object overlaps enable the algorithm to remove spurious categories and poses.

In Sect. 2 we discuss a selection of related work. In Sect. 3 we discuss the proposed algorithm, and in Sect. 4 we discuss how the algorithm is implemented. In Sect. 5 we discuss the HOOC data set, and in Sect. 6 we discuss the application of the presented algorithm to the HOOC data set. Finally, in Sect. 7 we give conclusions.

2   Related Work

There are many publications on object detection, pose estimation, and scene completion, which are topics relevant to this work. This section contains the most related work.

A classic approach to object categorization and pose estimation is to use object features such as SIFT features [20,21], or learned features [22,23]. These features can be used to find correspondences, identify parts, or to generate global descriptors for object classification [24]. However, these require RGB or intensity images to identify features, and a training set of RGB images of the objects of interest in order to construct a feature set. Training RGB images are not accessible in the HOOC data set due to an absence of RGB camera calibration information. There has been some research into identifying analogous features in depth images [25], which could potentially form part of an alternative approach to object categorization and pose estimation. Another approach is to use a set of RGB (or RGB-D) images and associated poses as templates, and compare test images to template images directly [26].

It is possible to measure the 3D geometry and RGB texture of objects using an apparatus such as a depth sensor and a turntable. These dense RGB-D measurements can then be used to construct a model and extract features specific to the object to maximise performance. Hinterstoisser et al. [16] presented an approach using templates consisting of RGB image gradients and depth image normal vectors of each object at a number of viewpoints to identify objects in RGB-D images. 6D pose was then refined using the depth data. Their method was dependent on possessing exact object representations in order to generate templates.

Brachmann et al. [4] presented an approach that trained decision forests to estimate pixel-wise category probabilities and poses based on local RGB-D features. They also experimented with pure depth features which did not perform as well. They generated pose estimates by associating object coordinates with the leaves of the decision forest, relying on the fact that their test objects did not possess RGB-D symmetries under rotation. The depth data and pixel probabilities were then used to decide whether to discard a pose via a designed energy function. Krull et al. [17] extended their previous work by replacing their designed energy function with a CNN which again evaluated individual poses. We adapt their decision trees for estimating pixel category probabilities but do not use the decision forests to directly estimate object poses, as the generic models, symmetric objects, and the lack of RGB data does not allow this. Unlike their approach we also do not attempt to detect a single object of a specific category and estimate its pose, but instead search for all objects belonging to categories of interest and use an energy function for the global scene to refine the set of potential object poses. By performing this for all objects simultaneously we compensate for the lack of specific object information.

Sun et al. [27] presented an approach using Hough voting to detect objects and estimate poses from RGB and RGB-D images. Depth was used to address challenges involving object scales in images and so was used to correct image patches for object distance, but the primary features used by the algorithm were RGB image patches. Tejani et al. [28] and Doumanoglou et al. [29] combined Hough voting with decision forests, in conjunction with other techniques.

Song and Xiao [18] presented an approach for object detection from depth data only, but did not focus on object pose. Similarly to this work, they used generic object models in the detection process. However, they used designed features as inputs to support vector machine (SVM) classifiers, and trained a classifier for each synthetic training object pose. They also adopted a 3D sliding window and processed the depth data in 3D form, rather than the approach in this work which operates on depth images directly. Song and Xiao later presented a CNN-based approach [11] which instead operated on RGB-D data.

Gupta *et al.* [5,10] proposed an algorithm for object categorization and 6D pose selection from RGB-D data. It used a CNN to detect objects using depth data converted to a geocentric coordinate system and RGB edge data, then a CNN to estimate object pose using normal vectors derived from the depth data, and finally the iterative closest point (ICP) algorithm to refine the pose. Interestingly, they demonstrated that their pose estimation CNN performed better when trained on synthetic data generated using generic object models than when trained on real data. Their algorithm successfully identified multiple categories of object in a single RGB-D image and produced 6D pose estimates. It was tested on a number of object categories and performed well on most of them. However, detection performance on geometrically simple objects such as desks (separate from tables) and boxes was poor, and this carried through to the pose estimation. Similarly to this work, they partially trained their algorithm on synthetic data generated using generic models and produced full 6D pose estimates for multiple instances of multiple categories for a single image. However, they relied on RGB data for object categorization.

The previously discussed algorithms adopted a local approach processing single objects. Guo *et al.* [19] examined the global scene instead, but with a different goal. Rather than performing object categorization and finding poses, Guo *et al.* estimated a complete 3D geometric representation of a scene including occluded regions, but did not attempt to decompose the scene into individual objects with specific categories and poses. Instead, generic objects were selected from a library irrespective of object category, and positioned such that the collection of objects matched the depth and appearance data and minimized object overlap in order to provide an estimate of the *occluded* scene geometry. Their use of global scene optimization and object overlap is similar to this work, but they also use RGB appearance data in their optimization function.

Finally, there are works that explore physical relations. Zheng *et al.* [30] proposed a method of forming 3D volumes from RGB-D images by projecting onto a voxel representation and executing a physical simulation to calculate parts that must be connected for the scene to be stable. Contacts between objects, and physical stability in general, is a property that could be used to extend the joint parsing stage of the algorithm in future work. Jia *et al.* [31] also examined supports and stability in RGB-D images, but used 3D blocks to represent objects rather than using a voxel representation. 3D blocks may not be an appropriate representation for some categories of object.

3 Method

The algorithm presented here consists of two stages: estimating a number of pose candidates for each object category, and selecting a globally consistent subset of those pose candidates. Fig. 1 illustrates this process.

Estimating Pose Candidates. The task of estimating pose candidates for each category was adapted from the approach of Brachmann *et al.* [4] in that a decision forest is used to estimate category probabilities for each pixel in each

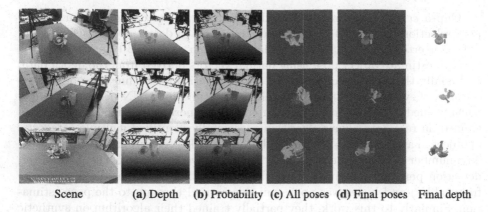

Scene   (a) Depth   (b) Probability   (c) All poses   (d) Final poses   Final depth

Fig. 1. The processing stages of the algorithm shown for the first scene containing 10 objects. The algorithm calculates pixel probabilities for each object category (**b**) using depth images acquired from multiple views (**a**), generates a number of pose candidates for each category using the pixel probabilities and depth images (**c**), and then selects a subset of pose candidates to match the depth images and pixel probabilities and to minimise the physical overlap between objects (**d**). The rows correspond to different camera views.

available depth image. However, the situation in this work differs significantly from that tackled by Brachmann *et al.* in several ways:

- They assumed a single view of a scene, whilst we consider one or sparse multiple views of a scene acquired from very different viewpoints.
- They used RGB-D data, whilst we use only depth data.
- They used detailed RGB-D information of the exact objects present in the scenes to create object models, whilst we use generic object models which do not correspond exactly to the objects imaged in terms of shape or general size, and not at all in terms of color.
- They searched for instances of a specific object category in each scene, whilst we do not assume knowledge of which categories are present in any scene.
- They searched for individual objects in isolation, whilst we search for all objects present in the scene.
- They used annotated data for training, whilst we have none.

In order to use all viewpoints we modify each decision forest to make decisions based upon all of the available views of the scene, and train a separate decision forest for each view but which uses features constructed from all views. Using multiple views enables truly 3D features to be learnt. Training these features requires the relative positions and orientations of the cameras to be known. This limits the general applicability of the multi-view features, but there are a number of cases where fixed cameras are standard, such as industrial environments and security cameras. A potential alternative approach would be to use features derived from point clouds combined from all views, but the use of the structure in two dimensional depth images provide computational advantages over unstructured three dimensional point clouds. The computational burden of training a decision forest for a view increases linearly with the number of views available, and a decision forest must be trained for each available view.

We train the decision forests by generating synthetic depth data for all of the views for random subsets of the generic object models placed in random positions in the scene. Because of the generic object models, lack of RGB data, and object symmetry, we cannot use the decision forests to estimate an object pose directly with any reliability. Instead we use the decision forests to segment pixels belonging to an object fragment in all of the available views, and convert the pixel depths into points in 3D space. A fitting process then estimates the 6D pose for the generic object model associated with the object fragment points.

Selecting a Globally Consistent Subset of Pose Candidates. The first stage of the approach produces a set of candidate object category and pose pairs from detected object fragments. This set should contain the set of correct poses, but the majority of the set candidates will be false. The second stage of the approach is to take the set of pose candidates and reduce the set to the true set of pose candidates or at a minimum to a globally consistent set of pose candidates. A globally consistent set of pose candidates is one that is consistent with the depth data and pixel category probabilities, and includes no or minimal volume overlap between objects.

Use of this information can enable discrimination between pose candidates for which the object is expected to be significantly occluded. The consistency requirements with respect to depth data and pixel category probabilities account for positive visibility (parts of the pose candidates that *should* be visible), and also negative visibility (parts of the pose candidates that *should not* be visible). The requirements that pose candidate volumes do not overlap and that the set of pose candidates and environment match well with the visual data in general can act as a natural constraint on solution complexity (subset size), particularly in the case where multiple camera views can minimize the occluded region. However, an artificial constraint on complexity could potentially be added for single view scenes.

The joint parsing algorithm combines object and background depth discrepancy, pixel category probabilities, and object volume overlap into an energy function which converts the task into an optimization problem. This is a combinatorial optimization problem as solutions to this problem are sets of objects. It is not practical to evaluate all of the possible subsets because there is a computational cost to evaluating the energy function, and the number of possible subsets also grows with the size of the full pose candidate set. Consequently it is necessary to find an approximately or locally optimal solution. A genetic algorithm (GA) [32] is used to find these solutions.

GAs can be attractive optimization algorithms because they are not necessarily greedy and so can avoid local optima, and because the nature of the crossover operation used to generate new solutions can preserve subsets of the existing solution. This can be beneficial because the relations between objects in a scene are likely to be local to a large extent. For example, three objects in close proximity are likely to largely determine each other's visibility. Removing one of those objects would then greatly modify the effect of the remaining two objects on the energy function, but not necessary objects further away. Therefore, once this subset of three objects have been identified, the subset should ideally persist as a single unit, so that the subset members are either all present in a solution or none are present. Doing so would simplify the optimization problem. An appropriately designed GA crossover operation can achieve this to an extent.

At the completion of the GA, a pose candidate subset with a locally minimum observed energy function value is retained, regardless of the iteration of the algorithm at which it was encountered. This is treated as the final output of the approach. See Fig. 1 for an example of the stages of the process.

4   Algorithm Implementation

The decision forest (DF) features were modified so that a pixel in the camera view associated with the DF defines the center of bounding regions in all camera views, and individual features can arise from sub-features within these regions in any of the camera views. The DF training process was modified to maximize information gain for sub-features in any of the views. The features for each decision tree were trained from a set of 500 synthetic scenes containing random subsets of the generic object models. The models were placed upright in the scene in a manner that ensured that there would be no physical overlap between objects. To prevent overfitting of the probability distributions in the leaves of the trees, the probability distributions of the leaves were estimated using a different set of 500 random synthetic scenes once the decision tree features had been learnt through the initial training.

The lack of RGB information and generic object models prevents the use of the DF for initial pose estimation as performed in the Brachmann *et al.* algorithm [4]. Instead the pixel category probabilities and bounding regions in each view (for a given chosen central pixel) were used to extract probable 3D points in space to which a uniformly sampled version of the generic object mesh was registered using the ICP algorithm. Central pixels were sampled from the pixel category probability images for all views. In each scene a total of 200 pose candidates were sampled for each object category. Each pose candidate was generated with a random fixed size and a random pose which was optimized using the ICP algorithm. The 5 best pose candidates for each category were added to a pose candidate set and presented to the joint parsing portion of the algorithm.

The joint parsing energy function used to quantify the global consistency of a pose candidate subset incorporates depth images discrepancies, pixel-based category probabilities, and object percentage volume overlap. The energy function itself is of the following form:

$$E(D, P, V; \tilde{D}, d_{max}) = \frac{1}{N_{pixels}} \sum_{i=1}^{N_{pixels}} \frac{1}{d_{max}} \min(\left|d_i - \tilde{d}_i\right|, d_{max}) +$$

$$\frac{1}{N_{pixels}} \sum_{i=1}^{N_{pixels}} (1 - p_i) + \quad (1)$$

$$\frac{1}{N_{objects}} \sum_{i=1}^{N_{objects}} v_i$$

Where $\tilde{D}$ is the set of measured pixel depths of the true scene, D is the set of calculated pixel depths of the current pose candidate subset, d_{max} is a maximum limit on the pixel depth discrepancy, P is the set of pixel category probabilities corresponding to the current pose candidate subset and background, V is the set of of fractional volume overlaps calculated for each pose candidate based of the volume fraction overlapping with any of the other pose candidates within the current subset, N_{pixels} is the number of pixels, and $N_{objects}$ is the number of pose candidates within the current subset. The first term in Eq. 1 calculates the average pixel depth discrepancy. The discrepancy at each pixel is limited to a maximum value of d_{max} (chosen to be 100 mm in this case) as distances larger than this are likely to result from incorrect categories or missing objects. In these cases the discrepancies may be large, but small changes in their magnitudes should not influence the optimization process because the degree of discrepancy between the measured depth and the depth generated from an incorrect pose candidate does not carry any information beyond that the pose candidate is incorrect.

The energy function here is similar to that of Guo et al. [19], except that where Guo et al. include a RGB-based appearance term we include a categorization probability term. However, the categorization probability term can be thought of as a depth-based local appearance term as it contains the probability that a local depth patch belongs to a certain category.

The optimization process is performed by a GA which modifies a population of 100 pose candidate subsets in an iterative manner. The population is initialized randomly so that each individual within the population contains an average of 10 pose candidates. At each iteration, the energy function value is calculated for each individual and the top 20 % of individuals are retained in the new population. A further 20 % of individuals are randomly retained in the new population via sampling, with a probability proportional to the inverse of their energy function values. 10 % of the new population is generated entirely randomly. Finally, 50 % of the new population is generated from the old population. Roulette selection using the energy function values is used to select two individuals from the old population to generate each member of the new population. The two individuals are combined using random three point crossover to form a new individual and then this individual is randomly mutated so that each pose candidate is added or removed with a given probability. This probability is initially high to encourage global search, and is reduced at each iteration.

5   The HOOC Data Set

The presented algorithm was tested on the highly occluded object challenge (HOOC) data set [33]. Each scene within the HOOC data set consists of three views of a table on which a number of objects are placed. The objects are placed on the table in close proximity to one another, including in some cases being stacked, which results in significant object occlusion. See Table 1 for quantitative measures of object visibility. These objects originate from a number of categories, and generic object models are available for each category. See Fig. 2 for some examples. Depth images and depth camera calibration data are provided for each of the views. RGB images are also provided, but these are not registered with the depth images so are for reference only and cannot be used within the approach. Human annotated ground truth categories and poses are provided for the test scenes, but no annotated training data is provided. As such this data set is uniquely complex and presents a great challenge. We contacted the creators of the data set and were provided with the data set and with the ground truth category and pose annotations.

Table 1. Examples of object visibility for each camera in the first scene containing 20 objects in the HOOC data set. The fractional pixel visibility is the fraction of the total image pixels associated with an object in isolation that are still visible in the presence of other objects. The fractional surface area visibility is the fraction of the total surface area of an object visible to the camera in the presence of other objects. The total fractional surface area visibility is the fraction of the total surface area of an object visible to at least one camera.

Object	Fractional pixel visibility			Fractional surface area visibility			
	1	2	3	1	2	3	Total
Teacup	0.86	1.00	0.69	0.18	0.36	0.20	0.49
Frying pan	0.55	0.52	0.64	0.24	0.21	0.29	0.47
Banana	0.50	0.57	0.76	0.24	0.26	0.33	0.47
Ball	0.89	0.32	1.00	0.40	0.17	0.47	0.68
Spatula	0.73	0.55	0.82	0.36	0.29	0.40	0.54
Tube	0.92	0.72	0.75	0.24	0.19	0.20	0.49
Sellotape core	1.00	0.96	1.00	0.35	0.45	0.47	0.71
Stapler	0.45	0.43	1.00	0.12	0.12	0.26	0.39
Glass	0.69	0.72	0.76	0.22	0.27	0.26	0.61

In detail, the HOOC data set contains 5 scenes each containing 10 objects on a table, and 4 scenes each containing 20 objects on a table. Every object within a given scene is of a different category, and there are a total of 25 object categories. A generic object model is provided for each of the 25 categories. Three Kinect II cameras are placed approximately at the vertices of an equilateral triangle with

Fig. 2. Generic object models. From left to right: teacup, frying pan, banana, ball, spatula, tube, Sellotape core, stapler, glass.

the scene in the center. Intrinsic and extrinsic calibration data is provided for each depth camera, but not for each RGB camera. The depth images contain significant spherical distortion which primarily affects the background, and the calibration data was used to correct each of the depth images using Bouguet's camera calibration toolbox [34].

A number of properties of the HOOC data set complicate the process of scene understanding. Firstly, a number of the generic object models match poorly with the associated real object. Small objects can be lost within the noise of the depth sensor, which is significant. Some objects, such as the jug, are translucent, and the recorded depth contains large systematic error that is different for each camera view. Many objects are partially occluded in each scene. The presence of three camera views reduces occlusion but does not remove it entirely.

Figure 3 shows an example from the jug category. This category exhibits many of the challenges associated with the HOOC data set. The jug is translucent, and this drastically affects the quality of the resulting depth data. The point cloud image shows the 3D points associated with the jug from the three camera views as seen from above. The points should form an approximate cylinder, but in practice do not resemble a cylinder due to the interactions of the depth camera light source with the translucent object. The generic mesh of the jug has a different width to height ratio and the shape, position and size of the handle is different. The generic mesh also contains a top surface that is not present in the actual object. Once processed to be closed, the mesh diverges further from the true object.

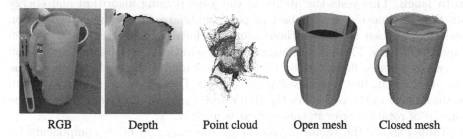

| RGB | Depth | Point cloud | Open mesh | Closed mesh |

Fig. 3. The jug category. From left to right, the images show a RGB image of the jug, a depth image of the jug, the 3D points associated with the jug in three registered camera views as viewed from above, the generic mesh of the jug, and a closed version of the generic mesh of the jug.

The generic object models for the dustpan and tray object categories were incompatible with object overlap calculation and so the dustpan and tray categories were excluded from the experiments, leaving a total of 23 object categories.

6 Experiments

The approach was applied to the scenes in the HOOC data set. The algorithm performance was tested using the full set of pose candidates generated from the DF. This consisted of 5 pose candidates for each of the remaining 23 categories (excluding the dustpan and tray categories), resulting in a total of 115 pose candidates. The joint parsing performance was separately tested specifically by modifying the full set of pose candidates by replacing the worst pose candidate of each ground truth category with the ground truth pose candidates themselves, resulting in a set of 115 pose candidates containing 10 or 20 ground truth poses depending on the scene.

The HOOC data set is uniquely complex and challenging. The combination of depth data without RGB data, noisy imaging using Kinect II, an absence of human category and pose annotations for training, three viewpoints, generic object models, and occluded objects makes the challenge extremely difficult. Algorithm performance must be considered in that context. These unique properties of the HOOC data set also mean that most of the existing state-of-the-art algorithms for simultaneous object categorization and pose estimation are incompatible with the HOOC data set and so cannot be directly compared with the presented approach.

Table 2 shows the categorization performance of the algorithm. The algorithm identifies instances of 44 % of the ground truth labels in the scene on average. When the pose for the label is required to be in spatial proximity of the ground truth pose (within a translation distance of half of the ground truth object size), the accuracy reduces to 29 %. Table 3 shows the categorization performance of the algorithm when using pose candidate sets modified to contain the ground truth labels. This tests the ability of the joint parsing algorithm and energy function to choose a good subset of pose candidates. Here the categorization performance rises to 62 % without requiring locality, and rises to 56 % when requiring locality. These results suggest that the initial pose candidate generation process is a major limitation on performance. Figure 4 shows the output of the algorithm for the first scene involving 20 objects. Pose rotation error is not shown because many of the objects in the HOOC data set contain symmetries and the concept of rotation error in this context is unclear.

Table 4 shows the values of the energy function and of its components for the selected pose candidate subset in the case where ground truth poses are not available and in the case where the ground truth poses are available, and for the ground truth pose set itself, in that order. The overall energy function value favors the ground truth poses and the best subset with the option to choose ground truth poses. The depth component of the energy function favors the ground truth poses. The probability and overlap components both favor the

Table 2. Categorization performance on the HOOC data set. The fraction of the ground truth categories found is listed, as is the fraction of ground truth categories where the ground truth pose center differs from the estimated pose center by less than half of the generic model size. Finally, the number of categories found that do not belong to set of ground truth categories is listed. The localized ground truth fraction is the most important quantity, and the ideal value is 1.

	Scene								
	10 (1)	10 (2)	10 (3)	10 (4)	10 (5)	20 (1)	20 (2)	20 (3)	20 (4)
Ground truth	0.40	0.50	0.33	0.50	0.33	0.47	0.56	0.44	0.44
Localized ground truth	0.20	0.50	0.22	0.50	0.22	0.32	0.22	0.28	0.17
False categories	5	8	2	5	7	1	1	2	2

best subset without the option to choose ground truth poses. The overall energy function value suggests that subsets in the case where ground truth poses are available perform similarly to the set of ground truth poses themselves, but both sets consistently outperform the set of poses where ground truth poses are not available.

Clear patterns are observed in each of the components: depth discrepancy, pixel category probability, and object overlap. As might be expected, the depth component consistently favors the set of ground truth poses. However, this is not the case for the both the pixel category probability and object overlap components, where the set of poses where ground truth poses are not available outperforms the other two. This suggests that discrepancy between the generic models and actual objects may be significant. The probability component results from similarity between local depth features in the scene and local depth features on the pose candidates, which suggests that the algorithm is better able to match

Table 3. Categorization performance on the HOOC data set when the ground truth poses are added to the input set of the joint parsing algorithm. The fraction of the ground truth categories found is listed, as is the fraction of ground truth categories where the ground truth pose center differs from the estimated pose center by less than half of the generic model size. Finally, the number of categories found that do not belong to set of ground truth categories is listed. The localized ground truth fraction is the most important quantity, and the ideal value is 1.

	Scene								
	10 (1)	10 (2)	10 (3)	10 (4)	10 (5)	20 (1)	20 (2)	20 (3)	20 (4)
Ground truth	0.50	0.88	0.44	0.60	0.56	0.63	0.67	0.67	0.67
Localized ground truth	0.30	0.88	0.44	0.60	0.56	0.58	0.56	0.61	0.56
False categories	4	5	2	6	5	0	3	2	1

Object set labels   Object set depth

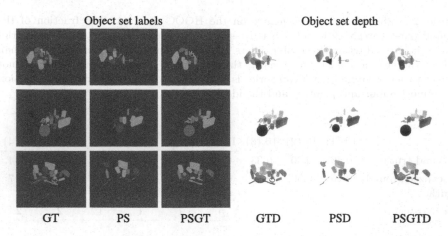

GT   PS   PSGT   GTD   PSD   PSGTD

Fig. 4. The output of the algorithm for scene 20(1). From left to right: ground truth object category labels (**GT**), pose candidate subset labels (**PS**), pose candidate subset with ground truth labels (**PSGT**), ground truth object depth (**GTD**), pose candidate subset depth (**PSD**), and pose candidate subset with ground truth depth (**PSGTD**). The rows correspond to different camera views.

these features by using poses other than the ground truth poses, and given the categorization results (see Table 2) other categories entirely. The object overlap component supports this interpretation as the ground truth pose set all have significant overlap. Object overlap may cause difficulty for a human annotator, as the annotator is concerned with visible discrepancies, while object overlaps are not obvious to the eye.

In this context, improvements to the DF stage are likely to provide the greatest improvement to general algorithm performance. However, the discrepancy between generic object models and actual objects would continue to affect per-

Table 4. Energy function values for chosen subsets. Each triple of numbers is in the order: the best subset without the option to choose ground truth poses, the best subset with the option to choose ground truth poses, and the set consisting of all ground truth poses. In all cases, lower values indicate a better solution, and the number in bold is the best of the triple.

Scene	Energy function	Depth component	Probability component	Overlap component
10 (1)	1.4007, 1.3973, **1.3944**	0.6199, 0.6094, **0.5994**	**0.7798**, 0.7877, 0.7901	0.0011, **0.0002**, 0.0050
10 (2)	1.3611, **1.3558**, 1.3559	0.5835, 0.5799, **0.5744**	**0.7751**, 0.7751, 0.7799	0.0025, **0.0008**, 0.0015
10 (3)	1.3772, 1.3586, **1.3550**	0.6000, 0.5702, **0.5670**	**0.7768**, 0.7852, 0.7838	**0.0003**, 0.0032, 0.0042
10 (4)	1.3417, 1.3321, **1.2913**	0.5588, 0.5360, **0.5124**	**0.7749**, 0.7822, 0.7789	0.0080, 0.0139, **0.0000**
10 (5)	1.3919, **1.3795**, 1.3842	0.6025, **0.5787**, 0.5827	**0.7876**, 0.7988, 0.7976	**0.0017**, 0.0020, 0.0039
20 (1)	1.3598, 1.3392, **1.3348**	0.5961, 0.5503, **0.5236**	**0.7637**, 0.7820, 0.7906	**0.0000**, 0.0069, 0.0207
20 (2)	1.3562, **1.3399**, 1.3875	0.5663, 0.5411, **0.5207**	**0.7899**, 0.7971, 0.8053	**0.0000**, 0.0018, 0.0615
20 (3)	1.3777, **1.3354**, 1.3459	0.5976, 0.5347, **0.5341**	**0.7801**, 0.7968, 0.8023	**0.0000**, 0.0039, 0.0094
20 (4)	1.3664, **1.3289**, 1.3320	0.5902, 0.5453, **0.5298**	0.7759, **0.7741**, 0.7835	**0.0004**, 0.0095, 0.0186

formance. A potential solution would be to randomly locally perturb the geometry of the generic object models when generating synthetic training data to increase variety. The use of a technique such as deformable models [15] and a priori statistical information of category shape variation would allow this to be performed in a more principled manner. Alternatively, additional generic models from an external source could be included in the training process. The integration of a physics engine into the synthetic training data generation process would allow the production of a wider variety of physically consistent pose sets, which may also increase performance.

An alternative direction which could be pursued in addition to adding shape variety would be to include additional sources of information. For example, the jug is difficult to image because its translucency results in different systematic error in each view. However, the 2D silhouette of the object is unaffected, and could be used. Additionally physical contacts could be included, but this would also be affected by generic model inaccuracy.

7   Conclusion

In this work we have demonstrated that it is possible to an extent to categorize sets of objects and estimate poses in scenes with occlusion where there are no annotated images and only generic object models are available. This was performed by estimating pixel category probabilities using local depth features and generating a large number of pose candidates according to those probabilities. The set of pose candidates was then reduced to a final subset that was consistent with the measured depth and pixel category probabilities, and contained a minimum of overlap between objects. However, there is much room for improvement. Future work would include incorporation of physical contacts into the joint parsing algorithm, and improvements to the DF technique to generate superior initial pose candidates. Replacement of the DF with a Hough Forest [28,29] or CNN may be appropriate. Further, ideally the two stages of the algorithm would be combined to simultaneously optimize categorizations, poses, and pose sets.

Acknowledgments. We acknowledge MoD/Dstl and EPSRC for providing the grant to support the UK academics' involvement in a Department of Defense funded MURI project through EPSRC grant EP/N019415/1. This work was also supported in part by EU H2020 RoMaNS, 645582.

References

1. Hejrati, M., Ramanan, D.: Analyzing 3D objects in cluttered images. In: Advances in Neural Information Processing Systems, pp. 593–601 (2012)
2. Lim, J.J., Pirsiavash, H., Torralba, A.: Parsing IKEA objects: fine pose estimation. In: Proceedings of the IEEE International Conference on Computer Vision, pp. 2992–2999. IEEE (2013)

3. Yoruk, E., Vidal, R.: Efficient object localization and pose estimation with 3D wire-frame models. In: Proceedings of the IEEE International Conference on Computer Vision Workshops, pp. 538–545 (2013)
4. Brachmann, E., Krull, A., Michel, F., Gumhold, S., Shotton, J., Rother, C.: Learning 6D object pose estimation using 3D object coordinates. In: Fleet, D., Pajdla, T., Schiele, B., Tuytelaars, T. (eds.) ECCV 2014. LNCS, vol. 8690, pp. 536–551. Springer, Heidelberg (2014). doi:10.1007/978-3-319-10605-2_35
5. Gupta, S., Girshick, R., Arbeláez, P., Malik, J.: Learning rich features from RGB-D images for object detection and segmentation. In: Fleet, D., Pajdla, T., Schiele, B., Tuytelaars, T. (eds.) ECCV 2014. LNCS, vol. 8695, pp. 345–360. Springer, Heidelberg (2014). doi:10.1007/978-3-319-10584-0_23
6. Peng, X., Sun, B., Ali, K., Saenko, K.: Learning deep object detectors from 3D models. In: Proceedings of the IEEE International Conference on Computer Vision, pp. 1278–1286 (2015)
7. Krizhevsky, A., Sutskever, I., Hinton, G.E.: Imagenet classification with deep convolutional neural networks. In: Advances in Neural Information Processing Systems, pp. 1097–1105 (2012)
8. Long, J., Shelhamer, E., Darrell, T.: Fully convolutional networks for semantic segmentation. In: Proceedings of the IEEE Conference on Computer Vision and Pattern Recognition, pp. 3431–3440 (2015)
9. Zhang, N., Donahue, J., Girshick, R., Darrell, T.: Part-based R-CNNs for fine-grained category detection. In: Fleet, D., Pajdla, T., Schiele, B., Tuytelaars, T. (eds.) ECCV 2014. LNCS, vol. 8689, pp. 834–849. Springer, Heidelberg (2014). doi:10.1007/978-3-319-10590-1_54
10. Gupta, S., Arbeláez, P., Girshick, R., Malik, J.: Aligning 3D models to RGB-D images of cluttered scenes. In: Proceedings of the IEEE Conference on Computer Vision and Pattern Recognition, pp. 4731–4740 (2015)
11. Song, S., Xiao, J.: Deep sliding shapes for amodal 3D object detection in RGB-D images. CoRR abs/1511.02300 (2015)
12. Shotton, J., Sharp, T., Kipman, A., Fitzgibbon, A., Finocchio, M., Blake, A., Cook, M., Moore, R.: Real-time human pose recognition in parts from single depth images. Commun. ACM 56(1), 116–124 (2013)
13. Karpathy, A., Toderici, G., Shetty, S., Leung, T., Sukthankar, R., Fei-Fei, L.: Large-scale video classification with convolutional neural networks. In: Proceedings of the IEEE Conference on Computer Vision and Pattern Recognition, pp. 1725–1732 (2014)
14. Pepik, B., Stark, M., Gehler, P., Schiele, B.: Multi-view and 3D deformable part models. IEEE Trans. Pattern Anal. Mach. Intell. 37(11), 2232–2245 (2015)
15. Zia, M.Z., Stark, M., Schiele, B., Schindler, K.: Detailed 3D representations for object recognition and modeling. IEEE Trans. Pattern Anal. Mach. Intell. 35(11), 2608–2623 (2013)
16. Hinterstoisser, S., Lepetit, V., Ilic, S., Holzer, S., Bradski, G., Konolige, K., Navab, N.: Model based training, detection and pose estimation of texture-less 3D objects in heavily cluttered scenes. In: Lee, K.M., Matsushita, Y., Rehg, J.M., Hu, Z. (eds.) ACCV 2012. LNCS, vol. 7724, pp. 548–562. Springer, Heidelberg (2013). doi:10.1007/978-3-642-37331-2_42
17. Krull, A., Brachmann, E., Michel, F., Ying Yang, M., Gumhold, S., Rother, C.: Learning analysis-by-synthesis for 6D pose estimation in RGB-D images. In: Proceedings of the IEEE International Conference on Computer Vision, pp. 954–962 (2015)

18. Song, S., Xiao, J.: Sliding shapes for 3D object detection in depth images. In: Fleet, D., Pajdla, T., Schiele, B., Tuytelaars, T. (eds.) ECCV 2014. LNCS, vol. 8694, pp. 634–651. Springer, Heidelberg (2014). doi:10.1007/978-3-319-10599-4_41

19. Guo, R., Zou, C., Hoiem, D.: Predicting complete 3D models of indoor scenes. CoRR abs/1504.02437 (2015)

20. Lowe, D.G.: Object recognition from local scale-invariant features. In: Proceedings of the IEEE International Conference on Computer Vision, vol. 2, pp. 1150–1157. IEEE (1999)

21. Martinez, M., Collet, A., Srinivasa, S.S.: Moped: a scalable and low latency object recognition and pose estimation system. In: IEEE International Conference on Robotics and Automation, pp. 2043–2049. IEEE (2010)

22. Wohlhart, P., Lepetit, V.: Learning descriptors for object recognition and 3D pose estimation. In: Proceedings of the IEEE Conference on Computer Vision and Pattern Recognition, pp. 3109–3118 (2015)

23. Crivellaro, A., Rad, M., Verdie, Y., Moo Yi, K., Fua, P., Lepetit, V.: A novel representation of parts for accurate 3D object detection and tracking in monocular images. In: Proceedings of the IEEE International Conference on Computer Vision, 4391–4399 (2015)

24. Drost, B., Ulrich, M., Navab, N., Ilic, S.: Model globally, match locally: efficient and robust 3D object recognition. In: Proceedings of the IEEE Conference on Computer Vision and Pattern Recognition, vol. 1, p. 5 (2010)

25. Holzer, S., Shotton, J., Kohli, P.: Learning to efficiently detect repeatable interest points in depth data. In: Fitzgibbon, A., Lazebnik, S., Perona, P., Sato, Y., Schmid, C. (eds.) ECCV 2012. LNCS, vol. 7572, pp. 200–213. Springer, Heidelberg (2012). doi:10.1007/978-3-642-33718-5_15

26. Hodaň, T., Zabulis, X., Lourakis, M., Obdržálek, Š., Matas, J.: Detection and fine 3D pose estimation of texture-less objects in RGB-D images. In: IEEE/RSJ International Conference on Intelligent Robots and Systems, pp. 4421–4428. IEEE (2015)

27. Sun, M., Bradski, G., Xu, B.-X., Savarese, S.: Depth-encoded hough voting for joint object detection and shape recovery. In: Daniilidis, K., Maragos, P., Paragios, N. (eds.) ECCV 2010. LNCS, vol. 6315, pp. 658–671. Springer, Heidelberg (2010). doi:10.1007/978-3-642-15555-0_48

28. Tejani, A., Tang, D., Kouskouridas, R., Kim, T.-K.: Latent-class hough forests for 3D object detection and pose estimation. In: Fleet, D., Pajdla, T., Schiele, B., Tuytelaars, T. (eds.) ECCV 2014. LNCS, vol. 8694, pp. 462–477. Springer, Heidelberg (2014). doi:10.1007/978-3-319-10599-4_30

29. Doumanoglou, A., Kouskouridas, R., Malassiotis, S., Kim, T.K.: Recovering 6D Object Pose and Predicting Next-Best-View in the Crowd. ArXiv e-prints, December 2015

30. Zheng, B., Zhao, Y., Yu, J., Ikeuchi, K., Zhu, S.C.: Scene understanding by reasoning stability and safety. Int. J. Comput. Vis. **112**(2), 221–238 (2015)

31. Jia, Z., Gallagher, A., Saxena, A., Chen, T.: 3D-based reasoning with blocks, support, and stability. In: Proceedings of the IEEE Conference on Computer Vision and Pattern Recognition, pp. 1–8 (2013)

32. Fogel, D.B.: An introduction to simulated evolutionary optimization. IEEE Trans. Neural Netw. **5**(1), 3–14 (1994)

33. Walas, K., Leonardis, A.: UoB highly occluded object challenge (UoB-HOOC). http://www.cs.bham.ac.uk/research/projects/uob-hooc/. Accessed 11 Mar 2016

34. Bouguet, J.Y.: Camera calibration toolbox for matlab (2004)

W18 – Local Features: State of the Art, Open Problems and Performance Evaluation

Preface

Welcome to the Proceedings for the **Workshop on Local Features: State of the Art, Open Problems and Performance Evaluation**, held in conjunction with the European Conference on Computer Vision on October 10th 2016.

Local features are at the centre of many fundamental computer vision problems. While local features have been subject of study in computer vision for almost twenty years, recent significant progress in this area has led to substantial improvements in many computer vision tasks including registration, stereo vision, motion estimation, matching, retrieval, recognition of objects and actions. With the advent of modern deep learning techniques, an area of particular interest is the development of learnable local feature descriptors. While this direction has already proved to be quite fruitful, there are still many challenges left for a variety of problem classes, including defining appropriate training sets, evaluation protocols, and benchmarks.

Following the success of two previous editions in conjunction with CVPR 2009 Miami, and ECCV 2012 Florence, this year's workshop promotes a technical discussion on methods to construct and learn better local features as well as new approaches to a rigorous and realistic evaluation of their performance.

The workshop also includes a Challenge on a newly introduced Benchmark. We provide a dataset of image sequences and local patches with ground truth. This dataset is accompanied by a benchmarking suite that evaluates the performance of local descriptors and interest point detectors. Researchers are encouraged to download the dataset from https://github.com/featw and report their descriptor's performance in future communications.

The workshop programme includes invited talks (Iasonas Kokkinos *Ecole Central Paris*, Vincent Lepetit *Technical University Graz*, and Stefano Soatto *UCLA*), presentations by the organizers on recent developments in the area of local features, results of the benchmark evaluation as well as a poster session of the accepted papers.

We would like to thank the reviewers who submitted high-quality assessments in a short period of time, the authors for their hard work in submitting high quality papers and contributing to the workshop. We hope that you enjoyed the event and see you all at the next edition!

Kind regards/Vriendelijke Groeten

October 2016

Vassileios Balntas
Karel Lenc
Jiri Matas
Krystian Mikolajczyk
Tinne Tuytelaars
Andrea Vedaldi

The CUDA LATCH Binary Descriptor: Because Sometimes Faster Means Better

Christopher Parker[1], Matthew Daiter[2], Kareem Omar[3], Gil Levi[4], and Tal Hassner[5,6(✉)]

[1] University of Oslo, Oslo, Norway
[2] Nomoko AG, Zürich, Switzerland
[3] University of Alabama in Huntsville, Huntsville, AL, USA
[4] Tel Aviv University, Tel Aviv, Israel
[5] Information Sciences Institute, USC, Los Angeles, CA, USA
[6] The Open University of Israel, Ra'anana, Israel
talhassner@gmail.com

Abstract. Accuracy, descriptor size, and the time required for extraction and matching are all important factors when selecting local image descriptors. To optimize over all these requirements, this paper presents a CUDA port for the recent Learned Arrangement of Three Patches (LATCH) binary descriptors to the GPU platform. The design of LATCH makes it well suited for GPU processing. Owing to its small size and binary nature, the GPU can further be used to efficiently match LATCH features. Taken together, this leads to breakneck descriptor extraction and matching speeds. We evaluate the trade off between these speeds and the quality of results in a feature matching intensive application. To this end, we use our proposed CUDA LATCH (CLATCH) to recover structure from motion (SfM), comparing 3D reconstructions and speed using different representations. Our results show that CLATCH provides high quality 3D reconstructions at fractions of the time required by other representations, with little, if any, loss of reconstruction quality.

1 Introduction

> *Quantity has a quality all its own*
> Thomas A. Callaghan Jr.

Local features and their descriptors play pivotal roles in many computer vision systems. As such, research on improving these methods has been immense. Over the years, this effort yielded progressively more accurate representations. These improvements were often demonstrated on standard benchmarks designed to measure the accuracy of descriptor matching in the presence of various image transformations and other confounding factors. It remains unclear, however, if the improved accuracy reported on these benchmarks reflects better, more useful representations when used in real world computer vision systems.

Take, for example, recent attempts to use deep learning for image feature representation (e.g., [10,26,40]). There is no question that given sufficient training

© Springer International Publishing Switzerland 2016
G. Hua and H. Jégou (Eds.): ECCV 2016 Workshops, Part III, LNCS 9915, pp. 685–697, 2016.
DOI: 10.1007/978-3-319-49409-8_57

data and computational resources deep learning methods can achieve astonishing accuracy. Hence, using them to obtain local descriptors can result in better representations and by so doing impact a wide range of computer vision systems.

But using deep learning for feature description and matching does not come without a price: Most of these methods are computationally expensive and even with graphical processing units (GPU), are relatively slow. Even after extraction, their dimensions and floating point values makes them slow to match. Finally, they require substantial training data which can be difficult to provide.

These limitations should be contrasted with evidence that accuracy, though important, is not the only property worth considering when choosing descriptors. For example, simultaneous localization and mapping (SLAM) methods were shown to obtain better 3D reconstructions for the same computational effort by increasing the amount of feature points per keyframe [29]. This suggests that computationally cheaper features are more desirable for these systems. Consequently, state of the art SLAM techniques [21] use ORB [25] rather than more accurate but computationally expensive representations such as SIFT [19]: Doing so allows for a greater number of features to be extracted without compromising reconstruction accuracy. In fact, even classification systems appear to benefit from having more features over higher feature accuracy, as reported by [22].

One side effect to the success of deep learning is that the hardware enabling it – GPU processors – is now becoming standard on systems running computer vision applications, including even consumer cellphone devices. Beyond deep learning, these GPUs can also be used to accelerate extraction and matching of older, so-called *engineered* descriptors. These representations may not reach the same benchmark performances as deep learning techniques, but their extraction on the GPU offers a potential trade off between accuracy and run time. In particular, faster descriptor extraction and matching allows for more descriptors to be used and consequently better overall system performances.

GPU accelerated features were considered in the past. We, however, focus on a particular binary descriptor: the *Learned Arrangement of Three Patches* (LATCH) [18]. It was recently shown to offer a compromise between the high accuracy, low speeds of floating point representations such as SIFT [19], and the low accuracy, high speeds of binary descriptors (e.g., ORB [25], BRIEF [8]). Beyond these properties, its design also happens to neatly fit GPU processing.

Our contributions are: (1) We describe CLATCH, a CUDA port for LATCH, enabling descriptor extraction and matching directly on the GPU. (2) We embed CLATCH in the OpenMVG library [20], along with a fast, GPU based Hamming distance, brute force descriptor matcher. Finally, (3) we compare SfM 3D reconstructions on scenes from [23] using SIFT, recent deep learning based representations and our CLATCH. These show that CLATCH reconstructions are comparable or even better than those obtained with other representations, yet CLATCH requires a fraction of the run time of its alternatives. Importantly, to promote reproducibility, the code used in this paper is publicly available from the project webpage: www.openu.ac.il/home/hassner/projects/LATCH.

2   Related Work

Due to their key role in many computer vision systems, local feature descriptors are extensively studied. A comprehensive survey is therefore outside the scope of this paper. Below we provide only a cursory overview of this topic.

Floating Point Representations. For nearly two decades now, SIFT [19] is very likely the most widely used local image descriptor. It and the representations that followed (e.g., SURF [6]) represent the region around an image pixel using a vector of typically 128 floating point values. This vector is often a histogram of measurements extracted from the image, most commonly various functions of the local intensity gradients.

Binary Descriptors. Despite the success of the older floating point representations, a prevailing problem was their extraction time and dimensionality (which, in turn, affected their storage and matching time). In response, binary descriptors were proposed as low dimensional, efficient alternative representations. These typically assign descriptor values by quick, pixel intensity comparisons.

One of the first binary descriptors was the Binary Robust Independent Elementary Features (BRIEF) [8], soon followed by the Oriented fast and Rotated BRIEF (ORB) descriptor [25] which added rotation invariance, the Binary Robust Invariant Scalable Keypoints (BRISK) [17] which used a more effective pixel sampling pattern, and the Fast REtinA Keypoint descriptor (FREAK) [1] which sampled intensities using a pattern similar to the one found in human retinas. The Accelerated-KAZE (A-KAZE) was suggested in [2]. It builds on the earlier Local Difference Binary (LDB) descriptor [38,39] by computing the binary descriptor values from mean image intensities over a range of patch sizes. The binary online learned descriptor (BOLD) [4] improve accuracy yet retain high processing speeds. Finally and very recently, the LATCH binary descriptors were proposed in [18]. We defer discussion of LATCH to Sect. 3.

Hybrid binary/floating-point methods were also suggested. One example is LDA-Hash [30] which extracts SIFTs, projects them to a discriminative space and applies a threshold to obtain binary descriptors. DBRIEF [34] instead uses patch intensities directly, BinBoost [16,33] learns a set of hash functions corresponding to each bit in the final descriptor and PR-proj [27] uses learning and dimensionality reduction to produce compact binary representations. The computational effort required to extract these descriptors is similar to (if not greater than) floating point descriptors. The representations, however, are short binary vectors and so matching and storing them is relatively efficient.

Computing Local Descriptors on the GPU. Of course, we are not the first to propose porting local feature extraction to the GPU. To our knowledge, nearly all these efforts used the GPU to aid in extracting *floating point descriptors*, including GPU-SIFT (see, e.g., [13,28,36,37]) and GPU-SURF [32]. These methods all used GPUs in portions of the extraction process. For example, [36] used the GPU only to compute convolutions, all other stages performed on the CPU. In addition, and more importantly, the gain in performance reported by these methods are modest and do not approach the speeds of contemporary binary descriptors, let alone our CLATCH.

Interestingly, the only available GPU *binary descriptor* is CUDA ORB, implemented by OpenCV [14]. As we later discuss, due to the nature of GPU processing, the run time advantage of ORB over the more accurate LATCH descriptor when computed on the CPU, vanishes on the GPU.

Deep Features. Following the remarkable success of deep learning in computer vision, it is no surprise that these methods are also being applied to feature point description. Convolutional Neural Networks (CNN) were used in a number of previous attempts to learn local descriptor representations [3,10,26,40].

In most cases, a Siamese deep network is trained with hinge loss [10,26,40]. The training set used in these cases consists of positive and negative labeled patch pairs. Metric learning is then used to improve matching. Finally, [3] proposed an efficient CNN design, bringing processing speeds down substantially. As we later show, their run time is still slower than our proposed approach.

3   CUDA LATCH

3.1   Preliminaries

The LATCH Feature Descriptor. LATCH was recently introduced in [18] and is available as part of the OpenCV library since ver. 3.0 [14]. Its design was inspired by the observation that *pure* binary descriptors such as BRIEF and ORB produce their values by comparing pairs of pixel intensities, a process which can be sensitive to local noise. To address this, these methods used various smoothing techniques before pixel values were compared. Smoothing, however, has the adverse effect of losing important high frequency image information.

Rather than smoothing the image and then comparing single pixel values, LATCH computes its binary values by comparing pixel *patches*. The LATCH descriptor for image pixel $\mathbf{p} = (x, y)$ is computed by selecting $t = 1..T$ patch triplets, one for each LATCH bit. For triplet t, three pixels are selected in the region around $\mathbf{p}$: an *anchor* pixel $\mathbf{p}_{t,A}$ and two *companion* pixels $\mathbf{p}_{t,1}$ and $\mathbf{p}_{t,2}$. The $k \times k$ pixel patches, $\mathbf{P}_{t,A}, \mathbf{P}_{t,1}$, and $\mathbf{P}_{t,2}$ centered on each of these three pixels are extracted. Finally, bit t in the LATCH descriptor for $\mathbf{p}$ is set by comparing the Frobenious norm of the anchor to its two neighbors, as follows:

$$LATCH(\mathbf{p}, t) = \begin{cases} 1 & \text{if } ||\mathbf{P}_{t,A} - \mathbf{P}_{t,1}||_F^2 > ||\mathbf{P}_{t,A} - \mathbf{P}_{t,2}||_F^2 \\ 0 & \text{otherwise} \end{cases}. \tag{1}$$

The triplets LATCH uses are fixed but are not arbitrary: Triplets are selected during training using the data set from [7], which contains same/not-same labeled image windows. Triplets were chosen by considering how well their bits correctly predicted the same/not-same labels over the entire training set. To prevent choosing correlated triplets, following [1,25], triplets are skipped if their predictions are correlated with those of previously chosen triplets.

In their work [18], LATCH contained 512 bits (selected triplets) each one representing triplets of 7×7 patches. At matching time, its computational requirements were obviously equal to those of any other 512 bit binary descriptor. Due to the use of patches and multiple Frobenious norms, extracting LATCH was slower than pure binary descriptors of the same size. Experiments reported in [18], however, showed that the increase in extraction time was small. This was balanced by improved accuracy which bested existing binary descriptors, sometimes rivaling even larger floating point representations.

The GPU Architecture and Non-blocking Programs. Though the specific architectural designs of GPU processors changes from generation to generation, all have several multiprocessors. A CPU can launch *non-blocking* (parallel) GPU programs on these multiprocessors, referred to as *kernels*. That is, while a kernel is being executed on the GPU, the CPU is free to pursue other tasks and similarly, memory transfers to and from the GPU can take place without blocking either CPU or GPU. This property is extremely important when designing computer vision systems using the GPU: It implies that if the GPU extracts descriptors independently of the CPU, *the CPU is free to perform higher level processing*. Related to the SfM application considered here are optimizations for recovering transformations [11] and/or multiple view stereo for scene structure [9].

Some previous attempts to port descriptors to the GPU used it only for parts of the descriptor extraction process, using the CPU for others and requiring multiple memory transfers between processors [28,36]. This at least partially explains why these attempts showed only modest run time improvements over their original, CPU implementations. As a design goal, we therefore limit the use of the CPU and any communications between it and the GPU when extracting and comparing our descriptors.

Why LATCH? LATCH was selected for following reasons.

- **Memory Access vs. Computation.** The emphasis in GPU processing on raw arithmetic power results in memory access patterns often being the determining factor in performance rather than the actual computation. LATCH requires more processing than pure binary representations (e.g., [1,2,8,17,25]) and therefore requires more CPU time to compute than they do. The memory transfer requirements of LATCH, however, are very similar to these other descriptors and hence it stands to gain more on the GPU.
- **Limited Conditional Branching.** As mentioned above, GPUs are optimized for processes which have few, if any, conditional branching; under these circumstances, modern GPUs are capable of up to 10 Tera-FLOPS. Most pure binary descriptors are therefore well suited for GPU processing, whereas porting more complex representations to the GPU is less trivial.
- **Binary String Comparisons.** LATCH is a binary representation. Like other binary representations, it can be matched using fast Hamming distance comparisons. These can further be performed extremely fast on the GPU.

Finally, as demonstrated in the tests reported by [18], LATCH outperforms other binary descriptors making it ideally suited for our purposes.

3.2 Implementing LATCH with CUDA[1]

We have ported the LATCH representation to CUDA 8, building on the original LATCH OpenCV C++ implementation. In all our evaluations, CLATCH representations were extracted from 64×64 pixel windows, using mini-patches of 8×8 pixels giving a 64-byte feature vector.

To minimize CPU processing, differently from [18], we use the Features from Accelerated Segment Test (FAST) [24] feature detector. FAST is already available on the GPU as part of the OpenCV [14] library. Given a detected oriented keypoint, $\mathbf{p} = (x, y, \theta)$ we extract LATCH from a 64×64 intensities window around this point. This process is described next.

Parallelizing LATCH on the GPU. GPU kernels include several identical, concurrently-executing, non-interacting *blocks*. Each one consists of groups (*warps*) of 32 threads. In our implementation, a CLATCH kernel sequentially computes 16 descriptors per block. While the region of interest for one interest point is being processed, the next one is prefetched to pipeline the processing.

A single descriptor is extracted by multiple warps in each block. Each warp independently computes sixteen patch triplets, $[\mathbf{P}_{t,A}, \mathbf{P}_{t,1}, \mathbf{P}_{t,2}]$, four at a time, without any explicit synchronization during the main computation. All told, two blocks of 32 warps, each one containing 32 threads (total of 2048 threads) are processed at a time per multiprocessor. This coarse granularity was chosen to maximize performance across a variety of GPU architecture generations.

Memory Optimization. Given the FAST orientation for an image region, the rotated 64×64 pixel rectangle is loaded into shared memory as an upright square of single-precision floats. We use texture memory accesses to efficiently load and process these values. Our implementation eliminates bank conflicts, with warp divergences or branches kept to a minimum. Thus, processing proceeds without if statements or communications between different warps. This is achieved by strided access patterns of patches and careful padding of shared memory, and is critical to CLATCH's high performance.

Specifically, patch comparisons are performed as follows. A warp simultaneously processes four triplets. Each thread (in a warp of 32 threads) performs two squared-distance comparisons per triplets in the F-norm of Eq. 1. Then, fast warp shuffle operations are used to quickly sum the result from all pixel pairs in a novel, optimal manner. The original LATCH implementation used 7×7 pixel patches. We use 8×8 patches instead as this implies 64 values which can be handled concurrently with no extra computation costs. To further optimize this process, instruction level parallelism was exploited by manual loop unrolling and carefully arranging operations to prevent stalls due to data dependency.

---

[1] For brevity, only implementation highlights are provided. For more details, please see the code available from: www.openu.ac.il/home/hassner/projects/LATCH.

Weighing Pixels in LATCH Patches. Each pixel within a patch can optionally be given a unique weight at no overhead. This is due to the GPU's emphasis on cheap fused-multiply-add operations. We use this property to simulate the original LATCH patch size of 7×7 by setting the relevant weights to zero, obtaining the exact same representation as the original LATCH. Another potential use for this feature, not tested here, is applying Gaussian weights to patch pixels thereby better emphasizing similarity at the patch center vs. its outer pixels.

4 SfM Using CLATCH and OpenMVG

LATCH (and consequently CLATCH) were shown to be slightly less accurate than some of the more computationally heavy, floating point descriptors. It is not clear, however, how these differences in accuracy affect the overall accuracy and speed of an entire, descriptor-intensive computer vision system.

To this end, we test CLATCH vs. other descriptors on the challenging task of 3D SfM reconstruction. Our goal is to see how the final reconstruction and the time required to compute it are affected by the choice of descriptor. We use the OpenMVG, multiple view geometry library [20], modifying it to include self-contained CUDA streams and a GPU based, brute force Hamming matcher. These are detailed next.

CUDA Integration. The kernel launching mechanism employed by CUDA on its default stream disables concurrent launches of feature detection kernels. We therefore modified the CLATCH descriptor and matching code to exclusively operate off of self-contained streams. Doing so allowed the GPU to concurrently execute feature detection and description kernels across multiple images at once, as well as perform feature matching.

Descriptor Matching on the GPU. Our tests compare the use of our binary descriptors with existing floating point representations. In all cases, we used the GPU to compute the descriptor distances. Because CLATCH is a binary representation, Hamming distance is used to compute similarity of CLATCH descriptors. To this end, we developed our own GPU based Hamming distance brute force matcher and integrated it into OpenMVG. To provide a fair comparison, distances between floating point representations were computed using the standard OpenCV GPU based L2 distance routine.

Each block of our Hamming-based brute force matching kernel processes half a probe descriptor per thread, though each descriptor is distributed throughout a half warp so that each thread holds parts of 16 probe descriptors. Gallery descriptors are alternatively prefetched into and processed from two shared memory buffers without intermediate synchronization. As the Hamming distance between each pair of probe and gallery descriptors is computed, partial results are distributed through a half warp. This calls for a simultaneous reduction of several independent variables, which minimizes the number of additions and warp shuffles to be performed.

First, each thread halves the number of variables it must reduce by packing two variables into the lower and upper 16 bits of a 32 bit integer. Then, pairs of threads simultaneously exchange their packed variables in a warp shuffle, and sum the result with their original variable. This results in pairs of threads with variables holding identical values. The threads again pair off in the same manner, but exchange and sum a different variable. The same pairs of threads now have two variables with identical values, so the second of each pair of threads overwrites the first packed variable with the second, before each thread discards the second packed variable. This results in every thread in a warp having a unique value in the same variable, which allows efficient participation in subsequent warp shuffles until the reduction is complete. This novel method requires only 16 additions to compare 16 descriptor pairs, while the standard warp reduction pattern would require 80.

5 Experiments

Descriptor Extraction Run Time Comparison. The CLATCH descriptor is identical to LATCH and so their accuracy on different benchmarks are the same. We therefore refer to the original paper for a comparison on standard benchmarks of LATCH and other representations [18].

By using the GPU, CLATCH is much faster to extract. This is demonstrated in Table 1, which provides a comparison of the run times reported for extracting many popular existing feature point descriptors compared to CLATCH. We report also the processor used to extract these representations and a price estimate for the processor in case of GPU based methods.

Evident from the table is that even on affordable GPU hardware, extraction run times are orders of magnitude faster than standard representations on the CPU and even other GPU representations (the only exceptions are the far less accurate CUDA ORB and the floating point representation CUDA SURF). PN-Net [3] in particular, is designed to be a very fast deep learning based descriptor method, yet even with more expensive GPU hardware, it is more than an order of magnitude slower to extract than CLATCH. More importantly, all floating point representations, including CUDA SURF and PN-Net, require more time to match their bigger, real valued representations.

SfM Results. We use the incremental SfM pipeline implemented in OpenMVG, with its default values unchanged. We compared the following descriptors in our tests: SIFT [19], often the standard in these applications, the deep learning based features, DeepSiam and DeepSiam2Stream from [40], the fast deep feature representations, PN-Net from [3] and our own CLATCH.

All descriptors used the CUDA FAST feature detector with the exception of SIFT which, for technical reasons, used its default DOG based detector. Following incremental SfM, point cloud Densification [5], Mesh Reconstruction [15] and Mesh Refinement [35] were applied to produce the final reconstructions visualized in Fig. 1.

Tests were performed on publicly available sets of high resolution photogrammetry images from [23], which include $5,616 \times 3,744$ (or $3,744 \times 5,616$) pixels

Table 1. Run time analysis. Mean time in microseconds for extracting a single local descriptor. For GPU descriptors we provide also the GPU models used to obtain these results and their estimated price. CPU results were all measured by [18] on their system. [a]CUDA ports for SURF and ORB are implemented in OpenCV [14]; their speeds were measured by us. [b]Run times and hardware specs provided in the original publications. [c]Time for extracting and matching a descriptor pair was reported as ×2 SIFT extraction time. [d]Run time reported in [3].

Descriptor	Extraction μS	GPU
SIFT [19]	3290	-
SURF [6]	2110	-
CUDA SURF [6][a]	0.9	GTX 970M ($280 usd)
LDA-HASH [30]	5030	-
LDA-DIF [30]	4740	-
DBRIEF [34]	8750	-
BinBoost [16,33]	3290	-
BRIEF [8]	234	-
ORB [25]	486	-
CUDA ORB [25][a]	0.5	GTX 970M ($280 usd)
BRISK [17]	59	-
FREAK [1]	72	-
A-KAZE [2]	69	-
LATCH [18]	616	-
DeepSiam [40][b,c]	6580	Titan ($650 usd)
MatchNet [10][d]	575	Titan X ($1,000 usd)
CNN3 [26][b]	760	Titan Black ($1,100 usd)
PN-Net [3][b]	10	Titan X ($1,000 usd)
Our CLATCH	0.5	GTX 970M ($280 usd)

in each image. Table 2 summarizes these results, providing the final scene reprojection RMSE and the total time for descriptor extraction, matching and SfM reconstruction. All these tests were run on our GTX 1080 GPU.

Reconstruction run time is dominated by the brute force, nearest neighbor matcher. Hence, the gaps in run times between the different methods are smaller than those in Table 1. Nevertheless, reconstructions with CLATCH required a fraction of the time for the runner up (PN-Net) and far less than the others.

Reprojection RMSE, is low for all methods and is typically around half a pixel. Although these errors fluctuate between the different methods and scenes, these differences are often below 0.1 pixels. Considering the high resolutions of the input images, these differences are negligible.

Table 2. Quantitative SfM reconstructions. Results on the eight scenes from [23], comparing various representations with our CLATCH. We report reprojection errors and the time required to extract, match and estimate shape for the various descriptors. All results measured on the same hardware. CLATCH run times are substantially faster than its alternatives despite similar qualitative results (see Fig. 1.)

	Avignon	Bouteville	Burgos	Cognac Garden	St. Jacques	Mirebeau	Murato	Poitiers
Number of images	11	26	9	12	20	22	43	33
SfM Scene RMSE (in pixels)								
SIFT [19]	0.475	0.405	0.495	0.438	0.498	0.478	0.533	0.690
DeepSiam [40]	0.533	0.489	0.422	0.566	0.535	0.489	0.533	0.547
DeepSiam2stream [40]	0.505	0.457	0.419	0.536	0.522	0.459	0.496	0.529
PN-Net [3]	0.538	0.462	0.493	0.554	0.536	0.482	0.531	0.533
Our CLATCH	0.556	0.414	0.466	0.478	0.400	0.466	0.494	0.454
Total time for descriptor extraction, matching and incremental SfM (in seconds)								
SIFT [19]	174.30	454.13	143.728	155.61	296.431	401.64	958.778	1206.10
DeepSiam [40]	172.49	596.07	130.72	146.49	347.576	416.01	943.841	812.39
DeepSiam2stream [40]	269.39	922.95	226.123	301.67	628.03	739.629	1750.535	1379.80
PN-Net [3]	49.56	210.60	50.12	56.02	122.29	167.51	372.28	311.18
Our CLATCH	18.91	69.07	15.907	19.089	27.877	47.534	86.377	61.868

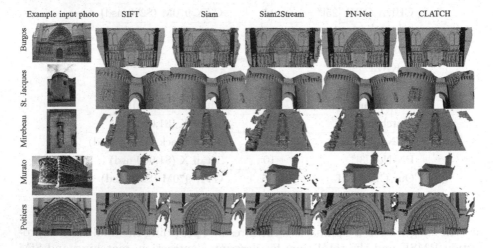

Fig. 1. Qualitative SfM reconstructions. Results showing the output of the same SfM pipeline on five of the eights scenes from [23], comparing the use of SIFT [19], Siam and Siam2Stream from [40], PN-Net [3] and our CLATCH. These results show only minor differences in output 3D shapes, despite the substantial difference in run time required for the different representations (see Table 2).

Finally, Fig. 1 additionally provides qualitative results, showing rendered views of our reconstructions. Evident from the figure is that despite large differences in run time, qualitatively, the reconstructions appear very similar.

6 Conclusions

In descriptor matching intensive application, such as SfM, accuracy per descriptor is sometimes balanced by the speed required to extract and match the descriptors. Taking advantage of this, we present CLATCH, a CUDA port for the LATCH binary descriptor. Although CLATCH descriptor accuracy in standard benchmarks may fall slightly behind other representations, particularly recent deep learning based methods, they are far faster to extract and match. CLATCH thereby provides a fast and accurate alternative means for 3D reconstruction.

From a technical point, an outcome of this work is openly available code for extremely fast feature extraction and matching and a pipeline for SfM allowing convenient interchange of feature descriptors, including deep methods. This implementation can be improved in many ways. For one thing, our use of the FAST detector [24] does not provide scale invariance. CLATCH, however, can easily be extracted at multiple scales, potentially improving its accuracy. Use of CLATCH in other applications where descriptors are extracted and matched in large quantities, is also a priority. One particularly appealing example is dense pixel matching [12,31] where the CLATCH may be an alternative to methods such as PatchMatch [5], providing similar run times without compromising spatial smoothness.

References

1. Alahi, A., Ortiz, R., Vandergheynst, P.: FREAK: fast retina keypoint. In: Proceedings of Conference on Computer Vision Pattern Recognition, pp. 510–517. IEEE (2012)
2. Alcantarilla, P.F., Nuevo, J., Bartoli, A.: Fast explicit diffusion for accelerated features in nonlinear scale spaces. In: British Machine Vision Conference (BMVC) (2013)
3. Balntas, V., Johns, E., Tang, L., Mikolajczyk, K.: PN-Net: conjoined triple deep network for learning local image descriptors. arXiv preprint arXiv:1601.05030 (2016)
4. Balntas, V., Tang, L., Mikolajczyk, K.: BOLD-binary online learned descriptor for efficient image matching. In: Proceedings of Conference on Computer Vision Pattern Recognition, pp. 2367–2375 (2015)
5. Barnes, C., Shechtman, E., Finkelstein, A., Goldman, D.: PatchMatch: a randomized correspondence algorithm for structural image editing. Trans. Graph. 28(3), 24 (2009)
6. Bay, H., Tuytelaars, T., Gool, L.: SURF: speeded up robust features. In: Leonardis, A., Bischof, H., Pinz, A. (eds.) ECCV 2006. LNCS, vol. 3951, pp. 404–417. Springer, Heidelberg (2006). doi:10.1007/11744023_32
7. Brown, M., Hua, G., Winder, S.: Discriminative learning of local image descriptors. Trans. Pattern Anal. Mach. Intell. 33(1), 43–57 (2011)
8. Calonder, M., Lepetit, V., Strecha, C., Fua, P.: BRIEF: binary robust independent elementary features. In: Daniilidis, K., Maragos, P., Paragios, N. (eds.) ECCV 2010. LNCS, vol. 6314, pp. 778–792. Springer, Heidelberg (2010). doi:10.1007/978-3-642-15561-1_56

9. Furukawa, Y., Ponce, J.: Accurate, dense, and robust multiview stereopsis. Trans. Pattern Anal. Mach. Intell. **32**(8), 1362–1376 (2010)
10. Han, X., Leung, T., Jia, Y., Sukthankar, R., Berg, A.C.: MatchNet: unifying feature and metric learning for patch-based matching. In: Proceedings of Conference on Computer Vision Pattern Recognition, pp. 3279–3286 (2015)
11. Hassner, T., Assif, L., Wolf, L.: When standard RANSAC is not enough: cross-media visual matching with hypothesis relevancy. Mach. Vis. Appl. **25**(4), 971–983 (2014)
12. Hassner, T., Liu, C.: Dense Image Correspondences for Computer Vision. Springer, Cham (2015)
13. Heymann, S., Müller, K., Smolic, A., Froehlich, B., Wiegand, T.: SIFT implementation and optimization for general-purpose GPU. In: WSCG (2007)
14. Itseez: Open source computer vision library (2015). https://github.com/itseez/opencv
15. Jancosek, M., Pajdla, T.: Exploiting visibility information in surface reconstruction to preserve weakly supported surfaces. International Scholarly Research Notices 2014 (2014)
16. Lepetit, V., Trzcinski, T., Fua, P., Christoudias, C.M., et al.: Boosting binary keypoint descriptors. In: Proceedings of Conference on Computer Vision Pattern Recognition (2013)
17. Leutenegger, S., Chli, M., Siegwart, R.Y.: BRISK: binary robust invariant scalable keypoints. In: Proceedings of International Conference on Computer Vision, pp. 2548–2555. IEEE (2011)
18. Levi, G., Hassner, T.: LATCH: learned arrangements of three patch codes. In: Winter Conference on Applications of Computer Vision (2016)
19. Lowe, D.G.: Distinctive image features from scale-invariant keypoints. Int. J. Comput. Vis. **60**(2), 91–110 (2004)
20. Moulon, P., Monasse, P., Marlet, R., et al.: openMVG. An open multiple view geometry library. https://github.com/openMVG/openMVG
21. Mur-Artal, R., Montiel, J., Tardós, J.D.: ORB-SLAM: a versatile and accurate monocular slam system. Trans. Robot. **31**(5), 1147–1163 (2015)
22. Nowak, E., Jurie, F., Triggs, B.: Sampling strategies for bag-of-features image classification. In: Leonardis, A., Bischof, H., Pinz, A. (eds.) ECCV 2006. LNCS, vol. 3954, pp. 490–503. Springer, Heidelberg (2006). doi:10.1007/11744085_38
23. Perrot, R.: Set of images for doing 3D reconstruction. https://github.com/rperrot/ReconstructionDataSet
24. Rosten, E., Drummond, T.: Machine learning for high-speed corner detection. In: Leonardis, A., Bischof, H., Pinz, A. (eds.) ECCV 2006. LNCS, vol. 3951, pp. 430–443. Springer, Heidelberg (2006). doi:10.1007/11744023_34
25. Rublee, E., Rabaud, V., Konolige, K., Bradski, G.: ORB: an efficient alternative to SIFT or SURF. In: Proceedings of International Conference on Computing Vision, pp. 2564–2571. IEEE (2011)
26. Simo-Serra, E., Trulls, E., Ferraz, L., Kokkinos, I., Fua, P., Moreno-Noguer, F.: Discriminative learning of deep convolutional feature point descriptors. In: Proceedings of International Conference of Computer Vision, pp. 118–126 (2015)
27. Simonyan, K., Vedaldi, A., Zisserman, A.: Learning local feature descriptors using convex optimisation. Trans. Pattern Anal. Mach. Intell. **36**(8), 1573–1585 (2014)
28. Sinha, S.N., Frahm, J.M., Pollefeys, M., Genc, Y.: GPU-based video feature tracking and matching. In: Workshop on Edge Computing Using New Commodity Architectures, vol. 278, p. 4321 (2006)

29. Strasdat, H., Montiel, J.M., Davison, A.J.: Visual SLAM: why filter? Image Vis. Comput. **30**(2), 65–77 (2012)
30. Strecha, C., Bronstein, A.M., Bronstein, M.M., Fua, P.: LDAhash: improved matching with smaller descriptors. IEEE Trans. Pattern Anal. Mach. Intell. **34**(1), 66–78 (2012)
31. Tau, M., Hassner, T.: Dense correspondences across scenes and scales. Trans. Pattern Anal. Mach. Intell (2014, to appear)
32. Terriberry, T.B., French, L.M., Helmsen, J.: GPU accelerating speeded-up robust features. In: Proceedings of International Symposium on 3D Data Processing, Visualization and Transmission (2008)
33. Trzcinski, T., Christoudias, C.M., Lepetit, V.: Learning image descriptors with boosting. Technical report, Institute of Electrical and Electronics Engineers (2013)
34. Trzcinski, T., Lepetit, V.: Efficient discriminative projections for compact binary descriptors. In: Fitzgibbon, A., Lazebnik, S., Perona, P., Sato, Y., Schmid, C. (eds.) ECCV 2012. LNCS, vol. 7572, pp. 228–242. Springer, Heidelberg (2012). doi:10.1007/978-3-642-33718-5_17
35. Vu, H.H., Labatut, P., Pons, J.P., Keriven, R.: High accuracy and visibility-consistent dense multiview stereo. IEEE Trans. Pattern Anal. Mach. Intell. **34**(5), 889–901 (2012)
36. Warn, S., Emeneker, W., Cothren, J., Apon, A.: Accelerating SIFT on parallel architectures. In: International Conference on Cluster Computing and Workshops, August 2009
37. Wu, C.: SiftGPU: a GPU implementation of scale invariant feature transform (SIFT). http://cs.unc.edu/ccwu/siftgpu
38. Yang, X., Cheng, K.T.: LDB: an ultra-fast feature for scalable augmented reality on mobile devices. In: 2012 IEEE International Symposium on Mixed and Augmented Reality (ISMAR), pp. 49–57. IEEE (2012)
39. Yang, X., Cheng, K.T.: Local difference binary for ultrafast and distinctive feature description. Trans. Pattern Anal. Mach. Intell. **36**(1), 188–194 (2014)
40. Zagoruyko, S., Komodakis, N.: Learning to compare image patches via convolutional neural networks. In: Proceedings of Conference on Computer Vision Pattern Recognition (2015)

Sensor Fusion for Sparse SLAM with Descriptor Pooling

Philipp Tiefenbacher[✉], Julian Heuser, Timo Schulze,
Mohammadreza Babaee, and Gerhard Rigoll

Institute for Human-Machine Communication,
Technical University of Munich, Munich, Germany
{philipp.tiefenbacher,reza.babaee,rigoll}@tum.de,
j.heuser@mytum.de, schulzetimo@gmx.net

Abstract. This paper focuses on the advancement of a monocular sparse- SLAM algorithm via two techniques: Local feature maintenance and descriptor-based sensor fusion. We present two techniques that maintain the descriptor of a local feature: *Pooling* and *bestfit*. The maintenance procedure aims at defining more accurate descriptors, increasing matching performance and thereby tracking accuracy. Moreover, sensors besides the camera can be used to improve tracking robustness and accuracy via sensor fusion. State-of-the-art sensor fusion techniques can be divided into two categories. They either use a Kalman filter that includes sensor data in its state vector to conduct a posterior pose update, or they create world-aligned image descriptors with the help of the gyroscope. This paper is the first to compare and combine these two approaches. We release a new evaluation dataset which comprises 21 scenes that include a dense ground truth trajectory, IMU data, and camera data. The results indicate that descriptor pooling significantly improves pose accuracy. Furthermore, we show that descriptor-based sensor fusion outperforms Kalman filter-based approaches (EKF and UKF).

1 Introduction

Handhelds are ubiquitous and are usually equipped with a video camera which enables the integration of simultaneous localization and mapping (SLAM). Handhelds also include additional sensors, the inertial measurement units (IMUs), which can improve the SLAM accuracy [1].

The combination of the video capture and the additional sensor data requires a multi-sensor fusion. This is commonly achieved by Kalman filters [2–4]. Besides the Kalman filter approaches, a vision-based approach exists that improves the image descriptor via the gyroscope data [5]. This work compares the sensor fusion via an unscented Kalman filter (UKF) with the sensor fusion via gravity-aligned feature descriptors (GAFD) [5]. Both approaches are integrated into the parallel tracking and mapping (PTAM) algorithm [6].

Furthermore, we change the patch-based PTAM matching to a descriptor based matching, e.g., SIFT [7]. Image feature detection aims at detecting salient

© Springer International Publishing Switzerland 2016
G. Hua and H. Jégou (Eds.): ECCV 2016 Workshops, Part III, LNCS 9915, pp. 698–710, 2016.
DOI: 10.1007/978-3-319-49409-8_58

positions in images at which descriptors are extracted that are robust in terms of scale and rotation. This modification allows us to propose two new descriptor maintenance techniques for an improved matching and tracking accuracy.

In summary, the contributions of this work are the following: *(a)* a new dataset for the evaluation of SLAM algorithms, *(b)* a new descriptor maintenance technique for higher pose accuracy, *(c)* a two-way sensor fusion technique by combining UKF with GAFD.

2   Related Work

The PTAM [6] algorithm belongs to the keyframe-based monocular SLAM methods. It differs from the filtering-based approaches [8]: The knowledge of the system is not represented by a probability distribution but by a subset of images (keyframes) and map points. The PTAM map constitutes a sparse scene representation since only patches of salient image points are incorporated. Sparse SLAM approaches usually allow for faster computation than dense SLAM approaches. Recent works such as ORB-SLAM [9] show that sparse-SLAM techniques can outperform semi-dense ones [10].

Direct visual odometry (VO) techniques utilize the full image information. For instance, dense tracking and mapping (DTAM) [11] is able to reconstruct the map in much more detail than the sparse SLAM techniques but the computational complexity is still too demanding to achieve real-time performance on handhelds. The so called semi-dense techniques [10, 12] calculate dense depth maps covering all image regions with non-negligible gradient. Optimized versions of this technique [13] run in real time on handhelds.

Our work integrates IMU output into a sparse SLAM technique. Several works already targeted the integration of inertial sensors into SLAM approaches by using Kalman filters. For example, Omari et al. [14] reviewed an optical flow-based visual system coupled with inertial measurement units. Their unscented Kalman filter (UKF) considered gyroscope and accelerometer measurements. Tiefenbacher et al. [1] used the IMU data as control input for the UKF. Furthermore, a motion model based on the a priori estimate of the UKF was presented. Aksoy and Alatan [2] focused on the uncertainty modeling for a Kalman filter which was combined with a tracking system similar to PTAM.

Besides the sensor fusion via Kalman filters, few works incorporated the IMU data directly into the visual descriptors. Kurz and Benhimane [5] proposed the gravity-aligned feature descriptors (GAFD) that align the orientations of local feature descriptors, e.g., SIFT [7] and SURF [15], to the gravitational force obtained from the gyroscope. They showed that GAFD increases the number of successfully matched features since the descriptors become not just invariant to orientation but, more importantly, distinguishable. Guan et al. [16] presented gravity-aligned VLAD features [17] to incorporate the same advantages as in [5]. Our work is the first that combines and evaluates both ways of sensor fusion: Filter- and feature-based fusion.

3   Descriptor-Pooled PTAM with Sensor Fusion

PTAM separates tracking and mapping into two threads. After map initialization, the positions of FAST [18] corners are used to extract patches. These patches are saved into the map and successively tracked. In each new frame, a motion model delivers a prior pose estimate. Then template matching between new patches and the warped patches of the map is applied for those patches which fulfill the epipolar constraint. A pyramid-based [19] matching approach leads to a coarse-to-fine pose estimation and accelerates execution time. The map is updated via keyframes in case of too few successful matches. The following sections present the adaption of PTAM to descriptor-based matching and the two main contributions: Local descriptor update strategies and sensor fusion through adaption of local descriptors or a Kalman filter.

3.1   Tracking and Mapping

The matching over pixel intensities of warped patches is exchanged with scale- and rotation-invariant keypoint descriptors. A guided nearest neighbor search identifies the best keypoints for map initialization, tracking and the mapping process. The number of pyramid levels have been reduced from four to three, since the forth level is too blurred to detect meaningful corner-based (FAST) keypoints. The two-stage coarse-to-fine tracking process is preserved. At the lowest pyramid level, we extract at most 1850 keypoints.

The advanced map stores multiple keypoints, called map points, for every keyframe. The map points hold the mapping to their descriptors. Multiple descriptors for each map point are permitted. We implemented and evaluated the descriptor-based PTAM using the prominent SIFT [7] and efficient ORB [20] descriptors. The 128-/32-dimensional descriptors are matched via euclidean and Hamming distances, respectively.

3.2   Descriptor Update

We investigate on three different descriptor maintenance strategies. The first and most trivial strategy is to keep the descriptor d of a map point p_m fixed to the descriptor of its source keyframe k_{source}. The source keyframe is the keyframe that initially creates the map point. The descriptor is given by

$$d_{p_m} = d_{k_{source}}. \tag{1}$$

The second strategy computes the *bestfit* descriptor d of a map point p_m. Since multiple keyframes of the map may contain measurements of the same map point, the best fitting descriptor minimizes the sum of the distances to all other descriptors that are linked to this map point p_m. It is given by

$$d_{p_m} = \min_i \sum_{j, j \neq i} \|d_i - d_j\|_{L2 \text{ or Hamming}}; \qquad d_i, d_j \in D \tag{2}$$

with D being the set of descriptors associated with the map point.

The third strategy computes temporally pooled descriptors. *Pooling* describes the combination of feature descriptors at nearby locations with the goal to achieve a joint feature representation "that preserves important information (intrinsic variability) while discarding irrelevant details (nuisance variability)" [21]. Dong and Soatto [22] showed that domain-size pooling of gradient histogram descriptors improves the matching performance significantly. However, this benefit comes with higher computational cost since multiple descriptors with different domain-sizes have to be computed for nearby locations.

We propose a *pooling* over time instead of nearby locations. Thus, a (median) *pooling* occurs over all descriptors that are linked to one map point p_m but captured at different points in time, i.e., different keyframes. For that purpose, we generate a sorted list for each entry of a descriptor and select the middle value, which easily removes outliers.

The descriptor of a particular map point is updated whenever a new keyframe is added that contains a measurement of the map point. In consequence, only a small computational overhead is introduced by this new descriptor update technique. Furthermore, the mapping process tries to refine map points in other keyframes that have not been searched before or have been rated as a bad measurement. If the mapping process is successful in this search, the descriptor of the corresponding map point will be updated. The entire descriptor update is handled by the mapping thread.

3.3 Sensor Fusion

Kalman Filter-Based Fusion. In order to project map points into the current frame, a motion model has to predict a prior pose. The precision and stability of the motion model has a direct influence on tracking performance. For our experiments, we make use of the PTAM motion model (PMM) and the findings in [1].

PMM consists of a decaying velocity model. It can be formalized using exponential coordinates

$$P_i = \exp(\tau_i) \cdot P_{i-1} \tag{3}$$

with the decaying linear and angular velocity being

$$\tau_i = 0.9 \cdot (0.5 \cdot \tau_{i-1} + 0.5 \cdot \ln(P_{i-1} \cdot P_{i-2}^{-1})). \tag{4}$$

This motion model is used for both PTAM and the PTAM+ [1] variants. For the latter, an unscented Kalman filter (UKF) additionally updates the final PTAM pose leading to a posterior pose estimate (similar to [1]). The state vector is identical to [1]. It has 26 dimensions and contains, among others, the IMU-to-world attitude, the position and velocity vectors as well as the gravity vector. The employed UKF update was most stable in estimating the attitude [1], since the UKF keeps track of the gravity vector. We do not make use of the accelerometer measurements as those tend to corrupt the position estimate of SLAM quadratically.

Gravity-Aligned Feature Descriptors (GAFD). We utilize the IMU data in the tracking and mapping process by aligning the descriptors to the gravity vector [23] prior to matching. This creates distinguishable descriptors for congruent features that would not be distinguishable with the basic algorithms, e.g., SIFT. We track the gravity vector in the fixed world frame with a UKF. For every frame, the gravity vector g_C in the moving camera frame is updated via

$$g_C = {}^C R_W g_W \tag{5}$$

with the gravity vector g_W in the world frame and the world to camera rotation matrix ${}^C R_W$. The gravity vector is projected onto the image plane by applying the camera model and the intrinsic camera calibration matrix K. Its 2D-orientation in the image plane is computed with respect to the location of the keypoint. The final 2D-projection of the gravity vector $d = [d_u, d_v, 0]^T$ at a pixel $p = [u, v, 1]^T$ is computed by

$$d = p' - p \tag{6}$$

with

$$p' = [u', v', 1]^T = \frac{1}{1 + g_{C_z}}(p + K g_C). \tag{7}$$

Finally, the orientation angle of the gravity-aligned descriptor is given by

$$\theta = \arctan \frac{d_v}{d_u}. \tag{8}$$

4   Dataset

Publicly available datasets lack either gyroscope and accelerometer data [24,25] or a dense ground truth trajectory [26]. Hence, we recorded new scenes including these data. Furthermore, we focused on recording fast movements and pure rotations which are very challenging for most visual SLAM approaches. The new dataset consists of 21 scenes that we make available at http://www.mmk.ei.tum.de/sensorintegrationslam/. A professional external tracking system by *ART* provides the ground truth of 21 motion trajectories. The tracking system includes

Fig. 1. Camera capture of scene 1 (left), scene 15 (center) and scene 18 (right). These captures are picked to illustrate the environment. The other scenes are recorded in the same environment.

Table 1. Absolute values of each low-level feature for each scene and the corresponding cluster assignment.

	Transl. distance [m]	Rot. distance [deg]	Transl. vel. [m/s]	Rot. vel. [deg/s]
Scene 1	23.823 (*Low*)	3948 (Mod.)	0.2362	39.1384
Scene 2	27.549 (*Low*)	6318 (**High**)	0.2908	66.7306
Scene 3	22.319 (*Low*)	4522 (Mod.)	0.2205	44.6794
Scene 4	46.718 (Mod.)	2967 (*Low*)	0.4590	29.1496
Scene 5	46.33 (Mod.)	4672 (Mod.)	0.5331	53.7486
Scene 6	59.747 (**High**)	2730 (*Low*)	0.6453	29.4867
Scene 7	56.13 (**High**)	2560 (*Low*)	0.6219	28.4292
Scene 8	54.74 (**High**)	6245 (**High**)	0.5968	68.0944
Scene 9	46.144 (Mod.)	4296 (Mod.)	0.6090	56.6942
Scene 10	63.447 (**High**)	4609 (Mod.)	0.7079	51.4246
Scene 11	33.078 (*Low*)	2235 (Low)	0.4229	28.5781
Scene 12	41.227 (Mod.)	2470 (*Low*)	0.4019	24.0790
Scene 13	46.492 (Mod.)	3748 (Mod.)	0.4795	38.6584
Scene 14	49.472 (Mod.)	4573 (Mod.)	0.5683	52.5257
Scene 15	18.942 (*Low*)	1662 (*Low*)	0.4083	35.8284
Scene 16	25.225 (*Low*)	3442 (Mod.)	0.3314	45.2329
Scene 17	39.73 (Mod.)	3379 (Mod.)	0.3496	29.7341
Scene 18	23.54 (*Low*)	1866 (*Low*)	0.3153	24.9886
Scene 19	10.534 (*Low*)	963.4 (*Low*)	0.2352	21.5068
Scene 20	38.262 (Mod.)	5101 (Mod.)	0.3475	46.3317
Scene 21	50.414 (Mod.)	5998 (**High**)	0.4563	54.2867

five high-resolution cameras that record the trajectories at a sampling rate of 60 Hz. The mobile device is equipped with passive markers. In order to validly compare the SLAM-based tracking results with the external tracking system, a hand-eye calibration between markers and the camera has been applied [27]. Besides the ground truth trajectory, each scene consists of a 20 Hz grayscale camera capture with a resolution of 640 × 480 and 60 Hz IMU readings (gyroscope and accelerometer) obtained from a "Microsoft Surface 2 Pro". Figure 1 illustrates camera captures of three different scenes.

In order to characterize each scene in more detail, we extract scene properties of the provided ground truth motion trajectory. The first and last 10 % of the frames are discarded for every scene, since they are either needed for the map initialization or the tracking already failed. Then we perform k-means clustering on the euclidean distances of each scene property (1D) with three cluster centers (low, moderate and high). The chosen scene properties are the overall translation distance (TD) and the overall rotation distance (RD). The velocities are proportional to the corresponding distances since each scene has a duration of 100 to 120 s.

Table 1 depicts the absolute values of the low-level features of each scene as well as the corresponding clusters. It is important to note that the number of scenes per cluster is not equally distributed. For instance, in RD only three of the 21 scenes belong to the *High* cluster, while 8 scenes are matched to the *Low* cluster. The cluster *TD High* starts at 54.74 m until 63.45 m, while the range of the *TD Low* cluster lies between 10.53 m and 33.08 m. The average translation velocities range from 0.22 m/s to 0.71 m/s, while the average rotation velocities range from 21.51 deg/s to 68.08 deg/s.

5   Results

The evaluations consider the first 350 frames of every scene due to tracking failures. The patch versus descriptor matching as well as the sensor fusion techniques are only evaluated via the absolute trajectory error (ATE), since the results are already very distinctive. Both ATE and rotation error are computed for the descriptor update techniques. We calculate the quaternion-based rotation error of Gramkow [28] for every frame. Afterwards, we averaged the rotation error per scene. The clusters results displayed in the figures depict the median of the averaged rotation errors. The ATE is computed via the publicly available script of [25].

5.1   Patch Versus Descriptor Matching

In Fig. 2, we compare the ATE results of the scenes that were trackable by all approaches. It can be seen that the patch-based PTAM performs similarly to ORB-PTAM with a slight advantage in scene 14. The gravity-aligned (GA)-ORB-PTAM performs better than the standard ORB-PTAM in 6 of 7 scenes. Moreover, the gravity-aligned features mostly improve tracking in cases of pure rotation trajectories (see *RD High* in Fig. 3). The SIFT-PTAM algorithm completely fails to track in those cases. That is why only this small subset could be evaluated here. Furthermore, SIFT-PTAM leads to higher ATE than ORB-PTAM in every tested scene.

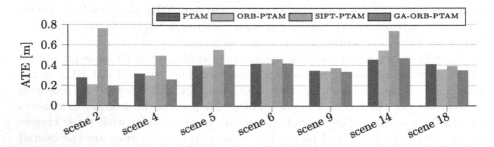

Fig. 2. The ATE [m] of patch-based versus descriptor-based matching.

5.2   Descriptor Update Techniques

For the evaluation of the descriptor update techniques, the original PTAM algorithm is adapted to ORB-PTAM with GAFD and without. No Kalman filter for a posterior update is used. Moreover, the size of set D of the associated descriptors is not limited for *pooling* and *bestfit* (see Eq. (2)). Figure 3 consists of 6 different trajectory clusters, however, the scenes 2, 7, 11, 15, 17, and 22 are excluded due to tracking errors in the *source* descriptor technique. It can be seen that the ATEs do not differ much except for GAFD and non-GAFD descriptor updates. GAFD produces the smallest error in every cluster. Considering only the GAFD versions, the *pooling* reaches slightly lower errors than the other descriptor update strategies. Moreover, the new descriptor techniques perform only worse than the *source* technique for the *RD High*. For the non-GAFD versions, there is no clear difference and source even performs best in *RD Low*.

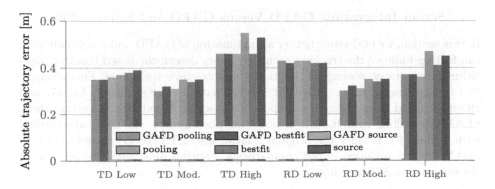

Fig. 3. The ATE [m] of the descriptor maintenance techniques for GAFD and non-GAFD extensions. Only the ORB descriptor is used for this comparison.

Figure 4 presents the rotational pose error (RPE). The rotational pose errors differ more significantly between the techniques. Here, *pooling* leads to a rotation error reduction compared to the *bestfit* and the *source* techniques except for *RD High*. There, the *bestfit* technique produces a lower RPE than *pooling*, whereas the *pooling* technique performs best in 5 of 6 cluster. In two clusters (*TD Mod* and *RD Low*) the *bestfit* approach leads to worse results than the *source* technique.

The local descriptors without the GAFD extension never state the best results. Additionally, the error variations between the descriptor maintenance techniques are much larger without GAFD than with GAFD. This shows that GAFD stabilizes the local features on the one hand, but on the other hand, outlines the importance of the descriptor maintenance technique, i.e., pooling, in case of non-GAFD. There is no relation between the clusters and the descriptor maintenance techniques.

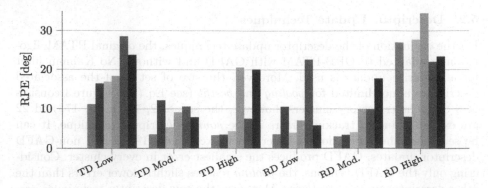

Fig. 4. Rotational pose errors (RPE) [deg] of the GAFD- and non-GAFD ORB features for different descriptor maintenance techniques. Same color scheme applies as in Fig. 3.

5.3 Sensor Integration: GAFD Versus GAFD and Kalman Filter

In this section, we evaluate whether a combination of GAFD and a Kalman filter can further improve the tracking accuracy. Every descriptor-based tracking algorithm incorporates *pooling* as descriptor maintenance technique. Furthermore, 17 of 21 scenes have been used for the evaluation. The scenes 7, 11, 17, and 19 either failed to initialize the map or the tracking failed after a certain time. SLAM algorithms that include a posterior pose update via UKF are marked with a plus (+). Besides the original PTAM, also PTAM+ [1] as well as EKF-SLAM [29] are included in our comparisons. Figure 5 illustrates the ATE of all clusters and SLAM techniques.

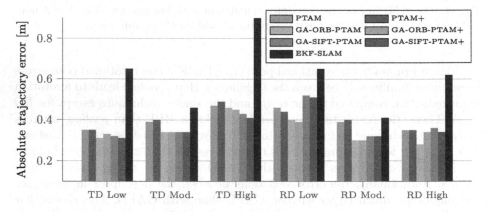

Fig. 5. Absolute trajectory errors [m] of GAFD versus GAFD and UKF (+).

The EKF-SLAM algorithm achieves the worst performance in all clusters. The GA(FD)-ORB-PTAM tracker shows the lowest error in 4 out of 6 clusters. Thus, GA-ORB-PTAM is the best algorithm in this comparison. The additional

UKF (+) for a posterior pose update does improve accuracy only for the clusters *TD High* and *RD Low*, whereas the ATE increases in the cluster with large rotations *RD High*. The GA-ORB-PTAM presents a recognizable smaller error than GA-ORB-PTAM+, which might be caused due to the accumulation of the error in the Kalman filter. This is expected since the gravity-aligned features stabilize the matching in these cases, whereas algorithms such as PTAM and also ORB-SLAM [9] struggle to identify the correct trajectories. The original PTAM algorithm is outperformed in every cluster.

The SIFT descriptor produces higher trajectory errors than the ORB descriptor, especially in *RD Low*. This is related to the fact that SIFT was unable to detect enough keypoints, while FAST produced enough keypoints for the ORB descriptor extraction and matching. It is of interest that for the GA-SIFT implementations an additional UKF (+) improved the tracking accuracy. Thus, a posterior pose update based on the sensor data is more beneficial in case of larger trajectory errors.

6   Computational Costs

The functional runtimes of every frame have been calculated and averaged over all sets. Table 2 depicts the function runtimes of keypoint extraction (KE), descriptor extraction (DE), tracking (T), relocalization (R) and motion model (MM). The experiments have been carried out on an Intel Core i7-4600U (2 cores @ 2.1 GHz).

Table 2. Mean runtimes of different PTAM approaches [ms].

	PTAM	PTAM+	ORB PTAM+	GA-ORB PTAM+	GA-SIFT PTAM+
KE	3.99	4.36	9.83	5.33	488.10
DE	-	-	26.11	16.78	646.08
T	18.21	19.10	13.37	10.07	7.03
R	1.18	1.69	2.17	0.72	2.19
MM	2.09	1.16	1.1	0.64	1.38
Total	25.47	26.30	52.60	33.54	1144.79

It can be seen that the descriptor-based versions perform slightly faster in the tracking stage (T) than their patch-based counterparts. The patch-based PTAM variants create warped patches on four pyramid levels, while the descriptor-based PTAM considers only three pyramid levels. The descriptor-based versions involve a computationally expensive descriptor extraction (DE) stage, which can be completely omitted in the patch-based versions.

Interestingly, ORB-PTAM+ is more time consuming than GA-ORB-PTAM+. The GAFD version allows to detect duplicated keypoints, which are erased prior to the descriptor extraction, thus saving time. The SIFT versions have been parametrized with a smaller number of keypoints to extract (~1000 keypoints), therefore, the matching process is faster in the tracking stage compared to ORB. The total runtimes show that GAFD-ORB-PTAM is around 6 ms slower than the original PTAM algorithm which runs the fastest (25.47 ms), but GAFD-ORB-PTAM is still real-time capable (~32 ms). The SIFT variant is not of practical use even though the number of keypoints has been limited.

7   Conclusion

We proposed two new descriptor maintenance techniques, temporal *pooling* and *bestfit*. The (median) *pooling* technique produced the highest rotational pose accuracy and the lowest absolute trajectory error. Moreover, the new techniques also increased tracking accuracy in combination with gravity-aligned (GA) features, but were even more beneficial when GA features were missing as in cases that lack gyroscope data. The local descriptors without gravity alignment varied much more revealing potential for further improvements. For the sensor fusion, we revealed that a posterior update with a UKF did not improve tracking accuracy if the sensor information is already included into the local features. While still real-time capable, the GA-ORB-PTAM algorithm performed better than the original PTAM, PTAM+ (UKF) as well as EKF-SLAM. Thus, we recommend to use gravity-aligned descriptors instead of incorporating the gyroscope data in a Kalman filter.

Future work should try to find even better maintenance techniques for the feature descriptors. For example, the descriptors could be selected based on a trade-off between the current velocity (motion blur) and viewing angle (texture quality).

References

1. Tiefenbacher, P., Schulze, T., Rigoll, G.: Off-the-shelf sensor integration for mono-SLAM on smart devices. In: Proceedings of the Conference on Computer Vision and Pattern Recognition Workshops, pp. 15–20. IEEE (2015)
2. Aksoy, Y., Alatan, A.A.: Uncertainty modeling for efficient visual odometry via inertial sensors on mobile devices. In: Proceedings of the International Conference on Image Processing. IEEE (2014)
3. Julier, S.J., Uhlmann, J.K.: A new extension of the Kalman filter to nonlinear systems. In: Proceedings of Signal Processing, Sensor Fusion, and Target Recognition, vol. 3068, pp. 182–193 (1997)
4. Servant, F., Houlier, P., Marchand, E.: Improving monocular plane-based SLAM with inertial measures. In: Proceedings of the International Conference on Intelligent Robots and Systems, pp. 3810–3815. IEEE (2010)
5. Kurz, D., Benhimane, S.: Inertial sensor-aligned visual feature descriptors. In: Proceedings of the Conference on Computer Vision and Pattern Recognition, pp. 161–166. IEEE (2011)
6. Klein, G., Murray, D.: Improving the agility of keyframe-based SLAM. In: Forsyth, D., Torr, P., Zisserman, A. (eds.) ECCV 2008. LNCS, vol. 5303, pp. 802–815. Springer, Heidelberg (2008). doi:10.1007/978-3-540-88688-4_59

7. Lowe, D.G.: Distinctive image features from scale-invariant keypoints. Springer Int. J. Comput. Vis. **60**(2), 91–110 (2004)
8. Montemerlo, M., Thrun, S., Koller, D., Wegbreit, B.: FastSLAM 2.0: an improved particle filtering algorithm for simultaneous localization and mapping that provably converges. In: Proceedings of the International Joint Conference on Artificial Intelligence, pp. 1151–1156. IEEE (2003)
9. Mur-Artal, R., Montiel, J., Tardos, J.D.: ORB-SLAM: a versatile and accurate monocular SLAM system. IEEE Trans. Robot. **31**(5), 1147–1163 (2015)
10. Engel, J., Sturm, J., Cremers, D.: Semi-dense visual odometry for a monocular camera. In: Proceedings of the International Conference on Computer Vision, pp. 1449–1456. IEEE (2013)
11. Newcombe, R.A., Lovegrove, S.J., Davison, A.J.: DTAM: dense tracking and mapping in real-time. In: Proceedings of the International Conference on Computer Vision, pp. 2320–2327. IEEE (2011)
12. Engel, J., Schöps, T., Cremers, D.: LSD-SLAM: large-scale direct monocular SLAM. In: Fleet, D., Pajdla, T., Schiele, B., Tuytelaars, T. (eds.) ECCV 2014. LNCS, vol. 8690, pp. 834–849. Springer, Heidelberg (2014). doi:10.1007/978-3-319-10605-2_54
13. Schöps, T., Engel, J., Cremers, D.: Semi-dense visual odometry for AR on a smartphone. In: Proceedings of the International Symposium on Mixed and Augmented Reality, pp. 145–150. IEEE (2014)
14. Omari, S., Ducard, G.: Metric visual-inertial navigation system using single optical flow feature. In: Proceedings of the European Control Conference, pp. 1310–1316. Springer (2013)
15. Bay, H., Ess, A., Tuytelaars, T., Van Gool, L.: Speeded-up robust features (SURF). Elsevier Comput. Vis. Image Underst. **110**(3), 346–359 (2008)
16. Guan, T., He, Y., Gao, J., Yang, J., Yu, J.: On-device mobile visual location recognition by integrating vision and inertial sensors. IEEE Trans. Multimed. **15**(7), 1688–1699 (2013)
17. Jégou, H., Douze, M., Schmid, C., Pérez, P.: Aggregating local descriptors into a compact image representation. In: Proceedings of the Conference on Computer Vision and Pattern Recognition, pp. 3304–3311. IEEE (2010)
18. Rosten, E., Drummond, T.: Fusing points and lines for high performance tracking. In: Proceedings of the International Conference on Computer Vision, vol. 2, pp. 1508–1515. IEEE (2005)
19. Burt, P., Adelson, E.: The Laplacian pyramid as a compact image code. IEEE Trans. Commun. **31**(4), 532–540 (1983)
20. Rublee, E., Rabaud, V., Konolige, K., Bradski, G.: ORB: an efficient alternative to SIFT or SURF. In: Proceedings of the International Conference on Computer Vision, pp. 2564–2571. IEEE (2011)
21. Boureau, Y.L., Ponce, J., LeCun, Y.: A theoretical analysis of feature pooling in visual recognition. In: Proceedings of the International Conference on Machine Learning, pp. 111–118 (2010)
22. Dong, J., Soatto, S.: Domain-size pooling in local descriptors: DSP-SIFT. In: Proceedings of the Conference on Computer Vision and Pattern Recognition, pp. 5097–5106. IEEE (2015)
23. Kurz, D., Benhimane, S.: Handheld augmented reality involving gravity measurements. Elsevier Comput. Graph. **36**(7), 866–883 (2012)
24. Geiger, A., Lenz, P., Urtasun, R.: Are we ready for autonomous driving? The KITTI vision benchmark suite. In: Proceedings of the Conference on Computer Vision and Pattern Recognition, pp. 3354–3361. IEEE (2012)

25. Sturm, J., Engelhard, N., Endres, F., Burgard, W., Cremers, D.: A benchmark for the evaluation of RGB-D SLAM systems. In: Proceedings of the International Conference on Intelligent Robot Systems, pp. 573–580. IEEE (2012)
26. Ovrén, H., Forssén, P.E.: Gyroscope-based video stabilisation with auto-calibration. In: Proceedings of the International Conference on Robotics and Automation, pp. 2090–2097. IEEE (2015)
27. Bianchi, G., Wengert, C., Harders, M., Cattin, P., Szkely, G.: Camera-marker alignment framework and comparison with hand-eye calibration for augmented reality applications. In: Proceedings of the ISMAR, pp. 188–189 (2005)
28. Gramkow, C.: On averaging rotations. Springer J. Math. Imaging Vis. **15**(1–2), 7–16 (2001)
29. Civera, J., Grasa, O.G., Davison, A.J., Montiel, J.M.M.: 1-Point RANSAC for extended Kalman filtering: application to real-time structure from motion and visual odometry. ACM J. Field Robot. **27**(5), 609–631 (2010)

An Evaluation of Local Feature Detectors and Descriptors for Infrared Images

Johan Johansson[1], Martin Solli[2]([✉]), and Atsuto Maki[1]

[1] Royal Institute of Technology (KTH), Stockholm, Sweden
{johanj4,atsuto}@kth.se
[2] FLIR Systems AB, Täby, Sweden
martin.solli@flir.se

Abstract. This paper provides a comparative performance evaluation of local features for infrared (IR) images across different combinations of common detectors and descriptors. Although numerous studies report comparisons of local features designed for ordinary visual images, their performance on IR images is far less charted. We perform a systematic investigation, thoroughly exploiting the established benchmark while also introducing a new IR image data set. The contribution is two-fold: we (i) evaluate the performance of both local float type and more recent binary type detectors and descriptors in their combinations under a variety (6 kinds) of image transformations, and (ii) make a new IR image data set publicly available. Through our investigation we gain novel and useful insights for applying state-of-the art local features to IR images with different properties.

Keywords: Infrared images · Local features · Detectors · Descriptors

1 Introduction

Thermography, also known as infrared (IR) imaging or thermal imaging, is a fast growing field both in research and industry with a wide area of applications. At power stations it is used to monitor the high voltage systems. Construction workers use it to check for defective insulation in houses and firefighters use it as a tool when searching for missing people in buildings on fire. It is also used in various other contexts for surveillance.

In the field of image analysis, especially within computer vision, the majority of the research have focused on regular visual images. Many tasks there comprise the usage of an interest point or feature detector in combination with a feature descriptor. These are, for example, used in subsequent processing to achieve panorama stitching, content based indexing, tracking, reconstruction, recognition etc. Hence, local features play essential roles there, and their development and evaluations have, for many years, been an active research area, resulting in rich knowledge on useful detectors and descriptors.

A research question we pose in this paper is how we can exploit those local features in other types of images, in particular, IR spectral band images, which

© Springer International Publishing Switzerland 2016
G. Hua and H. Jégou (Eds.): ECCV 2016 Workshops, Part III, LNCS 9915, pp. 711–723, 2016.
DOI: 10.1007/978-3-319-49409-8_59

has been less investigated. The fact that IR images and visual images have different characteristics, where IR images typically contain less high frequency information, necessitates an independent study on the performances of common local detectors in combination with descriptors in IR images. In this context, the contributions of this paper are:

(1) the systematic evaluation of local detectors and descriptors in their combinations under six different image transformations using established metrics, and

(2) a new IR image database (http://www.csc.kth.se/~atsuto/dataset.html).

1.1   Related Work

For visual images several detectors and descriptors have been proposed and evaluated in the past. Mikolajczyk and Schmid [1] carried out a performance evaluation of local descriptors in 2005. The local descriptors were then tested on both circular and affine shaped regions with the result of GLOH [1] and SIFT [2] to have the highest performance. They created a database consisting of images of different scene types under different geometric and photometric transformations, which later became a benchmark for visual images.

A thorough evaluation of affine region detectors was also performed in [3]. The focus was to evaluate the performance of affine region detectors under different image condition changes: scale, view-point, blur, rotation, illumination and JPEG compression. Best performance in many cases was obtained by MSER [4] followed by Hessian-Affine [5,6] and Harris-Affine [5,6].

Focusing on fast feature matching, another evaluation [7] was performed more recently for both detectors and descriptors: the comparison of descriptors shows that novel real valued descriptors LIOP [8], MRRID [9] and MROGH [9] outperform state-of-the-art descriptors of SIFT and SURF [10] at the expense of decreased efficiency. Our work is partly inspired by yet another recent evaluation [11] involving exhaustive comparisons on binary features although those are all for visual images.

IR images have been studied in problem domains such as face recognition [12,13], object detection/tracking [14,15], and image enhancement of visual images using near-infrared images [16], to name a few. With respect to local features, a feature point descriptor was addressed for both far-infrared and visual images in [17] while a scale invariant interest point detector of blobs was tested against common detectors on IR images in [18]. This work however did not use the standard benchmark evaluation framework which kept itself from being embedded in comparisons to other results.

The most relevant work to our objective is that of Ricaurte et al. [19] which evaluated classic feature point descriptors in both IR and visible light images under image transformations: rotation, blur, noise and scale. It was reported that SIFT performed the best among several considered descriptors in most of their tests while there is not a clear winner. Nevertheless, unlike their studies on visual images, the evaluation was still limited in that it did not test different combinations of detectors and descriptors while also opting out view-point changes. Nor was it based on the standard evaluation framework [1,3].

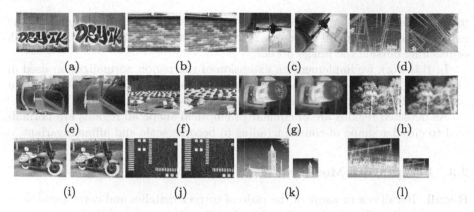

Fig. 1. Examples of images, under various deformations, that are included in the data set. Each image pair consists of a reference image, left, and a test image, right. (a,b) Viewpoint, (c,d) rotation, (e,f) scale, (g,h) blur, (i,j) noise, (k,l) downsampling.

To the best of the authors' knowledge, a thorough performance evaluation for combinations of detectors and descriptors was yet to be made on IR images.

2 Evaluation Framework

The benchmark introduced in [1,3] made well established evaluation frameworks for measuring the performance of detectors and descriptors. We thus choose to use those to ensure the reliability and comparability of the results in this work.

2.1 Matching

To obtain matching features we use nearest neighbours (NN). To become a NN match the two candidates have to be the closest descriptors in descriptor space for both descriptors. The distance between features are calculated with the Euclidean distance for floating point descriptors whereas the Hamming distance is applied to binary descriptors.

Further, a descriptor is only allowed to be matched once, also known as a putative match [11]. Out of the acquired matches, correct matches are identified by comparing the result to the ground truth *correspondences*. The correspondences are the correct matching interest points between a test image and a reference image. For insight in how the ground truth is created see [1].

2.2 Region Normalization

When evaluating descriptors a measurement region larger than the detected region is generally used. The motivation is that blob detectors such as Hessian-Affine and MSER extract regions with large signal variations in the borders. To increase the distinctiveness of extracted regions the measurement region is increased to include larger signal variations. This scale factor is applied to the extracted regions from all detectors. A drawback of the scaling would be the risk of reaching outside the image border.

In this work we implement an extension of the region normalization used in [3] (source available) to expand the image by assigning values to the unknown area by bilinear interpolation on account of the border values.

As detected regions are of circular or elliptical shape all regions are normalized to circular shape of constant radius to become scale and affine invariant.

2.3   Performance Measures

Recall. Recall is a measure of the ratio of correct matches and correspondences (defined in [1]). The measure therefore describes how many of the ground truth matches were actually found.

$$Recall = \frac{\#Correct\ matches}{\#Correspondences} \tag{1}$$

1–Precision. The 1–Precision measure portrays the ratio between the number of false matches and total number of matches (defined in [1]).

$$1 - Precision = \frac{\#False\ matches}{\#Putative\ matches} \tag{2}$$

Matching Score. MS is defined as the ratio of correct matches and again the number of *detected features* visible in the two images.

$$Matching\ Score = \frac{\#Correct\ matches}{\#Detected\ features} \tag{3}$$

2.4   Database

We have generated a new IR image data set for this study. The images contained in the database can be divided into the categories *structured* and *textured* scenes. A textured scene has repetitive patterns of different shapes while a structured scene has homogeneous regions with distinctive edges. In Fig. 1, examples of structured scenes are presented in the odd columns of image pairs and those of textured scenes in the even columns of image pairs. Out of the standard images, captured by the cameras, the database is created by synthetic modification to include the desired image condition changes. An exception is for view-point changes where all images (of mostly planar scenes) were captured with a FLIR T640 camera without modification. The database consists of 118 images in total.

Deformation Specification. The image condition changes we include in the evaluation are six-fold: view-point, scale, rotation, blur, noise and downsampling.

- Images are taken from different view-points starting at 90° angle to the object. The maximum view-point angle is about 50–60° relative to this.
- Zoom is imitated by scaling the height and width of the image using bilinear interpolation. The zoom of the image is in the range ×[1.25–2.5] zoom.
- Rotated images are created from the standard images by 10° increments.
- Images are blurred using a Gaussian kernel of size 51 × 51 pixels and standard deviation up to 10 pixels.
- White Gaussian noise is induced with increasing variance from 0.0001 to 0.005 if the image is normalized to range between 0 and 1.
- Images are downsampled to three reduced sizes; by a factor of 2, 4 and 8.

2.5 Implementation Details

Local features are extracted using OpenCV [20] version 2.4.10 and VLFeat [21] version 0.9.20 libraries. OpenCV implementations are used for SIFT, SURF, MSER, FAST, ORB, BRISK, BRIEF [22] and FREAK [23] while Harris-Affine, Hessian-Affine and LIOP are VLFeat implementations. Unless explicitly stated the parameters are the ones suggested by the authors.

IR images are loaded into MATLAB R2014b using FLIR's Atlas SDK. When loaded in MATLAB the IR images contain 16 bit data which are quantized into 8 bit data and preprocessed by histogram equalization.

To calculate the recall, MS and 1–Precision, this work utilizes code from [3].

Parameter Selection. VLFeat includes implementations of Harris-Laplace and Hessian-Laplace with the possibility of affine shape estimation. To invoke the detectors functions there are parameters to control a peak and edge threshold.

The peak threshold affects the minimum acceptable cornerness measure for a feature to be considered as a corner in Harris-Affine and equivalently a blob by the determinant of the Hessian matrix in Hessian-Affine. According to the authors of [5] the used value for the threshold on cornerness was 1000. As no similar value is found to the Hessian-Affine threshold it is selected to 150. With the selected threshold the number of extracted features is in the order of magnitude as other detectors in the evaluation. The edge threshold is an edge rejection threshold and eliminates points with too small curvature. It is selected to the predetermined value of 10.

Regarding the region normalization, we choose a diameter of 49 pixels whereas 41 pixels is chosen arbitrary in [1]. The choice of a larger diameter is based on the standard settings in the OpenCV library for the BRIEF descriptor.

3   Evaluation Results

This section presents the results of combinations of the detectors and descriptors which are listed in Table 1. The evaluation is divided into floating point and binary point combinations, with the exceptions Harris-Affine combined with ORB and BRISK, and SURF combined with BRIEF and FREAK. The combination of Harris-Affine and ORB showed good performance in [11], while BRISK is combined with Harris-Affine as the descriptor showed good performance throughout this work. SURF is combined with binary descriptors as it is known to outperform other floating point detectors in computational speed. Combinations which are also tested in the evaluation on visual images in [7].

Evaluated combinations are entitled by a concatenation of the detector and descriptor with hes and har being short for Hessian-Affine and Harris-Affine. In case of no concatenation, e.g. orb, both ORB detector and descriptor are applied.

The performances are presented in precision-recall curves for the structured scenes, Fig. 2, and for the textured scenes, Fig. 3. We also present the average results of both scene types in recall, precision and MS for each transformation. Here the threshold is set to accept all obtained matches as a threshold would be dependent on descriptor size and descriptor type.

3.1 Precision-Recall Curve

Recall and 1–Precision are commonly combined to visualize the performance of descriptors. It is created by varying an acceptance threshold for the distance between two NN matched features in the descriptor space. If the threshold is small, one is strict in acquiring correct matches which leads to high precision but low recall. A high threshold means that we accept all possible matches which leads to low precision, due to many false positives, and a high recall since all correct matches are accepted. Ideally a recall equal to one is obtained for any precision. In real world applications this is not the case as noise etc. might decrease the similarity between descriptors. Another factor arises while regions can be considered as correspondences with an overlap error up to 50 %, hence descriptors will describe information in areas not covered by the other region. A descriptor with a slowly increasing curve indicates that it is affected by the image deformation.

3.2 Results

View-Point. The effect of view-point changes on different combinations is illustrated in Fig. 2a and b for the structured scene in Fig. 1a, while the results of the textured scene in Fig. 1b are presented in Fig. 3a and b. The average of the performances against perspective changes in the structured and textured scenes are presented in Table 2a.

From the result it is clear that the performance varies depending on the scene and the combination. In the structured scene all combinations show dependency to perspective changes by a slow continuous increase in recall. Best performances among floating point descriptors are obtained by mser-liop and hes-liop.

Table 1. Included binary and floating point detectors and descriptors. Binary types are marked with (*)

Detectors		Descriptors	
Hessian-Affine	SURF	LIOP	BRISK*
Harris-Affine	BRISK*	SIFT	FREAK*
MSER	FAST*	SURF	ORB*
SIFT	ORB*	BRIEF*	

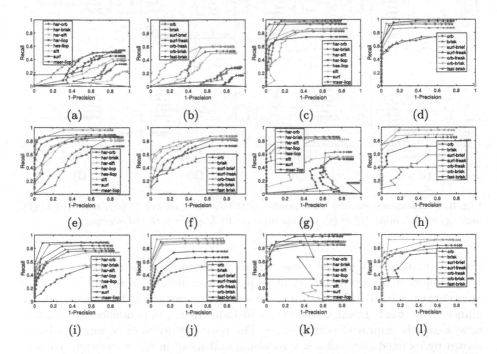

Fig. 2. Performance against view-point (a) & (b), rotation (c) & (d), scale (e) & (f), blur (g) & (h), noise (i) & (j), downsampling (k) & (l) in *structured scenes*.

Among binary combinations the best performance is obtained by orb-brisk, for both scenes, with results comparable to the best performers in the floating point family of combinations. Consecutive in performance are orb and orb-freak indicating how combinations based on the ORB detector outperform other binary combinations based on BRISK and FAST.

Rotation. The results of the combinations due to rotation are illustrated in Fig. 2c and d, for the structured scene in Fig. 1c, and in Fig. 3c and d, for the textured scene in Fig. 1d. The average results are presented in Table 2b.

We observe that the overall performance is much higher for rotation than for view-point changes. The majority of combinations has high performance in both

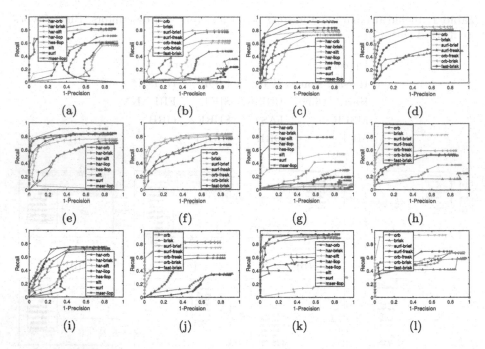

Fig. 3. Performance against view-point (a) & (b), rotation (c) & (d), scale (e) & (f), blur (g) & (h), noise (i) & (j), downsampling (k) & (l) in *textured scenes*.

the structured and textured scene. Figure 2d shows an illustrative example of how different detectors and descriptors perform in different setups. For example `surf-brief`, with BRIEF known to be sensitive to rotation, has a poor performance while `surf-freak` and `surf`, still indicating a dependence to rotation, have a greatly improved performance. The poor performance of `surf-brief` is shown by its fixed curve at a low precision and recall in the lower right corner.

Overall best performance is achieved by `hes-liop` followed by `har-liop` among floating point combinations, while for binary methods best performance is obtained by `orb-brisk`, `orb` and `orb-freak`.

Scale. The effects from scaling are shown in Fig. 2e and f for the structured scene in Fig. 1e, and in Fig. 3e and f for the textured scene in Fig. 1f. The average results are presented in Table 2c.

The combinations show a stable behavior with similar performance in both scene types. Among floating point combinations, best performance is achieved by `mser-liop` succeeded by `hes-liop`. The top performers within binary combinations are `surf-brief`, `orb-freak` and `orb-brisk`.

Blur. The results of combinations applied to images smoothed by a Gaussian kernel can be seen in Fig. 2g and h for the scene in Fig. 1g, and in Fig. 3g and h, for the scene in Fig. 1h. Combinations average results are presented in Table 2d.

Best performance among floating point combinations is attained by `surf`, outperforming other combinations in stability, which is visualized by a horizontal precision-recall curve. It is followed by `sift` and `hes-liop`. Overall best performance can be found in the category of binary combinations, with `surf-brief` as the top performer, outperforming floating point combinations. The consecutive performers are `orb-brisk` and `orb` which achieve best performance among corner based combinations, with comparable or better results than blob based combinations.

Table 2. Average performance when using NN as matching strategy by the measures: precision, recall and Matching Score (MS).

(a) Viewpoint

Combination	Precicion	Recall	MS
har-orb	19.6	40.8	19.6
har-brisk	22.9	47.3	22.9
har-sift	21.5	45.1	21.5
har-liop	26.3	54.9	26.3
hes-liop	41.8	62.8	41.8
sift	14.6	39.6	14.6
surf	31.7	44.0	31.7
mser-liop	30.1	71.1	30.1
orb	39.2	56.2	39.2
brisk	20.7	42.2	20.7
surf-brief	37.6	51.8	37.6
surf-freak	27.8	38.2	27.8
orb-freak	38.1	55.3	38.1
orb-brisk	43.0	62.1	43.0
fast-brisk	15.4	28.6	15.4

(b) Rotation

Combination	Precicion	Recall	MS
har-orb	59.1	76.8	59.1
har-brisk	63.7	82.5	63.7
har-sift	61.3	79.6	61.3
har-liop	74.1	96.2	74.1
hes-liop	84.9	95.5	84.9
sift	44.2	76.4	44.2
surf	62.7	75.3	62.7
mser-liop	67.0	88.0	67.0
orb	76.6	87.4	76.6
brisk	37.7	63.5	37.7
surf-brief	7.2	8.4	7.2
surf-freak	54.7	65.7	54.7
orb-freak	71.4	81.5	71.4
orb-brisk	79.2	90.4	79.2
fast-brisk	61.6	75.0	61.6

(c) Scale

Combination	Precicion	Recall	MS
har-orb	44.6	75.7	44.6
har-brisk	45.8	82.9	45.8
har-sift	48.0	81.5	48.0
har-liop	53.6	90.9	53.6
hes-liop	65.0	91.0	65.0
sift	57.5	83.4	57.5
surf	60.7	81.2	60.7
mser-liop	74.2	97.0	74.2
orb	60.5	82.1	60.5
brisk	35.1	59.6	35.1
surf-brief	64.8	86.6	64.8
surf-freak	54.8	73.2	54.8
orb-freak	62.8	85.5	62.8
orb-brisk	62.7	84.9	62.7
fast-brisk	11.2	13.3	11.2

(d) Blur

Combination	Precicion	Recall	MS
har-orb	19.5	30.9	19.5
har-brisk	29.8	47.8	29.8
har-sift	20.2	32.0	20.2
har-liop	24.5	38.4	24.5
hes-liop	53.7	57.3	53.7
sift	35.7	60.9	35.7
surf	63.4	66.7	63.4
mser-liop	24.4	33.0	24.4
orb	60.4	71.0	60.4
brisk	21.5	53.4	21.5
surf-brief	82.4	86.5	82.4
surf-freak	62.8	66.0	62.8
orb-freak	38.7	45.6	38.7
orb-brisk	67.9	79.6	67.9
fast-brisk	33.1	34.2	33.1

(e) Noise

Combination	Precicion	Recall	MS
har-orb	51.9	65.2	51.9
har-brisk	67.9	85.8	67.9
har-sift	51.1	64.1	51.1
har-liop	68.7	86.8	68.7
hes-liop	76.5	88.8	76.5
sift	45.7	72.9	45.7
surf	73.5	80.7	73.5
mser-liop	69.2	86.5	69.2
orb	81.7	91.0	81.7
brisk	47.5	62.3	47.5
surf-brief	79.1	86.9	79.1
surf-freak	69.6	76.5	69.6
orb-freak	76.1	84.7	76.1
orb-brisk	83.8	93.4	83.8
fast-brisk	63.0	65.1	63.0

(f) Downsampling

Combination	Precicion	Recall	MS
har-orb	47.6	68.2	47.6
har-brisk	59.4	86.2	59.4
har-sift	51.0	73.5	51.0
har-liop	60.8	88.6	60.8
hes-liop	65.3	88.3	65.3
sift	26.9	36.7	26.9
surf	78.2	85.8	78.2
mser-liop	39.5	72.0	39.5
orb	28.3	53.2	28.3
brisk	15.9	42.7	15.9
surf-brief	82.4	90.5	82.4
surf-freak	61.5	67.8	61.5
orb-freak	27.2	50.5	27.2
orb-brisk	29.8	55.8	29.8
fast-brisk			

Noise. The performance of combinations applied to images with induced white Gaussian noise is presented in Fig. 2i and j for the structured scene in Fig. 1i. The corresponding results for the textured scene in Fig. 1j are shown in Fig. 3i and j. The average results of the two scenes against noise are presented in Table 2e.

The overall performance for various combinations is relatively high. Best performance among floating point combinations are attained by `hes-liop` and `surf`, stagnating at about the same level of recall in the precision-recall curves for both scenes and in Table 2e. The overall best performance in the case of induced noise is achieved by `orb-brisk` followed by `orb` and `surf-brief` showing better performance than the floating point category.

Downsampling. Last, we evaluate the effect on combinations caused by down-sampling and present the results in Fig. 2k and l for the structured scene in Fig. 1k. For the textured scene in Fig. 1l the results are presented in Fig. 3k and l. The obtained average results for NN matching are presented in Table 2f.

Studying the precision-recall curves of floating point methods and Table 2f, the best performers on downsampled images are `surf`, `hes-liop` and `har-liop` and `har-brisk`. Among binary methods the best performance is obtained by `surf-brief`, with better results than `surf`, with `surf-freak`, `orb-brisk` and `orb` to come after. MSER does in Fig. 2k reach a 100 % recall which can be explained by that very few regions are detected.

4   Comparisons to Results in Earlier Work

4.1   IR Images

The most related work in the long wave infrared (LWIR) spectral band [19] shows both similarities and differences to the results in this work. Best performance against blur is in both evaluations obtained by SURF. For rotation and scale best performance is achieved by SIFT in the compared evaluation while LIOP, not included in mentioned evaluation, shows highest robustness to the deformation in this work.

Among binary combinations [19] presents a low performance for ORB and BRISK with their default detectors. In this work the low performance of the combination of BRISK is observed while the combination of ORB is a top performer among binary methods. An important difference between these two evaluations is that we have performed a comparison of numerous detector and descriptor combinations, which have led to the conclusion of a good match of the ORB detector and BRISK descriptor.

4.2   Visual Images

In the evaluation of binary methods for visual images in [24], it is obvious how the combination of detector and descriptor might affect the performance. When evaluating descriptors with their default detectors, BRISK and FREAK perform much worse than when combined with the ORB detector. Best overall performance was obtained by ORB detector in combination with FREAK or BRISK descriptors and ORB combined with FREAK is the suggested combination to use. In this work we have observed that BRISK with its default detector performed worse, in most categories the worst, compared to when in combination with the ORB detector while the combination of ORB and FREAK has lower performance in the LWIR spectral band. With the high performance of the combination of ORB and BRISK we can conclude that the choice of combination has large effect on the performance both in visual images and IR images.

Another similarity is the high performance by Hessian-Affine with LIOP in [8] and in this work as well as by the combination of SURF which shows high performance in both spectral bands.

5   Conclusions and Future Directions

We have performed a systematic investigation on the performance of state-of-the-art local feature detectors and descriptors on infrared images, justified by the needs in various vision applications, such as image stitching, recognition, etc. While doing so, we have also generated a new IR image data set and made it publicly available. Through the extensive evaluations we have gained useful insight as to what local features to use according to expected transformation properties of the input images as well as the requirement for efficiency. It should be highlighted that the combination of detector and descriptor should be considered as it can outperform the standard combination. As the consequence of our comparisons at large, Hessian-Affine with LIOP, and SURF detector with SURF descriptor have shown good performance to many of the geometric and photometric transformations. Among binary detectors and descriptors competitive results are received with the combination of ORB and BRISK.

Compared to the most relevant work by Ricaurte et al. [19] this work evaluated performances against viewpoint changes, the LIOP descriptor, float type detectors as Hessian-Affine and Harris-Affine including different combinations of detectors and descriptors, filling the gap of evaluations for IR images.

In future research we will extend the study from those hand crafted features to learning based representations such as RFD [25] as well as those [26,27] obtained by deep convolutional networks which were shown to be very effective for a range of visual recognition tasks [28–30]. Fischer et al. [31] demonstrated that those descriptors perform consistently better than SIFT also in the low-level task of descriptor matching. Although the networks are typically trained on the ImageNet data set consisting of visual images, it will be interesting to see if such a network is applicable to extracting descriptors in IR images (via transfer learning), or one would need yet another large data set of IR images to train a deep convolutional network. Nevertheless, the study in this direction is beyond the scope of this paper and left for the subject of our next comparison.

References

1. Mikolajczyk, K., Schmid, C.: A performance evaluation of local descriptors. TPAMI **27**(10), 1615–1630 (2005)
2. Lowe, D.G.: Distinctive image features from scale-invariant keypoints. IJCV **60**(2), 91–110 (2004)
3. Mikolajczyk, K., Tuytelaars, T., Schmid, C., Zisserman, A., Matas, J., Schaffalitzky, F., Kadir, T., Gool, L.: A comparison of affine region detectors. IJCV **65**(1-2), 43–72 (2005). http://www.robots.ox.ac.uk/~vgg/research/affine/
4. Matas, J., Chum, O., Urban, M., Pajdla, T.: Robust wide baseline stereo from maximally stable extremal regions. In: BMVC, pp. 36.1–36.10 (2002)
5. Mikolajczyk, K., Schmid, C.: An affine invariant interest point detector. In: Heyden, A., Sparr, G., Nielsen, M., Johansen, P. (eds.) ECCV 2002. LNCS, vol. 2353, pp. 128–142. Springer, Heidelberg (2002). doi:10.1007/3-540-47969-4_9
6. Mikolajczyk, K., Schmid, C.: Scale & affine invariant interest point detectors. IJCV **60**(1), 63–86 (2004)

7. Miksik, O., Mikolajczyk, K.: Evaluation of local detectors and descriptors for fast feature matching. In: ICPR, pp. 2681–2684 (2012)
8. Wang, Z., Fan, B., Wu, F.: Local intensity order pattern for feature description. In: ICCV, pp. 603–610 (2011)
9. Fan, B., Wu, F., Hu, Z.: Rotationally invariant descriptors using intensity order pooling. TPAMI **34**(10), 2031–2045 (2012)
10. Bay, H., Ess, A., Tuytelaars, T., Van Gool, L.: Speeded-up robust features (SURF). Comput. Vis. Image Underst. **110**(3), 346–359 (2008)
11. Heinly, J., Dunn, E., Frahm, J.-M.: Comparative evaluation of binary features. In: Fitzgibbon, A., Lazebnik, S., Perona, P., Sato, Y., Schmid, C. (eds.) ECCV 2012. LNCS, vol. 7578, pp. 759–773. Springer, Heidelberg (2012). doi:10.1007/978-3-642-33709-3_54
12. Li, S., Zhang, L., Liao, S., Zhu, X., Chu, R., Ao, M., He, R.: A near-infrared image based face recognition system. In: 7th International Conference on Automatic Face and Gesture Recognition, pp. 455–460 (2006)
13. Maeng, H., Choi, H.C., Park, U., Lee, S.W., Jain, A.: NFRAD: near-infrared face recognition at a distance. In: International Joint Conference on Biometrics, IJCB, pp. 1–7 (2011)
14. Strehl, A., Aggarwal, J.: Detecting moving objects in airborne forward looking infra-red sequences. In: Proceedings IEEE Workshop on Computer Vision Beyond the Visible Spectrum: Methods and Applications, pp. 3–12 (1999)
15. Broggi, A., Fedriga, R., Tagliati, A.: Pedestrian detection on a moving vehicle: an investigation about near infra-red images. In: Intelligent Vehicles Symposium, pp. 431–436. IEEE (2006)
16. Zhang, X., Sim, T., Miao, X.: Enhancing photographs with near infra-red images. In: CVPR, pp. 1–8 (2008)
17. Aguilera, C., Barrera, F., Lumbreras, F., Sappa, A.D., Toledo, R.: Multispectral image feature points. Sensors **12**(9), 12661–12672 (2012)
18. Ferraz, L., Binefa, X.: A scale invariant interest point detector for discriminative blob detection. In: Paredes, R., Cardoso, J.S., Pardo, X.M. (eds.) IbPRIA 2015. LNCS, vol. 9117, pp. 233–240. Springer, Heidelberg (2009). doi:10.1007/978-3-642-02172-5_31
19. Ricaurte, P., Chilán, C., Aguilera-Carrasco, C.A., Vintimilla, B.X., Sappa, A.D.: Feature point descriptors: infrared and visible spectra. Sensors **14**(2), 3690–3701 (2014)
20. Bradski, G.: OpenCV, open source computer vision. Dr. Dobb's Journal of Software Tools (2000)
21. Vedaldi, A., Fulkerson, B.: VLFeat: an open and portable library of computer vision algorithms (2008). http://www.vlfeat.org/
22. Calonder, M., Lepetit, V., Strecha, C., Fua, P.: BRIEF: binary robust independent elementary features. In: Daniilidis, K., Maragos, P., Paragios, N. (eds.) ECCV 2010. LNCS, vol. 6316, pp. 778–792. Springer, Heidelberg (2010). doi:10.1007/978-3-642-15561-1_56
23. Alahi, A., Ortiz, R., Vandergheynst, P.: FREAK: fast retina keypoint. In: CVPR, pp. 510–517 (2012)
24. Figat, J., Kornuta, T., Kasprzak, W.: Performance evaluation of binary descriptors of local features. In: Chmielewski, L.J., Datta, A., Kozera, R., Wojciechowski, K. (eds.) ICCVG 2016. LNCS, vol. 9972, pp. 187–194. Springer, Heidelberg (2014). doi:10.1007/978-3-319-11331-9_23

25. Fan, B., Kong, Q., Trzcinski, T., Wang, Z., Pan, C., Fua, P.: Receptive fields selection for binary feature description. IEEE Trans. Image Process. **23**(6), 2583–2595 (2014)
26. Balntas, V., Johns, E., Tang, L., Mikolajczyk, K.: PN-Net: conjoined triple deep network for learning local image descriptors. CoRR abs/1601.05030 (2016)
27. Simo-Serra, E., Trulls, E., Ferraz, L., Kokkinos, I., Fua, P., Moreno-Noguer, F.: Discriminative learning of deep convolutional feature point descriptors. In: ICCV (2015)
28. Zeiler, M.D., Fergus, R.: Visualizing and understanding convolutional networks. In: Fleet, D., Pajdla, T., Schiele, B., Tuytelaars, T. (eds.) ECCV 2014. LNCS, vol. 8693, pp. 818–833. Springer, Heidelberg (2014). doi:10.1007/978-3-319-10590-1_53
29. Donahue, J., Jia, Y., Vinyals, O., Hoffman, J., Zhang, N., Tzeng, E., Darrell, T.: Decaf: a deep convolutional activation feature for generic visual recognition. In: ICLR (2014)
30. Girshick, R.B., Donahue, J., Darrell, T., Malik, J.: Rich feature hierarchies for accurate object detection and semantic segmentation. In: CVPR (2014)
31. Fischer, P., Dosovitskiy, A., Brox, T.: Descriptor matching with convolutional neural networks: a comparison to SIFT. arXiv:1405.5769 (2014)

Evaluating Local Features for Day-Night Matching

Hao Zhou[1(✉)], Torsten Sattler[2], and David W. Jacobs[1]

[1] University of Maryland, College Park, MD, USA
hzhou@cs.umd.edu, djacobs@umiacs.umd.edu
[2] Department of Computer Science, ETH Zurich, Zurich, Switzerland
sattlert@inf.ethz.ch

Abstract. This paper evaluates the performance of local features in the presence of large illumination changes that occur between day and night. Through our evaluation, we find that repeatability of detected features, as a de facto standard measure, is not sufficient in evaluating the performance of feature detectors; we must also consider the distinctiveness of the features. Moreover, we find that feature detectors are severely affected by illumination changes between day and night and that there is great potential to improve both feature detectors and descriptors.

Keywords: Feature detector · Day-night image matching · Performance evaluation · Illumination changes

1 Introduction

Feature detection and matching is one of the central problems in computer vision and a key step in many applications such as Structure-from-Motion [18], 3D reconstruction [3], place recognition [20], image-based localization [27], Augmented Reality and robotics [7], and image retrieval [17]. Many of these applications require robustness under changes in viewpoint. Consequently, research on feature detectors [8,10,12,13,24,25] and descriptors [2,6,16,22] has for a long time focused on improving their stability under viewpoint changes. Only recently has robustness against seasonal [19] and illumination changes [21,24] come into focus. Especially the latter is important for large-scale localization and place recognition applications, *e.g.*, for autonomous vehicles. In these scenarios, the underlying visual representation is often obtained by taking photos during daytime and it is infeasible to capture large-scale scenes also during nighttime.

Many popular feature detectors such as Difference of Gaussians (DoG) [6], Harris-affine [9], and Maximally Stable Extremal Regions (MSER) [8], as well as the popular SIFT descriptor [6] are invariant against (locally) uniform changes in illumination. However, the illumination changes that can be observed between day and night are often highly non-uniform, especially in urban environments (*cf.* Fig. 1). Recent work has shown that this causes problems for standard feature detectors: Verdie *et al.* [24] demonstrated that a detector specifically trained

© Springer International Publishing Switzerland 2016
G. Hua and H. Jégou (Eds.): ECCV 2016 Workshops, Part III, LNCS 9915, pp. 724–736, 2016.
DOI: 10.1007/978-3-319-49409-8_60

to handle temporal changes significantly outperforms traditional detectors in challenging conditions such as day-night illumination variations. Torii *et al.* [20] observed that foregoing the feature detection stage and densely extracting descriptors instead results in a better matching quality when comparing daytime and nighttime images. Naturally, these results lead to a set of interesting questions: (i) to what extent is the feature detection stage affected by the illumination changes between day and night? (ii) the number of repeatable features provides an upper bound on how many correspondences can be found via descriptor matching. How tight is this bound, *i.e.*, is finding repeatable feature detections the main challenge of day-night matching? (iii) how much potential is there to improve the matching performance of local detectors and descriptors, *i.e.*, is it worthwhile to invest more time in the day-night matching problem?

In this paper, we aim at answering these questions through extensive quantitative experiments, with the goal of stimulating further research on the topic of day-night feature matching. We are interested in analyzing the impact of day-night changes on feature detection and matching performance. Thus, we eliminate the impact of viewpoint changes by collecting a large dataset of daytime and nighttime images from publicly available webcams [5][1]. Through our experiments on this large dataset, we find that: (i) the repeatability of feature detectors for day-night image pairs is much smaller than that for day-day and night-night image pairs, meaning that detectors are severely affected by illumination changes between day and night; (ii) for day-night image pairs, high repeatability of feature detectors does not necessarily lead to a high matching performance. For example, the TILDE [24] detector specifically learned for handling illumination changes has a very high repeatability, but the precision and recall of matching local features are very low. A low recall shows that the number of repeatable points provides a loose bound for the number of correspondences that could be found via descriptor matching. As a result, further research is necessary for improving both detectors and descriptors; (iii) through dense local feature matching, we find that there are a lot more correspondences that could be found using local descriptors than are produced by current detectors, *i.e.*, there is great potential to improve detectors for day-night feature matching.

2   Dataset

Illumination and viewpoint changes are two main factors that would affect the performance of feature detectors and descriptors. Ideally, both detectors and descriptors should be robust to both type of changes. However, obtaining a large dataset with both types of changes with ground truth transformations is difficult. In this paper, we thus focus on pure illumination changes and collect data that does not contain any viewpoint changes. Our results show that already this simpler version of the day-night matching problem is very hard.

---

[1] Please find the data set at http://www.umiacs.umd.edu/~hzhou/dnim.html.

Fig. 1. Images taken from 00:00–23:00 in one image sequence of our dataset.

The AMOS dataset [5], which contains a huge number of images taken (usually) every half an hour by outdoor webcams with fixed positions and orientations, satisfies our requirements perfectly. [24] has collected 6 sequences of images taken at different times of the day for training illumination robust detectors from the AMOS dataset. However, the dataset has no time stamps and some of the sequences have no nighttime images. As a consequence, we collect our own dataset from AMOS. 17 image sequences with relatively high resolution containing 1722 images are selected. Since the time stamps of the images provided by AMOS are usually not correct, we choose image sequences with time stamp watermarks. The time of the images will be decided by the watermarks which are removed afterwards. For each image sequence, images taken in one or two days are collected. Figure 1 gives an example of images we collected.

3   Evaluation

3.1   Keypoint Detectors

For evaluation, we focus on the keypoint detectors most commonly used in practice. We choose DoG [6], Hessian, HessianLaplace, MultiscaleHessian, Harris-Laplace and MultiscaleHarris [9] implemented by vlfeat [23] for evaluation. Their default parameters are used to determine how well these commonly used settings perform under strong illumination changes. DoG detects feature points as the extrema of the difference of Gaussian functions. By considering the extrema of the difference of two images, DoG detections are invariant against additive or multiplicative (affine) changes in illumination. Hessian, HessianLaplace and MultiscaleHessian are based on the Hessian matrix $\begin{pmatrix} L_{xx}(\sigma) & L_{xy}(\sigma) \\ L_{yx}(\sigma) & L_{yy}(\sigma) \end{pmatrix}$, where L represents the image smoothed by a Gaussian with standard deviation σ and L_{xx}, L_{xy}, and L_{yy} are the second-order derivatives of L. Hessian detects feature points as the local maxima of the determinant of the Hessian matrix. Hessian-Laplace chooses a scale for the Hessian detector that maximizes the normalized Laplacian $|\sigma^2(L_{xx}(\sigma) + L_{yy}(\sigma))|$. MultiscaleHessian instead applies the Hessian detector on multiple scales of images and detects feature points at each scale

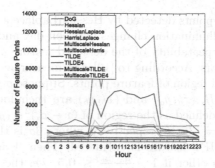

Fig. 2. The number of feature points detected at different time

independently. HarrisLaplace and MultiscaleHarris extended the Harris corner detector to multiple scales in a similar way to HessianLaplace and Multiscale-Hessian. The Harris corner detector is based on the determinant and trace of the second moment matrix of gradient distribution. All these gradient based methods are essentially invariant to additive and multiplicative illumination changes.

We also included the learning based detector TILDE [24], since it is designed to be robust to illumination changes. We use the model trained on the St. Louis sequence as it has the highest repeatability when testing on the other image sequences [24]. TILDE detects feature points at a fixed scale. In this paper, we define a multiple scale version by detecting features at multiple scales, denoted as MultiscaleTILDE. Feature points are detected from the original image and images smoothed by a Gaussian with standard deviation of 2 and 4. When TILDE detects feature points from the original image, the scale of it is set to be 10. Accordingly, the scale of detected feature points from those three images are set to be 10, 20 and 40. As suggested by [24], we keep a fixed number of feature points based on the resolution of the image. For the proposed MultiscaleTILDE, the same number of feature points as that of TILDE are selected for the first scale. For other scales, the number of feature points selected are reduced by half compared with the previous scale. In modified versions, we include 4 times as many points as suggested, naming these TILDE4 and MultiscaleTILDE4 respectively.

3.2 Repeatability of Detectors

In this section we address the question: **to what extent are feature detections affected by illumination changes between day and night?** by evaluating how many feature points are detected, and how repeatable they are. First we show the number of detected feature points at different times of the day for different detectors in Fig. 2. The numbers are averaged from all 17 image sequences in our dataset. The number of feature points for TILDE is the same across different times, since a fixed number of feature points are extracted. For the other detectors, fewer feature points are detected at nighttime. Especially, the number of feature points detected by HessianLaplace and MultiscaleHessian are affected most by illumination changes between day and night.

We then use the repeatability of the detected feature points to evaluate the performance of detectors. According to [10], the measurement of repeatability is related to the detected region of feature points. Suppose σ_a and σ_b are the scale of two points A and B, (x_a, y_a) and (x_b, y_b) are their locations, the detected regions μ_a and μ_b are defined as the region of $(x - x_a)^2 + (y - y_a)^2 = (3\sigma_a)^2$ and $(x - x_b)^2 + (y - y_b)^2 = (3\sigma_b)^2$ respectively, where 3σ is the size of one spatial bin from which the SIFT feature is extracted. Then A and B are considered to correspond to each other if $1 - \frac{\mu_a \cap \mu_b}{\mu_a \cup \mu_b} \leq 0.5$, $i.e.$ the intersection of these two regions are larger than or equal to half of the union of these two regions. This overlap error is the same as the one proposed in [10] except that we do not normalize the region size. This is because if the detected regions do not overlap, we cannot extract matchable feature descriptors; normalizing the size of the region would obscure this. For example, two regions with small scales may be judged to correspond after normalization. However, the detected region from which the feature descriptor is extracted may not overlap at all, making it impossible to extract feature descriptors to match them.

Some of the images in our dataset may contain moving objects. To avoid the effect of those objects, we define "ground truth" points and compute the repeatability of detectors at different times w.r.t. them. To make the experiments comprehensive, we use daytime ground truth and nighttime ground truth. Images taken at 10:00 to 14:00 are used to get the daytime ground truth feature points (and 00:00 to 02:00 together with 21:00 to 23:00 for nighttime ground truth feature points). We select the image that has the largest number of detected feature points and match them to those in other images in that time period. A feature point is chosen as a ground truth if it appears in more than half of all the images of that time period. Figure 3(a) and (b) shows the number of daytime and nighttime ground truth feature points detected for different detectors respectively. We notice that though Fig. 2 shows the number of detected feature points for TILDE4 at daytime is the second smallest among all the detectors, the number of daytime ground truth feature points of TILDE4 is larger than 6 detectors. This implies that the feature points detected by TILDE4 for daytime images are quite stable across different images.

We use these ground truth feature points to compute the repeatability of the chosen detectors over different times of the day. Thus, repeatability is determined by measuring how often the ground truth points are re-detected. Figure 3(c) and (d) show that the repeatability of features for nighttime images w.r.t. nighttime ground truth is very high for all the detectors; this is because the illumination of nighttime images are usually quite stable without the effect of sunlight (cf. Fig. 1). For comparison, the repeatability of daytime images w.r.t. daytime ground truth is smaller and the performance of different detectors varies a lot. Moreover, both Fig. 3(c) and (d) show that the repeatability of day-night image pairs is very low for most detectors, which implies that detectors are heavily affected by day-night illumination changes. The drop-off between 05:00–07:00

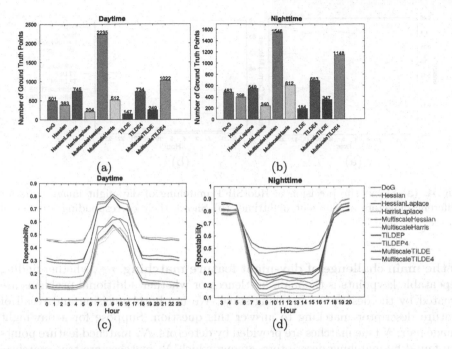

Fig. 3. (a) and (b) Show average number of daytime and nighttime ground truth feature points for each detector respectively. We show repeatability of different detectors at different times of the day w.r.t. (c) Daytime and (d) Nightime ground truth feature points. Please note time periods that are used to compute the ground truth feature points are excluded for fair comparison.

and 17:00–18:00 is caused by illumination changes between dusk and dawn. The peaks of the repeatability, as 09:00 in Fig. 3(c) and 03:00 and 20:00 in Fig. 3(d), appear because they are close to the time from which the ground truth feature points are computed. Among all the detectors, both single scale and multiple scale TILDE have high repeatabilities of around 50 % for day-night image pairs. This is not surprising since the TILDE detector was constructed to be robust to illumination changes by learning the impact of these changes from data. Based on the fact that nearly every second TILDE keypoint is repeatable, we would expect that TILDE is well-suited for feature matching between day and night.

3.3 Matching Day-Night Image Pairs

In theory, every repeatable keypoint should be matchable with a descriptor since its corresponding regions in the two images have a high overlap. In practice, the number of repeatable keypoints is only an upper bound since the descriptors extracted from the regions might not match. For example, local illumination changes might lead to very different descriptors. In this section, we thus study the performance of detector+descriptor on matching day-night image pairs. We try to answer the question **whether finding repeatable feature detections**

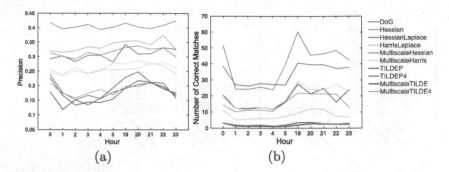

Fig. 4. (a) Shows the precision of RootSIFT matching of day-night image pairs for different detectors at different nighttime. (b) Shows their corresponding number of correct matched feature points.

is the main challenge of day-night feature matching, *i.e.*, whether finding repeatable keypoints is the main bottleneck or whether additional problems are created by the descriptor matching stage. We use both precision and recall of feature descriptor matching to answer this question. Suppose for a day-night image pair, N true matches are provided by detectors. N_f matched feature points are found by matching descriptors, among which N_c matches are true matches. Then the precision and recall of detector+descriptor are defined as N_c/N_f and N_c/N, respectively. Precision is a usual way to evaluate the accuracy of matching by detector+descriptor. Recall, on the other hand, tells us what is the main challenge to increase the number of matches. A low recall means improving feature descriptors is the key to getting more matches. On the contrary, feature detection is the bottleneck for getting more matches if a high recall is observed, but still an insufficient number of matching features are found.

For each image sequence, images taken at 00:00–05:00 and 19:00–23:00 are used as nighttime images and those taken at 09:00–16:00 are daytime images. One image is randomly selected from each hour in these time periods and every nighttime image is paired with every daytime image to create the day-night image pairs. As the SIFT descriptor is still the first choice in many computer vision problems, and its extension, RootSIFT [1] performs better than SIFT, we use RootSIFT as the feature descriptor. To match descriptors, we use nearest neighbor search and apply Lowe's ratio test [6] to remove unstable matches. The default ratio provided by vlfeat [23] is used in our evaluation. In practice, the ratio test is used to reject wrong correspondences but also rejects correct matches. The run-time of subsequent geometric estimation stages typically depends on the percentage of wrong matches. Sacrificing recall for precision is thus often preferred since there is enough redundancy in the matches.

The precisions of matching day-night images for all the detectors at different daytimes are shown in Fig. 4(a). We found that though different versions of TILDE have the highest repeatability among all the detectors, in general, they have the lowest precision. There are more than 20 % drop in precision w.r.t.

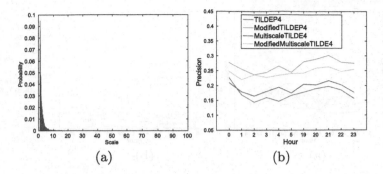

(a)   (b)

Fig. 5. (a) Shows the histogram of scales for correctly matched RootSIFT features using DoG as detector. (b) Compares the precision of TILDE4 and MultiscaleTILDE4 with small and large scales.

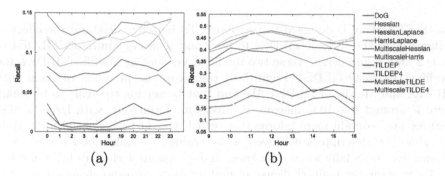

(a)   (b)

Fig. 6. (a) Shows the recall of RootSIFT matching of day-night image pairs for different detectors at different nighttimes. (b) Shows the recall of RootSIFT matching of day-day image pairs for different detectors at different daytimes.

DoG in most cases. This shows that a higher repeatability of a detector does not necessarily mean better performance for finding correspondences, and detectors and descriptors are highly correlated with each other for matching feature points. As shown in Fig. 4(b), the number of correct matches detected by RootSIFT for all the detectors are quite small. Even for detectors like DoG, which has the highest precision, only 20–40 correct matches can be found. As a result, for applications that need a large number of matches between day-night image pairs, the performance of these detector+descriptor may not be satisfactory.

Another interesting finding from Fig. 4 is that the multiple scale version of TILDE, MultiscaleTILDE4, does not have a higher precision compared with TILDE4. One possible reason may be that the scales of features detected by MultiscaleTILDE4 are set to 10, 20 and 40, which are too large. Figure 5(a) shows that most of the correctly matched features of DoG+RootSIFT have scales within 10. This is because within a smaller region, the illumination changes between day and night images are more likely to be uniform, to which the

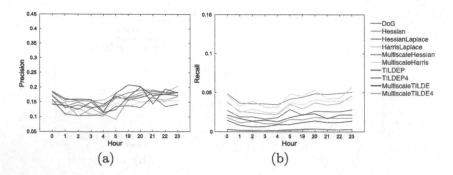

Fig. 7. (a) Shows the precision of matching of day-night image pairs for different detectors at different nighttime using cnn feature. (b) Shows the recall of matching of day-night image pairs for different detectors at different nighttime using cnn feature.

RootSIFT feature is designed to be robust. To better understand the effect of scales, we set the scale of TILDE4 to be 1 and scales of MultiscaleTILDE4 to be 1, 2 and 4, and denote these two modified versions as ModifiedTILDE4 and ModifiedMultiscaleTILDE4. Figure 5(b) compares the precision of them with TILDE4 and MultiscaleTILDE4. We find that by setting the scale to be small, there is around 5 %–10 % increase in precision. Intuitively, with larger scales, features may contain more information, which should be beneficial for matching. However, descriptors will need to be trained to make good use of those information, especially when robustness under viewpoint changes is required.

To examine the main challenge of finding more correspondences, the recall of these detectors for matching day-night image pairs is shown in Fig. 6(a). We find that the recall of each detector is very low. As a consequence, **one way to improve the performance of day-night image matching is to improve the robustness of descriptors to severe illumination changes**. As shown in Fig. 6, a much higher recall can be noticed for day-day image pairs, meaning that RootSIFT is robust to small illumination changes at daytime. However, it is not so robust to severe illumination changes between day and night. The low recall of day-night image pairs implies that there are a lot of "hard" patches from which RootSIFT cannot extract good descriptors.

With the development of deep learning, novel feature descriptors based on convolutional neural networks have been proposed. Many of them [4,15,26] outperform SIFT. We choose the feature descriptor proposed in [15] as an example to evaluate the performance of the learned descriptor+detector. [15] is chosen since their evaluation method is Euclidean distance, which can be used easily in our evaluation framework. Figure 7 shows that this CNN feature performs even worse than RootSIFT+detectors. One reason is that [15] is learned from the data provided by [2], which mainly focus on viewpoint changes, and illumination changes that are small. Though [15] shows its robustness to small illumination changes as in DaLI dataset [14], it is not very robust to illumination changes between day and night in our dataset.[2]

4 Potential of Improving Detectors

In this section, we try to examine **the potential of improving feature detectors** by fixing the descriptor to be RootSIFT.

Inspired by [20], we extract dense RootSIFT features from day-night image pairs for matching. When doing the ratio test, we select the neighbor that lies outside the region from which nearest neighbor's RootSIFT feature is extracted to avoid comparing similar features. Figure 8(a) and (b) show the precision of dense RootSIFT matching and the number of matched feature points. Though the precision is not improved compared with the best performing detector+RootSIFT, the number of matched feature points improves a lot. This means that there are a lot of "easy" RootSIFT features that could be matched for day-night image pairs. However, we find that the matched RootSIFT features tend to cluster. Since detectors would usually perform non-maximum suppression to get stable detections, in the worst case, only one feature could be detected from each cluster. As a result, the number of these matched features is an upper bound that cannot be reached. Instead, we try to get a lower bound on the number of additional potential matches that could be found. To achieve that, we count the number of connected components for those matched RootSIFT features and show the result in Fig. 8(c). Taking DoG as an example, we show the number of connected components that contain no correct matches found by detector+RootSIFT in Fig. 8(d). We found that matches found by detector+RootSIFT have almost no overlap with the connected components of the matched dense RootSIFT, meaning that there is great potential to improve feature detectors. Moreover, we notice that there are generally 10 - 20 connected

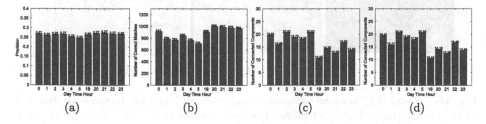

(a)   (b)   (c)   (d)

Fig. 8. (a) Shows the precision of matching dense RootSIFT for day-night image pairs at different nighttimes. (b) Shows the number of correct matches of dense RootSIFT for day-night image pairs. (c) Shows the number of connected components of matched points at different nighttime. (d) Shows the number of connected components that contain no matched points of DoG+RootSIFT.

---

[2] We also tried to tune the descriptor using day-night patch pairs, but were not able to increase the descriptor's performance.

(a)   (b)

Fig. 9. (a) Correct matches of DoG+RootSIFT. (b) Correct matches of dense RootSIFT.

components found by dense RootSIFT. This is in the order of correct matches we could get for day-night image matching shown in Fig. 4.

Figure 9 shows an example of correct matches found by DoG+RootSIFT and dense RootSIFT. For this day-night image pair, DoG+RootSIFT can only find 4 correct matches whereas dense RootSIFT can find 188 correct matches. Figure 10 shows the detected feature points using DoG for the day and night images and their corresponding heat map of cosine distance of dense RootSIFT. The colored rectangles in Fig. 9(b) and those in Fig. 10(a), (b) (c) are the same area. It is clearly shown that the cosine distances of points in that area between day and night images are very large, and Fig. 9(b) shows that they can be matched using dense RootSIFT. However, though many feature points can be detected in the daytime image, no feature points are detected by DoG for the nighttime image[3]. As a result, matches that could be found by RootSIFT are missed due to the detector. In conclusion, a detector which is more robust to severe illumination changes can help improve the performance of matching day-night image pairs.

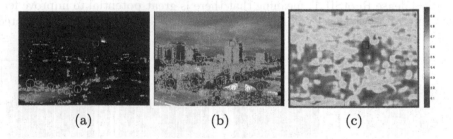

(a)   (b)   (c)

Fig. 10. (a) and (b) Shows an example of nighttime and daytime image with detected feature points using DoG. (c) Shows the heat map of the cosine distance of dense RootSIFT for (a) and (b). (Color figure online)

---

[3] The area in the rectangle of the night image actually has a lot of structure, it appears to be totally dark due to low resolution.

5   Conclusion

In this paper, we evaluated the performance of local features for day-night image matching. Extensive experiments show that repeatability alone is not enough for evaluating feature detectors. Instead, descriptors should also be considered. Through the discussion about precision and recall of matching day-night images and examining the performance of dense feature matching, we concluded that there is great potential for improving both feature detectors and descriptors. Thus, further evaluation with parameter tuning and advanced descriptors [11] as well as principal research on the day-night matching problem is needed.

References

1. Arandjelović, R., Zisserman, A.: Three things everyone should know to improve object retrieval. In: CVPR (2012)
2. Brown, M., Hua, G., Winder, S.: Discriminative learning of local image descriptors. IEEE Trans. PAMI **33**(1), 43–57 (2011)
3. Furukawa, Y., Ponce, J.: Accurate, dense, and robust multiview stereopsis. IEEE Trans. PAMI **32**(8), 1362–1376 (2010)
4. Han, X., Leung, T., Jia, Y., Sukthankar, R., Berg, A.C.: MatchNet: unifying feature and metric learning for patch-based matching. In: CVPR (2015)
5. Jacobs, N., Roman, N., Pless, R.: Consistent temporal variations in many outdoor scenes. In: CVPR (2007)
6. Lowe, D.G.: Distinctive image features from scale-invariant keypoints. IJCV **60**(2), 91–110 (2004)
7. Lynen, S., Sattler, T., Bosse, M., Hesch, J., Pollefeys, M., Siegwart, R.: Get out of my lab: large-scale, real-time visual-inertial localization. In: RSS (2015)
8. Matas, J., Chum, O., Urban, M., Pajdla, T.: Robust wide baseline stereo from maximally stable extremal regions. In: BMVC (2002)
9. Mikolajczyk, K., Schmid, C.: An affine invariant interest point detector. In: Heyden, A., Sparr, G., Nielsen, M., Johansen, P. (eds.) ECCV 2002, Part I. LNCS, vol. 2350, pp. 128–142. Springer, Heidelberg (2002)
10. Mikolajczyk, K., Tuytelaars, T., Schmid, C., Zisserman, A., Matas, J., Schaffalitzky, F., Kadir, T., Gool, L.V.: A comparison of affine region detectors. IJCV **65**(1/2), 43–72 (2005)
11. Mishkin, D., Matas, J., Perdoch, M., Lenc, K.: WxBS: wide baseline stereo generalizations. In: BMVC (2015)
12. Morel, J.M., Yu, G.: ASIFT: a new framework for fully affine invariant image comparison. SIAM J. Img. Sci. **2**(2), 438–469 (2009)
13. Richardson, A., Olson, E.: Learning convolutional filters for interest point detection. In: ICRA (2013)
14. Simo-Serra, E., Torras, C., Moreno-Noguer, F.: DaLI: deformation and light invariant descriptor. IJCV **115**(2), 136–154 (2015)
15. Simo-Serra, E., Trulls, E., Ferraz, L., Kokkinos, I., Fua, P., Moreno-Noguer, F.: Discriminative learning of deep convolutional feature point descriptors. In: ICCV (2015)
16. Simonyan, K., Vedaldi, A., Zisserman, A.: Learning local feature descriptors using convex optimisation. IEEE Trans. PAMI **36**(8), 1573–1585 (2014)

17. Sivic, J., Zisserman, A.: Video Google: a text retrieval approach to object matching in videos. In: ICCV (2003)
18. Snavely, N., Seitz, S.M., Szeliski, R.: Photo tourism: exploring photo collections in 3D. ACM Trans. Graph. (TOG) **25**, 835–846 (2006)
19. Suenderhauf, N., Shirazi, S., Jacobson, A., Dayoub, F., Pepperell, E., Upcroft, B., Milford, M.: Place recognition with convnet landmarks: viewpoint-robust, condition-robust, training-free. In: RSS (2015)
20. Torii, A., Arandjelović, R., Sivic, J., Okutomi, M., Pajdla, T.: 24/7 place recognition by view synthesis. In: CVPR (2015)
21. Triggs, B.: Detecting keypoints with stable position, orientation, and scale under illumination changes. In: Pajdla, T., Matas, J.G. (eds.) ECCV 2004. LNCS, vol. 3024, pp. 100–113. Springer, Heidelberg (2004)
22. Trzcinski, T., Christoudias, M., Lepetit, V., Fua, P.: Learning image descriptors with the boosting-trick. In: NIPS (2012)
23. Vedaldi, A., Fulkerson, B.: VLFeat: an open and portable library of computer vision algorithms (2008). http://www.vlfeat.org/
24. Verdie, Y., Yi, K.M., Fua, P., Lepetit, V.: TILDE: a temporally invariant learned DEtector. In: CVPR (2015)
25. Wu, C., Clipp, B., Li, X., Frahm, J.M., Pollefeys, M.: 3D model matching with viewpoint-invariant patches (VIP). In: CVPR (2008)
26. Zagoruyko, S., Komodakis, N.: Learning to compare image patches via convolutional neural networks. In: CVPR (2015)
27. Zeisl, B., Sattler, T., Pollefeys, M.: Camera pose voting for large-scale image-based localization. In: ICCV (2015)

Image Correspondences Matching Using Multiple Features Fusion

Song Wu$^{(\boxtimes)}$ and Michael S. Lew

The Leiden Institute of Advanced Computer Science, Leiden University,
Leiden, Netherlands
{s.wu,m.s.lew}@liacs.leidenuniv.nl

Abstract. In this paper, we present a novel framework which significantly increases the accuracy of correspondences matching between two
images under various image transformations. We first define a retina
inspired patch-structure which mimics the human eye retina topology,
and use the highly discriminative convolutional neural networks (CNNs)
features to represent those patches. Then, we employ the conventional
salient point methods to locate salient points, and finally, we fuse both
the local descriptor of each salient point and the CNN feature from the
local patch which the salient point belongs to. The evaluation results
show the effectiveness of the proposed multiple features fusion (MFF)
framework and that it improves the accuracy of leading approaches on
two popular benchmark datasets.

Keywords: Salient points methods · Convolutional neural networks ·
Correspondences matching

1 Introduction

Vision applications such as 3D object reconstruction [1], image stitching [2] as
well as object tracking in video sequences [3,4] mainly rely on the correct correspondences matching across images.

The determination that whether a pair of salient points is correctly corresponding to each other is a quite challenging task. This is mainly due to the
existing scale, rotation, and viewpoint transformations between the compared
images. The past decades witnessed the effectiveness of salient point methods
to this issue. The salient point methods firstly locate extrema (the candidate
salient points) in the image scale space, and then generate a local descriptor
to characterize each salient point. Finally, the nearest neighbor point obtained
by the similarity measure is determined as the correspondence. A representative
salient point method is SIFT [5], which detects the salient points in Difference-
of-Gaussians scale space, and uses the orientation histogram of gradient to represent these obtained salient points. Most of other efforts (such as SURF [6],
KAZE [7] were presented to improve the efficiency or accuracy of salient points
localization. The SURF method makes use of a box-filter to approximate to

© Springer International Publishing Switzerland 2016
G. Hua and H. Jégou (Eds.): ECCV 2016 Workshops, Part III, LNCS 9915, pp. 737–746, 2016.
DOI: 10.1007/978-3-319-49409-8_61

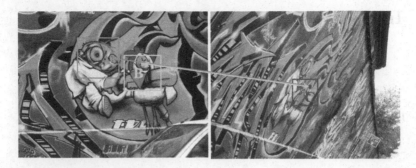

Fig. 1. Two salient points share the same nearest neighbor point between the compared images. However, the green line is a false match, and the yellow line is defined as a correct match. This is because the similarity of yellow patch is better than green patch when compared to the blue patch. (Color figure online)

the commonly used Laplace of Gaussian (LoG), and further employs the integral image to speed up the box-filter based scale space construction. The recent KAZE employs a nonlinear scale space and combines with the Additive Operator Splitting (AOS) and special conductance diffusion to reduce noise. The nonlinear scale space could retain the object boundary structure and generate more accurate positions for salient points. Furthermore, the local binary representations were proposed with the advantages of fast computation and low memory requirements (BRIEF [8], ORB [9], BRISK [10], and FREAK [11]). The generation of local binary descriptors is mainly based on the pair-wise intensities comparison in a pre-defined structure. However, the local binary descriptors focus primarily on improving the speed and storage rather than the precision.

The goal of this paper is to improve the accuracy of correspondences matching from salient point methods. We propose a novel multiple feature fusion (MFF) framework in this paper and it shows the robustness to the challenging transformations (such as the rotation and perspective changes). Our framework is motivated by the theory of global precedence that humans perceive the global structure before the fine level local details. As illustrated in Fig. 1, the proposed framework combines the low-level local feature of salient point together with the high-level feature in its surrounding patch in the pre-defined global structure to establish the correct correspondences matching.

There are two important roles in the proposed framework: one is how to define the global structure in the image, and the other one is what kinds of features are appropriate to represent these patches in the pre-defined global structure. Specifically, we employ a retina inspired sampling pattern to construct a retina patch-structure in the image. The retina sampling pattern could effectively mimic the topology of the retina in human vision system. Moreover, inspired by the fact that the image representations built upon convolutional neural networks (CNNs) [12] have strong discrimination, we choose to describe these patches via high-level CNN features. The performance evaluation on two popular benchmark datasets demonstrated that the proposed MFF framework could significantly increase the accuracy, stability, and reliability of correspondences matching under various image transformations, especially for the rotation and perspective changes.

The rest of the paper is organized as follows: Sect. 2 gives a brief review of related works. The construction of the proposed MFF framework is presented in Sect. 3. In Sect. 4, we describe the datasets and evaluation criterion in the experiment. The performance results of the MFF are shown in Sect. 5, and conclusions are given in Sect. 6.

2 Related Work

Because of the high performance of deep convolutional neural networks in various computer vision applications, the CNNs based image correspondences matching is receiving increasing attention. Fischer et al. [13] extracted salient regions in an image via MSER detector. The extracted regions were normalized to a fixed resolution and then passed through a pre-trained convolutional neural network, and the output of the last layer in the CNN is used to represent the patch. Long et al. [14] and Tulsiani el al. [15] proposed to predict the salient points based on the convnet features from the output of CNN architecture. The recent methods mainly focus on the supervised learning schemes. Zagoruyko et al. [16] and Han et al. [17] used a Siamese network architecture which minimizes a pairwise similarity loss of annotated pairs of raw image patches to jointly learn the features of local patches as well as the similarity metric for these local patches. The triplet network [18] employs the triplet ranking loss which can preserve the relative similarity relations of learn features to represent local patches. The framework introduced in this paper fuses the low-level local feature from each salient point and the high-level CNN feature from the patch it belongs to in order to achieve accurate correspondences matching.

3 Multiple Feature Fusion Framework

3.1 Retina Sampling Pattern Review

The retina sampling pattern has been widely used in various computer vision applications [11,19], and those approaches made good use of the topology of human retina inspired by neuro-biology research. The topology of human retina reveals that the spatial distribution density of cone cells in the human retina decreases exponentially with the distance metric from the center of retina. As the illustration of the cones density in Fig. 2(a), our approach employed the similar retina topology to define the patches structure in the image. As shown in Fig. 2(b), different size of blocks are placed at the image domain with high sampling density in the center area. The advantages of the proposed retina patch-structure are as follows: small numbers of patches (43 patches) cover almost all image domain which offers a good trade-off between accuracy and efficiency towards to the CNN features extraction; the size of the block is calculated

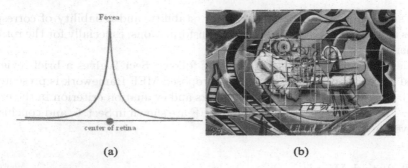

(a)   (b)

Fig. 2. (a) The illustration of the density distribution of cones in the human retina. (b) The retina patch-structure in the image domain.

respected to the log-polar and high density patches in the center image domain such that more details could be captured in the center area. Additionally, the overlapping between two patches in the retina pattern structure aims to increase the matching performance.

3.2   High Level Feature from CNNs

The motivation to utilize the output from a pre-trained CNN to represent the retina patch-structure stems from several properties of CNN features: First, the discrimination power of a CNN feature is significantly high and it outperforms those manually designed features in various computer vision applications by a large margin; Second, the CNN features are transferrable: some projects [20,21] have demonstrated that the pre-trained networks still work well when they are applied to other vision tasks different from the datasets they were trained on.

The performance evaluation is based on a popular network architecture presented in Krizhevsky et al. [12] (AlexNet), which was trained on 1.2 million images from the ILSVRC2012 for classification (note that other high performance networks such as VGGNet, GoogleNet can also be used in the proposed framework.). The AlexNet network architecture consists of five stacked convolutional layers followed by normalization layers and pooling layers as well as two fully connected layers and a softmax classifier on top. Each fully connected layer contains 4096 neurons, and we use the CAFFE implementation [22] to extract the activations from the last two fully connected layers to represent each patch (referred to as fc6, fc7 and with the dimensional of 4096, respectively).

3.3   Multiple Features Fusion Framework

Towards to the local features of salient points and CNN features from the patches in the retina sampling pattern, we propose a novel feature fusion framework. For a specific salient point $P(x, y)$ in image I, first, we calculate its local descriptor f, which is invariant to scale, rotation, and noise (such as SIFT, SURF, etc.). Then we calculate the distance between salient point position and the center of each retina patch to determine which patch the salient point belongs to. Finally each salient point is assigned a feature set: $F_{P(x,y)} = \{f, fc6_i, fc7_i\}$, where $i \in N$, which means $P(x,y)$ belongs to the ith patch in the retina patch-structure and N is the total amount of retina patches.

As the large variation in the value distribution from the directly obtained CNN features, the normalization operation is necessary. Inspired by the normalization of rootSIFT [23] which is more distinctive than SIFT, we apply the same normalization to the original CNN features, which exerts the feature vectors $L1$ normalization and then square root.

We define the similarity measure $S(P,P')$ to determine if two salient points $P(x,y)$, and $P'(x',y')$ is a correspondence as following:

$$S(P,P') = \exp(s(f,f')) \times (s(fc6_i, fc6'_i) + s(fc7_i, fc7'_i)) \tag{1}$$

where the $s(.)$ denotes the Euclidean metric, and we use an exponential function in order to emphasize the distance of two salient local descriptors.

Moreover, taking into the consideration that the existing overlaps in the proposed retina patch-structure, we use multiple assignment (MA) strategy to each salient point, which means that each salient point will be assigned K CNN features from its K nearest patches centers, and the similarity measure $S(P,P')$ is then updated as:

$$S(P,P') = \exp(s(f,f')) \times \sum_{i,j=1}^{K} (s(fc6_i, fc6'_j) + s(fc7_i, fc7'_j)) \tag{2}$$

The performance of correspondences matching in Fig. 3 demonstrated the strength of our MFF in the cases of challenging perspective transformations in comparison to the popular SIFT, and rootSIFT.

4 Experiment Setup

In this section, we conduct experiments to show the effectiveness of the proposed MFF framework. The accuracy of correspondences matching is evaluated on the MFF-rootSIFT and MFF-SURF, which applied our novel framework and compared with the leading popular approaches: SIFT, SURF, rootSIFT. The experimental environment for the evaluation is: Intel quad Core i7 Processor (2.6GHz), 12GB of RAM, and NVIDIA GTX970 with 4GRAM. The parameters of each compared salient point methods were set to the defaults and our MFF implementation is available online at: http://press.liacs.nl/researchdownloads/.

4.1 Datasets

The evaluation of correspondences matching is performed on two benchmark datasets (Mikolajczyk and Schmid [24] and Fischer et al. [13]), which both provided the ground-truth homography between the reference image and the transformed image. The first dataset contains eight groups, and each group consists

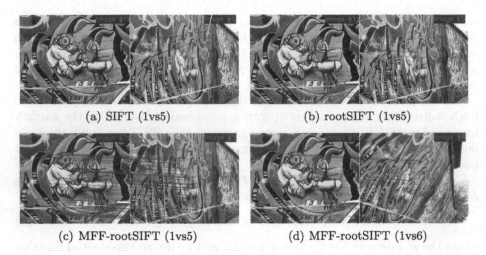

(a) SIFT (1vs5)   (b) rootSIFT (1vs5)

(c) MFF-rootSIFT (1vs5)   (d) MFF-rootSIFT (1vs6)

Fig. 3. Illustration of correspondence matching, the MFF is applied on rootSIFT and compared to SIFT, rootSIFT on challenge affine object detection (graffiti 1vs5, graffiti 1vs6 proposed by Mikolajczyk and Schmid [24]). Our framework exactly located the position of object after homography estimation by the RANSAC.

of six image samples (total 48 images) with various transformations (rotation, viewpoint, scale, JPEG compression, illumination and image blur). Considering the small scale of the dataset offered by Mikolajczyk and Schmid [24], a large dataset provided by Fischer et al. [13] is also employed in the evaluation. It contains 16 groups and each group contains 26 images (total 416 images) which are generated synthetically by applying 6 types of transformations (zoom, blur, illumination, rotation, perspective and nonlinear).

4.2   Evaluation Criterion

As MFF is a framework to increase the correspondences matching, we use the defined formula (2) to establish the correspondences. While for the compared salient point methods, KD-tree index is established and the Nearest Neighbor Distance Ratio ($NNDR$) is used as the matching strategy to find the similar descriptors. $NNDR$ defines that two points will be considered as a match if $\| D_A - D_B \| / \| D_A - D_C \|$, where D_B is the first and D_C is the second nearest neighbor to D_A. The $NNDR$ matching threshold is set to 0.8 in the experiment.

To further determine whether a match is correct or not, we enforce a one-to-one constraint so that a match is considered as a correct only if its matching point is geometrically the closest point within the defined pixel coordinate error. For two compared images I and I', let the set of all matches as:

$$M = \{p_i \leftrightarrow p'_j | m(p_i, p'_j)\} \tag{3}$$

where $m(p_i, p'_j)$ denotes the two matches satisfy the correspondence requirement. We need to note that different points in image I could be projected to the same point in image I (many-to-one matches), even though only one single best match is returned for each point in reference image, and then we refine them to one-to-one match by accepting only the p_i with the smallest distance measure.

$$M_{refine} = \{p_k \leftrightarrow p' \in M | k = \arg \min_i m(p_i, p')\} \tag{4}$$

and the final correct matches are evaluated by the ground-truth homography:

$$correct\_match = \{p_i \leftrightarrow p'_j | D(H(p_i), p'_j) < \varepsilon\} \tag{5}$$

where $D(H(p_i), p'_j)$ is the position error after the ground-truth homography H projection for the point in image I, and in all cases, the ε is set to 3 pixels.

Following the common practice in evaluation protocols, we use the amount of correct matches as a criterion, which computes the total number of correct correspondence matches between two compared images.

5   Evaluation Results

In this section, we apply our MFF framework on the local features of SIFT, rootSIFT and SURF and present the detailed comparison performance on two benchmark datasets.

Impact of multiple assignment size: We first analyse the impact of the size of MA. Table 1 shows that the increasing size of MA marginally improves the performance of matching accuracy on both datasets. As a large value of MA size accordingly introduces noise, the value of MA size is set to 2 in the experiment.

Table 1. The average number of correct matches under different MA size settings.

MA size	Accuracy on dataset [24]		Accuracy on dataset [13]	
	MFF-SIFT	MFF-SURF	MFF-SIFT	MFF-SURF
1	575	381	2181	889
2	589	410	2344	990
3	588	408	2354	990

Evaluation results: We first evaluate the performance of each method on the dataset proposed by Mikolajczyk and Schmid [24]. The number of correct matches and the results under perspective, scale and rotation changes are shown in Fig. 4, and they clearly illustrates the effectiveness of our proposed MFF framework. Note that the MFF-rootSIFT obtained the highest number of correct matches in all cases, and MFF-SURF also obtained better performance than original SURF method.

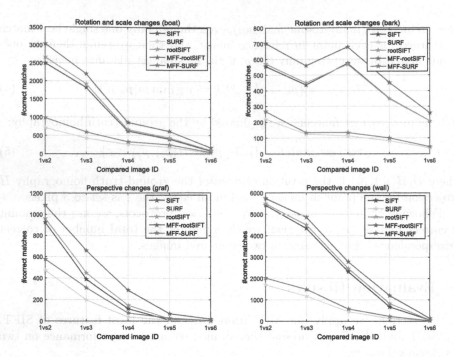

Fig. 4. Evaluation results on the viewpoint, rotation and scale changes based on the dataset provided by Mikolajczyk and Schmid [24].

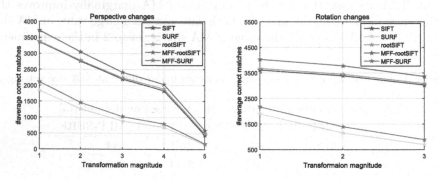

Fig. 5. Evaluation results on the viewpoint and rotation transformation based on the dataset of Fischer et al. [13].

We then evaluate all these approaches on a large scale dataset designed by Fischer et al. [13]. We use the average score of correct matches to measure the performance, and the evaluation results under two challenging transformations of viewpoint and rotation are shown in Fig. 5. It can be observed that similar tendency are demonstrated compared to the results illustrated in Fig. 4, and this further demonstrates that the MFF can significantly increase the matching accuracy under various transformations. The evaluation results in Figs. 4 and 5 both show that the proposed MFF framework is effective and can significantly improve the accuracy of correspondences matching when combined with the traditional salient point methods.

6 Conclusions

This paper propose a novel MFF framework. It firstly computes a retina inspired patch-structure and locates the salient points in an image. Then the MFF fuses the local descriptor of each salient point and the CNN feature extracted from the patch around the salient point. The experimental results demonstrate the effectiveness of the proposed framework and it yields higher accuracy in correspondences matching under the viewpoint, scale and rotation changes.

Acknowledgments. We are grateful to the support of NVIDIA for this work.

References

1. Rothganger, F., Lazebnik, S., Schmid, C., Ponce, J.: 3d object modeling and recognition using local affine-invariant image descriptors and multi-view spatial constraints. Int. J. Comput. Vis. **66**(3), 231–259 (2006)
2. Yang, X., Wang, M.: Seamless image stitching method based on ASIFT. Comput. Eng. **39**(2), 241–244 (2013)
3. Yang, H., Shao, L., Zheng, F., Wang, L., Song, Z.: Recent advances and trends in visual tracking: a review. Neurocomput. **74**(18), 3823–3831 (2011)
4. Gauglitz, S., Höllerer, T., Turk, M.: Evaluation of interest point detectors and feature descriptors for visual tracking. Int. J. Comput. Vis. **94**(3), 335–360 (2011)
5. Lowe, D.G.: Distinctive image features from scale-invariant keypoints. Int. J. Comput. Vis. **60**(2), 91–110 (2004)
6. Bay, H., Ess, A., Tuytelaars, T., Van Gool, L.: Speeded-up robust features (SURF). Comput. Vis. Image Underst. **110**(3), 346–359 (2008)
7. Alcantarilla, P.F., Bartoli, A., Davison, A.J.: KAZE features. In: Fitzgibbon, A., Lazebnik, S., Perona, P., Sato, Y., Schmid, C. (eds.) ECCV 2012. LNCS, vol. 7577, pp. 214–227. Springer, Heidelberg (2012). doi:10.1007/978-3-642-33783-3_16
8. Calonder, M., Lepetit, V., Strecha, C., Fua, P.: BRIEF: binary robust independent elementary features. In: Daniilidis, K., Maragos, P., Paragios, N. (eds.) ECCV 2010. LNCS, vol. 6314, pp. 778–792. Springer, Heidelberg (2010). doi:10.1007/978-3-642-15561-1_56
9. Rublee, E., Rabaud, V., Konolige, K., Bradski, G.: Orb: an efficient alternative to sift or surf. In: 2011 IEEE International Conference on Computer Vision (ICCV), pp. 2564–2571. IEEE (2011)
10. Leutenegger, S., Chli, M., Siegwart, R.Y.: Brisk: Binary robust invariant scalable keypoints. In: 2011 IEEE International Conference on Computer Vision (ICCV), pp. 2548–2555. IEEE (2011)
11. Alahi, A., Ortiz, R., Vandergheynst, P.: Freak: fast retina keypoint. In: 2012 IEEE Conference on Computer Vision and Pattern Recognition (CVPR), pp. 510–517. IEEE (2012)

12. Krizhevsky, A., Sutskever, I., Hinton, G.E.: Imagenet classification with deep convolutional neural networks. In: Advances in Neural Information Processing Systems, pp. 1097–1105 (2012)
13. Fischer, P., Dosovitskiy, A., Brox, T.: Descriptor matching with convolutional neural networks: a comparison to sift (2014). arXiv preprint arXiv:1405.5769
14. Long, J.L., Zhang, N., Darrell, T.: Do convnets learn correspondence? In: Advances in Neural Information Processing Systems, pp. 1601–1609 (2014)
15. Tulsiani, S., Malik, J.: Viewpoints and keypoints. In: 2015 IEEE Conference on Computer Vision and Pattern Recognition (CVPR), pp. 1510–1519. IEEE (2015)
16. Zagoruyko, S., Komodakis, N.: Learning to compare image patches via convolutional neural networks. In: Proceedings of the IEEE Conference on Computer Vision and Pattern Recognition, pp. 4353–4361 (2015)
17. Han, X., Leung, T., Jia, Y., Sukthankar, R., Berg, A.C.: Matchnet: Unifying feature and metric learning for patch-based matching. In: Proceedings of the IEEE Conference on Computer Vision and Pattern Recognition, pp. 3279–3286 (2015)
18. Kumar, B., Carneiro, G., Reid, I.: Learning local image descriptors with deep siamese and triplet convolutional networks by minimising global loss functions (2015). arXiv preprint arXiv:1512.09272
19. Wu, S., Lew, M.S.: RIFF: Retina-inspired invariant fast feature descriptor. In: Proceedings of the ACM International Conference on Multimedia, pp. 1129–1132. ACM (2014)
20. Razavian, A., Azizpour, H., Sullivan, J., Carlsson, S.: CNN features off-the-shelf: an astounding baseline for recognition. In: Proceedings of the IEEE Conference on Computer Vision and Pattern Recognition Workshops, pp. 806–813 (2014)
21. Yosinski, J., Clune, J., Bengio, Y., Lipson, H.: How transferable are features in deep neural networks? In: Advances in Neural Information Processing Systems, pp. 3320–3328 (2014)
22. Jia, Y., Shelhamer, E., Donahue, J., Karayev, S., Long, J., Girshick, R., Guadarrama, S., Darrell, T.: Caffe: Convolutional architecture for fast feature embedding. In: Proceedings of the ACM International Conference on Multimedia, pp. 675–678. ACM (2014)
23. Arandjelović, R., Zisserman, A.: Three things everyone should know to improve object retrieval. In: 2012 IEEE Conference on Computer Vision and Pattern Recognition (CVPR), pp. 2911–2918. IEEE (2012)
24. Mikolajczyk, K., Schmid, C.: A performance evaluation of local descriptors. IEEE Trans. Pattern Anal. Mach. Intell. **27**(10), 1615–1630 (2005)

Learning Local Convolutional Features for Face Recognition with 2D-Warping

Harald Hanselmann$^{(\boxtimes)}$ and Hermann Ney

Human Language Technology and Pattern Recognition Group,
RWTH Aachen University, Aachen, Germany
{hanselmann,ney}@cs.rwth-aachen.de

Abstract. The field of face recognition has seen a large boost in performance by applying Convolutional Neural Networks (CNN) in various ways. In this paper we want to leverage these advancements for face recognition with 2D-Warping. The latter has been shown to be effective especially with respect to pose-invariant face recognition, but usually relies on hand-crafted dense local feature descriptors. In this work the hand-crafted descriptors are replaced by descriptors learned with a CNN. An evaluation on the CMU-MultiPIE database shows that in this way the classification performance can be increased by a large margin.

Keywords: Face recognition · 2D-warping · Convolutional neural network

1 Introduction

2D-Warping tries to find a warping mapping between two given images. One of the images serves as source image and the other as target image. The warping mapping assigns each pixel in the source image a matching pixel in the target image. This mapping is optimized according to a given warping criterion (energy function). A similarity measure can be defined based on the assumption that images of the same class can be warped easier than images of different classes. The latter can then be used for e.g. nearest neighbor classification [17]. This approach has achieved very good accuracies for face recognition, especially with large pose variances (e.g. [12]).

The warping criterion is usually composed of two parts, local descriptor similarity and a smoothness term that incorporates the 2D-dependencies of the pixels in a local neighborhood. In the past, mostly hand-crafted features such as SIFT [22] have been used as local descriptors. However, this work aims to learn the local features using a Convolutional Neural Network (CNN). Lately, a lot of different methods learning a feature embedding by using a siamese architecture and a contrastive loss [24,28,30,31]. We use a similar approach to learn a regular grid of local feature vectors that can then be used as input to the 2D-Warping based recognition algorithm.

© Springer International Publishing Switzerland 2016
G. Hua and H. Jégou (Eds.): ECCV 2016 Workshops, Part III, LNCS 9915, pp. 747–758, 2016.
DOI: 10.1007/978-3-319-49409-8_62

1.1   Related Work

In the past, several methods have been proposed that use 2D-Warping for image recognition [17,35] or face-recognition in particular [1,3,4,9,12,23,26]. These methods mostly differ in how the warping criterion is defined and optimized, but usually use hand-crafted features such as SIFT [22] to describe the images. In this paper we use the algorithm proposed in [12]. The related work with respect to convolutional features for face recognition and 2D-Warping can be divided into the following parts.

First, there is work related to CNNs and Face Recognition. Similar to many areas of computer vision CNNs also had a large impact on face recognition [13,33,37]. While there are approaches taking pose-invariance into account specifically (e.g. [38]), most related to our work are the approaches where a face embedding is learned by optimizing a similarity measure between the face images. This can be done by training a siamese architecture with a contrastive loss [5]. In [28] this has been extended to a triplet-loss (this could be considered a siamese architecture with three streams). The training can be improved by including a classification loss that is trained jointly with the contrastive loss [30], or successively [24]. In [31] additional supervisory signals are included at lower levels of the CNN. However, none of these methods evaluate using features extracted from the lower levels of the CNN in combination with 2D-Warping for face recognition.

Second, there is work related to CNNs and 2D-Warping. The work published in [21] is very closely related to our work. Here the effectiveness of convolutional features for 2D-Warping is demonstrated for the task of keypoint matching with 2D-Warping, but the network is trained in a single-stream architecture without contrastive loss. There has also been research to learn convolutional features for stereo-vision [39,40]. The CNN is applied on each location resulting in a feature vector as output, which can then be used by a 2D-Warping algorithm as local cost. Usually rectified images are assumed and the warping is done only in the horizontal dimension and no joint training of classification and contrastive loss is applied. In [20] a conditional random field is optimized for depth estimation from a single image. By using a CNN small image patches are mapped to a single depth value which is then used to construct the energy function and the parameters are learned jointly.

Finally, there is work related to CNNs for local descriptor learning. These methods are similar to the methods mentioned in the first part but are not specifically for face recognition and focus on learning patch-similarity. One example is [29] where a siamese architecture is used to learn discriminative features for image patches. In [25] the features are learned unsupervised and in [11] a metric network is included that learns a probability that two input patches are similar.

2   2D-Warping

In this section we briefly review 2D-warping or image matching in compliance with [26]. The approach aims to find a matching between local feature descriptors

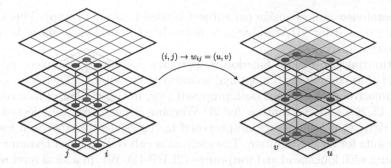

Fig. 1. 2D-Warping: the red feature descriptor is mapped with respect to the horizontal and vertical neighbor. The blue areas indicate the hard monotonicity and continuity constraints. (Color figure online)

of two images while respecting a local cost function and neighborhood dependencies. To this end a mapping function is searched that receives a set of local feature vectors of the first image (the source image) as input and maps them to the corresponding set of feature vectors from the second image (the target image). The local features are extracted using a regular grid of dimension $I \times J$ for the source and $U \times V$ for the target image. As a result, the source image is defined as $X \in \mathbb{R}^{I \times J \times D}$ and the target image is defined as $R \in \mathbb{R}^{U \times V \times D}$ where D is the dimension of the feature descriptor. The warping mapping w then maps each pixel of X to a pixel of R:

$$(i,j) \to w_{i,j} = (u,v) \quad \forall (i,j), \; i \in \{1,\ldots,I\}, \; j \in \{1,\ldots,J\} \qquad (1)$$

A local cost function $dist(\cdot)$ returns a score measuring the similarity of two local descriptors. In this work the l1-norm is used as local cost function. The neighborhood dependencies are realized using a smoothness term $T(\cdot)$ that penalizes large disparities in the mapping of pixels within a local neighborhood. As in [26] we use the l2-norm applied with respect to the vertical and horizontal predecessor as penalty function in addition to hard monotonicity and continuity constraints that limit the possible displacements of neighboring pixels [35]. These choices have been shown to work well for face recognition [12,26].

Finally, by combining the local cost and the smoothness term the following optimization criterion or energy function can be defined:

$$E(X, R, \{w_{ij}\}) = \sum_{i,j} \left[dist(x_{i,j}, r_{w_{ij}}) + T(w_{i-1,j}, w_{ij}) + T(w_{i,j-1}, w_{ij}) \right]. \quad (2)$$

In the context of classification 2D-Warping can be used in a nearest neighbor classifier to compensate small intra-class variations [17]. Each training (gallery) image is warped to the test (probe) image and the resulting energy is used as a similarity measure. Computing the energy between the probe image and a large number of gallery images can be costly, but in face recognition often only one frontal-view gallery image per subject is used (mugshot-setup). This case is especially suited for 2D-Warping as a normalized frontal-view image is a very good source image.

Optimizing the energy function in Formula 2 is an NP-complete problem [16] and thus computing the optimal solution is intractable. Therefore, several approximative methods have been proposed (e.g. in the context of face recognition [2,12,26]) and the runtime for 2D-Warping depends on the selected algorithm. Here we use the algorithm proposed in [12], since this approach leads to good results for face recognition. The method is called Two-Level Dynamic Programming with lookahead and warprange (2LDP-LA-W). In a local level several candidates for the optimization of a column are computed while on a global level the best sequence of such candidates is found. The procedure is guided by a lookahead that gives a rough estimate of not yet optimized parts of the image and the warprange restricts the possible displacements of each pixel (w.r.t. to their absolute position). The complexity of this algorithm depends on the image and feature dimensions [12]. The local distances are cached in a pre-processing step to avoid multiple computations of the same distance [9]. For the final runtime the choice for the spatial dimensions I, J, U and V is most important. Ideally, they should be kept as small as possible while not sacrificing too much spatial information.

2.1   Features for 2D-Warping

A crucial step in building a nearest neighbor classifier based on 2D-Warping is the choice of the features. In the past mostly handcrafted features such as SIFT [22] have been used. E.g. in [12] the authors extract a SIFT descriptor based on a regular grid. The descriptor is then reduced using PCA [15] and normalized by the l1-norm. For an input with spatial dimension $I \times J$ this results in a 3D structure of dimension $I \times J \times D$ with a D-dimensional feature descriptor at each spatial position $(i, j) \in I \times J$ (c.f. Fig. 1). As demonstrated in [21], the output of a single convolutional layer of a CNN can be interpreted in the same way, if the output of a single filter has a dimension of $I \times J$ and the layer has D feature maps. These features can then be used directly to optimize Formula 2. This means the CNN is applied just once on the input image and all local features are extracted directly from the output of one convolutional layer [21].

For face-recognition with the mug-shot setup and a focus on pose-invariance, self-occlusions in the probe images caused by rotations can be compensated by using just the left or the right half of the gallery image [3]. The half-images are generated after the convolutional features have been extracted by simply cutting the feature-maps in half.

3   CNN-Model

Our model is based on a simplified version of the well known GoogLeNet [32]. This deep network implements several 'Inception'-modules, which use parallel

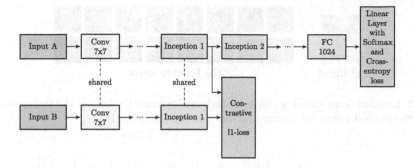

Fig. 2. The siamese CNN model based on GoogLeNet with an early contrastive loss.

convolutional layers with different kernel-sizes, concatenated to generate one combined output. GoogLeNet uses three classification loss functions at different depths of the network. We simplify the model by using the layers up to the first loss function. This includes the first three inception modules. As 2D-warping needs sufficient spatial dimension to work well, we select the output of one of the earlier convolutional layers as feature input to the 2D-Warping, specifically we use first inception module. The corresponding output is composed of 256 feature-maps with spatial dimension 28 × 28. As in [30] a contrastive loss is added to the classification loss leading to a siamese architecture [5]. However, we attach the contrastive loss to the output of the first inception module, since this is the layer we will be using later for feature extraction. For such a siamese architecture the training data is composed of positive and negative pairs of images (A, B). For a positive pair the two images have the same class $(A_c = B_c)$ while for a negative pair the class differs. We use each image A for the cross-entropy loss while image B serves as additional supervisory signal to minimize positive and maximize negative distances. The final layout of the model is shown in Fig. 2.

3.1 Contrastive L1-Loss

The input to the contrastive loss is the output of a convolutional layer with spatial dimension $I \times J$ and D feature maps. The first step is to normalize the features. As described in Sect. 2, the entries at a specific position in the feature maps are interpreted as the local feature vectors [21]. For this reason we apply a position-wise normalization using the l1-norm:

$$\hat{A}_{i,j,d} = \frac{A_{i,j,d}}{\|A_{i,j}\|_1} = \frac{A_{i,j,d}}{\sum_{d'} |A_{i,j,d'}|} \tag{3}$$

The actual loss function is based on the contrastive loss proposed in [30], but as in [5] we use the l1-distance to calculate the distance between two images and as in [27] a positive margin is included. The local loss for an image pair (A, B) is given by

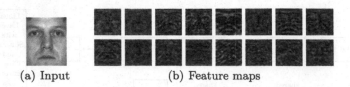

| (a) Input | (b) Feature maps |

Fig. 3. Learned features using the described architecture. Shown are the features-maps with the highest mean activation (gamma has been increased).

$$L_n(A, B) = \frac{1}{E_{max}} \cdot \begin{cases} \frac{1}{2}\max(0, \|\hat{A} - \hat{B}\|_1 - m_p)^2 & \text{if } A_c = B_c \\ \frac{1}{2}\max(0, m_n - \|\hat{A} - \hat{B}\|_1)^2 & \text{else} \end{cases} \qquad (4)$$

where m_p and m_n are margins that regulate the influence of positive and negative pairs. This helps to avoid that the training focuses too much on optimizing pairs of the same class that already have a low distance and pairs of different class that already have a large distance, respectively. This loss function adds two more hyper-parameters to the training procedure, but both can simply be set to the mean distance. Additionally, we normalize the loss using the maximal possible distance E_{max}, which is known at this point due to the position-wise l1-normalization. The contribution of the contrastive l1-loss to the overall loss is weighted by a parameter λ.

Figure 3 shows examples of features learned using the described model. We show the feature maps with the highest mean activation.

4   Experimental Evaluation

We implement the contrastive l1-loss with position-wise l1-normalization using the open source framework Caffe [14]. To evaluate the 2D-Warping algorithm 2LDP-LA-W (c.f. Sect. 2) we use the software provided with [12].

The experimental evaluation is done using the CMU-MultiPIE database [10]. The database contains over 700,000 images recorded in four different sessions and with variations in pose, illumination and facial expression, the former two are especially challenging. There are 15 different poses ranging from $-90°$ to $+90°$ rotation in yaw and 20 different illumination conditions (c.f. Fig. 4). There are two special poses emulating a surveillance camera view by including a small amount of tilt. To be able to compare with [12] we use the same pre-alignment, i.e. all images are cropped and normalized based on manual landmarks and pose information using the method proposed in [8].

We use two different settings. Setting 1 is designed to evaluate the method with respect to variations in pose [8]. Images from the first recording session are divided into a training and a test set. The first 100 subjects are used for training (c.f. Sect. 4.1), while the remaining 149 subjects are used for testing. The illumination is kept constant for this setting which leaves 2086 test images. In setting 2 the method is evaluated with respect to pose and illumination simultaneously.

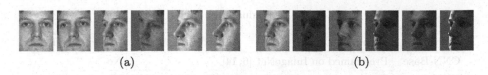

(a)   (b)

Fig. 4. Example images of the CMU-MultiPIE database. Different poses are shown in (a) and varying illumination is shown in (b).

The splitting of train and test subjects is the same as in setting 1, but for setting 2 all illuminations except the front flash (19 in total) are used, while the poses are reduced to those that range from $-45°$ to $+45°$ rotation (6 different poses). Overall there are 16,986 test images in this setting. In both settings one frontal view image per subject with neutral illumination is used as gallery which means we only have gallery image for each subject (mug-shot setup). In both settings, the trained CNN models have not seen the classes to be recognized before.

4.1 Training

We evaluate several different models, an overview is given in Table 1. The baseline model (CNN-Base) is trained on ImageNet [6] and provided with Caffe [14]. Initializing with these weights we finetune models using the CASIA WebFace [37] and the CMU-MultiPIE database (CNN-ft). From the CASIA WebFace we select the subjects with more than 60 images and create 1000 random pairs (A, B) for each subject. Half of the 1000 pairs are positive, the other half are negative pairs. In total there are 4,874,000 image pairs for 4874 subjects. Additionally, we use the 30,000 images from the training set provided by the two settings for the CMU-MultiPIE. For each of the 100 subjects we again generate random pairs and merge this with the training set provided by the CASIA WebFace database. Since the latter has much more classes we use 10,000 pairs for each subject such that the training set is not dominated too much by the CASIA WebFace database. The model CNN-ft is finetuned using only a cross-entropy loss. This means the model defined in Sect. 3 is reduced to the first stream and we only use the images A of the image pairs. This model is trained for 1,000,000 iterations with a batchsize of 32 and a base learning rate of 0.003. The learning rate is reduced gradually with a step-size of 100,000 iterations. We evaluate the model after each 100,000 iterations using a small holdout-set from the CMU-MultiPIE images and select the best one for our experiments. Furthermore, a model using both cross-entropy and contrastive loss (CNN-ft-CL) is trained. For this, we use the same number of iterations as the best CNN-ft model and the same hyper-parameters. The additional hyper-parameter λ to weight the contribution of the contrastive loss is set to 0.1.

We also evaluate training the models from scratch using only data from CMU-MultiPIE (CNN-M and CNN-M-CL). Since we have less data than in the previous case we reduce the number of iterations and the step-size for adjusting

Table 1. Evaluated models.

Name	Training database	Contrastive loss
CNN-Base	Pre-trained on ImageNet [6, 14]	No
CNN-ft	Finetuned from CNN-Base, WebFace, MultiPIE	No
CNN-ft-CL	Finetuned from CNN-Base, WebFace, MultiPIE	Yes
CNN-M	MultiPIE	No
CNN-M-CL	MultiPIE	Yes

the learning rate and evaluation. To have a better starting point for the distances in the contrastive loss, CNN-M-CL is finetuned from the best CNN-M model.

Apart from the different models there are also different ways to extract the features. As mentioned earlier, for 2LDP-LA-W we extract the features after the first inception layer (Inception 1 in Fig. 2). For comparison we also extract features at the last layer before the cross-entropy loss is applied, which is a fully connected layer of dimension 1024 (FC 1024 in Fig. 2). We use these vectors in a nearest-neighbor classifier with l1-distance (NN-l1) and without 2D-Warping (the spatial dimension is 1×1 at this point). Note that at this point we can not match left and right halves of the gallery anymore, since no spatial information is left.

4.2   Results Setting 1: Pose

The first evaluation with respect to robustness against pose variation is done using setting 1. The results are given in Table 2. We specifically compare our approach to the result reported in [12] using 2LDP-LA-W with SIFT features. For the latter, the authors use a 68×86 grid to extract feature vectors of dimension 30 (reduced by PCA). In our case, the feature dimension is with 256 much larger, but the spatial dimension is only 28×28.

It is surprising that applying 2LDP-LA-W with the out-of-the-box features CNN-base already achieves a slightly better result than with the SIFT features, even though no training with respect to a face recognition task has been performed. However, the models trained on face recognition database yield a significant improvement, especially when using the contrastive loss. While training the model from scratch using only the data from the MultiPIE database already achieves a large improvement over the previous approaches, the best result is achieved by finetuning CNN-Base with the WebFace and MultiPIE databases. Using the features extracted at the last fully connected layer does not work as well for setting 1, since the variation in pose can not be compensated, which demonstrates the need for more sophisticated spatial normalization than offered by the pooling layers included in the CNN.

More detailed results for all 14 test poses in setting 1 are given in Fig. 5. While most methods achieve close to 100 % accuracy on the images with 60° or less rotation in yaw, the more challenging poses prove difficult to handle,

Table 2. Setting 1: Results reported in accuracy[%].

Method	Total without surveillance	Total
PLS [8]**	90.5	90.0
MLCE [19]*	92.1	-
2LDP-LA-W + SIFT [12]	90.2	91.5
2LDP-LA-W + CNN-Base	91.7	91.7
2LDP-LA-W + CNN-ft	92.7	93.2
2LDP-LA-W + CNN-ft-CL	**95.5**	**96.1**
2LDP-LA-W + CNN-M	89.3	88.6
2LDP-LA-W + CNN-M-CL	94.0	94.6
NN-l1 + CNN-ft-FC1024	71.6	70.0
NN-l1 + CNN-ft-CL-FC1024	71.9	71.0

*Different pre-alignment.
**Different illumination.

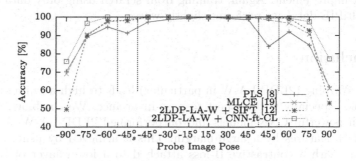

Fig. 5. Setting 1: results for each pose. The poses marked as -45_s° and 45_s° are the special surveillance poses.

especially the poses with 90° rotation. On these two poses our approach with 2LDP-LA-W and CNN-ft-CL features achieves the most improvements.

4.3 Results Setting 2: Pose and Illumination

We also evaluate robustness with respect to illumination to see how well the large variations in lighting contained in the CMU-MultiPIE database are learned. The results are given in Table 3. The evaluation only includes the best performing model from setting 1 (also on this task, the other models did not achieve competitive performance). Additionally we evaluated the effect of a normalization with respect to illumination [34], which is also used by the best performing state-of-the-art method [7]. While the features extracted with CNN-ft-CL lead to good results, it is evident that the variation with respect to the difficult lighting conditions was not learned to full extend. Normalizing the gallery and test images

Table 3. Setting 2: results reported in accuracy [%].

Method	$-60°$	$-45°$	$-30°$	$-15°$	$+15°$	$+30°$	$+45°$	$+60°$	Total
Ridge regression [18]*	-	63.5	69.3	79.7	75.6	71.6	54.6	-	-
RL-LDA [41]*	-	67.1	74.6	86.1	83.3	75.3	61.8	-	-
CPF [38]*	-	73.0	81.7	89.4	89.5	80.4	70.3	-	-
AQI-GEM [36]*,**	-	79.0	90.3	97.0	98.3	94.7	87.4	-	-
PBPR [7]*	**90.9**	**97.9**	**99.4**	99.0	**99.9**	**99.2**	**98.2**	**87.8**	**96.6**
2LDP-LA-W									
+ CNN-ft-CL	72.8	79.5	85.8	92.9	95.4	90.1	81.6	71.8	83.7
+ Norm [34] + CNN-M-CL	77.0	91.6	96.1	98.0	99.2	97.6	90.6	79.7	91.2
+ Norm [34] + CNN-ft-CL	85.5	94.7	98.6	**99.5**	99.8	99.0	92.6	86.5	94.5

* Different pre-alignment.
** Automatically detected landmarks.

and finetuning the model further on normalized images (MultiPIE only) yields a significant improvement. Again, training from scratch using only data from the CMU-MultiPIE database performs slightly worse.

5   Conclusion

Using 2D-Warping (2LDP-LA-W in particular) leads to high accuracies for face recognition, especially with respect to pose-invariance. We combined this approach with powerful CNN-models and outperformed 2LDP-LA-W with hand-crafted SIFT features by a large margin. This is achieved by using a siamese architecture with a contrastive l1-loss attached to a lower layer of the CNN-model, whose features are the input to the warping algorithm.

For future work it would be interesting to evaluate, if the distance used in the contrastive-layer can be replaced by a warping distance directly. This might lead to problems with the runtime, but a simple warping method such as zero-order warping [17] would be fast enough. It would also be interesting to evaluate if advances such as the triplet loss [28] lead to further improvements.

References

1. Arashloo, S.R., Kittler, J.: Efficient processing of MRFS for unconstrained-pose face recognition. In: IEEE Biometrics: Theory, Applications and Systems (BTAS), pp. 1–8 (2013)
2. Arashloo, S.R., Kittler, J.: Fast pose invariant face recognition using super coupled multiresolution markov random fields on a GPU. Pattern Recogn. Lett. **48**, 49–59 (2014)
3. Arashloo, S., Kittler, J., Christmas, W.: Pose-invariant face recognition by matching on multi-resolution MRFS linked by supercoupling transform. Comput. Vis. Image Underst. **115**(7), 1073–1083 (2011)

4. Castillo, C.D., Jacobs, D.W.: Wide-baseline stereo for face recognition with large pose variation. In: IEEE CVPR, pp. 537–544 (2011)
5. Chopra, S., Hadsell, R., LeCun, Y.: Learning a similarity metric discriminatively, with application to face verification. In: IEEE CVPR, pp. 539–546 (2005)
6. Deng, J., Dong, W., Socher, R., Li, L.J., Li, K., Fei-Fei, L.: ImageNet: a large-scale hierarchical image database. In: IEEE CVPR, pp. 248–255 (2009)
7. Ding, C., Xu, C., Tao, D.: Multi-task pose-invariant face recognition. IEEE Trans. Image Process. 24(3), 980–993 (2015)
8. Fischer, M., Ekenel, H.K., Stiefelhagen, R.: Analysis of partial least squares for pose-invariant face recognition. In: IEEE Biometrics: Theory, Applications and Systems (BTAS), pp. 331–338 (2012)
9. Gass, T., Pishchulin, L., Dreuw, P., Ney, H.: Warp that smile on your face: optimal and smooth deformations for face recognition. In: IEEE Automatic Face and Gesture Recognition (FG), pp. 456–463 (2011)
10. Gross, R., Matthews, I., Cohn, J., Kanade, T., Baker, S.: Multi-pie. Image Vis. Comput. 28(5), 807–813 (2010)
11. Han, X., Leung, T., Jia, Y., Sukthankar, R., Berg, A.C.: MatchNet: unifying feature and metric learning for patch-based matching. In: IEEE CVPR, pp. 3279–3286 (2015)
12. Hanselmann, H., Ney, H.: Speeding up 2D-warping for pose-invariant face recognition. IEEE Autom. Face Gesture Recogn. (FG). 1, 1–7 (2015)
13. Hu, G., Yang, Y., Yi, D., Kittler, J., Christmas, W., Li, S., Hospedales, T.: When face recognition meets with deep learning: an evaluation of convolutional neural networks for face recognition. In: IEEE International Conference on Computer Vision Workshops, pp. 142–150 (2015)
14. Jia, Y., Shelhamer, E., Donahue, J., Karayev, S., Long, J., Girshick, R., Guadarrama, S., Darrell, T.: Caffe: convolutional architecture for fast feature embedding. arXiv preprint arXiv:1408.5093 (2014)
15. Ke, Y., Sukthankar, R.: PCA-SIFT: a more distinctive representation for local image descriptors. In: IEEE CVPR, vol. 2, pp. II–506 (2004)
16. Keysers, D., Unger, W.: Elastic image matching is NP-complete. Pattern Recogn. Lett. 24(1–3), 445–453 (2003)
17. Keysers, D., Deselaers, T., Gollan, C., Ney, H.: Deformation models for image recognition. IEEE Trans. Pattern Anal. Mach. Intell. 29(8), 1422–1435 (2007)
18. Li, A., Shan, S., Gao, W.: Coupled bias-variance tradeoff for cross-pose face recognition. IEEE Trans. Image Process. 21(1), 305–315 (2012)
19. Li, S., Liu, X., Chai, X., Zhang, H., Lao, S., Shan, S.: Maximal likelihood correspondence estimation for face recognition across pose. IEEE Trans. Image Process. 23(10), 4587–4600 (2014)
20. Liu, F., Shen, C., Lin, G.: Deep convolutional neural fields for depth estimation from a single image. In: IEEE CVPR, pp. 5162–5170 (2015)
21. Long, J.L., Zhang, N., Darrell, T.: Do convnets learn correspondence? In: Advances in Neural Information Processing Systems, pp. 1601–1609 (2014)
22. Lowe, D.G.: Distinctive image features from scale-invariant keypoints. Int. J. Comput. Vis. 60(2), 91–110 (2004)
23. Mottl, V., Kopylov, A., Kostin, A., Yermakov, A., Kittler, J.: Elastic transformation of the image pixel grid for similarity based face identification. In: ICPR, pp. 549–552 (2002)
24. Parkhi, O.M., Vedaldi, A., Zisserman, A.: Deep face recognition. Br. Mach. Vis. Conf. 1, 6 (2015)

25. Paulin, M., Douze, M., Harchaoui, Z., Mairal, J., Perronin, F., Schmid, C.: Local convolutional features with unsupervised training for image retrieval. In: IEEE International Conference on Computer Vision, pp. 91–99 (2015)
26. Pishchulin, L., Gass, T., Dreuw, P., Ney, H.: Image warping for face recognition: from local optimality towards global optimization. Pattern Recogn. 45(9), 3131–3140 (2012)
27. Sadeghi, F., Zitnick, C.L., Farhadi, A.: Visalogy: answering visual analogy questions. In: Advances in Neural Information Processing Systems, pp. 1873–1881 (2015)
28. Schroff, F., Kalenichenko, D., Philbin, J.: FaceNet: a unified embedding for face recognition and clustering. In: IEEE CVPR, pp. 815–823 (2015)
29. Simo-Serra, E., Trulls, E., Ferraz, L., Kokkinos, I., Fua, P., Moreno-Noguer, F.: Discriminative learning of deep convolutional feature point descriptors. In: IEEE International Conference on Computer Vision, pp. 118–126 (2015)
30. Sun, Y., Chen, Y., Wang, X., Tang, X.: Deep learning face representation by joint identification-verification. In: Advances in Neural Information Processing Systems, pp. 1988–1996 (2014)
31. Sun, Y., Liang, D., Wang, X., Tang, X.: DeepID3: face recognition with very deep neural networks. arXiv preprint arXiv:1502.00873 (2015)
32. Szegedy, C., Liu, W., Jia, Y., Sermanet, P., Reed, S., Anguelov, D., Erhan, D., Vanhoucke, V., Rabinovich, A.: Going deeper with convolutions. In: IEEE CVPR, pp. 1–9 (2015)
33. Taigman, Y., Yang, M., Ranzato, M., Wolf, L.: DeepFace: closing the gap to human-level performance in face verification. In: IEEE CVPR, pp. 1701–1708 (2014)
34. Tan, X., Triggs, B.: Enhanced local texture feature sets for face recognition under difficult lighting conditions. In: Zhou, S.K., Zhao, W., Tang, X., Gong, S. (eds.) AMFG 2007. LNCS, vol. 4778, pp. 168–182. Springer, Heidelberg (2007). doi:10.1007/978-3-540-75690-3_13
35. Uchida, S., Sakoe, H.: A monotonic and continuous two-dimensional warping based on dynamic programming. In: ICPR, pp. 521–524 (1998)
36. Wu, Z., Deng, W.: Adaptive quotient image with 3D generic elastic models for pose and illumination invariant face recognition. In: Yang, J., Yang, J., Sun, Z., Zheng, W., Feng, J., Shan, S. (eds.) CCBR 2015. LNCS, vol. 9428, pp. 3–10. Springer, Cham (2015)
37. Yi, D., Lei, Z., Liao, S., Li, S.Z.: Learning face representation from scratch. arXiv preprint arXiv:1411.7923 (2014)
38. Yim, J., Jung, H., Yoo, B., Choi, C., Park, D., Kim, J.: Rotating your face using multi-task deep neural network. In: IEEE CVPR, pp. 676–684 (2015)
39. Zagoruyko, S., Komodakis, N.: Learning to compare image patches via convolutional neural networks. In: IEEE CVPR, pp. 4353–4361 (2015)
40. Zbontar, J., LeCun, Y.: Stereo matching by training a convolutional neural network to compare image patches. J. Mach. Learn. Res. 17, 1–32 (2016)
41. Zhu, Z., Luo, P., Wang, X., Tang, X.: Deep learning identity-preserving face space. In: IEEE International Conference on Computer Vision, pp. 113–120 (2013)

Improving Performances of MSER Features in Matching and Retrieval Tasks

Andrzej Śluzek[✉]

ECE Department, Khalifa University, Abu Dhabi, United Arab Emirates
andrzej.sluzek@kustar.ac.ae

Abstract. MSER features are redefined to improve their performances in matching and retrieval tasks. The proposed SIMSER features (i.e. *scale-insensitive* MSERs) are the *extremal regions* which are maximally stable not only under the *threshold* changes (like MSERs) but, additionally, under *image rescaling* (smoothing). Theoretical advantages of such a modification are discussed. It is also preliminarily verified experimentally that such a modification preserves the fundamental properties of MSERs, i.e. the average numbers of features, repeatability, and computational complexity (which is only multiplicatively increased by the number of scales used), while performances (measured by typical CBVIR metrics) can be significantly improved. In particular, results on benchmark datasets indicate significant increments in *recall* values, both for descriptor-based matching and word-based matching. In general, SIMSERs seem particularly suitable for a usage with large visual vocabularies, e.g. they can be prospectively applied to improve quality of BoW pre-retrieval operations in large-scale databases.

Keywords: MSER features · Scale invariance · Multi-scale image pyramid · Keypoint matching · Image retrieval

1 Introduction and Background

MSER features (originally proposed in [1] and computationally improved in [2]) continue to attract attention of machine vision researchers and practitioners. In comparison to other affine-invariant features, their main advantages are: (1) moderate computational complexity and the algorithmic structure suitable for hardware implementations, e.g. [3,4], and (2) a good identification of significant image parts usually combined with high repeatability under typical image distortions (as reported in [5]).

Nevertheless, some disadvantages of MSER features have been identified. In particular, MSERs have limited performances on blurred and/or textured images. Both cases are actually related to the image scale, since blur (which can distort shapes of extracted MSERs) is equivalent to image down-scaling, e.g. [6]. Similarly, shapes of fine texture details can vary irregularly under image rescaling. Protruding fragments of non-convex MSERs are particularly vulnerable to scale variations (as discussed in [7]).

© Springer International Publishing Switzerland 2016
G. Hua and H. Jégou (Eds.): ECCV 2016 Workshops, Part III, LNCS 9915, pp. 759–770, 2016.
DOI: 10.1007/978-3-319-49409-8_63

Thus, a number of papers have been addressing the issue of *actual* insensitivity of MSER features to scale variations. A simple approach (based on the original concept of MSER detection) is proposed in [8]. The authors just detect MSERs in a pyramid of down-scaled images, and keep all of them (after removing near-duplicate MSERs which reappear at different scales). More recently, combinations of the original MSER algorithm with other techniques have been proposed to improve performances of MSER detection. For example, in [7], alternative stability criteria for moment-normalized extremal regions are applied to improve affine-invariance for blurred areas. In [9], MSERs are detected over saliency maps (highlighting boundaries) of images. Again, the primary objective is to improve robustness to blur.

In this paper, we also strive to correct the above-mentioned inadequacies of MSER features and, subsequently, to improve reliability of MSER-based image matching/retrieval. The main objective is to preserve, as much as possible, the original principles of MSER detection and, therefore, our approach is closer to the ideas outlined in [8] rather than to more complicated improvements proposed in other papers.

In general, instead of detecting maximally stable extremal regions in 1D space of intensity thresholds (the original MSER algorithm) the proposed method identifies extremal regions which are maximally stable both under the threshold changes and under the scale variations (i.e. blur). We demonstrate that such a switch to a 2D space only moderately increases computational complexity, while performances (evaluated by most typical metrics of images matching) can be significantly improved. We also illustrate on simple analytical examples that intuitive notions are better satisfied by the proposed model than by the original MSER model.

Section 2 of the paper presents formal details of the proposed algorithm, and illustrates selected effects resulting from this theoretical model. A limited scale experimental verification of the algorithm's performances is presented in Sect. 3. Concluding remarks are included in Sect. 4.

2   Mathematical Models

2.1   Standard MSER Detection

Maximally stable extremal regions have been defined in [1] as black (or white) areas of a thresholded image which only insignificantly vary under threshold changes. Formally, a binarized region $Q(t)$ (where t indicates its threshold level) is considered MSER if the growth rate function $q(t)$ defined by the derivative of the region area over the threshold values:

$$q(t) = \frac{\frac{d}{dt}\|Q(t)\|}{\|Q(t)\|},\tag{1}$$

reaches a local minimum ($\|\cdot\|$ indicates the region area).

In practice, Eq. 1 is substituted by one of its discrete approximations:

$$q(t_j) = \frac{\|Q(t_j) - Q(t_{j-1})\|}{\|Q(t_j)\|} \quad \text{or} \quad q(t_j) = \frac{\|Q(t_{j+1}) - Q(t_{j-1})\|}{\|Q(t_j)\|}, \quad (2)$$

where the difference $t_j - t_{j-1}$ defines the threshold increment Δt.

The above formulas apply to both dark and brigth MSERs (for the latter, images should be inverted).

A number of other parameters is used to control stability of MSER detection and to reduce the nesting effects (e.g. caused by blurs), see [1,2].

2.2 SIMSER Features

The proposed improvements of MSER features are motivated by the results from several papers (see Sect. 1) which indicate that taking into account multiple resolutions (image blurring) may improve performances. Since (to the best of our knowledge) no formal model of MSER detection in multiresolution images seems to exist, we propose *scale-insensitive maximally stable extremal regions* (SIMSERs) model which extends the mechanism of MSER detection into a 2D space $Threshold \times Scale$. Although the name *scale-insensitive* sounds redundant because MSERs are supposed to be scale-invariant by default, we can argue that such a name modification highlights improvements in the *actual* invariance of these features to rescaling (blurring) effects.

Given an image presented over a range of scales $s \in S$ (i.e. a family of images) and binarized using a range of thresholds $t \in T$, an extremal regions $Q(s,t)$ (where s defines the current scale and t indicates the current binarization threshold) is considered SIMSER, if two growth rate functions $q_1(s,t)$ and $q_2(s,t)$ defined by the partial derivatives of the region area over s and t jointly reach the local minimum there:

$$q_1(s,t) = \frac{\frac{\partial}{\partial t}\|Q(s,t)\|}{\|Q(s,t)\|}, \quad (3)$$

$$q_2(s,t) = \frac{\frac{\partial}{\partial s}\|Q(s,t)\|}{\|Q(s,t)\|}. \quad (4)$$

To illustrate the concept of region stability under blurring (scaling), Fig. 1 shows evolution of a selected dark extremal region over a number of scales.

2.3 Theoretical Advantages of SIMSERs

Advantages of SIMSERs can be preliminarily discussed using two test images, with rectangular and triangular intensity profiles, correspondingly. The images are shown in Fig. 2 (1D case is selected to simplify calculations).

MSER features are extracted from these images at minima of the growth rate function $q(t)$ (see Eq. 1), while SIMSERs are extracted at joint minima of two growth rate functions $q_1(s,t)$ and $q_2(s,t)$ (see Eqs. 3 and 4). For SIMSER

Fig. 1. A sequence of dark extremal regions over a number of neighboring scales (with the same threshold). The framed central region is maximally stable under scale changes, and may be eventually identified as SIMSER (if it is also maximally stable in the threshold dimension).

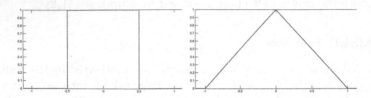

Fig. 2. Two 1D images with rectangular and triangular intensity profiles. The range of intensities is $\langle 0; 1 \rangle$.

extraction, the family of multi-scale images (where scale s ranges from 0 to ∞) is created using simple image averaging $i_s(x) = \frac{1}{2s} \int_{x-s}^{x+s} i(\zeta)d\zeta$, i.e. $s = 0$ represents the original image and larger scales correspond to more smoothing.

For the rectangular intensity profile (left image in Fig. 2):

$$q(t) = 0 \ , \quad q_1(t,s) = \frac{4s}{1 + 2s(1 - 2t)} \quad \text{and} \quad q_2(t,s) = \frac{|2 - 4t|}{1 + 2s(1 - 2t)}. \quad (5)$$

Therefore, the number of extracted MSERs is either infinite or zero (depending on the interpretation of zero values of $q(t)$), while SIMSER is detected only once for $t = 0.5$ and $s = 0$, i.e. the image should not be smoothed and the threshold is at half of the maximum intensity. Such a result is intuitively more plausible.

For the triangular intensity profile (right image in Fig. 2), $q(t) = \frac{1}{1-t}$ reaches the minimum only once for $t = 0$. Intuitively, MSER should be rather detected somewhere at non-zero threshold. The functions $q_1(s,t)$ and $q_2(s,t)$, however, have too joint minima (details are not presented because of complex and tedious mathematical analysis). First, SIMSER is detected for $t = 0$ and $s = 0$ (which is identical to MSER above), while the second SIMSER exists for $t = 0.5$ and $s = 0.5$, i.e. the image should be slightly smoothed and thresholded at half of the maximum intensity. Again, SIMSER detection results seem to be more complete and plausible.

2.4 Implementation Details and Computational Complexity

The numerical schemes for computing $q_1(s,t)$ and $q_2(s,t)$ growth rate functions in discretized $Threshold \times Scale$ space are basically the same (following Eq. 2), i.e.

$$q_1(t_j, s_k) = \frac{\|Q(t_j, s_k) - Q(t_{j-1}, s_k)\|}{\|Q(t_j, s_k)\|} \text{ or } q_1(t_j, s) = \frac{\|Q(t_{j+1}, s_k) - Q(t_{j-1}, s_k)\|}{\|Q(t_j, s_k)\|},$$

$$\tag{6}$$

$$q_2(t_j, s_k) = \frac{\|Q(t_j, s_k) - Q(t_j, s_{k-1})\|}{\|Q(t_j, s_k)\|} \text{ or } q_2(t_j, s_k) = \frac{\|Q(t_j, s_{k+1}) - Q(t_j, s_{k-1})\|}{\|Q(t_j, s_k)\|}.$$

$$\tag{7}$$

In line with recommendations from the original MSER papers and Matlab, we use in the subsequent experiments the threshold increment $\Delta t = 3$ (for images with 256 levels of intensity).

The scale-space increments follow the standards of multi-scale image processing (e.g. [10]), i.e. the original image is repetitively convolved with a smoothing filter equivalent to halving the image resolution. The minimum equivalent image size is assumed 64 because 32 pixels is a default (in Matlab) minimum size of MSER features, and we assume (somehow arbitrarily) that the largest MSER should not cover more than a half of an image. Thus, the number of scales NS is defined by

$$NS = 1 + \lfloor \log_2(n/64) \rfloor, \tag{8}$$

where n is the image resolution.

For example, for images of VGA resolution 640×480 the recommended number of scales is 13.

Based on the structure of Eqs. 6 and 7, we can preliminarily claim that computational complexity of SIMSER detection is the same as the complexity of MSER detection (subject to the multiplication by the number of scales NS, which is considered constant and as such it does not affect the theoretical estimate), i.e. $O(n \times log(log(n)))$ or $O(n)$ (the former based on [1], and the latter given in [2]).

The only issue is to verify whether the growth rate function $q_2(t_j, s_k)$, which does not exist in the original MSER algorithm, has the same or lower computational complexity. The problem is that the extremal regions over the sequence of threshold values are always nested, while the extremal regions over the sequence of scales generally do not nest (an illustrative example is given in Fig. 3), i.e. the topology of extremal regions may unpredictably change under image smoothing. Nevertheless, a simple algorithm has been proposed to track correspondences between extremal regions in the neighboring scales and to (simultaneously) compute the growth rate function $q_2(t_j, s_k)$. A commented pseudo-code of this algorithm is shown at the end of the paper. It is deliberately not optimized (a more

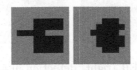

Fig. 3. Evolution of a dark extremal region over two neighboring scales (smoothing removes sharp fragments). The regions intersect significantly, but there is no nesting in either direction.

practical variant is outlined in [11]) to clearly illustrate its $O(n)$ complexity. This pseudo-code corresponds to the left expression in Eq. 7.

3   Preliminary Experimental Evaluation

SIMSER features have been experimentally compared to MSERs using several aspects of their performances. In general, the objective was to evaluate gains achieved by using SIMSERs instead of MSERs. Therefore, the results are given *relatively* to the corresponding MSER results (which are considered references with unit values).

3.1   General Properties

First, we established relations between numbers and distributions of SIMSER and MSER features in typical images. Experiments have been conducted on a large number of images (including benchmark datasets used in other experiments mentioned below), and the conclusions are as follows:

1. The numbers of SIMSER features are generally similar to the numbers of MSERs, even though SIMSERs are found from a multi-scale pyramid of images. The average number of SIMSER features is 109 % of the average number of MSERs (with very few cases outside 80 %–130 % range).
2. SIMSER features are generally better concentrated in the areas of higher visual prominence (see an example in Fig. 4) which suggests that SIMSERs are more likely to maintain their numbers under image distortions. Using a collection of near-duplicate images (including the benchmark dataset at [12]) distorted by illumination changes, blur, JPEG compression, rotation and scaling, we found that the standard deviation of SIMSER numbers within the same image under diversified distortions is, in average, lower by 38 % than the standard deviation of MSER numbers.
3. It seems the numbers of SIMSERs are less sensitive to *MaxAreaVariation* parameter which is used (see the Matlab notation at [13]) to define acceptable minima of growth rate functions.

Fig. 4. MSER (left) and SIMSER (right) detection in an exemplary image. To maximize the number of features, *MaxAreaVariation* parameter was not restricted.

3.2   Keypoint Detection and Matching

We have used three popular metrics to compare performances of SIMSERs and MSERs. First, keypoint *repeatability* is evaluated. Subsequently, reliability of keypoint matching is estimated using *precision* and *recall* parameters. Although these two parameters evaluate primarily performances of keypoint descriptors, they can be instrumental in assessing keypoint detectors as well. *Precision* and *recall* can be compared using the same descriptor over keypoints extracted by alternative detectors. We have adopted this approach, with SIFT descriptor computed over MSER and SIMSER features. SIFT (in RootSIFT variant) has been selected because of its popularity and good performances. Results based both on matching SIFT descriptors (vectors) and matching SIFT-based *visual words* are discussed; the latter for the practical importance.

Repeatability. Repeatability of MSERs and SIMSERs was compared on a popular dataset [12] which provides homographies between *the-same-category* images, so that the ground-truth keypoint correspondences can be identified similarly to [5]. It was found that both types of features have practically the same repeatability (actually, repeatability of SIMSERs is slightly higher by a statistically negligible margin of 2.4 %).

Matching (Keypoint Descriptors). *Precision* and *recall* of keypoint matching was evaluated on the same dataset [12]. First, SIFT descriptors are matched by the *one-to-one* (O2O) method (using the *mutual nearest neighbor* approach) which is considered a recommended setup returning the most credible matches, e.g. [14].

As seen in the first row of Table 1, SIMSERs outperform MSERs by a wide margin (both in *recall* and *precision* values). An illustrative example given in Fig. 5 shows a larger number of true correspondences (and fewer incorrect matches) for SIMSERs than for MSERs.

Matching (Visual Words). In actual applications (e.g. CBVIR) keypoints are represented by visual words so that *precision* and *recall* based on matching visual words are more significant in practice. Various sizes of visual vocabularies can be

Table 1. Comparative performances of matching SIMSER and MSER features using SIFT descriptors/words (the results obtained for MSERs are represented by the reference value 1.0).

Method	Precision	Recall
O2O - SIFT descriptors	2.42	2.34
M2M - 32M SIFT words	0.39	**11.22**
M2M - 1G SIFT words	0.46	**12.78**

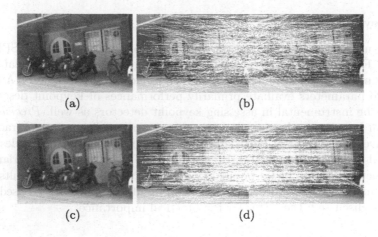

Fig. 5. A pair of near-duplicate images (a, c), and their O2O matching results for SIFT descriptors over MSERs (b) and SIMSERs (d).

used, but large vocabularies (at least a few million words) are recommended in several important works, e.g. [15,16], to provide sufficient *precision* (even though *recall* may suffer). Therefore, we performed tests focusing on very large vocabularies (vocabularies of 32 million and 1 billion words are used as examples). To minimize the computational costs of vocabulary building and word assignment, such large vocabularies are defined using a technique somehow similar to simplified *binary* embedding, where the numerical value of the code is considered the word number. Somehow surprising results (showing huge improvements in *recall* values) for those two exemplary vocabulary sizes are given in the lower part of Table 1.

The results of Table 1 can be interpreted in the context of Fig. 4 which shows that SIMSER regions (i.e. their best-fit ellipses) tend to nest more frequently than MSER ellipses (especially in most contrasted parts of images).

While nested MSERs are undesirable because they create a number of near-identical descriptors, nested SIMSERs are more useful since they represent visual data in diversified scales. Thus, their descriptors are usually sufficiently distinctive to be quantized into different words. As a result, several alternative words are found to represent what effectively is the same visual content. When near-duplicate image fragments are matched, chances are much higher that some of those alternative words are identical. An illustrative example is given in Fig. 6.

Those alternative visual words may, nevertheless, cause a drop of *precision*, as seen in Table 1 and Fig. 6. In our opinion, this is acceptable because for large vocabularies *precision* is usually so high that even if it drops by half (or more) it can still be considered satisfactory (especially if combined with a huge improvement in *recall*).

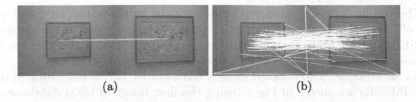

(a)   (b)

Fig. 6. In (a), MSER features of two images are matched using a vocabulary of 32M words. *Precision* is 100 %, but *recall* is very low. In (b), the same vocabulary is used to match SIMSERs. *Precision* is lower, but *recall* improves dramatically.

3.3   Image Matching

Finally, performances of SIMSERs and MSERs have been compared in a typical CBVIR task, i.e. retrieval of near-duplicate images. A popular UKB dataset (see [17,18]) was selected because of its regularity (classes of similar images do not intersect, and each class consists of exactly 4 images).

Using the same very large vocabularies of SIFT-based words of 32 M and 1G words (mentioned in Sect. 3.2), *bag-of-words* (BoW) histograms are built over MSER and SIMSER features and used for pre-retrieval of images ranked by the similarity of their BoW's to the query BoW. Individual images randomly selected from each class are used as queries.

Because our analysis is not targeting any particular database, BoW normalization requiring database statistics (e.g. *td-idf*, [19]) cannot be applied, and we use histograms of *absolute* word frequencies. We selected a simple *histogram intersection* measure of histogram similarities (proposed in [20]), where the distance between two histograms H_1 and H_2 over *Voc* vocabulary is defined by

$$d(H_1, H_2) = \sum_{w \in Voc} min(H_1(w), H_2(w)), \tag{9}$$

which nicely corresponds to the intuitive notion of similarity between images.

The results shown in Table 2 give the relative values *mean average precision* (*mAP*) for SIMSER-based approach (MSER-based results are considered unit-valued references). Again, two vocabulary sizes (i.e. 32 M and 1G words) are used, and *mAP* is computed for two different scenarios. First, *mAP* is evaluated from all retrieved images, and in the second scenario only 20 top-ranked images are taken into account.

Table 2. Relative *mean average precision* (*mAP*) of UKB image retrieval using two large vocabularies over SIMSER features (the corresponding MSER-based results are consider references with 1.0 value).

Scenario	mAP for 32M vocabulary	mAP for 1G vocabulary
All retrieved images	1.57	1.63
Only 20 top-ranked images	2.25	2.36

The results indicate significant improvements, in particular for fixed numbers of pre-retrieved images. This is because for large vocabularies *precision* of SIMSERs is much lower than for MSERs (see Table 1) so that the total number of pre-retrieved *false-positive* images would be larger for SIMSERs.

As an example, 8 top-ranked images retrieved by BoWs built over MSERs and SIMSERs are shown in Fig. 7 (using the first image of UKB database as a query).

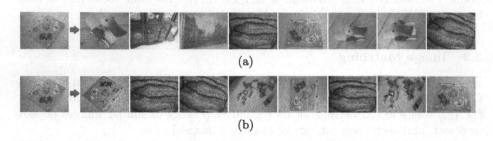

(a)

(b)

Fig. 7. Top-ranked retrievals for the first UKB image (note that in UKB each query has only three relevant images). In (a), BoW built over MSERs is applied, while in (b) BoW is built over SIMSERs. The same vocabulary of 1G words is used in both cases.

4   Conclusions

In the paper, MSER features are redefined to improve their performances, primarily in matching and retrieval tasks. Novel SIMSER features (i.e. *scale-insensitive* maximally stable extremal regions) are presented as an alternative to MSERs. SIMSERs are detected at joint local minima of two growth rate functions (in the *threshold* dimension and in the *scale* dimension), i.e. they are extremal regions which are maximally stable not only under the *threshold* changes (like MSERs) but, additionally, under *image rescaling* (smoothing). The proposed feature detector has the same complexity as MSER detector (subject to the multiplicative factor corresponding to the number of employed scales).

It has been verified that other important characteristics, namely the average numbers of features in images and repeatability of features, are practically the same for SIMSERs and MSERs.

However, CBVIR-related performances, i.e. *recall* and *precision* of keypoint matching, and *mean average precision* of image retrieval, are significantly improved for SIMSERs. In particular, results on a benchmark dataset indicate that SIMSERs are recommended in conjunction with huge-size visual vocabularies, for which they achieve a tenfold increase of *recall* over MSERs. This is an important property, because dramatically lowering *recall* has been detrimental to the usage of huge visual vocabularies (which, otherwise, are recommended for large-scale CBVIR applications).

Apart from typical CBVIR tasks, SIMSERs can prospectively replace MSERs in other applications. For example, we envisage that image segmentation could be one of such areas, because multiple-scale MSERs are explicitly used there (e.g. [21]) or MSER-like structures are exploited as a supplementary tool (e.g. [22]).

Pseudo-code for computing $q_2(t_j, s_k)$ growth rate function

```
Input: Im1(M,N), Im0(M,N)
% two binary images of M*N size (at two neighbouring scales)
Input: Rs1(M,N), Rs0(M,N)
% two labeled images of M*N size
Input: SoR1(K1), SoR0(K0)
% list of region sizes (K1 regions in Im1 and K0 regions in Im0)
Storage: Ints(K1,K0) <- zeros
% size of intersections between regions from Im1 and Im0
Output storage: q2(K1) <- large value
% q2 function for Im1 regions initialized with very large values
Output storage: previous(K1) <- zeros
% the numbers of the corresponding regions from the previous scale

for i = 1:M
  for j = 1:N
    if Im1(i,j)==Im0(i,j)
        Ints(Rs1(i,j),Rs0(i,j))++;
    endif
  endfor
endfor
for i = 1:M
  for j = 1:N
    temp = SoR1(Rs1(i,j))+SoR0(Rs0(i,j)) - 2*Ints(Rs1(i,j),Rs0(i,j));
    temp = temp/SoR1(Rs1(i,j));
    if temp < q2(Rs1(i,j)) && Ints(Rs1(i,j),Rs0(i,j)) > 0
        q2(Rs1(i,j)) = temp; previous(Rs1(i,j)) = Rs0(i,j);
    endif
  endfor
endfor
```

References

1. Matas, J., Chum, O., Urban, M., Pajdla, T.: Robust wide baseline stereo from maximally stable extremal regions. In: Proceedings of British Machine Vision Conference, pp. 384–393 (2002)
2. Nistér, D., Stewénius, H.: Linear time maximally stable extremal regions. In: Forsyth, D., Torr, P., Zisserman, A. (eds.) ECCV 2008. LNCS, vol. 5303, pp. 183–196. Springer, Heidelberg (2008). doi:10.1007/978-3-540-88688-4_14
3. Kristensen, F., MacLean, W.: Real-time extraction of maximally stable extremal regions on an FPGA. In: Proceedings of IEEE Symposium on ISCAS 2007, pp. 165–168 (2007)
4. Salahat, E., Saleh, H., Sluzek, A., Al-Qutayri, M., Mohammed, B., Ismail, M.: A maximally stable extremal regions system-on-chip for real-time visual surveillance. In: Proceedings of 41st IEEE Industrial Electronics Society Conference, IECON 2015, pp. 2812–2815 (2015)

5. Mikolajczyk, K., Tuytelaars, T., Schmid, C., Zisserman, A., Matas, J., Schaffalitzky, F., Kadir, T., Gool, L.V.: A comparison of affine region detectors. Int. J. Comput. Vis. **65**, 43–72 (2005)
6. Lindeberg, T.: Scale-space theory: A basic tool for analyzing structures at different scales. J. Appl. Stat. **21**, 224–270 (1994)
7. Kimmel, R., Zhang, C., Bronstein, A.M., Bronstein, M.M.: Are MSER features really interesting? IEEE PAMI **33**(11), 2316–2320 (2011)
8. Forssén, P.E., Lowe, D.G.: Shape descriptors for maximally stable extremal regions. In: Proceedings of 11th IEEE Conference on ICCV 2007, pp. 1–8 (2007)
9. Martins, P., Carvalho, P., Gatta, C.: On the completeness of feature-driven maximally stable extremal regions. Pattern Recogn. Lett. **74**, 9–16 (2016)
10. Lindeberg, T.: Feature detection with automatic scale selection. Int. J. Comput. Vis. **30**, 77–116 (1998)
11. Sluzek, A., Saleh, H.: Algorithmic foundations for hardware implementation of scale-insensitive MSER features. In: Proceedings of 59th IEEE MWSCAS Symposium, Abu Dhabi (2016, accepted)
12. Mikolajczyk, K.: http://www.robots.ox.ac.uk/~vgg/research/affine/
13. MathWorks®: http://www.mathworks.com/help/vision/ref/detectmserfeatures.html
14. Zhao, W.L., Ngo, C.W., Tan, H.K., Wu, X.: Near-duplicate keyframe identification with interest point matching and pattern learning. IEEE Trans. Multimed. **9**(5), 1037–1048 (2007)
15. Philbin, J., Chum, O., Isard, M., Sivic, J., Zisserman, A.: Object retrieval with large vocabularies and fast spatial matching. In: Proceedings of IEEE Conference on CVPR 2007, pp. 1–8 (2007)
16. Stewénius, H., Gunderson, S., Pilet, J.: Size matters: exhaustive geometric verification for image retrieval. In: Proceedings of 12th European Conference on ECCV 2012, Florence, vol. II, pp. 674–687 (2012)
17. Stewénius, H.: http://www.vis.uky.edu/stewe/ukbench/
18. Nistér, D., Stewénius, H.: Scalable recognition with a vocabulary tree. In: Proceedings of IEEE Conference on CVPR 2006, vol. 2, pp. 2161–2168 (2006)
19. Sivic, J., Zisserman, A.: Video google: a text retrieval approach to object matching in videos. In: Proceedings of 9th IEEE Conference on ICCV 2003, Nice,vol. 2, pp. 1470–1477 (2003)
20. Swain, M., Ballard, D.: Color indexing. Int. J. Comput. Vis. **7**(1), 11–32 (1991)
21. Oh, I.-S., Lee, J., Majumder, A.: Multi-scale image segmentation using MSER. In: Wilson, R., Hancock, E., Bors, A., Smith, W. (eds.) CAIP 2013. LNCS, vol. 8048, pp. 201–208. Springer, Heidelberg (2013). doi:10.1007/978-3-642-40246-3_25
22. Wang, G., Gao, K., Zhang, Y., Li, J.: Efficient perceptual region detector based on object boundary. In: Tian, Q., Sebe, N., Qi, G.-J., Huet, B., Hong, R., Liu, X. (eds.) MMM 2016. LNCS, vol. 9517, pp. 66–78. Springer, Heidelberg (2016). doi:10.1007/978-3-319-27674-8_7

W20 – The Second International Workshop on Video Segmentation

Preface

The second International Workshop on Video Segmentation (IWVS) was held in Amsterdam, Netherlands on October 10th, 2016, in conjunction with the European Conference on Computer Vision (ECCV). This is the second edition of the workshop, followed after the successful first IWVS in 2014 in Zürich. Video segmentation could be of crucial importance for building 3D object models from video, understanding dynamic scenes, robot-object interaction and a number of high-level vision tasks. The theme of this workshop is *How can video segmentation support learning?* which focuses on the conjunction between video segmentation and recent advances in deep learning for recognition and perceptual organization.

The workshop consisted of 5 invited talks, 7 talks from submitted work, 1 presentation of the recently published DAVIS video segmentation dataset, and a panel discussion. 6 of the submissions are present in this conference proceedings. The workshop had received 10 valid submissions from 5 countries. The submissions were of very high quality. These submissions were reviewed by at least 2 separate organizers. An external reviewer was contacted and provided the review for a paper outside the expertise of the organizers. We would like to thank all the authors who submitted to the workshop as well as the external reviewer for their time and effort.

The 6 papers in this proceedings covered many aspects of video segmentation, such as video segmentation based on spatial-temporal voxels, 3D point cloud video segmentation, image boundaries for video segmentation, fence segmentation and video semantic segmentation. The invited talks were presented by Dr. Michael Black from Max Planck Institute for Intelligent Systems, Dr. Vittorio Ferrari from University of Edinburgh, Dr. Michal Irani from Weizmann Institute of Science, Dr. Jitendra Malik from University of California - Berkeley and Dr. Stefano Soatto from University of California - Los Angeles. These invited speakers have also attended the panel discussion. We would like to thank the ECCV 2016 workshop chairs (Herve Jegou and Gang Hua) and workshop publication chair (Albert Ali Salah) for their support and feedback. We would also like to thank all the invited speakers, authors who presented at the workshop and the attendees. The workshop acknowledges the support from the US National Science Foundation (IIS-1320348, IIS-1464371).

Thomas Brox
Katerina Fragkiadaki
Fabio Galasso
Fuxin Li
James M. Rehg
Bernt Schiele
Michael Ying Yang

Improved Image Boundaries for Better Video Segmentation

Anna Khoreva[1]([✉]), Rodrigo Benenson[1], Fabio Galasso[2], Matthias Hein[3],
and Bernt Schiele[1]

[1] Max Planck Institute for Informatics, Saarbrücken, Germany
khoreva@mpi-inf.mpg.de
[2] OSRAM Corporate Technology, Munich, Germany
[3] Saarland University, Saarbrücken, Germany

Abstract. Graph-based video segmentation methods rely on superpixels as starting point. While most previous work has focused on the construction of the graph edges and weights as well as solving the graph partitioning problem, this paper focuses on better superpixels for video segmentation. We demonstrate by a comparative analysis that superpixels extracted from boundaries perform best, and show that boundary estimation can be significantly improved via image and time domain cues. With superpixels generated from our better boundaries we observe consistent improvement for two video segmentation methods in two different datasets.

| Video | TSP superpixels [7] (117 spx) | gPb$_\mathcal{I}$ superpixels [2] (101 spx) | Our superpixels (101 spx) |

Fig. 1. Graph based video segmentation relies on having high quality superpixels/voxels as starting point (graph nodes). We explore diverse techniques to improve boundary estimates, which result in better superpixels, which in turn has a significant impact on final video segmentation.

1 Introduction

Class-agnostic image and video segmentation have shown to be helpful in diverse computer vision tasks such as object detection (via object proposals) [18,19,25, 32], semantic video segmentation (as pre-segmentation) [9], activity recognition (by computing features on voxels) [37], or scene understanding [21].

Both image and video segmentation have seen steady progress recently leveraging advanced machine learning techniques. A popular and successful approach consists of modelling segmentation as a graph partitioning problem [12,22,29],

© Springer International Publishing Switzerland 2016
G. Hua and H. Jégou (Eds.): ECCV 2016 Workshops, Part III, LNCS 9915, pp. 773–788, 2016.
DOI: 10.1007/978-3-319-49409-8_64

where the nodes represent pixels or superpixels, and the edges encode the spatio-temporal structure. Previous work focused on solving the partitioning problem [6,16,30,41], on the unary and pairwise terms of the graph [14] and on the graph construction itself [24,33,38].

The aim of this paper is to improve video segmentation by focusing on the graph nodes themselves, the video superpixels. These nodes are the starting point for unary and pairwise terms, and thus directly impact the final segmentation quality. Good superpixels for video segmentation should both be temporally consistent and give high boundary recall, and, in the case of graph-based video segmentation, for efficient runtime should enable to use a few superpixels per frame which is related to high boundary precision.

Our experiments show that existing classical superpixel/voxel methods [1,4, 7] underperform for graph-based video segmentation and superpixels built from per-frame boundary estimates are more effective for the task (see Sect. 5). We show that boundary estimates can be improved when using image cues combined with object-level cues, and by merging with temporal cues. By fusing image and time domain cues, we can significantly enhance boundary estimation in video frames, improve per-frame superpixels, and thus improve video segmentation.

In particular we contribute:

- a comparative evaluation of the importance of the initial superpixels/voxels for graph-based video segmentations (Sect. 5).
- significantly improved boundary estimates (and thus per-frame superpixels) by the careful fusion of image (Sect. 6.1) and time (Sect. 6.2) domain cues.
- the integration of high-level object-related cues into the local image segmentation processing (Sect. 6.1).
- state-of-the-art video segmentation results on the VSB100 [15] and BMDS [6] datasets.

2   Related Work

Video Segmentation. Video segmentation can be seen as a clustering problem in the 3D spatial-temporal volume. Considering superpixels/voxels as nodes, graphs are a natural way to address video segmentation and there are plenty of approaches to process the graphs. Most recent and successful techniques include hybrid generative and discriminative approaches with mixtures of trees [3], agglomerative methods constructing video segment hierarchies [16,30], techniques based on tracking/propagation of image-initialized solutions [4,7] and optimization methods based on Conditional Random Fields [8]. We leverage spectral clustering [28,35], one of the most successful approaches to video segmentation [2,12,22,24,29] and consider in our experiments the methods of [14,15].

The above approaches cover various aspects related to graph based video segmentation. Several papers have addressed the features for video segmentation [6,16,30] and some work has addressed the graph construction [33,38]. While these methods are based on superpixels none of them examines the quality of the respective superpixels for graph-based video segmentation. To the best of our knowledge, this work is the first to thoroughly analyse and advance superpixel methods in the context of video segmentation.

Superpixels/Voxels. We distinguish two groups of superpixel methods. The first one is the classical superpixel/voxel methods [1,4,7,26]. These methods are designed to extract superpixels of homogeneous shape and size, in order for them to have a regular topology. Having a regular superpixel topology has shown a good basis for image and video segmentation [3,16,31,33].

The second group are based on boundary estimation and focus on the image content. They extract superpixels by building a hierarchical image segmentation [2,10,20,32] and selecting one level in the hierarchy. These methods generate superpixels of heterogeneous size, that are typically fairly accurate on each frame but may jitter over time. Superpixels based on per-frame boundary estimation are employed in many state-of-the-art video segmentation methods [14,21,39,41].

In this work we argue that boundaries based superpixels are more suitable for graph-based video segmentation, and propose to improve the extracted superpixels by exploring temporal information such as optical flow and temporal smoothing.

Image Boundaries. After decades of research on image features and filter banks [2], most recent methods use machine learning, e.g. decision forests [10,17], mutual information [20], or convolutional neural networks [5,40]. We leverage the latest trends and further improve them, especially in relation to video data.

3   Video Segmentation Methods

For our experiments we consider two open source state-of-the-art graph-based video segmentation methods [14,15]. Both of them rely on superpixels extracted from hierarchical image segmentation [2], which we aim to improve.

Spectral Graph Reduction [14]. Our first baseline is composed of three main parts.

1. *Extraction of superpixels.* Superpixels are image-based pixel groupings which are similar in terms of colour and texture, extracted by using the state-of-the-art image segmentation of [2]. These superpixels are accurate but not temporally consistent, as only extracted per frame.
2. *Feature computation.* Superpixels are compared to their (spatio-temporal) neighbours and affinities are computed between pairs of them based on appearance, motion and long term point trajectories [29], depending on the type of neighbourhood (e.g. within a frame, across frames, etc.).
3. *Graph partitioning.* Video segmentation is cast as the grouping of superpixels into video volumes. [14] employs either a spectral clustering or normalised cut formulation for incorporating a reweighing scheme to improve the performance.

In our paper we focus on the first part. We show that superpixels extracted from stronger boundary estimation help to achieve better segmentation performance without altering the underlying features or the graph partitioning method.

Segmentation Propagation [15]. As the second video segmentation method we consider the baseline proposed in [15]. This method does greedy matching of superpixels by propagating them over time via optical flow. This "simple" method obtains state-of-the-art performance on VSB100. We therefore also report how superpixels extracted via hierarchical image segmentation based on our proposed boundary estimation improve this baseline.

4   Video Segmentation Evaluation

VSB100. We consider for learning and for evaluation the challenging video segmentation benchmark VSB100 [15] based on the HD quality video sequences of [36], containing natural scenes as well as motion pictures, with heterogeneous appearance and motion. The dataset is arranged into train (40 videos) and test (60) set. Additionally we split the training set into a training (24) and validation set (16).

The evaluation in VSB100 is mainly given by:

Precision-recall plots (BPR, VPR): VSB100 distinguishes a boundary precision-recall metric (BPR), measuring the per-frame boundary alignment between a video segmentation solution and the human annotations, and a volume precision-recall metric (VPR), reflecting the temporal consistency of the video segmentation result.

Aggregate performance measures (AP, ODS, OSS): for both BPR and VPR, VSB100 reports average precision (AP), the area under the precision-recall curves, and two F-measures where one is measured at an optimal dataset scale (ODS) and the other at an optimal segmentation scale (OSS) (where "optimal" stands for oracle provided).

BMDS. To show the generalization of the proposed method we further consider the Berkeley Motion Segmentation Dataset (BMDS) [6], which consists of 26 VGA-quality videos, representing mainly humans and cars. Following prior work [23] we use 10 videos for training and 16 as a test set, and restrict all video sequences to the first 30 frames.

5   Superpixels and Supervoxels

Graph-based video segmentation methods rely on superpixels to compute features and affinities. Employing superpixels as pre-processing stage for video segmentation provides a desirable computational reduction and a powerful per-frame representation.

Ideally these superpixels have high boundary recall (since one cannot recover from missing recall), good temporal consistency (to make matching across time

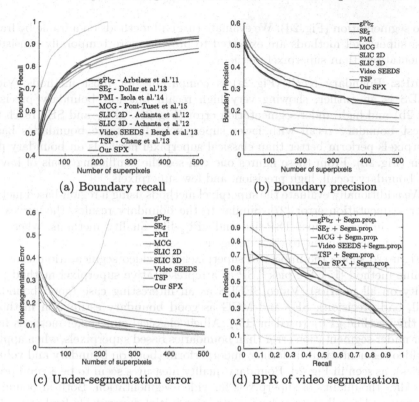

(a) Boundary recall

(b) Boundary precision

(c) Under-segmentation error

(d) BPR of video segmentation

Fig. 2. Comparison of different superpixel/voxel methods, and their use for video segmentation. VSB100 validation set. SPX: superpixels. Segm. prop.: segmentation propagation [15] (see Sect. 3).

easier), and are as few as possible (in order to reduce the chances of segmentation errors; to accelerate overall computation and reduce memory needs).

In this section we explore which type of superpixels are most suitable for graph-based video segmentation.

Superpixel/Voxel Methods. Many superpixel/voxel methods have been explored in the past. We consider the most promising ones in the experiments of Fig. 2. SLIC 2D/3D [1] is a classic method to obtain superpixels via iterative clustering (in space and space-time domain). TSP [7] extends SLIC to explicitly model temporal dynamics. Video SEEDS [4] is similar to SLIC 3D, but uses an alternative optimization strategy. Other than classic superpixel/voxel methods we also consider superpixels generated from per-frame hierarchical segmentation based on boundary detection (ultrametric contour maps [2]). We include gPb$_\mathcal{I}$ [2], SE$_\mathcal{I}$ [10], PMI [20] and MCG [32] as sources of boundary estimates.

Superpixel Evaluation. We compare superpixels by evaluating the recall and precision of boundaries and the under-segmentation error [27] as functions of the average number of superpixels per frame. We also use some of them directly for video segmentation (Fig. 2d). We evaluate (use) all methods on a frame by frame basis; supervoxel methods are expected to provide more temporally consistent segmentations than superpixel methods.

Results. Boundary recall (Fig. 2a) is comparable for most methods. Video SEEDS is an outlier, showing very high recall, but low boundary precision (Fig. 2b) and high under-segmentation error (Fig. 2c). $gPb_\mathcal{I}$ and $SE_\mathcal{I}$ reach the highest boundary recall with fewer superpixels. Per-frame boundaries based superpixels perform better than classical superpixel methods on boundary precision (Fig. 2b). From these figures one can see the conflicting goals of having high boundary recall, high precision, and few superpixels.

We additionally evaluate the superpixel methods using a region-based metric: under-segmentation error [27]. Similar to the boundary results, the curves are clustered in two groups: TSP-like and $gPb_\mathcal{I}$-like quality methods, where the latter underperform due to the heterogeneous shape and size of superpixels (2c).

Figure 2d shows the impact of superpixels for video segmentation using the baseline method [15]. We pick TSP as a representative superpixel method (fair quality on all metrics), Video SEEDS as an interesting case (good boundary recall, bad precision), $SE_\mathcal{I}$ and MCG as good boundary estimation methods, and the baseline $gPb_\mathcal{I}$ (used in [15]). Albeit classical superpixel methods have lower under-segmentation error than boundaries based superpixels, when applied for video segmentation the former underperform (both on boundary and volume metrics), as seen in Fig. 2d. Boundary quality measures seem to be a good proxy to predict the quality of superpixels for video segmentation. Both in boundary precision and recall metrics having stronger initial superpixels leads to better results.

Intuition. Figure 1 shows a visual comparison of TSP superpixels versus $gPb_\mathcal{I}$ superpixels (both generated with a similar number of superpixels). By design, most classical superpixel methods have a tendency to generate superpixels of comparable size. When requested to generate fewer superpixels, they need to trade-off quality versus regular size. Methods based on hierarchical segmentation (such as $gPb_\mathcal{I}$) generate superpixels of heterogeneous sizes and more likely to form semantic regions. For a comparable number of superpixels techniques based on image segmentation have more freedom to provide better superpixels for graph-based video segmentation than classical superpixel methods.

Conclusion. Based both on quality metrics and on their direct usage for graph-based video segmentation, boundary based superpixels extracted via hierarchical segmentation are more effective than the classical superpixel methods in the context of video segmentation. The hierarchical segmentation is fully defined by the estimated boundary probability, thus better boundaries lead to better superpixels, which in turn has a significant impact on final video segmentation. In the next sections we discuss how to improve boundary estimation for video.

6 Improving Image Boundaries

To improve the boundary based superpixels fed into video segmentation we seek to make best use of the information available on the videos. We first improve boundary estimates using each image frame separately (Sect. 6.1) and then consider the temporal dimension (Sect. 6.2).

6.1 Image Domain Cues

A classic boundary estimation method (often used in video segmentation) is $gPb_\mathcal{I}$ [2] ($\mathcal{I}$: image domain), we use it as a reference point for boundary quality metrics. In our approach we propose to use $SE_\mathcal{I}$ ("structured edges") [10]. We also considered the convnet based boundary detector [40]. However employing boundaries of [40] to close the contours and construct per-frame hierarchical segmentation results in the performance similar to $SE_\mathcal{I}$ and significantly longer training time. Therefore in our system we employ $SE_\mathcal{I}$ due to its speed and good quality.

Object Proposals. Methods such as $gPb_\mathcal{I}$ and $SE_\mathcal{I}$ use bottom-up information even though boundaries annotated by humans in benchmarks such as BSDS500 or VSB100 often follow object boundaries. In other words, an oracle having access to ground truth semantic object boundaries should allow to improve boundary estimation (in particular on the low recall region of the BPR curves). Based on this intuition we consider using segment-level object proposal (OP) methods to improve initial boundary estimates ($SE_\mathcal{I}$). Object proposal methods [18,19,25, 32] aim at generating a set of candidate segments likely to have high overlap with true objects. Typically such methods reach $\sim 80\,\%$ object recall with 10^3 proposals per image.

Based on initial experiments we found that the following simple approach obtains good boundary estimation results in practice. Given a set of object proposal segments generated from an initial boundary estimate, we average the contours of each segment. Pixels that are boundaries to many object proposals will have high probability of boundary; pixels rarely members of a proposal boundary will have low probability. With this approach, the better the object proposals, the closer we are to the mentioned oracle case.

We evaluated multiple proposals methods [18,25,32] and found RIGOR [18] to be most effective for this use (Sect. 6.1). To the best of our knowledge this is the first time an object proposal method is used to improve boundary estimation. We name the resulting boundary map OP ($SE_\mathcal{I}$).

Globalized Probability of Boundary. A key ingredient of the classic $gPb_\mathcal{I}$ [2] method consists on "globalizing boundaries". The most salient boundaries are highlighted by computing a weighted sum of the spatial derivatives of the first few eigenvectors of an affinity matrix built based on an input probability of boundary. The affinity matrix can be built either at the pixel or superpixel level. The resulting boundaries are named "spectral" probability of boundary, $sPb\,(\cdot)$. We employ the fast implementation from [32].

Albeit well known, such a globalization step is not considered by the latest work on boundary estimation (e.g. [5,10]). Since we compute boundaries at a single-scale, sPb (SE$_\mathcal{I}$) is comparable to the SCG results in [32].

Re-training. Methods such as SE$_\mathcal{I}$ are trained and tuned for the BSDS500 image segmentation dataset [2]. Given that VSB100 [15] is larger and arguably more relevant to the video segmentation task than BSDS500, we retrain SE$_\mathcal{I}$ (and RIGOR) for this task. In the following sections we report results of our system trained over BSDS500, or with VSB100. We will also consider using input data other than an RGB image (Sect. 6.2).

Merging Cues. After obtaining complementary probabilities of boundary maps (e.g. OP (SE$_\mathcal{I}$), sPb (SE$_\mathcal{I}$), etc.), we want to combine them effectively. Naive averaging is inadequate because boundaries estimated by different methods do not have pixel-perfect alignment amongst each other. Pixel-wise averaging or maxing leads to undesirable double edges (negatively affecting boundary precision).

To solve this issue we use the grouping technique from [32] which proposes to first convert the boundary estimate into a hierarchical segmentation, and then to align the segments from different methods. Note that we do not use the multi-scale part of [32]. Unless otherwise specified all cues are averaged with equal weight. We use the sign "+" to indicate such merges.

Boundary Results When Using Image Domain Cues. Figure 3 reports results when using the different image domain cues, evaluated over the VSB100 validation set. The gPb$_\mathcal{I}$ baseline obtains 47 % AP, while SE$_\mathcal{I}$ (trained on BSDS500) obtains 46 %. Interestingly, boundaries based on object proposals

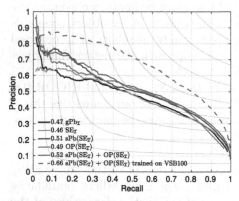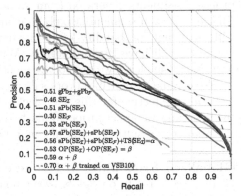

Fig. 3. Progress when integrating various image domain cues (Sect. 6.1) in terms of BPR on VSB100 validation set.

Fig. 4. Progress when integrating image and time domain cues (Sect. 6.2) in terms of BPR on VSB100 validation set.

OP $(\mathrm{SE}_\mathcal{I})$ from RIGOR obtain a competitive 49%, and, as expected, provide most gain in the high precision region of BPR. Globalization sPb $(\mathrm{SE}_\mathcal{I})$ improves results to 51% providing a homogeneous gain across the full recall range. Combining sPb $(\mathrm{SE}_\mathcal{I})$ and OP $(\mathrm{SE}_\mathcal{I})$ obtains 52%. After retraining $\mathrm{SE}_\mathcal{I}$ on VSB100 we obtain our best result of 66% AP (note that all cues are affected by retraining $\mathrm{SE}_\mathcal{I}$).

Conclusion. Even when using only image domain cues, large gains can be obtained over the standard gPb$_\mathcal{I}$ baseline.

6.2 Temporal Cues

The results of Sect. 6.1 ignore the fact that we are processing a video sequence. In the next sections we describe two different strategies to exploit the temporal dimension.

Optical Flow. We propose to improve boundaries for video by employing optical flow cues. We use the state-of-the-art EpicFlow [34] algorithm, which we feed with our $\mathrm{SE}_\mathcal{I}$ boundary estimates.

Since optical flow is expected to be smooth across time, if boundaries are influenced by flow, they will become more temporally consistent. Our strategy consists of computing boundaries directly over the forward and backward flow map, by applying SE over the optical flow magnitude (similar to one of the cues used in [11]). We name the resulting boundaries map $\mathrm{SE}_\mathcal{F}$ ($\mathcal{F}$: optical flow). Although the flow magnitude disregards the orientation information from the flow map, in practice discontinuities in magnitude are related to changes in flow direction.

We then treat $\mathrm{SE}_\mathcal{F}$ similarly to $\mathrm{SE}_\mathcal{I}$ and compute OP $(\mathrm{SE}_\mathcal{F})$ and sPb $(\mathrm{SE}_\mathcal{F})$ over it. All these cues are finally merged using the method described in Sect. 6.1.

Time Smoothing. The goal of our new boundaries based superpixels is not only high recall, but also good temporal consistency across frames. A naive way to improve temporal smoothness of boundaries consists of averaging boundary maps of different frames over a sliding window; differences across frames would be smoothed out, but at the same time double edge artefacts (due to motion) would appear (reduced precision).

We propose to improve temporal consistency by doing a sliding window average across boundary maps of several adjacent frames. For each frame t, instead of naively transferring boundary estimates from one frame to the next, we warp frames $t_{\pm i}$ using optical flow with respect to frame t; thus reducing double edge artefacts. For each frame t we treat warped boundaries from frames $t_{\pm i}$ as additional cues, and merge them using the same mechanism as in Sect. 6.1. This merging mechanism is suitable to further reduce the double edges issue.

Boundary Results When Using Temporal Cues. The curves of Fig. 4 show the improvement gained from optical flow and temporal smoothing.

Optical Flow. Figure 4 shows that on its own flow boundaries are rather weak ($SE_{\mathcal{F}}$, $sPb(SE_{\mathcal{F}})$), but they are quite complementary to image domain cues ($sPb(SE_{\mathcal{I}})$ versus $sPb(SE_{\mathcal{I}}) + sPb(SE_{\mathcal{F}})$).

Temporal Smoothing. Using temporal smoothing ($sPb(SE_{\mathcal{I}}) + sPb(SE_{\mathcal{F}}) + TS(SE_{\mathcal{I}}) = \alpha$) leads to a minor drop in boundary precision, in comparison with $sPb(SE_{\mathcal{I}}) + sPb(SE_{\mathcal{F}})$ in Fig. 4. It should be noted that there is an inherent tension between improving temporal smoothness of the boundaries and having better accuracy on a frame by frame basis. Thus we aim for the smallest negative impact on BPR. In our preliminary experiments the key for temporal smoothing was to use the right merging strategy (Sect. 6.1). We expect temporal smoothing to improve temporal consistency.

Object Proposals. Adding $OP(SE_{\mathcal{F}})$ over $OP(SE_{\mathcal{I}})$ also improves BPR (see $OP(SE_{\mathcal{F}}) + OP(SE_{\mathcal{I}}) = \beta$ in Fig. 4), particularly in the high-precision area. Merging it with other cues helps to push BPR for our final frame-by-frame result.

Combination and Re-training. Combining all cues together improves the BPR metric with respect to only using appearance cues, we reach 59 % AP versus 52 % with appearance only (see Sect. 6.1). This results are better than the $gPb_{\mathcal{I}} + gPb_{\mathcal{F}}$ baseline (51 % AP, used in [14]).

Similar to the appearance-only case, re-training over VSB100 gives an important boost (70 % AP). In this case not only $SE_{\mathcal{I}}$ is re-trained but also $SE_{\mathcal{F}}$ (over EpicFlow).

Figure 2 compares superpixels extracted from the proposed method ($\alpha + \beta$ model without re-training for fair comparison) with other methods. Our method reaches top results on both boundary precision and recall. Unless otherwise specified, all following "Our SPX" results correspond to superpixels generated from the hierarchical image segmentation [2] based on the proposed boundary estimation $\alpha + \beta$ re-trained on VSB100.

Conclusion. Temporal cues are effective at improving the boundary detection for video sequences. Because we use multiple ingredients based on machine learning, training on VSB100 significantly improves quality of boundary estimates on a per-frame basis (BPR).

7   Video Segmentation Results

In this section we show results for the state-of-the-art video segmentation methods [14,15] with superpixels extracted from the proposed boundary estimation. So far we have only evaluated boundaries of frame-by-frame hierarchical segmentation. For all further experiments we will use the best performing model trained on VSB100, which uses image domain and temporal cues, proposed in

Sect. 6 (we refer to $(\alpha + \beta)$ model, see Fig. 4). Superpixels extracted from our boundaries help to improve video segmentation and generalizes across different datasets.

7.1   Validation Set Results

We use two baseline methods ([14,15], see Sect. 3) to show the advantage of using the proposed superpixels, although our approach is directly applicable to any graph-based video segmentation technique. The baseline methods originally employ the superpixels proposed by [2,13], which use the boundary estimation $\mathrm{gPb}_{\mathcal{I}} + \mathrm{gPb}_{\mathcal{F}}$ to construct a segmentation.

For the baseline method of [14] we build a graph, where superpixels generated from the hierarchical image segmentation based on the proposed boundary estimation are taken as nodes. Following [14] we select the hierarchy level of image segmentation to extract superpixels (threshold over the ultrametric contour map) by a grid search on the validation set. We aim for the level which gives the best video segmentation performance, optimizing for both BPR and VPR.

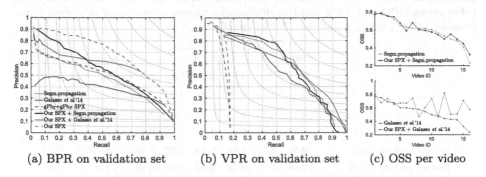

(a) BPR on validation set   (b) VPR on validation set   (c) OSS per video

Fig. 5. VSB100 validation set results of different video segmentation methods. Dashed lines indicate only frame-by-frame processing (see Sect. 7.1 for details).

Figure 5 presents results on the validation set of VSB100. The dashed curves indicate frame-by-frame segmentation and show (when touching the continuous curves) the chosen level of hierarchy to extract superpixels. As it appears in the plots, our superpixels help to improve video segmentation performance on BPR and VPR for both baseline methods [14,15]. Figure 5c shows the performance of video segmentation with the proposed superpixels per video sequence. Our method improves most on hard cases, where the performance of the original approach was quite low, OSS less than 0.5.

7.2   Test Set Results

VSB100. Figure 6 and Table 1 show the comparison of the baseline methods [14,15] with and without superpixels generated from the proposed boundaries, and with state-of-the-art video segmentation algorithms on the test set of

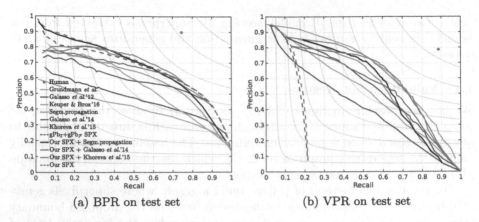

(a) BPR on test set   (b) VPR on test set

Fig. 6. Comparison of state-of-the-art video segmentation algorithms with/without our improved superpixels, on the test set of VSB100 [15]. Dashed lines indicate only frame-by-frame processing. See Table 1 and Sect. 7.2 for details.

Table 1. Comparison of state-of-the-art video segmentation algorithms with our proposed method based on the improved superpixels, on the test set of VSB100 [15]. The table shows BPR and VPR and length statistics (mean μ, standard deviation δ, no. clusters NCL), see Fig. 6 and Sect. 7.2 for details.

Algorithm	BPR			VPR			Length	NCL
	ODS	OSS	AP	ODS	OSS	AP	$\mu\,(\delta)$	μ
Human	0.81	0.81	0.67	0.83	0.83	0.70	83.2(40.0)	11.9
Grundmann et al. [16]	0.47	0.54	0.41	0.52	0.55	0.52	87.7(34.0)	18.8
Galasso et al.'12 [13]	0.51	0.56	0.45	0.45	0.51	0.42	80.2(37.6)	8.0
Yi and Pavlovic [41]	0.63	0.67	0.60	**0.64**	**0.67**	0.65	35.83(38.9)	167.3
Keuper and Brox [22]	0.56	0.63	0.56	**0.64**	0.66	**0.67**	1.1(0.7)	962.6
Segm. propagation [15]	0.61	0.65	0.59	0.59	0.62	0.56	25.5(36.5)	258.1
Our SPX + [15]	**0.64**	**0.69**	**0.67**	0.61	0.63	0.57	22.2(34.4)	216.8
Spectral graph reduction [14]	0.62	0.66	**0.54**	0.55	0.59	**0.55**	61.3(40.9)	80.0
Our SPX + [14]	**0.66**	0.68	0.51	**0.58**	**0.61**	**0.55**	70.4(40.2)	15.0
Graph construction [24]	0.64	**0.70**	0.61	0.63	0.66	**0.63**	83.4(35.3)	50.0
Our SPX +[24]	**0.66**	**0.70**	0.55	**0.64**	**0.67**	0.61	79.4(35.6)	50.0

VSB100. For extracting per-frame superpixels from the constructed hierarchical segmentation we use the level selected on the validation set.

As shown in the plots and the table, the proposed method improves the baselines considered. The segmentation propagation [15] method improves ~ 5 percent points on the BPR metrics, and $1 \sim 2$ points on the VPR metrics. This supports that employing temporal cues helps to improve temporal consistency across frames. Our superpixels also boosts the performance of the approach from [14].

Video   GT   [15]   Our   [14]   Our
                                        SPX+[15]   SPX+[14]

Fig. 7. Comparison of video segmentation results of [14,15] with our proposed super-pixels to one human ground truth. The last row shows a failure case for all methods.

Employing our method for graph-based video segmentation also benefits com-putational load, since it depends on the number of nodes in the graph (number of generated superpixels). On average the number of nodes is reduced by a factor of 2.6, 120 superpixels per frame versus 310 in [14]. This leads to ∼45 % reduction in runtime and memory usage for video segmentation.

Given the videos and their optical flow, the superpixel computation takes 90 % of the total time and video segmentation only 10 % (for both [14] and our SPX + [14]). Our superpixels are computed 20 % faster than $gPb_\mathcal{I} + gPb_\mathcal{F}$ (the bulk of the time is spent in OP $(\cdot)$). The overall time of our approach is 20 % faster than [14].

Qualitative results are shown in Fig. 7. Superpixels generated from the pro-posed boundaries allow the baseline methods [14,15] to better distinguish visual objects and to limit label leakage due to inherent temporal smoothness of the boundaries. Qualitatively the proposed superpixels improve video segmentation on easy (e.g. first row of Fig. 7) as well as hard cases (e.g. second row of Fig. 7).

As our approach is directly applicable to any graph-based video segmenta-tion technique we additionaly evaluated our superpixels with the classifier-based graph construction method of [24]. The method learns the topology and edge weights of the graph using features of superpixels extracted from per-frame seg-mentations. We employed this approach without re-training the classifiers on the proposed superpixels. Using our superpixels alows to achieve on par per-formance (see Fig. 6 and Table 1) while significantly reducing the runtime and memory load (∼45 %). Superpixels based on per-frame boundary estimation are also employed in [41]. However we could not evaluate its performance with our superpixels as the code is not available under open source.

BMDS. Further we evaluate the proposed method on BMDS [6] to show the generalization of our superpixels across datasets. We use the same model trained

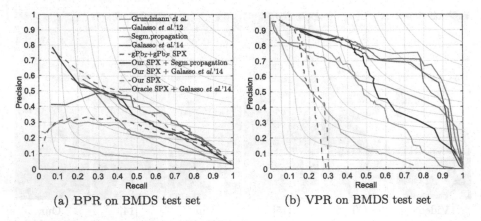

(a) BPR on BMDS test set   (b) VPR on BMDS test set

Fig. 8. Comparison of state-of-the-art video segmentation algorithms with the proposed superpixels, on BMDS [6]. Dashed lines indicate only frame-by-frame processing (see Sect. 7.2 for details). (Color figure online)

on VSB100 for generating superpixels and the hierarchical level of boundary map as validated by a grid search on the training set of BMDS. The results are presented in Fig. 8. Our boundaries based superpixels boost the performance of the baseline methods [14,15], particularly for the BPR metric (up to 4–12 %).

Oracle. Additionally we set up the oracle case for the baseline [14] (purple curve in Fig. 8) by choosing the hierarchical level to extract superpixels from the boundary map for each video sequence individually based on its performance (we considered OSS measures for BPR and VPR of each video). The oracle result indicates that the used fixed hierarchical level is quite close to an ideal video-per-video selection.

8   Conclusion

The presented experiments have shown that boundary based superpixels, extracted via hierarchical image segmentation, are a better starting point for graph-based video segmentation than classical superpixels. However, the segmentation quality depends directly on the quality of the initial boundary estimates.

Over the state-of-the-art methods such as $SE_\mathcal{I}$ [10], our results show that we can significantly improve boundary estimates when using cues from object proposals, globalization, and by merging with optical flow cues. When using superpixels built over these improved boundaries, we observe consistent improvement over two different video segmentation methods [14,15] and two different datasets (VSB100, BMDS). The results analysis indicates that we improve most in the cases where baseline methods degrade.

For future work we are encouraged by the promising results of object proposals. We believe that there is room for further improvement by integrating more semantic notions of objects into video segmentation.

References

1. Achanta, R., Shaji, A., Smith, K., Lucchi, A., Fua, P., Suesstrunk, S.: Slic superpixels compared to state-of-the-art superpixel methods. In: TPAMI (2012)
2. Arbeláez, P., Maire, M., Fowlkes, C.C., Malik, J.: Contour detection and hierarchical image segmentation. In: TPAMI (2011)
3. Badrinarayanan, V., Budvytis, I., Cipolla, R.: Mixture of trees probabilistic graphical model for video segmentation. In: IJCV (2013)
4. Bergh, M.V.D., Roig, G., Boix, X., Manen, S., Gool, L.V.: Online video seeds for temporal window objectness. In: ICCV (2013)
5. Bertasius, G., Shi, J., Torresani, L.: Deepedge: a multi-scale bifurcated deep network for top-down contour detection. In: CVPR (2015)
6. Brox, T., Malik, J.: Object segmentation by long term analysis of point trajectories. In: Daniilidis, K., Maragos, P., Paragios, N. (eds.) ECCV 2010. LNCS, vol. 6315, pp. 282–295. Springer, Heidelberg (2010). doi:10.1007/978-3-642-15555-0_21
7. Chang, J., Wei, D., Fisher, J.W.: A video representation using temporal superpixels. In: CVPR (2013)
8. Cheng, H.-T., Ahuja, N.: Exploiting nonlocal spatiotemporal structure for video segmentation. In: CVPR (2012)
9. Dai, J., He, K., Sun, J.: Convolutional feature masking for joint object, stuff segmentation. arXiv: 1412.1283 (2014)
10. Dollár, P., Zitnick, C.L.: Fast edge detection using structured forests. In: TPAMI (2015)
11. Fragkiadaki, K., Arbelaez, P., Felsen, P., Malik, J.: Learning to segment moving objects in videos. In: CVPR (2015)
12. Fragkiadaki, K., Shi, J.: Video segmentation by tracing discontinuities in a trajectory embedding. In: CVPR (2012)
13. Galasso, F., Cipolla, R., Schiele, B.: Video segmentation with superpixels. In: Lee, K.M., Matsushita, Y., Rehg, J.M., Hu, Z. (eds.) ACCV 2012. LNCS, vol. 7724, pp. 760–774. Springer, Heidelberg (2013). doi:10.1007/978-3-642-37331-2_57
14. Galasso, F., Keuper, M., Brox, T., Schiele, B.: Spectral graph reduction for efficient image and streaming video segmentation. In: CVPR (2014)
15. Galasso, F., Nagaraja, N.S., Cardenas, T.Z., Brox, T., Schiele, B.: A unified video segmentation benchmark: annotation, metrics and analysis. In: ICCV (2013)
16. Grundmann, M., Kwatra, V., Han, M., Essa, I.: Efficient hierarchical graph-based video segmentation. In: CVPR (2010)
17. Hallman, S., Fowlkes, C.: Oriented edge forests for boundary detection. In: CVPR (2015)
18. Humayun, A., Li, F., Rehg, J.M.: Rigor: recycling inference in graph cuts for generating object regions. In: CVPR (2014)
19. Humayun, A., Li, F., Rehg, J.M.: The middle child problem: revisiting parametric min-cut and seeds for object proposals. In: ICCV (2015)
20. Isola, P., Zoran, D., Krishnan, D., Adelson, E.H.: Crisp boundary detection using pointwise mutual information. In: Fleet, D., Pajdla, T., Schiele, B., Tuytelaars, T. (eds.) ECCV 2014. LNCS, vol. 8691, pp. 799–814. Springer, Heidelberg (2014). doi:10.1007/978-3-319-10578-9_52

21. Jain, A., Chatterjee, S., Vidal, R.: Coarse-to-fine semantic video segmentation using supervoxel trees. In: ICCV (2013)
22. Keuper, M., Brox, T.: Point-wise mutual information-based video segmentation with high temporal consistency. arXiv:1606.02467 (2016)
23. Khoreva, A., Galasso, F., Hein, M., Schiele, B.: Learning must-link constraints for video segmentation based on spectral clustering. In: Jiang, X., Hornegger, J., Koch, R. (eds.) GCPR 2014. LNCS, vol. 8753, pp. 701–712. Springer, Heidelberg (2014). doi:10.1007/978-3-319-11752-2_58
24. Khoreva, A., Galasso, F., Hein, M., Schiele, B.: Classifier based graph construction for video segmentation. In: CVPR (2015)
25. Krähenbühl, P., Koltun, V.: Geodesic object proposals. In: Fleet, D., Pajdla, T., Schiele, B., Tuytelaars, T. (eds.) ECCV 2014. LNCS, vol. 8693, pp. 725–739. Springer, Heidelberg (2014). doi:10.1007/978-3-319-10602-1_47
26. Levinshtein, A., Stere, A., Kutulakos, K.N., Fleet, D.J., Dickinson, S.J., Siddiqi, K.: Turbopixels: fast superpixels using geometric flows. In: TPAMI (2009)
27. Neubert, P., Protzel, P.: Evaluating superpixels in video: metrics beyond figure-ground segmentation. In: BMVC (2013)
28. Ng, A.Y., Jordan, M., Weiss, Y.: On spectral clustering: analysis and an algorithm. In: NIPS (2001)
29. Ochs, P., Malik, J., Brox, T.: Segmentation of moving objects by long term video analysis. In: TPAMI (2014)
30. Palou, G., Salembier, P.: Hierarchical video representation with trajectory binary partition tree. In: CVPR (2013)
31. Papazoglou, A., Ferrari, V.: Fast object segmentation in unconstrained video. In: ICCV (2013)
32. Pont-Tuset, J., Arbeláez, P., Barron, J., Marques, F., Malik, J.: Multiscale combinatorial grouping for image segmentation, object proposal generation. arXiv:1503.00848 (2015)
33. Ren, X., Malik, J.: Learning a classification model for segmentation. In: ICCV (2003)
34. Revaud, J., Weinzaepfel, P., Harchaoui, Z., Schmid, C.: EpicFlow: edge-preserving interpolation of correspondences for optical flow. In: CVPR (2015)
35. Shi, J., Malik, J.: Normalized cuts and image segmentation. In: TPAMI (2000)
36. Sundberg, P., Brox, T., Maire, M., Arbelaez, P., Malik, J.: Occlusion boundary detection and figure/ground assignment from optical flow. In: CVPR (2011)
37. Taralova, E.H., Torre, F., Hebert, M.: Motion words for videos. In: Fleet, D., Pajdla, T., Schiele, B., Tuytelaars, T. (eds.) ECCV 2014. LNCS, vol. 8689, pp. 725–740. Springer, Heidelberg (2014). doi:10.1007/978-3-319-10590-1_47
38. Turaga, S.C., Briggman, K.L., Helmstaedter, M., Denk, W., Seung, H.S.: Maximin affinity learning of image segmentation. In: NIPS (2009)
39. Vazquez-Reina, A., Avidan, S., Pfister, H., Miller, E.: Multiple Hypothesis Video Segmentation from superpixel flows. In: Daniilidis, K., Maragos, P., Paragios, N. (eds.) ECCV 2010. LNCS, vol. 6315, pp. 268–281. Springer, Heidelberg (2010). doi:10.1007/978-3-642-15555-0_20
40. Xie, S., Tu, Z.: Holistically-nested edge detection. In: ICCV (2015)
41. Yi, S., Pavlovic, V.: Multi-cue structure preserving MRF for unconstrained video segmentation. In: ICCV (2015)

Point-Wise Mutual Information-Based Video Segmentation with High Temporal Consistency

Margret Keuper[✉] and Thomas Brox

Department of Computer Science, University of Freiburg,
Freiburg, Germany
{keuper,brox}@cs.uni-freiburg.de

Abstract. In this paper, we tackle the problem of temporally consistent boundary detection and hierarchical segmentation in videos. While finding the best high-level reasoning of region assignments in videos is the focus of much recent research, temporal consistency in boundary detection has so far only rarely been tackled. We argue that temporally consistent boundaries are a key component to temporally consistent region assignment. The proposed method is based on the point-wise mutual information (PMI) of spatio-temporal voxels. Temporal consistency is established by an evaluation of PMI-based point affinities in the spectral domain over space and time. Thus, the proposed method is independent of any optical flow computation or previously learned motion models. The proposed low-level video segmentation method outperforms the learning-based state of the art in terms of standard region metrics.

1 Introduction

Accurate video segmentation is an important step in many high-level computer vision tasks. It can provide for example window proposals for object detection [12,27] or action tubes for action recognition [13,14].

One of the key challenges in video segmentation is on handling the large amount of data. Traditionally, methods either build upon some fine-grained image segmentation [2] or supervoxel [33] method [9,10,21,22,35] or they consist in the grouping of priorly computed point trajectories (e.g. [19,24]) and transform them in a postprocessing step into dense segmentations [25]. The latter is well suited for motion segmentation applications, but has general issues with segmenting non-moving, or only slightly moving, objects.

Indeed, image segmentation into small segments forms the basis for many high-level video segmentation methods like [9,22,35]. A key question when employing such preprocessing is the error it introduces. While state-of-the-art image segmentation methods [2,3,18] offer highly precise boundary localization, they usually suffer from low temporal consistency, i.e.,the superpixel shapes and sizes can change drastically from one frame to the next. This causes undesired flickering effects in high-level segmentation methods.

In this paper, we present a low-level video segmentation method that aims at producing spatio-temporal superpixels with high temporal consistency in a

© Springer International Publishing Switzerland 2016
G. Hua and H. Jégou (Eds.): ECCV 2016 Workshops, Part III, LNCS 9915, pp. 789–803, 2016.
DOI: 10.1007/978-3-319-49409-8_65

Fig. 1. Results of the proposed hierarchical video segmentation method for frame 4, 14 and 24 of the ballet sequence from VSB100 [10]. The segmentation is displayed in a *hot* color map. Note that corresponding contours have exactly the same value. Segmentations at different thresholds in this contour map are segmentations of the spatio-temporal volume.

bottom-up way (Fig. 1). To this aim, we employ an affinity measure, that has recently been proposed for image segmentation [18]. While other, learning-based methods such as [3] slightly outperform [18] on the image segmentation task, they can hardly be transferred to video data because their boundary detection requires training data that is currently not available for videos. However, in [18], boundary probabilities are learned in an unsupervised way from local image statistics, which can be easily transferred to video data.

To generate hierarchical segmentations from these boundary probabilities, we build upon an established method for low-level image segmentation [2] and make it applicable to video data. More specifically, we build an affinity matrix according to [18] for each entire video over space and time. Solving for the eigenvectors and eigenvalues of the resulting affinity matrices requires an enormous amount of computational resources. Instead, we show that solving the eigensystem for small temporal windows is sufficient and even produces results superior to those computed on the full system. To generate spatio-temporal segmentations from these eigenvectors according to what has been proposed in [2] for images, we need to generate small spatio-temporal segments from the eigenvectors. We do so by extending the oriented watershed transform [2] to three dimensions. This is substantial since, apart from inferring object boundaries within a single frame, it also allows us to predict where the same objects are located in the next frame. We achieve this without the need to compute optical flow. Instead, temporal consistency is maintained simply by the local affinities computed between frames and the smoothness within the resulting eigenvectors. Once we have estimated the spatio-temporal boundary probabilities, we can apply the ultrametric contour map approach from [1] on the three-dimensional data.

We show that the proposed low-level video segmentation method can compete with high-level learning-based approaches [22] on the VSB100 [10,29] video segmentation benchmark. In terms of temporal consistency, measured by the region metric VPR (volume precision recall), we outperform the state of the art.

1.1 Related Work

Image Segmentation. An important key to reliable image segmentation is the boundary detection. Most recent methods compute informative image boundaries with learning-based methods, either using random forests [8,17] or convolutional neural networks [4,5,23,31]. Provided a sufficient amount of training data, these methods improve over spectral analysis-based methods [2,18] that defined the state of the art before. However, the output of such methods provides a proxy for boundary probabilities but does not provide a segmentation into closed boundaries.

Actual segmentations can be built from these boundaries by the well-established oriented watershed and ultrametric contour map approach [1] as in [2,3,18] or, as recently proposed, by minimum cost lifted multicuts [20].

Our proposed algorithm is most closely related to the image segmentation method from [18], where the PMI-measure has been originally defined. The advantage of this measure is that is does not rely on any training data but estimates image affinities from local image statistics. We give some details of this approach in Sect. 3.

Video Segmentation. The use of supervoxels and supervoxel hierarchies has been strongly promoted in recent video segmentation methods [7,16,32,33]. These supervoxels provide small spatio-temporal segments built from basic image cues such as color and edge information. While [32] tackle the problem of finding the best supervoxel hierarchy flattening, [16] build a graph upon supervoxels to introduce higher level knowledge. Similarly [9,21,22,35] propose to build graphs upon superpixel segmentations and use learned [21,22] information or multiple high-level cues [35] to generate state-of-the-art video segmentations.

In [11], an attempt towards temporally consistent superpixels has been made on the bases of highly optimized image superpixels [2] and optical flow [6]. Similar to the proposed method, [11] make use of advances in image segmentation for video segmentation. However, their result still is a (temporally more consistent) frame-wise segmentation that is processed into a video segmentation by a subsequent graph-based method. In the benchmark paper [10], a baseline method for temporally consistent video segmentation has been proposed. From a state-of-the-art hierarchical image segmentation [2] computed on one video frame, the segmentation is propagated to the remaining frames by optical flow [6]. The relatively good performance of this simple approach indicates that low-level cues from the individual video frames have high potential to improve video segmentation over the current state of the art.

In [28] an extension of the method from [2] to video data has been proposed. In this work, the temporal link is established by optical flow [6] and the pixel-wise eigensystem is solved for the whole video based on heavy gpu parallelization. Temporally consistent labelings are computed from the eigenvectors by spectral clustering into a predefined number of clusters, thus avoiding to handle the problem of temporal gradients.

In contrast, our method neither needs precomputed optical flow nor does it depend on solving the full eigensystem. Instead, temporal consistency is established by an in-between-frame evaluation of the point-wise mutual information [18]. Further, we extend the oriented watershed approach from [2] to the spatio-temporal domain so we can directly follow their approach in computing the ultametric contour map [1] and thus infer the number of segments. In this setup, we can show that solving the eigensystem for temporal windows even improves over segmentations computed from solving the full eigensystem.

2   Method Overview

The proposed method is a video segmentation adaptation of a pipeline that has been used in several previous works on image segmentation [2,3,18] with slight variations. The key steps are given in Fig. 2. We start from the entire video sequence and compute a full affinity matrix at multiple scales. Eigenvectors are computed for these scales within small overlapping temporal windows of three frames. On the three-dimensional spatio-temporal volumes of eigenvectors, spatial and temporal boundaries can be estimated. These can be fed into the ultrametric contour map hierarchical segmentation [1] adapted for three-dimensional data.

3   Point-Wise Mutual Information

We follow [18] in defining the point-wise mutual information (PMI) measure employed for the definition of pairwise affinities. Let the random variables A and B denote a pair of neighboring features. In [18], the joint probability $P(A, B)$ is defined as a weighted sum of the joint probability $p(A, B; d)$ of features A and B occurring with a Euclidean distance of d:

$$P(A, B) = \frac{1}{Z} \sum_{d=d_0}^{\infty} w(d) p(A, B; d). \tag{1}$$

Here, Z is a normalization constant and the weighting function w is a Gaussian normal distribution with mean-value two. The marginals of the above distribution are used to define $P(A)$ and $P(B)$. To define the affinity of two neighboring points, the direct use of this the joint probability has the disadvantage of being biased by the frequency of occurrence of A and B, i.e. if a feature occurs frequently in an image, the feature will have a relatively high probability to co-occur with any other feature. The PMI corrects for this unbalancing:

$$\mathrm{PMI}_\rho(A, B) = \log \frac{P(A, B)^\rho}{P(A)P(B)}. \tag{2}$$

In [18], the parameter ρ is optimized on the training set of the BSD500 image segmentation benchmark [2]. We stick to their resulting parameter choice of $\rho = 1.25$.

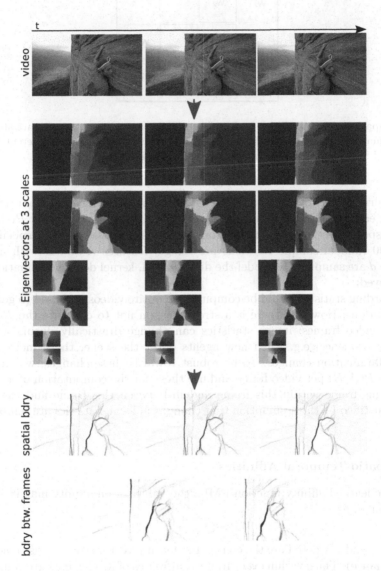

Fig. 2. Workflow of the proposed method for temporally consistent boundary detection. From an image sequence, temporally consistent eigenvectors are computed at multiple scales. While the spatial boundaries indicate object boundaries for every frame, boundaries in-between frames indicate the changes over time. In the example sequence, the *rock climbing* sequence from the VSB100 [10,29] training set, the dominant change over time in the first frames is the camera motion.

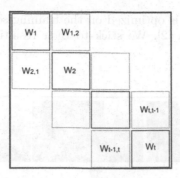

Fig. 3. Spatio-temporal affinity matrix. The affinities within every frame are stored in the sub-matrices on the diagolal (blue), the affinies between points in different frames are stored in off-diagonal submatrices (red). (Color figure online)

The crucial part of the point-wise mutual information measure from [18] that makes it easily applicable to unsupervised boundary detection is that $P(A, B)$ is learned specifically for every image from local image statistics. More specifically, for 10000 random sample locations per image, features A and B with mutual distance d are sampled. To model the distribution, kernel density estimation [26] is employed.

According statistics could be computed on entire videos and used to generate segmentations. However, there is a strong reason not to compute the $P(A, B)$ over all video frames: image statistics can change drastically during a video or image sequence, e.g. when new agents enter the scene, the camera moves or the illumination changes. To be robust towards these changes, we chose to estimate $P(A, B)$ per video frame and use these for the computation of affinities within this frame within this frame and in-between this frame and the next. This is justified by the assumption that changes in local statistics are temporally smooth.

3.1 Spatio-Temporal Affinities

From the learned affinity function PMI_ρ, the values of an affinity matrix W can be computed as

$$W_{i,j} = e^{\text{PMI}_\rho(\mathbf{f}_i, \mathbf{f}_j)} \tag{3}$$

at points i and j, where $\mathbf{f}$ are the considered feature vectors (in our case color and local variance). Thus, within every frame t, affinities of its elements are computed according to the estimated $\text{PMI}_{\rho,t}$ for color and local variance of every pixel to every pixel within a radius of 5 pixels. Within every frame t and its successor $t + 1$, affinities are computed according to $\text{PMI}_{\rho,t}$ for every pixel in frame t to every pixel in frame $t + 1$ within spatial distance of 3 pixels, and, for every pixel in frame $t + 1$ to every pixel in frame t within the same distance. The result is a sparse symmetric spatio-temporal affinity matrix W as given in Fig. 3.

4   Spectral Boundary Detection

Given an affinity matrix W, spectral clustering can be employed to generate boundary probabilities [2,18] and segmentations [9,11,22] according to a balancing criterion, more precisely, approximating the normalized cut

$$\text{NCut}(A, B) = \frac{\text{cut}(A, B)}{\text{vol}(A)} + \frac{\text{cut}(A, B)}{\text{vol}(B)}, \tag{4}$$

with $\text{cut}(A, B) = \sum_{i \in A, j \in B} w_{ij}$ and $\text{vol}(A) = \sum_{i \in A, j \in V} w_{ij}$.

Approximate solutions to the normalized cut are induced by the first k eigenvectors of the normalized graph Laplacian $L_{\text{sym}} = I - D^{-\frac{1}{2}} W D^{-\frac{1}{2}}$, where D is the diagonal degree matrix of W computed by $d_{ii} = \sum_{j \in V} w_{ij}$.

However, the computation of eigenvectors for large affinity matrices rapidly becomes expensive both in terms of computation time and memory consumption. To keep the computation tractable, we can reduce the computation to small temporal windows and employ the spectral graph reduction [9] technique.

Spectral Graph Reduction. Spectral graph reduction [9] is a means of solving a spectral clustering or normalized cut problem on a reduced set of points. In this setup, the matrix W defines the edge weights in a graph $G = (V, E)$. Given some pre-grouping of vertices by for example superpixels or must-link constraints, [9] specify how to set these weights in a new graph $G' = (V', E')$ where V' represents the set of vertex groups and E' the set of edges in between them such that the normalized cut objective does not change. They show on low-level image segmentation as well as on high-level video segmentation the advantages of this method.

Since we want to remain as close to the low-level problem as possible, we employ a setup similar to the one proposed in [9] for image segmentation. More specifically, we compute superpixel at the finest level produced by [3] for every frame, which builds upon learned boundary probabilities from [8]. In order not to lose accuracy in boundary localization, [9] proposed to keep single pixels in all regions with high gradients and investigate the trade-off between pixels and superpixels that is necessary. Similarly, we keep single pixels in all regions with high boundary probability.

Multiscale Approach and Boundary Detection. Since it has been shown in the past that spectral clustering based methods benefit from multi-scale information, we build affinity matrices also for videos spatially downsampled by factor 2 and factor 4. In this case, no pixel pre-grouping is necessary. For all three scales, we solve the eigensystems individually and compute the smallest 20 eigenvalues and according eigenvectors (compare Fig. 2). Note that these eigenvectors are highly consistent over the temporal dimension: corresponding points in different frames have very similar eigenvector values. We upsample these vectors to the highest resolution and compute oriented edges in 9 directions, with the standard oriented

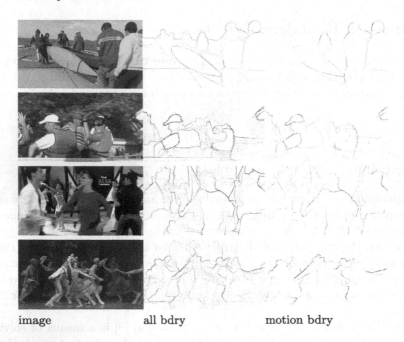

image   all bdry   motion bdry

Fig. 4. Examples of boundary estimates (center) and motion boundary estimates (right) on three sequences of VSB100 [10,29] (*arctic kayak*, *riverboat*, and *salsa*). The motion boundaries can be directly derived from the proposed method.

edge filters in 8 sampled spatial orientations and only one temporal gradient, i.e. there is no mixed spatio-temporal gradient. Depending on the frame-rate, using finer orientation sampling would certainly make sense. However, on the VSB100 dataset [10,29], we found that this simple setup works best. Examples of our extracted boundary estimates are given in Fig. 4. Visually, the estimated boundaries look reasonable and are temporally highly consistent. They form the key to the final hierarchical segmentations.

Evaluation of Temporal Boundaries. On the BVSD [29] dataset, benchmark annotations for occlusion boundaries were provided. This data can be used as a proxy to evaluate our temporal boundaries. Occlusion boundaries are object boundaries that occlude other parts of the scene - as opposed to within-object boundaries. In [29], the importance of motion cues for such occlusion boundaries has been pointed out. In fact, our temporal boundaries indicate boundaries separating regions within one frame that will undergo occlusion or disocclusion between this frame and the next. Thus, they can only provide part of the necessary information for object boundary detection. To extract this motion cue from our data, we apply a pointwise multiplication of the spatial boundaries at frame t with the temporal boundaries between frame t and its two neigh boring frames. Thus, if an object does not move in one of the frames, the respective edges are removed. Examples of the resulting motion boundary estimates are given in Fig. 4.

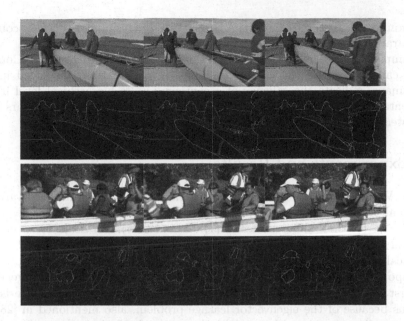

Fig. 5. Resulting UCMs from the proposed method on the sequences *arctic kayak* and *riverboat* of the VSB100 [10,29] dataset. We show the UCM value in frames 1, 11, and 21 while these actually extend over the full lengths of the sequences. Especially in the high levels of the hierarchy, the segmentations are very consistent.

When we evaluate on the closed boundary annotations of this benchmark with the benchmark parameters from BSDS500 [2], we get a surprisingly low f-measure score of 0.34 with the best common threshold for the whole dataset, 0.41 if we allow individual thresholds per sequence. The reason might be the relatively low spatial localization accuracy of our boundaries. We ran all our experiments on the *half resolution* version of the VSB100 benchmark such that, to evaluate on the annotations from [29], boundary estimates need to be upsampled.

5   Closed Spatio-Temporal Contours

Given spatio-temporal boundary estimates, closed regions could be generated by different methods such as region growing, agglomerative clustering [15], watersheds [30] or the recently proposed minimum cost lifted multicuts [20]. In [1] a mathematically sound and widely used (e.g. in [2,3,11,18,28]) setup for the generation of hierarchical segmentations from boundary probabilities and an initial fine-grained segmentation is given. The therein defined Ultrametric Contour Map provides for a duality between the saliency of a contour and the scale of its disappearance from the hierarchy.

The approach from [1] can directly be applied to three-dimensional data. The difference is that the region contours are now two-dimensional curves that meet each other in one-dimensional curves or points. Each one-dimensional curve is common to at least three contours. As in the two-dimensional case, every contour is separating exactly two regions.

Sample 2Dslices from the resulting three-dimensional Ultrametric Contour Maps can be seen in Fig. 5. The brightness of the contour, displayed in *hot* color maps, indicate the saliency of a contour, i.e. its hierarchical level in the segmentation. Over all frames of the videos, the resulting closed contours have consistent saliency.

6   Experiments and Results

Setup. We compute PMI-based affinity matrices W_s on color and local variance within all frames and between every frame and its successive frame as described in Sect. 3.1 for three different scales (1, 0.5 and 0.25). For scale 1, we employ spectral graph reduction [9], reducing the number of nodes by factor 12–15. At each scale s, we solve the eigenvalue problems of the normalized graph Laplacians corresponding to W_s for overlapping temporal windows with stride 1 to generate the first 20 eigenvectors. The best choice of the temporal window size is not obvious because of the eigenvector leakage problem, also mentioned in [28]. In the spectrally reduced graph, spatial leakage is probably low [9], so we we hope for an accordingly low temporal leakage and choose a larger temporal window of size 5, while we solve the eigenvalue problem for smaller temporal windows of length 3 for scales 0.5 and 0.25. The resulting eigenvectors are resampled to the original resolution. The average oriented gradients on these eigenvectors for the multiscale boundary estimates we use. We compare the 3D ultrametric contour maps computed from these boundary estimates to those computed on only the original scale with spectral graph reduction. For the original scale, we also compare to the results we get by solving the eigensystem on the full video without temporal windows.

Evaluation. In order to allow for a direct comparison to state-of-the-art methods [9,22] We evaluate the proposed video segmentation method on the *half resolution* version of the VSB100 video segmentation benchmark [10,29]. It consists of 40 train and 60 test sequences with a maximum length of 121 frames. Human segmentation annotations are given for every 20th frame. Two evaluation metrics are relevant in this benchmark, denoted as boundary precision and recall (BPR) and the volume precision recall (VPR). The BPR measures the accuracy of the boundary localizations per frame. Image segmentation methods usually perform well on this measure, since temporal consistency is not taken into account. The VPR is a region metric. Here, exact boundary localization is less important, while the focus lies on the temporal consistency. This is the measure on which we expect to perform well.

Results. The results of our PMI-based video segmentation are given in Fig. 6 in terms of BRP and VPR curves for 51 different levels of segmentation granularity, which is the standard for the VSB100 video segmentation benchmark.

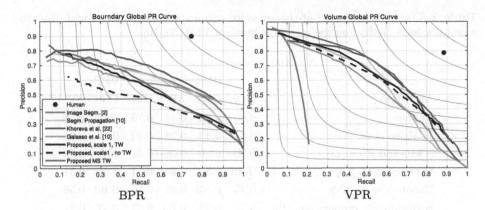

Fig. 6. Results on the general benchmark of the VSB100 [10,29] dataset. While the proposed method performs worse than the state of the art in terms of boundary precision and recall (BPR), we outperform all competing methods on the region metric VPR.

Table 1. Comparison of state-of-the-art video segmentation algorithms [9–11,16,22, 25,34] with the proposed low-level method. It shows the boundary precision-recall (BPR) and volume precision-recall (VPR) at optimal dataset scale (ODS) and optimal segmentation scale (OSS), as well as the average precision (AP). The algorithms marked with (*) have been evaluated on resized video frames to 0.5 of the original resolution.

VSB100: general benchmark						
	BPR			VPR		
Algorithm	ODS	OSS	AP	ODS	OSS	AP
Human	0.71	0.71	0.53	0.83	0.83	0.70
*Galasso et al. [11]	0.52	0.56	0.44	0.45	0.51	0.42
*Grundmann et al. [16]	0.47	0.54	0.42	0.52	0.55	0.52
*Ochs and Brox [25]	0.14	0.14	0.04	0.25	0.25	0.12
*Keuper et al. [20]	0.48	0.51	0.27	0.37	0.39	0.22
Xu et al. [34]	0.40	0.48	0.33	0.45	0.48	0.44
*Galasso et al. [9]	0.62	0.65	0.50	0.55	0.59	0.55
*Khoreva et al. [22]	**0.64**	**0.70**	**0.61**	0.63	**0.66**	0.63
Segmentation propagation [10]	0.60	0.64	0.57	0.59	0.62	0.56
IS - Arbelaez et al. [2]	0.61	0.65	0.61	0.26	0.27	0.16
Oracle & IS - Arbelaez et al. [2]	0.61	0.67	0.61	0.65	0.67	0.68
*Proposed MS TW	0.56	0.63	0.56	**0.64**	**0.66**	**0.67**

In terms of BPR, all our results remain below the state of the art. There can be several reasons for this behavior: (1) Competitive methods that are based on per image superpixels usually compute these superpixels on the highest possible resolution [9,22], while we start from the *half resolution* version of the bench-

Table 2. Comparison of state-of-the-art video segmentation algorithms with the proposed low-level method on the motion subtask of VSB100 [10].

	VSB100: motion subtask					
	BPR			VPR		
Algorithm	ODS	OSS	AP	ODS	OSS	AP
Human	0.63	0.63	0.44	0.76	0.76	0.59
*Galasso et al. [11]	0.34	0.43	0.23	0.42	0.46	0.36
*Ochs and Brox [25]	0.26	0.26	0.08	0.41	0.41	0.23
*Keuper et al. [20]	**0.49**	0.52	0.27	0.54	0.60	0.37
*Khoreva et al. [22]	0.45	**0.53**	0.33	0.56	**0.63**	0.56
Segmentation propagation [10]	0.47	0.52	**0.34**	0.52	0.57	0.47
IS - Arbelaez et al. [2]	0.47	0.43	0.35	0.22	0.22	0.13
Oracle & IS - Arbelaez et al. [2]	0.47	0.34	0.35	0.59	0.60	0.60
*Proposed MS TW	0.41	0.43	0.29	**0.58**	0.58	**0.58**

mark data. (2) The number of eigenvectors we compute might be too low. In our current setup, we compute the first 20 eigenvectors per matrix. The optimal number to be chosen here varies strongly depending on the structure of the data as well as the employed affinities. (3) Most importantly, by the definition of our boundary detection method, we force these boundaries to be temporally consistent. However, temporal consistency is not at all required for this measure. If our boundaries show some amount of temporal smoothness, this might cause the boundaries to be slightly shifted in an individual frame.

On the VPR, the proposed method benefits from the temporal consistency it optimizes and outperforms all previous methods in the three aggregate measures ODS (meaning, we choose one global segmentation threshold for the whole dataset), in OSS, which allows to choose the best threshold per sequence, and average precision (AP). Respective numbers are given in Table 1. This gives rise to the conclusion that the proposed segmentations are indeed temporally consistent.

In Fig. 6, we also plot the result we get if we only use boundary estimates from the original resolution without using multiscale information (depicted in black). As we expect, the segmentation quality remains below the quality we get with the multiscale approach. However, we did not know a priori what to expect from solving the eigensystem for the entire videos without applying temporal windows (dashed black line). To do so actually requires large amounts of memory (>512 Gb) for most sequences. The results actually remain clearly below those computed with temporal windows. In fact, the eigenvectors we compute on the small temporal windows show high temporal consistency while those computed on the whole video are subject to temporal leakage of the eigenvectors, meaning that values in the eigenvectors within a region can change smoothly throughout the sequence, resulting in decreased discrimination power.

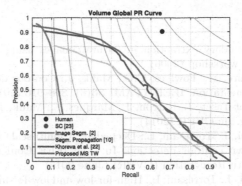

Fig. 7. Results on the motion subtask the VSB100 [10,29] dataset in terms of the region metric VPR.

The best results in Table 1 are those from the oracle case, where the individual image segments from [2] are temporally linked based on the ground truth. The numbers indicate the best result one could achieve on the benchmark, starting from the given image segmentation.

Results on Motion Segmentation. Since our segmentations claim to be temporally consistent even under significant motion in videos, we also performed the evaluation on the motion subtask of VSB100. For this motion subtask, only a subset of the videos, showing significant motion, is evaluated. Non-moving objects within these videos are not taken into account. Results are reported in Table 2 and Fig. 7. As for the general benchmark, our results are outperformed by the state of the art on the BPR but improve over the state of the art in terms of temporal consistency, measured by the region metric VPR.

7   Conclusions

We have proposed a method for computing temporally consistent boundaries in videos. To this end, the method builds spatio-temporal affinities based on point-wise mutual information at multiple scales. On the video segmentation benchmark VSB100, the resulting hierarchy of spatio-temporal regions outperforms state-of-the-art methods in terms of temporal consistency as measured by the region metric VPR. We believe that the coarser hierarchy level can help extract high-level content of video. The finer hierarchy levels can serve as temporally consistent spatio-temporal superpixels for learning based video segmentation or action recognition.

Acknowledgments. We acknowledge funding by the ERC Starting Grant Video-Learn.

References

1. Arbelaez, P.: Boundary extraction in natural images using ultrametric contour maps. In: CVPR workshop (2006)
2. Arbeláez, P., Maire, M., Fowlkes, C.C., Malik, J.: Contour detection and hierarchical image segmentation. IEEE TPAMI **33**(5), 898–916 (2011)
3. Arbeláez, P., Pont-Tuset, J., Barron, J., Marques, F., Malik, J.: Multiscale combinatorial grouping. In: CVPR (2014)
4. Bertasius, G., Shi, J., Torresani, L.: Deepedge: A multi-scale bifurcated deep network for top-down contour detection. In: The IEEE Conference on Computer Vision and Pattern Recognition (CVPR) (June 2015)
5. Bertasius, G., Shi, J., Torresani, L.: High-for-low and low-for-high: Efficient boundary detection from deep object features and its applications to high-level vision. CoRR abs/1504.06201 (2015). http://arxiv.org/abs/1504.06201
6. Brox, T., Malik, J.: Large displacement optical flow: descriptor matching in variational motion estimation. IEEE TPAMI **33**(3), 500–513 (2011)
7. Chang, J., Wei, D., III, J.W.F.: A video representation using temporal superpixels. In: IEEE Computer Vision and Pattern Recognition Conference on Computer Vision (2013)
8. Dollár, P., Zitnick, C.L.: Structured forests for fast edge detection. In: ICCV (2013)
9. Galasso, F., Keuper, M., Brox, T., Schiele, B.: Spectral graph reduction for efficient image and streaming video segmentation. In: CVPR (2014)
10. Galasso, F., Nagaraja, N., Cardenas, T., Brox, T., Schiele, B.: A unified video segmentation benchmark: Annotation, metrics and analysis. In: ICCV (2013). http://lmb.informatik.uni-freiburg.de//Publications/2013/NB13
11. Galasso, F., Cipolla, R., Schiele, B.: Video segmentation with superpixels. In: ACCV (2012)
12. Girshick, R.: Fast R-CNN. In: Proceedings of the International Conference on Computer Vision (ICCV) (2015)
13. Gkioxari, G., Malik, J.: Finding action tubes. In: CVPR (2015)
14. Gkioxari, G., Girshick, R., Malik, J.: Actions and attributes from wholes and parts. In: ICCV (2015)
15. Gonzalez, R.C., Woods, R.: Digital Image Processing, 2nd edn. Prentice-Hal, Upper Saddle River (2002)
16. Grundmann, M., Kwatra, V., Han, M., Essa, I.: Efficient hierarchical graph based video segmentation. In: IEEE CVPR (2010)
17. Hallman, S., Fowlkes, C.C.: Oriented edge forests for boundary detection. In: CVPR (2015)
18. Isola, P., Zoran, D., Krishnan, D., Adelson, E.H.: Crisp boundary detection using pointwise mutual information. In: ECCV (2014)
19. Keuper, M., Andres, B., Brox, T.: Motion trajectory segmentation via minimum cost multicuts. In: ICCV (2015)
20. Keuper, M., Levinkov, E., Bonneel, N., Lavoue, G., Brox, T., Andres, B.: Efficient decomposition of image and mesh graphs by lifted multicuts. In: ICCV (2015)
21. Khoreva, A., Galasso, F., Hein, M., Schiele, B.: Learning must-link constraints for video segmentation based on spectral clustering. In: GCPR (2014)
22. Khoreva, A., Galasso, F., Hein, M., Schiele, B.: Classifier based graph construction for video segmentation. In: CVPR (2015)
23. Kokkinos, I.: Pushing the boundaries of boundary detection using deep learning. In: arxiv, International Conference on Learning Representations (ICLR) (2016)

24. Ochs, P., Malik, J., Brox, T.: Segmentation of moving objects by long term video analysis. IEEE TPAMI **36**(6), 1187–1200 (2014)
25. Ochs, P., Brox, T.: Object segmentation in video: a hierarchical variational approach for turning point trajectories into dense regions. In: ICCV (2011)
26. Parzen, E.: On estimation of a probability density function and mode. Ann. Math. Statist. **33**(3), 1065–1076 (1962)
27. Ren, S., He, K., Girshick, R., Sun, J.: Faster R-CNN: towards real-time object detection with region proposal networks. In: NIPS (2015)
28. Sundaram, N., Keutzer, K.: Long term video segmentation through pixel level spectral clustering on GPUs. In: ICCV Workshops (2011)
29. Sundberg, P., Brox, T., Maire, M., Arbelaez, P., Malik, J.: Occlusion boundary detection and figure/ground assignment from optical flow. In: CVPR (2011)
30. Vincent, L., Soille, P.: Watersheds in digital spaces: an efficient algorithm based on immersion simulations. IEEE TPAMI **13**, 583–598 (1991)
31. Xie, S., Tu, Z.: Holistically-nested edge detection. CoRR abs/1504.06375 (2015). http://arxiv.org/abs/1504.06375
32. Xu, C., Corso, J.: Evaluation of super-voxel methods for early video processing. In: Proceedings of IEEE Conference on Computer Vision and Pattern Recognition (2012)
33. Xu, C., Whitt, S., Corso, J.: Flattening supervoxel hierarchies by the uniform entropy slice. In: Proceedings of the IEEE International Conference on Computer Vision (2013)
34. Xu, C., Xiong, C., Corso, J.J.: Streaming hierarchical video segmentation. In: Fitzgibbon, A., Lazebnik, S., Perona, P., Sato, Y., Schmid, C. (eds.) ECCV 2012. LNCS, vol. 7577, pp. 626–639. Springer, Heidelberg (2012). doi:10.1007/978-3-642-33783-3_45
35. Yi, S., Pavlovic, V.: Multi-cue structure preserving MRF for unconstrained video segmentation. CoRR abs/1506.09124 (2015). http://arxiv.org/abs/1506.09124

Can Ground Truth Label Propagation from Video Help Semantic Segmentation?

Siva Karthik Mustikovela[1], Michael Ying Yang[2]([✉]), and Carsten Rother[1]

[1] Technische Universität Dresden, Dresden, Germany
{siva_karthik.mustikovela,carsten.rother}@tu-dresden.de
[2] University of Twente, Enschede, Netherlands
michael.yang@utwente.nl

Abstract. For state-of-the-art semantic segmentation task, training convolutional neural networks (CNNs) requires dense pixelwise ground truth (GT) labeling, which is expensive and involves extensive human effort. In this work, we study the possibility of using auxiliary ground truth, so-called *pseudo ground truth* (PGT) to improve the performance. The PGT is obtained by propagating the labels of a GT frame to its subsequent frames in the video using a simple CRF-based, cue integration framework. Our main contribution is to demonstrate the use of noisy PGT along with GT to improve the performance of a CNN. We perform a systematic analysis to find the right kind of PGT that needs to be added along with the GT for training a CNN. In this regard, we explore three aspects of PGT which influence the learning of a CNN: (i) the PGT labeling has to be of good quality; (ii) the PGT images have to be different compared to the GT images; (iii) the PGT has to be trusted differently than GT. We conclude that PGT which is diverse from GT images and has good quality of labeling can indeed help improve the performance of a CNN. Also, when PGT is multiple folds larger than GT, weighing down the trust on PGT helps in improving the accuracy. Finally, We show that using PGT along with GT, the performance of Fully Convolutional Network (FCN) on Camvid data is increased by 2.7 % on IoU accuracy. We believe such an approach can be used to train CNNs for semantic video segmentation where sequentially labeled image frames are needed. To this end, we provide recommendations for using PGT strategically for semantic segmentation and hence bypass the need for extensive human efforts in labeling.

1 Introduction

Semantic segmentation is an extensively studied problem which has been widely addressed using convolutional neural networks (CNNs) recently. CNNs have been shown to perform extremely well on datasets such as Pascal VOC [9], NYU-D [33], CityScapes [7], etc. For efficient performance of CNNs, there are certain characteristics of training data which are required: (i) the ground truth (GT) training data needs dense pixelwise annotations which requires an enormous amount of human effort. For instance, an image in the Cityscapes dataset takes

© Springer International Publishing Switzerland 2016
G. Hua and H. Jégou (Eds.): ECCV 2016 Workshops, Part III, LNCS 9915, pp. 804–820, 2016.
DOI: 10.1007/978-3-319-49409-8_66

about 1.5 h for dense annotation [7], (ii) the training data has to be diverse in the sense that highly similar images do not add much information to the network. Such diversity in training data helps better modelling of the distribution of test scenarios.

For semantic video segmentation, continuous annotation of consecutive frames is helpful rather than annotations of discrete and temporally separated frames. In such a case it is again extremely expensive to obtain dense pixelwise annotation of consecutive images in the video. To this end, we arrive at an important question: can auxiliary ground truth training data obtained by using label propagation help in better performance of a CNN-based semantic segmentation framework?

In this work, we explore the possibility of using auxiliary GT, to produce more training data for CNN training. We use the CamVid dataset [5] as an example, which contains video sequences of outdoor driving scenarios. But the methodology can be easily applied to other relevant datasets. The CamVid has training images picked at $1fps$ from a $30fps$ video, leading to one GT training frame for every 30 frames. We propagate the GT labels from these images to the subsequent images using a simple CRF-based, cue integration framework leading to *pseudo ground truth (PGT)* training images. It can be expected that the new PGT is noisy and has lower quality compared to the actual GT labeling as a result of automaitc label propagation. We train the semantic segmentation network FCN [24] using this data. In this regard, we explore three factors of how the PGT has to be used to enhance the performance of a CNN.

1. *Quality* - The PGT labeling has to be of good quality in the sense that there should not be too much of wrong labeling.
2. *Diversity* - The PGT training images have to be different compared to the GT images, in order to match the potential diverse test data distribution.
3. *Trust* - During the error propagation, the PGT has to be weighted with a trust factor in the loss function while training.

Further, we systematically analyze the aforementioned dimensions through extensive experimentation to find the most influential dimension which improves the performance of the CNN. We perform experiments with two main settings. First, where equal number of PGT and GT training samples are present. Second, the number of samples of PGT is multiple folds larger than GT training samples. Our baseline is obtained by training the FCN only on the GT training images which stands at 49.6 %. From our experiments, we have found that adding PGT to the GT data and training the FCN helps in enhancing the accuracy by 2.7 % to 52.3 %.

The main contributions of this work are:

– We perform exhaustive analysis to find the influential factors among *Quality, Diversity* and *Trust* which affect the learning in the presence of PGT data. We conclude that PGT images have to be diverse from the GT images in addition to their labeling to be of good quality. Trust on PGT data should be sufficiently low when there is multiple folds of PGT than GT data.

– We provide application specific recommendations to use PGT data, taking the above factors into account. In the case of semantic video segmentation, when PGT is multiple folds larger than GT, it is advisable to have a low trust on PGT data. In case of image semantic segmentation, diverse high quality PGT data helps in improving the performance.

Detailed discussions are further presented in experimental section (Sect. 4).

2   Related Work

Semantic video segmentation has received growing interest in the last few years, as is witnessed by its increasing number of works both in foreground/background segmentation [10,11,13,16,21,22,26,27,30,34,36,38,40] and multi-class semantic segmentation [2–4,23]. We will focus our review on the later.

The influential label propagation method in [4] jointly models appearance and semantic labels using a coupled-HMM model in video sequences. This method was extended to include correlations between non-successive frames using tree structured graphical models in [2]. [3] presents a mixture of temporal trees model for video segmentation, where each component in the mixture connects super-pixels from the start to the end of a video sequence in a tree structured manner. While [2,3] adopt semi-supervised learning fashion for learning the pixel unaries, our method is principally different to their approach. In [2,3], they first set the pixel unaries to uniform distributions, use inference technique to estimate the pixel marginal posteriors, and then do iterative inference. We first generate PGT to train a neural network using combined GT and PGT data and perform the forward pass for the inference. Furthermore, since dynamic objects are ignored in the evaluation of [2,3], we don't know how good their approach applies to these object classes. While it has been shown experimentally in [2,3] that unaries learned in semi-supervised manner can help improve segmentation accuracy, we have performed thorough analysis of using PGT. [15] proposes to learn spatiotemporal object models, with minimal supervision, from large quantities of weakly and noisily tagged videos. In [20], the authors propose a higher order CRF model for joint inference of 3D structure and semantic labeling in a 3D volumetric model. [23] proposes an object-aware dense CRF model for multi-class semantic video segmentation, which jointly infers supervoxel labels, object activation and their occlusion relationship. Unlike aforementioned methods, we use PGT data for learning the CNN model to perform the inference.

Recently, CNNs are driving advances in computer vision, such as image classification [19], detection [14,41], recognition [1,28], semantic segmentation [12,24], pose estimation [35], and depth estimation [8]. The success of CNNs is attributed to their ability to learn rich feature representations as opposed to hand-designed features used in previous methods. In [25], the authors propose to use CNN for object recognition exploiting the temporal coherence in video. Video acts as a pseudo-supervisory signal that improves the internal representation of images by preserving translations in consecutive frames. [17] proposes a semi-supervised CNN framework for text categorization that learns embeddings of text regions with unlabeled data and labeled data. A number of recent approaches, including Recurrent CNN [32] and FCN [24], have shown a significant boost in accuracy by adapting state-of-the-art CNN based image classifiers to the semantic segmentation problem. In [29] the authors propose to build their model on FCN and develop EM algorithms for semantic image segmentation model training under weakly supervised and semi-supervised settings. The authors show that their approach achieves good performance when combining a small number of pixel-level annotated images with a large number of image-level or bounding box annotated images. This has been confirmed by [31,37], where [37] addresses the problem of training a CNN classifier with a massive amount of noisy labeled training data and a small amount of clean annotations for the image classification task, and [31] propose to use image-level tags to constrain the output semantic labeling of a CNN classifier in weakly supervised learning fashion. For semantic video segmentation, since obtaining a massive amount of densely labeled GT data is very expensive and time consuming, we analyze the usefulness of auxiliary training data. In [39], the authors propose an interesting approach that takes into account both the local and global temporal structure of videos to produce descriptions, which incorporates a spatial temporal 3D CNN representation of the short temporal dynamics. One could extend current 2D CNN model to 3D temporal CNN for video segmentation, but this is out of the scope of this paper.

3   Our Approach

In this section we discuss the details of our approach to generate PGT data, sorting schemes of PGT data and training the CNN.

3.1   Pseudo Ground Truth Generation Using Label Propagation

CamVid Dataset. The CamVid [5] dataset consists of video sequences of outdoor driving scenarios which is the most suitable dataset for our setting. It consists of 11 semantic classes namely *Building, Tree, Sky, Car, Sign, Road, Pedestrian, Fence, Pole, Sidewalk, Bicycle.* The video sequences in this dataset are recorded at $30fps$. We use these sequences to extract individual image frames at the same rate for Pseudo Ground Truth Generation. The Ground Truth labeling exists for 1 frame of every 30 frames per second. This frame can be leveraged to propagate the GT labels of that frame to the following frame using the approach described below (Fig. 1). The training set for CamVid contains M images ($M = 367$).

Pseudo Ground Truth Generation. Given a Ground Truth labeling S^t for a frame I^t in the training set, we propagate the semantic labels S^{t+1} of that frame to the next frame I^{t+1} in the sequence. The labeling of this new subsequent frame in the sequence, S^{t+1} is called *Pseudo Ground Truth (PGT)*. We follow an approach similar to [6], but use additional smoothness terms and a different inference scheme. A graphical model is formulated using optical flow and texture cues.

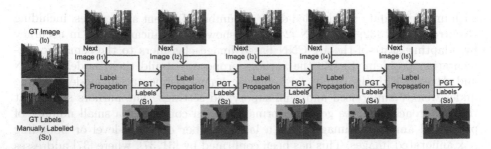

GT Image
(I0)

Next
Image (I1)   Next
Image (I2)   Next
Image (I3)   Next
Image (I4)   Next
Image (I5)

Label
Propagation   PGT
Labels
(S1)   Label
Propagation   PGT
Labels
(S2)   Label
Propagation   PGT
Labels
(S3)   Label
Propagation   PGT
Labels
(S4)   Label
Propagation   PGT
Labels
(S5)

GT Labels
Manually Labelled
(S0)

Fig. 1. Illustration of generating Pseudo Ground Truth data.

The labeling with optimal energy corresponds to the PGT S^{t+1} of the considered subsequent frame I^{t+1}. The energy of the graphical model is defined as follows,

$$E(S^{t+1} \mid S^t, I^t, I^{t+1}) = U^M(S^{t+1}, S^t, I^t, I^{t+1}) + \lambda^1 U^C(S^{t+1}, I^{t+1}) + \lambda^2 V^s(S^{t+1}, I^{t+1})$$

where U and V denote the unary and pairwise potentials in the model. The motion unary term U^M defines the potential when a pixel $z_n{}^{t+1}$ in I^{t+1} takes a label from one of the incoming flow pixels $z_{n'}{}^t$ from I^t whose flow terminates at $z_n{}^{t+1}$. The motion unary is defined as

$$U^M(S^{t+1}, S^t, I^t, I^{t+1}) = \sum_n \sum_{n' \mid z_{n'}{}^t \in f(z_n{}^{t+1})} w(z_{n'}{}^t, z_n{}^{t+1})(1 - \delta(S_n^{t+1}, S_{n'}{}^t))$$

where δ is the Kronecker delta and $f(z_n{}^{t+1})$ is the set of pixels in I^t which have a forward optical flow terminating at $z_n{}^{t+1}$. The function w defines the similarity of RGB histograms between two small image patches around $z_n{}^{t+1}$ and $z_{n'}{}^t$, measured using KL-Divergence. The appearance unary term U^C computes the log probability of a pixel $z_n{}^{t+1}$ belonging to one of the label classes. We learn a Gaussian Mixture Model for the texture of each semantic class using only the GT labeling of the first image(I^0) of that particular sequence. U^C is defined as

$$U^C(S^{t+1} \mid I^0, S^0) = \sum_n -\log P(z_n{}^{t+1} \mid \mu_0, \textstyle\sum_0)$$

where μ_0 is the mean and $\sum_0$ is the variance of the GMM over I_0. P gives the likelihood of $z_n{}^{t+1}$ belonging to a certain class. The pairwise term V^s is a generic contrast sensitive Potts model. V^s is given by

$$V^s(S^{t+1}, I^{t+1}) = \sum_{z_m, z_n \in c} dis(m,n)^{-1}[s_{z_m} \neq s_{z_n}] \exp(-\beta(h_{z_m} - h_{z_n})^2)$$

where z_m, z_n are two connected pixels, $dis(.)$ gives the euclidean distance between m and n, $[\phi]$ is an indicator function which takes values 0, 1 depending on the predicate ϕ, s_{z_m} is the label of z_m and h_{z_m} is the color vector of z_m. β is a constant chosen empirically. The inference is performed using mean-field approximation [18].

We start the label propagation using the reference frame as I^0, which is the Ground Truth training frame, and S^0, its corresponding semantic labeling. The labels are propagated till the 5th frame in the sequence. Figure 1 gives an illustration of the label propagation. The labeling S^{t+1} obtained after the inference is the so-called *Pseudo Ground Truth* labeling for the frame I^{t+1} using the reference labeling for I^t. In this way, for every GT labeled frame in the 367 image training set, we propagate the labeling to the next 5 consecutive frames obtained from the sequence. To this end, the total number of PGT frame labelings obtained is 1835. We can as well propagate the labels to the backward frames. We assume that we get similar kind of PGT and experimental results in such a case as well.

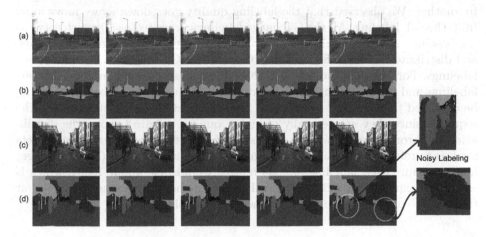

Fig. 2. Quality of some PGT labelings. (a), (c) are sequence of images. (b), (d) are corresponding labelings. (b) shows an example of good quality PGT label propagation for a sequence, while (d) shows a case where there is much noisy labeling in the PGT. A zoomed-in version of the last image in the sequence (d) illustrates the noisy labeling.

3.2 PGT Data

The focus of this work is to determine the right kind of PGT data that needs to be added to the GT to enhance the performance of CNN. As mentioned before, there are three factors of considering a PGT labeling while learning the CNN.

1. The quality of the labeling should be good. As it can be seen from Fig. 2(d), the PGT labeling for an image can be erroneous. On the other hand, labeling can also be reliable enough (Fig. 2(b)). This presents a situation where the right kind of high quality PGT must be chosen.
2. An important requirement in the learning of CNNs is that the data should be as diverse as possible. This aids in better modeling of the distribution of test images, which we assume are diverse. Hence, the images appearing in the later part of the sequence can be expected to enhance the performance of the network.

3. Because of the noise in the PGT labeling, the data may not be completely trusted when training a CNN for semantic segmentation. Hence, the gradient obtained during back propagation for a PGT has to be scaled appropriately.

The above mentioned criteria form the basis for sorting the PGT data using various schemes as mentioned below.

Visual Rating Based on Labeling Quality. The quality and the noise in the PGT labeling differs from image to image (Fig. 2) and we would like to choose the PGT data with high label quality. To achieve this, the PGT labelings are manually rated, based on their visual quality, ranging from 1 to 9. The labelings are checked for class label consistency, e.g. label drift from one semantic region to another. We observed that the labeling quality goes down as we move away from the GT labeling. All the GT image labelings are rated as 10 which serve as the baseline. Further, all the PGT labelings are sorted according to their rating and distributed into 5 different sets (PGT_R1 to PGT_R5) each containing 367 labelings. For instance the first set, PGT_R1 contains the highest quality 367 labelings and PGT_R2 contains the next best high quality 367 labelings. It could be expected that the first set PGT_R1 majorly contains the first images in the sequence since they are generally of higher quality. Figure 3 shows the distribution of chronological images in each set. We call these as visually sorted sets for future reference. Rating 1835 images took about about 2 h (4-5 sec/image) for a human. Dense labelling of 1835 images would take about 1000 h which is extremely expensive. We believe that the performance enhancement achieved at the expense of minimal human effort here is valuable.

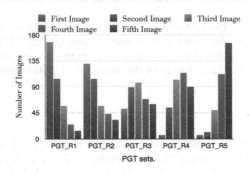

Fig. 3. Distribution of sequence of images in each visually sorted set.

Sequential Grouping. In this scheme, we group all the PGT labelings by their chronological order (PGT_S1-PGT_S5). For instance, PGT_S1 contains all the 1st labelings in the sequence and PGT_S2 contains all the 2nd labelings in the sequence. We call these as sequential sets. In this case PGT_S4, PGT_S5 can be expected to contain the most diverse images compared to the GT images because they appear later in the sequence.

3.3   Trust on PGT While Learning

As mentioned in Sect. 3.2, the PGT data cannot be completely trusted when it is being learnt. To address this, we scale the gradient obtained while back propagating the error through the CNN by a trust factor less than 1. Let the trust factor for a PGT labeling be t_f. The new update rule for the Stochastic Gradient Descent is then

$$\theta' := \theta - \eta t_f \nabla J(\theta) \quad if \quad S \in PGT \tag{1}$$

$$\theta' := \theta - \eta \nabla J(\theta) \quad if \quad S \in GT \tag{2}$$

where θ are the weights of the network, η is the learning rate and $\nabla J(\theta)$ is derivative of the loss function and S is the semantic labeling upon which the loss is being computed. Effectively, the trust factor scales the magnitude of the gradient because the direction of the gradient cannot be completely relied upon, when learning a PGT image. In the experiments, we used trust factors varying from 0.5 to 1. A value of $t_f = 1$ means that the PGT is trusted completely. All the GT labelings have a trust factor of 1 by default. We also tried using a separate trust factor for each class by scaling the trust factor by the number of pixels of a certain object label. Since, it did not show any improvement in our experiments, we decided to use a single constant.

Training. We use the standard implementation of FCN [24] in all the experiments. We train the FCN using SGD with momentum and our modified update rule. We use a batch size of 1, with learning rate of 1^{-9} with a momentum 0.99 and weight decay of 5^{-4}. We initialize the FCN with weights of VGG-16 network. For the whole set of experiments, we need 60 GPUs for about 210 h. Requirement of such resources is a major hindrance and hence we limit to experiments using only 5 consecutive frames.

4   Experiments

In this section, we evaluate our approach using various experiments and further present a discussion of the results. As explained above, we consider two schemes for sorting PGT data, i.e. through visual sorting and sequential sorting. Below we discuss two different experimental setups, when adding the 5 sets individually to the GT, and when accumulating the 5 sets with the GT.

4.1   Overall Performance

We first train the FCN only using the GT Training data, consisting of 367 images. This gives an average class IoU accuracy of 49.6 %. We consider this as the reference baseline. Table 1 gives a detailed comparison of all the class IoU accuracies and the average IoU. From Table 1, it can be seen that the FCN trained with extra PGT outperforms the FCN trained only on GT in all the classes. In this case, the PGT set is PGT_S4 with trust factor = 0.9. The average IoU accuracy is 52.3% which is higher compared to 49.6% in case of baseline FCN. For classes like *Bicycle, Sidewalk, Fence, Car* our model provides a commendable performance boost. Figure 5 shows some qualitative results of labeling obtained on test frames by our trained model.

Table 1. Semantic segmentation performance of our approach compared to an FCN trained only on GT data.

Approach	Building	Tree	Sky	Car	Sign	Road	Pedestrian	Fence	Pole	Side walk	Bicycle	Avg IoU
FCN (Only GT)	70.5	63.1	84.8	61.9	19.1	89.8	19.8	30.9	6.5	70.1	29.3	49.6
Ours (GT+PGT_S4 t_f=0.9)	72	65.6	84.6	64.6	20.8	90.6	24.9	38.8	8.0	71.8	33.9	52.3

4.2   Effect of Ambiguous Labeling of Images

In this experiment we want to analyze the effect of ambiguity in the semantic labeling of extremely similar images. We performed a preliminary experiment in which the PGT is produced just by using the labels of the first frame directly for all the successive frames. This is the most naive way of propagating labels from the base frame to the next 5 frames. We trained the FCN with GT and PGT containing either all the first frames or all second frames etc. We observed the accuracy sharply decreases as we move away from GT image in the following manner - 50.7 (GT+1st frames), 50.6 (GT+2nd frames), 50.2, 49.9, 49.7 (GT+ 5th frames). This is because the labeling that comes from the first frame GT is more erroneous when applied to the later frames.

Further, we performed another experiment where the labels of the first image are jittered and applied to the same image again. Unlike the above experiment, jittered labels are applied to the same image. To achieve this, we dilate the object labels along their borders by a very small amount followed by a minor random shift of 2-4 pixels. This simple technique creates an ambiguous labeling along the borders, effectively leading to a jitter of all semantic object labels. Effectively, such ambiguous labels mimic the labels that are a result of label propagation where they are generally erroneous, at the borders of the semantic objects. For each image-labels pair I_n-S_n in the GT set, we create 3 such ambiguous labelings $(I_n$-S_n^1, I_n-S_n^2, I_n-$S_n^3)$. Further, three training sets are created (AGT_1, AGT_1-2, AGT_1-3). AGT_1 contains the GT training data and the set of all first ambiguous labelings for each image. Likewise, AGT_1-3 contains the GT data, and all the ambiguous labelings for each image. Essentially, we are trying to analyse the effect of ambiguous labeling for a set of extremely similar images. We train the FCN using various trust factors for PGT data ranging from 0.5 to 1. From this experiment (last column of Table 2), it can be observed that the addition of multiple folds of ambiguous labels for a set of extremely similar images reduces the accuracy (AGT_1 to AGT_1-3). This is because of the addition of extremely similar images to the CNN with more ambiguous labeling which corrupts the learning of CNN. This effect would further be useful in explaining certain phenomena in the experiments below. The average accuracies are marginally more than 49.6 % (baseline) for AGT_1, AGT_1-2. The reason is that, effectively, we are increasing the number of epochs for which the CNN is trained when we are using the same image set repeatedly.

Table 2. Accuracies for various FCNs trained on ambiguously labeled data.

Trust factor/ Tr. Set	0.5	0.6	0.7	0.8	0.9	1	Avg. Acc
AGT_1	50.1	50.1	50	50.2	50.3	49.2	50.0
AGT_1-2	50.1	50	50.3	50.1	50.1	49.9	50.0
AGT_1-3	48.5	48.7	49.2	49.1	49.4	49.2	49.0

4.3 FCN Trained Using Separate PGT Sets

(A) Sequentially Sorted PGT Sets. In this experiment, we train the FCN with training sets containing 734 images which consist of GT (367 images) and one of the PGT_S training sets (367 images). As described in Sect. 3.2, there are 5 PGT sets in this experiment, each consisting of 1st, 2nd, 3rd, 4th and 5th images in the sequence starting from the GT image. We train the FCN using various trust factors for PGT data ranging from 0.5 to 1. In all these experiments, the trust on the GT training set is fixed to be 1. Table 3(a) outlines the accuracies for each training set over various trust factors. Following are the observations of this experiment:

Trust Factors: From Table 3(a) it can be observed that there is no clear trend in the effect of trust factors on the learning of CNN, particularly when a single set of PGT is added to the training. For example, in the case of GT+PGT1, $t_f = 0.6$ performs the best with an accuracy of 51.5, while $t_f = 0.5$ performs the best in case of GT+PGT2. In case of GT+PGT4, $t_f = 0.9$ gives the highest accuracy of 52.3 % and the other trust factors lead to similar accuracies in the range of 51.3 % to 51.5 %. This can be attributed to the extreme non-convexity of the function space of CNNs, due to which the scaling of magnitude of the gradient could lead to a different local minima. For this reason, to compare the effect of various training sets, we average the accuracies due to various trust factors (see last column in each table).

PGT Sets: It can be seen that the accuracy for a training set averaged over trust factors is the highest (51.5 %) when the training set contains all the 4th images in the sequence. Further, the average accuracy declines to 51.4 % when the set of all the 5th images is included in the training set. Fig. 4 shows the trend of average accuracy of the network when different sequentially sorted PGT sets are added to the training data. It can be clearly seen that the accuracy increases as the PGT images are farther away from the GT images and further drops when set of 5th images is added. This can be attributed to the fact that the PGT sets with 4th and 5th images are very different compared to those in the GT images and the labeling in the 5th set is lower in quality. Effectively, the 4th set aids in providing diverse high quality data and adding more information to the network. Effectively, if there is a better label propagation algorithm which can reliably propagate labels to farther images in the sequence, we conjecture that a later image would help in providing more information to the CNN and hence further enhance the performance of CNN.

From the above observations, it can be concluded that, in learning a CNN, the effect of using a high quality diverse PGT set (e.g. 4th set) is more prominent than the effect of a trust factor on a PGT set, in a case where the number of PGT images is the same as the number of GT images in the training data.

Table 3. Accuracies for various trust factors of training the FCN with GT images and an additional set of equal number of PGT images.

(a)Accuracies for Sequential Sets

Trust Fac./ Tr. Set	0.5	0.6	0.7	0.8	0.9	1	Avg. Acc
GT+PGT1	50.7	51.5	51.2	50.8	50.6	49.5	50.7
GT+PGT2	52.1	51.2	50.2	51.5	50.4	51.3	51.1
GT+PGT3	51.5	51.4	50.5	51.1	50.9	51.1	51.1
GT+PGT4	51.4	51.4	51.3	51.3	**52.3**	51.3	51.5
GT+PGT5	51.2	52.1	51.2	51.5	51.1	51.4	51.4

(b)Accuracies for Rated Sets

0.5	0.6	0.7	0.8	0.9	1	Avg. Acc
49.7	49.3	48	50.2	50.9	50.7	49.8
49.8	48.9	49.4	49.5	49.8	48.7	49.4
51.2	50.7	51.2	50.5	50.3	49.4	50.5
51.5	50.8	50.2	50.3	50.1	50.5	50.5
50.9	50.9	50.1	50.1	51.5	50.6	50.6

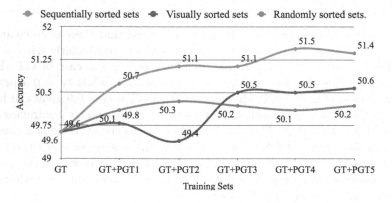

Fig. 4. Graph shows the average accuracy change upon varying the PGT set added to training along with GT. Green curve indicates the accuracies in case of sequentially sorted sets. Blue curve indicates the accuracies in case of visually sorted sets. Orange curve indicates the accuracies for randomly sorted sets. (Color figure online)

(B) Visually Rated PGT Sets. In this experiment, we train the FCN with training sets containing 734 images which consist of GT (367 images) and a PGT_R training sets (367 images). PGT_R1 contains the highest quality PGT labeling followed by PGT_R2 which contains the next highest quality PGT labeling, and so on. We train the FCN using various trust factors for PGT data ranging from 0.5 to 1. The trust on the GT training set is fixed to be 1. Table 3(b) outlines the accuracies for each training set over various trust factors. The following are the observations of this experiment. It can be seen that all 30 FCN models trained on GT+PGT perform better than our baseline which indicates that there is an improvement in performance of FCN when PGT data is used.

Trust Factors: There is no clear trend in the effect of trust factors on the learning of CNN. As mentioned above, the extreme non-convexity of the function space of CNN may prevent us from explicitly analyzing the effect of trust factors.

PGT sets: The accuracy for a training sets averaged over trust factors increases as we present the PGT sets PGT_R1 to PGT_R5. The PGT labeling in PGT_R5 is lower in quality compared to those in PGT_R1, but the accuracy is higher for PGT_R5 compared to that of PGT_R1. This could seem to be counter intuitive, but upon further analysis the trend is explicable. Consider Fig. 3 where the constitution of chronological images in visually sorted sets is depicted. It can be observed that the sets starting from the PGT_R3 majorly consist of later images than the earlier images in the sequence. Hence, the diversity of training data increases as we proceed to later sets.

Label ambiguity: It can be seen that the average accuracies for visually sorted sets (Fig. 4) are lower than those of sequentially sorted sets. This might as well seem to be unreasonable because the PGT labeling in visually sorted sets are of high quality. However, there is an important detail to notice here. These initial images are extremely correlated and similar. The presence of multiple highly correlated images and label ambiguity for these brings down the accuracy. While in the case of sequentially sorted images, only one of the highly correlated images in the sequence is present for each image in the GT.

From the above observations, it can be clearly concluded that the presence of diverse PGT images plays a stronger role in enhancing the accuracy of CNNs, rather than high quality images, particularly when the label propagation is done for shorter sequences. To this end, we conjecture that the quality of images could play a considerable role when the label propagation is done for longer sequences. Such an effect can already be seen in the case of sequentially sorted PGT sets where the accuracy for PGT_S5 is less than that of PGT_S4. This can be clearly attributed to the fact that the label quality in PGT_S5 is less than that of PGT_S4.

(C) Randomly Selected Sets. In this setting, we divide the set of all the PGT data randomly into 5 sets each containing 367 images. An image-label sample belongs to only one set in these five sets. As it can be seen in Fig. 4(orange plot), the average accuracies do not majorly change when the PGT sets are changed.

While in cases of sets 3, 4, 5 of the sequential and visually sorted images, the accuracies are higher than those of randomly selected sets. This again is for the reason that there is no major steer of selection of diverse high quality labeling in a randomly assigned set. Clearly, this experiment again reinforces the necessity of selection of diverse good quality labeling to improve the performance of CNN.

4.4   FCN Trained Using Accumulated PGT Sets

In this section we describe the experiments where the PGT sets are accumulated for training the FCN (Table 4). For instance, Set 1 contains the GT, first PGT set and the second PGT set. The last set contains GT and all the PGT sets. Note that the ratio of PGT samples to the GT samples goes up as we proceed. So the last set contains 5 times as many PGT samples as the GT samples. Similar to above section, we present two experiments where we accumulate sequentially sorted sets (Table 4(a)) and visually rated sets (Table 4(b)). We train the FCN using various trust factors for PGT data ranging from 0.5 to 1. The trust on the GT training set is fixed to be 1.

Trust Factors: The last row in Table 4 contains the average accuracy over all the datasets for a given trust factor. Unlike the earlier observation in Sect. 4.3 where the trust factors analysis did not show a clear trend, here it can be seen that lower trust factors help to produce better accuracies compared to higher trust factors. As seen from the last row (Table 4(a)), the average accuracy constantly declines from 50.2 % to 49.2 % when the trust factor is varied from 0.5 to 1 for sequentially sorted sets. Also, it can be seen from the last row (Table 4(b)), that the average accuracy constantly declines from 50.6 % to 48.6 % when the trust factor is varied from 0.5 to 1 for visually ranked sets. Note that even in the presence of multiple folds of noisy PGT samples in the training set, the FCN performs at an average accuracy of 50.6 % when the trust factor is set to a sufficiently low value.

From the above observations, we conclude that the trust factor for the PGT data should be low enough when the number of PGT samples is considerably higher than that of GT samples.

Visual Rating: The first columns of Tables 4(a,b) present an interesting observation. When the trust factor is sufficiently low ($t_f = 0.5$), the accuracy for each set in Visually Rated accumulation is in general higher than or equal to the accuracy in case of Sequential accumulation. The reason for lower accuracy of sequentially sorted accumulated sets is again due to label ambiguity as discussed before. For example, when the first and second sequentially sorted sets are added to the GT, there is a high correlation among the 1st, 2nd and 3rd images of the sequence and the effect of ambiguous labeling occurs (as discussed in Sect. 4.2). Of course such kind of correlated images are present in the visually sorted sets as well and would come up during accumulation. But in the initial sets, for some GT images, there are no images of that sequence till PGT_R3, PGT_R4, PGT_R5. This means there is no ambiguous labeling effect due to these images. This brings us to a conclusion that visual rating helps when the PGT data is

Table 4. Accuracies of various training experiments when the PGT data is accumulated for each training. GT+(PGT1-5) contains all the PGT sets 1,2,3,4,5.

Trust Factor/ Tr. Set	(a) Accuracies for accumulated Sequential sets						(b) Accuracies for accumulated Rated sets					
	0.5	0.6	0.7	0.8	0.9	1	0.5	0.6	0.7	0.8	0.9	1
GT+PGT(1-2)	50.1	48.9	50.1	49.1	48.3	48.4	50.3	49.3	49.9	51	48	48.4
GT+PGT(1-3)	49.6	50.3	50	50.4	49.2	50.5	50.7	49.4	49.5	49.8	49.7	48.5
GT+PGT(1-4)	51.5	50	50	48.5	49.7	48.3	51.5	50.6	50.3	48.1	49.4	48
GT+PGT(1-5)	50.3	50.9	50.1	49.8	49.6	48.5	50.3	50.9	50.1	49.8	49.6	48.5
Average IoU	50.2	49.8	49.6	49.6	49.5	49.2	50.6	50.3	50.3	49.9	49.4	48.6

accumulated and the number of PGT images is multiple folds higher than GT images. Evidently, accumulation does not explicitly help to enhance the accuracy over training with separated sets. The maximum accuracy achieved in both the cases is 51.5 %. But clearly, this experiment suggests that such kind of accumulated training with sequences of images for semantic video segmentation can help when there is usage of PGT data. Additionally, we conjecture that even better results can be obtained by adapting the trust factors to individual images based on label quality and other potential factors.

Fig. 5. Qualitative performance of our system. First row-Images. Second row-Output of FCN trained with GT+PGT_S4, trust factor = 0.9. Third row-ground truth.

5   Conclusions

In this work, we have explored the possibility of using *pseudo ground truth* (PGT) to generate more training data for CNN. The main contribution is to systematically analyze three aspects of how the PGT has to be used to enhance the performance of a CNN-based semantic segmentation framework. From our experiments, we make the following conclusions: (a) When the number of PGT samples and GT samples is comparable, it is important to use diverse PGT data compared to GT images which also has good quality of labeling; (b) When the number of PGT samples is multifold compared with GT, the trust on the PGT samples should be sufficiently low; (c) Accumulation of PGT data does not explicitly help in improving the performance of semantic segmentation by a considerable amount. But it is important to note that in cases such as video processing, sequential labeled data has to be presented to the CNN and our experiments show that PGT can be used in such cases with a sufficiently low trust factor and it does not worsen the performance. To this end, we recommend that diverse high quality PGT should be used when one has to improve the performance of semantic segmentation. In case PGT is being used for semantic video segmentation, we recommend that the trust on PGT is kept to a low value. Additionally, there are many exciting avenues for future research. One direction is to improve the PGT data generation itself. As the experiments have shown, we believe that even better results can be achieved when the so-called trust factors are individually adapted to the data in case of PGT accumulation. For instance, each frame, or even each pixel, receives a different trust factor, potentially also conditioned on the image content and other information. Another direction of research is to compare and complement our approach for data augmentation to other common strategies for data augmentation.

Acknowledgements. This project has received funding from the European Research Council (ERC) under the European Unions Horizon 2020 research and innovation programme(grant agreement No. 647769) and DFG (German Research Foundation) YA 351/2-1.

References

1. Agrawal, P., Girshick, R., Malik, J.: Analyzing the performance of multilayer neural networks for object recognition. In: Fleet, D., Pajdla, T., Schiele, B., Tuytelaars, T. (eds.) ECCV 2014. LNCS, vol. 8695, pp. 329–344. Springer, Heidelberg (2014). doi:10.1007/978-3-319-10584-0_22
2. Badrinarayanan, V., Budvytis, I., Cipolla, R.: Semi-supervised video segmentation using tree structured graphical models. PAMI **35**(11), 2751–2764 (2013)
3. Badrinarayanan, V., Budvytis, I., Cipolla, R.: Mixture of trees probabilistic graphical model for video segmentation. IJCV **110**(1), 14–29 (2014)
4. Badrinarayanan, V., Galasso, F., Cipolla, R.: Label propagation in video sequences. In: CVPR (2010)
5. Brostow, G.J., Shotton, J., Fauqueur, J., Cipolla, R.: Segmentation and recognition using structure from motion point clouds. In: Forsyth, D., Torr, P., Zisserman, A. (eds.) ECCV 2008. LNCS, vol. 5302, pp. 44–57. Springer, Heidelberg (2008). doi:10.1007/978-3-540-88682-2_5
6. Chen, A.Y.C., Corso, J.J.: Propagating multi-class pixel labels throughout video frames. In: WNYIPW (2010)

7. Cordts, M., Omran, M., Ramos, S., Rehfeld, T., Enzweiler, M., Benenson, R., Franke, U., Roth, S., Schiele, B.: The cityscapes dataset for semantic urban scene understanding. In: CVPR (2016)
8. Eigen, D., Puhrsch, C., Fergus, R.: Depth map prediction from a single image using a multi-scale deep network. In: NIPS, pp. 2366–2374 (2014)
9. Everingham, M., Gool, L., Williams, C.K., Winn, J., Zisserman, A.: The PASCAL visual object classes (VOC) challenge. IJCV 88(2), 303–338 (2010)
10. Fragkiadaki, K., Zhang, G., Shi, J.: Video segmentation by tracing discontinuities in a trajectory embedding. In: CVPR (2012)
11. Giordano, D., Murabito, F., Palazzo, S., Spampinato, C.: Superpixel-based video object segmentation using perceptual organization and location prior. In: CVPR (2015)
12. Girshick, R., Donahue, J., Darrell, T., Malik, J.: Rich feature hierarchies for accurate object detection and semantic segmentation. In: CVPR (2014)
13. Godec, M., Roth, P.M., Bischof, H.: Hough-based tracking of non-rigid objects. In: ICCV (2011)
14. Gupta, S., Girshick, R., Arbeláez, P., Malik, J.: Learning rich features from RGB-D images for object detection and segmentation. In: Fleet, D., Pajdla, T., Schiele, B., Tuytelaars, T. (eds.) ECCV 2014. LNCS, vol. 8695, pp. 345–360. Springer, Heidelberg (2014). doi:10.1007/978-3-319-10584-0_23
15. Hartmann, G., et al.: Weakly supervised learning of object segmentations from web-scale video. In: Fusiello, A., Murino, V., Cucchiara, R. (eds.) ECCV 2012. LNCS, vol. 7583, pp. 198–208. Springer, Heidelberg (2012). doi:10.1007/978-3-642-33863-2_20
16. Jain, S.D., Grauman, K.: Supervoxel-consistent foreground propagation in video. In: Fleet, D., Pajdla, T., Schiele, B., Tuytelaars, T. (eds.) ECCV 2014. LNCS, vol. 8692, pp. 656–671. Springer, Heidelberg (2014). doi:10.1007/978-3-319-10593-2_43
17. Johnson, R., Zhang, T.: Semi-supervised convolutional neural networks for text categorization via region embedding. In: NIPS (2015)
18. Krähenbühl, P., Koltun, V.: Efficient inference in fully connected CRFs with Gaussian edge potentials. In: NIPS, pp. 109–117 (2011)
19. Krizhevsky, A., Sutskever, I., Hinton, G.E.: Imagenet classification with deep convolutional neural networks. In: NIPS, pp. 1097–1105 (2012)
20. Kundu, A., Li, Y., Dellaert, F., Li, F., Rehg, J.M.: Joint semantic segmentation and 3D reconstruction from monocular video. In: Fleet, D., Pajdla, T., Schiele, B., Tuytelaars, T. (eds.) ECCV 2014. LNCS, vol. 8694, pp. 703–718. Springer, Heidelberg (2014). doi:10.1007/978-3-319-10599-4_45
21. Lee, Y.J., Kim, J., Grauman, K.: Key-segments for video object segmentation. In: ICCV (2011)
22. Li, F., Kim, T., Humayun, A., Tsai, D., Rehg, J.M.: Video segmentation by tracking many figure-ground segments. In: ICCV (2013)
23. Liu, B., He, X.: Multiclass semantic video segmentation with object-level active inference. In: CVPR (2015)
24. Long, J., Shelhamer, E., Darrell, T.: Fully convolutional networks for semantic segmentation. In: CVPR (2015)
25. Mobahi, H., Collobert, R., Weston, J.: Deep learning from temporal coherence in video. In: ICML (2009)
26. Nagaraja, N.S., Schmidt, F.R., Brox, T.: Video segmentation with just a few strokes. In: ICCV (2015)
27. Ochs, P., Brox, T.: Object segmentation in video: a hierarchical variational approach for turning point trajectories into dense regions. In: ICCV (2011)

28. Oquab, M., Bottou, L., Laptev, I., Sivic, J.: Learning and transferring mid-level image representations using convolutional neural networks. In: CVPR, pp. 1717–1724 (2014)
29. Papandreou, G., Chen, L., Murphy, K.P., Yuille, A.L.: Weakly-and semi-supervised learning of a deep convolutional network for semantic image segmentation. In: ICCV (2015)
30. Papazoglou, A., Ferrari, V.: Fast object segmentation in unconstrained video. In: ICCV (2013)
31. Pathak, D., Krähenbühl, P., Darrell, T.: Constrained convolutional neural networks for weakly supervised segmentation. In: ICCV (2015)
32. Pinheiro, P., Collobert, R.: Recurrent convolutional neural networks for scene labeling. In: ICML (2014)
33. Silberman, N., Hoiem, D., Kohli, P., Fergus, R.: Indoor segmentation and support inference from RGBD images. In: Fitzgibbon, A., Lazebnik, S., Perona, P., Sato, Y., Schmid, C. (eds.) ECCV 2012. LNCS, vol. 7576, pp. 746–760. Springer, Heidelberg (2012). doi:10.1007/978-3-642-33715-4_54
34. Tang, K., Sukthankar, R., Yagnik, J., Fei-Fei, L.: Discriminative segment annotation in weakly labeled video. In: CVPR (2013)
35. Toshev, A., Szegedy, C.: Deeppose: Human pose estimation via deep neural networks. In: CVPR, pp. 1653–1660 (2014)
36. Wu, Z., Li, F., Sukthankar, R., Rehg, J.M.: Robust video segment proposals with painless occlusion handling. In: CVPR (2015)
37. Xiao, T., Xia, T., Yang, Y., Huang, C., Wang, X.: Learning from massive noisy labeled data for image classification. In: CVPR (2015)
38. Yang, Y., Sundaramoorthi, G., Soatto, S.: Self-occlusions and disocclusions in causal video object segmentation. In: ICCV (2015)
39. Yao, L., Torabi, A., Cho, K., Ballas, N., Pal, C.J., Larochelle, H., Courville, A.C.: Describing videos by exploiting temporal structure. In: ICCV (2015)
40. Zhang, D., Javed, O., Shah, M.: Video object segmentation through spatially accurate and temporally dense extraction of primary object regions. In: CVPR (2013)
41. Zhang, N., Donahue, J., Girshick, R., Darrell, T.: Part-based R-CNNs for fine-grained category detection. In: Fleet, D., Pajdla, T., Schiele, B., Tuytelaars, T. (eds.) ECCV 2014. LNCS, vol. 8689, pp. 834–849. Springer, Heidelberg (2014). doi:10.1007/978-3-319-10590-1_54

3D Point Cloud Video Segmentation
Based on Interaction Analysis

Xiao Lin[✉], Josep R. Casas, and Montse Pardàs

Image Processing Group, Technical University of Catalonia (UPC), Barcelona, Spain
james.lin.xiao@tsc.upc.edu

Abstract. Given the widespread availability of point cloud data from consumer depth sensors, 3D segmentation becomes a promising building block for high level applications such as scene understanding and interaction analysis. It benefits from the richer information contained in actual world 3D data compared to apparent (projected) data in 2D images. This also implies that the classical color segmentation challenges have recently shifted to RGBD data, whereas new emerging challenges are added as the depth information is usually noisy, sparse and unorganized. In this paper, we present a novel segmentation approach for 3D point cloud video based on low level features and oriented to the analysis of object interactions. A hierarchical representation of the input point cloud is proposed to efficiently segment point clouds at the finer level, and to temporally establish the correspondence between segments while dynamically managing the object split and merge at the coarser level. Experiments illustrate promising results for our approach and its potential application in object interaction analysis.

Keywords: Object segmentation · 3d point clouds · Dynamic split and merge management · Object interactions

1 Introduction

Segmentation is an essential task in computer vision. It usually serves as the foundation for solving higher level problems such as object recognition, interaction analysis and scene understanding. Traditionally, segmentation is defined as a process of grouping homogeneous pixels into multiple segments on a single image, which is also known as low level segmentation. The obtained segments are somehow more homogeneous and more perceptually meaningful than raw pixels. Based on that, the concept of semantic segmentation/labeling is proposed. It is devoted to segment an image into regions which *ideally* correspond to meaningful objects in the scene. To achieve this goal, high level knowledge is usually incorporated into the segmentation process, such as object models [2] exploited in constrained scenes, accurate object annotations required in the initialization [12,16] and large databases containing fully annotated data in, for instance, label transfer approaches such as [9]. These approaches yield outstanding segmentation results; however, most computer vision applications involve

© Springer International Publishing Switzerland 2016
G. Hua and H. Jégou (Eds.): ECCV 2016 Workshops, Part III, LNCS 9915, pp. 821–835, 2016.
DOI: 10.1007/978-3-319-49409-8_67

large amounts of data with different types of scenes containing several objects, which difficult the adaptation to generic scenes of those methods based on manual initialization or predefined/learned object models.

To generalize the methodology from constrained situations, larger attention has been drawn on investigating the spatial relation between segments and their temporal correspondences when temporal video (stream) data is available. A bunch of methods focusing on the spatio-temporal relation between segments are proposed [1,3–6,15]. These methods mainly focus on tackling two problems: a higher level representation, which abstracts the raw data from scratch, and a method to establish the spatio-temporal correspondences. Several methods employ a generic model to represent the objects in the scene. Husain et al. [6] maintains a quadratic surface model to generally represent the object segments in the scene. The model is then updated along the sequence to obtain the final segmentation result. But it is difficult to handle objects with large displacement in successive frames. Similarly, a Gaussian Mixture Model (GMM) is used in [8] to represent the objects, while the model is incrementally updated for new frames in the sequence. However, it establishes the correspondence between the object model and the point cloud in the new frame by using the Iterative Closest Point (ICP) technique, which may lead to the accumulation of registration errors in the object model due to the deformation of the objects. More generally in scene representation, Richtsfeld et al. [13] propose to represent the 3D point cloud with a graph of surface patches detected in the scene, such as planes and non-uniform rational B-splines (NURBs). A SVM based learning process is then employed to decide the relation between surface patches for a sub-sequent graph cut segmentation. Grundmann et al. [3] use a graph-based model to hierarchically construct a consistent video segmentation from over-segmented frames. Similarly, Hickson et al. [5] extend the method to RGBD stream data. But the over-segmentation for each frame in these two approaches is still calculated independently, without the temporal coherence constraint, which may lead to a temporal inconsistency problem due to changes of corresponding over-segments in different frames. Abramov et al. [1] perform label transfer in the pixel level between frames by using optical flow. Then, they minimize the label distribution energy in the Potts model to generate labels for objects in the scene. This establishes the temporal correspondences in the pixel level, which makes the approach highly rely on the performance of optical flow estimation.

Motivated by the problems mentioned above, we propose a segmentation algorithm based on the definition of objects as "compact point clouds" in the 3D-space plus time domain. However, point clouds corresponding to an object can break into different compact sub-clouds due to occlusions, or can merge with compact point clouds corresponding to other objects, producing a single compact point cloud, when they become spatially close (object interaction). Our system aims to produce a robust spatio-temporal segmentation of the point clouds by analyzing their connectivity to define the objects according to the evidence observed up to a given temporal point. Our primary contributions are:

- We propose a novel tree structure representation for the point cloud of the scene which allows us to temporally update the similarities between nodes in the tree
- We propose to approach the temporal correspondences establishment task by a labelling assignment problem regarding the tree structure.
- A dynamic management of object splits and merges is exploited in our approach for generating a better segmentation result based on all low-level features available
- An over-segmentation method based on the compactness of the connection between neighboring super voxels in the graph is proposed.

The rest of the paper is organized as follow. In Sect. 2 we explain how the 3D point cloud segmentation problem is modeled. Sections 3 and 4, present the framework of the proposed segmentation approach and show experimental results, respectively. Finally, Sect. 5 discusses the results and yields conclusions.

2   Problem Modeling and Definition

In this section, we explain how the 3D point cloud segmentation task is modeled by the proposed tree structure.

2.1   Tree Structure Representation of the Point Cloud

Given a stream of RGBD data, our goal is to segment the foreground point cloud in each frame into meaningful sub-clouds and associate these sub-clouds in consecutive frames to maintain the trajectories for them without explicit object models or accurate initialization. More precisely, we represent the input point cloud as a graph G (shown in Fig. 1(b)) with a super-voxel approach [10]. Nodes in the graph are homogeneous sub-cloud patches and edges define the spatial connections among patches. In this manner, the connectivity of a point cloud is interpreted as the connectivity in the corresponding graph representation. The set of connected nodes in the graph corresponds to the compact parts of the input point cloud, which we call blobs (shown in Fig. 1(c) and marked in different colors). Then a tree structure with 4 levels varying from coarse to fine is exploited to represent the input point cloud at different scales of object-connectivity. Figure 1(a) shows the constructed tree structure for the point cloud data in the second row. The root of the tree represents the scene. The second level of the tree is the object level, in which each node stands for an object proposal. The next level, named component level, is employed to handle potential splits and merges of point clouds representing these objects. An object is represented by more than one component if it splits in different blobs in the graph. Components from different objects can be part of the same blob, because of the interactions between objects. Splits and merges of components are managed by maintaining the similarities among object components along time, which provides a temporally coherent way to obtain object proposals based on point cloud

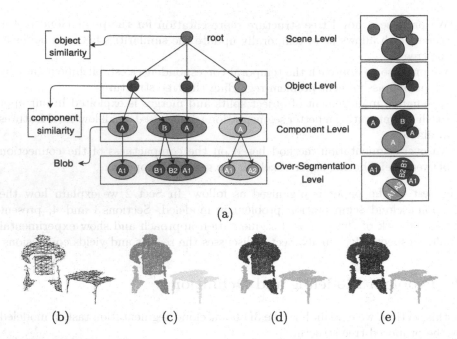

(a)

(b)   (c)   (d)   (e)

Fig. 1. An example of tree structure representation. (a) A tree structure representation of the input point cloud data. (b) The graph built on the input point cloud. (c) Blobs in the input point cloud. (d) Components for each object. (e) Objects segmentation obtained from the tree structure.

connectivity. The final level of the tree is the over-segmentation level. We over-segment components using normalised cut in their graphs in order to correctly establish correspondences between trees along time and update its structure, that is, the temporal coherent assignment of labels to the segmented objects. Note that three kinds of labels are used in Fig. 1(a) to differentiate the nodes in the tree while showing their relationships, which are object label (color), component label (alphabet) and segment label (number). We aligned the color used in Fig. 1(a) with the real point cloud data plots (Fig. 1(c) and (e)). In Fig. 1(e), we present the object segmentation result obtained in this tree structure, while Fig. 1(d) shows the components of each object from the point cloud view. Figure 1(c) presents the blobs in the input point cloud which is related to the ellipses marked with the same color in Fig. 1(a).

2.2   Tree Structure Creation

Taking the point cloud in frame t as input data, we abstract it with super voxels, using the method proposed in [10]. The graph representation simplifies the input data by grouping homogeneous points on the point cloud into super voxels while preserving the boundary information. Then, a graph G is constructed regarding the spatial connectivity between super voxels. We group the point cloud into

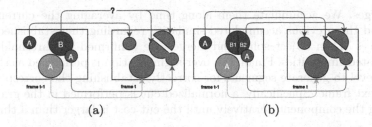

Fig. 2. An example of temporal inconsistency problem. (a) The problem when establishing the correspondence between components in the previous frame and blobs in the current frame. (b) Using the segments instead of components solves this problem.

blobs by detecting the connected components in the graph. The tree in the first frame is created by simply taking the detected blobs as the objects, as no prior information about the objects is provided. Accordingly, we create one component for each object and over-segment each component into segments. Apart from the first frame, the tree is built in a bottom-up way, starting at the component level. First, a correspondence is made between the connected components of the graph (blobs) in the current frame and the segments at the over-segmentation level of the tree structure in the previous frame. This over-segmentation level is employed to avoid temporal inconsistency problem. Figure 2(a) shows an example of it, where the component B of the blue object in frame $t - 1$ splits into two blobs in frame t. In this case, no correct association is found between components and blobs. The problem may be tackled by over-segmenting the component B of the blue object into segments $B1$ and $B2$ (shown in Fig. 2(b)) and associating the segments in frame $t - 1$ with blobs in frame t. Establishing the correspondence between the blob labels and the segments is a problem of assigning M_b blob labels to M_s segments. This is a nonlinear integer programming problem which is solved using a Genetic Algorithm to minimize an energy function which is composed of three terms: one for representing the appearance changes E_a, one for the displacements E_d and the other one E_o for the penalty when objects move out of the scene.

A further segmentation is needed when segments that correspond to different objects in the previous frame are assigned to the same blob. A restricted graph cut method is employed to segment the graph of the blob by minimizing a segmentation energy function, in which we consider the degree that a graph cut fits the current data while being coherent with the minimum cut in the previous frame. Once the current segmentation is done, the components and objects in the current tree are created initially from it regarding the previous tree structure.

To dynamically manage object splits and merges along time, we maintain similarities between nodes at the component and object level respectively and update the tree based on it. The component similarities are measured among components which belong to the same object while the object similarities are measured among objects. These similarities are computed considering spatial distance and appearance difference, which reveal the likelihood of object splits

and merges. We accumulate them along time by averaging the current similarity and the previous accumulated similarity regarding the established correspondences. Then object splits and merges are confirmed by thresholding the
accumulated similarities. Finally, an over-segmentation is performed at the component level to generate segments for correctly establishing the correspondence
to the next frame. Specifically, a normalized cut is performed in the graph representing the component iteratively until the cut cost is larger than a threshold.

3   Graph Based Dynamic 3D Point Cloud Segmentation

In this section, we present the frame work of the proposed approach including
data acquisition and initialization, temporal correspondences establishment and
segmentation, the proposed dynamic management of object splits and merges
mechanism and the over-segmentation method.

3.1   Data Acquisition and Initialization

We can transform the per-pixel distances provided in an RGBD image into a
3D point cloud $C_I \subseteq R^3$ using camera parameters. We focus on the interest
area of the foreground cloud $C_{fg} \subseteq R^3$ in 3D space. Taking the foreground
point cloud at frame t as input data, a graph representation is constructed
$f(C_{fg}) \to G(v, e)$ via a graph building method f, where v is the set of vertices
or nodes and e the edges of the graph. The super voxel method introduced in [10]
is employed as the graph building method f in our approach. It aggregates
points on the point cloud into homogeneous sub-cloud patches (super voxels)
with respect to the point proximity and appearance similarity while preserving
the boundary information. Then a graph G is built for the super voxels regarding
their adjacency. The connectivity of C_{fg} is interpreted as the connectivity on
G. Our system is initialized by building the tree structure for the first frame.
Nodes in the tree are denoted as N_{level}^i, where we specify which level the node
belongs to and its node number in this level. Each node is described by its
related point cloud and graph $N_{level}^i \sim (C_{level}^i, G_{level}^i)$, where $C_{level}^i \subseteq C_{fg}$ and
$G_{level}^i \subseteq G$. A node for the tree root is created as $N_{sc}^1 \sim (C_{fg}, G)$. As mentioned
in Sect. 2.2, we base the construction of the tree for the first frame only on
the connectivity of the input point cloud. Thus, we extract blobs from C_{fg} by
detecting connected components on graph G. Each blob is treated as one object
proposal while accordingly we create one object node N_o^i in the tree. For each
object node, one component node N_c^i is created. Components are over-segmented
into M_s segments via an over segmentation method $OSeg(N_c^i) \to \{N_s^1 \cdots N_s^{M_s}\}$.

3.2   Correspondences Establishment and Segmentation

Apart from the first frame, we create the current tree structure with respect
to the tree in the previous frame Tr'. Similarly, a graph G is obtained for the
current point cloud and blobs are detected on G. Then, the tree building process

is started by establishing the correspondences between the current data and Tr'. Associating a set of labels to another set of labels is treated as an assignment task, in which we optimize different assignment proposals with respect to an energy function. Since the problem scale increases exponentially with the number of labels, it is critical to limit the number of the labels. Therefore, we propose to assign the blob labels in the current frame to the segments in the previous tree Tr'. The blobs represent the few compact sub-clouds of the input point cloud. Assigning blob labels to segments reduces the problem scale while it respects the spatial disconnection between the compact sub-clouds, which may coincide with the object boundaries. The problem now becomes a task of assigning M_b blob labels in the current frame to M_s' segments in the previous frame. To cope with the situation when objects go out of the scene, we employ a virtual blob B_{out} which stands for the space out of the interest area and does not represent any point cloud. Then, the assignment energy function is defined as:

$$E_{ass}(A) = E_a + E_d + E_o \tag{1}$$

where A is an assignment proposal which maps a segment label in the previous frame l_s' to a blob label l_b in the current frame, $A\left(l_s'\right) \to l_b$. E_a stands for the summation of the energy of the appearance difference between the set of the point clouds $C_s^{j'}$ related to the segment $N_s^{j'}$ and the point cloud C_b^i related the blob B_i, where the segment label $l_s^{j'}$ is associated to the blob label l_b^i regarding the assignment A. The appearance difference is measured by comparing the number of points $NoP\left(\cdot\right)$ on the point cloud.

$$E_a(A) = \sum_{i=1}^{M_b} \left| NoP\left(C_b^i\right) - \sum_{A\left(l_s^{j'}\right)==l_b^i} NoP\left(C_s^{j'}\right) \right| \tag{2}$$

E_d is the summation of the energy of the displacement which is calculated by measuring the Hausdorff distance $dist_h\left(\cdot\right)$ between the point cloud $C_s^{j'}$ and the point cloud C_b^i, where $A\left(l_s^{j'}\right) == l_b^i$.

$$E_d(A) = \sum_{i=1}^{M_b} \sum_{A\left(l_s^{j'}\right)==l_b^i} dist_h\left(C_s^{j'}, C_b^i\right) \tag{3}$$

E_o is the summation of the distance between the point cloud of the segment $N_s^{j'}$, which is associated with blob B_{out}, to the closest boundary bd_i. The boundaries are predefined planes which are also used in the data acquisition step in Sect.3.1. The distance is calculated as the Euclidean distance $(dist_e\left(\cdot\right))$ from the centroid of the point cloud of the segment to the closest boundary plane.

$$E_o(A) = \sum_{A\left(l_s^{j'}\right)==l_b^{out}} \min_{bd_i \in Boundary} \left(dist_e\left(C_s^{j'}, bd_i\right)\right) \tag{4}$$

Optimizing this energy function is a nonlinear integer programming problem. We employed the Genetic Algorithm to solve it.

After the best assignment A^* is obtained, the blobs in the current frame are associated with segments in the previous frame. A further segmentation is needed when segments that correspond to different objects in the previous frame (according to the previous tree $T_r{}'$) are assigned to the same blob. Given a blob $B_i \sim (C_b^i, G_b^i)$ and the M unique object labels related to the associated segment labels $\{l_s^j \mid A^* (l_s^j) == l_b^i\}$, our goal is to segment the graph G_b^i into M parts. To this end, we employ the restricted graph cut approach proposed in [17] to seek for the minimal cut on graph G_b^i, which further segments this blob considering both spatial/feature homogeneity and the temporal consistency. The minimal cut is obtained by minimizing a segmentation energy function with the way introduced in [7]. The energy function for graph cut is usually defined as the summation of the data energy and the smoothness energy ($E(L) = E_{data} + E_{smooth}$), where L stands for the label proposal for the graph. The data energy is an unary energy term representing the degree that the label proposal fits the current data. The smoothness energy is a pair-wise energy which manages the label smoothness between nodes in the graph. The method proposed in [17] introduces a novel smoothness energy term considering the label smoothness regarding not only the current data but also the minimal cut obtained in the previous frame.

The further segmentation performed on the blob with segment labels related to multiple object labels yields the object partitions for this blob while establishing their correspondences to the objects in the previous tree. As mentioned in Sect. 2.1, an object is represented by more than one component if it splits in different blobs, in the current or previous frames. Thus, for each object partition in the blobs, we create one component for the related object. Accordingly, the correspondences between the current components and the components in the previous tree are made. Note that there is no correspondence established for the newly generated components in the current tree. In this step, the first three levels of the current tree structure are initially built regarding the established correspondences to the previous tree at each of the three levels.

3.3   Dynamic Management of Merge and Split

Given the current tree obtained in the last step, an object proposal is implicit at the object level. This object proposal for the current input data is temporally coherent with the object proposal in the previous frame. However, it may not be a correct object proposal, since no accurate initialization is guaranteed at the beginning of this process in our approach. That is to say, this object proposal needs to be further analyzed, in order to cope with the errors in the previous information. In this case, we exploit the established correspondences and analyze the behaviors of related nodes in trees along time. More specifically, we compute the similarities among the components corresponding to the same object, which forms a similarity matrix for each object in the tree. The object similarities are computed among objects in the tree producing an object similarity matrix.

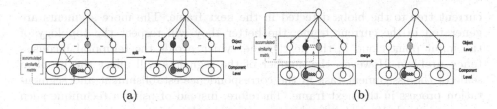

(a)   (b)

Fig. 3. Example of dynamic management of split (a) and merge (b)

In our approach, the similarity between node N^i and N^j is defined as the Euclidean distance between their related point clouds in Eq. (5).

$$Sim\left(N^i, N^j\right) = \begin{cases} 0 & dist_e\left(C^i, C^j\right) > \psi \\ 1 - \frac{dist_e\left(C^i, C^j\right)}{\psi} & otherwise \end{cases} \tag{5}$$

Note that here the Euclidean distance between two point clouds is calculated as the distance between the closest point pair from them. ψ is a normalizing factor. Afterwards, the similarities are accumulated along time by averaging them with the corresponding accumulated similarity in the previous frame, in order to dynamically manage the merges and splits of objects in the scene on the fly. The accumulated similarity reveals the likelihood of object splits and merges regarding the evidence observed up to the current frame. Thus, the decisions for split and merge are made by thresholding the accumulated similarity regarding two thresholds, Th_{split} and Th_{merge}. Figure 3 shows an example how the object merge and split are dynamically managed. Specifically, a split for an object node is confirmed when a set of its child component nodes have all the accumulated similarities smaller than Th_{split} with respect to the rest of the child component nodes. Then a new object node is created as the parent node of the split component nodes. In Fig. 3(a), the red component node splits from its parent object node and a new object node marked in blue is created as its new parent. A merge between object nodes is confirmed when they are physically connected while the accumulated similarities between them are larger than Th_{merge}. In Fig. 3(b), a merge is confirmed between the blue object node and the green object node which is physically connected with each other. The nodes are merged to the one with the larger number of the points on the related point cloud (the green node). Their child component nodes are all connected to the green object node in the tree. Then the blue object node is removed from the tree.

3.4 Over Segmentation

The first three levels in the current tree structure are built and updated in the last two steps. In this section, we introduce an over segmentation process in order to build the forth level of the tree. In the over-segmentation level, we generate segments for each component in the current tree. This is treated as the preparation for establishing the correspondence between segments in the current tree to the blobs detected in the next frame. The more segments are generated in the current frame, the better they will respect the topology of the input point cloud in the next frame, which avoids the temporal inconsistency problem. However, the number of the segments will affect the problem scale of the assignment task in the correspondence establishment and segmentation process in the next frame. Therefore, instead of using a technique such as super voxel [10] which finely over-segments the point cloud, we propose a relatively coarser over-segmentation method to tackle this problem. Pratically, in the related graph $G_c^i(v,e)$ of a component node N_c^i, we define the touching points for connected nodes in G_c^i. The touching points TP_j^i from the node v^i to the node v^j is computed as the number of the points in v^i which have the closest Euclidean distance lower than a threshold Th_{tp} to v^j. The touching points TP_i^j from v^j to v^i is defined in the same manner. The number of touching points reveals the compactness CC between connected nodes in the graph, which is defined as:

$$CC\left(v^i,v^j\right) = \frac{NoP\left(TP_j^i\right)}{NoP\left(v^i\right)} + \frac{NoP\left(TP_i^j\right)}{NoP\left(v^j\right)} \tag{6}$$

where $NoP\left(\cdot\right)$ stands for the number of the points in a graph node. We believe that any split of the point cloud will gradually lead the decrease in the number of touching points at the splitting position on the graph. Then the edges in the graph are weighted by CC and a normalized cut approach [14] is performed on the graph iteratively, which yields one segment node in each iteration until the cut cost is larger than a threshold Th_{mc}. In this manner, the component is iteratively over-segmented into segments at the positions which are less compact in the graph, which may coincide with the splits in the next frame.

4 Experiments

4.1 Segmentation Result Evaluation

To evaluate our approach from the 3D point cloud segmentation perspective, we select 4 sequences with 3D point cloud ground truth labeling in the human manipulation data set [11]. Each of them contains 200 frames. These 4 sequences vary from single attachment to multi-attachments, low motion to higher motion,

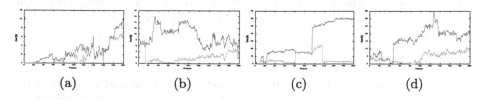

| (a) | (b) | (c) | (d) |

Fig. 4. (a)-(d) present the segmentation results for sequence 1-4, shown as percentage of error points (vertical axis) per frame (horizontal). Red: GDS, Blue: GS. (Color figure online)

double attached objects to multiple attached objects. The task of this experiment is to segment objects from the scene. The evaluation metrics is 3D segmentation accuracy (3D ACCU) proposed in [18] which computes the fraction of a ground truth segment that is correctly classified in our approach. Since the super voxel based graph representation method organises the input point cloud with voxels in 3D producing a down sampled point cloud, while the ground truth is labeled in the original cloud, we find K nearest neighbors for a point on the down sampled point cloud from the ground truth labeling and use majority voted label among K nearest neighbors as the ground truth labeling for this point.

Figure 4 shows the segmentation results of these 4 sequences. In each sub-figure, we plot the percentage of segmentation error against the frame number. We compare the segmentation performance of our graph based dynamic segmentation approach (GDS) with the graph based segmentation method (GS) proposed in [17] which provides a temporally coherent segmentation for RGBD stream data. The red lines in Fig. 4 stand for the result of GDS while the blue lines stand for the result of GS. As mentioned in Sect. 3.2, GS is also integrated in our approach producing temporally coherent segmentation for blobs with more than one unique object labels. Thus, the comparison between them shows the importance of introducing the dynamic management of object split and merge mechanism. Particularly, GDS outperforms GS in all the 4 sequences shown in Fig. 4, which proves that the dynamic management mechanism contributes in the low level to the better segmentation of actual objects in the scene. GDS achieves an overall foreground 3D point cloud segmentation 3.92 % mean segmentation error. In Fig. 4(c), we observe a dramatic increase (from 2.5 % to 15 %) in the segmentation error for GDS (red line). This is caused by the error in dynamic management of object merge and split. Figure 5(d)–(f) show 3 key frames in this process, where objects are marked in different colors. The left arm of the human body in blue is confirmed to split from the torso in frame 81 due to the persistent self-occlusion. The self-occlusion breaks the human body into two compact point clouds (the left arm and the rest), which gradually decreases the accumulated similarity till the split is confirmed in frame 81. However, these two point clouds reattach to each other in frame 103, which continuously increases the accumulated similarity between them, till they are confirmed to merge in frame 136. Figure 5(j)–(l) in the second row present another example, in which our system is incorrectly initialized in frame 1 (part of the torso marked in red is treated as one object because of the spatial disconnection caused by occlusion). They reattach to each other in frame 8 and get merged in frame 14 due to the dynamic management mechanism. These two examples illustrate the robustness of our system regarding the errors in previous frames while showing that our approach does not rely on an accurate initialization.

For comparison, we employ 3 more sequences proposed in [6] and perform our approach against the Adaptive Surface Models based 3D Segmentation method (ASMS) in [6]. ASMS maintains a quadratic surface model to generally represent the object segments in the scene. The model is updated along the sequence by finding and growing the overlapping area to obtain the final segmentation

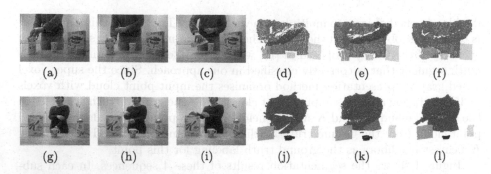

Fig. 5. Examples of dynamic management of merge and split. (a)–(c) present the color images of frame 81,103 and 136 in sequence 4, (d)–(f) show the segmentation results in these frames. (g)–(i) present the color images of frame 1,8 and 14 in sequence 2, (j)–(l) show the segmentation results in these frames. (Color figure online)

result. To adapt our approach to the scenes in these 3 sequences, we remove the background point cloud by using a plane fitting technique to extract foreground point clouds as input data. Figure 6 shows a quantitative comparison between GDS and ASMS in these 3 sequences. Sequence 1 contains a scenario of a human hand rolling a green ball forward and then backward with the fingers. Sequence 2 involves a robot arm grasping a paper roll and moving it to a new position. Sequence 3 describes a scenario in which the human hand enters and leaves the scene, displacing the objects rapidly. The comparison results show that the proposed GDS approach outperforms ASMS in all the 3 sequences. Specifically, Fig. 6(c) shows an example of the drawback in ASMS. The spikes in the blue curve are caused by rapid object movement, which leaves little or no overlap of corresponding segments for ASMS. However, our method has the robustness to rapid movements, since the correspondences establishment problem is treated as the optimization of an assignment energy.

Apart from the sequences used in the quantitative evaluation experiments, we employ 5 more sequences without ground truth labeling, recorded by ourselves with scenes displaying interactions in human manipulation scenes. Figure 7 shows some qualitative results of our approach from 4 sequences. For each sequence, we

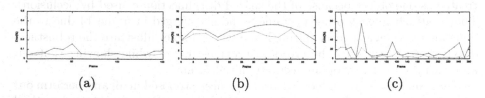

Fig. 6. Quantitative result of GDS (in red) and the ASMS (in blue) for the 3 sequences provided in [6]. From left to right, sequence 1–3. (Color figure online)

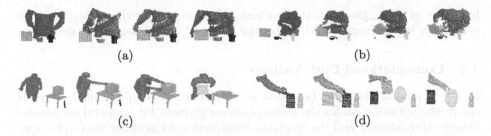

(a)   (b)

(c)   (d)

Fig. 7. Qualitative results of the proposed method: (a)–(b) from human manipulation dataset in [11], (c) from data recorded by ourselves and (d) from data in [6].

uniformly sample 4 frames and show the segmentation result from our approach. More visual results are available on https://imatge.upc.edu/web/node/1806.

4.2 Interaction Detection

Our approach is also capable to obtain the interactions between objects, which is implicit in the tree structure. As mentioned in Sect. 1, an interaction between objects is defined as a state when they become spatially close. In our method, an interaction is detected when a blob is related to more than one unique object label. An example of an object interaction is shown in Fig. 8(a), where an interaction between a human body and a box is detected and marked as the black line connecting them. Based on this definition, we manually label the object interaction occurring in the 4 sequences used in the first experiment and calculate the times of interactions between objects in the scene detected by the proposed method. Figure 8(c) shows the interaction detection result in each sequence, where the top of each bar shows the number of interactions in the ground truth, the red line stands for the true positive detections in our approach and the blue line stands for the false positive detections. Our approach detected 742 truth positive interactions over 980 labeled interactions in the ground truth. We notice that the number of false positive detections in sequence 3 is relatively high. This is mainly caused by the errors in dynamic management of object split and merge process. Figure 8(b) shows the segmented point cloud in a frame of sequence 3, where an interaction is detected between the arm in blue and the

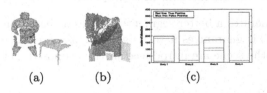

(a)   (b)   (c)

Fig. 8. (a) An example of object interaction. (b) An example of false positive detections (c) Interaction detection evaluation for 4 sequences from [11]

juice box in green. However, the arm and the torso are not correctly merged as one object in this frame, which makes the detected interaction a false detection.

4.3 Computational Cost Analysis

In our approach, there are two main parts where the computational power is spent: the optimization for the multi-labels assignment for temporal correspondences establishment and the graph cut technique used in either the further segmentation or the over-segmentation process. The main problem of approaching the temporal correspondences association by a multi-labels assignment problem is the computation complexity. The problem scale increases exponentially when the number of labels grows. However, the number of the labels is controlled in our approach by finding a suitable over-segmentation level so that we can achieve the assignment task in a small problem scale while not leading to the temporal inconsistency problem. In the experiments, generally 20 segments and 5 blobs are involved in the assignment task in each frame. The graph cut technique used in our approach has the reported computation complexity $O\left(v^2 \cdot sqrt\left(e\right)\right)$ where v stands for the number of vertices and e the number of edges on the graph.

5   Conclusion

In this paper, we have introduced a graph based dynamic 3D point cloud segmentation method, which works at low level with a tree structure representation for segmenting generic objects in RGBD steam data. We have evaluated the performance of the proposed approach with a human manipulation data set and also compared it with the method proposed in [6]. Our approach achieves an overall 3.92 % 3D point cloud segmentation error while outperforming in the comparison experiment. Our contribution can be summarized in 3 points:

- firstly, we proposed a novel over-segmentation method based on the compactness of the connection between neighboring super voxels on the graph
- then a novel tree structure representation for the scene is proposed, which allows to temporally update the similarities between nodes in the tree
- the temporal correspondences establishment task is approached by a labelling assignment problem that takes into account the appearance and displacement of the components. Based on the tree structure, a dynamic management of object splits and merges mechanism is proposed

Our approach generates a better segmentation result based on all low-level features available. This guarantees it to be generic, as no explicit or learnt model of the objects or the scene are introduced in the proposed method.

Acknowledgement. This work has been developed in the framework of the project TEC2013-43935-R, financed by the Spanish Ministerio de Economa y Competitividad and the European Regional Development Fund (ERDF).

References

1. Abramov, A., Pauwels, K., Papon, J., Wörgötter, F., Dellen, B.: Depth-supported real-time video segmentation with the kinect. In: 2012 IEEE Workshop on Applications of Computer Vision (WACV), pp. 457–464. IEEE (2012)
2. Felzenszwalb, P.F., Girshick, R.B., McAllester, D., Ramanan, D.: Object detection with discriminatively trained part-based models. IEEE Trans. Pattern Anal. Mach. Intell. **32**(9), 1627–1645 (2010)
3. Grundmann, M., Kwatra, V., Han, M., Essa, I.: Efficient hierarchical graph-based video segmentation. In: 2010 IEEE Conference on Computer Vision and Pattern Recognition (CVPR), pp. 2141–2148. IEEE (2010)
4. He, X., Zemel, R.S., Carreira-Perpiñán, M.: Multiscale conditional random fields for image labeling. In. In CVPR 2004. vol. 2, p. II-695. IEEE (2004)
5. Hickson, S., Birchfield, S., Essa, I., Christensen, H.: Efficient hierarchical graph-based segmentation of RGBD videos. In: CVPR2014, IEEE Computer Society (2014)
6. Husain, F., Dellen, B., Torras, C.: Consistent depth video segmentation using adaptive surface models. IEEE Trans. Cybern. **45**(2), 266–278 (2015)
7. Kolmogorov, V., Zabin, R.: What energy functions can be minimized via graph cuts? IEEE Trans. Pattern Anal. Mach. Intell. **26**(2), 147–159 (2004)
8. Koo, S., Lee, D., Kwon, D.S.: Incremental object learning and robust tracking of multiple objects from rgb-d point set data. J. Vis. Commun. Image Represent. **25**(1), 108–121 (2014)
9. Liu, C., Yuen, J., Torralba, A.: Nonparametric scene parsing via label transfer. Pattern Anal. Mach. Intell. **33**(12), 2368–2382 (2011)
10. Papon, J., Abramov, A., Schoeler, M., Worgotter, F.: Voxel cloud connectivity segmentation-supervoxels for point clouds. In: 2013 IEEE Conference on Computer Vision and Pattern Recognition (CVPR), pp. 2027–2034. IEEE (2013)
11. Pieropan, A., Salvi, G., Pauwels, K., Kjellstrom, H.: Audio-visual classification and detection of human manipulation actions. In: 2014 IEEE/RSJ International Conference on Intelligent Robots and Systems (IROS 2014), pp. 3045–3052. IEEE (2014)
12. Ren, X., Malik, J.: Tracking as repeated figure/ground segmentation. In: Computer Vision and Pattern Recognition, 2007. pp. 1–8. IEEE (2007)
13. Richtsfeld, A., Mörwald, T., Prankl, J., Zillich, M., Vincze, M.: Segmentation of unknown objects in indoor environments. In: 2012 IEEE/RSJ International Conference on Intelligent Robots and Systems (IROS), pp. 4791–4796. IEEE (2012)
14. Shi, J., Malik, J.: Normalized cuts and image segmentation. IEEE Trans. Pattern Anal. Mach. Intell. **22**(8), 888–905 (2000)
15. Shotton, J., Winn, J., Rother, C., Criminisi, A.: *TextonBoost*: joint appearance, shape and context modeling for multi-class object recognition and segmentation. In: Leonardis, A., Bischof, H., Pinz, A. (eds.) ECCV 2006. LNCS, vol. 3951, pp. 1–15. Springer, Heidelberg (2006). doi:10.1007/11744023_1
16. Tsai, D., Flagg, M., Nakazawa, A., Rehg, J.M.: Motion coherent tracking using multi-label MRF optimization. IJCV **100**(2), 190–202 (2012)
17. Xiao, L., Josep, C., Montse, P.: 3d point cloud segmentation oriented to the analysis of interactions. In: 24th European Signal Processing Conference (EUSIPCO 2016), IEEE (2016) (Accepted and to be published)
18. Xu, C., Corso, J.J.: Evaluation of super-voxel methods for early video processing. In: 2012 IEEE Conference on Computer Vision and Pattern Recognition (CVPR), pp. 1202–1209. IEEE (2012)

Deep Learning Based Fence Segmentation and Removal from an Image Using a Video Sequence

Sankaraganesh Jonna[1]([✉]), Krishna K. Nakka[2], and Rajiv R. Sahay[2]

[1] Department of Computer Science and Engineering,
Indian Institute of Technology Kharagpur, Kharagpur, India
sankar9.iitkgp@gmail.com

[2] Department of Electrical Engineering, Indian Institute of Technology Kharagpur,
Kharagpur, India
krishkanth.92@gmail.com, sahayiitm@gmail.com

Abstract. Conventional approaches to image de-fencing use multiple adjacent frames for segmentation of fences in the reference image and are limited to restoring images of static scenes only. In this paper, we propose a de-fencing algorithm for images of dynamic scenes using an occlusion-aware optical flow method. We divide the problem of image de-fencing into the tasks of automated fence segmentation from a single image, motion estimation under known occlusions and fusion of data from multiple frames of a captured video of the scene. Specifically, we use a pre-trained convolutional neural network to segment fence pixels from a single image. The knowledge of spatial locations of fences is used to subsequently estimate optical flow in the occluded frames of the video for the final data fusion step. We cast the fence removal problem in an optimization framework by modeling the formation of the degraded observations. The inverse problem is solved using fast iterative shrinkage thresholding algorithm (FISTA). Experimental results show the effectiveness of proposed algorithm.

Keywords: Image inpainting · De-fencing · Deep learning · Convolutional neural networks · Optical flow

1 Introduction

Images containing fences/occlusions occur in several situations such as photographing statues in museums, animals in a zoo etc. Image de-fencing involves the removal of fences or occlusions in images. De-fencing a single photo is strictly an image inpainting problem which uses data in the regions neighbouring fence pixels in the frame for filling-in occlusions. The works of [1–4] addressed the image inpainting problem wherein a portion of the image which is to be inpainted is specified by a mask manually. As shown in Fig. 1(a), in the image de-fencing problem it is difficult to manually mark all fence pixels since they are numerous

© Springer International Publishing Switzerland 2016
G. Hua and H. Jégou (Eds.): ECCV 2016 Workshops, Part III, LNCS 9915, pp. 836–851, 2016.
DOI: 10.1007/978-3-319-49409-8_68

Fig. 1. (a) A frame taken from a video. (b) Segmented binary fence mask obtained using proposed CNN-SVM algorithm. (c) Inpainted image corresponding to (a) using the method of [2]. (d) De-fenced image corresponding to (a) using the proposed algorithm.

and spread over the entire image. The segmented binary fence mask obtained using the proposed algorithm is shown in Fig. 1(b). These masks are used in our work to aid in occlusion-aware optical flow computation and background image reconstruction. In Fig. 1(c), we show the inpainted image corresponding to Fig. 1(a) obtained using the method of [2]. The de-fenced image obtained using the proposed algorithm is shown in Fig. 1(d). As can be seen from Fig. 1(c), image inpainting does not yield satisfactory results when the image contains fine textured regions which have to be filled-in. However, using a video panned across a fenced scene can lead to better results due to availability of additional information in the adjacent frames.

Although, there has been significant progress in the area of lattice detection [5,6] and restoration of fenced images/videos [6–10], segmentation of fence or occlusion from a single image and de-fencing scenes containing dynamic elements are still challenging problems. Most of the existing works assume global motion between the frames and use images of static scene elements only [8–10]. Initial work related to image de-fencing has been reported by Liu et al. [7], wherein fence patterns are segmented via spatial regularity and the fence occlusions are filled-in using an inpainting algorithm [2]. Recent attempts for image de-fencing [9,10] use the parallax cue for fence pattern segmentation using multiple frames from a video. However, these works [9,10] constrain the scene elements to be static. Another drawback of [9] is that if the scene does not produce appreciable depth parallax fence segmentation is inaccurate. A very recent image de-fencing algorithm [6] exploits both color and motion cues for automatic fence segmentation from dynamic videos.

The proposed algorithm for image de-fencing uses a video captured by panning a camera relative to the scene and requires the solution of three sub-problems. The first task is automatic segmentation of fence pixels in the frames of the captured video. Importantly, unlike existing works [6–10], we propose a machine learning algorithm to segment fences in a *single* image. We propose to use a pre-trained convolutional neural network (CNN) for fence texel joint detection to generate automatic scribbles which are fed to an image matting [11] technique to obtain the binary fence mask. Note that sample portions of images marked with yellow colored squares shown in Fig. 1(a) are treated as fence texels in this work. To the best of our knowledge, we are the first to detect fence texels using a pre-trained CNN coupled with an SVM classifier. Secondly, we estimate the pixel correspondence between the reference frame and the additional frames using a modified optical flow algorithm which incorporates the knowledge of location of occlusions in the observations. It is to be noted that existing optical flow algorithms find the relative shift only between pixels *visible* in two frames. Accurate registration of the observations is critical in de-fencing the reference image since erroneous pixel matching would lead to incorrect data fusion from additional frames. The basic premise of our work is that image regions occluded by fence pixels in the reference frame are rendered visible in other frames of the captured video. Therefore, we propose an occlusion-aware optical flow method using fence pixels located in the first step of our image de-fencing pipeline to accurately estimate background pixel correspondences even at occluded image regions. Finally, we fuse the information from additional frames in order to uncover the occluded pixels in the reference frame using an optimization framework. Since natural images are sparse, we use the fast iterative shrinkage thresholding algorithm (FISTA) to solve the resulting ill-posed inverse problem assuming l_1 norm of the de-fenced image as the regularization prior.

2 Prior Work

The problem of image de-fencing has been first addressed in [7] by inpainting fence pixels of the input image. The algorithm proposed in [12] used multiple images for de-fencing, which significantly improves the performance due to availability of occluded image data in additional frames. The work of [12] used a deformable lattice detection method proposed in [5] for fence detection. Unfortunately, the method of [5] is not a robust approach and fails for many real-world images. Khasare et al. [8] proposed an improved multi-frame de-fencing technique by using loopy belief propagation. However, there are two issues with their approach. Firstly, the work in [8] assumed that motion between the frames is global. This assumption is invalid for more complex dynamic scenes where the motion is non-global. Also, the method of [8] used an image matting technique proposed by [11] for fence segmentation which involves significant user interaction. A video de-fencing algorithm [9], proposed a soft fence segmentation method where visual parallax serves as the cue to distinguish fences from the unoccluded pixels. Recently, Xue et al. [10] jointly estimated the foreground masks and obstruction-free images using five frames taken from a video. Apart from the image based techniques, Jonna et al. [13] proposed a multimodal approach for image de-fencing wherein they have extracted the fence masks with the aid of depth maps corresponding to the color images obtained using the Kinect sensor. Very recently, our works [14,15] addresses the image de-fencing problem. However, the drawback of both the methods [14,15] is that they do not estimate occlusion-aware optical flow for data fusion.

The proposed algorithm for image de-fencing addresses some of the issues with the existing techniques. Firstly, we propose a machine learning algorithm using CNN-SVM for fence segmentation from a *single* image unlike existing works [6,9,10], which need a few frames to obtain the fence masks. Importantly, unlike the works of [9, 10], the proposed algorithm does not assume that the scene is static but we can handle scenes containing dynamic elements. For this purpose, we propose a modified optical flow algorithm for estimation of pixel correspondence between the reference frame and additional frames after segmenting occlusions.

3 Methodology

We relate the occluded image to the original de-fenced image using a degradation model as follows,

$$\mathbf{O}_m \mathbf{y}_m = \mathbf{y}_m^{obs} = \mathbf{O}_m [\mathbf{F}_m \mathbf{x} + \mathbf{n}_m] \tag{1}$$

where $\mathbf{y}_m$ are observations containing fences obtained from the captured video, $\mathbf{O}_m$ are the binary fence masks, $\mathbf{F}_m$ models the relative motion between frames, $\mathbf{x}$ is the de-fenced image and $\mathbf{n}_m$ is Gaussian noise. As described in Sect. 1, the problem of image de-fencing was divided into three sub-problems, which we elaborate upon in the following sub-sections.

3.1 Pre-trained CNN-SVM for Fence Texel Joint Detection

The important property of most outdoor fences is their symmetry about the fence texel joints. Referring to Fig. 1(a), we observe that fence texels appear repetitively throughout the entire image. Convolutional neural nets (CNN), originally proposed by [16], can be effectively trained to recognize objects directly from images with robustness to scale, rotation, translation, noise etc. Recently, Krizhevsky et al. [17] proved the utility of CNNs for object detection and classification in the ILSVRC challenge [18]. Since real-world fence texels exhibit variations in color, shape, noise, etc., we are motivated to use CNNs for segmenting these patterns robustly.

Convolutional neural networks belong to a class of deep learning techniques which operate directly on an input image extracting features using a cascade of convolutional, activation and pooling layers to finally predict the image category. The key layer in CNN is the convolutional layer whose filter kernels are learnt automatically via backpropagation. The commonly used non-linear activation functions are sigmoid, tanh, rectified linear unit (ReLU) and maxout [19] etc. The pooling layers sub-sample the input data. Overfitting occurs in neural networks when the training data is limited. Recently, a technique called Dropout [20] has been proposed which can improve the generalization capability of CNNs by randomly dropping some of the neurons.

However, since CNNs use supervised learning they need huge labeled datasets and long training time. A possible solution to this problem is to use transfer learning [21, 22], wherein pre-trained models are used to initialize the weights and fine-tune the network on a different dataset. One can also preserve the pre-trained filter kernels and re-train the classifier part only. In this work, we used a CNN pre-trained on ImageNet [18] as a feature extractor by excluding the softmax layer.

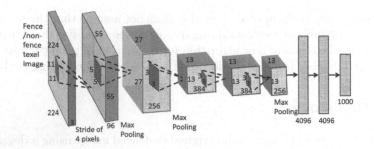

Fig. 2. The architecture of the pre-trained CNN [17].

The architecture of the CNN in Fig. 2 trained on ImageNet contains five convolutional layers followed by three fully-connected layers and a softmax classifier. Max-pooling layers follow first, second and fifth convolutional layer.

In Fig. 3(a), we show the 96 filter kernels of dimensions $11 \times 11 \times 3$ learned by the first convolutional layer on input images. In this work, we propose to use CNN as a generic feature extractor followed by a support vector machine classifier (CNN-SVM). A given RGB input image is resized to $224 \times 224 \times 3$ and fed to the proposed CNN-SVM a feature vector of size 4096 is extracted from the seventh fully-connected layer.

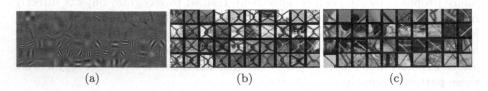

| (a) | (b) | (c) |

Fig. 3. (a) 96 learned filter kernels of size $11 \times 11 \times 3$ extracted from the first convolutional layer. (b) Sample fence texel joints. (c) Examples of non-fence texel joints.

An SVM classifier has been trained to detect fence texels using on these features of dimension 4096 extracted by the pre-trained CNN from a dataset of $20,000$ fence texel joints and $40,000$ non-fence texel sub-images. In Figs. 3(b) and (c), we show samples of fence texel texels and non-fence texels, respectively. During the testing phase, a sliding window is used to densely scan the test image shown in Fig. 4(a) from left to right and top to bottom with a stride of 5 pixels. The overall workflow of the proposed fence segmentation algorithm is shown in Fig. 4. Detected fence texels are joined by straight edges as shown in Fig. 4(b). In Fig. 4(c) we show the response obtained by Canny edge detection [23] algorithm after dilating the preliminary fence mask shown in Fig. 4(b) and treated as background scribbles. The combination of both foreground and background scribbles is shown in Fig. 4(d), wherein foreground scribbles are obtained by erosion operation on the image in Fig. 4(b). We fed these automatically generated

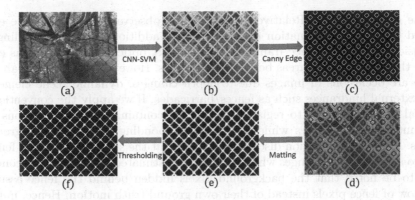

Fig. 4. Schematic of fence mask segmentation.

scribbles to the method of [11] and obtain the alpha map in Fig. 4(e). Finally, the binary fence mask shown in Fig. 4(f) is generated by thresholding the alpha map obtained from [11].

3.2 Occlusion Aware Optical Flow

The image alignment problem becomes more complex when real-world videos contain dynamic objects. Handling motion boundaries and occlusions in videos for optical flow computation is still challenging. Internal occlusions due to the layered dynamic objects and external occlusions such as fences make the problem tougher. In some practical applications of computer vision such as view synthesis, image de-fencing, etc. we need to compute the correspondence of all pixels between two images despite occlusions. Many algorithms for estimating optical flow are proposed in the literature [24–27], which are based on modifications of the basic variational framework proposed by Horn et al. [28] addressing its various shortcomings. Recently, significant progress has been made in order to compute dense optical flow in a robust manner [25,29,30]. The state-of-the-art optical flow algorithms [24,25] integrate descriptor matching between two images in a variational framework. It is due to a robust function in the variational framework that the algorithm in [24] can handle small internal occlusions. However, it fails to tackle large external occlusions. The algorithm of [29] computes dense correspondence between images by performing sparse-dense interpolation under contour and motion boundary assumption. An occlusion aware optical flow algorithm is proposed by [31], wherein occlusions in images are handled using a three-step procedure. Initially, the method in [31] estimates occlusion-ignorant optical flow. Subsequently, occlusions are computed using this unreliable optical flow. Finally, the algorithm in [31] corrects the optical flow using estimated occlusions.

The basic cue behind the proposed image de-fencing algorithm is that occluded image data in the reference frame is uncovered in additional frames of the captured video. Relative motion among observations needs to be estimated to fuse the information uncovered in the additional images for filling in occlusions in the reference frame. State-of-the-art optical flow algorithms estimate the flow of *visible* areas between two images. However, as described above, there are occlusions in images due to depth changes, dynamic scene elements and external hindrances such as fences/barricades. If we apply the conventional optical flow algorithms to register two images containing fence occlusions we encounter two difficulties while aligning corresponding fence and background pixels. Firstly, large motion discontinuities exist at the spatial location of fences due to abrupt depth changes which corrupt the estimated optical flow. Secondly, it is to be noted that the background pixels hidden behind the fence assume the flow of fence pixels instead of their own ground truth motion. Hence, in this work we modify the motion associated with fence pixels to that of surrounding background pixel motion in order to reveal the occluded pixel information in the warped adjacent frame.

In this paper, we re-formulate the optical flow algorithm of [32] to fit our application of image de-fencing. Akin to [32], coarse to fine optical flow is estimated using an incremental framework in Gaussian scale-space. Note that we have already obtained the binary fence mask $\mathbf{O}_m$ corresponding to the segmented fence pixels in the observation $\mathbf{y}_m$. We insert this mask $\mathbf{O}_m$ as occlusion operator inside the optical flow framework to deal with the motion inaccuracies at fence locations. At the fence locations data cost is assumed to be zero and only smoothness term in Eq. (3) guides optical flow estimation. We assume sparse gradient prior (modeled using l_1 norm) for both horizontal and vertical velocities. At every scale, the optimized values are up-scaled and used as initial estimate at the next fine scale.

Suppose $\mathbf{w} = [u, v]$ be the current estimate of horizontal and vertical flow fields and $\tilde{y}_r, \tilde{y}_t$ be the reference and t^{th} adjacent images, respectively. Under the incremental framework [32,33], one needs to estimate the best increment $d\mathbf{w} = (du, dv)$ as follows

$$E(du, dv) = \arg\min_{d\mathbf{w}} \| \mathbf{F}_{\mathbf{w}+d\mathbf{w}}\tilde{y}_t - \tilde{y}_r \|_1 + \mu \| \nabla(u + du) \|_1 + \mu \| \nabla(v + dv) \|_1$$

(2)

where $\mathbf{F}_{\mathbf{w}+d\mathbf{w}}$ is the warping matrix corresponding to flow $\mathbf{w} + d\mathbf{w}$, ∇ is the gradient operator and μ is the regularization parameter. To use gradient based methods, we replace the l_1 norm with a differentiable approximation $\phi(x^2) = \sqrt{x^2 + \epsilon^2}$, $\epsilon = 0.001$. To robustly estimate optical flow under the known fence occlusions we compute the combined binary mask $\mathbf{O} = \mathbf{F}_{\mathbf{w}+d\mathbf{w}}\mathbf{O}_t || \mathbf{O}_r$ obtained by the logical OR operation between the reference fence mask and backwarped fence from the tth frame using warping matrix $\mathbf{F}_{\mathbf{w}+d\mathbf{w}}$. To estimate the optical flow increment in the presence of occlusions we disable the data fidelity term by incorporating $\mathbf{O}$ in Eq. (2) as

$$E(du, dv) = \arg\min_{d\mathbf{w}} \| \mathbf{O}(\mathbf{F}_{\mathbf{w}+d\mathbf{w}}\tilde{y}_t - \tilde{y}_r) \|_1 + \mu \| \nabla(u+du) \|_1 + \mu \| \nabla(v+dv) \|_1$$

(3)

By first-order Taylor series expansion,

$$\mathbf{F_{w+dw}}\tilde{y}_t \approx \mathbf{F_w}\tilde{y}_t + \mathbf{Y}_x du + \mathbf{Y}_y dv \tag{4}$$

where $\mathbf{Y}_x = diag(\mathbf{F_w}\tilde{y}_{t_x})$, $\mathbf{Y}_y = diag(\mathbf{F_w}\tilde{y}_{t_y})$, $\tilde{y}_{t_x} = \frac{\partial}{\partial x}\tilde{y}_t$ and $\tilde{y}_{t_y} = \frac{\partial}{\partial y}\tilde{y}_t$. We can write Eq. (3) as

$$\underset{dw}{\arg\min} \parallel \mathbf{OF_w}\tilde{y}_t + \mathbf{OY}_x du + \mathbf{OY}_y dv - \mathbf{O}\tilde{y}_r) \parallel_1 + \mu \parallel \nabla(u+du) \parallel_1$$
$$+ \mu \parallel \nabla(v+dv) \parallel_1 \tag{5}$$

To estimate the best increments du, dv to the current flow u, v we equate the gradients $\left[\frac{\partial E}{\partial du}; \frac{\partial E}{\partial dv}\right]$ to zero.

$$\begin{bmatrix} \mathbf{Y}_x^T\mathbf{O}^T\mathbf{W}_d\mathbf{OY}_x + \mu L & \mathbf{Y}_x^T\mathbf{O}^T\mathbf{W}_d\mathbf{OY}_y \\ \mathbf{Y}_y^T\mathbf{O}^T\mathbf{W}_d\mathbf{OY}_x & \mathbf{Y}_y^T\mathbf{O}^T\mathbf{W}_d\mathbf{OY}_y + \mu L \end{bmatrix} \begin{bmatrix} du \\ dv \end{bmatrix}$$
$$= \begin{bmatrix} -Lu - \mathbf{Y}_x^T\mathbf{O}^T\mathbf{W}_d\mathbf{OF_w}\tilde{y}_t + \mathbf{Y}_x^T\mathbf{O}^T\mathbf{W}_d\mathbf{O}\tilde{y}_r \\ -Lv - \mathbf{Y}_y^T\mathbf{O}^T\mathbf{W}_d\mathbf{OF_w}\tilde{y}_t + \mathbf{Y}_y^T\mathbf{O}^T\mathbf{W}_d\mathbf{O}\tilde{y}_r \end{bmatrix}$$

where $L = \mathbf{D}_x^T\mathbf{W}_s\mathbf{D}_x + \mathbf{D}_y^T\mathbf{W}_s\mathbf{D}_y$, $\mathbf{W}_s = diag(\phi'(|\nabla u|^2))$ and $\mathbf{W}_d = diag(\phi'(|\mathbf{OF_w}\tilde{y}_t - \mathbf{O}\tilde{y}_r|^2))$. We define $\mathbf{D}_x$ and $\mathbf{D}_y$ are discrete differentiable operators along horizontal and vertical directions, respectively. We used conjugate gradient (CG) algorithm to solve for dw using iterative re-weighted least squares (IRLS) framework.

3.3 FISTA Optimization Framework

Once the relative motion between the frames has been estimated we need to fill-in the occluded pixels in the reference image using the corresponding uncovered pixels from the additional frames. Reconstructing de-fenced image $\mathbf{x}$ from the occluded observations is an ill-posed inverse problem and therefore prior information for $\mathbf{x}$ has to be used to regularize the solution. Since natural images are sparse, we employed l_1 norm of the de-fenced image as regularization constraint in the optimization framework as follows,

$$\hat{\mathbf{x}} = \underset{\mathbf{x}}{\arg\min} \left[\sum_m \parallel \mathbf{y}_m^{obs} - \mathbf{O}_m\mathbf{F}_m\mathbf{x} \parallel^2 + \lambda \parallel \mathbf{x} \parallel_1 \right] \tag{6}$$

where λ is the regularization parameter.

Since the objective function contains l_1 norm as a regularization function, it is difficult to solve Eq. 6 with the conventional gradient-based algorithms. Here, we employed one of the proximal algorithms such as FISTA [34] iterative framework to handle non-smooth functions for image de-fencing. The key step in FISTA iterative framework is the proximal operator [35] which operates on the combination of two previous iterates.

Algorithm 1. FISTA image de-fencing
***

1: **Input:**$\lambda, \alpha, \mathbf{z}_1 = \mathbf{x}_0 \in \mathbb{R}^{M \times N}, t_1 = 1$

2: **repeat**

3:     $\mathbf{x}_k = prox_\alpha(g)(\mathbf{z}_k - \alpha \nabla f(\mathbf{z}_k))$

4:     $t_{k+1} = \frac{1+\sqrt{1+4t_k^2}}{2}$

5:     $\mathbf{z}_{k+1} = \mathbf{x}_k + \left(\frac{t_k-1}{t_{k+1}}\right)(\mathbf{x}_k - \mathbf{x}_{k-1})$

6:     $k \leftarrow k + 1$

7: **until** $(\| \mathbf{x}_k - \mathbf{x}_{k-1} \|_2 \leq \epsilon)$
***

The proximal operator is defined as the solution of the following convex optimization [36]

$$prox_\alpha(g)(x) = \arg\min_y \{g(y) + \frac{1}{2\alpha} \| y - x \|^2\} \tag{7}$$

If $g(y)$ is l_1 norm, then $prox_\alpha(g)(x) = max(|x| - \lambda\alpha, 0)sign(x)$. The gradient for data matching cost f is given as follows

$$\nabla f(\mathbf{z}) = \sum_m \mathbf{F}_m^T \mathbf{O}_m^T (\mathbf{O}_m \mathbf{F}_m \mathbf{z} - \mathbf{y}_m^{obs}) \tag{8}$$

4   Experimental Results

Initially, we report both qualitative and quantitative results obtained using the proposed fence segmentation algorithm on various datasets. Subsequently, we show the impact of accounting for occlusions in the incremental flow framework. Finally, we report image de-fencing results obtained with the FISTA optimization framework. To demonstrate the efficacy of the proposed de-fencing system, we show comparison results with state-of-the-art fence segmentation, and de-fencing methods in the literature. We used only three frames from each captured video for all the image de-fencing results reported here using the proposed algorithm. For all our experiments, we fixed $\lambda = 0.0005$ in Eq. 6. We ran all our experiments on a 3.4 GHz Intel Core i7 processor with 16 GB of RAM.

4.1   Fence Segmentation

For validating the proposed algorithm for fence segmentation, we have evaluated our algorithm on state-of-the-art datasets [9,10,37]. We also show segmentation results on a proposed fenced image dataset consisting of 200 real-world images captured under diverse scenarios and complex backgrounds. We report quantitative results on PSU NRT [37] dataset and qualitative results on [9,10,37] datasets. As discussed in Sect. 3.1, we have extracted features from 20,000 fence, 40,000 non-fence texel images using a pre-trained CNN to train an SVM classifier. The trained classifier is used to detect joint locations in images via a sliding window protocol. We compare the results obtained using a state-of-the-art lattice detection algorithm [5] and the proposed algorithm on all the datasets.

Initially, in Fig. 5(a) we show a fenced image from the PSU NRT dataset [37]. Fence texels are detected using our pre-trained CNN-SVM approach and are jointed by straight edges, as shown in Fig. 5(f). Note that all fence texels are detected accurately in Fig. 5(f). In contrast, the method of [5] failed completely to extract the fence pixels as seen in Fig. 5(k). The output of Fig. 5(f) is used to generate foreground and background scribbles which are fed to the image matting technique of [11]. The final binary fence mask obtained by thresholding the output of [11] is shown in Fig. 5(p). Next, we have validated both the algorithms on image taken from a recent dataset [10] shown in Fig. 5(b). In Fig. 5(g), we show the fence texels detected using our pre-trained CNN-SVM approach and joined by straight edges. In contrast, the method of [5] failed completely to extract the fence pixels as seen in Fig. 5(l). The output of Fig. 5(g) is used to generate scribbles as outlined in Sect. 3.1. These foreground and background scribbles are fed to the image matting technique of [11]. The final binary fence mask obtained by thresholding the output of [11] is shown in Fig. 5(q). Finally, we perform experiments on images from the proposed fenced image dataset. Sample images taken from the dataset are shown in Figs. 5(c)–(e). In Figs. 5(h)–(j), we show the fence segmentations obtained using the proposed pre-trained CNN-SVM algorithm. We observe that the proposed algorithm detected all the fence texel joints accurately. The lattice detected using [5] are shown in Figs. 5(m)–(o). We can observe that the approach of [5] partially segments the fence pixels in Fig. 5(m). Note that in Fig. 5(o) the algorithm of [5] completely failed to segment fence pixels. The final binary fence masks obtained by thresholding the output of [11] are shown in Figs. 5(r)–(t).

A summary of the quantitative evaluation of the fence texel detection method of [5] and the pre-trained CNN-SVM based proposed algorithm is given in Table 1. The F-measure obtained for [5] on PSU NRT [37] dataset and proposed fenced image datasets are 0.62 and 0.41, respectively. In contrast, F-measure for the proposed method on PSU NRT dataset [37] and our fenced image datasets are 0.97 and 0.94, respectively.

Table 1. Quantitative evaluation of fence segmentation

	NRT database [37]			Our database		
Method	Precision	Recall	F-measure	Precision	Recall	F-measure
Park et al. [5]	0.95	0.46	0.62	0.94	0.26	0.41
pre-trained CNN-SVM	0.96	0.98	**0.97**	0.90	0.98	**0.94**

4.2 Optical Flow Under Known Occlusions

To demonstrate the robustness of proposed optical flow algorithm under known occlusions, we use frames from videos of fenced scenes in [6, 9, 10]. We show two frames from a video sequence named "football" from [9] in the first column

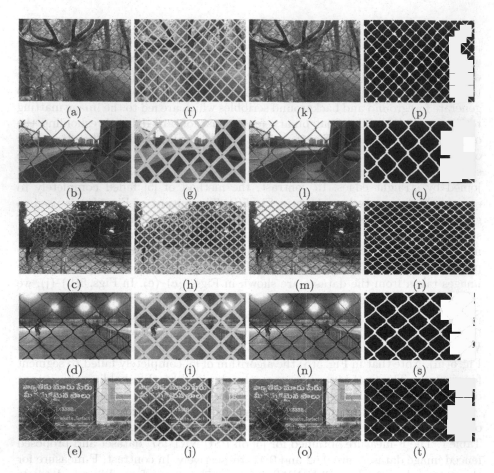

Fig. 5. First column: sample images from NRT [10,37] and proposed fenced image datasets, respectively. Second column: fence masks generated using the proposed pre-trained CNN-SVM algorithm. Third column: fence detection using [5]. Fourth column: final binary fence masks corresponding to images in the first column obtained by generating scribbles using fence detections in images of the second column which are fed to the method of [11].

of Fig. 6. The video sequences named "fence1" and "fence4" are taken from the work of [10]. Two frames from each of these videos are shown in second and third columns of Fig. 6, respectively. Video sequences named "lion" and "walking" are taken from [6] and a couple of observations from each of them are depicted in fourth and fifth columns of Fig. 6, respectively. In the third row of Fig. 6, we show the color coded optical flows obtained using [24] between respective images shown in each column of first and second row of Fig. 6. Note that the images shown in third row of Fig. 6 contain regions of erroneously estimated optical flow due to fence occlusions. In contrast, the flow estimated using proposed algorithm

Fig. 6. First and second row: frames taken from videos reported in [6,9,10]. Third row: optical flow computed between the first and second row images using [24]. Fourth row: de-fenced images obtained using the estimated flow shown in the third row. Fifth row: occlusion-aware optical flow obtained using the proposed algorithm.

under known fence occlusions are shown in the fifth row of Fig. 6. Note that the optical flows estimated using the proposed method contain no artifacts.

4.3   Image De-Fencing

To demonstrate the efficacy of the proposed image de-fencing algorithm, we conducted experiments with several real-world video sequences containing dynamic background objects. In Figs. 7(a), (d), (g), and (j), we show the images taken from four different video sequences. The fence pixels corresponding to these observations are segmented using the proposed pre-trained CNN-SVM and the approach of [11]. In Figs. 7(b), (e), (h), and (k), we show the inpainted images obtained using [2] which was the method used for obtaining the de-fenced image after fence segmentation in [6]. Note that we can see several artifacts in the inpainted images obtained using [2]. De-fenced images obtained using the proposed algorithm are shown in Figs. 7(c), (f), (i), and (l), respectively. We observe that the proposed algorithm has effectively reconstructed image data even for dynamic real-world video sequences. Also, note that for all the results shown in Figs. 7(c), (f), (i), and (l) we used only three observations from the captured video sequences.

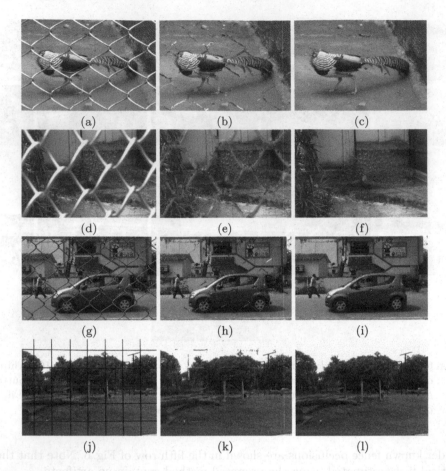

Fig. 7. First column: one frame each taken from challenging real-world videos. Second column: inpainted images obtained using exemplar-based image inpainting algorithm [2] which was the approach used in [6] for image de-fencing. Third column: de-fenced images obtained using the proposed algorithm corresponding to images in the first column.

Next, we compare the proposed algorithm with recent state-of-the-art methods [6,9,10]. In Fig. 8(a), we show the de-fenced image obtained using [9]. The corresponding result obtained by the proposed algorithm is shown in Fig. 8(e). Note that the de-fenced image obtained in [9] is blurred whereas the proposed algorithm generated a sharper image. We show a cropped region from both Figs. 8(a) and (e) in the last row to confirm our observation. In Figs. 8(b) and (f), we show the de-fenced results obtained by [10] and the proposed algorithm, respectively. The de-fenced image obtained using the method in [10] is distorted at some places which is apparent in Fig. 8(b). In contrast, the fence has been removed completely with hardly any distortions in the result shown in Fig. 8(f), which has been obtained using our algorithm. A cropped region from both Figs. 8(b) and (f) are shown in the last row to prove our point. The defenced images obtained using a very recent technique [6] are shown in Figs. 8(c) and (d), respectively. These results contain several artifacts. However, the defenced images recovered using the proposed algorithm hardly contain any artifacts as shown in Figs. 8(g) and (h). A cropped regions from Figs. 8(c) and (d) and Figs. 8(g) and (h) are shown in the last row for comparison purpose. Since we use only three frames from the videos, our method is more computationally efficient than [9,10] which use 5 and 15 frames, respectively.

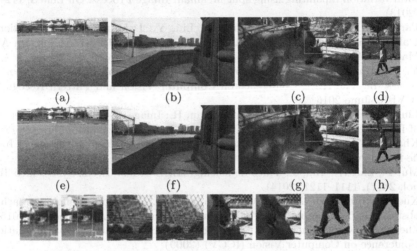

Fig. 8. Comparison with state-of-the-art image/video de-fencing methods [6,9,10] using video sequences from their works. (a) De-fenced image obtained by [9]. (b) Recovered background image using [10]. (c), (d) Inpainted images obtained by [2] which was the method used in [6]. (e)–(h) De-fenced images obtained by the proposed algorithm using occlusion-aware-optical flow shown in fifth row of Fig. 6. Last row: Insets from the images of first and second rows, respectively, showing the superior reconstruction of the de-fenced image by our algorithm.

5   Conclusions

In this paper, we proposed an automatic image de-fencing system for real-world videos. We divided the problem of image de-fencing into three tasks and proposed an automatic approach for each one of them. We formulated an optimization framework and solved the inverse problem using the fast iterative shrinkage thresholding algorithm (FISTA) assuming l_1 norm of the de-fenced image as the regularization constraint. We have evaluated the proposed algorithm on various datasets and reported both qualitative and quantitative results. The obtained results show the effectiveness of proposed algorithm. As part of future work, we are investigating how to optimally choose the frames from the video for fence removal.

References

1. Bertalmio, M., Sapiro, G., Caselles, V., Ballester, C.: Image inpainting. In: Proceedings of ACM SIGGRAPH, pp. 417–424 (2000)
2. Criminisi, A., Perez, P., Toyama, K.: Region filling and object removal by exemplar-based image inpainting. IEEE Trans. Image Process. **13**(9), 1200–1212 (2004)
3. Hays, J., Efros, A.A.: Scene completion using millions of photographs. ACM Trans. Graph. **26**(3), 1–7 (2007)
4. Papafitsoros, K., Schonlieb, C.B., Sengul, B.: Combined first and second order total variation inpainting using split bregman. Image Process. On Line **3**, 112–136 (2013)
5. Park, M., Brocklehurst, K., Collins, R., Liu, Y.: Deformed lattice detection in real-world images using mean-shift belief propagation. IEEE Trans. Pattern Anal. Mach. Intell. **31**, 1804–1816 (2009)
6. Yi, R., Wang, J., Tan, P.: Automatic fence segmentation in videos of dynamic scenes. In: The IEEE Conference on Computer Vision and Pattern Recognition (CVPR) June 2016
7. Liu, Y., Belkina, T., Hays, J., Lublinerman, R.: Image de-fencing. In: Proceedings of IEEE Conference on Computer Vision and Pattern Recognition, pp. 1–8 (2008)
8. Khasare, V.S., Sahay, R.R., Kankanhalli, M.S.: Seeing through the fence: Image de-fencing using a video sequence (2013)
9. Mu, Y., Liu, W., Yan, S.: Video de-fencing. IEEE Trans. Circts. Syst. Video Technol. **24**(7), 1111–1121 (2014)
10. Xue, T., Rubinstein, M., Liu, C., Freeman, W.T.: A computational approach for obstruction-free photography. ACM Trans. Graph. **34**(4), Article no. 79 (2015)
11. Zheng, Y., Kambhamettu, C.: Learning based digital matting. In: International Conference on Computer Vision (ICCV) (2009)
12. Park, M., Brocklehurst, K., Collins, R.T., Liu, Y.: Image de-fencing revisited (2010)
13. Jonna, S., Voleti, V.S., Sahay, R.R., Kankanhalli, M.S.: A multimodal approach for image de-fencing and depth in painting. In: Proceedings of International Conference on Advances in Pattern Recognition, pp. 1–6 (2015)
14. Jonna, S., Nakka, K.K., Sahay, R.R.: My camera can see through fences: a deep learning approach for image de-fencing. In: 2015 3rd IAPR Asian Conference on Pattern Recognition (ACPR), pp. 261–265, November 2015
15. Jonna, S., Nakka, K.K., Khasare, V.S., Sahay, R.R., Kankanhalli, M.S.: Detection and removal of fence occlusions in an image using a video of the static/dynamic scene. J. Opt. Soc. Am. A **33**(10), 1917–1930 (2016)
16. Lecun, Y., Bottou, L., Bengio, Y., Haffner, P.: Gradient-based learning applied to document recognition. Proc. IEEE **86**(11), 2278–2324 (1998)
17. Krizhevsky, A., Sutskever, I., Hinton, G.E.: Imagenet classification with deep convolutional neural networks. Adv. Neural Inf. Process. Syst. **25**, 1097–1105 (2012)
18. Deng, J., Dong, W., Socher, R., Li, L.J., Li, K., Fei-Fei, L.: ImageNet: a large-scale hierarchical image database. In: CVPR09 (2009)
19. Goodfellow, I.J., Warde-farley, D., Mirza, M., Courville, A., Bengio, Y.: Maxout networks. In: ICML (2013)
20. Srivastava, N., Hinton, G., Krizhevsky, A., Sutskever, I., Salakhutdinov, R.: Dropout: a simple way to prevent neural networks from overfitting. J. Mach. Learn. Res. **15**(1), 1929–1958 (2014)
21. Donahue, J., Jia, Y., Vinyals, O., Hoffman, J., Zhang, N., Tzeng, E., Darrell, T.: Decaf: a deep convolutional activation feature for generic visual recognition. CoRR abs/1310.1531 (2013)

22. Vedaldi, A., Lenc, K.: Matconvnet - convolutional neural networks for MATLAB. CoRR abs/1412.4564 (2014)
23. Canny, J.: A computational approach to edge detection. IEEE Trans. Pattern Anal. Mach. Intell. PAMI **8**(6), 679–698 (1986)
24. Brox, T., Malik, J.: Large displacement optical flow: descriptor matching in variational motion estimation. IEEE Trans. Pattern Anal. Mach. Intell. **33**(3), 500–513 (2011)
25. Xu, L., Jia, J., Matsushita, Y.: Motion detail preserving optical flow estimation. IEEE Trans. Pattern Anal. Mach. Intell. **34**(9), 1744–1757 (2012)
26. Brox, T., Bruhn, A., Papenberg, N., Weickert, J.: High accuracy optical flow estimation based on a theory for warping. In: Pajdla, T., Matas, J. (eds.) ECCV 2004. LNCS, vol. 3024, pp. 25–36. Springer, Heidelberg (2004). doi:10.1007/978-3-540-24673-2_3
27. Liu, C., Yuen, J., Torralba, A., Sivic, J., Freeman, W.T.: SIFT Flow: dense correspondence across different scenes. In: Forsyth, D., Torr, P., Zisserman, A. (eds.) ECCV 2008. LNCS, vol. 5304, pp. 28–42. Springer, Heidelberg (2008). doi:10.1007/978-3-540-88690-7_3
28. Horn, B.K., Schunck, B.G.: Determining optical flow. Technical report, Cambridge, MA, USA (1980)
29. Revaud, J., Weinzaepfel, P., Harchaoui, Z., Schmid, C.: EpicFlow: edge-preserving interpolation of correspondences for optical flow. In: Computer Vision and Pattern Recognition (2015)
30. Weinzaepfel, P., Revaud, J., Harchaoui, Z., Schmid, C.: Deepflow: large displacement optical flow with deep matching. In: Proceedings of International Conference on Compututer Vision, pp. 1385–1392, December 2013
31. Ince, S., Konrad, J.: Occlusion-aware optical flow estimation. IEEE Trans. Image Process. **17**(8), 1443–1451 (2008)
32. Liu, C.: Beyond pixels: exploring new representations and applications for motion analysis. Ph.D. thesis, Massachusetts Institute of Technology (2009)
33. Liu, C., Sun, D.: On Bayesian adaptive video super resolution. IEEE Trans. Pattern Anal. Mach. Intell. **36**(2), 346–360 (2014)
34. Beck, A., Teboulle, M.: A fast iterative shrinkage-thresholding algorithm for linear inverse problems. SIAM J. Imag. Sci. **2**(1), 183–202 (2009)
35. Barbero, A., Sra, S.: Fast Newton-type methods for total variation regularization. In: ICML, pp. 313–320. Omnipress (2011)
36. Parikh, N., Boyd, S.: Proximal algorithms. Found. Trends Optim. **1**(3), 123–231 (2014)
37. PSU NRT data set: http://vision.cse.psu.edu/data/MSBPLattice.shtml

Clockwork Convnets for Video Semantic Segmentation

Evan Shelhamer[✉], Kate Rakelly, Judy Hoffman, and Trevor Darrell

UC Berkeley, Berkeley, USA
{shelhamer,rakelly,jhoffman,trevor}@cs.berkeley.edu

Abstract. Recent years have seen tremendous progress in still-image segmentation; however the naïve application of these state-of-the-art algorithms to every video frame requires considerable computation and ignores the temporal continuity inherent in video. We propose a video recognition framework that relies on two key observations: (1) while pixels may change rapidly from frame to frame, the semantic content of a scene evolves more slowly, and (2) execution can be viewed as an aspect of architecture, yielding purpose-fit computation schedules for networks. We define a novel family of "clockwork" convnets driven by fixed or adaptive clock signals that schedule the processing of different layers at different update rates according to their semantic stability. We design a pipeline schedule to reduce latency for real-time recognition and a fixed-rate schedule to reduce overall computation. Finally, we extend clockwork scheduling to adaptive video processing by incorporating data-driven clocks that can be tuned on unlabeled video. The accuracy and efficiency of clockwork convnets are evaluated on the Youtube-Objects, NYUD, and Cityscapes video datasets.

1 Introduction

Semantic segmentation is a central visual recognition task. End-to-end convolutional network approaches have made progress on the accuracy and execution time of still-image semantic segmentation, but video semantic segmentation has received less attention. Potential applications include UAV navigation, autonomous driving, archival footage recognition, and wearable computing. The computational demands of video processing are a challenge to the simple application of image methods on every frame, while the temporal continuity of video offers an opportunity to reduce this computation.

Fully convolutional networks (FCNs) [1–3] have been shown to obtain remarkable results, but the execution time of repeated per-frame processing limits its application to video. Adapting these networks to make use of the temporal

---

E. Shelhamer et al.—Authors contributed equally.

Electronic supplementary material The online version of this chapter (doi:10.1007/978-3-319-49409-8_69) contains supplementary material, which is available to authorized users.

G. Hua and H. Jégou (Eds.): ECCV 2016 Workshops, Part III, LNCS 9915, pp. 852–868, 2016.
DOI: 10.1007/978-3-319-49409-8_69

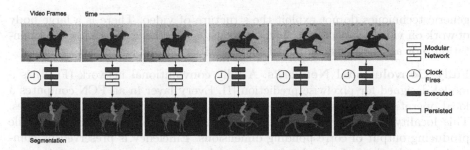

Fig. 1. Our adaptive clockwork method illustrated with the famous *The Horse in Motion* [9], captured by Eadweard Muybridge in 1878 at the Palo Alto racetrack. The clock controls network execution: past the first stage, computation is scheduled only at the time points indicated by the clock symbol. During static scenes cached representations persist, while during dynamic scenes new computations are scheduled and output is combined with cached representations.

continuity of video reduces inference computation while suffering minimal loss in recognition accuracy. The temporal rate of change of features, or feature "velocity", across frames varies from layer to layer. In particular, deeper layers in the feature hierarchy change more slowly than shallower layers over video sequences. We propose that network execution can be viewed as an aspect of architecture and define the "clockwork" FCN (c.f. clockwork recurrent networks [4]). Combining these two insights, we group the layers of the network into stages, and set separate update rates for these levels of representation. The execution of a stage on a given frame is determined by either a fixed clock rate ("fixed-rate") or data-driven ("adaptive"). The prediction for the current frame is then the fusion (via the skip layer architecture of the FCN) of these computations on multiple frames, thus exploiting the lower resolution and slower rate-of-change of deeper layers to share information across frames (Fig. 1).

We demonstrate the efficacy of the architecture for both fixed and adaptive schedules. We show results on multiple datasets for a pipelining schedule designed to reduce latency for real-time recognition as well as a fixed-rate schedule designed to reduce computation and hence time and power. Next we learn the clock-rate adaptively from the data, and demonstrate computational savings when little motion occurs in the video without sacrificing recognition accuracy during dynamic scenes. We verify our approach on synthetic frame sequences made from PASCAL VOC [5] and evaluate on videos from the NYUDv2 [6], YouTube-Objects [7], and Cityscapes [8] datasets.

2   Related Work

We extend fully convolutional networks for image semantic segmentation to video semantic segmentation. Convnets have been applied to video to learn spatiotemporal representations for classification and detection but rarely for dense pixelwise, frame-by-frame inference. Practicality requires network acceleration, but generic techniques do not exploit the structure of video. There is a large body of work on video segmentation, but the focus has not been on *semantic* segmentation, nor are methods computationally feasible beyond short video shots.

Fully Convolutional Networks. A fully convolutional network (FCN) is a model designed for pixelwise prediction [1]. Every layer in an FCN computes a local operation, such as convolution or pooling, on relative spatial coordinates. This locality makes the network capable of handling inputs of any size while producing output of corresponding dimensions. Efficiency is preserved by computing single, dense forward inference and backward learning passes. Current classification architectures – AlexNet [10], GoogLeNet [11], and VGG [12] – can be cast into corresponding fully convolutional forms. These networks are learned end-to-end, are fast at inference and learning time, and can be generalized with respect to different image-to-image tasks. FCNs yield state-of-the-art results for semantic segmentation [1], boundary prediction [13], and monocular depth estimation [2]. While these tasks process each image in isolation, FCNs extend to video. As more and more visual data is captured as video, the baseline efficiency of fully convolutional computation will not suffice.

Video Networks and Frame Selection. Time can be incorporated into a network by spatiotemporal filtering or recurrence. Spatiotemporal filtering, i.e. 3D convolution, can capture motion for activity recognition [14,15]. For video classification, networks can integrate over time by early, late, or slow fusion of frame features [15]. Recurrence can capture long-term dynamics and propagate state across time, as in the popular long short-term memory (LSTM) [16]. Joint convolutional-recurrent networks filter within frames and recur across frames: the long-term recurrent convolutional network [17] fuses frame features by LSTM for activity recognition and captioning. Frame selection reduces computation by focusing computational resources on important frames identified by the model: space-time interest points [18] are video keypoints engineered for sparsity, and a whole frame selection and recognition policy can be learned end-to-end for activity detection [19]. These video recognition approaches do not address frame-by-frame, pixelwise output. For optical flow, an intrinsically temporal task, a cross-frame FCN is state-of-the-art among fast methods [3].

Network Acceleration. Although FCNs are fast, video demands computation that is faster still, particularly for real-time inference. The spatially dense operation of the FCN amortizes the computation of overlapping receptive fields common to contemporary architectures. However, the standard FCN does nothing to temporally amortize the computation of sequential inputs. Computational concerns can drive architectural choices. For instance, GoogLeNet requires less computation and memory than VGG, although its segmentation accuracy is worse [1]. Careful but time-consuming model search can improve networks within a fixed computational budget [20]. Methods to reduce computation and memory include reduced precision by weight quantization [21], low-rank approximations with clustering, [22], low-rank approximations with end-to-end tuning [23], and kernel approximation methods like the fast food transformation [24]. None of these generic acceleration techniques harness the frame-to-frame structure of video. The proposed clockwork speed-up is orthogonal and compounds any reductions in absolute inference time. Our clockwork insight holds for all layered architectures whatever the speed/quality operating point chosen.

Semantic Segmentation. Much work has been done to address the problem of segmentation in video. However, the focus has not been on semantic segmentation. Instead research has addressed spatio-temporal "supervoxels" [25,26], unsupervised and motion-driven object segmentation [27–29], or weakly supervising the segmentation of tagged videos [30–32]. These methods are not suitable for real-time or the complex multi-class, multi-object scenes encountered in semantic segmentation settings. Fast Object Segmentation in Unconstrained Videos [28] infers only figure-ground segmentation at 0.5 s/frame with offline computed optical flow and superpixels. Although its proposals have high recall, even when perfectly parallelized [29] this method takes >15 s/frame and a separate recognition step is needed for semantic segmentation. In contrast the standard FCN computes a full semantic segmentation in 0.1 s/frame.

3 Fast Frames and Slow Semantics

Our approach is inspired by observing the time course of learned, hierarchical features over video sequences. Drawing on the local-to-global idea of skip connections for fusing global, deep layers with local, shallow layers, we reason that the semantic representation of deep layers is relevant across frames whereas the shallow layers vary with more local, volatile details. Persisting these features over time can be seen as a temporal skip connection.

Measuring the relative difference of features across frames confirms the temporal coherence of deeper layers. Consider a given score layer (a linear predictor of pixel class from features), ℓ, with outputs $S_\ell \in [K \times H \times W]$, where K is the number of categories and H, W is the output dimensions for layer ℓ. We can compute the difference at time t with a score map distance function d_{sm}, chosen to be the hamming distance of one hot encodings.

$$d_{\mathrm{sm}}(S_\ell^t, S_\ell^{t-1}) = d_{\mathrm{hamming}}(\phi(S_\ell^t), \phi(S_\ell^{t-1}))$$

Table 1 reports the average of these temporal differences for the score layers, as computed over all videos in the YouTube-Objects dataset [7]. It is perhaps unsurprising that the deepest score layer changes an order of magnitude less than the shallower layers on average. We therefore hypothesize that caching deeper layer scores from past frames can inform the inference of the current frame with relatively little reduction in accuracy.

The slower rate of change of deep layers can be attributed to architectural and learned invariances. More pooling affords more robustness to translation and noise, and learned features may be tuned to the supervised classes instead of general appearance.

While deeper layers are more stable than shallower layers, for videos with enough motion the score maps throughout the network may change substantially.

Table 1. The average temporal difference over all YouTube-Objects videos of the respective pixelwise class score outputs from a spectrum of network layers. The deeper layers are more stable across frames – that is, we observe supervised convnet features to be "slow" features [33]. The temporal difference is measured as the proportion of label changes in the output. The layer depth counts the distance from the input in the number of parametric and non-linear layers. Semantic accuracy is the intersection-over-union metric on PASCAL VOC of our frame processing network fine-tuned for separate output predictions (Sect. 5).

Score layer	Temporal difference	Depth	Semantic accuracy
`pixels`	.26 ± .18	0	-
`pool3`	.11 ± .06	9	9.6%
`pool4`	.11 ± .06	13	20.7%
`fc7`	.02 ± .02	19	65.5%

For example, in Fig. 2 we show the differences for the first 75 frames of a video with large motion (left) and with small motion (right). We would like our network to adaptively update only when the deepest, most semantic layer (`fc7`) score map is likely to change. We notice that though the intermediate layer (`pool4`) difference is always larger than the deepest layer difference for any given frame, the `pool4` differences are much larger for the video with large motion than for the video with relatively small motion. This observation forms the motivation for using the intermediate differences as an indicator to determine the firing of an adaptive clock.

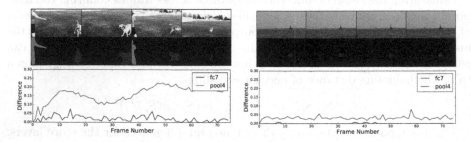

Fig. 2. The proportional difference between adjacent frames of semantic predictions from a mid-level layer (`pool4`, green) and the deepest layer (`fc7`, blue) are shown for the first 75 frames of two videos. We see that for a video with lots of motion (left) the difference values are large while for a relatively static video (right) the difference values are small. In both cases, the differences of the deeper `fc7` are smaller than the differences of the shallower `pool4`. The "velocity" of deep features is slow relative to shallow features and most of all the input. At the same time, the differences between shallow and deep layers are dependent since the features are compositional; this motivates our adaptive clock updates in Sect. 4.3 (Color figure online)

4 A Clockwork Network

We adapt the fully convolutional network (FCN) approach for image-to-image mapping [1] to video frame processing. While it is straightforward to perform inference with a still-image segmentation network on every video frame, this naïve computation is inefficient. Furthermore, disregarding the sequential nature of the input not only sacrifices efficiency but discards potential temporal recognition cues. The temporal coherence of video suggests the persistence of visual features from prior frames to inform inference on the current frame. To this end we define the clockwork FCN, inspired by the clockwork recurrent network [4], to carry temporal information across frames. A generalized notion of clockwork relates both of these networks.

We consider both throughput and latency in the execution of deep networks across video sequences. The inference time of the regular FCN-8s at ∼100 ms per frame of size 500 × 500 on a standard GPU can be too slow for video. We first define fixed clocks then extend to adaptive and potentially learned clockwork to drive network processing. Whatever the task, any video network can be accelerated by our clockwork technique. A schematic of our clockwork FCN is shown in Fig. 3.

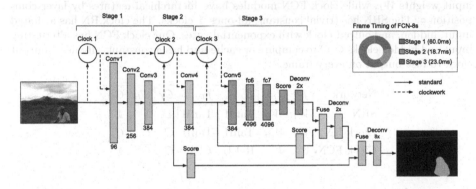

Fig. 3. The clockwork FCN with its stages and corresponding clocks.

There are several choice points in defining a clockwork architecture. We define a novel, generalized clockwork framework, which can purposely schedule deeper layers more slowly than shallower layers. We form our modules by grouping the layers of a convnet to span the feature hierarchy. Our networks persists both state and output across time steps. The clockwork recurrent network of [4], designed for long-term dependency modeling of time series, is an instance of our more general scheme for clockwork computation. The differences in architecture and outputs over time between clockwork recurrence and our clockwork are shown in Fig. 4.

While different, these nets can be expressed by generalized clockwork equations

$$y_H^{(t)} = f_T \left(C_H^{(t)} \odot f_H(y_H^{(t-1)}) + C_I^{(t)} \odot f_I(x^{(t)}) \right) \tag{1}$$

$$y_O^{(t)} = f_O \left(C_O^{(t)} \odot f_H(y_H^{(t)}) \right) \tag{2}$$

with the state update defined by Eq. 1 and the output defined by Eq. 2. The data $x^{(t)}$, hidden state $y_H^{(t)}$ output $y_O^{(t)}$ vary with time t. The functions f_I, f_H, f_O, f_T define input, hidden state, output, and transition operations respectively and are fixed across time. The input, hidden, and output clocks $C_I^{(t)}, C_H^{(t)}, C_O^{(t)}$ modulate network operations by the elementwise product $\odot$ with the corresponding function evaluations. We recover the standard recurrent network (SRN), clockwork recurrent network (clock RN), and our network (clock FCN) in this family of equations. The settings of functions and clocks are collected in Table 2.

Table 2. The standard recurrent network (SRN), clockwork recurrent network (clock RN), and our network (clock FCN) in generalized clockwork form. The recurrent networks have learned hidden weights W_H and non-linear transition functions f_T, while clock FCN persists state by the identity I. Both recurrent modules are flat with linear input weights W_I, while clock FCN modules have hierarchical features by layer composition $\circ$. The SRN has trivial constant, all-ones $\mathbb{1}$ clocks. The clock RN has a shared input, hidden, and output clock with exponential rates. Our clock FCN has alternating input and hidden clocks $C, \overline{C}$ to compute or cache and has a constant, all-ones $\mathbb{1}$ output clock to fuse output on every frame.

Network	f_I	f_H	f_O	f_T	C_I	C_H	C_O
SRN	W_I	W_H	TanH	TanH	$\mathbb{1}$	$\mathbb{1}$	$\mathbb{1}$
Clock RN	W_I	W_H	TanH	TanH	C	C	C
Clock FCN	$\circ$	I	ReLU	I	C	$\overline{C}$	$\mathbb{1}$

Inspired by the clockwork RN, we investigate persisting features and scheduling layers to process video with a semantic segmentation convnet. Recalling the lessened semantic rate of deeper layers observed in Sect. 3, the skip layers in FCNs originally included to preserve resolution by fusing outputs are repurposed for this staged computation. We cache features and outputs over time at each step to harness the continuity of video. In contrast, the clockwork RN persists state but output is only made according to the clock, and each clockwork RN module is connected to itself and all slower modules across time whereas a module in our network is only connected to itself across time.

4.1   Execution as Architecture

Clockwork architectures partition a network into modules or stages that are executed according to different schedules. In the standard view, the execution of an architecture is an all-or-nothing operation that follows from the definition of the network. Relaxing the strict identification of architecture and execution instead opens up a range of potential schedules. These schedules can be encompassed by the introduction of one first-class architectural element: the clock.

A clock defines a dynamic cut in the computation graph of a network. As clocks mask state in the representation, as detailed in Eqs. 1 and 2, clocks likewise mask execution in the computation. When a clock is on, its edges are intact and execution traverses to the next nodes/modules. When a clock is off, its edges are cut and execution is blocked. Alternatives such as computing the next stage or caching a past stage can be scheduled by a paired clock C and counter-clock $\overline{C}$ with complementary sets of edges. Any layer (or composition of layers) with binary output can serve as a clock. As a layer, a clock can be fixed or learned. For instance, the following are simple clocks of the form $f(x, t)$ for features x and time t:

- 1 to always execute
- $t \equiv 0 \pmod 2$ to execute every other time
- $\|x_t - x_{t-1}\| > \theta$ to execute for a difference threshold

4.2 Networks in Time

Having incorporated scheduling into the network with clocks, we can optimize the schedule for various tasks by altering the clocks.

Pipelining. To reduce latency for real-time recognition we pipeline the computation of sequential frames analogously to instruction pipelining in processors. We instantiate a three-stage pipeline, in which stage 1 reflects frame i, stage 2 frame $i - 1$, and stage 3 frame $i - 2$. The total time to process the frame is the time of the longest stage, stage 1 in our pipeline, plus the time for interpolating and fusing outputs. Our 3-stage pipeline FCN reduces latency by 59 %. A 2-stage variation further balances latency and accuracy.

Fixed-Rate. To reduce overall computation we limit the execution rates of stages and persist features across frames for skipped stages. Given the learned invariance and slow semantics of deep layers observed in Sect. 3, the deeper layers can be executed at a lower rate to save computation while other stages update. These clock rates are free parameters in the schedule for exchanging inference speed and accuracy. We again divide the network into three stages, and compare rates for the stages. The exponential clockwork schedule is the natural choice of halving the rate at each stage for more efficiency. The alternating clockwork schedule consolidates the earlier stages to execute these on every frame and executes the last stage on every other frame for more accuracy. These different sets of rates cover part of the accuracy/efficiency spectrum.

The current stages are divided into the original score paths of the FCN-8s architecture, but they need not be. One could prioritize latency, spatial refinement, or certain output classes by rebalancing the computation. It is possible to partially compute a span of layers and defer their full execution to a following

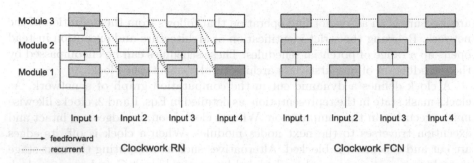

Module 3

Module 2

Module 1

Input 1   Input 2   Input 3   Input 4   Input 1   Input 2   Input 3   Input 4

→ feedforward
····· recurrent   Clockwork RN   Clockwork FCN

Fig. 4. A comparison of the layer connectivity and time course of outputs in the clockwork recurrent network [4] and in our clockwork FCN. Module color marks the time step of evaluation, and blank modules are disconnected from the network output. The clock RN is flat with respect to the input while our network has a hierarchical feature representation. Each clock RN module is temporally connected to itself and slower modules while in our network each module is only temporally connected to itself. Features persist over time in both architectures, but in our architecture they contribute to the network output at each step. (Color figure online)

stage; this can be accomplished by sparse evaluation through dynamic striding and dilation [34]. In principle the stage progression can be decided online in lieu of fixing a schedule for all inference. We turn to adaptive clockwork for deciding execution.

4.3 Adaptive Clockwork

All of the clocks considered thus far have been fixed functions of time but not the data. Setting these clocks gives rise to many schedules that can be tuned to a given task or video, but this introduces a tedious dimension of model search. Much of the video captured in the wild is static and dynamic in turn with a variable amount of motion and semantic progression at any given time. Choosing many stages or a slow clock rate may reduce computation, but will likewise result in a steep decline in accuracy for dynamic scenes. Conversely, faster update rates or fewer stages may capture transitory details but will needlessly compute and re-compute stable scenes. Adaptive clocks fire based on the input and network state, resulting in a responsive schedule that varies with the dynamism of the scene. The clock can fire according to any function of the input and network state. A difference clock can fire on the temporal difference of a feature across frames. A confidence clock can fire on peaks in the score map for a single frame. This approach extends inference from a pre-determined architecture to a set of architectures to choose from for each frame, relying on the full FCN for high accuracy in dynamic scenes while taking advantage of cached representations in more static scenes.

$$\text{threshold clock } \|x_t - x_{t-1}\| > \theta \qquad \text{learned clock } f_\theta(x_t, x_{t-1})$$

The simplest adaptive clock is a threshold, but adaptive clocks could likewise be learned (for example as a temporal convolution across frames). The threshold can be optimized for a specific tradeoff along the accuracy/efficiency curve. Given the hierarchical dependencies of layers and the relative stability of deep features observed in Sect. 3, we threshold differences at a shallower stage for adaptive scheduling of deeper stages. The sensitivity of the adaptive clock can even be set on unannotated video by thresholding the proportional temporal difference of output labels as in Table 1. Refer to Sect. 5.3 for the results of threshold-adaptive clockwork with regard to clock rate and accuracy.

5   Results

Our base network is FCN-8s, the fully convolutional network of [1]. The architecture is adapted from the VGG16 architecture [12] and fine-tuned from ILSVRC pre-training. The net is trained with batch size one, high momentum, and all skip layers at once.

In our experiments we report two common metrics for semantic segmentation that measure the region intersection over union (IU):

- mean IU: $(1/n_{cl}) \sum_i n_{ii} / \left(t_i + \sum_j n_{ji} - n_{ii} \right)$

- frequency weighted IU: $\left(\sum_k t_k \right)^{-1} \sum_i t_i n_{ii} / \left(t_i + \sum_j n_{ji} - n_{ii} \right)$

for n_{ij} the number of pixels of class i predicted to belong to class j, where there are n_{cl} different classes, and for $t_i = \sum_j n_{ij}$ the total number of pixels of class i. We evaluate our clockwork FCN on four video semantic segmentation datasets.

Synthetic Sequences of Translated Scenes. We first validate our method by evaluating on synthetic videos of moving crops of PASCAL VOC images [5] in order to score on a ground truth annotation at every frame. For source data, we select the 736 image subset of the PASCAL VOC 2011 segmentation validation set used for FCN-8s validation in [1]. Video frames are generated by sliding a crop window across the image by a predetermined number of pixels, and generated translations are vertical or horizontal according to the portrait or landscape aspect of the chosen image. Each synthetic video is six frames long. For each seed image, a "fast" and "slow" video is made with 32 pixel and 16 pixel frame-to-frame displacements respectively.

NYU-RGB Clips. The NYUDv2 dataset [6] collects short RGB-D clips and includes a segmentation benchmark with high-quality but temporally sparse pixel annotations (every tenth video frame is labeled). We run on video from the "raw" clips subsampled 10X and evaluate on every labeled frame. We consider RGB input alone as the depth frames of the full clips are noisy and uncurated. Our pipelined and fixed-rate clockwork FCNs are run on the entire clips and accuracy is reported for those frames included in the segmentation test set.

Youtube-Objects. The Youtube-Objects dataset [7] provides videos collected from Youtube that contain objects from ten PASCAL classes. We restrict our attention to a subset of the videos that have pixelwise annotations by [35] as the original annotations include only initial frame bounding boxes. This subset was drawn from all object classes, and contains 10,167 frames from 126 shots, for which every 10th frame is human-annotated. We run on only annotated frames, effectively 10X subsampling the video. We directly apply our networks derived from PASCAL VOC supervision and do not fine-tune to the video annotations.

Cityscapes. The Cityscapes dataset [8] collects frames from video recorded at 17 hz by a car-mounted camera while driving through German cities. While annotations are temporally sparse, the preceding and following input frames are provided. Our network is learned on the `train` split and then all schedules are evaluated on `val`.

5.1   Pipelining

Pipelined execution schedules reduce latency by producing an output each time the first stage is computed. Later stages are persisted from previous frames and their outputs are fused with the output of the first stage computed on the current frame. The number of stages is determined by the number of clocks. We consider a full **3-stage pipeline** and a condensed **2-stage pipeline** where the stages are defined by the modules in Fig. 3. In the pipelined schedule, all clock rates are set to 1, but clocks fire simultaneously to update every stage in parallel. This is made possible by asynchrony in stage state, so that a later stage is independent of the current frame but not past frames.

Table 3. Pipelined segmentation of translated PASCAL sequences. Synthesized video of translating PASCAL scenes allows for assessment of the pipeline at every frame. The pipelined FCN segments with higher accuracy in the same time envelope as the every-other-frame evaluation of the full FCN. Metrics are computed on the standard masks and a 10-pixel band at boundaries.

16 pixel shift	Time (% of full)	Mean IU	fwIU	Mean IU-bdry	fwIU-bdry
3-Stage Baseline	59 %	9.2	52.6	6.1	9.4
3-Stage Pipeline	59 %	56.0	76.5	44.6	42.9
2-Stage Baseline	77 %	22.5	64.7	16.6	21.9
2-Stage Pipeline	77 %	**63.3**	**81.7**	**52.3**	**51.0**
Frame oracle	100 %	65.9	83.6	57.0	56.3
32 pixel shift	Time (% of full)	Mean IU	fwIU	Mean IU-bdry	fwIU-bdry
3-Stage Baseline	59 %	9.2	52.6	6.0	9.4
3-Stage Pipeline	59 %	45.5	67.4	37.7	36.0
2-Stage Baseline	77 %	22.4	62.8	16.2	21.7
2-Stage Pipeline	77 %	**57.8**	**76.6**	**46.6**	**45.1**
Frame oracle	100 %	65.6	82.6	55.8	55.3

To assess our pipelined accuracy and speed, we compare to reference methods that bound both recognition and time. A frame oracle evaluates the full FCN on every frame to give the best achievable accuracy for the network independent of timing. As latency baselines for our pipelines, we truncate the FCN to end at the given stage. Both of our staged, pipelined schedules execute at lower latency than the oracle with better accuracy for fixed latency than the baselines. We verify these results on synthetic PASCAL sequences as reported in Table 3. Results on PASCAL, NYUD, and YouTube are reported in Table 4.

Our pipeline scheduled networks reduce latency with minimal accuracy loss relative to the standard FCN run on each frame without time restriction. These quantitative results demonstrate that the deeper layer representations from previous frames contain useful information that can be effectively combined with low-level predictions for the current frame.

Table 4. Pipelined execution of semantic segmentation on three different datasets. Inference approaches include pipelines of different lengths and a full FCN frame oracle. We also show baselines with comparable latency to the pipeline architectures. Our pipelined network offers the best accuracy of computationally comparable approaches running near frame rate. The loss in accuracy relative to the frame oracle is less than the relative speed-up.

Schedule	Time (% of full)	NYUD		Youtube		Pascal Shift 16	
		Mean IU	fwIU	Mean IU	fwIU	Mean IU	fwIU
3-Stage Baseline	59 %	8.1	22.2	12.2	74.2	9.2	54.7
3-Stage Pipeline	59 %	25.1	38.0	58.1	87.0	56.0	76.5
2-Stage Baseline	77 %	16.5	32.1	21.5	7.8	22.5	64.7
2-Stage Pipeline	77 %	**26.4**	**39.5**	**64.0**	**89.2**	**63.3**	**81.7**
Frame oracle	100 %	31.1	45.5	70.0	91.5	65.9	83.6

We show a qualitative result for our pipelined FCN on a sequence from the YouTube-Objects dataset [7]. Figure 5 shows one example where our pipeline FCN is particularly useful. Our network quickly detects the occlusion of the car while the baseline lags and does not immediately recognize the occlusion or reappearance.

5.2   Fixed-Rate

Fixed-rate clock schedules reduce overall computation relative to full, every frame evaluation by assigning different update rates to each stage such that later stages are executed less often. Rates can be set aggressively low for extreme efficiency or conservatively high to maintain accuracy while sparing computation. The **exponential clockwork** schedule executes the first stage on every frame then updates following stages exponentially less often by halving with each stage. The **alternating clockwork** schedule combines stages 2 and 3, executes

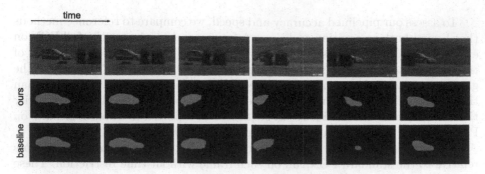

Fig. 5. Pipelined vs. standard FCN on YouTube video. Our method is able to detect the occlusion of the car as it is happening unlike the lagging baseline computed on every other frame.

the first stage on every frame, then schedules the following combined stage every other frame.

A frame oracle that evaluates the full FCN on *every* frame is the reference model for accuracy. Evaluating the full FCN on *every other* frame is the reference model for computation. Due to the distribution of execution time over stages, this is faster than either clockwork schedule, though clockwork offers higher accuracy. Alternating clockwork achieves higher accuracy than the every other frame reference. See Table 5.

Table 5. Fixed-rate segmentation of translated PASCAL sequences. We evaluate the network on synthesized video of translating PASCAL scenes to assess the effect of persisting layer features across frames. Metrics are computed on the standard masks and a 10-pixel band at boundaries.

16 pixel shift	Clock Rates	Mean IU	fwIU	Mean IU-bdry	fwIU-bdry
Skip frame baseline	(2,2,2)	63.0	81.5	60.2	52.2
Exponential	(1,2,4)	61.4	80.4	50.5	49.1
Alternating	(1,1,2)	**64.7**	**82.6**	**54.8**	**53.7**
Frame oracle	(1,1,1)	65.9	83.6	57.0	56.3
32 pixel shift	Clock Rates	Mean IU	fwIU	Mean IU-bdry	fwIU-bdry
Skip Frame Baseline	(2,2,2)	59.5	77.9	49.4	48.2
Exponential	(1,2,4)	55.5	74.7	46.3	44.8
Alternating	(1,1,2)	**61.9**	**79.6**	**51.7**	**50.6**
Frame oracle	(1,1,1)	65.6	82.6	55.8	55.3

Exponential clockwork shows degraded accuracy yet takes 1.5× the computation of evaluation on every other frame, so we discard this fixed schedule in favor of adaptive clockwork. Although exponential rates suffice for the time

Table 6. Fixed-rate and adaptive clockwork FCN evaluation. We score our network on three datasets with an alternating schedule that executes the later stage every other frame and an adaptive schedule that executes according to a frame-by-frame threshold on the difference in output. The adaptive threshold is tuned to execute the full network on 50 % of frames to equalize computation between the alternating and adaptive schedules.

Schedule	NYUD		Youtube		Cityscapes	
	Mean IU	fwIU	Mean IU	fwIU	Mean IU	fwIU
Skip frame baseline	27.7	41.3	65.6	89.7	62.1	87.4
Alternating	28.5	42.4	67.0	90.3	**64.4**	**88.6**
Adaptive	**28.9**	**43.3**	**68.5**	**91.0**	61.8	87.6
Frame oracle	31.1	45.5	70.0	91.4	65.9	83.6

series modeled by the clockwork recurrent network [4], these rates deliver unsatisfactory results for the task of video semantic segmentation. See Table 6 for alternating clockwork results on NYUD, YouTube-Objects, and Cityscapes.

5.3   Adaptive Clockwork

The best clock schedule can be data-dependent and unknown before segmenting a video. Therefore, we next evaluate our adaptive clock rate as described in Sect. 4.3. In this case the adaptive clock only fully processes a frame if the relative difference in `pool4` score is larger than some threshold θ. This threshold may be interpreted as the fraction of the score map that must switch labels before the clock updates the upper layers of the network. See Table 6 for adaptive clockwork results on NYUD, YouTube-Objects, and Cityscapes.

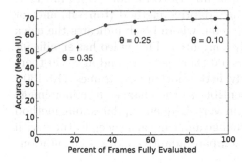

Method	% Full Frames	Mean IU
Adaptive [$\theta = 0.10$]	93%	70.0
Adaptive [$\theta = 0.25$]	52%	68.3
Adaptive [$\theta = 0.35$]	21%	59.0
Frame Oracle	100%	70.0

Fig. 6. Adaptive Clockwork performance across the Youtube-Objects dataset. We examine various adaptive difference thresholds θ and plot accuracy (mean IU) against the percentage of frames that the adaptive clock chooses to fully compute. A few corresponding thresholds are indicated.

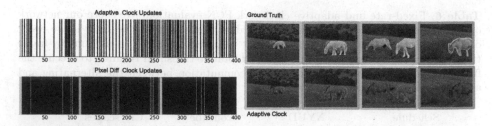

Fig. 7. An illustrative example of our adaptive clockwork method on a video from Youtube-Objects. On the left, we compare clock updates over time (shown in black) of our adaptive clock as well as a clock based on pixel differences. Our adaptive clock updates the full network on only 26 % of the frames, determined by the threshold $\theta = 0.25$ on the proportional output label change across frames, while scheduling updates based on pixel difference alone results in updating 90 % of the frames. On the right we show output segmentations from the adaptive clockwork network as well as ground truth segments for select frames from dynamic parts of the scene (second and third frames shown) and relatively static periods (first and second frames shown).

We experiment with varying thresholds on the Youtube-Objects dataset to measure accuracy and efficiency. We pick thresholds in $\theta = [0.1, 0.5]$ as well as $\theta = 0.0$ for unconditionally updating on every frame.

In Fig. 6 (left) we report mean IU accuracy as a function of our adaptive clock firing rate; that is, the percentage of frames the clock decides to fully process in the network. The thresholds which correspond to a few points on this curve are indicated with mean IU (right). Notice that our adaptive clockwork is able to fully process only 52 % of the frames while suffering a minimal loss in mean IU ($\theta = 0.25$). This indicates that our adaptive clockwork is capable of discovering semantically stationary scenes and saves significant computation by only updating when the output score map is predicted to change.

For a closer inspection, we study one Youtube video in more depth in Fig. 7. We first visualize the clock updates for our adaptive method (top left) and for a simple pixel difference baseline (bottom left), where black indicates the clock is on and the corresponding frame is fully computed. This video has significant change in certain sections (ex: at frame ∼100 there is zoom and at ∼350 there is motion) with long periods of relatively little motion (ex: frames 110–130). While the pixel difference metric is susceptible to the changes in minor image statistics from frame to frame, resulting in very frequent updates, our method only updates during periods of semantic change and can cache deep features with minimal loss in segmentation accuracy: compare adaptive clock segmentations to ground truth (right).

6   Conclusion

Generalized clockwork architectures encompass many kinds of temporal networks, and incorporating execution into the architecture opens up many strategies for scheduling computation. We define a clockwork fully convolutional network for video semantic segmentation in this framework. Motivated by the stability of deep features across sequential frames, our network persists features across time in a temporal skip architecture. By exploring fixed and adaptive schedules, we are able to tune processing for latency, overall computation time, and recognition performance. With adaptive, data-driven clock rates the network is scheduled online to segment dynamic and static scenes alike while maintaining accuracy. In this way our adaptive clockwork network is a bridge between convnets and event-driven vision architectures. The clockwork perspective on temporal networks suggests further architectural variations for spatiotemporal video processing.

References

1. Shelhamer, E., Long, J., Darrell, T.: Fully convolutional networks for semantic segmentation. In: PAMI (2016)
2. Eigen, D., Fergus, R.: Predicting depth, surface normals and semantic labels with a common multi-scale convolutional architecture. In: ICCV, pp. 2650–2658 (2015)
3. Fischer, P., Dosovitskiy, A., Ilg, E., Häusser, P. Hazş, C., Golkov, V., van der Smagt, P., Cremers, D., Brox, T.: Learning optical flow with convolutional networks. In: ICCV (2015)
4. Koutník, J., Greff, K., Gomez, F., Schmidhuber, J.: A clockwork RNN. In: ICML (2014)
5. Everingham, M., Van Gool, L., Williams, C.K.I., Winn, J., Zisserman, A.: The PASCAL visual object classes (VOC) challenge. IJCV **88**(2), 303–338 (2010)
6. Silberman, N., Hoiem, D., Kohli, P., Fergus, R.: Indoor segmentation and support inference from RGBD images. In: Fitzgibbon, A., Lazebnik, S., Perona, P., Sato, Y., Schmid, C. (eds.) ECCV 2012. LNCS, vol. 7576, pp. 746–760. Springer, Heidelberg (2012). doi:10.1007/978-3-642-33715-4_54
7. Prest, A., Leistner, C., Civera, J., Schmid, C., Ferrari, V.: Learning object class detectors from weakly annotated video. In: CVPR, pp. 3282–3289. IEEE (2012)
8. Cordts, M., Omran, M., Ramos, S., Rehfeld, T., Enzweiler, M., Benenson, R., Franke, U., Roth, S., Schiele, B.: The cityscapes dataset for semantic urban scene understanding. In: CVPR (2016)
9. Muybridge, E.: The Horse in Motion. Library of Congress Prints and Photographs Division, Washington, D.C. (1882)
10. Krizhevsky, A., Sutskever, I., Hinton, G.E.: Imagenet classification with deep convolutional neural networks. In: NIPS (2012)
11. Szegedy, C., Liu, W., Jia, Y., Sermanet, P., Reed, S., Anguelov, D., Erhan, D., Vanhoucke, V., Rabinovich, A.: Going deeper with convolutions. In: CVPR (2015)
12. Simonyan, K., Zisserman, A.: Very deep convolutional networks for large-scale image recognition. In: ICLR (2015)
13. Xie, S., Tu, Z.: Holistically-nested edge detection. In: ICCV (2015)
14. Ji, S., Xu, W., Yang, M., Yu, K.: 3D convolutional neural networks for human action recognition. PAMI **35**(1), 221–231 (2013)
15. Karpathy, A., Toderici, G., Shetty, S., Leung, T., Sukthankar, R., Fei-Fei, L.: Large-scale video classification with convolutional neural networks. In: CVPR, pp. 1725–1732 (2014)

16. Hochreiter, S., Schmidhuber, J.: Long short-term memory. Neural Comput. **9**(8), 1735–1780 (1997)
17. Donahue, J., Anne Hendricks, L., Guadarrama, S., Rohrbach, M., Venugopalan, S., Saenko, K., Darrell, T.: Long-term recurrent convolutional networks for visual recognition and description. In: CVPR, pp. 2625–2634 (2015)
18. Laptev, I.: On space-time interest points. IJCV **64**(2–3), 107–123 (2005)
19. Yeung, S., Russakovsky, O., Mori, G., Fei-Fei, L.: End-to-end learning of action detection from frame glimpses in videos. In: CVPR (2016)
20. He, K., Sun, J.: Convolutional neural networks at constrained time cost. In: CVPR (2015)
21. Vanhoucke, V., Senior, A., Mao, M.Z.: Improving the speed of neural networks on CPUs. In: Proceedings of the Deep Learning and Unsupervised Feature Learning NIPS Workshop, vol. 1 (2011)
22. Denton, E.L., Zaremba, W., Bruna, J., LeCun, Y., Fergus, R.: Exploiting linear structure within convolutional networks for efficient evaluation. In: NIPS, pp. 1269–1277 (2014)
23. Jaderberg, M., Vedaldi, A., Zisserman, A.: Speeding up convolutional neural networks with low rank expansions. In: BMVC (2014)
24. Yang, Z., Moczulski, M., Denil, M., de Freitas, N., Smola, A., Song, L., Wang, Z.: Deep fried convnets. In: ICCV (2015)
25. Grundmann, M., Kwatra, V., Han, M., Essa, I.: Efficient hierarchical graph-based video segmentation. In: CVPR, pp. 2141–2148. IEEE (2010)
26. Xu, C., Corso, J.J.: Evaluation of super-voxel methods for early video processing. In: CVPR, pp. 1202–1209. IEEE (2012)
27. Shi, J., Malik, J.: Motion segmentation and tracking using normalized cuts. In: ICCV, pp. 1154–1160. IEEE (1998)
28. Papazoglou, A., Ferrari, V.: Fast object segmentation in unconstrained video. In: ICCV, December 2013
29. Fragkiadaki, K., Arbelaez, P., Felsen, P., Malik, J.: Learning to segment moving objects in videos. In: CVPR, June 2015
30. Hartmann, G., et al.: Weakly supervised learning of object segmentations from web-scale video. In: Fusiello, A., Murino, V., Cucchiara, R. (eds.) ECCV 2012. LNCS, vol. 7583, pp. 198–208. Springer, Heidelberg (2012). doi:10.1007/978-3-642-33863-2_20
31. Tang, K., Sukthankar, R., Yagnik, J., Fei-Fei, L.: Discriminative segment annotation in weakly labeled video. In: CVPR, pp. 2483–2490. IEEE (2013)
32. Liu, X., Tao, D., Song, M., Ruan, Y., Chen, C., Bu, J.: Weakly supervised multi-class video segmentation. In: CVPR, pp. 57–64. IEEE (2014)
33. Wiskott, L., Sejnowski, T.J.: Slow feature analysis: unsupervised learning of invariances. Neural Comput. **14**(4), 715–770 (2002)
34. Yu, F., Koltun, V.: Multi-scale context aggregation by dilated convolutions. In: ICLR (2016)
35. Jain, S.D., Grauman, K.: Supervoxel-consistent foreground propagation in video. In: Fleet, D., Pajdla, T., Schiele, B., Tuytelaars, T. (eds.) ECCV 2014. LNCS, vol. 8692, pp. 656–671. Springer, Heidelberg (2014). doi:10.1007/978-3-319-10593-2_43

W25 – 1st International Workshop on Virtual/Augmented Reality for Visual Artificial Intelligence (VARVAI)

Preface

Welcome to the Proceedings for the 1st International Workshop on Virtual/Augmented Reality for Visual Artificial Intelligence (VARVAI) held in conjunction with the European Conference on Computer Vision (ECCV) and the ACM Multimedia Conference (ACMMM) on October 16th, 2016. We are currently observing a strong renewed interest in and hopes for Artificial Intelligence (AI), fueled by scientific advances that can efficiently learn powerful statistical models from large data collections processed on efficient hardware. Computer Vision is the prime example of this modern revolution. Its recent successes in many high-level visual recognition tasks, such as image classification, object detection, and semantic segmentation are thanks in part to large labeled datasets such as ImageNet and deep learning algorithms supported by new and more appropriate hardware such as GPUs. In fact, recent results indicate that the reliability of models might not be limited by the algorithms themselves but by the type and amount of data available. The release of new and more sophisticated datasets has indeed been the trump card for many recent achievements in computer vision and machine learning. Therefore, in order to tackle more challenging and general Visual AI (VAI) tasks, such as fine-grained global scene and video understanding, progress is needed not only on algorithms, but also on datasets, both for learning and quantitatively evaluating generalization performance of visual models. In particular, labeling every pixel of a large set of varied videos with ground truth depth, optical flow, semantic category, or other visual properties is neither scalable nor cost-effective. Such labor-intensive ground truth annotation process is, in addition, prone to errors. The purpose of this workshop is to provide a forum to gather researchers around the nascent field of Virtual/Augmented Reality (VR/AR or just VAR) used for data generation in order to learn and study VAI algorithms. VAR technologies have made impressive progress recently, in particular in the fields of computer graphics, physics engines, game engines, authoring tools, or hardware. Although mostly designed for multimedia applications geared towards human entertainment, more and more researchers (cf. references below) have noticed the tremendous potential that VAR platforms hold as data generation tools for algorithm/AI consumption. In light of the long-standing history of synthetic data in computer vision and multimedia, VAR technologies represent the next step of multimedia data generation, vastly improving on the quantity, variety, and realism of densely and accurately labeled fine-grained data that can be generated, and needed to push the scientific boundaries of research on AI.

Antonio M. López
Adrien Gaidon
Matthijs Douze
German Ros
David Vázquez
Eleonora Vig
Hao Su

Learning Markerless Human Pose Estimation from Multiple Viewpoint Video

Matthew Trumble[✉], Andrew Gilbert, Adrian Hilton, and John Collomosse

Centre for Vision Speech and Signal Processing (CVSSP), Univeristy of Surrey,
Guildford, UK
matthew.trumble@surrey.ac.uk

Abstract. We present a novel human performance capture technique capable of robustly estimating the pose (articulated joint positions) of a performer observed passively via multiple view-point video (MVV). An affine invariant pose descriptor is learned using a convolutional neural network (CNN) trained over volumetric data extracted from a MVV dataset of diverse human pose and appearance. A manifold embedding is learned via Gaussian Processes for the CNN descriptor and articulated pose spaces enabling regression and so estimation of human pose from MVV input. The learned descriptor and manifold are shown to generalise over a wide range of human poses, providing an efficient performance capture solution that requires no fiducials or other markers to be worn. The system is evaluated against ground truth joint configuration data from a commercial marker-based pose estimation system.

Keywords: Deep learning · Pose estimation · Multiple viewpoint video

1 Introduction

Performance capture is used extensively within the creative industries for character animation and visual effects. Current performance capture requires the actor to wear a special suit either augmented with retro-reflective markers (e. g. Vicon, Optitrack), or illustrated with high contrast multi-scale fiducials (e. g. ILM Fractal suit) from which an estimate of human pose is derived, usually as a sequence of skeletal joint angles. The use of unsightly markers prohibits co-capture of the pose with principal footage (i. e. roll visible in the final production), requiring multiple takes and so time and expense. Furthermore, many commercial performance capture systems require a large number of specialist cameras (typically infra-red) to be setup which takes time and restricts shooting to artificially lit locations. The contribution of this paper is a technique to estimate human pose sequences from the principal footage, using a set of synchronized video sequences shot from multiple static views. The acquisition of multiple viewpoint video (MVV) on-set is commonplace, and so this represents a practical cost saving to production. The proposed algorithm is the first to leverage deep convolutional neural networks (CNNs) to obtain a robust 3D human pose estimate from volumetric data recovered from MVV footage.

© Springer International Publishing Switzerland 2016
G. Hua and H. Jégou (Eds.): ECCV 2016 Workshops, Part III, LNCS 9915, pp. 871–878, 2016.
DOI: 10.1007/978-3-319-49409-8_70

2   Related Work

Human pose estimation (HPE) is the task of estimating either a skeletal pose or a probability map indicating likely positions of skeleton limbs. HPE commonly begins with the localization of people in images. The localization problem can be solved by background subtraction [1,2] or in cluttered scenarios, sliding window classifiers can robustly identify the face [3] or torso [4] to bootstrap limb labelling and subsequent pose estimation. Following localization, pose estimation can be approached either by (a) top-down fitting of an articulated model, via optimizing joint parameters and evaluating the correlation of the fitted model with image data; or (b) detection-led strategies in which body parts are labeled independently and their poses integrated to estimate full body pose in a bottom-up manner.

Following the results of Krizhevsky et al. [5], the benefits of deeply learned convolutional neural networks (CNN) have been explored for both 2D HPE [6] and more general 3D object pose estimation [7,8] within photographs. Deeply learned descriptors have recently shown promise in estimating 2D limb positions within very low-resolution images of human pose [9]. Yet although the problem of aligning pairs of 3D human body poses has been explored using deep learning [10], the estimation of 3D pose from MVV remains largely unexplored. Arguably the most closely related work is that within free-viewpoint video reconstruction where skeletal pose may be recovered by manually attaching limbs to vertex clustered in a tracked 4D mesh [11]. Other methods reliant on frame to frame tracking use a CNN for body part detections in 2D which are fused into 3D pose [12]. However both tracking and detection are reliant upon strong surface texture cues and absence of surface deformation.

3   Markerless Pose Estimation

Our approach accepts a multiple viewpoint video (MVV) sequence as input, shot using synchronised calibrated cameras surrounding the performance. A geometric proxy of the performer is built for each frame of the sequence via an adapted form of Grauman et al.'s probabilistic visual hull (PVH) [13] over a grid of voxels of resolution $5\,\mathrm{cm}^3$, computed from soft foreground mattes extracted from each camera image using a chroma key.

A dynamic threshold is applied to the voxel distribution to normalise against appearance variation between performers and across datasets. This is computed by analysing the voxel occupancy distribution to identify the background noise level. The proxy is then resampled into a log-polar representation $\mathcal{S}(\phi, \theta)$, quantizing longtitude and latitude into N regular intervals, aggregating voxels from the subvolume of the PVH within a particular distance interval from the centroid, and fed into a convolutional neural network (CNN) configured for a supervised classification task. The use of a log-polar representation follows successes in prior work on human 3D mesh alignment [14] and general 3D object retrieval [15] that employ spherical histogram representations to match on coarse shape. We investigate removal of phase information by computing a frequency domain (DFT)

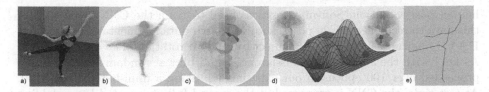

Fig. 1. Overview of proposed technique. MVV is captured (a) and a geometric proxy/PVH built (b). The PVH is sampled into log-polar form at multiple scales and passed through a CNN to learn a rotationally invariant descriptor (c). A non-linear manifold embedding of the combined CNN and joint angle space (d) is learned under supervision to regress a pose estimate (e).

representation of each row of the spherical histogram, and considering only the complex i.e. frequency magnitude. Similar to classical Fourier Descriptors this results in a shorter descriptor invariant to rotation of signal.

The CNN is trained using labeled examples of several distinct poses exercising the full range of typical human motion. Descriptors are extracted from the second fully connected layer of the network and a non-linear manifold embedding learned over a combined space of the CNN descriptors and joint angle estimates (Subsect. 3.2). The manifold enables pose regression from descriptors derived from each MVV frame. Figure 1 illustrates the full pipeline.

3.1 CNN Training

Our CNN adapts the architecture of [5] and is illustrated in Fig. 2. Similar to modern image classification work, which now extensively employs CNNs, we sample a high-dimensional descriptor from the second fully connected layer following training convergence. We evaluate (Sect. 4) fully connected layers of 1024 (1K) and 4096 (4K) leading to descriptors of similar dimension. The CNN was trained to perform a supervised pose classification task using a purpose-built dataset of labeled MVV footage comprising ~25 k multiple-view frames from 8 cameras. 25 individuals in a variety of clothing were filmed executing repetitions of 20 distinct poses following the Vicon "Range of Motion" (ROM) sequence used to calibrate commercial motion capture equipment to exercise all major modes of

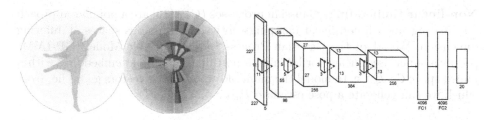

Fig. 2. Architecture of the proposed CNN (right) operating over the multi-scale log-polar representation parsed from MVV (left) and normalised against appearance variation via the dynamic thresholding operation (middle).

human pose variation. Soft-max loss was used to train the CNN using 80 % of this data to recognize the 20 poses, subject to two data augmentation strategies: **DA1:** Longitude Jitter. $\mathcal{S}(\phi, \theta)$ subject to random rotation of $\theta = [0, 2\pi]$. **DA2:** As DA1 with the addition of Gaussian noise and blur at random scale. Training proceeded over 100 epochs in our experiments, using a mini-batch size of 200. At test time, the CNN is truncated at the second fully connected layer yielding a vector of convolutional feature responses $\mathcal{C}$ that serves as our pose descriptor.

3.2 Joint Manifold Embedding

We perform human pose estimation via supervised learning in which a correlation is learned between exemplar pairs of descriptors (in CNN space $\mathcal{C}$) and a vector of 21 skeletal joint angles expressed in quaternion form (we denote this space $\mathcal{Q} \in \Re^{21 \times 4}$). We investigate three approaches to the generalisation of these sparse training correspondences to a dense mapping $\mathcal{C} \mapsto \mathcal{Q}$ suitable for inferring performer pose $P \in \mathcal{Q}$ from a query point $c \in \mathcal{C}$ derived from MVV at test time.

Nearest Neighbour (Baseline). The naïve approach to creating a dense mapping is to snap a query pose descriptor to the closest $c_i \in \mathcal{C}$ i. e. perform a nearest neighbour lookup to obtain pose estimate P_{nn}. This can be implemented in real-time (i. e. 25 frames/second) using a kd-tree pre-built over c_i. Under this approach no constraints are imposed to guard against invalid poses, since no generalisation beyond training is performed.

Piecewise Linear Embedding (Baseline). A linear subspace model is learned local to each c_i based on the local K most proximate training samples c'_j where $j = \{1..K\}$. We construct this model as an undirected graph connecting c_i to c'_j, forming a piecewise linear manifold over $\mathcal{C}$ covering likely poses and (linear) interpolations between similar poses. In our experiments $K = 5$ provides a balanced trade-off between speed and accuracy. We estimate the pose P_{ple} under this model as $P_{ple} = \sum_{j \in J} d(c, c_j) q_j$, where $d(a, b)$ is a value proportional to geodesic distance between two points on the graph manifold, and J is the set of K nearest neighbours to c in $\mathcal{C}$.

Non-linear Embedding. Gaussian processes (GP) [16] are a popular approach for creating smooth non-linear mappings between continuous spaces of differing dimension. We adopt the Gaussian Process Latent Variable Model (GP-LVM) [17] as a supervised means for learning a non-linear manifold embedding within joined space $\mathcal{C} \times \mathcal{Q}$ i. e. to model the manifold upon which vectors $[c_i\ q_i]$ lie, from which we can generate a pose estimate P_{nle}.

4   Experiments and Discussion

Pose Classification Experiments. We evaluated the CNN architecture under the two proposed data augmentation strategies on direct CNN classification and a non-linear SVM classifier using the FC2 descriptor. The mean average precision (MAP) score over the test data is shown in Table 1. Comparing augmentation strategy **DA2** against the **DFT** encoding of the log-polar representation, performance increases around 5 %. However when the FC2 layer is used as descriptor in conjunction with an SVM, there is a 12 % increase of classification performance. Much of the remaining limited confusion occurs between left and right variants of the pose classes. The high performance of FC2 derived descriptors implies the CNN has not only learned strong pose discrimination but that we are able to use it to produce a descriptor for pose estimation.

Table 1. Classification accuracy of DFT and CNN based descriptors

Descriptor type	Classifier	MAP (%)
DFT	SVM	75.62
4K CNN+DA1	CNN	77.55
4K CNN+DA2	CNN	80.97
4K CNN+DA2	SVM	**87.99**

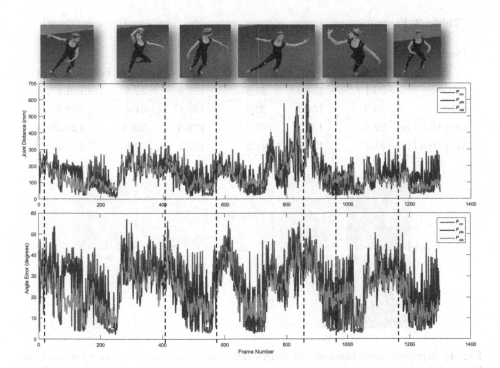

Fig. 3. Comparing total joint position and angular error of the three manifold embedding techniques over the *Ballet* dataset.

Pose Estimation Experiments. To evaluate the pose estimation accuracy, we used a hybrid dataset *Ballet* comprising five MVV sequences, totalling 9434 frames, each of which were accompanied by ground-truth measurement of 21 skeletal joint angles, produced by a professional motion capture engineer using a Vicon motion capture system. Figure 3 (top row) illustrates sample frames. We applied the optimal descriptor (CNN+DA2) learned on the *ROM* dataset to this dataset to extract pose descriptors.

The three manifold embeddings of Sect. 3.2 were learned using 4 of the 5 MVV sequences in *Ballet* with the remaining sequence used for testing. Table 2 shows the results of the three approaches, for different descriptor dimensionality and with or without the dynamic threshold (**DynThrs**). Two metrics are used to evaluate performance, the average angular error between the estimated quaternion angle of each joint and its groundtruth, and the average positional error, via simple euclidean distance. Dynamic thresholding the representation uniformly reduces error both in terms of joint angle and location. Without appropriate data scaling via this method, the log-polar representation poorly encodes extremities of the performer containing expressive arm and leg movements.

Although a general trend rewarding higher dimensionality is observed in P_{nn} and P_{ple}, this is not true for the non-linear embedding via GP-LVM where

Table 2. Estimation error: avg. angular error (deg); avg. location error (mm)

Descriptor	P_{nn}		P_{ple}		P_{nle}	
	Angle Err	Joint Err	Angle Err	Joint Err	Angle Err	Joint Err
1K	26.1	154.5	25.3	152.6	22.8	139.2
4K	23.2	136.1	22.9	140.1	21.4	132.2
1K+DynThrs	22.5	128.1	21.2	124.5	**20.3**	**122.9**
4K+DynThrs	21.7	124.9	21.5	127.5	20.8	129.8

(a)

(b)

Fig. 4. Representative examples of source data and corresponding pose estimations. From left to right: Source MVV frame; Ground truth (Vicon); Nearest-neighbour (P_{nn}); Piecewise linear embedding (P_{ple}); Non-linear GP-LVM embedding (P_{nle}). Frames sampled at (a) 582 and (b) 660 from *Ballet*.

the best performing configuration is a dimensionality of 1k (with dynamic thresholding). Figure 3 quantifies per frame error for each of the three manifold techniques over this best-performing descriptor. Not only does the non-linear embedding result in a lower average error under both metrics, but the graph also reflects a more temporally coherent estimate. Figure 4 provides qualitative comparisons via representative examples of pose estimates from each of the three approaches.

5 Conclusion

We presented a technique for markerless performance capture from MVV. A CNN was trained to discriminate between a broad range of motions using volumetric data derived from the MVV sequence. We reported experiments indicating that the pose descriptors learned by the CNN performed strongly in both pose classification and at pose estimation (regression). Furthermore, we demonstrated that the robustness of pose estimation was greatly improved by modeling the manifold of likely poses in the CNN descriptor space via a GP-LVM.

Future work will consider the fusion of additional forms of sensor data, such as wearable inertial sensors, to further enhance accuracy. On-axis rotation of limbs (e.g. wrist) are poorly captured by a silhouette-based representation (visual hull) whereas such movements may be captured with ease using inertial sensors. Although a prior toward valid poses is implicit within the learned manifold, explicit kinematic constraints might also be built in to further refine accuracy. The use of synthetic 3D animation data to boost the training set could also prove valuable. Nevertheless, we believe such improvements are unnecessary to demonstrate the potential for deep learning in pose estimation from MVV.

Acknowledgements. The work was supported by the REFRAME project, InnovateUK grant agreement 101854. The Ballet dataset is courtesy of the EU FP7 RE@CT project.

References

1. Zhao, T., Nevatia, R.: Bayesian human segmentation in crowded situations. In: Proceedings of the Computer Vision and Pattern Recognition, vol. 2, pp. 459–466 (2003)
2. Aggarwal, A., Biswas, S., Singh, S., Sural, S., Majumdar, A.K.: Object tracking using background subtraction and motion estimation in MPEG videos. In: Narayanan, P.J., Nayar, S.K., Shum, H.-Y. (eds.) ACCV 2006. LNCS, vol. 3852, pp. 121–130. Springer, Heidelberg (2006). doi:10.1007/11612704_13
3. Viola, P., Jones, M.: Robust real-time object detection. Int. J. Comput. Vis. **2**(57), 137–154 (2004)
4. Eichner, M., Ferrari, V.: Better appearance models for pictorial structures. In: Proceedings of the British Machine Vision Conference (BMVC) (2009)
5. Krizhevsky, A., Sutskever, I., Hinton, G.: Imagenet classification with deep convolutional neural networks. In: Proceedings of the NIPS (2012)

6. Toshev, A., Szegedy, C.: Deep pose: human pose estimation via deep neural networks. In: Proceedings of the CVPR (2014)
7. Wu, Z., Song, S., Khosla, A., Yu, F., Zhang, L., Tang, X., Xiao, J.: 3D shapenets: a deep representation for volumetric shapes. In: Proceedings of the CVPR (2015)
8. Wohlhart, P., Lepetit, V.: Learning descriptors for object recognition and 3D pose estimation. In: Proceedings of the CVPR (2015)
9. Park, D., Ramanan, D.: Articulated pose estimation with tiny synthetic videos. In: Proceedings of the CHA-LEARN Workshop on Looking at People (2015)
10. Wei, L., Huang, Q., Ceylan, D., Vouga, E., Li, H.: Dense human body correspondences using convolutional networks. CoRR abs/1511.05904 (2015)
11. Huang, P., Tejera, M., Collomosse, J., Hilton, A.: Hybrid skeletal-surface motion graphs for character animation from 4d performance capture. ACM Trans. Graph. (ToG) **34**(2), Article No. 17 (2015)
12. Elhayek, A., de Aguiar, E., Jain, A., Tompson, J., Pishchulin, L., Andriluka, M., Bregler, C., Schiele, B., Theobalt, C.: Efficient ConvNet-based marker-less motion capture in general scenes with a low number of cameras. In: 2015 IEEE Conference on Computer Vision and Pattern Recognition (CVPR), pp. 3810–3818. IEEE (2015)
13. Grauman, K., Shakhnarovich, G., Darrell, T.: A Bayesian approach to image-based visual hull reconstruction. In: Proceedings of the CVPR (2003)
14. Huang, P., Hilton, A., Starck, J.: Shape similarity for 3D video sequences of people. Int. J. Comput. Vis. **89**, 362–381 (2010)
15. Makadia, A., Daniilidis, K.: Spherical correlation of visual representations for 3D model retrieval. Int. J. Comput. Vis. **89**, 193–210 (2009)
16. Rasmussen, C.E., Williams, C.: Gaussian Processes for Machine Learning. MIT Press, Cambridge (2006)
17. Lawrence, N.: Probabilistic non-linear principal component analysis with Gaussian process latent variable models. J. Mach. Learn. Res. **6**, 1783–1817 (2005)

Virtual Immortality: Reanimating Characters from TV Shows

James Charles[(⊠)], Derek Magee, and David Hogg

School of Computing, University of Leeds, Leeds, UK
{j.charles,d.r.magee,d.c.hogg}@leeds.ac.uk

Abstract. The objective of this work is to build virtual talking avatars of characters fully automatically from TV shows. From this unconstrained data, we show how to capture a character's style of speech, visual appearance and language in an effort to construct an interactive avatar of the person and effectively immortalize them in a computational model. We make three contributions (i) a complete framework for producing a generative model of the audiovisual and language of characters from TV shows; (ii) a novel method for aligning transcripts to video using the audio; and (iii) a fast audio segmentation system for silencing non-spoken audio from TV shows. Our framework is demonstrated using all 236 episodes from the TV series Friends ($\approx$ 97 h of video) and shown to generate novel sentences as well as character specific speech and video.

Keywords: Visual speech · Video synthesis · Video alignment

1 Introduction

For many years humans have been enthralled with recording people and their activities using e.g. sculpture, paintings, photographs, video and sound. We strive to modernize the existing set of recording methods by building a generative computational model of a person's motion, appearance, speech, language and their style of interaction and behavior. This model is trained from unconstrained prerecorded material of a person but grants one with the ability to generate *brand-new* and *interactive* content, effectively rendering the person virtually immortal. Uses of such a system include a natural interface between human and computer, possibly putting a face and personality to existing voice-only assistants such as Apple's Siri, Microsoft's Cortana or Amazon's Alexa. Such a model could also be used as an effortless way to generate ground truth audiovisual data for training AI interactive systems.

A system capable of learning to generate virtual talking avatars of characters appearing in TV shows is proposed. Such a task is very challenging due to different camera angles, shot changes, camera motion, scale variations, lighting,

---

Electronic supplementary material The online version of this chapter (doi:10.1007/978-3-319-49409-8_71) contains supplementary material, which is available to authorized users.

G. Hua and H. Jégou (Eds.): ECCV 2016 Workshops, Part III, LNCS 9915, pp. 879–886, 2016.
DOI: 10.1007/978-3-319-49409-8_71

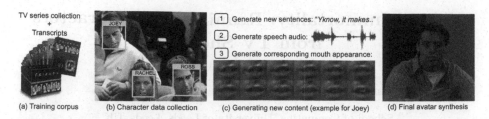

Fig. 1. System overview for learning to generate a virtual talking avatar of a target TV show character. Example shown for the *Friends* TV series and the character *Joey*. See text for details.

appearance changes and background audio, e.g. music and laughter. Transcripts (a written record of character dialog) supplement the videos and are used to help form training labels. However, as they contain no timing information, using them to infer where, who and when someone is talking on screen is non-trivial.

Related Work. Our work is most closely related to visual text to speech systems, which take a sentence, in the form of text, and synthesize speech audio and a visual head with corresponding mouth motion. Our virtual model is a 2D rendering of a character [31] and is trained to generate visual speech using a concatenative unit selection system [15,32] where short clips of mouth motion, called dynamic visiemes [30], are stitched together to form the visual signal. A similar approach is also taken for the audio [4]. Traditionally, visual speech systems are built from data captured in controlled environments [1,29]. However, in our case the audiovisual data from TV shows is unconstrained and not designed for the task of training a visual speech system. Our work also differs from previous methods as a model of character language is trained for producing new sentences in character specific style. Furthermore, we also produce background video content including upper body motion and gestures. For illustrative purposes throughout this paper, we train our generative audiovisual and language model on *Joey* from the popular TV show *Friends*, allowing him to say new sentences in his own style and voice. Next we give an overview of the system.

2   System Overview

A high level overview of our system is illustrated in Fig. 1. Our goal is to build a system capable of learning to generate new audiovisual content of a chosen TV character (the *target*) from a TV show, in the form of a moving, gesturing and speaking 2D avatar. A collection of episodes and transcripts from a popular TV show, Fig. 1(a), can provide a large training corpus (e.g. over 200 episodes of video for *Friends*) for learning a generative model of the avatar. Our system automatically labels audio and video with phonetic boundaries, character face bounding boxes with character names, and facial landmarks, as shown in Fig. 1(b) and Fig. 2(a). From this, our generative model is trained.

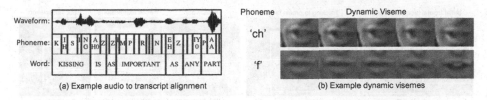

Fig. 2. Audio to transcript alignment and dynamic visemes.

Novel avatar content is produced for a target character, as shown in Fig. 1 (c)–(d), by: (1) first generating new short sentences sampled from a character specific language model. Then, corresponding audiovisual data is generated in a two phase approach [17] whereby (2) the text is converted to a phonetic sequence with phoneme durations and an audio signal is generated. (3) the visual speech engine uses this phonetic information for producing the visual element of the avatar, synthesizing a video of mouth appearance. Finally, mouth synthesis is blended on to a moving background of the target, showing the full face together with upper body and background scene, as if the target were performing and gesturing in the original TV show, example frame in Fig. 1(d).

3   Character Data Collection

Data collection is non-trivial and involves multiple stages of processing: (i) Muting of non-spoken audio, (ii) phonetically labeling the speech, (iii) face detection and tracking, (iv) automatic character labeling, (v) facial landmark detection, and finally (vi) producing phonetic databases (units of speech audio) and visemic databases (units of mouth appearance) for each character. From these databases new audiovisual content can be generated. Each of these stages is now explained in detail.

Muting Non-spoken Audio. A critical task for training our speech synthesizer is first detecting spoken audio. In TV shows, speech is mixed with background noise, e.g., music, traffic noise and in particular canned/audience laughter. Speech audio is automatically detected and background noise muted prior to further audio analysis. Although prior work on this exists for radio broadcasts [26], news broadcasts [16] and feature films [3], speech detection in TV shows is a very different domain. Comedy shows exhibit canned/audience laughter more so than in films. Also, one should leverage the consistent nature of episodes, i.e., same characters, same environments and similar music scores, to help improve speech detection. To this end, we build a speech detection system capable of generalizing well across episodes, yet trained from only one manually labeled episode. A sliding window classifier (random forest) labels the speech into spoken and non-spoken audio. The audio is represented with Mel Frequency Cepstral Coefficients (MFCCs), common in automatic speech recognition [18,20].

Aligning Transcripts to Video (Using Audio). Time-aligned transcripts act as supervisory labels for training our system. In particular, previous works

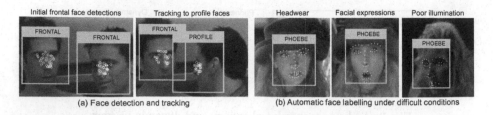

(a) Face detection and tracking   (b) Automatic face labelling under difficult conditions

Fig. 3. Face detection, tracking and automatic labeling with character names.

use subtitle aligned transcripts for learning to recognize and label characters in movies and TV shows [6,9,14,21]. Subtitles have words missing and the timing is rather ad-hoc and does not provide accurate timing level information necessary for learning visual speech systems where phoneme-level precision is required. Instead, we align the transcripts to speech audio, producing much greater timing precision and accuracy. Transcripts are force-aligned to speech only audio for each episode using dynamic programming and an American-English language model, as in [24]. Alignment results in word and phoneme boundaries, as shown in Fig. 2(a).

Face Detection and Tracking. An online multi-face detection and tracking system produces face tracks for all episodes. Highly confident face detections [33] initialize the face tracking. Face bounding boxes are tracked [25] to the next frame by tracking keypoints in the box center (Fig. 3(a) white circles). Boxes are tracked from frame to frame provided enough keypoints (>3) are matched, and the previous box covers at least 90 % of the tracked box. By tracking points only in the center of the face we limit the possibility of tracking background points and circumvent drifting, particularly between shots. While only frontal faces are detected, tracking leads to profile faces being captured (Fig. 3(a)). Note, this stage can produce tracks for main characters as well as supporting actors.

Automatic Character Labeling. Automatic labeling of characters in TV shows has received much attention over the years [6–8,10,14,21,23]. Our approach here is similar in principle to the founding work by Everingham *et al.* [9] where subtitle-aligned transcripts were used. However, we demonstrate that improved precision from audio aligned transcripts leads to a relatively simple and accurate approach while also removing the need for visual speech detection. As in [21], we automatically label whole face tracks from ConvNet based face features [22]. To initialize, we transfer character labels from the aligned transcripts to solitary face tracks (no other faces on screen). A multi-class linear SVM classifier is trained in an iterative manner to solve the labeling problem for the remaining face-tracks. At each iteration the classifier is trained from current labels and then applied to *all* tracks. Only easy tracks (high classifier confidence) are labeled. At each iteration, progressively more tracks become labeled. We found 8 iterations sufficient. One classifier per episode is initially trained and later a single classifier per series is trained from current labels and applied across every episode of that series. In this way, knowledge about appearance variation (e.g. changes in lighting) can be shared across episodes (example variations in appearance shown for the character *Phoebe* from *Friends* in Fig. 3(b)). Empirically it was found that training in this manner led to better results than simply training only one classifier from all data in the series.

Dynamic Visemes. As in [30] we generate dynamic, concatenative units of visual speech called *dynamic visemes*. In our case a dynamic viseme is a small video clip of mouth appearance capturing coarticulation. A one-to-many mapping from phoneme to viseme is formed by building a database per character, example visemes for the character *Joey* from *Friends* are shown in Fig. 2(b). Mouths are detected using a facial landmark detector [2], example landmark detections are shown as white dots in Fig. 1(b) and Fig. 3(b). RGB pixel values for each frame of the dynamic viseme is represented as a set of PCA coefficients. The PCA model is trained from all frames over all visemes, one model per target character. The previous and next phoneme in the phonetic sequence is also assigned to each viseme, providing contextual features. We next describe how to train our model and generate the virtual avatar.

4   Text to Visual Speech

Language Model. New sentences in the style of the target character are generated with a deep Long Short Term Memory (LSTM) [12] Recurrent Neural Network (RNN). Each letter of the sentence is generated given the previous letter [11,13,28]. RNNs capture long-range dependencies between letters to form words and sentence structure. In our case, a letter-level modeling approach is more appropriate than a word-level language model [19,27] as it has the ability to learn person specific spelling and sentence structure, such as "yknow" meaning "you know". A two hidden layer network with 128 nodes at each hidden layer is trained with backpropagation through time (unrolled to 50 time steps).

Text to Speech (TTS). Speech audio is generated using a cluster unit selection based method [5] and trained from the phonetic labeling of the audio. At run time, input text is converted to a phonetic sequence and for each phoneme a corresponding unit of audio is selected based on the phonetic context and word position. A speech waveform is generated by stringing the selected audio units together. We use the Festival auditory speech synthesizer [4] software for building and running the TTS model.

Visual Speech. Generating visual speech follows a similar approach to generating speech audio, except phonetic duration (from the TTS) guides the synchronization of mouth motion with the speech audio. Concatenating dynamic visemes together (in time) forms visual mouth motion. Visemes are selected based on their phonetic label and context and visual smoothness is enforced by matching the PCA coefficients of the last frame of one viseme to the first frame of the next, optimized using the Viterbi algorithm. A post processing method of temporal smoothing is applied. The number of frames for each viseme is either linearly upsampled or downsampled to match the phonetic duration.

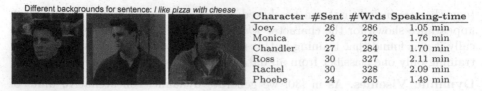

Character	#Sent	#Wrds	Speaking-time
Joey	26	286	1.05 min
Monica	28	278	1.76 min
Chandler	27	284	1.70 min
Ross	30	327	2.11 min
Rachel	30	328	2.09 min
Phoebe	24	265	1.49 min

Fig. 4. Left: example frames of avatar *Joey* showing same sentence with different backgrounds. Right: Table of average word/sentence statistics per episode.

Avatar Synthesis. A *moving* background section of video (containing only the target character in a frontal facing pose, perhaps gesturing) acts as a canvas for "pasting" on a generated mouth video over the targets mouth. The mouth video is scaled and rotated according to facial landmarks on the background video and blended using alpha mapping. The coloring of the mouth video is altered to match the color of the background mouth using histogram specification. Generated speech-audio is combined with the video to form the final synthesis.

5   Avatar from Friends

The framework is applied to the TV show *Friends* where we "virtually immortalize" the character *Joey*. A demo video can be viewed at http://tinyurl.com/ztvgeat.

Dataset. Audiovisual material is obtained from The Friends complete collection DVD boxset of 236 episodes in total, each episode approx. 22 mins in length. The first 3 seasons (73 episodes) are processed for data collection. Various statistics of the data extracted from automatic data collection is shown in Fig. 4.

Training. Episode 2 from season 1 was manually labeled with speech and non-speech for training the speech detector. All other training processes are fully automatic given the transcripts. The language model is trained from sentences with 5–10 words across all 236 episodes (1857 sentences in total).

Generating New Video and Speech. Example new generated sentences sampled from the language model include: "Hey Ross do you want me to talk to some lady" and "I want to do something wrong" more examples are in the supplementary material. Example generated output frames of *Joey* saying the new sentence "I like pizza with cheese" is shown in Fig. 4, produced using various moving backgrounds.

6   Summary and Extensions

We have presented a semi-supervised method for producing virtual talking avatars of celebrities from TV shows. Given only the transcripts and one manually segmented episode (3 h of manual work) one can process data from all episodes for any chosen character fully automatically. The character *Joey* from

Friends was "virtually immortalized" in a generative model, enabling him to say new sentences in his style and appearance. We plan to improve the rendering of the avatar and extend our model to include interaction with real people and also between avatars.

Acknowledgments. We thank Andrew Zisserman for useful discussions.

References

1. Anderson, R., Stenger, B., Wan, V., Cipolla, R.: Expressive visual text-to-speech using active appearance models. In: Proceedings of the CVPR (2013)
2. Asthana, A., Zafeiriou, S., Cheng, S., Pantic, M.: Incremental face alignment in the wild. In: Proceedings of the CVPR (2014)
3. Benatan, M., Ng, K.: Cross-covariance-based features for speech classification in film audio. J. Vis. Lang. Comput. **31**, 215–221 (2015)
4. Black, A., Taylor, P., Caley, R., Clark, R., Richmond, K., King, S., Strom, V., Zen, H.: The festival speech synthesis system (2001). http://www.cstr.ed.ac.uk/projects/festival/
5. Black, A.W., Lenzo, K.A.: Building synthetic voices. Language Technologies Institute, Carnegie Mellon University and Cepstral LLC (2003)
6. Bojanowski, P., Bach, F., Laptev, I., Ponce, J., Schmid, C., Sivic, J.: Finding actors and actions in movies. In: Proceedings of the ICCV (2013)
7. Cinbis, R.G., Verbeek, J., Schmid, C.: Unsupervised metric learning for face identification in TV video. In: Proceedings of the ICCV (2011)
8. Cour, T., Sapp, B., Nagle, A., Taskar, B.: Talking pictures: temporal grouping and dialog-supervised person recognition. In: Proceedings of the CVPR (2010)
9. Everingham, M., Sivic, J., Zisserman, A.: "Hello! My name is... Buffy" - automatic naming of characters in TV video. In: Proceedings of the BMVC (2006)
10. Everingham, M., Zisserman, A.: Automated detection and identification of persons in video using a coarse 3-D head model and multiple texture maps. IEE Proc. Vis. Image Sig. Process. **152**(6), 902–910 (2005)
11. Graves, A.: Generating sequences with recurrent neural networks. arXiv preprint arXiv:1308.0850 (2013)
12. Hochreiter, S., Schmidhuber, J.: Long short-term memory. Neural Comput. **9**(8), 1735–1780 (1997)
13. Karpathy, A.: The unreasonable effectiveness of recurrent neural networks. http://karpathy.github.io/2015/05/21/rnn-effectiveness/. Accessed 25 July 2016
14. Köstinger, M., Wohlhart, P., Roth, P.M., Bischof, H.: Learning to recognize faces from videos and weakly related information cues. In: Proceedings of the Advanced Video and Signal-Based Surveillance (2011)
15. Liu, C., Yuen, J., Torralba, A.: Sift flow: dense correspondence across scenes and its applications. In: IEEE PAMI (2011)
16. Lu, L., Zhang, H.J., Jiang, H.: Content analysis for audio classification and segmentation. IEEE Trans. Speech Audio Process. **10**(7), 504–516 (2002)
17. Mattheyses, W., Verhelst, W.: Audiovisual speech synthesis: an overview of the state-of-the-art. Speech Commun. **66**, 182–217 (2015)
18. Mermelstein, P.: Distance measures for speech recognition, psychological and instrumental. Pattern Recogn. Artif. Intell. **116**, 374–388 (1976)

19. Mikolov, T., Karafiát, M., Burget, L., Cernocký, J., Khudanpur, S.: Recurrent neural network based language model. In: Interspeech (2010)
20. Mogran, N., Bourlard, H., Hermansky, H.: Automatic speech recognition: an auditory perspective. In: Mogran, N., Bourlard, H., Hermansky, H. (eds.) Speech Processing in the Auditory System. Springer Handbook of Auditory Research, vol. 18, pp. 309–338. Springer, Heidelberg (2004)
21. Parkhi, O.M., Rahtu, E., Zisserman, A.: It's in the bag: stronger supervision for automated face labelling. In: ICCV Workshop: Describing and Understanding Video and the Large Scale Movie Description Challenge (2015)
22. Parkhi, O.M., Vedaldi, A., Zisserman, A.: Deep face recognition. In: Proceedings of the BMVC (2015)
23. Ramanathan, V., Joulin, A., Liang, P., Fei-Fei, L.: Linking people in videos with "Their" names using coreference resolution. In: Fleet, D., Pajdla, T., Schiele, B., Tuytelaars, T. (eds.) ECCV 2014. LNCS, vol. 8689, pp. 95–110. Springer, Heidelberg (2014). doi:10.1007/978-3-319-10590-1_7
24. Rubin, S., Berthouzoz, F., Mysore, G.J., Li, W., Agrawala, M.: Content-based tools for editing audio stories. In: ACM symposium on User Interface Software and Technology (2013)
25. Shi, J., Tomasi, C.: Good features to track. In: Proceedings of the CVPR (1994)
26. Sonnleitner, R., Niedermayer, B., Widmer, G., Schlüter, J.: A simple and effective spectral feature for speech detection in mixed audio signals. In: Proceedings of the International Conference on Digital Audio Effects (2012)
27. Sundermeyer, M., Schlüter, R., Ney, H.: LSTM neural networks for language modeling. In: Interspeech (2012)
28. Sutskever, I., Martens, J., Hinton, G.E.: Generating text with recurrent neural networks. In: Proceedings of the ICML (2011)
29. Taylor, S., Theobald, B.J., Matthews, I.: The effect of speaking rate on audio and visual speech. In: Proceedings of the ICASSP (2014)
30. Taylor, S.L., Mahler, M., Theobald, B.J., Matthews, I.: Dynamic units of visual speech. In: Proceedings of the ACM SIGGRAPH (2012)
31. Tiddeman, B., Perrett, D.: Prototyping and transforming visemes for animated speech. In: Proceedings of the Computer Animation (2002)
32. Verma, A., Rajput, N., Subramaniam, L.V.: Using viseme based acoustic models for speech driven lip synthesis. In: Proceedings of the Multimedia and Expo (2003)
33. Viola, P., Jones, M.: Rapid object detection using a boosted cascade of simple features. In: Proceedings of the CVPR (2001)

Light Source Estimation in Synthetic Images

Mike Kasper$^{(\boxtimes)}$, Nima Keivan, Gabe Sibley, and Christoffer Heckman

University of Colorado, Boulder, USA
{michael.kasper,nima.kevian,gsibley,christoffer.heckman}@colorado.edu

Abstract. We evaluate a novel light source estimation algorithm with synthetic image data generated using a custom path-tracer. We model light as an environment map as light sources at infinity for its benefits in estimation. However the synthetic image data are rendered using spherical area lights as to better represent the physical world as well as challenge our algorithm. In total, we generate 55 random illumination scenarios, consisting of either one or two spherical area lights with different intensities and positioned at different distances from the observed scene. Using this data we are able to tune our optimization parameters and determine under which conditions this algorithm and model representation is best suited.

Keywords: Light source estimation · Path-tracing · Synthetic data

1 Introduction

Computer vision is often referred to as the "inverse graphics" problem. This is because many of the equations and relations used in computer vision find their roots in the understanding of image formation and light interaction. However, the complete process of image formation is mainly ignored in most applications of computer vision. For instance, simulating light as it propagates through a scene is traditionally accomplished by means of ray-casting. This method ignores subsequent interactions a ray of light may have with the scene, instead terminating the ray on the first collision with a surface.

As a result of such simplifications, many visual quantities such as light position, sensor characterization and in-scene surface properties are irrecoverable. Ideally these quantities could be estimated as properties of the scene through simulating the propagation of light and employing optimization, requiring a lightweight but powerful simulation stack for graphics modeling.

In this work, we build on [7] to develop a light source estimation algorithm that includes light source location correction based on photometric differences and has the capability to extend to in-scene surface property estimation, a critical step toward semantic scene understanding. This algorithm relies heavily on leveraging synthetic data in order to calculate cost functions and to isolate individual aspects of the problem such as capturing realistic shadow diffusion and light reflection from in-scene surfaces. A visual sample of the results from our method are shown in Fig. 1.

© Springer International Publishing Switzerland 2016
G. Hua and H. Jégou (Eds.): ECCV 2016 Workshops, Part III, LNCS 9915, pp. 887–893, 2016.
DOI: 10.1007/978-3-319-49409-8_72

Fig. 1. *Left*: synthetic reference image. *Middle*: our rendered result after light source estimation. *Right*: photometric error image.

2   Method

Our approach relies on a custom image rendering system to compare synthetic data with our generative model's output for scene reconstruction. The synthetic data generation includes the encoding of scene geometry, albedo and 3D light positions. Results from our light source estimation system are compared with these synthetic results and guide an optimization over light position.

2.1   Image Rendering

To render our scene we have developed a path-tracer using NVIDIA's OptiX ray-tracing library. We employ a custom path-tracer due to our need to calculate analytical derivatives of the *light transport equation* (LTE) in order to guide later optimization. The LTE describes how radiance emitted from a light source interacts with the scene. Formally, we compute the exitant radiance L_o leaving a point p in direction ω_o as:

$$L_o(\mathrm{p},\omega_o) = L_e(\mathrm{p},\omega_o) + \int_{\mathcal{H}^2} f(\mathrm{p},\omega_o,\omega_i) L_i(\mathrm{p},\omega_i) |\cos\theta_i| \mathrm{d}\omega_i \tag{1}$$

where L_e is the radiance emitted at point p in direction ω_o. The integral term evaluates all the incident radiance L_i arriving at point p over the unit hemisphere $\mathcal{H}^2$, oriented with the surface normal found at p, and subsequently reflected in the direction ω_o. The function f evaluates the *bidirectional reflectance distribution function* (BRDF) found at point p. The BRDF defines the amount of radiance leaving in direction ω_o as a results of incident radiance arriving along the direction ω_i. Finally, θ_i is the angle between the surface normal found at p and ω_i. Using Monte Carlo integration we can rewrite Eq. (1) as the finite sum:

$$L_o(\mathrm{p},\omega_o) = L_e(\mathrm{p},\omega_o) + \frac{1}{N}\sum_{i=1}^{N} \frac{f(\mathrm{p},\omega_o,\omega_i) L_i(\mathrm{p},\omega_i)|\cos\theta_i|}{p(\omega_i)} \tag{2}$$

where $i = 1,\ldots,N$ is the number of samples drawn from the distribution described by the *probability density function* (PDF) p.

To compute the final pixel intensity I, we integrate the intensity of all rays $i = 1, \ldots, M$ arriving at our synthetic sensor (of the form of Eq. (2)). Using Monte Carlo integration we can evaluate this with the finite sum:

$$I = \frac{1}{M} \sum_{i=1}^{M} L_o(\mathrm{p}_i, \omega_o) \tag{3}$$

where p_i refers to the point where a ray originating from our sensor and traveling along ω_o first intersects with the scene. For more information on path-tracing and the LTE see [12].

2.2   Synthetic Data Generation

Scene Geometry. In this work we operate on a static 3D scene representing a tabletop with several items placed on its surface as seen in Fig. 1. This scene is constructed to afford interesting illumination conditions without addressing pathological factors such as the presence of mirrors, etc. The 3D geometry was captured from a real scene using KinectFusion [11] with an Asus Xtion Pro 3D sensor. While any scene constructed with 3D modeling software would suffice, we use a captured real-life scene so that we may compare results between real and synthetic data in future research.

Albedos. To render scenes under different illumination conditions it is necessary to associate surface albedos (i.e. color devoid of any shading information) with the 3D geometry. The problem of separating albedos and shading information found in images, often referred to as *intrinsic image decomposition*, is the subject of a rich field of ongoing research [2–4]; to obviate this challenge we assume albedo associations are known, although this knowledge need not be perfect accurate. Utilizing synthetic data allows us to both modulate the accuracy of the albedo map as well as address correcting it within our framework, as a topic of future work.

Area Lights. We employ spherical area lights to provide an arbitrary source of illumination in our synthetic reference images. Crucially, this representation of light used in rendering reference images is distinct from the environment map light we are estimating as described in Sect. 2.3. This enables us to assess how well our environment map-based light model can represent more complex illumination scenarios.

2.3   Light Source Estimation

Environment Light. As mentioned in Sect. 2.2 we model light using an environment map [6,9]. Instead of sampling points in 3D space as used with area lights, with environment map lighting we sample directions. This representation works well for approximating lights located further from the observed scene.

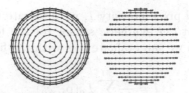

Fig. 2. Visualization of environment light discretization with a top-down view on the left, and a side view on the right. The light depicted here consists of 21 rings and 522 total points.

While many works have considered in-scene lighting examples [8,10], we instead focus on out-of-scene sources [1,5,13,14]. To compute the incident radiance L_i arriving at a point p we trace a ray with origin p in some direction ω. If the ray is unobstructed by the scene geometry, point p will receive the full radiance traveling along ω as determined by the environment map.

To compute the radiance emitted by the environment map along a given direction, we first discretize a unit sphere into a finite number of uniformly spaced points. We perform the same discretization as described in [6] for the entire sphere. The resolution of this discretization is indicated only by the number of desired rings. The spacing of points around each ring is computed to be as close to the inter-ring spacing as possible, as seen in Fig. 2. When tracing a ray along a given direction we determine the nearest-neighbor direction from the discretized environment map and return its associated RGB value λ as the emitted radiance.

Direction Sampling. To render a scene illuminated by an environment map we must sample a direction each time a ray intersects the scene. We perform importance sampling by sampling environment map directions that are more likely to contribute a larger amount of light. To achieve this we constructed a 2D probability distribution function that reflects the current environment light parameters as described in [12], however with the small modification to handle the unique discretized structure of the our environment map. It is from this 2D PDF that we can compute the probability of the sample $p(\omega)$.

Light Transport Derivatives. To estimate the environment light parameters we need to compute the Jacobian of partial derivatives of color channel α of each pixel I with respect to each environment lighting parameter λ. We first drop the $L_e(p, \omega)$ term from Eq. (2) as there is no point p on the surface of environment map that emits light. We then define a visibility function $V(p, \omega)$ which equates to 1 if the ray leaving from point p in direction ω is not obstructed by the scene geometry, and 0 otherwise. We now define the partial derivative of the intensity of color channel α at p with respect to the light source color channel α as:

$$\frac{dI_\alpha}{d\lambda_\alpha}\bigg|_p = \frac{1}{N} \sum_{i=1}^{N} \frac{f(p, \omega_o, \omega_i) V(p, \omega_i) |\cos \theta_i|}{p(\omega_i)}, \tag{4}$$

for which we then sum over the incident rays $1, \ldots, M$ to obtain the derivative of per-channel pixel intensity.

Optimization. We employ sequential Monte Carlo (sMQ) to estimate the parameters of our environment light. For each iteration we sample the scene according to the currently-estimated lighting parameters and compute the Jacobian of the LTE. We then perform gradient descent with backtracking until we have converged on a new set of lighting parameters. We continue this process until the optimization has converged, as indicated by the Wolfe conditions on gradient magnitude.

3   Results

We evaluated the proposed light source estimation algorithm to determined what environment map resolution can best represent a wide-variety of lighting conditions. For this we constructed 55 scenes illuminated by either one or two randomly placed, spherical area lights and rendered two synthetic reference images for each scene. We then replaced the area light with an environment light, uniformly initialized all environment map intensities to be near zero, and computed the LTE derivatives sampling the scene 512 times per pixel. For each scene we ran our light source estimation algorithm using 13 different environment map resolutions for a total of 715 different trials. While rendering the synthetic reference images only took 1–2 s, an entire optimization typically took 4–5 min to

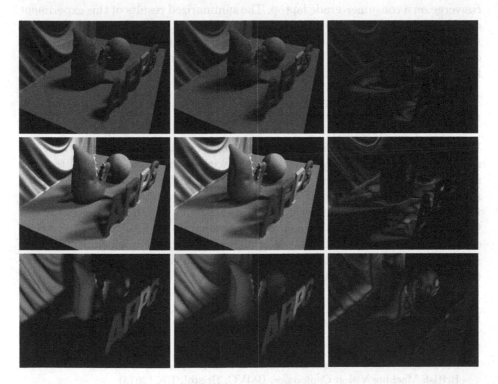

Fig. 3. Visual comparison of three different illumination scenarios. The left column shows the synthetic reference images, the middle column our estimation, and the right column their photometric error.

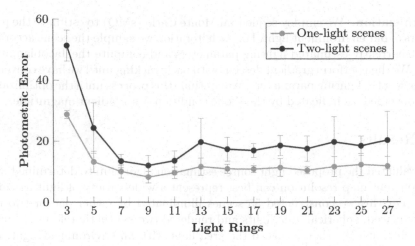

Fig. 4. Photometric error between reference image and rendered estimate for an environment light with the indicated number of rows. All images are rendered at 128×96. Mean and standard deviation computed for 55 different illumination scenarios.

converge on a consumer-grade laptop. The summarized results of this experiment can be seen in Fig. 4. Surprisingly a relatively coarse resolution of 9 light rings achieved the best results. However we suspect that for the higher-resolution models, 512 samples per pixel was insufficient and the resulting variance hindered their optimization.

4   Conclusions and Future Work

We have presented an algorithm that generates synthetic visual data in a 3D environment and developed a generative model with output that is refined through an optimization procedure over light position. We have also demonstrated a robust and efficient method of generating high-quality synthetic visual datasets which may be used to guide semantic scene understanding through optimization. Our results suggest that in-scene property estimation tasks may be successfully executed in an efficient optimization framework. In future work we will demonstrate full path-tracing and shadow detection within the postulated environment map to improve the accuracy of our estimation.

References

1. Boom, B., Orts-Escolano, S., Ning, X., McDonagh, S., Sandilands, P., Fisher, R.B.: Point light source estimation based on scenes recorded by a RGB-D camera. In: British Machine Vision Conference, BMVC, Bristol, UK (2013)
2. Chen, Q., Koltun, V.: A simple model for intrinsic image decomposition with depth cues. In: International Conference on Computer Vision, pp. 241–248. IEEE (2013)

3. Duchêne, S., Riant, C., Chaurasia, G., Moreno, J.L., Laffont, P.Y., Popov, S., Bousseau, A., Drettakis, G.: Multiview intrinsic images of outdoors scenes with an application to relighting. ACM Trans. Graph. **34**, 1–16 (2015)
4. Hachama, M., Ghanem, B., Wonka, P.: Intrinsic scene decomposition from RGB-D images. In: International Conference on Computer Vision, pp. 810–818. IEEE (2015)
5. Hara, K., Nishino, K., Ikeuchi, K.: Multiple light sources and reflectance property estimation based on a mixture of spherical distributions. In: 10th IEEE International Conference on Computer Vision (ICCV 2005), 17–20 October 2005, Beijing, China, pp. 1627–1634 (2005). http://doi.ieeecomputersociety.org/10.1109/ICCV.2005.162
6. Jachnik, J., Newcombe, R.A., Davison, A.J.: Real-time surface light-field capture for augmentation of planar specular surfaces. In: International Symposium on Mixed and Augmented Reality, pp. 91–97. IEEE (2012)
7. Keivan, N., Sibley, G.: Generative scene models with analytical path-tracing. In: Robotics Science and Systems (RSS) Workshop on Realistic, Repeatable and Robust Simulation (2015)
8. Knorr, S.B., Kurz, D.: Real-time illumination estimation from faces for coherent rendering. In: Proceedings IEEE International Symposium on Mixed and Augmented Reality (ISMAR2014), pp. 113–122 (2014)
9. Lalonde, J.F., Matthews, I.: Lighting estimation in outdoor image collections. In: International Conference on 3D Vision, pp. 131–138. IEEE (2014)
10. Meilland, M., Barat, C., Comport, A.: 3D high dynamic range dense visual slam and its application to real-time object re-lighting. In: 2013 IEEE International Symposium on Mixed and Augmented Reality (ISMAR), pp. 143–152. IEEE (2013)
11. Newcombe, R.A., Izadi, S., Hilliges, O., Molyneaux, D., Kim, D., Davison, A.J., Kohli, P., Shotton, J., Hodges, S., Fitzgibbon, A.: KinectFusion: real-time dense surface mapping and tracking. In: Proceedings of the 2011 10th IEEE International Symposium on Mixed and Augmented Reality, pp. 127–136. ISMAR 2011. IEEE Computer Society, Washington, D.C. (2011). http://dx.doi.org/10.1109/ISMAR.2011.6092378
12. Pharr, M., Humphreys, G.: Physically Based Rendering, Second Edition: From Theory To Implementation, 2nd edn. Morgan Kaufmann Publishers Inc., San Francisco (2010)
13. Takai, T., Maki, A., Matsuyama, T.: Self shadows and cast shadows in estimating illumination distribution. In: 4th European Conference on Visual Media Production, 2007, IETCVMP, pp. 1–10, November 2007
14. Zhou, W., Kambhamettu, C.: Estimation of illuminant direction and intensity of multiple light sources. In: Heyden, A., Sparr, G., Nielsen, M., Johansen, P. (eds.) ECCV 2002. LNCS, vol. 2353, pp. 206–220. Springer, Heidelberg (2002). doi:10.1007/3-540-47979-1_14

LEE: A Photorealistic Virtual Environment for Assessing Driver-Vehicle Interactions in Self-driving Mode

Saad Minhas[1], Aura Hernández-Sabaté[2(✉)], Shoaib Ehsan[1],
Katerine Díaz-Chito[2], Ales Leonardis[3], Antonio M. López[2],
and Klaus D. McDonald-Maier[1]

[1] University of Essex, Colchester, UK
[2] Computer Vision Center and Universitat Autónoma de Barcelona,
Barcelona, Spain
aura@cvc.uab.cat
[3] University of Birmingham, Birmingham, UK

Abstract. Photorealistic virtual environments are crucial for developing and testing automated driving systems in a safe way during trials. As commercially available simulators are expensive and bulky, this paper presents a low-cost, extendable, and easy-to-use (LEE) virtual environment with the aim to highlight its utility for level 3 driving automation. In particular, an experiment is performed using the presented simulator to explore the influence of different variables regarding control transfer of the car after the system was driving autonomously in a highway scenario. The results show that the speed of the car at the time when the system needs to transfer the control to the human driver is critical.

Keywords: Simulation environment · Automated driving · Driver-vehicle interaction

1 Introduction

The last few decades have seen a dramatic increase in the number of vehicles utilizing Advanced Driver Assistance Systems (ADAS), such as intelligent headlights [3], lane change assistance [2], and even the first attempts of automatic driving systems [6,14,15,18]. Although currently far from having feasible totally automated driving systems, there are several intermediate levels of driving automation for on-road vehicles, according to the SAE international standard J3016 [12], based on the system core functionality. Its level 3 specifies that the automated driving system performs all aspects of dynamic driving task with the expectation that the driver will recover the car's control when required. Thus, the human driver can perform other activities while the system is driving autonomously. This gives rise to an important question: At which moment and how can the automated driving system return the control to the driver?

© Springer International Publishing Switzerland 2016
G. Hua and H. Jégou (Eds.): ECCV 2016 Workshops, Part III, LNCS 9915, pp. 894–900, 2016.
DOI: 10.1007/978-3-319-49409-8_73

The answer to this question depends on several aspects, such as the activity of the driver, his/her general state and possible reaction, the particular state of the environment and the current action of the car. All these aspects should be carefully analyzed without compromising road security, and hence require a simulated environment for research, development and testing purposes.

This paper presents a low-cost, extendable and easy-to-use (LEE) simulation environment which allows to explore autonomous driving research. To demonstrate its utility, an experiment is performed using this simulator by designing two scenarios where the driver is alerted by a visual and acoustic alarm and asked to take over the control. Regardless of the activity of the driver, perception reaction time (PRT) has to be taken into account before making any decision [10], among other variables. Moreover, the reaction times pertaining to arm and feet are different [11]. Several variables are examined in this paper, such as the speed of the car at that moment, the reaction time of the arms (needed to reach the steering wheel) and the reaction time of the feet (needed to reach the brake pedal). The results show that the speed of the car at the time of triggering the alarm is critical. It can be observed that PRT of arms are greater than PRT of feet, which should be taken into account in further analysis. Figure 1(a) shows the driver simulator hardware setup while Fig. 1(b) provides a screenshot of the simulation recording with all the variables taken into account.

(a)   (b)

Fig. 1. Simulator hardware (a) and an example of the simulation recording (b).

2   Related Work

Simulation Environments. The first interactive driving simulator was introduced in 1960 [5]. TRAFFIS is an industrial grade driver simulator relying on a reconfigurable approach [1]. Similarly, 3xD is a driver-in-loop multi-axis driving simulator. The VTI's simulator consists of a partial car mock-up, hydraulic movement and a moving screen [9]. These simulators are high-cost and bulky requiring specialist dedicated hardware, with a Toyota's simulator costing in the region of 30 million pound sterling [17].

Perception Reaction Time. PRT of human drivers is an active research area within the driving performance domain, where it plays an important role in road incidents [4,7,8]. Green [4] highlights that the most important variable is driver's expectation. Jurecki et al. [7] confirm that reaction time is approximately a linear function of Time To Collision (TTC). Svetina [13] concludes that mean reaction time and inter-individual variability progressively increases with age. It is worth mentioning here that all these studies are carried out on active users while actually driving a vehicle.

3   Simulation Environment

This section presents the simulation environment 'LEE'. For building an efficient and inexpensive simulator, a custom workstation equipped with an Intel i7 processor, an NVIDIA GTX Titan Graphics card with 12GB of usable VRAM, two HD monitors, a HD Webcam and a Logitech G27 Wheel and pedal Set are used. On the software side, Autodesk 3DS Max is used to model and develop virtual assets for the driver simulator. This includes the driver's car, other traffic cars as well as road surfaces. Adobe Photoshop is used in the creation of 2D elements, which includes detailing on the modelled cars as well as the road sections. Finally, Unity3D is used to tackle the interactive challenges of the simulator.

Fig. 2. Road surface. Road sections (top row), Unity3D road environment (middle row) and road model dimensions (bottom row).

Major 3D assets that are created involve the vehicular models and the environment assets. The vehicle models provided by the Mission Group [16] and the traffic cars are then processed to optimize them for real-time applications. This includes stripping down any unwanted details on the models. In particular, the interiors of these vehicles are reduced quite substantially as they are never seen in the actual application. A Mazda 3 has been chosen as the model. The driver car's interior is also optimized to resemble the real life counterpart as close as possible.

The road surface is modelled in 3dsmax by using reference imagery from the internet. It is loosely based on a three lane section of M25 motorway around London. In order to keep the modular aspect of the environment intact, only two road sections are produced, a straight road section consisting of 100 meters, and an angular portion of 25 degrees. These two road sections help in creating different looking road environments within Unity3D. Basic trees are populated on either side of the road and a suitable sky environment is added to further enhance the realism of the virtual environment. The finished 3D assets including the vehicles and the road sections are then imported into Unity3D. The two road sections are cloned into multiple copies and are put together to form a looping M25 environment, which is approximately 4 miles long and is used as a base for the virtual world experiments. Figure 2 shows the road surface, including the two road sections at the top, the complete environment within Unity3D in the middle and the complete road model dimensions at the bottom.

(a)   (b)

Fig. 3. Virtual world. (a) Traffic simulation and (b) Main car interior rig

The traffic cars are populated by using a third party plugin called ITS (Intelligent Traffic System). Cars can be seen maneuvering throughout the virtual environment, overtaking other traffic vehicles and maintaining their specific lanes. The system is rigged in such a manner that the left most lane would have a speed of no more than 55 mph and will have a greater number of lorries, whereas the middle lane would have a 60 mph limit with medium and small sized cars. Finally, the right most lane has a speed limit of 70 mph. The cars that are populated do not necessarily keep a constant speed and it varies from car to car for producing a more realistic traffic simulation. The cars also stop when they detect a blockage in front of the road. The simulations are random every time the application is executed, hence giving a realistic and unperceived situation with every new session. Figure 3(a) shows the traffic system in action.

The main car model requires the most amount of rigging, as this needs to be an area where the driver would be interacting the most. Main components of the interior of the car are rigged in a realistic manner (Fig. 3(b)). This includes rigging the steering wheel, RPM needle, pedals and a fully functional Adaptive Cruise Control System. Moreover, the general car physics rig is based on the standard Unity3D Car Controller model. This gives a definitive advantage over the future upgrade of the physics model. The rear view mirrors reflect a virtual camera that is projected on the surface of the mirrors via Render to Texture approach. Finally, the main car has a fully functional Autonomous Driver mode which has the capacity of maintaining a particular distance from the car in front by using the primary proximity zone. It can also brake hard when the car in front enters the secondary proximity zone. Figure 4 shows how the Adaptive Distance Awareness works in the driver simulator.

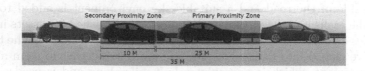

Fig. 4. Autonomous proximity sensor model

4   Application

Experimental Setup. While the car is running in autonomous mode, two different scenarios are defined in this experiment using LEE: (1) the subject is not looking at the road, but attentive with hands on the wheel, which serves as a baseline so that other scenarios can be used to compare the results for evaluation; (2) the subject is on the phone checking social media. In both cases, once the car detects a road block at a random distance ahead, it triggers an alarm, at which point the subject has to take back control in order to avoid a crash. LEE records the video of the subject, and several variables involved in the process, such as Hands/Feet PRT and the speed at which the alarm was triggered.

A total of 10 subjects aged between 26 and 62 years were involved in the experiment. Each trial contains 12 sessions, 6 for each scenario. The distance at which the road block is detected is set to 60 meters in 3 sessions and 80 meters in the other 3. We have compared the hands and feet PRT by means of the computation of their ranges (mean ± std) and have also explored the influence of some of the variables recorded such as Hands/Feet PRT and speed.

Results and Analysis. The subjects were found to keep the wheel in a static position unchanged from the Autonomous mode was in, thus in this context, the driver appears to concentrate on control of the pedals first. This result is also evident when we compare the Hands/Feet PRT of both the scenarios, in which Hands PRT are significantly greater than Feet PRT. Table 1 summarizes the ranges for Hands/Feet PRT in both scenarios.

Figure 5 shows the influence of three variables, Hands/Feet PRT and speed, where blue and red colors show crash/no crash results, respectively. Dots and

Table 1. Comparison of Hands/Feet PRT in both scenarios

	Hands	Feet	p-value
1st scenario	1.67 ± 1.61	1.26 ± 0.45	0.0034
2nd scenario	2.71 ± 1.91	1.42 ± 0.34	8.41×10^{-8}

circles represent results for scenario 1 and scenario 2, respectively. It can be observed that the speed of the car when the alarm was triggered is a determinant variable in both scenarios since we can appreciate two separate clusters in the speed direction. As opposed to this, two separate clusters in the direction of feet or hands PRT cannot be seen.

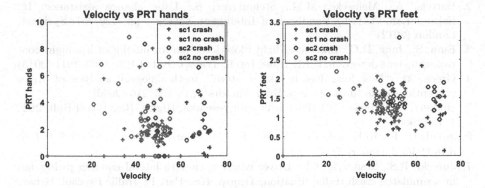

Fig. 5. Speed against PRT in both scenarios (Color figure online)

5 Conclusion and Future Directions

This paper has presented an affordable, customizable and easy-to-use simulation environment for facilitating research on driver-vehicle interaction for level 3 autonomous driving. The simulator is designed to be deployed at any location with the minimum amount of hardware peripherals, which significantly reduces the cost of the entire setup.

The results of an experiment at small scale, performed to highlight the utility of LEE, show that the speed of the car at the transfer moment is critical for ensuring vehicle safety. Distance to the front car is not a 100 % plausible variable, because there are situations where a driver would steer clear of any cars, or the initial distance before the road block between the front car and the user car is quite large. In future, we plan to increase the number of scenarios as the cognitive load of the driver is another variable that should be taken into account.

Besides, there are more potential uses of LEE to improve the perception engines of self-driving cars, such as driver state recognition and PRT prediction in function of both external (road, traffic, environment, weather, lighting...) and internal (driver, passengers, car configuration...) situations. As well, another question arises, how to maintain and check the driver attentiveness during self-driving? Computer vision and Artificial Intelligence will play a crucial role in the particular case of monitoring the driver and recognizing her/his attentiveness and general state and deciding how to transfer the car's control. LEE will allow to do all the tests in a road safety manner, which will be approached further.

Acknowledgements. This work is supported by the Spanish MICINN project TRA2014-57088-C2-1, by the Secretaria d'Universitats i Recerca del Departament d'Economia i Coneixement de la Generalitat de Catalunya (2014-SGR-1506).

References

1. Abdelgawad, K., Abdelkarim, M., Hassan, B., Grafe, M., Gräßler, I.: A modular architecture of a PC-based driving simulator for advanced driver assistance systems development. In: 2014 15th International Workshop on Research and Education in Mechatronics (REM), pp. 1–8. IEEE (2014)
2. Bartels, A., Meinecke, M.M., Steinmeyer, S.: Lane change assistance. In: Eskandarian, A. (ed.) Handbook of Intelligent Vehicles, pp. 729–757. Springer, London (2012)
3. Eum, S., Jung, H.G.: Enhancing light blob detection for intelligent headlight control using lane detection. IEEE Trans. Intell. Transp. Syst. **14**(2), 1003–1011 (2013)
4. Green, M.: "How long does it take to stop?" methodological analysis of driver perception-brake times. Transp. Hum. Factors **2**(3), 195–216 (2000)
5. Hulbert, S., Wojcik, C.: Driving simulator research. Highw. Res. Board Bull. **261**, 1–13 (1960)
6. Jitsukata, E., Kobayashi, S., Tamura, K.: Automatic driving system. US Patent 6,169,940, 2 January 2001
7. Jurecki, R.S., Stańczyk, T.L.: Driver reaction time to lateral entering pedestrian in a simulated crash traffic situation. Transp. Res. Part F: Traffic Psychol. Behav. **27**, 22–36 (2014)
8. Jurecki, R.S., Stańczyk, T.L., Jaśkiewicz, M.J.: Driver's reaction time in a simulated, complex road incident. Transport 1–11 (2014). http://dx.doi.org/10.3846/16484142.2014.913535
9. Knutsson, U.K.: Swedish national road and transport research institute. IATSS Res. **27**(2), 88–91 (2003)
10. Kuang, Y., Qu, X., Weng, J., Etemad-Shahidi, A.: How does the driver's perception reaction time affect the performances of crash surrogate measures? PLoS One **10**(9), e0138617 (2015)
11. Martin, S., Ohn-Bar, E., Tawari, A., Trivedi, M.M.: Understanding head and hand activities and coordination in naturalistic driving videos. In: 2014 IEEE Intelligent Vehicles Symposium Proceedings, pp. 884–889. IEEE (2014)
12. SAE levels driving automation: http://cyberlaw.stanford.edu/blog/2013/12/sae-levels-driving-automation. Accessed 29 July 2016
13. Svetina, M.: The reaction times of drivers aged 20 to 80 during a divided attention driving. Traffic Inj. Prev. (2016, in press)
14. Tesla driver dies in first fatal crash while using autopilot mode. https://www.theguardian.com/technology/2016/jun/30/tesla-autopilot-death-self-driving-car-elon-musk. Accessed 29 July 2016
15. Tesla says autopilot involved in second car crash. http://www.bbc.com/news/technology-36783345. Accessed 29 July 2016
16. The Mission. http://www.themission.co.uk/news/bigdog-goes-virtual-for-mazda2-launch/. Accessed 29 July 2016
17. Toyota's Driving Simulator Review. http://www.telegraph.co.uk/motoring/roadsafety/6598418/Toyotas-30-million-drivingsimulator-review.html. Accessed 29 July 2016
18. Zhang, W., Mei, T., Liang, H., Li, B., Huang, J., Xu, Z., Ding, Y., Liu, W.: Research and development of automatic driving system for intelligent vehicles. In: Sun, F., Hu, D., Liu, H. (eds.) Foundations and Practical Applications of Cognitive Systems and Information Processing. AISC, vol. 215, pp. 675–684. Springer, Heidelberg (2014). doi:10.1007/978-3-642-37835-5_58

Enhancing Place Recognition Using Joint Intensity - Depth Analysis and Synthetic Data

Elena Sizikova[1]($\boxtimes$), Vivek K. Singh[2], Bogdan Georgescu[2], Maciej Halber[1], Kai Ma[2], and Terrence Chen[2]

[1] Department of Computer Science, Princeton University, Princeton, USA
sizikova@cs.princeton.edu
[2] Medical Imaging Technologies, Siemens Medical Solutions Inc., Princeton, NJ, USA

Abstract. Visual place recognition is an important tool for robots to localize themselves in their surroundings by matching previously seen images. Recent methods based on Convolutional Neural Networks (CNN) are capable of successfully addressing the place recognition task in RGB-D images. However, these methods require many aligned and annotated intensity and depth images to train joint detectors. We propose a new approach by augmenting the place recognition process with individual separate intensity and depth networks trained on synthetic data. As a result, the new approach requires only a handful of aligned RGB-D frames to achieve a competitive place recognition performance. To our knowledge, this is the first CNN approach that integrates intensity and depth into a joint robust matching framework for place recognition and that evaluates utility of prediction from each modality.

1 Background

Visual place recognition is a task of detecting when two images in an image sequence depict the same location, possibly under camera viewpoint or illumination-related appearance changes [14]. This is a challenging problem in computer vision that is particularly important for intelligent autonomous robot systems. For instance, such systems include (but are not limited to) robots that need to map their positions in space, accurately localize themselves within their environment, and detect when they revisit a previous location. Typically, matches are determined based on similarity of image pairs from widely available and inexpensive RGB-D sensors, such as Kinect. This task is particularly challenging since the RGB appearance of a surface can vary dramatically with viewpoint and lighting. Moreover, depth appearance can have dropouts, noise, and other artifacts that hinder the extraction of repeatable features. Finally, long traversal trajectories contain thousands of scans which require efficient image search strategies.

Electronic supplementary material The online version of this chapter (doi:10.1007/978-3-319-49409-8_74) contains supplementary material, which is available to authorized users.

© Springer International Publishing Switzerland 2016
G. Hua and H. Jégou (Eds.): ECCV 2016 Workshops, Part III, LNCS 9915, pp. 901–908, 2016.
DOI: 10.1007/978-3-319-49409-8_74

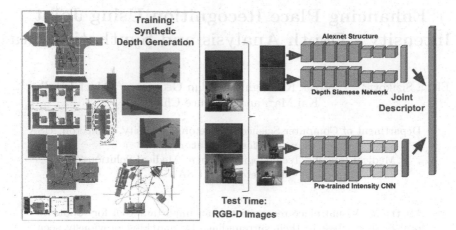

Fig. 1. Overview of the joint depth intensity CNN place recognition system. We use synthetic 3D models of office and living rooms [6] to train a depth Siamese CNN network. We then learn to match the network feature responses on unseen real depth images with intensity feature responses from a pre-trained CNN [25] to obtain a viewpoint-invariant RGB-D descriptor for place recognition.

Convolutional Neural Networks (CNN) have been recently shown to outperform methods relying on handcrafted features in place recognition tasks [1]. Furthermore, [10,20] compare performance of convolutional network layers, and conclude that the middle layers of networks trained for related tasks such as semantic place categorization [25], are especially suitable to address this problem. However, such methods are effective only in scenes with viewpoint-independent surface appearances and where training data with intensity image correspondences are available.

Due to illumination changes, color information can be ambiguous, which leads to a natural question of how effectively depth information can be used to resolve ambiguities. Previous studies indicate that depth is somewhat inferior to intensity for place recognition [17]. However, such findings are based on a Bag of Words model [13], which produces descriptors that are, in turn, hand-tuned rather than trained on data. Recently, [5,8,9] showed that joint RGB-D networks outperform intensity only methods for object detection. Depending on the definition of a 'place match', the problem of place recognition often does not have a sufficient amount of annotated and aligned RGB-D training data to train joint CNN models, and thus it is unclear how much each available modality contributes to performance. At the same time, synthetic depth data was shown to be very useful for dense semantic labelling [6] and for object detection [8], where it is complementary to intensity, but often cannot be directly used to improve joint models due to lack of RGB annotations.

In this paper, we investigate the performance of a depth CNN trained on synthetic depth images for an indoor place recognition task. We obtain training data by synthesizing depth images from computer graphics models of scenes

[6], by simulating camera movement along user generated realistic movement trajectories. At training time, the network learns to predict 3D overlap in synthetic depth; while at testing time, it is used to evaluate overlap on real data, in combination with a RGB-D CNN descriptor. We combine the two modalities in a robust matching framework and evaluate the relative contribution of each method using robust statistical analysis. Finally, we release a large dataset of synthetic trajectories with per-frame extrinsics annotations.

2   Approach

We introduce a CNN for matching pairs of RGB-D images that can be used to enhance place recognition under limited data availability. Although CNNs are known to be effective for RGB image matching [21], there are no joint RGB-D indoor place recognition systems. This is due to the fact that existing indoor datasets such as [18,23] lack the per-frame annotations and RGB-Depth sensor alignments which are necessary to train a larger model.

To address this issue, we synthesize a set of trajectories in computer graphics models of rooms that are then used to create synthetic depth frames. We train a CNN on pairs of the synthetic depth images to learn a match predictor (depth images that overlap significantly). Finally, at testing time, we combine that CNN with one trained on RGB images to recognize matches between real RGB-D images, and evaluate the statistical contribution of each component.

The key idea behind this approach is that synthetic 3D models can be used to produce sufficient amount of depth data to train a CNN, and that it is not necessary to have access to a large collection of aligned RGB and depth images to construct a joint predictor. Although a similar methodology has been used previously for object detection [5,8,16,22], it has never been employed for indoor place recognition.

3   Overview

We evaluate the capacity of joint intensity and depth place recognition method in improving recognition of previously visited places. Our input data consists of a sequence of RGB-D scans, where the correspondences between depth and RGB are known. The scans are acquired as the robot moves along a trajectory and its sensors periodically take snapshots of the current state.

In the next section, we describe the details of network training and descriptor extraction from each RGB-D frame.

3.1   Synthetic Dataset

We employ scenes from the SceneNet dataset [6] to draw custom trajectories and to generate synthetic depth scans to be used as training data for the network. Overall, we generated 134 unique trajectories for the bathroom, living room, and office scenes, where each trajectory circles the room several times to create a variety of realistic loop closure examples. Each trajectory is created by drawing two Bezier curves that circle around a room (see Fig. 1). The first curve represents the camera location, and the second curve represents a set of points that the camera observes. Camera movement is animated along these paths, producing a sequence of camera poses and corresponding 640 × 480-pixel depth frames simulated from a pinhole camera. The trajectories are intended to mimic the way an experienced user would scan the room – i.e., the motion is smooth, every scene object is viewed from multiple viewpoints, with varying time spent in different parts of the scene. The resulting trajectories contain 3,000 camera viewpoints each, and we use every 10-th viewpoint for training.

3.2   Depth Descriptor

Depth descriptors are extracted by calculating depth features from a CNN trained on depth data. Since our goal is to detect same objects under different viewpoints, we use 3D point overlap as a similarity estimator. Note that this is a more challenging metric than translation along the camera trajectory (which is often used for evaluation in place recognition systems), because the same overlap amount allows larger camera pose differences between frames. However, since selected frames are typically passed to a geometric alignment algorithm to generate pairwise transformations, a large amount of overlap is a suitable predictor that the correct transformation will be predicted.

We compute overlap O for each scan pair (i, j) as $O = (P_i \cap P_j) / \max\{P_i, P_j\}$, where P_i and P_j are sets of 3D points in each frame, and the union is the set of points within a threshold ϵ of each other ($\epsilon = 7.5$ cm in all experiments). Normalizing overlap by the maximum number of points ensures that if one of the scans captures a small portion of the other, a case which is visually ambiguous, this example is not selected for training.

Training Setup. Each example given to the network for training is a pair of depth images and a label. We generate the set of all pairs of depth images for each trajectory. Each example is assigned a positive label if the 3D overlap between these images is greater than T; otherwise a negative label is assigned. This threshold represents our confidence that such a network yields visually similar pairs, but with sufficient room for viewpoint changes. In our experiments, we find that choosing T of 75 % yields the most visually recognizable selections as determined by an observer. We also balance the number of positive and negative examples from each training trajectory. Overall, the training data consists of 1, 442, 252 depth image pairs, where depth is encoded using the HHA encoding [4], which is known to be compatible with popular existing CNN architectures. Training process is performed in the Caffe library [11].

Network Architecture and Loss. We use a Siamese CNN architecture [3] with two Alexnet branches to learn pose-invariant descriptors. The Siamese architecture equipped with a Contrastive Loss function is known to be especially suitable for distance metric learning from examples [3]. We compare the outputs of several bottom layers and obtain the best performance from the $fc6$ layer which we then use for joint descriptor calculations. To evaluate the quality and amount of our synthetic depth data, we train the network from scratch using stochastic gradient descent with $100,000$ iterations.

3.3 Intensity Descriptor

We employ a pre-trained CNN for descriptor extraction on intensity images, trained for semantic place categorization [25]. In particular, we use an AlexNet CNN trained on 205 scene categories of Places Database (2.5 million images) [25]. We also compare the Caffenet implementation [11]; however, we find PlacesNet layer $fc6$ to be superior (see Supp. Material), echoing conclusion of [20].

3.4 Learning a Joint Descriptor

Given two RGB-D frames, our goal is to estimate their distance. Because the distances between only the depth or only the intensity parts may be unreliable, we combine the distances from both modalities using a robust joint model, which we describe below. Given a pair of frames F_p and F_q, we start by extracting depth and intensity descriptors, (d_p, i_p) and (d_q, i_q), respectively. We then use a small set of aligned RGB-D frames to estimate the joint parameters of the model. In particular, let $D = ||d_p - d_q||$ and $I = ||i_p - i_q||$ be distances in the depth and intensity descriptor spaces, respectively. Our goal is to estimate overlap O as a function of D and I. We consider two models where O is either a linear or polynomial function of D and I, that is, $O \sim D + I$ (1) and $O \sim D + I + D \times I$ (2). Both models are highly sensitive to atypical observations and outliers. To reduce outlier impact, we use a robust MM-type estimator, which is known to deliver highly robust and efficient estimates, to obtain model parameters [12,15,24]. Given aligned data from any trajectory (we used ICL Living Room Sequence 3), we estimate coefficients of (2) using 100 bootstrap iterations (i.e. sampling with replacement). In each polynomial model, we balance the number of overlapping and non-overlapping pairs. We describe the statistical properties of these models and their evaluation on a place recognition task in the next section.

4 Evaluation

Model Assessment. Our analysis indicates that both linear terms (Depth and Intensity) and the crossterm ($D \times I$) are highly statistically significant), and thus all three terms contain meaningful addition in explaining variation of O. The relationship follows our hypothesis that overlap decreases with increasing distances between the intensity or between depth images (we provide values of the coefficients and standard deviations in Suppl. Material). In addition, we compare the mean adjusted R^2 values from models $O \sim D$ (density only), $O \sim I$

(intensity only), $O \sim I + D \times I$ (intensity and depth, non-robust), and $O \sim I + D \times I$ (intensity and depth, robust), which result in the adjusted R^2 values of 0.30, 0.68, 0.69, and 0.70, respectively. These findings indicate importance of each component to explain variability of our system and superiority of the polynomial model $O \sim I + D \times I$. Additionally, the mean coefficients from the robust model perform well across all test datasets, while the mean coefficients from the non-robust model perform substantially worse (see Supp. Material). These findings indicate sensitivity of a conventional estimators to outliers and importance of using a more robust MM-estimator.

Place Recognition Results. The goal of our work is to provide a robust view-invariant RGB-D place recognition descriptor, and we evaluate of our method on trajectories from three publicly available benchmark datasets, namely, ICL-NUIM [7], TUM RGB-D [19], and Sun3D [23]. All datasets are pre-processed in the same way as the training dataset to obtain 3D overlap pairs (subsampled to every 10th frame and depth converted to HHA encoding). The ability of descriptors to recognize the same location can be evaluated by F-scores. We calculate the precision and recall at equally spaced thresholds between the smallest and the largest descriptor distances of all pairs of scans, for each combination of method and dataset (so that predicted positives are pairs whose descriptor distances are below this threshold, selected among all non-consecutive scan pairs). In each dataset, the true positive pairs are those pairs of frames which have a small overlap in 3D space (less than 30 %, the threshold used in geometric alignment algorithms [2]). The F-scores are calculated from precision and recall for all thresholds and for all methods, and the top score is selected for each method.

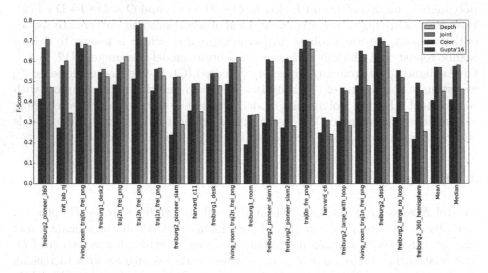

Fig. 2. Best F-scores obtained by each model (under its optimal parameters).

Figure 2 shows the top F-scores of each method in each dataset. The joint object detection method of [5] consistently ranks lower than both Placesnet [25] and DepthAlexnet (synthetic data only), which is expected without additional fine-tuning. DepthAlexnet outperforms Placenet [25] in 4/20 cases, and the joint model outperforms Placesnet [25] in 12/20 cases, and performs comparably well in others. Interestingly, DepthAlexnet outperforms method of [5] in many cases, suggesting that depth can be a good predictor on its own when sufficient synthetic data is available for training.

5   Conclusion and Future Work

We propose a novel outlier resistant place recognition descriptor in RGB-D. We show that synthetic depth can be employed to train view-invariant CNNs that are useful for place recognition tasks. We also show that combining descriptors from depth and intensity images shows improvement over intensity-only based place recognition, even when only a few aligned RGB-D trajectories are available for training.[1]

References

1. Chen, Z., Lam, O., Jacobson, A., Milford, M.: Convolutional neural network-based place recognition. arXiv preprint arXiv:1411.1509 (2014)
2. Choi, S., Zhou, Q.Y., Koltun, V.: Robust reconstruction of indoor scenes. In: CVPR (2015)
3. Chopra, S., Hadsell, R., LeCun, Y.: Learning a similarity metric discriminatively, with application to face verification. In: CVPR (2005)
4. Gupta, S., Girshick, R., Arbeláez, P., Malik, J.: Learning rich features from RGB-D images for object detection and segmentation. In: Fleet, D., Pajdla, T., Schiele, B., Tuytelaars, T. (eds.) ECCV 2014. LNCS, vol. 8695, pp. 345–360. Springer, Heidelberg (2014). doi:10.1007/978-3-319-10584-0_23
5. Gupta, S., Hoffman, J., Malik, J.: Cross modal distillation for supervision transfer. In: CVPR (2016)
6. Handa, A., Pătrăucean, V., Badrinarayanan, V., Stent, S., Cipolla, R.: Understanding real world indoor scenes with synthetic data. In: CVPR (2016)
7. Handa, A., Whelan, T., McDonald, J., Davison, A.J.: A benchmark for rgb-d visual odometry, 3d reconstruction and slam. In: ICRA (2014)
8. Hoffman, J., Gupta, S., Darrell, T.: Learning with side information through modality hallucination. In: CVPR (2016)
9. Hoffman, J., Gupta, S., Leong, J., Guadarrama, S., Darrell, T.: Cross-modal adaptation for rgb-d detection. In: ICRA (2016)
10. Hou, Y., Zhang, H., Zhou, S.: Convolutional neural network-based image representation for visual loop closure detection. arXiv preprint arXiv:1504.05241 (2015)
11. Jia, Y., Shelhamer, E., Donahue, J., Karayev, S., Long, J., Girshick, R., Guadarrama, S., Darrell, T.: Caffe: convolutional architecture for fast feature embedding. In: ACM MM (2014)

---

[1] Disclaimer: The outlined concepts are not commercially available. Due to regulatory reasons their future availability cannot be guaranteed.

12. Koller, M., Stahel, W.A.: Sharpening wald-type inference in robust regression for small samples. Computational Statistics and Data Analysis **55**, 2504–2515 (2011)
13. Konolige, K., Bowman, J., Chen, J., Mihelich, P., Calonder, M., Lepetit, V., Fua, P.: View-based maps. Int. J. Robot. Res. **29**, 941–957 (2010)
14. Lowry, S., Sunderhauf, N., Newman, P., Leonard, J.J., Cox, D., Corke, P., Milford, M.J.: Visual place recognition: a survey. IEEE Trans. Robot. **32**, 1–19 (2016)
15. Salibian-Barrera, M., Yohai, V.J.: A fast algorithm for S-Regression estimates. J. Comput. Graph. Stat. **15**, 414–427 (2006)
16. Papon, J., Schoeler, M.: Semantic pose using deep networks trained on synthetic RGB-D. In: ICCV (2015)
17. Scherer, S.A., Kloss, A., Zell, A.: Loop closure detection using depth images. In: ECMR (2013)
18. Silberman, N., Hoiem, D., Kohli, P., Fergus, R.: Indoor segmentation and support inference from RGBD images. In: Fitzgibbon, A., Lazebnik, S., Perona, P., Sato, Y., Schmid, C. (eds.) ECCV 2012. LNCS, vol. 7576, pp. 746–760. Springer, Heidelberg (2012). doi:10.1007/978-3-642-33715-4_54
19. Sturm, J., Magnenat, S., Engelhard, N., Pomerleau, F., Colas, F., Cremers, D., Siegwart, R., Burgard, W.: Towards a benchmark for RGB-D slam evaluation. In: RSS RGB-D Workshop on Advanced Reasoning with Depth Cameras (2011)
20. Sünderhauf, N., Dayoub, F., Shirazi, S., Upcroft, B., Milford, M.: On the performance of convnet features for place recognition. arXiv preprint arXiv:1501.04158 (2015)
21. Wang, J., Song, Y., Leung, T., Rosenberg, C., Wang, J., Philbin, J., Chen, B., Wu, Y.: Learning fine-grained image similarity with deep ranking. In: CVPR (2014)
22. Wohlhart, P., Lepetit, V.: Learning descriptors for object recognition and 3D pose estimation. In: CVPR (2015)
23. Xiao, J., Owens, A., Torralba, A.: SUN3D: a database of big spaces reconstructed using SfM and object labels. In: ICCV (2013)
24. Yohai, V.J.: High breakdown-point and high efficiency robust estimates for regression. Ann. Stat. **15**, 642–656 (1987)
25. Zhou, B., Lapedriza, A., Xiao, J., Torralba, A., Oliva, A.: Learning deep features for scene recognition using places database. In: NIPS (2014)

UnrealCV: Connecting Computer Vision to Unreal Engine

Weichao Qiu[✉] and Alan Yuille

Johns Hopkins University, Baltimore, MD, USA
qiuwch@gmail.com, alan.l.yuille@gmail.com

Abstract. Computer graphics can not only generate synthetic images and ground truth but it also offers the possibility of constructing *virtual worlds* in which: (i) an agent can perceive, navigate, and take actions guided by AI algorithms, (ii) properties of the worlds can be modified (e.g., material and reflectance), (iii) physical simulations can be performed, and (iv) algorithms can be learnt and evaluated. But creating realistic virtual worlds is not easy. The game industry, however, has spent a lot of effort creating 3D worlds, which a player can interact with. So researchers can build on these resources to create virtual worlds, provided we can access and modify the internal data structures of the games. To enable this we created an open-source plugin *UnrealCV* (Project website: http://unrealcv.github.io) for a popular game engine Unreal Engine 4 (UE4). We show two applications: (i) a proof of concept image dataset, and (ii) linking Caffe with the virtual world to test deep network algorithms.

1 Introduction

Computer vision has benefited enormously from large datasets [7,8]. They enable the training and testing of complex models such as deep networks [13]. But performing annotation is costly and time consuming so it is attractive to make synthetic datasets which contain large amounts of images and detailed annotation. These datasets are created by modifying open-source movies [2] or by constructing a 3D world [9,17]. Researchers have shown that training on synthetic images is helpful for real world tasks [11,14,16,18,21]. Robotics researchers have gone further by constructing 3D worlds for robotics simulation, but they emphasize physical accuracy rather than visual realism. This motivates the design of realistic *virtual worlds* for computer vision where an agent can take actions guided by AI algorithms, properties of the worlds can be modified, physical simulations can be performed, and algorithms can be trained and tested. Virtual worlds have been used for autonomous driving [5], naive physics simulations [1] and evaluating surveillance system [19]. But creating realistic virtual worlds is time consuming.

The video game industry has developed many tools for constructing 3D worlds, such as libraries of 3D object models. These 3D worlds are already realistic and the popularity of games and Virtual Reality (VR) drives towards even

© Springer International Publishing Switzerland 2016
G. Hua and H. Jégou (Eds.): ECCV 2016 Workshops, Part III, LNCS 9915, pp. 909–916, 2016.
DOI: 10.1007/978-3-319-49409-8_75

greater realism. So modifying games and movies is an attractive way to make virtual worlds [5]. But modifying individual games is time-consuming and almost impossible for proprietary games. Hence our strategy is to modify a game engine, so that all the games built on top of it can be used. We develop a tool, UnrealCV, which can be used in combination with a leading game engine, Unreal Engine 4 (UE4), to use the rich resources in the game industry. UnrealCV can also be applied to 3D worlds created for virtual reality, architecture visualization, and computer graphics movies, provided they have been created using UE4. More precisely, UnrealCV provides an UE4 plugin. If a game, or any 3D world, is compiled with this plugin then we can create a virtual world where we can access and modify the internal data structures. This allows us to connect AI programs, like Caffe, to it and use a set of commands provided by UnrealCV to obtain groundtruth, control an agent, and so on. Figure 1 shows a synthetic image and its ground truth generated using UnrealCV.

We stress that we provide an open-source tool to help create new virtual worlds, which differs from work which produces a single virtual world [5] or creates synthetic datasets [9,17]. We hope that our work can help build a bridge between Unreal Engine and computer vision researchers.

Fig. 1. A synthetic image and its ground truth generated using UnrealCV. The virtual room is from technical demo RealisticRendering, built by Epic Games. From left to right are the synthetic image, object instance mask, depth, surface normal

2   Related Work

Virtual worlds have been widely used in robotics research and many robotics simulators have been built [12,20]. But these focus more on physical accuracy than visual realism, which makes them less suitable for computer vision researchers. Unreal Engine 2 (UE2) was used for robotics simulation in USARSim [3], but UE2 is no longer available and USARSim is no longer actively maintained.

Computer vision researchers have created large 3D repositories and virtual scenes [4,6,10,15]. Note that these 3D resources can be used in the combined Unreal Engine and UnrealCV system.

Games and movies have already been used in computer vision research. An optical flow dataset was generated from the open source movie Sintel [2]. TORCS, an open source racing game, was converted into a virtual world and used to train an autonomous driving system [5]. City scenes were built [9,17] using the Unity game engine to produce synthetic images. By contrast, UnrealCV extends the functions of Unreal Engine and provides a tool for creating virtual worlds instead of generating a synthetic image/video dataset or producing a single virtual world.

3 Unreal Engine

A game engine contains the components shared by many video games, such as rendering code and design tools. Games built using a game engine combine components from the engine with the game logic and 3D models. So modifying a game engine can affect all games built on top of it.

Fig. 2. Images produced by UE4, (a) (b) An architectural visualization and an urban city scene from Unreal Engine marketplace. (c) An open-source outdoor scene KiteRunner. (d) A digital human from the game Hellblade, shown in the conference GDC2016

We chose UE4 as our platform for these reasons: (I) It is fully open-source and can be easily modified for research. (II) It has the ability to produce realistic images, see Fig. 2. (III) It provides nice tools and documentation for creating a virtual world. These tools integrate well with other commercial software and well maintained. (IV) It has a broad impact beyond the game industry and is a popular choice for VR and architectural visualization, so high-quality 3D contents are easily accessible.

4 UnrealCV

UE4 was designed to create video games. To use it to create virtual worlds, a few modifications are required: (I) The camera should be programmably controlled, instead of by the keyboard and mouse, so that an agent can explore the world. (II) The internal data structure of the game needs to be accessed in order to generate ground truth. (III) We should be able to modify the world properties, such as lighting and material.

UnrealCV extends the function of UE4 to help create virtual worlds. More specifically, UnrealCV achieves this goal by a plugin for UE4. Compiling a game with the plugin installed embeds computer vision related functions to produce a virtual world. Any external program can communicate with this virtual world and use a set of commands provided by UnrealCV to perform various tasks. For example, the command `vget /camera/0/rotation` can retrieve the rotation of the first camera in the scene.

Architecture. UnrealCV consists of two parts. The first is the UnrealCV server, which is embedded into a virtual world to access its internal data structure. The second is the UnrealCV client whose function is provided by a library which can be integrated into any external program, like Caffe, enabling the program to send commands defined by UnrealCV to the server to perform various tasks. The architecture is shown in Fig. 3.

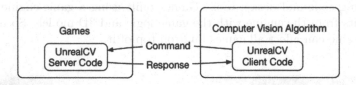

Fig. 3. The UnrealCV server is an UE4 plugin embedded into a game during compilation. An external program uses the UnrealCV client to communicate with the game.

The UnrealCV server is an UE4 plugin. After installing the plugin to UE4, the UnrealCV server code will be embedded into a game during compilation. The server will start when the game launches and wait for commands. The UnrealCV client uses a socket to communicate with the server. We implemented the client code for Python and MATLAB. Socket is a method of communicating between programs and is universal across programming languages and operating systems. So it is easy to implement a client for any language and platform that can support socket.

The server and client communicate using a plain text protocol. The client sends an UnrealCV command to the server and waits for a response. The command can be used to do various tasks. It can apply force to an object; can modify the world by changing the lighting or object position; can get images and annotation from the world. For example, the commands `vget /camera/0/image` and `vget /camera/0/depth` can get the image and depth ground truth. The command will save image as PNG file and return its filename. Depth will be saved as high dynamical range (HDR) image file, since the pixel value of PNG is limited within $[0\ldots255]$. The command `vset /camera/0/position 0 0 0` sets the camera position to $[0, 0, 0]$. An UnrealCV command contains two parts. The first part is an action which can be either `vget` or `vset`. The `vget` means getting information from the scene without changing anything and `vset` means changing some property of the world. The second part is an URI (Uniform Resource Identifier) representing something that UnrealCV can control. The URI is designed in a hierarchical modular structure which can be easily extended.

Features. The design of UnrealCV gives it three features:

Extensiblity: The commands are defined in a hierarchical modular way. Setting the light intensity can be achieved by `vset /light/[name]/intensity` to change the light color, a new command `vset /light/[name]/color` can be added without affecting the existing commands. UnrealCV is open-source and can be extended by us or other researchers.

Ease of Use: Since we provide compiled binaries of some virtual worlds, such as a realistic indoor room, using UnrealCV is as simple as downloading a game and running it. Hence researchers can use UnrealCV without knowledge of UE4. The design supports cross-platform and multi-languages (Python, MATLAB). It is straightforward to integrate UnrealCV with external programs and we show an example with Caffe in Sect. 5.

Rich Resources: UnrealCV only uses the standard Application Programming Interface (API) of UE4, making it compatible with games built with UE4. We will provide virtual worlds with UnrealCV integrated and also host a model zoo to share virtual worlds created by the community.

5   Applications

In this section we created a virtual world based on the UE4 technical demo RealisticRendering[1] which contains an indoor room with sofa, TV, table, bookshelves, floor lamp, etc. The virtual world can be downloaded from our project website. We demonstrate two applications of this virtual world in this section.

Generating a Synthetic Image Dataset. We use a script to generate a synthetic image dataset from the virtual world. Images are taken using random camera positions. The camera is set to two different heights, human eye level and

Fig. 4. Images with different camera height and different sofa color. (Color figure online)

Algorithm 1. Generate a synthetic image dataset from a virtual world

```
vget /objects ;                                    // Get objects information
for all camera position do
    /* Set the virtual camera position                              */
    vset /camera/0/location [x] [y] [z];
    vset /camera/0/rotation [yaw] [pitch] [roll];
    /* Get image and ground truth                                   */
    vget /camera/0/image;
    vget /camera/0/depth, vget /camera/0/object_mask;
end
```

---

[1] https://docs.unrealengine.com/latest/INT/Resources/Showcases/RealisticRendering/.

a Roomba robot level. The lighting, material property and object location can also be changed to increase the variety of the data, or to diagnose the strengths and weaknesses of an algorithm. Images with different camera height and sofa color can be seen in Fig. 4. Ground truth, such as depth, surface normals and object instance masks, is generated together with the images, shown in Fig. 1. The ability to generate rich ground truth is particularly useful for training and testing algorithms which perform multiple tasks and for detailed understanding of a scene. The UnrealCV commands used to generate this synthetic image dataset are shown in Algorithm 1. The synthetic images are on our website and a tutorial shows how to generate them step-by-step.

Diagnosing a Deep Network Algorithm. We take a Faster-RCNN model[2] trained on PASCAL and test it in the virtual world by varying rendering configurations. The testing code uses the UnrealCV client to control the camera in the virtual world and the Faster-RCNN code tries to detect the sofa from different views. We moved the position of the camera but constrained it to always point towards the sofa shown in Fig. 4. We got the object instance mask of the sofa and converted it into ground truth bounding box for evaluation. Human subject can easily detect the sofa from all the viewpoints. The Average Precision (AP) result shows surprisingly large variation as a function of viewpoint, see Table. 1. For each az/el combination, the distance from the camera to the sofa was varied from 200 cm to 290 cm. The symbol "-" means the sofa is not visible from this viewpoint. More generally, we can vary parameters such as lighting, occlusion level, and camera viewpoint to thoroughly test an algorithm.

Table 1. The Average Precision (AP) when viewing the sofa from different viewpoints. Observe the AP varies from 0.1 to 1.0 showing the sensitivity to viewpoint. This is perhaps because the biases in the training cause Faster-RCNN to favor specific viewpoints.

Elevation	Azimuth				
	90	135	180	225	270
0	-	0.713	0.769	0.930	0.319
30	0.900	1.000	0.588	1.000	0.710
60	0.255	0.100	0.148	0.296	0.649

6   Conclusion

This paper has presented a tool called UnrealCV which can be plugged into the game engine UE4 to help construct realistic virtual worlds from the resources of the game, virtual reality, and architecture visualization industries. These virtual worlds allow us to access and modify the internal data structures enabling us

---

[2] We use the implementation: https://github.com/rbgirshick/py-faster-rcnn.

to extract groundtruth, control an agent, and train and test algorithms. Using virtual worlds for computer vision still has challenges, e.g., the variability of 3D content is limited, internal structure of 3D mesh is missing, realistic physics simulation is hard, and transfer from synthetic images remains an issue. But more realistic 3D contents will be available soon due to the advance of technology and the rising field of VR. As an industry leader, UE4 will benefit from this trend. UnrealCV is an open-source tool and we hope other researchers will use it and contribute to it.

Acknowledgment. We would like to thank Yi Zhang, Austin Reiter, Vittal Premachandran, Lingxi Xie and Siyuan Qiao for discussion and feedback. This project is supported by the Intelligence Advanced Research Projects Activity (IARPA) with contract D16PC00007.

References

1. Battaglia, P.W., Hamrick, J.B., Tenenbaum, J.B.: Simulation as an engine of physical scene understanding. Proc. Nat. Acad. Sci. **110**(45), 18327–18332 (2013)
2. Butler, D.J., Wulff, J., Stanley, G.B., Black, M.J.: A naturalistic open source movie for optical flow evaluation. In: Fitzgibbon, A., Lazebnik, S., Perona, P., Sato, Y., Schmid, C. (eds.) ECCV 2012. LNCS, vol. 7577, pp. 611–625. Springer, Heidelberg (2012). doi:10.1007/978-3-642-33783-3_44
3. Carpin, S., Lewis, M., Wang, J., Balakirsky, S., Scrapper, C.: USARSim: a robot simulator for research and education. In: Proceedings 2007 IEEE International Conference on Robotics and Automation, pp. 1400–1405. IEEE (2007)
4. Chang, A.X., Funkhouser, T., Guibas, L., Hanrahan, P., Huang, Q., Li, Z., Savarese, S., Savva, M., Song, S., Su, H., et al.: ShapeNet: an information-rich 3D model repository. arXiv preprint arXiv:1512.03012 (2015)
5. Chen, C., Seff, A., Kornhauser, A., Xiao, J.: DeepDriving: learning affordance for direct perception in autonomous driving. In: Proceedings of the IEEE International Conference on Computer Vision, pp. 2722–2730 (2015)
6. Choi, S., Zhou, Q.Y., Miller, S., Koltun, V.: A large dataset of object scans. arXiv preprint arXiv:1602.02481 (2016)
7. Deng, J., Dong, W., Socher, R., Li, L.J., Li, K., Fei-Fei, L.: ImageNet: a large-scale hierarchical image database. In: IEEE Conference on Computer Vision and Pattern Recognition, CVPR 2009, pp. 248–255. IEEE (2009)
8. Everingham, M., Van Gool, L., Williams, C.K., Winn, J., Zisserman, A.: The Pascal Visual Object Classes (VOC) challenge. Int. J. Comput. Vis. **88**(2), 303–338 (2010)
9. Gaidon, A., Wang, Q., Cabon, Y., Vig, E.: Virtual worlds as proxy for multi-object tracking analysis. arXiv preprint arXiv:1605.06457 (2016)
10. Handa, A., Patraucean, V., Badrinarayanan, V., Stent, S., Cipolla, R.: SceneNet: understanding real world indoor scenes with synthetic data. arXiv preprint arXiv:1511.07041 (2015)
11. Hattori, H., Naresh Boddeti, V., Kitani, K.M., Kanade, T.: Learning scene-specific pedestrian detectors without real data. In: Proceedings of the IEEE Conference on Computer Vision and Pattern Recognition, pp. 3819–3827 (2015)
12. Koenig, N., Howard, A.: Design and use paradigms for Gazebo, an open-source multi-robot simulator. In: Proceedings of the 2004 IEEE/RSJ International Conference on Intelligent Robots and Systems, (IROS 2004), vol. 3, pp. 2149–2154. IEEE (2004)

13. Krizhevsky, A., Sutskever, I., Hinton, G.E.: ImageNet classification with deep convolutional neural networks. In: Advances in neural information processing systems, pp. 1097–1105 (2012)
14. Marin, J., Vázquez, D., Gerónimo, D., López, A.M.: Learning appearance in virtual scenarios for pedestrian detection. In: 2010 IEEE Conference on Computer Vision and Pattern Recognition (CVPR), pp. 137–144. IEEE (2010)
15. Mottaghi, R., Rastegari, M., Gupta, A., Farhadi, A.: "What happens if..." learning to predict the effect of forces in images. arXiv preprint arXiv:1603.05600 (2016)
16. Peng, X., Sun, B., Ali, K., Saenko, K.: Learning deep object detectors from 3D models. In: Proceedings of the IEEE International Conference on Computer Vision, pp. 1278–1286 (2015)
17. Ros, G., Sellart, L., Materzynska, J., Vazquez, D., Lopez, A.M.: The SYNTHIA dataset: a large collection of synthetic images for semantic segmentation of urban scenes. In: Proceedings of the IEEE Conference on Computer Vision and Pattern Recognition, pp. 3234–3243 (2016)
18. Su, H., Qi, C.R., Li, Y., Guibas, L.J.: Render for CNN: Viewpoint estimation in images using CNNs trained with rendered 3D model views. In: Proceedings of the IEEE International Conference on Computer Vision, pp. 2686–2694 (2015)
19. Taylor, G.R., Chosak, A.J., Brewer, P.C.: OVVV: using virtual worlds to design and evaluate surveillance systems. In: 2007 IEEE Conference on Computer Vision and Pattern Recognition, pp. 1–8. IEEE (2007)
20. Todorov, E., Erez, T., Tassa, Y.: MUJoCo: a physics engine for model-based control. In: 2012 IEEE/RSJ International Conference on Intelligent Robots and Systems, pp. 5026–5033. IEEE (2012)
21. Vazquez, D., Lopez, A.M., Marin, J., Ponsa, D., Geronimo, D.: Virtual and real world adaptation for pedestrian detection. IEEE Trans. Pattern Anal. Mach. Intell. **36**(4), 797–809 (2014)

Author Index

Printed in the United States
By Bookmasters